Battle of the Arctic

Battle of
the Arctic

*The Maritime Epic of
World War Two*

HUGH SEBAG-MONTEFIORE

WILLIAM
COLLINS

William Collins
An imprint of HarperCollins*Publishers*
1 London Bridge Street
London SE1 9GF

WilliamCollinsBooks.com

HarperCollins*Publishers*
Macken House, 39/40 Mayor Street Upper,
Dublin 1, D01 C9W8, Ireland

First published in Great Britain in 2025 by William Collins

2

ISBN 978-0-00-833577-9 (Hardback)
ISBN 978-0-00-833578-6 (Trade paperback)

Set in Minion Pro by Six Red Marbles UK, Thetford, Norfolk

Printed and bound in Great Britain by CPI Group (UK) Ltd, Croydon

*For Aviva Burnstock, my wife, and for Saul,
Esther and Abraham, my children*

Contents

Introduction

Lots of books have already been written about the Arctic, or Russian, convoys – the groups of ships that carried supplies to the Soviet Union during World War 2, which are at the heart of any description of the Battle of the Arctic. Most of these books either concentrate on the victories and errors of the British admirals who guarded the convoys, and their thrusts against the German warships sent to attack them, or they focus on the elements, and the resulting discomfort for sailors forced to steam their ships through mountainous seas in freezing gales.

But the Battle of the Arctic is not just about the Royal Navy and its efforts to shepherd ships past the waiting Germans, while doing their best to avoid storms and floating icebergs. Without minimizing their contribution, there is another aspect of the story which has never been properly explored, or understood by the general public. It involves the forgotten heroes of the Arctic convoys: the officers, armed guards and the ordinary civilian seamen, mostly from Britain and America, but also from other countries including Holland, Norway, Poland, and Russia, condemned to carry on steaming their merchant ships slowly through the icy waters to and from Russia, even though they knew that at any moment they might be sunk. That was not a very enticing prospect given that the seas were so cold that a man might freeze to death after just five minutes of immersion.

The scale of what was asked of the Allies' seamen during the passage of these Arctic convoys was staggering. The Arctic convoys rarely travelled alone: for much of the time they were watched by the crews of sinister enemy spy planes, which once in touch could, given a fair wind, circle them 24/7. Messages sent by these 'stalkers' to the German commanders in occupied Norway meant that convoy participants, whose ships had been armed, had to be constantly on their guard; a fleet of enemy warships might appear over the horizon at any moment.

The German method of communicating also facilitated attacks by swarms of hostile torpedo bomber planes and U-boat wolf packs, whose speed relative to the merchant ships, which typically lumbered along at just 8 knots (9 mph), made it possible for the pursuers to catch up more or less whenever they were summoned.

The super-efficient German search-and-sink system would have presented the Allies' navies with major headaches even in the most temperate of climates. Travelling as they had to, through ice and snow, squalls and even hurricanes, resulted in almost intractable complications.

Even during the dark months, light from the beautiful multi-coloured 'northern lights' – flickering shafts of light that lit up the sky – would at times, inconveniently for the Allies, provide just what the U-boat commanders needed to locate the convoys through their periscopes once the wolf packs were near enough to the merchant ships or escorts to put in an attack. In the Arctic there are also numerous natural decoys which confused the most alert of the merchant ship crews and the sailors aboard their escorts. Spouts of water or a dark form moving through the water could so easily be taken for a passing whale only for a gunner to discover too late it was a U-boat. There were also numerous false alarms on account of Arctic mirages which dramatically increased the apparent height of objects such as icebergs. It did not take many such cries of wolf for complacency to set in, leaving a ship's crew vulnerable when a real U-boat came along. The merchant ships' vulnerability was exacerbated when as frequently happened in the Arctic, the Allies' escorts' compasses and submarine detection equipment (Asdic) did not function reliably.

There were other factors that impeded the merchant ships' progress. Although all the Arctic convoys, hemmed in by the ice anchored in the North Pole, had to pass through the same arc of the Barents Sea – to the north and south of the appropriately named Bear Island (located between the summer ice edge and Norway's North Cape), each sailing after the first 11 'PQ' (east-going) Arctic convoys required that a different challenge had to be overcome.

Each time a group of aid carrying merchant ships set out for Russia from Iceland or Scotland, there had to be a fresh rolling of the dice by the British admirals, who were in charge of the predominantly but by no means entirely British protection forces cobbled together in order to give the escort the best chance of prevailing (at various times the Royal Navy was stiffened by support supplied by the American, Canadian, Polish, Norwegian and Free French navies). It became increasingly difficult for the commanders of these protection forces to select the permutations that would surprise or defeat the Germans, on account of the convoys having to be run again and again and again.

The Germans very nearly succeeded in their quest to stop the Arctic convoys. Anyone who has either read about Arctic convoy PQ17, or seen Jeremy Clarkson's BBC documentary about it, will know how close the Germans came in July 1942 to sinking every single merchant ship in the group. In the wake of the controversial decision made by the British First Sea Lord Admiral Sir Dudley Pound to scatter the convoy, depriving it of the cover provided by Allied warships, for fear it might be about to be attacked by Germany's giant battleship *Tirpitz*, the number of the convoy's merchant ships carrying aid which were abandoned or sunk following attacks by the Luftwaffe or by U-boats rose to 22 out of 33 which had participated following PQ17's initial stages.

It has become 'fashionable' to vilify Admiral Pound for the part he played in this disaster. With the benefit of hindsight his decision seems at first sight to have been one of the most heinous mistakes made by a British naval commander during the war. No less a commentator than Stephen Roskill, the official historian of the war at sea, has indicated that he could see no justification for it. His verdict probably would have been supported by just about every Arctic convoy participant had they been asked at the time. Jeremy Clarkson in his 2014 documentary appears to be saying the same thing.

However, a detailed re-examination of what Pound knew at the time, including what he could glean from specific Enigma decrypts which have become public since Roskill's official history of the war at sea was published, and which were also not cited in the documentary, could lead one to a very different conclusion. It cannot be denied that, as highlighted by Clarkson, when making his decision concerning PQ17, Pound was overworked, exhausted, and probably already disabled to some extent by the brain tumour that would kill him. The orders he gave to the convoy escort were ambiguously phrased. However, that does not mean his decision to scatter the convoy was wrong. Given his knowledge at the time, he appears to have had good reason to scatter PQ17. Readers who wish to decide for themselves whether Pound has been unfairly lampooned and castigated by historians and documentary film makers during the decades that have followed his momentous action should read this book's Chapter 17, and the case for supporting Pound's decision laid out in Note 5 in this book's conclusion (Chapter 44).

That said, one can understand why the Russians, who were not privy to Pound's reasoning, were upset by what had occurred. It looked to them as if while they were losing thousands of men every day on the Eastern Front, the Allies were not even prepared to support them by throwing into the fray the relatively small number of sailors in their warships, who had scarpered at the first sign they might encounter serious opposition. The result as seen through Russian eyes was that the much-needed aid had been needlessly consigned to the bottom of the Barents Sea.

Previous books have described Stalin's negative reaction to what he regarded as Pound's faint-hearted decision, disapproval which is echoed in the diaries written by Ivan Maisky, the Soviet Union's London-based ambassador. From the Russian viewpoint, it was all the more unforgiveable because it was made at a time when the Allies were also refusing to reduce the strength of the German opposition in the East by opening up a second front in the West. But the available histories have not been able to pronounce on whether this view was confined to the Kremlin and Russia's embassies. Thanks to documents brought to my attention and made available by staff working in Archangel's Northern Maritime Museum, I have been able to shine a light that goes a bit deeper into the Russian mindset. These documents in Archangel's archives highlight the disgust that was expressed by other Russian leaders at the way the Allies' warship commanders had behaved.

Russian exasperation was not just fuelled by the attitudes of the admirals in charge of the Allies' warships. The documents in Archangel also include a bitter denunciation of the way the Allies' merchant navies conducted themselves following the PQ17 scatter order. Some of the merchant seamen were cowards, according to the Russians. Concerning the actions of one ship, the political head of the Soviet Union's Northern Fleet wrote: 'Does it not make you feel sick to see such reckless behaviour?' These Russian documents, combined with the relevant Enigma decrypts and the US reports relating to the same incidents which are in the principal archives in America, in Washington D.C. and Maryland, have enabled me to describe the fall out from the PQ17 disaster in a much more balanced way than has been the case in some previous publications (see Chapters 1 and 17–24).

Whatever the rights and wrongs concerning PQ17, the Allies at times had good reason to feel equally frustrated by Russian behaviour. Stalin's apparent ingratitude notwithstanding efforts made on the Russians' behalf to protect subsequent Arctic convoys was provocative to put it mildly. After learning that the Allies had lost no less than 10 merchant ships in one day thanks to raids by U-boats and the Luftwaffe during the September 1942 Arctic convoy (PQ18), and then that a relatively modest British force had heroically held off an attack by the much larger warships fielded by the German fleet during the first stages of the December 1942 Battle of the Barents Sea, Churchill was appalled when the following month Russia's ambassador Maisky, without crediting the extremely plucky actions by the Royal Navy, effectively accused him of failing to keep his word concerning future convoys. It seemed there was nothing that could be done to dissipate Russian mistrust.

Churchill's outrage has been mentioned in previous histories. What has been less well documented is what lay behind his indignant response to this slur: his knowledge that the British seamen were one hundred per cent committed to the Russian cause. No-one who has read all the available reports concerning the actions by the Royal Navy during the Battle of the Barents Sea can doubt that its response to the threat posed by the German fleet was anything but resolute. British sailors were sorely tried. Here is not the place to describe in detail the nightmarish scenes that unfolded in two of the four HMS ships hit by shells fired from the German heavy cruiser *Admiral Hipper* during the battle while their crews were attempting to protect east-going Arctic convoy JW51B. Suffice it to say that the gory aftermath of the shelling would not have been out of place aboard the flagship *Victory* after Admiral Horatio Nelson was mortally wounded during the 1805 Battle of Trafalgar. All is explained in this book's Chapter 33.

Even those readers, like me, who were read bedtime stories as a child about Nelson, leading to a lifelong belief that the courage of Britain's most celebrated admiral would never be matched, might at least concede that the destroyer *Onslow*'s Captain Robert Sherbrooke came close during this fight. His exploits, which ended with him like Nelson losing an eye, and their decisive effects are depicted in Chapter 32.

Equally stirring, although based on flimsier evidence, are the events affecting the minesweeper *Bramble*, the third ship the German gunners hit during the battle. Because *Bramble* went down with all her crew, there are no available reports by any of them that can be quoted. This, and the fact that the attack on her was not witnessed from other Allied ships, has persuaded the writers of previous histories to relegate her crew's passing to the barest of mentions, although some have speculated that the British seamen who spotted the flashes made by gunfire over the horizon, may have been observing traces of what amounted to her valiant last stand. Fortunately, *Hipper*'s captain's previously unpublished account of the initial attack on *Bramble* came to light in the course of my research, and I am pleased to be able to publish brief extracts from it, thereby drawing back the curtain a little on what transpired, something that has only been possible by taking the reader to the very edge of reported history.

Readers who notwithstanding the above are of the opinion that Churchill may have been too quick to criticize Stalin and his ambassador Maisky for taking the Allies' aid for granted, should before making a judgement about this appreciate that the British prime minister also had in mind the other travails lived through by British seamen in the course of protecting previous Arctic convoys. Whether or not his aides had filled him in on the specific experiences of those who had – and had not – survived the flooding below decks aboard the cruisers *Trinidad* and *Edinburgh* (see Chapters 5 and 10) when these ships were torpedoed in March and April 1942, or the carnage on board the destroyers *Foresight* and *Forester* when, although outgunned, their captains nevertheless faced down the German warships attacking them at the beginning of May 1942 by advancing towards them (see Chapter 11), Churchill, who had served as the First Lord of the Admiralty during World War 1 as well as at the beginning of World War 2, would almost certainly have taken into account the terrible suffering that he would have known must have been part and parcel of these engagements.

As indicated at the beginning of this introduction, the battles fought by the Allies' crews in their warships and armed freighters during the World War 2 Arctic convoys have been referred to in previous books. The classic accounts are Richard Woodman's *Arctic Convoys 1941–1945,* and the Naval Staff History *The Royal Navy And The Arctic Convoys.* Between them the authors of these works have covered all the principal actions. Both books are remarkable. They have opened up a previously neglected area of history by shining a light on actions that without their investigations and write-ups might never have been given the attention they deserved.

However, like the majority of such histories which seek to cover the myriad of actions of a campaign without exception, this has been successfully achieved at a price. The only way the authors have managed to fit every relevant event into booklets or volumes that are not too long is by judicious abridgement, in the course of which many of the most dramatic experiences have been summarized in a few paragraphs or even sentences.

Not wishing merely to repeat what has already been carried out so expertly, I have approached the subject in a different way. Following what I have done when writing my previous books about well-known subjects, I have covered all the most important events, but by leaving out other actions which have not been covered in accessible colourful accounts, I have left space for the most vivid stories that have not always been given the oxygen of detailed exposition in previous publications. My object has been to give the reader some idea of what it was like to be involved in the great events portrayed even if some of the happenings during the Battle of the Arctic have as a result regretfully been excluded. Perhaps this will persuade the relatives of those veterans who participated in the Arctic convoys, but whose more dramatic accounts have not previously been made available, to bring them to my attention, thereby making it possible for them to be quoted in subsequent editions of this book.

My desire to include in my narrative the most compelling actions has taken me in unexpected directions. I have devoted a substantial number of pages to the experiences of the merchant seamen after their ships were sunk or abandoned during Arctic convoys. For the reason given above, although this aspect of the Battle of the Arctic was covered in Richard Woodman's book, he excluded the rich tapestry of vicissitudes the survivors lived through.

This has given me the chance to honour many of the men whose valour has been relatively unknown compared with that exhibited in World War 2's better known campaigns. The gap between what had happened and what has been published was particularly wide in relation to the aftermath of the battles fought in March 1942 during Arctic convoy PQ13. The detailed personal accounts mentioning first the traumatic sinkings during that convoy, and then the terrible hardships in the lifeboats lowered from the British freighter *Induna,* were a revelation.

The search within America for diaries and letters relating to this stage of the Battle of the Arctic engagements was if anything even more rewarding. Here I was to find in the papers possessed by the families of two teenagers who were aboard the American freighter *Effingham* when she was sunk by a U-boat during PQ13, letters and diaries that had not only never been published previously, but which also could be characterized as containing a complete set of Arctic convoy experiences.

As well as the frankest confessions one is ever likely to read about ruthless behaviour in the lifeboats, one sees in these documents how the boys, who began their journeys as innocent ingénues, were within a matter of months transformed, thanks to shabby treatment by their own government as much as by the aggression of their enemy, into disappointed, world-weary veterans. As if that was not punishment enough, the documents highlight the anguish suffered by the parents of one of the boys. A heartbreaking yearning note written by the mother of one of the teenagers after learning her son had not been seen since the sinking reveals how the Arctic convoys had an effect that spread well beyond those participating in them. One's sense of outrage on her behalf is all the keener when it is revealed that her misery could have been avoided if only communications between Russia and England had been more efficient. Her son had in fact been rescued shortly before the letter of condolence was sent to her by the US Navy.

The whole unedifying story of how she and the boys were treated, together with a complete guide to the tales of torment recorded by those who survived the sinkings during PQ13, appear in Chapters 6 and 7.

The fact that American seamen feature so prominently in the stories of those who survived in the Arctic following merchant ship sinkings and abandonings is not surprising given that after the first Arctic convoys, the largest contingent of merchant ships carrying aid to the Soviet Union came from the US. Nevertheless, partly with the aim of stressing the cosmopolitan nature of the aid to Russia operations, as well as underlining that there was equivalent resilience demonstrated by seamen participating from other nations, I have also described – in Chapters 7 and 23 – the astonishing adventures of the Norwegian and Dutch seamen who endured equally long days in lifeboats.

Readers of a sensitive disposition should be warned that reaching dry land in a lifeboat that had sailed through the Arctic did not necessarily equate to deliverance. Some of the seamen either because of their age, or their clothing and footwear, were more affected by the freezing cold than others, and were afflicted by frostbite. This has led me on to describe another part of the Battle of the Arctic that has not been adequately profiled in past works: the steps that were taken to counteract the hellish conditions encountered in the Russian hospitals, especially the one in Murmansk, where many of the injured merchant seamen were confined after they reached the Russian mainland. Other authors have disclosed that the facilities were unsatisfactory, and that frostbitten limbs were amputated without general anaesthetics being administered. What has not been explained in previous books was that the conditions were so dire that Lady (Juliet) Duff, an aristocratic friend of Lady Churchill, was driven to mount a one-woman crusade back in England until urgent efforts were made to insist they should be improved (see Chapters 8 and 26).

Coupled with the shock of seeing shipmates being given such primitive medical care in Russia, the merchant seamen who reached the northern ports also had to contend with their bafflement at the unenthusiastic way they were greeted by most of the locals even though so much had been sacrificed in order to deliver the aid. This anti-westerner bias in Russia has been reported in many of the books about the Arctic convoys. Excluded from previous publications is the evidence contained in documents in the Archangel archives confirming what lay behind the hostility. It is consistent with a report in a British archive about how the NKVD operated in Archangel. Any Russian who became too friendly with a 'foreign' seaman was liable to be interrogated by the NKVD, and either press ganged into being an informer, imprisoned or exiled. The western seamen were also liable to be punished. Some of the rowdiest seamen ended up serving their time in a gulag labour camp and were only let out because

Churchill had intervened. It was in these Russian documents that I found the scathing comments about the Western seamen which I have quoted, and the evidence of the crackdown enforced by that city's authorities which was aimed at counteracting the allure of the westerners and the products they handed out to young Russian women in return for favours (see Chapters 25 and 35).

Lest anyone should be under the misapprehension when reading the aforementioned chapters that they have appreciated the full extent of the distress experienced by the merchant seamen who took aid to the Arctic, they should go on to take a look at Chapters 30 and 31 where another low-light of the supply of aid to Russia is explored. The boats from two of the aid bearing merchant ships, the British *Chulmleigh* and the Russian *Dekabrist*, which during a suspension of the convoys had been travelling to Russia independently during November 1942, ended up in deserted areas on Arctic islands. The lifeboat occupants effectively became castaways for protracted periods, living from hand to mouth in conditions that resembled those that had greeted the likes of Willem Barentsz, the eponymous sixteenth-century Dutch explorer, who in 1596–7 was himself cast away with his shipmates on Novaya Zemlya, the Arctic archipelago at the eastern end of the sea named after him. It was tantamount to a death sentence for many of the Arctic convoy castaways, who had to endure at best scurvy and at worst a close to starvation diet in unheated animal trappers' huts where they were stalked by polar bears.

The story of how *Chulmleigh*'s men survived for the best part of two months in an isolated area of Spitzbergen during the winter of 1942–3 is not a new topic. However, previous publications have been forced to rely for the most part on an official report without consulting the personal account by one of the ship's gunners, who was particularly instrumental in the group's survival. I was therefore lucky to come across the son of Richard Peyer, the gunner in question, who sent me the harrowing chronicle his father had written, thereby enabling me to be the first to include extracts of it in a publication.

It is an appropriate time to be telling not just Richard Peyer's story, but also the story of all the crews who participated in the attempt to ferry aid to Russia via the northern route during World War 2. This is partly because the last of the youngest men who took part are reaching the end of their lives, making it likely that the majority of the personal accounts they have written as well as the records of their verbal statements have been brought to my attention, being now in the public domain. While researching this book, I was for example fortunate enough to be able to talk to Lieutenant Commander John Manners DSC concerning his memories of Arctic convoy PQ18, before he died having lived to the age of 105 (see Chapter 27). As I finished the editing of this book, the oldest living person whose account is quoted in it was the 101 year old Vice Admiral Sir Thomas Baird (see Chapter 13 for his memories of the day when the cruiser *Trinidad* was sunk).

The second reason why this book is timely is because it has been written during the Russian conflict with Ukraine at a time when the latter country, on the receiving end of an invasion, has been receiving military aid from the West. Thanks to the refiguration of alliances since World War 2, that means Ukraine is in the same position relative to the West as Russia was during the years 1941–5.

That triggers interesting as well as significant comparisons between the situation during World War 2 and what is happening today. It is important to note there are major differences as well as similarities between then and now. One of the most significant differences is that because this time there is no enemy separating the Western countries from their besieged ally, there has been, at least initially, no need to fight a battle in order to deliver the aid supplied. Another difference is that unlike the situation during World War 2, it is difficult to see the prospect of aid during the 2020s enabling the victim to defeat the aggressor. If there was anything approaching a sustained counter-attack by Ukraine's Western allies, Russia could simply threaten to go nuclear, an option that was of course not open to the Germans during World War 2.

Among the similarities is the way the Soviet Union's Joseph Stalin and Ukraine's President Volodymyr Zelensky both re-framed the supply of military aid as the invasions of their countries progressed. To start with, both of them showed nothing but gratitude for the support from their Western allies. However as their fronts stabilized, there was a comparable shift in the narratives coming out of Moscow and Kyiv. Following the shift, rather than feeling they must beg for the aid, both Stalin and Zelensky reverted to stating it was the West's duty to supply it because the

Soviet Union during 1941–5, and Ukraine during 2022–5, were effectively fighting as the West's proxies.

As has already been mentioned above, this change of emphasis upset Churchill. It also frustrated Anthony Eden, the British Foreign Secretary, who at one point during World War 2 likened Stalin's ambassador Maisky to Oliver Twist, because whatever the Soviet Union was given, Maisky would always ask for more. Those who follow the news in modern times will not need reminding that similar pleas coming from Zelensky have also annoyed the Americans. During that infamous meeting at the White House in February 2025, Vice President J. D. Vance and President Donald Trump publicly accused Zelensky of ingratitude.

One of the most significant contrasts between then and now is that Churchill and Roosevelt during World War 2 knew that however ungracious Stalin was, they needed him on their side if they were to defeat Germany, which they were determined to do, without huge losses. Whereas today's American electorate have apparently, whether or not they intended it, voted in favour of trying to appease Putin by electing a president who, at least in the first instance, appeared to regard friendship with Russia as his principal aim. Trump's realization that Putin was 'playing' him, and seemed to have no interest in ending the war with Ukraine on acceptable terms, has only come to the fore shortly before this book was completed.

Prior to this latest epiphany, an unforeseen present-day gloss was being put on the supply of aid to Stalin including through the Arctic convoys. Rather than pointing out the similarity of the supply of aid to the Soviet Union during World War 2 and the modern-day supply of aid to Ukraine, Trump's focus on a reset of the American relationship with Russia resulted in him stating that the success of the World War 2 alliance with the Soviet Union (he might have added warts and all) was a good reason for him to only support Ukraine up to a point, giving him the opportunity to cosy up to Putin.

The reason this was an unanticipated way of framing the World War 2 alliance was because it turned on its head the previously unchallenged principle that the West should support the victim against the aggressor. The main reason for telling Stalin in 1941 that aid was to be provided was to stop the Soviet Union being overrun. It would be the ultimate irony if a re-telling of how that same aid came to be given were to be used today as a political tool enabling Trump to convince Americans that the US should gang up with Putin's Russia in order to humiliate Ukraine, thereby humbling a heroic Western ally who has been attacked without what most European people would regard as justification.

And it might still happen. Trump is nothing if not capricious. His belated pivot to a position of giving Ukraine committed military support may not last if Putin does eventually decide to end the shooting on terms that are unfavourable as far as Ukraine is concerned. It still remains to be seen if all that fortitude and willingness to sacrifice lives during the Battle of the Arctic, in order to prove that the West will never allow nations to benefit from their bullying, will in the long term be shown to have achieved anything.

Note for Readers

Glossary
The most frequently used words or expressions in this book which might be unfamiliar to general readers are explained in the Glossary, located after the Maps section, which follows on from the main text near the end of this book. There is a separate section in it for German words.

Abbreviations
Abbreviations and the locations of German and American sources referred to are explained in the Abbreviations section, which precedes the Notes section near the end of this book.

Maps
The main text and notes in this book have been calibrated so that those who wish to can follow the locations of the actions described by looking at the maps which have been placed after this book's main text. Notifications of which maps are relevant for particular chapters are placed at the beginning of each chapter. However please note that Map 1, which displays most of the theatre where the events in this book took place, is relevant to most of the chapters even though some of the beginning of chapter notifications do not refer to it. An explanation about both the spelling of place names used in this book, and the references to the German grid system which was used by its navy, can be found in a note at the beginning of the Maps section.

Times

Subject to the next sentence, unless a specific 'time zone' is specified for a particular message or event, the time zone applicable to the events in each chapter is Greenwich Mean Time + 2 hours (GMT + 2). However if a different time zone is specified at the beginning of a particular chapter, that time zone is applicable for the events in that chapter unless a different zone is indicated for a particular message or event.

In some cases where the extract from a document or message quoted includes details of a time zone, it is expressed by placing an 'A' after the time specified if the reference is to GMT + 1 hour, by placing a 'B' after the time specified if the reference is to GMT + 2 hours, or by placing a 'C' after the time specified if the reference is to GMT + 3 hours.

It might help readers who do not think of times with reference to GMT, to know broadly speaking that at the time of writing: the UK uses GMT during winter, and GMT + 1 hour during summer, whereas the east coast of America uses GMT − 5 hours during winter, and GMT − 4 hours during summer.

Sometimes it is hard to know whether the time mentioned on an original message refers to the time it was drafted, or the time when it was transmitted. Where this ambiguity is relevant but unresolved even after looking at other sources, I have stated that the message in question was 'timed' with the specified time.

Edited Quotations

Where in order to make it easier to understand a quotation I have inserted one or more words, I have placed these words in square brackets. Where in order to explain a quotation I have inserted one or more words, I have placed them in round brackets. I have taken the liberty of using for quotations whatever punctuation makes the words easy to understand. I have inserted three dots where words in a quotation have been omitted.

Merchant Ship Positions in Convoys

The following descriptions of how I have expressed ship positions within convoys and how I have referred to convoy columns assume I am facing the way the convoy is travelling. In accordance with the practice in most official World War 2 reports, I have expressed ship positions within convoys by specifying a string of figures which first state the column where the ship was located relative to the area of sea on the left of the whole convoy, and which then state the row of the convoy where the ship was located relative to the area of sea in front of the convoy. Thus if I specify a ship was in convoy position 15, I am saying it was in the 1st column i.e. the column on the extreme left of the convoy, row 5 i.e. the 5th row from the area of sea in front of the convoy. If I just refer to a column without also specifying the row i.e. I refer to the 2nd column, I am writing about the 2nd column from the area of sea to the left of the column on the convoy's extreme left. When reading about convoys PQ16, 17 and 18 readers might find it useful to consult these convoys' formation diagrams in the Appendices, located after the Maps section and the Glossary, near the end of this book.

Holds in Merchant Ships

I have followed the practice aboard particular merchant ships in this book of referring to the front hold as No. 1, the next towards the back as No. 2, and so on.

Lifeboats in Merchant Ships

Reports by merchant ship officers which specify which lifeboats are used often refer to the starboard lifeboat and jolly boat as 1 and 3, and the port equivalent as 2 and 4.

Gun Turrets in Warships

I have wherever appropriate followed the practice aboard particular warships mentioned in this book of naming their main armament gun turrets with reference to a letter of the alphabet, or a word beginning with one of those letters. Typically the front turret aboard a British warship in this book is referred to as 'A' and aboard a German warship it is referred to as 'Anton', with the next turret further back being 'B' aboard a British warship, and 'Bruno' aboard a German warship. Typically aboard a British warship in this book the furthest back turret is referred to as 'Y', and the next turret further towards the front is referred to as 'X'.

1

Break Up

Main Action: 4 July 1942
The big attack on Arctic convoy PQ17

(See Maps 1 and 13, and PQ17's formation diagram)[1]

At 8.21 p.m. on 4 July 1942 a distant buzzing was heard.[2] Listening intently, their hearts in their mouths, were the sailors on the bridges and decks of 33 British, American, Dutch and Soviet merchant ships that were steaming slowly north-eastward through the freezing cold waters of the Barents Sea.[3]

It was a sound they had been dreading. It was not long before they realized the distinctive noise emanated from the engines of some twenty-three German Heinkel 111 torpedo bombers that were fast approaching from the south.[4] The big air attack, that for several days had been the main topic of conversation for all the Allies' seamen in the convoy, was about to begin.

The huge lumbering freighters that were about to be attacked north-east of Bear Island (see 6A in Map 1, 5 in Map 13 and Note 5 for location) were the key elements of Arctic convoy PQ17.[5] Like the vessels in PQ17's sixteen predecessors, the convoy's merchant ships were supposed to be carrying tanks, aircraft, and an assortment of other vehicles, weapons, equipment and raw materials manufactured or made available in America and Britain, from the assembly point in Iceland to the Soviet Union.

It was part of the aid promised by Britain's Prime Minister Winston Churchill and America's President Franklin D. Roosevelt so that it could be used by Joseph Stalin's forces against their common adversary, Adolf Hitler's Nazi Germany. Only now, all of a sudden, the convoy's destination, the northern Russian port of Archangel (Arkhangelsk), still some 800 miles to the south-east, seemed a world away.

Although the merchant ships, which were lined up in nine spaced-out columns, were bristling with guns, and the convoy was ringed by British and American warships under the overall command of Britain's Royal Navy, the freighters' crews knew full well they now faced an existential threat. If they failed to come up to the mark, all that effort since they had last raised their anchors in Hvalfjord (Hvalfjörður), on the west coast of Iceland, seven days earlier, would have been for nothing.

They had already been sorely tested. For much of the period commencing on 1 July 1942, when the convoy had been sighted by the Germans for the first time, their every move had been made under the watchful eyes of the crews in German Blohm & Voss 138 spy planes.[6] These monstrous aircraft with their dipped fuselages, raised wings and uplifted snouts, which made them look like a cross between an angry insect and a predatory pterodactyl from the age of the dinosaurs, had repeatedly circled the convoy and signalled their location back to the Luftwaffe bases in occupied northern Norway, some 300 miles away.

That was enervating. But not nearly as disturbing as the recurrent thought that a devastating knockout blow might be struck by the Luftwaffe at a time of the Germans' choosing. The guns on the decks of the merchant ships and escorts, the gunfire coming from the American destroyers being particularly effective, had already batted away three tentative raids (see Note 7 for the American contribution).[7] The first, on 2 July, which was made by around six torpedo carrying seaplanes, ended with their torpedoes being dropped miles away, no scalps for the Germans and the loss of one aircraft.[8] Admittedly the second attack during the early hours of 4 July had resulted in an American merchant ship being torpedoed. But it was a one-off strike by a single plane that had just got lucky – the plane had swooped down through a gap in the clouds taking the escorts by surprise – rather than a sign that the convoy's defences were overwhelmed, leading to fears the torpedoing would be repeated.[9]

The emotions that these attacks, and a third limp raid made during the afternoon of 4 July, induced were nothing compared with the fear tinged with excitement generated when the enemy finally appeared in force, or the blind panic demonstrated by at least some of the merchant seamen as they came face to face with the realization that they might be minutes away from annihilation.[10]

Ensign Howard Carraway, a 24-year-old US Navy officer from South Carolina in charge of his ship's armed guard, was well placed to view this and more from one of his gunners' action stations in the rusty old Panamanian-flagged freighter SS *Troubadour*. She was chugging along at the back of the convoy's second column (see PQ17's formation in Appendix A).[11] Afterwards he described the moment when he first appreciated that a large group of aircraft were advancing towards them in the following terms:

'I was relieving half the gun crew . . . when the Carpenter, using a pair of glasses, called to me to look to the south: (he said) there was a plane headed straight in. I looked, and saw three. Big, black, fast, the noise of their . . . motors already audible. They were coming in on our starboard quarter.

' "Man your guns!" I yelled, and scampered for the bridge. Once there, I glanced over [to] the horizon with my glasses, and saw not three, nor six, but twelve of them . . .

'I turned to look at the Commodore's ship, ironically named the *River Afton* (after the peaceful Scottish stream in the famous Robert Burns poem "Afton Water", as Carraway, who had studied English literature at university, had understood) and saw the dreaded JG signal hoisted. It was late, but it told us we were doing the proper thing. It . . . [was] code for "Prepare for instant action".

'I . . . told [the gunners] . . . to hold fire until they were in close, then to give 'im hell . . .'[12]

Hauptmann Bernd Eicke, commander of the 23 Heinkel 111 torpedo bombers from the 1st wing of Kampfgeschwader (KG) 26 which had all of a sudden appeared over the horizon, has also commented on his thoughts and fears at this pivotal moment. The German pilots had good reason to be anxious. They had been flying perilously close to the water in order to avoid detection, and they would have to continue on their low flight paths if the launching of their torpedoes was to be effective. The following extract from Hauptmann Eicke's report highlights how this spelt danger for attacker and those targeted alike:

'After the southernmost escort ship broadcast the alarm, I noticed what was lying straight ahead of us: the superstructures of an enormous convoy. A mass of funnels and hulls rose up out of the haze.

'I gave the order to attack when we were around 10 kilometres away. The two waves flying behind me came up to the left and right of my wave. This created an open quarter circle, allowing us to make a kind of pincer attack.

'[But] while still a long way from the target, we were greeted with murderous defensive gunfire. We had not only to contend with the ships' flak; there were also huge pillars of water rising up from the sea towards us, created by the shells fired at us by the British . . . [warships]. Some were so close, one felt one could just reach out to touch them.'[13]

That did not deter Leutnant Konrad Hennemann, the 22-year-old pilot of the first Heinkel to reach the merchant ships. After approaching PQ17 from the rear, he courageously flew up between the ships constituting the convoy's 4th and 5th columns, whose masters like all the freighter captains had been instructed to stay some 600 yards away from the ships in the next columns. Then when just 200 yards from the starboard side of SS *Navarino*, the British merchant ship in the second row of the 4th column, his aircraft's two torpedoes were released. This amounted to point blank range for such a well-trained crew.[14]

'As the aircraft approached, I put the helm hard over to port in an effort to upset his attack,' *Navarino*'s Captain Archibald Kelso reported afterwards. 'As I was doing so, someone shouted 'Torpedo!'' I ran out and saw a torpedo approaching the ship 45 degrees abaft my beam. I was hoping that as the ship was swinging . . . the torpedo . . . might miss . . . but unfortunately she was not quick enough . . . and the torpedo . . . struck the ship amidships under the bridge.'[15]

There was an explosion that threw up a fountain of water, and the ship 'immediately took a list of 30 to 40 degrees [to port] so that the bilge keel came right out of the water on the starboard side,' Kelso concluded. However according to Carraway, while observing this act of German heroism: 'a yell [of jubilation] went up. A red glow was seen growing ever larger in [Hennemann's] . . . forward hull. A trail of black smoke slid from it . . . He dove straight into the water [in front of the convoy], tracers from the forward ships' guns still pouring into his flaming carcass.'[16]

In the words of radio operator Robert Henderson, who was stationed in the American merchant ship SS *Washington* at the front of the convoy's second column and observed the climactic end to Hennemann's suicide mission at close quarters: the plane flew across the convoy 'at an altitude of about seventy-five feet', and after dropping its torpedoes, it 'continued across our bow and was a blazing torch when it hit the water.'[17]

The downing of the German plane elicited contrasting responses. Captain Willem Sissingh, the 48-year-old master of the SS *Paulus Potter*, the Dutch ship at the front of the convoy's left column, was prompted by his crew's reaction to this event to write in his after the action report: 'War transforms every man into an animal . . . On the ship there was enthusiastic applause even as the men in the plane were burning alive.'[18]

But that was afterwards. As the crews in the merchant ships were helping their gunners to reload their guns, there was no time for such fastidiousness. Carraway was so buoyed up by this early victory, the fact that three of the planes approaching his ship from behind the convoy had turned tail, and by the powerful booming sound made by the guns attached to two Russia-bound tanks on *Troubadour*'s deck which his gunners had commandeered, that he could not resist playing an active part in the defence of his ship. He fired his own relatively puny machine gun at another aircraft, ignoring for a moment the rabble that were effectively running amok all around him. He later reported how:

'. . . all the crew, except a few of the faithful black gang slaving in the heat below, were running around the deck, yelling and screaming in all their forty tongues, looking like demons, as will men . . . [with] addled brains, . . . in their bundled arctic clothing, clumsy life jackets, [and] silly [anti-]shrapnel helmets.'[19]

So preoccupied was he with the fast-moving plane in his sights that he was not even diverted from his shooting by what he referred to as another 'loud tearing explosion' which he later identified as the noise made by the torpedoing of the SS *William Hooper*, an American Liberty ship, at the back of the convoy's first column, a few hundred yards away from his ship's port side. 'The torpedoes had hit her near the stern on the starboard side', he reported. 'The whole after end of the ship was blown to hell. Some of her explosive cargo must have been hit.'

His report continues: '[But] then my knees buckled, my heart crowded my tonsils, my blood turned to water, and fear gripped me. Headed straight for our side was . . . [another] torpedo . . . What chilled me so was the . . . [anticipated] point of contact, directly below me under the bridge to starboard. I . . . screamed . . .: "Torpedo on the starboard beam!", hopped from the pill box and headed for the after tank . . . where two men were trapped if the torpedo went off. And it must go off!

'I stuck my head into the wheel house and yelled "Hard a-port!" in an effort to turn the ship's head away from the torpedo's track. But I couldn't stay to follow it up, for the two men aft in the tank were on my mind. I was scared stiff, but I ran, faster I think in all the heavy clothing and boots than I had ever run on a . . . track, (a judgement which really meant something, coming as it did from Carraway, a keen runner and before the war the sports editor on the local newspaper in his home town in South Carolina). On reaching the tank, I yelled to the boys there . . . to "get out, torpedo!" They didn't hear me, and I started to climb the tank, but looked and saw the torpedo a scant fathom (two yards) from the ship's hull. I dropped to my knees, grasped a nearby hatch cover and held on waiting for the explosion.

'Kneeling thus, as if in prayer, for a few seconds, and hearing nothing, the unbelievable dawned on me. By some miracle, the thing had either missed the ship, or had failed to go off.

'I leapt to my feet and scrambled back forward to my gun. When I got to the bridge deck, I saw the crew watching the port side blabbering crazily . . . The torpedo was now on the port side, travelling in an arc towards the ship's side somewhere astern. A Portuguese and [a] Spaniard were standing at the rail, stark terror on their faces, waving the torpedo away, repeating some phrase in their native tongues that could only mean "Go away!" It was pitiful, their terror, but the sincerity of their pleas was touching – and [in retrospect at least] funny.

'When I saw what was happening, I felt a swell of pride. Bill Lawson, a big blond kid from Virginia . . . was keeping the torpedo away from the ship by the simple method of firing burst after burst of machine gun fire just ahead of it as it turned towards the ship, deflecting it away.

'Up atop the bridge, the Captain was helping by yelling orders to his helmsman, manoeuvring the ship away from the deadly little iron fish. Both of them were cool, collected, logical. The only two such on the ship.' This was praise indeed, given that in his diary before setting off from Iceland, Carraway had written off *Troubadour's* 34-year-old master George Salvesen as a dull 'squarehead', a man who 'is 100% Norwegian . . . and is scornful of America and Americans, as well as any other nationality except Norwegians.' But Carraway would not be the first to revise his first impressions of a fellow human being in a life and death situation. That was certainly how Carraway regarded it, as is made clear by the next words in his account.

'I was desperate . . . This was one of those torpedoes designed to travel in a 100 yard circle and it must be avoided. Back on the bridge I manned my gun and waited. In a few moments I saw the track cross our stern and head for me again. I sighted my gun on it and let fly . . . at its nose, hoping to set it off, or sink it before it could reach us again. Before the pan was fired out, I saw her nose turn up and vanish. She was sunk. The *Troubadour* was saved. It was hard to believe, but there it was.'

Carraway's was far from the only account by men in the Allies' merchant ships which described their witnessing a near miss.[20] Nor were the escorts immune. HMS *Keppel's* Commander Jack Broome reported how his destroyer 'under full helm, avoided a torpedo by inches.'[21] But perhaps the most remarkable survival story on the side of the Allies that day occurred after a torpedo was fired at the starboard side of the Soviet tanker *Azerbaijan*, the 4th vessel in the convoy's 6th column. In the words of her captain, Vladimir Nikolaevich Izotov, as the missile hit, 'our ship shuddered violently, a loud explosion was heard, and the whole stern of the ship . . . was hidden behind a mass of [linseed] oil and diesel fuel thrown upwards into a huge column that was higher than the mast and which was blazing at the top. The ship abruptly veered to the left, and then leant over to her right.'[22]

Yet rather than panicking and immediately ordering his men to abandon ship, which might well have been the reaction of the majority of masters in the convoy had they seen such a terrifying sight from the bridges of their ships, Izotov coolly waited to see whether the situation really was irrecoverable. He was rewarded for his bravery when within minutes, the column of oil and scalding steam subsided. Then he set about issuing the orders that would enable the vessel to continue on her journey.

One group of men was ordered to move the content of one of

Azerbaijan's starboard holds to the port side in order to counteract the list. The engineer repaired one of the engines that had been damaged by the explosion, and the men who had fallen into the sea when their life-boat had been lowered prematurely and clumsily, were picked up. At around 8.45 p.m., about half an hour after sustaining what at first appeared to be catastrophic damage, Izotov was in a position to order his engineers to go full steam ahead so that they could start the long haul that was designed to see them catch up with the convoy.

Some of the German Heinkel crews survived in spite of living through equally dangerous circumstances. Eicke, whose plane had reached the back of the convoy, had been so impressed by the clouds of steam and smoke, and the huge fireball, issuing forth out of *William Hooper* as he had pulled his plane up to avoid the ship's mast that he temporarily dropped his guard. Seconds later he had been brought back to his senses when his radio operator reported that some of the smoke he could see was being made by his own plane. Thick white smoke was billowing out of his right engine which was on fire. 'I glanced at the instruments,' Eicke reported later. 'The oil pressure was dropping. The temperature was rising.'

There was nothing for it but to break off the attack immediately. He eventually switched off the burning motor, and he and his crew only made it back to the base at Bardufoss after dropping out of the plane the ammunition drum, and even its armour-plated panels to lighten the plane's load.[23]

Given the intensity of the defensive fire emanating out of the Allies' ships' guns, it was not surprising that some of the other German pilots also came to grief. The 32-year-old Roger Hill, the lieutenant commander in charge of the British destroyer HMS *Ledbury*, which formed part of the protection force on the convoy's starboard side, later wrote: 'Up to this time of the war, I had never seen such a barrage put up against an air attack. The whole sky round the convoy was a mass of bursting shells, with the black bursts remaining in the sky. Tracers were going in all directions, and the sea [was] boiling with the falling shrapnel. The noise of the gunfire was continuous, and in the centre [of the convoy there was a] . . . great pall of black smoke, slowly rising where a ship loaded with arms and ammunition had been hit.'[24]

The confusion – and cruelty – of war was highlighted by the following extract from the report by the 32-year-old actor Douglas Fairbanks Junior, who in his capacity as aide to the commander of USS *Wichita*, one of four cruisers in the 1st Cruiser Squadron that was shadowing the convoy, was looking on from five miles away: 'A plane is falling in flames. It crashes. Great blinding flash of fire hundreds of feet high, then black smoke. Big cheer from *Wichita*. Like being in the bleachers at a ball game: "Go get the bastards!" Now we hear the explosion and the sickening whoosh of the fire. Looks like a ship is hit badly. Fat smoke curling upwards. Yes, it is a ship. Now another plane dives in flames: another Nazi bites the dust.'[25]

No-one has better described what it was like to be on the receiving end of all this shelling and flak when flying at just 20 to 25 metres above the sea than the 27-year-old Leutnant Georg Kanmayer. In his account he related what occurred when he recklessly flew his plane too close to the American destroyer USS *Wainwright* which was located on the convoy's starboard bow between 3,000 and 4,000 yards away from the nearest merchant ship: '[As soon as] I came within the range of the destroyer *Wainwright*, I was surrounded by pillars of water. My aircraft swayed as if drunk because of the shells exploding near me, [and] my radio stopped working after being hit.

'When I was close enough, I dropped one of my torpedoes [and] I can still recall how at that point someone in the plane remarked that we were doing OK. It was at that precise moment that I heard a terrible noise, and for a few seconds I was unable to see anything except splinters and dirt.

'When I could see again, I noticed that my aircraft was flying straight at the destroyer. The plane's left engine and the hydraulic oil that had leaked into the cockpit were on fire, and my body was also being burned by the flames. All the windows and instruments in the aircraft had been shattered.

'Our mechanic . . . came to my aid. I indicated with my head that I was still conscious. On seeing this, he ran to the back of the plane to fetch the fire extinguisher which I used to put out the flames on me. I realized at that point the index finger on my left hand was in a terrible state, and was only connected to my hand by a piece of skin.

'While I pulled the plane up to the right in a steep curve, my observer shot at the destroyer with the 2 cm cannon, and it was then that the aircraft was hit in its oil tank.

'In the meantime my mechanic had dropped the second torpedo as an emergency measure, but I could not extinguish the fire as the air rushing into the plane directed the flames into the middle of the plane . . .'

In the end Kanmayer decided there was no option but to turn off his left engine and endeavour to crash land his plane in the sea. This he managed to do after bouncing a few times, no mean feat given that when he hit the water, he was still travelling at around 125 miles per hour.

The impact of the landing threw him out of his seat, and left him nursing a broken left hand to add to the injury to his finger. But the action ended well for him, and the other three men in his crew, because after they had climbed out of the wrecked Heinkel into its floating rubber dinghy, they were approached by *Ledbury* and rescued by her crew. The British destroyer's Lieutenant Commander Hill was so impressed by the German pilot's bravery that he refused to comply with the normal rule that forbids the making of any detour to rescue a fallen enemy in U-boat infested waters lest such an act jeopardize the safety of the warship's crew. Also, like one of those merciful jousting knights one reads about from ancient times, he nobly felt it behoved him to save the four Germans because notwithstanding *Keppel*'s Commander Broome's subsequent statement that the American destroyer had been responsible, Hill believed it was *Ledbury*'s guns, rather than *Wainwright*'s, which had shot down Kanmayer's plane.[26]

Kanmayer's aircraft was one of four Heinkels that failed to make it back to Bardufoss after the attack. Equally significant was that of those that did return, there were hardly any that were not damaged.[27] This reduced the likelihood that the mass attack could be repeated. What must have been particularly galling for the German commanders was the realization that they had been masters of their own misfortune. Their faulty tactics had lessened their chances of success: the firepower focusing on the Heinkel torpedo bombers could have been reduced if the other Luftwaffe unit sent to attack the convoy had been able to deploy at the same time as Eicke's group rather than arriving on the scene earlier.[28] That is not to denigrate what the armed guards and gunners in the Allies' ships had achieved, for the men protecting PQ17's merchant ships had shown how difficult it was to decimate a well-disciplined convoy from the air.

That lesson made what happened next, while the convoy was still heading in a north-easterly direction towards the relative security provided by the ice edge, so difficult to comprehend (see 6B in Map 1, 6 in

26

Map 13 and Note 29 for the location, to the south-east of Hope Island).[29] Some minor details in the following account by *Ledbury's* Roger Hill have been justly challenged (see Note 30), but no-one disputes the fundamental thrust of what he said took place shortly before 10.30 p.m. that night, less than two hours after the last aircraft had flown away to the south-west: 'The Commodore hoisted a string of flags. The Yeoman knelt down, and using his big telescope, called out the letters for someone to write down. Then he looked them up in the code book, and said to me: "The Commodore's Chief Yeoman has made a proper balls-up this time; the signal means: Convoy is to scatter."

' "Put the answering pendant at the dip," I replied (which means: your signal not understood, and makes the originator check it). I saw that the destroyer near me had also got the answering pendant at the dip.

'The Commodore's ship lowered the flags, and then hoisted the same ones again ... At the same time [Commander] Jackie Broome in [the destroyer HMS] *Keppel,* came up on the radio telephone: "To all destroyers: Strike!, repeat Strike!" '[30] That was the pre-arranged code, which when circulated without a time of origin, warned all destroyers to get ready to receive the order to join *Keppel* immediately.[31]

' "Christ!" I thought, "Here we go. Surface attack by the *Tirpitz* (the German battleship)." And I searched the horizon with my glasses.'[32]

Shortly afterwards, prompted by Broome, Hill issued the order to go full steam ahead to join *Keppel*.[33] Within minutes, *Keppel* followed by the five other destroyers under Broome's command, was pulling out ahead of the convoy so that they could all head off to the south-west together, the direction from which their crews expected *Tirpitz* would appear. But before they made their final move, Broome ordered his chief yeoman to use his most powerful signal searchlight to send a message to Rear Admiral Louis Hamilton, commander of the cruiser force, which was now clearly visible a few miles to the north-east, and which was surging southwards too.[34] Hamilton approved Broome's proposal that the six destroyers should link up with Hamilton's Cruiser Squadron One.[35] Then off they went together towards Norway, with lookouts on every ship scouring the horizon with binoculars for signs of the fearsome German battlegroup which at least some expected to spot on the horizon at any minute.[36]

It seems likely that many of the sailors in the Allies' two converging forces believed at the time that what they were doing was not only right, but that it was heroic. However even then, there were some in the Allies' warships who reviled what they were witnessing. 'We hate leaving PQ17,' Douglas Fairbanks wrote in his diary. 'It looks so helpless . . . The ships are going round in circles, turning this way and that like so many frightened chicks . . . Is the German Fleet out? If so, what of it? That's what we came up for, isn't it?' Later, once he had realized that they were not going to meet up with *Tirpitz* after all, his diary struck an even glummer chord: 'The wind is out of our sails. We try and tell ourselves that there must have been good reasons for us to have avoided further action . . . [But] the men feel ashamed and resentful.'[37]

Fairbanks' gloss represented the charitable interpretation. Howard Carraway in SS *Troubadour* evidently felt he and his men had been betrayed: 'Brought into the middle of the fire and [only] then told there was no water,' was the caustic complaint he scribbled in his diary.[38]

But it was not just the abandonment that was causing upset. Some of the men in the ships left behind, who had seen how aircraft and U-boats had been stalking the convoy ever since it was first sighted, were terrified they were being cut loose and left to die. 'We're better off as we are,' wailed Sidney Kerslake, the 22-year-old coxswain on the armed trawler *Northern Gem* when he heard the new orders. 'On our own we have no chance at all.' His youth and the thought of missing virtually all his adult life made the prospect of death particularly horrific. He later admitted that he had only controlled his emotions because he felt it was expected of him on account of his responsible position.

However, even he lost it when another young member of the crew kept repeating over and again: 'We'll never make it', or words to that effect. 'I literally had to shake him by the shoulders to get him to stop saying what most of us were thinking,' wrote Kerslake. The young coxswain only adopted a more fatalistic attitude when it dawned on him that he was possibly becoming downcast for no good reason. 'I thought: "We are a small ship on a very large ocean, and with a bit of luck, we should take some finding."'[39]

No such sense of proportion was in evidence in the Soviet Union's take on the action up to this point, once it became known. In an excoriating critique of their allies' conduct, the following passages appeared in a letter that the head of the political department of the Soviet Union's Northern Sea Fleet wrote to his country's Political Department Commissar:

'At the captains' conference [in Iceland just before PQ17 set out], the English bragged that the convoy was to be protected by a strengthened escort, and that there was therefore no need to be afraid of any attacks from the air . . . In theory with this strength, it was possible to repel a large attack . . . However something strange occurred. As soon as the planes arrived, the military vessels immediately turned around and steamed off in the opposite direction, "heroically" abandoning the merchant ships . . . In this way the British "warriors" saved their own skins . . . As the convoy was being dispersed, they said [to those they were supposed to be protecting] "Save yourselves if you can." '[40]

So what was this strange event to which the Northern Sea Fleet's political department chief alluded? Was it that Britain, an island nation famed for her navy, had allowed her fleet to become so antiquated, that even when reinforced by American warships, it was no match for *Tirpitz*, Germany's gigantic new battleship? Or was it that the British admirals, aided and abetted by their American partners, were at best refusing to take risks to aid another country, or, at worst, were running scared? Or was there something else going on behind the scenes, which was so secret that no-one was saying anything about it?

2

To Russia with Love

Main Action: 21–31 August 1941
Operation Dervish: the first Arctic convoy

(See Map 1)

The first of the convoys carrying supplies to north Russia following Germany's 22 June 1941 invasion of the Soviet Union (the German Operation Barbarossa) could not have been more different from PQ17. It was a relatively small, low-key affair. Codenamed Operation Dervish, one Dutch and five British merchant ships plus a fleet oiler left Hvalfjord (Whale fiord), north of Reykjavik, on the west coast of Iceland on 21 August 1941, and accompanied by a close escort of three destroyers, three minesweepers and three trawlers reached Archangel ten days later.[1]

It was also watched over during part of its journey by an aircraft carrier and two cruisers screened by three destroyers, but their presence turned out to be unnecessary.[2] The convoy was not opposed by any of the German surface ships which would eventually be based in occupied Norway whose presence there would later make the passage to northern Russia such an ordeal.

It can even be said that the journey, later dubbed the worst in the world, was for some a positively pleasurable experience. This was particularly the case for the men and women travelling in the passenger/cargo liner *Llanstephan Castle*. She doubled up as the convoy's commodore ship, as well as being the troopship for around five hundred personnel from the RAF's 151 Wing. They were going to Russia so that they could teach the Russians how to erect, fly and maintain Hurricane aircraft which were being given to the Soviet Union.[3] *Llanstephan Castle* was also carrying the likes of the Polish Legation staff and their wives who were on their way to Moscow. Most of these passengers were relaxed enough to make the most of the ship's facilities which were up to the standard one might have expected to find in a luxury liner in peacetime.

Because the liner's previous voyage had been to South Africa, where she had been re-victualled, the half a dozen dishes on the menu for breakfast included items such as butter and jam, eggs, and grapefruit which had not been readily available in England for more than a year.

The passengers also included a journalist, and the well-known Polish artist Feliks Topolski, who according to one account went 'skipping about the ship like a cheerful gnome and never ceasing drawing.'[4] The other passengers played deck games, watched boxing and concerts, and attended a series of lectures about Russia's history and culture, past and present. They were also able to observe some of the natural Arctic phenomena which, unbeknown to them, would play a significant role in the fighting that was to come.

In his account of the journey, Flight Lieutenant Hubert Griffith, 151 Wing's adjutant, mentions that he and the other passengers saw what he referred to as a school of whales 'spouting'. He does not appear to have registered that the presence of such creatures would one day pose a threat to exhausted Arctic convoy escort commanders who would have to make split-second decisions on whether their asdic (sonar) equipment had detected a mammal or a U-boat.

Similar comments could be made concerning Griffith's observations about the sun. He wrote: 'The sun hardly set at all: walking around the boat deck at midnight, the rim of the sun was seen to have set just below the horizon, and half an hour later, it was on the point of rising.' Little thought appears to have been given to the danger this never-ending daylight would represent for those sailing merchantmen and escorts alike as they attempted to travel along this same route in Arctic convoys during subsequent summers.[5]

Morris Mills, a 16-year-old deck officer trainee, who was making his first ever trip in the merchant ship SS *New Westminster City*, would never forget what impressed him most of all. In the account of his wartime experiences he wrote: 'The voyage was quite pleasant with sunny days and a moderate sea. Nearing the Arctic ice fields [however], the temperature . . . plunge[d] at night time, as I found to my cost. There was a magnificent display of Aurora Borealis, and Captain Harris decided to give us a lecture [about it]. We were mustered on the afterdeck and [I] foolishly turned out with only a seaman's jersey. Within minutes I was chilled to the bone.'

Apparently the discomfort was worth it. 'The Northern Lights were spectacular,' Mills' account continues, 'shafting the Arctic skies with a dazzling array of . . . rainbow colours, flashing and darting through the heavens, reflecting on the seas like sparkling jewels. Dull grey ships would momentarily be transformed into glittering gems, as the myriad splendour darted over their fat, ugly forms.'[6]

While engaged in such ecstatic contemplation, it was probably hard to appreciate that when summer changed to winter, these same lights could make all the difference between life and death if you were being hunted by a ship or U-boat on a moonless night.

There was likewise no opposition to the other supply operation unleashed while Dervish was drawing to an end. Another aircraft carrier left Scapa Flow (the Royal Naval base in the Orkneys) on 30 August 1941, and then steamed, supported initially by a cruiser and three destroyers, part of the way towards north Russia. When they and their reinforcements had shaken off the German aircraft in the fog in the vicinity of Hope Island (south-east of Spitzbergen), the two dozen Hurricane fighter aircraft, operated by the part of the RAF's 151 Wing on board the carrier, were on 7 September flown off and landed on the airfield near Vaenga (now known as Severomorsk), a base in north Russia's Kola Inlet, near Murmansk.[7]

The aircraft, along with 24 crated Hurricanes carried by the Dervish vessels, at first flown by their British pilots, and subsequently by the Russians they trained, were to protect the north Russian jetties, harbours and bays which would eventually act as reception centres for the aid being transported in the course of subsequent convoy operations.[8] Although the first Arctic convoys delivered their supplies to Archangel and its satellite ports, once the coming winter froze the waters leading up to them, Murmansk in the Kola Inlet would become the drop-off point until the thaw the following year. The Dervish minesweepers were to form another part of the convoy set up. They, or their replacements, were to remain in north Russia, and would be used to protect the waters near the bases, and to assist further out to sea if convoys needed to be helped, for example if they were attacked.

The delivery of the Dervish convoy aid and the supporting aircraft was only a beginning, but it was a symbol of Britain's, and her allies', intent. It represented one of the first major attempts to bring succour to the besieged Soviet Union, although much pro-Russia activity on the political and diplomatic fronts and a couple of abortive attempts to attack German shipping near the Norwegian and Finnish coasts had preceded it.

It had not taken long for Britain to declare how it would react to the German gambit. Starting at 9 p.m. on the night of the invasion, Winston Churchill, Britain's 66-year-old prime minister, had broadcast on the BBC a pro-Soviet Union speech that had enraptured Ivan Maisky, Russia's 57-year-old ambassador in London.[9] Although it included the words: 'No-one has been a more consistent opponent of Communism than I have for the last twenty-five years', it also included the declaration 'that we shall give whatever help we can to Russia and the Russian people'.[10]

It was doubly important because the first reaction by the 59-year-old Franklin D. Roosevelt to the invasion was relatively muted: the American president, no doubt fearing a backlash from the public as well as isolationist politicians if he made a rousing speech to match Churchill's, decided to make do by commenting on 24 June 1941, in response to a question posed at a White House press conference: 'We are going to give all the aid that we can to Russia.'[11]

Churchill's speech was to be backed up by a written declaration of intent. On 7 July 1941, in his first telegram to Joseph Stalin, the Soviet Union's 62-year-old leader, after the start of the invasion, Britain's prime minister had written: 'We shall do everything to help you that time, geography and our growing resources allow.'[12] He had also agreed to the signing of the 12 July 1941 'Agreement for Joint Action' stating that Britain and the Soviet Union would help each other in the war against Germany, and neither would unilaterally make peace.

But these were just words, and they were not very encouraging words when read alongside Churchill's 20 July 1941 telegram rejecting Stalin's suggestion sent two days earlier that Britain should seek to divert German forces from the East by invading northern France. In the same telegram,

Churchill warned Stalin he should 'realize the limitations imposed upon us by our resources and geographical position'.[13] The fact that five days later Churchill wrote to Stalin to say that the War Cabinet had agreed, as a one-off, to send the Soviet Union as soon as possible 200 American Tomahawk fighter aircraft only served to highlight the failure by the Western allies to set up a regular supply of arms and equipment on which Stalin's forces could rely.[14]

Given that by 16 July 1941 the German Army, apparently unstoppable, had already captured the city of Smolensk, just 230 miles from Moscow, it is possible that nothing along these lines would have been arranged by Britain and America in time to make a difference, had it not been for the dramatic intervention of Harry Hopkins, Roosevelt's 50-year-old personal envoy to London. Hopkins feared that Stalin might be tempted to make terms with Hitler unless he was convinced that his putative partners would give meaningful ongoing material support. Hopkins also believed that nothing relating to the Soviet Union would be agreed at the meeting between Roosevelt and Churchill that had been scheduled for the following month unless Stalin first answered some direct questions about the Soviet Union's chances of successfully resisting the invasion.

With that in mind, on 25 July 1941 Hopkins, who was staying with Churchill at Chequers, the British prime minister's country retreat in Buckinghamshire, sent an urgent telegram to the President. Hopkins proposed that he should fly out to see Stalin at once, adding persuasively: 'I think the stakes are so great that it should be done. Stalin would then know in an unmistakeable way that we mean business on a long term supply job.'[15]

It also made sense from an American point of view. It would have been foolhardy to send out arms and other supplies to the Soviet Union if it was about to be overrun. This was very much on the cards according to many officials both in Washington and London.[16]

Roosevelt quickly gave Hopkins the green light, and Churchill wrote to Stalin that Hopkins was on his way.[17]

However, a hastily arranged trip over such a great distance, part of it passing within striking distance of the enemy, was challenging to say the least. The Soviet Union's Ambassador Maisky has described how on Sunday 27 July, he received an urgent summons to meet up with John Gilbert (Gil) Winant, the American ambassador in London. They met at the Soviet

Union's embassy. There Maisky was told that Hopkins and two colleagues needed visas stamped in their passports immediately. Hopkins was already on the way to Euston station with his companions so that they would be in time to catch a flight from Invergordon, Scotland to Archangel.

Maisky did not have the necessary visa stamps, which were kept in the consulate, so instead he improvised, and wrote a message in the passports authorizing Hopkins and his team to pass any Soviet frontier without examination of luggage as diplomatic persons. The passports were then rushed to the station and thrust into Hopkins' hands just as the train began to move.[18]

The journey to Scotland was just the first stage of their journey. It was followed by a gruelling 24-hour flight in a Catalina flying boat which had to pass within a hundred miles of occupied Norway. It was a risky venture. Even if not intercepted by the Luftwaffe, there was no guarantee that the sickly Hopkins would arrive in a fit state to talk to anyone, let alone the Soviet Union's premier. Partly as a result of having survived stomach cancer, Hopkins was emaciated, and in normal circumstances would have been judged to be in no fit state to undertake such an arduous flight.

He was freezing cold for much of the journey and when he became too exhausted to sit beside the machine gun near the back of the plane usually operated by the observer, he lay shivering on a stretcher laid out on the aircraft's floor. Not surprisingly he was a wreck by the time the plane touched down in the Soviet Union. But after flying on to Moscow, he summoned up the strength to meet Stalin.[19]

They met for the first time on 30 July 1941, and then again the following day. The Soviet leader evidently captivated him. Hopkins would later describe Stalin as 'an austere, rugged determined figure in boots that shone like mirrors, stout baggy trousers and snug-fitting blouse. He has no ornament, military or civilian. He's built close to the ground . . . He's about five feet six, about a hundred and ninety pounds (13 stone 8 pounds) . . . There is no small talk in him . . . He speaks no English but as he shot rapid Russian at me, he ignored the interpreter, looking straight into my eyes as though I understood every word that he uttered . . . If he wants to soften an abrupt answer . . . he does it with that quick, managed smile that can be cold but friendly'.[20]

Whatever the truth behind this apparently hagiographic pen portrait, or Stalin's concluding throwaway comment: 'Give us anti-aircraft guns and the aluminium (to be used for constructing tanks and aircraft), and we can fight for three or four years', Hopkins in his subsequent report, written after the long journey back to Scapa Flow, warned Roosevelt: 'No information given [by Stalin] . . . was confirmed by any other source.'[21]

Such confirmation appeared to be neither here nor there as far as Hopkins was concerned, who was prepared to give Stalin's word about the numbers and staying power of his forces and equipment the benefit of the doubt. He wrapped up his report to the President with Stalin's overriding message: 'He asked me to tell the President that, while he was confident that the Russian Army could withstand the German Army, the problem of supply by next spring would be a serious one and that he needed our help.'[22]

Hopkins arrived back just in time to join Churchill in the battleship *Prince of Wales*, which on 4 August set out for Placentia Bay, Newfoundland, where the meetings between the British prime minister and Roosevelt were to take place.[23]

It was in the course of these meetings that the two leaders not only accepted the wording of what became known as the Atlantic Declaration, a statement of general principles regulating their conduct in the war, and decided that America would take over the escorting of Atlantic convoys between America and Iceland, but they also agreed in principle that Britain and America really should support the Soviet Union.[24]

Convinced by Hopkins' report that the Soviet Union was not a lost cause, a joint telegram was sent to Stalin on 14 August 1941 confirming their wish to sign up to a long-term commitment to give him the supplies that he craved. It was proposed the details should be hammered out in a conference to be convened in Moscow.[25]

Stalin wrote back to confirm that he would be happy to host the conference. But as days passed without any concrete action having been taken on the Western allies' side to firm up the conference dates, it became clear that a protest was in order.

It was in these circumstances that Maisky, alarmed by the complacency that still held sway in Britain, evidenced by the crowds of British workers who he had seen setting out for a day at the beach during the 2 August 1941 bank holiday, and the dearth of instructions from Moscow, decided he must take matters into his own hands.

During his meeting on 26 August 1941 with Eden, he gathered that while there was no chance of Britain complying with the Soviet Union's request to open up a second front in the near future, it was still sensible to carry on requesting it since the British foreign secretary was evidently so embarrassed by not being able to take the requested action that he was all the keener to be seen to offer assistance by way of supplying weapons. He realized that was all the more the case if Churchill and Eden were led to believe that if the Soviet Union did not get such support, they might become demoralized and enter into peace negotiations with Germany.

Maisky passed on these impressions to Moscow. This was the catalyst for what happened next. Stalin, egged on by Maisky, wrote on 3 September to Churchill and told him that since Hopkins' visit 'the position of the Soviet troops has deteriorated . . . We have lost the greater part of the Ukraine, and the enemy is now at the gates of Leningrad'. The 'unpleasant consequences' listed by the Soviet leader included the loss of aluminium works and motor and aircraft factories which he said 'weakened our power of defence capacity and placed the Soviet Union in a position of mortal peril'.

He went on to say that the position could only be remedied if the Western allies opened up a: 'second front . . . in the Balkans or France which would be able to divert from the Eastern Front some 30 to 40 German divisions', and if the Soviet Union was given '30,000 tons of aluminium at the beginning of October, and a minimum monthly delivery of some 400 aircraft and 500 tanks . . . Without these two forms of help the Soviet Union may either be defeated or weakened to such an extent that for a long period, it may not be in a position to help its allies by active operations'.[26]

This telegram was to have electrifying results. Although nothing would have induced Churchill to order the operations mentioned by Stalin while his chiefs of staff were saying they were not viable, which was the case at the beginning of September 1941, the British prime minister's suspicion that the Russians might be thinking about throwing in the towel helped to persuade him that he had to come up with a positive response. This was in spite of his initially telling Maisky, in the course of a passionate debate when they met on 4 September, that it would be impossible to supply what was being demanded. Churchill's negative attitude was in part fuelled by resentment. 'Don't forget that only four months ago we stood alone against Germany, and didn't know whose side you were on,' was the substance of what the British prime minister blurted out. But it was also prompted by the realization that Britain had to keep back a sufficient supply of weapons for her own forces (see Chapter 44 for how British forces lost out through arms being demanded by and supplied to the Soviet Union). Stalin was in effect asking for every single tank that Britain was manufacturing, Churchill told the Soviet ambassador.[27]

In Churchill's 5 September reply, he stated that Britain could manage to send half of the tanks and aircraft requested without expecting any payment, and he hoped America would provide the other half. He also promised to ask Roosevelt to expedite the arrival in London of the American representatives so that the conference in Moscow could be rapidly convened.[28]

Roosevelt was more than happy to comply with this request once he heard talk of the Russians giving in. And so it was that during the evening of 28 September 1941, Roosevelt's 50-year-old envoy Averell Harriman, a very rich American banker turned politician, and the equally prosperous 62-year-old press baron Max Aitken, better known as Lord Beaverbrook, Britain's Minister of Supply, ended up sitting down with the Communist Stalin and Vyacheslav Molotov, the 51-year-old People's Commissar of Foreign Affairs, in the Kremlin. Harriman later recalled Stalin as being shorter and broader than anticipated, wearing a heavy black moustache shot with grey, and dressed in a simple mottled brown tunic without decorations.[29]

Given that the Allies' wealthy negotiators represented everything communists were supposed to revile, Beaverbrook and Harriman appear to have been a strange choice. Although Beaverbrook had burnished his pro-Soviet credentials by organizing a 'Tanks for Russia Week' in British armament factories the week before the Moscow conference (workers were told all tanks produced during the week would be sent to Russia), the talks had some sticky moments.[30] After being disarmed by Stalin's frank disclosure of the Soviet Union's vulnerabilities during the first meeting – Stalin admitted Moscow 'certainly would have fallen' if Hitler had concentrated his attack on the Russian capital rather than attacking on three fronts – the next evening, according to Harriman: 'Stalin gave the impression that he was much dissatisfied with what we were offering. He appeared to question our good faith . . . "The paucity of your offers clearly shows that you want to see the Soviet Union defeated" . . . he said.'[31]

Harriman noted afterwards: 'It was deeply discouraging', although his diagnosis concerning what had led to such an abrupt volte-face was questionable. He believed Stalin was hostile because he was 'trying to trade' or 'to smoke us out'. It was just as likely that the cause of the hostility was the Soviet leader's plunging morale in the wake of yet more defeats on the battlefield.

Moscow may have been temporarily spared following Hitler's inexplicable decision at the end of July 1941 to stop his Army Group Centre's advance towards the Russian capital so it could assist the attacks to its north and south. However, during the last half of September 1941 the Red Army had to regroup because of another disaster. Kiev in the Ukraine, to the south, was encircled by German forces. Some 665,000 Soviet prisoners were taken. Stalin was to blame since he only permitted Soviet forces to retreat after it was too late. Coming as it did barely a month after around 300,000 Soviet prisoners were taken following the fighting in the Smolensk region, it would not have been surprising if this latest episode had pushed Stalin near to the edge.[32]

The suspicion that the Russian leader's bitterness was prompted by natural desperation would certainly have lined up with other available evidence. Harriman's account reveals that when reporting on the second meeting, Beaverbrook wrote to Churchill: 'Stalin was very restless, walking about and smoking continuously, and appeared to both of us to be under an intense strain.'[33]

The situation cannot have been helped by the fact that Stalin, who spoke to Harriman and Beaverbrook in Russian via an interpreter, had this unnerving habit of not looking them in the eye when talking to them.[34]

Fortunately for the Allies, whatever the cause of Stalin's sullen, resentful comments on 29 September 1941, the next evening (30 September) friendly relations were re-established. Stalin proceeded to graciously accept what he was being offered even though by then he had yet another reason to be distracted.[35] On the morning of 30 September 1941 the German Army Group Centre forces had resumed their advance towards Moscow as part of Operation Typhoon.[36] The final terms confirming what Harriman and Beaverbrook had offered Stalin and Molotov were included in what was referred to as the First or Moscow Protocol. It was signed on 2 October 1941.[37]

The Protocol included a clause promising that Britain and America would each supply 200 aircraft and 250 tanks per month during the period 1 October 1941 to 30 June 1942, a huge commitment particularly for Britain, who until American factories increased their output, would have to make up for any shortfall coming from America. In some cases, supplies from America originally earmarked for Britain were to be diverted so that they could instead be sent to the Soviet Union. But it answered Stalin's plea that he be given this armour to add to the 1,400 tanks he stated the Soviet Union could manufacture each month.[38] The Protocol also provided for other military equipment to be supplied such as anti-aircraft guns, anti-tank guns and lorries in addition to raw materials. The latter included steel and aluminium.

But it was a provision in the Protocol confirming what was finally agreed on 1 October 1941, the day after the last meeting with Stalin, which was to impose what would become the biggest obligation of all. Beaverbrook and Harriman had both insisted that Britain and America would only be obliged to make the supplies available at centres of production in their own countries. But when Molotov asked whether that meant Britain and America would not help with transportation to Russia, Beaverbrook chipped in: 'We will help, but we can't guarantee delivery.'[39]

Thus with a stroke of the pen, the starting gun was fired on a commitment which would in time result in Britain and America being sucked into a series of naval skirmishes, designated by some the Battle of the Arctic. Apart from its location, it was little different to the much better-known Battle of the Atlantic, only this battle was designed to provide a lifeline for the Soviet Union.

Beaverbrook's concession cannot have been unexpected in London. Even as Stalin and Molotov during the night of 1–2 October celebrated what had been agreed, at a huge banquet thrown in their visitors' honour in the Kremlin's Catherine the Great room, ten of the Western allies' merchant ships, which with an oiler constituted the core of the first of the Arctic convoys given the prefix 'PQ' (PQ1), were sailing from Iceland to Archangel with, amongst other aid, 193 fighter aircraft on board (see Note 40 for the origin of the prefix PQ – and of the linked prefix QP).[40]

Churchill, all the keener to stress that he was going to make the aid count because he knew Stalin would still be disappointed he was not getting the second front he really wanted, wrote to the Soviet leader on 6 October, four days before Beaverbrook and Harriman's return to London: 'We intend to run a continuous cycle of convoys leaving every ten days.'[41] There was to be no suggestion that the bulk of the aid should at this early stage be sent to the Soviet Union via the much safer, but much longer and therefore slower route which, if selected, would have involved merchant ships going round the Cape of Good Hope, up the east coast of Africa, and ending up at ports at the northern end of the Persian Gulf. Even had the 12,000-mile journey by ship from the American east coast to the Persian Gulf been an option notwithstanding the availability of the much shorter northern route which involved sailing around 2,800 miles from the US to Britain and then 3,000 miles from Britain via Iceland to the nearest of the northern Russian ports, there was the additional obstacle that road and railway connections between the Persian Gulf ports and the Soviet Union had yet to be developed sufficiently to make the transport of aid using them viable Stalin, who had first pointed this out during his July 1941 meetings with Harry Hopkins, had at the same time ruled out the bulk of the supplies being shipped to Vladivostok. One objection to that route being used was that it was likely to be opposed by the Japanese. It was also much too far away from the front to be practicable, Stalin had said.[42]

The undertaking to send what amounted to no less than three convoys per month was not the only positive news Churchill made known to Stalin. It was eventually agreed that Britain would not charge the Soviet Union for the military aid it was supplying, such as arms, tanks and aircraft, unless Britain had paid a third party for the items in question. That apart, the Soviet Union only had to pay Britain for non-military aid, such as raw materials and machine tools, after credit was given for the materials which the Soviet Union in her turn gave to Britain (the materials given to Britain would be loaded into the Allies' merchant ships, which were it not for such supplies, would be returning to Iceland empty apart from the ballast necessary to weigh the vessels down to give them stability).[43] Roosevelt likewise ruled that no immediate payment would be payable for American aid; it was said to be supplied under so-called 'lend-lease' terms, although the President would eventually state he would decide what that meant in the Soviet Union's case when the war ended (see Note 44 for financial arrangements at the end of the war, and see explanation of lend-lease in the Glossary).[44]

It is highly likely that Churchill's desire to support Russia with such an open hand was partly boosted by a wish to hold together his cabinet as well as to satisfy the public. There had been a groundswell of public opinion in favour of Britain supporting Russia. Fired up by articles in the press, including in Lord Beaverbrook's newspapers such as the *Daily* and *Sunday Express*, and demonstrations around the country, there was for a time mounting pressure on the government to save Russia by opening a second front, as requested by Stalin.[45]

This pressure reached its zenith during the early stages of the Germans' renewed advance towards Moscow during October 1941. It prompted Lord Beaverbrook, in the course of a stormy meeting of Britain's War Cabinet's Defence Committee on 20 October 1941, to allege that the country's Chiefs of Staff were insisting they must 'wait until the last button has been sewn on the last gaiter before we launch an attack', and he attacked Churchill for not standing up to them.

The secretary of the meeting reported Lord Beaverbrook's outburst thus: 'He wished to take advantage of the rising temper in the country for helping Russia. Others didn't. He wanted to make a supreme effort to raise production so as to help Russia. Others didn't ... He wished the Army to act in support of Russia. The Chiefs of Staff didn't. The line of cleavage between himself and his colleagues and the Chiefs of Staff was complete.'[46]

That may have been the case, but as it turned out Lord Beaverbrook was too late with his protest. Government public opinion surveys revealed that shortly before he spoke up against Churchill, public enthusiasm for a second front had waned dramatically. Potential agitators appear to have been put off trying to force the government to open a second front by the publication in mid-October 1941 of Lord Gort's despatch about the Dunkirk disaster, which reminded them what was likely to happen again if Britain attacked before her and her allies' armies were ready.[47]

In the short term at least, Churchill's willingness to comply with the obligation to supply aid to Russia, as specified in the First Protocol, also provided just enough meat to keep his fiery colleague – and the public – onside.[48]

3

First Blood

Main Action: 17 January 1942
Sinking of HMS Matabele, PQ8

(See Map 1)
GMT + 3

When Churchill wrote to Stalin on 6 October 1941 to tell him the pro-posed frequency of the convoys, he omitted to mention the unfortunate individuals in Britain's Merchant Navy, who would have to man most of the first convoys' merchant ships, and who in the first instance at least would become the main victims of the British prime minister's largesse.

Admittedly the Merchant Navy got off to a flying start. Six more con-voys (PQ1 to PQ6) made the journey to north Russian ports before the Germans sank their first Arctic convoy ship, in January 1942. The arrival of these convoys meant that prior to the end of 1941, 50 shiploads of aid which had been picked up in Britain or Iceland were dropped off in the northern Russian ports, if one includes the cargo carried by the Dervish ships in that total.[1] A substantial proportion of the hold and deck space in these 50 ships was taken up by more than 400 tanks and 400 aircraft which they had transported, most of them supplied by Britain.[2]

Although this was less than the 750 tanks and 600 aircraft (250 tanks and 200 aircraft per month) that Britain had undertaken to hand over during the last quarter of 1941 when signing the Moscow Protocol,

Churchill's government had broadly speaking complied with the agreement. More or less in line with its obligation to make the specified number of tanks and aircraft available in England, along with some extra tanks it had agreed to supply in England in order to reduce the American quota, most of 'the shortfall', i.e. the tanks and aircraft which Britain was obliged to make available in Britain during the last quarter of 1941 minus the tanks and aircraft which had actually reached Russia by the end of 1941, was made up of tanks and aircraft which by the end of 1941 had either been set aside to be transported to Russia during January 1942, or if not already by the end of 1941 on Arctic convoy ships afloat, were by that date in the process of being loaded onto ships that were to form part of subsequent Arctic convoys.[3]

The only substantial infringement of the Protocol's terms at this juncture was by the Americans, whose ability to make available its monthly quota of 250 tanks and 200 aircraft had been obstructed by its own forces' increased requirements in the wake of Pearl Harbor. That excuse did not go down well with the Russians.[4] Although on 5–6 December 1941, having repulsed the German thrust towards Moscow, the Red Army, reinforced by units brought up from the east of the Soviet Union, had counter-attacked, for some time no-one could be sure how costly that would be either on the ground or in the air.[5] That explains why as far as the Soviet Union's leadership was concerned the supplies from the West remained critical.[6]

This was the backdrop to the Russian demand for the ongoing transportation of the aid being provided by Britain and America. The feasibility of delivering the requested supplies was a different question. Because of the lack of opposition, these early journeys to and from northern Russia during 1941 were manageable. But with such large amounts of aid fuelling the Soviet Union's defiant defence and counter-attacks, it was obvious it would only be a matter of time before the Germans would react.

So who were these merchant seamen on whom the Soviet Union was going to have to depend? While the officers and especially the masters of British merchant ships were in many cases interchangeable with captains and officers of the smaller Royal Navy ships – some former merchant ship officers belonged to the Royal Naval Reserve (a category set up to provide 'employment' for professional civilian officers and seamen), and during the war commanded the smaller HMT (anti-submarine trawlers) and HMS ships – the often less ambitious junior merchant seamen could be very different from their Royal Navy counterparts.

Although like their equivalents in the Royal Navy, many were tempted to work in ships because they had been brought up near the sea or the ports where ocean going ships docked, or because their fathers or grandfathers had been sailors, the Merchant Navy also provided a haven for those who would not have been welcome in HMS vessels. This included men who for whatever reason might not have fitted in to an institution where youth, an athletic physique and a willingness to submit to discipline were all-important.[7]

One of the attractions of the Merchant Navy was its less stringent discipline and the fact it had turned its back on what was often referred to as the 'spit and polish' culture that was so much part of a career in the Royal Navy. It did not matter what the men in the Merchant Navy looked like, or within reason how eccentrically they behaved, as long as they could do their jobs and could put up with the lifestyle and conditions.

When they signed up to the Merchant Navy, they had to be able to endure a claustrophobic existence below decks, the monotony of an uneventful long journey, as well as terror when the wind got up and the sea became rough. They also had to be able to put up with living alongside the other men sharing their quarters, who were often full of testosterone and spoiling for a fight.

As if that was not bad enough, if you had to sail in the Arctic, you had to factor in extra privations and hardships, such as the inability to wash in running water because the pipes in the ship were frozen. Then there was the ice lining the walls inside their mess decks. When it was that cold, men could not safely go out on deck without dressing up like Arctic explorers. Heavy duffel coats with hoods, extra sweaters, long johns and two pairs of thick socks worn under sea boots were de rigueur, as were mittens.

If you happened to pick up a metal object while in the open air in such freezing cold conditions, you could say goodbye to the skin on your hands which would stick to it. Heaven help anyone who in the low temperatures prevailing in the Arctic fell or was forced to jump into the sea, for example if a relatively lightly armed merchant ship was torpedoed. Survival time was predicted to be less than five minutes, although there were cases of men, usually those under the age of 30, who could survive for longer. That was not much consolation if you happened to be 60 or even 70 years old. Unlike the Royal Navy, the Merchant Navy did not make old age a barrier to service during the war.

Many of these hardships also had to be endured by the sailors serving in the HMS ships which escorted the Arctic convoys. However, at least their ships which were better armed were less likely to be sunk. A typical so-called Defensively Equipped Merchant Ship (DEMS) used by Britain's Merchant Navy may have possessed her own guns, which were manned by Royal Navy personnel and men from the Army's Royal Artillery Maritime Regiment, referred to as DEMS gunners, but during the first series of Arctic convoys some of their weapons were unsuitable for the task in hand. Many of the freighters during these early convoys had one quite impressive looking 4-inch gun (similar in size to those aboard British minesweepers and some of the older British destroyers) mounted aft. But while it might prove useful if a surfaced U-boat was targeted, because it could not be elevated sufficiently, it could not be used to help repulse the anticipated mass attacks by German aircraft, the main hazard that could not be neutralized by convoy escorts. Some of the much smaller machine guns also deployed on board most merchantmen would prove to be less than ideal for a different reason. The .50 calibre machine guns, that fired projectiles half an inch in diameter, were only moderately effective once planes were as near as 500 yards away, by which time it was often too late to stop them dropping their torpedoes. While the .30 caliber machine guns fired bullets roughly one third of an inch in diameter that could not penetrate the German planes' armour at any distance.[8]

Another positive feature of service in the Royal Navy was that the enforced discipline meant that bullies in HMS ships were for the most part kept under control.

The fact that a junior merchant seaman needed to be tough was confirmed by handsome American Dalton Munn in his revealing account of life as a 20-year-old armed guard in – and off – SS *Larranga* (sometimes referred to as *Larranaga*), the very first American freighter to travel in a World War 2 convoy to north Russia. As it happened, American ships were not included in Arctic convoys until after the 7 December 1941 Japanese attack on US warships at Pearl Harbor, which led to declarations of war between America and Nazi Germany as well as Japan. *Larranga* was to arrive in Murmansk on 18 January 1942 along with most of the other merchant ships in Arctic convoy PQ8.

Munn was not strictly a member of the Merchant Marine (the US version of the Merchant Navy). Armed guards such as Munn were US Navy personnel placed in American merchant ships with a view to protecting them with the guns installed on their decks. That made them the American equivalent of the British DEMS gunners. Munn's outsider status appears to have loosened his tongue, enabling him to describe his Merchant Marine shipmates with some objectivity.

He did not hold back. One of his early diary entries, written shortly after his ship left the docks in Boston Harbor on the night of 6–7 December 1941 for the first leg of what he termed 'the most dangerous adventure of my career', summed up his first impressions of *Larranga*'s Merchant Marine crew in one sentence: 'I've never seen such a bunch of cutthroats in my life.'

His diary carried on: 'I see [why] . . . I [need to] wear my 45 everywhere I go. We were told to expect trouble because this is a union crew, and they have some beef. We are ordered to see that none that come aboard can go ashore again . . . Every damned one is drunk as hell and fighting.'[9]

What made his diary distinctive was the way it lifted the lid on the roughness of life on board a merchant ship. According to Munn, *Larranga*'s crew did not wait for the Arctic leg of their journey to show what they were made of. The fighting on board started while the vessel was sailing in convoy across the Atlantic. One entry recalls how a week into the journey, the carpenter's mate 'beat the hell out of our mess boy'.[10] It was just one of a series of fights between members of the crew during the long trip, which culminated with the Filipino steward attacking the Portuguese saloon messman with a knife and hammer.[11] It was a feature of life in a merchant ship that the crew was nothing if not cosmopolitan, which added to the difficulties of those on board.

As for the captain, Munn alleges he lost the convoy on this, the ship's preliminary voyage across the Atlantic from Nova Scotia to Iceland, because he was also drunk. The captain was subsequently taken off the ship because his foot was crushed between the ship and the side of a motor launch that was bringing him back from a trip to the mainland in Iceland, where *Larranga* was waiting for PQ8 to set off on its journey to the Soviet Union.[12]

Taken in isolation, the events described by Munn might make one wonder how the crew in *Larranga*, and in many of the other ships which were also home to misfits and violent oddballs, ever delivered their cargoes to the Soviet Union. But then if one thinks about it, one realizes that a more genteel set of characters might not have had the strength and courage necessary to survive the ordeals and sacrifices that were all part and parcel of a merchant seaman's life in a freezing cold war zone.

Focusing on the unsavoury also ignores the uplifting relationships Munn forged with some of the like-minded men he befriended in the ship, as they bonded through having to make the most of their difficult situation. There was something to be said for putting together a group of young men, who as Munn confirmed, all wanted the same thing: 'A bottle and a woman.'[13]

Also it would be wrong to assume that all merchant seamen were as pugilistic and good for nothing as some of Munn's prose suggests. An analysis of accounts of life in other merchant ships suggests that while many ships had a few bullying troublemakers of the sort mentioned by Munn, most merchant seamen who served in the Arctic convoys were skilful and hard working, and as peace loving as they were brave. If the bullies really got out of hand in a ship, and threatened to disrupt the officers' relations with other members of the crew, the master could always ask the authorities in a port to step in. That is precisely what happened during the lead up to one of the convoys during the summer of 1942 when the master of the American merchant ship *Silver Sword* complained in a report sworn in front of the American Vice Consul in Iceland that 'serious trouble' had boiled over in his ship's steward's department involving the ship's second cook and a utility man. It came to a head because, as the master reported, 'someone threw the 2nd cook's artificial leg over the side' of the ship into Reykjavik harbour. The 'insubordinate' men quickly learned there were limits even in the relatively lax Merchant Marine. The American Vice Consul in Iceland had them discharged from the ship and sent back to America.[14]

The fact that the relatively few bad apples led to both the British and American merchant navies being besmirched, some would say unfairly, was also down to rivalry between the regular naval ratings and the junior merchant seamen. There was a perception that even allowing for disparities in employment conditions – for example there was a time when the merchant seaman's pay was stopped on the day their ship was sunk – merchant seamen's weekly wages were far higher than what was earned by those serving in the regular navies. This could lead to a lot of bad mouthing by the regular seamen, some of whom appeared to feel if they could not be as well paid, they could at least get their just deserts in other ways, such as being rewarded for their superior discipline by having a better reputation.

Whatever the truth concerning the brickbats thrown at the Allied merchant seamen, basic levels of discipline and courage were to become more and more important. At the beginning of 1942 there was to be a step change. On the second day of the new year, the German U-boat *U-134* sank the SS *Waziristan*, one of two freighters, grandly referred to as convoy PQ7A, that had begun its journey to Russia with two trawlers as escorts. Unfortunately for her crew, she was not protected by any escort at the time she appeared in the sights of the U-boat; she was alone, having missed the scheduled rendezvous with a couple of minesweepers which were supposed to take the PQ7A ships under their wing after the armed trawlers departed.[15]

Tragically, none of the 47-man crew survived to tell the tale of what had happened. However, there was one positive as long as you were not one of *Waziristan's* crew. The inability to repulse the ambush and the failure to rescue survivors could be explained by the lack of an escort, a comforting point if that was possible when so many lives had been lost, because it did not suggest that the convoy system was broken.

There were no such pros discernible when two ships in PQ8 – an eight-merchant ship convoy protected by a cruiser, two destroyers and two minesweepers – were in their turn torpedoed by *U-454* on 17 January 1942.[16] *U-454* was one of three U-boats, in the group referred to by the Germans as Ulan, deployed against PQ8, the first time such a group had been unleashed against an Arctic convoy.[17] The torpedoing occurred during the last lap of the journey to Murmansk as the convoy steamed westward, parallel to the Russian coast, just a few miles to the east of the entrance to the Kola Inlet. (Rather than approaching the inlet directly from the north, which would have been the shortest route, Arctic convoys usually made landfall to the east of the Inlet, and then travelled westward until they reached its mouth.)

The first incident took place around 20 miles to the east of Cape Teriberski (which is itself east of the mouth of the Kola Inlet) where the convoy's commodore's ship, SS *Harmatris,* was torpedoed at 7.55 p.m. on her starboard side behind the fore peak.[18] At the time the merchant ships had been moving west-north-west in single file, with *Harmatris* at the front of the line. Their escorts were spread out to the front and rear and on both sides. The convoy had received no notice there were U-boats about, which partly explains why there was some debate after the torpedoing concerning whether she had been damaged by a mine.[19] A brief, unsuccessful search was made in case a U-boat was responsible.

It certainly was not in the interest of Kapitänleutnant Burckhard Hackländer, the 27-year-old commander of *U-454*, to resolve this question by making his presence known. He appears to have believed he needed all the help he could get. When he recorded his attack plan in his war diary, he commented: 'It would be better if I could attack with the Northern lights behind me, but going to the south to make that happen would take too long. It would also mean the boat would be hemmed in between the coast and the convoy'.[20] He had been forced to do his best in the circumstances, and still ended up hitting the merchant ship.

Luckily for the people of the Soviet Union, who were waiting for the 8,000 tons of supplies *Harmatris* was carrying, neither the first torpedo which came from her starboard seaward side, nor the subsequent explosion which damaged her port side was sufficient to sink her. All the crew, who had abandoned ship after the second explosion, went back on board to make sure *Harmatris* could be towed into port, which she eventually was three days later.

The long struggle to bring her in was not helped by the weather. Although the Kola Inlet was supposed to be temperate relative to Archangel, by the time she reached the safety of the harbour, in the words of *Harmatris'* master, 'everywhere ice and snow covered the ship to a depth of 1 foot'.[21]

Ironically, most of the men in the destroyer HMS *Matabele*, which temporarily moved away from the westward bound convoy to protect *Harmatris* after the merchant ship was torpedoed, would also end up as U-boat victims. At 11.27 p.m. that same night, after the destroyer had left *Harmatris* in order to once more take up her station about a mile away from the starboard side of the north-westward bound convoy, some of the crew in HMS *Somali*, on the other side of PQ8, heard the sound of an underwater explosion and saw a red flash.

Somali's Captain Donald Bain and two other *Somali* officers initially thought it emanated from the tanker *British Pride* at the front of the line of merchant ships, but as *Somali* was swiftly steered around the front of the tanker, bringing *Matabele* into view, they saw the destroyer was very nearly stopped with dark smoke or steam emerging from her engine room. A flashed signal from her bridge or decks indicated she had been torpedoed, and two rockets her crew shot over the sea to the north were perhaps intended to signify that was the direction from where the torpedoes which had hit her had been fired.[22] A *Matabele* survivor would later affirm she had been struck by a torpedo abreast her galley on her starboard side.[23]

This latest firing of torpedoes at the convoy should have come as no surprise to at least some in its escort. Shortly before 11 p.m. a report from the Admiralty had been received in *Trinidad,* the cruiser which until the *Harmatris* incident had been escorting PQ8, and in *Somali* stating that U-boats were operating near the Kola Inlet.[24] Although *Trinidad* had left the area after those on board had heard the explosion that damaged *Harmatris*, there was a case for her captain to order his telegraphist to break radio silence in order to make sure that the rest of the escort had the same information. But this was not done.

There was another circumstance that might have helped the U-boat crew. At the time *Matabele* was torpedoed, the convoy was around 10 miles to the north-east of the Cape Teriberski lighthouse, a useful aid for navigation, but one which could potentially get in the way of any attempt by shipping to approach the inlet without being noticed. In spite of the fact it was dark, any vessel to the north of the convoy's starboard side would have been able to see the merchant ships and their escort silhouetted against the light. [25]

The following extract from the official report on the incident describes the surge of activity which Ernest Higgins, an ordinary seaman in *Matabele,* witnessed beside X gun mount when the torpedo struck (X gun mount was the furthest forward of the two 4.7-inch gun mounts aft): 'First Lieutenant Britten rushed up from the wardroom and ordered [the] . . . crew to close all magazine access hatches . . . During this time cries for help were heard [and] men were seen in the water. Efforts were made to release the Carley floats . . . but the slips were frozen, no hammer was available and no one had a knife.'[26]

After realizing that this precluded their abandoning ship in a controlled manner from near the back of the ship where they were standing,

Higgins with some other ratings had just begun to move towards the front of the ship, when as the report put it: 'a wall of flame swept them back', apparently following a violent second explosion, probably the result of the B gun magazine blowing up.[27]

The ship quickly broke into two parts. Higgins later described how as the stern portion sank, he and two other ratings jumped over the side and swam away from the ship. There were around 50 other men who had also made it into the sea. The three men were joined by two others.

In an effort to save the trio of men with them who could not swim very well, Higgins and Ordinary Seaman William Burras swam over to a coiled-up life-saving net they had spotted floating in the water, and pushed it back to where the other men had been. Unfortunately they had taken too long. As the *Matabele* survivors' report confirmed, by the time they returned to where they had started, the three diffident swimmers had 'disappeared'.[28]

When the minesweeper HMS *Harrier*, which had been leading the convoy westward, arrived on the scene some 20 minutes after the second explosion, leaving to *Somali*'s crew the difficult task of searching for the U-boat, notwithstanding the unforgiving conditions that made the hunt using its sonar equipment next to impossible, there was still hope that a substantial number of survivors might be picked up. Although all that could be seen of *Matabele* at this point was 20 feet of the bow sticking out of the water, *Harrier*'s crew heard shouts.[29]

It is likely that these were the last cries made by drowning seamen. Only three men were pulled out of the water, one of whom died.[30] The other two were Higgins and Burras. They had also heard the fading calls for help which were some way away from them, and they too might have given up and drowned if *Harrier* had not appeared when she did.

Afterwards, Higgins recalled swimming over to *Harrier* and grabbing a net hanging over her side, but in the words *of Matabele*'s survivors' report, he 'remembers no more', until he came to after being rescued.[31] Burras also lost consciousness in the water, only coming to his senses the following day.[32] The fact that he and Higgins were the only survivors meant that the remaining 236 *Matabele* officers and ratings had died, which would turn out to be, if only by a small margin, the largest loss of life arising out of the sinking of one of the Allies' ships in the course of the Arctic convoys.[33]

During the rescue, *Somali*'s crew carried on searching for the U-boat. But as *U-454*'s Kapitänleutnant Hackländer confirmed later, the many star shells shot up into the air by the convoy escorts did not enable them to pinpoint where he was hiding. As a result, he and his crew in *U-454* were able to 'beat a hasty retreat in a NNE direction'.[34]

The U-boat's departure enabled the remaining PQ8 merchant ships to escape without further losses. However, a significant corner had been turned. The U-boat arm of the Kriegsmarine (the German Navy) had tasted the blood that had been spilt in the approaches to the Kola Inlet, and its appetite whetted, it was inevitable that sooner or later its boats would be back for some more.

4

Flight of the Albacores

Main Action: 9 March 1942
Hunt for Tirpitz, PQ12

(See Maps 1, 2, 3 and 4)

Even before the first Arctic convoy ships were sunk in PQ7 and 8, both German and British politicians and admirals were gearing up for what they realized would be quite a fight.

Showing admirable prescience, as early as 4 January 1942 Admiral Sir Jack Tovey, the 56-year-old commander-in-chief of the Home Fleet had written to the Admiralty, which was headed by the 64-year-old First Sea Lord Admiral Sir Dudley Pound (the most senior officer in the Royal Navy): 'From March until about June, the ice limit will still compel the routeing of the convoys south of Bear Island, within about 150 miles of the enemy occupied coast and 200 miles of Banak aerodrome. But they will be deprived of the protection they now receive from the long dark hours and bad flying conditions of winter . . . It must be assumed that the enemy will make a serious attempt to stop them.'[1]

He was right. Minutes of the meeting at Wolfsschanze (the Wolf's Lair, as Hitler's headquarters near Rastenburg, East Prussia, were known) between the 57-year-old Adolf Hitler and Grossadmiral Erich Raeder, the 65-year-old Oberfehlshaber der Kriegsmarine (commander-in-chief of the German Navy), at the end of December 1941, show there was already talk then about 'transferring *Tirpitz* (the battleship) to Trondheim (Norway)' with a view to opening up the possibility of 'attacks against the convoy route Britain-Iceland-White Sea', as well as to give German forces the capacity to repulse what Hitler would over the coming years again and again characterize as the inevitable Allied attacks on Norway. This transfer, and the desirability of a subsequent transfer to Norway of other German capital ships, was given the green light by the Führer at their subsequent meeting on 12 January 1942.[2]

Although some of these German warships were put out of action before they could be deployed from Norway, notably the battlecruisers *Scharnhorst* and *Gneisenau,* which were damaged by mines during the 11 February 1942 attempt to move them from Brest, France to Norway via Germany (the so-called Channel Dash), by 24 February 1942, a threatening German naval force was stationed in the Norwegian fjords near Trondheim.[3]

Tirpitz, which had duly entered a fjord near Trondheim on 16 January 1942, was a handful in her own right, putting it mildly. She was a 274 yards long by 39 yards wide monster whose main armament consisted of eight 15-inch guns in four two-gun turrets. She displaced some 50,000 tons of water, a significant part of her weight being the result of the exceptionally strong armour protecting the battleship's 'citadel'. In places this armour was 12.6 inches thick.[4] Relative to this ship, that could justifiably be referred to as the pride of the Kriegsmarine, the light cruiser HMS *Kenya,* the largest British ship that was to form part of the close escort for PQ12, the next Arctic convoy to be targeted, was a mere minnow. The 185 yards by 20 yards wide *Kenya* displaced around 10,000 tons – her armour's thickness not exceeding 3.5 inches, and strove to protect convoy PQ12 with a relatively unimpressive main armament consisting of twelve 6-inch guns in four three-gun turrets (cruisers carrying 6-inch guns are usually classified as 'light'). It helps to give some context to these dimensions when they are viewed alongside the vital statistics of a typical World War 2 merchant ship, which viewed in isolation might themselves have appeared pretty massive. SS (Steam Ship) *Empire Byron,* one of the PQ12 freighters, measured around 138 yards long by going on 19 yards wide.

Tirpitz was supported in Norway by the 'pocket battleship' *Admiral*

Scheer (a warship some have likened to a heavy cruiser but whose main armament consisted of 11-inch guns rather than the 8-inch guns found on most heavy cruisers) and at least five destroyers.

Notwithstanding the damage sustained by the two German battle-cruisers, it was no wonder given the arrival in Norway of all these warships that as preparations were being made for the passage of the east-going PQ12 and the west-going convoy QP8, Tovey should see the need to ring alarm bells again. On 25 February 1942, just days after *Admiral Scheer* had joined *Tirpitz* near Trondheim, he wrote to Admiral Pound: 'I must repeat my anxiety for both convoys . . . I presume a disaster would have serious political repercussions.'[5]

This reference to the political arena was doubtless intended to strike the loudest possible chord with Churchill. It was less than a month since the British prime minister had felt obliged to demand a vote of confidence in the House of Commons in order to face down those detractors who believed the government's decision to supply military aid to the Soviet Union was unwisely depriving British forces in action in the Middle and Far East of the equipment they needed to prevail. Although he had won that vote, the force of these same detractors had been strengthened after Singapore, which had been starved of the arms necessary for it to be defended, had fallen to the Japanese, a loss that was so demoralizing that some of Churchill's own supporters were wondering whether his popularity could ever be regained.

However, Tovey's plea was less persuasive than he might have wished. Churchill, who would have faced equally dangerous political opposition if he had not carried on supporting Russia, ruled that the convoys should go ahead, and Tovey had to do what he could to protect them. As PQ12's 16 merchant ships left Iceland's Hvalfjord on 1 March 1942 – with QP8's 15 merchant ships at Tovey's request leaving Kola Inlet on the same day – Tovey had plans in place to protect both convoys in the Jan Mayen Island to Bear Island area, where he believed the German warships based in the fjords near Trondheim were most likely to locate their attack.[6]

Tovey's plans involved providing distant cover for the convoys with the Home Fleet's most powerful ships. They included the two battleships HMS *Duke of York,* and *King George V* where he flew his flag, which were slightly smaller and less heavily armed than *Tirpitz* (the British battleships

measured 248 yards by 34 yards, displaced some 36,000 tons and were protected by: ten 14-inch guns in two quadruple-turrets and one twin-turret,
and in places, armour that was 14.7 inches thick), a battlecruiser (the British version had the kind of powerful guns usually seen in a battleship – in
this case the main armament included three twin 15-inch gun turrets – but
with lighter armour than is normally seen in a battleship), an aircraft carrier (*Victorious*), two cruisers and a screen of 12 destroyers.[7] It was the first
time it had been deemed necessary to protect an Arctic convoy in this way.
The idea was that after setting out in two groups, they would meet up, and
then cruise south of the routes followed by PQ12 and QP8, which would be
protected close up by the usual, much smaller and lighter escorts that had
previously been used to guard the convoys.

In PQ12's case, as well as the cruiser *Kenya* mentioned above, which
split off from the Home Fleet to reinforce the forces accompanying the
convoy, the close escort consisted of a couple of destroyers plus several
whalers, whereas the close ocean escort for QP8 was even skimpier: two
minesweepers and two corvettes plus support from two Soviet destroyers
until the convoy reached 30° East (to the east of the meridian that runs
through Norway's North Cape, and Hope Island).[8] QP8 was also to be
covered from afar by the cruiser *Nigeria*.[9]

These were only plans, however. The best of plans were the hostage to
good fortune and the other side's moves. The first German move that
appeared to set things off for them in the right direction involved one of
their aircraft. Shortly after 12.30 p.m. on 5 March 1942 the crew of a
German Focke-Wulf 200 Condor reconnaissance plane reported that
they had spotted PQ12 as it headed north-east around 70 miles south of
Jan Mayen Island (see 1A in Map 2).[10]

The report sparked off a surge of activity in Norway, as well as in Germany. Admiral Hubert Schmundt, the Admiral Nordmeer (Northern
Waters) based in Norway, ordered four U-boats to form up in a line ahead
of the convoy (see Map 2 for approximate positions where U-boats were
told to patrol).[11] But it was the discussion concerning the German surface
fleet which posed the greatest threat. It culminated with Hitler giving his
consent to a German battlegroup under the command of the 50-year-old
Vizeadmiral Otto Ciliax, Befehlshaber der Schlachtschiffe (BdS – commander of battleships) who was to fly his flag in *Tirpitz*, going out from

the Trondheim area to attack the convoy.[12] The German battleship was to be screened by three destroyers. The battlegroup then sailed at midday on 6 March.

In the first instance, Tovey had no way of knowing what the Germans were doing. But at around 7 p.m. that night Lieutenant Dick Raikes, in command of the British submarine *Seawolf*, which was patrolling outside the northern exit from Trondheimfjord, as he would later describe it, 'sighted the foretop and funnel top' of a large ship.[13] 'I closed at maximum underwater speed,' he wrote, 'but never got within 10 miles of her. Had I done so, I doubt if I'd be writing this, because we learned later she was escorted by a number of destroyers and a host of aircraft.'

Although he cautiously stated in his signal sent around an hour and a half later that he had seen a battleship or 8-inch cruiser, he subsequently affirmed in his written report: 'I was certain in my own mind that it was the *Tirpitz*.'[14]

Tovey received news of Raikes' sighting shortly after midnight on 6–7 March. He decided to position his group of ships south of PQ12 so that at daybreak on 7 March the torpedo bombers in *Victorious* could thoroughly search the area through which the warship seen by Raikes must pass if she was to intercept the convoy.

That made sense in theory. But less in practice. It conveniently failed to answer the all-important question: were the planes and air crews in *Victorious* up to carrying out the missions Tovey had in mind for them? Incredible as it may sound to those of us who are used to hearing about the RAF's invincible Spitfires and Hurricane fighters and its Flying Fortress (Lancaster) bombers, the Fleet Air Arm, which shortly before the outbreak of World War 2 had taken over from the RAF the responsibility for all flying done from warships, was still sending its crews into battle in biplanes. That is, planes with two wings on each side of the fuselage, that most of us associate with what the Royal Flying Corps pilots flew during World War 1.

Fortunately, those in *Victorious* during the passage of PQ12 and QP8 were Fairey Albacores rather than the even more primitive Fairey Swordfish aircraft, known derogatively as 'Stringbags' because of their capacity for carrying all sorts of cargo. But that was not saying much, as was confirmed after the war by Sub-Lieutenant Charles Friend, one of the Albacore observers during PQ12.

In his account he explained that 'the Albacore was like a first-class version of the Swordfish because it had a more powerful engine . . . and the air gunner had twin Vickers K guns instead of a single Lewis . . . but it was still a fixed undercarriage biplane'. Its top speed when level flying was around 170 miles per hour, which made it up to 100 miles per hour slower than the fastest of the Heinkel torpedo bombers that were subsequently brought into the Arctic theatre by the Germans.

A crucial improvement, given the freezing cold temperatures north of Norway, was that unlike the situation in a Swordfish, the Albacore's crew members were in enclosed heated cockpits. But Friend's description of the plane highlights the air of obsolescence that hung over what some referred to disrespectfully as 'the Applecore'. According to Friend, little had been done to update the archaic communication systems: 'Between . . . [the pilot] and the observer was a long petrol tank. In the Stringbag, if the pilot had forgotten to plug in his Gosport [speaking] tube, one simply reached over and banged his head to attract his attention, but in Albacores, we all carried a long garden cane to reach forward past the tank to tap him on the shoulder. The ultimate refinement of the device was an empty Very cartridge tied on the end in which to place a written note to the pilot.'

This low-tech approach was needed because of the rule prohibiting the use of the wireless to communicate routine information to the other two members of the crew. The wireless was strictly out of bounds for this purpose except 'to report the enemy or in dire emergency'. When communicating with ships or other aircraft, the Aldis lamp was the recommended device. That was when the likes of Friend were not signalling morse code with a swung forearm, known as zogging.

It says a lot that according to Friend, 'the greatest single enhancement of aircrew comfort was the "P-tube", a portable urinal. In the Stringbag we had, in desperate straits, to make do by filling the empty containers of aluminium dust markers or flame floats, flinging them overboard after use. It was important to throw them over the right side, because over the wrong one, the slipstream opened them and showered the contents back into the cockpit.'[15]

It was through employing these primitive planes that Tovey hoped to find and neutralize the ships that were after the convoy on the morning of 7 March.[16] But as he reported later, there was a snag: 'By great misfortune, for this search would almost certainly have located the *Tirpitz*, severe icing conditions . . . [and] low visibility . . . were experienced and no air reconnaissance was possible all day.'[17]

* * *

Victorious' aircraft were far from being the only victims of the Arctic weather at the beginning of March 1942. Long before they reached the Commander-in-Chief's proclaimed danger area, the ships in the west-going convoy QP8 also underwent a terrific buffeting. They included the American freighter *Larranga*, now on the way back to Iceland. We know from the diary written by Dalton Munn, *Larranga's* armed guard mentioned in Chapter 3, that on 4 March he was already cursing the 50-mile-an-hour headwind and the 25 foot high waves which made it impossible for his ship to keep up with the other ships in the convoy. Munn's diary entry for that day includes the words: 'This ship seems as though she'll break in two any minute for we are travelling light. The propellers are out of the water half the time.'

There was no let up from the wind the next day, and on 6 March there was an even more acute crisis after the ship's engines cut out, apparently because of a broken steam line. This prompted Munn to write: 'Axtell (Ensign Harold Axtell, head of *Larranga's* armed guard) has told us to put on all our clothes and stand by to abandon ship! We are completely help-less and expect to be torpedoed at any second.'

However, after all the talk in his diary about womanizing and getting drunk, when push came to shove Munn stood up to be counted, volunteering to man one of the ship's guns so that if a U-boat did approach as others on board took to the lifeboats, there would be someone in place who could attempt to repulse it. His courage was all the more admirable because of his misgivings which also appear in the diary. What he realized might end up being the very last entry read: 'God only knows I am scared, but I hope I'll have the chance to fight to the last. I hope I'll have the nerve to blow my brains out rather than freeze or drown for I won't have the chance to get to a life boat.'

He could not have known as he recorded what could have been his final testament on 6 March that on 7 March a snowstorm would descend, unpleasant in itself, but representing an answer to the prayers of the entire ship's company since it hid the ship until her engines were repaired.[18]

* * *

Further to the west, the crews in PQ12's ships had encountered problems of a different kind, although they were also affected by the vagaries of nature. During the evening of 6 March, those on board registered that the convoy's north-easterly course was taking their vessels into the ice. The only saving grace according to Captain Michael Denny, commander of the cruiser HMS *Kenya,* which had joined the close escort, was that it was 'loose pack ice'.

However, it was sufficient to damage the escorting destroyer *Oribi,* and frightening enough to induce Captain Denny to conclude: 'After experience with PQ12, I would never take a convoy anywhere near ice, accepting almost any other risk in preference'.[19]

The ice forced the convoy during the night of 6–7 March to alter the course it had been following, which had featured in all the German calculations made since the initial sighting by the Focke-Wulf crew, to a south-easterly direction. Tiresome as it seemed at the time, the change of direction, which was followed by a second change of course, back to the north-east, the next morning (7 March), was to have unexpectedly positive consequences.

Firstly, the new courses meant that at 1 p.m. on 7 March, PQ12 and QP8 met 'head on', according to Captain Denny, some 200 miles southwest of Bear Island (see 3 in Map 2), enabling the sailors in the two convoys to exchange intelligence about the ice. 'A perfect gridiron was executed in visibility one mile,' Denny reported later.[20]

Secondly, had the changes of course not been made by PQ12, it might well have been sighted by lookouts in *Tirpitz* following the next important development (see below). That was the case notwithstanding the warning from the Admiralty, apparently based on *Seawolf's* signal the night before, which told Captain Denny at around 5 p.m. during the afternoon of 7 March that 'Enemy surface forces may be in the vicinity of PQ12', and which instructed him to turn the convoy to the north.[21]

* * *

In the meantime, the crews in Ciliax's battlegroup had encountered their own problems. That morning (7 March) he had instructed the commanders of the three German destroyers to spread out and sweep north-westward towards the interception area specified by Kiel-based Generaladmiral

Rolf Carls, the 56-year-old commander of Marinegruppenkommando Nord, in the orders he had sent to Ciliax (see 2 in Map 2 for the expected interception point).[22] Little did Ciliax and his men realize that the interception area, which they thought had been worked out with such precision after taking into account the predicted speed and course of the convoy, had used as a base incorrect coordinates.

For some reason the Focke-Wulf crew which had flown over PQ12 on 5 March had specified they had seen the convoy some distance to the west of where the convoy appears to have been located at the time in question (see Note 23 for specifics of the German mistake).[23] Consequently, even allowing for the alteration in PQ12's route mentioned above, the area targeted by Ciliax was to the west of where the convoy was likely to be located at the relevant time. Unaware that they had been misled, the German destroyer commanders complied with Ciliax's command to proceed north-westward, while he headed on a parallel course on their left in *Tirpitz* (see Map 2).

Much of what later went wrong for the Germans sprang from this error, although they did not immediately appreciate they had made a mistake, or its negative consequences. Prior to that link being made, the Germans had more bad luck that had nothing to do with their misstep: a major prize was missed when *Z 25*, the starboard German destroyer, passed a few miles ahead of the west-going QP8 without seeing it since it was concealed due to the low visibility. Thus the delays to QP8's progress caused by the weather may have ended up saving its merchant ships. However, shortly after 4 p.m. on 7 March, as the three destroyers approached the meeting point for the German warships specified by Ciliax, a lookout in *Z 25* reported seeing smoke in the distance to their north. The smoke was belching out of the funnel of a west-going steamer.

It might have been sensible for the German destroyer commanders to have skirted round the ship with a view to checking whether she was a straggler attempting to catch up with the east-going or west-going convoy. Instead they sped towards her. It took an hour for the destroyers to advance close enough to exchange signals with her. On the steamer a flag was raised that revealed she was the *Ijora* from Leningrad. The signaller in the German destroyer *Friedrich Ihn* replied, using his flags to signal her to stop and not to send any radio messages. This was accompanied by the firing of a shell in front of the merchant ship's bows before the destroyers' radio disruption equipment was activated.

That was another mistake. At around 5.30 p.m. the Russian telegraphist in *Ijora* reacted by sending out a raider distress message which included the words: 'Gunned, gunned, *Ijora* gunned . . . 7235 N 1050 E.' (See 4 in Map 2 for location specified in *Ijora's* signal.)

The defiant response provoked action by the German destroyer commanders in their turn. They ordered their gunners to open fire, and after a number of shells and torpedoes had been fired and depth charges thrown, the merchant ship slowly sank leaving behind a solitary survivor on a raft who was picked up by the crew in *Friedrich Ihn*. He confirmed that *Ijora* was an empty ship on the way to England, perhaps hoping to emphasize the pointless slaughter that had just been perpetrated.[24]

But the rest of *Ijora's* crew may not have died in vain. Her telegraphist's signal echoed around the Arctic. As well as being registered in *Kenya*, which as indicated above was with PQ12, it had also been passed to Tovey in *King George V* after it had been picked up in one of his destroyers.[25] However it left him facing a dilemma concerning where to look for the powerful German battlegroup. The Admiralty had by this time confirmed it included *Tirpitz*.[26]

On the one hand, he was inclined to believe that the Germans would be so terrified that *Ijora's* message would lead to the sailing of the Home Fleet, and the German battlegroup being attacked and outnumbered, that *Tirpitz* would be rushed back to Trondheim. On the other hand, shortly after seeing *Ijora's* signal, he had received 'Ultra' messages from the Admiralty that pointed to the conclusion that because *Tirpitz* had made plans for a long operation to the east of Bear Island, that is where he should look for her.[27]

An Ultra was the name given to an Admiralty signal derived from information in a German message enciphered on an Enigma coding machine that had been decoded by British codebreakers at Bletchley Park, the codebreaking centre near what is now Milton Keynes. Each Ultra was sent out to the Home Fleet using an unbreakable 'one time pad' (one-off coding table). Because Ultras provided insight into the Germans' undoctored thinking, they were treated with the greatest respect.

That may explain in part why Tovey in the first instance believed he should at least allow for *Tirpitz* being near Bear Island rather than near

Trondheim. Another reason was that after the attack on *Ijora,* the Fleet's direction-finding equipment had pinpointed a signal coming from an unidentified vessel near where the Soviet ship appeared to have been attacked. To the untutored eye of someone like Tovey, it was quite reasonable to wonder whether this mystery vessel was *Tirpitz,* which he did.

However, after the war it was disclosed that it would have been quite evident to anyone who had been studying wartime signals sent from German warships that this was more likely than not made by another vessel. If messages were sent by Germany's surface warships that did not wish to be found, they were usually, if not invariably, short and to the point. This one was relatively long.

Tovey's misinterpretation of the wireless bearings would not have mattered had he not been apprised of another signal some three hours later made by a vessel to the south of the first. Tovey immediately jumped to the conclusion that it might also have been made from *Tirpitz,* and if he was correct, she was heading southward, that is back to Trondheim, after all.[28]

As a result, rather than heading towards Bear Island with the whole fleet, at 9 p.m. on 7 March, he hedged his bets by ordering six of the seven destroyers still with the Fleet to place themselves between the unidentified vessel and *Tirpitz's* home port while the rest of the Fleet carried on northward (five destroyers had previously peeled off for various reasons).[29]

A record of the atmosphere in the aircraft carrier *Victorious* at this critical juncture has been summed up in the following entry in 832 Squadron's war diary under the heading 'Excitement ran high': 'At 2100 in the ante-room, the usual "gen session" was held. We all thought that at last our chance had come, and that we would be given the honour of attempting to sink the mighty battleship *Admiral Von Tirpitz.* We were at half an hour notice of taking off, and as we lay down in the ante-room to get as much rest as possible, we were expecting at any moment to be called upon.'

However, as the Squadron's war diarist noted: 'At midnight the ship altered course to the westward . . . We all thought the flap was over.'[30]

It was, for the moment. Tovey, now separated from the bulk of his destroyer force, but with the other British warships in tow, had moved northward for a while just in case some new evidence of *Tirpitz's* whereabouts came in, only to backtrack in the face of the realization that he might be exposing his capital ships, stripped of their destroyer screen, to the growing risk of being attacked by U-boats in the area near Bear Island for no reason. He eventually retired to the south-west once it was obvious that the destroyers' interception gambit had failed.[31] By this stage, all seven of the destroyers which had remained at Tovey's beck and call had been sent away from the Fleet to refuel.[32]

The British destroyers had punched into thin air because Ciliax had indeed decided, notwithstanding his concern that *Ijora*'s signal might have persuaded those in charge of the convoy to change course or to turn back, to proceed eastward of Bear Island following the merchant ship's sinking. He intended to then loop around so that he could proceed westward down the estimated convoy route the next day (8 March) in the hope that he might yet meet PQ12 coming up it.

However, it soon became apparent that he too had made mistakes. So eager had he been to reach the interception area specified by Admiral Carls in the 6 March order, that he had rashly failed to halt his advance northward during his first night at sea in order to refuel the three German destroyers. When it was too rough to refuel them on his second night, or during the morning of 8 March, he was forced to send them back to Norway for their oiling.[33]

Not only did that mean that he lost the ability to make a wide sweep when he turned towards the west on the morning of 8 March (as shown in Map 3), which was one reason why PQ12's progress south of Bear Island that afternoon went unnoticed, but it also meant he had to send signals to the destroyers, either directly or via Carls, to tell their commanders where to meet up with him once their fuel tanks had been replenished. It was to be this signalling which would so nearly lead to his undoing.

The first such signal Ciliax had sent to the German destroyers nominated a rendezvous between Bear Island and Norway's North Cape.[34] But after he finally decided to call off the search for the convoy during the evening of 8 March, he nominated a second meeting point north-west of the southern tip of the Lofoten Islands, where the destroyers were to meet him at 8 a.m. on 9 March (see 1A in Map 3).[35]

It was unfortunate for Ciliax that at the time notification of this change was received by Carls, who shortly after 11.30 p.m. on 8 March repeated back to Ciliax the rendezvous location, the codebreakers at Bletchley Park had reduced the time it took to decode the German Enigma messages intercepted to three hours or less. The previous day it had been taking them around 12 hours to read the German Enigma messages. So it was that this crucial message from Carls, and similar messages from Carls to those in charge in two of the German destroyers, were intercepted by the British codebreaking operation before midnight on 8 March, and translated decrypts of them were sent to the Admiralty's Operational Intelligence Centre at around 2 a.m. on 9 March. The corresponding Ultra winged its way towards Tovey shortly before 3 a.m (see Note 36 for Bletchley Park's description of Carls' messages referring to the all-important rendezvous).[36]

The Admiralty's Ultra reached Tovey within an hour of it being sent, whereupon he had his fleet of ships wheeled to the south-east.[37] This was necessary (as can be seen from the Home Fleet's track in Map 3) because by the time he read the Ultra, he had already ordered the commanders of the ships in his fleet to head back towards the north-east, after he had been tipped off by a previous Ultra that *Tirpitz* was still operating near Bear Island.[38] However, the Bletchley Park codebreakers' coup did not guarantee a British victory. Because Tovey's ships had moved so far away from the Norwegian coast during 8 March, leaving them around 200 miles away from *Tirpitz* when the final turn to the south-east was made, there was no chance they could reach the rendezvous in time (the rendezvous was to take place around five hours after the turn to the south-east).[39] That is how it came about that not only the fate of the operation but also the prospects of the whole programme of sending aid via the northern route to Russia came to depend on the outdated Albacore planes about to be flown off *Victorious*.

After the British Fleet had been travelling south-eastward for going on an hour, Tovey passed on what he had gleaned from the Admiralty about *Tirpitz*'s movements to Captain Henry Bovell, *Victorious*' 49-year-old commander. By then an additional Ultra had been sent from the Admiralty specifying another point through which *Tirpitz* was supposed to pass, after the rendezvous location mentioned above, on the way back to Trondheim (see 1B in Map 3).[40]

Bovell replied to Tovey's request for an action plan: 'Propose fly off searching force of six aircraft at 0630 (a.m. 9 March GMT + 1; 7.30 a.m.

GMT + 2) to depth of 150 miles . . . Fly off striking force of 12 as soon as ranged about 0730 (GMT + 1; 8.30 a.m. GMT + 2).'[41]

Although the Albacore crews were still asleep or resting, they had been warned that they might be needed. 'We had orders to sleep ready dressed and ready for any emergency,' 832 Squadron's war diarist wrote afterwards. 'We were all woken up at 0530 (GMT + 1; 6.30 a.m. GMT + 2), and we knew something was in the wind. Apparently a signal had been received early that morning giving a position of the *Tirpitz*.'[42]

Charles Friend, who like all his 832 and 817 Squadron comrades was not privy to the breaking of the German naval Enigma code or the Ultras, later recalled how astounded they were by the accuracy of the intelligence they were given: 'I saw a signal in the Operations Room from the C-in-C which said in effect that *Tirpitz* would be in a stated position just off Vestfjord, which leads up to Narvik . . . at eight o'clock. My memory tells me that it also said what course she would be steering, and at what speed, because I remember thinking that to have such prior knowledge Admiral Tovey must have had a spy on board *Tirpitz*.'[43]

But there was a fly in the ointment. The command of the strike force that was ordered to attack *Tirpitz* was entrusted to Lieutenant Commander Bill Lucas, who had been brought in to replace 832 Squadron's previous commanding officer.

This was worrying. According to Friend, Lucas was 'an unknown quantity' with 'limited torpedo-spotter-reconnaissance experience'. During Lucas' short time with the Squadron, he had demonstrated a tendency to disregard junior officers' advice even if they had carried out the manoeuvre in question before. Given that Lucas had, as Friend confirmed, not 'practiced flying with us as a strike squadron', and that more experienced pilots were participating, including 817 Squadron's commanding officer who had previously been decorated with a Distinguished Flying Cross, putting Lucas in charge was controversial. It was to be a decision which those responsible would live to regret.

Having said that, the operation started smoothly enough. By around 7.45 a.m. on 9 March, the very moment when *Tirpitz* was approaching the compromised meeting point to find trusty escort destroyer *Friedrich Ihn* waiting for her, the six Albacores in the search force (three from 832 Squadron and three from 817 Squadron) were airborne, having taken off slightly later than originally proposed, and were starting out on their respective journeys, their courses ranging from 105° to 155°.[44]

So confident was *Victorious'* Captain Bovell that the searchers would find the battleship that the strike force consisting of 12 Albacores (seven from 832 Squadron, and five from 817 Squadron) armed with torpedoes were sent on their way at around 8.30 a.m., on a preliminary course of 134°, even before the first sighting reports came in.[45]

Charles Friend was in one of 832 Squadron's strike force planes. His account does not tell us whether before take-off he and his fellow pilots, observers and gunners (three men per plane) saw Tovey's stirring call to arms sent to *Victorious*. It read: 'A wonderful chance which may achieve most valuable results. God be with you.'[46]

Those in the strike force did not have long to wait before they received the intelligence they needed. They had barely been in the air for half an hour when at around 9 a.m. the first report from the 832 Squadron contingent in the search force came in. The crew in pilot Sub-Lieutenant Tommy Miller's plane had seen the battleship steaming southward, with *Friedrich Ihn* off her starboard bow, near where they had been told the German battleship would be located (see Note 47 and 2 in Map 3 for position).[47]

Miller's plane's appearance to the north had not gone unnoticed. After the war, Commander Gerhard Bidlingmaier, *Tirpitz's* navigating officer, described how he was stationed in the ship's chartroom writing up his log when Tommy Miller's plane was spotted by a lookout.

The first Bidlingmaier knew about it was when he heard the shout: 'Aircraft astern!' He rapidly dashed onto the bridge and ordered the officer of the watch to increase the battleship's speed and to prepare the ship's aircraft for launching.[48]

Meanwhile, alarm bells rang throughout the ship calling men to their action stations. The officers who returned to *Tirpitz's* bridge included her commander Captain Friedrich Karl Topp and Ciliax. They realized they were about to be targeted by aircraft flown off an aircraft carrier. An aircraft like Miller's in such a location was obviously carrier based. The best way to prevent an attack by more planes carrying torpedoes was to fly off one of *Tirpitz's* Arado planes in the hope that the German plane could shoot down the shadowers. That explains why the battleship's southward course was maintained until the plane was catapulted off. Then both German ships were turned towards the east with the object of entering the safety of Vestfjord, or at least fleeing as close to the coast as possible so that they could be protected by land-based German aircraft before the British strike force reached them.

The Arado once launched was quick to chase after the British shadowers, and its guns were duly fired at them, wounding a member of one of the British crews in his thighs. But with so much cloud about, it was no easy task to catch up with another plane. Notwithstanding the Arado pilot's best efforts, the shadowers escaped retribution, and remained in touch with the German battleship and her escort until the strike force arrived on the scene.[49]

That took place at around 9.45 a.m. when the observer in Lucas' plane spotted *Tirpitz* about 20 miles away to the south-east. But it soon became apparent to Friend, whose plane was following behind Lucas', that the whole formation was going to have trouble catching up.

He described the chase as a 'disheartening experience'. The Albacores, he said, were 'flying . . . against a thirty-five knot wind . . . to a target which was steaming . . . at twenty-five knots. Our closing speed was therefore [reduced to] thirty knots, about the speed at which one carelessly drives in a built-up area.'

This might not have mattered if everything else had gone according to plan. Lucas' strategy was to have the four sub-flights, each consisting of three aircraft, climb from the 500-feet level at which they had been flying prior to the sighting, to 3,500 feet where they would be hidden by the clouds, thereby concealing their approach.

However the sudden ascent caused problems. 'Ice began to form on our wings during the climb,' Friend observed. This could have become dangerous if they had been forced to remain in the clouds for too long. It was in these circumstances that Lucas waved goodbye to his initial plan to mount a conventional attack.[50]

Friend, and for that matter every member of the crews in the two squadrons, knew that 'the normal theory of the torpedo attack . . . was that all aircraft should get down to the dropping level of fifty to a hundred feet as nearly together in time as possible to drop their torpedoes in a fan-shaped pattern across [the target's] . . . bows to make it as difficult as we could for [the targeted ship] . . . to comb the [torpedo] tracks.'[51]

This also gave the attacking aircraft the best chance of avoiding the attacked ships' flak. According to Friend: 'The greatest danger to us occurred during the few seconds of aiming and firing, when the pilots were flying straight and level, very low and very slow. The optimum range for dropping was between eight hundred and a thousand yards.'

If they all dropped their torpedoes simultaneously, they could all turn away at once and they could, said Friend: 'present a maximum number of elusive targets for the defending gunners'.[52]

However, in the heat of the moment, Lucas chose to abandon all that – even though, as Friend recalled, it was on that, that 'the training of our pilots, not to mention the setting of the torpedo sight was based'. After registering the maddeningly long time it was taking to catch up, Lucas out of the blue gave the order that each sub-flight could attack independently.

Then, when suddenly faced with an unexpected gap in the clouds, and the realization born of noticing that *Tirpitz's* gunners did not open fire at them, that if he went in immediately, he would take those in the battleship by surprise, Lucas decided that he and the others in his sub-flight should do just that.[53] At 10.18 a.m. Lucas ordered his sub-flight's crews to make their move (see 3 in Map 3 and Note 54 for location).[54]

Friend later recalled how, 'to the astonishment of everyone else', the three Albacores in Lucas' sub-flight suddenly dipped down so that the three planes could drop their torpedoes 'on *Tirpitz's* port beam, leaving the other three [sub-flights on the battleship's starboard side] badly placed should she turn to port, which she forthwith did' (see Map 4 for track of Lucas' sub-flight consisting of aircraft 4A, 4B and 4C, starting from 1 in the map, relative to *Tirpitz's* course).

It is not clear whether Lucas' sub-flight's torpedoes missed because they were dropped from too far away, or whether it was because *Tirpitz* turned just quickly enough to escape out of harm's way. Whatever the reason, a story has circulated over how the turn by the battleship came to be made: there was apparently a conflict of views on *Tirpitz's* bridge over which way she should turn in order to avoid the dropped torpedoes. Topp requested a turn to port, only for Ciliax to countermand the order and demand a turn to starboard. Topp is then alleged to have said to Ciliax, 'I am in command of this ship sir, not you. Helmsman, obey my orders. Hard a port!'[55]

The helmsman obeyed his commander's order, and the ship swung to port. This meant the nearest sub-flight which before the turn had been on the ship's starboard side was now behind the battleship. The pilots of these planes chased after the battleship and dropped their torpedoes while on the battleship's port quarter but they also missed (see Map 4 for track of sub-flight consisting of aircraft 4G, 5M and 5H, starting from 2 in the map, relative to *Tirpitz*'s course).

The final pirouette by *Tirpitz* to starboard completely wrongfooted the remaining two sub-flights. The crews in these planes which were just about to reach a position that would have enabled them to launch their torpedoes from the classic position ahead of *Tirpitz*, at a stroke found themselves forced to fire their torpedoes from the starboard side of the ship where the defensive gunfire was strongest. 'Their dropping positions were unfavourable for attaining hits,' concluded Lucas afterwards (see Map 4 for track of sub-flights consisting of aircraft 4M, 4P and 4R, and 5B, 5C and 5L, which had all started from near 3 in the map, relative to *Tirpitz*'s course).[56]

Two of these unfavourably placed Albacores were shot down, with one crashing into the water almost directly in front of the onrushing battleship. Bidlingmaier claimed he saw the pilot of one of them climbing onto the fallen aircraft's tail piece and then waving at the Germans on board the battleship as *Tirpitz* thundered past.[57]

The failure of the attack from *Tirpitz*'s starboard side meant that Tovey had shot his bolt unsuccessfully. When the last British planes departed shortly after 10.30 a.m., *Tirpitz* was still afloat, although luck had played its part (see 3 in Map 3 for approximate place where the British aircraft completed their attack).[58] According to Topp's report, one torpedo only missed the battleship by a few metres.[59] Afterwards Ciliax, in a conciliatory gesture, if the legend is to be trusted, turned to Topp and said words to the effect of: 'Well done, captain. You fought your ship magnificently.' Then he took off his own Iron Cross and pinned it onto the front of Topp's uniform.[60]

The atmosphere back in *Victorious* where the surviving Albacores landed at around 11.30 a.m. was much more downbeat. The gloom persisted until *Victorious* made it back to her base on 11 March. According to 832 Squadron's war diarist, once at anchor back in Scapa Flow, 'the

Captain saw all officers . . . in the Wardroom . . . He said . . . that there was no excuse for our "failure", that he considered the material we used satisfactory, that the weather conditions were perfect, and he thought our failure was due solely to the fact that the attack was unsynchronized and not pressed far enough home. We were dismissed, and spirit ran pretty low (no mention at all was made as regards our losses). We all expected to be de-rated in the very near future.'[61]

They might have been bucked up a bit if they had been congratulated for participating in an operation which after all had seen the two convoys arrive safely. On the same day they were scolded, QP8 reached Iceland without further loss, and the next day the first batch of PQ12's merchant ships arrived in the Kola Inlet. All of PQ12's ships would eventually make it to their destination.[62]

Perhaps a fairer verdict on the Albacores' performance would have been along the lines of what was in the signal which *Victorious'* Captain Bovell made to Tovey during the evening of 9 March, after the fighter aircraft in the aircraft carrier failed to lay a finger on any of the three Junkers 88 bombers whose crews tried to sink Bovell's ship on the way back to Scapa Flow.[63] Bovell thanked Tovey for his condolences concerning the lost Albacore crews, adding, 'we feel we have let you down'. But he tacked onto the end of his apology one of the lessons learned in the course of the operation: 'As regards the fighters, I am afraid one cannot catch hawks with sparrows.'[64]

5

Tit for Tat

Main Action: 29 March 1942
The cruiser Trinidad which shot herself, PQ13

(See Maps 1, 5, 6 and 7)

The unsuccessful attack on *Tirpitz* during the passage of PQ12 provoked contrasting responses by the admirals in the British and German navies. In his after the action report, the Home Fleet's Admiral Sir Jack Tovey wrote: 'It was evident that even if [*Tirpitz*] . . . had not been damaged, she had received a salutary fright to deter her from future adventures against the northern convoy route.'[1]

This reading of the likely German response to *Tirpitz*'s escape was at least partially correct. In the minutes of the 12 March 1942 meeting between Hitler and Grossadmiral Raeder, convened the day before Tovey's conclusions were written, there was a report by Raeder stating that 'our naval forces should be held back at first. They should only be deployed after the enemy's exact position and strength has been accurately ascertained by air reconnaissance, and when there is sufficient support by the Air Force'. However, this appeared to be contradicted by Raeder's statement in the same report that when Arctic convoys were sighted, 'all forces available must be used unconditionally for the important task of disrupting the shipment of supplies to Russia'.[2]

It was in the context of this confused German declaration that the next confrontation in the Arctic between the opposing naval forces was to take place. Once again it would be set against the desire by the Germans to intercept an Arctic convoy. On this occasion the merchant ships targeted would be the tanker and 18 other merchant ships, plus three whalers, in convoy PQ13. It was a convoy, most of which had originally sailed to Iceland from Loch Ewe, the assembly point in north-west Scotland, but which finally set out from Hvalfjord on 20 March 1942 after a false start. From there, like most Arctic convoys starting from Hvalfjord, it travelled northward up the west coast of Iceland, only finally turning towards the north-east after passing Iceland's northernmost cape.[3]

Bad weather was another common factor that affected both PQ12 and PQ13, although the gale PQ13 encountered to the east of Jan Mayen Island on 25 March, as it headed in a north-easterly direction, was so extreme, the ships in the convoy were scattered.

John Dodds, a 24-year-old officer in HMS *Fury*, one of the two destroyers which with the light cruiser *Trinidad* provided the core of PQ13's escort during the first half of its journey, did not mince his words when on 25 March he wrote in his contemporaneous diary, addressed to his girlfriend Margaret: 'During the night (of 24–25 March) we ran into some very rough sea, and before dawn broke, there was a terrific storm blowing. Also a blinding snowstorm. When daylight did eventually come, we found ourself absolutely alone. We took a sight and found that during the night we had been blown at least 50 miles off our course, and where the convoy is God only knows.'[4]

Dodds' diary bears witness to 26 March not being much better. 'We . . . [have] been looking for the convoy all day, but not a trace of it anywhere,' Dodds recorded at the end of the day. By the morning of 27 March the strength of the storm had subsided, but the ships of the convoy appear to have been scattered over some 150 miles.[5] That was not the only problem.

'This morning there . . . [was] 3–4 feet of solid ice all over the ship,' Dodds wrote on 27 March. 'The seamen were hacking it away with pickaxes, for it gives us too much top weight. If we do a bad roll, it is possible that we would not come up, and we do not particularly want that to happen because that water out there is none too warm! . . . We found one ship this afternoon . . . We have taken her under our wing and [are now] looking for the other 17!'[6]

Dodds would not have been surprised to learn that the crews in the British warships were not the only ones looking over the high waves through which they were ploughing. Even as they searched, U-boat lookouts, peering through the gloom, were also trying to locate the convoy's ships, as well as those in the westbound convoy QP9 (said to have consisted of 19 merchant ships), which had left the Kola Inlet on 21 March.[7]

At the time when Dodds was writing about his and his shipmates' search, unbeknown to Marinegruppenkommando Nord's Generaladmiral Rolf Carls, there were only three U-boats in the vicinity. The fourth, *U-655*, which was supposed to be there, had been neutralized south of Bear Island on 24 March. A QP9 escort, the minesweeper *Sharpshooter*, had happened to come across her with her guard down.

Minutes later *U-655* was being stalked and rammed, and once that had taken place, it was all over in a moment. After the ramming 'she drifted aft,' *Sharpshooter*'s Lieutenant Commander David Lampen reported, 'until one cable clear, when she turned turtle and . . . sank by the stern with her bows coming clear of the water.' The men inside did not have a chance.[8]

This depletion of the U-boat arm's scarce resources being used to search for PQ13 was exacerbated by the Germans' decision to only permit Admiral Hubert Schmundt, the 53-year-old Admiral Nordmeer (Northern Waters), to command the U-boats covering the north-western section of the northern route after PQ13 was found. Until that occurred, the four U-boats controlled by Schmundt remained cooped up near the Kola Inlet rather than being deployed along with the U-boats controlled by Carls to the north-west, where they were really needed.[9]

In the event, this administrative shortsightedness would not be decisive, although it took a certain amount of good fortune favouring the Germans for them to be able to thwart the ingenuity of the British codebreaking efforts. Bletchley Park's codebreakers were able to read Admiral Carls' 25 March 1942 Enigma-encoded message addressed to the commanders of the four U-boats he referred to as Gruppe Zieten, telling them to form up south-east of Bear Island.[10] Not surprisingly Carls wanted them to patrol within the 228-mile 'pinch point' that ran between the southernmost rocks of Bear Island and North Cape, the northernmost cliff in German occupied Norway, the narrowest channel north of Norway through which the convoys had to pass. But there were not enough U-boats available to achieve a complete blockade. Carls' orders only contemplated the U-boats at his disposal occupying a small section near the northern end of the channel. This enabled the Admiralty during the night of 26–27 March to issue instructions, which if complied with, would have steered the PQ13 ships to the south-east, enabling them to evade the area mentioned in Carls' message.[11] It was the second time during the passage of PQ13 that a change to the convoy's route had been ordered thanks to British code-breakers deciphering orders sent to U-boats.[12] However on this, the second occasion, the scattering of the convoy as a result of the storm made it impossible for Bletchley Park's latest coup to be exploited immediately. It was in these circumstances that some of the convoy's ships were to be sighted by a lookout in a Gruppe Zieten U-boat after all.

At 7.02 a.m. precisely on 28 March 1942, a *U-209* lookout all of a sudden spotted through the falling snow the distinctive dark silhouettes of two of PQ13's merchant ships plus what looked like two escorts (these ships were from the group of PQ13 merchant ships subsequently referred to as the western group – see Note 13 and 1 in Map 5 for the names of the ships in this group and the location where ships from the group were sighted).[13]

Forty-eight minutes later, one of those eerie morse code messages composed by Kapitänleutnant Heinrich Brodda, *U-209*'s 28-year-old commander, was floating through the ether on its way to Admirals Carls and Schmundt to tell them what had transpired.[14] It was that message, bolstered by a German reconnaissance aircraft sighting of the group of PQ13 ships subsequently referred to as the eastern group, that set the scene for what took place next (see names of ships in the eastern group and sighting position of this group in Note 15 and 2 in Map 5).[15]

As soon as Brodda's message was received by Schmundt in Kirkenes, plans were made to send three destroyers to attack the convoy's eastern group referred to above. The eastern group was the target because Schmundt had been given to understand that one of the escorts with the western group might be a cruiser, whereas he had gathered that the eastern group was guarded by ships that might be more easily overcome.[16]

In fact the cruiser *Trinidad* was not tied to either of the two groups. During 28 March and the early hours of 29 March she and the destroyer HMS *Fury* had been sailing from one group to the other, and to the south of both of them, in an attempt to provide a screen against the German surface fleet (see 1 in Map 6 indicating where *Trinidad* was operating). Thanks to a series of tip-offs on 27 March by the Admiralty based on the decrypts of German Enigma messages supplied by Bletchley Park's codebreakers, *Trinidad*'s 45-year-old Captain Leslie Saunders had learned that a raid by three German destroyers might be imminent.[17]

That is not to say that Saunders knew exactly when the German destroyers would appear. Leading up to the German destroyers' departure from Kirkenes, Bletchley Park's codebreakers were taking between 12 and 24 hours to read German Enigma messages.[18] This delay explains why, although British equipment intercepted Admiral Schmundt's message sent shortly after 1.30 p.m. on 28 March stating that German destroyers would be departing from Kirkenes approximately an hour later so that they could attack the convoy, the signal was not decrypted until it was too late.[19]

Germany's 8th Destroyer Flotilla's three destroyers, Zerstörer 24, Zerstörer 25 and Zerstörer 26 (*Z 24*, *Z 25* and *Z 26*), under the command of the 43-year-old Kapitän zur See Gottfried Pönitz, who was flying his flag in *Z 26*, duly left Kirkenes at 2.30 p.m. on 28 March.[20] Although they of course represented nothing like the threat *Tirpitz* had posed for vessels of PQ12, the fact that the main armament on the decks of each destroyer consisted of four 5.9-inch guns – similar in power if not quantity to the guns in a light British cruiser – meant they were not to be underestimated. They sailed in a northerly direction for more than seven hours before turning, when north-north-east of the Kola Inlet, to make a sweep towards the west where they hoped to find the convoy (see Maps 5 and 6).[21]

Hans-Jürgen Meyer-Brenkhof, a 20-year-old midshipman in *Z 26*, later recalled the rough conditions he and his shipmates were having to endure when at around 11.30 p.m. that night they struck silver if not gold.[22] 'I was in the crow's nest up the front mast of the ship looking out for the enemy. *Z 26* was lurching 45 degrees to the left and then to the right. You can imagine how that felt up in my nest. Then all of a sudden I heard what sounded like a honking noise on the port side in front of us. I reported it using the microphone to the duty officer. The reply came back. "Greetings from the commander. But we are not on the Kurfürstendamm (a Berlin street) now!" They did not believe me. However, the honking sound did not stop, and when I reported it again, the Flotilla changed course towards it.'[23]

It turned out that the noise had emanated from the lifeboats full of men which had moved away from the floating wooden boxes, planks of wood and other wreckage, all that remained of the British merchant ship *Empire Ranger*. After being separated from the other merchant ships in the convoy by the storm, she had sunk well to the north-east of Norway's North Cape at around 8.30 p.m. on 28 March after being attacked by a German aircraft (see 2 and 3 in Map 6).[24] That probably explained the mysterious flash the watching seamen in the German destroyers had seen on the horizon earlier that night.[25] The 61 survivors were rescued by the crew of *Z 24* before she followed her sister ships westward. Buoyed up by their discovery, their crews were already continuing the hunt for the rest of the convoy.[26]

Approximately two hours later, at 1.35 a.m. on 29 March, a second solitary ship, that had likewise been separated from the other ships in PQ13 by the storm, was spotted from *Z 26* (see 4 in Map 6).[27] It was the Panamanian-flagged merchant ship SS *Bateau*. Once again midshipman Meyer-Brenkhof played a leading role in what followed. As part of his training, he was ordered to fire the torpedo that was supposed to sink her. 'It shot out of its tube and went on its way,' he wrote, 'only for the commander of the ship, who was an artillery expert, to become impatient when there was no quick explosion. However no sooner had the commander given his gunnery officer permission to fire at the ship than we heard a deafening blast which showed I had hit her after all.'[28]

But his relief turned to horror when shortly afterwards he heard what he described as the 'terrible cries issuing from the mouths of our American comrades who were attempting to swim away from the ship in the burning water'.

Viktor Gernhard, who was watching from *Z 25*, described what transpired: 'The merchant ship slowly rolled over onto its side. Then its stern pointed up in the air as the bow disappeared into the sea, and there was a hissing sound as a cloud of steam shot up. We clearly saw the propeller rotate a couple of times before the ship slipped vertically into the waves and was lost forever.

'All the men on the deck and even the men who had been in the boiler room came over to watch the dramatic scene, and that's when they heard the screams. They were horrifying animalistic screams. Our commander Korvettenkapitän Heinz Peters immediately ordered that the survivors should be rescued. We heard them crying out: "Germans, help! Help!"

'To those of us watching, it was a nightmarish vision. Some of the sunk ship's crew were lying on floating objects they had grabbed. Others protruded from the sea, only supported by their life jackets. Again and again we heard the same shattering cry.'

According to Gernhard, strenuous efforts were made to rescue as many men as possible. *Z 25*'s Korvettenkapitän Peters himself took charge of the rescue efforts, leaning over the side of the ship so that he could order the necessary adjustments to both the rudder and the engines. While he did this, the 3rd watch officer shouted in English to the floating men instructing them to swim closer to the destroyer, and one man from *Z 25*'s crew allowed himself to be suspended from a rope over the water so that he could grab the few men who passed within his reach.

But as Gernhard observed, 'it soon became clear that the shipwrecked men were too weak to help themselves. And even though the ship went back and forth, the men in the water were swept away so that their cries became fainter and fainter.'

Nevertheless, Gernhard was shocked when he heard Korvettenkapitän Peters shouting down from the bridge: 'First Officer and Oberbootsmann (Chief Petty Officer). Stop the rescue. Hurry up!'

This seemingly callous termination of the rescue operation, which in spite of all their best efforts had only resulted in the picking up of six men, prompted Gernhard to end his account of the incident with the following fatalistic summing up: 'As our propellers sprang into action – we'd been left behind by the other destroyers – the inhuman screams of the men who were being left in the water could still be heard: "Germans, help!" However no one could help them now because the war knew no mercy.'[29] Forty-two of the men making up *Bateau*'s crew and armed guard were later registered as missing following the sinking.[30]

It is possible that *Z 25*'s Korvettenkapitän Peters was persuaded he should leave the drowning seamen in the water because of an order issued by Admiral Schmundt. The German Admiral Nordmeer's command that the ships in the Flotilla should sail to the south-east if they did not find the rest of the convoy near where they were, reached the destroyers shortly after *Bateau* was sunk.[31]

Schmundt's instructions were obeyed (see Map 6), only for the destroyers' commanders to receive a counter order at around 6.30 a.m. that same morning (29 March) telling them that some ships from the convoy had been sighted from *U-376* to the east of where the destroyers had started their south-easterly detour.[32] The German ships sped up to the northern latitude line signposted by the U-boat, and then at around 9.20 a.m. they turned towards the west once more.[33]

It was at this point that Kapitän Pönitz made what midshipman Meyer-Brenkhof branded 'a fundamental error, which would condemn many of our comrades to die a heroic death for the Fatherland'.[34] In an attempt to ensure that their crews would stay in touch in the snowy and foggy conditions, Pönitz had the commanders of the three destroyers advance in single file behind *Z 26*.[35] This was done rather than having the three ships spread out so that they could move forward side by side. The obvious disadvantage of the single file formation was that the front ship would foul the range of the following ships if an enemy appeared ahead.

In view of this, Pönitz might have thought twice before giving this order had he realized that the cruiser *Trinidad*, backed by the destroyer *Fury*, was fast approaching through the semi-impenetrable fog and falling snow from what was effectively, if not precisely, the opposite direction (as shown in Map 7, the south eastward course of the British cruiser and the westward course of the German destroyers converged).[36] However, in fairness to him, at the time he had no way of knowing that a British cruiser was coming towards him. In fact he had reason to believe that was not the case. He had been told that most of the escorts guarding the PQ 13 group he was targeting were to the south of the convoy, giving any ships like those in his flotilla that advanced towards the merchant ships from the east the chance to make their raid without encountering effective opposition.[37] He may also have been influenced by the fact that the radar in *Z 24* and *Z 25* was not working, leaving these ships vulnerable if they encountered an unexpected ambush while not shielded by *Z 26*'s radar.[38]

There was an even more fundamental problem that could not be fixed whichever formation he chose. Detecting the enemy with radar, as was the case in *Z 26* as the British and German ships converged, did not get you very far if you could not exploit the detection quickly enough.[39] It was to take the rapid response by the well-drilled crew in *Trinidad* following its detection of the German destroyers to bring home to the unfortunate seamen in *Z 26* the speed of exploitation that was required.

The first alert in *Trinidad* occurred at 9.42 a.m. (still 29 March), when an able seaman seated in front of one of *Trinidad's* radar sets reported seeing an echo on his screen at a distance of six and a half miles, the relative bearing being 79°. Two minutes later *Trinidad's* radar was showing that the distance had come down to a little over five miles, the relative bearing being 92°.[40]

The British cruiser's Captain Saunders would not have been human if at this critical point his heart was not beating a little faster than usual. Because he knew the approximate whereabouts of all the convoy's escorts, including the three destroyers, one British (HMS *Oribi*) and two Russian, which had joined the protection force earlier that morning, he could be pretty sure that if the vessels detected on his ship's radar were not merchant ships, they must be hostile.[41]

That explains why shortly after 9.50 a.m., when the three 'shapes' spotted through the mist and sleet-like snow, on a bearing of 64°, some two and a half miles away, were identified as being destroyers, Saunders' gunnery officer with his captain's permission was immediately able to order the men operating *Trinidad's* twelve 6-inch guns to 'Open fire!' (see 1 and 2 in Map 7 and Note 42 for *Trinidad's* approximate positions during this stage of the engagement).[42]

By all accounts the first broadside fired at the leading German destroyer, *Z 26*, fell short. But before the return of fire from *Z 26* could find the right range and direction, *Trinidad's* next salvo had slammed into the German ship amidships. This, Saunders reported later, 'started a fire, with much flame and smoke stretching between the mainmast and the after funnel.'[43] Viktor Gernhard, still in *Z 25*, at the back of the German line, described the sudden transformation from hunter to hunted in the following terms: 'I saw a flash directly in front of us, and then flames leapt up from *Z 26*. The ship had evidently been hit. We were paralysed by shock and horror, as rooted to the spot, we stared at what was unfolding before our eyes. I could see the flames and the billowing smoke as *Z 26* sped off into the snow.'[44]

By this time, after firing at Z 26 less successfully three more times, *Trinidad*'s guns had swivelled round to engage Z 24, the second ship in the ill-advised line. It took some time for the Germans on the receiving end to comprehend what was happening. 'We were puzzled by the howling whistling sounds that followed,' Gernhard reported, 'until we saw the 20-metre high columns of water between us and Z 24 ... which were accompanied by the continuous sound of thunder that was rolling over the sea.' Z 25's Korvettenkapitän Peters quickly realized that his ship and Z 24 were being shelled, and would almost certainly share Z 26's fate if they did not take evasive action.

It may have been this thought that persuaded him and Z 24's Korvettenkapitän Martin Saltzwedel, after ordering the firing of torpedoes and guns (two shells hit *Trinidad* aft on her port side), to scurry away to the north. Saunders was relieved to see them go; he later confessed he feared that *Trinidad* might only have been able to engage one of the two ships if they had both turned on him.[45] The gunners in HMS *Fury*, which was behind *Trinidad*, and who were unable to see the German ships through the mist when the shooting started, would have been unable to intervene.[46]

Undeterred, Saunders ordered his crew to give chase to the north-west where one of the German destroyers, which he would later discover was Z 26, had disappeared. Some 15 minutes later, as Saunders later reported, 'black smoke was seen, shortly followed by a shape of a ship, from which it was coming.'[47] Those in the British cruiser were further encouraged by the sight *of Trinidad*'s shells hitting the ship ahead, and the realization that the German ship's rear guns had stopped firing. German men dead and alive were seen floating in the water as *Trinidad* swept past them in hot pursuit.

In what appeared to be a last display of defiance as *Trinidad* caught up, Z 26 ceased her zigzagging shortly after being hit on her port side below the bridge and aft, and wheeled to starboard, as if like a wounded stag, she was preparing to fight her pursuer to the finish at close quarters. At this point the German destroyer was about a mile away relative to *Trinidad*'s port bow. But if a last-ditch stand was her captain's intention, he clearly no longer had the means to make an impact. After a token single salvo from her surviving front guns, she turned away once more.[48]

It was at this critical stage of the battle, with *Z 26* languishing in the sea at *Trinidad*'s mercy, that the tables were cruelly turned, at least from the British viewpoint. According to Saunders, 'the torpedo officer reported: "All torpedoes fired Sir." He had a covering permission to fire if in a melée he saw a suitable target. But our only target was stern on to us, presenting no target at all, so I said: "What at?" He indicated the enemy, and I told him it was a bloody waste of torpedoes!'[49]

Saunders' account goes on to describe what he witnessed next: 'Immediately after this exchange, a lookout reported: "Torpedo on the port bow!" Looking over the side, a torpedo was breaking surface only 200 yards away and [was] heading straight for us.' If the legend is accurate, this prompted *Trinidad*'s captain to say: 'It looks remarkably like one of ours.'[50]

If Saunders really said this, it was an astute statement: it was later discovered that possibly because of the icy conditions, after only one of the torpedoes 'fired' by *Trinidad* had left its tube, this unleashed torpedo, although aimed at *Z 26*, had turned around in mid-flight, and had come speeding through the water towards the port side of the ship that had fired it.[51]

Although the wheel in *Trinidad* was put hard over to port in order to avoid the missile speeding towards the cruiser, it was too little, too late, and in Saunders' words, 'it hit just forward of the bridge, drenching us with dirty sea water.' (See 2 in Map 1, 4A in Map 7 and Note 52 for the location.)[52] The following account by Frank Pearce, a member of one of *Trinidad*'s gun crews, was less phlegmatic: 'The explosion . . . momentarily lifted the ship, and a huge column of black oily water rose into the air, covering everybody on the compass platform and lookout positions on the port side. The torpedo had exploded in the Royal Marines Barracks, flooding the forward Boiler Room, destroying the forward Damage Control Headquarters and killing instantly numbers of officers and ratings in these spaces.'[53]

It also trapped men in *Trinidad*'s transmitting station, the section of the ship where all information is processed that has a bearing on where the guns are pointed in order to hit a spotted target. This section was deep down in the bowels of the ship – on the third 'deck' down from the top deck, that is two decks down from the marines' mess deck where the torpedo had exploded. This was potentially disastrous. The transmitting station was particularly vulnerable because it and the sections above it were flanked on their port and starboard sides by fuel tanks positioned just inside the ship's hull.

It is hard to convey the terror experienced by those trapped below the top deck in the flooded areas of a torpedoed ship. The physical conditions can be likened to, if not equated with, those endured by men imprisoned inside the hull of a sinking submarine. In both cases the trapped men would be lying if they said they were not petrified by the prospect of being drowned or suffocated before they were rescued. That is why, when following the explosion, a wave of water swept through the ship's forward boiler room, carrying the two surviving stokers in the room to the foot of the escape ladder, they could not be blamed for fearing the worst. There they had to wait in the dark, waist deep in seawater, half-deafened by the piercing scream made by the escaping steam that had scalded their skin, fearing that at any minute the water would rise up and drown them. Fortunately, the exit hatch at the top of the ladder was eventually opened, permitting them to get out.[54]

We have been given an even more graphic description of the ordeal suffered by the men trapped *in Trinidad*'s transmitting station thanks to an account by George Lloyd, one of that section's only four survivors. Lloyd, then aged 28, was one of 21 musicians who were manning the processing machinery in the transmitting station when the explosion of the torpedo severed any contact between his section and the gun turrets.

'Warrant Officer Gould, who was in charge, shouted to me to try to telephone the bridge,' Lloyd reported later, 'but the lines were dead. Gould then ordered a sailor to go to the bridge and report our condition.' In spite of the fact that a small amount of oil had already begun to trickle down the ladder that was the only way of leaving the transmitting station, the sailor managed to climb up, followed by another man.

Lloyd's account continues: 'Oil . . . [had] started to come through the hatch (at the top of the ladder at a faster rate). I moved a few yards to the other side of the main room to get away from it. As the oil became a strong cascade, Gould shouted: "Shut the hatch!" No one moved. Everyone seemed to be completely paralysed and stayed glued to his position. The picture of these silent men standing motionless, the cold black oil engulfing their bodies, the tiny emergency light bulb giving its dim light . . . is a picture that will always live with me.

'Again Gould shouted: "Shut the hatch!" The oil was now up to our groins. Thomas (Lou) Barber, our solo cornet went to the ladder . . . [but] was knocked backwards . . . by the force of the oil. He tried again. I went after him and pushed. He took the worst of the oil and swallowed a lot.' However, somehow the two men made it out through the hatch, and then barely conscious, struggled up to the top deck.

There, as Lloyd lay gasping for air like a beached fish, he heard the voice of another sailor on the deck below, shouting: 'Anybody below? Anybody below?', and only wished he could direct the shouting sailor to the transmitting station. But for precious minutes he could not do or even say anything, and by the time he had recovered enough to stand up, the men whom he had left behind had long since drowned in the oil that had flooded into the section from the adjacent tank. The hatch at the top of the ladder leading out of the transmitting station had slammed shut, crushing the man who had attempted to follow Lloyd, in the process breaking this man's back and blocking the exit. Lloyd was the last man in the section to escape.[55]

The explosion of the torpedo that had stopped *Trinidad*, leaving her with fires raging below her top deck, and with a list of 17 degrees to port, resulted in a second reprieve for the surviving men in *Z 26*.[56] However, it was only to be temporary. By steaming off into the fog, *Z 26* managed to evade *Fury*, whose commander had, on seeing *Trinidad* stopped, elected to take up the chase where the British cruiser had left off.[57]

But *Z 26* ended up passing the port side of the group of seven PQ13 merchant ships (the western group so designated in Note 13 plus one more merchant ship), which along with one of the convoy's trawlers and one of PQ13's whalers was approaching from north-west of the site where *Trinidad* had first fired at the German destroyers (as shown in Map 7). The fleeing German destroyer's crew were fortunate not to be set upon once more there and then. They were spotted from the destroyer HMS *Eclipse* which was sailing about a mile in front of the merchant ships, with one of the recently arrived Russian destroyers on either side of her. The only reason *Z 26* was permitted to sail by unchallenged by the crew in the British destroyer was because *Eclipse's* 32-year-old Lieutenant

Commander Edward Mack thought the passing ship he was looking at was British.

Mack knew from the first enemy report he had received from *Trinidad,* and the sound of gunfire, that the British cruiser had been in action against German destroyers. But he at first suspected that *Z 26,* whose silhouette he saw through the mist, was *Trinidad*.[58]

Before he could verify this, his attention was diverted by the appearance of another warship, which loomed up out of the snow and proceeded to fire at *Eclipse* (see 5A and 5B in Map 7).[59] It turned out it was *Fury,* some of whose gunners had mistaken *Eclipse* for either the German ship (*Z 26*) that *Fury* had been pursuing, or one of *Z 26*'s sister vessels.

'For some minutes chaos reigned in the destroyer screen,' *Eclipse*'s Mack commented drily later, preferring to gloss over the frustration that evidently boiled over at the time.[60] Fortunately for the British sailors in both destroyers, no harm was done, because all the gunners who fired missed their targets. But as one of the men who had been near *Fury*'s B-gun later reported: 'as . . . [*Eclipse*] was passing very close to our starboard side, there came a stream of expletives from the bridge'.[61]

After the confusion involving the two British destroyers was resolved, Mack had *Eclipse* turned to the west in order to link up with the other warship, which he still thought was *Trinidad*. The warship he had seen had by this time disappeared in that direction.

But closer inspection, when the distance between the two ships had been reduced because of *Eclipse*'s superior speed to around 800 yards, revealed, among the mysterious ship's other features, a small reddish ensign on her yardarm. This was sufficient to tell Mack she was German, although he would have received corroboration, had he needed it, if he had looked up in his confidential books the *Z 26* call sign 'Z.U.' which a signaller in the mystery ship had flashed at *Eclipse,* evidently believing the British destroyer to be German.

Without more ado, Mack immediately gave the order to open fire (see 6A in Map 7 for location). However, rather than tying *Z 26* down, this merely resulted in her turning tail. As Mack later reported: 'A running battle through the snow now ensued, with the enemy endeavouring to work to the south making smoke, while *Eclipse* tried to cut him off, and at the same time bring her aft guns to bear. The enemy was obviously damaged and made little effort to reply to our fire, only occasional guns being fired.'[62]

The chase carried on for no less than half an hour, with Mack endeavouring to keep his ship to the rear of Z 26 so that his gunners could carry on raining their shells into the German ship, while Z 26, whose rear guns were out of action, could not bring her front guns to bear on the British destroyer.

Then at 11.20 a.m., after a particularly heavy hit forward near the bridge, Z 26 at long last slowed down and came to a halt, leaving her a sitting duck, at a British warship's mercy for the second time that day. Mack later reported: 'His stern was almost awash, and there was a considerable shambles aft and amidships with smoke rising from it. Forward there was a large hole in the ship's side below B-gun . . . She had a list of about 10 degrees to port.'[63]

Josef Hirsch, a 19-year-old stoker in Z 26, who had also been responsible for loading the shells onto the lifts that carried them up to one of Z 26's guns, later recalled: 'While the ship's engines were running, we could carry on trying to get away. But after heavy hits to the engine room, that was no longer possible.

'The men from the engine room who could still walk came out of it with horrific mutilations, looking as if they had been boiled. The [boiling hot] steam . . . had had a terrible effect on them. Dead men lay everywhere. Even our sick bay had been hit. Our doctor lay on the companionway to the bridge. A comrade next to me, close to my fighting station, was also dead.'[64]

Another young sailor, who had taken cover along with midshipman Meyer-Brenkhof behind a searchlight on Z 26's deck, was not just dead. Meyer-Brenkhof later related how 'the poor boy had been torn apart by a shell that had landed near us', adding, 'I survived because I was protected from the blast by the searchlight.'

However, the lives of those who had survived the blasts of the shells were still in jeopardy: 'The whole ship . . . [seemed to be] on fire,' Meyer-Brenkhof reported. Because of this, as he recalled: 'the metal deck plates were very hot, and there was a danger the heat would reach the ammunition chamber'. That particular threat was only averted after Meyer-Brenkhof and the ship's 1st Officer scooped up water from the sea using one of the ship's coffee pots attached to a rope so that they could pour it onto the steaming plates.[65]

Meyer-Brenkhof's account gives another sailor the credit for an even more heroic act. This man deactivated the torpedo that was hanging out of one of Z 26's torpedo tubes, thereby saving the survivors and the ship from the kind of explosion that had resulted in such suffering in *Trinidad*.[66]

But all such efforts to save life and limb would have been in vain if the surviving men in Z 26 had not had a second helping of good fortune. When *Eclipse* finally drew level with the stopped German destroyer, which was just 1,200 yards away from the destroyer's port side, three of the British ship's torpedoes were by mistake fired ahead rather than at the German vessel.[67] That explains why Z 26 was still afloat when, as Mack reported: 'Eclipse ran up past . . . [Z 26's] starboard side and . . . turned across [the] bows of [the] enemy and came down her port side on reciprocal course in order to fire [the] remaining torpedo' that was to constitute the coup de grâce.[68]

Unfortunately for Mack, the short delay required to perform this manoeuvre not only scuppered his chances of claiming the first sinking of a German warship in the Battle of the Arctic, but very nearly ended up with his own ship being sunk. For just as he lined up his ship for this final shot, the snow stopped falling and the fog lifted, revealing the presence around two miles to the east of the other two German destroyers on *Eclipse*'s disengaged starboard beam.

Their crews had been searching for Z 26 ever since they had separated following *Trinidad*'s initial ambush. Within seconds of the sighting, those in *Eclipse* saw the flashes made by the German destroyers' guns, and heard the crashing sound as shells struck home (see 7A and 7B in Map 7 for Z 24's and Z 25's location).

It was fortunate for Mack and his crew that as they in their turn fled, snow had started to fall again to the north-west. Unfazed by the smoke pouring out of his vessel, he quickly gave the order to go full speed ahead in that direction, and although it meant relinquishing the chance of sinking Z 26, he was now just grateful he could hide his ship in the welcoming arms of the snowstorm.[69]

However he did not make good his escape before one 5.9-inch shell had crashed into the supply lobby of *Eclipse*'s X gun aft. The result was two men were burned so badly they later died of their wounds, while another man was wounded so severely that his smashed-up foot and the bottom four inches of his leg had to be amputated in an emergency operation carried out at the site of the explosion.[70]

Eclipse's departure enabled the two German destroyers to approach *Z 26*. It was decided that *Z 25* should go as close to the wrecked ship as was possible with a view to conducting the main rescue operation, while *Z 24* was given the task of searching for those survivors in the water who had been swept away from their ship, while at the same time watching out for enemy vessels.

Afterwards Viktor Gernhard described what he witnessed as *Z 25* moved closer to *Z 26*, stopping around 20 yards away. He saw what he termed: 'A moving sight. Thick clouds of smoke were billowing up into the air above the ship. Its superstructure had been shot up and burned out. The three aft guns had been smashed. The section near where the depth charges were stored [at the back of the ship] was on fire. A torpedo with its head still attached was hanging half out of a torpedo tube. There were yawning black holes all over the ship's hull and superstructure. The destroyer's deck was littered with debris and bodies. The crew for the 2 cm flak gun at the front of the ship lay spread-eagled over their weapon. [However] on the front mast, the war flag still fluttered on the yard arm . . . In contrast to what had been heard during the drama [of the battle] everything was now very quiet.'

Gernhard also noticed that 'while dotted around the upper deck there were some survivors tending the wounded, others were already in the sea, or on floats and rubber dinghies, their brightly coloured life jackets standing out against the grey green water.'[71]

There, according to Meyer-Brenkhof, another deadly battle was being fought over the raft which he threw into the sea shortly before he followed it into the water. 'The raft became a battlefield,' he reported, 'as men fought each other for the privilege of boarding it. No comradely spirit was to be seen. It was the survival of the fittest. I remained in the water . . . and held onto the raft . . . This saved my life. Of those who climbed onto the raft, none survived.' This was because although the water was freezing cold, it was nothing compared with the temperature of the air.

Even so, Meyer-Brenkhof was so cold that he lost consciousness before he was rescued, and he was lucky he could be revived.[72] According to Gernhard, reviving the rescued men, who quickly lost the ability to help themselves, became more and more difficult as the minutes ticked by, and he began to see men he knew well floating lifeless down the side of his ship. When there was no sign of life in the last twelve men picked up, they were dumped onto the floor of a washroom in *Z 25*, a gruesome reminder of the horrors of war for anyone, like Gernhard, who stumbled upon them.[73]

Even more upsetting was what followed in the sea when the order was finally given to take the German destroyers back to Kirkenes, leaving *U-376* to rescue the relatively few survivors who had been missed by the surface ships. Meyer-Brenkhof has revealed that some of the men floating near the ships were sucked into the water churned up by the vessels' propellers, and if any were living, they were chopped up while still alive.[74] In any case, they certainly could not be included in the 80 survivors rescued by the German destroyers, and the eight saved by *U-376*.[75]

Prior to the destroyers' departure, the stern of *Z 26* sank lower and lower into the water, and the ship's list to port became more and more pronounced. That was the cue for Pönitz, who had remained on board along with the ship's commander and first officer, to trigger the explosion that would ensure nothing would be left of the vessel for the enemy. They then swam over to *Z 25*.[76] As Gernhard noted, at 11.57 a.m.: '*Z 26* sank stern first and her bow pointed up in the air. Then there was a jolt, and *Z 26* with her war flag still flying vanished. That left us feeling deeply moved, as we remembered our comrades who had not managed to get out of the wreck, and as we thought about the boiler room men who died in the machine rooms.'[77]

As for *Trinidad*, her safety was prioritized over that of the convoy's western group. Her Captain Saunders ordered the commanders of two of the convoy's escorts to protect her. As the damaged cruiser struggled to make it to Russia, she was escorted initially by *Fury*, and subsequently by *Oribi* and the minesweeper *Harrier*. The latter ship's commander had been ordered by the SBNO North Russia to join the rescue party so she could help bring *Trinidad* in. *Trinidad* eventually made it to the Kola Inlet under her 'own steam', arriving at the mouth of the inlet at 10.30 a.m. on 30 March.[78]

On the way, during the evening of 29 March, her torpedo officer, Lieutenant Commander Dent, noticed that an indicator was lit up on the compass platform on the bridge. It told him that the generator in the low power room underneath the flooded marine mess deck where the torpedo had exploded was still working, something that could not have been possible if the room was flooded. This combined with the knocking that was heard led to the conclusion that the men in the room must be alive. Arrangements were quickly made to pump the water out of the marine mess deck. When the two men who had been incarcerated stepped out, their reappearance was greeted as one of those miracles which at the time seemed so extraordinary, but which were to prove remarkably commonplace during the life and death struggles in the Arctic that were to come. It was at least some compensation for all the heartbreaking scenes that those fortunate enough to have survived following the torpedoing of the cruiser had been forced to witness.[79]

6

Abandoned

Main Action: 30 March 1942
The sinking of SS Induna and SS Effingham, PQ13 part 2

(See Map 5)

It is sad to say that the blood shed in the course of the fighting between the two sides' warships during the mid-stages of PQ13 only represents half of what went wrong as far as the Allies were concerned. Arguably those who served in the convoy's merchant ships and who were forced to endure the consequences of having no escort to speak of after the majority of the Allies' warships departed, suffered even more harrowing hardships.

One of the Americans who was to be affected in this way was Bernard Covington, a 17-year-old armed guard from South Boston, Virginia. It is clear from the following extract from the letter he wrote to his parents on 19 January 1942, before he embarked on the preliminary 4,000-mile journey taking him from America's east coast to Iceland, that he had no idea how bad things would get during PQ13:

'Dear Mama and Daddy,

I am in Boston [Massachusetts] now. They are loading the ship. I don't know where we are headed. They gave us winter clothing, and someone says we are headed for Russia. I am aboard the SS *Effingham*, a good-sized freighter. We have plenty of machine guns and 1 four-inch. The chow is really good. We have nice cabins. Four boys to each. There are seven of us boys, 1 petty officer and 1 ensign, and one Radio Operator. Ten navy men in all . . . Don't worry about me as we can shoot straight, and will have a convoy also.'[1]

Almost, but not quite as green, was Britain's 17-year-old Morris Mills, all 6 foot 3 inches of him. In spite of his tender years, PQ13 was to be his second trip to northern Russia in the British merchant ship SS *New Westminster City*. The first had been when participating in the uneventful Operation Dervish in August 1941 (see Chapter 2).

The German failure to place any obstacles in the path of that first Arctic convoy had only served to reinforce Mills' feeling that going to sea, even if that entailed travelling all the way to faraway Russia, was merely another way of satisfying that same thirst for adventure that had made him want to become a sailor in the first place.

In the course of writing his memoirs after the war, he described how that had come to pass. In a bid to follow in the footsteps of his grandfather, who had been a petty officer in the Royal Navy, he had when just 13 years old, tried to run away to sea without obtaining permission from his parents, only to be sent home by the police. He had subsequently persuaded his parents to let him sign on as an apprentice trainee deck officer in the Merchant Navy.[2]

Mills' enthusiasm was not dented by the rough reception he was given by his *New Westminster City* shipmates. The memoirs also describe how for example he had to prove himself by fighting another member of the crew.[3] But perhaps most terrifying of all, leaving aside for a moment the aftermath of the German attacks on his ship, was the great PQ13 storm referred to in the previous chapter. In his memoirs he described it in the following unforgettable terms:

'The noise of the wind was indescribable, howling and screaming like a banshee . . .

'The deeply laden ships pitched and rolled in the mountainous seas and would sink into the valleys of enormous waves with just their topmasts visible. Then [they were swept up in] the tortuous climb to the next wave pinnacle, revealing their salt encrusted, scarified hulls, with racing propellers, before falling with a shuddering crash into the next trough . . .

'It was awesome to see the ship drive into and under these gigantic waves, then slowly, agonizingly, shuddering like a trapped animal, struggle to lift her head from under the colossal weight of water. Huge seas cascaded over her fo'c'sle and poured down the length of the ship. At times I . . . thought we had been overwhelmed and were sinking . . .

'[The] thunderous seas poured over and down the decks, finding their ways into ventilators and cabins . . . [Below decks] we lived with several inches of water swilling around the cabin . . .

'[While above decks] watchkeepers and gunners rapidly became ice-sculptured silhouettes, moving lethargically. The warm air they breathed out immediately froze into tiny icicles around the slits of their headgear. Eyelids were constantly brushed to stop them freezing together; hairs in the nostrils became icicles that pierced the nose when rubbed. Only later, after thawing out [did] one . . . [feel] the pain.'[4]

Such was the force of the gale, it was no surprise that at least one ship foundered in it. That appears to have been the fate of *Sulla*, one of the three whalers accompanying the convoy, which was last seen during the night of 24–25 March 1942, shortly before the gale scattered the ships. The inconclusive evidence all pointed to her having turned turtle due to an accumulation of ice on her superstructure that could not be chipped away sufficiently because of the weather.[5]

So extreme were the conditions that young Mills could not stop himself sharing his fears about their survival prospects with *New Westminster City*'s second mate. Only for the 2nd mate to reply: 'Aye lad, but it will get a bloody sight worse when this gale moderates – we'll be easy pickings for the U-boats.'[6]

That second mate certainly knew what he was talking about, although it was the Luftwaffe, following the initial sighting of the convoy during the morning of 28 March, as mentioned in the previous chapter, who would draw the first blood.

Shortly after 1 p.m. that afternoon the pilots of two German planes stumbled across the Panamanian-flagged merchant ship SS *Raceland*, whose master, Sverre Brekke, and first and second mates were Norwegian, as were a substantial proportion of her crew. At the time she was unaccompanied by any other vessels. Because of boiler and rudder wire troubles, she was straggling some distance away from the two main blocks of merchant ships that had formed up after the storm had died down (see Chapter 5 and its Notes 13 and 15).[7]

Details of subsequent events are sparse in the British and American archives. However, an account based on the memory of Herman Torgersen, the ship's Norwegian steward, combined with a report compiled by other survivors, has explained how the ship came to be targeted when she was between Norway's North Cape and Bear Island.

Torgersen remembers how when the ship's siren sounded the alarm, as the German planes approached, he turned to the Canadian man who was sorting through the potatoes with him in the provisions room, and said: 'Now we're for it.'

Torgersen had the presence of mind to grab a pair of high-on-the-leg sheepskin-lined boots before he dashed up to the top deck, but he failed to take an extra pair of socks with him, an oversight which would have unpleasant ramifications later on.

However, he had been right to move quickly. Unlike some of the merchant ships in PQ13, *Raceland* had no guns on board which were powerful enough to repulse a determined attack. Consequently the German pilots were able to swoop down in their planes so that their bombs could be dropped from just 30 metres above the sea. At least one bomb dropped into the water near *Raceland*'s starboard side; the blast from the resulting explosion breached the ship's hull, the engine room was flooded, and the crippled ship heeled over to port.

The order was given to abandon ship, and two lifeboats, one under the command of *Raceland*'s first mate containing some 15 men, and one under the command of her second mate containing around 18 men, were launched. The remaining men on board (around 16) had to make do with two smaller aluminium boats. One was commanded by Sverre Brekke, who nobly turned down the chance to take a seat in one of the much more robust wooden lifeboats.

Because the ship did not sink immediately, Brekke ordered Torgersen and another man to go back on board to collect food, preserved milk and blankets, a difficult task since the electricity generators on the ship were no longer functioning and the provisions room was in total darkness.

After they had returned to their lifeboat, Brekke insisted that all four boats should stay where they were. It seems that he was hoping that waiting near the abandoned ship gave them the best chance of being rescued. But at around 10 p.m. that night, *Raceland* finally went down. The explosion that followed sent a tall column of fire shooting up into the sky.

That settled it. Brekke ordered the men to row towards Murmansk with all the boats tied together, an ambitious target given that they were still hundreds of miles from their destination. Rowing commenced, but with general trepidation. There was a fear that the two smaller boats would not stay afloat if there was another storm.[8]

However, at least no-one would claim that the Royal Navy was to blame. When *Raceland*'s crew permitted the ship to lag behind the convoy, albeit involuntarily, they were in effect divesting themselves of the escorts' protection.

The same could not be said concerning the crews in the merchant ships in PQ13's two main groups. After *Trinidad* was torpedoed, and after *Eclipse* was damaged by the German destroyers' shells, as described in Chapter 5, the so-called western group of merchant ships (listed in Chapter 5's Note 13) at a stroke lost the core of the protection force that had been guarding them when it was decided that *Trinidad* needed to be escorted to the Kola Inlet by the two undamaged British destroyers that had been with PQ13. Although *Eclipse* could proceed alone, she was no longer fit to act as an escort. The result was that the western group, even though still escorted by the two Russian destroyers, had no meaningful protection against U-boats; neither of these warships had asdic equipment fitted (ASDIC was the anti-submarine detection system that used sonar to track U-boat movements).[9]

Morris Mills, whose *New Westminster City* had joined the western group, would later reveal how 'naked and undefended' he personally felt, after he along with the others in the western group of vessels had within minutes of the last shots being fired seen *Trinidad*, once their proud protector, 'with a huge hole in her from which smoke and flames poured'.[10]

The merchant ships referred to in Chapter 5's Note 15 as PQ13's eastern group were even harder done by. Unlike the western group, they did not even have escorts which could protect them against enemy aircraft. It was a shameful state of affairs that reduced the armed guard commander in SS *Dunboyne*, an American merchant ship in this group, to writing the following words into his war diary in three consecutive entries covering 29 and 30 March: 'Still no escorts'.[11]

To add insult to injury, crews operating the merchant ships in the eastern group were eventually burdened with having to look after *Silja*, another of the whalers that was to be donated to the Soviet Union, but which did not have sufficient fuel to make it to Murmansk unaided.[12]

It was *Silja*'s deficiencies which were to lead to the next disaster. After repulsing a raid by a German aircraft on 28 March, which damaged and stopped the Panamanian-flagged merchant ship *Ballot*, the Bofors 40 mm (ca. 1.5 inch) gun mounted on the British SS *Induna* – the only merchant ship in the convoy to possess such an effective anti-aircraft weapon – being particularly instrumental in the defence, the remaining ships making up the eastern group had avoided further opposition by heading northward into the ice. On the way *Silja* had run out of fuel. That is how it came about that *Induna* ended up towing her. During the morning of 29 March *Induna* was left behind by the other merchant ships in the group after the ice field, in which she lay, 'solidified', temporarily trapping her. Her crew managed to extricate her that afternoon, whereupon *Induna*, after taking on board the 16 seamen *Silja* had previously taken off the damaged *Ballot*, was finally able with *Silja* in tow to proceed in the general direction taken by the other eastern group ships towards the Kola Inlet.

It was at this critical juncture, during the night of 29-30 March, that the very long chain used to tow *Silja* broke, without it immediately being noticed, because of the worsening weather. Rather than immediately abandoning her, *Induna*'s 32-year-old master, William Collins, insisted their journey to the south should be interrupted while they searched for her – flashing lights and blowing whistles – for no less than eight hours, before he finally gave up at around 5 a.m. on 30 March.[13] Thus he squandered the chance to bring his ship and her crew through what some might have characterized as the most dangerous part of their journey under the protective cloak of darkness. Admittedly he attempted to make amends by ordering his chief engineer and firemen to spare nothing in their attempts to drive the ship through to Murmansk as quickly as possible, 'buying' the firemen's compliance by handing out extra-large glasses of rum and whisky.[14]

But by then, the most propitious moment for running the gauntlet through the eight U-boats which Admiral Schmundt had lined up across the approaches to the Kola Inlet was past.[15] One of those who would live to rue the consequences was Austin Byrne, a 20-year-old DEMS gunner from Bradford, known as 'Titch' because of his diminutive stature. In the following extract from an interview he gave after the war, he recalled in his broad Yorkshire accent the events he witnessed from one of *Induna*'s gun pits beside the bridge, when shortly after 8 a.m. that same morning (30 March) the ship's headlong dash for the home straight was abruptly terminated (see Note 22 and 6 in Map 5 for approximate location):

'I was feeling peckish. I were ready for my breakfast. There's this great big bang, a flash and a shudder. Nobody has to tell you what it is. Mate were in chart room, and he come dashing out, and the skipper come dashing out. And the Mate said: "I'll see." And he dashed down aft. He looked over the well deck. He come back . . . and he saluted the skipper and he said: "She's torpedoed in the starboard quarter, Sir. Torpedo in number 5 hold, big fire, and she's going down by the stern." . . . The skipper said: "Sound abandon ship, Mr Mate."

'The sea were all on fire astern, the stern were all on fire. There were people screaming aft. I dashed to my lifeboat and I was the first there. I were in the port boat. I remember seeing . . . a gunner that were older than us . . . jump off from the stern into the flaming sea because the wind were taking the flames from the petrol right over the stern.

'Robinson, the other Bradford lad, he came through the flames. Then Mate said: "Right boy, in the boat. Good luck to you".'[16]

There were no women in *Induna*, but her first mate let pass all the seamen who in a different context might have counted as children. They included the 16-year-old cabin boy James Anderson, the 25-year-old Malcolm Robinson, the other young gunner mentioned by Byrne, and also R. Bennett, a seaman from SS *Ballot* who had been badly burned as he ran through the flames in order to reach the lifeboats.[17]

In the course of his post-war interview Byrne related how: 'This lad put his hands on the side of the boat and screamed and left his flesh there . . . We pulled him in.'[18]

Byrne and Robinson could count themselves as lucky. An after the action report by Evan Rowlands, *Induna*'s second mate, stated that although the few gunners who had been up on deck escaped, 'unfortunately the torpedo struck almost directly under the gunners' accommodation, and the other gunners are missing, probably being burned.'[19]

More men would have followed the youngsters into the boat if that had been permitted. According to Byrne, 'they were all shouting, and there were some going to rush the boat. The Mate said to the 3rd Mate: "Get the panic bar." He picked a piece of metal up . . . about 4 foot long, about one inch square, and he just turned round and said: "Who's first?", and with that they all fell back.'[20]

It is hard to know why the 1st Mate would not permit any more men to climb into the boat. Possibly he feared that if it was full, it might sink as it was being dropped down into the sea. It was on the weather side of the ship. The waves certainly banged it against the side of the ship on the way down.

Whatever the reason, this lifeboat that was built to take around 25 men was lowered to the sea with just nine men aboard. Left behind were not just those who had been denied a seat in the boat, but also those who had not been able to make it onto the boat deck before it was lowered.

One of these men was the 22-year-old Scottish engineer officer Bill Short, who had been inside his cabin when the torpedo struck, and who only arrived at his allotted lifeboat station after the boat had been launched. On seeing that he had literally missed the port boat, he rushed round to the starboard boat, only to see that it had already been launched too, with a full complement of survivors aboard.

When he was interviewed after the war, he remembered at this point bumping into a young radio officer, who had also been stranded following the launch of the starboard lifeboat. The radio officer asked him what he was going to do. Short said he did not know. On hearing this, the radio officer ran forward to see if he could help to launch the jolly boat, or cut adrift some rafts. This, said Short, galvanized him into seeking a way out for himself. He carried on, his measured way of talking and the calming effect of his Scottish lilt contrasting with the frenetic events he was describing:

'All I could hear was the people in the starboard lifeboat shouting at me to jump . . . I knew the temperature was . . . below zero, the boat deck was awful high, and I had the old type of lifebelt on which if I hit the water the wrong way could break your neck. But something gave me the courage . . . to jump. And I did jump. I must have been in the water for 2 or 3 minutes . . . I managed to scramble somehow . . . with the lifebelt to get reasonably close to the lifeboat . . . It was so cold that when I was pulled into the lifeboat, I was crying like a baby. I'd acute cramp across every part of my body . . . It was a shock to the whole nervous system.'[21]

But he did well to take the plunge when he did. Some time later,

Kapitänleutnant Karl-Friedrich Marks, the 27-year-old commander of *U-376*, who had ordered the firing of the first fan of three torpedoes at the merchant ship shortly after *Induna* had appeared out of the mist to the north-east of the Kola Inlet, ordered his men to take the U-boat to the surface and then to fire the torpedoes that he hoped would constitute the coup de grâce.[22]

Whether it was thanks to *U-376*'s torpedo, or the blowing up of the ship's boiler, Bill Short's report states that seconds after he heard an explosion, 'she went bow up ... and I have a recollection of ... people clambering up as high as they could to the bow of the *Induna*, hoping by some means or other that they could be rescued. But they were all sucked down when the *Induna* went under, and none of them survived. So in actual fact I was the last person off the *Induna*.'[23]

Those who disappeared into the deep with *Induna* were not to be the only PQ13 seamen who were to come to a sticky end on 30 March. As if there had not already been enough bloodshed for one day, the crew and armed guards in another ship would soon find themselves in a U-boat's sights in the area north of the Kola Inlet (for the approximate location, see Note 24, and 7 in Map 5).[24] The threatened merchant ship was the American SS *Effingham*, one of the eastern group of ships that had left *Induna* the previous day when the latter ship had become stuck in the ice. By this stage (30 March) there were just three ships in what remained of the group. The master of the fourth ship had elected the previous day to travel alone.

Charles Hewlett, *Effingham*'s master, was so traumatized by what happened next that he was deemed incapable of making a full report.[25] However Charles Hunnefield, a 17-year-old member of *Effingham*'s crew, wrote a detailed account of some of that day's most traumatic events in his diary, which he filled in after reaching dry land under the heading 'A Day I'll Never Forget'.

The most lively section in it starts with the words: 'Mon. 30 We were sailing along at 10 knots that eventful morning, *Effingham*, *Dunboyne* and ... [*Mana*], when at exactly 10.30 am a terrific blast shook the ship, knocking me on deck just as Danny asked me if there was any signs of enemy planes around.

'Immediately I ran out [on] deck in [a] sort of daze. Looking at the *Dunboyne*, I saw the letter Z flying, which in the code meant enemy aircraft in [the] vicinity. I thought a plane must have dropped an egg near the Effie. I couldn't believe Effie could ever get hit, so I started for my gun station, when Effie started to take a terrible list. I then soon realized that the SS *Effingham* had been torpedoed. I . . . started for the foc'sle to get some heavy gear, but was pushed back as the other sailors were running out. The ship started to list some more, and then I said, "To hell with gear; get to a lifeboat." '

Hunnefield's diary entry goes on to describe how after being ordered to board the starboard boat, on the opposite side to where the torpedo had hit, the boat was lowered with him in it; how the ship, that was still moving forward, left the boat floundering in her wake in what Hunnefield referred to as the 'raging' sea, and how a U-boat surfaced and then fired another torpedo at the ship before submerging.

If the 30 March entry written by *U-435*'s Kapitänleutnant Siegfried Strelow is accurate, it seems likely that his boat was only responsible for the second batch of torpedoes fired at *Effingham*. If that is correct, another U-boat commander, who has not been identified, should be credited with the first strike on *Effingham*, leaving the way open for *U-435*'s crew to shoot the missiles representing the coup de grâce.

Their efforts were nothing if not effective. According to Strelow, at least one of *U-435*'s torpedoes exploded under *Effingham*'s bridge shortly before 12.30 p.m.[26]

'Immediately the *Effie* split in two, and sank in 30 sec,' wrote Hunnefield, adding: 'Meanwhile the . . . [*Mana* and] *Dunboyne* . . . left us. It was a sickening sight to see them on the horizon leaving us in the freezing Barents Sea. However this is war, and they can't risk picking [us up] lest they get a tin fish too.' His only consolation was that he and his shipmates in the lifeboat were not entirely alone; the ship's other lifeboat, full of survivors, was spotted about a mile away.

This was reassuring. The men in the boats would not have been the first to assume there was safety in numbers. However, if they thought that they were now over the worst, they were mistaken. Their ordeal, and that of the occupants of the other lifeboats scattered across the Barents Sea that Monday afternoon, was only just beginning.[27]

7

Thirty-Two Men in a Boat

Main Action: 30 March–6 April 1942
In the lifeboats of SS Raceland,
SS Effingham and SS Induna, PQ13 part 3

(See Map 5)

Before SS *Induna* disappeared beneath the waves north-east of the Kola Inlet at around 8.30 a.m. on 30 March 1942, one of her radio operators had tapped out the following radio message in morse code: 'Induna torpedoed. Cheerio', preceded by longitude and latitude coordinates. Another more desperate message followed nine minutes later: 'Induna torpedoed. On fire aft and sinking. Am abandoning ship.'[1]

But for those who had abandoned ship, the distress signals provided no reassurance. There was no morale boosting certainty that the coordinates specified were correct, no confirmation they had been received and no confidence that even if read, someone would heroically come to rescue them.

Demoralization was most marked in the lifeboat where the conditions were worst. It is hard to imagine conditions could have been much worse than in *Induna's* starboard lifeboat. According to engineer officer Bill Short, there were at first so many men (at least 32) in the boat designed for 25, 'it was like sardines in a tin'.[2] What made it worse, he added, was for much of the time it was 'waterlogged'. They were 'just sitting in water'.[3]

Having said that, the first crisis in the boat was self-inflicted. *Induna's* steward thought he was doing the boat's occupants a favour when he doled out mugs of whisky. He might just as well have handed round arsenic. Those who imbibed more than a mouthful, fell asleep and then died in the perishing cold. Around seven passed away during the first night in the boat.[4]

'All we could do was drop the bodies over the side,' Short reported afterwards, 'because we had to lighten the boat as much as we could.' The only exception was a member of the crew, who had been so badly burned by the fire in *Induna's* engine room that when she had been abandoned, he had been laid down in the water at the bottom of the boat. He was one of the men who expired that first night, but as Short recalled, 'we couldn't get him out . . . He was frozen stiff', and attached to the bottom of the boat.

Those who survived had to endure freezing limbs and an insatiable thirst, probably exacerbated by their eating the pieces of chocolate that were passed round in order to stave off hunger and to give the trapped men energy. Some tried to row the boat in an attempt to restore diminishing circulation, but most of those who did this had such cold hands, it was all they could do not to drop the oars. Men who licked the ice that formed on the boat's gunwales were just asking for more trouble. Short remembered afterwards how their tongues swelled up because of the salt.

'One chap went mad,' Short recalled. 'He was ready to jump over the side . . . Even weak as we were, we had to try to stop him.'[5] But it was a losing battle. They could not watch him all the time. According to another post-war account, written by Jimmy Campbell, at the time a 15-year-old steward's boy, the mad man believed he was on the way 'to the pub to meet his mates' and he eventually calmly 'stepped off' into the sea and was gone before anyone could lift a finger.[6]

There was not much chance of anyone in the boat doing anything very vigorous after a couple of days. 'We were more dead than alive,' Short confessed later, and because the water pump did not work efficiently in Arctic temperatures, the water level in the boat rose remorselessly until it was within a few inches of the top of the gunwale. According to Short: 'It was only the buoyancy tanks that were keeping the lifeboat afloat.'[7]

Conditions in the other *Induna* boat could not have been more different – apart from the occupants likewise being tormented by the inability to slake their thirst. Even Austin Byrne's remedy – drinking his own urine – only provided temporary relief. The main reason why the men in this boat were so much better off was because there were relatively few sailors in it. That made it easier to move around.

Psychology also played its part. Whereas hopes of a favourable outcome for those in *Induna*'s starboard boat faded a bit more each time another man passed away (15 of the men in the starboard boat died before they could be rescued), one suspects it was difficult for most of the men in the ship's port lifeboat not to be swept along by Austin Byrne's infectious optimism. A larger than life, cheeky chappie character at the worst of times, notwithstanding the cold, he remained a human dynamo to the last. One moment he was rowing, the next he was bailing out water and the next, he was putting up the sail.

It did not hurt that he really believed what he told the others about their chances. He assured them that at the admittedly slow speed at which the boat was moving through the water, they would nevertheless make the 120 miles, which he estimated was their distance from Russia, in around six days. He would later confirm he never doubted they could survive that long, provided of course the boat stayed afloat and the cold did not kill them.

That was by no means a given for all of them. The seaman from *Ballot,* whom Byrne referred to as 'the American', had been so badly burned that his fingers could no longer be straightened. His hands resembled an animal's claws. They could not even hold a cigarette. When he wanted a smoke, Byrne had to light the cigarette for him and place it in his mouth. According to Byrne, the American barely moved except when smoking. Most of the time, he sat immobile on a seat in the middle of the lifeboat, only kept alive in spite of the freezing cold because someone had had the kindness to give him the use of a spare duffel coat that had found its way into the boat.

James Anderson, the 16-year-old Scottish cabin boy was also a worry. He was as sure they would not make it as Byrne was certain they would, and according to Byrne 'he seemed to get further and further into himself as cold bit him'.

That comment is revealing for what it says about the need for shipwrecked sailors to keep warm, as is the description of what Byrne was wearing. When Byrne was interviewed after the war, he stated that one of the main reasons why he and Malcolm Robinson, the other young gunner in the boat, were able to keep going was that they wore adequate clothing. This is how Byrne described his getting dressed routine in *Induna*: 'I had a pair of ordinary socks, a pair of tropical socks and two pairs of seaboot socks on. Then I had me long johns on. Then I had me pants on. Then I'd two jumpers. And a scarf. And me gloves. Then I had me leather sheep-skin jacket on. Then me lifejacket. And a balaclava. Then I put me heavy duffle coat on. The heavy duffle coat had elastic in the arms . . . And a hat on top of the balaclava.' That was all on top of his outer footwear: 'huge' seaboots, which he said were themselves critical to his survival.[8]

But Byrne realized that no clothing would have saved them had they not also had good fortune when it really mattered. When during the third day after the sinking, he dropped into the sea the bucket they were using to bail out the boat, Robinson saved the day by grabbing it before it floated away. When the next day the boat sunk lower and lower in the water because of the large mass of ice that had collected on the ropes that were hung around the outside of the lifeboat, there just happened to be an axe to hand that enabled them to chip it off.[9]

After incidents like that, only a fool would have denied their fate was still hanging in the balance. They might have been somewhat comforted, however, had they known that they and their *Induna* shipmates were not the only ones in boats off the Russian coast after sending out an SOS. An SOS, albeit one that was received by the PQ13 commodore without coordinates, had also been sent out from the American ship *Effingham,* whose torpedoing shortly after *Induna,* to the south-east of where the British merchant ship sank, was mentioned at the end of the previous chapter.[10]

The fortunes of the men in *Effingham*'s two lifeboats would to a great extent mirror those of the survivors in *Induna*'s boats, the smaller number of men in the *Effingham*'s port boat 'enjoying' better conditions that those in the packed starboard boat. The experiences of the 18 men cast away in *Effingham*'s port lifeboat would feature a few months later in an article in the American newspaper *South Boston News*. Entitled 'Bernard Coving-ton's Story of His Adventures', it is evidently based on the account given to the writer of the article by the same 17-year-old Bernard Covington whose naively optimistic letter is quoted at the beginning of the previous chapter.[11]

It seems likely that the article was sanitized in places so as not to deter other young Americans from serving in merchant ships. It certainly contains some positive details. According to the journalist who wrote up what happened to the lifeboat's occupants: 'Food in the lifeboat was adequate. They had concentrated foods and condensed milk. Water proved a problem though, for the very first night, all the water they had in their boat froze solid. Later, on the third day, they began cutting up their boat, and they cut the seats out and made a fire by which they melted the water.'

Continuing in the same vein, the article stated that although there were 'terrible . . . hardships', the men in the boat 'took them in true Navy fashion. Once Bernard and his best pal were under a blanket which they had to give up to a dying man.'

However, in the following extract from the article, even if one ignores the racist language of the day that today we find so objectionable, there is just a hint that some in the boat might have been treated less well than others, leaving the reader wondering if in that sense, something had gone on that was not quite right: 'They rowed all of the first day. Then after that, they used sails. The very first night, a Negro mess boy froze to death. After that two other Negroes and one white man froze.'

It was only years afterwards that another man who had been in the boat, while writing a private letter to a relation of one of the drowned *Induna* men, revealed that the 'blacks who froze to death . . . were the warmest dressed . . . in our boat. After they died, we took their heavy clothes, and dumped them overboard.'[12] This leads one to at least question whether the black men in the boat were disadvantaged in some other way.

The *South Boston News* article hints at even darker deeds perpetrated in the ship's starboard boat, where it states 'a coloured cook went mentally insane and cut himself up with a butcher knife'.

At the time the article appeared, and for many years afterwards, there was no way, short of buttonholing a survivor, of discovering whether everyone in that boat was equally at risk, or whether because of their race, black seamen were discriminated against. It is only very recently, with the discovery of the diary written by Charles Hunnefield, the 17-year-old whose description of the sinking of *Effingham* is quoted in the previous chapter, that it has become possible to probe a little deeper.

There can be no doubt that all the men in *Effingham*'s starboard life-boat suffered whatever the colour of their skin. Just reading the following words in the diary about Charles Hunnefield's first hours in the boat, makes one shiver: 'The only clothes I had on was my jersey, heavy pants and aviation boots. No coat or hat or gloves . . . Immediately my hands started to freeze, so I put some whale oil on . . .'

The stream of consciousness-style chronicle that follows, part of which is reproduced below, highlights the nature of the ordeal that most of the men in the boat had to endure: 'All of us are thinly clad except the men who were on watch . . . Jimmy, the oiler, has no shoes or stockings . . . The seas come crashing at our boat . . . sending spray and sea all over us, and after a while freezes . . . My feet are soaking wet and cold . . . Everybody is seasick . . . [The] crew is groaning and cryin'. I'm praying for God [to] help us . . .'

Nevertheless, at sunset they had their supper: malted milk tablets, chocolate and pemmican, before huddling together for warmth, and falling asleep.

As we know from Bill Short's account mentioned earlier, the last two words, which would be comforting in most circumstances, are full of hidden menace in the context of seamen striving to survive in a boat in the Arctic. Sure enough, the following passage from Hunnefield's subsequent entries, written under the heading 'Tue. 31', disclosed the macabre consequences, already referred to in the context of the Covington account in the *South Boston News* article: '1st Cook is dead, laying at our feet in the bilge. All night we put our feet on him to keep them out of the water. We finally got him up to toss him overboard, when we noticed his guts were hanging out of him, for he had committed suicide during [the] night. Over he went.'

The fact that another dead man, 'frozen stiff', was also thrown over the side does not conceal the disrespectful way the 30-year-old chief cook's corpse was treated, or quieten the fear that he was given harsher treatment in the first place once it was known he was fading because he was a black man.[13]

It was all the more the pity because that day things began to look up. There was some respite from the previous day's stormy weather, as is registered in Hunnefield's optimistic next entry: 'Sea calm, so started to rig up the sail. We got it up, and [are now] heading for shore – [it matters not whether it's] Finland or Russia as long as it's land . . .'

However, evidently another merciless clear out of those who had been struck down overnight was still necessary. Hunnefield's account of the steps they took concerning one poor soul left little to the imagination: 'Dragged Gus (the 19-year-old mess boy) out of bilge and dropped him over the side. Personally I think he was still alive. But nevertheless he was freezing to death anyways . . .'

During that day Hunnefield noted there was a recognizable pathway to death which was prompting survivors to adapt their behaviour accordingly. First the condemned man would lose all sense of proportion and start insisting they were all going to die, or he would act crazily, before finally expiring. By that time his neighbours would be watching hungrily for his last breath, and as soon as he died, there would be a race to pick him clean of everything he had. His boots and overcoat were invariably long gone before he was heaved over the side. With or without their clothes, 'they all sink like a rock' Hunnefield observed grimly.[14]

And so it went on. But the hellish torture inflicted by the extremes of nature on those in the lifeboats during the days following the sinkings of *Raceland*, *Induna* and *Effingham* should not distract us from the relatively unobstructed progress made by most of the crews in the other PQ13 merchant ships after the thwarted attack by the three German destroyers. The remaining 14 merchant ships from the convoy all made it into the Kola Inlet by midnight during the night of 30–31 March, apart from one ship which arrived early the next morning.[15] The successful ships included *Ballot*.[16] Even the whaler *Silja* reached the Kola Inlet eventually, albeit not under her own steam; she was found afloat with her engines stopped by the destroyer HMS *Oribi*, and towed to Polyarnoe, the Soviet naval base in the Kola Inlet, by the minesweeper HMS *Harrier*, arriving there on 31 March.[17]

Nor should the frightful conditions in the lifeboats lead us to conclude that those who had abandoned ship were condemned to sail forever through the icy waters in a kind of perpetual purgatory, although that was evidently what it felt like for at least some of the men whose time in their lifeboat stretched beyond a day or two. At around 8.30 p.m. on 2 April, the 17 remaining survivors in *Induna*'s starboard lifeboat, who by this time had sighted land, while being too weak to reach it, saw Russian aircraft overhead.[18] According to Bill Short: 'We spotted two planes . . . and the planes circled around . . . We waved to the best of our ability.

'It did not seem all that long before this Russian ship appeared . . . It came alongside and they dropped a ladder down . . . but we were too weak . . . So the Russian seamen had to come down and help us on the deck.'[19]

The Russian ship was the minesweeper *TSh-36*. After the war, her commander Sergey Antropov explained how they had found Short's lifeboat: 'A Hurricane aircraft appeared . . . waving its wings to show it was a friend . . . The pilot was pointing to the north-east. We headed that way. After a short time we saw . . . a lifeboat.'

The minesweeper's commissar Ivan Bogdanenko would later describe what was done after all the survivors were taken on board: 'There was another body in the boat. Part of his body was embedded in the ice. I said to my commander: "We can't leave him like this. Let's bring him on board [too]." '

Bogdanenko's report also includes a description of the living: 'Their coats and sweaters were covered with ice, while their gloves were actually inside blocks of ice because they had had to use them to bail out water from the lifeboat. The ship's doctor and I cut off their boots . . . with a knife, and turned away our eyes in horror when we saw how their skin was pulled off at the same time.'[20]

The rescue operation was not without its hitches. Jimmy Campbell, the 15-year-old steward boy, has recalled how as the Russians arrived on the scene, 'I was sitting with my left hand on the [lifeboat's] gunwale to prevent being thrown all over the place; when I was lifted from the lifeboat, four fingers of my [left] hand stayed attached to the gunwale of the lifeboat.'[21]

All nine in *Induna's* port lifeboat, and 14 out of the 18 who had been in *Effingham's* port lifeboat, including Bernard Covington, were also picked up by other Russian ships on the same day.[22]

Charles Hunnefield was one of the 17 survivors out of the 23 men who had originally been in *Effingham's* starboard lifeboat; they had already been rescued by the minesweeper HMS *Harrier* during the afternoon of 31 March.[23] Given that two men had been killed when *Effingham* was torpedoed, and 10 of the men in her lifeboats died, her total losses were 12 men out of 43 who had been on board the ship.[24] A higher proportion of the 66 men who had been aboard *Induna* died. Some 25 went down with the ship, and 15 men succumbed in the starboard lifeboat before it was found, so that the total number of deaths up to that point was 40.[25]

It is tempting to conclude that the men who had endured such arduous torment in *Induna's* and *Effingham's* lifeboats, in some cases over several days, could not have been more sorely tried. However, their trials are arguably trumped by what happened to the survivors from SS *Raceland*.

The *Raceland* boats had barely started out on their long journey before they were separated by a storm. The two smaller aluminium boats could not have lasted long. Herman Torgersen, the Norwegian steward in the starboard lifeboat, reported that tell-tale wreckage was spotted within an hour of the storm starting.

Torgersen's own survival was threatened by the action of the first engineer, a handsome Dane. All of a sudden he appeared to lose his senses, and after throwing the compass into the sea, draped his arms around the steward's legs in the act of dying. Because his arms quickly froze in this position, Torgersen had to struggle for several hours before he could escape the deadly embrace. Only then could the corpse be heaved overboard.

During the nine days Torgersen's lifeboat was at sea, more than twice the time the *Effingham* and *Induna* boats were afloat, there were deaths every day, usually after the dying man lost his mind.

One man all of a sudden ripped off his long sheepskin boots and dangled his feet in the cold sea saying, 'This is delightful. Now I'll get warm.' He died five minutes later. Another jumped into the water; he was hauled back on board but died shortly afterwards. A third man seized the axe that was in the boat and waved it around threateningly, while wildly yelling out a song before finally becoming silent forever.

As the days passed, more and more men began to see and hear mirages of imaginary honking rescue ships. In the end, no-one dared to talk about what they were experiencing.

Eventually even the 2nd Mate Johannessen, who had been expected to lead the survivors until the bitter end, lost his mind. He experienced devastating cramps, and then began to hit a dead Canadian mess boy who was lying in the bottom of the boat; by the time this occurred, nobody had the strength to throw the dead overboard.

Torgersen would later explain that his secret for surviving in one piece was down to performing what he referred to as 'gymnastics with my arms and legs; they weren't still for a moment', except presumably when he was sleeping. Even so, by the time they reached Auvær, a small island some 70 miles north-west of Tromso (Tromsø) on 6 April, his feet were black and swollen. He was one of the five survivors who were lucky enough to be spotted there by a passing Norwegian fisherman, but he was the only one of them who did not have to have his legs amputated because of frostbite after they became prisoners of war.[26]

Less is known about the agonies experienced by the occupants of the second *Raceland* lifeboat, which according to a German report dated 2 April 1942 had landed in the fjord north of Sørvær in Norway's Sørøya island. It is likely that the torment suffered in this boat matched what had occurred in Torgersen's boat. When the second boat landed, there were some 7 survivors on board, but also approximately the same number of corpses.[27]

It took some time for news of the rescue of men from the boats to filter through to the survivors' families.

On 9 April, seven days after Bernard Covington was rescued, a telegram was sent to his parents in South Boston, Virginia stating: 'The Navy Department deeply regrets to inform you that your son Charlie Bernard Covington Jr seaman second class US Navy is missing following action in the performance of his duty and in the service of his country . . .'[28]

This led to a report in a local paper stating: 'C. B. Covington received notification . . . today that his son C. Bernard Covington, Jr, had been killed in action.'[29]

It may well have been this report which prompted a friend to write a letter to Bernard junior's parents stating: 'I am thinking and praying about you tonight. I am so sorry for you both; wish so much there was something I could do or say that would help . . .

'Be brave. Go to our heavenly Father. He alone can help us over such sorrows.'[30]

It was clearly not the only such letter that was sent. Bernard Covington's heartbroken mother marked the event by writing the following note: 'I'll never forget April 9 1942 when my husband walked in about 9 o'clock with the telegram that read missing in action in performance of his duty. The neighbours, relatives, friends and pastor coming to extend their sympathy. Pots and vases of flowers filling the house, letters, cards and telephone calls from ones that couldn't come, reporters from newspapers, all trying to say maybe he got picked up.

'My head and mind both cried out: you hear and read of these things. It might happen once in 1,000 times, but it would never happen to me. At night I would see him by his gun.'[31]

The best part of a month had passed since the first telegram before 'the miracle' his mother believed would never happen actually came to pass: Bernard Covington's parents received a telegram dated 4 May 1942 stating: 'The Navy Department is glad to inform you that son Charlie Bernard Covington Jr seaman second class US Navy previously reported missing following action in the performance of his duty is now reported to be a survivor . . .'[32]

One of Bernard Covington's first steps when he later arrived back in the USA was to apply to be transferred from the US Armed Guard. 'I will keep on trying to get anything except merchant ships,' he assured his parents in a letter, while at the same time admitting 'to get a transfer you have to know President Roosevelt and Sec. Navy Knox personally I think.

'I was talking to a British sailor . . . and he has had 4 ships shot from under him . . . So why should I kick if one is shot from under me (that's probably what the officers here think)?'[33]

A Charles Hunnefield diary entry was also critical: 'The crews wouldn't mind fighting the enemy if they would only give us adequate protection.' This presumably meant not leaving a convoy to run the gauntlet of the enemy without any escort. But it also entailed providing guns with more punch than the .30 and .50-calibre machine guns for use against attacking aircraft. 'We found out they're no damned good,' he wrote, referring to the general consensus that the guns supplied were just 'pea shooters' whose bullets bounced off the planes they hit unless they happened to hit a vulnerable spot.

He also wanted gunners to have shields for every gun like the British. 'But our government thinks that our gunners are made of steel; flying shrapnel will just bounce off us! It just proves that [our] government don't give a damn about its men or its ships. Just as long as the cargo gets there.'[34]

Hunnefield's complaints could have caused the Allies a major headache if his views had been made public, as could the way Covington and his family had been treated by the US Navy. They could have made it much more difficult to recruit seamen to man the merchant ships being sent from America to the Soviet Union. But both families were effectively muzzled.

Much more influential were the opinions expressed within the Berlin-based German Naval Staff (Seekriegsleitung – abbreviated form: Skl) on 30 March 1942. After confirming that five enemy ships had been sunk, the Skl's Operations Division's war diarist wrote: 'However this success does not make up for the loss of *Z 26* with a large part of her crew, which is especially unfortunate, given the few destroyers available . . .

'We must . . . hold back our few surface forces all the more during the conditions such as prevailed . . . when due to the weather there was no air reconnaissance, and it was impossible to gain an absolutely clear picture of the number of enemy forces and their positions.'[35]

The British response to the imminent arrival of the bulk of PQ13 was equally downbeat. The cruiser *Kenya*'s Captain Michael Denny told General Mason Macfarlane, head of the military mission in Moscow, who visited him in his ship in the Kola Inlet, that he was not optimistic about the future. It was not just the difficulty of operating at such low temperatures that was causing concern; since he arrived in the Kola Inlet, the average temperature had been -12 °C with a low of -18 °C. In his report Captain Denny wrote: 'I mentioned to him that the safe and timely arrival of PQ convoys might develop into a task requiring virtually the whole strength of the Home Fleet, in fact a major naval operation similar to the passage of Malta bound convoys.'

The General responded by stating that the armaments being sent to Russia 'were a mere drop compared with what Russia was now producing . . . , and . . . should the convoy[s] become a grave embarrassment to the proper conduct of the naval war, Joe Stalin was a big enough man to appreciate that fact if it were to be represented to him, and accept an interruption until a more favourable situation developed.'[36]

8

A Different Kind of Operation

Main Action: 3 April 1942 – and aftermath
In the Russian Hospital, Murmansk

(See Maps 1 and 23)
GMT + 3

If the men in PQ13's merchant ships which had steamed into Murmansk's harbour on 30–31 March 1942 believed they were home and dry, and were going to be thanked by the Russians, they were in for a rude awakening.

According to *New Westminster City*'s Morris Mills: 'The ship secured to a rough wooden quay. There were no brass bands, no cheering crowds or flag waving. The shore gang, resembling bundles of old rags, sullenly took our ropes and wires to the bollards, avoiding eye contact. It was as though we didn't exist. Were they aware we had been through hell to bring them these vital war supplies?

'No sooner were we tied up than a squad of armed soldiers came aboard and stationed themselves around the ship. We could not fail to notice two sentries posted on the gangway.'[1]

The appearance on subsequent days of lines of manacled prisoners, and bedraggled civilians, many of them women, who were to unload the ship, and the brutal way the Russian soldiers dispersed any Soviet workers who had the temerity to gather round the area opposite the ship's galley so that they could scrounge food, only strengthened Mills' impression that they had moved into alien territory. As did the soldiers' threats shouted at those soft-hearted crew members who attempted to intervene.

But that was nothing compared to the 'welcome' they received from the German bombers, some of which were based in the Luostari aerodrome near Petsamo, Finland, which was only some 50 miles to the west.[2] Every few hours another wave would come flying over the hills overlooking the Kola Inlet in the hope they could flatten the town and make the port unusable.

Shortly before 9 p.m. on 3 April 1942 there was yet another raid by around 20 German bombers.[3] This time Murmansk's so-called Fish Port where *New Westminster City* and *Empire Starlight*, another PQ13 merchant ship, were tied up was targeted. Both were hit. Four bombs landed on Mills' ship, including one that according to the radio operator Ted Starkey, who was acting as assistant to a gunner, made a 'neat hole' in the bridge about two yards from where he was standing but which exploded lower down inside the ship.[4] The explosion from this bomb 'only' caused him what he subsequently stoically referred to as 'slight damage' – it flung him against the guns beside which he was standing, breaking his left arm and knocking him senseless. It was discovered afterwards that the gunner who he had been assisting did not have a mark on his body, but he was so shocked by the explosion that he became insane.[5]

The effect on Mills in his cabin three decks down from where Starkey was standing was equally catastrophic: he woke up just in time to see what he described as a 'vivid blue flash' and a 'column of flame' which was accompanied by a 'colossal roaring sound', presumably the noise made by the bomb blast as it swept away the bulkhead separating his cabin from the one next door 'revealing for a split second the horrified face of the Radio Officer'. Mills ended up being thrown 'into a corner and showered with burning debris'.

'The conflagration of flames, the hideous sounds of metal being torn apart mixed with the cries and screams of the wounded drove me to a mad desperation,' wrote Mills. 'Frantically I tore myself free of burning wreckage, and hurled myself through a jagged hole where once the door had been. Out on the open deck, I ran blindly for several yards before collapsing . . . The bridge was a burning inferno, and I could feel my skin scorching. I was quite rational, and knew I had to get to somewhere safer, so pulled myself upright only to fall down. "This is bloody stupid," I thought. "What's wrong with me?" Then I saw my left foot had been smashed to a bloody pulp, and was only connected to my leg by strips of sinew, the white bone protruding at the bottom.'

Only then did he feel the agonizing pain. But the following extract from the account in his memoirs discloses that his main preoccupation was the nature of his life-changing injury: 'I was terrified the foot was going to drop off, and sat cradling the bloody object in my hands, the hot blood pumping out through my fingers.'[6]

He was eventually found by the ship's Captain Harris, who quickly had a heaving line wrapped around him so that he could be lowered over the side of the ship onto the quay.[7]

Mercifully he lost consciousness before he was transported to the Murmansk hospital where Arctic convoy victims were to be treated. The next thing he remembered was coming to in one of the hospital's operating theatres. Beside him stood a figure wearing a blue uniform, who he later learned was a Russian Merchant Navy officer. 'He was gripping my hand very hard,' Mills recalled, 'his face inches from my own. "You very bad," he said in broken English. "Me very sorry." Shaking his head [he said] "Foot bad – must cut." He made a chopping motion with his hand. "You lose much blood. I give you blood."'

Minutes later an ether mask was clamped over Mills' face and once again he lost consciousness.

His first sensation next time he came to was searing pain, which was swiftly followed by the discovery that his left foot had been amputated. However, the following recollections in his memoirs concerning the immediate aftermath and the following weeks suggest that it was the psychological impact which was hardest to bear: 'Gradually I became aware of my situation. Pain, misery and the realization I had been crippled overwhelmed me . . .'

But over the next days and weeks it would be the conditions where he was being treated that would preoccupy him. As another extract from his memoirs makes clear, the building where he had been taken had not been used as a hospital in peacetime: 'I was . . . in the assembly hall of a school that had been turned into a hospital . . . containing some sixty beds, inches apart, occupied by merchant navy survivors . . . All around were cries and groans of the wounded. The foul stench of suppurating wounds, and the stinking sickly smell of [soon to be] amputated frostbitten limbs bore down on one's senses . . . All clean air had been excluded by the boarded up windows.'[8]

The merchant seamen he referred to were, in the first instance at least, those who needed treating following their being rescued from the PQ13 lifeboats (see Chapter 7). Unlike Mills, whose case was an emergency, it took some time before they realized the full extent of the sacrifice they had made in order to help the Russians. This was explained by *Induna*'s Austin Byrne, who through the medium of a series of post-war interviews including the one already alluded to in Chapters 6 and 7, was to become one of two unofficial spokesmen for all those who sustained life-changing injuries during PQ13.

The beginning of the process that would end with all the *Induna* boat survivors coming to terms with the damage that had been done took place in one of the Russian ships that had rescued them. While Byrne was complying with a request made by a member of the Russian ship's crew to help undress James Anderson, the 16-year-old *Induna* cabin boy, Byrne was horrified to see 'he was black way above his waist' from the feet up. When the Russian helping him saw this, he ushered Byrne away, indicating the boy was too far gone to be saved.[9]

But it was not just the cabin boy. On reaching the hospital, they were taken to a bathroom where, after they had stripped off, they were washed by the Russian nurses. It was then that Byrne noticed that one of the legs of another of his shipmates was 'black way up'. *Induna*'s 44-year-old chief steward, Jerry Lanning, who was placed in the assembly hall bed next to Byrne, was also in a bad way. 'His legs were black and all colours to above his knees: blues, greens, bits of red, shiny like patent shoes,' Byrne recalled. 'Later both his legs were amputated.'[10]

The second unofficial spokesman for the PQ13 survivors was *Induna*'s engineer officer Bill Short, whose testimony about the sinking of the ship and the subsequent journey in one of her lifeboats was also featured in the previous two chapters. Included in one of his post-war interviews is the following account of what he termed the very 'basic' treatment he received at the hospital for his frostbitten limbs:

'They had to take me down to a makeshift operating theatre when they discovered the gangrene . . . It was a large classroom . . . There were six tables [in it] . . . I was placed on [one of these tables] . . . and there was a white cloth placed in front of me . . . [Then] someone said in broken English: "We're going to take your legs off." So they went ahead and took my legs off. I'd no general anaesthetic. I've only a vivid recollection of . . . an excruciating pain . . . [before] I passed out . . .

'They had literally chopped my legs off as if you'd cut a piece of meat right through. And the bones and everything else were sticking out . . . They'd cut channels in my legs to let the gangrene poison seep out.

'The only answer the Russians had for gangrene was "Chop it off". And that's what they did.'[11]

But the amputation was just the preamble to something which in the short term was much worse. After their operations, both Short and Mills were regularly subjected to the agonizing removal of their dressings, which were fabricated out of what Mills described as 'a stiff paper like material'.[12] 'There is only one way to describe the dressings,' Short reported. 'They were pure hell. It was like taking paper off of raw meat . . . When they took them off, I used to yell. You could not stop yourself.'[13]

According to Mills, 'it normally took three nurses to change the dressing, one to hold you down, one to hold the stump in a vice-like grip, and the other nurse to swab and pick away at the stump'. If the nurse doing the holding was not being attentive, there could be consequences that would have been unthinkable in a Western hospital. In the following extract from his memoirs, Mills described what occurred when the nurse doing the picking touched a sensitive nerve, causing his stump to twitch so violently that it thumped against the underside of a nearby trolley, sending the instruments that had been on it crashing all over the room:

'The Army Doctor in attendance came rushing over . . . Fumbling under his white coat, he withdrew an enormous service pistol, pointing [it] with a trembling hand straight between my eyes, screaming a torrent of abuse. I tried to shut my eyes to blot out the spectre of having my brains blown out, but could not [drag] . . . my . . . gaze away from the trembling finger curled around the trigger . . . Then, regaining some semblance of control, he stormed out of the room.'[14] The dressing procedure was then resumed as if nothing out of the ordinary had taken place.

The gun-pointing was just the most extreme of a number of acts by the hospital staff that the merchant seamen would probably never have encountered had they been cared for in London. The Russian nurses were particularly partial to pushing a rubber pipe down the throats of anyone who had frostbite so that tepid water poured into the top end could defrost any ice that had formed in the patient's stomach. Then there was the Russians' use of burning hot goose grease in a jar that was placed upside down on the patient's chest, which was believed to be another way to heat up the inner organs after a man had been frozen.

The Russian nurses also liked to treat their patients with enemas. This was resisted by some of the British contingent. In one of his interviews, Austin Byrne recalled how in a desperate attempt to avoid having a tube inserted up his anus following his arrival in the hospital, when he saw what the nurses were inflicting on the other men in the assembly hall, he fled to the toilet, and would not allow it to be flushed until the nurses had inspected the faeces which, notwithstanding the near starvation diet in the boat, he somehow forced out.

It has to be said that it was not just the patients who were appalled by their treatment in the hospital. No-one was more critical than John Ballantyne, the destroyer *Ashanti*'s 27-year-old surgeon lieutenant, who for a short period during June 1942 was the acting Base Medical Officer in the Kola Inlet.[15] The official report he wrote contained the following damning indictment: 'No words of mine can [adequately] describe the deplorable conditions under which the patients [in this hospital] were treated. "Bloody awful" in its literal sense is the nearest I can get!'[16]

When assessing the treatment of frostbite, and surgical procedures following gangrene or sepsis, one of the hospital's main tasks in relation to the PQ13 survivors rescued from the lifeboats, he wrote: 'The Russian doctors seem to lack the very fundamentals of medical and surgical practice.' He complained that when carrying out amputations, the Russians liked to make their cut through the line of demarcation, the infected area between the gangrenous and healthy tissue, a practice which was likely to result in more infection, requiring another amputation later.

He was equally scathing about the Russian post-operative dressing procedure so hated by Mills and Short, which he branded 'medieval'. It was done, he said, 'without anaesthesia on the ground floor of the hospital (two floors down from the ward housing the PQ convoys survivors) under conditions vaguely simulating a dungeon where no screams could be heard'.[17]

Probably because of shortages, pain relief was regarded as a luxury. Another British surgeon lieutenant, writing in May 1942, pointed out that: 'In cases where the duration of the operation exceeds that of the [local] anaesthetic, re-injection ... is rarely seen. The patient feels progressively more pain but the operation proceeds, the patient being held if necessary'.[18]

It should be stated however that there was no suggestion by any of the surgeons quoted that the Russians gave their own men preferential treatment. Ballantyne was of the opinion that 'the low standard of medical practice ... [is] due to the fact that they assess the value of human life at a lower value than we do. They therefore hold the view that if a man becomes a casualty, he is no longer of use to his country, and a minimum of time and expense is wasted upon the patient.'

This analysis was backed up by the treatment of a Russian soldier that was observed by Mills. The man he said 'had an evil sack of pus hanging from his stomach wound. The woman army doctor ordered him to stand to attention. Then taking up a surgical knife slit the stomach releasing the stinking pus to run down his leg. The man swayed but pulled himself together when the doctor snarled at him. A rough dressing was applied and he was dismissed.'

Those were just the complaints about the hospital's medical care. Ballantyne also lambasted the shortage of nurses, which meant that patients often had to make do without the level of support they needed: According to Ballantyne: 'If a patient wished to open his bowels at a mealtime, then he did so, without screens around his bed.'

Not that anyone in his senses would voluntarily eat the food. Ballantyne described it as 'nauseating, a type of gelatinous bread, rice and yak,' adding, 'its poorness in quality and the unappetising way in which it was served defy all description'.[19]

And that was without asking how patients could be expected to eat when there was a foul odour pervading the air as a result of the primitive sanitary arrangements, and when 'overriding all was the fearful stench of sepsis'.[20]

As if the jeopardy arising from the Russian medical and administrative shortcomings were not sufficient, an extra dimension was tacked on as a result of the frequent bombing raids. 'This hospital ... stands on a hill dominating the town,' wrote Ballantyne, 'its vast white walls making an obvious landmark ... No visible red crosses were shown on its roof.' Because of this, it was almost inevitable that it would sooner or later become a target. Even before this happened, the explosions made by the bombs which were being dropped during what Ballantyne referred to as the 'frequent raids' literally made the hospital rock.

'Naturally ... [the patients] were terror stricken,' wrote Ballantyne, 'to such an extent that absence of arms and legs proved no hindrance to their diving under their beds, as a result of which as often as not they injured and hurt themselves, and would have to have their wounds redressed,' with all the agony that entailed.[21]

Mills in his memoirs recorded how the medical staff would run for the air raid shelters when the German aircraft attacked, leaving the patients to fend for themselves, adding: 'One night [when this occurred], a Polish seaman with terrible stomach wounds fell out of bed and lay writhing ... on the floor, his life blood spreading an obscene stain ... We shouted, screamed, bang[ed] objects on the floor, to no avail. He took an incredibly long time to die, ranting and raving ... In the morning the nurses came and took the body away.'[22] Nobody asked any questions.

Mills and Short appear to be the only amputees whose detailed accounts of their treatment in Murmansk in the immediate aftermath of PQ13 are freely available to the public. But a document to be found in the National Archives in Maryland, America contains a list of nine other Allied seamen who thanks to their service during PQ13 and subsequent amputations in Russia almost certainly endured similar hardships.[23] *Ballot*'s 45-year-old bosun Peter Hyde, who was excluded from the list, possibly because he 'only' had his ten toes amputated, was subsequently quoted in *The Boston Globe* in the USA, saying, 'Thank God I still have my hands. You should see some of the other fellows.'[24]

This comment was probably a veiled reference to among others, Carlos Luz, a Portuguese seaman, who like Hyde had transferred from *Ballot* to *Induna* via *Silja* before making it into *Induna*'s starboard lifeboat. The National Archives Maryland list reveals that because of frostbite, his hands were amputated as well as his legs. But Short has reported that he was nevertheless 'an inspiration to us all. That man used to walk around on his knees.'[25] Notwithstanding his disability, he somehow managed to entertain the other patients in the Russian hospitals where he was cared for by playing a harmonica. Such snapshots put a positive gloss on his true feelings. According to Geoff Jelbart, another patient who was in hospital with him, 'during the day he was the happiest fellow in the ward ... but at night when I couldn't sleep, I would hear his broken-hearted sobbing. I believe he had a wife and several children in Portugal'.[26]

After the first frenetic rush to save the rescued seamen from the ravages of gangrene, the tension in the assembly hall dropped. This gave the young men in the hospital the opportunity to joke and misbehave like rowdy schoolboys. Some of their ribaldry was in the worst possible taste. It sometimes amounted to iniquitous racism and bullying. Because their diet – which almost invariably consisted of rice and bread, with yak thrown in only occasionally – was so monotonous, a lot of their joking revolved around food. Short recalls how when told meat was on the menu, one of them would quip: 'Someone is going to have an amputation today'.[27]

Jimmy Campbell, *Induna*'s 15-year-old cabin boy, who had part of his right leg and his left foot amputated, and who, as already mentioned in Chapter 7 lost four fingers of his left hand, as well as losing the ability to bend the fingers of his right hand, later remembered the larking around that occurred after a nurse in the hospital found the time to put him into a hot bath, with his bandaged hands and what remained of his two heavily bandaged legs hanging over the side:

'I was lying there with my mind miles away, when I became conscious of a lot of giggling, and the nurse talking to someone behind me. She must have been telling them who I was and why I was there, because the next minute, I was surrounded by about twenty naked women. I ... had never seen a naked woman. My eyes were popping out of my head, and because I couldn't get my bandages wet, I couldn't cover myself. The girls obviously noticed [my excitement] because they started laughing and giggling, and were talking nine to the dozen [until] my nurse said something to them, and they all returned to their showers.' He was later told they were Red Army girls who defended the surrounding area with ack-ack (anti-aircraft) guns.[28]

Thus these mutilated sailors, who for a time had feared they would never experience normal life again, discovered that there was something to live for after all. And rather than wishing they could be allowed to die without ever seeing their families and loved ones again, they began to wonder when it would be their turn to go home.

9

Saved by the Bell

Main Actions: 11 and 16 April 1942
Sinking of Empire Cowper and Empire Howard, QP10 and PQ14

(See Map 1)

At the British Chiefs of Staff meeting on 1 April 1942, while some of PQ13's seamen in their lifeboats were still counting the cost of participating in the so-called Murmansk Run, the First Sea Lord Admiral Sir Dudley Pound noted the 'increased difficulties of running convoys to Northern Russia.' This he said was because: 'The German Air Force had been considerably strengthened in Norway. There were also the German Naval units based in Norwegian waters and in addition some 10 U-boats ...' Taking into account the threat posed by these German forces, he concluded: 'The present month was the most difficult due to the inability to take the more northerly route until the ice melted.'[1]

The ice could certainly be correctly regarded as the convoys' enemy number 2, if not number 1. Within days of the next convoy, PQ14 (around 25 merchant ships) setting out from Hvalfjord, Iceland, on 8 April 1942, a combination of damage caused by the nine-foot-deep ice encountered, the failure by the crews of some ships to see a change of direction signal made by the commodore, and the difficulty in following the other ships in front because of fog had whittled down the convoy to a rump of just eight merchant ships.[2] The damaged and the lost returned to Iceland whereas the intrepid eight carried on. They were protected by the light cruiser *Edinburgh,* the ship in which the 18th Cruiser Squadron's Rear Admiral Stuart Bonham Carter flew his flag, six destroyers, four corvettes and two armed trawlers.[3]

It was this group of vessels which was sighted south-west of Bear Island by the crew in a German Focke-Wulf reconnaissance plane on 15 April.[4]

U-boats were soon on the convoy's tail, the bearings of their signals first being registered on the escorts' high frequency direction finding (HF/DF) equipment during the early hours of 16 April.[5] The escorts' commanders' reaction did not always receive the approbation of the merchant ship crews. Concern was raised in the commodore's ship *Empire Howard* at the way two of the destroyers had at 2.20 p.m. that day turned away from their positions in the escort screen protecting the PQ14 freighters to stage a counter-attack.

'The Commodore (Eric Rees) said to me at the time that he hoped the destroyers were not being decoyed away from the convoy,' Captain John Downie, *Empire Howard*'s 36-year-old master, recalled later, in his report. He evidently took what the commodore said seriously. Who would not have, after hearing it spoken by a man with Eric Rees' experience? As well as spending a lifetime at sea, the 55-year-old commodore had achieved renown for having been on duty in the liner *Carpathia* when on 15 April 1912 her crew had rescued the survivors from the sunk *Titanic,* almost exactly 30 years to the day before Rees' most recent warning was voiced.

Rees was right to be worried. Half an hour later, when the convoy, by now formed up into four columns of two ships, was a short distance to the south-east of Bear Island, that is well inside what the destroyer *Bulldog*'s Commander Maxwell Richmond referred to as 'the U-boat danger area', Downie felt the ship – the leader of the 3rd column from the left – shudder three times (see Note 6 for location).[6] His report confirms: 'We were struck by a torpedo in the boiler room on the starboard side, followed by a second torpedo seconds later which struck the ship in the engine room, followed 10 seconds later by a third torpedo which struck the ship between No. 4 and 5 holds.

'The first torpedo burst the boilers and the ship became enveloped in steam and smoke. The second torpedo shattered the engines, whilst the third torpedo caused the magazine to explode and completely shattered the after part of the vessel.'

It was clear that the ship's crew were going to have to swim for it since she was going down fast, and as Downie stated, 'the explosion had blown all the boats back on board in pieces'.

'I stepped into the water from the lower bridge, and scrambled as far away from the ship as I was able,' Downie reported. 'I had not got very far before the bow of the ship reared up and the ship slid under rapidly stern first.'[7]

It is likely that Downie, like most men who served in the Arctic, had been told *ad nauseam* that it was impossible to survive more than a few minutes in icy water. In his report he specified that the water temperature was 29 °F (about -1.6 °C). But he was of the opinion that it was not the cold which did for many of the crew (see Note 8 for casualty statistics).[8] 'Whilst we were swimming about, the escorting destroyers were dropping depth charges amongst us,' he wrote. 'I think the concussion from them was directly responsible for the deaths of many of the men as several of the men were [subsequently] picked up with broken necks.'

He believed that might have explained why the commodore did not survive: 'Commodore Rees . . . was spoken to in the water by my Second Officer soon after the ship sank. He was trying to smoke a cheroot . . . and appeared to be perfectly all right when last seen. Shortly after this, the destroyers were dropping the depth charges and it may be possible that he was [also] killed by concussion.'

Downie's report goes on to state that he believed the death toll was tragically increased still further because of what happened after he and the other 'survivors' were rescued by the crews of the trawlers *Northern Wave* and *Lord Middleton*: 'We were all given a small amount of spirits on board the trawlers . . . One man on board the *Northern Wave* and eight of the men on the *Lord Middleton* . . . went to sleep and did not wake up again. A signal from a medical officer of an escort vessel warning the officers of both trawlers against giving spirits to the survivors was received too late, as the spirits had already been given when it was received.'[9]

One can understand why Downie would have reached the conclusion he did. However, while some post-war evidence and analysis has backed up what the medical officer advised, other conclusions, including those taking into account the experiments involving hypothermia carried out during World War 2 in Dachau concentration camp, have suggested that there might also have been other reasons for the deaths of *Empire Howard*'s men after they were rescued. One respected post-war hypothesis recorded in a medical journal, which cites the case of the *Empire Howard* deaths post-rescue on the grounds that it is a classic case of men dying after immersion in cold water, suggests that it was the lowering of arterial blood pressure rather than the alcohol which might well have been responsible.[10]

The dispatching of *Empire Howard* could well have been the first of many sinkings had not the other ships in the convoy had good fortune. As well as having the benefit of being a small group of merchant ships guarded by enough escorts to have protected a 25-ship convoy – the original British escort group was swelled still further by the arrival on the scene of two Russian destroyers on the morning of 17 April, and four British minesweepers the following day – PQ14 also was very lucky with the weather. This was a game changer given that clear skies at this time of year, when there were no hours of darkness – the darkest period was twilight at midnight – would have been lethal.[11]

By the time during the afternoon of 17 April that the Luftwaffe finally arrived in force bent on pulverizing the convoy, the fine weather that had made the remaining seven ships a tempting target during the previous two days had been replaced by thick fog. As a result, although the merchant ship and close escort crews heard the German planes flying overhead, the Luftwaffe pilots did not catch a glimpse of one PQ14 ship that afternoon, and after an hour of fruitless searching, they flew back to Norway. The weather also led to the cancellation of an operation by German destroyers, which had been sent out to intercept the convoy. This cleared the way for PQ14's ships to coast sedately into the Kola Inlet, and eventually to Murmansk, on 19 April without being troubled by further opposition.[12]

Most of the men in the 15 merchant ships which as part of the west-going convoy QP10 had sailed from the Kola Inlet on 10 April 1942 (16 sailed but one turned back), that is two days after PQ14 had set out, were eventually to have similar good fortune with the weather.[13] But they were not to know it was coming until after they and their escorts had been put through their paces (at the time of the most intense attacks on 13 April – three days before the main attack on PQ14 – QP10's close escort consisted of five destroyers, two armed trawlers and a minesweeper, while the cruiser HMS *Liverpool* covered the convoy in the first instance at least from afar in case the German surface fleet put in an appearance; two Russian destroyers and a minesweeper left the convoy on 12 April).[14]

Their problems and peace of mind were not helped by the Soviet Union's failure to live up to the promise made by Admiral Arseni Golovko, commander-in-chief of the Soviet Union's Northern Fleet, to provide long-range fighter protection during the first part of QP10's journey, and by the Russians' ineffective anti-submarine measures.[15]

Commenting on Golovko's boasts about the efficacy of his submarines, the cruiser HMS *Liverpool*'s Captain William Slayter later wrote: 'He appeared to take a distinctly optimistic view of the success of the Russian anti-submarine operations outside the Kola Inlet. The patrol craft have not as yet been fitted with asdics, though this is in hand, and it appears to be the accepted view that if a U-boat is sighted, it is only necessary to drop a fair number of depth charges in the neighbourhood to ensure its destruction.'[16]

Notwithstanding the Russian shortcomings, Slayter apparently remained optimistic about the convoy's prospects. To the consternation of the PQ13 survivors on board, before the cruiser eventually met up with QP10 – the link up between *Liverpool* and QP10 was delayed until 15 April so as not to provide another target within the convoy for U-boats and aircraft – he gave a stirring speech over the ship's loudspeakers stating that he was hoping that the German cruiser *Admiral Hipper* would come out so that he could sink her. He added that he would do the same to the *Tirpitz* if she crossed their path.[17] Apparently there was to be no holding back just because the cruiser was carrying 21 tons of gold bullion, representing part payment for the non-military goods that had been supplied to the Soviet Union.[18]

The 11 survivors from SS *New Westminster City* who found themselves taking passage in the British ship SS *Empire Cowper*, and the 18 survivors from *New Westminster City* travelling in the British SS *Harpalion* during QP10 would have been even more disturbed had they realized at the beginning of the voyage what they were to be in for.[19]

It did not take those in *Empire Cowper*, in convoy position 43 (4th column from left, in row 3), long to find out. At about 2 p.m. on 11 April, while the convoy, then located around 100 miles north-east of the Kola Inlet, was still heading north-westward towards the ice, before making the turn towards the west that would enable QP10 to head towards Iceland, two of the German aircraft, which had been circling, attacked from port and starboard simultaneously (see Note 20 for location).[20]

Although the plane darting in on Empire Cowper's starboard side was hit and had black smoke pouring out of one of its engines, its crew kept the aircraft on course.[21]

According to Empire Cowper's 21-year-old Thomas Errington, who at the time was the ship's fourth engineer officer: 'This aircraft dived to about mast height, and [the pilot] waved as he went past. But [it] never regained height and crashed in the sea.' However, before it went down on the port side of the convoy, its crew managed to drop three bombs, one of which in the words of Errington 'fell directly down the coal bunker and . . . exploded right in the bowels of the ship . . . in front of the boilers . . . Hence one of the firemen died later through lumps of coal being buried in his face.'[22] Another died on the spot before he could be evacuated.[23]

What was observed by distant onlookers, who were spared the screams and mayhem in the ship's boiler room, was nothing if not spectacular.

'I saw an enormous sheet of flame rise in the air, seemingly enveloping the whole ship,' reported an officer in the minesweeper escort HMS Speedwell.[24] The destroyer Oribi's Commander John McBeath, the senior officer of the escort, agreed that the prognosis for those on board the merchant ship did not at first look promising. The ship 'appeared to go up in a sheet of flame 200 feet high', he wrote in his official report, only to qualify his record of his initial perception by noting: 'When the flame and smoke cleared, the ship inexplicably appeared to be still intact, with a small amount of smoke coming from aft.'[25]

Nevertheless, perhaps not surprisingly given these fearsome pyrotechnics, there was a rush in some quarters to leave the ship more rapidly than was safe. Such was the confusion and panic caused by the escaping steam that the first lifeboat lowered was not level, with the result that the six occupants fell into the sea and were drowned.[26] Fortunately, the rest of the abandonment went well, and all but nine of the 57 crew and gunners and the 11 passengers survived. The casualties included the scalded fireman whose injuries were so severe, he passed away after having been taken on board the trawler which picked up the survivors.[27]

Spirits within the convoy were lifted, however, by the sight of some of the planes which had attacked that afternoon departing with smoke or flames coming out of their engines, in addition to at least two which according to British witnesses had been shot down.[28]

Moreover, those grimacing sailors in the leading destroyer *Punjabi*, who in temperatures recorded at -8 °C, had to leave their messes on 12 April to chip off the ice that had accumulated from frozen spray on their A (front) gun, were surely more upbeat once they realized that the arrival of the bad weather had its advantages.[29] The strong northerly wind and snow showers that day grounded the German aircraft for many hours, with the result that until that evening there was no German plane shadowing the convoy.

Not that this temporary reprieve changed much. The fact there was no darkness meant that once the German aircraft returned to the fray, it was impossible to make an evasive alteration of course without being observed.[30]

It was in that context that the next attack on the convoy took place. Shortly after 1 a.m. on 13 April, shortly after the convoy, then north of Kirkenes, changed from its north-western course towards the west, the Soviet merchant ship *Kiev*, the second ship in the convoy's second column, was in her turn shaken by a violent explosion as she was struck on her starboard side by two torpedoes near her seventh hold.[31] This was followed by two more loud bangs around 25 minutes later when the Panamanian *El Occidente*, the leading ship in the starboard column, was also hit on her starboard side by two torpedoes (see Note 32 for location).[32]

Given the mayhem the torpedo strike on *Kiev* had unleashed during the seven minutes between the moment when the torpedo exploded and the sinking of the ship (occupants of two of the lifeboats ended up in the water, and other men dived into the sea because, for a time, rope connecting another lifeboat to *Kiev* could not be cast off), it is astonishing to discover that only four men from *Kiev*'s crew were not rescued. A female cleaner from the ship who expired soon after being rescued increased the number killed to five.[33]

Things ended less well concerning *El Occidente* which sank stern first just two to three minutes after being hit. Although the crew in the minesweeper *Speedwell* picked up 32 of the Panamanian ship's 45-man crew, seven of the rescued men were so cold after being immersed in the icy water that they passed away, bringing the death count to 20.[34]

At 5.40 a.m., the first of that day's complement of Junkers 88 bombers arrived.[35] The intensity of the bombing of the remaining ships in the convoy, which started shortly after 6 a.m., has been captured in the following words written by the destroyer *Fury's* John Dodds in his journal: 'The first four came [and] dropped their bombs, and before they left, their place was taken by four more. And so it went on . . . I have never been in such a determined bombing in my life, and I hope I shall never see the like of it again. It was unnerving.'[36] Although of around 20 aircraft in the raid, six Junkers 88s were lost, the bombing continued until the last of the surviving aircraft finally departed at 10.40 a.m. leaving two damaged British ships straggling in the convoy's wake to the north of North Cape.[37]

One of the damaged ships, *Beacon Street*, was able to catch up after counterbalancing the water that had rushed in where she was holed. But the other, *Harpalion*, ended up being abandoned, and then shot up by *Fury's* gunners. According to the report by *Harpalion's* Captain Henry Williams, his ship was last seen 'blazing fiercely and sinking rapidly.'[38]

Harpalion was to be the last German QP10 scalp. At first sight this was encouraging from the Allies' point of view. The fact that QP10 eventually made it back to Iceland on 21 April having only lost four ships, in spite of such sustained attacks from the air as well as some hit and run strikes from U-boats, was interpreted by some to confirm that the convoy system was working for the Allies and all was well. This was the case, notwithstanding the restricted visibility that assisted the convoy for much of the time after the 13 April air raid.[39] Indeed D. A. Casey, QP10's commodore, was so buoyed up by what he had overseen, he concluded in his report: 'Convoys accompanied by anti-submarine and anti-aircraft escorts should be able to make the passage without unduly heavy losses.'[40]

However *Liverpool's* Captain Slayter's gloss on the same events was decidedly pessimistic. His negative thoughts were apparently coloured by the Arctic mirages he and his lookouts had seen while covering QP10 which highlighted the danger posed by the lurking U-boats. (On two occasions they had spotted what looked like the tall funnel of a trawler or cargo ship at a distance of some 8 miles, only for it to become obvious as they drew closer that what they had in fact observed were relatively low level U-boat conning towers transformed into something that appeared to be much higher by the Arctic conditions.) And that was before the threat posed by the Luftwaffe was even considered.

Near the end of his report he stated: 'It was only providentially foul weather at the right moments that limited the losses of QP10, a convoy of only 15 ships, to four.' Bearing that in mind, he recommended 'that convoys to north Russia should be held up until the ice clears sufficiently to allow ships to be routed well north and east of the Norwegian coast permitting them to stay well away from the nearest German aerodromes.'[41]

His conclusion was echoed by Rear Admiral Stuart Bonham Carter, who as explained above had been in charge of the PQ14 escort. In his report he wrote: 'The remains of PQ14 were extremely lucky in the weather . . .

'Under present conditions with no hours of darkness, continually under air observation for the last four days, submarines concentrating in the bottle necks, torpedo attack to be expected, our destroyers unable to carry out a proper hunt or search owing to the oil situation, serious losses must be expected in every convoy.'[42]

It is interesting to note however, that just when British naval commanders were citing the absence of hours of darkness as a reason why the convoys were becoming more risky, their opponents were also stating that it made their job more difficult. The German Seekriegsleitung war diary entry for 18 April states that the absence of darkness as well as the strength of the British escort force and the bad weather were together responsible for the 'meagre results'.[43]

10

David and Goliath

Main Action: 30 April 1942
The torpedoing of HMS Edinburgh, QP11

(See Maps 1, 8 and 9)

On 23 April 1942, just days before the scheduled departure of the next pair of convoys, members of the Chiefs of Staff Committee received a report from Admiral Sir Jack Tovey 'recommending that no further convoys should be despatched until the ice conditions would permit a more evasive routeing, or if this was unacceptable that the convoys should be limited to 20 ships'.[1]

Taking into account Tovey's reasoning without fully endorsing his recommendation, the next day the War Cabinet, responding to Admiral Pound's additional statement about how many convoys per month were possible, ruled that the number of convoys sent each month would be reduced to three every two months (compared with four – PQ12, PQ13, PQ14 and the scheduled PQ15 – during the two calendar months March and April), and the number of ships in each convoy would not exceed 25.[2]

These constraints on what could be sent to the Soviet Union were not popular in America. On 26 April 1942, Roosevelt sent a telegram to Churchill telling him how 'greatly disturbed' he was by the 'political repercussions' of this decision. What worried him was that the large accumulation of American ships in Icelandic ports due to the return there of 16 ships from PQ14 threatened to deny the Soviet Union the benefit of US aid prior to the launching of the next German offensive on the Eastern Front. 'I do hope . . . you can review again the size of immediate convoys so that the stuff now backed up in Iceland can get through,' he wrote, adding, 'I hope that in any conversations Eden may have with the Russian ambassador, they may be confined to telling him the difficulties, and urging their cooperation in bringing the convoys in, rather than any firm statement about the limit to the number of ships that can be convoyed . . . It seems to me that any word reaching Stalin at this time that our supplies were stopping for any reason would have a most unfortunate effect.'[3]

Churchill replied two days later stating that the number of convoys was not negotiable. 'We are at our utmost strain for convoy escorts,' he wrote. But influenced no doubt by a desire to remain in step with American as well as British public opinion, a substantial proportion of which was in favour of helping the Soviet Union as much as possible, as well as by the desirability of fostering good relations both between himself and Roosevelt and between Britain and Stalin, he included in his telegram the following concession: 'One convoy limited to 25 ships (PQ15) has just sailed . . . We are ready to consider in the light of the experience with this convoy whether the number of merchant ships in future convoys can be increased to as many as 35.'[4]

The sop to public opinion may have been thought necessary in the wake of the pro-second front speech Lord Beaverbrook – who by this time had resigned from Churchill's cabinet – had given at the Waldorf Towers in New York on 23 April 1942. Because it had been approved by Roosevelt, and broadcast all over America, it threatened to spark off another round of pro-invasion of France rhetoric in the media in London.[5]

It was against the background of the transatlantic correspondence that the final arrangements for QP11, the next west-going convoy, were made. It was to consist of more escorts than merchant ships.

The 13 merchant ships in the convoy were to be protected, at least during the first part of its journey, by a close escort including no less than 17 warships: the cruiser *Edinburgh* under the command of the 18th Cruiser Squadron's Rear Admiral Stuart Bonham Carter, six British destroyers, four corvettes, four minesweepers plus two of the Soviet Union's destroyers, and an armed trawler.[6] That was without counting the warships of the Home Fleet – for the first time an Arctic convoy was to be bolstered by American warships (US warships with the Fleet consisted of four destroyers, two cruisers, and the 242 yards long by 36 yards wide battleship USS *Washington* with her nine 16-inch guns giving her even more firepower by way of main armament than both *Tirpitz* and the British battleships in the Home Fleet) – which would be watching over both QP11 and the east-going PQ15 from south-west of Bear Island.[7]

Edinburgh also had another role to play. Like some of the other British cruisers returning to Iceland from Russia before her, she was to carry gold ingots that were to go towards the money the Soviet Union owed to the Allies for non-military supplies. The way it was delivered to the ship as she lay anchored in Vaenga Bay, around 13 miles north of Murmansk in the Kola Inlet, was very cloak and dagger. *Edinburgh*'s Arthur Start, a supply petty officer, recalled being awakened in the middle of the night a few days before the convoy set off by the sound of a bugle. He and his men were told to go to the starboard waist of the ship. Start has described how astonished they were by what they saw:

'The scene was like something from a film. Secured along the starboard side were two barges, and at vantage points aboard were about a score of Russian soldiers armed with Tommy guns held at the ready. On our own ship . . . were . . . our own Royal Marines . . . As we watched, a tarpaulin covering the barge's cargo was drawn back to reveal . . . ammunition boxes. The natural assumption . . . was that these contained small arms ammunition. But [if so], why . . . such security . . .? [Also] the boxes, rope handled, were extremely heavy, each needing two men to lift them. In the dull grey . . . light of the Arctic . . . night, we carried those boxes all the way up to the flight deck, and there lowered them down [using] . . . ropes through a shaft . . . to the bomb room three decks below.'[8]

What was in the boxes was only revealed when one of them was dropped, according to Royal Marine Bill Miles. As he recalled, 'It crashed down, just missing me, and there in front of me and the others were [some . . .] gold bars.'[9]

The box was quickly repaired and the bars were placed back inside it before it was in its turn hoisted up to the flight deck and then lowered down to the bomb room. But when during this operation it began to sleet, and the red stencilling on the boxes dripped onto the snow on the ship's decks leaving behind a trail of crimson, this was taken as an inauspicious omen. A seaman expressed the views of many when he turned to an officer and remarked, 'It's going to be a bad trip sir.' As saw it, the Russian gold was 'dripping with blood'.[10]

However, such premonitions were not passed on to the wounded survivors from convoys past, 28 of whom were brought on board *Edinburgh*.[11] Most were accommodated in the ship's recreation spaces on the forecastle deck, but the worst cases were carried down to the sickbay on the starboard side of the confusingly named upper deck (one deck down from the forecastle deck) where they were each allocated a 'bunk' cot.[12] They included Morris Mills (last referred to in Chapter 8), who basked in what he referred to as the 'efficiency, cleanliness, order, good food and medicine. Above all, the wonderful cheerful esprit de corps of the Royal Navy.' After he had been given clothing and washed, the ship's surgeon came over and asked to see his stump, adding: 'It's all right lad; I'm [just] going to give you a shot to kill the pain.'[13]

The convoy eventually left Murmansk during the morning of 28 April 1942, and passed out of the Kola Inlet at around 1 p.m. *Edinburgh* followed in its wake, sailing from Vaenga at 9.30 p.m. that night. As the ship accelerated away from Russian soil, Morris Mills luxuriated in the feeling that he was safe at last. He later wrote: 'Laying in my cot, warm, fed and partially sedated, I felt the ship dip her head into the seas, and felt a wonderful sense of suffocating joy surge through my body . . . I was going home on one of the most powerful ships in the British Navy . . .

'The following morning Rear Admiral . . . Stuart Bonham Carter, . . . commanding 18th Cruiser Squadron, paid us a visit in the sick bay. A burly figure in a heavy naval coat, . . . the Admiral was full of bonhomie and confidence as he spoke with each of us. Before leaving, he made a short speech [which was along the following lines]: "Well lads, you know we are escorting Convoy QP11 . . . I don't think our German friends are going to let us pass without a fight, so you must prepare yourselves for action. But never fear, you are in the hands of the Royal Navy, and we'll get you back safely." '[14]

Mills' morale was only dented by some emergency surgery he witnessed which took place a few yards from his cot. One of the other men in the sickbay was a survivor from a ship that had sunk during a previous convoy. The gangrene in his leg had become life threatening. He would surely die if the leg was not amputated. A screen was placed around the operating table, but Mills was able to see the surgeon and his assistants over the top of it from his cot which, being the top one of two bunks, was elevated well above the deck.

'The sickbay was deathly quiet except for the clink of instruments and the subdued voices of the medical team,' Mills remembered later. 'Then came the harsh rasp of the saw as the surgeon cut through the bone, invoking a visceral stabbing pain to shoot through my stump, as I suffered with the patient . . .

'The sight of the severed limb being taken away . . . drove me into a frenzy of self-pity . . . From being a healthy . . . [seventeen] year old, bursting with energy and full of the joys of life, I had been reduced to a helpless cripple. At that moment I did not care if I lived or died.'[15]

Of course, although one suspects the 52-year-old Rear Admiral would have been full of sympathy for the likes of Mills, whose prospects had been undermined so cruelly after the maiming, his main preoccupation after departing from the Kola Inlet was on how to protect as many of those participating in QP11 as was feasible. There were soon signs that the peace experienced as the convoy's participants enjoyed their first hours at sea might be short lived. Just minutes after *Edinburgh* joined the convoy during the morning of 29 April, the crew in a German reconnaissance plane sighted QP11's ships.[16] By the night of 29–30 April, QP11 was being shadowed by U-boats.[17]

Bonham Carter appreciated the danger this posed. He later wrote: 'In view of the slow speed of the convoy, it was my policy to keep clear, and this I did by proceeding ahead some 15 to 20 miles on different courses, zigzagging at the highest speed permitted by the state of the sea, turning to make contact every few hours.'[18]

It was just unfortunate that on 30 April, while *Edinburgh* was taking a detour looping around to the north-west in order to stay clear not just of the convoy – which by this time was heading towards the west (see Map 8) – but also of a U-boat brought to his attention by a signal sent from the destroyer *Bulldog,* he found himself approaching another U-boat which unbeknown to him lay in his path (as shown in Map 9).

It was *U-456*. Her 27-year-old commander Kapitänleutnant Max-Martin Teichert had been watching *Edinburgh*'s progress on and off ever since she first appeared over the horizon during that morning (30 April). The sighting had prompted him to send an urgent message back to base shortly before midday including the location, around 250 miles north-west of Murmansk, and the words: 'Cruiser, Belfast class, westerly course, high speed, extreme zigzags . . . Teichert.'[19]

Shortly after he sent his message, 'the cruiser' disappeared from sight. But around half an hour later, she reappeared. Teichert once again recorded *Edinburgh*'s movements, writing in his war diary: 'Cruiser is approaching on a bearing of 120° . . . zigzagging on a course of approximately 300° . . . She rapidly looms up on the horizon.'[20]

But tragically, at the metaphorical end of the day, it was Bonham Carter, not Teichert, who made the final critical adjustment that would make all the difference. 'At 1555, knowing submarines were in the vicinity, I sent for the Captain in the Plotting Office to discuss the best action,' he wrote in his report.

After a discussion, Bonham Carter decided that it was now safe to turn to the south-west with a view to turning back towards the convoy afterwards, little realizing that would present *Edinburgh*'s broadside to the U-boat that was stalking her.[21] The turn was duly made (see 3 in Map 9).

'Wunderbar (Marvellous)!' was the comment later inscribed in *U-456*'s war diary by Teichert to describe his delight on observing the cruiser's change of course, although he was having to rely on his vessel's hydrophone equipment as much as on the very blurred image he could see through the blotches on the lens of his periscope. At around 4.15 p.m., minutes after seeing what had occurred, he gave the order to fire three torpedoes at the enormous target that had unexpectedly presented itself to him at a range of just over 1,000 metres (see 3A in Map 1, 1 in Map 8, and Note 22 for location of torpedoing).[22]

Knowledge concerning the impact made by the first explosion as one of *U-456*'s torpedoes smashed into *Edinburgh*'s starboard side near the aft section of the stoker's mess amidships (forrard of the ship's funnels and aircraft hangar), depended on where you were in the ship (see Note 23 for explosion site in ship).[23] Norman Sparksman, a seaman in his early twenties who was on the platform deck, that is third deck down from the top open-air forecastle deck, in the aft high-angle transmitting station (on the ship's port side, aft of the funnels, well to the rear of the first explosion), would later write about feeling 'a muffled bump as if the ship had hit something solid, and a slight roll as she leaned over and then righted again'.

He added: 'I have a distinct recollection of hearing one of the more experienced sailors muttering: "That was a fuckin' tin fish!" A few seconds later, the second torpedo struck the starboard side of the ship [at its rear end] with much more dramatic effect.' According to Sparksman, there was 'an enormous bang with much rattling and scraping of metal, and all the lights went out leaving us in complete darkness. The ship gave such a heave, we all lost our footing and fell on the deck.'[24] During the first minutes afterwards, before emergency lighting kicked in, the only light in the transmitting station was provided thanks to Sparksman, as he put it, 'pedalling furiously' on what he described as 'a bicycle frame bolted to the deck with a belt drive from the back "wheel" to a dynamo on the deck.'[25]

It is not surprising there was such upheaval inside the ship. Part of *Edinburgh*'s back end had been sheared off (more would finally break off around two hours after the explosion), and the remainder was scrunched up like the wreck of a car that has been involved in a head-on crash. Gone was the rudder and two of the ship's propellers, while the top deck had curled up like the 'lid' on an opened sardine tin, and had come to rest sticking up in the air, masking the barrels of the main armament position known as Y gun turret (the back turret).[26]

Commander Jocelyn Salter, the 40-year-old officer in charge in *Foresight*, one of four destroyers (two British and two Russian) subsequently sent by the destroyer *Bulldog*'s Commander Maxwell Richmond (the convoy escort's senior officer) to ward off any further attacks on *Edinburgh*, would later write: 'We found her in a very poor state . . . She looked like a scorpion about to attack. The whole of the quarter deck was peeled back.'[27]

If Sparksman was lucky to avoid being vaporised by the explosion of the second torpedo, John Kenny, a 19-year-old signals decoder, was equally fortunate that the marines' mess compartment on the ship's lower deck (second deck down from the open-air 'forecastle' deck) where the signallers and the telegraphists' mess was located, was separated by a sturdy bulkhead from the seamen's mess (for'ard of the marines' mess), which along with the stokers' mess forrard of it, seems to have taken the brunt of the blast made by the first explosion.[28]

In his post-war memoirs Kenny described how in the minutes leading up to the attack 'those of us awake were sitting at the mess deck table drinking tea. There was a terrific flash and two tremendous bangs that almost merged into one, and the lights went out. Time seemed to stand still, like a film stopped suddenly, and in the dim light coming from the deck hatch [overhead], I saw through the thick smoke a . . . wide crack in the midships' bulkhead which ran from the roof to the floor (at the for-rard end of the marines' mess).

'For what seemed an age we still sat at the table. Then the shock wave passed and we were galvanized into action, and started running around the large mess deck waking people up; incredibly a large number had slept through the explosion.'[29]

Once it was realized that there was ample time to get out of the mess deck, the initial feelings of panic subsided. An orderly queue was formed, and the men calmly took their turn to climb up the ladder in the centre of the mess deck to the upper deck. Last out was Alan Higgins, an 18-year-old wireless operator and message decoder, who had slipped on the mixture of oil and water that had soaked the mess deck, thereby ensuring that he was at the back of the queue.

Referring to the movement of *Edinburgh* after the explosions, he later wrote in his memoir: 'The ship felt as though she was clasped in a trembling hand which was turning it over to the starboard side at a steep angle . . . I had to crawl on hands and knees, holding on to the legs of the clothes lockers to make progress. You can imagine how slowly the queue moved as, one by one, the men squeezed through the one small hatch.'[30]

He would never forget what he heard as he clambered up the ladder: 'As I climbed up, I was hearing faint cries for help coming from the . . . [seamen's] mess [forrard] behind the next bulkhead. Someone was saying over and again, "Please will someone help me." Another voice cried out, "Oh Mum! Oh Mum!" They were words that would haunt Higgins, and give him survivors' guilt, for the rest of his life because, shocked as he was by what he heard, he had obeyed the unspoken command known to all defeated soldiers and sailors, 'every man for himself', and thinking about number one, he had just kept on climbing.[31]

At least he could climb. That was a solace denied to Morris Mills, who until the torpedo struck, was still counting his lucky stars in the ship's sickbay. One minute he was sipping the tea that had been brought to him by the sickbay rating. The next, following the explosions which had caused such devastation in the stokers' and seamen's messes, one deck down from the sickbay, albeit a short distance to the rear of it, all hell broke loose. 'Following the explosions, there was a split second's silence,' he recalled in his memoirs, 'then the all too familiar cries and screams of the wounded. Panic broke out in the sickbay, as thick oily smoke reeking of cordite belched through the alleyways, filling our confined space. I felt sure I was going to die, but was terrified of dying like a rat caught in a metal box . . .

'I desperately struggled to pull myself over the cot side in order to fall to the deck . . . I had almost made it when a sailor rushed in and hoisted me onto his shoulder. "It's alright mate – I've got you," [he said] . . . He battled his way through a milling crowd of seamen up several iron ladders and laid me on the open deck. He . . . [then] returned below to rescue others.'

Mills would later refer to the seaman as 'a true unsung hero', but if the truth be told, this selfless angel had almost killed the apprentice deck officer with his kindness. 'Owing to the violent manner necessary to get me from below, my various wounds had all burst open. Yet again, I could feel the hot blood pumping from my stump,' Mills remembered afterwards. 'I might have bled to death, but for the fact . . . [that because it was so cold] even the spurting blood became bloody icicles.' However, before pain and fear became overwhelming, he lost consciousness. When he next came to, he was lying shoulder to shoulder with many others in an officers' wardroom, having been wrapped in blankets after his wounds had been redressed. There he weakly lay, listening to another rating, who was trying to explain that although the ship had lost her stern, and the U-boat was still at large, everything was going to be all right.[32]

Mills, as well as Sparksman, Higgins and Kenny, had survived thanks to the requirement that each discrete section in a warship should be separated with watertight bulkheads and hatches from other areas. It was this principle that permitted the hell-like scenes below decks witnessed by Leading Stoker Leonard Bradley to occur, without many of those in other sections being any the wiser. Bradley had been chatting to his friend Taff Harrington, an amateur boxer, in the stokers' mess deck on the lower deck, when the torpedo exploded in the oil tank beneath them. This is how he described what ensued:

'The whole mess deck split in two, and as the lights went out, Harrington and I . . . [and some other men] fell straight through into the storage tank, which was partially filled. The emergency lighting failed to come on, and we were down there in complete darkness, floundering around in oil and water. In the blackness, with men around screaming and shouting, I managed at last to get a footing, and started to make my way towards where I thought the hatch might be.

'As I moved, I heard Taff Harrington near me. I called out "Taff!" and he grabbed me. The oil was now pouring in fast from burst pipes in adjoining tanks and rising up to our shoulders. Harrington tried to hold [on to] my hand, but it slipped, and he . . . [drowned] in the oil . . .

'All this time I was swallowing oil. Gradually . . . [it] found its level and stopped rising, [and] everything went very quiet. The hatch above us was sealed, and we had no idea if the ship was afloat, partly submerged or at the bottom of the . . . [sea]. We must have been there nearly an hour when "the miracle" [we had been praying for] happened. The hatch was prised open, and three stokers came down with ropes and pulled us to safety.'[33]

But it was still far from certain the cruiser would remain afloat. While measures were taken to counterbalance the list to starboard by pumping water into the cruiser's port side tanks, *Foresight*'s Commander Salter was trying to fathom how it would be possible to take a warship to safety when she had no capacity to steer. Eventually, *Edinburgh* was reduced to tacking from side to side by using alternate propellers.[34]

These difficulties did not constrain *Edinburgh*'s 41-year-old Captain Hugh Faulkner, who gave an encouraging speech to those of the crew who could be mustered on the ship's flight deck. 'I told them I had high hopes of getting the ship back to harbour,' he wrote afterwards. On hearing this, they cheered, a response he later conveyed to his superiors by stating in his official report: 'The way they responded to these remarks convinced me that my hopes were shared by them all.'[35]

One suspects however that his apparent positivity was dampened somewhat by the realization that a substantial number of his crew had already lost their lives. In his post-war memoir, Jack Thwaite, who at the time of the torpedoing was serving in *Edinburgh* as a 'boy' signalman, mentioned the following revealing incident. It showed that losses were ongoing:

'During the evening of 30th April, the bridge was contacted by one of the boy seamen who was down in the telephone exchange (in the supposedly flooded area of the platform deck – which is the third deck down from the ship's open-air deck). Neville Holt had been off watch, and had gone down to the telephone exchange to see his mate. He must have been knocked out by the initial explosion, and when he regained consciousness, the section was in darkness.

'He had called the bridge on the voice pipe. The Captain answered him, and reassured Holt, telling him it might be a bit before they got him out, but in the meantime they would try and get some food to him. Someone was on the voice pipe all the time talking [to him] and encouraging him. He complained of being very tired, and was told to try and get some sleep. He never spoke to us again. The Captain's theory was that CO_2 from the cold room next to the exchange had seeped through the door and quietly, and mercifully, suffocated the boy.'[36]

Faulkner's morale boosting words notwithstanding, *Edinburgh*'s chances of making it back to port were not good. Shortly after 6 p.m. on 30 April, Teichert had sent Admiral Schmundt (Admiral Nordmeer) back in Kirkenes an update on the situation.[37] Despite doubts raised over the use of their warships offensively following the loss of *Z 26* during PQ13, the Germans acted quickly. Shortly before 1 a.m. on 1 May, Zerstörergruppe Nordmeer consisting of the three German destroyers *Z 24, Z 25* and *Hermann Schoemann*, under the command of the 42-year-old Kapitän zur See Alfred Schulze-Hinrichs, who flew his flag in the latter ship, set out from Kirkenes.[38]

They were to attack both QP11 and *Edinburgh*. However, as they advanced on their north-western course (see Map 8), there was debilitating indecision about which was to come first. This was because during their deployment, Schmundt's knowledge concerning the whereabouts of their targets was twice lost and regained.[39] However, the switching and the emphasis that both targets should be hit worried those in the Seekriegslei-tung who were watching from the sidelines. They were to ask subsequently whether it had stopped Schulze-Hinrichs being able to focus on either.[40]

This flaw was exacerbated by Schmundt's instruction that if Zerstörer-gruppe Nordmeer encountered stout defence, the German destroyers' crews were to distract the British warships in order to enable the U-boats to attack. In the light of what was to happen over the next 24 hours, it is tempting to question whether this was taken as a veiled permission to react to opposition by not going in for the kill.[41]

11

Sitting Ducks

Main Action: 1 and 2 May 1942
The sinking of HMS Edinburgh, QP11

(See Maps 1, 8, 10 and 11)

At around 1.30 p.m. on 1 May 1942, when the convoy QP11 was still south-east of Bear Island (but well to the west of where *Edinburgh* had been torpedoed), a signalman in HMS *Amazon*, a destroyer on the starboard side of the convoy, saw a light winking on the corvette HMS *Snowflake*, which was on QP11's port side. The signal stated that ships had been detected via *Snowflake*'s radar where there should not have been any, to the south (see 3 on Map 8 for where this took place).[1]

Minutes later an alert lookout in the destroyer HMS *Beverley*, one of the other escorts on the port side, reported that the shapes visible on *Snowflake*'s radar screen, to the south-south-west, were enemy warships.[2] After seeing both of these signals, Commander Maxwell Richmond, the 41-year-old New Zealander in *Bulldog*, had his crew take his ship at full speed from the starboard bow to the port bow of the convoy. He then ordered the commanders of the other three destroyer escorts to: 'Join me.'[3]

The destroyers' commanders immediately abandoned their anti-submarine stations to the north and south of the convoy, and had their ships take their allotted places behind *Bulldog*, all the while releasing smoke to conceal the merchant ships, most of whose masters had obeyed

144

the commodore's instruction to turn from their westerly course so that they could sail towards the north-east. So quick was the British destroyers' deployment, that at 2 p.m. *Bulldog,* with the German warships still around five miles away, was able to head off to the south-west followed by *Beagle, Amazon* and *Beverley* in that order.

This was all part of the pre-arranged plan, agreed with the escort commanders before the convoy set out, to place the destroyers between any German surface ships that turned up and the convoy, and to obscure the battlefield with smoke. Another part of Richmond's plan still had to be put into effect. He realized the ships in his game group were relatively lightly armoured and armed compared to the German destroyers, whose type he believed he had identified (in fact as previously stated in Chapter 5, two of the German ships – *Z 24* and *Z 25* – carried four 5.9-inch guns, making their main armament almost as powerful as that carried by light cruisers such as *Edinburgh,* and only one – Hermann Schoemann – carried the 5-inch guns he had suspected).

Three of the destroyers under his command mounted two 4.7-inch guns and the fourth, *Beverley,* one of the ancient 'four-stackers' (four-funneled destroyers) purchased from America, mounted three 4-inch guns, of which only two could be fired in a broadside. Given the disparity, he concluded his best hope of holding the Germans up was to keep them at arm's length.

It was with that in mind that shortly after he observed the flash of the enemy's guns as they opened fire at 2.07 p.m. (see 2A and 2B in Map 10 for the relative positions at this juncture), more than matching the shells that flew out of his own ships' guns, he first led the vessels under his command round to the east, putting them on a parallel course with the German destroyers which had also been turned in that direction (see movements during the battle in Map 10), and he then insisted that the four British destroyers should fire their torpedoes. Although he realized that torpedoes were unlikely to cause the German ships any problems when fired from around five miles, he hoped the sight of them might serve as a deterrent. If the German ships came too close, they should be ready to take the consequences.[4]

However, it was the British ships which were in jeopardy. The following extract from the report written by *Amazon*'s 33-year-old Lieutenant Commander Nigel Roper reveals how close the Germans came to sinking his ship – presumably as the British destroyers headed to the east during the initial engagement – with their first salvos:

'More than one German destroyer's salvos were falling in line with *Amazon*, as a few seconds after a complete salvo (four splashes seen) landed within 100 yards, short, another salvo fell not much further over . . .

'A splinter pierced the starboard side of the wheelhouse, fatally wounding a rating . . . and shattering the glass and woodwork of the steering scuttles in the wheelhouse. *Amazon* altered about 20° towards the enemy in an endeavour to draw their salvos over, but straddling continued. A hail of splinters was spraying the upper deck, and after B gun had fired three rounds, three members of the gun crew . . . were wounded.'

It was only after both the German and the British ships had turned away from each other that Roper discovered why there had been no response from his torpedo section when the order 'Ready starboard!' had been given. Petty Officer Charles Green, the torpedo gunner's mate, had been hit so fairly and squarely by a splinter, that in the words of the subsequent recommendation for a decoration: 'his right arm was all but severed at the shoulder'. No. 1 of the torpedo crew had also been wounded. However, Roper and the others on the bridge were none the wiser until the first action was over, because 'the "talking" switch of the communications number's telephone was switched to "off" early in the engagement'.

In spite of his terrible injury, Green survived. He was rushed to the sickbay where, once again in the words of the decoration recommendation, the arm 'was cut off by the Medical Officer with a pair of scissors'.[5] Green was afterwards commended because 'despite . . . [his] weakness due to loss of blood and pain, he managed to smile and keep up the spirits of the other casualties . . . It was impossible to attend . . . [his] wound properly owing to danger of exposure to blood poisoning, and . . . [he] endured this period with the greatest courage.'[6]

While preparing for the Germans' next assault, the British destroyers fell back on the convoy and made more smoke in a renewed effort to conceal the merchant ships. However, it was too late for one of them. 'On nearing the convoy, No. 33's bows were seen rearing up vertically before her final plunge,' Roper reported, adding: '*Lord Middleton* had reported that No. 33 (the Soviet merchant ship *Tsiolkovsky*) had been torpedoed a few minutes earlier, and that she was picking up survivors.'[7]

There were to be precious few of them. Only 15 of her crew were saved, a testament to the plunging temperatures near to the ice at this time of year, which were as low as -10 °C out of the water.[8]

There was little time for the British destroyer crews to catch their breath. Shortly after 2.30 p.m. the German destroyers were sighted again, this time approaching from the south-south-east. Once again they were met by the four British destroyers, whose crews opened fire at the same time as the Germans when the two forces were around seven miles apart (see 5A and 5B in Map 10 for their approximate relative positions).

Amazon was in the thick of it once more. 'It again appeared as if [the] enemy were concentrating . . . on *Amazon*,' Roper reported. 'Within less than a minute of [the] fall of first enemy salvos, a shudder and wave of blast on the bridge indicated that . . . [the] superstructure had been hit. Through the voice-pipe, the only surviving member in the wheelhouse managed to say: "Somebody take the wheel. I can't!" I ordered "Stop starboard!", while Sub-Lieutenant McDonald ran down to the wheelhouse to take the wheel. Climbing over the debris, and the bodies of the coxswain and the telegraph man, he found that the ship was still answering the wheel, which although badly splintered, had had a quite remarkable escape.

'The shell had glanced off the port Oerlikon [20 mm cannon] mounting and burst on the plating below the sliding wooden door of the wheelhouse.

'By the time the ship had been conned back to the original course, the remainder of the destroyers had turned away to starboard and were making smoke. The enemy had also turned away, and had evidently been too busy to notice our temporary loss of control.'[9]

Amazon ended up being relegated to the back of the line of the British destroyers so that in spite of having no surviving compass, she could remain as part of the destroyer group without being in the way. Nevertheless, some pretty rudimentary measures had to be taken. Because the German shelling had severed most of the wiring from her wheelhouse and from her bridge, a human chain was formed so that messages could be passed to her engine room.

During the attacks 'the convoy continued steaming . . . right up into the ice,' wrote QP11's commodore, Captain William Lawrence, master of SS *Briarwood*. 'We steamed for about 5 miles, and then found a pool within the ice field which we sailed round for the rest of the afternoon. During this time a submarine came up outside the ice, and fired his 4-inch gun, but his shooting was ineffective. He stood by outside the ice to wait for us to come out, and every time the escorts came up, he would dive, coming up again as soon as they went away.'[10]

The merchant ships would only escape from their icy prison when the destroyers came to release them following the departure of the German trio.

The three German destroyers were gone by around 6.15 p.m., having straddled the British destroyers on several occasions, and narrowly missed one of the British ships with a torpedo, in the course of the five separate attacks (see Map 10 for attack details).[11] They had to move on if they were to have enough ammunition to target *Edinburgh,* and any vessels protecting her, with a viable attack.[12]

The return to business as usual enabled *Bulldog's* Commander Richmond to congratulate the other British escorts' commanders and crews for a job well done, whereupon one of these commanders is said to have messaged him back: 'I should hate to play poker with you!'[13]

* * *

It was certainly the case that *Edinburgh* was no longer the soft option she might have been had she been attacked by the Zerstörergruppe Nordmeer warships first. As the three German destroyers ploughed through the waves and the snow during the Arctic night in an effort to reach their next objective, 170 miles to the south-east, before breakfast the next day, a growing gaggle of supporting ships was gathering around the British cruiser.[14] They included a Russian gunboat and tug, and three British minesweepers which had been sent out from the Kola Inlet. Given the pre-existing presence of the destroyers *Foresight* and *Forester,* that meant the cruiser had seven escorts with her by the time the three German destroyers made their initial assault shortly before 6.30 a.m. on 2 May (see 4 in Map 8 for location).[15]

Foresight's Commander Jocelyn Salter later stated that the first indication that *Edinburgh* and her protection force were under attack was 'the sound of gunfire and the sight of flashes and splashes. Nothing was visible otherwise,' he reported.[16]

Salter's advance to the north-north-east (shown in Map 11), in order to identify the source of the flashes, quickly helped him establish why the Germans were for much of the time out of sight. As Salter put it, 'all three enemy destroyers were playing hide and seek in the snow and their own smoke screens . . . Their tactics were to dart in, fire a few rounds and then make smoke and retire under it. Owing to this and to the snow squalls which were constantly coming down, no mobile enemy ship was in sight at any time for more than about two minutes on end.'[17]

The German risk-averse tactics could not have been more different to *Edinburgh*'s Captain Faulkner's more robust approach. Faulkner ordered the slipping of the wires that had attached the cruiser to the minesweeper *Gossamer* and the tug, so that *Edinburgh* could move at speed through the sea without constraint. Even though she could only steam to port in circles, the fact she could do so at eight knots made her a much more elusive target than if she was attached to other ships.[18]

Then rather than focusing on keeping as far away from the German guns as possible – and meekly accepting that none of her main armament could be fired because as a result of the torpedoing, her gunners had no access to the electronic devices that normally helped them to fire her guns accurately – Faulkner enterprisingly went onto the offensive.

This involved him leaning over the front of the bridge, and shouting out orders concerning which way to point the guns so that Robert Howe, the lieutenant who was looking out of the manhole at the top of B turret, could direct the gunfire by the turret's three 6-inch guns locally.[19]

The result was one of those remarkable acts which can change the course of an entire battle. Korvettenkapitän Heinrich Wittig, the 37-year-old commander of the German destroyer *Hermann Schoemann*, has recorded how the first salvo, which at around 6.40 a.m. was spat out of the guns operated from *Edinburgh*'s B gun turret, landed around 100 yards from the starboard side of his ship. However, he says shells from the second salvo smashed into his ship's two engine rooms: 'The engine on the port side stopped working,' he reported, adding: 'Shortly afterwards the starboard engine stopped. All engines needed to move . . . the ship had now failed.'[20]

There was no avoiding the conclusion that as far as the Germans were concerned, this was a disappointing disaster. Until that point, the Germans had held all the aces, even if they were reluctant to play them.

Provided there were no unexpected distractions or obstacles, the bigger German ships with more powerful guns were always likely to prevail over the less well-armed British destroyers. However, the transformation of *Hermann Schoemann* into a sitting duck changed all that. From that moment, the crews in the other German destroyers had a real excuse to go on the defensive so that they could rescue their comrades, including the Zerstörergruppe Nordmeer commander.

Before that could be achieved, they had to take the sting out of the British counter-attack. In the best traditions of the Royal Navy, *Forester*'s 33-year-old Lieutenant Commander George Huddart had positively galloped into battle. He courageously, or rashly depending on your point of view, had his destroyer dash towards the German ships in the north notwithstanding that her front 4.7-inch guns could not be used because they were iced up (see Map 11 for a visual record of *Forester*'s and *Foresight*'s movements). That meant he could only have *Forester*'s main armament fire at the Germans when the 'A' arcs of the after guns were opened (in other words when his ship was turned to one side or the other so that the rear guns could be deployed). However, just as he had the *Forester* turned to starboard at around 6.50 a.m. so that the destroyer's torpedoes could be unleashed from a distance of two and a half miles, which they were successfully, his ship was hit by the murderous fire of the German destroyers' 5.9-inch and 5-inch guns.

The damage was catastrophic. It was impossible for anyone in the ship to see whether the torpedoes they had fired had struck home because of the mass of steam that shot up into the air, the consequence of one of the German shells reaching *Forester*'s No. 1 boiler room. Even more problematic was that, deprived of steam, the ship's engines ground to a halt, and *Forester* ended up wheeling round clockwise and stopping facing towards the west, which meant that she was also a spitting, but nevertheless a sitting, duck.

Even her spitting was curtailed. X gun (in front of the back main armament gun in the ship) was also hit and put out of action, as was B gun (the gun behind *Forester*'s front main armament weapon). Moreover, metal from the same shell that had hit B gun killed Lieutenant Commander Huddart, who like *Edinburgh*'s Faulkner, had been leaning over the front of the bridge in an attempt to encourage his gunners. Next in line to take command was *Forester*'s 23-year-old First Lieutenant, Jack Bitmead. But his period in command might have ended within minutes when some of the torpedoes fired by all three German destroyers came racing towards his ship.

Bitmead's after the action report does not disclose the horror he surely must have felt when he observed two of these torpedoes approaching. He merely states they passed under *Forester*'s hull, and makes the point that one of them might have gone on to hit *Edinburgh* which was still steaming around in circles to the south.[21]

Whether or not this theory was correct, shortly before 7 a.m. Bonham Carter and Faulkner in *Edinburgh* saw no less than four German torpedoes about three miles away which were approaching the cruiser's starboard side. As *Edinburgh* at that moment was being turned to port, they hoped the ship's stern would be facing the oncoming missiles by the time what the Germans had fired came near to the ship. If the potential target was reduced in size in this way there was a good chance the torpedoes would miss. But the turn (shown in Map 11) became so rapid that although one ran ahead of the ship and two missed her stern, the remaining torpedo homed in on the very part of the ship which was most damaging for those on board: the port side, opposite the cracked bulkhead separating the marines' mess and the seamen's mess. This was one of the most vulnerable spots following the damage to the ship caused by the first torpedo hit two days earlier (see Chapter 10).[22]

As the torpedo struck, *Edinburgh*'s signalman Jack Thwaite, who was also watching, heard a 'vast explosion', and he would later recall in his memoir how he was drenched by the 'huge sheet of water [which] shot over those of us standing on the Flag deck'.[23] Commander Eric Hinton in the minesweeper *Harrier* referred to the torpedo that struck *Edinburgh* 'creating a mast-high column of water . . . causing her to list heavily to port'.[24]

On board *Edinburgh* the shock waves from the blast were so intense that they knocked out Jack Higgins, who was near the galley on the upper deck (one deck below the top open-air deck). He had rashly, given his previous near-death experience below decks in the aftermath of the first torpedo hit two days earlier (described in Chapter 10), gone down in the hope he might get something to eat.

When he came to, he saw he was at the foot of another of those ladders which constituted the nearest escape route for so many of *Edinburgh's* seamen following the torpedoings. Only this time, there was an armoured hatch at the top which was firmly shut. Because the way forward was also blocked, he decided he must move towards the stern. In a daze he staggered off in that direction through the gloom and dust, and would have stepped into the large hole that unbeknown to him had been blasted in the deck outside the galley, had not a cook, who stepped out of the galley just in front of him, beaten him to it. The cook was never seen again, but in falling to his death, he had saved Higgins' life, who had survived, almost literally, by the skin of his teeth for the second time in three days.

Or had he? For Higgins was still trapped, with seemingly no way out of the metal prison where he was encaged. Then, just as he was beginning to give up hope of ever escaping, the hatch at the top of the ladder was finally opened, and he heard an incredulous voice asking: 'What are *you* doing down there?' He didn't wait to think up a crushing response, but clambered up the ladder as quickly as he could in case another emergency would see it slammed shut again before he could climb out.[25]

This third torpedoing of *Edinburgh,* which eventually left her with a 17° list to port, meant that there were now two British sitting ducks.[26] *Forester* might well have been the first to sink had not Salter come to her aid. Within the space of 20 minutes, between around 7 and 7.20 a.m., he had *Foresight* streak across the battlefield, going from east to west and back again on two occasions so her gunners could fire at the German ships whose shells were getting close to striking *Forester,* notwithstanding *Forester's* crew's ongoing resistance. *Forester's* gunners were firing, whenever a German ship appeared, using Y gun (the rear gun), her one working main armament weapon.[27]

On each occasion *Foresight's* guns were fired at them, the German ships in question retired, only to appear again shortly afterwards. On the way back to the east on the second occasion, Salter took *Foresight* almost as close to the two British destroyer crews' German tormentors as *Forester* had ventured at 6.50 a.m., with similar results. Like *Forester's* torpedo section, *Foresight's* torpedomen fired torpedoes at the German targets as Salter's ship closed in on them, and as with *Forester,* a German shell landed in one of *Foresight's* boiler rooms, severing two main steam pipes. This hit at around 7.24 a.m. brought her to a halt shortly afterwards, and left her listing to starboard, with two large holes in her starboard side, around a mile and a half to the south-west of where *Forester* lay.[28]

The moment when *Foresight* was hit, and the aftermath, was later described by Joseph Fowells, at the time the destroyer's 26-year-old torpedo officer: '*Foresight* shuddered and stopped . . . We knew what had happened. We had been hit in the boiler room and lost steam . . . A leaden feeling of dread replaced the exhilaration of the fight . . . I think everyone except the Captain and the Engineer . . . was certain we were finished. [In the short term at least] there was nothing we could do.'[29]

For eleven long minutes the three British warships languished in the sea at the mercy of *Z 24* and *Z 25*, the two German ships that had not been immobilized.[30] 'It is little short of a miracle that both ships (*Foresight* and *Forester*) survived,' Salter wrote afterwards in his after the action report. 'There is no shadow of a doubt they ought to have finished us off. Providence was undoubtedly on our side.'

It was not just that *Foresight* could not be moved. As was the case with *Forester*, three-quarters of her main armament was not working properly. Her only main armament weapon that could be relied upon was X gun (the gun forrard of the aft Y gun), evidently not enough on its own to silence the German destroyers' guns. *Foresight*'s other guns kept icing up, and could only be fired from time to time during the battle. 'We were repeatedly straddled, and much shrapnel was bursting almost overhead,' Salter wrote afterwards, adding: 'I personally saw one shell passing close over my head, and several other officers and men in other parts of the ship had a similar experience.'[31]

Curiously the ship's plight appeared to galvanize Salter. As some people do when facing up to a disaster that cannot be averted, he smiled at his fellow officers and looked positively happy. Joseph Fowells afterwards recalled how by way of contrast, he himself was inconsolable. 'As I went down to the chart room to collect the secret books which were to be thrown over the side on doomed ships, I thought to myself that . . . unless some miracle happened, I was dead . . . [But] as I came on deck there was a shout from the port lookout: "*Forester*!" *Forester* was moving.'[32]

Sure enough the 'miracle' that Salter – and Fowells – had referred to had come to pass. At 7.35 a.m. *Forester*'s engines had been started up, and even as Fowells watched, she was steaming in front of his stricken ship concealing her from the Germans with her smoke. Fowells' account goes on to describe the dramatic change that *Forester*'s resurrection had brought about: 'Blanketed by the smoke, a great calm descended as though the battle had moved to a great distance. We could no longer see the flashes of the enemy's guns, or the splashes of their shells. For some minutes *Forester* steamed madly between us and the [German] destroyers blazing away at the enemy with her one gun.'

Then at 8.15 a.m. Fowells witnessed another historic moment. 'The engineer arrived on the bridge. "Ready to go sir", he announced, saluting in the less than military style that engineers affect. "Thank you Chief," said the captain . . . And we were off.'[33]

It is impossible to know who to praise most for saving the two British destroyers. The contribution of Lieutenant Robert Howe, the *Edinburgh* officer who stood with his head sticking out of the top of the cruiser's B turret so that he could tell the gun team how to aim their guns, has already been mentioned. But *Foresight*'s survival owes much to the action of Stoker Petty Officer John Bain, who insisted on remaining in the ship's No. 3 boiler room when she was hit so he could shut off critical valves. He collapsed afterwards, and was so badly burned that he later passed away. He was one of the nine men in *Foresight* who lost their lives during the 2 May action but the only one who was awarded the Albert Medal.[34]

It is also worth highlighting the remarkable symmetry in the minds of the commanders of some of the two sides' ships. While *Forester*'s Lieutenant Bitmead was being forced to come to terms with the unpleasant thought that his ship would be boarded and captured by the Germans, and *Foresight*'s Commander Salter was wondering how it was possible the German destroyers had not sunk all the British ships, similar thoughts were running through the minds of the German destroyer commanders. *Hermann Schoemann*'s Korvettenkapitän Heinrich Wittig later wrote he just could not understand why one of the British ships, which had come so close to the German vessels, had not managed to administer the coup de grâce by shooting a torpedo into his ship.

Wittig's pessimistic outlook was doubtless influenced by his misreading of the balance of power remaining on the battlefield. In his after the action report, Wittig proudly refers to the perspicacious way he was able to name the different kinds of British destroyers that Zerstörergruppe

Nordmeer was facing, little realizing that of the five ships he identified as destroyers, three were mere minesweepers with relatively small-calibre 4-inch guns. These minesweepers could have been swept away by the 5.9-inch guns on *Z 24*'s and *Z 25*'s decks.[35]

So keen were the German destroyer commanders to cut their losses and run, that during the crucial period when the three largest British warships in the vicinity were immobilized, the German group did next to nothing to exploit their success. Instead they spent the hour and a half after *Hermann Schoemann* had been hit striving to engineer a situation which would permit *Z 25* to pin back the British warships and to cover the area with smoke so that *Z 24* could rescue the German destroyer's crew. So out of touch were they with what had happened on the other side of the battlefield, they did not even realize that *Edinburgh* had been torpedoed a third time.

Of course that suited Rear Admiral Bonham Carter, who on realizing that *Edinburgh* might break into two halves at any moment, gave the order to abandon ship.[36] The evacuation began at 7.20 a.m., around five minutes before *Foresight* was hit. The minesweeper *Gossamer* which came alongside the British cruiser's starboard side ended up with around 440 of the rescued men. The minesweeper *Harrier* which closed *Edinburgh*'s port side took the remainder (around 350 men).[37]

There were some difficult moments. Morris Mills found himself being tempted by a sailor to board the minesweeper *Harrier* via a metal object that was jutting out from *Edinburgh*'s side. 'The surface was rough and jagged,' Mills wrote afterwards, 'and several times I struck my raw stump causing it to haemorrhage a fine spray of blood.' But he made it across, and was swiftly seen to by *Harrier*'s surgeon, who applied a tourniquet, and gave him a shot of morphine to deaden the pain.'[38]

The last man off was Captain Faulkner, who boarded *Harrier* at around 7.45 a.m., after being assured that all survivors had left before him. Notwithstanding the valuable treasure still aboard *Edinburgh*, he was instructed by Bonham Carter that the cruiser must be sunk. A message was sent to *Foresight* instructing Salter to sink *Edinburgh* with the destroyer's last torpedo.

Joseph Fowells has recorded the 'no pressure' comment tacked onto the instruction to fire the torpedo at the cruiser that was handed down to him by Salter: ' "If you miss, I'll never speak to you again," said the captain, and I think for the moment he meant it. He took out his watch to time the run of the torpedo, and after the allotted time [following the firing of the torpedo], put it away with as grim an expression on his face as I have seen. Then there was the noise of an explosion and a great cascade of water. "I think your watch needs adjusting Sir," I said. "It must be all these explosions!" '[39]

The deed was done at 8.52 a.m., over an hour after *Harrier* had completed the ship's evacuation. 'The ship then sank in about two minutes,' Bonham Carter reported. 'She rolled over to port, her back broke . . . and the fore part broke off where the first and third torpedoes had hit . . . The last seen of her was her bows rising vertically in the air and then disappearing' (see 3B in Map 1, 4 in Map 8 and Note 40 for approximate location).[40]

If anyone had any regrets about the gold ingots still sitting untouched since they were placed in the cruiser's bomb room, no-one gave voice to them in the ship's official reports. Like some latter day sacrifice to appease the gods, the Russian gold had been consigned to nature and left to sink with all that baser ship metal to the bottom of the Barents Sea. That task completed, the remaining British ships hotfooted it to Murmansk.[41]

Before *Edinburgh* sank, the Germans in *Z 24* and *Z 25* also made good their escape after sinking their own sitting duck. They asked *U-88*'s commander to rescue the survivors they could not quickly pick up before their departure. Out of *Hermann Schoemann*'s crew of around 375 men, only eight had been killed, a remarkable result in the circumstances that compared favourably to the 57 killed in *Edinburgh,* even if one adds onto the German total the five men killed in *Z 25* when in the course of the battle, her radio room was hit by a shell.[42] The death tolls in the British destroyers – *Forester* 11 killed; *Foresight* 9 killed – were likewise on the low side relative to what might have been expected in ships fought to a standstill while still being targeted by enemy guns.[43]

After their arrival in the Kola Inlet, the British destroyers had to be patched up before they could be taken back to Iceland and the UK. They also had to be cleaned. As Salter recalled in an interview he gave many years later: 'I always remember after we got back to Murmansk, I was walking on the upper deck, and there were bits of my poor old chief stoker all over the after superstructure. He'd been just blown to smithereens poor chap. It was all rather frightful.'[44]

As for the convoy QP11, over which they had all been fighting, it had a relatively peaceful passage after the action on 1 May, and reached Reykjavik on 7 May.[45]

After returning to Kirkenes, Kapitän zur See Schulze-Hinrichs wrote a stinging rebuke aimed at the commanders who had been naive enough to send just three destroyers against such a strongly protected convoy. They had behaved like 'enthusiastic amateurs', he said.[46]

Didn't they know that the destroyer is a ship made for reconnaissance and for escorting heavy ships such as battleships? Unlike battleships, destroyers could not absorb being hit by the enemy's shells, something that was bound to happen when taking on well-protected convoys. And it was all the more unwise to send them on operations where the enemy had superiority since it would be difficult to recover them if they were damaged.

He might have been even more indignant had he read Admiral Schmundt's own complaint about the urgent message Schulze-Hinrichs had sent after departing from the battlefield, calling on all U-boats in the area to rescue the men he had left behind from the sea. Schmundt, impractical as ever, would have preferred it if he had been asked to organize an orderly rescue which did not disrupt other operations. Schmundt only did not countermand the cry for help because, he said, 'it would have diminished our sailors' trust in their leaders'.[47]

Notwithstanding Schulze-Hinrichs' denigration of the tactics employed, Captain Wagner, the Seekriegsleitung's head of operations, after reading the British admission that *Edinburgh* had been sunk, came up with a more nuanced way of analysing what had been achieved and learned. He mistakenly believed that as well as sinking *Edinburgh* and damaging two destroyers, four merchant ships had been sunk, which he said was an 'excellent' result. However, he as good as admitted that the operation represented a strategic defeat because it had proved that there was virtually no point attacking the convoys with destroyers. Such attacks he said would rarely be successful if the enemy could always stack up superior forces against them.[48]

12

Friendly Fire

Main Action: 3 May 1942
Attack by the Luftwaffe, PQ15

(See Map 8)

While the commanders of the surface fleets of both sides were still digest-
ing the lessons learned from the fighting during the passage of QP11, the
seamen in the Allies' vessels that were participating in PQ15 were having
to prepare to ward off Germany's other forces.

PQ15's 23 merchant ships (fifteen American, seven British and one
Panamanian-flagged merchant vessels), plus two icebreakers, one from
Russia and the other from Canada, had departed from Hvalfjord, Iceland
on 26 April 1942.[1] At the time it was hard to know whether or not most of
its freighters would get through to Russia, and the same applied in respect
of any future convoys. That explains why news of PQ15's progress was
awaited with such interest in both Britain and America. As mentioned in
Chapter 10, PQ15 had effectively been designated by Churchill as a 'guinea
pig' convoy, whose outcome would have a bearing on how many merchant ships could in future 'safely' be protected by the British and
American warships available for that purpose.

Two of the PQ15 American vessels were so-called Liberty ships, their
presence in the PQ15 line up being the start of what was to become a
growing trend to ferry cargo to Russia in such ships. There were good

reasons for this. Liberty ships were merchant vessels built to a standard design using what were then regarded as revolutionary building techniques (for example, their constructors used assembled prefabricated sections, and time-consuming riveting was replaced by labour-saving welding) so that they could be rolled off the production lines in America much more quickly than would have been the case had they been constructed using conventional methods. Another advantage, particularly at a time when there was a limit on the number of merchant vessels that could be placed in a convoy, was their size. They were around 147 yards long by 19 yards wide at their broadest point. Their gross tonnage (a measure of their internal volume rather than of their weight) was around 7,000 tons, giving them a larger capacity than the majority of merchant vessels used in the early Arctic convoys (the range of gross tonnages in PQ15 ran from around 3,000 to around 7,500 tons, with the majority falling into the 4,500 to 6,000 gross tonnage category).[2]

The surviving merchant ship manifests specifying their cargo suggest that many of the PQ15 merchant ships were carrying around 5,000 tons of aid, with the largest loads being in excess of 7,500 tons. A comparison of the consultable manifests discloses what was probably typical. The manifest for one American ship in the convoy, in addition to a long list of items that covered a sheet-and-a-half of paper, included 15 medium tanks (together weighing 390 tons), 80 one-and-a-half to two-and-a-half ton Studebaker, Ford and Chevrolet trucks (weighing 425 tons in total), and 13,000 aluminium 'pieces' (weighing 286 tons).[3] The aluminium was particularly significant because although not something that could be used against German forces immediately on delivery, it was what was needed if Soviet factories were to be able to manufacture their own aircraft, and tank engines (it was used in the construction of the engine of the T-34 tank, which was arguably the most effective Russian 'armour'). That explains why it was one of the main items Stalin had requested when ten months previously Harry Hopkins had made that game-changing flight to Moscow in order to find out among other things what would keep the Soviet Union in the war (see Chapter 2).

Such items were to be expected. Perhaps more surprisingly the same ship was carrying what can best be described collectively as a large amount of food. Her manifest reveals that the flour, eggs, canned meat and pork 'fat backs' carried weighed in at going on 1,000 tons, making food account for more cargo weight than the tanks and trucks, a trend that is repeated in the other available manifests.

The tonnage carried on each ship was also relevant because of the way it affected the discussions between Churchill and Roosevelt over how many ships should be included in each Arctic convoy (see Chapter 10). Churchill's 28 April 1942 telegram to Roosevelt had pointed out that while it might be ideal to send 'Uncle Joe' as much aid as the Americans had already either sent across the Atlantic, or had stockpiled for the benefit of the Soviet Union, it was the arms and other goods America was obliged to supply by the end of June 1942 under the First Protocol (last mentioned in Chapter 2) which was most critical.

As Churchill informed Roosevelt, Britain's war transport minister estimated that the remaining American pre-July 1942 commitment under the First Protocol, excluding the relatively small amount of cargo that could be sent to the Soviet Union via the Persian route, amounted to 290,000 tons. Given that well-packed merchant ships could on average carry 6,000 tons each, that meant the outstanding goods which America had undertaken to supply could be placed into 290,000 tons/6,000 tons = approximately 48 ships.[4] That fitted in nicely with the three convoys of 25 ships 'every two months' (i.e. 75 ships over the two-month period) that Churchill said Britain could live with whatever happened to PQ15. He had been told Britain would need 24 of the 75 ships for the First Protocol supplies that the country had undertaken to supply by 30 June 1942, leaving more than the 48 ships required for American aid.[5]

Churchill's promises linked to these figures notwithstanding, there was always the chance that the commitment to Russia would become unachievable if the rate of sinkings during Arctic convoys all of a sudden shot up. Maximizing the number of escorts was crucial. By the time PQ15 encountered its first serious opposition, during the early hours of 3 May, its merchant ships were guarded by a close escort that included an auxiliary anti-aircraft cruiser (*Ulster Queen,* the first time such a ship, with high-angle 4-inch anti-aircraft guns, had accompanied an Arctic convoy), six destroyers, three minesweepers and three armed trawlers.[6]

The crews in the two cruisers that had sailed with it for a few days under the command of the 10th Cruiser Squadron's Rear Admiral Harold

Burrough were by that stage watching over both PQ15 and QP11 from afar so that they could protect them in the case of attack by large surface forces, while at the same time they themselves stayed out of reach of any U-boats that might be circling the convoy.[7] Admiral Burrough's report does not expressly record his and his crew's feelings when during the night of 1–2 May they were ordered by the Admiralty to remove themselves from the U-boats' likely orbit. But Burrough did refer to there being 'some excitement' on 1 May when what a jumpy lookout mistook for a group of U-boats, or a flotilla of German surface ships, in the distance, turned out on closer inspection to be icebergs.[8]

By then the submarine *Sturgeon,* which had also accompanied the convoy for more than two days, had also departed, but not before on the way to the position east of Iceland where she, an oiler and another destroyer were to meet up with the convoy, she had been machine-gunned by a 'friendly' aircraft, that had evidently mistaken her for a U-boat.[9] Such friendly fire was to become a recurring theme during the passage of PQ15.

For what it was worth, extra protection for the convoy could also be provided by the specially adapted Hurricane aircraft which could be launched off PQ15's catapult aircraft merchant ship (CAM ship), the first time such a vessel had sailed in an Arctic convoy. This ensemble was a poor substitute for the aircraft carrier whose presence was known to be required, not only because there was only one aircraft, but also because after its mission, the aircraft could not land on the CAM ship's deck but had to be crash-landed in the sea.

However, before any of the close protection forces could be tested against the Germans, a tragic accident took place within the Home Fleet while carrying out its distant covering duties in relation to PQ15 and QP11.

The accident occurred in thick fog north-east of Seidisfjord (Seyðisfjörður), the Arctic convoy escorts' assembly base on Iceland's east coast, at around 3.45 p.m. on 1 May when a botched attempt was being made by an officer in the destroyer *Punjabi* to move the vessel closer to where the Fleet's capital ships were advancing in single file.[10] Rather than ending up parallel to the capital ships, which would have been desirable, he mistakenly had the destroyer steered directly into the path of the battleship *King George V,* which was haring along at 18 knots, with catastrophic consequences. *King George V*'s bows cut through the port side of *Punjabi*'s hull abreast the destroyer's X gun (the gun forrard of the back Y gun), and came out the other side, cutting the destroyer in two.

Some of the men in *Punjabi*'s aft section jumped into the sea before she sank. But their lives were then in jeopardy because of two violent explosions, apparently caused by the destroyer's depth charges blowing up. *Punjabi*'s Stoker Petty Officer Robert Ellis, who had rushed up on deck on the front section to see what he termed 'the gigantic side of the battleship passing right through us', also saw how one officer 'was blown . . . up in the air for at least 50 feet'. According to Ellis, he was 'a fine figure of a man, about 6 feet 4 inches [tall], and his long body . . . with his arms thrown out hurtling into the air . . . made quite an impression'.[11]

Those in the water who escaped being blown up by depth charges also risked being mown down by the capital ships behind *King George V*, as was explained by the destroyer's Sub-Lieutenant Synnot: 'Looking up, I saw (the cruiser) USS *Wichita* bearing down on me from about 70 feet away. I struck out to get clear, but was only about six feet off when she came up to me. I remained at about this distance on my back all the way along the starboard side experiencing very little wash.'[12]

But it is likely that at least some of the men who made it into the water were harmed by the effects of the fuel oil released from *Punjabi*'s tanks. Robert Ellis stated: 'It was an awful sight to see them trying to jerk themselves up [from the oil] into the [clear] water as they slowly suffocated.'[13]

The death toll from the oil, the depth charges and the 'friendly' ramming by *King George V* eventually reached 50 men which was around 20 per cent of *Punjabi*'s crew.[14] The majority of the crew were picked up by other nearby destroyers. As for *King George V*, although her hull was damaged, she was able to carry on with the Fleet until replaced by the battleship *Duke of York* the next day.[15] Nevertheless, the loss of the destroyer and so many of her crew in such circumstances was a bitter blow, made even more unpalatable because it could have been avoided. The subsequent court martial ruled that *Punjabi*'s Commander John Waldegrave was at fault for not supervising the manoeuvre, and his Lieutenant Leonard Hollis, who had been the officer of the watch, had been negligent.[16]

The extent of the losses following this accident became even harder to bear when another of the Allies' vessels sustained losses due to friendly fire in different circumstances a day later. The root cause this time was a series of technical problems in the Polish submarine *Jastrząb*, one of the Allies' four submarines whose crews were supposed to be keeping watch south of the convoy's route. Because of this, Lieutenant Commander Bolesław Romanowski, her 32-year-old captain, did not realize his vessel was straying to the north of where he had been ordered to patrol.[17] It would not have mattered had the convoy, which had been heading north-eastward with the aim of passing to the south of Bear Island, not changed its course unexpectedly to the south.[18] PQ15's course alteration enabled it to steer clear of a couple of U-boats whose location had been betrayed by the decryption of an Enigma message at Bletchley Park.[19] However, the resulting converging of the two Allied forces led to the following tragic consequences.

At around 8 p.m. on 2 May, when the submarine was south-south-west of Bear Island, Romanowski saw two ships through his periscope which he took to be British (only later did he discover the ships' true identities and their location relative to PQ15: they were the Norwegian destroyer HNorMS *St Albans,* another of the four-stackers which Britain purchased from America at the beginning of the war before transferring her on to the Norwegian Navy, and the British minesweeper *Seagull,* on the convoy's port bow (see Note 20, and 5 in Map 8 for approximate location).[20] His first reaction after seeing the destroyer steam past in the falling snow was to tell his crew their submarine must submerge.[21] But when he was informed that one of the 'British' ships appeared to have locked her asdic onto *Jastrząb*'s hull, he ordered his crew to take the submarine up to periscope depth so a flare could be fired. This was duly done, but as he would relate many years later, it did not have the desired effect:

'I saw [through the periscope] something which is every submarine commander's nightmare: A ship with its bow jutting straight up, and its pronounced bow wave, was charging towards us.

'I knew what that meant. It would not be long before the very effective British depth charges would be exploding around us.

'Making an effort to keep my voice as calm as possible, I gave the orders: "Full steam ahead. Dive to 300 feet!"

'[Even as we dived] we could hear the ship approaching. At first there was a rapidly growing rumble. Then it became like roaring thunder and finally like a fast train going through a tunnel.

'All of a sudden *Jastrząb* was shaken. We heard the sound of breaking glass and hissing, followed by the short and sharp bangs made by the exploding depth charges which were like a gun being fired. Water came down through the seals round the submarine's hatches.'

Romanowski's account describes how, after firing a second flare, he told his men they must change course to avoid the next group of depth charges about to be dropped. Afterwards he and his crew brought the submarine to the surface again. The hatches giving access to the bridge were opened quickly, and Romanowski without a second thought followed the British signaller who was part of *Jastrząb*'s crew up the ladder although he could hear the sound of the bullets fired by the British guns splashing in the water around them.

'I reached the bridge,' he reported, 'but tripped over the body of the British signaller. I quickly got up, only to feel a sharp pain in my legs. I collapsed onto the bridge seat.'

For the moment at least there was no escape. Gunfire emanating from the minesweeper *Seagull*, on the port side of the submarine, was raking the water and hitting *Jastrząb*'s hull, while the destroyer *St Albans* on her starboard side, whose gunners were also firing, was steaming towards the helpless submarine as if intent on ramming her. On seeing this, Romanowski shouted down to the control room: 'All crew on deck!'

As the other members of the crew in their turn rushed up the ladder leading to the bridge, another British signaller on *Jastrząb*'s bridge flashed a recognition signal with an Aldis lamp. Although this silenced the guns in the minesweeper, Romanowki's account, an extract from which is laid out below, makes it clear that he believed his men were still being targeted by a gunner in the destroyer, although she had in the meantime pulled up.

'Men were being bowled over on the bridge, their white sweaters stained with blood. Some lay still, while others were trembling, so shocked were they by what they were witnessing.'[22]

Romanowski's recollections have been corroborated by Stanisław Olszowski, who at the time was a 22-year-old sub-lieutenant. This is what he witnessed after he finally made it out through *Jastrząb*'s hatches:

'When I reached the right side of the bridge, I was amazed to see what looked like an American destroyer rocking in the waves so close to *Jastrząb* that she blotted out a third of the horizon . . . Something was flashing from the destroyer's bridge wing. Oh God! It was a machine gun. I suddenly felt a sharp pain in the upper part of my chest. Grunting, I fell to my knees . . . I saw there were also two bullet wounds on my left arm, although I had not felt myself being hit.

'I could hear the machine gun chattering, and at the same time the groans and curses of the wounded. Then the gunfire stopped, and we heard a voice amplified by a megaphone asking: "Are you Germans?" Those who could shouted back in unison: "We are Polish!"'

But for some, the ceasefire had come too late. According to Olszowski: 'Chief Petty Officer Czub was lying face down; he had a large hole in his back. He appeared to be dead. Able Seaman Czerwiński's face was covered with blood and he was examining his hanging arm. When Leading Seaman Kędziora staggered towards me . . . I saw there were three or four holes in his abdomen, and one in his belt. I tried to smile at him, but I realized he was a gonner.

'Then I saw Niedzielski, the Able Seaman who (before the action) had told me his (worrying) dream about wild swans, lying on the bridge (superstitious Polish people used to believe that dreams about white swans meant that there would be a disaster), and I also saw Martin Dowd, the Royal Navy signalman, whose body was draped over the side of the bridge with an Aldis lamp beside it. Lieutenant Anczykowski was trying to get up, although one of his legs was bent forwards at an abnormal angle. He was sitting on a bench and was attempting to bring his leg back into line with both hands.

'The commanding officer, also wounded, was sitting on the upper part of the bridge. Next to him was the ship's flag under which several men were lying . . . There was . . . blood everywhere.'[23]

Eventually a dialogue was started up between the crews in the three ships. Arrangements were made to evacuate the submarine. Then she was sunk by the minesweeper *Seagull*'s gunfire, and heartfelt apologies were proffered by Lieutenant Commander Charles Pollock, *Seagull*'s captain, to Sub-Lieutenant Andrzej Guzowski, the only *Jastrząb* officer who was not wounded, after he was taken aboard the minesweeper.[24] The wounded were taken on board *St Albans*.

After *St Albans* caught up with the convoy, an attempt was made to close in on *Ulster Queen* in the hope that the severely wounded could be placed in the anti-aircraft ship's more voluminous sickbay. Unfortunately, at the moment of the approach, *Ulster Queen*'s crew were busy in view of an air raid alert, and the transfer did not happen either then or later. It is not known whether this had a negative effect on the men's care. Two of the severely wounded from *Jastrząb* died that night.[25]

Seagull's captain, who had given the order to cease fire as soon as he saw the letters (P551) emblazoned on the submarine's conning tower, was later exonerated from all blame. As PQ15's senior officer, escort stated, the two British escorts were on the port side of the convoy 'in waters in which it was a certainty that many enemy submarines were operating, and they could afford no hesitation in their attack.'[26] Romanowski was also found to be not culpable.[27]

However, Commander Skule Storheill, the 34-year-old Norwegian commander of *St Albans,* was blamed for not knowing about and recognizing the smoke flares that were to be used by nearby submarines.[28] After the action, it had come to light that before any of the Polish seamen had been shot, Storheill had seen the yellow smoke produced by *Jastrząb*'s flares but had mistaken it for the smoke made by the calcium flares he used to mark the position of a depth charge attack. Storheill only gave the order to cease fire after his liaison officer pointed out that the submarine was not a U-boat. 'I ceased fire at once,' he reported, 'and then made the terrible discovery that I had been firing at an Allied submarine.'[29]

* * *

Meanwhile, insulated from these events, which for all their tragic repercussions were essentially sideshows, the crews in the merchant ships and in the other escorts constituting PQ15 remained on the alert ready to ward off the attacks which they suspected might be made at any minute by the Germans. The convoy had been sighted by the crew of a German aircraft for the first time shortly before midnight during the night of 30 April–1 May.[30] During the evening of 1 May, the escorts and merchant ships had repulsed a half-hearted attack made by six Junkers Ju 88 bombers. One aircraft was shot down.[31]

But for all the Allied gunners' success in the face of this first attempt to disrupt the convoy, those in PQ15's escorts had reason to fear that the Germans would not just leave it at that. What really frightened R. Struben, second-in-command in the anti-aircraft cruiser *Ulster Queen,* was the news gleaned from the crew in QP11's escort *Bulldog* as the two convoys passed each other during the morning of 2 May that the Germans had used aircraft carrying torpedoes to attack them, a significant development since it was believed to be the first time such tactics had been used in the Arctic.[32] 'Whenever *Ulster Queen* was at sea, I used to include in my nightly prayers a special one for the safety of our ship's company, and during [PQ15] . . . that particular prayer became very earnest indeed,' Struben admitted later.[33]

However, even Struben could not have envisaged the way his worst fears would be realized. One of *Ulster Queen*'s most valued assets, in addition to her high-angle guns, was her radar. There was an expectation that with it switched on, her crew would be able to warn the other escorts before any German aircraft approached the convoy. So it was disappointing when at around 1.30 a.m. on 3 May, as the convoy, by this time located south of Bear Island, steamed eastward, six more aircraft materialized in front of the convoy without any warning (see Note 34, and 6 in Map 8 for location).[34]

As far as at least some of the escort commanders were concerned, one moment there was nothing to be seen ahead of the convoy, and there was not a blip to disturb the stillness on the radar screen in *Ulster Queen.* The next moment there was what Captain Jack Eaton, the 39-year-old commanding officer of the destroyer *Somali,* described as 'six aircraft resembling Heinkel 111s . . . at a range of about 6,000 yards flying across the front of the convoy in single line ahead'.

According to Eaton, in contrast to the previous attack from the air, this time the German aircraft crews barely gave the gunners in British escorts the chance to catch their breath: 'Within a few seconds of being sighted, they turned 90° together into line abreast and came straight for the convoy, the centre of the formation being slightly on its starboard bow.'[35]

The gunners in *Somali* and the other escorts in the screen on the southern side of the convoy quickly opened fire, as did every merchant ship who could safely get a shot in while the aircraft were close enough, and some who could not.[36] The Soviet Union's icebreaker *Krassin* was picked out as being one of the worst culprits in this regard by Captain J. Smith, master of the convoy's commodore ship, the British SS *Botavon*, whose position at the front of the middle column made it one of the most dangerous spots in the five-column formation: '*Krassin* which was stationed close to us (it was the second ship in the column to the right of the column led by *Botavon*) was so anxious to engage the enemy that he was firing across our bridge in his eagerness,' Smith complained afterwards.[37]

According to W. L. Cruickshank, master of the CAM ship *Empire Morn*, which was at the front of the convoy's right-hand column, friendly fire across his bow was one of the reasons why he vetoed the suggestion that his Hurricane should be flown off. 'It would have been suicide to have done so,' he stated afterwards.[38]

It was the sound of all this shooting, added to the noise of the ringing alarm bell, which had Struben jumping down from the top bunk in his cabin, and scurrying up to his action station by the pom-poms (40 mm – 1.6 inch – anti-aircraft guns on 4-gun mounts), aft in *Ulster Queen*, like a scalded cat. 'The midnight twilight was turning to gloomy Arctic day,' he recalled afterwards, highlighting that there was constant daylight in the Arctic at this time of year, 'and I could make out aircraft flying low over the sea. I knew they must be torpedo bombers. The starboard pom-poms which had been at action stations let fly as the enemy were crossing our bows, while the crew of the port mounting clattered up from below, and trained on the foremost bearing to lie in wait.

'Within seconds a target appeared, and the four barrels played their deliberate staccato tune, pumping out a stream of tracered shells,' justifying their nickname 'the Chicago Piano'.[39]

They were far from being the only guns firing at one of the German aircraft, whose pilot had the temerity to streak across in front of the leaders of the merchant ship columns, as if positively inviting their gunners to hose their bullets into his Heinkel 111's fuselage.

According to the master of SS *Cape Race* (the front ship in the second column): 'The plane offered a target so large that it filled our gun sights, and it banked on its side in an endeavour to edge away, but the range was so short that our tracers could plainly be seen entering the fuselage of the machine. Immediately afterwards it crashed into the sea on my port bow.'[40]

'We opened fire at it, shooting off its port wing. It then burst into flames and crashed into the sea,' wrote the master of SS *Southgate* (the leading ship in the port column).[41]

But as the following extract from Struben's account demonstrates, his gunners celebrated as if they alone deserved the credit for downing this plane: 'As the Heinkel crashed into the sea, the young sailors at the gun cheered and danced on the little platform of the mounting . . . My megaphone failing to penetrate their excitement, I clambered down from my perch and reached across the pom-pom platform, grabbing their ankles to attract their attention, and the gun was soon firing again.'[42]

However, all the defensive gunfire in the world was not going to deter some of these courageous German airmen from launching their torpedoes, and it was the ships in the front row of the convoy which were, as was so often to be the case during the months ahead, the victims. Before Captain Smith's 'Hard to starboard' order could take *Botavon* (front of the third column) out of the line of fire, he saw a torpedo which had narrowly missed *Empire Morn*'s bow (front of starboard column) approaching the starboard side of his ship.[43] It 'appeared to circle in towards us', he reported, adding that 'it struck my ship amidships in the after end of No. 2 hold'.

The result according to Captain Smith was: 'a very loud explosion, and a large column of water was thrown into the air', leaving the ship listing to starboard, and settling by the head.

Seconds later, if that, Captain John Henderson, Master of the British SS *Jutland*, at the front of the column on *Botavon*'s right, found himself watching the progress of the torpedo, which after it narrowly missed *Empire Morn*'s stern, turned out to have his ship's name written on it.[44] He later described how: 'I watched as it struck the water about 100 yards off our starboard bow and 100 yards ahead. I could see the bubbles of the wake quite clearly as it crossed our bows. Then it turned to port in a semi-circle, with a radius of about 150 yards, finally striking . . . [my] ship on the port quarter, the opposite side from which it had been released . . . The poop was completely wrecked [and] . . . a great deal of debris . . . was thrown up . . . An American [passenger] named Mr Weinstein was asleep in his cabin, which was at the after end of the poop, and he was no doubt killed by the explosion.'[45]

But it was to be the devastating consequences of a torpedo hitting the British SS *Cape Corso*, the second ship in the convoy's port column, seconds after the other two ships were torpedoed, which has come to define the horror felt by all from the convoy who witnessed the events of 3 May. No account in the public domain has ever been identified which precisely pinpoints how the *Cape Corso* torpedo came to be fired. All that is known is that it went underneath the stern of *Cape Race*, the leading ship in the second column, and then struck *Cape Corso* just aft of amidships on her starboard side, between the engine room and No. 3 hold.[46]

The result could not have been more traumatic. Struben, whose ship was some distance to starboard, marooned as *Ulster Queen* was between the convoy's central column and the column to its right, later recalled: 'Suddenly there was a thunderous explosion, overwhelming the racket of gunfire, and an inferno of flaming smoke burst out of that ship, followed by an irregular succession of less terrible detonations.' He watched transfixed as within minutes, as he later related: 'her stern went under, while her bows reared up briefly as she sank. Three or four men were visible on her foc'sle, but of the rest of the crew [there was] not a sign, as she disappeared beneath the icy waters in the eerie northern light.'[47]

Jack Whyte, who was watching from his vantage point on the icebreaker *Montcalm* (the second ship in the convoy's second from left column, making her one of the closest vessels to *Cape Corso*), described afterwards what he saw of the catastrophe: 'There was a . . . flash . . . We all dropped to the deck, and . . . a terrible explosion followed. Debris started falling, and then the wave of heat hit us. It was all over in a minute. One ship and crew. The next minute, nothing! All gone. It was a shattering experience.'[48]

Incredibly there were six survivors. Kenneth Allen, who was one of them, would have been burned alive if the attack had taken place an hour earlier. He had just come off watch, and was probably one of the men whom Struben saw standing on the forecastle after the torpedo struck the ship. Allen later recalled: 'When I heard the explosion . . . I looked up at the bridge and it was a mass of flames. I saw two of the officers try to jump, but they were on fire and didn't make it . . . The ship was loaded with tanks and planes, but also a great deal of aviation spirit . . . and ammunition. It sank in two minutes. There was no hope of getting lifeboats or rafts away, and those of us that were saved [survived] by jumping into the water.'[49]

The second engineer George Waddingham was another of the lucky six. If he had not stepped up from his cabin for a last breath of fresh air before going to sleep, he would also surely have perished. Instead he was on deck, and may have been the only survivor who saw the torpedo approaching. He estimated that it would hit amidships, and was surprised when it hit between the engine room and No. 3 hold, that is aft of the engine room. That led him to question afterwards whether the ship's master, in a last desperate move to save the crew, had ordered the ship to be turned to port, and it was that which led to the torpedo hitting *Cape Corso* further aft than Waddingham had been expecting.

Waddingham's official report of the incident laid out below, delivered in short staccato sentences, is disturbingly stripped of any emotion, but it reveals he did his best to get out of harm's way, and gives a sense of what he witnessed afterwards: 'I made a dash for the port side, and a second later was thrown off my feet as the torpedo struck . . . In a very few seconds the whole of the after part of the ship was a blazing inferno . . .

'I saw one of the sailors rushing from the after part of the ship, his duffel coat pulled well over his head . . . He dived overboard. A fireman came from aft, his clothes ablaze like a human torch. I tore his clothes off him, then decided it was time I dived overboard too. I did not see this fireman again. I dived overboard . . . When I came up, I saw the deck was under water, and the poop just an island. I saw the 3rd Mate trying to lower the port jolly boat . . . A second later I saw the ship sink . . . just two minutes after the explosion.

'There was one sailor in the port jolly boat [when it went down with the ship]. He had his leg caught in the wreckage strewn all over the boat, and as the wreckage came to the surface, the sailor came up too. He managed to get clear of the wreckage and swam away.'

As for Waddingham, he was rescued by one of the convoy's armed trawlers, as was Kenneth Allen and another member of the crew who may have been one of the men Waddingham saw escape from the ship. The other three survivors were picked up by a destroyer. The remaining 50 crew and gunners must have been killed.[50]

The one consolation, apart from the survival of the six *Cape Corso* men, was that only one man was lost on the other two ships torpedoed that day. The remainder, having assembled in lifeboats, were picked up by two of the trawler escorts and by the destroyer *Badsworth*.[51] The latter destroyer was also given the task of sinking the disabled *Botavon*.[52] There was no need to do anything further in respect of *Jutland*. She sank without further assistance from anyone some twelve minutes after she had been hit.[53]

Shocked as the crews in the merchant ships and escorts were by the mayhem that had been produced by just six German aircraft, and fearful that encouraged by their success, the Germans would follow up with a mass attack that could not be resisted, the ships in the convoy continued making progress eastward with their gunners on high alert. 'We … expected heavy losses before we should reach Murmansk,' Struben recalled.[54]

However, what he did not appreciate was that the Germans had only just begun to drip feed their torpedo bomber crews and their Heinkel 111 torpedo carrying aircraft up to their bases in northern Norway. Enigma decrypts told the intelligence boffins at Bletchley Park that there were only nine crews in Bardufoss during the eastward passage of PQ15.[55] That, combined with the deteriorating weather which so often protected the convoys during these early days, served to prevent Struben's and his comrades' worst forecasts being realized.

Early on 4 May, the skies became overcast just as the bombers were about to reach their goal 'in the uncannily sudden manner of the Arctic', Struben reported, 'and we heard the baffled enemy rumbling to and fro above us, hoping for a break to dive through', until they departed empty handed.[56]

After another 24-hour stretch when reduced visibility along with heavy snow and gales grounded the German planes, he recalled 'the sense of relief after our 10 day ordeal as we steamed past the snow clad hills in the Kola Inlet to an anchorage off the Russian naval base a few miles below the port itself.'[57]

He cannot have been alone in feeling that way. The merchant ships and escorts may have arrived at the ports in and around Murmansk on 5 and 6 May without further loss, but as *Somali*'s Captain Jack Eaton would subsequently remind those on high: 'the escort were fortunate in having weather conditions which on the whole favoured the defence rather than the attack'.

As far as he was concerned 'given reasonable weather conditions . . . it will not be possible to prevent the convoy being continuously shadowed and reported by submarines and aircraft during the later part of the passage to Murmansk'.

Sending a CAM ship such as *Empire Morn,* as was done with PQ15, would not neutralize the growing threat, he said, since it could only ward off the German spy planes 'for a very short period'. The only answer was to have an auxiliary aircraft carrier accompany future convoys, since the fighters on such a ship could 'give a far longer measure of air support with the added advantage that this support could be maintained'.[58]

13

Coup de Grâce

Main Action: 14–15 May 1942
Sinking of HMS Trinidad

(See Map 1)

Even as a gale and a heavy snowfall were masking the progress of PQ15 through the Barents Sea – the second consecutive convoy to the Soviet Union which had benefited from the bad weather in this way – a political storm was brewing between London, Washington and Moscow.

Roosevelt had evidently been less than overjoyed at seeing his request for more aid to be sent to Russia being brushed off with statistics about the smallest number of ships and convoys that could be sailed while complying with America's obligations under the First Protocol (see Chapter 12's reference to Churchill's 28 April 1942 telegram). Referring to Churchill's proposal in the same telegram that the ships that had been left stranded in Iceland following their failure to make it to Russia in PQ14, as well as those that were still crossing the Atlantic, should be unloaded and repacked so that more aid could be fitted into each ship than was currently the case, and so that the repacked ships only carried cargo which had the highest priority, Roosevelt replied on 30 April 1942: 'I am very anxious that ships not be unloaded and reloaded in England because it would leave . . . [a] very disquieting impression in Russia.' In an effort to 'break the log jam of ships already loaded or being loaded for

Russia . . . prior to 1 June' which he said amounted to 107 ships if one also included ships being loaded in the USA as well as those being loaded in England, he wanted Churchill to fit in an additional convoy in May.[1]

However, for once Churchill, who had until this point always been in favour of sending as much aid to the Soviet Union as he could, put his foot down, writing on 2 May 1942: 'With great respect what you suggest is beyond our power to fulfil . . . Our transatlantic escorts are already too thin.' And after citing the damage to HMS *Trinidad* (during PQ13) and *King George V* (during PQ15), as well as the torpedoing of HMS *Edinburgh* during the QP11 convoy being run even as he wrote, his telegram continued: 'I beg you not to press us beyond our judgment in this operation . . . I can assure [you] Mr President we are absolutely extended and I could not press the Admiralty further.'[2]

In order to maintain good relations with his ally, Roosevelt backed down on receiving Churchill's firm rebuff.[3] But his prediction that Stalin would not be very happy if the supplies were delayed was borne out when the Soviet Union's leader on 6 May 1942 sent a telegram asking Churchill whether he could ensure that the 90 merchant ships which were either in Iceland or on the way to Iceland from America reached the Soviet Union before the end of May.[4] It was a reasonable demand given that even as he wrote, the Red Army was preparing for its next large-scale offensive. Russian generals hoped the offensive, which commenced six days later, would forestall the imminent German push towards the East, while enabling the Soviet Union to take back the city of Kharkov in the Ukraine. At the time neither Stalin nor Churchill could have known the Soviet attack was doomed to failure whether or not the American aid was expedited, leaving the way open for the Germans to launch their equally ill-fated Operation Blue on 28 June 1942, which would come to a jarring halt at Stalingrad.[5]

This inability to predict the outcomes of the great events unfolding on the Eastern Front enabled the British prime minister to stick to what his chiefs of staff had advised was feasible with a clear conscience, while at the same time not provoking Stalin's wrath with an outright refusal to comply with his demands. Rather than there and then disclosing the reduced number of convoys and merchant ships that were going to be sent, Churchill diplomatically replied: 'We are resolved to fight our way through to you with the maximum amount of war materials', even though the presence of German surface ships meant each convoy was 'a serious fleet operation'.

However, Churchill in the same telegram turned the tables on Stalin, requesting that the Soviet Union should play her part by 'increasing the assistance given by the USSR naval and air forces in helping to get these convoys through safely'.[6] The response from Russia was not very promising. Stalin's 13 May reply, sent the day after the start of the Soviet advance towards Kharkov, included the warning: 'Our naval forces are very limited' and 'our air forces in their vast majority are engaged at the battle front'.[7]

Churchill's correspondence with Stalin during the first half of May 1942 also alluded to the challenges which the Luftwaffe posed to any attempt to protect the Arctic convoys.[8] In the eyes of some of those who had escorted the most recently arrived convoys, this was even more pressing than the danger on account of the presence in Norwegian ports of Germany's surface fleet.

'It is in the air that our greatest weakness lies,' *Bulldog*'s Commander Maxwell Richmond wrote in his after the action QP11 report, echoing fears concerning the Luftwaffe voiced by *Somali*'s Captain Jack Eaton, adding: 'Whilst the enemy know exactly where the convoy and its escorts are located, we . . . receive no warning of impending air attack.'[9]

If their comments had only been heeded before the next Allied naval operation on the Murmansk run – the attempted repatriation of three of the warships that had been damaged during PQ13 and QP11 – then the Royal Navy might have been spared another of the Battle of the Arctic's great disasters.

To be fair, other factors militated against delaying the return of the warships. *Foresight*'s Commander Jocelyn Salter found his heart was softened by the 'appalling smell' encountered when he visited his destroyer's wounded in the Murmansk hospital, and the patients' pleas they should be taken home as soon as possible.[10]

Trinidad's Captain Leslie Saunders had at first adopted a more robust approach towards his ship's crew. He evidently believed some stiffening was required before volunteers went down below decks to remove the corpses and body parts in relation to the 32 men categorized as dead or missing. 'I endeavoured to help them face it by accompanying them, and explaining that they must regard the remains as merely cast off matter, and that the souls had moved on to another plane,' he wrote later.[11] It was probably just as well his pep talk was bracing. Some of what they found was shocking.

But it was the primitive facilities laid on for Saunders' demoralized crew while the cruiser was repaired in the dry dock at Rosta, some two and a half miles to the north of Murmansk, and the fear that she might be targeted and sunk while waiting to return to her British base, that may have persuaded those in charge of the deployment of warships that *Trinidad* should as quickly as possible be sent back to the West.

Shortly before midnight during the night of 13–14 May 1942, she weighed anchor under the overall command of the 18th Cruiser Squadron's Rear Admiral Stuart Bonham Carter, so that she could be steamed out of the Kola Inlet along with the four destroyers accompanying her during the calm weather prevailing, enabling them to make their escape at 21 knots. The destroyers included the partially repaired *Foresight* and *Forester*.[12] On board the cruiser were around 80 to 100 passengers, consisting for the most part of survivors from *Edinburgh* and from various sunk or abandoned merchant ships.[13]

Bonham Carter and Saunders had been told there would be Russian air support during the first 200 miles of their voyage, but within the first hour of leaving the Kola Inlet, the Russian aircraft disappeared.[14]

It was not long before the Germans were capitalizing on this shoddy teamwork. By 8.30 a.m. on 14 May the crew in a German aircraft had not only found the ships which were still heading northward towards the ice, but the plane was circling round the convoy while the crew sent out homing signals.[15] 'We knew what to expect,' wrote Thomas Baird, who at the time was a 17-year-old midshipman in *Trinidad*. His duties included acting as lookout while doing stints in the ship's crow's nest, from where he was able to watch the unsuccessful attempts to throw the German reconnaissance snoopers off the scent by steaming the British warships into low-lying snow clouds.[16]

When shortly before 7 p.m. that night no less than four shadowers appeared, the tension in the cruiser began to rise exponentially. By this time *Trinidad*, having reached the ice to the north of the Kola Inlet, was heading west-north-westward into the danger area.[17] A babble of voices was heard coming out of the cruiser's crowded canteen and recreation space where the Indian merchant seamen among the passengers were praying for deliverance.[18]

'The suspense of doing nothing but wait was almost unbearable,' wrote Frank Pearce, the able seaman whose previous appearance in this book's narrative is in Chapter 5. Describing what he witnessed from his action station on *Trinidad*'s bridge his account continues: 'Then (when southeast of Bear Island) out of the southern sky we heard them. At first a low whisper, merging into a rhythmic hum like a swarm of angry bees. The familiar drone of Junker[s] planes grew [louder as they came] closer and closer. Anxiously our eyes peered into the scattered haze high above us. At the guns, fingers tensed round the triggers as the noise increased.

'Just before 10 o'clock [p.m.] they came at us. Formations of [Ju] 88s screamed down at near vertical angles, to pull out from their dives at incredibly low levels as they released their bombs. We watched with tight throats as the groups of bombs came toward us, nearer and nearer, to miss by only a few feet on one side or the other. Then came the mighty explosions and towering sheets of water falling across the ship.'[19]

Pearce attributed the planes' failure to sink the ship immediately to Captain Saunders' astute handling of the cruiser. Saunders had her swinging from port to starboard and vice versa in anticipation of the fall of each 'stick' of bombs. But during the sustained attack that lasted for around one hour, Pearce observed that 'no one dared express the thought uppermost in our minds: just how long could the welded repairs take the battering from these near misses? Each explosion followed by a shower of shrapnel sent a massive shudder through the ship, but still the plates held.'[20]

Not that *Trinidad* was the only or even the main target at this juncture. '(The destroyer) HMS *Matchless* received the greatest attention,' Baird remembered afterwards. 'But in spite of several near misses, she came through intact. One stick dropped so close astern of (the destroyer) *Somali* that she was completely obscured from our view by the spray. I thought she had received a direct hit, but amidst the clouds of sea water and bomb fragments, a line of tracer bullets could be seen going up towards the attacking aircrafts, and *Somali* appeared out of it continuing on her way entirely untouched.'[21]

Having survived unscathed until around 10.30 p.m., it seemed as though *Trinidad* might somehow pull through, as she had when bombed during PQ13.[22] But this time there was a difference.

Because the Germans now had access to torpedo aircraft, they were able to stage what might be termed a pincer manoeuvre, only there were to be three arms to this attack rather than two. It started with eight torpedo aircraft flying in towards *Trinidad* on her starboard bow. They were 'flying very low', Saunders noted, adding, 'These circled round to the stern at a range of about five miles and split into groups.' One group of four aircraft turned round, and after starting by retracing their original route, cut in in a line abreast to make their attack from *Trinidad*'s starboard quarter. While they were dropping their torpedoes at a distance of around two to three miles from the cruiser, another group of two aircraft advanced as if to attack from the port quarter.[23]

Saunders, unfazed, believed he could easily deal with torpedoes spotted while they were so far away. He had the ship turned to port, thereby presenting a small target to the oncoming missiles dropped by the larger starboard group. Sure enough, after the ship changed her course, he and the other crew members on and around the bridge watched at least two of the torpedoes rush harmlessly past on *Trinidad*'s starboard side. But as Thomas Baird, who was watching from the compass platform noticed, Saunders had not catered for the third arm of the pincer which appeared on what was now the ship's starboard quarter:

'Just as I was beginning to think we had succeeded, . . . I heard the familiar sounds of a bomber diving to the attack. It emerged from the clouds into a blaze of machine gun, pom-pom and Oerlikon fire. But still it came on, far closer than any of the others had. Soon the barrage had its effect, and before its bombs were dropped, the fuselage had caught alight.

'I saw the four bombs clearly as they were released from the aircraft. One of them seemed to be coming straight for the compass platform . . . Everyone lay down flat on the deck and waited. There followed a series of terrific explosions which rocked the ship . . .'[24]

Frank Pearce has also given us what he remembered of the attack. His account mentions 'the overpowering roar of the plane's engines', 'the scream of the wobbling bombs coming straight for us', and 'the feeling of terror and despair welling up inside [us]'. When the bombs landed, it was, he said, like 'an earthquake which blinded the senses, metal shattering everywhere, the bridge deck leaping, hurling us in all directions'.

These directions are indicated more precisely by what he wrote about the bombing's aftermath: 'I found . . . I was lying on the opposite side of the bridge to where I had been standing . . . A quick glance round showed me the gunnery officer with blood streaming down his face, the officer of the watch lying prone, . . . the captain falling back inboard to the deck from the bridge screen on to which he had been blown, and the signalmen picking themselves up in various stages of stupor.'[25]

Saunders' memoirs describe this near-death experience more phlegmatically: 'I was standing on the same side of the bridge (that is on the port side where one of the bombs landed), and must have been lifted off my feet by the blast, and had a momentary blackout, because all I remember is dazedly landing with my behind on top of the bridge screen and fortunately facing inboard, from which position I was able to jump down to my feet. The others on the bridge were picking themselves up, except for one, the officer of the watch, who was lying prone face downwards. He was always a stupid officer, and my immediate thought was: "It would be you who would make a nuisance of himself by getting himself killed." I told two signalmen to pull him out of the way, but he forthwith pulled himself up, none the worse.'[26]

Those on the bridge had got off lightly. Although two of the bombs from this plane, which had dived down towards the ship's starboard side, were near misses beside the port side of the forecastle, the other two were to spell doom for Trinidad and for those of her crew unfortunate enough to be in or near the latter two bombs' paths. One of these bombs appears to have hit the Admiral's sea cabin in the bridge superstructure, and after passing through the canteen on the forecastle deck (level with the top open-air deck), ended up exploding near the port side of the ship either in the lower deck (two down from the top open-air deck) or between the stokers' petty officers' and petty officers' messes on the upper deck (one down from the top open-air deck).

Another appears to have detonated against or just inside the ship's starboard side in line with the bridge, and may have been responsible for the blasting in of the temporary patch that had been fixed to the starboard side of the hull between lower and upper decks, as well as the ship's subsequent list to starboard.

The explosion of these two bombs was to have catastrophic consequences. Men in the magazine or the cordite handing room for B gun turret (the second turret from the front of the ship) were drowned almost instantaneously when these compartments were flooded before they could be evacuated. The man in the wrecked B turret tasked with shouting down to those below to come up, reported back that there was no reply; all he could hear was the rushing sound of water as it cascaded in.[27]

The explosion inside the ship on the port side resulted in a huge crater being formed in the forecastle and upper decks (top open-air deck and the deck under the open-air deck respectively) in front of the bridge superstructure with a fire blazing inside it. It was the inability to quickly douse this fire because the fire main (water supply for the hoses) was out of action which eventually led to the flames spreading between the decks and becoming uncontrollable.[28]

'I had to decide whether to continue steaming and thereby fan the flames, or to stop,' Saunders wrote in his memoirs. 'As I could see more torpedo bombers preparing for another attack, I decided to keep going. Their torpedoes missed, but the fire [eventually] reached such serious proportions that I had to reduce speed, and finally to stop. This was of little avail. The fire quickly became a raging inferno, and started coming up through the forecastle deck and the bridge structure, the flames licking up through the hatchway. We were forced to evacuate the bridge . . . The situation was clearly hopeless. I decided to cut our losses and gave the order to prepare to abandon ship. Rear Admiral Bonham Carter most readily agreed. By means of a bicycle contraption on the quarterdeck (which, as already mentioned in Chapter 10 in relation to the torpedoing of *Edinburgh*, when pedalled created the necessary electricity) I warned the senior officer of our destroyer escort.'[29]

After that, it was just a matter of waiting as the four destroyers approached *Trinidad*'s quarter deck one by one, with *Forester* being the first in line and taking off the wounded shortly after 11.30 p.m. and leaving *Somali* to bring up the rear. The latter ship approached *Trinidad* at about 1 a.m. on 15 May with a view to taking the officers and Captain Saunders himself, as well as the last of the crew.

The abandonment was helped along by two of *Trinidad*'s gunners, who remained at their posts and fired their guns at a torpedo plane which came skimming over the waves towards them on the port quarter. The firing of the guns had the desired effect. The plane was jerked off its course before bursting into flames and crashed into the sea. The kill was greeted by a loud cheer from the watching seamen.[30]

At around 1.15 a.m. on 15 May, *Matchless'* captain was ordered to sink the ship with his torpedoes. It took three. Baird, who was watching from *Somali,* noted that after the third torpedo struck, 'the bows went under, and the stern came up until it was at right angles with the water. Then it went right over and disappeared completely' (see 4 in Map 1 and Note 31 for approximate location).[31] According to Saunders, one officer and 62 ratings went down with the ship, along with an unknown number of merchant seamen who were travelling in the ship as passengers.[32] Pearce states that as far as he knows, few of the merchant seamen who were in or near the canteen when the ship was bombed escaped with their lives.[33]

The lost officer was the 22-year-old Lieutenant John Boddy. Saunders' report describes how in spite of being flattened and stunned by the explosions which appear to have detonated while he was beside the hatch leading down to the stokers' mess on the lower deck, ten minutes later he was seen raising himself to his hands and knees, and crawling towards that hatch from which shouts for assistance were emanating. On the way, he asked a rating whether he would help him rescue these men. Boddy was never seen again by any of the survivors, which led Saunders to conclude that rather than running for his life, he must have died while attempting to save those in the stokers' mess, who were in danger of being cooked alive by the fires that were raging between the decks. It was an act of heroism among many that day. 'He had been married only a week before we sailed from Devonport,' Saunders commented later, 'and I had attended his wedding. I got him the Albert Medal posthumously.'[34]

After the sinking, the depleted force rushed off to the west. On the way, they were intercepted at around 1 p.m. that same day (15 May) by a group of ships which those on board the destroyers initially believed was the enemy. In fact it was four cruisers from the 10th Cruiser Squadron, of which *Trinidad* had been a part.[35] Twelve Junkers Ju 88s attempted to bomb them that evening.[36] But thanks to the robust defensive fire, and a bit of luck, there were no more casualties, and after the planes eventually departed, the British warships steamed on peacefully to the east coast of Iceland, arriving at Seidisfjord at around 12.20 a.m. on 17 May.[37]

14

Suck it and See

Main Action: 25–26 May 1942
Air raid and first sinking, PQ16 part 1

(See Map 12, and PQ16's formation diagram)[1]

The successful strikes by the German bombers against PQ15 and *Trinidad* during the first half of May 1942 led to another re-assessment of future Arctic convoys' prospects. On 16 May 1942, the First Sea Lord Admiral Sir Dudley Pound was the instigator behind a memorandum signed by all three chiefs of staff pointing out to the War Cabinet how dangerous it was to carry on transporting aid to northern Russia while everything was stacked against them.

The chiefs of staff did not pull their punches. Their memorandum started: 'The arrival of 23(sic) ships out of 25 in P.Q. 15 will we think have given a false impression as regards the possibility of getting convoys through to north Russia (in fact 22 of PQ15's ships made it to Russia).

'The experience of *Trinidad* has shown that unless the weather is unsuitable for flying, the chances of even a ship steaming 18 knots getting through without being attacked from the air are very remote, taking into consideration the restricted area which is available at the present time owing to ice conditions and the fact there are no hours of darkness in this latitude.'

It went on to say that because there were currently over 100 bombers in northern Norway backed up by reconnaissance aircraft including the dreaded Focke-Wulf planes, and because of the 'efficiency of the enemy' in bringing their air superiority to bear once the convoys had been located, 'it seems probable . . . that future convoys will be subjected to such a heavy scale of attack that only a small proportion of the ships of the convoy will reach their destination'.

Their conclusion could not have been clearer: 'In our view therefore it would be better to defer the sailing of the convoys until the ice has receded further to the northward, and our convoys can not only be routed further from the Norwegian coast, but can also make use of evasive tactics.'

This, they said, meant cancelling the next two convoys, including PQ16 which was scheduled to depart on 18 May 1942, since the ice would not be likely to have receded sufficiently until 1 July.[2]

The short time remaining before PQ16 was supposed to sail added to the tension at the meeting of the War Cabinet on 18 May where this recommendation was discussed. The arguments for and against postponing the convoys were complicated by events on the Eastern Front. Unfortunately for those merchant ship crews who ended up having to run the gauntlet of what the Luftwaffe had lined up for them, by 18 May events were not going the Russian way in the Ukraine. It had been hoped that the Red Army would deprive the Germans of the springboard for the expected thrust towards the Caucasus in the south by retaking Kharkov. But the viability of the Soviet offensive that had commenced on 12 May was still hanging in the balance. Whatever might have been the decision if the Soviet offensive had gone well, the fact that the Red Army's resources had all of a sudden become so stretched made it very hard for Churchill and the War Cabinet to back the safety-first approach being contemplated.

That being the case, it is no surprise to see that the minutes of the meeting record the Prime Minister expressing the view that: 'It was our duty to fight these convoys through whatever the cost. The Russians were engaged in a life and death struggle against our common enemy. There was little we could do to help them except by maintaining the flow of supplies by this northern route. In the last convoy 22 out of 25 ships had got through in spite of our apprehensions, and this time we might again do better than we feared.'

However, Stalin was to be 'strongly urged' to bomb the aerodromes in northern Norway, and he was to be warned of the consequence of PQ16 coming to grief. As Churchill explained to Stalin in his 19 May 1942 telegram: 'If luck is not with us, and the convoy suffers very heavy losses, the only course left to us may be to hold up the further convoys until we get more sea room when the ice recedes to the northward in July.'[3]

One of those who believed he would be among the likely victims if PQ16 suffered heavy losses was the 38-year-old Lieutenant Graeme Ogden, skipper of the trawler *Lady Madeleine.* An old Etonian amateur sailor who had joined the Royal Naval Volunteer Reserve (the category that catered for sailing enthusiasts as well as complete beginners), he had been given to understand that he was not someone whose views about tactics, even if pertaining to his own vessel's self-preservation, would be given much sway by the professional sailors in charge of the convoy. At least some of the regular naval officers to whom he reported before being instructed to join PQ16's escort had let it be known that amateurs such as him were regarded in some quarters as more of a hindrance than a help. His usefulness as an officer was called into question even more vehemently by one middle ranking regular officer after learning that Ogden's family had made their money from their cigarette business, trade during the early war years being regarded by some British officers as a breeding ground for men who were not as well equipped for the rigours of leadership as those hailing from a wealthy aristocratic lineage.[4]

The deficiencies of the ship Ogden commanded also affected his state of mind. The vital statistics of an old-fashioned coal burning armed trawler did not automatically inspire confidence. Because *Lady Madeleine* was armed with a 4-inch gun for'ard, and a twin half-inch Vickers machine gun aft plus two Lewis light machine guns (.303 calibre) for use on the bridge, and had been fitted up with anti-submarine asdic equipment and depth charge throwers, she was classified as a convoy escort in spite of her status as a former fishing vessel and her relatively small stature (she was 195 foot long, with a beam of 32 feet).[5] But if it came to an attack by the German surface fleet or the Luftwaffe, it was evident she would not be much more effective than the merchant ships she had been brought in to protect.

That might explain why during the lead up to the departure of PQ16, Ogden was studiously in denial about the vulnerability of Arctic convoy escorts, and referred to the gossip about damage to warships during the previous pair of convoys as 'ugly rumours'. His complacency only fell away when, as he wrote in his memoirs, the day before PQ16's original departure date, he saw incontrovertible evidence of what he had previously dismissed as impossible while chugging around Reykjavik's harbour:

'Across our bows steamed two F-class destroyers (HMS *Foresight* and HMS *Forester*). These ships were near wrecks. Their masts were down, their sides holed, their smoke stacks askew. They bore the scars of German shells, and their own gun turrets were a shambles . . . It was a grim reminder of what might be in store for us. We returned to Hvalfjord . . . in rather a chastened mood.'[6]

He was, he recalled, cheered up 'somewhat' however by the reassuring words spoken by the 52-year-old Rear Admiral Sir Harold Burrough, commander of the 10th Cruiser Squadron, who was to be in charge of the protection of PQ16, at the pre-convoy conference attended by escort commanders as well as by masters of merchant ships, during the morning of 20 May.[7] PQ16's departure had been delayed for a couple of days. According to Ogden, Admiral Burrough informed the conference 'in the traditional bluff naval style . . . that we had little to fear, as the escort for this convoy was the most powerful ever to be sent on a north Russian convoy. He, with four cruisers, would be near us all the way up and battleships would be covering the convoy as a distant screen.'[8] This was double the number of cruisers Burrough had had under his command when escorting PQ15 (see Chapter 12).

Ogden was equally impressed by the 38-year-old Commander Richard Onslow, the senior officer in charge of the convoy's close escort, although Onslow was a man whom Ogden had at first underrated. First impressions told Ogden that Onslow was 'a most charming person: tall, elegant and well dressed . . . complete with a monocle . . . I felt he would be more at home in White's (the Club), in St James' Street, than the Arctic.' However, once Ogden had seen how accurately Onslow described to the escort commanders, at another conference, what they were likely to face, and what they must do if they were to cope, he was already saying to himself: 'how wrong I was!'[9]

Ogden explains in his memoirs how he eventually decided it would be best to pass on what he had learned to his crew: 'I . . . told them in their own language what they were in for, and what I expected of them. I made it clear that their best chance of survival was instant obedience to my orders, whatever might befall us, and that I would not have any nonsense from anybody.'[10]

PQ16 finally sailed from Hvalfjord during the evening of 20 May.[11] Churchill had been as good as his word to Roosevelt: it consisted of 35 merchant ships, including 1 Dutch vessel, 20 American, 7 British, 4 Soviet, and 3 Panamanian-registered vessels.[12] Ogden's recollection was that the ships were given their marching orders when 'Commodore Gale in the [SS] *Ocean Voice* blew a long blast on his ship's siren.'[13] Alexander Werth, the BBC's 41-year-old Russia correspondent, who was a passenger in the convoy's SS *Empire Baffin,* later recalled that: 'It had rained that day. But as we were sailing out of the fjord, the sun broke through the black clouds resting heavily on the hills, and a glorious rainbow appeared above the grey choppy sea. I felt a strange elation at the good omen.' However, he would later deride himself for being naively superstitious, admitting that 'many others in our convoy must have welcomed . . . [it], and among them, some of those who were never to see land again.'[14]

Like most Arctic convoys, PQ16 was not protected by any of the larger warships when it first left the cover of Hvalfjord, accompanied only by its modest local escort. This might have had undesirable repercussions had the departure of the convoy not been delayed, or had the weather been fine. Because it was foggy, and because by 22 May no convoy had turned up south-east of Jan Mayen Island where the six U-boats designated Gruppe Greif (Griffen) had on 18 May been ordered to line up, Admiral Schmundt (Admiral Nordmeer) lost his nerve. Fearing that the next Russian convoy he had been expecting might have slipped through the net because of the restricted visibility, he instructed the U-boats' commanders to move to the north-east, not realizing that had he waited a little longer, the lightly protected freighters might have fallen into his original trap (see initial location of Gruppe Greif U-boats in Map 12).[15]

The chance to catch the convoy with such scant support would not recur. By early morning on 25 May, the nine-column convoy was not only protected by the four cruisers promised by Admiral Burrough at the pre-convoy conference along with their three supporting destroyers (Burrough flew his flag in the cruiser *Nigeria*), but it was also supported by an anti-aircraft ship, five more destroyers, four corvettes, three trawlers, two submarines and one minesweeper. There was also a tanker with its one destroyer screen, which was to refuel the convoy's escorts, and was then to switch over so it could refuel the west-going convoy's escorts before PQ16 reached what was generally accepted as the main danger area between Jan Mayen Island and Bear Island.[16]

Ogden would later recall how the arrival of four of the five destroyers that were to form part of the so-called 'through (to Russia) escort' during the early afternoon of 24 May was marked by *Ashanti*'s Commander Onslow being 'enough of a showman to steam right round the convoy to make sure his arrival had been noticed by all the merchantmen'.[17]

But Ogden confessed that his heart fell when, within an hour of the arrival of the cruisers, which showed up at around 6.30 a.m. on 25 May, the first German shadower aircraft, a Focke-Wulf 200 Condor, appeared and began to circle the convoy, well within sight, but outside the range of any of the ships' guns.[18]

The account in his memoirs continues: 'I realized with a sickening feeling ... there could be no escape. The barbed harpoon had been plunged into the whale's side, not to be withdrawn until its captors had killed it and its blood had turned the pale Arctic sea to crimson. As I watched this evil shadow through my glasses, I thought of it as a gigantic bat, a Fledermaus, a spectre consorting with a butcher, a Schlachter.'[19]

Nevertheless the Focke-Wulf, and the aircraft which replaced it, featured in a version of the humorous myth, or much-repeated joke, which appears in many of the detailed accounts written by Arctic convoy veterans, and particularly in those penned by PQ16 survivors. The story goes – and it appears to have been sincerely believed by at least some who told it – that various captains of ships in the convoys asked their signalmen to flash messages to the crews of the shadowers to tell them that their going round and round was making them dizzy. Would they mind circling in the opposite direction? On receiving this request, the shadowers changed the direction of the circling, after replying, 'Anything to oblige'.[20]

Less amusing was the information passed to Onslow by his opposite number in west-going QP12 (initially 15 ships excluding escorts), which had set out from the Kola Inlet on 21 May, as the two convoys chugged past each other east of Jan Mayen Island during the early afternoon of 25 May.[21] Onslow was informed that QP12 had been shadowed by at least one U-boat. Within an hour of being told this, a U-boat was sighted from one of PQ16's escorts.[22] Although for some time after the sighting, this U-boat was the fugitive as she was chased and targeted by PQ16's escorts and their depth charges, there was no mistaking the sense that all of a sudden the lives of everyone involved with PQ16 had become that much more insecure.

QP12 also brought with it other bad news. It was with great sadness that Admiral Burrough learned from QP12's senior destroyer commander what had transpired earlier that day.[23] During the early hours of 25 May, the appearance of aircraft that proceeded to shadow QP12 had tempted Captain Dan McGrath, the senior officer of the escort in the anti-aircraft ship *Ulster Queen*, to try to shoot them out of the sky before they could summon the Luftwaffe units from northern Norway. Although R. Struben, his second-in-command, believed that three German planes was too many for the one available Hurricane on QP12's CAM ship *Empire Morn*, McGrath insisted that a signal should be sent to *Empire Morn*'s master requesting that its plane should be deployed.

Struben has written about how he watched the 'thrilling drama' that ensued after 'in a cloud of fiery rocket smoke, the fighter roared off the merchantman's fo'c'sle and soared behind the cover of an isolated cloud'. What made the situation so dramatic was that the German aircraft's crew appeared not to have seen the British plane. 'In a minute or two, we saw the Hurricane dive at full throttle out of the cloud onto the tail of the first unsuspecting enemy to send it hurtling into the sea,' Struben reported.

While the Hurricane's pilot, Flying Officer John Kendall, circled the convoy, he was instructed to make sure the 'job was complete'. According to *Empire Morn*'s master, W. L. Cruickshank, Kendall radioed back to say that he could see the wrecked plane and a dinghy close by, but no crew. 'I take it they must have gone down with their plane,' Cruickshank reported. He added, 'The other two must have realized that a Hurricane was about, for they made off for home to report.'[24]

Struben's account describes what happened next. After the encounter with the German aircraft, Kendall 'circled round *Ulster Queen* to . . . report his petrol was nearly finished, and that he was about to ditch the

Hurricane. Had the clouds been high enough, Kendall would have gained a safe height for parachuting, and then baled out near the rescue trawler . . . But he jumped from under the clouds . . . , and we watched in horror as he struck the water before the parachute had had time to open. Of course he was killed.'[25]

Struben's report suggests that the deployment that ended in Kendall's death did not achieve anything since one of the shadowers returned. There was no disputing Cruickshank's assessment of Kendall's courage however, contained in the following epitaph. Kendall, he said, had 'showed his mettle against the Hun . . . The attack was magnificently carried out with skill and daring against superior numbers . . . We all regret the loss of a fellow countryman, a gallant fighter and a hero.'[26]

A different strategy was adopted concerning the PQ16 shadowers. It was decided that *Empire Lawrence*, PQ16's CAM ship, should hold on to her Sea Hurricane until a bombing raid materialized. There was not long to wait.

Alexander Werth appears to have recorded the moment when, shortly after 8.30 p.m. that night (25 May), as PQ16 continued sailing on its course of 25°, south-west of Bear Island, torpedo bombers appeared in the distance for the first time (see 3 in Map 12 and Note 27 for approximate attack location).[27] They came in, he said, 'on the starboard side, low above the water. Three – four – five, then three more, then four or five after that, further to the right. We were all on deck [by this time] . . . and we counted and watched. Eleven, twelve, thirteen. Something was already happening ahead of us . . . The . . . cruisers . . . and the destroyers on the edge of the convoy were firing like mad . . . and the sky was . . . dotted with specks of smoke from the flak shells.'[28]

It was in an attempt to forestall the port arm of the attack that the Hurricane in *Empire Lawrence*, which was sailing in convoy position 11 (the 1st column from the left side of convoy, i.e. the convoy's extreme left column; 1st i.e. front ship), was unleashed against it.[29]

The order it should take off almost led to a fight between the two pilots in *Empire Lawrence*, who were in the middle of a change-over when the message arrived. The argument was soon over. The 20-year-old South African pilot Alastair Hay was in the cockpit when the plane was catapulted off the ship.[30]

'Its engines hum in a rising crescendo of sound,' wrote the Polish journalist Bohdan Pawłowicz, who was embedded with the crew of the Polish Navy's destroyer ORP *Garland*, the escort on the convoy's port beam. 'The pilot semi-circles round the convoy and makes off for the horizon where I can see torpedo planes approaching. He flies right into their midst. Smoke appears!'[31]

Most of those watching from the convoy could only pray that it was not their man who had been hit. It was not: his voice could still be heard over his link with *Empire Lawrence*. He stated he had shot down one plane and damaged another on the port side of the convoy.[32]

However, their excitement was quickly transformed into concern when he was heard reporting that he had been hit in one of his legs, and that his ammunition had run out. He then announced that he would bale out.

Pawłowicz in *Garland* was watching as the Hurricane returned to the convoy. 'As he approaches, some cargo ships open up with their machine guns,' Pawłowicz wrote. 'The pilot frantically dips his wings. "What? Don't they know their own plane!" I shout out . . . The Hurricane circles in a wide sweep. The pilot bales out . . . I see the white mushroom of his parachute slowly settling on the water, and simultaneously a motor boat reaches him.'

For now he was down, but he was not out, and a sailor in *Garland* was able to subsequently inform Pawłowicz, the pilot would live to shoot down more Germans.[33] Whatever his future prospects, his patrol only ended after he had successfully disrupted the port arm of the German attack.[34]

The torpedo bombers on the convoy's starboard bow were also thwarted. They were evidently put off by the barrage put up by the cruisers which had been rushed out in front of the merchant ships in time to repulse the attack. As a result, the German torpedoes were dropped too far away to trouble either escorts or merchant ships.

Stunned by all the banging sounds made by the warships' and merchant ships' guns, Werth and the other passengers with him silently watched the battle from amidships on their vessel. But all that changed when, as Werth recorded, 'Something happened.'[35] From where he was standing, it seemed that a cruiser's guns had hit one of the German planes, although assuming that the same incident is being talked about, gunners in *Ashanti* and *Volunteer*, the destroyers positioned to guard the convoy's port bow, were subsequently given the credit: according to Onslow's official report, the shot-down Junkers Ju 88 was one of three planes that in quick succession had dived on the convoy out of the sun on the port side, which *Volunteer* and *Ashanti* were guarding. The shot down pilot appears to have paid the price for having had the temerity to think his aircraft could pass through the curtain of fire emanating out of the guns in these destroyers without paying the price.[36]

As Werth watched the hit aircraft 'reel and swoop down' on the convoy's port bow, he noted the ecstatic reaction in his ship *Empire Baffin*, which at the time was in convoy position 21 (2nd column from left side of convoy; 1st, i.e. front, ship in column): 'It was like a football match . . . The RAF boys were shouting: "He's on fire! He's on fire! That's it! . . . He's down!"' After such gusto, the final act of the drama was incongruously unspectacular. 'The plane . . . slid into the water without much of a splash,' Werth recorded.[37]

Eventually at around 10.30 p.m. the other German planes slunk away.[38] After all that bombing, the only enemy casualty the Germans had to show for it was the American SS *Carlton*, the freighter in convoy position 14 (1st column from left, 4th row) which was seen to have smoke coming from her engine room.[39] The ship's main steam pipe had been fractured by the blast from a near miss, and her master was ordered to take her back to Iceland. She was first towed and later escorted by *Northern Spray*, one of the convoy's armed trawlers.

They, and the last of the German bombers, had not been long gone when crews in the remaining escorts found themselves being distracted by the kind of Arctic phenomena which so often intruded when convoys sailed near to the ice edge. A passage in the report by the commander of the corvette *Hyderabad*, sailing on the port bow of the convoy, explains how he feared his vessel's hull might be damaged as his ship steamed through an ice field consisting of small pieces of ice in between several larger pieces, some of which he said 'rubbed along the ship's side'.[40]

Even more alarmingly at 2.30 a.m. on 26 May, when around 200 miles south-west of Bear Island, *Ashanti*'s crew dropped depth charges on a suspected U-boat detected ahead of the convoy's sixth column, only for her commander, Richard Onslow, who had spotted what he referred to as an 'oval shaped slick in the water identical in appearance to those made by whales breaking surface . . . and observed frequently during the preceding twenty four hours', to insist it was a false alarm. 'I personally classified this contact as a whale', he confessed afterwards. His embarrassment was all the more acute when the events that followed suggested he had been mistaken. He felt he should have known better because U-boats had been in contact with the convoy since the previous afternoon.[41]

The observations around half an hour later of 18-year-old officer cadet Romuald Holubowicz, while standing watch on the port wing of the bridge in the American merchant ship SS *Syros*, nominally in convoy position 74 (column 7; 4th row in column), though lagging behind where she was supposed to be sailing, certainly called into question Onslow's judgement. 'I noted a plume of water rising up behind the ship abeam our convoy position, approximately 1,000 metres distant, and reported to the 3rd mate the oddity of what I thought was a fog buoy being streamed unnecessarily', Holubowicz reported later.

His account carries on: 'Suddenly the fog buoy changed direction, and began heading towards *Syros*. And immediately thereafter, I saw the wake of a torpedo heading straight at us. On seeing the track . . . I managed to throw the switch on the general alarm, but it was only seconds before impact, and therefore futile . . . Within a minute of sighting the torpedo track, *Syros* was struck amidships (port side), with a mighty explosion stopping the vessel dead in the water.' (See 4 in Map 12 and Note 42 for position of convoy when *Syros* was torpedoed.)[42]

A slightly more detailed description has been provided by Kapitänleutnant Heinz Bielfeld, the daring 25-year-old commander of *U-703*, who confirmed that two torpedoes hit the ship. The report he compiled after the attack describes how he deliberately had the U-boat submerged ahead of the convoy, and then had her set on a course so that *U-703* could run underwater between two of the three British destroyers lined up in front of PQ16. Thanks to Onslow's apparent misinterpretation of his destroyer's asdic, *U-703* appears to have ended up in one piece near the back of PQ16's third column. From there he was able to fire at the largest merchant ship he could see through his periscope, and ended up hitting *Syros* twice in quick succession.

His war diary entry continues: 'The torpedo detonations are so loud they can be heard by everyone in the boat . . . I see a tall white cloud of smoke followed by another one. Then the clouds of smoke spread out until they completely envelop the ship so that we can't see anything of her anymore.'[43]

Syros' ultimate fate may have been hidden from her executioner, but it should have been obvious to those on board that the ship was sinking. Nevertheless, Holubowicz prioritized the collection of his most treasured possessions, and raced down the ladder fastened to the starboard side of the bridge, in the hope he could make it to his cabin, stopping on the way to don a life jacket. It was only then that he came to his senses, and finally opted in favour of leaving everything behind so he could try to get back out on deck as quickly as possible.

By this stage 'the vessel was heavily listed to port', Holubowicz's account continues. 'I retraced my steps across the saloon's now greatly sloping deck to reach the open deck on the starboard side, at which moment, *Syros* began to . . . [sink] . . . As I was rushing through . . . I was deeply moved by the sight of the captain's mongrel dog cowering beneath the settee, . . . knowing there was nothing I could do to save it.

'As I stepped out on deck, I was . . . swept off my feet by the water . . . engulfing the ship . . . The ship, carrying me with it, [then] slipped below the surface . . .

'I did not have time to panic . . . I remember being quite relaxed, not even trying to hold my breath after going under, which . . . resulted in a stomach full of oily water. It was only when I . . . came to the surface . . . , and saw the convoy disappearing over my horizon that a feeling of abandonment . . . crept in.'

During the first minutes after the sinking, he only came across two other men. 'I saw another survivor nearby, and heard the moans of an injured crewman a short distance away,' he recalled later.[44] But surprisingly, given the speed at which *Syros* sank and the time (around 45 minutes) it took for those in the sea and on rafts to be collected by the crew in the minesweeper *Hazard*, as many as 30 of the 40 men who had been in *Syros* were picked up alive, although two of them succumbed within an hour of their rescue.[45]

One's heart must go out to those, and the families of those, who might have died unnecessarily. But at the same time, it is hard not to also spare a thought for Commander Onslow. Even if his initial mistaking a U-boat for a whale was partly responsible, he at least had the humility to acknowledge his shortcomings on this occasion. 'I have a far from happy conscience regarding the loss of SS *Syros*,' he would later admit in his report, 'as I now believe I may have been wrong in this classification, and that contact may in fact have been the U-boat that sank *Syros*.'[46]

That said, by the time the rescue had been completed, a new day was dawning. With the prospect that more raids would soon be coming at the convoy from under the sea and in the air, Onslow had to swallow the guilt he was feeling and get back to defending those freighters whose crews were still relying on him.

15

A Perfect Storm

Main Action: 27 May 1942
Luftwaffe hit 9 ships (6 sink), PQ16 part 2

(See Maps 1 and 12, and PQ16's formation diagram)[1]

The sinking of *Syros* did not just result in a freezing cold swim for those of her crew who were lucky enough to survive. Together with reports that a U-boat had fired a torpedo at one of his cruisers, it also persuaded the 10th Cruiser Squadron's Rear Admiral Harold Burrough that his force had outlived its usefulness as far as protecting PQ16 was concerned. Within half an hour of *Syros* being torpedoed, the four cruisers and their three-destroyer screen had departed.[2]

For a while their departure did not appear to make any significant difference. The six Gruppe Greif U-boats shadowing the convoy kept their distance, and the only raid by the Luftwaffe on 26 May was half-hearted. The merchant ships' crews would only realize later that it was the calm before the next day's storm. Whichever accounts you read about the events of 27 May, they are almost always prefaced by similar words to the following used by the BBC's Alexander Werth to introduce his version of what took place: 'I am not likely ever to forget this day . . .'[3]

The first of the overlapping factors that would coalesce to transform the events of 27 May 1942 into what for the Allies was to be a metaphorical perfect storm was the need to steer to the south to avoid what *Ashanti's*

Commander Richard Onslow described as the 'heavy and impenetrable pack ice . . . south of Bear Island'. After the long-suffering merchant seamen had wheeled their vessels to their right at 3.50 a.m. on the morning of 27 May, bringing them ever nearer to the Luftwaffe's aircraft bases in northern Norway, what helped them keep track of where they were was the sight of the appropriately named Mount Misery rearing up from Bear Island, around 60 miles away to the north.[4]

The second building block for the metaphorical storm was the Luftwaffe's determination to strike a decisive blow against the convoy on 27 May. With that in mind, they would deploy over a hundred aircraft before the end of the day.[5]

But even that was not enough on its own to justify the description. Air raids prior to 1 p.m. on 27 May were no more effective than the single half-hearted effort the day before. In the following extract from *Ashanti*'s Commander Richard Onslow's after the action report, he explained how it was the changed conditions after 1 p.m. which altered everything: 'In the cloudless period before 1300 all [Luftwaffe] formations were engaged . . . before attacking . . . This warned the pilots . . . that they had been spotted, and . . . that they must expect their targets to be ready with all they had got. Consequently all aircraft pulled out at heights up to 4,000 feet and scored no successes.

'When it clouded over, pilots became daring and pressed home their attacks to 1,000 feet on ships in convoy.'

This was possible because there were not only broken clouds at around 3,000 feet, but also what Onslow termed 'an intermittent filmy haze at about 1,500 feet' which he said made the aircraft 'very difficult to see'.[6]

The series of air raids that were eventually to make 27 May such an ordeal for those men on the receiving end began that day at around 11.15 a.m. when the convoy was heading towards the east (see 6 in Map 12, and Note 7 for the convoy's location when the first of these raids started).[7] No ships were sunk during the morning, but for most of the time there appeared to be little the convoy's escorts could do to stop the Ju 88s flying overhead, five to nine at a time, so that they could drop their bombs.

The bombers did not quite have it all their own way. At about 12.30 p.m., one of the Ju 88s that was queuing up to make its run-in was engaged by the gunners in *Ashanti*, located at the centre of the screen in front of the convoy's merchant ships. According to Commander Onslow, after the aircraft was hit, it 'swerved onto a course heading for home, and when about five miles from the ship, struck the water, paused a moment, tail in [the] air, then sank.'[8]

But that was to be the last moment of triumph the crews in the British escorts experienced that day, although a report describing actions ordered by Luftflotte 5, the Luftwaffe command unit responsible for aircraft based in Norway, would confirm that three of its aircraft were lost on 27 May.[9] Within half an hour of the crash landing of the aircraft shot down by *Ashanti*'s gunners, the clear skies had vanished, to be replaced by the clouds and haze which gave the German aircraft the cover they needed. Those thirty minutes were all it took for the tables to be turned.

The BBC's Alexander Werth in *Empire Baffin*, in convoy position 21 (2nd column from convoy's left; 1st, i.e. front, ship in column), was well placed to notice what he described as 'the first casualty' at around 1 p.m. that afternoon. It was the Polish escort ORP *Garland*, described by Werth as the 'pale blue and pale green destroyer' on the convoy's port beam, which following yet another attack by the circling German aircraft 'was smoking furiously, and signalling, signalling, signalling.'[10]

No account has been unearthed which describes the attack on this ship. Such was the intensity of the bombing leading up to it that Bohdan Pawłowicz, the 43-year-old Polish journalist on board *Garland*, who was supposed to be recording anything of note, admitted later that he had not even seen the plane whose bombs did the damage. His chronicle of events merely records what happened before and after the plane in question had passed overhead. He was, he wrote, just catching his breath after seeing three large fountains of water spring up between *Garland* and a nearby corvette, an indication that three bombs had fallen too close for comfort, when at about 1 p.m. he heard that distinctive long shrill whistle which those who hear it find it so alarming. His chronicle continues: 'Against the background of the smoke of previous explosions, I saw as in a nightmare, the dark spear-like shapes of four bombs. I instinctively huddled against the wall of the rangefinder.'

It seems it was that act of taking cover that sheltered him from the lethal metal splinters that hurtled across the ship's top deck shortly afterwards, lacerating anything, and anybody, that were in their path. They were the consequence of the explosion of the four bombs that fell into the sea a short distance to starboard of the ship's so-called No. 2 gun (2nd main armament gun from the front of the ship).[11] The fact they missed the ship did not appear to muzzle their effect. Pawłowicz's account, recalling his sensations immediately after the bombs blew up, reads: 'My eyes seemed filled with dust, [and] my open mouth had an unpleasant metallic taste. A huge pall of smoke and water covered the corvette, the convoy, and [seemingly] the whole world. "It's the end," I thought . . .'

However, once he had picked himself up, and worked out that the blood on his arm was not his own – it was dripping down from the director tower located above where he had been standing – he realized that he was not only still in the land of the living, but he had somehow escaped without any injury whatsoever. Others were less fortunate. As he would soon discover, it would be hard to find anyone else in the ship who did not at the very least have blood streaming down his face. Those whose cuts were superficial were able to carry on. However, the cacophony of moans issuing forth from the mouths of the many men who were severely wounded told him that something very serious had just taken place.

Nothing could be done for the No. 1 and No. 2 gun crews at the front of the ship. They had been wiped out by the nearest explosion, as had the two gunners who had operated the starboard Oerlikon. 'Their charred bodies lay, as they had fallen, among the smoking embers of the splinters which had killed them,' Pawłowicz recalled later, adding that he watched while a sailor covered up their remains with a blanket. At least 'they died quickly', the sailor said.

But Pawłowicz was able to comfort Pawel Płonka, his wounded cameraman, who had been filming the battle from his vantage point on the searchlight platform near where one of the explosions had caused so much damage. The blast had shattered the cameraman's right elbow. A member of *Garland*'s crew had informed Pawłowicz that Płonka had been found lying in a pool of his own blood, clutching the camera in his one usable hand, and had been taken to the stern along with the other wounded who were waiting to be treated. 'He didn't want to let go, said he must hand it over to you sir,' the rating told Pawłowicz, as they rushed to the back of the ship where his assistant was lying.

Clearly the repercussions arising out of so many men being wounded were not confined to the area adjacent to where the bombs exploded. 'I had to be careful amidships not to slip on the blood which seemed to cover the entire deck,' Pawłowicz reported.

The Polish journalist was able to fetch his assistant a glass of whisky, and to assure him that the camera was 'covered with blood, but safe and untouched'. But the following words in Pawłowicz's chronicle bear witness to his desire to do more for the injured cameraman. 'I went down to the mess which had been transformed into an operating theatre . . . I intended to ask when could . . . [Płonka] be brought down for further attention, but I remained rooted to the threshold . . . The surgeon was . . . amputating the second limb of some poor devil, and sealing the veins of the bloody stump with clips.' In spite of his concern, Pawłowicz could not bring himself to mention a mere broken arm.

Meanwhile frantic efforts were being made to sort out the situation at the front of the ship, where Pawłowicz had noted there was 'a cloud of evil smelling yellow-white smoke . . . rising upwards'. The explosion nearest to the front of the ship had lit a fire near the front guns, and the smouldering matting lying on the deck, combined with a burning smoke flare, was producing this thick smoke that told the crew of every German plane in the vicinity that *Garland* was for the moment winged and ready for the taking.

Two of *Garland*'s officers and some ratings risked their lives by rushing to throw the nearby shells, the matting and the flare into the sea, only for the smoke to be replaced by a cloud of steam which shot up to the height of the ship's funnel from a broken pipe in the engine room amidships.[12]

Eventually even that was brought under control, and that night the captain of the British destroyer *Achates* was instructed to lend his medical officer to the Polish ship.[13] In addition to the 21 men in *Garland* who had been killed outright by the blasts, there were 27 seriously wounded, some of whom would later expire. There were too many to be cared for by *Garland*'s surgeon acting alone.[14] If the crew in the British destroyer needed any evidence of the scale of the disaster, they only had to look at what was happening on *Garland*'s top deck as *Achates*' captain had his ship brought right up alongside her Polish counterpart so that the doctor could be transferred.

'We . . . were shocked to see the devastation,' *Achates'* First Lieutenant Loftus Peyton Jones wrote years later when describing the large numbers of casualties in his memoirs. 'They lay in groups on . . . [*Garland's*] shattered deck as her crew worked feverishly to clean up the mess. One young seaman was hosing down the quarterdeck as we approached, and we saw the ship's side becoming stained with blood. He stopped to pick something up, and we realized with horror that it was what remained of someone's arm.'[15]

The sailor was almost certainly not the only one in the convoy using a hose for that purpose that day, nor would he be the only one having to pick up his comrades' remains. No sooner had Werth in *Empire Baffin* been assured that *Garland* was going to carry on, and that her being hit was not the beginning of the end for all of them, than he caught sight of another ship in trouble, on the other side of the convoy, that had also been bombed at around 1 p.m., during the same raid.

It was the Soviet merchant ship *Starii Bolshevik*, which had been in convoy position 83 (8th column from convoy's left; row 3). 'Her foredeck was enveloped in clouds of smoke, and flames were bursting out of the hold,' Werth reported later. '"They're going to abandon her," somebody said. Were they? Yes, they were lowering their lifeboats. But no. She was still keeping up steam . . . [although] the clouds of smoke rising from her were growing larger and larger [until] her whole foc'sle was a cloud of black smoke. But still she went on, and through the smoke, one saw dim shapes of people running and doing something.'[16]

The fire in *Starii Bolshevik* was still raging when the destroyer HMS *Martin's* 32-year-old surgeon Ralph Ransome Wallis was invited on board in order to collect their severely wounded. Braving the bombs which were still being dropped between *Martin* and the Russian ship, he and his sick berth attendant were rowed across the 300 yards separating the two ships in a small whaler. When he climbed on board, he was surprised to be greeted by three Russian women.

They had evidently been briefed on why he had come, but had very different ideas on how badly wounded men should be lowered into a small boat. They proposed tying a rope around the men and then lowering them down over the side of their ship. However, they had no objection when he insisted the three worst cases were lowered on the

Neil Robertson stretchers (flexible canvas stretchers with straps to hold in the patient) that he and his attendant had brought with them.

Before leaving *Starii Bolshevik*, he surveyed the scene at the front of the ship. It was not looking good. 'The Russian ship had carried an anti-aircraft gun right up in her bow,' he reported in his memoirs. 'The bomb which had done the damage had landed on this, and blown a hole deep into the ship into which most of the wrecked gun appeared to have fallen. The ready use ammunition on the deck was burning fiercely, and smoke was pouring out of the ship from her forehold which appeared to be well alight. Round the jagged edge of the hole were some bits of badly burnt bodies, and a little further aft lay the twisted body of another seaman, very obviously dead.'

On seeing all this, Ransome Wallis beat a hasty retreat back to the boat where his team and the casualties were waiting for him, and trying not to look as if he was in too much of a hurry to get away, he waved farewell to the Russians, and ordered the sailors in the boat to row him back to *Martin* as quickly as possible. He later admitted that he had expected the Soviet ship to blow up at any minute.[17]

That did not happen, but her movements after being hit had started a kind of chain reaction which had negatively affected the crews in other ships. When the bomb hit her deck, her crew tried to comply with the convoy regulation which demanded that an incapacitated ship should move out of her allocated column so as not to block the ships behind her. However the Russian ship's veer to starboard forced SS *American Robin*, the ship in the next column to starboard bearing down on her (*American Robin* was in convoy position 94 – 9th column from convoy's left, row 4), to swing to starboard as well to avoid a collision. This at a stroke meant that the air defences surrounding the American ship SS *Mormacsul*, which had been in convoy position 84 (8th column from convoy's left, row 4), that is directly behind *Starii Bolshevik*, were reduced. Before her master was able to move her up to the position vacated by *Starii Bolshevik*, she was further isolated at around 1.15 p.m. by the diversion and eventual abandonment of SS *Alamar*, another American ship, which had been the next ship on the Russian ship's left, in convoy position 73 (7th column from convoy's left, row 3), following the explosion of a bomb that had landed a direct hit behind *Alamar*'s main mast.[18]

Fortuitously, this hit did not kill any of the crew, and there was only one casualty. However the movement and subsequent abandoning of the ship, combined with the moves by the other ships in the vicinity specified above, left the way clear for yet another group of seven Ju 88s, whose pilots were queuing up to carry out the next attack, to target *Mormacsul*. No less than three planes swooped down to bomb this one ship, and one of the bombs dropped exploded under the midship section of *Mormacsul*'s port side. The result was: 'a geyser of water and fuel oil gushed over the ship', according to the head of her armed guard, all electric power was abruptly shut down, and the ship could no longer be steered.

'Fear was evident in the actions of the crew that the explosive cargo would detonate,' the same armed guard noted, and when the ship's captain ordered that *Mormacsul* should be abandoned, the cutting of one of the falls regulating the descent of one of the lifeboats resulted in it capsizing and drifting off with four men clinging to its piping. That meant that those of her crew who had not already jumped onto one of the ship's liberated rafts, had to crowd into the starboard lifeboat, from which they were rescued by the corvette *Starwort* ten minutes later. The remaining nine survivors were picked up by a trawler. Three of the ship's crew were missing.[19]

Mormacsul herself only sank around 25 minutes after being hit, when she suffered the indignity of being rammed by the abandoned *Alamar* whose engines were still racing. According to *Lady Madeleine*'s Lieutenant Ogden, the trawler '*St Elstan* . . . nearly got run down by this blazing rogue elephant. An abandoned ship under steam was a menace and she had to be sunk.'[20] *Alamar* eventually sank stern first after being torpedoed by the British submarine *Trident* at around 2.20 p.m.[21]

Worse was to follow. Shortly after 2.45 p.m., by which time the convoy was heading north-eastward as part of the effort to distance it from the German aerodromes by hugging the edge of the ice, a bomb was dropped into the No. 2 hold of the CAM ship *Empire Lawrence* (in convoy position 11) where ammunition was stored. It exploded, prompting her master to order those on board to abandon ship because the vessel was sinking (see 5 in Map 1, 7 in Map 12, and Note 22 for the location).[22]

But as Lieutenant Ogden in *Lady Madeleine* would attest, the German bomber crews, not for the first time that day, had smelled blood. No sooner did he give the order to his crew to approach the wounded ship than he realized that he was also going to be impacted. 'I heard the cruel whine of bombers,' he recalled afterwards, 'and looking aft saw three of them diving on us.'[23]

In the course of a post-war interview, Eddie Grenfell, at the time a 22-year-old leading seaman, one of the radar operators in *Empire Lawrence*, confirmed that he heard the same sound. He also averred, as part of a lively account of the incident, all delivered in the same soft Scottish burr: 'We could see the bombs coming.'[24]

Then according to Werth, whose ship was in the very next column, to starboard of *Empire Lawrence*, there was 'a flash', and 'an explosion' coming from *Empire Lawrence* followed by an awesome sight: 'Like a vomiting volcano, a huge pillar of fire, smoke and wreckage shot two hundred feet into the air' before it 'slowly, terribly slowly . . . went down to the sea.'[25]

Even though they were not on the bombed ship, the explosion knocked Ogden and his second-in-command off their feet. 'The next thing I remember is that Geoff and I were rolling about on our backs on the deck of the anti-submarine bridge,' Ogden recalled. 'We were covered with falling wreckage and enveloped in suffocating brown smoke. I thought we had been hit.' But as he soon found out, '*Lady M* was untouched, although we were lying with our engines stopped the length of a cricket pitch away.'[26]

The same could not of course be said of *Empire Lawrence*. However in his account, Grenfell has highlighted the strange fact that although he was at its epicentre, he did not even hear the explosion. 'All I could remember was flying through the air,' Grenfell recalled later. 'Flying through the air with me . . . [were] huge shapes, chunks of metal . . . , and there was one that looked like the funnel of the ship . . .

'The next I knew I was in the water, and it was freezing . . . I went down. And, I heard about it later, the ship just exploded and went down with a great gush, and I was dragged down with it . . . I was in a tangle of ropes and everything . . . I was holding my breath. It was . . . dark green . . . And then I shot . . . to the surface . . .

'When this was discussed with people who'd saved us, they reckoned what had happened was that when the ship went down, her boilers burst when she was deeper in the water, and it was this rush of water that shot a lot of us to the surface . . . I was looking up and I could see the sea becoming clearer until it became white, as white as the sky, and then I came through.

'And then a dreadful thing happened. I'd reached the surface. My prayers had been answered, . . . [but] I started going down again . . . It was my right arm. It was going down . . . And then I kicked with my feet, and I came to the surface again, and I pulled my arm up, and I found that there was a hand hanging onto the arm of . . . [my] navy blue pullover. This was a body. He was dead. There was no doubt about that. His head was split right down the middle. I could see I could do nothing for him. I just undid his arm and pushed him off . . . Then I started swimming.'[27]

While he swam, those in the convoy who had seen the terrible eruption were also left to count the cost. It took some time for the smoke to waft away. Werth has described what he saw when it did: 'The little white . . . [ship, *Lady Madeleine*] was still there, . . . perhaps looking for improbable survivors. [But] the *Empire Lawrence* was gone. The surface of the water was littered with wreckage, planks, pieces of wood. And perhaps five seconds later, the black triangle of the bows, detached from the rest of the ship, came to the surface for a second, and sank forever . . .'[28]

One suspects that all lookers-on would have assumed that few, if any, could have lived through such a violent explosion. However, not only did Eddie Grenfell get picked up, but eventually at least 30 of the 68 men who had been in *Empire Lawrence* found a safe haven in the corvette *Hyderabad*, including some who were originally picked up by *Lady Madeleine*'s boats.[29] Lieutenant Ogden stated in his account of the incident that the crew in his ship were responsible for saving the lives of 16 men.[30]

Some of the most severely wounded in *Lady Madeleine* were passed over to the destroyer *Martin* so that they could be treated by her surgeon Ralph Ransome Wallis, who by this time had arrived back on the ship with the wounded from *Starii Bolshevik*. He has written movingly not only about the terrible injuries some of these men had sustained – they included a teenager who was paralysed from the waist down, a man whose broken leg had 'a series of grotesque angles in it', as well as two men with life threatening head injuries – but also about the psychological trauma they endured.

Many of them were terrified by the loud banging noises they heard below deck every time there was a nearby explosion in the water, but this applied in particular to the boy with the broken back, who would scream and shout whenever he was scared. 'I had the distasteful job of having to speak roughly to this boy to try to make him control himself,' Ransome Wallis confessed when all the fighting was over. The boy, he said, 'stared back at me in dumb misery, and I felt a brute as I climbed the ladder onto the upper deck, knowing that he could never do that any more.'[31]

There must have been a lot of rough speaking to the boy with the broken back if he screamed after every air raid. That afternoon, raid followed raid with alarming regularity, and one merchant ship after another fell prey to the debilitating results of what were dismissively referred to as 'near misses'. When at around 4.30 p.m. the American ship *City of Joliet*, in convoy position 62 (6th column from left of convoy, row 2), was the victim of a near miss starboard of her foremast, the ship was jolted so violently that most of the crew were knocked off their feet, and the No. 1 hold began to fill up with sea water. It was sixteen feet deep before pumping out stopped the level rising any further (see 8 in Map 12, and Note 32 for approximate location).[32]

Empire Baffin was also damaged by a very near miss. 'Like a great tidal wave, the pillar of water [that rose up] . . . swept over the ship,' Werth reported. 'The crockery came down with a crash in the pantry, and a flood of water came rushing from the deck into the smoke room' where the passengers were assembled. 'Several of us made for the lifeboats,' Werth admitted, 'wading ankle deep in water along the lower deck.'

They only stood down when they were confronted by the ship's captain, who shouted at them that it was all right, a phrase that was echoed reassuringly by *Empire Baffin*'s little engineer. For once the engineer, who was usually taciturn, was moved to engage voluntarily with the passengers. 'The engines are working. That's the main thing,' he said. 'In the engine room, they got a bit of a shock, but they are all right now. The firemen are fine . . . Only one of them refused to go down.'

However the smashed lifeboat that was dangling from a rope on the starboard side of *Empire Baffin*'s lower deck bore witness to the power of the explosion. Another near miss to starboard shortly afterwards emphasized once again that survival was now a lottery. 'We might as well have tried to sail through the Kiel Canal,' one passenger remarked lugubriously to Werth, while another opined: 'Dunkirk wasn't a patch on this!'[33]

Nevertheless, if the balance sheet of sinkings and attacks had remained as it was by the end of the raid terminating shortly after 4.30 p.m., no-one responsible for the convoy's security could have had any grounds for complaint. Three merchant ships sunk, and four damaged, plus a damaged destroyer was a relatively favourable result given that the Germans, whose KG 26 and KG 30 on 27 May deployed from their aerodromes in Norway's Banak and Bardufoss no less than 101 Ju 88s and seven Heinkel He 111s, had been bombing the convoy for the previous four hours almost without respite.[34]

For a while the Germans believed they had knocked out more ships than they had. However the truth, once it was known, would certainly give the Luftwaffe's commanders an additional reason to question whether their aircraft were up to what was being demanded of them.

Not that this stopped Billie, the steward in *Empire Baffin,* from railing against the disappearance of the cruisers, leaving PQ16's merchant ships to take the flak, just when things were hotting up.[35] Little did he know that the cruisers' disappearance was a masterstroke. Although the German surface fleet was put on standby during 27 May, time and again Admiral Schmundt (Admiral Nordmeer) noted in his war diary that he could not even think of deploying it against the convoy while he did not know where the cruisers, and the Home Fleet's aircraft carriers, were located.[36]

The complainers were on surer ground when they bewailed the lack of ammunition. By late afternoon, all the ships were having to ration their fire as stocks of shells and bullets plummeted. That, combined with the hole in the convoy's defences on the port side caused by *Garland* being neutered, was rightly or wrongly blamed for what happened during the final series of attacks that commenced at around 7.25 p.m. that evening (see 9 in Map 12, and Note 37 for the location where the raid culminating in hits on two merchant ships commenced).[37]

Once again *Empire Baffin* was in the thick of it. At around 7.45 p.m., when the convoy was around 60 miles east-south-east of Bear Island, Werth caught sight of a torpedo that had been unleashed by one of the He 111 torpedo bombers on the port side of the convoy 'darting up and down the waves'. 'I felt our ship suddenly give a sharp turn,' he wrote. It was just enough to ensure the missile missed *Empire Baffin*'s stern.[38] Thomas Chilvers, an International Brigade veteran, who happened to be manning *Empire Baffin*'s wheel at the crucial moment, described the moment in his diary thus: 'Someone shouted out, "Subs on the port bow!" but which turned out to be torpedoes dropped by planes. The Third Mate saw them coming and gave "Hard a starboard!" But the old man (the captain) in the starboard wing of the bridge gave "Hard a port!" . . . I ignored him, and swung in behind the *Lowther Castle* (in convoy position 31, the British ship to starboard of *Empire Baffin*) which got the torpedo.'[39]

Apart from the six blasts on the siren of the destroyer on the port bow of the convoy, the only warning given to *Lowther Castle*'s Captain Hugh Williams and his Chief Officer John Lomas, who had been standing watch on their bridge, was the sight of the torpedoes bearing down on them 25 seconds before they hit the ship. The two torpedoes penetrated the port side of the hull beside No. 1 and 2 holds.

'There was a tremendous amount of water thrown up when the torpedoes struck,' Lomas reported later. 'The explosions were not very loud, and sounded like dull thuds . . . The ship swung round to port, and on trying the steering gear, I found . . . it useless . . . The ship immediately started to settle by the head, so the Captain gave the order to abandon ship. By now No. 2 hold was on fire and blazing furiously.

'After seeing the *Empire Lawrence* blow up, I think the crew were shaken and keen to get away from the ship in case she blew up,' Lomas stated, adding, 'I went to my [life]boat [on the port side of the ship] but found that some of the firemen had panicked, and had let go the falls, allowing the boat to fall into the slings and become jammed on the Fish Plate.' It only reached the water after he pushed it away from the side of the ship so that its descent could be completed.

There was also a problem with the smaller boat on the starboard side of the ship occupied by the captain. Lomas later discovered that it was dropped into the water so quickly that all of its occupants were thrown into the sea. Although the other five men were saved, the captain, for the moment at least, was nowhere to be found.

It was almost midnight before *Honeysuckle*'s crew finally picked up the men from *Lowther Castle*'s boats.[40] The corvette's boat then set off under the command of her Sub-Lieutenant Roy Dykes to check one last time whether there was any trace of the captain on the starboard side of *Lowther Castle*. 'We proceeded to that side of the vessel,' he reported, 'and found the captain bent over the thwart of his lifeboat hanging on to the falls with his hands. But he was so frightened he would not listen to us. We tried to get him to swim, a matter of a few yards, . . . but he wouldn't do it. In the end we . . . had to abandon the attempt . . . on the approach of three Ju 88s which were circling.'[41] And so the captain was left to his fate.

There were comparable disasters in the course of the abandonment of SS *Empire Purcell* (which had been in convoy position 44), another British ship that was bombed during the evening series of raids, although her nemesis, as was the case for all ships hit that day apart from *Lowther Castle*, was a Ju 88. Repeating what had occurred in the aftermath of the *Lowther Castle* torpedoing, her No. 2 hold, which contained explosives as well as lorries and oil, caught fire after being hit by two bombs, and in addition her engine room was flooding, the result of a near miss beside No. 3 hold. This prompted the chief engineer to stop the engines. But it was once again the fear of an *Empire Lawrence*-style explosion that persuaded the captain R. Stephenson that the ship must be abandoned. That may also have been behind the disastrous lowering of the starboard after lifeboat. Whatever the cause, the front of the boat descended faster than its rear, and all the occupants ended up in the sea, six of them losing their lives.

The ship's port jolly boat reached the water all right in spite of having been previously damaged by the bombing, but it capsized after bumping into a passing raft, trapping its five occupants underneath. They were only saved after an able seaman dived under the boat and pulled them out one by one.[42] The report filed for *Hyderabad* states that as the corvette approached *Empire Purcell*, 'huge flames and bright yellow smoke blazed from forward of the bridge, and soon the whole bridge structure was on fire.' That notwithstanding, the corvette's Lieutenant Stuart Hickman reported that when he came across the men clinging to the bottom of the upturned boat, they 'were all lustily singing "Rule Britannia"'.[43]

Hyderabad's crew eventually picked up 26 survivors, and the crew in *Honeysuckle* rescued a few more after leaving *Lowther Castle*.[44] According to *Hyderabad*'s report, when she left the rescue area at around 9 p.m.:

'*Empire Purcell* was blazing furiously with flames leaping to a height well above the masts, and there was obviously no possible chance of saving the ship, loaded as she was entirely with inflammable and explosive cargo.'[45]

The situation was made even more bleak by the fact that even some of the other ships that were still afloat appeared to be on their last legs. The bombing at around 4.30 p.m. had left the commodore's ship SS *Ocean Voice*, in convoy position 51 (5th column from convoy's left; 1st, i.e. front, ship), afloat but on fire, with a gaping 20 foot by 10 foot hole beside her No. 1 hold, just two feet above the water line.[46] Although she had not sunk by 9.30 p.m. when the last German bombers disappeared, *Ashanti*'s Commander Onslow wrote that he 'had little hopes of her survival'. The same was true of *City of Joliet* which, after being bombed during the same raid as *Ocean Voice*, was settling by the bows. 'There seemed little prospect of the weather deteriorating to the extent necessary if the convoy was to become invisible from the air,' Onslow stated.

It was British understatement at its best therefore when, writing about the situation at the end of what must be counted as the most traumatic day of the Arctic convoys so far, Commander Onslow stated: 'With another three days to go and 20% of the convoy already lost, I felt far from optimistic.'[47]

Werth's concluding comments about that day were perhaps more indicative about what those participating on the Allies' side were feeling. Referring to the torpedoing and bombing of *Lowther Castle* and *Empire Purcell*, he wrote: 'We realized that this attack had perhaps been the deadliest of all. Far away two of our ships were blazing, and some small vessel was picking up the survivors . . . For a long time we could watch the two bonfires burning far away on the grey sea. I think everybody felt that this was about as much as any human being could stand in one day.'[48]

Empire Purcell eventually blew up at around 12.30 a.m. on 28 May.[49] There appears to be no British account in the public domain of how *Lowther Castle* ended her days.

Early the next morning (28 May) *City of Joliet* signalled that she was filling up with water, so Commander Onslow ordered a trawler to take off her crew. The merchant ship was to be left in a sinking condition (see 10 in Map 12 for approximate location).

But just when the Luftwaffe appeared to have the convoy on its knees, the Germans pulled back. On 29 May the U-boats were called off, and there were no more committed attacks by aircraft until the night of 29–30 May, by which time reinforcements had arrived in the form of the three Soviet destroyers *Grozni*, *Sokrushitelni* and *Kuibishev*, their anti-aircraft firepower more than compensating for the loss of *Garland*, which had been sent on ahead to the Kola Inlet so that her wounded could be taken to hospital.[50]

There were more near misses during this raid, but no more ships were damaged or sunk. PQ16's main branch reached Murmansk shortly before 7 p.m. on 30 May, whereas the smaller branch of the convoy, after being helped to cut through the ice by a Soviet icebreaker, and escorted part of the way by British minesweepers, made it to Archangel during the night of 1–2 June.[51]

16

Safe as Houses

Main Action: 27 June 1942
Sailing of convoy PQ17, PQ17 part 1

(See Map 13, and PQ17's formation diagram)[1]

The arrival in northern Russia of no less than 28 of the 35 merchant ships that had started out with PQ16 prompted the following backhanded compliment from the Commander-in-Chief of the Home Fleet Admiral Sir Jack Tovey on 19 June 1942: In spite of the convoy having been under 'air bombardment for six days' with 'virtually no fighter protection . . .' four-fifths of the merchant ships reached their destination. 'This success was beyond expectation.'[2]

He realized that the Arctic convoys were far from secure whatever German forces were deployed against them. But what worried him most in connection with PQ17, which was to be the next east-going Arctic convoy after the escorts temporarily let go by Tovey at the beginning of June 1942 for Operations Harpoon and Vigorous – to escort the latest supply convoys to Malta – had returned to the Home Fleet, was the German Fleet. If the Germans deployed *Tirpitz* and other surface ships to the east of where the Home Fleet could 'safely' operate, it could all get very messy. When debating what could be done about this with Admiral Sir Dudley Pound, the First Sea Lord, Tovey suggested PQ17 should sail back the way it had come once it reached the danger area, in the hope that this would tempt the *Tirpitz* group to follow, thereby enabling Tovey to spring a trap.[3]

That did not appeal to Pound, who stated that if *Tirpitz* did come out, he always had the option of ordering the convoy to scatter. At which point Tovey claims he uttered the prophetic words for which he will always be remembered, given the way PQ17 turned out: 'If you do that, it will be pure bloody murder!'[4]

The safe arrival of the aid in most of PQ16's ships also led to the Germans questioning their approach concerning the next Arctic convoy. Following the discovery that the commanders of the U-boats and Luftwaffe units had initially overestimated the number of ships sunk, and that the convoy had not been decimated after all, there was a growing realization that something new should be tried next time. The Luftwaffe's commanders had to face up to the finding that their tactics were not going to yield the knockout blow they had anticipated. Although unlike the better known single-engined and relatively small Ju 87 Stuka dive bomber aircraft (measuring around 11 metres long with a wing span of around 13 metres) which terrorized everyone they targeted with the noise made by their sirens, the larger twin-engined Ju 88A-4 bombers (around 14 metres long with a wing span of around 20 metres) deployed against PQ16 had the fuel capacity and range to enable them to reach convoys near the ice edge (their range that varied depending on what they carried was typically around 1,500 miles), their 4 man crews were evidently incapable of reliably hitting moving ships with their bombs.

This underlined the need, already realized by some, for a change. When planning attacks on later convoys, the desirability of increasing the number of torpedo bombers which would also be large enough to have the fuel carrying capacity to reach the convoys would be factored in. It was set against this determination that it was decided that when the Luftwaffe attacked the convoys after PQ16, it should employ a much higher proportion of the large twin-engined torpedo-carrying Heinkel He 111 H 6s – on account of their glazed 'greenhouse' noses, the most easily recognized German combat aircraft employed in the Arctic, as well as Ju 88A-4s that had been adapted so that they could also carry torpedos.

'However because these new tactics were by their definition untested, the way was opened for Grossadmiral Raeder to propose an alternative solution which at least offered the possibility of improving on the Luftwaffe's relatively lacklustre performance against PQ16. On 15 June 1942 he persuaded Hitler to allow Germany's capital ships to be used against PQ17. The plan, codenamed Rösselsprung (Knight's Move), was to feature an attack on the next Arctic convoy by two battle groups, one of which would be led by the 54-year-old Flottenchef und Befehlshaber der Schlachtschiffe (Fleet and Battleship Commander) Admiral Otto Schniewind who would fly his flag in *Tirpitz*. It was agreed, however, that the plan could only go ahead if Hitler's consent was obtained once the prevailing circumstances were known. No such consent was to be forthcoming unless the enemy's aircraft carriers, whose planes might reach the German surface ships during the operation, were put out of action. The operation would also not go ahead if there was a chance that superior enemy forces might intervene.[5]

Agreeing to these rules of engagement enabled Raeder to insist that sufficient reconnaissance by the Luftwaffe should be laid on, something its leaders had been reluctant to accommodate prior to Hitler's conditions being imposed.[6]

For a few days there was no direct way for British admirals or politicians to find out what Raeder and Hitler had agreed. But three days after Hitler's approval of the Rösselsprung operation, Henry Denham, the British naval attaché in Stockholm, Sweden sent a message to London warning that the Germans intended to use *Tirpitz* along with other warships to attack 'the next convoy'. Denham had graded the intelligence he was passing on 'A3', which reflected his belief that his source could not be more reliable, hence the 'A', and the intelligence itself was probably true, the latter being indicated by the '3'.[7] Only certain intelligence, such as much of what was seen in Enigma decrypts, was rated 'A1'. Denham's informant was Colonel Carl Björnstierna, who as head of the foreign section of Swedish intelligence, had access to the summaries of encrypted messages that passed by telex between the German naval commands in Norway and Berlin. The Swedes had secretly tapped the landlines used by the Germans for this purpose which passed through Oslo, and had broken the code being used.[8]

Denham's message was timely, coming as it did just one day after another scheme proposed by Tovey, aimed at luring *Tirpitz* into the arms of the Home Fleet, had been activated. It had been developed in the following circumstances. A German agent had been taken to Iceland in a U-boat. However on landing, the agent had handed himself in to the authorities without informing his German handlers. This had given Tovey the opportunity to ask British intelligence personnel to send messages that would appear to the German recipients to have been transmitted by the agent, who was referred to by the British as 'Cobweb'. One of these messages was sent on 17 June 1942. It stated: 'Friend from Reykjavik says that recently many merchant ships have entered Hvalfjord. Believe convoy leaving soon . . .'

The message was part of the so-called 'Plan Tarantula', a scheme that had been worked out with input from the Naval Intelligence Division's Commander Ewen Montagu, who a year later would mastermind Operation Mincemeat, the plan to plant misleading documents on a corpse with a view to deceiving the Germans about the Allies' intentions prior to the invasion of Sicily. Tovey hoped that the 17 June message, when combined with other messages from Cobweb, would persuade the Germans to use *Tirpitz* against a 'dummy' convoy (consisting of ships with no aid for Russia on board) that was to be sent out towards Norway during the passage of PQ17. If all went well, the dummy convoy would reverse its course before reaching Norway, and *Tirpitz* would then chase it until within range of Tovey's guns with fatal consequences for the German battleship.[9]

Provided Cobweb's message remained secret except for those in the know, the PQ17 merchant vessel crews would never realize it had been sent. If on the other hand it was ever disclosed, the merchant seamen, whose lives could have been jeopardized by the revelation in it, might with some justification have protested that the attempt to ensnare the German battleship was being prioritized over their safety, and that they were being used as bait.

The fact that the Germans would not be content with finding out about PQ17 by conventional means would not have surprised at least one of the merchant seamen whose ships were anchored in Hvalfjord during the latter half of June 1942, while awaiting the convoy's departure. Because Vladimir Nikolaevich Izotov, captain of the Soviet tanker *Azerbaijan*, was a Soviet citizen, he was used to the mindset which assumed that there were spies and enemies of the state everywhere. He suspected that the Germans would try to obtain intelligence from sympathizers and agents in Iceland. Cobweb's testimony shows that he was not far wrong.

Because of his suspicions, Izotov was upset by the lax security relating to PQ17. After he and his crew had courageously nursed their ship all the way to Archangel notwithstanding the attacks on PQ17, he would write a devastating critique of the inept attempts that were made by the Soviet Union's British allies to ensure the convoy's sailing remained under wraps. 'The [merchant] ships' crews were for the most part a rabble,' he reported. 'Their behaviour when ashore, and their drunkenness when given the opportunity to visit the Icelandic taverns, gave the Germans every chance of finding out about the convoy's ships.

'Already on June 23rd, three shots of vodka were loosening the tongues of staff from the war control department, and technical workers were being told unofficially and "secretly" that our convoy would sail on Saturday 27th June.

'On June 25th, the completely drunk captain of the port of Hvalfjord visited all the ships of the convoy, and was blabbering not only about its departure but also about its escort. There is a good chance there are spies even in the convoy's ships.

'On June 26th, in the evening, an announcement was made very loudly through a loud speaker that the convoy conferences would take place on June 27th in the morning, when this information should have been passed discreetly to each captain, and not shouted across the whole harbour using a megaphone!'[10]

It is hard to gauge from available sources to what extent Izotov's criticism was justified. In the report which the Hollywood actor Douglas Fairbanks Junior wrote about his time in USS *Wichita*, the American cruiser where Fairbanks was to be stationed while she escorted the convoy, he stated that: 'The necessity for maintaining the utmost secrecy regarding our forthcoming operation was forcibly impressed upon me.' However, he admitted the comings and goings of various British and American ship captains before the sailing, combined with the sight of so many laden merchant ships in the fjord, meant that 'the whole ship's company smells something in the wind'.[11]

He also confessed that while previously attached to the American battleship *Washington,* which was based in Scapa Flow with the rest of the Home Fleet, he had foolishly tried when tipsy to impress a pretty girl by showing her around Admiral Robert Giffen's quarters, which was just the kind of behaviour that might have spelled trouble if there really were spies about.[12]

What is known is that on the morning of 27 June 1942, a boat circulated around Hvalfjord picking up the PQ17 merchant ship captains and their radio operators. They were dropped off near the huts where the convoy conferences were to take place. There was to be one conference for the captains and a separate one for the radio officers.

This is Izotov's recollection of what was said at the captains' conference, which was held in a large new canteen in the partly built camp beside the fjord: 'The captain of the convoy explained the order in which the vessels would leave the harbour, the convoy formation and the important signals. The commander of the escorts spoke about the strong protection forces that would accompany the convoy. It was to be the strongest group of warships ever laid on for one of these convoys ... Surveillance of the sea around the convoy was to be carried out 14 hours a day by the hydroplanes flown off the cruisers. It was possible that those in the convoy might never see the cruisers. But they would always be within 15 to 20 miles of the convoy ... At the conference it was [also] announced that the convoy had nothing to fear, that we would arrive successfully and on the way we would sink a couple of (German) vessels if they came anywhere near the convoy.'[13]

At around 4 p.m. on 27 June 1942, the 35 merchant ships with aid for the Soviet Union on board, that were to form the nucleus of PQ17, raised their anchors and moved towards the entrance of Hvalfjord in single file.[14] The ships accompanying them included two British oilers, one of which would have to replenish the escorts' tanks en route to Russia before departing in order to refuel the escorts with the westbound convoy QP13. The number of PQ17's civilian ships that were supposed to sail through to Russia would eventually be swelled to 39 if one included the three rescue ships, two of which would join the convoy when the larger ships forming part of the through escort met up with the convoy.[15] Of the 35 merchant ships mentioned above, no less than 21 were American, 9 were British, 2 sailed under the Panamanian flag, 2 were Soviet, and 1 was Dutch. Their local escort during the first stage of the journey before they met up with the ocean escort was as usual dominated by some minesweepers and trawlers.

Izotov's account confirms that his ship passed through the gap in the nets that constituted the fjord's boom at 5.25 p.m. Douglas Fairbanks, watching from *Wichita,* memorably commented that 'as they passed us (in the fjord), they looked like so many dirty ducks waddling out to sea'.[16]

Two of the American merchant ships were forced to drop out after being damaged by the ice the convoy encountered in the fog early on, and the British oiler whose crew had been expecting to take her to Russia was also damaged, leading to the decision that she should link up with the westbound convoy, leaving the other oiler with the task of going all the way.[17]

The departure of two of the merchant ships brought with it some benefit: it served to improve the convoy's escort to merchant ship ratio, although it could not be said that even the complete complement of civilian ships originally scheduled to go through to Russia was inadequately provided for when it came to protection. By the time the rendezvous with the additional escorts would be kept on 30 June, the convoy's close-up through escort would include six destroyers, four corvettes, three minesweepers, four armed trawlers, two anti-aircraft ships and two submarines, an impressive 21 vessels, with additional support from the three previously mentioned rescue ships and a CAM ship (one of the 35 merchant ships mentioned above).[18]

Highlights of the last-minute preparations in the auxiliary anti-aircraft ship HMS *Pozarica* before sailing have been preserved for posterity because they were recorded by the embedded 35-year-old Fleet Street journalist Godfrey Winn, a popular columnist at the *Sunday Express* newspaper.

According to Winn, shortly before *Pozarica* weighed anchor during the afternoon of 29 June 1942 in Seidisfjord, the assembly point on the eastern coast of Iceland being used by some of PQ17's escorts, prior to their joining the convoy to the north-east of Iceland, her men were rallied by a stirring speech made by her commander, the 55-year-old Acting Captain Edward Lawford. His words contained none of the reassuring flannel that had been in the speeches delivered to the merchant ship captains at the conference two days earlier. Although he started off by likewise mentioning all those cruisers and battleships backing them up, the list was followed by a pregnant 'but' spoken so emphatically that everyone present realized that he was about to disclose the unvarnished truth. It was followed by a string of the obstacles they would have to overcome. They included 'twenty-four hours' daylight', 'no hope of cover of darkness', 'floating pack ice . . . which can be as great a headache as the subs', and last but not least 'attacks all the time', making their passage 'even more difficult' than what the previous convoy had endured. 'You don't need me to tell you that our allies in Russia are in desperate need,' he told them. 'This convoy will be . . . the largest yet to sail for North Russia . . . And it's *got* to get through,' he concluded, the emphasis on the word 'got' brooking no argument.[19]

Not long after the captain's speech, which ended with him formally saluting the listening men, *Pozarica*'s crew witnessed what some might have regarded as an even more memorable ceremony. Winn's chronicle has described how it was played out as the convoy's ocean escort, including *Pozarica*, sailed past the cruiser HMS *London*, which flew Rear Admiral Louis Hamilton's flag. The chronicle continues: 'As we gathered speed, there came the sound of the bugler on our bridge saluting the senior ships, and across the intervening water, the answering acknowledgement, while on both decks, theirs and ours, every man from the Admiral downwards [was] standing to attention . . . all united in that moment . . . [as we prepared ourselves] for whatever lay ahead.'[20]

Afterwards *Pozarica*'s captain, who Winn noticed all of a sudden looked ten years younger now that they were at sea, turned to him and said, metaphorically licking his lips: 'No more parties. *The* Party! Now you should have something really to write about.'[21]

The first incident Winn wrote up was the meeting with the convoy north-east of Iceland that took place the next day (30 June) at around noon.[22] As those on *Pozarica*'s top deck watched the merchant ships steam through the mist in their nine-column formation, Lawford ordered music to be played over the ship's loudspeakers to 'cheer them' up. For a few precious minutes the men on the deck of the nearest merchant ship, the American SS *Hoosier,* danced and threw their hats in the air to the tune of 'Anchors Away'. Then as the music came to an end, the jollity subsided, and all were on a war footing again.[23]

This was followed by a period of peace and quiet that was only broken by the sound of the ships at the front of each column from time to time blowing off steam to reveal their exact position to those following them. The sound reminded Winn of the lowing cattle in the Romney marshes. But even as he was beginning to wonder whether they might after all make it through another day or two without being molested, their luck was already running out.

During the afternoon of 30 June, QP13, the westbound convoy, was spotted by a German aircraft's crew north-east of North Cape. That told the German admirals that PQ17 must be south of Jan Mayen Island if what had happened during PQ16 was anything to go by, when the east and westbound convoys had passed each other between that island and Bear Island.[24] It also strengthened their belief that the 10 U-boats referred to by the Germans as Gruppe Eisteufel (Ice Devil), whose commanders had been ordered to line up to the south-east of Jan Mayen Island, were in the right area. If this was correct, all they had to do was to carry on patrolling, and with a bit of luck, PQ17 would 'bump into' one of them.[25]

As it turned out, the first threat to the PQ17 ships' sedate north-easterly progress did not emerge from under the water. The calm in *Pozarica* was interrupted the next day (1 July) at around 2.30 p.m., as the convoy passed to the east of Jan Mayen Island, when a call from the ship's radar officer told those on the bridge an aircraft was approaching (see 1 in Map 13, and Note 26 for location).[26] Through the fog they saw on the horizon a vision that Winn said 'sent a shiver down our spines': the distinctive silhouette of a Blohm & Voss 138 plane 'with her clumsy bat-like wings and her nose . . . tipped slightly towards the water as though she was smelling out her prey'.[27] Its presence dampened the spirits of everyone in the convoy. Now they had been spotted, it was surely only a matter of time before they would have to face up to the same level of bombing as what had been dropped on PQ16, not to mention probing attacks by those U-boats whose commanders had not already been tipped off concerning where to find PQ17. The crew in a PQ17 escort had previously sighted a U-boat that morning.[28]

Over the next 36 hours more bad news trickled in. A message from the Senior British Naval Officer in north Russia announced that Murmansk, PQ17's original destination, was in flames following another vicious bombing raid, and the convoy was being diverted to Archangel.[29] Then to cap it all, the merchant ships were ordered to fly their 'kites' (barrage balloons) which told them the first air attack was imminent. It was no wonder perhaps that in a rare display of emotion, during one of their meals together in Lawford's cabin, *Pozarica*'s normally reticent captain surprised Winn by all of a sudden dropping his guard and sounding off against the politicians whose incompetence had placed them in this vulnerable position.[30]

But when the first air raid took place north-east of Jan Mayen Island (see 2 in Map 13 for the location) between 6 and 6.30 p.m. on 2 July, it was an anti-climax; General-Leutnant Ernst-August Roth, Commander of Fliegerführer Lofoten (Luftwaffe commander covering the Lofoten Islands region), had restricted the aircraft he was willing to commit at this juncture to just seven Heinkel 115 torpedo float planes from 1./Küstenfliegergruppe 406.[31] Their pilots had gamely taken off for the long haul to the convoy, but when they caught sight of their target, they were for the most part unwilling to risk life and limb by coming in close within the reach of all that flak put up by merchant ships and escorts alike.[32] For those in *Pozarica*, the only manifestation that the convoy was in immediate danger was the sight of a solitary torpedo which sped harmlessly past them.[33]

Afterwards the inexperienced *Pozarica* crew members, who had made it no secret that they were dreading not being able to rise to the occasion of their baptism of fire, were so bucked up by the apparent ease with which the convoy had warded off the attack that many of them, their anxiety now forgotten, queued up on deck to witness a remarkable sight through a long telescope: the crew of the one shot-down German aircraft, whose pilot Herbert Vater was commander of the squadron, climbing aboard another plane that briefly landed in the sea beside them before taking to the skies again.[34] The destroyer *Keppel*'s Commander Jack Broome, the officer in charge of the close escort, was quick to give credit to the Americans in their midst for this single scalp. He commented afterwards: 'Unless this aircraft died of fright, I think it should be credited to [the destroyer] *U.S.S. Rowan*, who was seen at this time putting up a fine display of A.A. fire while approaching the convoy [from the cruiser force] to fuel.'[35]

The barrage put up by the escorts suggested that sinking PQ17's ships was not going to be easy. However, Winn sensed that *Pozarica*'s Captain

Lawford did not share his crew's complacent satisfaction. Had Lawford perhaps seen something sinister in the German aircraft's unwillingness to press home their attack? When they were eating a meal in the privacy of Lawford's cabin the next day (3 July), Winn found out what was bothering *Pozarica*'s commander. Lawford told Winn that he had received a signal telling him and the commanders of the other escorts that *Tirpitz* had left Trondheim, and then as far as British intelligence was concerned, had as good as disappeared.[36]

Lawford's displeasure was only too evident. According to Winn, *Pozarica*'s captain now had 'furrows on his face' and looked 'tired and grim'. When Winn, in an attempt to put the latest news into perspective, suggested that this might not be disastrous given that the Home Fleet was hopefully 'more than a match' for the German warships, Lawford, Winn reported, 'did not answer for a moment. He was looking beyond me, reliving the experience of thirty years at sea', and when he eventually replied, it was to suggest that it might be better to send the convoy back to Iceland 'while there was still time'.[37]

'I was astonished,' Winn commented later. But that may have been because no-one had thought to tell him before sailing the restrictions the Admiralty had imposed on the cruisers and on Tovey.

As stressed at the merchant vessel captains' conference, Rear Admiral Hamilton's force, known as Cruiser Squadron 1 (CS1) was a powerful group of warships. It contained four heavy cruisers (two of them American with nine 8-inch guns, and two of them British with eight 8-inch guns – and with no less than 11 on board aircraft shared out between them), and three destroyers (two of them American and one British). And at the very moment when Winn was disabused by Captain Lawford, they both hoped CS1 was not far away from their position. They would later find out the warships were concealed in the fog from German eyes and were sailing around 40 miles to the north of the convoy's port bow.[38]

But what Winn did not appreciate was that notwithstanding all the promises at the captains' conference, the time during which CS1 and the Home Fleet could protect the convoy was fast running out. For a start, Hamilton was under strict instructions not to let himself be drawn into a direct confrontation with Germany's giant battleship.[39] Also there was no question of the cruisers supporting the convoy all the way to Russia.

Unless the Admiralty changed Hamilton's instructions, CS1 was only allowed to go east of Bear Island if the convoy was threatened by a German force that did not include *Tirpitz*, and even in that case, it was not supposed to pass east of 25° East (the longitude line passing through Hope Island and just to the west of Norway's North Cape – see Map 13).[40]

Admittedly thanks to the reinforcement from America, the Home Fleet firepower deployed to cover PQ17 from afar was massive. Spearheaded by two battleships (*Duke of York* in which Tovey flew his flag and the American USS *Washington* whose main armament consisted of nine 16 inch guns), and the aircraft carrier *Victorious*, and including no less than three cruisers and ten destroyers (two of which were American), it was a much more potent force than anything the Germans could field against the convoy. However it was as constrained as CS1. After the 'Cobweb operation' was called off on 1 July because the Germans on two occasions did not spot the dummy convoy, Tovey was prepared to move the Fleet so that if called upon, *Victorious'* aircraft could cover PQ17 until it was a short distance to the east of Bear Island.[41] But as *Pozarica*'s Lawford may have been thinking, that was all very well if the attack came while the convoy was west of or a short distance to the east of Bear Island. If *Tirpitz* attacked after the convoy passed a long way to the east of Bear Island, what then?

17

Mind the Gap

Main Action: 4 July 1942
Enigma blackout, PQ17 part 2

(See Maps 1 and 13, and PQ17's formation diagram)[1]

The Luftwaffe was to attack PQ17 several times on 4 July 1942. The first raid took place at around 4.50 a.m. As the convoy headed eastward, northeast of Bear Island, an He 115 torpedo plane all of a sudden appeared out of a cloud on the right side of the convoy and launched a torpedo which slammed into the starboard side, amidships, of the American freighter *Christopher Newport*, in convoy position 81 (8th column from convoy's left; 1st, i.e. front, row), killing the three men on watch in her engine room (see 3 in Map 13, and Note 2 for approximate location).[2]

Her master's decision that the vessel must be abandoned – along with the 13 tanks and 178 aircraft that formed part of her cargo – because both her boilers had blown up, her engine and fire rooms were flooded, and 'nothing could be done to manoeuvre the ship', was to be controversial.[3]

Vladimir Izotov, the captain of the Soviet tanker *Azerbaijan*, in position 64 (6th column from convoy's left, 4th row), would later complain he saw only 'superficial damage' to the ship's starboard side and to where the starboard lifeboats had been hanging as he sailed on past. He was it seems well placed to make an accurate assessment. *Christopher Newport* had by this time come to rest near his column.[4] 'There was no sign of any fire, or of the ship sinking,' he observed, adding: 'yet the crew nevertheless quickly got into [the remaining] lifeboats . . . No investigation of the abandoned vessel's condition was made by the commanders of the convoy, or of the escort ships . . . The crew were picked up by a rescue ship.' In spite of the ship remaining buoyant, no attempt was made to reboard her.[5]

The incident provoked an equally irate response aboard the British anti-aircraft ship *Pozarica*, although for a different reason. When Winn arrived on the ship's bridge after being summoned from his bed to record the result of the first successful enemy action, he heard the yeoman criticizing, with plenty of expletives added, the crew in a nearby American merchant ship who were lowering her flag. 'The yellow [f]uckers!' he shouted. 'They can't take it.' Winn noted that the yeoman's face 'was a mirror of disgust'. Winn's chronicle of the episode concluded: 'No one else made any comment. We were all too horrified.' He wondered disconsolately what were the chances of their convoy making it all the way to Russia if the ships' crews were 'surrendering because one of their number had been torpedoed'.

But then a shout went up telling Winn, and the others on *Pozarica*'s bridge, to 'Look!' And when they did, they saw a sight that was wonderful to behold. Far from the ship surrendering, 'a new Stars and Stripes was being run up the masthead'. And it was not only in the neighbouring ship. As Winn's eyes travelled beyond, up and down the other columns in the convoy, he could see that all the other American ships, 'were carrying out the same manoeuvre'. According to Winn, it was 'a single united movement of such co-ordinated precision' that they might have been performing a well-rehearsed parade ground-style 'ceremony' that had been conducted like this since time immemorial. Whatever its pedigree, it was certainly a defiant display of their strength of purpose, timed to have the greatest effect on the morale of all who saw it. Not only did it make it clear that none of the Americans in the convoy were going to hide their nationality even if the Luftwaffe was intending to target them specifically. It was also a paean to all things American, a fitting tribute given it was 4 July, America's Independence Day. [6]

Winn, and for that matter all the convoy's sailors, would surely have been similarly cheered up had they seen the equally flamboyant messages which later that morning passed between the officers on the bridges of the British and American cruisers. The cruisers were still over the horizon to the north, out of sight of the merchant ships' crews and the crews of their close escorts.

The exchange was kicked off by the message the 51-year-old Rear Admiral Hamilton sent out at around 8 a.m. to the men in the American cruisers wishing them 'the best of hunting . . . on the occasion of your great anniversary'. It was just the kind of warm-hearted, morale-boosting gesture one might have expected from a naval officer who came from a family of naval leaders, and an aristocratic one at that. His father was an admiral, as was one of his grandfathers; two of his great uncles were earls. This meant that a desire to chase after both foxes and enemy ships was in his blood. Captain Harry Hill, the 52-year-old commander of the American cruiser *Wichita,* replied that it was an honour to be part of an operation 'in furtherance of the ideals which July fourth has always represented to us', before adding tongue in cheek: 'Celebration on this holiday always requires large fireworks displays. I trust you will not disappoint us.' Then replying to another message from the captain of HMS *Norfolk,* the second British cruiser, Hill responded: 'I think it is only fitting that you should celebrate Mother's Day!', alluding perhaps to his and his fellow Americans' perception that Britain, the mother country, had provided the inspiration for the values they were celebrating.[7]

But the elevated spirits on board the PQ17 escorts did not line up with the mood of those ultimately in charge of the convoy. There was rising tension in the Admiralty's Operational Intelligence Centre (the OIC) in central London. It was situated in the basement of the Citadel, the bomb-proof blockhouse located behind the old Admiralty building which stands in the street that is confusingly called Whitehall. There was a good reason for the increased anxiety level in the OIC. Although the Admiralty's intelligence officers who worked there would sooner or later have access to some of the German naval commanders' most secret signals thanks to the Bletchley Park codebreakers' ability to read the German naval Enigma messages, there was a delay in getting decrypted messages to the OIC because of one of the temporary codebreaking blackouts which occurred every time the Enigma settings were changed.

The settings were changed at midday every 48 hours, and most of the new settings were then used for the next pair of days, although a small number of the new settings were altered again after the first 24 hours of the 48-hour cycle. Each time the settings were changed, no German messages encoded using them could be read until the codebreakers worked them out, enabling them to break into the Enigma code again.

Working out the new settings adopted at the beginning of each 48-hour cycle typically took between 30 and 48 hours after they were used for the first time whereupon the codebreakers could decipher most messages sent during the first 24 hours of the cycle. The codebreakers would subsequently have to work out the smaller change to the settings made at the beginning of the second of the paired days. That could take another hour or two. Only then could all the transmitted messages encoded during the whole 48-hour period covered by the cycle be penetrated.[8]

But this was just one of the problems impeding the Admiralty. There was another obstacle which was to prove to be harder to iron out, perhaps because it was the result of two sets of diverging human characteristics which, unlike the mathematical puzzle posed by the Enigma, could not be reconciled.

In July 1942, the OIC officer who was responsible for collecting and analysing all the information relating to Germany's surface ships was the 37-year-old Paymaster Commander Norman ('Ned') Denning. He was a clever man from one of those British families where several siblings have been blessed with a particular talent that has enabled each of them to reach the top of the tree in his chosen profession. Ned was the younger brother of the high-flying barrister Tom Denning, KC, who would one day become Lord Denning, the best known judge in Britain. Their older brother, Reginald Denning, was a brigadier in the British army, who would end up being promoted to the rank of Lieutenant-General.

After the war, Ned Denning would himself become Director of Naval Intelligence, matching his brothers' rises in their fields. But in 1942, he was still reliant on others, who were older and arguably not always wiser when it came to the question of whether they should give free rein to his facility to analyse intelligence. Even so, he had done well since he had decided to start work at the Admiralty. In spite of his relatively tender years, and the fact that he owed his responsible position to administrative prowess rather than to having served at sea, by 1942 he had been given powers that he would never have dreamed of exercising when, with him as its only officer, the OIC was first set up in 1937. By the time the officers at the Admiralty were faced with the problem of deciding whether PQ17 was about to be attacked by the German surface fleet, he was the go-to man when it came to receiving and interpreting the relevant intelligence relating to the German Navy, including anything relating to this subject produced by the codebreakers at Bletchley Park. He was also allowed, whether off his own bat or after discussion with Rear Admiral Jock Clayton, the head of the OIC (official title Deputy Director Intelligence Centre), to send what he had gleaned to the admirals at sea without supervision, something that was once the preserve of Rear Admiral John Godfrey, the Admiralty's Director of the Naval Intelligence Division.[9]

If Ned Denning had been reporting to someone with a similar background, it is just possible that his ability to predict German behaviour from scraps of intelligence, would have been respected. But the First Sea Lord, Admiral Sir Dudley Pound, Denning's ultimate boss, had strikingly different characteristics that had been moulded by the kind of events that Denning had never experienced.

For a start, Pound knew what it felt like to be pressurized into agreeing to a deployment of ships that he knew was unsafe, and then to see the ships being sunk. In December 1941, he had reluctantly yielded to Churchill's demand that *Prince of Wales,* a modern battleship, should be sent to patrol near Singapore even though she was not to be accompanied by an aircraft carrier because none were available. Within days of her arrival, both she and the battlecruiser *Repulse* had been sunk by land-based aircraft, the very outcome that Pound had feared might come to pass if capital ships were deployed without adequate air cover. Among the 800 plus sailors who died was Admiral Sir Tom Phillips, a man Pound referred to 'as one of my greatest friends'.[10] It was only natural that this disaster on Pound's watch should have made him much more risk averse than someone like Denning, who had never been directly responsible for men's lives, and had not yet at least made a decision where he could be blamed for hundreds of deaths.

Perhaps even more significant was their difference of opinion concerning delegation. Denning, who owed his own fast progress within the OIC to his superiors' willingness to delegate, was very much in favour of carrying on in this vein. Pound on the other hand was an autocrat, who preferred to make every important judgement call himself. Even if he had been fighting fit and alert enough to appreciate that a subordinate could be relied upon day to day, such a man was hardly likely to defer to another man's expertise in a crisis.

And no-one could say that in 1942 Pound was fighting fit. His insistence that he must cover every base in person had contributed to his becoming burnt out. His exhaustion was partly caused by the discomfort he experienced as a result of the deterioration of his right hip. This both made it difficult for him to walk without a stick, and made it hard for him to get to sleep.[11]

But his habit of regularly working late into the night in an effort not to be overwhelmed by his enormous workload was also a contributing factor. He became famous within the Admiralty for summoning his subordinates to late night meetings. These gatherings, often in the early hours of the morning, were referred to as 'The First Sea Lord's Midnight Follies'. Afterwards, he would take what others might have described as a relatively brief nap without going home. Admiralty staff arriving for work at dawn would often be greeted by the sight of Pound padding around in his dressing gown on the way to have a bath.[12]

No wonder then that he would sit through meetings during his long days with his eyes closed so that no-one around the table would know whether he was asleep or awake. Whichever was the case, his subsequent orders often led participants to believe that he had made his mind up as to what to do before the meeting started.[13] The brain tumour which eventually forced him to retire a year later, may have been another of the reasons for his failing powers of concentration.

The temperature in the OIC first began to soar during PQ17 thanks to a couple of German messages sent during the night of 2–3 July 1942 that could not be decoded at Bletchley Park. They had been transmitted after the German telegraphist had used a procedure which gave the signals the highest level of security that was available. Known as 'Offizier', it effectively meant the original German text had been encoded twice, once with the Enigma machine set up with the settings for all standard naval Enigma messages sent in the Arctic during the 24 hours leading up to midday on 3 July, and once using settings specified in a secret table. When the naval Enigma settings for the period up to midday on 3 July were worked out by Bletchley Park, it was possible for the codebreakers to read who these Offizier messages were to and from, and the number of characters in the message, but apart from revealing that the messages had been 'Offiziered', and that they had been sent by radio, nothing else was known about them.

However, these details were enough to yield some alarming intelligence. Both of the 'decrypts' for these messages, which were forwarded to the OIC at around 9.30 a.m. on 3 July, showed that the signals had originally been copied to Admiral Otto Schniewind, the Flottenchef und Befehlshaber der Schlachtschiffe who, as mentioned in Chapter 16, flew his flag in *Tirpitz*. The fact they were sent to Schniewind by radio rather than by teleprinter told the OIC that the German battleship was almost certainly at sea. This was the first inkling the British Admiralty had that *Tirpitz* had left her anchorage at Trondheim, Norway, possibly with a view to attacking PQ17. At 10.17 a.m. on 3 July an 'Ultra' containing this information was sent to Admirals Tovey and Hamilton even though they were also at sea.[14]

This deduction about *Tirpitz* was corroborated by observations and photographs taken during a reconnaissance flight later that afternoon, which cleared the way for reports containing this information to be sent out to the commanders of all the PQ17 escorts.[15] It appears to have been these reports which according to Godfrey Winn upset *Pozarica*'s Captain Lawford (see Chapter 16).

Unfortunately for the intelligence officers at the Admiralty, and the seamen in the ships within PQ17, the doors that had swung open to permit the British to pick up this vital piece of information from the Germans, at that point slammed shut. At midday on 3 July the Enigma settings were changed, with the result that all links between the German naval commanders and Bletchley Park were abruptly if temporarily severed.

From that moment, everyone involved with the convoy from Admiral Pound downwards was on tenterhooks. When nothing had been heard about *Tirpitz*'s whereabouts during the remainder of 3 July, and the whole morning of 4 July, Pound sent a message permitting Hamilton to take his cruisers east of 25° East (the line which Hamilton's cruiser force was not to cross without authorization), provided that Tovey did not issue a counter order.[16]

As it turned out, Tovey did object vehemently. Pound's signal was completely contrary to the agreement Tovey had struck with the First Sea Lord concerning the limitations on Hamilton, which were designed to prevent a repetition of the HMS *Edinburgh* disaster (see Chapters 10 and 16). And now because of Pound's interference, Tovey felt obliged to break radio silence even though that risked betraying his and the accompanying Home Fleet's position at sea to the Germans. His signal sent at 3.12 p.m. on 4 July instructed Hamilton not to proceed east of 25° East unless the Admiralty assured the CS1 commander that *Tirpitz* could not be met.[17]

Of course, with *Tirpitz* still being at large and off the Admiralty's 'radar', no such assurance could be forthcoming. Eventually Hamilton, pulled in two directions by his two competing masters, ended up obeying neither to the letter. His response sent at 6.09 p.m. on 4 July stated that he intended to delay his turn, taking him back to the west, until around 10 p.m. that night. It was sent at a time when he had already passed well to the east of the 25° East line that Tovey did not want him to cross.[18]

If Hamilton hoped by delaying his response to Tovey's order that *Tirpitz* would have been located before the time came for him to move away, he was to be disappointed. When Pound had terminated the first of his discussions that evening with Denning in the OIC, which he did shortly after seeing the message containing Hamilton's decision, the available intelligence on the German battleship's whereabouts was no different to what it had been the previous day (see Note 19 for discussion timing).[19] According to Denning, during this first meeting: 'Pound [had] sat down on a stool in front of the main plotting table . . . Bletchley had not yet broken into the new keys (that had been used since midday 3 July). Almost immediately Pound asked what would be the farthest on position of *Tirpitz,* assuming she had sailed direct from Trondheim to attack the convoy . . . Someone . . . plotted a rough course, and estimated that she could by then be within striking distance of the convoy. I interjected that it was unlikely in any event that she would have taken a direct course from Trondheim Fjord, as she would almost certainly have made as much use as she could of the Inner Leads and proceed via Vestfjord. I also considered that she would put into Narvik or Tromso to refuel her escorting destroyers before setting out on a sortie.

'Pound gazed at the plot for some time . . . I broke into his apparent reverie to inform him that more definite information was possible within three or four hours when Bletchley would most likely have broken into the Enigma keys for the previous twenty-four hours (the twenty-four hour period commencing at midday on 3 July). Pound then left.[20]

Denning recalled that Pound had not been gone long when a call came through on an OIC scrambler telephone. It was Harry Hinsley, Denning's main contact in Bletchley Park's Naval Section, who wanted to tell Denning that the long-awaited break into the Enigma was imminent. It was sooner than expected because the search for *Tirpitz* had been officially rated 'a flap' resulting in it being given priority at Bletchley Park.[21]

The following holding message was therefore sent to Hamilton at 6.58 p.m.: 'Further information may be available shortly. Remain with convoy pending further instructions.'[22]

Minutes before this message to Hamilton was encoded using a one-time pad and sent, a teleprinter in the OIC had jerked into life, and had begun to spit out a series of decrypts, each summarizing a German message that had been encoded on an Enigma machine after midday on 3 July.

They had certainly been worth waiting for. One of the first that arrived on Denning's desk was the message originated by Admiral Schniewind and transmitted to Vizeadmiral Oskar Kummetz, the Befehlshaber der Kreuzer (the Admiral Commanding Cruisers) at 7.40 a.m. that morning (4 July). The decrypt of the text sent over to Denning at 6.59 p.m. on 4 July stated: 'Immediate. Arriving Alta 0900. You are to allot anchorages *Tirpitz* outer Vagfjord (as received). Newly arriving destroyers and torpedo boats to complete with fuel at once.'[23]

The receipt of this message answered a lot of questions. It did not just disclose where *Tirpitz* had stopped off after moving to the north. Combined with previous intelligence which indicated that the pocket battleship *Admiral Scheer* had left her base in Bogenbucht, near Narvik, it confirmed that the pocket battleship with Vizeadmiral Kummetz on board had also moved to Altenfjord (Altafjord). Unbeknown to the British at this time, *Lützow*, Kummetz's original flagship, had been left behind because she had been damaged on the way. But it begged the question: what had happened after *Tirpitz* and the destroyers had joined *Admiral Scheer* in Altenfjord at 9 a.m.?

Denning suspected another decrypt which had emerged from the teleprinter minutes earlier might provide the answer to the riddle. It referred

1. Above: President Roosevelt with Winston Churchill at one of the series of meetings off the coast of Newfoundland in August 1941 where it was agreed the West would send arms to Russia (see Chapter 2).

2. Right: Soviet Ambassador Ivan Maisky thanks British workers at a tank factory on 22 September 1941, during the 'Tanks for Russia' week referred to in Chapter 2.

3. Left: Averell Harriman (seated) and Lord Beaverbrook (leaning on the table) with Molotov between them at the 2 October 1941 signing of the Moscow Protocol (see Chapter 2). Harriman is also visible *2nd from right* in photo 1.

TANKS AND AIRCRAFT SENT TO THE SOVIET UNION

4. Left: A British Matilda tank bound for Russia is hoisted into the air so it can be loaded onto a merchant ship at Liverpool Docks on 17 October 1941.

5. Below left and 6. below: Publicity shots circulated to the British press showing tanks and crates containing other aid in Murmansk's port shortly after their arrival in North Russia.

7. Above: A British Hurricane fighter aircraft sent to Russia, in the airfield near the Kola Inlet's Vaenga.

8. Above and 9. above right: Arctic conditions endured on board the British cruiser *Sheffield* during December 1941.

10. Above: Another wintry scene on the deck of a British ship on Arctic convoy duty, during 1942.

11. Above right: An intrepid seaman poses in front of the British cruiser *Belfast*'s B gun turret barbette in November 1943.

12. Right: The iced-up guns of a British battleship on Arctic convoy duty.

13. Left: German Vizeadmiral Otto Ciliax (*on extreme left*), who was in command on board *Tirpitz* (*15.* pictured *below*) during her first Arctic sortie, and *16. bottom right* Generaladmiral Rolf Carls, his land-based superior officer (pictured *on left*), seen greeting members of the battleship's crew. However the two admirals endangered everyone on the ship because they failed to appreciate that their communications would betray *Tipitz*'s future position (see Chapter 4).

14. Below: Admiral Sir John Tovey, Commander-in-Chief of Britain's Home Fleet, who was confident his forces could sink *Tirpitz* if they caught up with the German battleship, but whose efforts were hampered by the weather and a misreading of German communications.

17. Above and 18. right:
Obsolescent Fairey Albacore
aircraft are shown sitting on and
taking off from carrier *Victorious'*
flight deck in scenes which were
similar to what took place during
the early morning of 9 March 1942.

19. Below: Wake left behind by
Tirpitz, as seen from one of the
attacking Albacores on 9 March
1942, as the German battleship was
steered away from the dropped
British torpedoes (see Chapter 4).

20. Right: *Tirpitz*'s Kapitän Karl Topp who
saved the ship and her crew by the prompt
evasive action he called for during the
9 March 1942 attack (see Chapter 4).

21. Above: The British cruiser *Trinidad* prior to participating in the protection of PQ13.

22. Above: The massive hole in *Trinidad*'s port side made by the explosion of her own torpedo which, during the battle with German destroyers on 29 March 1942, rather than hitting its German target boomeranged back to incapacitate the British cruiser (see Chapter 5).

23. Above right: George Lloyd, a musician who was one of just four men who escaped from *Trinidad*'s transmitting station after it was flooded following the torpedoing of the ship.

24. Right: The destroyer *Eclipse*'s Lieutenant Commander Edward Mack, whose attempts to sink the winged German destroyer Z 26 during the 29 March 1942 battle were interrupted by the appearance of the other two German destroyers which had previously been accompanying Z 26.

25. Left: Bernard Covington, a 17-year old armed guard from South Boston, in the US state of Virginia, who was reported missing following the torpedoing of his vessel, the American merchant ship *Effingham*, on 30 March 1942 during the passage of PQ13, but who was rescued after around four freezing days in a lifeboat.

26. Above: The British merchant ship *Induna* which, like *Effingham* (mentioned above), was torpedoed by a U-boat on 30 March 1942.

27. Right: Austin Byrne, a 20 year old from Bradford, who was serving as a gunner on *Induna* when she was torpedoed. He also survived in a lifeboat along with his shipmates for the best part of four days until they were rescued.

28. *Above*: Morris Mills, pictured here after he had survived his adventures in the Arctic, suffered life-changing injuries when his ship *New Westminster City*, which had been part of PQ13, was bombed while tied up in Murmansk's harbour (see Chapter 8). His left foot was subsequently amputated by a Russian surgeon while he was a patient in the Murmansk school, part of which is shown in photo 29. *on the right*, that had been converted into a hospital.

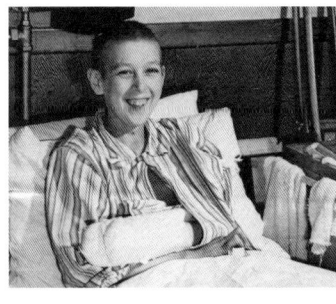

30. *Left*: Jimmy Campbell, the 15-year-old *Induna* steward, shown here recovering in a Scottish hospital from the injuries caused by the freezing conditions and frostbite he sustained while in one of *Induna's* lifeboats.

31. *Right*: Bill Short, pictured here after the war, by which time he had been fitted with artificial legs. He also suffered in the Murmansk hospital. As a result of the frostbite he sustained as a 22 year old in one of *Induna's* lifeboats after the sinking, both of his legs were amputated (see Chapters 6–8).

to a message sent at 12.40 a.m. the previous night (3–4 July) by Flieg-erführer Lofoten. The message revealed that at 12.15 a.m. that night (3–4 July) a German reconnaissance aircraft near the convoy had seen the following Allied warships: '1 battleship, 1 heavy cruiser, 2 light cruisers, 3 destroyers. Course 60 degrees.'[24]

Because this report referred to the same number of warships as were in Hamilton's CS1, Denning correctly assumed that it was Hamilton's cruisers and destroyers that had been spotted. As Denning's post-war account subsequently acknowledged, it was not surprising that one of the cruisers had been mistakenly referred to as a battleship: 'The Luft-waffe ship recognition handbook – of which we had captured a copy earlier in the war – classified warships under the number of funnels, and when modifications were made to the cruiser *London* changing her from a three-funnel to a two-funnel ship, she was invariably reported as a battleship.'[25]

His account carries on: 'The question was: what credence would the German Naval Staff place on this report?' If they really believed a battle-ship was near the convoy, they would very likely think twice before sending *Tirpitz* to take it on.

It was at this crucial juncture that Denning's and Pound's latent differences of opinion concerning the reliability of inferences from intelligence came to the fore. According to Denning: 'I was in the process of drafting an Ultra to the Commander-in-Chief Home Fleet and CS One based on the information in these two latest decrypts when . . . Pound [and some of his staff walked in] . . .

'Pound resumed his seat on the stool at the head of the plotting table, and enquired how long it would take for the destroyers to top up with fuel. I had already mentally calculated this at about three hours. Then he asked what was likely to be the speed of *Tirpitz*. I replied 25 or 26 knots provided the weather was favourable for the destroyers, but two or three knots less if the pocket battleships were also in contact.

'Taking up the dividers and using a smaller chart of the area for plot-ting, Pound remarked that if *Tirpitz* had sailed from Alta that morning, she could be up with the convoy about midnight (that very night, 4–5 July, i.e. assuming the meeting was at about 7 p.m. as specified in Note 26, in around five hours).[26]

'He then asked why I thought *Tirpitz* had not yet left Alta. I expounded what had happened during the *Tirpitz* sortie against PQ12 (when U-boats were told to keep away from the area where the *Tirpitz* was to operate). I pointed out that . . . no decrypt had been received ordering U-boats to keep clear of the convoy, and even now direction finding of U-boat transmissions showed that they were still very much in contact with the convoy. [Also] despite intensive air reconnaissance (the decrypts seen up to that point suggested that prior to midday 3 July and possibly even prior to midday 4 July) the Luftwaffe had not yet relocated Tovey's force.[27] They had indeed located the cruiser covering force . . . but the formation was reported as including a battleship.

'. . . Although Bletchley had not yet broken the Enigma from noon that day (4 July), the nature of the radio transmissions intercepted during the afternoon (of 4 July) revealed none of the characteristics normally associated with surface ships being at sea . . .

'There had been no sighting report from our own or Russian submarines patrolling off the North Cape.'

The others present asked and answered questions, but Denning recalls that Pound 'spoke very little'. He 'played idly with the dividers' and gave the impression he was 'sunk in thought'. He eventually 'got up to proceed to the U-boat tracking room'.

It is always hard to remember exactly what words were spoken long after the event. But Denning, writing his account years after the war, believed that his overall response to Pound's questioning was in substance: 'I was confident' *Tirpitz* was still in Altenfjord, but 'I could not give [an] absolute assurance' though '[I] fully expected to receive confirmation in the fairly near future when Bletchley had unbuttoned the new traffic (the German messages sent after midday 4 July).'[28]

This evidently was not enough to convince Pound, who would not let Denning pass on his inferences from the evidence to Tovey and Hamilton. The Ultra sent to the two admirals at 7.18 p.m. on 4 July stated truthfully, but, because it omitted Denning's gloss, misleadingly: 'C-in-C Fleet in *Tirpitz* arrived Altenfjord 0900/4th July. Destroyers and torpedo boats ordered to complete with fuel at once. *Admiral Scheer* was already present at Altenfjord . . .'[29]

What Denning called 'the new traffic' began to flow through from

Bletchley Park to the Admiralty at around 8 p.m. on 4 July.[30] It arrived in the OIC just minutes before PQ17 faced the big air attack north-east of Bear Island, described in Chapter 1.

The new traffic contained some worrying signs. Although a decrypt which emerged from OIC's teleprinter at 8.15 p.m. showed that Admiral Schmundt (Admiral Nordmeer), who was communicating with the U-boats near the convoy, had sent a message at 2.58 p.m. that afternoon referring to 'the battleship' with the warship group near the convoy, a reference which reinforced Denning's conclusion that the German commanders had not permitted *Tirpitz* to launch an attack, there was another message referring only to cruisers and destroyers being near the convoy, which pointed in the opposite direction.[31]

There are conflicting accounts about what happened next. There is Denning's version, and a version which was first outlined in *The Destruction of PQ17*, the classic account of the convoy, by David Irving. Denning's account goes as follows:

Denning remembers triumphantly reading shortly after 8.30 p.m. the decrypt of the following message originated at 11.30 a.m. that morning (4 July) by Admiral Schmundt and sent to the Eisteufel U-boats operating around the convoy: 'No own Naval forces in the Operational Area. Position of heavy enemy group not known at present . . . Recce is being operated.'[32] This told Denning that *Tirpitz* had almost certainly still been in Altenfjord at around noon, and that the German battleship had probably not been moved unless after the sending of the message the Home Fleet (the heavy enemy group) had been sighted.

Denning says he quickly passed the decrypt to Clayton, his boss, who was on the way to an urgent meeting convened by Pound. While Denning was waiting for Clayton to come back, Rodger Winn from the U-boat tracking room, who happened to be Godfrey Winn's older half brother, entered Denning's office, and looked at the Ultra which Denning was in the process of drafting. 'I was perturbed by his remarks,' Denning wrote later, adding: 'He said he understood from the discussions which had just taken place in his room that *Tirpitz* was already at sea, and there was some talk of dispersing the convoy.'[33]

It is at this point that Denning's account is interrupted, leaving those of us who want to know what happened afterwards with what Irving has written. According to Irving, the meeting attended by Clayton took place upstairs in Pound's office which overlooked Horse Guards Parade. It was a long room containing the kind of large table you might expect to find in any corporate boardroom, only in this case there was a chart laid out on it. None of the official minutes of the meeting are available for consultation, if any were written, and no contemporaneous private notes of what occurred have subsequently seen the light of day. According to a note Irving made after interviewing one of those who had been present, Pound asked each of the senior officers sitting around the table what he thought should be done. None of them wanted to see PQ17 dispersed except for Admiral Henry Moore, Vice Chief of the Naval Staff, who using the chart in the conference room and a pair of dividers, worked out that *Tirpitz* might reach the convoy in a matter of hours.[34]

After the others had spoken, Pound leaned back in his chair and closed his eyes. The few moments of silence that followed were broken when one of the young staff officers whispered irreverently to his colleague: 'Look, Father's asleep.' But if Pound was, he soon woke up, opened his eyes, and after holding up his hands as if to convey to those present that he was taking responsibility for what followed, he reached for his message pad and announced dramatically: 'The convoy is to be dispersed.'[35]

In his account, Denning explains how when Clayton returned to the OIC, they discussed Denning's fear that Pound was not taking into account all the known facts. Clayton agreed to talk to Pound again, but as Denning recalled: 'He was not away very long, and said to me on his return: "Father says he's made his decision, and is not going to change it now."'[36]

At 9.11 p.m., the following signal was sent by Pound to Hamilton: 'Most Immediate. Cruiser force withdraw to westward at high speed.'[37]

At 9.23 p.m. the next message sent by Pound was addressed to the commanders of all PQ17's escorts. It stated: 'Immediate. Owing to threat from surface ships convoy is to disperse and proceed to Russian ports.'[38] But when it was pointed out in London that the order to disperse would have permitted the merchant ships to proceed to their destination in groups, making them almost as vulnerable as if they had remained in convoy, Pound agreed that another signal should be sent. It was this signal which was to fire the starting gun on a controversy concerning whether Pound's order was justified, that would run for more than 80 years, but which more importantly would end up in the short term being a death sentence for so many ships and their crews (the controversy is explained in the Conclusion in Chapter 44). The signal stated: 'From Admiralty. Addressed Escorts of PQ17. Most Immediate. My 2123/4. Convoy is to scatter.'[39]

Shortly afterwards, Denning's assistant, Lieutenant Archie Hutchinson, who had recently come on duty, noticed yet another flaw in what had been sent out: 'I wonder what Turtle (Hamilton) will make of that,' he said, referring to the signal telling CS1 to withdraw. 'He'll think *Tirpitz* is on his tail. I wonder what will happen to the escort.'[40]

Hutchinson was right to be concerned. More than 1,500 miles away in the Barents Sea, south-east of Hope Island, the question about the escort was about to be considered by the 41-year-old Commander Jack Broome, who, as mentioned in Chapter 16, was the convoy's senior escort officer in the destroyer HMS *Keppel* (see 6B in Map 1, 6 in Map 13, and Note 41 for PQ17's position at this juncture).[41] The fact that he was the man in charge on the spot now that Hamilton had been ordered to head westward turned out to be significant.

Broome was not just any old destroyer commander. He was one of the smartest and wittiest in the service. No-one was more attuned than he was to the need for naval officers to act efficiently and to do their duty. He appears to have assumed that most of his peers and his superiors would also do their best while at the same time realizing that because of human failings, some of the men he worked with could not live up to his high standards unless they were given a push in the right direction. This nuanced interpretation of human nature was apparent to anyone who looked at his artwork. He was famous within the Navy for his irreverent and barbed cartoons that lampooned incompetent admirals and merchant seamen alike. Any naval officer like Hutchinson, who appreciated the shortcomings of the admirals dealing with PQ17, would have been sure to have recalled Broome's take on the commanders in the Admiralty as expressed in one of his cartoons that had been published in a journal. It featured a wall chart in the Admiralty's Operations room, in front of which a pretty 'wren' – as women in the Women's Royal Naval Service (WRNS) were known – at the top of a step ladder was plotting the route of an Arctic convoy. At the bottom of the ladder, a buffoonish admiral

was gazing appreciatively upwards, while to one side there were two dis-
approving WRNS officers, one of whom remarked acidly to the other:
'Either the Admiral routes the convoy further south, or Wren Jackson
goes into trousers.'[42]

It took some time for the Admiralty's last three signals to reach Broome
on his destroyer's bridge, even after they had been seen by *Keppel*'s telegraphist in the ship's radio room. They had been encrypted before being
sent, and had to be decoded by *Keppel*'s doctor-cum-decoder before they
could be read by the destroyer's commander.[43] The last two signals, which
Keppel's Dr McKendrick could see were marked respectively 'Immediate'
and 'Most Immediate', were decoded and sent up to Broome first.[44]

When Broome many years later was questioned during the court case
in which he successfully sued David Irving and his publisher for damages
concerning the libellous depiction of Broome's actions during PQ17, he
stated that the impact these last two signals had had on him was as start-
ling as if he had received 'an electric shock', so astonished was he by their
content (see Note 45 for a description of the court case).[45] As he wrote in
his official report: 'My impression on seeing the resolution displayed by
the convoy and its escort [in the face of the attacks by aircraft and U-boats]
was that provided the ammunition lasted, P.Q.17 could get anywhere.'

But then out of the blue this notification came in telling him there was
an elevated threat which they could not handle. Explaining how he processed this notification, he stated in his report: 'An order to scatter,
especially when made most immediate by signal following an order to
disperse, and thereby giving the impression of a situation developing
very rapidly, is in my impression given when the threat is imminent from
surface forces more powerful than the escort. By imminent, I mean that
the surface forces are in sight . . . We were all expecting therefore to see
either the cruisers open fire, or to see [enemy] masts appearing over the
horizon.'[46] He subsequently commented with reference to the attempts to
be the first to spot the German fleet: '*Keppel*'s bridge never contained binoculars working so hard or getting so hot!'[47]

After reading the last two signals at around 10.10 p.m. (still 4 July),
Broome quickly told his signalman that the scatter signal should be made
immediately. A white pendant with a red St George's Cross on it was
raised aloft on *Keppel*'s masthead. Receipt of the signal was confirmed by

those destroyer signalmen who accepted it by repeating the signal from their own mastheads. As for the commodore John Dowding in *River Afton*, he appeared to be indicating that he did not understand the signal by having his ship's scatter flag half hoisted. Broome ended up having to shout across to Dowding what had happened through a loud hailer after having his destroyer parked on the starboard side of the commodore's ship.

That turned out to be the prelude to his last duties concerning the convoy; first of all, Broome had a radio telephone message sent to the commanders of the other destroyers in the close escort using the single word 'Strike', the pre-arranged shorthand for the instruction they were to fall in behind *Keppel* as soon as he told them to act. Shortly afterwards, the commanders of all the other ships which formed part of the close escort were ordered to sail independently to Archangel. The two submarines were also told to act independently.[48]

Then, having confirmed to Dowding what was expected of him, and after sheering ahead of the convoy, Broome flashed one last farewell signal in *River Afton's* direction: 'Sorry to leave you like this. Goodbye and good luck. It looks like a bloody business.' Whereupon Dowding had his signalman flash back: 'Thank you. Goodbye and good hunting.'[49]

18

Consequences

Main Action: 4–5 July 1942
The convoy scatters, PQ17 part 3

(See Maps 1, 13 and 14)

Given that Commander Jack Broome believed that the powerful German battlegroup might appear from the south at any minute, rather than being a coward as implied by David Irving in the first edition of his book, Broome was actually acting courageously when he decided that he and his flotilla of destroyers should join CS1 with a view to intercepting the German surface fleet.

It was with that in mind that Broome at around 10.15 p.m. on 4 July 1942 sent Hamilton the following signal which because of its central position in the Broome against David Irving libel action, was to become almost as infamous as the scatter signal that had prompted it: 'Propose close escort destroyers join you.'[1]

Hamilton replied, 'Approved'. On seeing this, Broome and his destroyers tagged along behind the cruisers as CS1's warships passed in front of the convoy before turning to the west.

If there are any doubts about whether some, if not all, the British sailors in Broome's 1st Escort Group's destroyers thought as they sailed in the cruisers' wake that they were about to do battle with a superior enemy, they should be dispelled by the 4 July 1942 entry in the diary of John

Dodds, the 25-year-old officer in the destroyer HMS *Fury* who was first featured in this book in connection with PQ13 (see Chapter 5). As someone whose job it was to unravel all the messages that came in while he was on watch, no-one in his ship was better placed to appreciate the perceived precariousness of their situation. 'This afternoon we were told that the *Tirpitz* with other ships are steaming north to attack,' he wrote to his girlfriend, continuing: 'We . . . are now at full speed steaming . . . to intercept the naval force. *We* have got to do a torpedo attack . . . Now all we can do is wait. Some of us will be lucky, and some of us are going to get hurt if we meet [the Germans]. So just in case, goodbye my darling. I love you now and always. I have all your photos with me, so if I go, you come with me.'[2]

Nevertheless a question mark has ever since hung over the rightness or wrongness of the decisions made by those officers whose job it was to regulate the destroyers' action. Although Broome would afterwards state that he believed he had acted correctly given his knowledge at the time, he surely understood what were the likely consequences for the merchant ships and their crews. They were already in the U-boats' commanders' sights even before the scatter order. Had he not made his name as a cartoonist for that famous drawing, aimed at convincing merchant seamen who straggled behind convoys that they should do their best to keep up? It showed U-boats and German aircraft closing in on the straggler behind a convoy above the catch line: 'How To Join the Straggler's Club.'

It had been displayed in the canteen where the PQ17 pre-convoy conference was held as a reminder to the merchant ship masters of the consequences of not keeping up with the other ships in the convoy.[3] Yet here he was by his own action turning all the surviving merchant ships into stragglers.

At least Broome had the comfort of initially believing that he was doing his best to protect the merchant ships, which was more than could be said for some of the British naval officers under his command. Like the crew in the American cruiser *Wichita*, whose anguish concerning the retreat is recorded in Douglas Fairbanks' account (see Chapter 1), these British officers only reluctantly complied with their commanders' bidding. William O'Brien, who at the time had been a 25-year-old first lieutenant in the destroyer HMS *Offa*, would later comment: 'I can remember we sat on the bridge, . . . the Captain, the Navigator and I, and no doubt others, . . . and we debated ... pretending to break down and dropping back, and going to rejoin the convoy. To this day I blame myself for not pressing this policy to my captain. But always we came back to the belief that we could not be doing what we were doing without a purpose, and soon something more would be told to us and the enemy would appear. [But] nothing more was told to us, no enemy appeared, and the distance between us and the convoy opened steadily... [At that point we realized] we shouldn't be doing this. We should have stayed with the convoy ... [It was] broad daylight, little floes of ice [were] coming by us, ... looking beautiful in the serene flat calm glassy sea. And there we were, quitting. It's the most horrible recollection.'[4]

To his credit, *Pozarica*'s Captain Lawford's first impulse was to exploit the ambiguity within Broome's order to the escorts which were not destroyers (Broome had told them to proceed to Archangel 'independently'). But when Lawford proposed that *Pozarica*, backed by three corvettes and two trawlers, should be permitted to carry on guarding the ships within the two left-hand columns of the convoy which Lawford had been covering prior to the scatter order, his superior officer, the 53-year-old Acting Captain Jack Jauncey, commander of *Palomares*, the second anti-aircraft ship, ruled it out. That convinced Lawford that he should advise the masters of any merchant ships he encountered to follow his lead by heading for Admiralty Peninsula (Poluostrov Admiralteystva), the largest promontory on the northern of the two main islands that are part of the Novaya Zemlya archipelago, the nearest land within the Soviet Union to the east.[5]

Some of the merchant ship masters were equally unsure what was expected of them. Nowhere did the fog of war descend more confusingly than on board the Soviet Union tanker *Azerbaijan*. Because she had been left behind after being torpedoed, and had not quite caught up by the time the scatter flag was displayed on *River Afton*'s masthead, *Azerbaijan*'s captain, Vladimir Izotov was nonplussed when at about 10.30 p.m. he noticed that the ships in the convoy were no longer sticking to the nine-column formation that at the pre-convoy conference had been said to be so important (see 6B in Map 1 and 6 in Map 13 for where these events unfolded).

In Izotov's official report, he explained what he witnessed: 'The vessels of the convoy changed their course, and began to go off in different directions. The four columns on the left went to the left, and with them went the cruiser (sic – he was referring to the auxiliary anti-aircraft ship *Pozarica*) that had been in [or beside] the second column . . . and some corvettes. Columns 5 and 6 went on a course of 45 degrees (i.e. straight ahead, since that was the convoy's course prior to the scattering) . . . Columns 7, 8 and 9 turned to the right, effectively going to the east, and with them went the second cruiser (sic – he was referring to the auxiliary anti-aircraft ship *Palomares*) which had been travelling in between columns 8 and 9.'[6]

One cannot help but feel sympathy for this Russian captain, who along with his crew had battled so valiantly to carry out the necessary repairs and to catch up, only to observe their chance of regaining their position within the convoy disappearing into the distance.

They had certainly made an unforgettable impression. Even before the big air attack, they had made waves once it was realized *Azerbaijan's* crew was partly female. Godfrey Winn's account reveals that some of *Pozarica's* crew had taken to eyeing up the blonde woman they had spotted through their binoculars on the Russian ship's deck who was believed to be the bosun's mate. 'Some of the boys quite fancy her,' Winn informed *Pozarica's* commander.[7]

Within half an hour of the spectacular explosion after *Azerbaijan* was torpedoed, the action in the Soviet ship had prompted the whole gamut of emotions in the eyes of the fascinated beholders: first bafflement by the commander of the rescue ship whose offer to take off the crew was turned down.[8] Then opprobrium when there was a rumour that one of the eight men rescued from the water asked the rescue ship crew to hand his compatriots over to *Azerbaijan's* captain, presumably so that the 'deserters' could be punished for abandoning ship without permission.[9] And finally delighted approval from the decks of the other merchant ships when, within around half an hour of being torpedoed, *Azerbaijan* was seen to be moving north-eastwards again in a bid to overhaul the surviving ships in the convoy.

Izotov's report does not register any pleasure in connection with the respect he and his crew had earned. What he wrote is dominated by his disappointment at the callous way they were treated by the commanders of PQ17's escorts. Even before the convoy scattered, Izotov was frustrated by his inability to elicit a useful reply from one of the two British submarines within the escort in spite of her acknowledgement she had received his flashed signal requesting that the convoy should be slowed down so that *Azerbaijan* could catch up.

The reaction coming from the deck of the first escort which had approached *Azerbaijan* after the Soviet tanker had got under way again, was no more satisfactory. The destroyer in question may well have been *Keppel*. 'I went out astern of the convoy [after the mass attack by aircraft] to have a close look at the Russian,' Broome reported. If *Keppel* was the ship Izotov mentioned, Broome had underestimated what was expected of him. According to Izotov, no sooner had a signal been flashed from *Azerbaijan* specifying the Soviet vessel's best speed, than the escort whizzed off after the convoy, without offering any advice, assistance or even encouragement. Broome's record of his encounter with 'the Russian' was much more positive: 'Her crew were singing and smiling,' he recalled later, adding: 'A couple of lusty dames waved cheerfully from her bridge.'[10]

Izotov claimed he asked the crew of the next Allied warship that passed – possibly one of the minesweepers sent to sink the torpedoed *Navarino* and *William Hooper* – whether she might escort *Azerbaijan* until she caught up with the convoy. But the reply came back: 'The convoy is not going to re-form. I'm very sorry. Save yourselves. I advise you to carry on towards the north. Good luck.'[11]

On hearing this, Izotov finally realized that he could not rely on any of the escorts to protect him. If he and his crew were going to make it to the Soviet Union, they would have to manage on their own. Having reached that decision, he gave the order to head towards the north-east as quickly as possible.[12]

Some of the merchant ships, which like *Azerbaijan* and the other Soviet tanker *Donbass* started off heading north-east, were in the first instance intercepted and attacked, albeit unsuccessfully, by German aircraft acting alone. By way of contrast, those merchant ships that turned towards the north or north-north-west, soon found they were no longer being shadowed by the aircraft which had followed them after the implementation of the scatter order.

When Ronnie Crees, a British boy apprentice on the northbound Dutch ship *Paulus Potter*, went on watch at around midnight that night, he was amazed to discover that he and his shipmates were for the first time for eight days all alone. This was a surprise. As he later confessed in a post-war interview, the warships sailing away 'was a terrible thing in our eyes, especially on a Dutch ship, because the Dutchmen thought: "My God, the British Navy! Where's it going? Where's your navy going? Your brave navy."' But as Crees observed, although it was late at night (during the night of 4–5 July), 'the sun was shining . . . and the sky was blue. If I had had sunglasses I would have put them on. It was beautiful . . . The war seemed to be a long way away. I thought . . . this is not as bad as I thought it might be. We're on our own. It's nice and peaceful. Not another ship in sight . . . It was like a summer holiday just off Brighton.'[13]

But eventually, like all the other ships that had headed in the same direction, *Paulus Potter* reached the edge of the ice fields to the north, and was forced to turn towards the south-east, and once that happened, their fate was hanging in the balance because they were heading just where the German aircraft crews would be bound to look sooner or later.

Another merchant ship heading northwards that night was the Panamanian-flagged SS *Troubadour*. According to Howard Carraway, who as mentioned in Chapter 1, was the commander of her American armed guard: 'About midnight we ran into a light fog . . . Before the fog fell, we could see two ships near us. One was Harry Vawter's rusty old Hog Islander, the *Pan Kraft* (Harry Vawter, an old friend of Carraway, was the armed guard commander in *Pan Kraft* – see Glossary for 'Hog Islander'). Another was a big US freighter of 10,000 tons or more, the *Washington*. Behind us was a little trawler (*Ayrshire*), one of the escort. When it [the fog] lifted, only the trawler was there.

'He came alongside, told us to go to a certain point on the Spitzbergen group (of islands), and we would proceed [together] from there. He was carrying, he said, depth charges, two dual purpose guns, and [a] listening service (asdic, the sonar system used to search for U-boats). We agreed to accompany him, and we [both] sallied forth . . . The sun was high above the horizon, and the day as bright as it ever is in May in South Carolina. That was the first I had seen of it, although we had been in the "land of the Midnight Sun", and north of it, for more than a week. Bad weather had hidden it.'[14]

Carraway neglected to say that Leo Gradwell, the 42-year-old commander of *Ayrshire*, was sticking his neck out in proposing this arrangement, which amounted to a refusal to comply with Pound's scatter order. But that did not deflect the *Ayrshire* skipper. He may have had few formal naval qualifications. The most striking was a certificate of competency awarded by the Board of Trade as a master of a pleasure yacht in coastal waters. Like Graeme Ogden, the trawler commander featured in the chapters about PQ16, he had joined the Royal Naval Volunteer Reserve, the section of the British forces designed for amateur sailors. However, he had other qualities that few in the regular Navy possessed.

Unlike the majority of Royal Navy officers, who have it drilled into them that they must always obey their admirals, Gradwell, who had studied Classics at England's Oxford University before becoming a barrister, had been trained to question every statement that came his way, whether or not it came from a superior. Such rigour was combined with a keen desire to do what was right. This resulted in his belonging to that long line of Englishmen who will always refuse to obey orders which in their eyes are either misconceived, or which contravene natural justice. As far as he was concerned, the order that he should abandon ships with even less chance of surviving than his own failed to meet this high bar on both counts.

That explains why, after clubbing together with *Troubadour*, he also invited the masters of SS *Silver Sword* and SS *Ironclad*, two other Hog Islanders which happened to catch his eye as he followed the route northward to the ice and then along its edge south-eastwards, to come under his protection. Not that he had much to offer. Although the asdic equipment and depth charges on board made him a useful companion if a U-boat decided to have a go at them, he might turn out to be a positive liability if faced with the powerful guns in one of the German warships. He had ordered his men to stack up depth charges near the bow of his ship, transforming *Ayrshire* into a kind of floating bomb, which could be used to blast a hole in the hull of any warship it struck, but which could also blow not only his ship, but any nearby vessel, to kingdom come if the trawler was hit by a powerful shell.

However the wily Gradwell had a plan which was designed to minimize the chance of either him or his charges ever being put in that position. The ice might have appeared unpassable from a distance, but in the higher temperatures of the mid-summer months, it was melting, leaving behind floating fields of ice that might be penetrated by a ship like *Ayrshire* with a strengthened bow, or by the much heavier merchant ships accompanying him. If they could only work their way in far enough, they could hide away until the searching U-boats and aircraft had shot their bolts. Then they would have the ocean to themselves, and be able to make their way to the Soviet Union unimpeded.

It was a plan that appealed to the masters of the three merchant ships. But as William Carter, the commander of *Ironclad*'s armed guard, commented in his account, after the ships had stopped a few feet into the ice, the ships' commanders 'liked the defensive protection that the ice provided'. But they were not blind to the accompanying danger. Carter stated that: 'The major risk was that the long stretch of abnormally calm weather had to break some time. If a wind of much force came up from the south, we could be trapped in the ice and probably crushed.'[15]

No-one could deny that was a good argument. But like the ice in which they lay, it was not an immovable barrier that could never be overcome. Just as the ice would crack and give way if enough weight was placed on top of it, so this objection would be swept aside when the risk of taking no action became high enough. In the meantime they remained where they were, as Carraway in his diary described it: 'Not very far, but just enough in to keep the subs away and prevent torpedoes from planes having effect if they came.'[16]

It has to be said that this quartet of ships had been dealt a good hand. The ships which headed to the right after the scatter order, that is towards the east, had no means to 'keep the subs away', or for that matter the Luftwaffe when they, as Carraway put it, came 'a hunting'.[17] These ships were effectively heading straight into the lion's den.

One of the lions thirsting for blood was the 25-year-old Kapitänleutnant Heinz Bielfeld in *U-703*, the very same U-boat commander, who along with his crew, had opened the German score against PQ16 by sinking the American ship *Syros* (see Chapter 14). During the morning of 5 July 1942, he was quickly in a position to carry on against PQ17 where against PQ16 he had left off. He saw so many merchant ships heading his way at one point that it was hard for him to know which to attack first. He would eventually settle on the 6,645-ton British freighter *Empire*

Byron, which had been in convoy position 71 (7th column from left of convoy; 1st, i.e. front, row), one of the ships that Izotov had seen deviating to the right after the scatter order.

At around 8.20 a.m. on 5 July, by which time the vessel was around half of the way between the scatter point and Novaya Zemlya (see 1 in Map 14, and Note 18 for the German specification of the location), a torpedo fired from Bielfeld's U-boat slammed into *Empire Byron*'s port side alongside her No. 4 hold just forward of the main mast and exploded.[18] 'It was a very violent explosion, and the ship vibrated considerably,' reported *Empire Byron*'s 37-year-old master John Wharton, adding: 'Nobody reported seeing a flash as the torpedo struck, but a large column of water was thrown up.'[19]

The brunt of the blast appears to have come up through the gunners' accommodation in between decks in No. 4 hold, carrying with it all the beams and hatches from the hold. Explaining afterwards how it came about that six of the gunners were missing, Wharton reported: 'The deck was bulged about 2 feet directly over the gunners' accommodation, and the ladders from this accommodation were blown away. There was a rope ladder always kept in the companion way, and the gunlayer put this down into the accommodation and assisted two of the gunners up on deck. These men . . . said that as far as they knew the rest of the gunners in the accommodation were killed by the explosion.'[20]

Two engine room ratings also lost their lives in the explosion. But Wharton's second report suggests he was most affected by the fate of Richard Phillips, the ship's 3rd radio officer from Manchester, who at 18 years of age was young enough to have been Wharton's son: 'I sent the 3rd Radio Officer to the starboard lifeboat with the boat's portable radio set,' Wharton reported. 'When he . . . reached this boat, the Second Officer who was in charge ordered him into the boat, but he did not do so and insisted on returning to the bridge to see if he could be of any further use to me.' It was a very brave act. There was no time to lose since as Wharton confirmed 'the ship was sinking rapidly by the stern'. Wharton tried to save the teenager by directing him to get into the port bridge boat. But whereas the ship's two larger lifeboats were safely lowered into the sea even though the ship's engines could not be stopped and the ship continued to charge on forward, the starboard bridge boat capsized and the port bridge boat, with

Richard Phillips in it, was according to Wharton 'half swamped'. Wharton believed that the young man ended up in the sea and 'died from exposure and shock'.[21]

Wharton could count himself fortunate not to share his 3rd radio officer's fate. He was one of the nine men left on board after the last of the boats had been lowered. 'We went to the port raft on the after deck,' he recalled, 'but by this time the water was up to the rail, and the slipping gear for the raft was underwater. Luckily, I was wearing a strong pair of shoes, and managed to kick the slips adrift; and the remaining men floated off on this raft as the ship sank. I then swam after them and scrambled on to the raft.'[22]

They were around 100 yards away from the ship when there were explosions caused by what Wharton took to be two more torpedoes crashing into the ship under the funnel on the port side.[23] According to Wharton: 'When the water and smoke cleared, the ship had disappeared.'[24]

While Wharton and the other eight survivors on the raft were transferring into one of the lifeboats, their nemesis, *U-703*, emerged, and approached the other lifeboat that was around a mile away.

'I saw the submarine leave this boat and turn towards my boat,' Wharton would write later. 'I immediately took off my uniform coat and put it in the locker. The submarine came within about 10 yards and ordered us to go alongside . . . On the conning tower there was a soldier covering us with a tommy gun. A young officer . . . was on the after deck and he asked for the Captain. I told him I did not know where the Captain was, and that he was last seen on board the ship. He then noticed one of the passengers, Captain Rimmington (who, as Wharton had previously explained, was rather conspicuous with a white duffel coat over his uniform), and ordered him to board the submarine . . . The German then called across to us "We are keeping this gentleman." '[25]

It was the prelude to a performance that was to be repeated time and again by the crews of other U-boats that participated in the sinking of PQ17's merchant ships. According to Wharton, the German officer 'in perfect English' apologized for sinking the ship, but stated that supplying Russia was 'ridiculous', the implication being that he could not understand why the merchant seamen would want to support the communists, who were opposed to everything their Western allies stood for. However, he handed over a bottle of wine, a piece of German sausage and a small packet of biscuits, an action that appears to have been prompted by the desire to create useful propaganda rather than by innate generosity towards those who had lost their ship.[26] Wharton recalled afterwards that the donation of the goodies 'was recorded by a camera of the Cine Kodak type'.[27] Finally, the Germans wished the occupants of the lifeboat good luck and sped away on the surface.

On seeing they were to be left to their own devices, Wharton ordered his men to bring the three boats still afloat together, divided the men in the small boat between the two larger lifeboats so that all 61 survivors were in the two lifeboats (33 in Wharton's motor boat, which thanks to Richard Phillips also contained the portable wireless, and 28 in the Chief Officer's boat), and then ordered the first shifts of men to start rowing their boats towards the south-east.[28]

He was right to assume that their lives were in their own hands. Because the receiver on the ship's on-board wireless equipment had been damaged, it could not receive incoming signals, which meant he could not be sure that the distress signal sent before they abandoned ship had been heard. Wharton certainly had no grounds for expecting that the Germans in the U-boat would help them by informing potential rescuers on the British side where to find them.

Yet that is exactly what *U-703*'s Kapitänleutnant Bielfeld did, albeit unintentionally, when he had the German version of the following Bletchley Park decrypt, after it had been encoded on an Enigma machine, sent back to Admiral Hubert Schmundt (Admiral Nordmeer) in Narvik, Norway: 'HAVE SUNK 9000 TON EMPIRE BYRON AT AC2629 (see Note 18) CARGO BATTLE VEHICLES. PORT OF DESTINATION ARCH-ANGEL. HER CAPTAIN JOHN RIMINGTON (sic) ON BOARD AS PRISONER . . . CONVOY TOTALLY DISPERSED . . . AM PUR-SUING.' (*Empire Byron*'s cargo in fact included, amongst other aid, 30 tanks, 15 aircraft and six other vehicles.)[29] The decrypt containing the abovementioned translation of the decoded message was forwarded by Bletchley Park to the Admiralty that afternoon at 2.40 p.m.[30]

The ether was to become full of such signals as the day progressed. It took time for the Germans to marshal their forces for what was an unexpected development: the disappearance of most of the escort and the scattering of the convoy, leaving the isolated merchant ships at their mercy. There was only one other sinking that morning – at around 10.15 a.m. *U-88*'s crew torpedoed and sank the American merchant ship *Carlton*, which had been steered even more sharply to the right after the scatter order (see 2 in Map 14 and Note 31 for sinking position).[31] *Carlton* went down carrying amongst other aid 16 tanks and 124 other vehicles.[32]

However, during the afternoon of 5 July, and the night that followed, ship after ship was either immobilized and abandoned, or dispatched after being attacked by U-boats and or German aircraft. Luftflotte 5 had deployed the Ju 88s in the 3rd wing of KG30 based in Bardufoss in what was to be the first stage of an operation aimed at cutting off the supply of arms to the forces opposing the Germans on the Eastern Front by decimating the scattered convoy.[33]

Most of these abandoned and sunk ships had likewise been steered to the right sooner or later following the scatter order. Although their crews strove to achieve their top speeds, in some cases careering along at up to 13 knots, a marked improvement on the average of 8 knots they were ordered to maintain while in convoy, it availed them little. During the mid to late afternoon and early to late evening of 5 July, no less than seven PQ17 vessels were abandoned or sunk after attacks by the Luftwaffe and U-boats in a narrow finger of sea pointing eastwards towards the same Admiralty Peninsula on Novaya Zemlya's west coast which *Pozarica*'s captain had decided should be his ship's initial destination (see above). Four of the seven abandonings and sinkings took place during a thirty-minute feeding frenzy between 5.00 and 5.30 p.m. on 5 July.

Most of the abandonings and sinkings followed on from the ruthless bombing of these ships by the crews of Ju 88s with often three or more of these aircraft being lined up to attack their prey one after another, or sometimes simultaneously. If the aircraft did not actually sink the vessels by scoring a direct hit, they usually so terrorized the crews with their near misses that the men abandoned ship without any attempt being made to repair ruptured steam pipes or to pump out sea water from flooding holds and engine rooms. At least some of these abandoned vessels were then eventually dispatched thanks to torpedoes fired at them by any U-boat which happened to stumble across them.

Of the ships abandoned or sunk during the afternoon of 5 July and the night of 5–6 July, the American *Peter Kerr* (carrying 10 tanks, 4 aircraft and 305 other vehicles) and *Fairfield City* (carrying 26 tanks and 144 other vehicles), and the British rescue ship *Zaafaran* and oiler *Aldersdale* were the victims of aircraft; the American *Daniel Morgan* (carrying 18 tanks and 372 other vehicles) and the British *Earlston* (carrying 35 aircraft and 195 vehicles which were not tanks) were defeated by the combination of aircraft and U-boats mentioned above; and the American *Honomu* (carrying 39 tanks and 176 other vehicles) was sunk by a U-boat (once again refer to Map 14 which specifies approximate positions where they were attacked).[34]

Given the intensity of the bombing, there were remarkably few fatalities. Most of these ships were abandoned without anyone being killed. The largest death toll from these ships was 'just' seven from *Fairfield City*. Only three men from *Daniel Morgan* lost their lives, although aircraft are believed to have dropped an estimated 81 bombs on or near the ship, resulting in no less than 30 near misses.[35] Reports by *Daniel Morgan*'s master and armed guard commander make it clear that the large expenditure of bombs on this ship was down to the way the ship was 'kept swinging' from side to side each time she was targeted. Another reason was the deterrent effect of the dual purpose 3-inch gun at the front of the ship which kept the aircraft at a respectful height until the weapon was out of action near the end of the series of raids focused on her.[36]

The Luftwaffe may have been slower to target the merchant ships which had sooner or later headed north and north-north-east, but the freighters' departure in this direction had not gone unnoticed. Here the German aircraft crews would eventually find a tempting target: ships that had been creeping along the edge of the ice fields. One of the cosmopolitan mini convoys that had been formed after initial compliance with the scatter order had sought refuge there. It consisted of the Dutch ship *Paulus Potter* (carrying 34 tanks, 15 aircraft and 103 other vehicles), the American ship *Washington* (carrying 14 tanks, 10 aircraft and 220 other vehicles), and the British ship *Bolton Castle* (carrying 35 tanks, 20 aircraft and 136 other vehicles) without any escort in support.[37]

'It was nice to see other ships,' *Paulus Potter*'s Ronnie Crees commented in the course of his post-war interview, 'because although we'd seen no aeroplanes since the convoy split, we knew that they would come.' He was right. During the early afternoon of 5 July an aircraft finally appeared overhead. 'We thought that was it; we've been spotted,' reported Crees. 'He flew round us for a bit before flying away, presumably to report what he had found.'[38]

The first air raid targeting this group of ships later that afternoon was a half-hearted affair, with one aircraft dropping three bombs that fell twenty feet away from *Washington*. There was no immediate follow up.[39] However at around 5.45 p.m., the Luftwaffe arrived in force (see 8 in Map 14 for the approximate location). One of the seven Ju 88s dropped a bomb into *Bolton Castle*'s No. 2 hold which contained 300 tons of cordite, and Ronnie Crees who had been watching out of the corner of his eye while preparing to defend his own ship was stunned when he saw how 'she blew up'. There was a 'terrific explosion and she sunk very quickly', he reported later.[40]

What he appears to have observed was the flaring up of the 'sheet of flame' mentioned in the report by Captain John Pascoe, *Bolton Castle*'s master, accompanied by the loud bang caused by the cordite exploding. 'There was this great crash and a terrific shudder,' remembered William Kenyon, *Bolton Castle*'s 3rd radio officer, who was in the radio room at the time. 'Someone shouted "We've been hit!" . . . Then someone came in and said we were sinking; "that's the position". I sent it out three or four times . . . The whole . . . [ship] began tipping up, bow first . . . I came out. They'd already lowered the boats. I went aft along the deck and started to climb down the rope [into one lifeboat]. They were shouting, "Come on!" They were all ready to go.'[41] They had good reason to insist Kenyon should get a move on. 'We had just pulled away,' Pascoe wrote in his report, 'when the ship sank, bows first within 12 minutes of being hit.'[42]

Minutes later the bombers turned their attention to *Washington* and *Paulus Potter*. *Washington*'s crew were already jittery after observing what had happened to *Bolton Castle*. Although most if not all the bombs aimed at the American ship were near misses to starboard, her master Julius Richter saw that some of her deck cargo was on fire, and he feared what might follow if the explosives stored underneath went up before the ship sank. The explosions as the bombs hit the water had holed her hull. She was listing to starboard. When it was confirmed that the bombing had also put the steering gear out of action, Richter gave the order to abandon ship. Her crew did not need to be told twice. They left the vessel, and then rowed away so quickly that the last man into the lifeboats landed with half his body in the boat and the other half in the water.[43]

The rush to leave *Washington* permitted the German aviators to focus all their attention on *Paulus Potter*. Thanks to a combination of her gunners' fire power and the clever zigzagging ordered by her captain, she managed to survive for some time after she was first bombed, although on occasion the misses were frighteningly close. 'We had one bomb that was so near me that I got soaked through from the water descending from the bomb bursts,' Crees recalled afterwards.[44] But when yet another near miss damaged her steering, and her engine room began to fill up with water thanks to her hull being punctured below the water line, repeating what had done for *Washington*, Willem Sissingh, her Dutch master, ordered that she should be abandoned in her turn, which she was, with her crew using all of her four boats as well as some of her rafts.

Not that that was quite the end of the first part of their story. The pilot of one of the German planes decided he would dive down over the top of the lifeboats. 'I thought our moment had come,' Crees reported. 'I thought he was going to just fire straight into the boat at us . . . But he didn't fire at us thank God. He just dived over us a couple of times . . . We waved our arms at him and screamed and shouted and hurled our abuse . . . But he went away and didn't return.'[45]

19

The Good Samaritan

*Main Action: 5 July 1942
HMS Lotus' rescue mission, PQ17 part 4*

(See Maps 1, 13 and 14)

During the early hours of 5 July 1942, Ned Denning, who had taken the chance to have a bit of shuteye in the Admiralty's OIC, was woken to be told that some of his comments about *Tirpitz*'s movements were to be shared with Tovey and Hamilton after all.

The Ultra sent out to them at 2.38 a.m. on 5 July stated: 'It is not repeat not known if German heavy forces have sailed from Altenfjord but they are unlikely to have done so before 1200B/4. It appears that Germans may be in some confusion whether a battleship is in company with CS 1. Germans do not repeat not appear to be aware of position of C-in-C Home Fleet.'[1]

A subsequent post-war reading of the German naval commanders' war diaries has revealed that Denning's and Clayton's analysis of *Tirpitz*'s movements, as expressed or implied by the 2.38 a.m. Ultra, was one hundred per cent correct.

By around 9 a.m. on 4 July the core of the two German battlegroups, which had departed from Trondheim and Bogenbucht near Narvik at 8 p.m. on 2 July and at around 12.30 a.m. on 3 July respectively, were linked up in Altenfjord.[2] Missing from this northern base were the Narvik group's pocket battleship *Lützow,* and three destroyers from the Trondheim group, all of which unbeknown to the British, had been damaged on the way. But the battlegroups had remained in their northern base while the crews of Luftwaffe reconnaissance aircraft searched for the Home Fleet.[3]

That state of affairs did not last long. At 6.45 a.m. on 5 July the crew in a German aircraft spotted the Home Fleet around 240 miles west-north-west of Bear Island (see 7 in Map 13, and Note 4 for approximate location). Before touch was lost at around 8 a.m. that day, the Home Fleet was some 450 miles away from the nearest ships in the convoy.[4] That appeared to give the Germans the space they needed to carry out their Rösselsprung operation. After Hitler's consent had been obtained, an encoded 11.45 a.m. 5 July message from Schniewind to Carls (in command at Marine-gruppenkommando Nord) confirmed that the German Fleet would be ready to depart from the area near the island Rolvsøya, one of the water-ways leading out of Altenfjord, at 2.30 p.m. that afternoon (see Note 5).[5] Notwithstanding the abovementioned losses before it was deployed, the German Fleet, after its escorts turned back, was to include seven destroy-ers in addition to *Tirpitz,* the pocket battleship *Admiral Scheer* and the heavy cruiser *Admiral Hipper.*[6]

Even at this late stage there was a potential hitch that might have spelled disaster for the Germans. The 11.45 a.m. message from Schniewind to Carls mentioned above had been encoded on an Enigma machine using the settings that had already been worked out by the Bletchley Park codebreakers. If the message had been encoded just 16 minutes later, the new Enigma settings for messages encoded after midday 5 July would have been utilized, thereby making the signal 'secure' because the new settings would not be broken by the British for many hours. As it was, the message was read relatively quickly, and minutes before the scheduled departure time, a decrypt of it was rushed through to the Admiralty in London from Bletchley Park.[7] The corresponding Ultra was sent out to Tovey shortly after 3 p.m., only for Tovey to decide that he really was too far away to intervene given that by this time his destroyers needed to be refuelled.[8]

The same could not truthfully be said by the commanders of some of the Allies' escorts whose vessels had remained in the vicinity of PQ17, even if they believed their superiors' orders precluded their sailing alongside the merchant ships. During the worst of the onslaught on 5 July, commanders of one HMS ship and one rescue ship which were within 10 miles of an attacked and abandoned merchant ship and a sunk rescue ship had bravely diverged from their eastward courses to pick up survivors.[9] But they were the exception to the rule. Most of the mayday signals from the attacked merchant ships went unanswered.

In at least one case, the refusal by the commander of an HMS ship to turn back was the direct result of the instruction given to the escort commanders at the pre-convoy conference not to jeopardize the safety of their ships and crews by stopping to pick up survivors.[10] Rescuing was only to be carried out by the convoy's rescue ships.

However, just as in more recent times, great powers who have heard about a war of aggression against a faraway country have started off by refusing to intervene, only for the government of one of them to completely change its mind when the pain and barbarism witnessed has become too much to bear, so in the Barents Sea during the aftermath of the scatter order, a similar process was set in motion on the bridges of some of the escorts.

During the late afternoon of 5 July, while the anti-aircraft ship *Pozarica*, accompanied by the three corvettes *Lotus*, *La Malouine* and *Poppy*, was still heading for Novaya Zemlya's Admiralty Peninsula, two of the corvettes' commanders signalled to each other about whether they should go back to help the crews of the ships whose SOS's they had received.[11] Although Captain Lawford was said not to be in favour, *Lotus'* 32-year-old Lieutenant John Hall eventually decided he could not stand inaction any longer.

He would later reveal that what pushed him from rebellious talk into what could be described as a form of condoned mutiny was what he referred to in his report as: 'a very very loud SOS signal which could be heard from the loudspeakers all over the bridge'. It had been transmitted by SS *Pan Kraft*, one of the American merchant ships that, as confirmed by *Troubadour's* Ensign Carraway, had also sought refuge up near the ice. 'She was screaming for help,' Hall recalled, 'and said that she had been bombed and had abandoned ship.' (See 9 in Map 14, and Note 12 for location.)[12] He might also have acknowledged that as an ex-civilian mariner himself who had been called on to take command of a corvette by virtue of being a full time professional officer in the Royal Naval Reserve, he was particularly susceptible to appeals emanating from merchant ships.

Going back to assist *Pan Kraft* was certainly achievable. Her survivors were less than 30 miles away, and so could be reached after just over two hours' sailing to the north-west. Furthermore, going back was supported by his crew. In his account Hall mentions how he was particularly affected by the miserable countenance of a young signalman on the bridge, who on hearing all the distress messages coming in, had become 'green (not from sea sickness) and distressed'.

Shortly before 6.30 p.m., *La Malouine*'s Lieutenant Bidwell received Hall's abrupt order: 'Take over from me ... and attend on *Pozarica*'s orders. I am going back for survivors.'[13]

His action was all the more remarkable because while on the way to *Pan Kraft* Hall received the following 7.04 p.m. signal from Admiral Bevan, the Senior British Naval Officer, North Russia: 'At 1700B *Tirpitz* and *Admiral Scheer* 071 degs. 25' 023 degs. 40' (north-west of the North Cape), course 45 degs., 8 Destroyers in company. Russian s/m K 21 claimed 2 hits on Tirpitz with torpedoes.'[14] (See Map 13 for the route taken by the German battlegroup.) In other words, Hall was not only going into an area where U-boats and aircraft might strike at any moment, but there was also a real risk that if he did not complete his mercy mission smartly, and if the Russian submarine's claim turned out to be overstated, the German battlegroup might cut off his line of retreat to Novaya Zemlya.

That explains why, when shortly before arriving at the scene of the attack on *Pan Kraft* Hall encountered three of the PQ17 trawler escorts whose skippers were likewise inclined to rush to the aid of the merchant ship's crew, he advised them to head towards Novaya Zemlya while they could, leaving him to pick up the shipwrecked American sailors.[15]

Ironically, while no-one should be quick to criticize the actions of men in any bombed ship, Lieutenant Hall's rebellion may have been prompted by one of that day's least worthy causes. When shortly after 8.30 p.m. *Lotus* reached the *Pan Kraft*'s survivors in their four boats, he found that many were disgruntled; some complained later that their master and chief officer had abandoned ship without waiting for all their men to disembark, and without ensuring steps were taken to see whether the ship could be saved.[16]

The attack on *Pan Kraft* had been a hit and run affair. As the three attacking aircraft, the last of the 69 Ju 88s from KG 30 to participate in a successful air raid that day, passed over the ship from starboard to port at an altitude of around 4,000 feet, they had dropped nine bombs, of which three had landed around 20 feet from the port side of her Nos 1, 3 and 4 holds.[17] The blasts from these bombs had indeed ruptured steam and oil connections in various places around the ship, but nothing else in the ship had been damaged.

As a result of the failure of the two most senior officers to take responsibility for overseeing the abandonment, the ship's second officer was forced to stand in for them, and he was killed by machine gun bullets fired by an aircraft as he attempted to leave. The only other casualty was a man who appears to have been killed by a machine gun bullet while in one of the lifeboats.[18]

In his report, Lieutenant Hall stated that he resisted the temptation to send out a boarding party to see whether repairs could be carried out and Pan Kraft's engines restarted because he had been notified that U-boats were nearby. Having made that decision, he had no alternative but to order his gunners to try to sink the ship with its cargo, which included 10 tanks, two aircraft and 378 other vehicles.[19] In the short amount of time Hall gave them before giving the order to depart, they could not be certain that they had succeeded. After they had fired nine shells at the merchant ship with their 4-inch gun, *Pan Kraft* was left on fire fore and aft, while *Lotus* steamed away to the south-east.[20]

20

Just in Time

Main Action: 5 July 1942
Sinking of River Afton, PQ 17 part 5

(See Map 14)

At 2.30 a.m. on 6 July 1942 an attempt was made to circulate the following signal from Admiral Pound to all escorts which were still, nominally at least, in contact with PQ17: 'Attack by enemy surface forces is probable in next few hours. Your primary duty is to avoid destruction to enable you to return to scene of attack to pick up survivors after enemy have retired.'[1]

It was the first time since the convoy had been scattered that an Admiralty order had been issued countenancing HMS ships rescuing survivors.

But it would have been cold comfort to those left behind in merchant ships to know that a rescue operation might be mounted twenty-four to forty-eight hours after they took to their lifeboats, when what they really wanted was protection before their vessel was attacked and sunk.

One group of sailors who would have benefited more than most from a more humane deployment of the remaining PQ17 escorts were those manning Commodore John Dowding's ship *River Afton*. By the evening of 5 July 1942, she was heading on a south-easterly course away from the edge of the northerly ice fields towards Matochkin Strait (Matochkin Shar), the waterway that is between the two main islands within the Novaya Zemlya archipelago, and therefore to the south of the north island's Admiralty Peninsula, the haven recommended by *Pozarica*'s Captain Lawford following the scattering (see Chapter 18).[2]

However, at about 9 p.m. that evening a torpedo fired from *U-703*, the U-boat that had sunk *Empire Byron* that morning, hit *River Afton* on her port side beside the engine room (see 12 in Map 14, and Note 3 for location).[3] The explosion destroyed the port lifeboat. Perhaps it was the partial loss of the crew's means of escape that stirred up the panic that ensued.

According to Harold Charlton, *River Afton*'s 30-year-old Geordie master, the starboard lifeboat was 'rushed by the sailors, . . . firemen and gunners without orders' with disastrous consequences. He went on to describe how as it was being lowered to the water, 'a second torpedo struck the ship on the starboard side . . . blowing the stern portion off and sending the 4-inch gun into the air . . . The blast overturned the boat, throwing the occupants into the water, the majority of whom lost their lives.'[4]

'I saw the starboard [life]boat turned in the air,' wrote George Jamieson, another witness. 'It got chucked about 30 or 40 feet. There were [about] 14 of them in that boat. I saw some of them fall [out] as the boat was turning over. All that came up . . . were [about] four.'[5]

As *River Afton*'s stern slowly settled deeper into the water, the ship's port jolly boat was successfully lowered following Charlton's order to abandon ship, only for a second calamity to occur after Charlton became the last of the 14 men to board it. 'The ship had still about two knots way on her,' Charlton reported, 'and as the fore part of the boat was being dragged under and taking water, the painters had to be cut, but the boat caught the wreckage of the port motor lifeboat throwing the occupants into the water . . .

'I heard the Chief Officer shouting for help but could do nothing for him as it was an effort for me to keep afloat and swim in the cold water . . . My wet coat and briefcase on my back were weighing me under. AB Hanford attempted to rescue him, but had to give up in order to save himself.

'I managed to swim to the upturned boat, and got on to the keel . . . Lieutenant Cook (a Royal Navy passenger) . . . also got on to the [bottom of the] boat. "See if we can right it," I said. We rocked the boat, [and] the rock gathered momentum. Suddenly the boat righted. We clambered in over the stern . . . But the gunwale was well below [the surface of] the water . . .

'The bailer I knew was fastened to the keelson. I submerged to try and find it but the cold was too intense . . . However by standing in the fore-part of the boat, about five feet of the after end came out . . . and my ship's papers were lost in . . . [the successful] endeavour to use the case as a bailer.' Eventually the jolly boat was bailed out sufficiently for another man to be hauled on board.[6]

Charlton may have saved one member of his crew, but it had only been achieved by his failing to comply with the rule that requires the master to remain on his ship until everyone else has left it. He had abandoned *River Afton* while there was still a chance of saving John Wood, the 47-year-old second engineer who had been wounded in the engine room.

Fortunately, the commodore John Dowding had remained behind to marshal what forces were left on deck. They included Thomas Waller, the 19-year-old second cook, who in spite of the prospect that the U-boat would torpedo the ship again, descended into the shattered engine room so that he could tie a rope around the injured man. After much huffing and puffing, both men were then extracted through the engine room sky-light, and the injured man laid out on a stretcher on a small raft on the ship's deck.

It was not a moment too soon. Shortly afterwards *River Afton* was hit amidships on her starboard side by what *U-703*'s Kapitänleutnant Bielfeld would refer to as the 'coup de grâce' torpedo.[7] This exploded the ammu-nition in No. 3 hold. 'There was a violent explosion,' Charlton reported. 'This explosion caused a terrific flash. Clouds of smoke and debris blotted the ship from view. When cleared, I saw the ship had broken in two.'[8] Dowding has described how within two minutes of this third strike what remained of 'the ship rolled over to starboard and then sank vertically'.

However, a lot happened in that two minutes. According to Dowding, the raft on the upper deck with the wounded engineer on it, 'was carried across the ship, fouled the derricks and the hatches which were blown off by air below, and was capsized by the mast as the ship sank'.

'I swam to it,' wrote Dowding, 'and picked up the wounded engineer who was close to, and two young cooks.'[9]

Percy Grey, the 31-year-old chief steward has described how he and another man, who like him had also remained on board *River Afton* until the last minute to assist Dowding, had an even luckier escape: 'The vessel sank so quickly, we had no time to do anything, and were dragged under the water with the suction caused by the sinking. It seemed an eternity before I stopped going down, and it was only by struggling furiously that I finally reached the surface.'

Benjamin Coffey, the 24-year-old first cook, another man who had participated in the rescue of the engineer, was also dragged down. 'My lungs felt as though they were bursting,' he complained afterwards. 'I thought I was going to lose consciousness, but the boilers exploded and this helped me reach the surface again.'

Both men ended up on rafts that had survived the sinking.[10]

'Shortly after the ship sank, the submarine surfaced and closed a raft,' Dowding's account continues. After going through the usual routine, first seen following the sinking of *Empire Byron* that morning, a member of the U-boat crew advised the survivors to steer east towards Novaya Zemlya. Given that when the U-boat departed there were just four paddles split between five rafts and a dinghy, such impracticality prompted Dowding to remark drily in his report: 'Without any paddles [on some of the rafts] this would have been a difficult job!'[11]

Charlton was equally pessimistic about their chances: 'Having about 200 miles to go to make land, and no lifeboats, the position was rather grim,' he stated afterwards.[12] 'I think we knew that we could not last much longer in the intense cold . . . Frostbite was setting in. Our clothes were hard with ice. We sat huddled . . . It was strangely peaceful. No one seemed to fear death. The sea remained calm; God was being good. There were no complaints. No demand for food and water.'[13]

At least he and his men were spared the torment of having to witness prolonged suffering by the two members of the crew with the most severe wounds. Trapped as most of them were on rafts, without doctors or medication. there was not much that could be done for them. According to Charlton, the 36-year-old ship's fireman John Breene had sustained a head injury that was so extreme 'his brain protruded'. Charlton's account describes how in an attempt to stop him freezing to death, one of his shipmates 'held the poor man's frozen feet inside his shirt under the warmth of his armpits'. But it was to be all in vain; it was not long before he passed away. 'We laid him to rest . . . [in] the sea,' Charlton reported. 'We let him float [away] in [his] orange life jacket . . . [Then] we sang "Abide with me, fast falls the eventide." '[14]

The second engineer, who remained on the raft occupied by Dowding, also died. As for Thomas Waller, the heroic cook, he never made it onto the rafts or into Charlton's dingy. 'The last I saw of him was when he was standing near the point where the third torpedo hit us,' Percy Grey reported. 'I think he must have been killed by the explosion.'[15]

It was with their hopes fading fast that one last attempt to attract rescuers was essayed. Some smoke flares found on the rafts were lit. They did not look very promising to the demoralized soaking wet survivors whose extremities were already numb from the cold. 'The . . . thick reddish . . . smoke from these flares . . . never rose more than six feet above the water,' Dowding wrote in his report, although he added, 'It behoves one to try everything once.'[16]

How right he was. However unimpressive they seemed from close up, their apparent height from afar was enhanced as a result of the elevated mirage effect resulting from temperature inversion that often occurs in freezing cold Arctic conditions: unlike the normal situation in warmer climes, where the higher you get from the earth's surface, the colder it becomes, in the Arctic, the air near the water or ice often becomes colder than the air above it, and this can result in items near or on the water looking from a distance as if they are suspended in the air. Dowding in his report recalls how he and the other survivors were later told these seemingly unimpressive puffs of smoke appeared to those in HMS *Lotus*, which at that moment appeared from over the horizon, as 'pillars of smoke as from a ship on fire.'[17]

Although these pillars of smoke, viewed from HMS *Lotus,* were located in the direction where *Tirpitz* might have been expected, the fact they told John Hall that he had stumbled across more merchant seamen in trouble was enough for him. He immediately had his ship's course diverted so that he could steam to the rescue for a second time that day.[18]

Suspecting the U-boat that had caused all this misery might still be lurking nearby, he had *Lotus* approach *River Afton*'s jolly boat and rafts with extreme caution. Then he quickly had his crew pick up the 36 survivors, all that were left out of the 58 men who had been in *River Afton*.[19] According to Charlton, 'There was not time to take the dead engineer on board . . . The raft was his final resting place.'[20]

No sooner had the last survivor been brought aboard at around

2.45 a.m. on 6 July, than *Lotus'* engines roared into action, and she sped off once again towards the south-east.[21] No doubt the exact number of tanks and aircraft lost during that day were the last thing Hall would have wanted to think about. But statisticians back at the Admiralty would later conclude that the seven British merchant ships and seven US ships that were sunk or abandoned on 5 July were carrying 308 tanks, 178 aircraft and 2,218 other vehicles, the kind of numbers which if lost in the course of a land or air battle would have been adjudged a major setback if not a crippling defeat.[22]

The *River Afton* survivors were not the only men whose lives were saved as an indirect result of *Pan Kraft's* distress signal. The same desperate plea – 'Hit by bomb . . . SOS . . . 76°50' N 38°00' E' – wrapped up in that haunting morse code message, which had galvanized *Lotus'* Lieutenant Hall to return to the danger area where the lives of those in *River Afton* as well as *Pan Kraft* would be in jeopardy, also struck a disturbing note in the ears of those listening in on their radios in the quartet of ships to the north which had taken refuge in the ice.[23] It was the final movement of that symphony of sound that prompted *Troubadour's* Howard Carraway to sum up what he was hearing in the following pithy, and very American, way. 'All over the Arctic, German planes and subs were raising hell.'[24]

Even before hearing it, the signals picked up from other attacked ships were making him more and more anxious. In that day's diary entry for his wife, he wrote: 'The big *Washington* that I mentioned earlier was abandoned after being attacked within 50 miles of us.'[25] (The abandoning of *Washington* is described in Chapter 18.)

But it was the SOS signal announcing the attack on the much nearer *Pan Kraft* which pushed him and those in the other ships in the group over the edge.[26] 'It was Harry's ship,' Carraway noted in his diary, referring to his friend, 'the one I had been waiting to hear from . . .He was not more than 20 miles away according to his [stated] position, and we scanned the horizon for a sight of the ship or the planes . . .

'Wary now, the trawler skipper (Leo Gradwell) . . . told us to follow him into the ice to avoid the bombers, [which we did] . . . We were scared stiff. Planes were within . . . five minutes of us, and the trawler and our few guns were all the protection we had . . . We manned our guns and waited . . . Poor Sparks got very sick, and threw up over the rail from fear and excitement.

'After what seemed an eternity, an hour [or so] passed, and [then] there were no more distress signals. We breathed deeper, [and] felt more secure as we packed further into the ice fields [where] the cakes were getting bigger [and] the ice harder.'[27]

On the other hand, those below decks wondered whether saving themselves from the Luftwaffe would result in their falling victim to other terrors. 'Every moment it sounded as though the bulkhead would burst in under the pressure, or be cut clean . . . through, as by a giant tin opener,' wrote Walter Baker, one of two coders in *Ayrshire*. But fear of the German planes evidently trumped concern about the cutting properties of the ice. Notwithstanding Baker's concern, they somehow pressed on. His report continues: 'When the ice became really thick, our bows would rise up over it, and then the weight of the ship would force them down, crack it and on we would go.'[28]

Emboldened by the dying down of the distress signals coming from the south, or perhaps deterred by the thickening of the ice to the north, they eventually steered to the south-east and then stopped.

Leo Gradwell asked Richard Elsden, his first lieutenant, to walk across the nearby ice to talk to the other ships' crews in an attempt to boost their morale. It was while fulfilling this mission, that Elsden had the idea which was to produce one of PQ17's iconic images. The ships' relatively dark silhouettes stood out against the white ice. Why not camouflage with white paint the starboard sides of the ships which would be facing towards the south when the ships' bows were pointing eastwards, thereby making them harder to spot from the direction where aircraft were likely to appear, and why not complete the job by also painting their decks?[29] The idea was swiftly adopted by the commanders of all the ships.

'All hands turned to,' Carraway wrote. 'There were thirty and more brushes slapping white paint over our decks, housing, rails, boats, funnel, masts, forecastle, everywhere.'

Carraway has recorded how before the job was completed, 'the trawler came alongside. Her skipper (Gradwell) . . . and his first lieutenant, a kid in his twenties, both English to the core, came aboard for a war council. [Gradwell] . . . asked [*Troubadour's*] Captain Salvesen if he wanted to head south to Russia, or what. The Captain [Salvesen] said he thought we'd better go back into the ice as far as we could, finish the painting and let the excitement die down a little before we made a run for it . . . That was agreeable, and we headed once more into the ice.

'The other ships soon followed. About ten miles into the heavy stuff, we found an opening and stopped. The others stopped too, south of us, but within easy signalling distance.'

While they lay in this position, Carraway was given the chance to have a rest. When he woke up, he was so astounded by the spectacle, he was prompted to write in his diary: 'The ship was a mass of white. I never saw such a transformation.'[30]

The crews in the four ships had vied with each other to produce the best results. According to *Ironclad*'s William Carter, the steward in his ship 'went into the dirty laundry hampers, and got out sheets and table cloths. We spread these on the deck, and weighted them down with spare fire bricks used to repair the fire box of the boiler. They were also wrapped around the masts and secured in place by tying them with string.'

Paradoxically the sun, which usually tends to assist observation, only served to improve the blending-in effect. 'The glare from the bright sunlight was blinding,' Carter reported, 'with us surrounded by solid white ice for miles around. All of us were bothered somewhat by snow blindness. We all had dark goggles, but they would not stay clear of vapor, so we stopped using them . . . The ships were [only] about a hundred yards apart. [But] in the sun's glare from the ice, we could barely see each other.'[31]

Reassuringly even Gradwell, the group's leader, was satisfied with what they had done. Carraway noted in his diary: 'The trawler signalled us that we were very nearly invisible.'[32]

For the moment at least they were safe. But knowing they could not stay where they were forever, they soon began to wonder how long this blessed state could last.

To Add Insult to Injury

Main Action: 5 July 1942
In the minefield near Iceland, QP13

(See Maps 1 and 23)
Gossamer sinking: GMT + 3
QP13 sinkings: GMT

After all the torment suffered by PQ17's merchant seamen in the course of 5 July 1942, the last thing the officials in the British Admiralty and Ministry of War Transport wanted to see was another disaster on the same day. Yet partly as a result of their departments' own inefficiency during the run up to the westbound QP13's departure, that is what was to happen during the passage of that convoy.

It is possible that the repercussions from the bombing of Murmansk and the nearby bays in the Kola Inlet during the days leading up to 27 June 1942, when the bulk of the freighters participating in QP13 left the inlet, were partly to blame (QP13 consisted of 23 merchant vessels which sailed from Murmansk and another 12 from Archangel).[1] The bombing was so heavy that the British headquarters in Murmansk had to be moved to the town's outskirts. At the beginning of July 1942 Rear Admiral Richard Bevan, the Senior British Naval Officer North Russia, was moved to confirm that most of the town was 'in ruins'. His 2 July 1942 report that effectively formed part of his war diary confirmed: 'Incendiaries caused the many wooden structures to be burnt down, only rows of brick chimneys being left standing.'[2]

The damage was not confined to residences. During June 1942 three Allied merchant ships (the British *Empire Starlight*, and the American *Steel Worker* and *Alcoa Cadet*) which had reached northern Russia in previous convoys were sunk in the Kola Inlet by a mixture of bombs and mines dropped from German planes. The bombing near the Murmansk hospital became so intense that it had to be closed down, and all its patients moved to other hospitals near the Kola Inlet and in Archangel. British administrators in Murmansk were also preoccupied by the fallout from another acute emergency which occurred just three days before QP13, and PQ17, were due to sail.

At around 9 a.m. (Russian time: GMT + 3) on 24 June 1942, in the course of yet another bombing raid, the British minesweeper HMS *Gossamer*, which was anchored in the Kola Inlet's Mishukov Bay (near Mishukov Point, a short distance to the north-west of Murmansk – see Map 23), was hit.

At least one of the bombs struck *Gossamer* aft, the resulting explosion practically severing her stern from the front of the ship. Some 15 men were killed as a direct result of the explosion.

When *Gossamer* shortly afterwards began to tip over slowly to starboard, the survivors were ordered to abandon ship. According to *Gossamer*'s Lieutenant Commander Thomas Crease: 'The only two wounded men it was not possible to get away would undoubtedly have died anyhow, the one with a shattered spine, and the other with a very severe chest wound and two broken legs.' However, a handful of men ended up being drowned.[3]

One of the men who had a lucky escape was the 19-year-old asdic operator Geoff Jelbart, who hailed from Parkes, a town in New South Wales, Australia. 'Aussie', as he was known by his British crew mates, recalled when interviewed after the war how he was manning a pair of *Gossamer*'s Lewis guns when the German planes appeared: 'The [plane] . . . I remember mainly was one that seemed to be attacking *Hussar* (another minesweeper) . . . I can still see that plane levelling out after the attack on *Hussar* and . . . I was firing at that. Next I remember, I was about perhaps 30 feet up along the boat deck lying on my face with the guns . . . still strapped to me . . . I remember pushing myself up on my hands, and somehow I realized my legs wouldn't work. I can remember the blood squirting out of my right ear . . . I thought: "The bastards, they got me."

'(Able Seaman) . . . Wingfield came along, and he said: "Are you all right Aussie?" . . . I said: "My arms are all right, but I don't think my legs will work." . . . He had to undo the gun belt, and he got me [up] and slung me across his shoulder . . . I was just like a sack of spuds hanging over his shoulder, and I heard the First Lieutenant's voice saying: "Who've you got there Wingfield?" And he said "Aussie, Sir". He said "OK, put him in the boat."'

Jelbart must have blacked out at that point. When he next came to his senses, he registered that he was lying face down on a stretcher on the deck of *Hussar*'s wardroom, among the wounded who were deemed past saving: 'There was a stretcher alongside me with a bloke on it, and he was a real mess . . . I can remember thinking to myself: "I wonder who that is." [I could see] I could poke my finger into his brain as his head was mashed up.'

Jelbart only realized how terrible his own wounds must have appeared when he heard some of his friends from *Gossamer* asking how he was, and then saw the *Hussar* seaman who came to check on him go back to them shaking his head. As far as the *Hussar* crew were concerned, Jelbart, like the man lying beside him, was a goner. Only later did Jelbart discover that he was literally covered with blood from the top of his head to the bottom of his legs, thanks to the shrapnel thrown out by the explosion having pierced his flesh all over his body, front and back. His back had also nearly been broken in two places, which explains why at one point, he cried out for a cushion to be placed under his stomach to take the pressure off his spine. He was very nearly naked, since the blast from the explosion had ripped off most of his clothing apart from his belt and boots.

The man lying beside him died the next day. Whereas Jelbart and the other 13 severely wounded *Gossamer* survivors had the relative good fortune to be taken to what by all accounts was the best of the hospitals in the Kola Inlet, in Grasnaya (a few miles to the north-east of Murmansk). How he was transported there he never discovered, because he fainted before he was moved there, and when he next came round, he was lying in a hospital bed, bandaged from his neck down to the calves of his legs in blood-soaked bandages, sorry that he had ended up in such a state, but thankful he was not one of the 24 who had lost their lives.[4]

Whether or not the strain of dealing with the fallout of the *Gossamer* sinking distracted British administrators, they were less punctilious than usual during the days that followed. Significantly they committed the cardinal error of not briefing the American Captain James Hiss, master of SS *American Robin*, properly. He was not informed in advance he was to be the reserve commodore for QP13, let alone clearly told the location of the minefields the convoy would have to avoid.[5]

As a result, when on 4 July the 35-ship convoy was split into two, and the next day he was called on to lead the part of the convoy consisting of 19 ships past the minefield off Straumnes Point, north-west Iceland, on the way to Reykjavik, he had to rely on the minesweeper *Niger*'s Commander Arthur Cubison, the senior officer of the escort, to direct him where to go.[6]

That might not have mattered had Cubison himself, in the low visibility that obscured his vision at around 10 p.m. on 5 July, not mistaken an iceberg he came across off the coast for mainland Iceland, thereby prompting him to believe he and the two-column convoy following him were within the four-mile-wide safety zone off Straumnes Point, making it safe to proceed towards the west. Whereas in fact they were further away from the mainland, and therefore, unless they changed course towards the south, at risk of hitting the mines in the minefield laid in that area.

At around 10.45 p.m. (8.45 p.m. GMT) Cubison sent Hiss an urgent signal disclosing his mistake concerning the iceberg, and recommending the convoy should change course towards the south.[7]

Shortly afterwards Lieutenant Graeme Ogden, commander of the British trawler *Lady Madeleine*, which had previously escorted the eastbound PQ16 (see Chapters 14 and 15), and was now the escort on the westbound convoy's port beam, heard what he later described as a 'heavy muffled explosion'. His account continues: 'Looking round, I saw *Niger* . . . about half a mile off our port bow . . . had taken a . . . list, and was clearly in serious trouble.'

With engine racing, *Lady Madeleine* approached the sinking minesweeper at top speed. But she arrived too late for most of *Niger*'s crew. 'By the time we got to *Niger*, her bows were pointing skyward like a [sinking] toy boat,' Ogden wrote in his account. 'The part of her bottom which was above water was unharmed. I thought at the time an acoustic torpedo must have blown her stern off. Some of her crew were clinging to the nearly perpendicular foredeck, and others covered in black oil were hanging onto a Carley float some little way away. Within a minute, with a final hiss of escaping steam, she slid backwards into the hungry sea, and disappeared before our astonished eyes.'

Ogden still had the chance to save the lives of some of those who were in the sea. However, he described as 'heartbreaking' the attempt to rescue men whose bodies were as slippery as eels as a result of being immersed in the sunk ship's fuel oil. He would never forget how at one point, he had an arm around *Niger's* 'oil-covered Australian first lieutenant', the first and last of the minesweeper's officers whom he saw after the explosion, only for a wave to sweep the lieutenant away. As Ogden reported, *Niger's* second-in-command was 'never to be seen again'.[8] It was not just the minesweeper's officers who were lost. The official report chronicling the events of that night suggests that the number of *Niger's* crew who were rescued was as few as eight.[9] Another report states that 148 of the minesweeper's officers and ratings lost their lives as a result of the sinking.[10]

Ogden and his crew were far from being the only ones who were perplexed by what they witnessed that night. François Flohic, a young cadet in the Free French corvette *Roselys,* which had been guarding the starboard side of the convoy, would later describe how shortly before 11 p.m., in her turn, '*Roselys* was shaken by an explosion, and a fountain of water shot up into the air beside one of the merchant ships in the convoy, which began to sink. Nearby, other giant mushrooms of water sprang up out of the sea without any clues being displayed that might have revealed the whereabouts of any vessel that might have been the instigator of the explosions.'

Flohic's account confirms that rather than taking evasive action, *Roselys* was steered towards a merchant ship which was sinking around half a mile ahead, 20° to port of the corvette's original course. The account continues: '[On the way] I saw an eruption of water under the stern of the fifth ship in the [convoy's starboard] column, jolting it up in the air. Another column of water shot up in front of the vessel 100 yards behind the [fifth] ship, and a similar column went up under the eighth ship in the line. I could hear other explosions without being able to work out where the sound was coming from.'

Faced with what seemed to be a murderous attack, which had appeared from nowhere, the crews in the merchant ships were panic stricken. Some signalled torpedoes were passing under their hulls, while others fired with all their guns at what they took to be U-boats or surface ships they believed they had sighted through the mist.'[11]

In fairness it was not just the merchant seamen who thought they had seen traces of the enemy. *Lady Madeleine*'s Graeme Ogden attested afterwards that he too had seen 'the track and bubble wake of two torpedoes' which had prompted a member of his crew to yell out a warning to the trawler's helmsman.

Some of the escorts' crews were slower to react than others. The following explanation forms part of a post-war interview given by Norman Pickles, a radio operator in the British trawler *St Elstan*, which was behind the two columns of merchant ships: 'I was cleaning my teeth, leaning over the stern of the boat, and I looked up and there was a merchant ship halfway out of the water . . . [standing] perpendicular with the screw up in the air and the boat down as far as the bridge . . . I chose to ignore it. They'd been telling us about there being mirages up in the Arctic in these conditions, and I kept on cleaning my teeth. I had just finished cleaning my teeth and [was] going back up on deck [when] . . . the alarm bells rang.' Only then did he realize that the vision he thought was playing tricks on him was in fact the nightmarish reality.[12]

It is likely that Pickles was witnessing what one seaman would refer to as 'the spectacular death throes' of the American ship *Hybert*. What he described is certainly consistent with the following extract from the account by the cadet Romuald Holubowicz, who had been one of the distressed seamen in that ship being ferried back to Iceland after his own vessel *Syros* had been sunk during PQ16 (see Chapter 14). Following explosions near *Hybert*, he along with the crew had abandoned her. They then had the luxury of watching the ship go down from afar.

'We saw the vessel settling by the stern,' he recalled afterwards, 'and [then] saw a gradual reversal of the sinking attitude. Our last view of *Hybert* was seeing it standing perfectly upright on its bow end, with the entire hull from the bridge aft totally out of [the] water. After a majestic pause, the vessel seemed to give a final shudder, and slid quickly and arrowlike into the deep.'[13]

How fortunate *Hybert*'s crew and passengers were compared to those travelling in the American ship *Massmar*, whose passengers included all the survivors from *Alamar*, another of the ships sunk during PQ16. It did not help that both of *Massmar*'s lifeboats had been damaged in the course of the German air raids on Murmansk even before QP13 sailed. The failure to stage an abandon ship 'practice' before leaving port was also unwise.

Because of this latter omission, when there was an explosion under *Massmar*'s starboard side aft following on from the explosions near the other QP13 ships, there was no tried and tested escape plan, and in the words of William Gibson, the officer in charge of the *Alamar* armed guard: 'Pandemonium reigned.' One of the most costly mistakes was that too many people got into one lifeboat, and it sunk causing many to drown. The failure to prepare for the worst explains how it came about that *Massmar* ended up having the highest death toll for any merchant ship that was sunk on 5 July, or for that matter for any vessel participating in either QP13 or PQ17. No less than 45 of the men on board lost their lives in the course of this disaster.[14]

The number of crew members, armed guards and distressed seamen who lost their lives in the course of *Massmar*'s sinking was thankfully an exception to the rule in spite of the quantity of vessels impacted by the explosions. Five QP13 merchant ships were sunk or abandoned, including four American vessels, and two more were damaged. However, apart from *Massmar*, the only other merchant ship with substantial losses was the sunk Soviet ship *Rodina* (see Note 15 for other American ships' losses).[15] A Russian account states that of the 58 crew and passengers who had been travelling in *Rodina*, just 23 were picked up.[16]

Having said that, it might have been a very different story had it not been for the heroism exhibited by the captains and crews in the three remaining escorts, who continued their search for survivors notwithstanding their expectation that any minute they might find themselves on the end of a torpedo, shell or mine.

Given the escorts' vulnerability, it is no wonder the contribution made by the officers and men in the corvette *Roselys* was appreciated by the survivors so keenly. Her crew picked up no less than 179 men, more than the other two escorts added together.[17] In another extract from the account of the action by *Roselys*' cadet François Flohic, laid out below, there is a description of how the corvette's captain, Lieutenant de Vais-seau André Bergeret, organized the rescue:

'All the crew except those needed to manoeuvre the ship were assembled aft, where the deck is nearest to the water and where the rescue nets made it possible to pull individual men from the sea. To achieve this, because the sea was too rough to launch boats, [Bergeret] . . . had to move alongside the shipwrecked men one by one. The wind and waves made it hard . . . to pull this off at the first attempt. It had to be done quickly because those who had not choked to death through swallowing oil would not survive for long in the freezing water . . .

'It was not necessary to bother with some of them . . . Sadly some were floating face down in the water . . . One man in his hurry to escape from his lifeboat [to *Roselys*] had his skull crushed like a nut between the two hulls.

'At the same time there was . . . a humorous side to the drama. One man who was rescued declared in [his best] French: "Ne vous occupez pas de moi, je connais le chemin!" (Don't worry about me; I know the way) before going to the chief engineer's . . . cabin. It was the *City of Joliet*'s chief engineer who was heading for the bunk he had occupied [after his ship was sunk during PQ16] on the way out.'[18]

Norman Pickles was also able to see the funny side linked to one of the most tragic incidents of the night which he observed while *St Elstan* was rescuing survivors from the sinking Soviet ship *Rodina*. 'The [Soviet] crew were making for their own lifeboats. So we went alongside her and the lifeboats. Some of them were in the water . . . and two unfortunately were children. They were floating in the water, dead. I think probably what caused it was that, being children, they were only small, and they had full length life jackets on, so they were floating horizontally on the water, whereas normally with a life jacket, your head's out of the water. It was a sorry thing to see, but we got . . . these Russians on board, and the first thing that we did when they'd been in the water, they were taken down to the mess deck, stripped off, rubbed down and if possible given some dry clothing.

'One of the engineers came dashing up into the wheelhouse where the duty officer was, just outside my cabin, and he was in a panic. They'd been stripping these survivors down in the engineer's cabin aft. They'd stripped this one down and found she was a woman! "What are we to do with her?" [he had asked].'[19]

Eventually, the easily shockable engineer's blushes were spared, and the traumatized lady's immediate needs catered for when it was decided she could sit in the wardroom, and have the use of one of the junior officers' cabins. Pickles was later told her husband was a Soviet diplomat who was about to take up a new position abroad.

The search for survivors was eventually called off during the early hours of 6 July. Some initially thought German vessels were involved. But no German surface ships materialized. Also, analysis of Admiral Nordmeer's war diary after the war has not disclosed the involvement of any U-boats. That all goes to suggest that Rear Admiral Dalrymple Hamilton was correct when in his report of the tragedy, he wrote: 'There seems little doubt that the convoy had steamed into the eastern edge of the minefield.'[20]

In the circumstances, the Admiralty and the ships' crews just had to be thankful that the whole of the Reykjavik portion of the convoy had not been sunk. The 12 merchant ships, representing the bulk of the vessels from this portion of the convoy still afloat, reached Reykjavik during the evening of 6 July, and that night. The other two surviving ships went to a different Icelandic port. [21] All ships in the other branch of the convoy also made it safely to their destination, the bulk of them reaching Loch Ewe on 7 July.[22]

22

A Safe Haven

Main Action: 6–7 July 1942
Making for Novaya Zemlya, PQ17 part 6

(See Maps 13, 14 and 22)

Even while the dramatic scenes during the evening of 5 July 1942 that resulted in so much torment and heartache for the Allies were being played out off Iceland as well as in the Barents Sea, equally momentous events were taking place in Germany. Shortly after 8 p.m. that same evening, intelligence landed on the desk of the Marinegruppenkommando Nord's Admiral Carls in Kiel that was to change everything. It contained an astonishingly accurate translation of the report emanating from one of the Allies' ships that the German battlegroup spearheaded by *Tirpitz* had been sighted at 5 p.m. that afternoon heading towards the area still occupied by the remains of convoy PQ17.[1] It was precisely the same intelligence as that contained in the signal Admiral Bevan (SBNO North Russia) had circulated to the PQ17 escorts almost exactly an hour earlier (see Chapter 19, and its Note 14).

Before another hour had passed, another reported sighting by the Allies was on Carls' desk.[2] He immediately realized that this opened up the possibility that the Home Fleet would seek to catch up with the German battlegroup while it was chasing after the convoy. Although Carls was in favour of continuing with the operation even if it involved taking a risk, Grossadmiral Raeder disagreed. Raeder felt that attacking with his capital ships was no more likely to succeed than if the Germans relied exclusively on their U-boats and aircraft. That being the case, taking any risk whatsoever with the capital ships could not be justified. During the evening of 5 July, Admiral Schniewind was duly informed the attack was off.[3]

If the commanders of the British escorts still with the convoy could have been informed about this immediately, a lot could still have been done to protect the PQ17 merchant ships. However, although a message sent by the Germans shortly after 10 p.m. that night, which contained the confirmation that Rösselsprung had been cancelled, was duly intercepted and passed to the codebreakers at Bletchley Park, it was not decoded until the morning of 6 July, and it was the afternoon of that day before it was incorporated into an Ultra.[4] Possibly because it was thought necessary in order to conceal the source of this intelligence, the attempt to let the PQ17 escort commanders know they could rescue survivors was delayed until the evening of 6 July.[5]

A lot of water had passed under the escorts' bridges by then. Between 10 a.m. on 6 July and midday the following day, 11 of these escorts had made it to the area inside the entrance to the Matochkin Strait. It was the same narrow waterway separating Novaya Zemlya's north and south islands, which as mentioned in Chapter 20, had been the haven identified by *River Afton*'s master Harold Charlton before his and his crew's journey there had been cut off in mid-flight by *U-703*'s torpedoes. The sailors aboard some of the other fleeing merchant ships had been more fortunate. Five of these vessels joined the escorts there along with one of PQ17's rescue ships.[6]

At the time, their arrival in such a haven after all they had seen and heard must have appeared to their crews as nothing short of miraculous. However, the crews in the first groups of ships which arrived there were left in no doubt that they were still far from civilization; this could by no stretch of the imagination be called the Soviet Union proper. When *Pozarica* and her two accompanying corvettes nosed into the strait during the afternoon of 6 July, members of their crews, after seeing that *Palomares* had arrived before them, witnessed the kind of welcome from the few inhabitants they saw which they might have expected to encounter had they been in a liner steaming without prior notice into the harbour of a semi-deserted African island. The only difference was that here, they were overlooked by snow-covered hills and mountains, and there were patches of snow on the unexpectedly green foreground leading down to the water's edge.

The following extract from Godfrey Winn's account describes the main features he noticed as *Pozarica* edged gingerly past the isolated settlement they came across in a bay on entering the strait: 'A few bare wooden buildings in front of which were grouped a dozen men, two women and their children, and a pack of hunting dogs, all gazing out at us with curiosity tinged . . . with caution . . . They did not unbend so far as to wave a greeting. Instead they pointed the barrels of their guns at us.'[7]

Only after the settlement's reception committee consisting of a small band of Russians in a motorboat had chugged out to *Pozarica* with a tommy gun in its bows trained on the ack-ack ship, was there any indication that the British fugitives were among friends. Winn concluded his description of this stage of the proceedings by adding: 'In the end, the language difficulty was overcome by the usual international currency. A cigarette was offered and accepted. Smiles followed. All was well.'[8]

The next stage commenced with even better news. According to Winn, there was 'a spontaneous burst of cheering' in *Pozarica* when during that evening *Lotus* steamed into the strait carrying the *Pan Kraft* and *River Afton* survivors: 'Small and sturdy, the *Lotus* came slowly past,' Winn reported later, 'her very limited deck space packed tight with human salvage, many of whom were still wearing their lifebelts . . . One more proof that battle does go to the brave.'[9]

However, there was ongoing nervousness concerning what might happen if the Germans decided to blockade the strait's entrance, transforming the safe haven into a prison.[10] That might have been assuaged somewhat had they received the Admiralty's messages intimating that the German battlegroup had returned to its base and that picking up survivors was now officially permitted.[11] Unfortunately for those survivors who might have benefited, atmospheric conditions did not favour communications. While they were in the strait, no messages from London reached them. Although an attempt was made to communicate with the Admiralty via the local radio station near the entrance to the Matochkin Strait, there was no immediate response.[12]

Fear of what was lying in wait outside the strait persisted for those in the haven in spite of the dearth of mayday messages. On 6 July 'only' two PQ17 ships were sunk: US freighter *John Witherspoon,* which was torpedoed by *U-255* to the west of Novaya Zemlya's South Gusini Nos (Yuzhnyy Gusinyy Nos) at the southern end of the archipelago's west coast, and the American *Pan Atlantic,* when TNT on board blew up after she was bombed by an aircraft well to the west of Novaya Zemlya's west coast resulting in 26 fatalities (see 13 and 14 in Map 14, and Note 13 for approximate locations).[13] Whether any distress messages were sent, or whether if sent they were received by those who had by then reached Novaya Zemlya is hard to fathom given no mention of them is to be found in the relevant official reports.

Whatever was received, it was set against the context of the sense that those in the 'safe haven' were still in danger that the escorts' commanders decided that they must all head off to Archangel on 7 July without any effort being made to go looking for other ships, or the many lifeboats which were heading their way.[14]

Afterwards there would be time enough to argue over whether it was wrong to strive to save the five merchant vessels 'in the hand' rather than seeking out other orphan ships 'in the bush'. There was always a risk that all of the in-hand ships might be sunk if their escorts were too ambitious. But there were consequences. The attitude of the officers in charge in the safe haven, however understandable, was probably responsible for the sinking of the American *Alcoa Ranger* by *U-255* to the south of Novaya Zemlya's southern island's Moller Bay during the morning of 7 July, and the sinking of the American ship *Olopana* south-west of Novaya Zemlya's North Gusini lighthouse by the same U-boat during the early hours of 8 July in the course of which at least five men were killed (for locations see 15 and 17 in Map 14, and Note 15).[15]

It was the witnessing of the former sinking, and the subsequent pursuit northward by the U-boat involved, that persuaded the master of PQ17's CAM ship *Empire Tide,* who had spurned the chance to shelter in the Matochkin Strait the previous evening, to take refuge in Novaya Zemlya's Moller Bay (Zaliv Mollera), anchoring in what her master referred to as 'Nazizderik Roads at the back of Karmskulski Island' (Nayerdnik Reyd at the back of Ostrov Karmakul'skiy).[16] There was another small settlement nearby (Malyye Karmakuly) with a wireless station and an emergency hospital, making *Empire Tide* the nineteenth ship to find a relatively safe haven in a sparsely populated part of the archipelago (the eighteenth was the Soviet tanker *Azerbaijan*, which had not only made contact with the occupants of the settlement alongside the Russian Harbour (Russkaya Gavan') at the northern end of Novaya Zemlya's northern island, but had persuaded them to use the settlement's wireless station to request assistance in a message sent to Moscow via another port).[17]

The decision by the escorts' commanders to remove themselves from the danger area can also be 'blamed' for the sinking of another of the scattered ships by a U-boat, which in terms of the number of casualties, as well as the resulting suffering, can lay claim to be PQ17's biggest disaster.

Minutes before the 17 vessels crept out of the Matochkin Strait, which they did at around 7 p.m. on 7 July, the chances of the British SS *Hartlebury*, which had some time earlier steamed southward past the strait, making it to safety on her own was in jeopardy. Her crew were sailing her as fast as she could go towards the south, parallel to Novaya Zemlya's west coast, about 15 miles away from the shore. Her cargo included, amongst other aid, 36 tanks, seven aircraft and six other vehicles.[18]

Members of her crew may well have been hoping that having avoided the attention of the Germans so far, they might now be allowed to complete their voyage without further interference. However, unbeknown to anyone on board, *Hartlebury* was already a marked merchantman. During the early afternoon of 7 July, as *U-355* approached Novaya Zemlya, the U-boat's lookouts had spotted the smoke emitted from *Hartlebury*'s funnel. By late afternoon the U-boat had caught up with the merchant ship, and the German submarine's crew were tracking her every move.

At around 6.35 p.m., by which time *Hartlebury* was well to the southwest of what her master referred to as Novaya Zemlya's 'Britvin Light Head' (Mys Britvin), *U-355*'s 31-year-old Kapitänleutnant Günter La Baume gave the order to fire a fan of three torpedoes at the British merchant ship from around 2,000 yards (see 16 in Map 14, and Note 19 for location).[19]

The result could not have been better from the German point of view. *Hartlebury* was struck twice in quick succession under the bridge and beside her engine room on her starboard side, and then again on her starboard quarter a few minutes later.[20] Her back broken, she broke into three pieces and sank within a matter of minutes.[21] The aftermath that followed the shooting was to be more drawn out. It has been well documented. The torment endured by those members of her crew who survived, and the tragic deaths of some of those who did not make it in spite of successfully abandoning ship, have been immortalized in a series of vivid diary entries written after the event by Needham Forth, who was the ship's 20-year-old 3rd mate. More recently what happened to some of the other members of the crew has been described in an interview given by Peter Armstrong, who at the time of the sinking was a 17-year-old cadet in the ship.

Needham Forth's recollection of the minutes before and after the first torpedo struck were recorded in the following terms (his incomplete sentences have been filled out with words in square brackets and explanatory information in round brackets): '[I] had just relieved [the] 2nd Mate (the 25-year-old Harold Spence) for tea. [I had] walked out on [the] bridge, and . . . walked into [the blast from the first] torpedo which exploded immediately below [where I was standing. There was a] terrific crash, [and] everything [went] black . . . [as I] was drenched by [a] solid wall of water coming from [the] Monkey Island, bringing with it all kinds of debris. [I was] struck heavily on [the] head by something, and [although] stunned, my one [main] thought . . . [was] to get to the other side of [the] ship before the second . . . [torpedo] struck . . .

'[I] crawled through [the] wheelhouse . . . and got on [the] other side just as [the] second torpedo exploded. This time my feet left the deck . . . and I landed on my back. [The] Oerlikon gun nest collapsed, and pinned the Captain (George Stephenson) down. [He was] freed by [the] marine gunner, and [then] we all made a dash for the lifeboats . . .'

Needham Forth's account goes on to chronicle the events after he reached the ship's port lifeboat: 'Cadet (Cox) . . . let go the forward fall, sending the nose of the lifeboat crashing into the sea, where she filled right up, throwing several of the fools who had jumped into her into the water. This terrible accident caused a panic, as the starboard boat was already damaged . . . [Some of the seamen] dashed to the tiny jolly boat which was hastily dropped into the water . . . and she capsized under this weight . . .

'Meanwhile the Chief Mate . . . had gone straight to the (port) forward raft and got her into the water . . . But he was so engrossed in his task of letting the painter go, that he did not hear our cries to wait for us as we struggled with the confounded ladder. [Before we could climb down to it], the raft was . . . cut loose, so I decided my only hope was the port lifeboat, now full with water, and hanging by the after fall with several of the crew inside, and apparently dozens [nearby], shouting and crying in the water.

'[I] slid down a rope and got aboard . . .'[22]

'I [then] turned around, thinking Spence was going to follow me, but he hesitated . . . I suppose he was waiting for me to get off the bow line. And at that moment [either] somebody slipped it (or it was cut, possibly using the knife the Master said he threw down to the boat for that purpose), and we shot away.'[23]

Whichever event took place, Forth's diary entry concluded, 'we drifted astern leaving the poor 2nd Mate hanging on the ladder.'

According to Forth: '[We] hauled as many as we could aboard [the lifeboat], including the Captain, who had jumped overboard and swam to us.'

Their rescue efforts were impeded by the explosion made by the third torpedo. It 'struck home right abreast of us', said Forth, 'lurching the side of the ship right over us, and we all thought she was coming right over on [top of] us. AB Dixon, a worthless type of individual at any time, was shouting and screaming about us all being doomed etc . . . [However we] finally cleared the ship with only . . . minutes to spare.'

Yet the climax of the sinking drama was still to come. As the following extract from Forth's account makes clear, only then did he witness the shocking sight which would haunt him for the rest of his life: '[I] was horrified to see [Spence, the] 2nd Mate, [was] still on . . . [the ship. He] had taken off his coat, lifejacket and cap, [and had] resigned himself to his fate. [He] gave us a wave just before the ship folded up and went down.'[24]

Forth, interviewed later, said: 'Maybe he thought he could swim clear. But he didn't.'[25] It was, as Forth emphasized, 'a tragedy' because Spence was 'only just married'.[26]

One suspects the survivors on the chief mate's raft felt even more miserable after *U-355* surfaced and after the U-boat crew had talked to them. While going through the usual motions, the German U-boat crew told the shipwrecked sailors that all the other ships in the convoy had been sunk as well. Then they sailed away, leaving the survivors to make it to land as best they could.[27] Kapitänleutnant La Baume evidently did not think they would make it. After appraising the state of approximately 30 survivors he saw squatting in the 'not very seaworthy boat and rafts', his verdict was that 'it is questionable whether they will reach the coast given the wind blowing out to sea'.[28] The German failure to offer them a helping hand provoked Forth to comment: they were 'leaving us in a state [which] seemed at the time to be one of the cruelest things possible'.[29]

It is difficult to decide who out of around 13 men on another raft occupied by amongst others the teenage cadet Peter Armstrong, and the 17 men including Forth and the 42-year-old Captain Stephenson in the port lifeboat had the most traumatic experiences over the next hours.[30]

According to Armstrong, it was a case of the survival of the fittest on his raft: 'The ones who sat down succumbed to the cold, and they died the first night. I remained standing throughout the night. The (39-year-old 2nd) engineer (Joseph Tighe) and I stood facing each other with our arms round each other's necks, and that was the only way we could keep out of the water, which was very choppy . . . What he was doing was to recite the 23rd psalm all night. In the morning (8 July), he said to me: "I've got to sit down". So he sat down, and he died too. We just slid him over the side, and watched him float away.

'He was the seventh man on the raft to pass away,' Armstrong confirmed, 'leaving six of us. That made the raft a little more stable than it had been. The raft was floating higher.'[31]

Nevertheless, given the captain recorded in one of his reports that the water temperature was 32 °F (0 °C), it is surprising that Armstrong did not freeze to death.[32] He would later recall he was wearing: 'a pair of shoes, trousers, shirt, a blue boiler suit and a life jacket and that was it. The 2nd Engineer had a nice white cable stitched jumper, and he was floated off with his jumper. I've often thought it would have been very handy to have kept [it]. I didn't think of that [at the time].'

They drifted like this for many hours. What saved them on 8 July was something that must have seemed like divine intervention. 'We came across another raft [from the ship],' Armstrong explained later, 'with one of the crew and a dead gunner in with him. We put the dead gunner over the side, and we transferred to that raft which appeared to be undamaged. It had paddles, but you can't paddle a square object very efficiently. You can't make much headway. [However] once we met up with the other raft, we could sit down. In the raft there was condensed milk, pemmican and water.'

They then had another stroke of luck. Although they could not control

the raft, it drifted towards Novaya Zemlya, and on 9 July, they just happened to pass within sight of a lifeboat from another PQ17 freighter. The
ship was the American *Winston Salem,* which since the previous day, had
been grounded around two and a half miles from North Gusini Nos (Sev-
ernyy Gusinyy Nos), off the western coast of Novaya Zemlya's south
island (to the south of where *Hartlebury* had been sunk), where there was
an uninhabited lighthouse.[33] The lifeboat 'came . . . and picked us up, and
took us back to the ship,' Armstrong remembered. Then carrying on,
using the terminology that was acceptable in those days, he recalled:
'They hoisted the lifeboat up on its falls and its davits, level with the boat
deck. I stepped out, and went down in a heap. I can remember this big
negro picking me up, and taking me down to the accommodation. They
stripped us off and rubbed us down with alcohol, and we were on that
ship for about three days.'[34]

While Armstrong and the other six men on the raft were surviving
against all the odds, an equally desperate battle was being waged by those
who had ended up in the port lifeboat. From the moment Forth boarded
the lifeboat, it was partially submerged: 'All of us [were] up to our waists
in the icy water,' he recalled. After *Hartlebury* sank, he did his best to
make the boat habitable. 'I got an oar and tried to pull her head round . . .
but by myself it was hopeless. Everybody else [was] apparently resigned
to their fate . . .'

At this stage their prospects seemed irrevocably hopeless. The following words in Forth's account reveal how the culling started off:

'[The] crew began to die . . . First fireman Hutchinson, then the Mess
Boy, AB Clark, poor old Sibbitt (Sparks), then the 16-year-old cabin boy,
then AB Dixon and Hansen . . . These [men] were dead inside two hours,
and had to be unceremoniously pushed overboard to lighten the boat. A
little later Chief Engineer, galley boy [and] another fireman died, and by
midnight Chief and 2nd Stewards, Cook, a gunner and . . . Ordinary
Seaman . . . Jessen had also gone . . . All went the same way. [Each man]
became sleepy. [His] mind [began] wandering slightly, and then [came
the moment when his] eyes [were] glazing over [before finally arriving at
the] finish. Apparently not a bad death.'[35]

Captain Stephenson had a more decorous way of describing the action
taken when members of his crew passed away in this way, confirming in

one of his reports: 'I took the lifejackets off these bodies and buried them.'[36]

Forth's account continues: '[I was also in] very bad shape myself. [I] had stayed up to [my] waist in water trying to handle [an] oar for an hour, and I was slowly [becoming] aware of the fact that I was going the same way as the others. The water [was] having a stupefying effect on me. So I struggled out [of it], and scrambled up among the gang in [the] bows, where we huddled together with [the] boat rolling, and waves washing along her whole length. Everyone [was] cramped and frozen. [Our] feet [were] absolutely white and stiff.'[37]

As was the case in relation to Armstrong's raft, it took a bit of good fortune to turn the tide for those in the lifeboat. '[The] weather calmed down at midnight,' Forth wrote. 'There were now only 5 of us left . . . [However we] started bailing as soon as we could, and despite our condition, we quickly had the boat half emptied, and the mast and sail up [after a fashion – we] couldn't get the mast right up. But we got along OK.'

Nevertheless the following words in Forth's account show they were not out of the woods yet: 'Fireman [John] Storey, after being very useful [and] energetic in the bailing out, went off his head, and climbed overboard and was lost.'

As on Armstrong's raft, a second stroke of luck was needed before the survivors in the lifeboat could really say they were in control. '[We] sighted [a] "boat" about 2 a.m.,' Forth reported. 'It turned out to be a raft . . . with the Chief Mate and 8 others [on it. We] maneuvered alongside, and they piled aboard, bringing additional stores with them. They were all quite fit, and had [had] no casualties. [They] immediately . . . got to work, bailing the boat dry, [and] stepped the mast up properly.'[38]

'[We] (the 13 men now in the lifeboat), had [a] tot of brandy, biscuits, condensed milk and Horlicks tablets. Pretty soon [we] had the boat going along in fine style. [We] reached land either early morning [9 July] or [during the] evening [of 8 July – it was] impossible to tell with sun up all day.'[39] (*Hartlebury*'s Captain Stephenson's reports state it was the night of 8–9 July.)

They had made it to what they believed to be a small uninhabited island off the southern of Novaya Zemlya's two main islands. Once on dry land, they celebrated by rigging the sail so that it could serve as a tent, lighting a fire and cooking up a soup made out of the tins of pemmican in their emergency supplies along with some eggs they found. 'In spite of the eggs containing young birds, they tasted very good,' Captain Stephenson confirmed later.[40]

They remained in their makeshift camp for two nights, only making their next move after a third piece of good fortune. When the mist cleared at breakfast time on 10 July, a vessel was sighted in the distance which appeared to them to be stopped out at sea. They decided to row towards it in the lifeboat, and were greeted on their way by some of the sighted ship's crew in their own lifeboat. The *Hartlebury* men learned it was the same ship, *Winston Salem,* which was still aground on Novaya Zemlya's North Gusini Shoal, whose crew had rescued the men on Armstrong's raft.[41]

Some 20 out of the 59 men who had been in *Hartlebury* when she sank had made it to what amounted to another haven, if not yet to ultimate safety. The remainder had died, making her the sunk PQ17 ship with the largest number of losses (39).[42]

On the other hand, all things considered, most of the *Hartlebury* survivors had relatively minor injuries. 'All my crew were suffering from immersion feet,' Captain Stephenson wrote in one of his reports, 'and 4 men who were very badly affected were [eventually] flown from Pomorski Bay to Archangel. We were in the boat for 17 to 18 hours, but our feet did not commence to swell until after we landed at Archangel. We had doctored our feet as best we could whilst on the island, and only one man [after arriving in Archangel] had to be "operated on".'[43]

According to Needham Forth, the man requiring surgery was the assistant steward, one of the four survivors who had been in the port lifeboat from the very beginning, before they were rescued by the chief officer and the men on his raft. As for Forth's own feet, he had frostbitten toes all right, but they and his feet were saved because he had been able to put on the seaboots he had taken from the 33-year-old 2nd Radio Officer Herbert Sibbitt, before his corpse was dragged to the side of the boat and dropped into the sea.[44]

23

Home Run

Main Action: 7–15 July 1942
First Novaya Zemlya to White Sea convoy, PQ17 part 7

(See Maps 14 and 24)

As mentioned in Chapter 22, the 17-ship PQ17 'convoyette' (5 merchant ships, 11 escorts and a rescue ship), which it was hoped would have a straight uninterrupted run to Archangel, had set out from the Matochkin Strait during the early evening of 7 July 1942. Having said that, their passengers and crews might have been much less optimistic had they been privy to the torpedoing of *Hartlebury,* and the torment suffered in the aftermath.

The first event that told Godfrey Winn, one of the convoy's participants, it would not be plain sailing, occurred during the late afternoon on 8 July.[1] He, and everyone else in *Pozarica*'s petty officers' mess where he was standing, heard what he described as 'a crunching grinding noise . . . against the sides of the ship . . . like the grating of a giant's teeth', a sure sign they were surrounded by ice.

So pronounced was it, that it prompted one petty officer to squeeze the curled up fingers on one hand against his palms, and to blurt out: 'I saw a ship off Newfoundland broken in two just like that.'

When Winn reached the open-air deck, he was horrified to see 'ice as far as you could see in the fog, sheets and sheets of it'. His account carries on to explain that even while the captain 'tried to back out of the trap, a fresh block closed in behind us, so that we were assailed from all sides . . . Fifty yards away we could glimpse *Palomares* . . . [likewise] struggling helplessly to escape, turning now this way and now that, and all the time the ice closing tighter and tighter against her sides.'[2]

Far from being able to make a direct run to Archangel, there was an enormous ice barrier running from the north-west to the south-east in their path, every bit as unpassable as the one that had hemmed PQ17 in from the north. The ships ended up having to travel to the north and west until they reached the ice edge's westernmost point. Only then could they turn to the south once again.[3]

All but one of the ships, after being extricated from the ice, reached this westernmost point, but in so doing, the convoy was split into two main groups. The leading cluster of ships consisted of the two ack-ack ships, the three corvettes, one trawler, two of the five merchant ships and the rescue ship *Zamalek*.[4] The other group was led by two minesweepers, and also included two trawlers and two merchant ships, one of which, *Ocean Freedom*, had a flooded forepeak, the result of her hull having been holed by the ice.[5] The fifth merchant ship, which was nowhere to be seen, had returned to the Matochkin Strait, with the benefit of hindsight a wise decision considering what was to come.[6]

No sooner had the ice obstacle been cleared than Winn's heart missed a beat again when shortly before midnight during the night of 9–10 July he heard reports coming in telling *Pozarica*'s captain that aircraft had been detected by the ship's radar heading towards them, then more aircraft and then still more.

Within minutes around 15 aircraft were overhead, but flying so high that, as Winn recalled later, they looked like 'flies . . . with silver wings outstretched . . . apparently harmless'. As the following extract from his account makes clear, that was not the case: 'Above the . . . cacophony of all the [ship's] guns . . . , you could . . . hear the tiny brittle peevish sound of the bombs coming down . . . As the whining shrilled to its ominous climax, it was a relief even to close your eyes . . . and duck. The next instant, the ship started to rock in protest, and raising my head . . . I beheld a great water-spout astern. The first of our "near misses."'

Winn found some comfort in that from 10,000 feet, which was his estimate of the planes' altitude, 'a ship of our size would look no larger than a matchbox' (see Note 7 for escorts' commander's analysis).[7] But that did not appear to prevent the large body of aircraft coming close to sinking each of the ships in turn. Around 25 more aircraft turned up after the first wave of attacks.[8]

The rescue ship *Zamalek* appeared to be particularly fortunate, if a ship that came under a sustained attack could be described in such a way. 'Again and again she . . . [was] straddled, [and] . . . completely obscured by huge fountains of engulfing spray,' wrote Winn. 'Again and again one turned away, not wanting to witness the death of such a brave ship, and then a moment later, someone called out: "It's OK; she's still under steam." And by Jove she was, holding to her course . . . as though she was taking part in some peace time manoeuvre and the fantastic disturbance of the water had been caused by nothing more dangerous than a school of porpoises.'

The merchant ships were less fortunate. 'Hell, they've got her!' was the cry that told Winn that the American ship *Hoosier* was out of action, after one near miss too many caused her to drop out of line, when her engines cut out. A second merchant ship, *El Capitan,* soon went the same way.[9] In both cases there were no fatalities.[10] But with U-boats circling, a decision was made to try to sink the abandoned ships (see 20 and 21 in Map 14, and Note 11 for approximately where these ships were abandoned).[11]

Those in *Pozarica* had their much-criticized captain to thank for keeping the anti-aircraft ship out of trouble. 'I can see him now,' Winn wrote admiringly afterwards, 'looking up and waiting for the exact second when he sensed the bombs were actually leaving the plane, and then he'd make his decision . . . "Hard to Port" down the tube to Mac in the wheelhouse below, in a voice no louder than you would ask for a window to be opened in a railway carriage. "Hard to Starboard" . . . Instantly the ship would begin to swing round, . . . but so agonisingly slowly that you rose on the toes of your feet to try and increase her speed in turning from the line of the bomb aimer's sights.' Then as Winn's account attested, they all had to hold their breath and duck while listening to the 'whining of the bombs. Again and again and again.'[12]

It was around 4.30 a.m. on 10 July before the last of the aircraft had disappeared over the horizon.[13] By then Winn was so stunned, and in such agony as a result of a burst eardrum in one of his ears, that he was unable to celebrate his and the ship's survival with any vigour. But there was one last act that he could not bear to let his chronicling omit: 'The Captain gave orders to change direction slightly so that we should come alongside . . . [*Zamalek*].' Then, wrote Winn, Lawford announced over the loudspeakers, ' "Let's give them a cheer." The same second he was taking off his cap and waving it in salutation towards the strangers on the other bridge fifty yards away, who must surely have had their hearts warmed to hear cheer upon cheer echoing from fore to aft right along our ship's length.'

But that was not the end of it. Winn recounts how shortly afterwards those in *Pozarica* 'beheld a sight . . . that must have made them equally content. The *Zamalek* was dipping her ensign in recognition of the protection she had received, while the answering cheers rolled back from her own packed decks.'[14] By this stage she was host to more than 150 survivors.[15]

The respect *Pozarica*'s captain showed to Mac, whose responses to his commands had steered their ship out of harm's way so often that night, was all the more intense for its restraint: it consisted of a casual handshake as if to say: I knew I could rely on you and I was not disappointed.[16]

But the loss of the two merchant ships meant that the half of the convoyette escorted by the ack-ack ships and corvettes was now pointless from the Russians' point of view, since it brought with it no aid. The only positive, apart from rescuing the merchant seamen from the two abandoned ships, was that on 8 and 9 July, the escorts had stumbled across the lifeboats first of *John Witherspoon* and then of *Pan Atlantic*, the two American merchant ships sunk on 6 July.[17] As Winn observed, the first boat had a scarlet sail. 'Yet even so, five hundred yards away, the sail had been invisible in the fog. Another few minutes, and we should have been past and their last chance of survival . . . gone.'[18]

None of the ships comprising the other half of the convoy were lost. That was not through the Luftwaffe's want of trying. Although two of the 34 German Ju 88s from 1 and 2 wings of KG30 which were sent to sink the remaining freighters were shot down by their escorts, both the surviving merchant ships were damaged by very near misses, and one as a result had to be towed part of the way towards its destination.[19] The British merchant ship *Ocean Freedom* eventually made it to Bakaritsa, an Archangel anchorage, on 11 July with the 20 tanks and 15 aircraft which formed part of her cargo.[20] While the American *Samuel Chase*, which had 37 tanks and 108 other vehicles on board as part of her cargo, arrived in Molotovsk one day later.[21] The fact that none of the other merchant ships that had participated in the convoyette had arrived meant the grand total of delivered cargo for the first Novaya Zemlya-to-the-White Sea run was what was carried in these two merchant ships.

Perhaps that explains in part why there was no Russian reception committee laid on for the escorts' crews. After the long passage down the Dvina river, representing the last stage of their journey, prompting a signaller on the corvette *La Malouine* to note 'the strong pine smell' and to write in his diary: 'Nothing can be seen but timber at the water's edge, and behind that, pine forests', rather than being welcomed in Archangel, *Pozarica* was diverted to a wharf on Brevennik several miles away, which according to Winn was worse than a 'dump'. There was, he wrote: 'not a shop, not a café, not a house of any size'. The only signs of civilization consisted of 'a few miserable huts [and] a few old men in rags, who eyed our arrival as we tied up with an unchanging, uninterested stare that made us wonder why we had come at all'.[22]

There was no doubt that Stalin had been briefed on the PQ17 disaster. The following extract from the interim report Anastas Mikoyan, the Soviet minister for trade, sent to Stalin and Molotov on 9 July concerning what was referred to as 'the 17th convoy of ships from Iceland to Archangel' made for depressing reading:

'On 27th June 35 ships left Iceland, but two of them were damaged by the ice and returned to where they started. 33 ships were expected in Archangel. As at today's date, two have arrived, one Soviet, *Donbass* . . . and one British . . . (in fact the convoy's only Western merchant ship that had arrived at a Russian mainland port by the date of the report was the American *Bellingham*. She, and the 20 tanks and 105 other vehicles she was carrying along with other aid, reached Iokanka, near the entrance to the White Sea, on 8 July.[23] The British rescue ship *Rathlin* and *Donbass* reached Archangel on the day Mikoyan wrote the report).'[24]

Mikoyan added that he hoped more ships could be salvaged.[25] But the arrival of just two ships with the convoyette from the Matochkin Strait during the three days after he wrote his report made for an unpromising start.

It says a lot that arguably the greatest achievement of the West's merchant seamen who were supposed to be transporting the aid to Russia in PQ17 was the way they managed to row their lifeboats to Russia after abandoning their ships. It would be overegging it to state that the Barents Sea was full of such lifeboats. But there were many more than for example during PQ13; in excess of 40 lifeboats were successfully launched from PQ17's sunk and abandoned merchant ships.[26]

None of these survivors' travails have been described in more detail than those experienced in the lifeboats lowered from *Paulus Potter*, the Dutch ship that was one of the group of three freighters sunk or put out of action near the ice on 5 July (see Chapter 18). It seems appropriate to refer to them here, apart from anything else because they represent a continuation of the Dutch contribution to the history of the Arctic which had started centuries earlier. The reports about the exploits of *Paulus Potter*'s predominantly Dutch crew under the command of her Dutch master represent an appropriate homage to the eponymous Dutch explorer Willem Barentsz, their fellow countryman, whose sixteenth-century expeditions had led to the Barents name being given to the sea whose limits he had explored.

Some of the first tottering steps by *Paulus Potter*'s crew after abandoning ship are referenced in the following extract from the report by Captain John Pascoe, the 51-year-old master of the British ship *Bolton Castle*, who has written about how his own crew took to two of their lifeboats during the same air raid as that which led to *Paulus Potter* being abandoned: 'We . . . went over to the 4 lifeboats from the *Paulus Potter* . . . Her Captain [Sissingh] asked what I proposed to do, and I told him I should try and make the Murmansk coast, distant about 470 miles. He said that was too far, and he would try to reach . . . [Novaya Zemlya], only 370 miles away. This coast is deserted, and I did not want to risk landing in some uninhabited spot with no assistance available even though it might be nearer. So we agreed to part, and I set my course for Murmansk.'[27] *Bolton Castle*'s master was to be the odd man out. Julius Richter, the master of the American *Washington*, which as mentioned in Chapter 18 had been abandoned during the same raid, also agreed that the members of her crew who had clambered aboard two of her lifeboats should head towards Novaya Zemlya.

At first the mood in the Dutch boats was positive. Their morale was improved by the good weather, and by the way the boats were pulled swiftly through the waves by the lifeboat with a motor to which the other three lifeboats were attached.

Ronnie Crees, the young British apprentice, who initially thought they would be picked up quickly because the Royal Navy would come looking for them, recalled afterwards how he was so lighthearted at the start of their journey in the lifeboats that he even went so far as to crack a joke, only to be met by a censorious reply which highlighted the difference between the British and the continental use of humour: 'I said to the Steward, who was in the boat: "Chief . . . How about a bowl full of water so I can have a nice wash?" He said: "Ronnie, if you want water, you must wash over the side; we have water only for drinking", as if I didn't know it.'[28]

But *Paulus Potter*'s Captain Sissingh noticed how his men's high spirits were dampened when during the night of 5–6 July, they caught sight of a ship which turned out to be the American merchant ship *Olopana*. One might have expected such a sight to have cheered everyone up, but 'I noticed the mood on the boat worsened,' Sissingh reported later. It turned out the men did not want to be taken on board, putting them at risk of being attacked by aircraft again. Against his better judgement, Sissingh agreed to go along with what the majority wanted.

Sissingh's views were influenced by his privately held fears which he did not disclose to his subordinates. There was not enough fuel to enable the 'motor boat' to keep its motor running all the way to Novaya Zemlya. They would need to rely on the wind once the motor conked out. But what if the wind blew towards the north rather than towards the south? 'A southern wind would blow us back to the ice edge, and that would mean a swift death for us all,' he reflected.

He was also apprehensive, as in fact were many of his crew, especially after they were separated from the lifeboat with a motor, about their vulnerability while in thin-skinned lifeboats because of the dangers posed by the natural world that was all around them in the Arctic. There were several scares on this count. The boats were sometimes approached by seals whose heads poking out through the surface of the sea, looked just like U-boat periscopes. On other occasions they nervously watched pods of whales swimming alongside them, conscious that these huge mammals could so easily upset their relatively fragile boats.

Equally disturbing in a different way were the hallucinations which affected many of the men in the boats. Long before they reached land, they 'saw' beautiful mountains, houses and ships which tempted them to make for them. The hardest to resist was the sight of a pub, which many of the thirsty Dutchmen would have given almost anything to visit.

After they returned to civilization in England, Sissingh read a book entitled *A Guide To The Preservation Of Life At Sea After Shipwreck* published in 1943 by the Medical Research Council's Committee on the Care of Shipwrecked Personnel. It specified that people in lifeboats 'particularly in the northern latitudes, sometimes imagine they can see things which are not there . . . This is the same phenomenon as occurs in the desert, and if you experience it, it does not mean that you are out of your mind.'[29]

The book also contained a section on how to ration water, which Sissingh believed might, if he had only known about it, have provided a means to control the hallucinations. The writers of the book advised that to remain completely healthy for the time normally spent in a lifeboat, the ration for each person could be around half a litre each day.[30] Whereas the two half teacups a day which he allowed, basing the ration on his estimate that they might have to remain in the lifeboats for around 12 days, amounted to just 0.2 litres per day. After reading this, he concluded that it was the lack of water which had been the problem; as soon as they had enough to drink after reaching dry land, they had no more visions.[31]

Accounts relying on the recollections of members of *Paulus Potter's* crew do not appear to specify accurately when exactly they made it to Novaya Zemlya. The men in the three boats without a motor eventually reached the archipelago's northern island (they had previously lost touch with the boat with a motor). However, the diary written by Robert Henderson, a radio operator from SS *Washington*, whose boats were following a similar route at an equivalent speed, states that they first sighted land during the early hours of 11 July, although he says they had to travel another 80 miles or so down the west coast of Novaya Zemlya's northern island before they found a suitable spot for landing. They stepped onto dry land early the next morning. That means their first sight of land and their first landing occurred on the same days when ships from the first convoy from the Matochkin Strait reached Archangel and Molotovsk.

They had a lot to be grateful for. As had been the case with the three *Paulus Potter* boats which reached Novaya Zemlya, no-one in *Washington's* had died on the way to the archipelago. Nevertheless, Henderson complained that the time in between abandoning ship and landing had been 'a nightmare'. He added: 'There was plenty of grim reality out there in that vast ocean in a little open boat . . . There were 23 men in each boat, and we were so crowded that you couldn't stretch out at any time. Fellows started getting frozen feet a couple of days out. The deck engineer (Eddie Hall) was the first to discover that his were black, and others examined theirs and found them badly swollen . . . We had less than a blanket apiece, and at times we nearly froze. We had snow, rain, sunshine at midnight and almost every kind of weather condition imaginable. At the same time fellows were suffering with frostbitten feet, their faces were peeling from sunburn . . . Many were sea sick, and seasickness is much worse when there is nothing . . . [in] your stomach to come up. Our lips became dry and cracked, and at times we could hardly talk because our throats were so dry.'

As if that was not enough of a challenge, the men in *Washington*'s boats were also at risk on account of the same natural phenomena that had worried the men in the *Paulus Potter* boats. Henderson reported afterwards: 'We had the hell scared out of us when a whale came up so close to the side of the boat that we had to pull in our oars to keep from hitting him.'[32]

However, all these scares and torments would be quickly forgotten once they had climbed out of their boats onto the deserted section of Novaya Zemlya where they landed. Here they found fresh running water, driftwood that enabled them to make a fire, and birds they could catch. The birds were added to the stew which the steward cooked up using the tins of tomatoes and corn that were in the boats. He also made an acceptable hot drink out of the bars of chocolate from the lifeboats.

The plentiful food and drink gave them back their strength. After a couple of days, they got back into their boats again, and sailed on down the coast. On the way to their next stopping place, they met up with the men in the three *Paulus Potter* boats who had also sailed southward down Novaya Zemlya's western coast after a fortifying break on dry land. All five boats from the two ships that had ended up making it to the archipelago subsequently landed in a little cove that was some 70 miles from the *Washington* boats' first landing place. Here a feast was enjoyed by all, thanks to some of the men discovering they could catch local birds by dangling string nooses from the top of the cliffs, and then yanking them up when the unsuspecting birds put their necks into them. In this way over a hundred birds were caught, and they were all cooked on the six fires that were soon blazing.[33]

But still there was no sign of civilization. Apart from anything else, they needed to find a doctor and medication for two of the men whose feet were so painful they could no longer walk.

The next day the five boats set out on their longest journey since arriving on the archipelago. For the first time since they had landed, all their lives were in jeopardy again, because if they missed the island they were targeting, the next land mass was hundreds of miles away. About 12 hours after setting off they ran into fog, and then carried on blindly for around another 12 hours.[34] They might have had to follow the same route taken by the first Matochkin to Archangel convoy, had they not during the morning of 15 July, thanks to one of those 'lucky' chances so appreciated by Godfrey Winn, happened to hear what Henderson described as 'the whistle of a large steamer'. One can well imagine the relief of those in the boats on hearing this. 'We shouted, whistled, sent up flares and damned near went hysterical,' Henderson reported. 'She [then] tooted her whistle several times till we got close enough to see her.'[35] It was the very same *Winston Salem*, whose position marooned on the rocks near the North Gusini lighthouse, had now saved five more lifeboats full of desperate men from having to endure another epic journey, and what might well have ended up with a painful death for all of them.[36]

It was a great relief for all the men in the lifeboats when an American sailor looked over the side of the partially abandoned *Winston Salem* and saw them. 'They heaved us all up on deck,' *Paulus Potter*'s Ronnie Crees recalled later. 'We couldn't . . . [climb] up. They gave us coffee which we couldn't drink. They fed us . . . a sort of hash . . . And then I was carried into a cabin which seemed to me to be suffocatingly hot, and I was laid onto a bunk . . . I must have been in a filthy condition. My hands were black, my hair was encrusted with salt, my raincoat was thick with it . . . I didn't need a shave . . . I was too young for that . . . I went into some sort of stupefying sleep.'[37]

Early the next day a Soviet trawler turned up, and took all the remaining raft and lifeboat survivors, along with a ton of canned meat and dry beans, from *Winston Salem* to the Moller Bay settlement to the north near where *Empire Tide* which was still lying. There, a primitive form of triage was put into operation. Those who were critically ill were carried onto a Catalina flying boat that had landed nearby, and airlifted to Archangel so that they could be quickly transported to hospital. They included Eddie

Hall, *Washington*'s deck engineer, who in addition to the problems with his feet, now had what Henderson described as 'a bad cold on his stomach and was having internal haemorrhages'. Others, who like Crees could not walk, had in the short term to make do with what the settlement had to offer. 'They had to carry us up a hill over the ice,' Crees recalled afterwards. 'They were slipping . . . [Once there] we could lay down, which was lovely even though there were only bare boards. They gave us a few blankets . . . [and] at least we could drink . . . They had water.'[38]

It is hard to know whether the *Paulus Potter* and *Washington* sailors would have suffered less had their captains not insisted on taking them to the icy wastelands of Novaya Zemlya.

Reports from those in the two *Bolton Castle* lifeboats, who all made it to the Kola Inlet, suggest that while they shared many of the same experiences and torments, which included becoming very thirsty especially when rowing after the motor in the starboard lifeboat conked out, and sitting for most of the time with their feet in water, most of the men escaped the level of frostbite suffered by those who had abandoned the Dutch and American ships. 'A number of the men had swollen feet, and one or two suffered from frostbite, but most of the men could walk when we landed,' *Bolton Castle*'s master John Pascoe reported. This may have been because as he had anticipated, the temperature was higher near the Kola Inlet than it was near Novaya Zemlya, or for that matter where he and his men had abandoned ship. His report notes the temperature had been minus 1°C when they first climbed into the lifeboats, whereas it was around 4°C where they were rescued.

That is not to say that all was harmonious in both *Bolton Castle*'s boats. Pascoe would later report that 'the Arab firemen refused to do anything, and just lay in the bottom of the boat waiting to die . . . I punished them by reducing their ration of water, a terrible punishment for thirsty men after nearly 9 days in a boat.' In the event this tension between the black gang, many of whom hailed from Aden (modern day Yemen) and their Anglo-Saxon master, who lived in Cornwall, did not lead to fatalities. The 37 men in the lifeboat commanded by *Bolton Castle*'s chief officer were picked up by a Soviet ship around 50 miles north-east of the Kola Inlet on 13 July, while John Pascoe and the 33 men in his boat were just 3 to 4 miles off the Soviet coast when they were picked up 120 miles north-east of the Kola Inlet. They were dropped off at Polyarnoe, the Soviet naval base in the Kola Inlet, the next day.[39]

24

And Then There Were Eleven

Main Action: 6–24 July 1942
2nd Novaya Zemlya to Archangel convoy, PQ17 part 8

(See Maps 13, 14 and 22)

While the deeds chronicled in the previous chapters played out, the moment of truth had also arrived for the men in the Allies' ships further north. During the evening of 6 July 1942, amateur yachtsman Leo Gradwell had finally released his trawler *Ayrshire* and his three charges, *Silver Sword*, *Ironclad* and *Troubadour*, from their self-imposed hibernation in the ice fields where they had been waiting since the previous night (see Chapter 20). He had become worried that the wind that had blown up from the south would lead to the ships being gripped and imprisoned by the ice.[1]

His decision to sail eastward had also been influenced by the observation that although their move into the ice had certainly not been unimpeded, once they were several miles into it, they could see that there were places where it could be penetrated by ships such as theirs. This welcome development was highlighted in a more graphic manner by the following diary entry written by *Troubadour*'s Howard Carraway describing what he witnessed after they had set off: 'The surface of the ocean here is 4/5ths covered with ice. [There is] almost a solid mass of it. But it's melting and rotten, offering little resistance when our 10,000 tons rams into it at 8 knots.

'We have been grinding steadily on, sometimes north, sometimes east, then again south when the ice gets too heavy. Frequently the old ship shakes and rattles from stem to stern, as every timber in her creaks [when] we have failed to dodge a really big hard cake and have to smack her head on. But it's gradually getting thinner, the big ones more infrequent, as we work further south and east. Every hour takes us a few miles nearer our destination and further from the damned Jerry.'[2]

That may have been the case. But they had only remained beneath the German radar thanks to an additional slice of good fortune. 'At about 5 p.m. yesterday (7 July) a plane flew directly over us,' Carraway reported in his 8 July diary entry, 'invisible as we were to him for the fog. We went to battle stations for a few minutes, but soon forgot it since there was no chance of his having seen us.'[3]

This incident, combined with the ongoing fear they might be discovered at any minute, so spooked the captains of two of the merchant ships that when the group of vessels finally reached the western coast of Novaya Zemlya on 9 July, and paused in a deep bay to the north of Admiralty Peninsula for a conference, there were nascent signs of a rebellion.[4]

'One captain, of the *Silver Sword*, wanted to scuttle the ship and save the crew,' Carraway reported, adding: 'The captain of the *Ironclad* didn't disagree. But the Old Man (George Salvesen, the 34-year-old Norwegian master of *Troubadour*, already praised by Carraway for being 'admirable in the ice, standing in the bitter cold atop the bridge for a better view hour after hour' so that 'we were the only ship of the four to get through the stuff without a bent bow or dented side') got heated up about this ... He said he was not scuttling his ship. He was going to Archangel with the cargo (which included amongst other aid 18 tanks and 186 other vehicles), or be sunk on the way there. Lives, he said, could be lost in the attempt ... [However] if they wanted to go back, or scuttle, or do anything except head for Archangel, they could do it without his company. He would go alone. I was 100 per cent behind him. This rallied weakening spirits, and we ended by planning to be off ... [that very evening].'[5]

Thus one man's courage effectively 'rescued' *Ironclad*'s cargo, which included amongst other aid 10 tanks, 15 aircraft and 80 other vehicles, and also *Silver Sword*'s which included 10 tanks, 4 aircraft and 92 other vehicles.[6]

A day later, having first made contact with the Russian radio station near the mouth of the Matochkin Strait, the group were sitting pretty beside another small settlement, some seven miles up the strait, where they found the *Samuel Harrison*, the American merchant ship which had returned to the strait after becoming lost in the fog during the first Matochkin Strait to Archangel convoyette.[7] There they were able to link up on 13 July with a Catalina seaplane flown by a Russian pilot to whom Gradwell passed the following message so it could be transmitted to Rear Admiral Bevan, in Polyarnoe:

'The situation at present is that there are four [merchant] ships in the Matochkin Strait . . . The masters . . . are showing unmistakable signs of strain. I much doubt if I could persuade them to make a dash for Archangel without a considerably increased escort and a promise of fighter protection in the entrance to the White Sea. Indeed there has already been talk of scuttling the ships near the shore rather than go to what they consider, with only one escort, certain sinking. In these circumstances, I submit that increased escort might be provided, and that I may be informed as to how to obtain air protection.

'I intend to remain in Matochkin Strait until receipt of further orders, but I may move the ships further east in the Strait if I am satisfied it will offer further cover . . .'[8]

It was 15 July before these messages were received by Rear Admiral Bevan.[9] And the three British corvettes he ordered should set out from Archangel to Novaya Zemlya with a view to escorting all the PQ17 ships still in the strait, only did so during the night of 16–17 July. They reached yet another settlement near the south of Novaya Zemlya on 19 July by what *Lotus*' Lieutenant John Hall referred to as Byelushaya Bay (Guba Belush'ya), where some of *Olopana*'s survivors had landed (the sunk American ship previously referred to in Chapter 22). It was agreed that these survivors should travel to Archangel in a Russian merchant ship scheduled to leave the next morning.[10]

By then *Ayrshire* with her group of merchant ships had sailed further east up the strait, a move prompted by a Catalina's crew informing Gradwell that they had seen his vessels stationed in the anchorage near the local medical centre from outside the strait.[11]

After making their move, they anchored in a lead off the main channel.

According to Carraway, they were: 'with high hills and mountains on all sides, as snug as a bug'. His diary entry continues: 'There is a lot of snow and ice on the land here, and huge hunks are floating in the water . . . And it's cold, as bad as it was up in the ice floes. The land is perfect wasteland. There isn't a sign of habitation or vegetation . . . Other than a few lights and beacons along the channels' more tortuous bends, you'd never know man had ever been here before us.'[12]

However, once again it was only a temporary refuge. During the night of 19–20 July, the crews in the corvettes *Lotus*, *Poppy* and *La Malouine* found them after they had moved to another bay within the strait – along with *Azerbaijan*, which had joined Gradwell's vessels, having made the journey from Novaya Zemlya's Russian Harbour, escorted by the Soviet icebreaker *Murman*. The corvettes were the first HMS ships the men in this plucky little group had seen since the scatter order no less than 15 days earlier.[13]

The corvettes' crews found at least some of the group refreshingly upbeat. That was partly because of the fact there was an end in sight, but also because the weather had taken an abrupt change for the better. The day before, Carraway had written in his diary: 'Spring is coming to Novaya Zemlya! It has been pleasant today, even warm at times . . . I bathed, changed into lighter clothes and basked in the sun on deck all day with shirt collar open and sleeves rolled [up]'.[14]

It was decided they should depart quickly, and after picking up *Empire Tide*, which for some time had been waiting in Moller Bay, and which by this time had the remaining survivors on board from several of the sunk and abandoned merchant ships, the second PQ17 Mitochkin Strait to Archangel convoyette on 21 July was on its way.[15] This time there was no opposition, and the five merchant ships and the tanker duly reached the Dvina River leading to Archangel on 24 July before being sent to their various unloading jetties in and around Archangel and Molotovsk.[16]

Eventually *Winston Salem* was refloated after some of her cargo was transferred to a Soviet ship, and on 28 July she too made it to Molotovsk along with the aid she had been carrying, which included 25 tanks and 150 other vehicles.[17] She was the last of the nine PQ17 merchant ships to make it to the Soviet Union mainland; the arrival of the two Soviet tankers took the number of PQ17 ships carrying supplies that reached the Soviet mainland to 11. *Winston Salem*'s arrival meant that the number of

PQ17 ships sunk was limited to 24, including 22 carrying weapons, vehicles or aircraft – a terrible result, but not quite as bad as had at one time been feared.[18]

There was also the added consolation that for all the talk that two-thirds of the convoy had been sunk, and the fear that scores of men had died, men in lifeboats and on rafts, who had long since been given up for lost, for some time kept turning up alive.

Many of the men who spent long days in rafts and lifeboats either survived because they reached Soviet territory under their own steam, or because they happened to be seen by the crews of passing ships. But the 61 men in the two lifeboats launched from *Empire Byron*, the first ship sunk on 5 July, owed their rescue on 10 July, approximately midway between where their ship was sunk and the entrance to the White Sea, to the deliberate attempt by the crew in the corvette *Dianella* to find PQ17 survivors. *Dianella*, one of the first PQ17 escorts to reach the White Sea, had left Archangel at midnight during the night of 7–8 July pursuant to the order of Rear Admiral Bevan, her deployment representing a token and belated compliance with the Admiralty's 6 July order that efforts should be made to rescue survivors (referred to in Chapter 22).[19]

Others who owed their lives to British search efforts included the 21 men who had escaped on four rafts following the 5 July torpedoing of the American merchant vessel *Honomu* (mentioned in Chapter 18). They had to manage without their captain, who was taken away by one of the U-boats that were present at the sinking site. During the first days following the sinking, the rafts had been tied together and towed by the survivors in *Honomu*'s only usable lifeboat. That may explain how it came about that when they were spotted from a searching British Catalina aircraft around 320 miles north-north-east of the Kola Inlet, the report that was passed on during the early hours of 15 July to the officers in the minesweepers *Halcyon* and *Salamander*, two of the other PQ17 escorts which had made it to the Dvina River, near Archangel, mentioned five 'boats'. The two minesweepers reached the area indicated two days later, by which time the men in the lifeboat which had been pulling the four rafts had abandoned their charges and left the men on the rafts to their fate.

The problem the minesweepers faced was that they had to carry out their search in low visibility. As a result they searched for more than 24 hours without finding a trace of the survivors. However, when during the morning of 18 July they tested their guns, something they did routinely every day, the men on the *Honomu* rafts saw the flashes. About an hour later, lookouts on the minesweepers in their turn heard the sound of a revolver being fired, and saw a flash to the south. After the ships had been turned towards the flash, their crews spotted the rafts and rescued all the men.

Ironically, while the 21 men were saved, the minesweepers' crews could not find the men in *Honomu*'s lifeboat, who had abandoned the rafts for fear that if they had all stayed together no-one would have had a chance of reaching the coast. By the time the lifeboat was spotted on 28 July by a look out on U-209, some 200 miles to the south-west of where the rafts had been found, only 8 out of the 19 men who had been in it were still alive. Their survival was all the more miraculous given that, as they told their captors, they had gone several days without any drinking water.[20]

It is a sobering thought that even though *Honomu* and *Paulus Potter* were abandoned on the same day, the rescued *Honomu* men survived on their relatively unprotected rafts for around seven days after three of *Paulus Potter*'s lifeboats finally reached Novaya Zemlya (see Chapter 23), and the men in the *Honomu* lifeboat were only picked up by U-209's crew ten days after that.

But perhaps the most extraordinary survival story of all could have been told by the men who made landfall in a lifeboat launched from the American merchant ship *Carlton*, had they decided to tell it. As mentioned in Chapter 18, *Carlton* was the second ship to be torpedoed on 5 July. The prospects of all but two of the crew – the two men who were killed by the torpedo – were initially the same as for the *Honomu* survivors. They had to make do with a single lifeboat and four rafts. However, at that early stage of the operation, the Germans were keen to capture and interrogate those who had survived the sinkings. Within the first 12 hours of the sinking, no less than three German aircraft landed near the survivors, and then took off, carrying as many *Carlton* survivors as could be fitted in. Eventually the rafts were abandoned, and the remaining 17 men from *Carlton* huddled together in the lifeboat as they attempted to make it to the coast.

It was a long journey. A diary written by the *Carlton* armed guard Charles Mulchy hints at the torment these men endured as they struggled to keep going. He says they became very weak, and for much of the time they were freezing cold. The sea was often rough and the wind strong. The entry he wrote for the night of 17–18 July, shortly before the men on the *Honomu* rafts were rescued, highlights their unenviable situation: 'Water ration strict, men complaining of cold. First Assistant [Engineer] delirious. Morale of men not so good. At 2200 First Assistant Engineer George Pine died of exposure. Service was held by all hands as he was dropped into the sea.'[21]

Charles Blockston from *Baltimore*, a 23-year-old oiler in the boat, benefited from George Pine's demise, inheriting his overcoat. He would subsequently admit that it was this together with the spare pair of 'pants' donated by a living shipmate which helped him withstand the cold.[22]

They were to be in the boat for another seven days before they finally made it to Tufjord, a small fishing village on Rolvsøya, an island off the Norwegian mainland, on 24 July, the same day the second convoyette from Novaya Zemlya reached Archangel (see 8 in Map 13 for the *Carlton* survivors' landing place). Insult was added to injury when, after all their efforts, the Germans immediately took them prisoner.[23]

They appear to have been the last survivors off an abandoned PQ17 ship to make it to dry land without being rescued at sea. Their arrival in Tufjord was eleven days after the last PQ17 ship was sunk; that was the long since abandoned *Paulus Potter* which *U-255* sank with a torpedo on 13 July 1942.[24]

As far as the Germans were concerned that capped what had already been described in the 6 July entry of the Seekriegsleitung's operation division war diary as 'one of the most outstanding successes to be scored at one blow against enemy supply lines'. It was only a minor exaggeration to say, as was stated in the entry, that the convoy 'was almost completely annihilated . . . The strategic, physical and moral effect of this blow is similar to that of a lost battle.'[25]

This was the German verdict at a time when the Luftwaffe was already claiming it had sunk 19 ships, overshadowing the U-boats which were claiming they had sunk at least six ships. By 10 July the claimed totals had crept up to 20 and 16 respectively.[26]

On 12 July, Colonel General Stumpff, commander of Luftflotte 5, the Luftwaffe section responsible for Norway, claimed the scalps of 22 merchant ships. This prompted him to write to Reichsmarshall Göring: 'I beg to report the destruction of PQ17. During reconnaissance made on July 10th 1942 . . . not a single merchant ship was observed.'[27]

The incontestable German victory resulted in turf wars. Admiral Schniewind, the German Fleet commander, wanted to push the line that his battlegroup's sortie was the crucial element because it had scared away the British Home Fleet, and Marinegruppenkommando Nord's Admiral Carls also concluded in his final report that the sortie was the reason why the convoy scattered.[28] However, neither of these theories was supported within the Seekriegsleitung. Their final word on the subject was that because the convoy scattered before the sortie proper started, one could not say the battlegroup's movements caused the ships in the convoy to disperse. The real reason in their opinion was that the Luftwaffe's lethal air superiority made it impossible for the Home Fleet to protect the convoy, and once the cruisers became short of fuel and departed, the convoy was no longer viable.[29] Of course, as revealed in Chapter 17, the German theories were incorrect. But the German commanders would only find out the truth after the war when the story of the breaking of the Enigma code reached the public domain.

Not surprisingly the Soviets were as bitter as the Germans were jubilant. On 17 July 1942 Comrade Koltiakov, head of the Political Department of the Northern Sea Fleet, complained: 'The Americans, like the British, don't try to save their vessels when they sustain small insignificant damage. They are quick to get into their lifeboats to save themselves . . . It's no wonder the British and Americans marvel at how our sailors behave. They were amazed at how the crews in *Starii Bolshevik* (during PQ16) and *Azerbaijan* reacted . . . According to the American report, *Azerbaijan*'s crew did not panic and took all necessary measure in order to "heroically" save the tanker . . . This could be used as an example for the foreign sailors . . . to follow, but as it stands, they admire what we do, but do not follow suit.'[30]

Koltiakov went on in a subsequent letter not only to castigate the Royal Navy for running away (see his quote in Chapter 1), but he also enumerated what he took to be the most egregious examples of the Allies' merchant seamen's lack of commitment.

Concerning the abandoning of the American vessel *Washington* on 5 July, he wrote: 'Our comrades (passengers on board *Paulus Potter*) witnessed how quickly the British (sic) sailors abandoned the vessel which had been set on fire, and got into their lifeboats . . . while it was still afloat . . . The English (sic) did not attempt to save the vessel.'

He had similarly trenchant views concerning the abandonment of *Paulus Potter* after a series of near misses: 'The Dutch sailors became scared, and the English sailors on board intervened and said they must get ready the lifeboats. The lifeboats were immediately lowered, although at this time there was no damage, and there wasn't a single enemy plane in sight, as they had already dropped all the bombs they had carried . . . The crew started to get into the lifeboats . . . The vessel stayed afloat. It could have been saved.'

He also criticized the sailors in the American ship *Olopana* for temporarily abandoning their ship when they mistook a seagull for a German aircraft (on 5 July, in other words more than 48 hours before the ship, with the sailors back on board, had approached Novaya Zemlya and then been sunk – see Chapter 22). 'This shows how easily the American and British sailors are scared, and what cowardice they exhibit when there is a battle to be fought. It shows that the Americans and British have not yet learned to fight for the survival of their vessels and cargo. They do not yet have an ingrained hatred of the enemy.'

When referring to the subsequent sinking of *Olopana* on the night of 7–8 July, he wrote: 'Can we really believe the vessel was sunk [by the enemy]? It would be fair to speculate based on the previous evidence that the crew abandoned their vessel at the first sight of a scouting enemy plane.' (However see Note 31 for a different take on the *Olopana* crew's actions).

As for the *Winston Salem* sailors, who had abandoned their ship after it was grounded near Novaya Zemlya, and who had thrown the machine guns into the sea before going ashore (the ship is first referred to in Chapter 22), Koltiakov wrote: 'Does it not make you feel sick to hear about such reckless behaviour?'[31]

Koltiakov was far from being the only Soviet official to rant about the shortcomings of Russia's British and American allies before the last of the PQ17 merchant ships reached the White Sea. The 19 July 1942 report to Molotov by Admiral Nicolai Kuznetsov, People's Commissar of the Navy, stated: 'It was clear that the British were unwilling to risk their large ships even though the British Navy had superiority over the German Fleet two times over . . . The [defence of the convoy] operation was effectively just a case of the British going through the motions; the covering of the convoy by the main forces was a sham. And the strongest part of the convoy's close escort went to cover the Navy's main forces, leaving the merchant ships defenceless . . . The operation was unsuccessful due to its bad organization and the indecisiveness and cowardice of the British commanders. Our military attaché in England reports . . .that some of the Navy's officers and crews think that what the British Fleet has done is a disgrace.

'I think we should tell the British Government that the Admiralty has not acted efficiently, and suggest to the British Government they should take their Fleet commander in hand.'[32]

It is likely that Kuznetsov's report being delivered on 19 July 1942 was no accident. The previous day Churchill's 17 July telegram confirming that the next Arctic convoy must be suspended, had reached Stalin. Churchill's message had in its turn been triggered by the briefing the British prime minister had been given by his most senior admiral. In the course of the 13 July 1942 Defence Committee meeting, Admiral Pound had warned that the next convoy would face similar challenges to those which had led to the decimation of PQ17; the minutes stated that this meant 'he could not guarantee that a single ship would get through'. He said this at a time when it was believed that a maximum of eight ships from PQ17 would be saved, which would have resulted in around 500 tanks and 260 aircraft being lost.[33]

Pound's pessimism struck a chord with Churchill for the first time since the Arctic convoys began. The minutes of the meeting record Churchill as having stated: 'He had taken the view that if 50% of the ships of a convoy got through, it would be justifiable . . . but if the loss were heavier than that, it would be wrong to continue.'

That did not stop him as a last resort on 15 July running past Pound a possible solution to the problem that anyone else would have realized was unthinkable: escort the convoy all the way to Russia with no less than four aircraft carriers, at least five auxiliary aircraft carriers, two battleships and some 25 destroyers. 'If we can move our armada in convoy under an umbrella of at least a hundred fighter aircraft, we ought to be able to fight our way through and out again, and if a fleet action results so much the better.'

However, while theoretically possible, this extreme proposal ended up being rejected because, as Churchill conceded, it 'involved engaging a force vital to us, out of proportion to the actual military importance of the Arctic convoys'.[34]

Once that had been decided, there was nothing for it but to give the Russians the bad news, and after receiving confirmation that Roosevelt agreed, Churchill wrote to Stalin to tell him Pound's forecast, and that 'therefore with the greatest regret . . . we have reached the conclusion that to attempt the next convoy . . . would bring no benefit to you, and would only involve dead loss to the common cause.'

In the hope Stalin would agree they were taking a rational decision, Churchill in his telegram explained that the problem arose because: 'We do not think it right to risk our Home Fleet eastward of Bear Island . . . where it can be brought under the attack of the powerful German shore-based aircraft. If one or two of our very few most powerful battleships were to be lost . . . while the *Tirpitz* and her consorts, soon to be joined by the *Scharnhorst*, remained in action, the whole command of the Atlantic would be lost. Besides affecting the food supplies by which we live, our war effort would be crippled; and above all the great convoys of American troops across the ocean, rising presently to as many as 80,000 in a month, would be prevented and the building up of a really strong second front in 1943 rendered impossible.'

The only consolation he could offer immediately was the statement that the capacity of the 'trans-Persian routes' was expected to rise to 75,000 tons monthly by October 1942, and 95,000 tons and 100,000 tons of aid could be delivered to the Persian Gulf in September and October respectively excluding trucks and aircraft. Churchill added: 'If we can devise arrangements which give a reasonable chance of at least a fair proportion of the contents of the convoys reaching you, we will start them again at once. The crux of the problem is to make the Barents Sea as dangerous for German warships as they make it for ourselves. This is what we should aim to do with our joint resources.'[35]

Churchill's message would have been unwelcome at the best of times. However, coming as it did at the very moment when the German army, seemingly unstoppable as their forces converged on Rostov on the River Don, a staging post on the planned advance towards Stalingrad and the

Caucasus as part of Operation Blue, it was almost inevitable that it would receive a very frosty response.[36]

Sure enough, on 23 July, the day before the second Novaya Zemlya convoyette reached Archangel and Molotovsk, and more importantly the very day when triumphant German forces were entering Rostov's city centre, Stalin replied indignantly: 'Our naval experts consider the reasons put forward to justify the cessation of convoys . . . wholly unconvincing. They are of the opinion that with goodwill and readiness to fulfil contractual obligations, these convoys could be regularly undertaken and heavy losses . . . inflicted on the enemy . . . Of course I do not think that regular convoys . . . could be effected without risk or losses. But in war, no important undertaking could be effected without risk or losses.'

His experts also could not understand why the scatter order had been made.[37]

At the end of his letter, Stalin stated that he hoped Churchill would not be offended by his frank comments, but Soviet Ambassador Maisky, who had handed over the telegram, noted in his diary that Churchill was both 'depressed and offended' by what he had read. It did not help that, as Maisky noticed, Churchill 'must have had a drop too much whisky'. The British premier was particularly upset by the accusation that Britain had broken her contractual obligations which he disputed.[38]

In respect of the all-important military supplies requested by Russia, Churchill was strictly speaking correct. During the period covered by the First Protocol (1 October 1941 to 30 June 1942), Britain had dutifully made available at centres of production more than the promised 1,800 fighter aircraft, 2,250 tanks and 3,000 trucks. However, even though Britain had complied with the Protocol's clauses, there was no avoiding the fact that there was a shortfall in substance. For example at the time when Churchill and Maisky met, only 1,300 First Protocol aircraft, and 1,440 of the First Protocol tanks had actually arrived in Russia, and given that the Arctic convoys had been suspended, there was no chance in the short term at least of Britain's deliveries via the northern route catching up.

Nevertheless there was to be no admission in the first instance that Stalin had a point. The next day Churchill and his War Cabinet decided that no reply should be sent to Stalin to avoid 'a wrangle', and Maisky was to be told verbally why the British government was only stating the truth when it claimed that Stalin's charges were unfounded. Maisky was also to be given a fuller explanation as to why the convoys were being stopped.[39]

The need for a negative reaction to Stalin's message was to be superseded by the evolving situation on the ground out in Russia. By the time the War Cabinet convened on 27 July, Churchill's mood had been uplifted by the news that 10 merchant ships had reached the White Sea ports, and an eleventh was on the way there. Only two of the eleven were British. However, as Churchill pointed out, the arrival of that many ships meant overall 'practically one-third of the convoy had reached [its destination]. This was better than we had at one time expected.'

He was informed that if the last ship (*Winston Salem*) arrived safely, the convoy would have delivered 87 aircraft (with the British and American ship contributions being 53 and 34 respectively), 164 tanks (British and American contributions being 20 and 144 respectively) and 896 other vehicles (British and American contributions being 9 and 887 respectively) to the Soviet Union.

This was admittedly slim pickings compared with the 210 aircraft (British and American losses being 48 and 162 respectively), 430 tanks (British and American losses being 175 and 255 respectively), and 3,350 other vehicles (British and American losses being 499 and 2,851 respectively) lost. However, the relative success, compared with the zero deliveries Pound had been talking about, appears to have galvanized Churchill into suggesting that, after all, they should consider running another convoy in September.[40] Churchill's spirits may also have been uplifted by the surprisingly small number of PQ17 fatalities, although the convoy's final losses would only become known over the coming months (the final PQ17 death toll reported was around 155 men killed).

The British prime minister's positive frame of mind may well have been further influenced by the fact that notwithstanding the losses, at least Britain had done something right: the country had more than complied with the terms of the First Protocol insofar as they related to military supplies, something Churchill had been very keen to achieve given that the Western allies were not in the short term accommodating Stalin's second demand: to open that much talked about second front (see Note 41 for details of the First Protocol compliance).[41]

Maisky's diary records how at 12.30 a.m. on the night of 30–31 July, he received a phone call requesting he come to 10 Downing Street immediately. When he arrived, he could see that Churchill was completely transformed compared to how he had been when they had dealt with the fallout from Stalin's 23 July telegram. The British Prime Minister he recalled afterwards 'was in one of those moods when his wit begins to sparkle with benevolent irony, and when he becomes awfully charming'. Smiling, Churchill thrust a document towards Maisky, saying, 'Take a look. Is it any use?' Maisky speed read its content before blurting out: 'But of course! It's worth a great deal, a very great deal!'[42]

The piece of paper contained the next telegram Churchill wanted to send to Stalin. This time it contained only positive information. It started, 'We are making preliminary arrangements . . . to make another effort to run a large convoy to Archangel in the first week of September.

'I am willing, if you invite me, to come myself to meet you . . . I could then tell you plans we have made with President Roosevelt for offensive action in 1942 . . .

'I am starting for Cairo forthwith. I have serious business there, as you may imagine. From there I will, if you desire it, fix a convenient date for our meeting, which might so far as I am concerned, be between 10th and 13th August, all being well.'[43]

A supplementary message made it clear the offer of the convoy which contemplated sending 40 ships to the Soviet Union was conditional on Stalin ensuring that the 'air threat to the German surface fleet in the Barents Sea is such as to deter the latter from operating against the convoy.'[44]

Stalin wrote back the same day. He agreed to provide the necessary air cover, and he invited Churchill to come to Moscow on a day of his own choosing.[45]

25

The Red Carpet

Main Action: Late July 1942
Archangel hospitality

(See Maps 1 and 24)

While the last of the flotsam and aid ringing Novaya Zemlya's beaches and harbours was being gathered up and transported, the Allied seamen who had already reached the mainland were having their first tastes of the hostile, alien world they had entered. The passengers and crew in the PQ17 anti-aircraft ship *Pozarica* had noticed how strange everything was as early as 11 July 1942, while at the tail end of the first Novaya Zemlya convoyette they were still chugging down the Dvina river, before they had even stepped ashore at one of the ports in the vicinity of Archangel, their ultimate destination.

It was not just that women appeared to play an even more dominant role in every walk of life than was the case back in Britain. According to the signaller on one of the accompanying escorts, women sentries were seen patrolling the wood yards beside the river, scything in the fields they passed and rowing quite large boats with a boy or an old man at the tiller. Also, it was hard to avoid the impression that if something did not go according to plan, there would be unpleasant consequences of a kind unimaginable back home.

The influence this feeling of menace had on Russian citizens was highlighted by what happened while *Pozarica*'s crew were being directed on what path to follow as they proceeded downstream. One of the two Soviet 'pilots' who had come on board *Pozarica*, described by Godfrey Winn as 'Mongolian in type' wearing 'dull blue jackets . . . buttoned up at the throat, reminding one of Chinese coolies . . .' allowed the ship to run aground. *Pozarica*'s Captain Lawford was furious, and Winn observed how 'the object of his wrath, looking more like a coolie than ever, withdrew to the back of the bridge, where his companion continued to belabour him with hissing words . . . till he finally burst into a storm of hopeless hysterical weeping.'

'Why doesn't his chum stop yelling and take over?' Winn asked. *River Afton*'s Captain Charlton, who was taking passage in the ship following the sinking of his own, replied. 'Because he's not a pilot. He's simply here to watch how the other one manages and report accordingly.' The pilot, Charlton said, is 'for the high jump all right . . . He'll be sent for a long weekend in the Urals.' When Winn asked what that meant, Charlton responded: 'Haven't you heard that expression before? . . . Well you will, and many times if you stay here long enough.'

Sure enough, even before he and members of *Pozarica*'s crew were allowed off the ship for an extended run, Winn spotted at the docks at Molotovsk: 'gangs of workmen . . . chained to each other with overseers watching their progress . . . [The overseers had] a whip in one hand and a revolver at their belt.' He assumed they were guarding the much talked about 'political prisoners', whose very existence would have been a reason for Britain and America not to support the Soviet Union had there not been a war on.[1]

This was to be just one of a series of incidents, in Molotovsk and the other ports on the Dvina dotted around Archangel, which were to appal and disgust the visitors from the West. Perhaps the most shocking was the Soviet guards' reaction to seeing a Russian man, apparently driven half mad with hunger, run off with some food he had taken from a soup kitchen.

According to Sidney Kerslake, the coxswain in the PQ17 trawler *Northern Gem* quoted in Chapter 1, who at the time of the incident was on the bridge of his ship after she had been tied up at a wooden jetty on the Dvina river alongside what he referred to as 'Maimska' island: 'One of the guards shouted for him to stop, but the man either failed to hear the shouts or was too afraid ... and the guard who was carrying a sub-machine gun ... immediately opened fire with a short burst which hit the running figure squarely in the back.

'Killing in that way for such a small crime ... made my blood run cold,' Kerslake wrote later.[2]

Several similar incidents, albeit based on hearsay, are referred to in reports by other British and American sailors. Something else that upset the more squeamish of the visitors was the Russian habit of punishing perceived slackers among the 'chain gang' prisoners by making them take down their trousers and sit on the ice for up to four hours.[3] When word was received by Samuel Frankel, America's Assistant Naval Attaché who was based in Archangel, that this kind of punishment was taking place, he complained to a Soviet official, and as far as he knew, it never occurred again while American ships were in the port.[4]

That was more than can be said for the way the Russians treated the prisoners who in the course of their work were injured. William Carter, commander of the armed guard aboard *Ironclad* (one of the ships that was hidden in the ice during PQ17), tells of being alerted by a burst of gunfire near the docks at Molotovsk, and being told the prisoner lying on the ground before him, whose leg had been sliced off after falling under a rail car, had been shot by one of the Russian guards, thereby putting him out of his misery as if his life was of no more value than that of a wounded dog.[5]

Tales of such killings circulated freely among the merchant seamen. According to Kerslake, 'It ... made us more aware of the repeated warnings we received from our officers when we went ashore to stop dead when we heard a shout, and to stand still until we knew what it was all about.'[6] It is likely that it was thanks to such warnings that none of the Allies' sailors wandering around the streets of Archangel and Molotovsk, or for that matter Murmansk, were killed by the armed Soviet guards who had been instructed to control 'the foreigners'' movements. The small number of British sailors who were shot by trigger-happy guards lived to tell their tales.

However 'the foreigners' were not exactly made to feel welcome. Captain Harvey Crombie, the minesweeper commander whose ship *Bramble* had formed part of the local escort which greeted the first Matochkin Strait to Archangel convoyette, told Winn that no westerner was safe.

Although Crombie had been out in Russia for some time, he had been arrested and locked up for six hours just for going for a walk on the docks.[7]

But it was the more commonplace shunning of the seamen by the locals which members of the Allies' ships' crews tended to find most demoralizing. It started long before the PQ17 disaster. R. Struben, second-in-command of the anti-aircraft ship *Ulster Queen* which had arrived in the Kola Inlet with PQ15, has told how when he asked the way, having strayed into a building that he had mistaken for the Murmansk hotel Arctika, he was ignored. 'It was as though I were a ghost,' he reported, 'inaudible and invisible, or that there was a panel of thick plate glass between us. No one responded; all faces remained . . . blank.'

He would later conclude sardonically that 'the [Russian] comrades would have been horribly contaminated had they associated with a wicked bourgeois . . . even though he had just helped, at considerable inconvenience to himself, to bring them a large supply of weapons with which to defend their country!'[8]

This was no one-off. Godfrey Winn described witnessing similar standoffish behaviour at the Archangel theatre where he and a friend went to see a performance after PQ17. During the interval 'all the other theatre goers who had also come out for air took one look in our direction and then, almost ostentatiously, made for the far end of the balcony. It was like being sent to Coventry at school. We were as isolated as though we had the plague.'[9]

Things were not much better at the Archangel Interclub, one of several such institutions set up in the northern ports to provide a location where the foreign seamen could relax after their long voyages, and gain access to local culture. When Winn attended a dance night, he noted that the hostesses 'were behaving like the warders at a prison dance . . . They looked like robots. Hardly a smile, and certainly not a sign that they were enjoying the novel sensation of being held in the arms of a British sailor, out to kill in his tiddly suit, usually an irresistible combination the world over! . . . Clearly they had their orders – no fraternizing – and one had a sensation that all the time they were conscious of being watched by some female member of the Ogpu (name of Soviet secret police – until the mid-1930s), to be reported for any weakening, any show of real warmth towards the strangers in their midst.'[10]

An even more insidious way of stifling relations between the locals and the seamen was witnessed by John Beardmore, a junior sub-lieutenant in the corvette *Poppy* during PQ17, who after arriving in Archangel had struck up a friendship with Catrin, a young schoolteacher. He would later describe how during one of their meetings she brought along an English Literature textbook which was a potted version of Dickens' *Oliver Twist*, only it was written in the present tense:

'It was ... evident that the description of Fagin's kitchen, the slums, the poverty and crime were [being represented as] pictures of twentieth century London. I explained that this of course was not so ... She was incredulous [at first] but [eventually] believed me. Unfortunately she went away and told her friends. Sadly I never saw her again, but I learned that for her folly in listening to and repeating "false" western propaganda, she had been sent away.'[11]

During the years 1941 and 1942, Catrin was far from being the only woman who disappeared as if into thin air after being deemed to have become too close to a foreign sailor. One of the British naval officers based in Archangel in order to supply back up to the Russian end of the Arctic convoys, told Winn he had given six bars of chocolate to the Russian woman whom he had paid to clean his apartment. She gratefully thanked the officer for the gift, only to disappear the next day, never to reappear.[12]

Such happenings have tended to support the often referred to, but incorrect, assumption that in the northern Russian ports, it was impossible for there to be any meaningful relationships, let alone intimacy, between local women and the foreign seamen (this leaves aside the British convoy and aid administrators, many of whom went native during their long stays in the northern ports and took Russian girlfriends, or the foreign seamen who spent a few odd nights with Russian women classed by the Soviet authorities as 'prostitutes' – both of which are dealt with in Chapter 35). This is a fallacy which possibly only came to be accepted because many, apparently a majority, of those who visited the northern ports were never tempted or never indulged in such link ups. This is partly explained by the fact that intimate relationships between local women and the foreign seamen appear to have been confined to the White Sea ports. Witnesses have stated that if such relationships existed in Murmansk, they were not generally known about.[13]

On the other hand if you were young and reasonably good-looking, there certainly were some women in the White Sea ports who were not averse to going to bed with you. The American sailor Jim North, who hailed from Newtown Pennsylvania, was a hot blooded 19-year-old when he arrived in Molotovsk in the PQ17 merchant ship *Troubadour*. In the course of giving interviews after the war, he has openly described how he used cigarettes and chocolate to help him befriend and bed several of the women in the workers' barracks near the docks. When he first spoke to me, he appeared to be saying that he believed he had hit the jackpot. But he later admitted that after he had made love to the Russian girl whom he found most attractive – years after the war when he was interviewed by me, he recalled she was a 16-year-old blonde who was henpecked by the others – he never had sexual relations with her again because the next time he went to the barracks she was gone.[14]

26

The Blips

Main Action: 12–15 and 23 August 1942
Churchill goes to Moscow,
and a British hospital arrives in the Kola Inlet

Churchill's historic trip to Moscow, where he arrived on 12 August 1942, was made primarily so that he could break the news to Stalin in person that, for the moment at least, there was to be no second front.

But it was also meant to pre-emptively put a lid on any anger that might have been stirred up in the Kremlin concerning the suspension of the Arctic convoys.

He appeared to make a promising start. By all British – and American – accounts, during Churchill's first meeting with Stalin at the Kremlin that night, the British premier, with support from America's Averell Harriman, played a blinder.[1] After the briefest of preliminaries, Churchill informed the Russian leader there would be no invasion of France before spring 1943. And then, encouraged by Stalin's unexpectedly benign response, he announced the Anglo-American plan to seize the north coast of French Africa, so-called Operation Torch, which it was hoped would take place on or before 30 October 1942.

After illustrating the merits of this operation by waving in front of Stalin a drawing of a crocodile having what Churchill referred to as its 'soft belly' being pierced while it was distracted by feints towards its 'hard snout', the British prime minister had the satisfaction before they parted for the night of hearing the Soviet leader agree it was a 'good scheme'.[2]

The only problem was that Stalin had a habit of first playing the good cop, and then without warning, going to the opposite extreme, and being bitterly opposed to what he had previously philosophically accepted, if not approved.[3] It was a tactic previously witnessed by Averell Harriman when he and Lord Beaverbrook had visited the Kremlin in September 1941 (see Chapter 2), and it was repeated during the second evening meeting, on 13 August. In the course of this encounter Stalin was, as Harriman recalled, not just critical but 'really insulting'.[4] Churchill later recalled that Stalin said 'a great many disagreeable things'.[5]

First there was the bitter complaint that Britain was breaking the promise allegedly given to Molotov during his June 1942 visit to London to open a second front during the autumn of 1942. Then there was the querulous allegation that the West were only giving 'the remnants of equipment that could be spared', and that the decision to suspend the convoys until September represented 'an underestimate of the importance of the Russian front'. That was all the more unpopular after Churchill announced that there would have to be another suspension for the Torch operation.

But it appears to have been Stalin's hostility which irked Churchill more than anything. So much so that when the British prime minister saw the recently appointed 60-year-old Ambassador Sir Archibald Clark Kerr, an Australian-born Scot, the next morning, he said, as the ambassador noted in that day's entry in his account, 'he was damned if he would keep his engagement to dine with Stalin tonight'.

Although Churchill eventually attended the dinner in the Kremlin, he appeared to be signalling to Stalin that he was already metaphorically on his way home by dressing in what Clark Kerr described as 'a dreadful garment which he claims to have designed himself to wear during air raids in London, its advantage being that it slipped on easily and gripped itself shut. No fiddly buttons. It looked like a mechanic's overalls, or more still like a child's rompers . . . All the bourgeois Bolsheviks in uniform or in their . . . black suits stared in amazement!' That was just the first faux pas. According to Clark Kerr, Churchill's toast to Stalin was 'unduly brief and lacking in warmth. It was an occasion when, if he had cared, he might by more expansiveness have provoked much goodwill . . . He didn't.'

Clark Kerr's account of how he was forced to step in to save the day is self-serving, since it shows him in a good light, although it may well in substance at least be true. If so, it highlights, should readers need convincing, the extent to which personality can affect history. Anyone assessing it for accuracy needs to know that the raffish, bisexual British ambassador's ability to disarm irascible world leaders with his charm and small talk – what some might describe as the common touch – did not come from nowhere. His report to the Foreign Office describing his first March 1942 meeting with Stalin in the Kremlin leaves one in no doubt about that.

Confined as he was with Stalin and Molotov for two and a half hours in an underground Kremlin shelter after the air raid sirens went off, he not only managed to extract an admission from the infamously hard to please Russian premier that the Soviet Union top brass were pleasantly surprised at the way Britain had lived up to their promises of aid through the Arctic convoys, but he was also able to bond with the Russian leader on a more personal level.

The ice was broken by Clark Kerr, on seeing that Stalin was smoking a pipe in the shelter, bringing out his own pipes and tobacco so that they could compare notes on what they were smoking. There was apparently lots of sniffing and tugging at the tobacco strands with a view to comparing the British product with what was available in Moscow. 'Inevitably my tobacco went into Stalin's pipe and his into mine,' Clark Kerr reported. The British ambassador then expertly steered the conversation in directions that took it beyond anything that the ascetic teetotal Sir Stafford Cripps, his rather dry although well intentioned predecessor as ambassador, would have been able to bring to the table. There were, Clark Kerr confided: 'digressions into such matters as democracy and its weaknesses, love, the best way of handling it, . . . wives, . . . women in general . . . and the private habits of Chiang Kai Shek (Clark Kerr's previous posting had been as the British ambassador to China)', all laced with lots of jokes and laughter. The Soviet premier and the British ambassador parted if not as firm friends, with a lot more to bind them together than had been the case when their meeting had started.

If anything, softening up his own recalcitrant prime minister turned out to be the harder assignment of the two, although similar methods were employed. A key component was having a feel for the interlocutor's comfort zone, and being worldly enough, chameleon-like, to step into it. Clark Kerr's account of how this worked with Churchill starts with a description of the long drawn-out night of drinking, and interminable toasting of just about every Soviet soldier and bureaucrat at the banquet, undiluted by any attempt by Stalin at the dinner itself to establish any kind of rapport with the British leader. This, stated Clark Kerr, led to even more determined statements by Churchill the next day that 'he had had enough of Stalin' and he intended 'to pack up and go'.

According to Clark Kerr, Churchill only changed his mind after listening to his ambassador speaking some home truths while they walked around the grounds of the dacha where Churchill was staying. Clark Kerr says he pointed out that Churchill 'was an aristocrat and a man of the world' who was about to fall out with Stalin just because his pride had been hurt by this 'peasant who didn't know any better', who was 'rough and inexperienced . . . straight from the plough or the lathe', a man who unlike Churchill 'thought aloud, and in thinking aloud . . . said many harsh and offensive things'. Clark Kerr claims he reinforced his analysis of Stalin by observing that any falling out would have consequences: it was tantamount to condemning innocent men in the Allies' armed forces to die needlessly, as they surely would if the partnership of the West and the Soviets against Germany was not maintained.

Clark Kerr might have added that some allowance should be made for the extreme strain Stalin was under as the rampant German Army prepared to crown their successful launch of Operation Blue by besieging 'fortress' Stalingrad.

After a few protests from Churchill such as, 'The man has insulted me . . . I represent a great country and I am not submissive by nature . . . the man thinks he can upset my government and throw me out . . . From now on he will have to fight his battles alone', in the end the Prime Minister and his ambassador came to an understanding. It was agreed that Churchill would swallow his pride, and be prepared to come towards Stalin in the same way Stalin had tried to make up with him by accompanying the British prime minister after the dinner, as Churchill put it: 'an immense distance through corridors and staircases to the front door'. And so that such goodwill could be demonstrated, Churchill would pro-actively send a message to Stalin saying he wanted to talk to him again. 'Just the two of them . . . man to man.'[6]

And that is how it came about that the two men did meet up again, during the evening of 15 August, this time with just their interpreters present, and did manage to establish an understanding after all. To such an extent that afterwards, Stalin invited Churchill to come back to his private Kremlin apartment.

In such a relatively relaxed atmosphere, made even more so because they were served seemingly endless dishes by Stalin's housekeeper and because his red-haired daughter made an appearance, it was possible for Stalin to say anything he wanted without recrimination. Just weeks after the majority of PQ17's merchant ships had been sunk with going on 450 tanks on board (see Chapter 24), Stalin casually dropped into the conversation that the Red Army no longer needed any more tanks from his Western allies since Soviet production rates were sufficient. Instead the Soviets needed 20,000 to 25,000 lorries per month to carry their infantry around the battlefields.[7]

Also Stalin felt able to make what Churchill called 'a rough and rude remark' about the PQ17 disaster which reached the British prime minister in the following form: 'Mr Stalin asks,' said Pavlov (Stalin's interpreter) with some hesitation: 'Has the British Navy no sense of glory?'

Fortunately, from the point of view of good Anglo-Soviet relations Churchill was now in complete control of himself, and he batted away the provocation, replying simply: 'You must take it from me that what was done was right. I really do know a lot about the Navy . . .' And when Stalin replied: 'Meaning that I know nothing,' Churchill once again responded diplomatically: 'Russia is a land animal; the British are sea animals.'[8]

Early the next morning, following one final parade at the airport, the Liberators carrying Churchill and his party took off, signifying the end of a visit which in spite of the two leaders making up, had not led to a meeting of minds concerning the future.

It was against this background that a dispute blew up between the Soviet Union and Britain in relation to the medical treatment of the Allies' seamen in the northern ports.[9]

The issue first came to the fore a month before Churchill went to Moscow, as a result of outrage in London over the way the Allies' injured sailors were being treated in the Russian ports. News had seeped out after some of the wounded men had been shipped back to England in convoy

QP 13. Lady Juliet Duff, the 4th Earl of Lonsdale's 61-year-old daughter, who was a friend of the Churchills, objected. Her intervention was to be significant. Although most history books do not credit her with any great achievements, she used her social connections to make a difference. These connections stretched out in manifold directions. She was one of those women during the 1940s with access to many of the most powerful men and women in Britain, thanks to her and her family's relationships both before and during the war, with a large circle consisting of the rich and famous. Before the war, they included the former monarch King Edward VII. On 15 July 1942 she wrote to Lady Clementine Churchill, addressing her as 'Dearest Clemmie'. She wanted to know whether Lady Churchill would be prepared to use her influence 'to get a British medical unit sent to Murmansk'. Lady Duff evidently had a special interest in matters medical, borne out by her becoming a patron of the Red Cross, and the St. John Ambulance Association, as well as by her efforts to raise money for Charing Cross Hospital. That probably explains why she had been told about someone she described in her letter as 'a wireless operator in the Mercantile Marine who went there in a convoy', and who after his ship was sunk, visited 'the wretched survivors . . . taken to the Russian hospital, there being no English medical aid there'.

The reason why a British unit was needed, she said, was because: 'the conditions in this hospital are apparently appalling. It is filthy dirty, there are very few dressings, hardly any medical stores, and no drugs, so that the gravely wounded lie there groaning all day long.

'They are given only bread and rice to eat, and there are not even any toothbrushes, so primitive is the equipment.'

In case that was not enough detail to prompt action, her letter went on to explain that there was a danger the current situation might hamper the British war effort. 'Knowing what their fate will be if they become casualties, no one in the Merchant Navy ever signs on for a second voyage to Murmansk', she stated, adding: 'I do not know [the wireless operator] . . . personally. But his instructor at a wireless college, who is a great friend of mine, vouches for him as a thoroughly reliable boy, and not one to invent stories.'[10]

The reason why Clementine Churchill was targeted by Lady Duff was obvious to anyone who read the newspapers. Lady Churchill was the face of the Red Cross Aid to Russia Fund. It had raised from the British public, as well as from donors overseas, the millions of pounds required to pay for the medical equipment and drugs which were being sent to the Soviet Union.

The very next day Clementine Churchill wrote back to Lady Duff to assure her that she had mentioned the problem to her husband, and that he would ensure that the relevant enquiries were made.[11]

The enquiries proceeded on two fronts. One of several resulting chains of correspondence that were exchanged within government departments resolved around whether it was correct, as Lady Duff alleged, that sailors were refusing to go to Russia a second time because they were so put off by the state of the Russian hospitals.

Each time the civil servants came up with a rebuttal which did not quite hit the spot, Lady Duff wrote back again to make sure her point was not sidestepped by some petty bureaucrat who preferred to protect his back rather than give the injured men the treatment they deserved.[12] When she was informed by a civil servant that it was not hard to get men to go to Russia, she replied that while that might be true, 'very few are ready to go for a second time'. And when that was queried, she replied: 'of course no one minded so much doing the trip in winter, but that in summer, with practically no hours of darkness, they were attacked incessantly by planes all the way up the Norwegian coast'.[13]

While Lady Duff was upping the ante in England, in Russia two reports were prepared on hospitals in the Kola Inlet ports, including the ultra-critical assessment by the destroyer *Ashanti's* Surgeon Lieutenant John Ballantyne (quoted in Chapter 8). It was completed on 23 July 1942 and given to *Ashanti's* Commander Richard Onslow. Onslow quickly had it forwarded to Admiral Tovey with a note stating: 'I was unable to read this report without a feeling of shame that the conditions of our wounded in north Russia has so long remained neglected'.[14]

Tovey evidently agreed, because on 30 July he informed the Admiralty that the state of affairs was 'deplorable', and that equipment and personnel should be sent as soon as possible 'to establish a wholly British Hospital to care for British and Allied seamen'.[15]

Ironically, this edict was sent just when the care of the Allies' survivors was improving. Because the Murmansk hospital had been closed, and because most of the survivors were being cared for in Archangel, where the standard of the hospital accommodation was higher, the conditions experienced by PQ17's survivors were much better than those endured by the poor men injured during PQ13, and when HMS *Edinburgh* was sunk during QP11.

When Captain Guy Maund, the SBNO Archangel, was asked whether the medical conditions on his patch were adequate, he wrote back on 4 August 1942 saying that: 'The treatment and care of British sick and wounded, . . . while not coming up to British standards, is reasonably good.' However there were reservations: 'I do feel that they would be happier and better cared for in the hands of British doctors and nursing staff. Linguistic difficulties, Russian food . . . , such [practices] as head shaving, their somewhat crude methods and their indifference to alleviating pain, all tend to depress patients and to lengthen their convalescence.'[16]

The kind of crude methods he was talking about were described in the course of his post-war interview by Ronnie Crees, the *Paulus Potter* survivor, who had been taken to one of the Russian hospitals in Archangel after being transported from Novaya Zemlya's Moller Bay to Bakaritsa, near Archangel, in the CAM ship *Empire Tide*.

Before the survivors accompanying him were put on the train that took them to Archangel, they were shaved by a Russian woman. 'She shaved our hair off our heads . . . , under our arms and everywhere else,' Crees reported. 'And we were put into blankets and our clothes were taken away.'

When they reached the hospital, there was nothing much that could be done immediately. Crees would recall later: 'Our feet were so bad – at that time they were white, covered in blisters – I was just put in a bed with a cage over my feet . . . full of electric lightbulbs . . .

'One . . . day we were taken down for treatment . . . to a surgery . . . This was later on. After that stage of whiteness and blistering, the blisters burst, and the whiteness goes, and . . . the foot shrinks back (it was [at first] like a football) to something like normal size. The toes are black . . .

'[We were] sat round the edges of this room. None of us could . . . walk. In the centre of the room was a table . . . One by one, they took us up to this table, sat us on the table with our legs out in front of us on the table to examine the feet. We could see the scissors come out. And there'd be snip, snip. And something would fall into a bucket just below the table . . .

'When the first chap came back, we learned he'd lost two toes . . . They'd literally been cut off in front of us. The bone would be rotten. You wouldn't feel a thing. Then the next chap would go up, and he'd lose three toes, and someone would lose half a heel, and bits and pieces of the foot. I think they did it this way to give us a certain amount of Dutch courage.

'I was fortunate. I went up and they ummed and ahhed. But I never lost anything.'[17]

That put him in the minority. Although all the crew from the *Paulus Potter* survived – they were told on arrival in Russia proper, that the men in the ship's motorboat had also reached Archangel – several of the Dutch survivors had to have parts of their feet and legs amputated.

Their treatment by the surgeons was for many of them the most important part of their stays in hospital. But the pre and post-operative care, and the pared down diet, was not exactly what was conducive to their making a swift recovery.

'A lot of our bandages had been washed, and used again,' Crees stated in the course of his interview. 'You could see bandages hanging up in the yard to dry. They were stained . . . The food was appalling. The sausage seemed to smell. The soup was slices of black potato floating in water, highly seasoned to make it taste like soup . . . We complained bitterly . . . , but . . . we were told we were getting the best that they had . . .'

They probably gleaned this from the British doctor and his American colleague who visited them while they were laid up. It was the same pair of doctors who on 22 July 1942 had gone on a fact finding mission in the course of which they visited Archangel's morgue in order to organize the burial of Edward Hall (last mentioned in Chapter 23), the one man from the *Washington* lifeboats who had passed away after reaching the city.

The two doctors evidently believed the morgue was in a disgusting state. Their very frank report records that on entering there was 'a terrific stench'. The same document states that the room where they found the American seaman's corpse was 'generously splattered with blood, bits of intestines and brains, and the floors were filthy'.

But it was what they saw next door which gave them information of general interest. According to their report: 'On low tables . . . – all unclothed and piled [up] like cordwood – lay some one hundred and fifty dead Russians, from unborn babies weighing not more than three pounds, to quite elderly persons. The greater part had died of starvation, and the bones of the thick part of the thighs were merely covered with skin.'[18]

So that was it. The citizens of Archangel were struggling to make ends meet notwithstanding the famine that had descended on the town. The full extent of it only became generally known after the war when survivors were interviewed, and when the diary of the 54 year old Filadelf Parshinsky, a disabled out of work teacher, was published. In the diary he described how during the latter half of 1941, he managed to survive for a time on a near-starvation diet in wartime Archangel. Even when food was available in the shops, getting enough to eat was challenging to say the least. Galloping inflation had reduced the value of his pension by a factor of ten, leaving him with no choice but to subsist mainly on the relatively affordable soup and bread he was entitled to buy using his ration cards – when he could get it.

As anyone will know who has lived through epidemics or plagues, or at other times if food supplies are disrupted, when provisions come into the shops, they can only be accessed after standing in long queues. Parshinsky's experience was very much in line with this. He regularly had to queue up outside shops for many hours, an experience that was not improved when it had to be done for the best part of the day in the snow. Panic buying exacerbated shortages. Only the richer inhabitants were able to afford the inflated prices that put the more expensive food that was available in some shops out of the reach of those like Parchinsky with modest means. The acceptance of his lot was not made easier by his mistaken belief that food was being given to the Western allies in return for the weapons they were delivering to Archangel in their convoys. The Western seamen who visited Archangel's Intourist hotel were able, provided they paid the relatively high price, to have a filling, nourishing meal in its restaurant to supplement the more basic food available in their ships. But there was no mass-export of Russian foodstuffs of the kind Parshinsky appears to have imagined. On the other hand the queues that your average Russian in both Archangel and Molotovsk had to endure in order to get food, which Parshinsky describes, are corroborated by the Allied seamen's accounts. *Troubadour's* Howard Carraway for example included a paragraph in a diary entry covering what he witnessed towards the end of July 1942 which confirmed that there were what he referred to as 'little stations, soup kitchens' all over the place in these towns, where 'long queues of workers, ranging from old men and women to dirty little gamins, line up with buckets, pails, bottles etc, and a net bag for the bread.'

The food shortages led to Parshinsky taking extraordinary measures. In one entry, written during the winter of 1941 after not being able to access food for four days, he confessed: 'Today at midday I strangled my cat with a ribbon. It was suffering for about five minutes . . . I only undid the knot at 1 p.m. after the convulsions stopped, so I knew it would not come back to life.' In the days that followed, his diary describes in gruesome detail how he cut up the corpse, and then ate the cat's organs, and made soup out of its bones and head in order to supplement the meagre amounts of other food he was eventually able to acquire. He subsequently also killed and ate his other two cats. On 25 December 1941 he was driven to steal another from the street for a similar purpose, the latter being as he put it 'a grey cat that was very fat. Now I can lead a life of luxury!' he crowed in his diary entry for that day. He was evidently not the only Archangel citizen adopting such tactics. An entry in the war diary for the 126 Base Unit (the British army group responsible for training the Russians to use western tanks) stated that by mid-April 1942 all the dogs had disappeared from the streets.

Unfortunately Parchinsky did not survive the war. He may have been one of some 20,000 Archangel inhabitants who are believed to have died of hunger and disease during the winter of 1941–2, although it is possible that he died in a labour camp. He was arrested in January 1942 and given a long sentence after being convicted for his anti-Soviet pronouncements and actions.[19]

The challenges Russian civilians were facing only made it more important to lessen the impact on the Western seamen languishing in the city's hospitals.

The British hospital unit sent out on 17 August 1942 in the American cruiser *Tuscaloosa* might have achieved that end had all gone well. It was sufficient to create a 100-bed unit, for example, or two 50-bed units.[20] Rear Admiral Douglas Fisher, the new SBNO North Russia, eventually decided two-thirds should be allocated to Archangel, and the remaining one-third deployed in Vaenga in the Kola Inlet.[21]

The news that Tovey's edict was being put into action had by then been passed on by Clementine Churchill to Juliet Duff, who on 21 August wrote back: 'My dearest Clemmie. I was so thrilled when I got your letter, and I feel full of admiration for your genius in getting things done. It will make the whole difference to those wretched sailors to know that there will be a British medical unit at Murmansk to look after them.'[22]

However, Lady Duff had written too soon. Although *Tuscaloosa* with the necessary equipment on board safely reached the Kola Inlet on 23 August, and although it was then transported on two destroyers to Archangel, so that it could be divided there, the Soviet authorities would not allow it to be unloaded.

It turned out that the Soviet intransigence was because, while Admiral Miles at the British Mission in Moscow had on 10 August 1942 asked how best to obtain permission for a medical unit to be housed in Archangel, no-one had thought to actually apply for permission to land the medical personnel, stores and equipment. The official explanation given by those who looked into it was that there was a hurry to get it out to Russia while there was a ship going out there for another purpose.[23] However, possibly it was also because everyone at the British end was anxious to sort out the medical situation before Churchill returned from his travels – which he did on 24 August.[24]

If this was the explanation, one is led to the conclusion that while Lady Duff's back-channel approach had very effectively worked as a catalyst to ensure that the hospital problem was flagged, it had at the same time been counter-productive. Officials anxious to avoid being scolded by the Prime Minister, prompted by his wife, for being dilatory, may have felt goaded into acting against their better judgement before they had taken the necessary diplomatic steps. It would take months of further diplomacy before there was an abatement of the Russian anger that had been fired up by the way their approval had been taken for granted. Only then could the hospital issue be sorted.

27

Blitz

Arctic convoy PQ18, whose scheduling at the end of July 1942 had prompted such an enthusiastic response from Soviet Ambassador Maisky (see end of Chapter 24), was not permitted to depart until it was known what was the cost in terms of lost warships of Operation Pedestal.[2] This featured the protection of a convoy sent through the Mediterranean during the first half of August 1942 in order to supply Malta, a stronghold and naval base, whose occupation by British forces was of the greatest significance. During the operation more than half of the convoy's merchant ships were lost, along with several British warships, but Axis forces did not sink enough of the latter vessels to jeopardize the Home Fleet's ability to support the next Arctic convoy.[3]

PQ18 was also not given the go ahead before the many lessons learned over the preceding months were taken into account. By the time Churchill on 6 September 1942 sent Stalin a telegram confirming: 'Convoy PQ18 ... has started', there had been a major rethink concerning the measures that were necessary to secure the safety of Arctic convoys insofar as that was possible.[4]

Arctic convoys henceforth were not going to rely for protection against

German surface ships on the capital ships of the Home Fleet, which Tovey was still unwilling to risk east of Bear Island. Instead, convoys to and from Russia were to be guarded during the most dangerous parts of their journeys by an escorting force whose core would be a large gaggle of destroyers. In the case of Operation EV, the protection of PQ18 and the westbound QP14, this fighting force consisted of no less than 16 destroyers, one anti-aircraft cruiser (*Scylla*) in which Rear Admiral Robert Burnett flew his flag, one auxiliary anti-aircraft ship and, and most significantly of all, *Avenger*, an auxiliary aircraft carrier (a small-scale carrier of aircraft, also known as an escort or 'Woolworth' aircraft carrier, built by placing a flat flight deck on top of a merchant ship's hull). It was to be the first time such a carrier had escorted a Russian convoy.

For Operation EV the carrier was to be home to 12 ready to operate Sea Hurricane aircraft IBs (the carrier would also have on board six partially unassembled spares) manned by the Fleet Air Arm's 802 and 883 Squadrons, and three four-winged Swordfish aircraft manned by 825 Squadron. Tovey ruled that the carrier would in her turn be escorted by two more destroyers.

This was to be in addition to the convoys' close escort which would accompany each convoy all the way, after replacing the local escort once the convoy was at sea. By the time PQ18 met its first opposition, its close escort consisted of 2 destroyers, 4 corvettes, 4 trawlers, 3 minesweepers, 2 submarines and a second auxiliary anti-aircraft ship, all backed up by a rescue ship and 3 motor minesweepers.[5] The abundance of destroyers meant that when all were present, eight could during air raids drop back towards the convoy so that as well as the regular outer screen, German aircraft would also have to pass through an inner screen.[6]

Because PQ18's aid carrying shipping – one tanker and 39 other merchant vessels – plus its two escort oilers was in itself a sizeable armed group compared with what had gone before, the Germans were facing what could be described as a veritable armada. Of the 39 merchant ships excluding the aid bearing tanker, 21 were American, 10 were British, 6 were Soviet and 2 sailed under the Panamanian flag. They were hard to miss from close up once they were well on their way, formed up as they were in 10 columns (see the PQ18 formation diagram in Appendix C).[7]

That made it all the more important not to give the Germans any clues concerning where PQ18 might be located. In an attempt to hide the sailing of the convoy from the crews of German reconnaissance aircraft, most of the PQ18 merchant ships set out from Loch Ewe instead of from Iceland on 2 September 1942. The efforts to hide the convoy's early stages from prying eyes were however later criticized by Viacheslav Plavinski, the senior engineer in the Soviet vessel *Stalingrad*, one of seven ships carrying aid which set out from Iceland's Hvalfjord on 7 September, so that the two branches could merge off Iceland's west coast.[8]

According to Plavinski, by close of play on 5 September it would have been obvious to anyone watching the ships in the fjord that the Icelandic branch was about to set off: 'A couple of days before we departed, dozens of motorboats and other vessels began to circle our ship and the other vessels that were to form part of the convoy. Why else would that happen if the convoy was not preparing to depart?' he asked.[9]

His concerns were echoed in the following comment by E. Puzyreva, a translator from the Soviet consulate in London, who was to be a passenger in *Stalingrad*: 'When the day before we set off, we were returning to the *Stalingrad* (in Hvalfjord) in a motorboat after a visit to the town (Reykjavik), we went past some of the convoy's American vessels. Their sailors affably and nonchalantly shouted down to us from their decks: "Ahoy. Good evening. Be ready to set off tomorrow morning at 8 o'clock." '[10]

These Russian critics were not to know that the Germans did not on this occasion need to rely on such indiscretions. On 5 September 1942, an aircraft from one of the two squadrons of Hampden torpedo bombers which had been ordered to fly to Vaenga in the Kola Inlet with a view to protecting PQ18 from a Russian base, was shot down by gunners in a German ship near the port of Vardoe, in northern Norway. Although the Germans were not able to extract useful intelligence from the only survivor, secret documents retrieved from the plane confirmed that the convoy was about to depart from Hvalfjord.[11]

As if from the Allies' point of view that was not bad enough, the 7 September 1942 entry of the Seekriegsleitung's Operations Division's war diary contains a record of the decrypt of a signal sent by the Soviet 95th Naval Air Force Regiment specifying the dates when the convoy would pass through particular coordinates.[12] Armed with such precise intelligence, it was a simple task for the Germans to calculate when approximately the convoy had set out.

One suspects therefore it would not have surprised the staff within the Seekriegsleitung's Operations Division when it was reported that the crew in a Luftwaffe reconnaissance aircraft had tracked down and flown over the merged branches of the convoy off the northern coast of Iceland the very next evening.[13]

That was a good start from the German viewpoint. But a fleeting glimpse from the air provided no guide as to where the convoy would go during the following days. During the early hours of 12 September Konteradmiral Otto Klüber (the replacement Admiral Nordmeer) ordered the 7 U-boats that were available immediately to go to the area between Spitzbergen and Bear Island. However, it was only when there was a chance sighting of the convoy from a German aircraft later that day, approximately a third of the way to midway between Jan Mayen Island and the southern tip of Spitzbergen (that is, well to the south-west of where they had been ordered to line up), that Klüber was given the steer he needed to put the U-boats under his command permanently on the convoy's tail.[14]

This time the shadowing by the U-boats would not be cost free for the Germans. Although the convoy's escorts made several abortive anti-submarine attacks that day, that evening after dropping depth charges above a suspected U-boat, the destroyer HMS *Faulknor*'s crew heard a loud noise coming up from under the water that sounded like tanks being blown (see 1 in Map 15, and Note 15 for location).[15] After another charge was dropped, they observed what the British anti-submarine report states was 'a patch of strong-smelling oil' on the surface of the water. A sample taken was later proved to be diesel oil, prompting the writer of the above-mentioned report to rate this a 'very promising attack'.[16] Post-war analysis tells us they had sunk Kapitänleutnant Heino Bohmann's *U-88*, in effect a revenge sinking given that this was a vessel which had chalked up at least two victims during PQ17.

But any sense that the convoy's escorts might be gaining the upper hand did not last very long. Shortly before 10 a.m. on 13 September, when the convoy was still heading north-east towards Spitzbergen's south-west coast, lookouts in the American merchant ship *Virginia Dare*, in convoy position 82 (8th column from left side of convoy, row 2), reported seeing 'spouts of water' on her starboard quarter, just beyond convoy column 10, the line of ships on the convoy's extreme right (see 2 in Map 15, and Note 17 for approximate location).[17]

A few minutes later, as Lieutenant John Laird, commander of the armed guard in *Viriginia Dare* noted, apparently tongue in cheek, 'the whale spouted again', to be followed by the appearance of the strongest possible evidence that the splashing the lookouts had sighted was made by a lethal German U-boat rather than a relatively harmless Arctic mammal: the sight of the Soviet SS *Stalingrad*, in convoy position 103 (10th column from left, row 3), sinking after being hit on her starboard side amidships by an exploding torpedo.[18]

The explosion resulted in a number of fatalities. However, *Stalingrad*'s navigation officer Valentin Dartau, whose memories are recorded in a Russian journal, survived, if only just. His account describes how he cheated death because when prior to the attack he went down to his cabin, which would be impacted by the explosion, in order to have a rest after the end of his shift on the bridge, the ship's female cleaner was in the process of cleaning it. He decided to return to the bridge. Before he did so, the cleaner informed him that he was not the only one who was going to lose his beauty sleep; one of the pregnant women on board had just given birth to a baby boy.

Back on the bridge, the captain Anatoly Sakharov asked him to check the depth of the sea using the echo sounding device. Dartau informed him it was around 1,700 metres deep. On hearing this, Captain Sakharov, who was usually so positive, surprised Dartau by commenting gloomily: 'If it comes to it, it will be a long journey to the bottom.'

Dartau would never forget that uncharacteristically lugubrious comment because it was followed seconds later by the loud explosion on the starboard side of the ship which knocked over everyone on the bridge. The blast also shattered the glass in the wheelhouse, and part of the ship's superstructure collapsed, catching fire in the process.

Dartau's recollection was that he was the first on the bridge to stand up again. He saw at a glance that nothing could be done for the sailor on the bridge who had been on watch: he was lying pinned to the deck by a metal stand that had fallen on top of him.

For a moment Dartau was deafened by the roaring noise made by the water as it rushed through the gaping hole in the side of the ship. But eventually the distant sound of shouts and screams coming from other survivors became audible.

Seeing that the ship was sinking rapidly, Captain Sakharov quickly announced over the tannoy that everyone was to abandon ship, and then shouted the same message using his megaphone from both wings of the bridge.

Nevertheless Dartau descended to his cabin, only to discover on opening the door it was full of fumes and particles which might have suffocated him had he been asleep. As he clambered back onto the top deck, he stumbled over the bodies of some of the passengers who just two months earlier had survived the sinking of the Soviet ship *Rodina* during convoy QP13.

He eventually made it into the ship's starboard boat which had somehow avoided being damaged by the explosion, and he was rowed away from *Stalingrad*. The occupants had cut it very fine; they were just 30 metres away from her when they observed the ship sink stern first. When half the ship including the superstructure had become submerged, they heard the sound of the military vehicles and crates that had broken free from the wires holding them in place crashing towards the back of the ship. At one point near the end, the ship's bow was pointing vertically up towards the sky. The ship remained in this position for some 20 to 30 seconds, which made her look like a fisherman's float, and then with a hissing sound, she disappeared into the depths.

Passengers and crew who had either been killed by the initial explosion of the torpedo, or who had not been able to escape in time, disappeared with her. Those who died included the new-born baby. 87 of the passengers and crew were picked up by British ships including the 16 from Dartau's boat.[19]

Stalingrad was not to be the only ship torpedoed that morning. A few minutes later another torpedo sped past the stern of the American SS *William Moultrie*, in convoy position 83 (8th column from left, row 3), that is two columns to the left of *Stalingrad*, before a third torpedo, once again coming from the starboard side of the convoy, struck the American Liberty ship *Oliver Ellsworth*, in convoy position 105 (10th column from left, row 5 – that is two ships behind *Stalingrad*) on her starboard side between Nos. 4 and 5 holds, while she was jinking to the left and then to the right in order to avoid the sinking *Stalingrad*. *Oliver Ellsworth*'s crew had committed the cardinal error of allowing their vessel to straggle behind her allotted station.[20]

Once *Stalingrad* was hit, not even the kind of heroics that had helped nurse other seemingly lost Soviet causes to port in previous Arctic convoys could have saved her. By way of contrast Otto Buford, master of the American ship *Oliver Ellsworth*, was evidently critical about the way his ship was given up.[21]

In spite of certain members of the crew being as her master put it 'panicky', all but one man from his vessel safely abandoned ship and were picked up. Lieutenant John Kelly, *Oliver Ellsworth*'s armed guard commander, believed the missing man 'jumped off the stern while the propellers were still turning and he was caught in them'. Kelly's report also reveals that there might have been another fatality, had it not been for the 'heroism' of one of his armed guards who was trapped without a life jacket underneath an upturned lifeboat. The hero 'came to the surface for air', and then 'dove under and released John McKelvey, [a] deck cadet, . . . brought him to the surface, and pushed him on top of the boat'.[22]

But the ship herself was given up for lost, even though, after her entire stern had become submerged, the remainder of the vessel remained above the water because the engine room bulkheads held.[23] Her master Otto Buford believed his ship could have been towed to her destination had there been a tug with the convoy – he pointed out that 'liberty ships (like *Oliver Ellsworth*) simply cannot be sunk by one torpedo'. *Oliver Ellsworth* was sunk by the minesweeper HMS *Harrier* going on an hour following the torpedoings.[24]

The successful U-boat attacks, which subsequent investigation in German archives suggests were carried out by *U-408* and *U-589*, had taken place while the convoy escort was at its weakest since arriving in the danger zone. Although half of the 16-strong destroyer force had met up with the convoy with topped up tanks after refuelling in Spitzbergen's Bell Sound, by the time the first two merchant vessels were sunk, five destroyers and the anti-aircraft cruiser *Scylla*, with Admiral Burnett on board, had left the convoy, and would only return during the afternoon of 13 September, following their own refuelling jaunt in Bell Sound, too late to help in the ongoing battle to keep the U-boats in check.[25] Several U-boats made an appearance after the first attacks.[26]

There was to be no such excuse for the losses that happened next. They occurred during a series of raids by German aircraft during the afternoon of 13 September. The most effective raid took place at around 4.30 p.m. The convoy was by this time plodding eastward, well to the north-west of Bear Island. As its ships edged ever nearer to the area to the south of Spitzbergen's southern tip, they were set upon for the first time by what witnesses would later describe as anything between 42 and 45 aircraft (see 3 in Map 15, 7 in Map 1, and Note 27 for the location – and number of planes).[27]

John Manners, who at the time of the raid was a 27-year-old lieutenant aboard the destroyer HMS *Eskimo*, would never forget his trepidation when from his action station by the pom-pom guns aft he saw the planes approaching. And that was saying something for someone like him, who both before and after the war had played first-class cricket for Hampshire, and who as a result was used to standing firm when 'missiles' were being hurled at him. In his post-war memoirs he would write: 'Suddenly there was one of the most horrifying sights of the war. Along the whole horizon were aircraft flying just above the waves, wing tip to wing tip . . . below radar cover.'[28]

It was all the more terrifying because there was not one fighter from the escort carrier *Avenger* available to defend the convoy. The fighters that had been in the air before the attack had used up all their ammunition against the German snooper planes.[29]

All sorts of vivid images have been used to convey the horror of the scene unfolding before the eyes of the Allies' crews. The 55-year-old convoy commodore, Rear Admiral Edye Boddam Whetham, operating from SS *Temple Arch*, convoy position 61 (6th column from left; 1st, i.e. front, row), stated that the long line of incoming aircraft looked like 'a huge flight of nightmare locusts coming over the horizon.'[30] Captain Patton, master of SS *Ocean Faith*, in convoy position 71 (7th column from left; 1st, i.e. front, row), said they were 'like a lot of hornets.'[31]

'[The] planes came in flying low over the horizon on our starboard bow,' *Virginia Dare*'s Ensign John Laird wrote in his report. '[Some] crossed ahead and went in to attack the port side of the convoy . . . [Others] continued along the starboard horizon and came in when about abeam to starboard.'[32]

Eskimo and the other escorts in the convoy's screen had no means of stopping them. 'We fired with everything we'd got,' John Manners sighed wistfully when he told me long after the end of the war what he remembered. By then he had reached the ripe old age of 103, which meant I may well have been speaking to the last PQ18 officer alive who had witnessed the attack. However, his verdict on his ship's performance did not appear to have changed in all the years that had passed since that dismal day. 'We were firing at planes whizzing overhead at 200 to 300 miles per hour,' he told me, before concluding: 'Our shooting wasn't very accurate or effective. They just roared overhead.'[33]

By all accounts the same could have been said about much of the shooting emanating from the guns mounted on the merchant ships' decks. It did not help the convoy's defences that gunners aboard the freighters in columns 9 and 10 opened fire when the planes were out of range, Laird reported. The result, he said, was that 'by the time the planes were upon them, their rate and volume of fire was considerably less'.[34]

'They swept in . . . about 20 feet above sea level,' wrote Horace Bell, the chief radio operator in the rescue ship *Copeland,* located at the back of the convoy. He appears to have believed that no amount of fire would have repulsed them. In spite of the gunfire from the merchant ships, 'there was,' he said, 'no hesitation'.[35] The only evasive action taken by the aircraft was what one witness described as 'a hedge hopping manoeuvre'.[36]

According to Bell, the firing by so many of the merchant ships simultaneously concealed their targets somewhat: 'A pall of smoke hung like a curtain out on the starboard flank of the convoy, criss crossed by the bright red tracks of the tracers, and punctuated by the flash of the shell bursts . . . Every plane as it emerged from the haze became targets for the smaller weapons too.'

Nevertheless he was able to watch as 'each one, as it got into position, dropped two torpedoes, and swept off astern . . . a few [apparently] on fire'.[37]

One reason why notwithstanding the noisy defensive barrage, the German aircraft were not deterred effectively is hinted at in the following extract from a report by Ensign Daniel Rooker, Armed Guard Commander in the American SS *Campfire,* in convoy position 63 (6th column from left, row 3): 'Ships on the port side of the convoy did much of the firing, many of their shells landing on our decks . . . Machine guns from a friendly ship to port of us strafed our poop . . . wounding three of the armed guard . . . We were barely within range [of the aircraft], and we too wasted ammunition . . . by firing out of range.'

There was also the problem that most of the machine guns in American merchant ships such as *Campfire* were, as Rooker put it, 'of no use whatever'. He emphasized that the only guns on board that were effective against these low-flying planes were the 20 mm Oerlikons, and even they only worked at relatively close range: 'We were forced to wait until the planes were within a thousand yards in order to make our shots tell,' he complained. This was never going to pose a threat to most of the aircraft involved with this attack; the majority were dropping their torpedoes when around 1,500 to 2,000 yards from their targets.[38]

It is not surprising to hear that with torpedoes dropped at such close range there were several near misses in addition to the many hits.[39] The ships hit were mostly in the two columns on the extreme right side of the convoy, which were decimated, all but one of their remaining vessels being torpedoed – and worse. Before the aircraft departed, Bell witnessed what he described as: 'the most awe-inspiring sight, as a munition ship (*Empire Stevenson*) blew up. There wasn't a tremendous lot of noise – just a huge column of smoke and dull red flame lighting up the whole sky for a few seconds, and then silence. Everyone [who saw it] seemed momentarily stunned or fascinated, watching the smoke billowing upwards. Of the ship, not a trace remained.'[40]

Or to be absolutely accurate, as Lieutenant John Laird could see from the decks of *Virginia Dare*, still in convoy position 82, behind and to port of *Empire Stevenson*, which had been in convoy position 91 (9th column from left; 1st, i.e. front, row), the blown up 'ship . . . was suddenly enveloped in a tower of flame and smoke, and when that subsided, there was nothing there but an oily slick on the water'.[41]

Bell's account continues: 'I think it was our Bofors that first opened up again, and almost immediately everyone else got going, until we at last got a breather as the last torpedo bomber disappeared . . . ducking and weaving as he went.'[42]

The convoy the Luftwaffe left behind was noticeably smaller than the one they had attacked. The blowing up of *Empire Stevenson* had not just vaporized one whole ship. The blast had fractured so many steam valves, oil lines and instruments in the American ship *Wacosta*, in convoy position 92 (9th column from left, 2nd row – in other words the vessel behind the blown-up ship), that her engines stopped working. She fell behind the surviving ships, and it was not long before one of the follow-up waves of aircraft that penetrated the columns from the convoy's starboard beam, targeted her with a torpedo dropped from such close range, 30 feet away, that it landed directly on her No. 2 hatch, blasting a large hole in her deck and hull. In the circumstances it was astonishing that everyone on board was able to abandon ship safely before she sank around 30 minutes after being hit.[43]

As had happened during the 5 July 1942 attacks on ships during PQ17, there was an equally perplexing lack of any casualties on some of the other ships impacted during this cull of the vessels in PQ18's columns 9 and 10. They included the Panamanian *Macbeth*, in convoy position 102 (10th column from left, row 2), which according to an official report was 'rendered helpless' by two torpedoes dropped by a plane approximately 40 feet away from her starboard side, and the Panamanian *Africander*, in convoy position 94 (9th column, row 4), which was also incapacitated by two torpedoes that hit her starboard side before she sank a few minutes later.[44]

That is not to say that the attacks were not scary even in ships where few, if any, men were lost. The cargo in the No. 5 hold in the British ship *Empire Beaumont* in convoy position 41 (4th column from left; 1st, i.e. front, row) caught fire, and the tanks lashed to her deck were blown overboard after she was hit on her starboard side. The torpedo that hit her was the only one that hit a ship to the left of the convoy's column 7. Apart from one missing man, there were no casualties, yet ten of her gunners and crew jumped into the sea, preferring that to waiting for the lifeboats to be lowered. 'After having seen the *Empire Stevenson* blow up, they were a little panicky,' the ship's captain wrote in his understated official report which omitted to spell out that one good reason why the men were jittery was that the cargo on board included what the report referred to as 'explosives'. All but the one missing man were subsequently rescued.[45]

The 21 crew and armed guards who jumped into the sea after the American *John Penn*, in convoy position 73 (7th column, row 3), was struck had slightly more reason to panic, since the torpedo that hit their ship amidships on her starboard side during one of the later waves of the attack had killed three men in the engine room. The fact that *John Penn* was a Liberty ship which could not be sunk by a single torpedo was not a good answer to those who feared she might be torpedoed again. As it turned out, all but those in the engine room were rescued after she was abandoned.[46]

After the aircraft had departed and the survivors picked up, efforts were made by the minesweeper *Harrier*'s crew to sink *John Penn* and *Macbeth*, two of the three damaged ships they could see as the weather closed in, with gunfire. Neither attempt succeeded, capping a frustrating day for all concerned.

While this was going on, the weather had taken an even more extreme turn for the worst, and the convoy, which by this time was around nine miles to the east of where the bombing had taken place, was shrouded by the snowstorm that had set in ahead of *Harrier*. It was in these circumstances that the decision was made to leave the damaged ships floating so that *Harrier* could catch up. The abandoned Soviet vessel *Sukhona*, convoy position 104 (10th column, row 4), which was also out of sight because of the snow, was likewise not seen to sink.[47]

It seems that the only ship apart from *Empire Stevenson*, whose sinking during the attack represented a disaster in terms of loss of life as well as on account of the loss of the valuable cargo, was the American *Oregonian*, which had been in convoy position 101 (10th column from left; 1st, i.e. front, row). A report by her survivors states she was hit by three torpedoes 'nearly blowing the starboard side of the ship to pieces, flooding the engine room and causing the ship to take on a heavy list.' Twenty-eight men including all those in the engine room were lost out of a crew of 55.[48]

Her loss added to others sunk or abandoned on 13 September meant that U-boats and the Luftwaffe had in one day neutralized eight ships in the convoy's 9th and 10th columns, leaving in working order in those columns just one ship, *Mary Luckenbach* which had been in convoy position 93 (9th column from left, row 3). A total of ten ships had been lost during the day.

A scene of desolation was left behind following the air raid. *Empire Beaumont*'s master Captain D. J. Jones, reporting what he saw about an hour after the attack from the deck of the minesweeper that rescued him, stated: 'The last I saw of the s.s. *Beaumont* was . . . , when looking between the snow squalls, I saw the ship well down in the water and burning furiously.'[49] It would be some time before all traces of what had just occurred disappeared from view from the convoy's perspective. An American armed guard, whose ship continued towards the east with the rest of PQ18, reported that 'black smoke was visible as it went skyward until dusk'.[50]

At least one British officer was quick to identify what had to be done to prevent a recurrence. Commenting on his flawed tactics, Commander Anthony Colthurst, the 41-year-old officer in charge of the escort carrier *Avenger*, would later write: 'At the end of this unfortunate day, I realized that my operation of the ship and her fighters had been very wrong. At the start of it, I had not realized the heavy scale of the attack to which the convoy would be subjected, nor the duration of the attack. I had not appreciated the hopelessness of sending even four Sea Hurricanes to attack the heavily armed enemy shadowers. We had not learned to differentiate between small groups of shadowers and striking forces on the R.D.F. screen.

'I then decided . . . we must use them only to try to break up large attacking formations rather than to destroy individuals. Further that we must endeavour to maintain a continual cycle of sections taking off, landing on to re-arm and refuel, and taking off again. The achievement of this would avoid congestion in the carrier, and ensure that there were always some fighter sections ready to counter attack striking forces.'[51]

There were however a couple of positives the Allies could take from what had happened. Firstly in spite of Colthurst's error, *Avenger* herself had not been successfully targeted. Werner Klümper, commander of the 1st wing of Kampfgeschwader (KG) 26, whose aircraft based in Bardufoss constituted the first waves of the main strike force on 13 September, would later reveal that was because the airborne shadowers had failed to pinpoint in advance where in relation to the 10-column convoy *Avenger* was operating.[52] Secondly, the convoy had demonstrated its ships were not toothless. Afterwards Klümper had to accept that when attacking such a keenly defended mass of ships, it was almost inevitable some of his aircraft would be damaged or lost. Two of his He 111s crash-landed off the Norwegian coast on the way home, and another aircraft from KG26's 3rd wing also failed to make it back to base.[53]

But there had been another avoidable mistake by the Allies that had been significant. When on detecting the aircraft's approach prior to the big attack on 13 September, Commodore Boddam Whetham had ordered the convoy's masters to alter their course by 45° to starboard, which if complied with would have resulted in the merchant ships turning the narrowest part of their hulls towards many of the oncoming torpedoes, none of the masters of the ships in columns 9 and 10 had obeyed.[54]

It is quite likely that this inability to exert effective control over the ships in the convoy, combined with the not unreasonable expectation that there might be similar losses the next day, played its part in pushing Boddam Whetham towards the edge of the mental breakdown which would eventually overwhelm him once he arrived in the Soviet Union.[55] He certainly showed signs that he believed that some elements within the convoy had it in for him. In his official report, he focused much of his ire on the masters of the American and Panamanian ships in PQ18, especially on those whose vessels had accounted for six of the nine ships stationed in the right two columns at dawn on 13 September: 'The Americans in particular pay but scant attention to signals, know little of the importance of good station keeping, and do not as yet know anything about convoy work,' he complained.[56]

He had previously written in a letter penned while still at sea: 'These Americans must be persuaded to . . . realise that the Commodore's orders are given to get the convoy home safely, and not for [his] amusement, or to show his authority.'[57]

After the way the Americans had shown him up, it is perhaps not surprising that he did not take kindly to the master of *William Moultrie*, a US ship, requesting that his vessel should be moved from what following the 13 September attack was the very exposed eighth column to a safer position within the convoy in the place of a British ship carrying half the quantity of explosives. Boddam Whetham acceded to the demand, permitting the American ship to swap places with *Goolistan*, which had been in convoy position 74 (7th column from left, row 4), but wrote in his report: 'I informed [the] Master of *W[illiam]Moultrie* however that the only difference I could see between 4,000 tons of T.N.T. and 2,000 tons was a fractional part of a second should she be hit.'[58]

If Boddam Whetham was already feeling tense and exhausted because of the losses suffered during the big attack, one can understand how his anxiety might have increased exponentially thanks to subsequent events. There were two more probing raids by aircraft that day, and U-boats kept popping up all over the place.[59] That suggested there would be similar attacks the next day.

Knowing that the convoy was being sized-up in this way would have been hard for any convoy commodore to take in his stride. But for one whose mental health was being worn down by the constant challenges coming from his own side as well as by the exhaustion that was part and parcel of remaining on the alert for long periods at a stretch, the situation was becoming unbearable.

28

Turning of the Tide

Main Action: 14 September 1942
Massed air attack, PQ18 part 2

(See Maps 1 and 15)

Compared with the angst-ridden PQ18 commodore Rear Admiral Boddam Whetham, Robert Burnett, the 55-year-old rear admiral in overall control of the escorting of the convoy, who was flying his flag in the anti-aircraft cruiser *Scylla,* was a cheerful, ebullient fellow.

A stocky athletic man who had at one time been responsible for the Navy's physical training, Burnett's ready smile, his optimism and joie de vivre stood out and were a tonic to those serving under him, even to those who, thinking his positive side overdone, nicknamed him 'Bullshit Bob'.[1]

It was typical of the man that he was not at all put out by the more challenging weather conditions that he and his force had to face during the most dangerous part of their journey. Rather than bemoaning the fact that summer was already being overridden by fog and snow showers, after he had sailed into Spitzbergen's Bell Sound on 12 September 1942 during the PQ18 refuelling expedition (see Chapter 27), he did not focus on the difficulty of passing through a narrow entrance where there were very strong tidal streams. Instead, in his report, he extolled the 'magnificent glacier [that] could be seen leading down from the snow covered mountains to the sea'. He ignored what he described as 'a few small ice flows' in the sound that might have caused a less robust character to advise that the inlet should be avoided in the even colder climes that were to come.

He had an equally positive way of assessing the opposition that PQ18 was facing. Instead of dwelling on the frightening aspects of being targeted by the 40-plus torpedo bombers on 13 September, he reported that even though it was 'a decidedly unpleasant experience', it was 'exciting'. Likewise he had nothing but praise for the German pilots who had raided PQ18, writing in his report: 'What impressed me was the apparent countless number of attackers [and] the determination of attack ... I am convinced that nothing will prevent that number of attackers, gallantly led as they undoubtedly were, scoring many hits.'[2]

Waving aside frustration because the American merchant seamen had not obeyed the commodore's order to turn to starboard when the German aircraft attacked, the following words in his report characteristically take the glass half-full approach: 'Such a manoeuvre would only have thrown the convoy into confusion, and would not have reduced casualties. Indeed it would probably have increased them. The majority of the two starboard columns had gone, but I heaved a sigh of relief when I heard the *Rangers* (the convoy's oilers *Gray Ranger* and *Black Ranger*) were safe.'[3]

By the same token Grossadmiral Raeder, whose staff had twice requested that the Luftwaffe should focus on sinking any tankers the aircraft crews spotted within the convoy – so that the convoy escorts would run short of fuel – must surely have been pleased by what occurred at around 4.30 a.m. on 14 September: that was when, shortly after those in the convoy, as they proceeded eastward, had caught sight of Spitzbergen's South Cape to their north, *U-457* unleashed the torpedo that crashed into the port side of the tanker *Atheltemplar* beside her engine room (see 4 in Map 15, and Note 4 for the approximate location).[4]

After so much defending had been done in order to ward off the Luftwaffe the day before, it was a bit of a surprise to be targeted by a U-boat. The first *Atheltemplar*'s Captain Carl Ray knew of the *U-457*'s attack was when, as disclosed in his report, he heard a 'dull explosion'. However, it did not take him long to realize that the tanker, which appears to have been in convoy position 45 (4th column; 5th, i.e. back, row), would have to be abandoned. As well as blowing away the after port lifeboat, the explosion had stopped the engines and extinguished the lights below decks. Even more ominously the stern of the ship was settling. After he gave the abandon ship order, the majority of the crew climbed into two of the surviving lifeboats.

However, before the rest of the crew boarded the minesweeper that came alongside, shouts coming from down below were heard by the 2nd Engineer. Torches were quickly directed from a skylight into the engine room below. It did not look very promising. Through the steam and vapour it was possible to see that the water and fuel that had flooded in was already about 25 foot deep, well over the top of the engines. Fortunately, the would-be rescuers were not put off. An assistant engineer and a fireman, who had both been injured, were eventually spotted above the water line, and it was decided they needed to be pulled to safety.

James Reeves, the ship's chief officer, had a ladder lowered into the engine room and climbed down to assist the trapped men who were on beams. Reeves attached a line to the assistant engineer, and this man was hauled up. It was much harder to extricate the fireman, who as Ray reported, 'was a very heavy man and was soaked with oil . . . Owing to his weight and the oil on his clothes, the rope round . . . [him] slipped under his arms, and his arms were forced over his head, and when he was six or seven feet from the skylight, he slipped through and fell onto the beam, and being unconscious was unable to help himself.'

He was only saved because Reeves went down the ladder again and attached the line to the fireman's body more securely. Eventually the two injured men, the rescue party and all the men in the tanker's boats were picked up by the attending minesweepers, and after attempts to sink *Atheltemplar* failed, she was left burning.[5]

As had been the case the previous day, the U-boat attack was just the opening act of a series of actions that featured the British escorts chasing after the prowling German submarines. Shortly before midday, the wily 37-year-old Captain Harold Armstrong in HMS *Onslow*, crept up to within around a mile of one of these U-boats, south of the convoy, whose conning tower had been seen in the distance by the destroyer's masthead lookout. From there, Armstrong and his crew were able to use the destroyer's asdic to hunt for the U-boat after she submerged, attacking her again and again by dropping no less than nine patterns of depth charges within the space of around two hours (see 5 in Map 15, and Note 6 for location).[6] Three of the patterns resulted in what Armstrong described as 'oil, air bubbles, wreckage of wooden gratings and some green vegetables' appearing on the surface of the water, and an underwater explosion heard after the seventh attack told Armstrong that if they had not sunk the U-boat, they had almost certainly damaged it severely (it turned out that he had sunk *U-589*, which took with her the unfortunate shot-down four-man aircraft crew who had been 'rescued' after the air raid on PQ18 the previous day).[7]

At the time, this cut and thrust underwater battle during the first half of 14 September must have seemed all-important. However, the second phase of the main battle over PQ18 was still to come. At 1.35 p.m. that afternoon, as *Onslow* was completing her attacks on the U-boat, and Armstrong was receiving instructions from Burnett not to stay away from the convoy, whose eastward course was about to take it south of Hope Island, for too long, an alert was announced over *Scylla*'s radio: 'Enemy aircraft ahead!' (See 6 in Map 15, and Note 8 for approximate location.)[8]

Five minutes later, after it became clear that the branches of what would together constitute the first wave of 20-plus torpedo bombers were approaching from ahead, those listening in heard the even more stirring announcement: '[Our] fighters [are] in the air. [But] do not stop firing; they're not there yet.' (See Note 9 for number of attacking aircraft.)[9]

The calls to arms were appreciated so much because it showed that *Avenger*'s Commander Colthurst really had learned his lesson. No sooner had the incoming aircraft been detected than he had immediately set in motion his plan to fly off the nine Hurricanes he had ready waiting for just such an eventuality.[10] This, and the escort carrier's subsequent evasive action, reassured Admiral Burnett, who was watching from *Scylla*, a ship in an equally exposed position to that occupied by the carrier. When the first wave of German aircraft arrived, *Scylla* was stationed at the front of the fifth column of what was now an eight-column convoy, but she would later be rushed out in front of the merchant ships to meet the attackers involved in the follow-up attack head on.[11]

Nevertheless, at times Burnett evidently only had eyes for the carrier, remarking in his report: 'It was a fine sight to see *Avenger* peeling off

Hurricanes whilst streaking across the front of the convoy from starboard to port inside the [escort] screen with her [own] destroyer escort blazing away with any gun which would bear.' That was the case even though as he put it, he then had to watch *Avenger* 'being chased by torpedo bombers as she steamed down on [the] opposite course to the convoy to take cover'.[12]

Unlike the previous day, while dealing with the first wave of the big German attack on 14 September, Burnett and Colthurst were at least sitting in the driving seat, even if they could not be said to be fully in control. As Burnett reported, 'the attack was pressed home, but no ships were hit', although that was partly because those in the British warships were the beneficiaries of more than their fair share of good fortune. According to Burnett, '*Scylla* was continually under helm during this period to avoid torpedoes, several of which were observed to pass uncomfortably close'. *Avenger's* report reveals that while the carrier was certainly targeted, some of the torpedoes did not run after being dropped, and some German aircraft jettisoned their torpedoes after being chased away by the carrier's Hurricanes. *Avenger's* Commander Colthurst added that some of the German crews were put off by the gunfire emanating from the ships in the convoy, and dropped their torpedoes 'at long range'.[13]

There was the additional bonus that the Luftwaffe had losses (see Note 14 for losses recorded in German sources).[14] 'I myself saw one torpedo bomber crash on *Scylla's* port quarter just ahead of the convoy,' Burnett reported.[15] These losses, and the Luftwaffe's inability to capitalize on their success the previous day, prompted Burnett to label it 'a most gratifying action'.[16]

The Hurricane pilots could be particularly proud of what they had achieved using aircraft whose firepower, restricted by its reliance on relatively puny .303 guns, was known to be insufficient.[17]

One might have hoped that a convoy charged with the task of transporting Hurricanes equipped with an improved armament would in its turn be protected by aircraft with similar guns now that an aircraft carrier formed part of the escort. However, that was not the case, and those in the convoy had had to watch the depressing spectacle of no less than four of the fighters attempting to chase one of the German shadowers after the big attack on 13 September, only for one of the Hurricanes to be shot down. Its pilot, who died during the action, was the sole Fleet Air Arm fatality during the convoy. Although three other Hurricanes were shot down while defending the convoy during the 14 September attacks, their pilots baled out before their planes hit the water, and all of them were rescued.[18]

But what is not stated explicitly in official British and German documents was that British success overall on 14 September was assisted by Luftflotte 5's flawed tactics. Although Hitler himself had demanded that the Luftwaffe should focus all its efforts on 14 September on sinking the aircraft carrier with the convoy, the 22 aircraft from the first wing of KG26 led into battle by Werner Klümper, shortly after 1.30 p.m. that day, did so without an update telling them where *Avenger* was stationed relative to the convoy.[19]

The consequence of furnishing the Luftwaffe's strike arm with such poor intelligence is highlighted by the following extract from Werner Klümper's report: 'Thanks to the very good visibility, we initially saw in the distance the smoke made by the ships, then pieces of the ships' structures such as their masts and funnels, and finally the ships themselves. When I looked through my binoculars, I saw that the biggest ship was at the front of the convoy's central column. I was sure this was the aircraft carrier because I had not been told of any change to the convoy's formation.

'I ordered the aircraft to spread out so they could execute the planned pincer manoeuvre. After doing this, the distance between each aircraft was 500 to 800 metres.

'It was then that a message came over the radio announcing: "Watch out! Fighters ahead!"

'. . . I ordered the other pilots to stay in groups of 3 or 4 aircraft, but to stick to the planned formation. No sooner had I spoken, than I saw through my binoculars that the ship at the front of the convoy was not the aircraft carrier. It was a large freighter. I then spotted the aircraft carrier approximately in the middle of the convoy's northern column.

'I immediately informed the other crews, and ordered them to change the direction of their attacks accordingly. I did this in the full knowledge that the altered attack would be less effective; it would have taken too long to set up a new pincer movement.'[20]

So it was that the second of the massed torpedo bomber attacks during the period 13–14 September 1942, which Hitler and his commanders hoped would lead to the dismantling of the convoy's defences, was hobbled. Klümper went on to describe how as his unit approached, his links with the other aircraft were cut, and how as he avoided the British Hurricanes and the guns of a destroyer, he found himself having to fire at the carrier from a distance, which he took to be 1.5 kilometres, at an angle of 45°, not surprisingly with no apparent success. The other aircraft with him were equally unsuccessful.

The majority of the crews in the 25 torpedo bombers which reached the convoy at around 3.10 p.m. on 14 September were equally out of luck. Those unable to locate the carrier settled for targeting the merchant ships. But even that goal eluded most of them. Unlike the big attack the previous day, when several aircraft sped from the convoy's starboard side over its right columns permitting them to drop their torpedoes at what amounted to point blank range, only one or two handfuls of 14 September's second wave managed to reach the air space over PQ18's interior.

Not that entry into PQ18's air space helped them achieve anything like what had been pulled off on 13 September. The following extract from the report by Ensign John Laird, commanding officer of the armed guard unit in the Liberty ship *Virginia Dare* (apparently still in one of the convoy's right-hand columns), describes how a substantial number of those who did penetrate the area above the convoy came to grief: 'Six came madly down the columns . . . towards our end of the convoy flying only about 20 to 30 feet above the water, and hopping in a peculiar fashion.

'As the first came down between our column and the one to port, Chief Bosun Harshaw opened fire with his 20 mm (Oerlikon), setting the port engine afire, and the anti-aircraft ship astern to port finished him off.

'[As] the second plane attempted to pass between this ship and the ship ahead . . . Seaman 2nd class Graff opened fire with his 20 mm setting him afire. The plane . . . headed for our bow in a crash dive [but] the 3-inch/50 [calibre] followed him in . . . Seaman 2nd class Harmon fired [the gun] when the plane was at the point blank range of sixty yards, [and] the plane blew up.

'Three more . . . crossed our bow ridiculously close. Hits were scored on all three, and two were brought down . . . The planes crashed a little abaft our starboard beam about half a mile out.' (See Note 21 for comment on ships' positions within the convoy.)[21]

With planes flying in so fast, it is sometimes hard to know whether a witness is referring to an aircraft described in other accounts, resulting in double counting. That said, the next plane Laird says his men targeted was almost certainly one of those flown by a particularly fearless threesome of pilots mentioned in several witnesses' statements. The three aircraft appear to have cut in from the front of the convoy near the 6th column, and then sped obliquely in the direction of the starboard edge of the convoy with a view to torpedoing the ships in the 7th and 8th columns. The terrible consequences of what followed would inspire many who saw them to commit their recollections to paper.

The account by Horace Bell, who as during demolition of *Empire Stevenson* in the attack by the Luftwaffe the previous day, was watching from *Copeland* at the back of the convoy, states that 'the leader came in to about … 300 yards from one ship (the American *Mary Luckenbach*, which at least one witness suggests was in one of the right two columns) before dropping his torpedoes, and then swept on down the column. As he passed, the gunners raked him fore and aft, and bright tongues of fire flickered from his starboard engine. He dipped, recovered, dipped again, and it seemed to be just about to crash, when the torpedoes reached their mark, and the ship simply vanished. The plane broke up into small pieces, exactly like a well-shot clay pigeon, a fate shared by his next astern.

'In the stupefying moments of silence and inactivity that followed, we watched as an enormous column of smoke billowed upwards, slow, thick, black and ugly … till it reached the clouds at 3,000 feet, and then only, it began to drift to leeward.

'Gradually from the overhanging top, there drifted down dust, like a shower of rain against a sunset, and that was all. There was no tremendous report with it, just a deep awful rumble.'[22]

A description of the climax of the same event as seen from HMS *Milne*, a destroyer on the starboard side of the screen guarding the front of the convoy, is to be found in the following extract from the account written by midshipman Thomas Wells: 'There was a bright flash as [one of the German planes] … crashed into the superstructure, and a second's pause before a brilliant blood-red flame shot up to a good 300 feet.

A great scarlet flower, it slowly developed into pitch black smoke, which rose and expanded, fat and solid, with burning wreckage dropping from it. It grew and billowed silently upwards, spreading into the cloud above. Like some horrible black and grey fungus, it rose steadily, writhing like a living thing, so huge that the largest ships seemed dwarfed into little water beetles. Eventually its base lifted from the water, and a corvette steamed through the murk. The smoke thinned slowly, and diffusing into the cloud, making a vast brooding blackness which cast a shadow over the water.'[23]

There are several different versions of the events that led up to the explosion, in addition to those quoted above. Some for example say that the first of the three planes observed flying between the columns was shot down, and it was only the second that disappeared seemingly into thin air as *Mary Luckenbach* went up. But all who focused on these three planes inside the convoy agreed that not one of them emerged in one piece. The third plane was seen by some crashing into the sea near the rear of the convoy. And all witnesses described the same terrible funeral pyre with its unimaginable consequences for every man caught up in it.[24]

It was a sight that shocked everyone who saw it, matching the emotions unleashed when *Empire Stevenson* had exploded the day before. No-one who has seen the iconic photographs taken just seconds after *Mary Luckenbach* was blown up can doubt the impact of such a conflagration on witnesses observing it in real time. They had just seen a metal hulk measuring 392 feet by 54 feet, and 28 feet from deck to bottom, turned to dust as if by a magician's wand in the blink of an eye.

It took some blast to demolish such a substantial structure. The shockwave that spread out from the massive explosion was so powerful, it threatened to engulf all those in its path well beyond the confines of *Mary Luckenbach*. Official reports written by witnesses on at least five merchant ships in the vicinity have described its effects on them.[25]

Captain Hugh Macleod, the master of *Dan-Y-Bryn* (said by some to be the leading ship in column 8, possibly making her the ship to starboard of *Mary Luckenbach*'s bow) wrote: 'When *Mary Luckenbach* blew up, I thought the *Dan-Y-Bryn* had also been hit, as the explosion of the former vessel caused our engines to stop . . . The explosion knocked all our 4-inch and Bofors gun teams over on to the deck . . . I gave the signal: "Stand by the lifeboats!", but on examining the ship . . . I found no damage . . . , and we stood on again.'[26]

Captain Jay, the master of *Ocean Faith* (described by some as the leading ship in column 7, in other words possibly putting her directly in front of *Mary Luckenbach*'s patch), wrote: 'I was on the after end of the bridge at the time when I noticed ripples get up on the sea which must have been caused by the blast, and the next moment I was blown into the wheelhouse. I called to the Carpenter and a few other men to come in there too, and flying debris rained down . . . The Chief Officer was aft, alongside one of the guns, and he said that the men were thrown to the deck by the explosion . . . I have been torpedoed before, and realized our ship had not been hit, but . . . some of the men thought we had . . . Two of the firemen . . . completely lost their heads, and had thrown the falls off the pins and . . . dropped the starboard bridge lifeboat into the water . . .'[27]

But none of these ships were as badly affected as the American Liberty ship *Nathanael Greene*.[28] Lieutenant Roy Billings, head of the armed guard on *Nathanael Greene*, wrote in his report: 'How everyone topside [in *Nathanael Greene*] was not killed or injured seriously I don't know. It is impossible to put into words the force of the explosion, or the amount of debris that hit the ship . . . *The Mary Luckenbach* had blown up about 200 yards off our starboard quarter.

'My helmet and phones were blown off . . . All the cargo boxes on deck were smashed by the concussion . . . Ten doors and some bulkheads were blown down . . . The insides of many rooms . . . were a shambles. The cast iron ventilators buckled. Shrapnel and scraps [of metal] were covering the deck. A piece of . . . iron penetrated my starboard four-inch ready box and went through a shell [inside], missing the primer by less than an eighth of an inch. Glass ports were smashed. The "hospital" aft was practically demolished. The compasses were all out of adjustment. The pointer's platform on the 4-inch gun had completely disappeared . . .

'A side plate about two feet square was found on the deck. Bullets were picked up all over the deck, both tank ammunition from the *Luckenbach*, and bullets fired at us by the planes. Every splinter shield on the ship had bullet marks in it. Every gun station had been marked by shrapnel and bullets.'[29]

Yet as Billings confirmed: 'My men never showed the least sign of cowardice. Although scared stiff (and who wasn't?), they obeyed my orders to the letter and kept fighting.

'I had seen four torpedoes dropped by planes off the bow and thought we had been torpedoed. Boat stations were ordered by the Captain. The Second Mate ordered my men to let go the two forward life rafts, which they did. The engines had been stopped by the Master . . . The number two lifeboat was lowered . . .' But then a calm voice was heard. As Billings recalled, it was the First Assistant Engineer who 'came up from below and said everything was all right in the engine room'.

On hearing this, Billings ordered his men back to their guns. 'We then resumed our place in convoy that we had temporarily vacated,' he reported, before listing the surprisingly slight damage to personnel given the mayhem they had just lived through: 'Two of my men had been wounded, five of the merchant crew had received injuries, and one of the merchant crew was lost overboard.'[30]

Even the man overboard ended up in the land of the living. He would later be among the rescued seamen delivered by one of the convoy's minesweepers to *Scylla*, although for a time, some believed he was *Mary Luckenbach's* only survivor.[31] That was just one of those legends.[32] Those who stated that no-one on board *Mary Luckenbach* could have survived such an explosion were right. All 65 men on board perished in this terrible disaster.[33]

They were to be the only personnel lost by the Allies during the raid, or for that matter during that afternoon. Although there was to be another raid later that day, it achieved nothing.

That enabled Admiral Burnett to report, without opening himself up to the accusation he was being ridiculously upbeat, that 14 September was 'more encouraging from our point of view', a verdict that was bolstered by the confirmation that high-level bombers had not sunk any ships, and although German aircraft had fired an estimated 17 torpedoes at *Avenger*, none had connected.[34] Furthermore, *Avenger's* pilots were claiming they had shot down at least five German aircraft during that afternoon's air raids, and an analysis attached to Burnett's report claimed 14 German aircraft had been seen to crash during the two big torpedo bomber raids on 14 September as compared with just four during the large-scale raid the day before.[35]

Evidently, on this occasion the figures cited by the British commanders were not far out. German sources conceded that 12 to 14 aircraft were shot down during the big 14 September raids.[36]

Subsequent events would prove that in relation to PQ18, as well as in relation to other great battles in the Arctic that would be coming down the line, Burnett's positive view of the world was justified. During the next three days, the torpedo bombers which had wreaked such havoc on 13 September, and which threatened to do so again, were grounded by the bad weather.

By the time the next two torpedo bomber air raids were made on 18 September, the convoy was already at the entrance to the White Sea (see 8 in Map 15, and Note 37 for location).[37] Although the number of escorts protecting the convoy had been reduced by then (the support given to the convoy by four Russian destroyers could not match what had previously been offered by *Scylla*, *Avenger*, the 16 destroyers and one of the auxiliary anti-aircraft ships – which had departed during the afternoon of 16 September so that Burnett could mastermind the escorting of the westbound QP14), the air raids failed to have the desired impact.[38]

Whether this was principally because the Germans chose to approach PQ18 from the rear, a silent tribute to the effectiveness of the convoy's barrage against the guileless attack from the front during the second 14 September attack, even though the new tactics meant they were up against the guns of the anti-aircraft ship and Russian destroyer placed at or near the back of the convoy, or because the Luftwaffe units deployed were depleted on account of so many aircraft having been damaged on 14 September is hard to say.[39] The torpedoing of one American ship, *Kentucky*, during the first 18 September raid, and its subsequent sinking was really just a consolation prize for the Germans. It may have deprived the Russians of aid, but it did not result in loss of personnel (there were no casualties), or alter the fact that most of the convoy had got through.[40]

The destroyer *Impulsive*'s previous successful attack on a U-boat during the early hours of 16 September, shortly after PQ18 had changed its course to the south (see 7 in Map 15 for location) – the U-boat turned out to be *U-457*, which had sunk *Atheltemplar* two days earlier as well as one of the PQ17 ships – merely reinforced the general feeling that while the Allies had been given a bloody nose, they had ended up on top.[41]

After another half-hearted air raid on 21 September, most of PQ18's remaining merchant ships proceeded to the ports allocated to them, at Molotovsk, Bakaritsa and Archangel itself, although three ships that had become grounded during the bad weather only arrived in harbour between 25 and 27 September.

Once again the number of aid bearing ships that had made it to the Soviet Union – 27 out of the 40 that had set off – was unexpectedly high given all that had been thrown at them. Even more importantly, the ship-borne aircraft backed up with an abundance of destroyers and a sprinkling of anti-aircraft ships had proved to be the basis for a formula that could well prevail against future attacks by the Luftwaffe and U-boats. If the German surface ships could only be defeated, the Allies now knew the battle to support their Russian ally could be won.

29

So Near . . .

Main Action: 20–24 September 1942
Sinking of Leda and Somali, QP14

(See Map 15)

By the time the westbound QP14 (eventually comprising 15 merchant ships, including several from PQ17, and two of PQ17's rescue ships) departed from the Kola Inlet on 13 September 1942, its prospects, unbeknown to its participants, were already looking up.[1]

That morning Hitler had warned Grossadmiral Raeder not to take any risks with the German Fleet, and Raeder had subsequently decided to cancel the contemplated sortie by the cruiser *Admiral Hipper* and four destroyers from Altenfjord that had been about to target QP14.[2]

If Owen Morris, the captain of the PQ17 rescue ship *Zamalek*, had known of the cancellation before QP14 sailed, it might have increased still further the confidence he exhibited when before the voyage he talked to his more nervous passengers about the imminent trip. He told the 18-year-old Wim van Laar, who had lost most of his left leg as well as the toes on his right foot following his ordeal in one of the *Paulus Potter* lifeboats: 'You should not be frightened because God will be with us.' Van Laar was not religious, but the captain's optimism was infectious, and the crippled teenager's feverish anxiety was doused if not extinguished.[3]

It was harder to convince *Paulus Potter*'s captain Willem Sissingh, who had had all ten of his toes amputated after reaching Archangel, and was at first accommodated below decks in *Zamalek*'s makeshift hospital, an uncomfortable position for someone who knew only too well that most of the fatalities when ships were torpedoed involved those not in the open air. Even after he was given a berth above decks, he remained sceptical about whether it was sensible to rely on the warships protecting QP14 despite the assurance by a British naval officer that the statement that the convoy was going to have an exceptionally strong escort, repeating what had been said at the pre-PQ17 conference, was this time going to be more than hollow rhetoric.[4]

Historical records do not disclose the prevalence of views such as those held by Sissingh amongst the other PQ17 sailors going home in QP14's ships. But a report by Captain Guy Maund, the SBNO Archangel, gives one an indication of the state of mind of the merchant ships' crews. On 15 July 1942 he had reported: 'There is no doubt that their morale is badly shaken, and so far as American ships are concerned, there is a bitterness combined with panic. If P.Q.18 is to be sailed through into [the] Barents Sea without adequate protection . . . and another debacle results, it will be difficult to control the morale of Merchant Ship personnel . . .'[5]

Although what was promised in relation to QP14 did eventually prove to be correct, there was no accounting for what some refer to as the fog of war. The sighting of QP14 by the crew of a German aircraft for the first time during the morning of 15 September was the prelude to what could have been considered comic farce had not the consequences been so fraught with danger. At the time two Russian aircraft were also overhead, but for some reason their pilots did not spot the German plane they were supposed to be guarding against. The crew in a Russian destroyer, at that point with the convoy, could not communicate with them. In the end in a bid to alert them, a warning shot was fired at the German aircraft from the British destroyer *Middleton*, but as Captain Harvey Crombie, the commander of the British minesweeper *Bramble*, noted regretfully, 'This as I feared had exactly the opposite effect to that intended, and the Russian fighters disappeared home, probably complaining they had been fired at!'[6]

It was not the kind of action calculated to calm the jitters the passengers were experiencing at a time when the number of QP14 escorts was quite restricted. Until reinforcements arrived, the convoy's close protection force, excluding the local escort consisting of four minesweepers and two Russian destroyers – which would depart on 16 September, – was down to 2 British destroyers, 2 anti-aircraft ships, 4 corvettes, 2 minesweepers and 4 trawlers.[7]

That explains why until the escort was reinforced, some in the convoy's merchant ships pinned their hopes on the Arctic weather to conceal them from snoopers. 'We're all praying for snow . . .' *Troubadour*'s Howard Carraway noted in the 13 September entry in his diary.[8] Notwithstanding what *Zamalek*'s captain had said to *Paulus Potter*'s Van Laar about God, Carraway's prayers went unanswered for a while. However, by midnight during the night 16–17 September *Troubadour* was, as Carraway's diary thankfully confirmed, 'ploughing through an Arctic blizzard', which carried on for much of the next two days.

Carraway's desire to be hidden from prying eyes became all the more pressing because *Troubadour* ended up straggling behind the convoy and being shadowed. Shortly after the skies cleared on 19 September, he spotted what he at first took to be 'a blackfish' (a whale species that spouts from a hole in its 'beak'), but which he quickly realized to his horror was a torpedo that was speeding towards *Troubadour*'s stern. Seeing what was almost a carbon copy of the terror invoked during PQ17 following the targeting of his ship all over again, and the equivalent pandemonium on board, Carraway once again shouted out to his men to: 'Take cover!'

Once again they were saved in the first instance because the torpedo missed *Troubadour*. However the Royal Navy's determination to live up to their promises would also play its part. Before the U-boat returned for another shot, they received a reassuring message from Burnett's force, which after leaving PQ18 on 16 September (see Chapter 28) had by this time caught up with the main body of QP14. The message which had been sent in response to their distress message stated 'assistance is on the way'.[9]

At the time they were some 40 miles south of Spitzbergen, whose 'snow white mountain peaks' could be seen to the north, according to Carraway. Perhaps fearing that reinstating radio silence would in the circumstances be interpreted as ungrateful, *Troubadour*'s radio operator sent the following message to those who were deploying their fast approaching saviour: 'Thanks a million!', a signal so out of keeping with the British penchant for understatement, that Burnett appended to it, by way of explanation, 'The *Troubadour* hails from the United States.'[10]

Troubadour would eventually be escorted by the destroyer that came back to help her to Spitzbergen's Bell Sound. But by 19 September, Burnett had another problem on his plate: how to evade the U-boats that had been pursuing the main body of QP14 on and off, notwithstanding it had also been shielded at times from the shadowing by the opaque effects of the weather. Although the men in the ten U-boats ordered to search for QP14 would have struggled given the conditions to find the convoy on their own, the crew of a reconnaissance aircraft had tracked the merchant ships down on 18 September, and helped by the shared intelligence, during the early hours of 19 September a U-boat's lookout had finally sighted some of the escorts covering the west-going merchant ships.[11] An abortive attempt was made to escape from the U-boats' clutches by sending destroyers back to make them submerge while the convoy was wheeled to the north after it had passed Spitzbergen's South Cape (see Map 15). But following the turn, the convoy was once again sighted by the crew of an aircraft, and during the night of 19–20 September, it was realized that U-boats were shadowing the convoy again.[12]

U-435's 31-year-old Kapitänleutnant Siegfried Strelow, one of the U-boat commanders in contact, would later write: 'I concluded that because it was not very dark [for long], and because there was strong protection from escorts to the front and sides, it would be impossible to attack on the surface.

'It would also have been impossible to reach the front of the convoy in daylight because of the reconnaissance by aircraft, and the fact that the escorts were operating a long way from the convoy. I therefore decided to go ahead of the convoy in the dark [during the night of 19–20 September] with a view to attacking at dawn.'

That is precisely what he did. At around 6.30 a.m. on 20 September, when the convoy was west-south-west of Spitzbergen's South Cape travelling in a west-south-west direction, his crew unleashed a series of torpedoes, one of which travelled some 1,200 metres before homing in on the minesweeper *Leda*, behind one of the convoy's starboard columns (see 9 in Map 15, and Note 13 for location).[13] The fallout from the explosion of the torpedo, which tore into *Leda*'s boiler rooms through her starboard side, was observed around 30 seconds later by coxswain Sidney

Kerslake, whose trawler, the PQ17 escort *Northern Gem,* was a short distance behind *Leda* on the minesweeper's port side.

'I noticed a huge cloud of smoke come out of her funnel,' he wrote afterwards. '[Then] I saw a column of flame shoot upwards, and at the same time heard the crump of an explosion.'[14]

According to *Leda*'s 46-year-old Lieutenant Commander Arthur Wynne-Edwards, the 'violent explosion shook the ship [so brutally], I was unable to get out of the chart house for some five minutes as the door was jammed . . . When I did get out, the ship [already] had a list of about 20 degrees (to port). I climbed down from the bridge onto the upper deck, and it was perfectly obvious that there was no chance of saving the ship, as there was a very large hole amidships on the starboard side . . . The starboard side of the ship amidships was blown out completely from the boat deck to below the water line . . . The whole of the boat deck on the starboard side was missing, . . . and the funnel was split from top to bottom on the starboard side . . . She was gradually heeling further over.'[15]

Another officer reported: 'The ship was nearly [split] in two . . . There was no communication between fore and aft.'[16] This latter point was corroborated by a third officer who had been on the back half of the ship: he confirmed that 'smoke and flame[s] were coming out right across the ship . . . We appeared to be isolated.'[17]

Fortunately there were sufficient floats in the ship for the men who survived the initial blast. Three of the lifeboats were out of action. And the men at the front and back of the ship reacted quickly to the calls by the captain and the other officers to abandon ship. Nevertheless, the oil in the sea was so thick that in spite of *Northern Gem* and two other ships quickly coming to the aid of those who jumped into the water, some were drowned before they could be picked up.[18]

According to Kerslake, at least some survived because of his commander's refusal to obey inhumane orders: 'We had the rescue nets over the side [of the trawler] for them to climb up as quickly as was possible . . . As they did so, a destroyer came up our starboard side and shouted through her loud hailer for our skipper to get back to the convoy, for we were not supposed to stop to pick up survivors on the run back. Our skipper told him to f**k off, whereupon the destroyer's CO said he would report him when we arrived in port, though as far as I know nothing came of it.'[19]

That so many survived was also down to the warmer temperature in the sea (4 °C) compared with approaching -1 °C out of the water.[20] Of the 134 officers, ratings and merchant seamen on board, 'only' around 43 lost their lives.[21]

Leda's end came very quickly. Twenty minutes after the torpedoing, her back broke after she turned onto her port side, and she floated, as Wynne-Edwards put it, 'on her beam ends . . . with her bow and stern out of the water'. He reported that he remained on board the ship until the last, eventually 'jumping off her fore foot' into the sea, from where he was rescued.[22]

His bravery made it sound all the more unfair that the inquiry, subsequently set up to look into the sinking, led to him being rapped over the knuckles for what had occurred. Having read the inquiry findings, Admiral Bruce Fraser, on behalf of Admiral Tovey wrote: 'I consider the fact that *Leda* was not zig-zagging at the time to have been an error of judgment on the part of her Commanding Officer, and he has been informed accordingly.'[23]

The harshness of this verdict, with its apparent implication that Wynne-Edwards had been responsible, was highlighted when at around 8 p.m. that same day the destroyer *Somali* was torpedoed on the port side of her engine room even though she was zig zagging.[24]

Whatever the rights and wrongs in *Leda*'s case, a crucial factor in *Somali*'s was the decision to strip QP14 of the protection offered by the carrier *Avenger* and her aircraft. That decision was made by Burnett in the light of the discovery that notwithstanding the presence of so many escorts, the convoy's valuable escort carrier's safety was no longer a good bet. One catalyst for this realization was the torpedoing of one of the convoy's merchant ships. At 6.30 p.m. that evening (20 September, i.e. before *Somali* was targeted) the American *Silver Sword* was abandoned and sunk after being hit at least twice on her port side by torpedoes fired from a U-boat – which post-war records would identify as *U-255* (see 10 in Map 15, and Note 25 for location).[25] Although the torpedoing – and subsequent on-board explosion – had not resulted in any fatalities, other than the death of one man after he had been rescued, it underlined the danger which the U-boats posed to all of QP14's ships.

This was the case despite the best efforts by the crews in the two British submarines, which like the other members of Burnett's fighting force had switched from escorting PQ18 to guarding QP14.[26] During the afternoon of 20 September their crews tried and failed to launch a counter-attack against one of the U-boats seeking to follow QP14.[27]

Scylla and *Avenger,* escorted by three destroyers, left the convoy around an hour following the sinking of *Silver Sword,* after Burnett had been transferred to the destroyer HMS *Milne,* which for the moment was to remain with QP14.[28] It was set against the context of these precautions and actions that some 90 minutes after the attack on *Silver Sword,* those in *Somali* were in their turn exposed to the jeopardy of appearing in a U-boat's sights.

This time it was *U-703* commanded by the 26-year-old Kapitänleutnant Heinz Bielfeld which had done the stalking. His 20 September entries in *U-703*'s war diary confirm that his submarine was one of the vessels which *Avenger*'s aircraft had been chasing before the carrier departed. He had had to take his U-boat down into the depths three times during the afternoon after *U-703* had been spotted from aircraft on three occasions.

Unlike Strelow, although finally obtaining his chance to attack after the carrier's departure, Bielfeld miscalculated. 'Unfortunately I am not positioned far enough to the front,' he admitted when recording how at around 7.15 p.m. he had ascended to just below the water surface and had peered out through his periscope. 'I am on [the convoy's] port side and have to be content with attacking one of the escorting destroyers.'

That is how he came to target *Somali,* located around three and a half miles to port of the port beam of the convoy whose merchant ships were still doggedly chugging away on the same west-south-westerly course (see 11 in Map 15, and Note 29 for location).[29] *Somali* was in the process of turning to starboard as part of her zig zagging routine when shortly before 8 p.m. Bielfeld ordered his crew to fire three torpedoes at her at a distance of around 1,330 metres.[30]

The result of one of the torpedoes hitting *Somali* on the port side of her engine room, as seen from the bridge of Burnett's latest flagship *Milne,* then at the centre of the screen of destroyers at the front of the convoy, was so spectacular that it prompted the flagship's Midshipman Thomas Wells to write the following account of what he heard and witnessed in his diary:

'Someone exclaimed: "Look at *Somali*!" I saw a white column of water springing up abreast her second funnel . . . It grew into a mushroom-like shape and then collapsed, and she swung around to port with steam gushing out of her sides in a cloud. Still turning, she was completely shrouded in steam and came to a stop.'[31]

The explosion did not come as a complete surprise for all of *Somali's* crew. Some of them had received a last-minute warning. Around 30 to 45 seconds before the torpedo struck, *Somali's* asdic operator had pressed a buzzer to alert those on her bridge that he had detected a torpedo approaching from the port side. *Somali's* officer of the watch, prompted by her captain, had quickly called out 'Torpedo port: Hard a port!'[32]

Lieutenant Walter Williamson, the destroyer flotilla's anti-submarine officer, who had heard both the alarm hooter and the order to the helmsman via the loudspeaker in *Somali's* wardroom, later described how they had spurred him into action:

'I immediately ran up . . . to the upper deck, intending to close up to my anti-submarine station on the bridge. I ran forward on the starboard side. As I got abreast the [torpedo] tubes, the torpedo hit on the port side. I have a vague recollection of being thrown to the deck and surrounded by . . . debris. After some time, I got to my feet again . . . [I] could see nothing for dense clouds of steam. I tried to move away . . . but I was afraid of either falling into the hole [made by the explosion] or over the side [of the ship]. So I stood where I was, touching the guard rail until . . . the steam cleared away.

'I then observed that the torpedo tubes had vanished, and there was a large hole in the upper deck between the after funnel and the tube mounting, through which the remains of the engine room was visible.'[33]

Only after full visibility was restored, did Williamson, feeling in his own words 'a bit shaken', complete his interrupted journey to the bridge, where he arrived according to another witness, 'looking like a ghost covered in a white film' of dust.[34]

Somali's captain at the time, whose recommendations would play an important role in determining what action should be taken, was Lieutenant Commander Colin Maud, who had recently taken over the command of the ship after her previous commander had fallen sick. It had not taken the new commander long to make an impression. 'Mad' Maud was a larger than life 39-year-old. He was described by Acting Captain Richard Onslow, commander of the 6th Flotilla of Tribal Class Destroyers as well as *Ashanti*, as 'a great giant of a man, with a brick red face and a huge black beard. His voice and his laugh were as big as he was.'[35]

As is often the case, looks proclaimed the character. He was a bit of a maverick, who said what he thought, and to a large extent did as he pleased. His alcohol intake was vast, yet it did not appear to affect his ability to run his ship. He was worshipped by his men.[36] As Captain Onslow saw it, 'He was still a lieutenant commander (rather than a commander, like Onslow, who was one year younger than Maud) because their Lordships had never been quite able to reconcile promotion with his sometimes exaggerated sense of fun. Those . . . who may remember him two years later as Chief Beachmaster on D-Day, and the fear he struck into the soldiery with his huge presence, and still larger vocabulary, will know that this omission was very soon made good.'[37]

Before going to sea in *Somali* for the first time at the beginning of the month, Maud had been informed by the ship's engineer commander that in his opinion, the ship would not be seaworthy if three of her major compartments were flooded.

Inspection following the torpedoing told Maud this was exactly what had occurred; the explosion had blasted a hole in the port side of the engine room extending to about eight feet under the water line, and caused the internal bulkheads at either end of the engine room to buckle. As a result, within a few minutes, not only the engine room, but also the compartments to the front (the No. 3 boiler room) and to the rear (the gearing room) filled with sea water, and the entire ship listed around 15 to 20 degrees to starboard. It was later confirmed that five men had died in the first minutes following the strike.[38] The stern of the ship sank low in the water to such an extent that the starboard side of the quarter deck was almost level with the sea's surface.[39]

While the convoy continued on its course, Maud decided that he should evacuate as many of the crew as could be spared, while keeping enough men on board to ensure the ship could be towed by *Ashanti*. Sixty remained on board at first although some of those evacuated were sent back to the ship later. Progress after the towing started was slow; it was realized the 700-mile journey to Iceland's Akureyri would take five to six days. On one occasion the towing ceased temporarily after the towing cable and hawser broke.

But things looked up after *Ashanti*'s Sub-Lieutenant Terence Lewin, who some 40 years later would be Britain's Chief of the Defence Staff when Prime Minister Margaret Thatcher sent a taskforce to retake the Falkland Islands, showed his mettle. He was put in charge of a party sent out in *Ashanti*'s motor cutter to attach electricity cables to the tow lines in an attempt to provide electricity to *Somali* while she was still moving. On 22 September, with the cables once in place, the pumps in *Somali* were switched on, enabling water to be sucked out as fast as it leaked in. It was no mean feat since it involved Lewin and his men at a time when the water temperature was zero degrees immersing their arms in the sea on and off over many hours in order to do their work.[40]

By 23 September, officers in *Ashanti* and *Somali*, who had started by believing *Somali* only had an outside chance of being towed to Iceland, began to think that they might make it after all.[41]

And perhaps they might have, had it not been for what started off as a freshening of the wind during the night of 23–24 September that bore down on the two destroyers from the north-west. At the time the wind strength did not particularly bother either Maud or Onslow.[42] They were more concerned about what might happen if the weather worsened. Onslow even went so far as to go down the ladder to his sea cabin so that he could go to sleep. However, before dozing off, he noticed an unexplained sharp drop in the temperature that with the benefit of hindsight, he conceded later, should have rung alarm bells.

If it had led to anxiety, it would have been justified. While Onslow slumbered, the 29-year-old Lieutenant Moses Lee, the watch officer on *Somali*'s bridge, sensed something had gone badly wrong.

'At 0225 (according to Time zone A) I heard a loud cracking,' Lee told the subsequent *Somali* inquiry, 'and felt the ship roll to starboard. The Captain awoke and asked if the tow had parted. I looked aft and saw that the stern was rising out of the water, and told him that she had broken her back.

'Seas were then breaking over amidships, and she was listing heavily. The Captain ordered the Chief Yeoman to tell *Ashanti* to stop, but I think by this time the tow had parted.

'Most of the ratings . . . mustered on the port side of the forecastle, abreast the bridge, and officers either on the Upper bridge or Flag Deck . . . It appeared obvious that she would not right herself, and the list increased to about 70° to starboard. The upper deck appeared to be holding the fore and the after parts together.

'The Captain ordered everybody to blow up their lifebelts, and stand by to abandon ship. I took off my sea boots, sheepskin coat and gloves and blew up my lifebelt. The Captain then ordered abandon ship starboard. The list by that time was about 80 degrees . . .

'I walked down the port side of the bridge onto the ship's side, and assisted in the final clearing away of the port carley raft. There were only about six hands around this float at this time. We got the float into the water, and I took the painter, intending to hold it close to the ship for more hands to get in. However I was swept off my feet . . . [into the sea].'[43]

While all this had been going on, Onslow had been sleeping. He would later explain that the first he knew that anything was going wrong was when he was awakened in his sea cabin in *Ashanti* at around 3.30 a.m. (in other words 2.30 a.m. according to the A time zone which Lieutenant Lee had been using) by a call down the voicepipe, and told the tow had parted:[44] 'I was up the ladder and on the bridge in seconds. Looking astern, we could just see the blink of an Aldis lamp. The quarter deck reported that the tow had indeed gone, and they were having trouble in slipping the cable.'[45]

As if that was not trouble enough, it was at around this time that the bad weather that Onslow had been dreading all of a sudden swept down on them.[46] 'It came without warning,' Richard Onslow wrote afterwards. The wind, he recalled, was 'like a whirling dervish, shrieking and howling in the rigging, whipping off the crests of the rising waves, and driving them to leeward in an unbroken sheet of spindrift . . . Then came the snow driving horizontally, cutting our faces and our eyes, freezing on the decks and superstructure.'[47]

'I [nevertheless] turned *Ashanti* back without undue haste to investigate,' he wrote in his official report. His report continues: 'Due to the snow, it was not until I was close to *Somali* that I saw she had broken in half. Her bow was rising rapidly, and her company were dropping 100 feet or more from her forecastle head, as the fore part [be]came vertical.

I could see her captain on the port side of the bridge encouraging the remainder to jump.'

'I could not immediately place myself in a good position to pick up survivors, who mostly abandoned ship on the lee side of the ship. The Commanding Officer of (the trawler) *Lord Middleton,* who had been stationed astern, very gallantly put his ship close in under the wreck at the risk of it falling over on to him.'[48]

However, it was obvious that *Lord Middleton* could not pick up everyone, and Onslow was put under pressure to let *Ashanti* take a more proactive role:

' "Put her alongside Sir" said . . . (*Somali*'s officer who had earlier been transferred from his own ship to *Ashanti*) pleadingly.[49] His voice was tense, and when I glanced at him, so was his face. They were his shipmates hanging there . . . But I knew that any attempt to go alongside in that raging sea could only result in severe . . . damage to *Ashanti,* even without the handicap of the still trailing towing hawser. When I told him so, he turned away to hide his distress.'[50]

Who can blame him? It was a shocking sight. In *Somali*'s Lieutenant Lee's report, he stated that 'the whole of the forecastle from the bridge forward was clear of the water. It appeared to me that the stern had sunk and was pulling the bows down.'[51]

According to Maud, the end came when 'the after part broke away, and the fore end reared her forecastle head up vertically, washing the bridge personnel and myself, who had clustered around the port signalling projector, overboard to port.'[52]

Onslow admitted he did not himself see *Somali* finally disappear, because once *Ashanti* was free of the tow hawser, he was too busy manoeuvring her so that she could replicate *Lord Middleton*'s moves and thereby give *Ashanti*'s crew the opportunity to fish passing men out of the water. But others in *Ashanti* appear to have seen *Somali*'s last moments. According to Onslow's understanding of their reports, the front end of the ship 'settled lower and lower in the water, still vertical. As the waves reached the bridge . . . (Maud and another officer dropped) off their platform into the boiling sea. Then very quickly . . . [*Somali*] was gone.'[53]

Onslow's account reveals how all efforts were then focused on the rescue: 'I [had]signalled to the other two . . . [rescuing destroyers] to get to windward of me. In that weather it was hopeless to try to hold the ship head to sea. The only possible manoeuvre was to stay beam on, and by backing and filling, pick up as many as we could to leeward.

'It was heartbreaking work. The ship was rolling drunkenly, and we were drifting so fast that inevitably a few of those in the water were trapped under our bilge keel before we could grab them. And a few swept past our bow or stern, when to have moved the ship would have meant losing those we nearly had. We could only pray that the [destroyers] . . . to windward would see them . . . When we could see no more men to leeward, we worked round to windward again.'[54]

The following sections of Lieutenant Lee's report suggest that some of those who were rescued owed their survival to the way he directed them to the raft to which he had swum:

'I had a torch with me, and by sweeping the water with it[s beam], I attracted more to the raft, so many that it became . . . so overcrowded it was awash. I saw an empty raft between us and the ship, and told some of the hands to make for this. By this time, we saw the searchlights of at least three ships searching the water.

'*Lord Middleton* then appeared to windward, and eventually manoeuvred us alongside. They threw us a line, but at this juncture, the raft tipped, and I found myself in the water with four ratings holding on to me. I grasped three lines in succession, but was unable to climb to the trawler's gunwale. Eventually I reached a scrambling net, and was hauled aboard with, according to the trawler's crew, two ratings holding on to me.'[55]

In his report, Maud described some of his own efforts to be picked up: 'The water was so cold that I was quite unable to get my breath to speak for the first few minutes, but later on one became acclimatized. I swam to . . . a flotanet around which were about six seamen and Sub-Lieutenant Longhurst. The flotanet was still rolled up, and I tried to get at my knife to cut lashings but this was impossible; my hands were too cold . . .

'I found my voice again, and was able to try to stop some of the ratings nearby, who were wasting their energy shouting for help . . .

'*Lord Middleton* soon appeared, and we did our best to paddle toward her, but we missed her. Then HMS *Eskimo* came in sight, and we paddled alongside. Sub-Lieutenant Longhurst . . . managed to secure a line to the net, but I lost my grip as [the] net was hauled forward, and I floated aft down the ship's side.

'I managed to hold onto the sea ladder for some time, but an empty carley float drifted down the side and knocked me off . . . Shortly after this, I became unconscious.'[56]

But although down, he was not quite out, as was confirmed by the following statement by one of *Ashanti*'s officers: 'I was standing on . . . [*Ashanti*'s] bridge, when what looked like a walrus was sighted floating down towards us . . . [But that] seemed too extraordinary. [Then] someone realized it was in fact Colin Maud.

'His sheepskin coat was billowing out and his black beard was only too obvious. There was [immediately] a general exodus from the bridge to the iron deck. To get a frozen body of 15 stone onboard was not a simple problem, and there was nothing he could do for himself. He arrived alongside amidships, and a meat hook was slung over on a . . . davit. Three chaps went over the side . . . and [one] secured the hook in the back of his coat. The rest of us went half way down the ship's side to guide him up and ensure he did not fall back.'

After being revived, he was reported to be singing as he was taken aft, even though he had been in the sea for such a long time. His clothes had become embedded in the ice that had formed around them. The story goes that in spite of his ordeal, he was none the worse for wear once he had been warmed up because before falling into the sea, he had fortified himself by swigging the brandy in the hip flask that he liked to carry around in his pocket.[57] Whether or not this is an apocryphal tale, Onslow would later confirm that it was not long before Maud was standing beside him on *Ashanti*'s bridge as if nothing untoward had happened, telling him his version of *Somali*'s last minutes.[58]

Others were not so lucky. The same *Ashanti* officer has described how *Somali*'s first lieutenant 'reached our stern, but fell back and sank before he had been secured.'[59] According to Onslow, the only other 'survivor' rescued by *Ashanti*'s crew died shortly after being brought on board.[60]

He later added: 'Between us (the three destroyers) we covered the area until all hope was gone.'[61] They finished searching at around 5.45 a.m., although *Eskimo* remained in the vicinity until daylight.[62] Onslow concluded: 'The three of us could count the living on one hand, and it took some time to find out from the *Lord Middleton* how many she had. We had lost sight of her in the storm and could get no answer on the wireless, so we spent a very anxious time while we spread on a line of search to find her.'[63]

According to Onslow's 1942 report, *Lord Middleton* picked up one officer and 17 ratings, and he estimated that 40 to 50 of those in *Somali* lost their lives when she sank in addition to the five killed when the torpedo exploded. A subsequent report concluded that the total number of *Somali* fatalities was 82 officers and ratings.[64] He later commented: '"Thank God for the *Lord Middleton*" was our thought at the time. But we had lost some . . . gallant officers and men including our own "Doormouse" (Sub-Lieutenant J. M. Longhurst, an *Ashanti* officer who had been lent to *Somali*).'[65]

By the time *Ashanti* and the remaining destroyers rejoined the convoy at 8.30 a.m. on 24 September, QP14 and its escorts had already seen further action and sustained additional losses. On 21 September, as the merchant ships progressed towards the area west of Jan Mayen Island, the pilot of a circling Catalina aircraft had been forced to make a forced landing on the sea after a shell fired from the deck of the U-boat it had been targeting had pierced its petrol tank. Its crew were rescued by a destroyer.[66]

Less fortunate were some of those in the three ships attacked during 22 September: the American PQ17 veteran *Bellingham* with her cargo of iron ore, which had been the leading ship in the convoy's 6th (starboard) column, the British oiler *Gray Ranger* (which had been in convoy position 52 – 5th column, row 2), and the British *Ocean Voice* (in convoy position 31 – 3rd column, 1st, i.e. front, row) which had Commodore John Dowding on board along with her cargo of timber and paper. These three ships were all victims of torpedoes fired from *U-435*, around 45 miles west of Jan Mayen Island, from the starboard side of the convoy just an hour after Admiral Burnett's departure from QP14 in the destroyer *Milne* during the early morning of 22 September (see 12 in Map 15, and Note 67 for approximate location).[67] Given that *U-435* had already sunk *Leda*, that took her Kapitänleutnant Strelow's QP14 scalps to four.

The torpedoing of *Ocean Voice*, hit firstly on her starboard side underneath the passengers' accommodation in No. 5 hold at the back of the ship, and then again on her starboard side beside No. 1 hold at the front of the ship, before being sunk by a British destroyer after the crew and passengers had abandoned ship, demonstrated once again the perils of being in a commodore's freighter in the middle of the front row of a convoy.[68]

Although it has been hard to find detailed reports about the oiler's demise which extend beyond a statement of the number of her crew who were killed (an official report confirms there were 6 *Gray Ranger* fatalities), accounts written up by the commanders of the two rescue ships *Rathlin* and *Zamalek*, and by the survivors and commander of *Bellingham* and *Ocean Voice* respectively suggest that the overall loss of life in the latter two sunk merchant ships was also remarkably low. There were no *Bellingham* casualties.[69] Tragically, the one fatality among those travelling in *Ocean Voice* – which included 25 Russian passengers, 19 of them women and children, and 9 survivors following previous sinkings as well as the 58-man crew – was a baby Russian girl who had been born the day after the convoy set sail.

Not that the saving of these *Ocean Voice* passengers was a foregone conclusion. All ladders leading to their accommodation, which was in the No. 5 hold at the back of the ship, were smashed by the first torpedo's explosion. The passengers only escaped from the sea water that eventually filled up the hold thanks to three members of the crew, who helped them ascend rope ladders that were lowered, and carried to safety those who could not climb up. These passengers were then all put into the ship's two after lifeboats and rowed over to *Zamalek*.[70]

There they would find many of the traumatised passengers who had come all the way from Archangel. *Paulus Potter's* master Willem Sissingh admitted that it was much more frightening being a helpless survivor in a rescue ship when U-boats were about than being bombed while attempting to repulse repeated attacks by German aircraft on his own ship, which had been the case during PQ17. Speaking for all *Paulus Potter's* wounded on *Zamalek* during QP14, he summed it up by stating: 'We all lost our nerve on this convoy.'

The Dutch ship's Wim van Laar was also traumatised in a different way. Stationed as he was below decks near the operating theatre, he could not avoid witnessing the long-running battle fought by *Zamalek's* surgeon to save the life of a woman passenger, probably the one who had been brought on board after being injured when the first torpedo hit *Ocean Voice*. According to Van Laar, she was bleeding so heavily that she only survived thanks to the blood donated by sailors in the rescue ship.[71]

But the survivors' fears turned out to be unnecessary. There were to be no more QP14 sinkings. The remaining ships were saved partly because of the aggressive tactics employed by the escorts, and partly because of the safety-first approach adopted by the Germans. At 12.59 p.m. on 23 September Konteradmiral Klüber (Admiral Nordmeer) ordered the eight U-boats that had been attempting to catch up with QP14 after losing contact to terminate the operation against the convoy.

His war diary states he did this not only because he realized that British and American aircraft would be searching for the tell-tale signs of U-boats as the convoy neared Iceland's coast, but also because he suspected that the U-boat crews would be exhausted after being at sea for so long. Another factor he said was that 'it makes even more sense to stop operating against this convoy as it approached the coast because its cargo is less valuable than PQ18.'[72]

The ten vessels constituting the bulk of the surviving QP14 merchant ships, and the two rescue ships, escorted by the local escort of four corvettes and three trawlers plus three anti-aircraft ships, passed the Butt of Lewis (on Scotland's Island of Lewis in the Outer Hebrides) during the morning of 26 September, and those vessels going on to Loch Ewe arrived there later that day.[73] The two merchant ships that had become separated from the convoy also reached their desired destinations, *Troubadour* and *Winston Salem* arriving at Reykjavik and Loch Ewe respectively on 27 September.[74]

30

Castaway

Main Action: November 1942
The sinking of the independent ships including Dekabrist, part 1

GMT + 1
(See Map 1)

On 3 October 1942 Stalin sent an urgent request to Churchill. It started: 'I have to inform you that the situation in Stalingrad has deteriorated since the beginning of September,' and continued: 'The Germans were able to concentrate in this area great reserves of aviation, and in this way managed to secure superiority in the air of ratio 2:1. We had not enough fighters for the protection of our forces from the air. Even the bravest troops are helpless if they lack air protection. We particularly require Spitfires and Airacobras.'[1]

Stalin's telegram went on to ask that instead of the tanks and artillery the Allies were committing to supply under the Second Protocol, which once signed would determine total Western aid during the year commencing 1 July 1942 (the year that had already started), 'Great Britain and the USA . . . supply us with 800 fighters a month (approximately Great Britain 300 and the USA 500),' and confirmed 'such a help would . . . improve [the] position at the front.'[2]

In an equivalent telegram to Roosevelt sent four days later, he tacked onto his wishlist a monthly delivery of '8 to 10 thousand trucks, 5,000 tons of aluminium and 4 to 5 thousand tons of explosives', plus over the next 12 months, two million tons of grain and as much fats, food concentrates and canned meat as possible.[3]

These telegrams sent at what promised to be a turning point in the war not only highlighted Stalin's anxiety about the Soviet Union's precarious situation. They also revealed that he really was hoping that supplies from his Western allies would bide the Soviet Union over. As is pointed out in this book's Conclusion, there would come a time after the war when Russian propaganda would deny that any of the aid supplied by the Western Allies had been needed by the Soviet Union, or that it substantially helped the Red Army to defeat the Germans. However, this is arguably at odds with the combination of Stalin's October 1942 beseeching requests, and British and American compliance with them, if only in part.

Stalin's pleas for assistance were certainly made at a critical time on the Eastern Front. Although Soviet generals were already working on the plan for the great counter-attack that would commence in November 1942, and would culminate with the successful encirclement of all German forces involved with the attack on Stalingrad, Stalin could not be certain that this so-called Operation Uranus would succeed. At the beginning of October 1942, it was touch and go whether Stalingrad would even be in Soviet hands when Operation Uranus was ready.

In fact even as Stalin wrote, small groups of soldiers from the Red Army were fighting a series of desperate last-ditch rearguard actions in Stalingrad. They had to do this if they were to cling on to what at the time appeared to be an ever-decreasing series of perimeters on the western side of the River Volga that ran more or less from north to south down the east side of Stalingrad while German forces attacked from the west with renewed fury and vigour.[4]

Given the importance of these world-changing manoeuvres, it was awkward to say the least that even before the receipt of Stalin's entreaty, Churchill was discussing with Roosevelt the wording that should be used to inform the Russian leader that the Arctic convoys would have to be suspended again.[5] This time it was so that the necessary warships could be committed to the Torch operation, scheduled to take place in November 1942. It was in the context of the fear in Washington that Stalin might lose heart and give in if Churchill's draft was sent, that Roosevelt on

5 October 1942 wrote to Churchill: 'In so far as PQ19 is concerned . . . , we should not tell Stalin that the convoy will not sail . . . Let PQ19 sail in successive groups, comprising the fastest ships now loaded and loading for Russia. These groups would comprise two or three ships, each supported by two or three escorts, and sent at 24 or 48-hour intervals. They might have to go without the full naval covering support that would protect the convoy from the *Tirpitz* or heavy cruisers, but that must simply be a risk that we have to take . . .

'I think it is better that we take this risk than to endanger our whole relations with Russia at this time.'[6]

Two days later (7 October) Churchill replied: 'There is no possibility of letting P.Q.19 sail in successive groups with reduced escorts as you suggest. I append a note by the Admiralty on this subject.'[7] The Admiralty note explained why Roosevelt's proposal was impractical: 'Possibilities of evasion are slight as German air reconnaissance for north Russian convoys is very intensive, and anything in the nature of a group of ships would be continually shadowed . . . A group is more likely to draw attack by enemy surface vessels . . . Anything short of full covering support invites disaster both to the group and Naval forces . . . To send a total of 40 ships in groups of 2 or 3 ships with 2 or 3 escorts would employ as many escorts as were required for P.Q.18!'

That explains why the Admiralty was proposing: 'to sail about 10 ships from Iceland . . . during dark period 28th October to 8th November. These would sail singly at about 200 mile intervals . . . and rely on evasion and dispersion.'[8] The implication was that single ships would have a better chance of slipping through the net unnoticed, and even if spotted, would probably not be continuously shadowed until they were sunk.

However, Churchill wanted Roosevelt to take on board what those in the Admiralty perceived as the likely consequences of what they referred to as 'independent sailings'. According to the Admiralty: 'The voyage in anything but a full escorted convoy is so hazardous that it should only be undertaken by volunteers who clearly understand the risk. The chance of crews of stricken ships surviving when they take to their boats is remote.'[9] In case that was not clear enough, Churchill in his enclosing note to Roosevelt commented: 'Their sole hope if sunk far from help . . . [is] arctic clothing and such heating arrangements as can be placed in lifeboats.'[10]

After receiving this explanation, Roosevelt finally caved in, and agreed that Churchill should give Stalin what Churchill had called 'the blunt truth.'[11] That was contained in Churchill's 8 October telegram to Stalin, in which he stated that while because of Torch, 'naval protection . . . for escorted convoys . . . will be impossible until our impending operations are completed . . . , we intend in the meanwhile to do our best to send you supplies by the northern route by means of ships sailed independently. Arrangements have been made to sail ships from Iceland during the moonless period 28th October to 8th November. Ten of ours are preparing in addition to what Americans will do.'[12]

On the same day Roosevelt wrote to Stalin informing him he was taking measures calculated to increase the capacity of the Persian Gulf route.[13]

But apart from what was going to be sent in the independent ships, relatively little was on offer. Admittedly Churchill also promised to send by the Persian Gulf route 150 Spitfires with the equivalent of 50 more in the form of spares as a one-off reinforcement.[14] While Roosevelt in his 11 October message to Stalin stated: 'In October we will ship to you 276 combat planes . . .'[15] However, Churchill and Roosevelt were only agreeing to supply just over 40 per cent of the fighters that Stalin was hoping to receive in the month of October, and were putting no plans in place to satisfy the demand for fighters in subsequent months. Nevertheless, they were upset by the very negative Soviet reaction. On 19 October an article published in *Pravda* stated that England's harbouring of Rudolf Hess, the Nazi who in May 1941 had fled to Britain, meant that England was 'a refuge for gangsters'.

Such intemperate language in a publication controlled by the Soviet government so riled the British politicians, that Foreign Secretary Anthony Eden called in the Soviet Ambassador Maisky and informed him of his 'astonishment and keen displeasure' that language 'intolerable between allies' should have been used. According to Maisky, the Foreign Secretary 'was seriously agitated, anxious. He flushed, went pale and raised his voice to a high pitch on several occasions.'[16]

At least the *Pravda* article was out in the open, and could consequently be contradicted. Behind the scenes on the same day as the *Pravda* article was published, Stalin was writing to Maisky: 'We in Moscow have an impression that Churchill is set on Soviet defeat in order then to connive with . . . [Germany].' On 28 October in another message to Maisky, Stalin wrote: 'Churchill told us in Moscow that by early spring '43 one million Anglo-American forces would open a second front in Europe. But Churchill evidently belongs to those statesmen who give a promise easily, only to forget about it just as quickly, or insolently break it. He also vowed to bomb Berlin intensively throughout September and October. However he has not fulfilled his promise and did not even bother to inform Moscow of the reasons for non-compliance.'[17]

It was in the face of such negative thinking on the part of the Soviet Union's leader that the plan that was supposed to disarm Stalin kicked off. The first of the initial batch of 10 independent east-going merchant ships (five British, five American and one from the Soviet Union) eventually pencilled in to participate in 'Operation FB' set sail from Iceland's Hvalfjord on 29 October 1942. The remainder set sail one by one at the rate of two or three ships per day, with the last setting out during the first days of November.[18]

But it soon became clear that the Admiralty had been right to highlight their vulnerability. It did not take long for the Germans to draw their first blood. Shortly after 1.15 a.m. on 2 November two of the torpedoes fired from *U 586* struck the British *Empire Gilbert* when she was still south-west of Jan Mayen Island (see Note 19 for location).[19] *U-586*'s 27-year old commander Kapitänleutnant Dietrich von der Esch would later write that when he drew near where the merchant ship had been, all he could see were three 'Tommies clinging to a plank of wood, and six more on a raft'. He rescued the former, but the latter were abandoned, and probably froze to death or drowned in the water whose temperature was 1 °C. Nothing was heard again of the remainder of the 66 men who had been on board.[20]

Next to go was the American Liberty ship *William Clark*, which was also torpedoed and sunk south-west of Jan Mayen Island. The torpedoing took place at around 1 p.m. on 4 November, although in her case her nemesis was *U-354* (see Note 21 for location).[21] Although the five men in the merchant ship's engine room were killed when the torpedo exploded, the remainder of her crew managed to escape in three of her lifeboats. The 41 survivors in two of these lifeboats were subsequently picked up by the two trawlers summoned to the scene by the distress signals, but not before two men in one had died. The 17 men in the third boat were never found, and some of those who made it back to dry land complained bitterly that when they had volunteered, they had been deceived into thinking the trawlers patrolling on the route would be in contact every five hours, whereas it took three days for one of the trawlers to locate one of the boats.[22]

One suspects however that if the *William Clark* survivors had ever learned the fate of the third of the east-going independent merchant ships which crossed the path of a U-boat as part of Operation FB, they would have put a more positive gloss on their traumatic experiences. *Empire Sky* had reached Spitzbergen's South Cape when at around 7 p.m. on 6 November she was torpedoed by the crew in *U-625*. The German submariners were helped by the rays cast by the Aurora Borealis which happened to appear at the critical moment. Rather than permitting *Empire Sky's* crew to row away from their damaged vessel, the U-boat's 25-year-old commander Oberleutnant Hans Benker had another torpedo fired at the ship. The following extract from his war diary recorded the result:

'The ship goes up with a powerful explosion that turns the dark night into what looks like day. A column of fire rises up into the sky, and pieces from the wrecked ship fall back down into the water which gives it the appearance it is boiling. Many splinters land on our boat.

'A short time afterwards, the only evidence of the disaster is the smoke. The lifeboats have also vanished as if into thin air.'[23]

Backing up what Churchill had told Roosevelt about sunk independent ships' crews being on their own, Ensign Roger Wise, the armed guard commander in *Hugh Williamson*, another of the independent sailers, whose crew had only finished talking to *Empire Sky's* a few hours earlier, after the two ships had passed each other west of Spitzbergen, later reported that when *Empire Sky's* SOS message was heard, there was no thought of going to her rescue. The earlier Admiralty message which had instructed *Hugh Williamson's* master to be sure to pass Spitzbergen's South Cape during the night – implying there might be a German vessel in the vicinity – might have had something to do with it. 'We manned the guns and proceeded full speed ahead,' Wise wrote. His report continues: 'About twenty five minutes later we saw a huge red flare go up about ten to fifteen miles off our port quarter. This was accompanied by a low rumble, and immediately followed by three booms, apparently from a 4 or 5 inch gun.'[24] Then there was silence, and one can well imagine that the watching sailors thought 'there but for the grace of God go I'.

Given how close *Hugh Williamson* was to the action, she was certainly fortunate in not becoming *U-625*'s next victim. Her luck was to hold all the way to north Russia. Although the next morning her gunners were called on to ward off a Focke-Wulf aircraft whose crew attempted to bomb her, she was not attacked again, and made it to Molotovsk on 11 November, one of four independent ships participating in Operation FB to reach that port, and one of five to reach north Russia.[25] *Empire Scott,* which had set off on 2 November, dropped off her cargo in Murmansk. Three of the other ships participating in Operation FB returned to Iceland.[26]

All of these east-going ships which reached Russia also had the good fortune to sail clear of the route followed by the German cruiser *Admiral Hipper.* During the late afternoon of 5 November, *Hipper* accompanied by four destroyers set out from Altenfjord on a sortie referred to by the Germans as Hoffnung (Hope). Two of the Soviet ships sailing independently in a western direction were less fortunate (during the period 31 October to 5 December 1942 around nine Soviet ships set off from northern Russia with a view to reaching Iceland).[27] Both were sunk by the gunners in the destroyer *Z 27* on 7 November. Forty-three men were saved from the Soviet ship sunk by *Z 27* 260 miles south-east of Hope Island, the large number of survivors reflecting the speedy abandoning of the targeted ship without any resistance being offered. The crew in the tanker *Donbass,* a PQ17 veteran, which was intercepted 220 miles east of Hope Island, jeopardized their chances of survival by returning *Z 27*'s fire. Just 15 men and one of the five women in the crew were saved after the gunners in the Soviet ship tried to resist. There were 49 fatalities.[28]

But no-one assessing the success or failure of Operation FB can do so without taking into account the almost indescribable torment suffered by those from the other two east-going merchant ships which failed to make it to the north Russian ports.

German records confirm that the first of these ships to experience problems was the Soviet Union's *Dekabrist,* which sailed from Hvalfjord at the end of October 1942.[29] At 11.05 a.m. on 4 November, around two hours before *William Clark* (mentioned above) was hit, the Russian vessel was torpedoed by the crew of a German aircraft while *Dekabrist* was around

60 miles south of Hope Island. She sank the next day at 11.17 a.m. while still some 10 miles away from the island.[30]

But while those two matter of fact statements in Admiral Nordmeer's war diary suggest that the ship was subjected to two separate attacks, and that in between there was an abortive attempt to make it to the nearest dry land, they do not begin to convey the desperate efforts taken by her crew to save the ship, and the life and death struggle to survive that followed afterwards. For what happened to her and her crew before she was abandoned, we are beholden to the diary written by Stepan Polikarpovich Belyaev, the captain of the ship, who was in his late forties when the events described in it occurred, whereas the aftermath is chronicled particularly vividly in the recollections of Nadezhda Natalich, the ship's doctor, a young woman in her early thirties when the tragic events she wrote up turned her life upside down.[31]

According to Belyaev, their journey was uneventful until the morning of 4 November when they were approaching the meridian of Hope Island from the west. The turning point came when Maurice Sherbakov, the ship's radio operator, transcribed a message sent by a member of the English speaking crew of a ship sailing around 120 miles to the east, that is directly ahead of *Dekabrist*'s line of travel, stating she was being attacked by aircraft. The ship attacked may well have been the American *John Walker,* one of the other vessels participating in Operation FB, whose radio operator that morning sent a signal announcing she was being bombed by aircraft south-east of Hope Island.[32] Although the report by at least one of the aircraft crews, referred to in Admiral Nordmeer's war diary, stated the ship had been observed sinking, *John Walker*'s armed guard and crew in fact fought off the attack.[33] That was lucky for her sailors, as once again no other ship went to her aid; rather than rushing to rescue her, Belyaev immediately ordered his helmsman to try to evade the German planes by turning towards the north. But the attempt to stay out of harm's way was to no avail. Shortly afterwards *Dekabrist* was herself attacked by what Belyaev later described as nine torpedo aircraft and two dive bombers.

In what appears to have been a reprise to what happened when *Paulus Potter* was besieged during PQ17, for the best part of two hours, the aircraft were kept at bay by the ship's gunners and the just in time changes of course ordered by Belyaev. But *Dekabrist*'s firepower was weakened when bombs dropped by one of the dive bombers beside No. 1 hold put the bow gun out of action. That paved the way for three newly arrived torpedo bombers to attack simultaneously from the starboard side of the ship, safe in the knowledge that if the ship was turned towards them in order to present a narrow target, the stern guns on the ship would be also unable to fire at them for fear of hitting the ship's bridge.

Belyaev in his diary described the result: 'The first torpedo landed in the water, and we manoeuvred past it, and the second torpedo as well. But the third . . . hit the ship's forepeak . . . It was as if she had collided with an underwater rock. The vessel shook violently and sparks flew up into the sky.'

That proved to be the end of the attack. Or as Belyaev put it: 'The Fascists having completed their dirty work flew away.' They left the Russians with the task of trying to repair the damage. For many hours they tried to staunch the sea water that was pouring into the forepeak, and into No. 1 hold through the large hole in the ship's side made by the torpedo. However, although two seamen were at one point standing in the hold with water up to their necks, they could not attach a patch to the side of the hull, apart from anything else because the area around the cavity was no longer flat.

The explosions had also caused other leaks. Sea water gradually filled up No. 3 hold and the boiler rooms, and when in spite of the ship's tilt to port, the water reached the starboard boiler, it was also extinguished, and the huge engines, the beating heart of the ship, finally fell silent, leaving the ship to drift helplessly at the mercy of the waves and weather.

A British or American captain in these circumstances might have immediately given the order to abandon ship. With the wind becoming stronger every hour, and the ship's list increasing slowly but surely, there was a danger the ship would topple over before the lifeboats could be launched. For around four hours after the writing was on the wall for *Dekabrist*, Belyaev prevaricated, perhaps hoping against hope that one of the series of desperate signals sent out by his radio operator would result in a last-minute reprieve.

He did not find out until much later that although the signals were being received on at least two Soviet wirelesses, both were located in the Kara Sea, operated by those who were too far away to offer direct assistance.

The signals intercepted provided an unusually complete history of what was going on. First came the SOS sent out soon after the ship was torpedoed. Then in the late afternoon of 4 November the next message informed those tuning in: 'The vessel is tilting and it's getting worse. Water is coming into the engine room.' Shortly afterwards another message was broadcast: 'The vessel is sinking. We are preparing the lifeboats.' This was followed around four hours later by a notification that 'The crew are getting into the lifeboats' and then an hour later, shortly before midnight, Belyaev's telegraphist Maurice Sherbakov tapped out on his transmitter: 'This is my final message. I am leaving the vessel. Save us.'

After the war the radio operator who had been listening in from his ship in the Kara Sea told how he and his comrades carried on listening for some time after hearing this last pathetic cry for assistance. But the radio operator heard nothing further from *Dekabrist*, and although two Soviet submarines were sent to the spot mentioned in the signals where it was believed the ship had been torpedoed, they found no sign of either the ship or her crew.[34] It would be several years before the families of those who had served in the ship would discover what had happened to them.[35]

The abandoning of *Dekabrist* went smoothly. According to Nadezdha Natalich, everyone from the ship found a place in one of the four lifeboats. She even managed to take her cat with her in her lifeboat, which accommodated 19 of the crew including her, the captain and Sherbakov. The next morning those in all four boats could see *Dekabrist* was still afloat. Her mast could be seen poking out of the sea. But not for long. During the morning an aircraft appeared and sank the vessel with another bomb.

Those in the lifeboats bowed their heads sadly as the ship sank beneath the waves, Natalich reported, since the sinking of the ship represented the loss of what they feared might be their last link with what they regarded as home soil. What followed, at least for those accompanying Natalich, was another of those gruelling journeys in a lifeboat, similar to what had already been experienced by those seamen whose ships were sunk during PQ13 and PQ17. After a storm split up the four lifeboats, while they were heading on the captain's orders towards Murmansk, those in her boat never saw two of the other boats again, and they only met up with the occupants in the other boat once, near Hope Island, where both boats had ended up, before it too disappeared in a second storm. The men in these 'lost' boats never made it back to the Soviet Union; it is likely most of their occupants were either drowned or died of thirst or hunger.

Natalich recalled afterwards that sometimes falling snow helped to assuage the thirst of those in her boat, which came as a huge relief after their daily water ration fell from 100 grams to 50 grams and finally to a teaspoon. However, the relief was only transitory. Dehydration became so acute after being adrift for around 10 days, the Captain suggested they should cut open her cat. He seemed to be proposing they might drink its blood. Natalich in her account recalled how she retorted in substance: 'You will only do that over my dead body; while I'm alive I will not give up my cat.' Instead she came up with what was literally a more acceptable solution: 'I remembered I had heard somewhere that thirst could be quenched with urine,' she wrote. 'I told everyone about it. The Captain suggested I try it first to see if it worked. Then the others followed suit. It was very unpleasant, but it may have saved our lives.' She added: 'Some might think such details should not be revealed. But I think it's right that I don't hold anything back.'

She certainly kept to her word about that. Her accounts leave little to the imagination. Their suffering had continued for 14 days before the sight of a snow-covered mountain told them they were approaching what turned out to be Hope Island. Their boat was eventually washed up onto one of the beaches on Hope Island's east coast. First impressions were unfavourable. 'The Island . . . appeared harsh and gloomy,' Natalich wrote. 'There was not a tree or bush to be seen; all that could be seen was a land-scape covered with stones.' However, they were so feeble by this stage that any dry land was more than welcome. It was a huge relief to be able to scoop up handfuls of snow to quench their thirst.

Enough provisions were taken from the boat to satisfy their immediate needs. But although they lit a fire using the available driftwood, and fashioned a tent out of the boat's sail and oars, in the hope that the most disabled of them could be protected while some of the men went off in search of better shelter, those in the improvised campsite were buried alive by the first blizzard that engulfed the island after their arrival.

'I could feel I was being covered by snow,' Natalich wrote afterwards, 'but I was too weak to get up. I would have been suffocated by the snow, if it hadn't been for my cat, which kept pushing away the snow with its paws to make an air hole. But I only discovered this later. At the time I didn't see or hear anything. I was in a deep sleep . . . [When] the other men . . . returned, the place where the canvas had been located had been transformed into a mound of snow. Those underneath it had severe frost-bite and some had died. I was dug up by the sailor (Vasilli) Boradin. He had been calling out my name, but I hadn't heard him, and in the end it was the cat who attracted his attention.'

Long-term survival was another matter. Those gathered at the campsite near where they landed – which also included a ditch covered with wood where the more athletic sailors could squat – only realized it was feasible when the group of men who had been sent to look for shelter to the north returned with the news that on the island's east coast they had come across a wooden hut that had previously been occupied by animal trappers. However, reaching it involved walking over a mountain pass in deep snow; that explains why those who were unable to walk over such terrain because of their frozen feet, had to be left behind. The plan was to escort to the hut all those who were mobile, and then come back for the others the next day.

The journey to the hut was a struggle. 'I could barely stand up,' Natalich wrote. 'I had frostbite in my hands and feet. The sailors had to bind them up with cloths.' Nevertheless by walking very slowly, and after multiple stops for rests on the way, they somehow reached their destination. When they arrived, Natalich did not think it looked very promising. 'It was just a little old shed,' she recalled. 'The walls were dilapidated, and here and there we could put our hands through the holes. Inside there was a cast iron stove without a [working] chimney, and bunk beds. The floor was covered in ice.'

However, it was to be a life saver. Shortly after they – and a second group including the captain – arrived, a gale blew up. 'The shed shook and almost collapsed,' Belyaev noted in his diary. 'It was freezing cold. And when we closed the door, we almost suffocated from the smoke [coming out of the lit stove]. We lay on the floor, breathing through cloths.'

But when the wind died down, all the occupants were still in one piece and the hut was still standing. That was more than could be said for the even more rudimentary covers shielding the three men, including the radio operator Sherbakov, who had remained behind through not being able to walk, and the stoker who had volunteered to look after them. When those who could still walk had dug their way out of the snow that had settled on top of the wooden hut, permitting them to set out on their rescue mission, there was deep concern for those in the campsite.

Natalich, who had stayed in the hut, has described the scene when the would-be rescuers returned: 'They were exhausted. Their clothes were covered in ice. They silently dropped from their shoulders the bags of food that had . . . come from the lifeboat. Then I asked: "Where are the others?" The Captain answered: "They've been frozen to death." Only the stoker . . . was alive when they reached them . . . He himself died in the arms of his comrades.'

Captain Belyaev, Natalich and the remaining Russian survivors eventually had to come to terms with the realization that they would probably not be able to escape from the island under their own steam until the summer came. It was a bleak prospect. In such an environment, all advantages that scientific discoveries had given humanity were stripped away. They were reduced to eking out an existence that was little different to that experienced by the group of Dutch sailors, including the navigator Willem Barentsz, when they were marooned on Novaya Zemlya for a comparable amount of time in similar conditions some three and a half centuries earlier. After Barentsz's ship became trapped in the ice near the north of Novaya Zemlya in August 1596, the Dutchmen were forced to live for more than 10 months in the wooden hut they constructed – subsequently referred to as Het Behouden Huys ('free' translation: House of the Saved, but see Note 36) – until the improved summer weather in 1597 permitted those who survived to escape in small boats (see 1 in Map 22 for location).[36]

During that time these sixteenth-century explorers had to combat the same terrors, which are part and parcel of any Arctic winter in such a desolate spot, that the Soviet castaways encountered so many years later. A diary written by one of Barentsz's men described how in order to survive, they had to make do in spite of freezing blizzards that effectively transformed their abode into a kind of igloo. That meant enduring the deadly fumes of the fires they made inside in an attempt to keep warm, and repeated attacks by the circling polar bears as well as the ravages of scurvy, which may well have been what ultimately killed Barentsz himself at the beginning of their journey home.

Natalich's chronicles describe how even the shelter provided by the hut where they ended up could not save all the *Dekabrist* 'survivors' from the effects of the elements. One man died of pneumonia. Frostbite accounted for another. Two more men died of unexplained causes.

Co-existing with the polar bears represented another challenge. In one passage in her chronicles, Natalich wrote: 'When members of our crew died, we took off their clothes and wore them ourselves to keep warm. Then we took the corpses out into the snow. But that left them at the mercy of the bears.' She later recalled that when two of the four remaining survivors became incapacitated by scurvy, Borodin, one of those afflicted, urged her: 'Go and dig a grave for the two of us so that the bears do not take us like the others.'

In one of her accounts she describes how during her stay on the island, which was to carry on for 11 months: 'Bears . . . often came looking for us. The hut [during the winter months] was completely covered with snow so we could only get out through a hole which was excavated. The bears would climb onto the roof . . . We had a rifle . . . in the hut . . . The Captain made a hole in the door with a knife and killed a bear that had come too close for its own good with one shot. That gave us some meat to eat, and we were able to use the fat in our fire. We wrapped the fur round us to keep us warm. The carcass served as bait to catch Arctic foxes. We killed one of them and ate it . . . Then the Captain used the fur to make himself some socks using a needle fashioned out of wood.'

The killing of the bear did not represent the four survivors' only good fortune. For most of the time they were trapped on the island, there were only four mouths to feed because all the others had died. As a result the supplies designed to provide sustenance for all the men in a lifeboat went a long way, all the more so because the amount consumed each day was rationed. Having said that, the supplies they had brought with them would not have been sufficient had the survivors not also had access to a substantial amount of tinned food, bags of flour, rice and peas, barrels of salt, and petrol most of which they found either washed up near the beach where they had landed, or in a second hut which was on the island's east coast to the south of the landing site. They had also found a smaller amount of flour in the hut to the north of the landing site which was their original haven.

But the following extracts from Natalich's accounts, which appear to refer to the period before the remaining survivors were cut down to four, demonstrate that psychological wellbeing is as important for a long-term castaway as physical strength. 'While those that could went out on expeditions, I stayed in the hut and kept the fire going in the stove,' she wrote. 'I melted snow on the stove so I could feed the warm water to my patients. At the same time I wept because I could do so little to help those who were ill. What could I do when I had no medicine or nourishing food for them? And when I myself was feeling almost as bad as my patients because of my frostbitten hands and feet . . .

'I remember [on one occasion] sitting in the little hut with my patients and listening . . . to the sounds all around me. They included the sound of the ice cracking . . . And I thought I heard a woman screaming and a baby crying. It was a dark polar night. From time to time there were columns in the sky with many coloured strips – the northern lights – and I heard the roars of polar bears. I feared what would happen if my comrades who had left [on an expedition] were all killed.'

According to Natalich, such anxiety metamorphosed into fully fledged paranoia after the four remaining survivors had been on the island for many months. She disclosed it reached its most extreme form when Belyaev insisted on going a few miles to the south to see whether he could repair an old boat that had been discovered near the southern hut: 'I even started to be suspicious about what the Captain was doing. I suspected he had fixed the boat, and was going to sail off on his own and was going to leave us all to die where we were.'

These ruminations persisted even though it is unlikely that such an idea had ever entered Belyaev's head. Setting off alone in a small boat would have been foolish except as a last resort.

'Later [after being rescued] I was embarrassed that I had entertained such thoughts,' Natalich admitted. But at the time it was only natural, having seen so many dying around her, that even an educated professional such as Dr Natalich should lose hope, and come to believe she must sooner rather than later face up to her own mortality.

31

Rescued

Main Action: 5 November 1942–2 January 1943
The independent ships part 2, the Chulmleigh shipwreck

(See Map 1)

The second group of seamen who had to endure unspeakable hardship as a result of what had happened to their ship during Operation FB belonged to the team of gunners and crew of the British merchant ship SS *Chulmleigh*.

Like the master of the American ship *Hugh Williamson* (mentioned in the previous chapter), *Chulmleigh*'s 35-year-old master Daniel Williams, whose vessel had set out from Hvalfjord on 31 October 1942 with 58 men on board, had been instructed by the Admiralty to sail well to the north, when west of Spitzbergen, so that he could pass its South Cape in the dark.

However, on account of a navigational error, and the reduced visibility because of what Williams described as the 'heavy snowstorm raging', the attempt to comply failed. This was to spell disaster. While still to the west of Spitzbergen, *Chulmleigh* appears to have gone further north than Williams realized, so that when he doubled back with a view to passing south of South Cape during the night of 5–6 November, rather than proceeding well clear of it, the ship ended up going eastward following a route that was not sufficiently to the south of South Cape's southern tip.[1]

A window into the traumatic repercussions of this miscalculation has been made available not only thanks to the official report by Williams and David Clark, his 22-year-old 3rd Mate, but also through the account written by Richard Peyer, who at the time of the operation was a 23-year-old Lance Sergeant, one of nine DEMS gunners seconded to *Chulmleigh* from the Maritime Royal Artillery.[2]

As it turned out, Peyer was not on watch when shortly before midnight the disastrous events of the night of 5–6 November started to unfold. He would afterwards write:

'I went to bed at 7 pm, as I was to go on watch . . . [that night]. The next . . . I knew I was on the cabin deck, and the alarm bells were ringing . . . I had been flung out of my bunk by a sudden . . . [jolt]. I immediately seized my life jacket and rushed to my life-boat station. On arriving there, I . . . [was told] that we had struck a submerged rock . . .

'I returned to the cabin, and put on my sea boot stockings and a further pullover. While I was doing this, there was another lurch . . . I at once rushed to the life-boat in time to hear the ship's carpenter (Solomon Owens) shouting there was eighteen feet of water in No. 1 hold and that No.2 (hold) was . . . also leaking.'[3]

Daniel Williams later confirmed that the ship had not just struck a hard object, but she was 'firmly stuck amidships on . . . a . . . reef with the stern almost out of the water and the bow well down, the fore deck being almost awash . . . Owing to the swell, I was afraid she would break her back.'

A distress message was sent out, but when 90 minutes passed with no sign that anyone was coming to their aid, Williams gave the order to launch the lifeboats. His report confirms that the first he heard about the abortive launch and swamping of what he referred to as the 'No. 1 port lifeboat' was when: 'I heard a cry for help from the port side . . . I ran down the deck with my torch and saw two men in the water. I called to the crew in 'No. 2 port lifeboat' to pick them up, but the men appeared [too] dazed and took no notice.

'[This No. 2 port] . . . boat was still alongside [the ship], so I went down into it and managed to get hold of [one . . . of the men in the sea] with the assistance of the bo'sun and one of the apprentices. We had a terrible job getting this man into the boat as the others would not help us. But eventually we succeeded, and after having a drink of brandy, he was all right.

'I then tried to pick up the second man, a Royal Marine gunner, but when we reached him, he was floating with his head fallen forward into the water and appeared lifeless . . . I felt the man's pulse [while he was still in the water], but could feel nothing. Presumably he was dead [on account of] the water . . . [being] very cold. Eventually we had to give up the attempt and let him go.'

They also had to give up their hopes of rescuing the ship. After one more failed attempt to refloat *Chulmleigh* by restarting her engines, Williams eventually decided the ship would have to be abandoned. Then when the murky light which passed for daybreak at this time of year finally enabled them to see where they were going, the three remaining lifeboats containing the 57 survivors were rowed out of the semi-enclosed horseshoe-shaped lagoon they were in whose perimeter was divided from the open sea by sections of the reef.

Their departure at first sight appeared to be timely. As they rowed, a small group of German aircraft appeared, and at least two of the bombs they dropped hit the ship, causing a column of black smoke to rise up into the air.[4]

However, although this could only be established subsequently with the benefit of hindsight, leaving the area where the ship lay was a mistake. If Williams had insisted that the boats waited near the *Chulmleigh* wreck for a few more hours, they would surely have been spotted by the crew of the British submarine *Tuna*, and what followed could have been avoided. After receiving the SOS sent out by *Chulmleigh*'s Radio Officer, *Tuna*'s commander had rushed the submarine to the scene, arriving during the morning of 6 November. She only departed in her turn after her crew had seen there were no boats in the immediate vicinity. *Tuna*'s commander Lieutenant Raikes evidently did not think much of the *Chulmleigh* crew's chances. The comment he wrote in his war diary reads: 'It is possible survivors may have landed at South Cape. But the cold was intense, and I think they cannot have survived long.'[5]

After the German aircraft disappeared, Williams eventually had the men in the smaller of the three lifeboats transferred into the two larger boats so that there were 28 including Peyer in his boat, and 29 in the 1ˢᵗ Mate's boat. Williams told the men in both boats they should make for Barentsburg (around 150 miles away if they travelled northward up

Spitzbergen's west coast, and then sailed up a fjord to the east), which had been occupied by a small Allied force, and resupplied with provisions during PQ18.

After some ups and downs during the following days because of bad weather, it was agreed on 9 November that the lifeboat commanded by Williams, which had a motor, should go on ahead for the remaining 80 miles, and try to summon help for those in the other boat.

Writing later in his report about those left behind, Williams comforted himself by reporting: 'They all seemed quite fit and well, and very cheerful at that time.'[6] Little did he know as they separated that neither he or anyone else would ever see the men in the second boat again.

Shortly after the two boats split up, the weather changed, and it all of a sudden became much colder and much windier. For a time they found themselves having to do their best to keep their boat afloat in a gale. These conditions were too much for the vulnerable to bear. The 30-year-old Chief Steward was the first to lose control of himself. He 'became delirious', Williams reported.[7] Peyer's verdict was more judgemental. Describing this man's actions in his account, he wrote: 'The Chief Steward went mad and attempted to kill us!'[8] While that may literally have been true, the characterization of his behaviour by 3rd Mate David Clark was possibly more accurate. He said the men who were a problem 'refused to eat or drink, and were irritable and nasty-tempered if interfered with'.[9] Whatever the loss of control amounted to, Williams evidently did not hold it against the steward, reporting: 'We wrapped him in a spare coat and an extra blanket, but he died during the night.'[10] He was 'buried' at sea.[11]

Two days later the boat was within sight of Isfjord (Isfjorden), the waterway jutting into Spitzbergen's western coast and running eastward from the Denmark Sea to Barentsburg. But before they reached the fjord, there was a second casualty. As Peyer put it, 'The (34-year-old) Donkeyman (John Suttie) walked over the side of the boat, and had to be fished out of the water.'[12] Such behaviour was one of the first signs that delirium was setting in, a state from which some men never recovered.[13] Before they had travelled much further, Suttie had also passed away.[14]

Even more significantly, Williams had himself become delirious on 10 November, leaving David Clark, the 22-year-old 3rd Mate in charge. That was not very popular, especially when he insisted they must ration the drinking water.[15] In the end the extremely weak occupants of the boat were saved by the tide and waves which on 11 November swept them to the shore, a short distance north-east of Kapp Linné, which constituted Isfjord's entrance's southern lip (see Note 16 for location).[16]

Led by their revived captain, they then staggered over the snow to a group of three wooden huts they spied, inside which they were able to take shelter from the biting wind.[17]

After a long sleep, most of the men assembled in the largest of the huts. It 'was roughly ten feet wide by fifteen feet long,' wrote Peyer, 'and contained three bunks, a small table . . . [as well as a] stove.'

At first their prospects looked rosy, at least relative to what they had been before they landed. In one of the huts, they had found a small supply of coal which could be used when making a fire inside the stove. They also had access to matches to light the fire, two primus stoves with a small amount of oil that could be lit, and some food: tins of corned beef and biscuits.[18]

Unfortunately 'some of the men helped themselves to a large proportion of the rations we had discovered', wrote Peyer. 'These fellows were nearly all mentally unbalanced owing to the exposure and cold.'

They could perhaps be forgiven for at this stage believing that now they had landed, they could eat whatever they wanted because they were home as well as dry. It was only the day after Peyer and the 3rd Mate (Clark) had walked two miles to the west to a nearby lighthouse, only to find it deserted, that everyone understood the danger they were still in.

'The following day the Chief Engineer (Richard Colvin, aged 47) died,' Peyer reported later, 'and on taking a "census", we discovered that only the following were fit for . . . work: Gunners (Reginald) Whiteside, (James) Burnett, Swainston and myself.'

By the time they had been in the hut for two more days, making their stay there going on a week, there was also the sobering realization that now they had eaten up much of what they had found in the huts, and were having to rely on what they had brought with them, the clock regulating how long they could survive without starving if they were not rescued had started ticking (see Note 19 for analysis of dates specified).[19]

Nevertheless, there were still survivors who wanted more than the rationing permitted, and some of the provisions were stolen the first night they were retrieved from the lifeboat.

'I was able to stop this happening again by sleeping on top of the food supplies,' Peyer would write later. His action highlighted a change that had come into force without anyone expressly authorizing it. In an existential crisis such as that prevailing in the huts, the young gunners' fitness and vigour put them into pole position, enabling them to lord it over the others who, as Peyer confirmed, 'had become incapable of movement . . . It was necessary to feed and look after them in every way.' The main problem, according to Williams, were the older men's 'swollen feet and hands' from frostbite.[20]

The young turks now in charge believed the circumstances justified some extraordinary measures. None was more radical than the punishment meted out to those who threatened the group's common welfare. 'We were forced to remove (the 44-year-old Greaser Alfred) R[ei]d . . . to the other hut owing to his developing homicidal tendencies,' Peyer admitted, explaining action taken just over a week into their stay in the huts.[21]

This might not sound like a very severe sanction, until it is remembered that the other huts appear to have been colder inside than the main hut, if not completely unheated, and it is likely that coercion would have been required to ensure that Reid did not try to return from the icy cold 'prison' to which he had been banished. It is no surprise to read a confirmation in a subsequent entry in Peyer's account that Reid died a few days later. He had it seems been the victim of what amounted to a summary execution.

His death as well as the passing away of others before and after him also required some thinking outside the box. According to Robert Paterson, the 25-year-old Scottish Radio Officer: 'We buried each of our companions as they died. The only burial place we could get for them were clefts in the rocks. We laid their bodies in these clefts, and covered them with snow. The Captain conducted the burial services.'[22]

It seems likely that the predicament concerning what do about Reid served as a catalyst. Shortly after Reid's removal from the main hut, Peyer and Clark made a second attempt to seek help, this time aiming to reach the settlement at Barentsburg. But this attempt, around ten days after their landing in Spitzbergen (the attempt was made ca. 21 November) was no more successful than the first: 'We came across a huge ravine with its sides coated with ice, making descent impossible,' Peyer reported. 'On the way back we sat down to eat some food and have a drink of coffee which we had in a bottle, and we very nearly fell asleep, which is the great danger in these extremely cold climates. We returned to the hut roughly four hours . . . [after setting out] to find the ship's cook had died.'

Their disappointment at not being able to obtain assistance must have been tempered by the following event also recorded in Peyer's account: 'The next day (ca. 22 November) Reginald Whiteside discovered some flour in a hut about a mile away. It was a complete sack and was an invaluable discovery. Those of us who were fit enough set out to bring back as much as possible to our own hut.'

However, the discovery was counterbalanced by yet another fatality. Peyer's diary reported: 'One of the apprentices died during this day.'

The discovery of the flour was also followed by another ominous development. 'The following day (ca. 23 November) . . . Whiteside and I were the only two fit enough to carry on,' wrote Peyer. Peyer's account reveals however that even he was really walking wounded: 'I was unable to walk around [a lot] because of frostbite in my knee which made it extremely painful,' he reported. His write-up of the next day shows that, to add to his woes, he was suffering from what he described as 'severe pains in the stomach caused probably by the lack of food'.

But it was the rapid lowering of the air temperature which seems to have transformed the onset of disability into a fully-fledged cull. At one stage there was another person succumbing to the cold every other day. On what appears to have been 26 November, it was the mess boy. Two days later 'we met with [another] tragedy,' wrote Peyer. 'The Third Engineer (34-year-old James Wood) kicked our dinner all over the floor. The poor chap had lost his senses, and we were compelled to move him to the other hut' – which, as already explained, was tantamount to giving him a death sentence.

Equally upsetting was the fate of William Pounder, who at 16 years old was one of the two youngest sailors in *Chulmleigh*'s crew. Like his fellow apprentice, who had died a few days earlier, Pounder had never recovered from the strain the extreme cold imposed on his immature frame while in the lifeboat, and he passed away that same day.

At the time, there were so many men dying that William Pounder's death barely took up half a line in Peyer's account. Doubtless he was buried out in the snow along with all the other luckless seamen who could not last the course. However, perhaps because he was one of the youngest, the gravestone which would eventually be erected in his honour in a Tromso cemetery after his corpse was moved there subsequently, had the following touching tribute engraved on it:

'The only life he saw was school

One trip and just sixteen

The rest must be in heaven.'[23]

Pounder's passing was followed by such cold weather, that the next morning, as Peyer noted, 'We awoke to find the fjord entirely frozen over. It was so cold we had very great difficulty in lighting the fire and keeping ourselves warm during the day.'

The plummeting temperature may explain why two more men died before the next day dawned. 'We were now reduced to only twelve men and our food was getting very short,' Peyer wrote in his chronicle. The twelve survivors were swiftly reduced to eleven when that same evening, the 3rd Engineer James Wood, still shut away in the nearby unheated hut, succumbed to the cold.

The great freeze certainly was a killer. But it might have been slightly more palatable had it been accompanied by blue skies and sunshine, however watery. Sadly for those in the huts, even the daily Arctic twilight shortened as each day passed, until it finally petered out. The survivors' only respite then was the glow from the stove, while there was still wood to burn, and from the home-made lamps they made by punching a hole in the lids of flattish tins which they had filled with oil so that a protruding wick made of cloth could be slowly burned.[24]

The survivors' restricted access to any kind of light explains why when a natural phenomenon unexpectedly cut through the gloom, towards the end of the month, Peyer gave it the following rave review:

'After an extremely cold night with a very strong wind and snow falling, we awoke to find a glorious "morning" (ca. 30 November). The moon was shining brightly, and in the south, the sky was a little red. We had no daylight, but just a reddening in the south about midday. [However] the moon was nearly as good as sunlight on the snow and ice around us . . .'

The extra light, and the slightly warmer weather, albeit only for a day or two, appears to have inspired a reckoning. Peyer's account continues:

'We [now] had roughly enough [food] for fourteen days on our ration which was: . . . 1 tin [of] pemmican, 4 pieces [of] chocolate, 2 biscuits, and one packet [of] Horlicks tablets per man per day . . .

'Our main subject of discussion was food, our thoughts were about food all day, and during the "night", our dreams were likewise on the subject of food. Many a time one of us would wake up just at the critical moment when the food was being put into his mouth to find it was only a dream.'

In view of this, one can well understand why Peyer referred to the discovery of more food in yet another hut about a mile away during an attempt by the three other gunners to walk to Barentsburg as 'a wonderful find'. This led to one day (ca. 5 December) of 'fine meals' wrote Peyer. Afterwards he would recall with relish what was served up: 'Bacon and beans for breakfast, pemmican, biscuits and marmalade for lunch, corn beef and potatoes for tea, pemmican and biscuits for supper', although as he pointed out, 'the quantity of each of these was very small'.

But this was to be their last bonanza. They entered a kind of downward spiral as the middle of the month of December approached, from which it seemed almost inevitable the remaining ten men would be unable to escape (one more had died shortly beforehand). First 'we finished the last of the pemmican,' wrote Peyer, which he hailed as 'the most nourishing of all the foods we had had'. Then his account marked the day 'our tobacco supply was finished', a psychological blow since 'it provided something for us to do, and had taken our minds off the situation'.

Even more serious were the obstacles to their gathering sufficient wood to keep the fire in the stove burning. Their ability to collect enough wood from the ground around the hut had ended at the end of November as the supply of driftwood dwindled to zero. This had meant their only reliable means of finding wood was to extract it from the walls of one of the nearby huts, and then to cut it up.

Referring to another downturn in their situation during the lead up to Christmas, Peyer's account records how 'conditions became very much worse, and a gale started blowing with the snow drifting fairly thick. It began to pile up outside our hut, and we were afraid we would be unable to go out because of the drifts . . . The snow drifted to a depth of between two and three feet.'

Fortunately, the next day 'conditions were perfect', Peyer stated. 'The sky was clear, and the snow was frozen hard [so] . . . we were able to walk on it. We collected a large store of wood as we were afraid that we might get snowed up.' One suspects they were all the more relieved to be able to go outside of the hut during the following days because, as Peyer recalled, one of the firemen, 'who had been ill for a long time, had become much worse and was raving all the time'. The fireman's death shortly before Christmas meant there were now only nine *Chulmleigh* men who were still alive.

Striving to understand why these men had lasted so long might make for an interesting case study. However, as so often in such matters, one reason for their longevity was luck. In such frigid conditions, it was all the more ironic that if one ignores the ever-present risk of their perishing because of the cold and starvation, the nearest the survivors in the hut had come to extinction was when one man knocked over a petrol tank taken from the boat, and the petrol that ran out immediately caught fire. 'The whole hut was a mass of flames, and all thought it would be burned down,' Peyer reported. Only a panic-stricken stamping out of the flames saved the day and the fire was quickly extinguished. 'Fortunately the tank itself did not catch fire, or we should all have been blown up,' Peyer observed later.

But after the fire, they all had to face up to a slower, more insidious threat to life. As Christmas approached, in another reversal of the norm, at a time when there is usually food and good cheer a-plenty, their rations were remorselessly reduced. The edible provisions would have run out had it not been for the contribution made by *Chulmleigh's* 27-year-old able seaman Andrew Hardy. During the first half of the month he had recommended that they should use the flour found by Whiteside to cook what his mother, like him a Shetland Islander, referred to as 'floorie bannocks', a kind of pancake, made out of flour and water. 'Fortunately I was able to make the bannocks without moving,' Peyer noted, presumably recalling how he had endured the pain in his knee through gritted teeth.

These pancakes were very welcome but they did not provide much sustenance for a grown man. They 'were roughly the size of a digestive biscuit', Peyer recalled.

'Towards the end of December, the situation was becoming desperate,'

32. Above: *Edinburgh*'s Captain Hugh Faulkner (*left*) with Rear Admiral Stuart Bonham Carter (*right*) probably on board the cruiser. *Edinburgh* was torpedoed on 30 April 1942 while they were in charge (see Chapter 10). Kapitänleutnant Max-Martin Teichert (*33. above right*) was the commander of *U-456*, the U-boat whose crew fired the torpedoes. Teichert's initial reaction to seeing the cruiser in his sights was to write one word in his war diary: 'Wunderbar (Marvellous)!'

34. Right: *Edinburgh* after being torpedoed. One of the destroyer commanders remarked that her peeled-up quarter deck made her look as if she was a scorpion about to attack.

35. Below right: After learning what had happened to *Edinburgh*, Admiral Hubert Schmundt, Admiral Nordmeer, (pictured *on the left* with his assistant and Reinhart Reche, one of his most productive U-boat commanders *on the right*) found it hard to decide whether the three destroyers under his command should first attack the damaged cruiser, or whether they should initially head towards QP11, the convoy he was also targeting.

36. *Above*: Thanks to this photograph taken from the German destroyer *Z 24*, we can observe how *Z 25*'s making smoke in the distance concealed the crippled German destroyer *Hermann Schoemann* (in the middle ground) after she had been hit by a British shell during the 2 May 1942 battle between the rival surface forces.

37. *Below*: *Hermann Schoemann*'s men gather on deck after the battle referred to above as *Z 24* advances with a view to rescuing them. The rescue went well. Only eight of *Hermann Schoemann*'s crew lost their lives.

38. *Left*: This photo records the final stages of the minesweeper *Harrier*'s successful attempt to rescue the men still on board *Edinburgh* after the cruiser during the 2 May 1942 battle was hit by a third torpedo.

39. Left: In the Kola Inlet: members of *Trinidad's* crew can be seen on the cruiser's deck after the damage caused by the self-torpedoing had been repaired, while awaiting the order to depart.

40. Right: *Trinidad* is pictured here listing and smoking after being damaged for a second time. On this occasion she has been hit by bombs dropped from German planes in the course of their attack during the evening of 14 May 1942.

41. Above: A line up of the midshipmen learning the ropes on *Trinidad*. They include the 17-year-old Tom Baird (*on the right*), whose memories of the bombing which led to the sinking of the cruiser, are quoted in Chapter 13.

42. Right: *Trinidad's* Captain Leslie Saunders with his wife and oldest son standing in front of the gates at London's Buckingham Palace, where he had gone to be invested with a DSO, a just reward for his and his ship's crew's bravery during their encounters with the enemy.

43. *Above*: Gathering of the merchant ships in Iceland's Hvalfjord prior to the departure of PQ16 on 20 May 1942. They included the CAM ship *Empire Lawrence*, 44. pictured *right* at an earlier date.

45. *Below*: The British submarine *Trident* stands guard beside one of the PQ16 merchant ships as the convoy steams eastward.

46. Above: The PQ16 merchant ships steam past an iceberg, one of the occupational hazards that had to be taken in their crews' stride when their route took them near the ice edge.

47. Above: A Focke-Wulf 20 Condor reconnaissance aircraft. A German crew flying one of these machines caught up with PQ16 on 25 May 1942, prompting the commander of one of the armed trawlers with the convoy to describe it as a sinister bat which would deliver them into the hands of the 'butcher' who was searching for them.

48. Right: Bohdan Pawłowicz (*2nd from left*), the embedded Polish journalist aboard the Polish destroyer *Garland* during PQ16, who would later write an account of some of the traumatic events he witnessed.

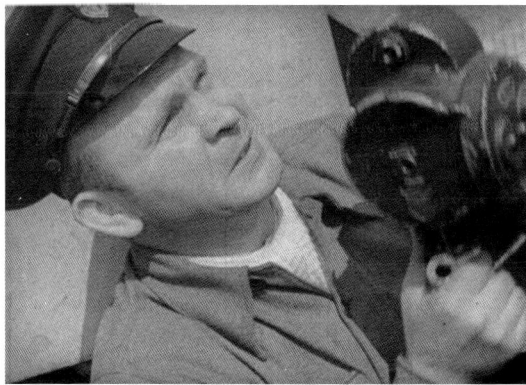

49. Left: Pawłowicz's cameraman Pawel Płonka aiming his camera in the general direction of the German aircraft, which during the 27 May 1942 air raids were whizzing overhead. He was later wounded following a near miss (see Chapter 15).

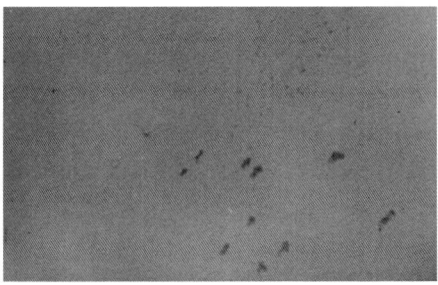

50. Left: In this blurred still, lifted from a Polish film featuring shots taken from *Garland*'s decks during PQ16, German aircraft are to be seen streaking over the convoy.

51. Below: This photograph taken from the corvette HMS *Honeysuckle* shows a stick of bombs dropped by a German aircraft falling uncomfortably close to one of the British submarines escorting the convoy, and to some of the nearby merchant ships. The submarine in question may well have been *Trident* whose commander courageously insisted he would take his chances along with the other surface escorts rather than diving each time enemy aircraft appeared.

52. Below: Another still from the film shot from *Garland* shows a merchant ship being targeted by the Luftwaffe during PQ16, probably in the course of one of the series of raids by aircraft on 27 May 1942.

54. Right: *Garland*'s starboard Oerlikon points skyward, but remains silent and unattended, beside the covered up corpses of its gunners. This photo is displayed in the book written by Pawłowicz where he describes seeing the gunners' charred corpses lying among the smoking embers of the splinters which had killed them during one of the 27 May 1942 air raids. Near misses during these raids ravaged *Garland* and her crew. The bodies of the gunners were eventually covered up, Pawłowicz reported, sparing the feelings of those readers who were afterwards shown a photo of the scene.

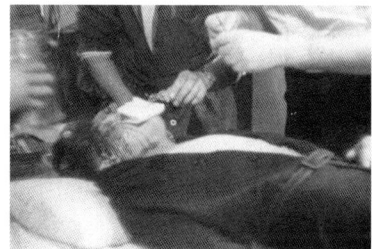

53. Above left: Another still taken from the *Garland* film. It shows one of the destroyer's crew, who was injured during one of the 27 May 1942 air raids, being operated on by the ship's surgeon. The film's commentary reveals that unfortunately this man was one of many who did not make it.

55. Below: A photograph of PQ16's SS *Empire Purcell* burning after she had been hit during one of the last air raids during 27 May 1942. The ship is seen behind the head of *Honeysuckle*'s gunner whose head and shoulders and the eyepiece he is looking through form the jagged silhouette in the foreground.

56. *Left:* Icy conditions encountered on board *Garland* while anchored off North Russia.

58. *Below*: The commanders of the Polish destroyer *Garland* (Lieutenant Commander Henryk Eibel – *left*) and the Polish submarine *Jastrząb* (Lieutenant Bolesław Romanowski – *centre*) seen here on one of *Garland*'s decks on the way back from Russia. The third man is *Jastrząb*'s Andrzej Guzowski.

57. *Above*: Sailors bury at sea one of the *Garland* seamen who was killed during the 27 May 1942 battle that claimed so many Polish lives.

59. *Above*: Destroyer A*shanti*'s Commander Richard Onslow seen here being rewarded for his action during PQ16: with his son Richard junior and wife Kathleen standing outside Buckingham Palace on the day he was invested with the bars to his DSO.

60. *Above*: Trawler *Lady Madeleine*'s Graeme Ogden with first wife Sheila and daughter Julia at the investiture at the Palace concerning his DSO in relation to his courageous action during Arctic convoys including PQ16.

Williams would later acknowledge in his report. 'Mr Clark (3rd Mate) and Able Seaman Hardy were both in a very bad condition; they were suffering from gangrene, as were several of the others, their feet and hands were discharging, and the smell was awful.'

Notwithstanding the bannocks, the food situation was also dire; each man was by this time only being given four bannocks per day, half the initial ration. 'I therefore decided to make a final attempt to get help, or die in the effort,' Williams wrote.

'The following morning the Captain, Whiteside and myself set out in the direction we had seen [some] lights from the lifeboat in our last attempt to obtain rescue,' Peyer recalled later. But it was too much for them in their weakened state.

'We covered about half the distance,' Williams reported 'when Whiteside for the first time broke down, and refused to go any further. Peyer was not very keen either, so I turned back with them, and it was as much as we could do to reach the hut. We collapsed on arrival.'

No-one could blame them. 'During the whole day we only had two bannocks each,' Peyer recalled.

When there was no more flour, 'we raked about to find something [else] to eat,' Radio Officer Robert Paterson remembered later. 'In a tin about the size of a biscuit tin, from which we had taken oil, there was a putrid piece of meat we believed was seal meat (blubber). It smelled vile.

'We cut it up into hunks, and hung these up outside the hut where they froze hard. This kept the meat from getting any worse. Once a day we had a cube of this stuff. It tasted wicked, but we had to eat it because it was the only thing to save us from death.'[25]

Williams has described how on 2 January 1943, Whiteside as usual 'went out to collect [the] firewood, as he was still in a comparatively good condition. But [he] soon came rushing back into the hut.' He left the door open, and was evidently 'absolutely terrified'. 'I could get nothing out of him,' Williams reported. 'We thought we were about to be attacked by bears.'

Had they looked out of the door, they might well have seen evidence to back up this supposition. Two creatures covered in white were creeping towards them. But rather than finding themselves being hunted by ravenous carnivores which wanted to devour them, they would soon discover that they had been stalked by two Norwegian soldiers dressed in white camouflage suits who would end up rescuing them. They had walked and skied all the way from Barentsburg on a trapping expedition.

The Norwegian soldiers were at first as alarmed as Whiteside when they heard voices emanating from the hut they were approaching. One of the Norwegians crept forward to investigate, while the second man positioned himself on what he took to be a frozen sand dune to protect with his gun the man moving towards the hut, only to discover that the 'dune' was in fact a frozen corpse dressed in a British uniform partially concealed under some snow.[26]

He advanced so as to join his friend outside the hut. When they opened the door, they were overwhelmed by the terrible smell. Their next impression was stunned amazement, the result of coming across so many men in a hut which until minutes before they had believed was deserted. Some of the men inside the hut were staring at them, while others at first sight appeared to be dead. In fact they were informed that all nine inside the hut were alive, although it took a while for both rescuers and rescued to make known their respective nationalities, and how best to communicate. Only after that had been sorted out, could plans be formulated and appropriate measures taken.

The subsequent rescue was carried out in three stages. First the two Norwegians escorted Whiteside and Burnett, the two gunners who could still walk, the 12 miles back to Barentsburg, although Burnett ended up being carried part of the way. The next day a rescue party with two sledges reached the hut; they were used to carry off Clark and Hardy, the two men in the worst state. That was saying something. According to Williams: 'We were all in a pretty bad condition . . . Our clothes were soaked with pus from gangrenous limbs, which caused a horrible stench.' Finally a day later, a third rescue party with sledges appeared that could transport the remaining five castaways, including Williams and Peyer.[27]

'During the journey, the Norwegians stopped the sledges so that we might [once again] admire the beauty of the Northern Lights,' wrote Peyer, adding apparently with tongue at least partly in cheek, 'I must confess that in the condition we were in, we did not appreciate the sight to the full!'

After the rescue one suspects the nine survivors must have longed to go home. Not being able to travel back to England immediately must have been particularly hard for David Clark (the 3rd Mate), all of whose fingers were amputated to save him from the gangrene that had taken hold because of the time his severe frostbite had remained untreated. Andrew Hardy also had a readjustment to make after frostbite led to his losing one of his toes. However, their isolation from normal society only came to an end when two cruisers, which came to Isfjord to drop off stores, picked them all up on 10 June 1943, and they were back in Scotland five days later, more than seven months after *Chulmleigh* sailed for northern Russia.[28]

It is pleasing to note that Williams never tried to take the credit for the survival of the *Chulmleigh* nine. He put down their coming through alive to the efforts of the four young army gunners, with particularly lavish praise being pointed in the direction of Peyer and Reginald Whiteside. By common consent Whiteside was a human dynamo, or as Williams described him, 'a really tough guy, a Liverpool docker in peacetime, only 4' 11", [who] suffered no ill effects at all'.[29]

Williams' wife had good reason to be equally grateful. During December 1942, she had attended his memorial service in Llangrannog, near Wales' Cardigan Bay, after being told he must have died.[30] Yet now he had returned to her as if from the dead.

It is unlikely that all the *Chulmleigh* survivors were as positive about what they had experienced. However, it is a moot point whether their suffering was as keenly felt as that endured by the last of the *Dekabrist* crew. The woman and three men from *Dekabrist* remained trapped on Hope Island for many long months after *Chulmleigh*'s nine survivors were rescued. In fact, they were still there when *Chulmleigh*'s men made it back home to Britain some five and a half months later.

The first attempt to rescue the *Dekabrist* four only came about in July 1943 after a German aircraft crew by some lucky chance spotted them while flying over the island. Oberleutnant Joachim Brünner, the 23-year-old commander of *U-703*, was ordered to take his submarine to investigate, and on 25 July *U-703*'s gunners fired warning shots when the vessel was located around a mile off the island's south-east coast near the more southerly of the two huts visited by *Dekabrist*'s survivors where Captain Belyaev was by this time living on his own. This was followed up by Brünner sending four armed men in a motor boat to the island to find out who was the man they could see waving at them.[31]

U-703's Leutnant Heinz Schlott, who led the boat party, later described what he saw when after first reaching the island and then the hut, they opened the hut's door: 'A man was standing in the middle of the room, with his hands up, looking absolutely terrified. He was of medium height . . . and had a shaggy beard that almost totally covered his face. He was emaciated to such an extent that his bones protruded. What hair he had left was grey . . . His clothes were held together with patches, his leather boots were cracked . . . His bright blue eyes looked at us with such a lack of guile that they evoked our sympathy.

'He put his index finger to his head, and made a movement as if pulling an imaginary trigger . . . I shook my head, and held out 2 cigarettes for him, which he took . . .'[32]

But who was this Arctic version of Robinson Crusoe, Schlott wanted to know. After a few exchanges, Schlott finally understood. As he stated in his account: 'Here standing before us was Captain Belyaev from the freighter *Dekabrist,* which had set out for Murmansk in the Soviet Union from Iceland's Reykjavik nine months ago . . .!'

There were to be more surprises. Belyaev astounded his German interlocutors by what he told them next about the three other survivors who were living in another hut further to the north. According to Schlott, Belyaev 'held up two fingers and said "Man", then one finger and said "Woman". When he said this, I wondered whether I had misunderstood him, and asked him to repeat what he had said. He then confirmed to an accompaniment of explanatory gestures that one of the survivors was indeed a woman, a "Miss Doctor".'

Schlott's account went on to say that before they went to find the other three, Belyaev made some more meaningful gestures after noticing the Germans were looking closely at the gun, and the bones and fur that in addition to various provisions were scattered in and around his hut: 'He once again held up 7 or 8 fingers saying [something that sounded like] "blibli" but meaning: "Icebears". Perhaps he feared the bones might be misinterpreted, and he might be accused of having only survived by eating his compatriots' corpses.

If Schlott and his men had such thoughts, they kept them to

themselves. Without any further interrogation, they escorted Belyaev back to their U-boat. Afterwards, guided by the Russian captain, they motored around two miles to the north, where they spotted the third hut they had seen that day on the island (the first was near the south of the island). Then the Germans fired more shots, and when the threesome inside the hut appeared, Belyaev instructed them through the U-boat's megaphone to row out to *U-703* in their small boat.

When they reached the U-boat, as Schlott's account noted, three more Robinson Crusoe-ish figures were greeted, and brought on board: 'a man who was about 50 years old, who was very thin, and obviously ill and weak; a woman who was [apparently] around 40 years old with . . . straggly hair, a plump broad face and intelligent eyes; and a younger man with Asian features, who had dark hair and who was taller than the others. All of them wore fur hats and were swathed in tattered and torn clothes.'

Although Brünner had been instructed to collect everyone on the island, he did not fancy taking the ill man as well as the others.[33] Eventually it was decided that he could not leave the ill man on the island by himself. The three latest arrivals would all have to go back to the hut, and Brünner would for the moment only take the Captain.

So it was that the two men and the woman doctor, who had already survived one winter against all the odds, were sent back to the island in their boat after it was filled up with provisions including vitamin tablets, bandages, paraffin, matches, cigarettes, chocolate and rum. 'We told them that we hoped we'd be able to pick them up on our way back, even though we had no idea whether we'd ever be able to do what we were saying,' wrote Schlott.

Belyaev was to become very popular in the U-boat. His departure did not go down so well on Hope Island. Although he had been living away from the others, his presence nearby had evidently had a unifying effect. The absence of his steadying influence appears to have upset the relative harmony that had persisted while he was available to lead by example.

This was not revealed to 'outsiders' until 7 October 1943 when Brünner, in compliance with another order, returned to Hope Island in *U-703* to pick up those he had left behind the first time. Once again Schlott was placed in charge of the landing party. He and another young sailor rowed over to the southern of the two huts that had been occupied, where they had previously picked up the Captain. There they found 'the woman doctor' (Natalich) and Borodin, the middle-aged man. There was no sign of the younger man, but after the two Russians were interrogated using sign language, they finally disclosed that the third man was in the northern hut.

The reason for their reluctance to tell the Germans where the third man was living would subsequently become clear. Leaving that question hanging in the air, Natalich and Borodin had been taken to the U-boat so that *U-703* could be moved up the island's east coast until she was near the northern hut. Schlott and his subordinate had then gone ashore again. 'The hut was dark and damp inside,' Schlott recalled later. 'We only saw the Russian after our eyes became accustomed to the light. He was lying like a dead man under a pile of blankets and clothes. His pulse was very weak. We put wood in the oven and used paraffin to help light it . . . This warmed up the hut, and we put the man near the oven and propped him up with blankets. What that poor soul needed more than anything was a sip of rum, but there was none of that in sight. [He had to make do with] a lit cigarette I gave him. We warmed up some snow in a pot on the stove. and an hour later, after he swallowed some of the warm water, he appeared to come back to life.'

However, their attempt to take him back to the U-boat undid all their good work. Again and again the surf pushed their rubber boat back to the shore, and by the time it finally reached the U-boat during the late afternoon, the Russian invalid was soaked. When he was at last brought onto the U-boat, he was clearly at death's door.[34]

Schlott would later recall that a lot of dark looks were cast in the direction of Natalich and Borodin for having abandoned their 'comrade' when he was in such a weak state. He duly died that night and was buried at sea. However, the lack of a common language appears to have precluded the conducting of any kind of inquiry there and then. Perhaps the key to the mystery was the simple fact that Natalich and Borodin had become a couple by the time they were rescued.[35] That being the case, it does not take much imagination to wonder whether they might have ganged up against the younger man for some undisclosed reason, or selfishly left him to his fate, either before or after he became ill, so that they might enjoy the privacy to which a married couple might in a normal civilized environment feel entitled.

Whatever the rights and wrongs of what took place on the island, the U-boat with Natalich and Borodin on board safely reached Harstad, Norway on 9 October 1943, and they, like Belyaev, ended up in a prisoner of war camp. When they stepped off the U-boat on arriving at the Norwegian port, they could not have been more grateful to the Germans who had rescued them, even though it was the U-boat crew's compatriots who had put their lives in jeopardy in the first place. Schlott recalls how one man Natalich tried to embrace as she left the U-boat would for the rest of his short life have to bear being the butt of jokes made by his comrades over the way he had pleased the Russian woman.

Their arrival brought to an end a dark episode in the delivery of aid to the Soviet Union. It had highlighted the British and American leaders' mindset concerning the Allies' merchant navies, which was not very sympathetic. Merchant ships' crews had been regarded as being as expendable as the Soviet soldiers on the Eastern Front whom their ships' cargo was supposed to support. That is not to say there was no good reason for treating them in this way. However, while it is no exaggeration to say that in the course of Operation FB, the Allies' merchant seamen were sacrificed in a good cause, it is only fair to point out that its main accomplishment appears to have been that it kept Stalin onside rather than materially assisting the Red Army.

Last Stand

The situation which had prompted the jeopardizing of merchant seamen's lives in Operation FB – Britain's inability to commit warships to the Arctic convoys – would soon pass. On 8 November 1942, Anglo-American forces under the overall leadership of America's Lieutenant General Dwight Eisenhower pulled off a successful start to the long awaited Torch operation by landing their armies in Morocco and Algeria (French North Africa).

The boost to morale in the West that this provided was only matched by the thrill brought about after it was learned that Rommel's forces in Egypt had been routed at the Battle of El Alamein which had reached its climax by 4 November 1942.[1]

With the Torch landings accomplished, came the opportunity to assist the Soviet Union again: a sufficient number of escorts were available for Churchill to inform Stalin that convoying could restart, which he did on 24 November 1942.[2] However, before the next east-going convoys could set out, other challenges facing the British and American navies which in the meantime had come to a head, were being surmounted. By mid-November 1942, a stark choice for those controlling the merchant ships still in Archangel had to be made. Either submit to their being locked in by the ice, which was already well over four inches thick in places, as temperatures plummeted to 10 °F (-12 °C), or try to get them back to the West by sending them to sea as soon as possible even though that would require them and their crews to brave the deteriorating weather.[3] The latter was preferred, and the unfortunate seamen left to deal with the consequences.

The following extract from the account by V. Shackleton, at the time a young British signalman on the PQ17 veteran minesweeper HMS *Salamander*, represents his recollection of the terrifying force 7 to 9 gale on 20–21 November, and the huge waves that it stirred up, which threatened to swallow not only him and his ship, but the whole of convoy QP15.[4] This was the west-going convoy containing 28 merchant ships – the majority ex-PQ18 – and a rescue ship that set out from Archangel on 17 November 1942: 'QP15 taught me . . . how helpless . . . man is when natural forces are released against him. I found that even the atheists who shirked all church parades were calling on God to deliver us from the fury of the elements . . .

'We were facing monstrous waves, nearly mast high . . . coming at us with the speed of an express train . . . [These] massive waves . . . hung high over the bridge like apartment blocks before breaking in great avalanches over the bows . . . Add[ed] to this ferocious onslaught, [we faced] the howling [of the wind] in the rigging.

'Continual noise and movement stretched . . . frayed nerves to breaking point . . . [There was] no relaxation of tension by night or day. Every seventh wave, we hit a "milestone". [Then] the bows rose [even] high[er], borne aloft by the huge wave. As it passed beneath the hull, the screws, [all of a sudden out of the water] raced. Then the bows crashed down with a hammer blow that shook every plate in the vessel . . .

'Below decks all was chaos. [There was] loose gear tumbling about . . . [in] inches . . . [of] seawater, as *Salamander* rose and fell, twisted and corkscrewed. The pendant hammocks, acting as clinometers, told of rolls of over 45 degrees, dipping to the limit of safety before reluctantly reversing the roll . . . [Seconds later the ship was] accelerating into the [next] trough, leaving [our] stomachs [seemingly] suspended in the region of the gullet.'

Shackleton's account reveals those in *Salamander* were forced to contemplate the likelihood of immediate extinction when one of the giant waves he had been talking about: 'carried away a mooring wire, which wrapped around the port screw, stopping the port engine. To keep *Salamander* in the teeth of the gale [heading into the waves], the Coxswain had to have maximum starboard wheel on, as our lone remaining engine sought to push us sideways into danger.'

There was 'apprehension and fear . . . in everybody's mind', Shackleton wrote afterwards. No-one liked to think what would be the result if the surviving propeller faltered, causing the ship to slew off to one side or the other, permitting the gigantic waves to beat down upon *Salamander*'s exposed flank. But 'then the miracle happened', Shackleton recalled. 'The sea . . . must have [been]reversing . . . the screw's blades, . . . untwisting the hawser from around the shaft. The slackness was noticed, and [the] First Lieutenant . . . manhandled the wire clear of the screws, and cast it over the side. Visible relief flowed over the whole crew, as the port engine answered the telegraph.'[5]

Somehow British escorts, and merchant ships alike, survived the storm that had scattered them. Many of them formed up again, and all but two merchant ships – the stragglers *Goolistan* and *Kusnetz Lesov* which sank after being torpedoed by U-boats with the result that all hands were lost – reached their destinations.[6]

However, one of QP15's Russian escorts turned out to be less hardy. The destroyer *Sokrushitelni,* which a later inquiry concluded had an inbuilt design fault, was on 20 November broken in two by the unforgiving combination of wind and waves after leaving the convoy to head for the Kola Inlet.[7] Although the majority of her crew were rescued from the forward part of the ship, a small number went down with the stern portion, and the 15 men, who as part of their effort to let others escape first, heroically remained on board until the bitter end, were also lost.[8]

The remainers did not include the ship's captain, and some of his most senior aides, who failed to comply with the rule that obliges such senior officers to stay in a sinking ship until they know everyone else has departed. It is unlikely their cowardice did them much good in the long term. An account by the *Sokrushitelni* sailor P. Nikiforov states that he was present when a tribunal handed down death sentences to the ship's captain and another officer, and witnessed the other transgressors being given 10-year prison sentences or being told they must serve in a penal battalion on the Eastern Front.[9] Nikiforov's account does not say whether the punishments were ever carried out.

Bad weather would also play its part in the sea battle that was fought during the passage of the east-going convoy JW51B, which had set out from Loch Ewe on 22 December 1942 (the new series of east-going Arctic convoys sent in line with Churchill's latest correspondence with Stalin, the first of which was JW51A, were given titles including the prefix 'JW', and the west-going convoys were given titles beginning with 'RA', for 'security reasons'. For the same reason, the first convoys in the series were allocated the number 51, which had no connection with the numbers used for previous convoys).[10]

The bad weather in question was yet another gale, on this occasion blowing from the north and north-west on 28–29 December. It scattered, delayed and diverted JW51B's 14 merchant ships, and reduced the number of JW51B's close-up escorts which got back in touch with the convoy's freighters that were reassembled when the wind died down. Because three of the escorts became separated from the bulk of the convoy, JW51B was left with a close escort consisting of just five destroyers, two corvettes and one trawler.[11] The other effect of the gale was to alter JW51B's route. Although 12 of the convoy's merchant vessels had been rounded up by these remaining escorts by the end of 30 December, they were formed up some thirteen miles to the south of the scheduled track.[12]

This position change brought with it damaging consequences which affected Rear Admiral Robert Burnett's Force R, consisting of his flagship, the light cruiser *Sheffield,* backed up by the light cruiser *Jamaica.* Having successfully covered the passage of JW51A, which after sailing from Loch Ewe on 15 December had reached Russia on 1942's Christmas Day, Force R had set out from the Kola Inlet on 27 December so as to be on hand on 31 December to protect JW51B when in the vicinity of 30° E (the meridian that runs a short distance to the east of Norway's North Cape). This was the area where the convoy would come closest to the German surface fleet's northern base, Altenfjord, during an Arctic twilight, making it the most likely place where it would be attacked by German warships. However, without Burnett realizing it, because of the diversion of JW51B,

Force R ended up at dawn on 31 December away from where the Rear Admiral wanted to be relative to the convoy.[13]

Previous information about JW51B had persuaded him that at 8.45 a.m., that is at first light, on 31 December, he had reached the ideal position for defending it (for details of his force's movements, and location at this time south-east of Bear Island, see Note 14, and Force R's course line and 1A in Map 16).[14] He had not at this stage sighted JW51B because he only arrived near where he expected to find the convoy in the dark. In Burnett's report written afterwards, he stated he had positioned Force R around 10 miles to the north of the convoy's pre-determined planned route so 'that during the short hours when there was visibility, I should have the advantage of light over any enemy that might appear', and 'I might ... avoid air reconnaissance which would lead the aircraft on to the convoy.'[15]

The only problem was that because of JW51B's deviation from what was expected, rather than being a short distance from the convoy, in a perfect position to intervene, Burnett's cruisers at dawn on 31 December, as he was about to find out, were around 25 miles to the north of it (see approximate relative positions at around 8.45 a.m. that morning at 1A and 1B in Map 17).[16]

That would not have mattered had the convoy not already been spotted by the Germans. The heaving merchant ships had first been sighted by a lookout in U-354, one of only two U-boats near the convoy route, at around 9.15 a.m. on 30 December, when JW51B was some 50 miles south of Bear Island.[17]

Finding the convoy in such foul weather was no mean achievement. The following extract from the entry in U-354's war diary written by Kapitänleutnant Karl-Heinz Herbschleb, her 32-year-old commander, highlights what he and his men had had to contend with: 'The fine snow that is falling and the waves that break over the boat make it hard to see anything clearly. The silhouettes (of the convoy's ships) are fuzzy even when close up so I can only see those which are nearest to me. The handrail on the bridge is encrusted with ice. The glass (through which he was looking) is wet and fogged up.

'But never mind all of that,' he wrote excitedly. 'We have found the convoy.' A brief message to that effect was sent to Admiral Klüber (Admiral Nordmeer) at 10.50 a.m.[18]

Herbschleb's notification set in train frantic efforts to obtain the necessary permission to let loose the German warships in anchorages and fjords in and around Altenfjord, some of which had been cooped up without taking any action for several months.

Ironically, the news that an operation was in the offing based on *U-354*'s sighting reached Hitler's headquarters at the very moment when Hitler was chairing a meeting in the course of which he scornfully criticized the Kriegsmarine for their inactivity. According to Vizeadmiral Theodor Krancke, Raeder's Permanent Representative at Hitler's headquarters, Hitler had even gone so far as to complain that the Kriegsmarine was a 'pale imitation of the British Navy', adding: 'The ships are not ready for combat; they lie in the fjords, utterly useless, like so much old iron.'

Krancke's notes reveal that another of those attending chipped in to say that no more convoys were being sent to Murmansk, implying that backed up Hitler's point. One suspects it must have been a relief therefore for Krancke to have at his fingertips just what was needed to silence the carping.

His account continues: 'I read [out] a teletype message from the Seekriegsleitung's Operations Division which stated it was intended to commit a Northern cruiser task force against a convoy that had been reported by our U-boats. The Führer asked whether the force could get there in time, and whether it could find the convoy. I replied this was possible, and went into details. In this way the Führer's previous questions [about the German Navy] were answered.'[19]

Meanwhile, there had been much discussion between Admiral Klüber and Marinegruppenkommando Nord's Admiral Rolf Carls concerning the size of the force that would be needed given the possibility that the convoy might be supported by cruisers.[20]

It was eventually agreed that the attack on the convoy (codenamed Unternehmung Regenbogen – Operation Rainbow), which was to be carried out under the command of the 51-year-old Vizeadmiral Oskar Kummetz, the Befehlshaber der Kreuzer (BdK – Cruiser Commander), would be made by the heavy cruiser *Admiral Hipper* and the pocket battleship *Lützow* plus the six destroyers of the 5 Zerstörerflotille (5th Destroyer Flotilla).

Its centrepiece was to be a pincer movement. If all went well, *Hipper* with Kummetz on board and three of the destroyers would attack the east-going convoy from the north-west. Then, after the British destroyers had moved to the north of the convoy to repulse the incursion, and after the merchant ships had turned to the south, that is away from the shooting, *Lützow* would swoop in with the other three destroyers from that direction and sink the merchant ships with hardly any opposition.[21]

For better or for worse, Kummetz's eight warships started their slow exit from Altenfjord during the late afternoon on 30 December.[22] Krancke noted in his account that the battlegroup's progress was mentioned during that evening's conference with Hitler: 'I reported that the task force had left port and would presumably locate the convoy in the early morning hours. The Führer emphasized that he wished to have all reports immediately, since, as I well know, he cannot sleep a wink when ships are operating. I passed this message . . . to the Operations Division of the Seekriegsleitung, requesting that any information be telephoned [through to me] immediately.'[23]

Judging by the copious notes in Kummetz's war diary, which appear to have been made on board *Hipper* as the German heavy cruiser sped northward, it seems that he too did not get much sleep that night. The notes reflect the worries and concerns of an anxious, cautious man, who on account of his hasty, pessimistic reaction to unfolding events, struggled to either relax, even in quiet moments, or to stick to decisions he had taken just a few hours earlier. That made him a very different proposition to his much more optimistic, even flamboyant opponent, Admiral Burnett (the British Rear Admiral's characteristics are described in Chapter 28).

That is not to say that the German Vizeadmiral did not have a positive side ingrained within his psyche. Kummetz, who evidently had strong ideas on how best to stage the attack, recorded in his war diary that he would not just approach the convoy any old how. He was going to creep up on it from behind. Like Admiral Burnett, he wanted his lookouts to be able to pick out the enemy easily at dawn against the brightening sky to the south. However, unlike the British Rear Admiral, he also jotted down what was negative. He was frustrated when told the accompanying German destroyers could not move through the waves any faster. He was also troubled by the realization that British radar had a longer range than the German attempt at equivalence.

As if these limitations were not impediment enough, he told the commanders of the German ships their crews only had his permission to switch on their so-called 'measuring devices' after 6 a.m. on 31 December, by which time they could expect to be approaching the convoy. Even then, they were not to use them for longer than two minutes every ten minutes, lest they be picked up on British radar screens. He gave this command notwithstanding the risk his battlegroup might as a result advance into thin air if the convoy changed its course.

In fairness to him it should be noted that some of the caution adopted by him during this operation was the result of his having been instructed via Admiral Nordmeer to exercise restraint, for example if he came up against 'an equal opponent'.

For a man who spent so much time and effort getting everything lined up, it must have been galling to admit afterwards that in spite of all this fore-thought, the only preparation that proceeded as planned was the initial deployment. At 2.30 a.m. on 31 December, the commanders of the ships in the German cruiser group obeyed his instruction to spread their vessels out into a long line, as discussed before their departure, with *Hipper* behind the three destroyers in the north, and *Lützow* behind the other three destroyers to the south. They then raked eastward in this formation, only for Kummetz around three hours later to hurriedly issue instructions to extend the line 20 miles to the south to take into account the latest report emanating from *U-354* that the convoy had changed its course from east to east-south-east.

However, no sooner had the new positions been taken up, than Kummetz appreciated that his acceptance of *U-354*'s update had been premature. At 7.18 a.m. (31 December) in spite of it still being dark, a lookout reported that two 'shadows' had been spotted to port ahead of *Hipper*. Commenting on this important development, Kummetz would subsequently inscribe into his war diary: 'These shadows are first spotted by a lookout on the forward mast. They then become visible from the Admiral's bridge [although] they are only visible from time to time.

'But they could be German destroyers which are out of position. I delay sounding the alarm until I get conclusive proof it really is the convoy, and pending that confirmation, I request that *Hipper* should turn towards the shadows to reduce the width of her (*Hipper*'s) silhouette.'

Minutes later another shadow was spotted, then another, then others. 'Six shadows can be seen,' Kummetz would note down eventually. 'It has to be the convoy.'

Shortly before 8 a.m. Kummetz finally agreed the alarm signal should be sent out (see Note 24, and the reference to 7.45 a.m. on the course line for *Hipper* and accompanying destroyers in Map 16 in order to know *Hipper*'s approximate location at this point).[24] However, the waiting game would continue for a while yet. *Hipper*'s 45-year-old Kapitän zur See Hans Hartmann was ordered to have the ship turned away temporarily, leaving it to the crew in *Friedrich Eckoldt*, the German destroyer carrying the 42-year-old Kapitän zur See Alfred Schemmel, the leader of the 5 Zerstörerflotille, to act as the convoy's shadower until dawn.

While the sailors in *Hipper* were metaphorically treading water, a very relieved Kummetz wrote in his war diary: 'Sighting the convoy has immediately lessened the tension. We are just in time to attack it during the day . . . I realize this opportunity may never come my way again. So I must seize my chance.

'I must act quickly, while at the same time taking care not to put the ships in the way of the enemy's torpedoes. This is all the more important [in the prevailing circumstances] because I have been given the [difficult] task of not taking any risks with the cruisers . . .

'While I have been lucky to sight the convoy, it would have been better if I had not made the first contact with my northern wing, or if I had spotted it an hour to ninety minutes earlier. *Lützow* is now around 75 miles to the south. She won't be able to reach the convoy until after the first attack at dawn.'[25]

That was not ideal. But it was a mere pin prick relative to a much more serious wound that Kummetz had avoided. As usual leading up to an important operation, the German admirals and circling U-boat commanders had not stinted in the sending of messages to each other, believing it would be safe to do so if what they transmitted was first encoded on an Enigma machine.

Had such signals been decoded straightaway after being delivered to Britain's Bletchley Park, it would have been obvious to all participating codebreakers and intelligence analysts alike that Kummetz's cruiser group was about to attack the convoy. Whether the sending of an Ultra message to that effect to Burnett in *Sheffield* would have prompted him to break radio silence, and whether that would have scared off the Germans, was never put to the test. It just so happened that, exactly as had occurred during the early stages of the operation against PQ17, at the most critical moment, when JW51B was in most danger, there was a codebreaking blackout. Once again the most incriminating German messages only finally became readable after the code was finally broken on 1 January 1943, too late to influence the German operation's outcome.

Although Kummetz may have been comforted somewhat by the belief his own messages were secure, it was not long before his anxiety levels increased abruptly again. This time it was because he was told that at 8 a.m. the on-board intelligence service had intercepted a mysterious – unreadable – message. 'It's possible that it's the convoy reacting to a sighting of *Hipper*,' he wrote pessimistically in his war diary. Then, as if spurred into action by the thought that he might not get the first shot in, he briskly issued the following order: '*Hipper* will attack from the north at first light.'[26]

As it turned out, the signal Kummetz's intelligence service had intercepted did not connote anything sinister. Even as the German ships loomed up in the darkness behind him, Captain Robert Sherbrooke, JW51B's 41-year-old senior close escort officer in the destroyer *Onslow*, which was patrolling a short distance in front of the convoy's port column as JW51B headed eastward, was still blissfully unaware that it was being stalked.

He had not even registered there were U-boats about. Although during the previous evening, a lookout in one of the other escorts had reported seeing a lurking U-boat that might have reported the convoy's position, and depth charges had been dropped by two destroyers, the verdict after the two hunting warships had returned to the convoy was that it had not been a German submarine after all.[27] It would be years before those British seamen who studied German records could confirm that the 'non-U-boat' was in fact none other than *U-354*.[28]

The incorrect verdict did not mean Sherbrooke was not expecting trouble. In fact he was so apprehensive, that shortly before the beginning of the 31 December 4 a.m. to 8 a.m. watch, he turned to Lew King, his Kiwi first lieutenant, and remarked that he had a feeling that this was the day when something was going to happen. King was then instructed to ensure that everyone in the ship had breakfast as soon as possible, and that all the seamen should be encouraged to change their underwear, a traditional Royal Naval instruction in the lead up to a fight.[29]

This prelude to the battle could not have been more timely. Even though the first streaks of light in the south were only expected at around 8.45 a.m., shortly after 8.15 a.m., while the convoy was still around 220 miles north-west of the Kola Inlet, a lookout in one of the British corvettes which was guarding the starboard side of the convoy in his turn spotted a couple of dark silhouettes. They were behind the merchant ships his ship was guarding. However, because the corvette's officers had been given to understand that two Russian destroyers were expected, her officers did not even report the sighting.[30]

The silhouettes were only reported to Sherbrooke at 8.30 a.m. after they were seen by a lookout in *Obdurate*, the British destroyer which was also on the starboard side of the convoy. Her commander was instructed to investigate. But it was about 9.30 a.m. before gunners in at least one of the three German ships, which by this stage were being tracked by the British destroyer's crew as the threesome moved first west then north-west, fired her guns at *Obdurate* at a distance of around four miles, thereby disclosing beyond a shadow of a doubt that the vessels were hostile.[31]

One witness to this engagement was the 20-year-old Alan Ross, at the time an unknown wireless operator rating in *Onslow,* who had interrupted his studies in Modern Languages at Oxford University to join the Navy, but who would one day become a well-known poet. 'I went out on deck,' he would write later in his memoir, 'but no sooner had I begun to breathe the snow-flecked air, than short sharp volleys of flame snorted across the horizon. Almost simultaneously the action station alarms – shrill, staccato rings – went off.'[32]

As they rang, *Obdurate* was already retreating towards the convoy. But Sherbrooke had not needed to wait for *Obdurate*'s commander's more detailed report. On seeing the flashes made by the guns, Sherbrooke had *Onslow* turned sharply to the west, that is down the northern side of the convoy, so that he would be well-placed to go to *Obdurate*'s assistance.[33]

The following extract from Ross' memoir captures the sense of urgency conveyed by Sherbrooke's reaction to the gunfire, which the young telegraphist was well placed to both feel and hear: 'By the time I was back in the W/T office, we had begun to keel over, swinging hard to port and picking up speed. From the bridge the Captain's voice came down the voice pipe: "Make to destroyers: Join me".'[34]

But before any of the warships summoned by Sherbrooke had a chance to make their presence felt, another urgent call was put out. This time it came from the mouth of the destroyer *Achates'* Lieutenant Commander Arthur Johns, demanding that his crew should live up to their pre-ordained responsibilities. They were to move the ship from the convoy's port quarter, where she had been sailing, to interpose her between the German guns and the back of the merchant ships. Then they were supposed to forget that she had once been a proud destroyer. She was to be transformed into a form of floating bonfire, making as much smoke as ever had been seen in a maritime conflagration until the 12 slow-moving freighters were out of sight at least as far as the Germans were concerned.[35]

But first *Achates'* men had to reach their action stations. George Charlton, the captain of the ship's hedgehog team on the forecastle deck (the exterior deck), was in the head (toilet) when *Achates's* alarms rang. 'I cannot write the adjectives that were said . . . not only by myself, but by all who were there . . .' Charlton wrote afterwards. '[We were] pulling up our long johns . . . thick woolen ones, [our] overalls over our thick woolen sweaters,' then putting on 'sheepskins plus gloves and mittens with a few puffs into our lifebelts.'[36]

That final touch suggests that at least some members of the crew appreciated the risks they were running, as in the words of the ship's 24-year-old First Lieutenant, Loftus Peyton Jones: 'dense clouds of thick black smoke started pouring from our funnel.'[37]

Perhaps it was as well that during those first heart-stopping minutes, nobody on the British side knew what they were up against. The penny would only drop some ten minutes after the German ships first fired their guns. We know that thanks to the testimony of Tom Marchant, the 34-year-old lieutenant commander who at the time was *Onslow's* second-in-command, as well as her torpedo officer. After the war he would describe the lead up to the moment when the scales fell from his eyes in the following terms:

'The rear of the convoy was approximately abeam of us . . . We could see . . . very little. [However] on stepping on the compass platform from the after end of the bridge . . . I was amazed to see a large shape, apparently bows on, away to the north-west . . . almost indiscernible in the dark horizon.

'Captain (D) (Sherbrooke, the captain of destroyers) had spotted this too. And course was altered about 30 [degrees] to starboard to bring the vessel right ahead, and speed increased to 25 knots. By now of course everyone was keyed up, for it was obvious that "summat was going on somewhere", or would be pretty soon. For three minutes nothing happened, except for [the taking of] an occasional range, which was with difficulty being obtained. And so far as light would permit of accuracy, the first was 14,000 [yards and] closing. Then suddenly the "object" dead ahead, which was considerably bigger than a destroyer, turned broadside on us, and almost simultaneously opened fire.

'The first salvo revealed her [class] identity . . . so far as I was concerned, for the eight flashes from the four symmetrically spaced twin turrets suggested *Hipper, Prinz Eugen* or *Lützow* (it was *Hipper*, whose main armament was eight 8-inch guns). Her first salvo fell in the vicinity of *Achates,* and thereafter broadsides were fired about every 25 seconds.'[38]

Hipper's gunfire would not go unanswered. Ross would later recall: 'We could hear [the following] orders coming from the Director to the TS (Transmitting Station): "All guns broadside. All guns load, load, load!"' Then he felt 'the ship shuddering and recoiling as each salvo spat into the darkness'.[39]

Unfortunately for the British close escort ship crews, the conditions were not in their favour. That was particularly the case for those in *Achates*, which attracted *Hipper's* gunners' attention because of all the smoke she was emitting, while not being concealed by it thanks to the west-north-westerly wind that blew the smoke to the south-east.[40] The smoke clouds covered up the merchant ships all right but left its emitter exposed.

The following words from *Achates'* Lieutenant Peyton Jones' memoir highlight how the destroyer's position was rendered even more dangerous on account of the distribution of the light: 'Though the southern sky was slowly lightening, to the north, the black snow clouds merged into the sea, leaving no horizon . . . Suddenly out of the blackness appeared . . . gunflashes, . . . and great fountains of water were thrown up a cable's length (around 200 yards) away . . . [They were made by] big shells . . . which exploded on impact.

'I felt the added vibration as the Captain increased speed, and the ship heeled under helm. Orders came down for guns to load, and we opened fire, though at extreme range. Then the next salvo arrived, much closer this time with eight huge splashes, some on either side of the ship. The enemy had found the range, and we had been straddled.'

There were, he said, two more salvos like that. Then at around 9.45 a.m., while the merchant ships, with *Achates* steering across their wakes, were still heading towards the east, the inevitable happened: there was a near miss on *Achates*' port side, abreast the bridge, which according to Peyton Jones, 'sent showers of splinters scything across the deck'. It also, he added, 'drenched the guns' crews in icy spray' (see 2 in Map 17 for the approximate location relative to the convoy where *Achates* at this stage was sailing).[41]

But that was nothing compared to the mayhem on the decks below. According to Peyton Jones: 'Many of the shell splinters had cut through the ship's side . . . The port side was riddled with holes, many of them on and even below the water line, and water was pouring in fast. Electric leads had been cut, and lockers and mess tables, broken loose from their fastenings, were sliding about all over the place. In the dim light it was difficult not to trip over the bodies of the killed and wounded.'

Peyton Jones' account also makes it clear there was much screaming and groaning by the latter before, with emergency lighting rigged, the ship's doctor was able to have the injured removed to the first aid post, after 'quieting the more seriously injured with shots of morphia'.

Patching up the damage to the ship's hull was not so easily accomplished, at least for the holes below the water line. It was eventually agreed that the stokers' mess deck, on the second deck down from the top open-air deck, along with the magazine and shell room below it, would have to be sealed off and left to flood even though that meant the ship proceeded henceforth trimmed down by the head.[42]

At first *Achates* was the only British ship targeted by *Hipper*'s guns, and even that was restricted to what could be achieved by the German gunners firing at the destroyer when there was more than eight miles of clear water separating the two vessels. Kummetz might have insisted *Hipper* was brought in closer had it not been for the way Sherbrooke had craftily persuaded the Germans that their cruiser might be torpedoed if they gave the British flotilla half a chance.[43] In fact, so successful was Sherbrooke's approach, or so nerve wracking was the prospect of punishment if *Hipper*'s crew did not comply with the German command that nothing should be done to put at risk their precious cruiser's safety, that a lookout on the cruiser's deck 'saw' a line of bubbles made by a torpedo streaking through the water even though no British torpedo had been fired.[44]

As the German cruiser looped round to the east, keeping well to the north of the convoy (see Map 17 for the general direction of travel), Sherbrooke had *Onslow,* and the other British destroyers following her, mirror *Hipper*'s movements while always remaining between the German cruiser and the merchant ships. The strategy worked for a while. Although during the early stages of the battle, every so often the Germans would manoeuvre *Hipper* so her teams of gunners could fire broadsides in the general direction of the merchant ships, she invariably remained more than 9,000 yards away from the British destroyers, putting her beyond the range of their torpedoes. This was living proof that Sherbrooke had correctly deduced that the Germans would be much more likely to keep their distance if the British destroyers did not fire their torpedoes, retaining the prospect that they would be used if *Hipper* did not take care.[45]

However, shortly after 10.15 a.m., by which time the commanders of two of the British destroyers had been instructed to reinforce the merchant ships following the freighters' turn to the south-east, *Hipper*'s gunners finally singled out Sherbrooke's ship. The threat was existential: either Kummetz or Hartmann had finally seen fit to loosen if not to wholly cut the shackles holding back the German cruiser. This time when *Hipper*'s guns were fired, they were only 8,500 yards (less than five miles) away from her target, the closest the German warship came to a British destroyer during the operation.[46]

Ross, who happened to be out on deck when the shelling of his ship began, would later write: 'As I walked aft to peer out in the half-light, we slewed violently [and I saw] repeated flashes of gunfire stabbing the horizon on our port beam.'[47] The first salvo fired on the correct bearing sailed 150 yards over *Onslow*'s forecastle, to be followed by a second in the same place.[48] By this stage *Hipper* was firing shells 'about every half minute', Marchant reported, and 'they were getting closer and closer'.[49]

It was not long before Ross, who had once again taken refuge in the W/T Room, realized that their luck must surely run out, and they would be hit; all he could do was to listen, transfixed, to the commentary being relayed down from the bridge, and pray. If Ross' recollection is accurate, the commentator's disembodied voice hid nothing, announcing in quick succession: 'Salvo coming towards ... going left ... going right ... coming towards![50]

'Hardly had the last words been uttered, than the ship seemed to heave up out of the water, rock wildly and then plunge,' Ross reported in his memoirs.[51] *Onslow*, which had been zig zagging violently, had not moved sufficiently out of the line of advance *Hipper*'s gun teams had been predicting, and had suffered the consequence: the near miss from *Hipper*'s sixth salvo, resulted in projectiles punching holes in the port side of *Onslow*'s torpedomen's mess deck and engine room (see 3 in Map 17 for *Onslow*'s approximate location relative to *Hipper* and the convoy when hit).[52]

According to Marchant: 'Soon after, one 8-inch shell of the 7th salvo exploded on the top of the funnel, splitting it open almost to the level of the upper deck, making a pepper dredge of the after side of the bridge ... completely wrecking the RDF (radar) hut.

'At this stage, the surviving RDF operator in a most calm, unperturbed and apparently unconcerned voice, yet with a touch of annoyance and regret, reported to the Gunnery Officer that he was afraid that further RDF ranges would not be forthcoming as the "set had blown up". His colleague was killed outright.

'At this time, I was standing facing approximately forward with the magnetic compass between Captain (D) (Sherbrooke) and me. I had no knowledge of any casualties having been sustained on the bridge, until odd sounds made me look round. Then I saw that Captain (D) had been hit in the face, and was in a pretty bad way ... . As far as I could see ... a splinter had ... passed over the bridge from the burst on top of the funnel and struck Captain Sherbrooke ... He was bleeding badly and ... his left eye was hanging down his cheek.

'Almost at the same time, though I cannot recollect any shock, we were hit immediately in front of the bridge under B and A guns (the main armament gun in front of the bridge, and the main armament gun for'ard of B gun respectively). B gun was put out of action, and most of its crew either killed or wounded. The shell under A gun had penetrated just below the upper (exterior) deck, and exploded on the mess deck (below), killing or wounding most of the forward damage control and repair party.

'Fire immediately broke out in the vicinity of both hits, and the ready use ammunition, which caught alight.'[53]

In short, Sherbrooke's ship was in a parlous state. According to the commander of *Orwell*, the destroyer following *Onslow*, Sherbrooke's ship looked 'wretched'.[54] Fortunately from the British point of view, in spite of being half-blinded, Sherbrooke had somehow managed to remain at his post long enough to have the ship turned away from her eastern course to starboard.[55] By all accounts she and her crew were also fortunate in that she was at least partially concealed by the clouds of smoke produced by the fires below her decks and her funnel.[56] That might explain why three more salvos fired by *Hipper*'s gun teams at this point narrowly missed her. Only then did *Hipper*'s gunners rotate their guns so that they were pointed at *Orwell*.[57]

Ominously, *Orwell* was also straddled by some of the first salvos *Hipper*'s gunners fired at her.[58] However, *Hipper*'s Kapitän Hans Hartmann's report reveals that minutes later he was distracted, and *Orwell* and *Onslow* were saved, not thanks to the arrival of the two British cruisers, which by this time were approaching from the north-north-west, but as a result of the sighting by the Germans of a British ship to the south-east that was not even part of the convoy's main fighting force.[59] Unbeknown to the sailors in *Hipper*, the ship they had spotted in the wintry gloom, and which they started to bombard at around 10.36 a.m., was the 245-foot-long minesweeper HMS *Bramble,* which prior to the arrival of the Germans had been sent out to round up some of the scattered merchant ships, and was now caught just over three miles away from what was to be her nemesis like a startled owl in a car's headlights as she was coming home to roost (see 4 in Map 17 for *Bramble*'s approximate location at this stage relative to *Hipper* and the convoy).[60]

Bramble's telegraphist's reaction to *Hipper* being sighted was to send out at 10.39 a.m. a mayday signal in the form of an enemy report. It consisted of just six digits and letters as in: '1CR/300' (1 Cruiser bearing 300 degrees).[61] But rarely has such a brief message been so pregnant with horror and suspense. It encapsulated the moment when, lost and lonely in the Arctic twilight, the crew in a diminutive minesweeper had just seen a monstrous 665-foot-long German heavy cruiser sail into view, from whose gunfire, in the absence of a miracle or a gutless surrender, there could be no escape. *Bramble* might just as well have been a lame gazelle spotted in the African bush by a hungry lion for all the hope she had of getting away once *Hipper*'s gunners targeted her.

As it turned out, the message appears to have only been intercepted by a telegraphist in one of the JW 51B escorts, which was not in a position to come to *Bramble*'s aid.[62] But at least that meant the crew members would not die without trace. The only other record of the ship's last moments is in the German chronicles of events.

These chronicles appear to suggest that the Germans in *Hipper* initially approached *Bramble* with almost as much caution as they had shown when facing up to all four of the convoy's free-ranging destroyers. 'At first we thought she was a corvette,' *Hipper*'s Hartmann reported, 'but then we decided she must be a destroyer. We fired at her with both heavy artillery and our heavy flak guns, while the enemy, who was very nippy, tried to get away by making frequent changes of course and by releasing smoke. However she was soon on fire, and we quickly began to catch up with her because her speed was reduced as a result of what we'd done to her.

'*Hipper* was then turned away to avoid being torpedoed. But when explosions and the fires showed how badly the other ship was damaged, *Hipper* was turned to the south so that she could at the same time finish her off, and approach the convoy. More salvos from *Hipper*'s artillery and flak were on target, and there were more fires and explosions. By the time our firing ceased at 11.10 a.m., it was clear the ship was mortally wounded.'[63]

33

We Must Take the Current When it Serves

Main Action: 31 December 1942
Battle of the Barents Sea, JW51B part 2

(See Map 17)
GMT + 1

Even as the tragic events on board *Bramble* were unfolding, members of the crew in the burning *Onslow* were already counting the cost of having taken on *Admiral Hipper*, the heavy German cruiser. According to *Onslow*'s Tom Marchant, who had replaced Sherbrooke as the destroyer's commander:

'The appearance of things produced a very alarming picture . . . We were . . . making thick black smoke . . . The ship was gradually taking up a list to port . . . The bridge was almost uninhabitable due to the choking smoke from the fires for'd. The noise (from the raised safety valve in the semi-destroyed funnel) rendered speech practically impossible. And then came a phone call from the engine room to say that there was a fire in one of the boiler rooms, and that water was making its way into the engine room.'[1]

Luckily for those on board, a mixture of preventative action and good fortune would save the ship's main engines, but for some time the crew in various compartments below decks found themselves caught up in what initially must have appeared to be an unwinnable battle against the debilitating effects of the flames and smoke.[2] Indications of the kind of conditions under which those below decks were operating, and the terrible injuries they were witnessing, are conveyed by the following extract from a post-war verbal account spoken, stream of conscious-style, by Thomas Hanley from Bolton, *Onslow*'s sick berth attendant:

'I go into the sick bay . . . and all the bunkheads were ablaze. We had to keep down on our knees because of the smoke. A fire party arrived and got a hose going . . . The fire . . . was put out in the sick bay. But there's fire down below.

'A "body" comes up the ladder (from the mess decks), pulling himself up with his hands. He has one leg shot off and the other is shattered below the knee . . . Most of his clothes [had been] blown off. I recognized him as the petty officer cook . . . He'd been down below in charge of the shell supplies which had been hit . . . [I] grabbed him, pulled him up, laid him on the deck, . . . made sure the arteries which were fractured were tied off. All you can do in a case like that is put a blanket under him, give him a shot . . . – in the Navy we had ampoules of morphine . . . – just push it in, squeeze it, put a mark on his wrist [to indicate] he has had a shot of morphine so he is not killed by morphine if someone else [with morphine] comes along . . .

'Then a message came from back aft: "Sick berth attendant wanted back aft. Urgent! Urgent! Casualties back aft!" I make my way along the . . . deck . . . I got down to the wardroom, where the secondary sickbay was . . . to find chaos . . . They started bringing bodies up from for'ard . . . The immediate job was to get rid of the dead. One came along, a leading stoker, one of my own mess . . . Put my hand under his head. My hand sinks into his brain. Doesn't affect you. Too much going on. He's dead. Take him away. I want the living. I don't want the dead.

'I'd filled the officers' cabins with the injured. There was a particular one, a leading hand . . . was not conscious but he was alive. I couldn't tell what was wrong with him. There wasn't a sign of injury, apart from one or two shrapnel holes. I try and examine him to see if there was any bleeding. But there wasn't. I pulled his arm across, and suddenly a spurt of blood almost hit the ceiling, so I had to stop the artery off . . . I eventually had to get to the doctor, and [I] said I've got one or two people I wasn't sure about.'[3]

But even Hanley's experiences slip into insignificance compared with what *Onslow*'s Alan Ross, the young wireless operator mentioned in the previous chapter, had witnessed below decks after he was ordered by Lieutenant King to fight the fire above the magazine at the front of the ship.

'I'm afraid we'll have to lock you in,' King had warned him after escorting Ross into the compartment where the fires were burning. 'We'll get someone to relieve you when we can . . . , but for the moment I'm afraid you're on your own . . . Try and get as close to the fires as you can.'

'The steel door . . . clanged shut behind him,' Ross wrote in his memoir. 'I adjusted my mask, wiped the eyepieces with my gloves and looked around. Spray from a huge hole in the port side was spurting in all directions. The noise from the raised safety valve overhead (in the funnel) was deafening, a concerted hiss of steam sharpened to the level of torture. For'ard above the magazine, a bonfire raged, its area of flame checked by the freezing swill at its base . . .

'I directed the hose in my hands towards the heat . . . I was waist-deep in water, and each time I moved, I stumbled on one of the bodies that rolled like sodden hammocks beneath me. Somewhere under my feet [the best part of] two whole gun crews, [which had been] wiped out, began to pile up with the increasing list of the ship. Occasionally a face washed through the surface, all expression sponged away from its features . . .

'The ship began to take on an even steeper list, and I could only train the hose by hanging on to a bulkhead. There were no lights, but in the glare from the advancing flames, the hair of the drowned drifted like seaweed . . . Several times as we lurched and I fell sideways, I had to lever myself upright on someone's body. I began to wonder . . . whether there might still be someone around me with some life in him . . . whom I could resuscitate into companionship. But the bodies were so heavy, their several sodden layers of clothing making them double their weight, that I soon gave up attempts to raise them . . .

'I began to have the illusion that I had entered a strange limbo, a kind of ante-room to death, accessible only to those whose fate had already been sealed. Would it be simpler just to lie down in the seawater with my unknown messmates and get it over and done with? Minutes went by, the buckling and blistering bulkheads crackling in the flames.'

At long last, he spied Lieutenant King beckoning to him, as Ross described it, 'like a ghost through the smoke'. Ross, who did not need summoning twice, stumbled out past the opened steel door after him. 'We're not out of the wood yet,' King confided in his best bedside manner after the steel door had been clanged shut behind them, 'but we're rejoining the convoy. You might give a hand with the baling . . .'[4]

It was at the same time as the desperate battle to extinguish the flames in *Onslow* was being fought that *Lützow* and her accompanying destroyers finally appeared to the south of the convoy. At 10.50 a.m., some fifteen minutes after *Hipper* had opened fire for the first time on the luckless *Bramble*, the German pocket battleship's radar told her commander that a group of vessels lay to the north of his ship, some of which were as near as three miles away. Was this the moment when Kummetz's trap would snap shut?

It might have been, had it not been for the restricted visibility and the risk averse focus that constrained the putting into effect of German plans by those in the front line. As *Lützow*'s 43-year-old Kapitän zur See Rudolf Stange noted in his war diary: 'Because of the failing light and the smoky horizon, it is not immediately clear whether it is friend or foe. So to avoid having to advance into the snow squalls and smoke to the south [of the convoy], I decide I should run alongside the convoy at a slow speed to look for better opportunities.'

Little did he realize as he made that fateful decision that he already had been given the best opportunity any German would be given that day to decimate the convoy. There are grounds for saying he should have seized the moment and rushed into action while he had the chance. Although his gunners would subsequently find they were able to target the merchant ships, which by that time were south-west of *Lützow*, the pocket battleship's crew quickly discovered that relying on radar in the already fading light was no substitute for firing using good old-fashioned eyesight.[5]

Equally significant errors were at the same time being committed by the Germans at the northern end of the battlefield. Error number one was Kummetz's decision shortly after 11 a.m. to leave the crew in the destroyer

Friedrich Eckoldt behind to finish off *Bramble* so that *Hipper* could carry on heading first south, and then south-west in the general direction of where the merchant ships were fleeing. For a man who appears to have set great store in the minimizing of risks, it is strange that he appears to have failed to anticipate how, once separated, the crews in the two German ships would be hampered by not knowing whether any vessel that approached them afterwards was German or British.[6]

That is said even though the decision to split up the northern German force did enable *Hipper*'s gunners, as the cruiser proceeded south-westward, to target the *Achates* again, shortly after 11.15 a.m., before the damaged British destroyer could escape from her position at the back of the convoy. This time *Hipper*'s gunners made a better job of it, notwithstanding that the distance separating the ships was, initially at least, not much reduced compared with what it had been during their first engagement. A shell from *Hipper*'s very first salvo crashed into the bridge of the British destroyer causing the kind of damage that every artillery officer in a warship longs for when targeting an enemy vessel. Even from seven miles away where the cruiser's guns were fired, it was possible to see that the front of *Achates* was on fire (see 5 in Map 17 for *Achates*' approximate location relative to *Hipper* and to the convoy when the British destroyer was damaged for a second time).[7]

Of course those aboard *Hipper,* being so far away, had not seen the half of it. *Achates*' Lieutenant Peyton Jones would subsequently write the following description of what he found after hurrying to the wheelhouse from where he had been standing on the upper deck when the shell struck:

'On arriving in the wheelhouse, it became obvious that the hit had been on the bridge above. The deckhead was bulging downwards, and a somewhat dazed coxswain . . . was endeavouring to revive the two telegraph men who lay . . . beside him.

'The usual way up to the bridge was barred, so stepping out onto the port Oerlikon platform, I clambered up the remains of the outside ladder. The familiar scene was unrecognizable: just a blackened shambles of twisted metal with the remains of a few identifiable objects sticking grotesquely out of the wreckage. There was no fore-end of the bridge . . . It was carried away.[8] Among this . . . jumble . . . were lying the mercifully unidentifiable remains of my shipmates (they included the Captain, Navigator, signalmen, lookouts and asdic operator) who had been standing there when the 8-inch shell burst among them. All had been wiped out, their lives instantly extinguished. Over this indescribably desolate scene hung the acrid smell of high explosive fumes and the sick stench of death.

'Further aft (on the bridge) the damage was less severe, although still effectively flattened as if by some giant hand. Here several men were lying, not all of them dead. I leant over Fred Barrett who had been directing the gun armament, but although he tried to speak, he was too badly wounded to tell me anything.

'From further aft still (on the bridge) appeared the Yeoman . . . stumbling and still dazed with shock, but able in halting words to tell me of the recent exchange of signals with *Obedient* (the commander of the destroyer *Obedient* had instructed *Achates'* Arthur Johns to take his winged ship to join the damaged *Onslow*, by this time out of harm's way, at the front of the convoy).'[9]

There was no time for sentimentality or commiseration. The ship which was circling to starboard at 28 knots had to be brought under control. 'There was a jagged hole in the [bridge] deck leading to the wheelhouse below,' Peyton Jones recalled. 'Through this I shouted to . . . [the Coxswain] to put the wheel amidships, and was much relieved to have his confirmation that the steering appeared to be undamaged. Our heel to port decreased as the ship slowly came round to a south-easterly course.'[10] It also helped that the ship's speed was reduced to 12 knots.[11] Not that this solved everything. 'All this time my view was much obscured by the smoke billowing up from a cordite fire which had broken out on B gundeck, immediately in front of the bridge,' Peyton Jones' account continues.[12]

Even more concerning was the fact that *Hipper's* gunners did not just hit *Achates* and leave it at that. Before they had done with her, the British destroyer had been straddled again, and then in spite of Peyton Jones' best efforts to have the ship dodge the next salvo by turning as he put it 'sharply to port', she had been hit again – this time on the port side underneath the bridge leading to mayhem in the transmitting station (the TS). According to Peyton Jones, 'the shell had torn a huge gaping hole in the ship's side before exploding in the seamen's bathroom putting the TS out of action'.[13] Evidently that applied to the TS's occupants as well. One man who visited the transmitting station afterwards would later report:

'I don't think anyone got out of there alive. I recall we were talking to one chap who said he couldn't move his legs. He lost consciousness and died as we were getting him free from the debris . . . We saw that both his legs had been taken off . . . [There were] bits of bodies all over the place.'[14]

The impact made by the shell's explosion, or possibly by a near miss, also fractured the after bulkhead of the previously flooded stokers' mess deck, leading to the flooding of the ERA mess deck aft of it. Also flooded was No. 2 boiler room. The one piece of good fortune for the ship's company was that the holes leading to No. 1 boiler room were relatively small, so that the inflowing water could be sucked out by a pump.[15]

No such good news was forthcoming in the vicinity of B gun. A man sent to investigate whether B gun could still be fired, reported back what he summed up as 'devastation'. There were he said 'bodies lying in all states . . . I looked at a number to see if anyone was still alive, but could not find anyone [who was still breathing].'[16] The gun itself had been immobilized.[17]

Achates ended up not just down by the head, but also listing 15 degrees to port, a state of affairs that might have tempted a more experienced captain to bow out of the fight. However Peyton Jones was not having any of that. 'I decided to ignore the earlier instructions (from *Obedient*'s Lieutenant Commander David Kinloch who was now in charge of the British destroyers) to join *Onslow*, and to resume our role as smoke layer, thus making the only effective contribution to the defence of the convoy of which we were now capable,' Peyton Jones reported afterwards.[18]

Not that *Obedient*'s Kinloch was in a position to scold Peyton Jones for his breach of discipline. After almost crippling *Achates*, *Hipper*'s gunners had at around 11.30 a.m. shot away *Obedient*'s aerials, while Kinloch's ship and the other destroyers with her were sailing between the cruiser, some six miles to their north, and the convoy to their south. That made it next to impossible for Kinloch to reliably communicate with the commanders of the other escorts (see 7 in Map 17 for the approximate relative locations of Hipper and *Obedient* when the latter ship was hit).[19]

But what finally did for the German attack was the result of another cardinal error by the Germans: *Hipper*'s officers and crew were caught minutes later totally unprepared for the attack coming from the German cruiser's disengaged (northern) side.

It was delivered by the 6-inch guns in *Sheffield* and *Jamaica*, which had at long last arrived on the scene from the north (see Note 20 for why the arrival of the British cruisers was delayed).[20] But it had been made possible by *Sheffield*'s and *Jamaica*'s radar. This had enabled the crews in the two British cruisers, while still too far away to see the German ships, to track *Hipper*'s progress as, following on from her initial contact with *Bramble*, she had turned from her easterly course to a southerly course, firing at *Bramble* again as she passed the minesweeper. Radar also enabled the two British cruisers' crews to pinpoint *Hipper*'s distance from them, and the moment when *Hipper* completed her turns to the west, thus placing herself with her disengaged broadside facing *Sheffield*'s and *Jamaica*'s guns.

For approximately two long minutes after observing a change of course, *Sheffield*'s captain, Andrew Clarke, permitted the tracking of *Hipper*, whose silhouette was by this time visible, to continue so that his ship could also be turned to starboard, thus removing her from *Jamaica*'s gunners' eyelines. Then with *Hipper* believed to be about seven miles away, he gave the order all those on the bridge had been waiting for: 'Open fire!' (see 8 in Map 17 for the approximate position where *Hipper* was located relative to the British cruisers when Force R's vessels opened fire).[21]

Petty Officer Fuller, who was on *Sheffield*'s bridge when the order was given, and when a similar command was given in *Jamaica*, later confirmed in the course of an interview: 'The [German] cruiser didn't know we were there until our shells straddled him . . . It was a real thrill to watch tracer shells soar through the air, and to see the terrific flash when they landed . . . We saw a salvo hit him. Everyone yelled . . .'[22]

As had been the case when *Hipper*'s shells rained down on *Achates*, Fuller was not just talking about one salvo from each cruiser. According to one witness, once the shooting started, the interiors of *Sheffield*'s gun turrets were a hive of activity, as the men inside worked 'like devils' to reload their guns so that they could be fired ideally at the rate of three per minute again and again and again.[23]

In fact, as the writer of *Sheffield*'s gunnery report confirmed: 'Fifteen salvos were fired [by us] before "Target A" turned [towards us] under cover of smoke made presumably by her screen. During this period while the range closed to 8,900 yards (5 miles), hits were observed from the Director Control Tower on the enemy's starboard quarter and amidships between the funnel and the mainmast.'[24]

Equally deadly from the Germans' point of view was *Hipper*'s inability to land any punches herself. During the first shocking moments when her crew unexpectedly found themselves being targeted, vital seconds ticked by while Hipper's turrets were rotated 180 degrees until they could be aimed at her tormentors. By the time her gun teams were ready to return fire, it was too late. As the writer of her artillery report confessed afterwards: 'After the second salvo [fired by *Hipper*'s gun teams], the target could not be seen . . . The radar was no help . . . The aft director was blinded by smoke from *Hipper*'s funnel and the burning aircraft hangar. In the front director, the optical screens were iced up . . . This may have been because of the columns of water thrown up into the air as high as the foremast by the enemy's shells which fell short, or it may have been because of the condensation as a result of the gases that were expelled from the funnel as the ship turned [to starboard].

'It took two and a half minutes to remove the ice. But this two and a half minutes, during which the enemy exploited his superiority, was critical. In that time, we were hit three times.'[25]

The first impact, from the shell which struck *Hipper*'s starboard side at around 11.34 a.m., before she had turned sufficiently to the north to narrow the breadth of the ship visible from the British cruisers, was the most serious; as a result, her No. 3 boiler room was flooded and *Hipper*'s maximum speed was reduced. The other shells struck the port side of the German cruiser a minute later as she turned; one set alight her aircraft hangar. The fire would be extinguished before it could endanger *Hipper*'s survival, but as observed above, it may have obstructed the German crew's ability to successfully target the enemy's ships.[26]

Admiral Burnett would later reveal what happened next: 'I turned to starboard . . . to conform [with *Hipper*'s turn].' It was then, as *Sheffield* and *Jamaica* turned first to the north and then to the east, that Burnett saw what he described as a 'destroyer . . . fine on the port bow in an ideal position for torpedo attack [on us]. I ordered HMS *Sheffield* to shift target to this destroyer, and course was altered . . . towards her to comb any possible tracks' (see 9 in Map 17 for *Friedrich Eckoldt's* approximate location when seen by Burnett).[27]

The precautions activated in *Sheffield* were eminently sensible. At least one lookout in *Friedrich Eckoldt*, which was the German destroyer sighted, had spotted one of the British cruisers. However, relative to Burnett's and his gunners' decisive response to the sighting of *Friedrich Eckoldt*, the reaction of the German 5 Zerstörerflottille's Kapitän Schemmel in *Friedrich Eckoldt* to the sighting of the British cruiser was pitiful. As a result of the earlier decision by Kummetz to separate his ships, Schemmel had evidently lost his grip on where the other German ships were located, as is proved by the following verbal exchange starting shortly after *Hipper's* gun turrets had rotated round to fire at *Sheffield* and *Jamaica*:

> **Friedrich Eckoldt to Hipper**: In which direction are you shooting?
> **Hipper**: To the north . . .
> **Eckoldt to destroyer Richard Beitzen**: Are you beside *Hipper*? How many destroyers are with *Hipper*? . . .Are you firing towards the south-west?
> **Eckoldt to Hipper**: I can see . . . a cruiser and a destroyer. Is that you? . . .Where are you relative to the convoy?
> **Hipper to Eckoldt**: I am north of the convoy . . .[28]

Those crew members in *Friedrich Eckoldt*, who had seen unidentified ships firing to the south-west, barely had time to digest the alarming implications of this exchange before they saw one of these ships, about two miles away, advancing rapidly towards them.[29] Meanwhile, as would later be confirmed by John Somers, at the time of the incident, a 23-year-old member of *Sheffield's* pom-pom crew who appears to have been standing on the British cruiser's exterior deck, *Sheffield's* forward guns were being swung round until they pointed directly at the German destroyer. The following extract from Somers' subsequent account of the next minutes reads: 'On the starboard signal bridge, just behind and above me, the Chief Petty Officer of Signals is flashing this ship on the Aldis lamp, and was flashed back by the oncoming ship . . . If something don't happen soon we will collide.'

Something did happen. The testimony of Petty Officer Fuller, who was still on *Sheffield*'s bridge, bears witness to the shooting by the British cruiser's guns that ensued: 'They blazed out with a terrific roar, and the first salvo caught him a smasher! Several more quick salvos set him on fire with smoke pouring from him.'[30]

That first hit provoked the following indignant protest:

Eckoldt **to** *Hipper*: You are shooting at me!

This complaint prompted the response laid out below from someone in the German destroyer *Richard Beitzen,* which had accompanied *Friedrich Eckoldt* on her journey to the east side of the battlefield, and which was now herself being targeted unsuccessfully by *Jamaica* as *Richard Beitzen* veered off to the south:

Richard Beitzen: No, that's an English cruiser![31]

Meanwhile the gap separating *Sheffield* from *Friedrich Eckoldt* carried on reducing. 'We were getting very close to him,' Fuller later reported: 'I remember the Captain saying: "Shall we ram him Sir?" The Admiral said "Yes, Ram!" When the pipe went "Stand by to ram!", you could almost feel the thrill going through the whole ship's company. However the destroyer was in such a mess that we did not have to ram him. We passed him, (the British cruiser having deviated her course to port, so that the German destroyer was nearest to *Sheffield*'s starboard side when the ships were side by side), . . . and our smaller guns finished him off.

'As we hauled out to port . . . we could see him sinking by the stern blazing furiously. The fire must have got hold of his box of pyrotechnics, and for a few minutes the sky was lit by red, white and green flares. Someone suggested he was signalling for help. And someone else on the back of the bridge said: "I should think he damn well is!"'[32]

However, some in *Sheffield* were less triumphant. Herbert Twiddy, at the time a 17-year-old boy on his first voyage, recalls how he and some others were let out of their gun turret: 'to see this dark grey wreck of a vessel, a short distance away, some 2–300 yards at most, listing over with her hull exposed, and with fires burning at various points along her deck. The upper deck short range weapons [in *Sheffield*] raked the burning deck with gunfire as she drifted astern of us into the darkness and oblivion. I cannot remember seeing any . . . signs of life on board . . . It was an eerie . . . ghostly vision . . . but the flames already dying as they were, seemed to illustrate the submissive though reluctant finality of a gallant foe.'[33]

What had been witnessed prompted *Sheffield*'s Alan Somers to write in his stream of consciousness post-war account: 'I will never forget [this]. I turn to my oppo. "Poor bastards," I said. "What a way to go! Either blown up, burnt, or frozen to death."'

Talking of gallantry, this account of *Friedrich Eckoldt*'s demise would not be complete without mentioning what may have been the final plucky rearguard action on board the British minesweeper *Bramble;* it may have played an important role in the ambush of the German destroyer. At 11.38 a.m., just minutes before the message from *Friedrich Eckoldt* complaining that *Hipper* was firing at her, *Obedient*'s David Kinloch, whose ship had remained between *Hipper* and the south-going convoy, observed traces of what appeared to be two separate actions going on over the north-east horizon. He believed the one more to the west was between two cruisers, and signified the welcome arrival of Force R. The one more to the east, he said, 'was between a heavy unit and a much smaller ship, which was firing a single gun and what appeared to be Pom-Pom tracer.'[34]

This battle to the east may well have been *Bramble*'s last stand as she faced up to *Friedrich Eckoldt*. Once again when assessing *Bramble*'s role, it is necessary to read between the lines. But if this is done, it summons up the haunting possibility, referred to in the official Admiralty Communiqué relating to her loss, that at least two of her 121 man crew (one from each of the two gun crews whose weapons were believed to have been seen firing) had survived the ruthless pounding the minesweeper had received from *Hipper*'s heavy artillery (see end of Chapter 32), and on seeing the approach of another large German warship, around an hour after having first being targeted by *Hipper*, had decided to go down fighting, knowing that at any second they were likely to be blasted to kingdom come.[35]

As for Kummetz, his realization that the remains of his battlegroup might end up being caught between a British cruiser and British destroyers persuaded him that he should order the German commanders to depart from the battlefield while they could. The order was duly given, and notwithstanding another exchange of fire, complied with.[36]

The Germans left behind an evolving tragedy. Shortly after 1 p.m., by which time *Achates'* boilers had stopped working and her list to port had reached 60 degrees, Peyton Jones finally realized the surviving crew must abandon ship. But before he gave the final order, as he described it in his memoir: 'the ship started to roll over onto her port side, and we were forced to climb over the edge of the bridge on to the side of the wheelhouse. Looking down into the wheelhouse passage, I saw Fred Barrett (the mute survivor following the explosion on *Achates'* bridge referred to in the abovementioned description of the second sustained attack on the destroyer) being helped by Able Seaman MacIver out of the Captain's sea cabin, and reaching down, we hauled them up beside us.

'We were now completely on our beam ends, and the sea was surging into the horizontal funnels and pouring through ventilator outlets, doors and hatches. I recall having time to unsling my binoculars from around my neck and hang them carefully on some convenient projection before the ship completed her capsize, and the sea surged over our heads.

'The water . . . was bitterly cold . . . , but it took a moment or two to penetrate my many layers of clothing . . . I struck out to get clear of the ship. [Then] looking back, I saw the dark outline of her screws and rudder as she slowly disappeared, stern pointing to the sky.'[37]

He later recalled how he had noted with satisfaction the number of rafts and Carley floats that had been launched into the sea before the ship sank, and how pleased he was to find that the emergency light in the float onto which he had climbed flashed so brightly, making him sure that the crew in the nearby trawler *Northern Gem* would see it. That was what gave him the confidence to tell the fifteen to twenty men who gathered around it that help was on its way, and to encourage the singing of that morale boosting song 'Roll Out The Barrel' which was often sung by shipwrecked seamen during World War 2.

Fortunately, *Northern Gem* reached them before too long, and soon men were being hoisted on board by the trawler's crew, some of whom were clinging to rescue nets hung over the gunwale. But many of the *Achates* men in the sea were beyond helping. One such case is mentioned in the following extract from the account by *Northern Gem's* Sidney Kerslake, the trawler's coxswain, whose previous attempts to rescue members of the minesweeper *Leda*'s crew, sunk during QP14, were profiled in Chapter 29:

'I saw a young lad drifting past the stern with his arm outstretched to catch a line; as I threw it to him, it dropped over his shoulders, but he seemed to have lost all the feeling in his body due to the cold. I screamed at him to hold on, but he could do nothing to help save himself. So I tried to throw several loops . . . around his arm [to no avail]. I distinctly heard him crying out for his mother. "Mother!" was the last word I heard, as he disappeared below the surface. I know I was crying myself with helplessness and frustration as I saw him go.'[38]

Peyton Jones felt his own body growing numb as he waited for his turn to be rescued from the water. He only recovered a little after climbing back onto the empty float that had capsized when everyone on it had crowded onto one side. Then after it ended up near to the trawler, he stood on its side and flung himself towards *Northern Gem,* hooking his arms over the gunwale as he reached her. Seconds later he felt himself being pulled on board.

'Getting up, I returned to the gunwale and looked over the side,' Peyton Jones recalled. 'A few scattered red lights [attached to life jackets] were still visible, but none were close to the ship, or appeared to be moving . . .'[39]

A few minutes later the trawler was shaken by a loud underwater explosion which was probably caused by the blowing up of *Achates*' depth charges. According to Kerslake: 'The surface of the sea shivered for a few moments, then burst into a boiling cauldron of confused froth. When it returned to its former state, there was no one left alive in the water . . . Six or eight bodies [came] floating past still with their lifejackets, on which glowed the red lights, but there was no sign of any life. They had either been killed by the explosion, or had succumbed to the frightful cold of the water.'[40]

Peyton Jones has written about how after being taken below, he slowly peeled off his soaking wet clothes. His account continues: 'As I lay in my bunk, I began to feel the agony of returning circulation to arms and legs, and others were also crying out in pain. Eventually all was quiet, and it was only then that the enormity of all that had happened that day swept over me. The loss of so many friends and shipmates, as well as the ship in which we had so proudly served, coupled I suppose with the trauma of the past few hours was too much, and I sobbed in anguish.'[41]

·It was later revealed that 80 men from *Achates* were picked up by *Northern Gem*'s crew, and a history of the destroyer states that 112 of the crew died during the battle and its aftermath.[42] It is at the same time heartwarming and humbling to hear that the men who were too badly wounded to make it up from below decks in *Achates* were not left alone when the ship rolled over. The Officers' Steward and the Canteen Manager refused to leave the wounded men they were looking after even though it meant they too went down with the ship.[43]

When *Northern Gem* caught up with the convoy, a request was sent for assistance, and in the half light of the next morning (1 January 1943), the trawler's skipper, Lieutenant Horace Aisthorpe, was ordered to approach the destroyer *Obdurate* to take her doctor on board.

That was an ambitious undertaking given that by this time the weather had taken a turn for the worse. According to Peyton Jones: 'The tiny *Northern Gem* corkscrewed up and down in the rising seas . . . It was blowing a moderate gale and both ships were yawing, rolling and pitching badly.

'Taking the wheel himself, Skipper Aisthorpe edged his ship close under *Obdurate*'s port quarter, and then with great skill steadily closed the gap to about ten feet. It was a tricky moment, as the decks of the two ships rose and fell, and the gap widened and narrowed as they rolled, while the foam flecked sea surged between them. Seizing his moment, Aisthorpe nudged the destroyer's well-fendered side, and the Doctor (Lieutenant Surgeon Maurice Hood) bravely jumped the eight feet down to the trawler's heaving deck . . . His bag followed and he was escorted below.'

He immediately set to work, using the forward mess deck as his surgery. 'I administered the anaesthetic, slowly dripping chloroform on to a face mask, or emptying a syringe into a vein,' Peyton Jones reported, 'whilst Mayer handed him his instruments. On the wildly gyrating deck, all three of us had to be anchored round the waist by two men each so that we could have both hands free. Someone held a specially bright torch to illuminate his work, whilst two more held the patient stretched out on one of the wooden mess tables.'

Improvising in this way, Hood was able to stabilize more than 10 of the wounded. Ironically the only man he could not save was *Achates*' Fred

Barrett (mentioned above) who did not have a mark on his body. Barrett's only communication with those trying to care for him since he was found lying on the bridge following the explosion of *Hipper*'s shell had been through what he could convey with what Peyton Jones referred to as 'the pleading in his eyes'. He was buried at sea the next morning.[44]

Northern Gem with the rest of the convoy reached the Kola Inlet the next day (3 January 1943) two days after *Onslow*'s arrival.[45] By then, *Onslow*'s 23 wounded were receiving the intensive care they so badly needed, even if it was limited to what was on offer in Russia.[46] Seventeen of her ratings died during or in the aftermath of the battle and were buried at sea.[47] The *Onslow* wounded were treated in the Royal Naval Auxiliary Hospital, the 75-bed British hospital with two doctors but no running hot water or reliable heating that had finally been permitted to open in Vaenga, some 18 miles north of Murmansk.[48]

A few days later Sherbrooke was told he had been awarded the Victoria Cross. Tovey's verdict on what *Onslow*'s commanding officer and the escorts under his command had achieved, which was circulated around three weeks later, contained the following approbation: 'That an enemy force of at least one pocket battleship, one heavy cruiser and six destroyers, with all the advantage of surprise and concentration, should be held off for four hours by five destroyers and driven from the area by two 6" cruisers, without any loss to the convoy, is most creditable and satisfactory.'[49]

In Germany, the action received a mixed reception. 'The enemy certainly won a tactical victory,' Grossadmiral Raeder commented, but 'the positive effect of the battle was it shows the enemy that we will take any opportunity to attack convoys in the Arctic, which means the enemy has to carry on using convoys to carry his supplies, protected by a strong escort ... Also the use of our cruisers and destroyers has given their crews valuable combat experience ...'[50]

However, Hitler was apoplectic. One can well imagine that even before what came to be known as the Battle of the Barents Sea, he was already in an extremely anxious state because of recent events on the Eastern Front: they had demonstrated the impossibility of rescuing General Friedrich Paulus' 6th Army, which was already on borrowed time having been surrounded west of Stalingrad in the wake of Russia's great counter-attack (Operation Uranus which had started on 19 November 1942), and which had then been denied the chance to break out of the encirclement by Hitler's order to remain in place.

History cannot tell us how much more frustrated he would have been had he only lived to read what Nikita Khrushchev wrote about Stalingrad in his post-war memoirs. Khrushchev highlighted the pivotal role played in the successful Soviet counter-attack by the large numbers of trucks supplied by the West. The vehicles, which had given the Red Army the capacity to quickly move troops, weapons and ammunition up to the front line, included those transported by the very Arctic convoys which Hitler's Kriegsmarine, for all its efforts prior to and during the Battle of the Barents Sea, had been unable to stop (see Note 51 for the number of UK produced trucks supplied to Russia).[51]

Hitler's bad mood was not improved by his having been initially led to believe the attack on JW 51B was a success, and by his subsequently having to wait a long time for the full disappointing story. The following analysis to be found in Vizeadmiral Krancke's notes is also germane. Krancke revealed Hitler's 'special emphasis on the fact that the action had not been fought to a finish. This, said the Führer, was typical of [crews in] German ships, and quite different from the way the [crews in] British ships would have behaved, who true to their tradition would always fight to the bitter end . . . The whole affair spelt the end of the German high seas fleet. I was to inform the Grand Admiral immediately that he was to come to see the Führer at once so that he could be informed in person of the Führer's irrevocable decision.'[52]

Krancke duly arranged with Hitler's Naval Adjutant that Raeder should come to the Führer's Wolfsschanze (Wolf's Lair) HQ, in Rastenberg, East Prussia, although the visit was delayed until 6 January 1943. Raeder later wrote about the meeting: 'For one whole hour Hitler . . . gave me a thorough dressing down. He reiterated his complaint about getting insufficient information. He went on to attack the Navy in a vicious and impertinent way . . .' Raeder was then asked to give his considered comments on Hitler's decision to scrap at least the seven largest ships in the German Fleet. The Grossadmiral subsequently complied, writing a long memorandum which was sent to Hitler on 15 January.[53] However, anticipating Hitler's refusal to listen to reason, he asked the Führer to accept his resignation, which Hitler eventually did.[54] The appointment of the 51-year-old Admiral

Karl Dönitz, who had been the Commander of the Kriegsmarine's U-boat force, as the new Commander-in-Chief of the German Navy to replace the 66-year-old Raeder was duly announced publicly on 30 January 1943.[55]

It was to be a fitting date to confirm the changing of the guard at the top of the Kriegsmarine, and not just because it was the 10th anniversary of Hitler's accession to power. The announcement coincided with the day when the remaining German officers with the recently promoted Field Marshal Paulus in the southern pocket of the besieged 'Kessel' (Cauldron), on the western outskirts of Stalingrad, finally decided that they must surrender, a result that as intimated above, was in no small way the consequence of the Kriegsmarine's failure under Raeder to stop the supply of aid to Russia.[56] The formal surrender by the leaders of all German troops in the southern pocket took place the very next day (31 January) with the surrender of the Germans in the northern pocket following on 2 February 1943. It was a humiliating defeat for the Germans, and given that just four months earlier Hitler's troops had appeared all set to take the city, one of the greatest and most significant turnarounds in history. After the surrenders, 22 generals and some 91,000 other German soldiers who had been fighting in and around Stalingrad were captured.[57]

34

Sacrifice

Main Action: 9–10 March 1943
Sinking of Puerto Rican and Richard Bland, RA53

(See Map 1)
GMT + 1

When a country is attacked, but is no longer facing extinction partly because of its successful utilization of foreign military aid against its supporters' common foe, it is tempting for it to regard the assistance from its allies which was at first regarded as a favour as more akin to a right.

That perhaps explains the Soviet ambassador Maisky's complaint to British Foreign Secretary Anthony Eden in January 1943 – even after it became known that Soviet troops were well on the way to winning a great victory at Stalingrad – that Churchill was not honouring his promise to send 30-ship Arctic convoys to Russia in both January and February 1943.

The complaint prompted Churchill to write to Eden on 9 January 1943: 'Monsieur Maisky is not telling the truth when he says I promised Stalin convoys of 30 ships in January and February. The only promise I have made is contained in my telegram of December 29 [1942] (it stated there would be 'a full convoy of 30 . . . ships . . . in January').[1]

'Maisky should be told that I am getting to the end of my tether with these repeated Russian naggings, and that it is not the slightest use trying to knock me about any more.'[2]

The next day Churchill sent a telegram to Stalin referring to 'the fine engagement fought by our light forces against heavy odds' in order to fight through the December convoy. It continued: 'Since it is clear from the experience of the last convoy that the enemy means to dispute the passage of further convoys by surface forces, it will be necessary immediately to increase our escorts beyond the scale originally contemplated for January . . . We have therefore had to revise our arrangements . . .'

Churchill went on to say that instead of running the January convoy in two parts, there would be one convoy of 19 ships on 17 January 1943, with another leaving on around 11 February consisting of 28–30 ships. Britain would also do her best to send a third convoy in March.[3]

As it turned out, Churchill's concern that the kind of attacks seen during JW51B might be repeated was not borne out in relation to any of the east or west-going Arctic convoys that sailed in January and February 1943, all of which eventually made their passage for one reason or another with significantly fewer ships than the 30 demanded by Maisky.[4] Efforts by U-boat crews to make their mark on these well-defended convoys were only rewarded with the sinking of one merchant ship, which was torpedoed by *U-255* on 3 February 1943 during the west-going RA52. This was in contrast to the U-boats' better fortunes against Soviet ships travelling independently between Russia and Iceland (during January 1943 U-boats sank two Soviet merchant ships and one icebreaker, the latter and one of the former also being a victim of the above and below-mentioned *U-255*).[5]

Notwithstanding the better than expected convoy balance sheet, there was evidently rising concern in America at the prospect that their boys might be put off signing up for the Merchant Marine on account of all the sinkings. In an attempt to boost morale, Russell Riddell, a 28-year-old American who had made it back home to Los Angeles having survived the sinking of *Syros* during convoy PQ16, was asked to appear in a series of scripted radio shows, giving him the chance to demonstrate that being sunk on a merchant ship was not by any means the end of the road. It would not have hurt the appeal of the Merchant Marine's reputation that during the final programme, broadcast on 2 February 1943, Riddell was interviewed by an admiring Ginny Simms, a glamorous actress and singer billed by the presenter as 'the sweetheart of Uncle Sam's Armed forces', reflecting her penchant for entertaining the troops. In the course of the interview, which was full of banter about whether 'Russ's' wife was going to rule the roost at his home, and about how he was 'just fine', and was smiling in spite of the fact that as Ginny Simms put it 'an enemy of democracy has blown his ship from under him', he was able to slip in that it was all worth it because it was helping the Russians. 'There's nobody can ever lick 'em. They're great!' he concluded.[6]

There were certainly no shortage of Americans for the first 30-ship Arctic convoy following Maisky's complaint. The west-going convoy, RA53, was predominantly American. It set out from Murmansk on 1 March 1943 (see Note 7 for composition).[7]

Complacency among the officers in the beefed-up number of escorts for this convoy – 13 destroyers, 4 corvettes and 2 trawlers plus anti-aircraft cruiser *Scylla* – was so high, possibly because of their apparent invincibility on the way out to Russia, that an initial claim made by a lookout in one of the merchant ships that there were U-boats about was discounted. The senior officer of the 3rd Destroyer Flotilla in the destroyer *Milne* noted: 'Whales had been encountered in this vicinity with J.W. 53, and no great credence was given to this report . . .'[8]

However the whale enthusiasts, after observing the 'noise' made by the communications between the crews in the five U-boats which were tracking the convoy, as well as the circlings of the Ju 88 and Blohm & Voss reconnaissance aircraft on the horizon, had long since eaten their words by the time the convoy, having passed south of Bear Island, reached the area south-west of Bear Island on 5 March.[9]

Shortly after 8 a.m. that morning, U-255's Kapitänleutnant Reinhart Reche, who by this time had one of the best records for a U-boat commander in the Arctic (as well as the sinkings mentioned above, his vessel had sunk three PQ17 ships, plus one during QP14), took action that led to his writing in his war diary: 'Submerged for the attack.' The entry carried on: 'After [going past] a destroyer a long way in front [of the merchant ships], come to the ring of close escorts. [Behind them] the columns of steamers are quite close together which does not leave me much room to turn. At the front of the middle column there is [another] destroyer. I will go for the steamer behind this destroyer.'

Then beside the entry for 9.26 a.m. he wrote: 'I fire three shots one after the other . . . The last ship [fired at] was very close . . .' (see Note 10 for location).[10]

The sight of *U-255*'s torpedoes speeding through the water towards the starboard side of American Hog Islander SS *Executive*, tucked in at position 52 (5th column, row 2), a mere 600 metres away from the U-boat according to Reche's calculation, resulted in a commotion: first there were six blasts on the steam whistle of the second ship in the convoy's sixth column to warn her compatriot; this was followed by the rat-tat-tat-tat of two machine guns fired by *Executive*'s Armed Guard in an attempt to destroy the fast approaching missile within the 40-odd seconds it took to travel from *U-255* to their ship. *Executive*'s 3rd Mate quickly shouted out 'hard left rudder!'

However, all was in vain. One of the torpedoes hit the starboard area of *Executive*'s hull between her No. 4 hatch and the engine room. The subsequent explosion threw two men overboard, killed the three men on watch down below, put out all lights in the ship and stopped the engines.[11]

Around 30 seconds later one of the other torpedoes fired from Reche's boat slammed into the starboard side of the No. 1 hold in *Richard Bland*, the Liberty ship in position 42 (4th column, row 2), on *Executive*'s left, before exploding.[12] Reche had come up trumps for the Germans once again.

Back on *Executive*, it seemed imperative that she needed to be abandoned quickly. She was settling and had developed a list to starboard. But prompt action turned out to be counter-productive. Gordon McAllister, the 1st Mate, described in his report how 'as soon as . . . boat [no. 4] was waterborne [with a few men on board], due to the excessive way upon the ship, and the hard left rudder, the boat sheered away from the ship's side [and] two men were lost as they attempted to enter the boat by going down the life lines.'

He also described how boat no. 2 'suffered a disastrous accident': its weight tore out the forward davit and the boat ended up lying upside down in the water. Of the five men who had been in it, only three were recovered.[13]

Tragically one of those lost had almost swum to a ladder running down the side of the ship when according to another report he 'let go of the lifeline and floated out of reach'.[14] All told, nine lives were lost, six unnecessarily. Although *Executive*'s after deck was awash when she was abandoned, the ship remained obstinately afloat even after being 'attacked' by an escort.[15]

By way of contrast, although the rush of water flooding into *Richard Bland*'s No. 1 hold had led to her bows sinking deeper into the water and the propellers at her stern almost coming out of it, slowing her down, reallocation of oil and water to different tanks rectified the situation sufficiently so that she was able to continue and catch up with the convoy. That was notwithstanding the one-inch-wide crack across the exterior main deck just forward of the flooded No. 3 hold which was the most worrying consequence of the explosion.[16]

Richard Bland's crew could just about cope with the other damage. The force of the explosion of the torpedo that had entered No. 1 hold from the starboard side appears to have been increased through coming into contact with that hold's cargo (relatively light arctic spruce lumber) with the result that as well as putting the 12 pounder gun up on deck at the front of the ship out of action, a hole was blasted in the port side of the ship, and the resulting semi-dislodged 4 foot square piece of the ship's hull plating was left sticking out. This acted as a kind of brake, not to mention its effect as an obstacle to normal steering.

However William Carter, who had travelled to Russia in Arctic convoy PQ17 as *Ironclad*'s Armed Guard commander, and who was going back to Iceland as a working passenger in *Richard Bland*, noticed how as she straggled behind the convoy during the heavy, force 8, gale blowing the next morning, 'the break in the main deck and down both sides began to open and shut as the ship rode over the . . . waves. Looking down from above, as we rode over a wave, the sides of the break in the main deck plating would separate as much as three inches. Then when we crossed over the trough, with a wave at each end putting upward pressure on our bow and stern, the edges of the crack would close. Sometimes . . . the edges would slide past each other. This was accompanied by a horrific noise that sounded like it came directly from the nether regions, and it caused the whole ship to convulse with a great shudder.'

Given the increasing size of the waves due to the foul weather and the fact that *Richard Bland* had straggled so much there was not another ship in sight, it is not surprising to learn that Carter as well as the majority of the crew believed they were doomed. 'We recognized we were beyond any reasonable possibility of help, even from the Almighty,' he would write later.[17]

Whether such calm resignation would have prevailed had they known the future fate of *JLM Curry*, another Liberty ship that had sailed with the convoy, is open to question. She had to be abandoned south-east of Jan Mayen Island on 8 March when the rough seas cracked her from upper deck to water line.[18]

The failure to rapidly round up the other stragglers after the gale force winds had moderated was to lead to the sinking of two more of the convoy's ships. The American *Puerto Rican* was some way behind the convoy, when at around 10 p.m. on 9 March, she was struck by a torpedo on the starboard side of her No. 5 hold which had been fired from *U-586* (see Note 19 for location analysis which puts the torpedoing probably some 100 miles, but possibly some 200 miles, north-east of Seidisfjord).[19]

August Wallenhaupt, the 26-year-old fireman who ended up being the only survivor, explained afterwards how at first there was no panic. 'I was in my bunk at the time with my clothes on . . . Lights went out when we were hit, but almost immediately were back on. Crew mustered at their stations in good order.'

However, as Wallenhaupt would explain, it was then that the problems started: 'Due to severe weather and ice coated conditions of boat deck, life boats, boat falls and equipment, we were able to lower away and launch but one boat.'[20] He later confirmed that the boats were frozen solid under up to 18 inches of ice, and the men had no tools to enable them to crack it. The men near each boat resorted to hurling themselves like human battering rams against the solid mass, sometimes shouting 'One-two-three' before two or more launched themselves simultaneously at it while taking care not to slip on the icy deck. Although some of the men had flashlights, much of this desperate action took place in the dark.

'It was like ramming your shoulder against the Empire State Building and expecting it to fall,' Wallenhaupt reported later.

He was fortunate in having been detailed to go to lifeboat no. 4, the rear boat on the ship's port side, because eventually around ten minutes after the torpedo struck, the ramming paid dividends and the ice restraining this boat gave way as he put it like 'the way a frozen tray breaks loose in an ice box'.[21]

The boat full of men was then lowered with Wallenhaupt, as pre-arranged during training, fending the boat away from the ship's side. But releasing its falls after the boat reached the water was another matter. Probably because of the ice, the after fall could not be released, and as a result when *Puerto Rican* sank, the boat which was still attached to her capsized.

'I threw myself . . . out of the boat,' Wallenhaupt reported, 'and . . . swam to a cork doughnut type life raft.' There he was joined by six other men from the capsized boat.[22]

All but one of the men on the raft were wrapped up in heavy coats, but none had put on the kind of rubber suit that Wallenhaupt was also wearing.[23] 'I had on heavy underwear, trousers, two pair[s] of heavy socks and two sweaters, and the rubber suit which gave great protection,' he would later confirm.[24] This was in marked contrast with one of the rescued men, an oiler, who, as was often the case for those seamen coming up from warm places such as boiler or engine rooms, was dressed in a relatively skimpy pair of dungarees over a denim shirt and not much else.

Not that even the warmest of coats was going to save them if they were on the raft for a long time. Water sloshed up between the lattice work which constituted its base so that those sitting in it were still for much of the time as good as sitting in up to two feet of icy cold water.

Shortly after they reached the raft, a more substantial wooden raft drifted in their direction. After he grabbed hold of it, Wallenhaupt allowed the five men who were still capable to clamber over his body onto it before he in his turn followed them. The other two had already expired.

At least they were out of the water, which was more than could be said for the rest of the crew, most of whom appear to have either gone down with the ship or to have not been able to get out of the water following the boat capsizing. At any rate Wallenhaupt did not see many of the crew after *Puerto Rican*'s disappearance. 'I saw one other raft of this type afloat after the vessel sank,' Wallenhaupt recalled. 'I [also] saw about ten men clinging to [the] upturned lifeboat.'[25]

During the night the six survivors huddled together in the centre of the wooden raft in a futile attempt to keep warm. Every so often water from the 30-foot-high waves swept over the raft's surface, causing the men to tumble in a heap on one side of it. Then began the process of seeing how the freezing cold weeded out the weakest of the men, who were either washed overboard in pairs or one by one.

Wallenhaupt would later dwell on how he battled to save one of the men who, after being swept overboard, managed to cling on to ropes attached to the raft. Wallenhaupt helped hold him in place by hooking his arms through the half-submerged man's. 'His eyes were only about ten inches from mine and we kept looking at each other,' Wallenhaupt remembered. 'His were sort of glazed, and he looked at me as though he wasn't really seeing me. Then he said: "Gee Auggie, can't you please help me?" I said, "I'm sorry, I can't do a thing." Then his strength gave out, and he slipped away.'[26]

While these terrible events were unfolding, *Richard Bland* was still some way behind the nucleus of the convoy, even though the convoy's commodore during the early afternoon of 10 March had decreed the bulk of RA53 must wait until the weather cleared before continuing southward down the east coast of Iceland. This was the route RA53 was to take before heading south-eastward towards its ultimate destination, Scotland's Loch Ewe.[27] *Richard Bland* had against all expectations of those aboard survived the great gale, and had reached the area around 35 miles away to the north-east of Langanes, the peninsula which juts out from the north-east tip of Iceland.

Making it through the storm was just one of the challenges the American Liberty ship had passed with flying colours. On her journey westward, she had passed through what *Ironclad*'s William Carter referred to as 'huge blocks of floating ice . . . as far as the eye could see'.[28] They had been broken off the ice edge by the storm, and while *Richard Bland* was in their midst, there had been a fear that one of them, driven towards the ship by the large waves, might puncture the ship's hull just as effectively as any U-boat's torpedo.

It was extremely disappointing therefore when, having made it past the drift ice without further damage, shortly after 4.30 p.m. on 10 March, their progress westward, and the peace Carter was at last enjoying on the ship's bridge, were interrupted by the lookout shouting out: 'Periscope on the port quarter!' (See Note 29 for location.)[29]

'I ran to the port wing of the bridge,' he wrote later, 'and just as I threw my binoculars up to my eyes, a torpedo exploded on the port side, just abaft the engine room in number four hold.'[30]

It was a killer blow, because with her engines no longer working courtesy of the explosion, two of her lifeboats out of reach (they had floated away when launched after the torpedo had hit the ship), and because of the list to port, her most powerful gun (the 4-inch gun mounted aft) unable to take on the circling U-boat, *Richard Bland* and those on board had been left in a kind of hellish limbo. She wallowed helplessly in the heavy sea, her lookouts' vision dimmed by the intermittent falls of snow, at the mercy of the lurking U-boat unless another ship intervened in response to *Richard Bland*'s transmitted SOS.

Although by 1943 the armed guard on board American merchant ships such as *Richard Bland* were being routinely equipped with up to eight 20 mm Oerlikon machine guns, which were generally acknowledged to be much more effective than the smaller calibre machine guns relied on previously, the new guns' range was restricted to around 1,000 yards (less than two-thirds of a mile). That made them a menace for German aircraft diving down to attack a convoy – as had been proved when they were instrumental in warding off the German bombers that had moved in on the convoy on 5 March, but of less worth against a U-boat, which could unleash torpedoes from a distance that made them impervious to the Oerlikons' defensive fire.[31]

Richard Bland's crew did not have to wait long before the U-boat, none other than Reche's *U-255* which had torpedoed the ship five days earlier, struck again. This time the single torpedo, fired some three hours after the first 'fan' of three that had been spat out earlier that afternoon, hit the starboard side of the ship beside the engine room below the bridge.[32] According to Carter, who at the time was standing on the open starboard wing of the bridge, 'a mass of flames' came roaring up from below decks, creating a barrier between the starboard and port sides of both the wheelhouse near where he was standing and the boat deck one level below. Shortly afterwards he saw that the vessel's structure by the crack just in front of the bridge had finally given way, and that the ship had broken into two parts.

Fortunately for him, by the time he noticed this, Carter had somehow been able to make it through the flames to the port side of the boat deck on the stern section, which was gradually sinking forward end first as the front section of the ship floated off. He was hoping to catch a lift in one of the two port side boats, which had not been launched after the first torpedo hit a few hours earlier. However, at first sight his prospects of getting away did not look very promising. When he reached the port side of the boat deck, he was dismayed to see that the forward boat was hanging down vertically from its forward davit.

After descending to the main deck, he saw the men who, as he would later describe it in his memoir, 'had been dumped out of the forward life-boat' into the water. Given that the sea temperature was a crippling -2 °C, so cold that the snow that had been falling had formed a kind of sludge on the surface of the water, this was evidently a fatal accident for anyone not picked up quickly.[33] His memoir continues: 'Now mostly inert bodies, they all floated face upward. This was a safety feature designed into our life preservers, that upon becoming immobile, a body automatically turned its face up to enable breathing and prevent drowning . . . This had been demonstrated by a swimmer, with strokes slowing to a final halt, face down in the water, then turning face up . . . It was a horrible thing to see happen to a shipmate, and I thanked the Lord that the failing daylight depersonalized the picture.'[34]

He thanked the Lord even more profusely after he managed to find a place in the rear port lifeboat, the last to be launched, and saw some of the crew in the sea beside it who had not been able to get in.

'There were two men hanging to the side [of the boat] by me,' Carter recalled in his official report. 'I tried twice to get them into the boat, but their clothing was so heavy, and the boat so crowded, that three of us were unable to haul them over the side. We held on to them as long as there was any use to hold on . . .'[35]

But he reserved his most heartfelt praise so that it might pay tribute to Wayne Baker, an armed guard who had served under Carter in *Ironclad* during PQ17. On seeing that the lifeboat was full, Baker refused to jump down into it in spite of being encouraged to do so by those already aboard. Instead he pulled out his sheaf knife, and helped to cut through the tangle of lines linking the boat to the ship, thereby ensuring the boat was clear of *Richard Bland* before she sank.

'Baker went down with the ship, preferring to sacrifice his own life rather than risk swamping the boat and costing the lives of 27 other men. I was among the men whose lives were saved by Baker's magnificent self-sacrifice,' Carter reported afterwards.[36] Baker would later be awarded the Navy and Marine Corps Medal, the highest American award for non-combat heroism.[37]

Richard Bland's chief engineer was also begged to jump, and was witnessed 'limping along . . . unable to do so because of infirmities. He must have been 70 years old or more,' wrote another witness. Perhaps it was him who the same witness saw 'standing erect on the sinking stern section . . . as the section made its final plunge.'[38]

Carter and his companions only had to endure one night in the boat. At around 7.30 a.m. the next day HMS *Impulsive*, one of two destroyers sent back from the convoy to look for them following the receipt of *Richard Bland*'s SOS, turned up and spotted their flashlight. Because the two other lifeboats that had been launched were also found, 35 of the 69 who had been on board *Richard Bland* were rescued.[39]

But those searching had still not found evidence that there were any *Puerto Rican*'s survivors even though they believed they had identified the location where the ship had gone down. Within hours of receiving *Puerto Rican*'s SOS, during the night of 9–10 March, the convoy's trawler *St Elstan* had passed by a waterlogged boat near a large oil slick before heading for home (see Note 40 for location).[40]

That condemned Wallenhaupt to a second and a third night on the raft. There was eventually only one other man with him. This other man was lying face down on the raft's wooden planks, his hair matted with ice. But when Wallenhaupt attempted to rouse him by nudging the recumbent man's head with his elbow, it became clear that the head was attached by ice to the raft. So was the rest of his body. The man had passed away.

Nevertheless the corpse's presence continued to help Wallenhaupt, who was protected from the bitter wind when he sheltered behind it. 'I didn't think of him as a dead human,' he would say later. '"It" was something frozen . . . something like a piece of earth or an anchor. By this time he was covered with at least ten . . . inches of solid ice.'[41]

On 12 March, which would turn out to be his last day on the raft, Wallenhaupt began to hear what sounded to him like other people speaking.

The only way he could drown out the voices was by praying, which he did repeatedly. That explains why, when at around 7 p.m. on that day, he heard the words 'Hello there!' again and again, he thought nothing of it.

But this time someone really was there. *Ironclad*'s William Carter happened to be watching when the destroyer *Impulsive*, with him aboard, approached Wallenhaupt's raft. 'It looked like it had been in the water for a long time,' Carter wrote afterwards. 'There were . . . piles of ice on the surface of the raft that we all assumed to be bodies. After making an asdic search all around and finding it clear of subs, *Impulsive* stopped beside the raft, and [a] . . . bosun's mate hooked the far side with a small grapnel hook to hold the raft against the side of the ship . . . Other bosun's mates held the raft steady with boat hooks . . . One of the . . . hooks happened to hit the raft within inches of the nearest of the . . . piles of ice, and "the ice" started moving . . . A bare hand reached out and grabbed the wooden handle . . . and started trying to pull upright the body to which the hand was attached . . . For me . . . it was akin to a religious experience. I saw an apparently dead body come alive.'[42]

Seconds later two men from *Impulsive* were fastening ropes around their own bodies and climbing down to the raft to help the man who was of course Wallenhaupt. Ropes were then attached to him, and with assistance from men on the ship's deck, he was finally lifted aboard.

The next he knew he was in the ship's sickbay being given sips of hot Bovril and water, and a shot of morphine. He was going to need that as the circulation came back into his limbs, if it did come back. His hands which were white from frostbite were terribly swollen. They were wrapped up in towels.

Later after arriving in Reykjavik, Iceland, Wallenhaupt was transferred to a US Army hospital, where his legs were hoisted on pulleys high above his head to stop the circulation returning too quickly.[43] But several weeks later, one of the doctors said to him: 'Wally, we're going to take 'em off tomorrow.' He had been expecting it, and was just hoping they would be able to save his hands.

He was given a spinal anaesthetic, but before he fell asleep, he felt the vibration of the electric saw. And when he awoke, his legs were gone, and so were all the fingers on his right hand down to the knuckles except for the thumb, and he had also lost all but one finger and his thumb on his left hand.[44]

But at least he had survived, making him the sole survivor out of the 65 men who had been in *Puerto Rican*.[45]

August Wallenhaupt's rescue represented the last momentous event linked to RA53's passage. The rest of the convoy reached Icelandic ports or the sea area adjacent to Iceland's coast between 10 and 12 March.[46] Even the forward part of *Richard Bland* reached home territory, being pulled in to Heradsfloi (Héraðsflói), a bay to the north of Iceland's Seidis-fjord, on 16 March.[47] The convoy's main body of 20 ships reached Loch Ewe, Scotland on 14 March.[48]

35

Culture Clash

Main Action: March–August 1943
Crackdown in Archangel

On 30 March 1943, Churchill wrote to Stalin: 'It is a great disappointment to President Roosevelt and myself that it should be necessary to postpone the March convoy ... We should hope to resume convoys in early September.'

The reasons cited by Churchill in his telegram for the suspension were that in addition to the scheduled offensive operations by Britain and America during the summer in the Mediterranean (in the first instance Operation Husky, the plan to invade Sicily), and alarming shipping losses sustained by the Western allies in the Atlantic: 'The Germans have concentrated at Narvik a powerful battle fleet consisting of *Tirpitz*, *Scharnhorst*, *Lützow*, one 6-inch cruiser and 8 destroyers. Thus the danger to the Russian convoys which I described in my message to you of July 17 last year have been revived in even more menacing form.'[1] There was no explicit reference to the fact that because of the final Soviet victory at Stalingrad, which had been sealed during the last days of January 1943, the supplying of aid was now less urgent, but one suspects that this cannot have been far from Churchill's thoughts.

Churchill however, realized that his decision would be a bitter blow for the Soviets, even though he was telling Stalin that the Americans would try to increase aid sent via the Pacific to Vladivostok, and that by August 1943 it was possible that monthly aid sent via the Persian Gulf would rise to 240,000 tons, an eightfold rise since the same time the previous year, exceeding the amount of aid that could be transported in a large Arctic convoy (a typical 30-ship convoy could be expected to carry some 180,000 tons). 'Will it mean a split with Stalin?' he nevertheless nervously asked Soviet Ambassador Maisky when they met the next day.[2] He was astonished and delighted therefore when Stalin's 2 April reply was relatively restrained.[3] Stalin said the decision was 'catastrophic' because 'transport via Pacific is limited . . . and southern route has a small transit capacity' but left it at that.[4]

But although on this occasion there was no immediate conflict between the countries' leaders, the Russians would find other ways to make their displeasure known: it would surface in the ratcheting up of the more nuanced struggle that was already being fought on the ground in the northern Russian ports, which was the main flashpoint where, when talking about the Allies, East met West.

If one leaves aside the irritation felt by the Russians due to the suspension of the convoys, and the other overarching reason for Russian exasperation with the West – the failure by the Western allies to open a second front – the clash in the northern Russian ports, which principally came to the fore in Archangel, appears to have been sparked off by two main causes.

The first was the Archangel local authorities' fear that their citizens' support for communism would tail off if contacts between ordinary Russians and the foreign forces in their midst went unchecked. Ever since the Arctic convoys started, there had been rumours that far from coming merely to provide aid, the British were intending to take over the city of Archangel, just as this had been attempted in 1918–19 after the communist Revolution during what was known as 'the North Russia intervention'. A report about the perceived ongoing threat compiled by Vsevolod Merkulov, the head of the People's Commisariat for State Security (the NKGB: Narodnyy komissariat gosudarstvennoy bezopasnosti), which would eventually end up on Stalin's and Molotov's desks, stated: 'Most of the people who spread the rumour pointed out that if the British did take over the Soviet North, their quality of life would be improved, shops would reopen and goods would be imported again.'[5]

It was regarded as being all the more dangerous because among those alleged to have been rumour-spreaders was Captain Guy Maund, the

SBNO Archangel. He, like many of those serving long term in Archangel with a view to administering the convoys and showing the Russians how to use the supplied aid, had a ready-made conduit into Russian homes given that notwithstanding the known Russian antipathy to relationships between Russians and foreigners, he had a Russian girlfriend.

Perhaps even more insidious from the Russian point of view was the second major concern voiced by Merkulov: that Russians' contact with relatively rich foreigners might tempt the citizens in Archangel to hand over state secrets. This was all the more likely, he pointed out, because: 'The British are able to ingratiate themselves with the local population by handing out tempting little gifts.'

It is necessary to appreciate what life was like for the majority of Allied seamen in Archangel during 1942–43 to understand what can perhaps best be described as this Russian paranoia. A diary written by Billie Moore, a young steward from the armed trawler *Daneman,* whose ship had docked in Solombala, the Archangel satellite port, after arriving in Russia with PQ18, is indicative. It reveals that if anyone had anything to fear from Allied seamen being allowed ashore, it was the visitors.

According to Moore, before he and his shipmates were allowed to take the ten-minute ride on a ferry from Solombala to Archangel, the captain 'assembled the crew . . . and warned them against the danger of (Russian) women – and the Russian wine called "Vodka" which is 50 per cent deadly poison to English people.' They were also told to watch out for pickpockets, which was lucky because no sooner had they arrived in the city than they were surrounded by a pack of Russian urchins, and he felt hands burrowing into his pockets. Another man who failed to take appropriate precautions during a later visit was less fortunate. He felt a sting in one of his buttocks. One of the children who had been jostling him had cut him with a razor blade while trying to get at what was in his trouser pocket.

It would have been clear to any of the visitors that there was a reason why there were so few young men about, leaving the way open for the crowds of boys to roam the streets without constraint. There was no chance of any of the Allied seamen not realizing that most of the 'missing' young men were at the front, and that the Red Army was leading the way in the fighting, because as Moore noted: 'there are loud speakers [attached to] every lamp post, and the natives hear news and music from 5 am to 11 pm when the broadcast finishes with . . . the Red Flag . . . the Russian national anthem.'

Because Moore's ship remained tied up at Solombala for two months, there would be plenty of scope to sample many other facets of Archangel life that would put him on his guard. The children who had at first tried to buy the sailors' chocolate and cigarettes soon switched to offering the same amount of roubles for a slice of bread. Hunger was obviously a major issue for many Archangel citizens. Many of the Russians Moore encountered were starving metaphorically if not literally. This had a marked effect on the average Russian's behaviour. All of a sudden all Russians started to demand food instead of money for services rendered. Moore was particularly impressed by the action of one 'young lady' who boarded *Daneman* to have lunch with the trawler's sailors. 'It must have been hunger that drove her down our mess decks into a crowd of lads,' he commented. That was the least of it. It was no secret that when a Russian died, there was a temptation to keep the frozen corpse in the loft, so that the family could carry on having access to the dead person's rations.

Such coping mechanisms became all the more prevalent as the temperatures experienced in and around Archangel plunged. During the summer Archangel could be compared to a ski resort off season. There was no snow to cover up the roads which for the most part consisted of wooden planks nailed to a raised wooden foundation. Only Archangel's main street was cobbled using granite slabs laid in sand. The pavements also consisted of planks of wood, and most of the houses outside the city centre were also wooden. During the summer the main inconveniences for the visitors stemmed from the unexpected number of mosquitoes, and the unpleasant smell which hung over the city because of the primitive toilets.

All this would change during the winter. By November 1942 the temperature was hovering around minus 10° Celsius. The river Dvina froze, and it became so cold that minutes after an icebreaker vessel had cut a pathway through the ice, the exposed water would freeze over again, enabling the locals who had stopped to allow the ship to pass to walk over the reformed ice. This presented Allied seamen such as Moore who wanted to go from Solombala to the city with a dilemma. They either had to stay on their ship and be bored, or to take their lives in their hands along with locals and walk to Archangel across the ice. If they chose the latter option, it was a bit like playing Russian roulette. Some of *Daneman's* crew told Moore that they had seen a young woman drown after she fell through the ice. 'They say the screams were terrible,' he wrote. 'One of the lads was going to rescue her but five men held him back. I suppose they just think it was one less to feed.'

If only the local authorities had seen all this through the likes of Moore's eyes, they might have been less on edge. They might for example have listened to the Allied officers who were worried that their men were being driven into contracting a venereal disease through sleeping with Russian women because there were not enough leisure activities laid on. Instead the Russian leaders saw risks where there were none. Pavel Malkov, the head of the Archangel NKVD (Narodnyy komissariat vnutrennikh del – Commissariat for Internal Affairs) at one point made a speech complaining that the British seamen were taking photographs of the street children as they 'queued up' with wads of rouble notes to buy the chocolate and cigarettes they were being offered so that the images could be published along with critical comments about Russia in English newspapers.

This comment appears to have been provoked by the Archangel authorities' third great concern resulting from the presence of foreign seamen in their city: that if their citizens' behaviour and standard of life did not match what the visitors expected to find in a civilized community, communism – and Russia – would be shown up on the world stage, leading at best to reduced respect and at worst to loss of influence and less good treatment. The authorities' dislike of the way the foreigners apparently looked down on them was only increased by the natural humiliation that any normal man experiences when he senses another person does not see him as an equal.

This sense that the foreigners did not respect Russians was in evidence from the moment British seamen (submariners) first appeared in Archangel. As early as mid-August 1941, the starving Filadelf Parshinky (last referred to in Chapter 26) was referring in his diary to 'a rumour they are going round our shops and are laughing at the sight of the empty shop windows and shelves.' It was obvious that nothing had changed when two years later, a Russian naval officer complained to a British lieutenant: 'It's a pity you don't salute us. But you obviously have a low opinion of us. You see us at our worst, when privation and hunger have reduced the morals of some of our people.'

Not that the Russian officer believed his opposite numbers in the West really were superior. He assumed that the smart uniforms worn by Western naval officers, and the Western cigarettes they smoked did not reflect what they had access to in London and New York, but were just produced in Russia as propaganda to show the Westerners and their political beliefs in a good light.

Based on what he had seen of the visiting seamen, he was able to assure his interlocutor that he was sure that the Soviet education system was better than anything on offer in Britain and America: witness the fact that, as he put it, 'your ratings indulge in vodka and women as soon as they come to a new port, whilst our ratings would go to inspect the museums and sights of a new town.' But notwithstanding the protestations about Russian superiority, it was clear that there was resentment at the way Russians were regarded by the foreign seamen, and anxiety it might not be to Russia's advantage.

These and other fears would fester as time passed. On 3 July 1943, at a time when there was growing tension at both high and low levels of Soviet government and society over the ongoing failure by the Allies to contribute in a meaningful way to the war effort – the Allies were still not sending aid via the northern ports let alone opening a second front – a series of strident anti-foreigner statements were made at a meeting of the bureau of Archangel's Communist Party committee headed by Georgii Ogorodnikov, the First Secretary of the Archangel region's Communist Party (the region's leader). One statement contained the chilling diktat that henceforth it should be a given that anyone with close links with the Western allies' seamen and representatives in Archangel 'was liable to disclose a lot of information that is secret'.

At this meeting the point was also made that the number of communists and *komsomol* (Communist youth) members with foreign acquaintances in the city was increasing, proof that the 'required vigilance to stop such contacts had slackened'. This trend was now to be reversed – subject to one major exception.[6]

The exception is hinted at in a report on NKVD activity in Archangel written by a British naval officer, who was a member of the British naval mission based in the town. The report confirms that Russian women in the city were being permitted to have relationships with foreign naval officers and seamen if this facilitated the attempt to extract valuable intelligence from Western sources.[7] However this relaxation of the general practice following the crackdown decision, the latter being aimed at stopping Russians from having intimate relationships with foreigners, came with strings attached. The report also makes it clear that once the NKVD had a woman acting under its control, there was no way out. One woman, whose dealings with the NKVD are profiled, was given in the words of the report: 'specific instructions how she was to behave with her English friend (a British Army interpreter), and she was to report at regular intervals. Moreover, she was warned on no account to tell him about the interrogation or of her future task.' The report then relates how when she told the NKVD she had decided to stop seeing the man, and that she wanted to leave Archangel, 'she was refused a visa to leave town; she was ordered to remain in Archangel and not break up the friendship.' Subsequently, the report continues, she was interrogated 'on a number of occasions' about what he said to her.'

The NKVD were to prove equally determined when it came to bringing to fruition the main aims of the crackdown. They appeared to believe there was no better way of starting to roll back the foreigners' infiltration into Russian society than by targeting those young Russian women in Archangel and Molotovsk who were willing to take the foreign seamen into their beds. Whether it was principally the physical attributes of the seamen which appealed to the women, or the fact that making the acquaintance of such men gave the women access to the food and products these sailors brought with them, which were otherwise unattainable in wartime Russia, the Arctic convoy sailors could hardly have been more popular in Archangel among a certain section of what was then referred to as the weaker sex. These women crowded around the foreign seamen in the parts of the city the foreigners frequented regularly like bees around a honeypot. They did this notwithstanding the well known danger, even before the crackdown, that contact with foreigners which went beyond providing a legitimate service could lead to complications if the NKVD intervened. Under cover NKVD agents were to be found lurking in every institution where the foreign seaman came into contact with Russians, including in the Archangel interclub, the Intourist hotel and theatre. Knowledge that this was the case had deterred a substantial proportion of the White Sea ports' populations from having such relationships.

But because the NKVD's enforcement of the no relationships with foreigners 'rule' (there was no explicit prohibition) even after the start of the crackdown was so patchy, apparently because it gave Malkov's men the opportunity to use as informers the women who slept with the seamen, the women who believed the rewards made the risk of having such relationships worth taking, carried on as before.

It was to be these women who would be amongst the first targets of the crackdown even though, as those Russians who moved in the right circles well knew, the foreigners consorting with them would also be affected indirectly. Those in authority in Archangel would not have been short of intelligence confirming that if local women were willing, the Arctic convoy seamen would not be able to resist the bait. According to reports written by a Mr Gluzman, the NKVD appointed manager of the Archangel Interclub, and by virtue of that position, as well informed as any other Russian when it came to assessing the Arctic convoy seamen's characters and behaviour, a substantial proportion of the British and American seamen in particular were 'uneducated . . . semi, or completely, illiterate . . . social outcasts', whose principal reason for joining the Merchant Navy in the first place was to earn a lot of money. However, as Gluzman pointed out, while away from home, it was alcohol that the foreign seamen valued most. Many seamen, Gluzman said, were 'prepared to hand over all their possessions to get it', and once they had it, they not only behaved like vandals, but were susceptible to the charms of Russian women, who were next on their shopping list.[8]

The Arctic convoy seamen were never paragons of virtue. But their bad behaviour was to become worse, making it all the more objectionable in the eyes of their Soviet hosts, after the suspension of the convoys following the arrival at the end of February and the beginning of March 1943 of the ships forming part of the February 1943 convoy (JW53). This was because many of the sailors were stuck in Russia for a long time with nothing constructive to occupy them.[9] It was on account of these men being marooned in Russia for so many months, that JW53 acquired its nickname 'the forgotten convoy'.

Gluzman found the British sailors' behaviour particularly galling. In one report he wrote: 'The British are arrogant . . . They think they are the most civilized people in the world.'[10] Yet as he pointed out in another report, they did everything possible to sabotage his attempts to ensure the club remained a class act where the seamen could be indoctrinated as much as possible with Russian propaganda. According to his report, 'Most of the foreign seamen behave as if they are in a capitalistic pub or club where the owner is motivated by the desire to keep his customers happy. For example they refuse to leave their coats and rubber boots in the cloakroom; they smoke in areas where this is prohibited . . .; they drink alcoholic drinks in the club (which was not allowed); they walk around and talk when films are being shown; they lie down full length on the sofas, and put their feet up on chairs. . .'

Even before the crackdown was accepted by the Communist Party committee, the NKVD's Malkov began to issue a string of charges against those women who were profiteering by acquiring products from the foreign seamen and then selling them at sky high prices in the Archangel and Molotovsk markets.

The charge sheets for some of the women who were prosecuted in this way are still to be found in Archangel's archives. They make for painful reading. Many of the women were lonely, having lost their husbands in the war. Some were supporting children. Others had contributed to the war effort by working as locksmiths, wagon greasers or in factories. All of them appeared to be in such a dire state financially that they would do almost anything to get their hands on the products supplied by the foreigners which would transform their lives if sold at high enough prices on the black market.

Yet it was these same pitiful women who were accused in batches, using such similar, formulaic wording that it seems likely that the iniquity of their actions, even judged by Soviet standards, may well never have been fully explored. The following extracts from one of the charge and punishment summaries issued in July 1943 in relation to one of the women, provides a sample of the kind of accusations levelled at all of them: 'She organized a den of debauchery'; 'she spent the night with foreigners'; 'the fee is cigarettes, soap and different products'; 'she sold them in the market at exorbitant prices'; 'evicted to Lensky district (some 500 miles east of Archangel's city centre) until the end of the war'.

The charge sheet for the woman in question, first name Anastasia, is representative of what is to be found in many of the accusations levelled against these women. It gives one a sense of how she and the others came to fall on hard times, and how they came into contact with the seamen. She had been born 30 years previously in Kramatorsk in the Donetz region of Donbas (in the east of the Ukraine) but had lived with her husband in Molotovsk until he had been shipped off to fight with the Red Army. The mini-brothel she had set up apparently had plenty of potential customers as long as there were foreign seamen in town. She had taken to moving in on them as soon as their ships arrived in the port. According to the charge sheet 'she used two girls with no occupation or residence. They speak English. She sent them out into the street to invite foreigners to her apartment. They spent the night with the foreigners.' What followed has been outlined above.[11]

Some reports in British archives are equally revealing on this topic. In one such document, there is a reference to a British signalman (surname Loades), who along with another signalman (surname Prior) had at first been imprisoned in the women's section of Archangel's prison after they had been arrested following a scuffle in the street at the end of November 1943.[12] While in the prison he was shown how he could use an aluminium mug wetted at the bottom, which when pressed against the wall of his cell could be used as an amplifier, enabling him to talk to the prisoner in the next cell. Through exploiting this newly learned method of communication, he was informed that one of the female prisoners next door had been given an eight-year sentence merely because, after her British boyfriend, a rating, departed, she was found with trifling gifts, such as the bars of chocolate he had given her.

While in prison, the same British signalman came across a 20-year-old girl called Anna, who had worked as a waitress in Archangel's state run Intourist hotel. Her only crime appears to have been getting pregnant while going out with an American merchant seaman in spite of being married to a Russian seaman.[13]

Such extreme punishments were not always deemed to be necessary. The same report referred to above about Archangel's NKVD mentions one woman working in the town's customs house, who was told she must choose between prison and her friendship with a foreigner. An NKVD agent said to her: 'You will not be able to keep up your friendship behind prison walls.' The report concluded, 'She had to submit.'

Similar tactics were employed by the Interclub's Gluzman, who according to the same report was feared more than many of those NKVD agents who wore the service's uniform. A trace of the way he viewed the dual role he had been allocated – encouraging foreign sailors to immerse themselves in Russian culture, and keeping them out of trouble – is to be found in the extract from one of his reports, which stated that even if the foreign seamen did not show any interest in Russian life: 'At least [while in the Club] they are not hidden away in a place where they cannot be observed.'

During 1943–44 evidence would be collected from informers about over 1,000 women in the Archangel region who had been with foreign seamen, plus another 150 whose intimate relationships with westerners based in the region were more stable and longer lasting.[14] The phenomenon was taken so seriously by the People's Commissar for State Security (Merkulov), that he wanted Stalin and Molotov to decide whether the value of the Western aid was such that it was worth putting up with the threat to Soviet security which these relationships represented.

A hard-hearted Allied leader could pity these women, whose mistreatment was collateral damage linked to the latitude given to the Arctic convoy seamen after their journeys, while at the same time realizing that when it came to clashes inside Russia, it was their effect on the war effort that must remain his principal concern.

That might explain why there is little evidence of senior officers based in the northern ports or Western politicians insisting there should be high-level objections to the crackdown. On the other hand, actions by the Russians that directly threatened the convoys elicited a much more determined response.

The undesirable effect of the Russians' more obstructive conduct was already an issue for the Western allies before the convoys were suspended. In February and March 1943, Anthony Eden and British Ambassador Archibald Clark Kerr had felt it was well within their rights to complain to both Molotov and Maisky about what the British Foreign Secretary referred to as the 'cumulative process of obstructiveness in connection with convoy protection'. When handing Maisky a memorandum specifying the obstructions, Eden warned the Russian Ambassador that 'we should have no alternative but to re-examine the whole question of the dispatch of future convoys' if the Soviet Government did not become more accommodating.[15]

The Soviet Foreign Minister's response had been conciliatory, at least up to a point, responding that while the British had overstepped the mark in the way they had been using their wireless sets in Russia, and in presuming they could without a permit use a piece of equipment in Russia that could jam the signals of German aircraft so that the enemy could not summon attacking forces (the local Soviet authorities had confiscated it), he was happy to give the British the permissions they had requested. However, Molotov refused to back down on the Soviet decision not to permit the RAF to fly the Hampden squadrons which Britain wanted based in northern Russia to provide air cover for future convoys east of Bear Island. It was this decision which presented Churchill with another reason to cancel the May 1943 convoy, which he did with the support of the Chiefs of Staff.[16]

There was also no movement by the Soviet Government on what had become known in British documents as the 'vexatious formalities', which after the arrival of the last Arctic convoy before the March 1943 suspension were enforced for the first time.[17] An updated list of such formalities compiled in March 1943 included for example the seemingly unreasonable insistence that Soviet authorities should be given notice each time a British ship or boat proceeded alongside one of the Allies' merchant ships in the Kola Inlet.[18]

Equally resented by those supporting the Western seamen in Russia were the long delays in distributing private mail as a result of Soviet insistence it should be censored, and the difficulties in obtaining permits to pass between the various British bases in the north Russia ports. These are just examples. There were many more complaints.[19]

Given that during much of 1943 no convoys were being run, one could argue that many of the 'formalities' were relatively unimportant inconveniences in the larger scheme of things. However there was a fear that petty resentments, if pushed too far, might blow up into something really damaging.

Evidence that feelings were running high is to be found in a report that was circulated in August 1943. Using language that suggests it might have been at least typed by an American secretary, the writer stated concerning recent football matches in Archangel between British and Russian teams: 'It is most regrettable that certain Britishers are apt to lose control of their tongues and forget all spirit of sportsmanship . . . Most foul language is used by the British spectators directed against the Russian referee and players. There is no objection to the base war cry, . . . but this foul language and insulting remarks are to cease . . . Try to remember that the spirit of sportsmanship amongst Britishers is not yet dead.'[20]

Given that the worst culprits at the England against Russia football matches in Archangel were said to be from 'amongst the British Services Shore Personnel', which included those at Base 126, the British unit operating near Archangel, tasked with showing the Russians how to use foreign tanks, it is likely that at least some of their ire related to the harsh Soviet treatment of Major Reith, the Base 126 commander. This was perceived by some to be part of the campaign of intimidation waged against British servicemen during the second half of 1943, with a view to changing Britain's foreign policy.[21]

Reith might never have fallen foul of the Soviet authorities, had he not had the temerity to complain in April 1943 about the theft of food from the British store at Ekonomia, one of Archangel's sub ports. Having said that, he had provoked the Russians by ignoring their desire not to let foreigners become too close to their citizens when he took up with a Russian woman who had his baby.

Nothing was heard from the local Archangel Narkomindel (People's Commissariat for Foreign Affairs) representative about Reith's complaint concerning the food for around three months after it was made. However, when the reply finally came through, it contained the counter-allegation that Reith and some other Base 126 staff had themselves picked up material from the store being discussed, and had either sold it in the market or had given it to their Russian women friends.[22]

In an attempt to prove that these allegations were baseless, a search was made by British officers of the apartments where Reith's girlfriend, and the Russian girlfriend of another British serviceman lived, without anything compromising being found. However a few weeks later, in August 1943, Clark Kerr in Moscow was informed that because the search of the flats had been contrary to Soviet law, Reith and two of the British searchers were to be expelled.[23]

In the meantime another row between the seamen and the Russians had come to the boil. On 17 June 1943 a Sergeant Ryan, a DEMS man from the merchant ship *Pontfield*, had been arrested at Murmansk's

Interclub for haranguing a Russian girl who refused to dance with him because she said it was too hot.

It did not help his cause that he swore at the police and cursed the Soviet government as he was taken to the police station. But he was released the next day, and it was only twelve days later that the master of *Pontfield* found himself face to face with Soviet policemen who had come to the ship to take Ryan away for questioning. The ship's master sought advice from a British official supporting the convoys as to whether he should comply.

The matter was referred to Rear Admiral Ernest Archer, the latest SBNO North Russia, who advised non-compliance, and the question whether Sergeant Ryan should be subject to the Soviet justice system was eventually discussed by Archer and Narkomindel's Comrade Timoshenko. Timoshenko's initial stance had been threatening: he had stated the police might arrest the entire ship if Ryan was not handed over. Timoshenko subsequently advised Archer that this difficulty, along with all the other British problems in Russia, would cease as soon as the Allies opened a second front.[24]

In the end, after several more threats that Ryan would be arrested, *Pontfield* was during July 1943 released with Ryan on board. But the kerfuffle was followed by an even more provocative example of the Soviet authorities using their police and judicial system to ratchet up the pressure on the British. On 17 July 1943, the Naval Mission in Moscow was informed that two sailors off the British merchant ship *Dover Hill,* who had been arrested for striking a Russian official in Ekonomiya, the Archangel subport, after being told not to smoke in a public place, were given jail sentences of five years and two years respectively.[25]

Although it was always hoped that these sentences might be reduced on appeal (they were in due course reduced to 18 months and 12 months), they were all the more upsetting from the British viewpoint because American sailors had committed similar misdemeanours without any Soviet response whatsoever. Admiral Archer cited the case of one American who had been brawling in Archangel's Interclub restaurant: 'He seized a Russian and shook him until his head nearly dropped off, and at the top of his voice told him just what he thought of Premier Stalin and the country in general, a tirade which lasted five minutes and culminated in specific and unmistakable but unmentionable directions as to what the Russians could do with each.'[26]

It is possible that there was a motive for the vilification of these British servicemen in addition to the one implied by Timoshenko's blunt insistence that it had something to do with getting the British to open a second front. They were not the only cases. Several other British seamen during the second half of 1943 were either imprisoned, and then released, or threatened with a trial for hooliganism. Showing that the British sailors and members of the missions and the base unit could not be relied on to behave well while no convoys were running certainly strengthened the hand of anyone striving to reduce the numbers of British servicemen in north Russia.

A battle had been fought for months over this issue. The Soviet authorities had stopped handing out visas to British servicemen, which meant if men were to go home on leave, they would not be able to return afterwards. The Soviet position was that there were too many British personnel in the north Russia ports. Whereas the British had countered that they in fact needed to increase their establishments so that they would be ready for when the convoys restarted.

In the course of 1943 there would be deadlock on both this point and concerning the vexatious formalities. At one point during the summer of 1943, Churchill was all for telling the British servicemen in the northern ports to ostentatiously make it known they were preparing to go home for good in the hope that fearing it would put an end to the convoys, the Soviet Government would fall into line.[27] But this plan was later shelved, because it was feared that should Churchill's bluff be called, Britain might end up having to send home men they needed to be in place, if not for future convoys, for a secret operation that was being planned that would make subsequent Arctic convoys feasible. Its purpose was to take out some of the German ships camped out in Altenfjord, whose presence there was stopping the aid being delivered via the northern route to Russia, thereby contributing to the poisoning of Anglo-Soviet relations.[28]

Eventually in August 1943 it was decided that the British Ambassador Archibald Clark Kerr should tell Molotov about the planned operation in the hope that once the Soviet Commissar of Foreign Affairs realized what was at stake, he might at least be persuaded to rein in the drive to reduce the number of British men who could remain in the north Russian ports in the short term.[29]

36

Churchill's Ultimatum

Main Action: 1 October 1943
Churchill's conditions for the resumption of the Arctic convoys

(See Map 16 inset)

The secret operation ('Operation Source'), whose disclosure to the Russians was meant to remove their objections to the maintenance of a substantial presence in the Kola Inlet and Archangel, was to be one of the most audacious and celebrated British actions of the war.[1]

Six miniature submarines that had been specially constructed for the operation were to be towed predominantly under the water by six normal-sized submarines all the way from the north-west coast of Scotland to the area off the north-west coast of Norway. Once there, the so-called midget 'X craft' were to be unleashed. Their four-man crews were then to proceed in the X craft up Altenfjord to the sub-fjords where it was hoped they would find *Tirpitz, Scharnhorst* and *Lützow* anchored behind anti-torpedo netting. If all went well, the X craft were to drop their saddle bag shaped charges, each weighing two tons, under the three ships, and then beat a hasty retreat before the German ships – or they – were blown up.

After much preparation, the submarines set out from Loch Cairnbawn to the north of Scotland's Loch Ewe, on 11 September 1943 with a view to the attack being carried out on 22 September.[2]

During the evening of 21 September 1943, even while the crews in the three midget submarines which had not been damaged, lost or forced to abort the mission, were making their final moves inside Altenfjord in preparation for the attack the next day, Molotov summoned Archibald Clark Kerr to his office in Moscow to talk to him about the ongoing convoy suspension.[3]

During the meeting, a note written by Molotov was handed to the British Ambassador. It asked why there had been no change of heart concerning the suspension when the reduced number of U-boats in the Northern Atlantic and the availability of escorts thanks to the Allies' increased strength in the Mediterranean in the wake of the successful invasion of Sicily and landings on the Italian mainland 'made a further postponement of convoys quite unjustifiable'. Given that the Red Army was currently attacking German units almost along its entire front, 'for the success of which every intensification and increase in supply of armaments and other materials was important', the Soviet Government, Molotov stated, 'insisted upon the urgent resumption of the convoys'.[4]

The note could not have been more timely. By the time Churchill was in a position to give the green light to the convoys, he knew from a Norwegian agent's report and Enigma decrypts that whatever the cost (he would eventually discover that in the course of the operation 10 British men lost their lives) Operation Source had been successful, in that *Tirpitz* had at least temporarily been put out of action.[5] He did not have to wait for the 1945 report, which confirmed that the charges dropped by two of the midget submarines near *Tirpitz* in Kaa Fjord (Kåfjord) had duly exploded, damaging the German battleship so significantly that a German war diary entry confirmed she would not be available 'for months' (see 1 in Map 16 inset for where *Tirpitz* was 'attacked' by the X craft, and Note 6 for other ways of spelling Kaa Fjord).[6] By then the commanders of the two X craft whose crews had dropped the charges that had done the damage had deservedly been awarded the Victoria Cross.[7] A mixture of Enigma messages, a Norwegian agent's report and air reconnaissance also told Churchill before the end of September 1943 that *Lützow* had left Norway.[8]

The removal from the area of the threat that had been posed by two of the three largest German warships paved the way for the running of the convoys. That gave the British prime minister the perfect opportunity to ask Stalin to improve the working conditions of the British seamen and administrators in northern Russia. He could now make the request from a position of strength.

On 1 October 1943 he wrote to Stalin: 'We are planning to sail a series of four convoys to North Russia in November, December, January and February, each of which will consist of approximately thirty-five ships . . . However I must put it on record that this is no contract or bargain, but rather a declaration of our solemn and earnest resolve.'

That was the carrot. It was followed with the stick: 'If we are to resume the convoys, we shall have to reinforce our establishments in North Russia . . . Your civil authorities have refused us all visas for men to go to North Russia, even to relieve those who are seriously due for relief. M. Molotov has pressed His Majesty's Government to agree that the number of British Service personnel in North Russia should not exceed that of the Soviet Service personnel in this country. We have been unable to accept this proposal since their work is quite dissimilar, and the number of men needed for war operations cannot be determined in such an unpractical way.'

Churchill went on to say he also wanted to send the small medical unit for Archangel that had previously been agreed. And he asked Stalin's assistance 'in remedying the conditions under which our Service personnel and seamen at present find themselves in North Russia' taking into account they were 'engaged in operations against the enemy . . . chiefly to bring Allied supplies to your country' putting them 'in a wholly different position from ordinary individuals proceeding to Russian territory'.

His telegram continues: 'We have already proposed to M. Molotov that as regards offences against Soviet law committed by personnel of the Services and of ships of the convoys, they should be handed over to the British Service authorities to be dealt with.'[9]

Stalin normally replied to Churchill's letters within a few days. This time there was an ominous silence for going on two weeks. When the Soviet leader finally replied on 13 October, it was far from the friendly response Churchill had been anticipating: 'I received your message . . .' Stalin wrote. 'However this communication loses its value by your statement that this intention to send Northern convoys to the U.S.S.R. is neither an obligation, nor an agreement, but only a statement which as it

may be understood is one the British side can at any moment renounce . . .
I must say that I cannot agree with such a posing of the question . . .
Supplies from the British Government to the U.S.S.R. . . . . cannot be considered otherwise than as an obligation, which by special agreement
between our countries, the British Government undertook in respect of
the U.S.S.R. which bears on its shoulders already for the third year the
enormous burden of struggle with the common enemy of the Allies . . .

'It is impossible to consider this posing of the question to be other than
a refusal of the British Government to fulfil the obligations it undertook,
and as a kind of threat addressed to the U.S.S.R.'

Stalin's telegram also contained little that was accommodating relating to the conditions facing British servicemen in the north Russian
ports. He was happy to let British servicemen censor their own mail, and
if there were 'small violations committed by British servicemen which
did not involve court procedure', British military authorities could deal
with them.

However, concerning Churchill's complaint that Britain's establishments in north Russia could not be brought up to strength, he disdainfully
wrote: 'I consider the principle of reciprocity and equality proposed by
the Soviet side for settlement of the visa question . . . to be a correct and
indeed a just one. The reference to the difference in the functions of the
British and Soviet military missions, and that the numbers of the staff of
the British military mission must be determined by the British Government only, I consider unconvincing.

'I do not see the necessity for increasing the number of British Servicemen in the north of the U.S.S.R. since the great majority of British
Servicemen who are already there are not adequately employed, and for
many months have been doomed to idleness.'

As if that was not negative enough, he went on to complain that some
of the servicemen already there had 'attempted in several cases to recruit
by bribery certain Soviet citizens for Intelligence purposes'. There was
also to be no give and take concerning the 'vexatious formalities'.[10]

Churchill, who had fought tooth and nail to persuade his advisers to
give Stalin as much aid as was possible, was extremely upset by Stalin's
sense of entitlement. It provoked a flurry of correspondence and action.

To Anthony Eden, who had fortuitously flown to Moscow for a tripartite foreign ministers conference, involving Britain, the US and the Soviet Union, Churchill wrote on 15 October 1943: 'This offensive reply has been received to our telegram about convoys . . . It would be a great relief to be freed from the burden of these convoys and to bring our men home from North Russia. If this is what they really mean and want, we ought to oblige them.'[11]

To Roosevelt, he wrote on 16 October: 'I have now received a telegram from U. J. (Uncle Joe) which I think you will feel is not exactly all one might hope for from a gentleman for whose sake we are to make an inconvenient, extreme and costly exertion.'[12]

Two days later, he summoned 38-year-old Fedor Gusev, the newly appointed Soviet ambassador in London who had replaced Maisky, and after the usual discussion that prime ministers have with the representatives of allies, he told him that he was leaving it to Eden to discuss the convoys with Stalin in person. Churchill in his memoirs wrote: 'I then handed back to the Ambassador an envelope. Gusev opened the envelope to see what was inside it, and recognizing the message, said he had been instructed to deliver it to me. I then said: "I am not prepared to receive it," and got up to indicate in a friendly manner that our conversation was at an end. I moved to the door and opened it.' Then after a brief conversation about Mrs Churchill's Russia fund, Churchill said his farewell and in his own words 'bowed him out'.[13]

The meeting Churchill had requested Eden should have with Stalin took place during the evening of 21 October 1943. In his post-war memoirs, Eden could only characterize the opening minutes as 'sticky'. His account continues: 'After some preliminaries, the Marshal said: "The Prime Minister is offended and will not accept my reply [to his telegram]. Well, let it be so."'

'He spoke glumly,' Eden remarked, also observing that: 'he still has that disconcerting habit of not looking at one as he speaks or shakes hands. A meeting with him would be in all respects a creepy and even a sinister experience if it weren't for his readiness to laugh, when his whole face creases and his little eyes open.'[14]

Eden protested that Britain wanted to be firm allies, and that Stalin had misunderstood what Churchill was trying to say concerning the supplies not being guaranteed. He was not saying the supplies, which it was hoped would amount to 860,000 tons in 140 ships, represented 'a gift', 'an act of favour' or 'charity' (Eden appears to have been alluding obliquely to the recently signed Third Protocol which stated that during the year July 1943 to June 1944, in addition to other specified aid for Russia, the Allies would use best endeavours to ship to Russia 200,000 tons per month via the northern route if not by the Persian Gulf route).[15] He was merely being careful not to mislead Stalin.[16]

At first Stalin would not give way, stating that he would not allow Britain to have more men in north Russia because there were already too many there with nothing to do apart from fighting with Soviet sailors. However then, according to Eden's report, he rowed back from that statement, saying 'that if our people would treat his people as equals, we could have as much personnel as we liked'.

It was eventually agreed that Eden would tell Molotov on the following day what he required to be changed, and they would then see whether they could accommodate what was requested.

He was as good as his word. The next day Eden telegraphed to Churchill: 'My talk with Molotov went well. He agreed to granting of visas for fresh men we need and for reliefs, and to meet us on other minor matters connected with convoys . . . Destroyers (whose sailing from UK bases Churchill had delayed in case there was no agreement) may therefore sail at once.'[17]

Molotov also agreed to see what could be done by way of seeking clemency for the two imprisoned sailors from *Dover Hill* (see Chapter 35).

Eden went on to report how before the meeting wound up, in a rare display of humility, which appeared to suggest that the Soviet leaders were extremely relieved that the delivery of aid was back on again, Molotov 'said that it was in the interest of his country to acquiesce in our proposals, for after all it was his government who was asking something of us, not the other way round'.[18]

Within a week of the meeting, Clark Kerr learned that the two *Dover Hill* prisoners were to be released.[19] During the first days of November, Molotov also confirmed his agreement that the British presence in the north Russia ports could be increased to 320 men with a 10 per cent uplift if necessary, which included those required to man a British hospital ward that could be set up in a Russian hospital in Archangel.[20]

There was still no final agreement on how the Soviet authorities would relax the 'vexatious formalities', or what would happen if a British serviceman was accused of a serious crime that the Soviets believed must be dealt with in their courts.[21] But for the moment those concerned felt it 'best to let matters take their course' and hope that in the improved atmosphere prevailing at the top, relations even if not pinned down with the precision one might expect to find in a legal document, could proceed in a more amicable way.[22]

Two men who would benefit in the long run from this laissez-faire approach were the signalmen Loades and Prior, who as mentioned in the previous chapter, had been given 1 and 4 year prison sentences respectively following a scuffle in an Archangel street. The official British report that described their experiences stated that rather than remaining confined in the Archangel prison where they were sent initially, they were taken on an 18 hour 250 mile train journey to the south, ending up in one of a group of camps which Loades afterwards stated, apparently mistakenly, was at a place called 'Yertzowa', but which was apparently at Yerzevo. This belonged to the network of Soviet labour camps which we now refer to as the gulag (the acronym for the Soviet institution Glavnoe Upravlenie ispravitel'no-trudovykh LaGerei – Main Administration of Corrective Labour Camps).

Here they were forced to work for several weeks on what amounted at times to a near starvation diet alongside the other inmates, many of whom stated they were political prisoners with no expectation they would ever be freed. Hearing this cannot have been very encouraging for Loades and Prior. Conditions were insalubrious. Loades reported that when they first arrived in the camp, the place where they were supposed to sleep was teeming with what he termed 'vermin', and as he described it, 'rats were running freely about the floors'.

Some of the prisoners had been working in Archangel before being sent to the camp. According to the report mentioned above, one of the inmates was a Russian captain who 'was until eighteen months ago a representative of the foreign trade department, connected with the unloading of incoming convoys. He claimed that the sentence of ten years imposed upon him was due to the fact that he was friendly with members of the British Naval Staff in Archangel'. Another prisoner, the report continued, was a woman who 'similarly claimed that she was in the camp because of her friendly attitude to members of the American Mission.' It would have been obvious to the writer of the report that Loades' testimony was opening a window into what had happened to all those Russians who had mysteriously disappeared from Archangel after becoming friendly with Allied staff in the city.

Their lives were not easy, even if the daily hard labour was put to one side. The picture Loades painted shows that normal life and expectations had to be forgotten while fitting into what was a parallel society. Rather than loving couples and the rule of law being the cornerstone on which life was built, all of the 1,000 plus prisoners stole whatever they could, and a substantial number of the 400 women belonged to the men best able to offer them protection. The report states: 'Some of the women were known as the mistresses of one man, who in exchange would look after them . . . The men who received parcels from home, or had a job that enabled them to steal more than everyone else were able to keep their own mistresses.' Many of the women who were not tied to a protector in this way became prostitutes, preferring to earn extra food by satisfying the men in the camp rather than by doing extra work.

Whether or not Loades and Prior would have survived in such a place throughout their sentence was not tested. Towards the end of March 1944, they were without any prior warning transported back to Archangel, and although Prior was locked up again for a while longer in the local prison, Loades was eventually just left in a street after being told to walk straight to the British mission. According to the report, 'By that time he was . . . frightened to such an extent that he misunderstood the instruction to mean that he was to walk in the middle of the road. Thus walking in the middle of the road from prison Loades arrived at the Mission in the afternoon of March the 28th.' Prior would also be let out before serving the bulk of his sentence, although around two more months passed before he was finally released.[23]

37

A German Tragedy – Act 1

Main Action: 26 December 1943
Battle of North Cape – the first engagements
with Scharnhorst, JW55B part 1

(See Maps 18 and 19)
GMT + 1

On 16 December 1943, the 55-year-old Admiral Sir Bruce Fraser, who had replaced Tovey as Commander-in-Chief of the Home Fleet, steamed into the Kola Inlet in his flagship, the battleship *Duke of York*. She was accompanied by the cruiser *Jamaica* and their screen of four British destroyers. It was the first time since the Arctic convoys had started that the Home Fleet had ventured this far east, and it constituted a show of force and commitment to the Soviet cause that it would have been hard to have bettered. All that was missing to make the event signify the support of Britain in her full pomp was the attendance of His Majesty King George VI himself, although this was remedied to some degree by the British sovereign featuring prominently in the alcoholic toasts at the formal lunch to which Fraser and the other admirals with him were invited.

However, Fraser had not come all this way east merely to fly the flag in this British outpost, and to establish a personal relationship with Vice Admiral Arseni Golovko, his 37-year-old opposite number in the Russian Northern Fleet. It also enabled him to protect the latest east-going convoy,

JW55A, at a time when it was conceivable the German Fleet might attack it even though the previous convoys had sailed through to Russia without mishap.

JW55A, which had set off from Scotland's Loch Ewe on 12 December 1943, was the third of the new series of east-going Arctic convoys promised by Churchill two months earlier in return for Stalin ameliorating the conditions of the Western allies' seamen in the north Russian ports (see Chapter 36).

Nevertheless, diplomacy was allowed to take its course. After anchoring at Vaenga, and hosting Golovko in the British battleship while a 45-man Russian dance and song group provided the entertainment, Fraser was the next day taken in a Russian boat to Polyarnoe, some 12 miles away, where he met up with Golovko again, this time in a Russian destroyer. On this occasion the Russians could not have been more hospitable. 'I pointed out a very nice metal anchor attached to an officer's watch chain, and it took but a nod from the Commander-in-Chief before he whipped it off and gave it to me,' Fraser reported afterwards. When Fraser later politely admired the black plate glass on the top of what he described as 'a great desk below a more than life size portrait of Marshal Stalin, floodlit with curtains at each side' in Golovko's Polyarnoe headquarters, the Soviet admiral likewise insisted that Fraser should take the desk plate home with him.

In the course of their subsequent good-humoured banter about what Fraser later referred to as this 'embarrassing ... oriental generosity', the same report states that he told Golovko that in that case he would have to be careful not to admire any of the Russian ladies 'as this might lead to complications'. At this, Golovko 'laughed delightedly', Fraser recalled, 'and said that he much admired my battleship!' This prompted Fraser, who in theory at least would have liked to reciprocate, to comment in his report: "There are however limits, and I felt sure that the Treasury would not have approved!"[1]

But his qualms did not mean his Russian hosts would be short changed. Little did Golovko know, as they laughed at the repartee, that at the back of Fraser's mind was his belief that the Home Fleet would soon be in a position to take on the German surface ships that had been causing the Allies so much concern, and if that occurred, Golovko and the Soviet Union might end up receiving a present whose significance would dwarf even the unimaginable donation of Britain's state of the art 745-foot-long battleship.

However, hard evidence that an attack on a convoy was brewing reached Fraser sooner than he might have expected. It was contained in a series of Ultra messages based on Enigma decrypts. The two Ultras sent to him on 23 December 1943, after he had left Russia and arrived back in the harbour at Akureyri, Iceland, warned him that JW55B, the 19 merchant ship convoy that had left Loch Ewe on 20 December 1943, had been sighted to the east of Iceland by the crew in a German reconnaissance plane on 22 December, and that the German Fleet had been ordered to be ready to depart if given three hours' notice (see 1 in Map 18, and Note 2 for sighting location).[2]

The secret nature of the intelligence derived from the German Enigma messages decrypted at Bletchley Park meant Fraser could not refer to the content of the Ultras in his official report. Instead he discreetly stated: 'I felt very strongly that the *Scharnhorst* would come out and endeavour to attack J.W. 55B.' Mindful that he would have to get a move on if he was to be in a position to protect the convoy, he sailed in *Duke of York*, escorted by the screen of four destroyers and the cruiser *Jamaica*, that very night (23–24 December).[3]

But even taking such decisive action brought him no peace of mind. He was tormented by the knowledge, relayed to him in a series of signals sent by the senior officer of the convoy's escort, that JW55B was from time to time being shadowed by German aircraft. As Fraser would later write in his report: 'Although German surface forces had never before made a sortie to the westward, the convoy which had reached the position 70°40' N 3°10' E (east of Jan Mayen Island – see 2 in Map 18) at 1200 (24 December), was entirely unsupported, and I was uneasy lest a surface attack should be made.'[4]

Not that the convoy and its close escort, which included 10 destroyers, 2 corvettes and a minesweeper, was to be entirely reliant on the Home Fleet (referred to by Fraser as 'Force 2') for reinforcement.[5] Support was also to be provided by the 10th Cruiser Squadron ('Force 1'), consisting of three cruisers. Force 1 was under the command of the redoubtable Vice Admiral Robert Burnett, the star if not the hero of the Battle of the Barents Sea (see Chapter 33), whose efforts then had been rewarded with a promotion. On this occasion he flew his flag in the cruiser HMS *Belfast*, a vessel that was destined not just to survive the engagement with German forces during JW55B, but also to carry on emphasizing the durability of British warships long after the end of war through its ending up as a museum ship on the Thames that even as I write can still be inspected by visitors. But although, as at the aforementioned battle, Burnett's cruisers were approaching the convoy from the east, after escorting the previous convoy to the Kola Inlet, Fraser knew Force 1, which had set out from Vaenga Bay during the early hours of 23 December, would be unable to reach a covering position that day.[6]

Fraser comforted himself by breaking radio silence during the early afternoon of 24 December and ordering that the convoy should be reversed for three hours. This he hoped would ensure that any German Fleet group that had gone out earlier than expected would reach the area near where JW55B was located after dark.[7]

He might have received additional consolation had he known the state of the German preparations. They were in turmoil due to differences of opinion about the role which the battlecruiser *Scharnhorst* should play. One might have thought that any German naval commander would have been thrilled at the prospect of being able to call on the firepower and speed of such a large, well-armed and protected ship – she was around 770 foot long (slightly longer than *Duke of York*) by around 100 feet wide, with nine 11-inch guns in three triple-gun turrets as her main armament, and 13 to 14-inch thick armour covering the central portion of the ship and the fronts of the gun turrets (*Duke of York*'s central armour was 14.7 inches thick), while retaining the capacity to cut through the water at 31 knots (three knots faster than Fraser's battleship).

That did not mean she was invincible. If it came down to a duel between the two ships, *Duke of York* was superior (see Chapter 4 for her statistics). That was particularly the case, as the Germans were about to find out, if it came to a contest where reliance on radar was critical. But given that there were supposed to be no German attacks on Arctic convoys unless the Home Fleet was too far away to intervene, *Scharnhorst*'s relative shortcomings might have seemed academic.

That probably explains why *Duke of York* was not the prime focus when doubts about *Scharnhorst*'s suitability for raids on Arctic convoys were voiced by the 45-year-old Konteradmiral Erich Bey, the experienced destroyer commander who had temporarily replaced Kummetz as Befehlshaber der Kampfgruppe (Battlegroup commander). Bey was to lead the sortie against JW55B, flying his flag in the battlecruiser. Disturbingly, long before the decision to attack JW55B was taken, he had declared that using *Scharnhorst* to attack Arctic convoys during the winter months was misconceived, writing in his war diary: 'Big ships can only bring their main armament to bear during the brief twilight . . . In the dark a "battleship" (which was how some Germans categorized *Scharnhorst*) will be in danger if attacked by destroyers . . . Destroyers . . . are the best bet for attacks on convoys during the winter.'

But even destroyers had their limits, he said, if the number that attacked did not match the number deployed by the British. He believed that given the likely size of the convoy escort, the five German destroyers available were too few to make an impact. He did not assert that there was a permutation of ships given the limited German resources remaining in Norway that would have a good chance of success in a raid on an Arctic convoy; he just knew an attack spearheaded by *Scharnhorst* backed by five destroyers was not it. As he concluded succinctly in his war diary: 'Using *Scharnhorst* with the destroyers in a night battle would not make up for the shortage of destroyers.'[8]

Bey's views were evidently respected, but they were not to be the last word. The 56-year-old Fleet commander Admiral Otto Schniewind, now also Dönitz's appointee as the leader at Marinegruppenkommando Nord, did what he could to square the circle between the use of *Scharnhorst* demanded by Dönitz and Bey's objections by initially suggesting a compromise solution. In his original draft order for the sortie, he proposed that while *Scharnhorst* should form part of the battlegroup, she would only be used in the event that the visibility was good when the time came to launch the attack.[9]

This took into account Bey's additional observation that, depending where the convoy was located when sighted, the German Fleet might end up having to move in on JW55B when there was no suitable 'hunting' light. According to Bey, to the north of 73° North 'where an attack is likely, there is no hunting light, which means that conditions are never suitable for the deployment of a heavy ship's artillery'.[10]

However, such a strategy merely highlighted Schniewind's naivety.

Even if Dönitz had not disclosed to Schniewind one aspect of the faustian pact he had made with Hitler – in February 1943 Hitler had been smooth-talked by Dönitz into cancelling the dismantling of the best of the capital ships, after all capital ships had been condemned to be scrapped in the wake of the Battle of the Barents Sea (see Chapter 33), and had agreed they could be used aggressively against the convoys – surely Schniewind should have guessed that Dönitz must have bought the Führer's change of mind with a quid pro quo. Dönitz had in fact promised that the reprieved capital ships would be used to attack the convoys at the first opportunity.[11]

In view of that, Schniewind's attempt to finesse the differences of opinion over *Scharnhorst* was never going to stand up to scrutiny. *Scharnhorst* was going to have to be used come what may. And once it was known that an east-going convoy had been sighted from a German aircraft, it was clear that the moment of truth was fast approaching. During the night of 24–25 December, the eight U-boats constituting the Eisenbart group, which the German admirals had entrusted with the task of making contact with the convoy on Christmas Day, were moved to the 120-mile patrol line to the south-west of Bear Island towards which JW55B was heading. The positioning could not have been bettered (it is shown in Map 18). Shortly after 10 a.m. on 25 December (Christmas Day), a brief message sent from Eisenbart's *U-601*, which had been placed near the centre of the line, confirmed that while the vessel was submerged, the convoy had passed overhead.[12]

That sighting, and the rash subsequent decision to send the German battlegroup on its way to exploit it that very day, notwithstanding the inability of the U-boats to remain in contact, was to bring the conflict that had been simmering within the various strands of the German naval command to a head. It boiled over shortly after *Scharnhorst* and the five accompanying destroyers had set off from Altenfjord on their mission during the early evening of 25 December, in the light of the forecast that there was to be a gale. 'I am worried about the extremely bad weather,' the 44-year-old Kapitän zur See Rudolf Peters, the Führer der Unterseeboote Norwegen (Commander of U-boats Norway) who was standing in for Konteradmiral Klüber (Admiral Nordmeer), wrote in his diary after sounding off about this to Schniewind in a telephone call that lasted from 7.15 to 8 p.m. that night. The entry in Peters' war diary continues: 'Although

I am hoping the U-boats will be in a patrol line across the Bear Island passage in good time tomorrow morning (26 December), it's unlikely that they will make contact during the night, let alone stay in contact, which is vital if the operation by the battle group is to succeed.'

There was another circumstance that worried Peters: the British, he said, would want to do whatever they could to guard against the possibility that the German Fleet would attack from the south. This would lead those in charge of the convoy to sail it as near to the northern ice as possible. In his diary, Peters explains why this spelt trouble: 'The further north it is attacked, the easier it will be for the British battle group – which has yet to be intercepted by our air reconnaissance, but which past experience . . . tells us is approaching – to intercept our forces.' If that was not argument enough against permitting the attack to proceed, Peters also pointed out that the inability because of the weather for the German reconnaissance planes to scour the ocean for the Home Fleet would make it impossible to know before Bey's force reached the convoy – which was scheduled to take place at dawn the next morning – whether Fraser's ships would be within striking distance. This led him to conclude: 'As a result the conditions required for the operation to go ahead . . . are not met as far as I can tell.'[13]

But even as Peters was telling Schniewind he thought the operation should be cancelled, Dönitz was circulating the following stirring exhortation explaining why the attack was needed:[14] 'The enemy is making it harder for our eastern army by sending a big convoy laden with food and arms to Russia. We must help . . .

'The tactical situation must be exploited with courage and skill. Partial success is not enough. Once the attack begins, it must be followed up. Our best asset is *Scharnhorst*'s superior gunpower. Therefore every effort must be made to bring these guns to bear. Destroyers must be used to make it happen.'[15]

At 8.30 p.m. Schniewind finally managed to pass on Peters' concerns to Dönitz via the Grossadmiral's 52-year-old Chief of Staff, Vizeadmiral Wilhelm Meisel. By this time Schniewind, who had never been keen on the operation, had also decided it was not advisable.[16] 'An operation in these conditions has too much going against it,' he wrote in the report summarizing his views, continuing: 'A decisive victory is unlikely. I therefore suggest the operation should be aborted. However if Germany's plight demands an operation be carried out in spite of these reservations, I propose that *Scharnhorst* should be sent out to attack the convoy without the destroyers.'[17]

Thus Schniewind weakly gave Dönitz's plan the green light even though it was opposed by the man who was to carry it out. It may be an exaggeration to say that never has a German commander gone into battle as unwillingly as Bey, but this cannot have been far from the truth.

Bey's frame of mind was underlined by another message sent by the acting Befehlshaber der Kampfgruppe. Shortly after 9 p.m. during the night of 25–26 December, Bey broke radio silence to tell Schniewind that in view of the weather he was encountering as he made his way out of Altenfjord: 'Use of destroyer weapons drastically impaired.'

Unfortunately for the Germans, although Peters in Narvik had Bey's warning just over an hour after it was sent, it did not reach Schniewind until after Dönitz had made his final decision based on what Schniewind had previously written to him.[18]

The Grossadmiral's final verdict was that the attack should go ahead, provided the Home Fleet was not spotted close to the convoy.[19] And at 12.35 a.m. on 26 December Schniewind received the follow-up message from Meisel telling him that Bey should be permitted to attack with *Scharnhorst* alone, if as a result of the rough sea the German destroyers were unable to function effectively.[20]

It was only later that Dönitz's flawed reasoning would become known. He was giving the go ahead partly because no British covering battlegroup had been detected and because the bad weather would hamper the light enemy naval forces as much as the German destroyers. But it was also partly because, as the Seekriegsleitung operations division's war diarist put it: 'It was possible to surprise the enemy since he had already passed two convoys through to Northern Russia unmolested by our forces.'[21]

Given that was how Dönitz was thinking, how horrified he would surely have been had he somehow been able to read the pair of Ultra messages that were sent by the British Admiralty to Fraser and Burnett some two hours after Schniewind had received the final confirmation of Dönitz's marching orders.

Contained within the haunting dots and dashes that at 2.17 a.m. 26 December were beeped over the air waves from the Admiralty in London to the admirals in the flagships of the two British forces approaching the convoy simultaneously from east and west there was an implicit warning concerning the impending attack. The Ultra started with the word: 'Emergency', and then carried on: '*Scharnhorst* probably sailed 1800A/25th December.'[22]

The details of the intercepted and decrypted German signal – an Enigma message sent by Bey at 5.15 p.m. on Christmas Day – on which the first Ultra was based followed a minute after the first Ultra was sent: 'A patrol vessel . . . was informed at 1715 that *Scharnhorst* would pass outward bound from 1800A/25th December.'[23]

The fact that Bletchley Park's codebreakers were able to decrypt the message so quickly (within 9 hours of the German signal being intercepted) was fortunate from the British viewpoint. Their contribution was all the more significant because of the failed attempt by Norwegian agents to warn the Admiralty that *Scharnhorst* had been seen leaving Lang Fjord where she had been anchored (see Note 24 for Norwegian agents' actions).[24] The Ultra signal, and another in the same vein, were to be of great assistance to the convoy's defenders. That was the case in spite of Fraser at the time he received them being only too aware that, these warnings notwithstanding, his warships, still ploughing through the very rough seas, of necessity well below their top speed, some 200 miles to the west of JW55B at 4 a.m. on 26 December, would be unable to reach the convoy in time to ward off the initial attack, if as seemed likely, it took place at the beginning of twilight that morning (see 3A-E in Map 18 for locations of both sides' ships at 4 a.m. 26 December; twilight times are described in Note 25).[25]

Knowing what was coming enabled Fraser to improve the merchant ships' chances remotely.[26] He did this by breaking radio silence again, at 4.01 a.m. and at 6.28 a.m. on 26 December, to order the destroyer *Onslow*'s Captain James McCoy, the senior officer in command of JW55B's close escort, to divert the convoy, which had been moving east-north-eastward, initially to the north and subsequently to the north-east.[27] In case that was not sufficient to hide JW55B from the Germans, he could only hope that his risk assessment the previous day had been well judged. He had then concluded that the ten original destroyers with the convoy reinforced by four more taken from the west-going convoy RA55A, combined with Burnett's Force 1, would have the necessary firepower to fend off the German battlegroup until the Home Fleet was in a position to intervene.[28]

Not that firepower alone was ever sufficient in itself. But on this occasion, as at the previous battle almost exactly a year earlier, it was to be backed up by what might be referred to as the Royal Navy's secret weapon: Burnett's seemingly unerring capacity, thanks to a mixture of intuition and rational thought, to position his ships where they could inflict the maximum damage on a superior enemy. The following extract from his after the action report describes how, on being instructed by Fraser's 6.28 a.m. 26 December message to close in on the convoy, he took care to place his ships, which at the time were to the south-east of JW55B, in an advantageous position: 'I altered course to 270° (heading west), my intention being to approach the convoy from the southward to avoid, in the event of action, steaming into the strong south-westerly wind and heavy seas, which outweighed the advantages of ensuring that the enemy would be between me and the light southerly horizon.'[29]

But he was once again helped by the Germans. Not only had they gone ahead with an operation by their surface fleet at a time when their U-boats were not shadowing the targeted convoy continuously. As a result they could not be sure the British would not divert the convoy away from its expected path, as Fraser had in fact done.

They had also failed to learn one of the key lessons that could be drawn from the Battle of the Barents Sea: it was dangerous in the Arctic winter to allow the capital ship to become separated from one or more of the supporting destroyers. On this occasion the separation took place after the German battlegroup, whose general direction of travel during the night of 25–26 December was north-north-eastward, at around 7 to 7.30 a.m. on 26 December reached the place which Bey believed would be in the path of the convoy. (This appears to have been based on the incorrect assumption that JW55B had carried on heading in the east-north-eastward direction reported by a U-boat on 25 December, starting from the convoy's position reported by a second U-boat during the early morning of 26 December.)[30]

Bey had then ordered the five destroyers to turn to port so that they could rake south-westward towards where he believed the convoy would be found. The destroyers were to proceed 10 miles ahead of *Scharnhorst* (the location where the German battlegroup turned to the south-west is shown at 4 in Map 18, and is described in Note 31).[31] Whether intentionally on Bey's instructions, or because of the rough seas whipped up by the south-westerly wind they were sailing into, *Scharnhorst* failed to keep in touch with the German vanguard, and visual contact once lost was never regained.

Given Bey's declared opposition, prior to setting out, to *Scharnhorst* getting in the way of the destroyers in poor visibility, it is tempting to see this as the maritime equivalent of Bey eating what had been served up with a very long spoon; it certainly had Bey's fastidious disdain for the use of capital ships in the Arctic in winter written all over it.

The upshot was that when at around 8.40 a.m. on 26 December *Scharnhorst* was detected, around 20 miles away to the north-west – more or less halfway between Force 1 and the convoy – by the cruiser *Belfast*'s radar, the German battlecruiser was all alone (see 5 in Map 18 for detection position, and 1A, 1B and 1C in Map 19 for respective relative positions of Force 1, *Scharnhorst* and JW55B at this time).[32]

Worse still from the German point of view, when at around 9.30 a.m. the gunners in *Norfolk*, another Force 1 cruiser whose radar was tracking *Scharnhorst*, opened fire at the battlecruiser after the German ship had ended up going on six miles to the cruisers' south, *Scharnhorst*'s crew were it seems taken by surprise (see 2A and 2B in Map 19 for relative positions of Force 1 and *Scharnhorst* respectively when *Norfolk*'s gunners opened fire).[33]

The encounter was to be unsatisfactory whichever side you were on. It ended minutes after it started, when *Scharnhorst* was turned away, without those great guns so extolled by Dönitz scoring so much as one hit.[34] Bey would later be criticized by Dönitz for not standing his ground and sinking his much less imposing opponent. If Bey had done his duty, the merchant ships would have fallen into his hands 'like ripe fruit', according to the Grossadmiral.[35]

But at least two of the 8-inch shells fired from *Norfolk* were on target.[36] One penetrated *Scharnhorst*'s deck on her port side between the 5.9-inch gun mounting and the port torpedo tubes and ended up in a seamen's mess deck without exploding. Nineteen-year-old Signalman Matrosenobergefreiter (Able Seaman) Helmut Backhaus, 38 metres up the battlecruiser's main mast on the lookout platform, nearly paid with his life for being in a position to describe what happened to the second of *Norfolk*'s shells that connected with the battlecruiser. 'I . . . felt the draught when the shell whistled right over me,' he recalled when interviewed about his experiences after the war. 'The . . . shot from the English ship dropped through the tower where two men were sitting. The shell then exploded. One man was killed. The other lost his leg, and the radar was destroyed.'[37]

Bey still had his destiny in his own hands however, as he had *Scharnhorst* wheeled away to the north-east, because Burnett made the controversial decision not to chase the German ship, an action he later justified with the following explanation: 'I was convinced he was trying to work round to the Northward of the convoy, and in view of the limit on my speed imposed by the weather, I decided to return to place myself between him and the convoy.'[38]

This fails to mention that intentionally breaking off radar contact with *Scharnhorst* by turning Force 1 to the north-west, as Burnett did at 10 a.m., was a brave call. It risked contravening one of the most fundamental rules all naval officers of the day were taught: never lose contact with the enemy unless you have a very good reason.

Belfast's 42-year-old Captain Freddie Parham witnessed how anxious Burnett was concerning what he had done. When Parham, by then an admiral himself, was interviewed after the war, he revealed that shortly after radar contact with the German battlecruiser was severed, Burnett 'sent for me. He was down in the chart house, one deck below the bridge. He himself worked entirely from the plot. I don't know that he ever came to the bridge . . . (For much of the time) there was nothing to be seen; it was pitch dark . . .

'He said to me, "Freddie, have I done the right thing?" I said . . . "I'm absolutely certain you have." Shortly after that (at 11.04 a.m.) we had a fairly snorting signal from the C-in-C, which said, roughly speaking: "How the hell do you think I'm going to bring her to action," or words to that effect.

'It was a terrible thing. Poor old Bob. He was a terribly emotional chap. He was jolly nearly in tears about it [although] I was able to reassure him.'[39]

Fraser's signal to Burnett was uncharacteristically harsh. Events during the day were to show that he was fundamentally a very kind man. However, during the morning of 26 December he had had a lot on his plate. The first reverse he encountered occurred shortly after 10 a.m. when *Duke of York* was still approximately 200 miles to the south-west of where *Scharnhorst*'s first engagement that day had been fought. He was informed that *Duke of York*'s radar had detected three German aircraft about eight and a half miles away which were shadowing Force 2 from the starboard quarter. One of them was overheard reporting back to base. This carried on for nearly three hours, all of which time Fraser must surely have been wondering whether that might be the cue for *Scharnhorst* to go scuttling back to her base, putting paid to his chances of catching up with the German battlecruiser (see 6 in Map 18, and Note 40 for the approximate location of the British ships detected).[40]

Bey might have ordered just that had it not been for another extraordinary lapse on the German side. Although Leutnant Helmut Marx, the captain of the Blohm & Voss 138 aircraft crew doing the signalling, duly reported the detection of a group of ships where none should have been, Oberst Ernst-August Roth, the commander of Fliegerführer Lofoten, failed to circulate 'the sighting' details immediately, and even when he did during the early afternoon, he failed to mention one of the ships detected was significantly larger than the others.[41]

Schniewind appears to have compounded Bey's intelligence deficit by failing to communicate with him adequately, or at all, concerning another ominous development: helped by the B-Dienst, the German Navy's interception of signals and codebreaking service, by around 11.15 a.m. on 26 December, staff at Marinegruppenkommando Nord had worked out that a ship, which appeared to be the cruiser whose guns had fired at *Scharnhorst* during the battlecruiser's earlier encounter, had reported making contact with the enemy to another mysterious ship. It was realized that the recipient of the message might be the commander of the expected heavy cover group.[42]

So it was that shortly before midday on 26 December, Bey, deprived of evidence or at least analysis concerning the approaching threat that should by this stage have been passed on to him, stripped of some of the protection that might have been offered had all his radar been in working order, and constrained by the push me-pull me orders from Dönitz and Schniewind prior to the attack that respectively urged reckless attack and safety first retreat simultaneously, terminated the long loop northward by turning to port in the hope he could target the convoy again.

This second attempt was to be no more successful than the first. Once again *Belfast*'s radar detected *Scharnhorst* before the crew in the German ship knew the whereabouts of her foe. At 12.05 p.m. radar operators in Burnett's flagship registered *Scharnhorst* some 17 miles to the north-east. The German battlecruiser was approaching the three British cruisers, which were positioned some ten miles to the north-east of the convoy (see Note 43, and 7 in Map 18 for approximate location, and 3A and B in Map 19 for Force 1's approximate position relative to *Scharnhorst*'s at this juncture).[43] Burnett's uncanny ability to place his ships exactly where they were most needed had stood him in good stead once again.

Shortly before 12.30 p.m. the cruisers' gunners, complying with Burnett's order, opened fire on the battlecruiser when she was just over six miles away (see 4A and B in Map 19 for approximate position of Force 1 relative to *Scharnhorst* at this stage).[44] But because the action took place during the last of the twilight hours that day, as *Sheffield*'s gunnery report confirmed. 'At no time could the target be seen clearly from the Director Control Tower, being merely a grey shape slightly darker than the background.'[45] Although there would subsequently be claims by members of the cruisers' crews that *Scharnhorst* was hit more than once, in the prevailing murk, no Force 1 personnel could know the extent of the impact. The gun teams in the three cruisers were eventually reduced to aiming impotently at the gun flashes coming from where *Scharnhorst* was believed to be located.[46]

By way of contrast, the silhouettes of the three British cruisers, which stood out against the light sky to the south, were only too visible from the battlecruiser.[47] As a result, on this occasion *Scharnhorst*'s shelling quickly drew blood, albeit not with her first salvos. *Sheffield* was struck by a piece of shrapnel described by one of her officers as 'about the size of a man's head' that hit her starboard side just below and aft of the bridge without causing significant damage or any injuries.[48]

But it was the targeting of *Norfolk*, picked out by *Scharnhorst*'s gunners on account of her, unlike the other two cruisers, not using flashless cordite, which was to be so traumatic.[49] The same *Sheffield* officer quoted above has told how in mid-battle, he observed what he described as a 'sickening red column of fire' which hung for around ten seconds over *Norfolk*'s X turret before subsiding (X turret being the furthest forward of the two twin 8-inch gun turrets aft). The flames had been ignited when one of the German ship's 11-inch shells penetrated the massive 'roller ring' at the base of the turret, on which it rotated, and after passing through to the other side, exited without exploding.

Although spared the catastrophic consequences of such a detonation, leading to an enormous secondary explosion caused by the contents of the magazine and shell room under the turret going up, some of the turret's occupants were killed, while others, who were not wearing flashproof protective equipment, were badly burned.[50] A witness has described seeing one of the latter, on fire from head to foot, run screaming out onto the deck. The burning man would have flung himself overboard to douse the flames, had he not been intercepted by an alert petty officer, who knocked him down, and then rolled him over and over until the fire that threatened to scorch the life out of him was extinguished.[51]

Norfolk's crew also had another stroke of good fortune. Had the other *Scharnhorst* 11-inch shell which ploughed into the cruiser's starboard side, hit the ship a little lower, it might have taken out the giant turbines powering the ship in her forward engine room on the platform deck (three decks down from the level of the top open-air deck at the front of the ship), and possibly the turbines in the adjacent aft engine room as well. That would have stopped the ship in her tracks, leaving her if not at Bey's mercy, at the mercy of any passing U-boat. As it was, in the words of one of the chief engine room artificers, it 'tore through the side of the ship and ripped up the deck . . . above us as if it were cardboard'.[52]

The first *Norfolk*'s 29-year-old stoker Bert Moth, in the secondary damage control headquarters on the cruiser's lower deck (the level above the engine rooms), knew of it was when he heard what sounded like a crashing car and an explosion coming from the next compartment. 'One of my mess mates standing with his back to the communicating door was thrown across the deck by the blast,' Moth stated during an interview later. 'The door was . . . opened. All was dark. Clouds of steam and smoke came issuing [forth] from within, along with cries for help.'[53]

This strike, like the one that hit X turret, resulted in fatalities (in total seven of *Norfolk*'s crew would die on account of the two hits).[54] And what Moth described as 'confusion' reigned, as men from four different sections rushed to the scene of this hit amidships to carry out repairs while, as Moth bore witness, 'the medical parties worked feverishly with our ill-fated casualties'.[55] But the worst of the damage was contained within the compartments directly affected, and was therefore manageable. Eventually all the wounded still in one piece were carried on stretchers to the two sickbays, including one rigged up aft in *Norfolk*'s wardroom.

That excluded those who were less fortunate. At least one member of the crew could not at first be located; when the ship's chaplain went looking for him, all that could be found was one of the missing man's disconnected arms, the only part of him that had survived the blast.[56]

Such carnage was shocking. But those witnessing it might have been facing something much worse had the weather been better, thereby ensuring that *Scharnhorst*'s crew had the time and space to fire at the three cruisers at her leisure from outside the range of the British ships' guns. Because of the restricted visibility, Bey appears to have come to the conclusion that he was facing heavier opposition than three cruisers. That at least was the excuse his telegraphist had transmitted to Schniewind.[57] It is also possible the low visibility led Bey to fear that if destroyers advanced unseen by him through the smoke, he might end up becoming the victim of their torpedoes. He would have been right had he been so concerned. At the beginning of the second action Burnett had instructed the commanders of the four destroyers with Force 1 to try to make a torpedo attack.[58]

Bey's turn away, that ultimately led to his fleeing to the south-east, foiled that plan. But it left Burnett with what if anything was an even more attractive option. Because the British Vice Admiral knew that *Scharnhorst* was on a converging course with the Home Fleet that was racing in from the south-west, he decided that British interests would best be served by playing a waiting game. He would shadow *Scharnhorst* using the cruisers' radar while remaining some seven miles behind the German ship, that is out of sight, while frequently updating Fraser on the battlecruiser's position.[59]

That fitted in very well with the plans being hatched by Fraser, who had perked up as soon as he learned from Burnett that the cruisers were in contact with *Scharnhorst* again. 'I knew now there was every chance of catching the enemy,' he would later write in his report.[60]

His caution was praiseworthy. There was still much that could go wrong. Although, as we have seen, Bey went into the second action with the cruisers without much insight into the opposition he was facing, by around 3.30 p.m. Marx's message had it seems finally reached him. According to Matrosengefreiter Günter Sträter, one of *Scharnhorst*'s gunners, who ended up being one of the few survivors, at around that time something akin to the following message was broadcast on the tannoy system around the ship: 'To All Stations: Radio message from the Luftwaffe. Reconnaissance aircraft reports enemy ship group 150 miles West 1100 hours. Look out for it!'[61]

It was not long after this announcement that Bey had a second chance to break away from the chain of linked events that were bearing him and his ship's company inexorably to their doom. Shortly after 4 p.m., first *Norfolk*'s crew had to reduce her speed because of a fire, and then *Sheffield*'s crew had to do the same when her port inner shaft went out of action.[62] This left *Belfast*, whose main armament like *Sheffield*'s consisted of 6-inch guns in four triple-gun turrets, in a vulnerable position; all of a sudden she found herself up against the 11-inch guns of *Scharnhorst* while only supported by destroyers. The disparity set off in her Captain Parham's mind some very anxious ruminations. He was well aware, as he confirmed in a post-war interview, that *Scharnhorst* 'need only have turned round for 10 minutes or less, and [could then have] blown us clean out of the water. Then of course she would have been lost to everybody, and absolutely safe to get home.'[63]

He need not have worried. Bey, probably blinded by the inadequacy of what remained of *Scharnhorst*'s radar, appears never to have wavered from his belief that he was outgunned. He was certainly no longer anticipating any assistance from the German destroyers. Shortly after 2 p.m. he had instructed their commander Kapitän zur See Rolf Johannesson to abort the search for the convoy, and to head back to base, perhaps the most sensible command any German had given since the operation started.[64]

Meanwhile Fraser was busy preparing for his first big fight in *Duke of York*. One of his most important tasks was to notify the commanders of the other Home Fleet ships – the cruiser *Jamaica*, and the destroyers *Savage* and *Saumarez*, *Scorpion* and *Stord* – when battle would be joined. Or as Fraser would put it in an interview after the war, the question was: 'whether we should have tea before the battle or wait till afterwards. We had tea before the battle.'[65]

Fraser also made it his business to bolster up the courage of all those around him on *Duke of York*'s bridge, and in nearby compartments. His

Flag Lieutenant Vivian Cox, who after the war became a well-known film producer, recalled how Fraser, on seeing that two young midshipmen were very nervous, 'found the time and the humanity to give them little nameless useless tasks to do to keep them busy, . . . at the same time . . . winking slightly to us to [make us] realise that [he knew] we also were slightly nervous. It was a real triumph of a single personality dominating a ship's company.'[66]

It was 4.17 p.m., not long after the dropping out of the two British cruisers, when *Duke of York*'s radar finally locked onto *Scharnhorst*, at a distance of some 25 miles on a bearing of 20 degrees (to the north-north-east). Given that by this time, the dim light available during twilight hours had long since petered out, and the only illumination, sufficient to provide visibility up to around five miles, was provided by whatever seeped through the clouds from the flickering northern lights, the need to 'hold bearing' via the radar was self-evident.[67] As the minutes passed, *Scharnhorst*'s south-south-eastern course combined with *Duke of York*'s converging movement from the south-west resulted in the range rapidly decreasing, a situation that prompted *Duke of York*'s 45-year-old Captain Guy Russell to point out: 'You know you can open fire any time you like now sir.' To which Fraser, calmly puffing his pipe responded: 'We'll wait while the enemy does not know we're there. The closer we get, the more certain we'll be.'[68]

At 4.37 p.m., as the countdown continued, the four Home Fleet destroyer commanders, whose ships forged ahead on *Duke of York*'s bows, were told to prepare to make a torpedo attack.[69]

However, the clock hands were moving round to 4.45 p.m. before Fraser at last decided the time had come. Only then was *Duke of York*'s course altered to east-north-east 'to open A arcs', and Burnett was instructed by Fraser to illuminate the battlecruiser. With the distance between the two opposing capital ships cut to around seven miles, first the gunners in *Belfast* and then those in *Duke of York* fired their starshell (see Note 70, and 8 in Map 18 for approximate location).[70]

Tony Ditcham, at the time a 21-year-old sub-lieutenant in the destroyer *Scorpion,* which along with the other three Fleet destroyers was between the British battleship and the German battlecruiser, later reported: 'When the starshell illuminated *Scharnhorst*, I could see her so clearly that I could see her turrets were fore and aft. And what a lovely sight she was at full speed. She was all at once obliterated by a wall of water from the *Duke*'s salvo. When she reappeared her guns wore a different aspect.'[71]

The following extract from the report written after the battle by Lieutenant Bryce Ramsden, who at the time was located in the high angle gun director on the cruiser *Jamaica*'s port side, shows that he was equally impressed: 'Even to us, now a thousand yards astern, the noise and concussion was colossal . . . The vivid spirt of flame lighted up the whole . . . [of *Duke of York*] for an instant, leaving a great drift of cordite smoke hanging in the air.'

The thunderous sound made by *Jamaica*'s own guns added to the general tumult. 'The concussion momentarily deafened me,' the overwhelmed Ramsden admitted later, 'and my vision was blurred by the shaking of the director, and the sudden flash . . . We could see the tracer shells coursing away like a swarm of bees bunched together, and could follow them as they curved gently down towards the target.'[72]

By all accounts *Jamaica*'s shells missed *Scharnhorst*. But the immediate consequence of Fraser's ship's first broadsides were gratefully chalked up. According to *Duke of York*'s gunnery officer, there were 'splashes [which] completely obliterated [the view of] *Scharnhorst*, and then there followed a greenish glow along her waterline where she had been hit.'[73]

Witnesses in *Scharnhorst*, quoted in reports in the British archives based on the memories of the *Scharnhorst* survivors, would later state that the damage from this first hit, which made a hole half a yard in diameter in *Scharnhorst*'s starboard side about two foot above the water line, was quickly patched up. But they also confirmed that during this first encounter with Force 2, *Scharnhorst*'s front 11-inch gun turret (referred to by the Germans as 'Anton') was hit and put out of action.

This hit generated general panic among those in the vicinity of the damage, once it was realized that the explosion had lit a fire, which was quickly spreading towards the magazine underneath the adjacent 11-inch turret further back (referred to by the Germans as 'Bruno'). Members of the gun teams immersed themselves up to their waists in the ice cold water pumped into Bruno's magazine to make it safe. This enabled them to move the ammunition away from the water before it was spoiled. However, the survivors' testimony bears witness to the strength of *Scharnhorst*'s armour. Terrifying as this incident was for all those concerned, it did not impede the battlecruiser's mobility one whit.[74]

Without showing so much as a metaphorical limp, before Fraser had the presence of mind to order a torpedo attack by the four Home Fleet destroyers, *Scharnhorst*'s crew had her wheeled round to port. Then she sped off towards the east, firing at the pursuing British ships, which included *Duke of York*.[75]

Fraser would later describe *Scharnhorst*'s fire as 'erratic to begin with'. Some of her first shells fell as much as a mile and a half away from the British battleship.[76] But paradoxically, as *Scharnhorst*'s superior speed increased the distance between the capital ships to around 10 miles, the accuracy of her 11-inch guns, brought into play whenever she in her turn opened A arcs by deviating to the side, noticeably improved. At times *Scharnhorst*'s shells rained down in the vicinity of *Duke of York,* and as Fraser later confessed, 'there were many near misses'.[77]

One of *Scharnhorst*'s shells smashed up Fraser's barge.[78] Another sliced a chunk out of the main mast behind *Duke of York*'s bridge, just inches below the feet of the two able seamen and the 27-year-old electrical officer, Lieutenant Harold Bates, in their cubby hole some 40 feet up from the battleship's top deck. Legend has it that when it was noticed that the radar was no longer working properly, Lieutenant Bates heroically climbed up the mast, and then manually restored the broken connection by holding two bits of broken wire together with his bare hands. Try as he might to explain what he really did (he climbed into the compartment above the cubby hole and turned the right levers until the aerials and gyroscope were aligned), he was forever acclaimed afterwards as 'Barehands Bates'.[79]

At around 6.20 p.m., after the distance between the opposing capital ships had risen to around 12 miles, the gunners in both *Scharnhorst* and *Duke of York* stopped firing. The mood in the British battleship, on her bridge and in her gun turrets alike, had by this time become despondent.[80] The most depressing moment of all was at around 6.40 p.m. when Fraser messaged Burnett: 'I see little hope of catching *Scharnhorst* . . . Am proceeding to support convoy.'[81]

38

Turning Point

Main Action: 26 December 1943
Battle of North Cape – sinking of Scharnhorst, JW55B part 2

(See Maps 1, 18 and 20)
GMT + 1

The 20-year-old gunner Sub-Lieutenant Henry Leach – a future First Sea Lord in the making (see Note 1), but on 26 December 1943, the officer in charge of *Duke of York*'s A gun turret – was one of many in Fraser's battleship who were bitterly disappointed at the turnaround of events during the early evening of 26 December.[1]

He was not to know it until long afterwards, but some of *Scharnhorst*'s crew were likewise beginning to believe that after all they might escape. Günther Sträter, the *Scharnhorst* gunner referred to in Chapter 37, later recalled how out of the blue, the battlecruiser's 42-year-old Kapitän zur See Fritz Julius Hintze broadcast over the sound system the following uplifting message: '*Scharnhorst* forever onwards!'[2]

But then, as Leach would later recall, everything changed again: 'Quite suddenly, the range steadied, and then the range counters started to tick down. It was almost like awakening from a bad dream. You realized if it went on like that, you were catching him up, and then you were in with a chance.'[3]

The reason for this unexpected transformation was that, unbeknown

500

to anyone in *Duke of York* at the time, *Scharnhorst* had been hit by one of the last of the British battleship's shells fired before her ceasefire. Some German witnesses believed it damaged one of the battlecruiser's propeller shafts.[4]

This was a shorthand way of saying that at least one of the ten 14 inch guns in *Duke of York*'s three turrets had spat out a 5 foot long shell weighing around three quarters of a ton, the shell's velocity as it left the gun barrel being some 2,400 feet per second. Then there had been a delay of some 25 seconds as it flew over the ten miles or so which at the time separated the British battleship from the German battlecruiser before either smashing into *Scharnhorst*'s hull aft or exploding in the water near her stern. Whatever the precise trajectory and impact point, a German witness is quoted in one of the survivors' reports as having stated that at about this time 'he felt the stern of the ship thrust upwards and thereafter noticed on his speed indicator a reduction from 29 to 22 knots', leading him to conclude that 'a hit had been obtained in the region of the screws.'

This gave the four Fleet destroyers, some six miles behind the battlecruiser, the opportunity to catch up.[5] Not only that. At 6.42 p.m. HMS *Scorpion*'s 35-year-old Lieutenant Commander Bill Clouston (the younger brother of the Canadian Commander Campbell Clouston, who had sacrificed himself so altruistically and heroically on the way back from France, after acting as piermaster during the 1940 evacuation of the British Expeditionary Force from Dunkirk) reported that the 2nd Sub-Division of destroyers, consisting of his own ship and the Norwegian *Stord*, which had been haring along at 30 knots, had 'undertaken' *Scharnhorst* as she fled in a south-easterly direction, and had reached the point five and a half miles to the south-east of the battlecruiser.[6]

It was a momentous announcement, signifying the prospect that the German ship could now be attacked simultaneously by the two destroyers speeding along in front of her as well as by the two destroyers racing up behind her (see Map 20 for the relative courses of the two sub-divisions of destroyers and the battlecruiser).

A more complete exposition by Clouston would have revealed that his sub-division was already cutting in towards the battlecruiser, on a north-easterly converging course, which if nothing changed, would have ensured that the destroyers bumped into *Scharnhorst* within a matter of minutes.

Clouston might have further raised the hopes of those on board the destroyers behind the battlecruiser if he had indicated that he was no longer just relying on radar; notwithstanding the darkness, *Scharnhorst* was as good as in his gun teams' sights. *Scorpion*'s Sub-Lieutenant Ditcham would later confirm that from his vantage point inside the destroyer's director control tower, above and behind her bridge, he saw what he described as 'a brief silhouette . . . of *Scharnhorst* . . . each time she fired at our two chums [to her rear]'.[7]

Even so, had Bey made the right decisions, he might still have managed to blast his way out of the trap into which he had fallen. A good start would have involved his gunners firing starshell above the area to the front and to the side of the line where his ship was advancing, in addition to the starshell they were shooting over the destroyers to their rear in an effort to facilitate their gunfire. Had they taken this precaution, the presence of *Scorpion* and *Stord* would probably have been disclosed as the two destroyers raced in on their north-easterly course, permitting Bey to at least try to take evasive action.

Instead, the battlecruiser's officers and crew alike carried on, seemingly unaware that danger was approaching out of the darkness off her starboard bows. Then, in an apparent attempt to open A-arcs so that all her most powerful remaining guns could fire at the two 1st Sub-Division destroyers (*Savage* and *Saumarez*), by this time also to her south but behind her, *Scharnhorst* was all of a sudden wheeled to starboard.[8]

The turn represented a catastrophic mistake. Bey could hardly have selected a more self-destructive manoeuvre. At a stroke, it presented the German ship's west-facing starboard broad side to *Savage* and *Saumarez*, which following the turn were off her starboard bows, and her east-facing port broad side to *Scorpion* and *Stord,* which after the turn were off her port bows. Or as *Scorpion*'s Sub-Lieutenant Tony Ditcham memorably put it: 'an onrushing target became a sitting bird.'[9] 'Thank God she's turning away!' *Scorpion*'s Lieutenant Commander Clouston remarked, when he clocked what was happening.[10]

Minutes later, first *Scorpion* and then *Stord* swooped in, enabling each ship's crew to fire eight torpedoes at the battlecruiser from as close as

2,100 and 1,800 yards respectively (see Note 11, and 9 in Map 18 for the approximate location of the final series of attacks on *Scharnhorst*; and 1A and 1B in Map 20 for the approximate relative positions of *Scorpion* and *Stord*, and *Scharnhorst* when these destroyers fired their torpedoes).[11] This was so near the target, compared to what the crews had been taught to expect in training, that a member of *Scorpion's* port team of Oerlikon gunners, perhaps inspired by the fear that his words might be his last, was moved to utter the immortal line: 'Out wires and fenders, we're going alongside the bastard!'[12]

British witnesses must have been disappointed in view of this to discover later that only one of the 16 missiles fired by *Scorpion* and *Stord* is believed to have hit *Scharnhorst*. A 'water-spout' seen shooting up into the air beside the battlecruiser's after superstructure was adjudged to indicate where and when this single torpedo struck home.[13] There was little doubt which ship's crew had fired it. It was spotted so soon after *Stord* fired her torpedoes, that her commander, Lieutenant Commander Skule Storheill, admitted it must have emanated out of *Scorpion's* tubes.[14]

Less is known about the course of the torpedoes fired at *Scharnhorst's* starboard side minutes after *Scorpion's* and *Stord's* gambit. *Savage's* torpedo team fired her complement of eight torpedoes from around 3,500 yards. The torpedo team in *Saumarez* then fired the only four torpedoes it had set up, albeit from what was alleged by some to be less than half the distance selected by *Savage*, as *Scharnhorst* rushed past her (see 2A and 2B in Map 20 for the approximate positions of *Savage* and *Saumarez* relative to *Scharnhorst* when these destroyers fired their torpedoes at the German battlecruiser).[15] Subsequent analysis suggested that at least three of the 1st Sub-Division destroyers' missiles struck home, although there was less certainty about the location of the hits, or concerning which destroyer's tubes were responsible. There is little doubt the strikes were significant. German survivors reported that these destroyers' torpedoes hit a boiler room and damaged another propeller shaft, slowing down the battlecruiser still further.[16]

It is difficult to appreciate the courage shown by the men who participated in this second batch of torpedo attacks without highlighting their context. Even before their final run-in, these destroyers were being targeted by *Scharnhorst*'s 5.9-inch and 4-inch gunners, as well as by occasional salvos fired by the 11-inch guns in *Scharnhorst*'s after turret.[17] However, as they advanced to torpedo, the noise of the firing at them from *Scharnhorst* reached a crescendo.[18]

Savage somehow made it through the shells and bullets without so much as a casualty, although one man's life was saved by his helmet.[19] *Saumarez* and her crew were less fortunate. During the final run-in, shortly before her torpedoes were fired, the British ship's starboard side was peppered with fragments after a shell fired from *Scharnhorst* landed nearby. At least one of these fragments reached *Saumarez*'s starboard engine, putting it out of action, and leaving the destroyer floundering.

Her inability because of this to speed away to safety appears to have been critical. Seconds after her torpedoes were fired, *Saumarez* was hit again. This time the shell fired by *Scharnhorst*'s gunners struck the British destroyer's director tower, killing most of its occupants, but sparing those on the bridge in front of it because, replicating what occurred when *Norfolk*'s X turret was hit, there was no explosion.

As a result *Saumarez*'s surviving crew were able to steer her away from the battlecruiser, following *Savage* to the north. But there was no escaping the question: had the outstanding bravery exhibited by *Saumarez*'s Lieutenant Commander Eric Walmsley been worth it, especially given the small number of torpedoes fired by his ship compared with the payloads launched from the other three destroyers? Nine of *Saumarez*'s crew died when *Scharnhorst*'s shells and shell fragments hit the destroyer, and two more men passed away afterwards. Also several members of her crew were seriously wounded.[20]

They included the 20-year-old stoker Kenneth Evans from near Neath, Wales, whose story is told here in order to underline the point that life-changing injuries are just as important as fatalities when quantifying the damage caused by a shell. Evans had started the day like any inquisitive young man in such circumstances, keen to see what a sea battle was like, only to end it so badly injured that it seemed almost inevitable he would remain a helpless cripple for the rest of his life.

When after the war, he was asked during a face to face interview to describe that terrible moment when he was wounded, while carrying shells from the lifts to one of *Saumarez*'s 4.7-inch guns, he said matter of factly, sugaring his gruesome tale with that distinctive sing-song lilt that is so characteristic of English spoken with a Welsh accent: 'You could see the tracers and everything coming at you . . . from the *Scharnhorst*. It was dark . . . We were up above the deck . . . I did not see . . . the shell that "hit" me . . . It just exploded. [There was] a blinding flash . . .

'Next thing I remember is turning to my side, and finding another boy alongside me, and unfortunately his stomach more or less was blown out like . . . When I first come to, I . . . couldn't feel anything. It was numbed . . . But when I became conscious of things . . . I couldn't feel my legs. I was dead scared . . . I thought both legs had been blown off.

'What had actually happened was . . . both . . . my legs . . . had been cut across, through the knees . . . I had [then] fallen . . . onto my legs. My legs were doubled under me . . . [I saw] all the blood and everything . . . One of the officers came up . . . I remember him giving me an injection . . . to kill the pain . . .

'The next thing I remember was lying on a stretcher down below deck with a drip in me . . . There were various stretchers alongside me. Some of [the men on] them were dead. Others were dying. . .'[21]

While testimony such as this leads one to question whether the heroic action taken by the commanders of all four destroyers was proportionate, in spite of it causing so much suffering, there is no doubt it broke the deadlock. After the destroyers' attacks, *Scharnhorst*'s progress southward was demonstrably slower than beforehand, enabling the larger ships in Fraser's Force 2 to catch up in their turn.[22]

The following extract from the account by *Jamaica*'s Lieutenant Bryce Ramsden (previously quoted in Chapter 37, concerning the first tussle between the two sides' capital ships) records the unforgettable minutes, as seen through the eyes of this impressionable young officer, just before and just after Fraser decided they were near enough to open fire on the battlecruiser again (see 3A and 3B in Map 20 for the position of *Duke of York* and *Jamaica* relative to *Scharnhorst* when these two British ships opened fire at 7.01 p.m.): 'We turned to starboard, the turrets following round, so that both ships presented a full broadside. I think I yelled, "Stand by again!" over the telephones, but my words were drowned by the deafening crash of gunfire. The tracer now appeared almost horizontal, so flat was the trajectory, as they rushed like fireflies to converge at a point in the darkness. Suddenly [there was] a bright-red glow, and in it the enemy was to be clearly seen for a brief moment. "She's hit! My God, we've got her!" I was yelling like one possessed . . . All over the ship a cheer went up, audible above the gunfire.

'I had risen, half standing in my seat, as the wild thrill took hold of me. Again the dull glow, and in its light, the sea was alive with shell splashes from an outpouring of shells. Great columns of water stood out clearly in the brief instant of light, and I could see smoke hanging over her.'[23]

It was just the beginning of that phase of the battle when the gunners in both Fraser's battleship and *Jamaica* were able to pound the battle-cruiser with broadside after broadside, initially from around six miles to *Scharnhorst*'s west, and eventually from around four miles to her south, at first without any return of fire.

This devastating exercise of unrestricted naval firepower, which was supplemented by *Belfast*'s gunners' contributions from the north (see 4A and 4B in Map 20 for *Belfast*'s and *Scharnhorst*'s relative positions at 7.15 p.m. when the British cruiser opened fire), continued for more than 15 minutes as *Duke of York* and *Jamaica* proceeded to the south, effectively herding *Scharnhorst* away from her southern course (see tracks in Map 20). It was quickly followed by British warship after British warship, either singly or in pairs, torpedo tubes at the ready, taking their turn to charge in and torpedo the stricken battlecruiser after she changed course again, meandering first northward and then towards the south-west, in what amounted to a collective coup de grâce.

Fraser sent *Jamaica* in first. She left *Duke of York*'s side at 7.19 p.m. (see 5 in Map 20) and then darted in to fire her port side torpedoes at around 7.25 p.m. from around two miles to the south of *Scharnhorst* (see 6A and 6B in Map 20). They missed.[24]

Minutes later, after Burnett had likewise been instructed by Fraser to 'finish her off with torpedoes', *Belfast* moved in on *Scharnhorst* from the north. *Belfast*'s after the action torpedo report stated, '*Scharnhorst* was clearly visible from the tubes, silhouetted against the clear sky.'

The German ship was a tempting target. The winged battlecruiser, which had started the day with the capacity to outrun all the British war-ships apart from the destroyers, was adjudged to be crawling along at a mere six knots. Three of *Belfast*'s torpedoes were fired from going on four miles to *Scharnhorst's* north (see 7A and 7B in Map 20). According to Burnett, 'about four minutes later, a flash was seen, and underwater explosions were heard'. This led to the subsequent claim that the cruiser's torpedo teams were responsible for one of the hits that did for the battlecruiser.[25]

The relative locations of the subsequent torpedo attacks by British destroyers, and finally *Jamaica,* are shown in 8A and 8B, 9A and 9B and 10 A and 10B in Map 20. Post-battle analysis carried out in order to determine what eventually sunk the German ship took into account a report that during this late stage, *Scharnhorst* 'was seen to be well on fire amidships', and that on her starboard side, 'two simultaneous red glows under water were seen aft, and a few seconds later two columns of water appeared to come from further forward'.[26] The analysis suggests that the torpedo attacks after 7.19 p.m. by the British cruisers and destroyers yielded some five hits.[27]

It was a sign of how severely *Scharnhorst* was damaged even before the post-7.19 p.m. torpedo attacks, that when her guns finally responded to *Duke of York's* and *Jamaica's* initial 7.01 p.m. shelling, it was for the most part via her secondary armament. The only 11-inch gunners putting up a spirited resistance were in her rear turret, referred to by the Germans as 'Caesar'. The 11-inch guns in the Anton turret had long since fallen silent, while those in the Bruno turret were only in action intermittently.[28]

Given all this shelling and torpedoing, it is surprising there was anyone left on board the battlecruiser who was still capable of standing up, let alone shooting. Appalling scenes are alluded to in the *Scharnhorst* survivors' reports (referred to in Note 29): they for instance refer to the 'frightful scenes of carnage' in the compartments above the armoured deck, where 'stretcher parties picked their way through ... mangled bodies swilling round in a mixture of blood and sea water'.[29]

Scharnhorst's Maschineobergefreiter (stoker) Helmut Feifer, who was just 20 years old at the time of the action, may have been describing the lead up to the abovementioned carnage when he recalled, in the course of an interview after the war, how he felt the ship being jolted while he was delivering a message below decks, and how at the time he could not be sure whether the vibrations were caused by the firing of his ship's own guns, or by the impact of the enemy's shells or torpedoes. He says he only discovered the grim truth on returning to the compartment above the armoured deck where his action station was located: 'My compartment had been hit . . . My comrades had been torn apart . . . Only one was still alive. He was on fire from head to toe. His hair was burning like a flaming torch.'[30]

Feifer somehow managed to extinguish the flames, only to be tortured by the sight of his burned comrade in agony. What he witnessed during the battle was all the more upsetting because the men killed in Feifer's compartment were just some of those below decks who lost their lives. More than 25 other men had to be sacrificed when yet another torpedo blast at the back of the ship caused irreparable damage. In order to protect the rest of the ship, the doors sealing off the aft section had to be locked, leaving those aft of them to their fate.

As one might have expected, the battlecruiser's sailors at their action stations in the open air were if anything even more vulnerable than those below decks. One of the *Scharnhorst* survivors' reports details 'how most of the gun crews on the port side seemed to be dead . . . [What was left of] their crews lay in grotesque attitudes all over the deck . . . slowly being washed overboard.'

At least those confined in *Scharnhorst*'s main armament gun turrets had some protection. The German gunners in *Scharnhorst*'s Bruno turret survived after a hit early on in the battle had put its ventilation and suction system out of action, but only just. According to one of the *Scharnhorst* survivors' reports, 'the whole turret filled with choking smoke every time the breeches were opened . . . It was impossible to see anything more than a yard away. This, combined with the motion of the ship in [the] heavy weather, rendered nearly every man in the turret violently seasick.'

Minutes before the end of the battle, the turret was finally put out of action as a result of a torpedo exploding. In the words of one of the *Scharnhorst* survivors' reports: 'The men from the magazines clambered up into the turret, only to find the doors had jammed . . . After frantic efforts, they only got one of them open, by which time *Scharnhorst* was already sinking, and water was coming up from below.'

Shortly before the last of the torpedo attacks triggered the order to abandon ship, the disembodied voice of *Scharnhorst*'s commander, Hintze, was once again heard making an announcement over the ship's sound system. This time it was valedictory: 'I shake you all by the hand for the last time. I have sent this signal to the Führer: "We shall fight to the last shell."'

Hintze was as good as his word. Although many of *Scharnhorst*'s guns were either destroyed, or were not manned during the worst of the shelling, the 11-inch guns in the rear turret carried on firing until the abandon ship order was given. By then it was obvious that *Scharnhorst*'s progressive listing to starboard would soon make it impossible to carry on firing, if that was not already the case.

The final abandoning of the ship was chaotic. None of the survivors had been pre-allocated an abandon ship station, and lifebelts were only hurriedly put on at the last minute by those who could find them. According to one of the *Scharnhorst* survivors' reports, 'two or three of the cadets attempted to jump into the water from the bridge, but misjudged the list, and crashed to the deck. A large number of men jumped overboard on the starboard side [only] to be sucked under, or knocked out by falling debris.'

Not everyone was so keen to get into the water. There were evidently some in *Scharnhorst*'s crew who had come to believe the myth that claimed the battlecruiser was unsinkable. As far as they were concerned, it was irrational to even contemplate swapping the 'safety' of her decks for the icy water. Others were in denial for different reasons. Interviewed after the war, Helmut Backhaus, the signalman referred to in Chapter 37, cited the case of a man from the engine room, who rang him up after the abandon ship order had been given. 'I shouted: "Stop what you're doing, and abandon ship". He said, "You must be crazy". He didn't understand even though the ship was listing.

'I repeated: "We have to abandon ship." [Then] I scrambled to remove my fur jacket and fur lined boots. I climbed over the parapet onto the enormous searchlight, and then I was in the water. It was freezing! I was struggling in the water when I saw *Scharnhorst*'s keel. She had turned over.'[31]

Matrosengefreiter (Ordinary Seaman) Helmut Boekhoff, who like Backhaus was just 19 years old at the time, told his post-war interviewer that he did not even have the chance to undress: 'By the time I got over to the starboard side, she just went . . . right over. I was slung right out into the water away from the ship. The first thing I thought about was: "Raft!". I'd got no life jacket . . . I saw . . . bits floating around, and the next thing I saw there was a piece of wood, and I just grabbed it.

'Someone grabbed hold of my boot, which I let go because if you don't let the boot go, you go with 'em. You couldn't save anybody because the moment you are in the water, all you think about is yourself . . . At that time I looked round, I saw the ship turn right round, and saw the propellers still turning because . . . the English had shot a star shot right across us. Then all of a sudden, I saw her going down, [and] come back up again. Then all of a sudden she finally went down. As she went down, I had this tremendous tremor in my stomach, [and] in my legs. There was a big explosion below, and by that time all I thought about was to get away, [to]get saved. When I looked round, I see these blokes, they're swimming between all these bits, and still shouting "Heil our Führer!" and "Scharnhorst. Hip hip hooray!" again and again. I thought, "Well, what a waste." '[32]

The attempt by those in the water to cheer each other up with their patriotic exclamations did not last long. According to Backhaus: 'All of a sudden the water became calmer. You could see the corpses floating face down. You knew they were dead.'[33]

Backhaus and the remaining German survivors would almost certainly have gone the same way had it not been for the early intervention of the crews in the British destroyers *Scorpion* and *Matchless*. Their arrival near the location where *Scharnhorst* was last seen – which was where she had been sighted through the smoke billowing out of her at 7.37 p.m. when *Jamaica*'s second batch of torpedoes had been fired at her – might have come too late, had not the men in both these destroyers reacted quickly after being presented with evidence suggesting the German battlecruiser had gone down.[34] *Scorpion*'s Lieutenant Commander Clouston later confirmed: 'At 1940 the radar reported that the echo, which had been getting smaller, had faded completely.'[35]

Dick Squires in *Matchless*, the other destroyer which had moved in to save survivors, appears to have been one of the last British sailors to see evidence of *Scharnhorst* afloat. When interviewed post-war, he admitted he only saw the dying traces of the battlecruiser in the distance: 'All we could see originally was a glow. She was well on fire . . . You could see her silhouette as we came nearer. Then the fire disappeared suddenly . . . One second she was there, and the next she was gone.' (See Note 36, and 10 in Map 1, and 9 in Map 18 for approximate location.)[36]

Sub-Lieutenant Rex Chard, *Scorpion*'s navigation officer, would later recall how in spite of the darkness, they knew when they arrived at the place where *Scharnhorst* had gone down: 'You could smell the fuel oil on the water, and hear voices, people shouting.' John Baxendale, a *Scorpion* able seaman, would never forget how they then 'switched searchlights on, and there they all were, floating round everywhere'.[37]

Scorpion's 20-year-old telegraphist John Wass, who went out on deck shortly afterwards, was amazed by the scale of the disaster. An hour earlier he had been praying that his own life and the lives of his shipmates would be spared as *Scorpion* narrowly missed being hit by *Scharnhorst*'s shells following the firing of *Scorpion*'s torpedoes. Yet here being played out before his eyes was the embodiment of a complete reversal. Rising and falling with the heavy swell, amidst pieces of wood, wooden gratings, and duckboards not to mention the oil were what looked like around 200 Germans, some on rafts, and some in the water, supported by life jackets with amber lights on them. 'One raft had a man on it with gold braid on his cuffs, as well as other men,' Wass recalled later. 'Seamen on our ship threw them a line. But they did not seize hold of it, and before anything could be done, they were swept away.'[38]

A report from *Scorpion* would later inform Fraser that 'the Captain' and 'the Commander' of *Scharnhorst* (possibly *Scharnhorst*'s First Officer Fregattenkapitän Dominick and Commander, Kapitän zur See Hintze) were seen in the water seriously wounded. 'The Captain was dead before he could be reached,' Fraser wrote in his battle report, adding 'the Commander grasped a life-line, but succumbed before he could be hauled in.'

It is easy to understand how Fraser, whose last view of *Scharnhorst* had been, as he described it, 'a dull glow through a dense cloud of smoke', was able to remain objective when it came to deciding how long it was safe to remain near the scene of the battle.[39] But *Scorpion*'s Sub-Lieutenant Rex Chard, who could not have been closer to the rescue effort, became quite emotional when he was later asked what he had witnessed, answering: 'You could see them giving up. Some were swimming and not making it, literally drowning in front of you, and you couldn't do any-thing about it.'[40]

At least one of the German survivors might have taken issue with that statement. The following extract from Günter Sträter's account of his rescue suggests he believed his rescuers could have done more: 'We even-tually drifted [on the raft] up to a stationary English destroyer (*Scorpion*) which had a net hanging down her starboard side. We climbed up to the deck on this. The English did not assist those who did not have the strength to climb up. As a result, three of those on our raft drowned.'[41]

There must have been several others who, like Sträter's lost compan-ions, fell at the last fence. *Matchless*' Tom Bethell recalled afterwards: 'We couldn't bring them all in. They was sliding back in the water.'[42]

Approximately 20 minutes after the rescuing started, Fraser messaged *Scorpion*'s Lieutenant Commander Clouston to ask whether he could confirm that *Scharnhorst* had sunk.[43]

At 8.20 p.m. Clouston replied: 'Survivors are from *Scharnhorst*', and then added ten minutes later: 'Survivors state *Scharnhorst* has sunk.'[44] That was good enough for Fraser, who quickly informed the Admiralty: '*Scharnhorst* sunk.'[45] The reply came back, presumably approved by Admiral Andrew Cunningham, who had several months previously replaced the then ailing Sir Dudley Pound as First Sea Lord: 'Grand. Well done.'[46]

Shortly afterwards the commanders of all the destroyers in the area were ordered to follow *Duke of York* to the Kola Inlet, even though that meant abandoning some of *Scharnhorst*'s crew, who might have survived had the rescue not been curtailed so abruptly.[47] By the time this signal reached Clouston, *Scorpion* had rescued just 30 Germans and *Matchless* had saved another six, a paltry haul compared with the 1,900-plus mem-bers of the crew who had been on board the battlecruiser.[48]

The order to depart was particularly resented by *Scorpion*'s John Baxen-dale, one of eight men in the destroyer who had been pulling the survivors out of the water: 'I was just about to pull another guy out, when we got the buzz that the U-boats were arriving. Well, naturally the Captain ups and out, so we had to leave them all there. We were nearly crying.'[49]

A redeeming feature from the Allies' viewpoint was that the tragic loss of life was in a good cause. Those travelling in JW 55B could now be sure they would not be attacked by surface ships. However, that did not mean they were home and dry. The convoy's Commodore Maitland Boucher at first feared that the focus on the sinking of the battlecruiser would leave the way open for the U-boats, which had been following JW55B. Conditions would certainly have assisted an underwater attack. The strong wind, high seas, occasional sleet and darkness, would have made it very hard to spot any U-boats which were stalking JW55B's merchant ships.

But as Boucher wrote in his report: 'These conditions suddenly changed. The wind and sea became calmer. The sky cleared, and the most extraordinary Northern Lights ever seen during the voyage illuminated the whole sky for some hours. Broad sinuous ribbons of very bright light streamed right across the sky from horizon to horizon, sometimes three or more together lighting up the whole sea. It seemed like supernatural aid in our favour . . . for it quite reversed the conditions for submarine attack, and may have saved the convoy.'[50]

Whether or not it was decisive, JW55B duly reached Russia prior to the end of the year, as did the warships in Forces 1 and 2.

The 16 wounded from *Norfolk* and the 11 from *Saumarez* were immediately rushed to the Royal Naval Auxiliary Hospital, which by this time was up and running in Vaenga. Although a vast improvement on facilities offered previously, the care could not match the treatment they would have received in a London hospital. Two of the *Saumarez* casualties died within hours of being admitted.[51]

Saumarez's Kenneth Evans only survived after being given transfusions using the blood donated by his shipmates. But nothing could be done to save his shattered right leg. Shortly after arriving at the Vaenga hospital, he was told it would have to be amputated under a local anaesthetic by one of the British surgeons.

Losing a limb in any circumstances is an ordeal. However the following description of the operation suggests that the bedside manner of those in Russia, who had been entrusted with the task of caring for wounded British seamen, was substantially improved compared with what the likes of Bill Short and Morris Mills had had to endure following their vessels' arrival in the Kola Inlet as part of PQ13 (see Chapter 8).

According to Evans, the operation was still frightening: 'Although they piled the blankets up on my chest . . . [so I could not] see what was going on, there were lights above the operating table where [thanks to the reflection] you could see action taking place, and you get the sound of sawing through bones . . . you could hear the sound of it . . . You didn't feel pain . . .

'I remember the anaesthetist standing alongside me . . . talking to me, and dropping things and asking me to count [them] to keep me occupied.'[52]

However not being put to sleep was to prove advantageous. The surgeon wanted to amputate Evans' left leg as well once he saw how badly the broken femur had been fragmented. He might have gone ahead and taken it off too, had Evans not remonstrated, and asked if he could be sent back to England to see if it could be treated successfully there. This was agreed provided Evans signed a note stating that he would be responsible if anything went wrong on the way home.

He was eventually sent back to Scapa Flow in one of the returning warships, along with the other wounded men, after being fitted with a Spica plaster (a plaster that covered not just his left leg but also the trunk of his body up to his chin) so that his broken bones were not further damaged on the way back. It was to be worth all the discomfort. After many operations, Evans' left leg was eventually saved. Not only that: thanks to painstaking experimentation and a lot of determined exercising, he was able to build it up, and with the aid of an artificial right leg, he was able to walk again.

Being willing to learn lessons from what had happened was not apparently something that appealed to the man ultimately responsible for Evans' injury – and for the deaths of so many German sailors. Dönitz never deigned to admit that he had erred in sending *Scharnhorst* out in such unsuitable conditions in spite of knowing that her radar equipment was so much less effective than that used by her foe. In his self-serving memoir, written after the war, he wrote: 'With a little more luck, everything might have turned out differently and with happier results . . . The story that the *Scharnhorst* in both engagements had been unable to locate the enemy and had simply been shot to pieces thanks to the enemy's superior radar is certainly and demonstrably false.'[53]

Schniewind by way of contrast was repentant. He was not going to let anything so catastrophic happen again on his watch. Two days after the sinking, he circulated a report laying out what amounted to sensible practice. It started with the words: 'These are the prerequisites for success . . .' But it was obvious to anyone on his staff who read between the lines that what followed implied a damning indictment of Dönitz's folly. There were to be no further sorties by the remaining heavy surface ships unless there was: 'Gap free reconnaissance and shadowing . . . , [and there would be] no deployment when enemy radar . . . can be exploited.' Because of the German shortage of aircraft, this he said counted out any action by surface forces except during daylight, and for the same reason he insisted: 'ambitious operations using heavy forces should only be carried out where we have a clear picture of the enemy units' location'. That he said would only be the case during the summer.

That did not mean he was advocating that the remaining heavy ships should be withdrawn from northern Norway during the winter. He was only backing what Raeder had said to Hitler before resigning. With that in mind Schniewind added: 'If we completely take away the threat of attack against the convoys in favourable circumstances, we will be allowing the enemy freedom to deploy his surface forces and especially his heavy ships wherever he wants . . . This could cause problems elsewhere.'[54]

However, there was an internal logic deficit in what he had written. If German surface forces were no longer being used during the winter months, it was likely that the British Admiralty would quickly realize what was happening and act accordingly. The significance could not have been more striking. The fact that the German naval commanders were being driven to such contortions in order to formulate their policy for the future underlined how comprehensive was their defeat. It would completely alter the balance of power in the Barents Sea during the months to come.

Lessons Learned

Main Actions: 25 and 30 January, 25 February and 30 April 1944
Sinking of Fort Bellingham, Hardy, Mahratta, and William
S. Thayer, JW56A and B, JW57, and RA59

GMT + 1

Paradoxically the reduced threat of attack by German surface ships after the *Scharnhorst* sinking did not in the first instance help the Allies quite as much as they might have wished. The Allied victory resulted in a level of complacency on the British side that did the Arctic convoy sailors a disservice. That explains how it came about that the 15 merchant ship convoy JW56A, which after a false start set out from Akureyri, Iceland on 21 January 1944, found itself squaring up to the 12 U-boats eventually made available by Kapitän Rudolf Peters, Führer der Unterseeboote Norwegen, with an inadequate close escort whose core was just nine destroyers. The convoy's escorts were under the command of the 26th Destroyer Flotilla's Captain Geoffrey Robson, who sailed in the destroyer *Hardy*. A distant covering force comprising two British cruisers, deployed in case German surface ships appeared, was not permitted to approach the convoy to provide additional anti-U-boat support.[1]

This failure to provide an adequate escort for the first leg of what was referred to in British documents as Operation FW, the protection of JW56A and B and RA56, would prove to be an expensive mistake. While the Germans also had limited resources at sea in the Arctic during the first weeks of January 1944 – there were in the first instance just six U-boats available for anti-convoy work – Peters made the most of these boats, referred to by him as Gruppe Isegrim (the name of the wolf in a series of medieval fables), by ordering them to lie in wait in the constricted Bear Island passage between that island and Norway's North Cape. He preferred to increase their interception chances by doing this even if it meant they would have fewer days to attack the convoy once it was located than if they made contact further to the west.

Peters' strategy would pay off. A lookout in one of the Isegrim boats duly sighted a convoy escort as JW56A approached the passage during the morning of 25 January 1944. Then, long before the appearance of all of the other six U-boats quickly summoned by Peters, some of the original six attacked.[2]

The first torpedoes unleashed missed their targets. However, in an ominous sign of things to come, shortly after 6.30 p.m. that same evening, the destroyer *Obdurate* was semi-crippled by the explosion made by a T5 torpedo fired by the crew in *U-360* (see Note 3 for location).[3] This was a new kind of torpedo: a German Navy Acoustic Torpedo that came to be known by Allied seamen as a 'gnat' and by Germans as a Zaunkönig (wren), whose charge was set off by the sound of the targeted ship's propellers.

Because the effects of the explosion, which went up some 20 yards away from the destroyer's starboard side, were relatively minor – some leaks and cracks affecting one engine – *Obdurate*'s crew managed to carry on driving their ship forward, albeit slowly.[4] But those in some of the now even less well-protected merchant ships were not to share *Obdurate*'s good fortune. No less than three of these vessels were to be torpedoed within the space of four hours as the convoy continued on its eastern path.[5] In case that number did not of itself provide its own message to Admiral Fraser, who was ultimately responsible for the Arctic convoys, he may have been further spurred on to take appropriate corrective action by the reports of the resulting suffering. Two of the torpedoings had tragic consequences.

The first such torpedoing occurred at around 8.15 p.m., that is in the dark, that same evening (25 January). *U-278*, aided by the flickering northern lights which improved the visibility, fired two torpedoes into the port side of the American Liberty ship *Penelope Barker*, in convoy position 12 (1st column, row 2 – see Note 6 for location).[6] In line with what happened in many of the attacks on merchant ships in the Arctic, the men in the engine room could not be saved. They were killed by the initial explosion. A premature death also awaited those other men who ended up in the sea, except for those who were rescued quickly.

One of the unlucky ones was the 24-year-old oiler Henry Teixeira, who had donned a rubber suit before jumping into the sea. Unfortunately for him, the precautions he had taken did not help him. Quite the reverse. According to several members of the destroyer *Savage*'s crew, who tried to fish him out of the water, Teixeira's suit 'was covered with fuel oil, and as he was attempting to climb the side of the destroyer . . . , he slipped back into the water and was caught in the destroyer's propeller'.[7] A post mortem report pointed out that it was the 'rubber suit without any place in which a boat hook could be inserted' which was the death of this man, 'who would otherwise have survived'.[8] He was one of the ten members of the 42-man crew who perished along with five of the 27 armed guards.[9]

Surgeon Lieutenant Maurice Hood (the same doctor who in the gale during the hours after the 31 December 1942 Battle of the Barents Sea, had leapt from *Obdurate* onto the trawler *Northern Gem*, so that he could care for the wounded – see Chapter 33) was also lost. He had boarded *Penelope Barker* two days previously to care for the American armed guard Henry Hazard, who was believed to be suffering from appendicitis. According to a report compiled afterwards, on hearing the abandon ship order, 'Dr Hood injected a sulfa derivative to prevent infection in case the appendix burst, and morphine to prevent pain. Ensign Wood and Dr Hood [then] dressed Hazard and walked him carefully to the [life]boat.' After doing that, Ensign Wood and Dr Hood went below again, apparently to assist others who had been wounded, but never re-emerged. They must have drowned when the ship sank stern first at around 8.25 p.m.[10]

John Crawley, an officer who served in the destroyer *Offa* while she was escorting JW56A, after the war recalled witnessing a similar level of commitment to saving lives exhibited by a sailor on his ship after the British merchant ship SS *Fort Bellingham*, in convoy position 31 (3rd column, 1st, i.e. front, row), was attacked. She was one of two merchant ships torpedoed by U-boats within a few minutes of each other shortly after midnight that night (see Note 11 for approximate location).[11] It beggars belief that anyone would have voluntarily entered the water in such freezing conditions, but as Crawley affirmed: 'A heroic AB torpedoman, [*Offa's*] Jimmy Green, attempted to rescue a . . . seaman by swimming out to him on a line. He [Green] was hauled back aboard the *Offa* unconscious.' The following extract from Crawley's account also commended the courage displayed by *Offa's* first lieutenant, who was in command of the destroyer's whaler: 'I can see her now, almost vertical, climbing the waves! . . . The First Lieutenant had made at least one . . . trip against orders, and was going away again, when the Captain yelled through the loud hailer: "Get bloody well inboard! Hoist whaler!" Knowing there were still survivors out there, I remember we yelled back, and cursed our Skipper.'[12]

To no avail. At around 3.20 a.m., after doing his best to sink both *Fort Bellingham* and the American *Andrew G. Curtin,* the second abandoned ship, *Offa's* much-criticized Lieutenant Commander Rowland Leonard ordered his crew to take the destroyer away from the scene while she was still in one piece. He later admitted he knew he was 'abandoning the *Fort Bellingham's* power-lifeboat and the men it carried', having previously cut short the attempt to rescue the British ship's survivors. 'I thought I had been lying stopped too long in a dangerous vicinity,' he explained.[13] In fairness to Leonard, another report states that he believed another ship would pick up the abandoned men.[14]

The men in this lifeboat were eventually written off as 'missing', which was all the more tragic because if they had remained on board *Fort Bellingham* until help arrived, they would have been saved along with the others who had waited. The single torpedo which had hit the ship on her port side beside the after end of her No. 3 hold, killed the two men in the flooded engine room. But although the ship settled, she was not actually sinking. *Fort Bellingham's* master reported later: 'I had given no orders to abandon ship . . . Obviously these men had panicked. They were under the impression that the cargo contained ammunition and feared a second torpedo.'[15] The failure to rescue the men in the lifeboat took the number who were not picked up to 39, out of the 75 who had been in the ship.[16]

There were to be no more sinkings before the merchant ships from

JW56A reached the Kola Inlet on 27 January.[17] However, the convoy's losses combined with intelligence derived from Enigma decrypts about the location of seven of the fifteen U-boats being assembled to attack JW56B, the next east-going convoy, which had set out from Loch Ewe on 22 January, shocked Fraser into changing his plans.[18] He was so perturbed that during 28 January, he diverted JW56B, with its 16 merchant ships (including 13 American vessels), to the north, in the hope this would delay its contact with U-boats.[19] That same day, he also insisted that the eight destroyers from the 26th Destroyer Flotilla which were still in working order after their work with JW56A, and which were scheduled to form part of the west-going RA56A's escort, should instead reinforce the nine destroyers originally allocated to JW56B.[20]

As was so often the case in the Arctic, where because of the ice to the north, it was hard to divert convoys away from both German reconnaissance aircraft and U-boat wolf packs effectively, Fraser's 28 January diversion of JW56B did not make much difference. The next morning the convoy was found by the crews in a Blohm & Voss 138 and in a U-boat.[21] By way of contrast, the fact that the British destroyer reinforcements reached JW56B, was to have a transformative effect.[22] Now for the first time since the start of the Arctic convoys, with the possible exception of PQ18, there was a substantial group of destroyers, unconstrained by defensive responsibilities, whose commanders had been given a licence to roam and attack aggressively wherever they detected U-boats operating.[23] It was a landmark event that was to have far reaching consequences. At a stroke, U-boat hunters became the hunted. But perhaps even more importantly, there was now a silver if not a gold standard for Arctic convoy protection, which could be followed from then on.

As a result, in contrast to what had transpired during the previous east-going convoy, not one JW56B merchant ship was lost, whereas one U-boat was sunk.[24] The U-boats' only success was the detonation during the early hours of 30 January of an acoustic torpedo near the starboard side of the back of the destroyer *Hardy*, which still carried Captain Geoffrey Robson, the 26th Destroyer Flotilla leader, as the convoy was proceeding south of Bear Island (see Note 25 for approximate location).[25] 'Bits of glowing red wreckage shoot up into the air twice as high as the mast,' *U-278*'s Oberleutnant Joachim Franze commented when he wrote up his war diary, adding: 'Just over a minute later, there is another blast, and the ship's silhouette is masked by a cloud of dark smoke'.[26]

The explosion was so powerful, it lifted the destroyer's 21-year-old Sub-Lieutenant Lloyd Stainer off the seat where he was sitting in his captain's sea cabin, and pitched him onto the deck. More significantly, because *Hardy*'s stern had been damaged so extensively, it was touch and go whether the destroyer could remain afloat for long enough for its crew to abandon ship in a measured way. After making it out into the open air, Stainer experienced what he described as 'the torture' of having to wait to be picked up off *Hardy*'s top deck while knowing that 'We had only a thin watertight bulkhead keeping out the ocean [at the back of the ship].' There was also the agony of not being able to help despite seeing where some of the crew were floating in the water. Their whereabouts, he said, were 'identified by the little red lights we all carried . . . There were very few of the red lights to be seen, but I could hear the pitiful cries for help.'

When eventually the destroyer *Venus* nosed up so that those remaining on board *Hardy* could jump across, Stainer remembered how the officers stood back while their men clambered to safety. Then, as he recalled afterwards: 'the Captain (Geoffrey Robson) simply called out: "Thank you gentlemen", thus releasing us to save ourselves.'

Stainer would never forget the aftermath, as they gathered in *Venus*' wardroom. There was the unexpected sound of another 'hefty explosion some way away from the ship. A few minutes afterwards, Captain Robson entered the wardroom to announce we had just torpedoed the *Hardy* so that her wreck would not be a hazard for other ships. With that he broke down in tears, to our embarrassment, and claimed he was a Jonah because he also lost his previous ship'.[27] This time he had lost 33 of *Hardy*'s crew; 16 officers and some 200 other ranks survived.[28]

The lessons learned during the passage of JW56B would be taken to heart with even more enthusiasm during the escorting of JW57, the next east-going Arctic convoy, which was to be the first stage of Operation FX (the protection of JW57 and RA57). JW57 was to be a massive enterprise, consisting of 43 merchant ships (30 American, 12 British and 1 Dutch), and 6 Russian minesweepers and chasers, as well as 2 oilers and a rescue ship. The convoy set out from Loch Ewe on 20 February 1944.[29] In addition to being allocated 20 destroyers, 4 corvettes, 2 frigates, and an anti-aircraft cruiser (*Black Prince*) in which escort commander Vice Admiral Irvine Glennie flew his flag – the abundance of escorts permitting four or more of them to be freed up so they could act as U-boat hunting groups outside the main convoy protection screen – JW 57 was also supported by the 11 Swordfish and 11 Grumman Wildcat fighter aircraft carried by *Chaser*, an auxiliary escort aircraft carrier, the first time such a vessel had accompanied an Arctic convoy since PQ18.[30] The use of the American-built Wildcats with their .5-inch guns instead of the Sea Hurricanes flown during PQ18 showed that the reports about the inadequacy of the latter's guns had been taken into account. The Wildcats were also about to earn praise for another characteristic. Unlike the Sea Hurricanes, they could be slammed down when landing on a pitching carrier flight deck in the roughest seas, and as the commander of *Chaser* put it, 'still come up smiling'.[31]

The addition of this new line of defence to the already impressive number of warships was to form the basis of the very efficient system that was to become the norm for future Arctic convoys. However, it could only work seamlessly if the weather permitted the carrier's aircraft to fly continuously. Because of the bad weather, they were grounded for much of 25 February.[32] That was awkward. The FdU's Kapitän Peters may have been frustrated at the way the convoy bypassed his original line of nine U-boats (Gruppe Werwolf) placed south-east of Jan Mayen Island (a change from the strategy adopted against JW 56A which had seen him place his boats in the Bear Island passage). But by working off frequent sighting reports by the crews of German reconnaissance aircraft, the first of which was on 23 February, he had managed to point the U-boats he had been able to deploy, which thanks to the formation of another group (Gruppe Hartmut – literally hard courage) had risen to 14, in the right direction. By the night of 24–25 February at least one U-boat was sustainably in touch and seemed likely to remain so.[33]

At around 8.55 p.m. during the evening of 25 February, as JW 57, still to the south-west of Bear Island, proceeded on its north-easterly course prior to its turn to the east, *U-990*'s Kapitänleutnant Hubert Nordheimer took advantage of a gap in the screen of escorts behind the convoy to fire an acoustic T5 torpedo at the destroyer *Mahratta* (see Note 34 for the location).[34] This ship was in the line of escorts that splayed out to starboard from the back of JW 57's starboard side.[35]

The result was violent to say the least. By all accounts there was a relatively quiet bang followed by a colossal boom, the latter probably being a secondary explosion set off by the first. It appears to have blown off the back of the ship. Lieutenant Commander Philip Bekenn, commander of *Impulsive,* a nearby destroyer, later confirmed: 'It was enormous! I thought the after magazine had gone up.'[36]

In one sense the events after the torpedoing mirrored what happened whenever a destroyer was successfully attacked by a U-boat. But this time there was a difference that took the incident from commonplace into the sphere of legend. The events affected even those like the destroyer *Wanderer*'s Sub-Lieutenant Dennis Foster, who was nowhere near where the action took place. He afterwards stated he initially registered the second explosion in *Mahratta* as 'a dull thud from the other side of the convoy' accompanied by 'a red glow' that 'lit up the low cloud'.[37]

Unusually, those in the most distant escorts were able to follow in real time communications between the commander of the torpedoed ship and the commander of the nearest destroyer. According to the post-war recollection of *Wanderer*'s Lieutenant Commander Reginald (Bob) Whinney: 'Up on the bridge I heard the educated and entirely calm voice – it could have been Drought, the Commanding Officer who had been at prep school and again at Dartmouth with me. "Have been hit by torpedo aft and am stopped" . . .' This, said Whinney, was followed by a series of equally restrained observations that culminated in one final report, delivered this time 'probably due to a fault in the R/T set' with 'an unhappy warble in the voice: "We are abandoning ship. We are sinking. We cannot last much longer." '[38]

Wanderer's Sub-Lieutenant Foster would later recall how *Mahratta*'s radio operator reported 'the hitting of a second torpedo over and over again' because, Foster said, 'the telegraphist's receiver (which if working properly would have enabled him to know his messages had been received) had been put out of action, his voice rising to a [peak] . . . until finally there was silence and we knew the end had come'.[39] Even more dramatic is the following extract from the post-war recollection of the incident by a sailor who had been on board the JW57 tanker *Daphnella*: 'The last thing they said was: "The water is now coming in through the door. It's rising higher . . ." It just stopped.'[40]

It seems possible that at least some of these memories of what was heard remotely may, like so many legends, have become slightly embroidered in the telling. That is an allegation that no-one could reasonably suggest in connection with the testimony of the appropriately named Jack Humble from Durham, who was just 18 when as a seaman on board *Mahratta* he found himself at the centre of the disaster.

It is no exaggeration to conclude from his verbal account, conveyed matter of factly with the kind of down to earth northern twang that one might expect to come out of the mouth of a Geordie from Newcastle, that when during the aftermath of 'the torpedoing' he realized the doors leading up from below decks, where he had been preparing for bed, to the upper open-air deck had been jammed by the explosions, he was terrified. 'You get that churning in your stomach . . . You think you're going down with your ship,' he admitted later.[41]

Eventually the blockage was cleared, and on making it up into the open air, he managed to step onto the ship's starboard side as *Mahratta* keeled over to port. Minutes later, her bows pointed up into the air and she sank stern first, barely giving him time to plop into the sea before she disappeared.[42] 'People were shouting: "Help!" Shouting for their mothers,' Humble reported when interviewed after the war, continuing: 'Then the shouts got less and less and less, until there was just the odd shout and then no shouts at all . . .

'In the water, I just kept myself moving, and just waited for my time to come. Till this voice said – I didn't know somebody was there: "I think I can see a ship. Let's swim towards it." I don't know who he was. But he probably helped to save my life really. I wouldn't have noticed that other ship . . . I swam towards the ship. The chap in front of me . . . I was swimming behind him . . . said, "I can't go any further." It had got to him, the cold. I felt the cold in the lower part of me stomach. When I got closer, I could see it was a destroyer . . . I shouted up. They threw a line over, but . . . because I was so cold and [because of] the oil fuel, I slipped off, and a wave took me away from the ship . . . I . . . thought that's it; I've had it . . . And then all of a sudden another wave came, and took me up the lower end of the ship, and they grabbed me.'

Humble would only later realize how lucky he had been to make it to the other ship. It was the destroyer *Impulsive*, whose commander had had to abort his ship's first attempt to approach *Mahratta* as a result of the deteriorating visibility caused by what was referred to in the report of proceedings as the 'blanketing snow'.[43] Humble was to be one of only 17 survivors. Notwithstanding the terrible weather, this was an astonishingly small proportion of the 236-man crew given that *Impulsive* was on hand as *Mahratta* sank.[44] It highlighted the terrible consequences of warships being sunk in the Arctic. The sinking of this one destroyer had resulted in the loss of more men than had been killed after no less than 24 merchant ships had been sunk or abandoned during PQ17 (see Chapter 24).

The total picked up might have been even smaller had it not been for the altruism of Peter McRae, *Mahratta's* 28-year-old surgeon, an accomplished all round sportsman, who before the war had played county cricket for Somerset. When after *Mahratta* sank, he realized that the Carley raft he was on was too crowded, he casually remarked, 'There's not enough room for us all', and slipped back into the water. Sadly he was not among those who were rescued. There cannot be many doctors who have embraced the spirit behind the Hippocratic Oath so wholeheartedly.[45]

As tragic as the events surrounding the sinking of *Mahratta* were, the ups and downs of JW57 were instructive. The combination of Allied aircraft and destroyers working in tandem was so effective that even though the sinking of the British destroyer gave Kapitän Peters a morale boosting lift, not one JW57 merchant ship was sunk by the 14 U-boats Peters deployed before the convoy reached Russian waters, which it did on 28 February.[46] This was partly because so as not to fall victim to the British anti-submarine tactics, Kapitän Peters was eventually forced to order his U-boat commanders, whose vessels were already partially disabled on account of iced-up guns and radar equipment, to stay out of harm's way by remaining underwater during daylight hours, and only to attack when it was dark.[47] This order was too late to help the crews in two of Peters' boats. He would later accept they must have been sunk after they failed to reply to his signals.[48]

The unequal dynamic between the two sides was to be repeated during the passage of RA57, the 31 merchant ship west-going convoy that departed from the Kola Inlet on 2 March 1944. The Allies' superiority was not surprising given that the close escort included most of the same ships that had protected JW57. This time a U-boat sneaked in to sink one merchant ship when the convoy was south-east of Bear Island, but for his pains, Peters lost another three U-boats, all of which were the victims of rocket projectiles fired from Swordfish, even though credit for one of the scalps had to be shared with the crew in a destroyer.[49]

The British aircraft crews from the Fleet Air Arm's 816 Composite Squadron, who had flown off the carrier during Operation FX, and whose participation had been crucial, would subsequently be hailed in the press for their magnificent determination and dedication. Vice Admiral Irvine Glennie, the head of the escort, stated: 'They never let me down once. They were so frozen after their flights that they had to be lifted out of the cockpits when they had landed.'[50]

But this glossed over that matters needed to be changed, even leaving aside the acknowledged fact that pilots were being asked to go up in Swordfish aircraft which had open-air cockpits. This, as Admiral Fraser appreciated, made them 'most unsuitable for Arctic conditions'.[51] The Swordfish, which at the time represented the Allies' main anti-U-boat threat during Arctic convoys, were being used in bumpy seas and foul weather, which led to their being damaged on landing. During Operation FX, concerns were raised that the pilots would run out of serviceable planes to fly.[52] At noon on 27 February during JW57, only six of the Swordfish on board the carrier were serviceable.[53] It was clear that if the U-boats were to be kept at bay in future, something had to be done to ensure more aircraft were available.

Fortunately for the merchant seamen in JW58, most of whom sailed from Loch Ewe on 27 March 1944 in what was to be the last east-going Arctic convoy before Operation Overlord, the invasion of France, Admiral Fraser was able to lay on what was required to protect the merchant ships in just about every way possible. Accompanying the convoy consisting of 48 merchant ships, an American cruiser which was to be donated to the Soviet Union, and one rescue ship, a record number of vessels for one Arctic convoy, for this, the first stage of Operation FY (the protection of JW58 and RA58), there were no less than 30 regular escorts – including the anti-aircraft cruiser *Diadem* in which the 10th Cruiser Squadron's Rear Admiral Frederick Dalrymple Hamilton flew his flag and 20 destroyers.[54] The level of air support was also unprecedented. Two escort carriers accompanied the ensemble, the first time this had been done. On board were 3 Swordfish, 12 Grumman Avenger torpedo bombers, adapted so they could drop depth charges, and 14 Wildcat fighters.[55] Although there were not enough Avengers available to replace all the Swordfish, and although there was not time to fit the Avengers up so they could carry rocket projectiles, which Swordfish crews had found so effective during RA57, the introduction of these new faster planes with their covered cockpits for the majority of the anti-U-boat work at least showed that things were moving in the right direction.

The sailing of such a big convoy would never have been attempted had it not been for the sinking of *Scharnhorst* which ruled out a large-scale attack by the German surface fleet. In other words, JW58's scale was a windfall of the Allies' Battle of North Cape victory. However, it was the deployment of the extra carrier and aircraft that was to make all the difference in the ongoing fight with the U-boats.

Now at long last there was a sufficient number of planes and carriers so that the aircraft in one carrier could bear the brunt of flying sufficient anti-submarine patrols, while the aircraft in the other could focus on hunting down the German airborne shadowers which had been homing in the U-boats, and which for that reason had been the bane of those participating in Arctic convoys for more than two years. If the crews operating from one carrier became overwhelmed, they could be helped by aircraft flying off the sister carrier. This new arrangement was to quickly bear dividends. Six shadowers were shot down by the JW58 Wildcats before the convoy reached Russia, without it losing a single ship.[56]

So devastating were these German losses that a Luftflotte 5 message was sent to the officers constituting the German Air Staff informing them that 'the shadowing of the latest ... convoy has shown that the aircraft available are no longer fit for purpose ... The Luftwaffe will not in future be able to give the U-boats the preliminary information it needs.'[57]

The carriers' aircraft were also responsible for sinking one of the three U-boats sunk during the convoy.[58]

That is not to say that everything went like clockwork for the Allies. One negative aspect of operating so many aircraft was that accidents became that much more likely. During the passage of the convoy, as well as one Wildcat being shot down by a U-boat's gunners, another aircraft, an Avenger, caught fire after crash landing on the carrier *Tracker*'s flight deck. The formal report describing the incident stated that the pilot, Sub-Lieutenant A. E. Ballantyne was 'very badly on fire' by the time he and his three-man crew got out of the plane, and although duffel coats were used to beat out the flames, 'the Pilot did not move after this'. The only compensation was that it might have been a lot worse. While mourning the officer's death, *Tracker*'s commander commented: 'Had this aircraft carried four depth charges, as well it might, the ship could probably have been a total loss.'[59]

The loss of the officer was not perceived as being the only negative development during the convoy. There was disappointment that the sinking rate relative to U-boat hunts, which did not match that obtained in the Atlantic, was not higher with so many escorts participating.[60]

However, that was not to compare like with like. The legendary Captain Freddie (Johnnie) Walker, whose record led to him being called 'King of the U-boat killers', and who led an escort group during JW58 with five sloops in it, pointed out that: 'Asdic conditions . . . were exceedingly bad. I had the humiliating experience of getting on to three U-boats at close range by sighting, radar etc, and of being utterly unable to make any asdic contact at all. It seems . . . there is a layer of water below which asdic detection of U-boats is impossible.'[61]

Nevertheless, even without effective asdic detection, the inner and outer rings of escorts that surrounded the convoy, supported by aircraft flying overhead, so terrorized the U-boat crews, that their vessels never came close enough to the merchant ships to have a chance of making an impact against JW58. Worse than that: as well as getting the merchant ships with all their aid through – JW58 arrived in the Kola Inlet on 4 April – the Germans were so focused on the actions of the escorts and their charges that crews of German U-boats and aircraft alike failed to spot the two fleet and four escort carriers that during the first days of April assembled with their escorting warships 120 miles north-west of Kaafjord, the sub-fjord off Altenfjord where *Tirpitz* lay.[62] On 3 April, 40 Barracuda bombers and 81 fighters flew off these carriers representing the core of Operation Tungsten, which culminated with *Tirpitz* being bombed in Kaa Fjord, and damaged again so that Germany's great battleship was out of action once more.[63]

The more or less equivalent escort to that laid on for JW58 also worked for the west-going RA58, which left Russia on 7 April 1944. However, there was to be a setback during the passage of the subsequent west-going RA59, the last Arctic convoy before the invasion of France, which departed from Russia on 28 April 1944 with 45 merchant ships. This can be partly explained by the relatively parsimonious allocation of escorts. The main difference for what was to be known as Operation FZ compared to the previous convoys was that the number of destroyers which along with the other escorts had been specially sent out to Russia from Scapa Flow to protect the convoy had been reduced to 16. They were to be supported by four Canadian frigates and a corvette.[64]

The setback certainly had nothing to do with any dereliction of duty by the aircraft crews operating from the two carriers. During one stretch, patrols launched from the carrier focusing on anti-U-boat cover (*Fencer*) remained airborne for 72 virtually consecutive hours. This was some feat given that the planes carried on flying in spite of the bad weather, only breaking off when the low visibility because of snow-storms, of which there were many, became impenetrable. Also because of the wind following the convoy, each time a new section of aircraft was flown off, the carrier had to be turned so that she was facing into the wind.[65] The intrepid work by the air crews paid off. In the course of the convoy, the aircraft sank three U-boats, including one caught on the surface by a Swordfish, no mean achievement for a plane written off for being too sluggish.[66]

Wildcat fighters flying off the carrier *Activity* also shot down one reconnaissance aircraft and appeared to cripple another.[67]

However, aircraft were not the answer to every situation. Because of the ineffectiveness of the asdic sets mentioned above, there was always the possibility that even the most vigilant of escort crews would let one or more U-boats through the net. This was all the more likely when a substantial U-boat force was able to get into position ahead of a convoy before the aircraft flown off the escorting Allied carriers could do anything about it. That just about sums up the context of the U-boat success that was to follow: the 12 U-boats in Gruppe Donner and Gruppe Teil, which had initially been waiting for an east-going convoy, were diverted into a line south-west of Bear Island, putting them in RA59's westward path, following a sighting by the crew in a German reconnaissance aircraft during the night of 28–29 April. By the late afternoon of 30 April the U-boats were already in their allotted positions.[68]

At around 8 p.m. that evening, as the convoy approached the line, *U-307*'s 33-year-old Oberleutnant Friedrich-Georg Herrle, perhaps benefiting from the asdic limitations mentioned by Johnnie Walker, infiltrated the two rings of escorts (see Note 69 for location).[69] This enabled his crew to fire three torpedoes, at least two of which powered into the starboard side of the American *William S. Thayer*, in position 33 (column 3, row 3) in the 12-column convoy.[70] Within minutes the freighter broke into two parts. The front section sank very quickly, leaving only the rear section afloat. It was listing to starboard, but carried on bobbing up and down in the waves until sunk by escorts some time later.[71]

Her master Daniel Sperbeck survived in spite of being on the bridge as the front section went down, since, as he put it, he just 'floated off'. But when analysing who else had made it, he made it clear it was curtains for anyone below the top deck in the forward section. After learning that the 3rd Assistant Engineer had said he was going to retrieve some possessions from his cabin for'ard, Sperbeck reported: 'If he did enter his room, there is no doubt he went down with the forward part of the ship.' Sperbeck had an equally negative tale to tell of a man who ran in the opposite direction, from the front of the ship towards the rear: 'He ran aft, and fell head first between the two parts of the ship. No one saw him after this time.'

Anyone, who like Sperbeck, climbed out of the water quickly after abandoning *William S. Thayer*, had a good chance of surviving because the master and crew in the *Robert Eden*, a merchant ship sailing at the back of the convoy, bravely came looking for them in spite of the danger. Many also survived for much longer than the minutes they had been told was the limit in such cold water because, as was noted by the commander of one of the circling destroyers, they were 'all floating in thick oil'.[72]

However, there were exceptions to this rule. Writing about the last sighting of Chin Wong, his ship's 3rd cook, Sperbeck reported: 'He was in the water; with one hand, he was holding on to one of the small rafts, while a member of the gun crew held on to his left hand. After he was in this position about one hour, he let go of the raft, and yanked away his hand that was being held by the gunner. He swam away and lowered his head into the water, holding it there. There is no doubt that he drowned.'[73]

Understandably, the attack spooked the Soviet seamen who were taking passage in the SS *John B. Lennon*, in the nearby position 24 (column 2, row 4) in the convoy, and as a result, their berths below decks left them feeling very vulnerable. They were just some of the Soviet sailors who were travelling to the West with RA59, so they could take possession of the warships the Soviet Union was being given. According to one of them, a G. Poliakov: 'We heard two loud explosions. On our vessel, action stations was sounded. The sound of boots could be heard running along the deck overhead. Our sailors climbed up onto the deck as well. Through clouds of smoke and steam we could see the Liberty ship sinking . . . However our ship just carried on sailing without making any detour . . .

'Some of the gunners in the merchant ships opened fire, mistaking ice flows and the crests of waves, and the fog buoys in the sea ahead of them for U-boat periscopes.'[74]

The First Cruiser Squadron's 51-year-old Rear Admiral Rhoderick McGrigor, who exercised his command of the escort while flying his flag in the anti-aircraft cruiser *Diadem,* also noted that equally suspicious as far as some trigger-happy gunners were concerned was 'a school of porpoises which passed through the columns'.[75]

Poliakov was summing up the mood that appears to have run through the crews in many of the convoy's ships when he wrote: 'On our ship, a ripple of fear touched crew and passengers alike.' However, the Soviet contingent in *John B. Lennon* eventually agreed to comply with the master's order that they go back below decks so as not to get in the crew's way after one of their officers quoted the Russian saying: 'When you go to a foreign monastery, you don't act as if you are at home'. What may have clinched it was the Russian officer pointing out that while their berths were below the water line, the jeopardy this presented was no more risky than that accepted every day by Russian submariners.

Nevertheless their nervousness revived after they were told that more than 20 Black Sea seamen had not been picked up following the torpedoing. Although the Russians in *John B. Lennon* did not know any of them, Poliakov wrote: 'Our hearts were saddened by the loss of every one of them.' American records reveal that 30 of *William S. Thayer*'s 69 crew and armed guards also perished.[76]

In case it is thought that some of the Russians in *John B. Lennon* were being unusually faint hearted, it is interesting to note that they were not alone in worrying that the U-boat commander who had attacked once successfully might come back for more. We will probably never know if this anxiety was justified. If it was, it is likely that any ardour stirred up in German submariners' breasts by the sinking and the continuous daylight all 'night', was only snuffed out because of the remarkable resolve of the carrier *Fencer*'s Acting Captain Wolf Bentinck. With a view to discouraging a renewed attack, he ordered that there should be what he afterwards referred to as 'maximum anti-submarine air effort' during the nine hours following the torpedoing which he considered essential 'to counter the initial success of the U-Boat pack'. His robust counter-measures appear to have had the desired effect. His report concluded: 'By 0600 (1 May) all [U-boats] were 20 miles astern.'[77] There were to be no more sinkings during RA59. Those ships whose destination was the Clyde arrived there on 6 May.

The carriers' and their aircraft crews' success did not go unnoticed. It prompted Admiral Fraser to pay a special tribute to them. In the following extract from his report he concluded: 'Operation FZ brings to an end a most successful season of winter convoys to North Russia. The arrival of so large a convoy . . . with only one casualty is a tribute both to the good conduct of the convoy and the escorts, and in this case to the great efforts of the escort carriers particularly.'[78]

40

Soviet Union's PQ17

Main Actions: 12 and 22 August 1944
U-boats' raid in the Kara Sea, Soviet convoy BD5,
and JW59 and RA59A

(See Map 22)

During August 1944, that is some three months after the suspension of
the Arctic convoys so that nothing should stand in the way of Allied shipping making a significant contribution to the invasion of France, the
German Navy found itself with enough resources to extend its operations
to the east of the Barents Sea. It was not the first time this had happened.
During the suspension of the Arctic convoys after the PQ17 disaster, the
German pocket battleship *Admiral Scheer* and several U-boats had in
August 1942 been sent to attack Russian ships with some success to the
east of Novaya Zemlya (Operation Wunderland).

One of the U-boat commanders sent eastward during this latest 1944
break was *U-365*'s Kapitänleutnant Haimar Wedemeyer, a nature loving
37-year-old with a very positive disposition. As he and his crew had sailed
U-365 around the northern end of Novaya Zemlya, and then southwards
past the eastern side of the archipelago, he had marvelled at the sea ice
which he said was 'swarming' with seals and polar bears. His account
discloses he had also greatly enjoyed seeing the vivid blue waters in the
far north, so different from the brackish muddier seas further south.

533

But all that was to sink into insignificance compared with what he saw during the late afternoon of 12 August 1944.

When he reached the area to the west of the Kara Sea's Ostrov Bely (White Island, a small piece of land which is separated from Russia's Siberian district's Yamal Peninsula by the narrow Malygin Strait – see Map 22), a lookout pointed out wisps of smoke on the horizon to the west. This was followed shortly afterwards by the appearance of the silhouettes of a funnel and masts, some of which had crow's nests. In an attempt to convey the sense of excitement that moved him and his crew as he positioned his vessel in order that they might attack the approaching ships, Wedemeyer would later write: 'We had often been at action stations in this boat. But we'd never been fortunate enough to find our enemy right in front of our torpedo tubes!'[1]

He would later find out it was a convoy referred to as BD5, whose name was derived from the Russian names of its two terminals. It was travelling to the east from Molotovsk in the White Sea (Beloye More in Russian) to the Kara Sea's Dikson, a staging post on the so-called Northern Sea Route (the latter being a portion of the 'Northeast Passage' between the Atlantic and Pacific Oceans), that passed along Russia's northern coastline, and which connected the country's ports at the western end of the Arctic with the Soviet Union's far east.

BD5 was tiny compared with those gigantic 1944 Arctic convoys referred to in the previous chapter. It consisted of just one freighter, the American *Ironclad,* which after her service during PQ17 had been donated to the Soviet Union and renamed *Marina Raskova,* and three trawlers converted into minesweepers. However, what made its safe arrival particularly important was that *Marina Raskova* was not just carrying supplies, such as flour and other food stuffs and equipment. In addition to her 55-man crew, she also had 364 passengers on board.[2] Among them were around 120 women and 20 children, most of whom were on their way to the various Northern Sea Route polar stations.[3]

The following extract from Wedemeyer's account makes it clear that as the submerged *U-365* crept forward from the side towards her passing prey, he only had eyes for the escorts, whose crews he realized might catch sight of his raised periscope at any moment. 'There is a single steamer . . . escorted by three escorts. One escort is moving forward in front [of the steamer], and the other two are around 600 metres away on either side . . . We carefully steam past the escort at the side [nearest us] . . . The vessel in front [of the steamer] passes, while we are still about 500 metres away. I shall never forget the scene: a relatively modern ship converted to act as a minesweeper and submarine chaser . . . Her Soviet flag is fluttering in the wind. Now she has passed, we can focus on the steamer . . . The quiet order is given: "Permission to fire salvo." '

Minutes later, after everyone in the U-boat had felt the jolt that occurred shortly before 7 p.m. when the fan of three torpedoes were fired simultaneously, they all felt what Wedemeyer referred to as 'the rumbling made by the detonation' as one of the missiles hit its target. His account continues: 'At the same time I see a column of water shoot up in the air amidships beside the steamer's engine room.' (See 8 in Map 22 and Note 4 for the approximate location.) [4]

After the explosion and the violent tremors, which were also registered by those in *Marina Raskova,* her panic-stricken passengers screamed, and rushed up to the top deck.[5] It took some time for the ship's crew to calm them down. But even the crew were shocked when they saw that *T-118,* the minesweeper in front of *Marina Raskova,* which had turned to come to their aid, had shortly afterwards likewise become the victim of an explosion. A member of *Marina Raskova*'s crew has described how *T-118* 'initially tilted to port. Then (the aft) half of the ship became submerged, leaving the other half sticking up out of the water. There followed another very loud explosion, probably her depth charges going up, and seconds later there was nothing to see apart from those of her crew who were either swimming in the water or supported by a floating pontoon; the ship herself had completely disappeared.'[6]

At the time, the prevailing view in the remaining minesweepers was that the two holed vessels had struck mines. Witnesses who saw the sinking of *T-118* appear to have been misled because the explosion from the acoustic T-5 torpedo fired at the minesweeper looked like what occurs when a mine is activated.[7] This misunderstanding was to contribute to the unfolding tragedy. Rather than carrying out a thorough and determined hunt for the U-boat, the crews in the two remaining minesweepers *T-114* and *T-116* had them moved to respectively two and a half miles away from the steamer's port and starboard sides, where they stopped so that boats carrying *Marina Raskova*'s passengers and crew could be brought to them.[8] The freighter's captain had reluctantly decided that because the engines were out of action, she must be abandoned.

Wedemeyer was to be pleasantly surprised when, after remaining submerged while his men manhandled into place fresh torpedoes, he ordered that the U-boat should ascend to periscope depth again. On arriving near the surface, he looked around the U-boat using his periscope, and noticed to his amazement that one of the escorts (*T-114*), which had stopped just a few hundred metres away from where he and his men had been working, far from continuing the search for a U-boat, had put down her anchor. 'It all adds up to making it impossible to miss her with our torpedo,' he wrote later.[9]

Whether he would have gone ahead and fired his torpedo at *T-114* if he had realized that many of the women and children from *Marina Raskova* had boarded this ship is left unsaid. In his account he confined himself to explaining the consequences of proceeding as he did, writing: 'The torpedo hits the Soviet warship astern. I see a blazing fire which engulfs the back of the ship . . . We feel the shock wave from the explosion hit our hull. We must have hit their magazine . . . The bows of the ship rise up until they are pointing at the sky. The crew can be seen jumping off, or perhaps they are wounded and are falling wounded into the sea. I only see one lifeboat. The others must have been blown up. Then the vessel capsizes and lies on its side . . . until eventually the bows disappear under the water.'[10]

What was observed by the Russian witnesses being rowed away from *Marina Raskova* appears to be in line with this. One reported: 'We heard a loud explosion and saw water shoot up into the air where *T-114* had been.'[11] When it came down, all that could be seen poking out of the water was the nose of the minesweeper and the cut-off stern. Even these wrecked remains were not visible for long.[12]

It would be some time before the scale of the tragedy would be fully understood. It was later discovered that one boat was able to rescue around 25 survivors, including five of the women and *T-114*'s Lieutenant Ivan Panasiuk.[13]

It is also unclear how long it took for *T-116*'s Lieutenant B. Babanov to realize that a U-boat's torpedoes rather than mines was behind the explosions. All that is certain is that before *U-365* could be manoeuvred into a position where it could attack Babanov's ship, he decided that discretion was the better part of valour, and left the area as quickly as he could.[14] And so it was that when it came to it, a Soviet ship had abandoned Russian seamen and their passengers, in a situation that was in principle not so very different from that encountered by the Royal Navy during PQ17, even if the scale, because there were fewer and less grand ships involved, was much smaller.

That may well not have excused Babanov as far as those abandoned were concerned, of which there were many. After *U-365*'s crew finally sank *Marina Rascova* with a torpedo at around 2 a.m. on 13 August, there were at least five boats holding survivors in the vicinity of the attack location.[15] It was only then that Wedemeyer appreciated the gravity of what had been perpetrated. 'Among the shipwrecked people there were . . . women,' he would later acknowledge in his account, 'dressed in drab but warm Russian weatherproof jackets. The survivors put their hands up. They seem to fear that we are going to shoot them with our machine gun.' But whatever one might think about whether it was acceptable for Wedemeyer and his crew to leave the Russian men and women in such an isolated cold spot in small boats, which is what Wedemeyer confirmed he had done, murdering helpless survivors was never the Germans' intention. Wedemeyer had the U-boat move away from the Russians in their boats without so much as communicating with these men and women he was in his turn leaving behind.[16]

That said, one suspects that Wedemeyer would have realized that at least some of those unfortunates left in the boats to fend for themselves would never see dry land again. If that was his premonition, he was correct. In the boat under the command of Ivan Vondrukhov, *Marina Raskova*'s 3rd navigator, two of the freighter's passengers died during the first three days after leaving the merchant ship, and their corpses were dropped over the side into the sea. A third man lost his mind and jumped into the sea of his own accord, and drowned.[17] But all was not lost. Babanov in *T-116* made it back to Khabarova, the base on the Russian mainland south-east of Novaya Zemlya, and raised the alarm. A gale descended over the Kara Sea during the days following the sinkings. However once the worst of the bad weather was past, aircraft were sent to look for those in the boats, and on 18 August the survivors, who had transferred from

Vondrukhov's boat into another of BD5's boats they had come across with only two men in it, were picked up west of Bely Island.[18]

That was two days after the boat that had saved 23 men and five women following the torpedoing of *T-114* had also been found by the Russian crew in an aircraft. This boat had reached dry land although the conflicting accounts make it hard to know whether they made it to Bely Island or to a deserted part of the Russian mainland near to the island.[19] But it was the fate of some 80-odd men and women who crowded into a large wooden boat, referred to as a 'kungas', which has attracted the interest of most historians who have written up the *Marina Raskova* story. Around 25 of them had died before the crew of one of the aircraft participating in the search located the boat and landed in the sea near the kungas six days after the *Marina Raskova* sinking.[20] The remainder might have been rescued there and then had not the first two men who jumped into the boat that was sent from the floating aircraft to the kungas contrived to capsize it. Although they were saved, the aircraft's boat was lost, and because the weather was deteriorating, the aircraft's pilot decided he had to take off there and then and return to his base, even though it meant leaving the majority of the survivors in the kungas behind.[21]

Because of the ongoing bad weather, four more days had passed before another pilot was able to resume the search. The kungas was duly found after a seven-hour flight, but after circling the boat for some nine hours while waiting for a ship that had been summoned to arrive, the Russian pilot, whose plane was getting low on fuel, had to take matters into his own hands. Notwithstanding the rough sea, he managed to land the plane, which according to some reports was a Catalina flying boat, near the kungas, and sent across a boat with two men from the aircraft in it.[22]

They were met by an unpleasant sight: around 20 corpses were lying in the bottom of the kungas with water lapping around them. Those who were still alive were no longer able to stand up. In hoarse rasping voices, they pleaded for a drink. There were pitifully few of them. It turned out there were only 14 survivors. One of them was Aleksandra Poroshina, the only female survivor from the kungas. The other woman who had been in the kungas had also died.[23]

This time all the living in the kungas were taken on board the plane.

However, in spite of the relatively small number of survivors, the aircraft was too heavily laden to take off. Eventually the pilot decided the only solution was to 'sail' the plane with the survivors in it to Bely Island. It took around 12 hours for them to reach the Malygin Strait, south of the island, and only then, having been located by the pilot of another plane, was another ship summoned. The survivors eventually ended up in Dikson. Their safe arrival meant that in the end the only boat with survivors in it that was never found was the *Marina Raskova*'s captain's boat. The men in the captain's boat were included in some 270 men, women and children who are believed to have died out of around 520 who had been on the three sunk ships.[24]

In the meantime, the Arctic convoying proper had resumed on 15 August 1944 with the sailing of JW59 from Loch Ewe on that day, thereby relegating the action in the area to the east of Novaya Zemlya to a sideshow once again. JW59 consisted of 31 merchant ships (18 American and 13 British), three tankers and a rescue ship as well as some submarine chasers, some destroyers and a battleship that were being donated to the Soviet Union. Its protection, the first part of Operation Victual (the support for JW59 and RA59A), was by a similar level of escorts and escort carriers as what had been laid on for some of the previous Arctic convoys (2 escort carriers, 1 cruiser and 17 other escorts), the only twist being that on this occasion the convoy leader, the 10th Cruiser Squadron's Vice Admiral Frederick Dalrymple-Hamilton, flew his flag in *Vindex*, one of the carriers.[25]

Given there had been no dramatic changes to the protection force, it is not surprising to find that even though the convoy was duly spotted by one of the five U-boats in the line up referred to by the Germans as Gruppe Trutz (Defiance), well to the south-west of Bear Island on 21 August, where some of them had been waiting for several weeks, the U-boats, pinned back as they were by the aircraft from the carriers, were only able to make an impact when something untoward occurred.[26] The slowing down of the sloop *Kite*, the escort covering the convoy's starboard quarter on 21 August, because of a technical problem, appears to have been such an event. Before it was fixed, while the convoy, around a third of the way between Jan Mayen Island and Bear Island, continued in a north-easterly direction, two of the torpedoes fired from *U-344* at around 6.40 a.m. that morning ended up blasting into her starboard side (see Note 27 for the location).[27] Ironically the problem that had led to what would turn out to be a disaster was the malfunctioning of the so-called foxer device dragged behind the ship, which was supposed to make such a loud noise as it was pulled through the water that it would act as a decoy, diverting the German acoustic homing torpedoes away from the ship's hull, rather than causing the ship to slow down so that she was vulnerable.[28]

The result was catastrophic. Within minutes, the ship appears to have turned onto her starboard side, and to have broken into two parts. One of the few who survived by jumping from the slanting port side of her hull into the water, and then being rescued by the crew in a destroyer, would later bear witness to how as he struggled to stay afloat, he saw *Kite*'s bows disappearing and her stern sticking up in the air. The stern also disappeared from view following two more loud bangs made when the ship's depth charges exploded.[29] The death toll was increased over what it would otherwise have been because although around 30 men made it off the ship, the thick oil combined with many not wearing lifebelts led to only 14 being recovered, five of whom expired within minutes. Only nine survived.[30]

As if to underline that this was a one-off, the crew in *U-344* were never given the chance to make it home so that they could celebrate their achievement. The very next day, she was sunk by one of *Vindex*'s Swordfish.[31] Two days later Wildcats from *Striker*, the other carrier, shot down a Blohm & Voss reconnaissance plane.

However, before the climax of the battle between the circling U-boats and the convoy's escorts could be played out, a strike by another U-boat against the other British force that was then at sea in Arctic waters was to spell out more death and destruction for the Allies. During the morning of 22 August 1944, the first wave of British aircraft that were to attack the repaired *Tirpitz* in Kaa Fjord had flown off the three Fleet aircraft carriers, which along with other vessels had assembled around 90 miles north of Altenfjord. The attacks represented the first of the series of bombing raids that were to take place during Operation Goodwood.[32]

While waiting to play their part, the escort carrier *Trumpeter* on the left, the cruiser *Kent* in the centre and the escort carrier *Nabob* on the right in a line abreast, and their screen of five frigates, whose general direction of travel was westward, had the misfortune to be spotted at around

5 p.m. that day by a lookout in *U-354*. The sighting was unexpected. The U-boat's officers had been told they should attack the east-going convoy, and they were on the way to where they hoped to do just that when they happened to stumble on the Operation Goodwood ships. Kapitän-leutnant Hans-Jürgen Sthamer, *U-354*'s 25-year-old commander, however, rose to the occasion. Around 15 minutes after the first sighting, his crew on his instructions fired a torpedo at what turned out to be the escort carrier *Nabob* while she, *Kent* and *Trumpeter* were just beginning the south-west leg of their zigzag. He was rewarded 21 seconds later when he saw what he described as 'a cloud' spring up into the air above *Nabob*, amidships.[33] Afterwards he observed that the aircraft carrier was listing 'a little' to starboard (see Note 34 for approximate location).[34]

The damage may have appeared insignificant from where Sthamer was standing, but the explosion, which according to a witness on board the targeted carrier sounded 'like a huge hammer hitting the side of the ship', left a gaping 50 by 40 foot hole in *Nabob*'s starboard quarter.[35]

Water surged inside the ship, and there are several accounts by survivors from the predominantly Canadian crew who had been swept off their feet as it reached them. Kenneth Scollan, an electrical artificer from Ontario, who at the time was in the pistol testing room four decks down, would tell the subsequent inquiry into the incident: 'The rush of water was very strong, just like standing in a strong river. The next thing I knew . . . my face was up against the . . . deck [above].'

Leading Seaman Adam Mckinley, who was fortunate enough to be in the port side section of the seamen's mess deck (three levels down from the flight deck) rather than on the starboard side next to the explosion, told the hearing which is referred to in the official record as the 'Enquiry': 'There was . . . a great tearing noise like very stiff paper being ripped. I imagine this was the bulkhead tearing open. I was then thrown down by a wave of water and oil which swept over me.' Mckinley only knew two men who had survived in spite of their being in the starboard side of the mess when the torpedo struck, and they, like Mckinley and Scollan, only escaped because they happened to end up within grasping distance of a ladder or hatch giving them a quick way up and out.[36]

No-one in the ship had a closer shave than Lieutenant James Goad from Toronto, who like Scollan was four decks down, where he was retrieving rum from the spirit room, when the surge reached him. All the members of the crew who were with him were drowned, and he would have been too had the water not picked him up and carried him through a number of open hatches to a higher deck, from where it was possible to stand on his own two feet, and then to find his own way up.[37]

There was no guarantee that even after such deliverance, those of *Nabob*'s crew who had survived the initial explosion and surge would make it off the ship safely. Members of the crew who assembled on the carrier's flight deck realized the U-boat might well attack again. They were right to be concerned. *U-354*'s Sthamer evidently wanted to go for a coup de grâce. But the acoustic T-5 torpedo his crew fired at about 5.25 p.m. instead blew the back off the frigate *Bickerton,* whose 40-year-old Commander Donald Macintyre, by turning her and two others from his 5th Escort Group towards where he believed the U-boat was hiding, had in effect sacrificed his ship, a reasonable decision given the frigate which had less than 200 men on board had screened a carrier carrying valuable aircraft, not to mention 840 men.[38] Although this was done deliberately, the moments after the impact were horrifying: 'The ship shuddered violently,' Macintyre reported, 'while a huge plume of water, in which could be seen depth charges and bodies, rose to a great height over the stern, and the ship then came to a standstill.'

At this most dangerous of times Macintyre temporarily lost control of his crew thanks to the loud blaring sound made by *Bickerton*'s siren being 'jammed full on', until it was finally silenced, and the 'choking fumes' released by the damaged smoke apparatus. But he was eventually able to venture aft to assess whether the ship could be saved. 'Passing some hideously shattered corpses, and burnt and wounded men, I found the stern had more or less disintegrated,' he wrote in his post-war memoirs. 'The ship lay with the remains of her stern under water, and a heavy list [to starboard].'[39] There had been many fatalities. According to his official report: 'All personnel stationed aft with the exception of one or two who were discovered wounded . . . were undoubtedly killed instantly by the explosion. It was not possible to identify individual bodies as they were badly mangled.'[40]

However, because the bulkhead aft of the engine room was still intact, the ship might have been towed back to port had there not been a more valuable vessel to protect. *Nabob*'s Canadian Captain Horatio Lay reported that although the interior of his ship was flooded up to the new water line, not only was the bulkhead aft of her engine rooms holding, but also her shaft propellers and rudder were intact.[41] On hearing this, Admiral Sir Henry Moore, who had replaced Admiral Fraser as Commander-in-Chief of the Home Fleet, and was flying his flag in the battleship *Duke of York*, agreed with Macintyre that *Bickerton* should be sunk, thereby allowing all ships to focus on escorting *Nabob*.[42]

Although it made sense, there were many heavy hearts as the frigate was abandoned and sunk by the destroyer *Vigilant*'s crew. More than 40 men had died in *Bickerton* alone. To that death toll had to be added the 21 who lost their lives in *Nabob* that day, including 11 who were Canadian.[43] What was to make the losses even more upsetting was the knowledge acquired in the coming days that all four British air raids during Operation Goodwood between 22 and 29 August 1944 had been failures. Although an Enigma decrypt would disclose that at least one 1,600 lb bomb dropped during the operation had passed through *Tirpitz*'s upper decks, it also revealed it only caused superficial damage because it failed to explode.[44]

The main problem for the Allies highlighted by the Operation Goodwood attacks was that while the Fleet Air Arm's Fairey Barracuda bombers could carry the 1,600 lb bombs that had the capacity to penetrate all *Tirpitz*'s decks (the lightest bomb that could), the top speed of these aircraft (around 240 mph) meant they were too slow to surprise the battleship's defenders. Each time Barracudas were deployed during Operation Goodwood, *Tirpitz* was concealed behind a smoke screen before these aircraft appeared overhead. The only Allied aircraft that reached the air space above Kaa Fjord during the operation before the smoke screen concealed the battleship – which is what Fleet Air Arm pilots flying the American-built Grumman Hellcat fighter-bombers (top speed around 390 mph) managed to engineer – were carrying lighter bombs, weighing as little as 500 lb, that could not penetrate all of *Tirpitz*'s decks.[45] In fact, one of the only positives to come out of the operation was that after a very slow journey, *Nabob* did eventually make it back to port, arriving at Scapa Flow on 27 August.[46]

Events after the *Nabob* torpedoing would explain why we will never know what Kapitänleutnant Sthamer and his crew in *U-354* were thinking as the damaged carrier escaped from their clutches. During the night of 23–24 August, while Sthamer and his men were endeavouring to make contact with JW59, their original target before they sighted Operation Goodwood's ships, *U-354* and another U-boat were spotted by the crew in a Swordfish aircraft, that had been flown off *Vindex,* when these U-boats were some 56 miles south-west of the south-east-going convoy. By this stage JW59 had already completed its passage to the east, and having reached the area to the north-east of North Cape, had turned to the south, as was necessary in order to approach its destination, the Kola Inlet. Two of the convoy's other escorts were summoned to where the U-boats had been seen.[47]

Sthamer and his men were unfortunate that the escorts summoned included the sloop *Mermaid,* whose 33-year-old commanding officer Lieutenant Commander John Mosse had prior to the sailing of JW59 been unjustly accused by Admiral Sir Max Horton, Commander-in-Chief Western Approaches, of trying to evade convoy duty by reporting his ship's engines needed to be checked. At the time Mosse hotly refuted the accusation. But he wondered later whether Horton was merely attempting to fire up his fighting spirit. If so, it was a clever ruse since it definitely had that effect.[48]

What the fired-up Mosse achieved during Operation Victual is described in his post-war account. The following extract from it takes up the story after *Mermaid* and the second escort had reached the spot where the U-boats had been sighted: 'I was swallowing a mug of cocoa at 0321/24 [August] when suddenly PING! – the sound [of the asdic sonar beam bouncing off a U-boat] I had been waiting to hear for five years. We took anti-GNAT precautions just in time. 90 seconds later a GNAT exploded close astern, followed a minute later by another.'[49]

But having narrowly avoided disaster, the tables were quickly turned and depth charges were dropped. Afterwards oil gushed up, and later bubbled to the surface, and this carried on for many hours afterwards. Promising though this was, when the British ships left the area, they had no proof that their depth charging had been successful (see Note 50 for the location).[50] It was only when German records became available after the war that it was established that a U-boat had certainly been sunk, and it was none other than Sthamer's *U-354.*[51]

JW59 duly reached Russia without further loss on 25 August, and RA59A, a relatively small convoy consisting of just nine merchant ships, which left the Kola Inlet on 28 August, was barely troubled by the three U-boats available west of Bear Island to attack it, an unsurprising result given that RA59A had the same escorts as the much larger JW59 in spite of the smaller convoy being easier to protect.[52] But on 2 September, HF/DF information suggested a U-boat was lying in wait to the south-east of Jan Mayen Island, around 50 miles to the west of the south-west-going convoy (see Note 53 for the location).[53] Aircraft from *Vindex* were directed towards it, and when the vessel submerged before it could be hit by rocket projectiles fired by the crew of the Swordfish which sighted it, escorts were once again summoned.[54]

The escorts' commander ordered that a creeping attack should be made. This involved three of the striking group in line abreast moving very slowly and quietly with main asdic switched off towards the site identified by the asdic of the directing ship some 600 yards behind them, and then simultaneously dropping depth charges when told by crew on the directing ship to do so. Mosse's *Mermaid* was the escort at the centre of the line of three, while the sloop *Peacock* participated as the director. '*Peacock* guided us rather like a ploughman with three horses,' Mosse explained later.[55]

Although there was no immediate evidence after this concerted attack to suggest that the U-boat had been damaged, about an hour later, following a thwarted attempt to line up another assault, there were three loud explosions, and after patterns of depth charges were dropped from *Mermaid* and then from *Peacock* over the area where the explosions had been observed, first bubbles, then some of the most grisly evidence imaginable floated to the surface.

The following gruesome details referring to what came up are contained in the report by Lieutenant Commander Dick Stannard, *Peacock*'s 42-year-old commanding officer, who as befitted a man who had been the first Royal Naval Reserve Officer to win the Victoria Cross, was not one to be squeamish:

'A gun's crew and ship's surgeon reported a human head passing down port side of ship. Some splintered wood was visible. Oil and wreckage was now coming to the surface practically alongside *Peacock*. Sea boat called away. The very pleasing sight of human bits and pieces were now visible, one nice large piece a few yards distance. The seagulls unfortunately robbed us of the smaller tit-bits; they could be seen having some very good pickings. For the next 20 minutes various odd things kept popping to the surface.'[56]

Much of this evidence was collected. Stannard's report states it included '1 pr of German leather trousers, 1 cushion, 1 glove . . . [and what the surgeon believed to be] 1 human lung (the ship's butcher said it did not come from an animal) . . . This has been bottled in a wardroom vase, and now reposes on C/O's mantlepiece.'[57] There could not have been clearer proof that the U-boat had been sunk. An entry in the war diary of Fregattenkapitän Teddy Suhren, now in post as Führer der Unterseeboote Norwegen, confirms it was the 31-year-old Kapitänleutnant Wolfgang Borger's *U-394*.[58]

There was to be no further contact with the Germans before RA59A reached port on 5 September without any losses.

Mosse subsequently wrote the following comments describing what transpired when he and *Peacock*'s Dick Stannard were called in to see Admiral Max Horton in Derby House after their ships had berthed in Gladstone Dock, Liverpool: 'Our reception this time was very different from the last. We went in together, Stannard clutching his gruesome jar of evidence, which he generously described as having been recovered from "*Mermaid*'s U-boat". He placed it on C in C's desk, and Max Horton waved it away with a shudder, and made me tell the story of both sinkings . . . No further reference was made to our engine noises.'[59]

The completion of Operation Victual represented another victory for the Allies, although there was still room for improvement. For example *Vindex*'s commander repeated the comment made following previous Arctic convoys that the Swordfish aircraft used on the carriers were usually too slow to be able to reach U-boats located using HF/DF.[60] This was a mere wrinkle in the larger scheme of things.

By way of contrast, well-informed Germans realized their prospects in the Arctic were now bleak. Fregattenkapitän Suhren, who could be relied upon to accurately disclose the prevailing pessimism at the Norwegian U-boat headquarters, conceded that while there was always a chance of sinking British warships provided the Germans were prepared to sacrifice some of their U-boats, there was no real prospect of their stopping the Arctic convoys as things stood. As was emphasized in one telling entry in his war diary: 'Only a line of U-boats placed ahead of the convoy will lead to success against the merchant ships. For that to happen, there would need to be offensive air reconnaissance.'[61]

Slaying the Dragon

Main Actions: 12 November and 13 December 1944
Sinking Tirpitz and U-365, RA62

(See Map 18 insert)
GMT + 1

The unsuccessful Operation Goodwood (referred to in Chapter 40) was to leave a dark cloud literally as well as metaphorically hanging over the attempts to protect subsequent Arctic convoys. The ongoing threat sprang from the continued presence in the Arctic of the battleship *Tirpitz*, which depending on the speaker's inclination, was nicknamed 'the beast' or 'the big bad wolf', but which might with more accuracy have been portrayed as the dragon that lay smoking in her lair.[1]

Not only did the failed Operation Goodwood attacks by the Fleet Air Arm bombers leave her still stationed in Kaa Fjord ready to pounce, but she had such well-honed defences by the second half of 1944 as to appear almost impregnable. Activation of these defences during Operation Goodwood had demonstrated that, no sooner did German lookouts or radar detect Allied aircraft flying towards her, than smoke began to belch forth from the smoke screen devices on her upper deck as well as from nearby ships and boats and from vantage points on the sides of Kaa Fjord in her vicinity. Within ten minutes of any alarm, she could be completely hidden from the crews of any aircraft that flew overhead, precluding a viable attack.

This seemingly insoluble problem was only solved thanks to input from Britain's most creative scientists and engineers. Leading the way was Barnes Wallis, the brilliant engineer behind the bouncing bomb which famously breached two German dams, thereby causing flooding in the Ruhr valley in May 1943. Barnes Wallis was also the inventor behind the bunker-busting 12,000 lb Tallboy bombs (going on 6 tons, more than seven times heavier than the heaviest bombs used during Operation Goodwood) which RAF commanders believed could be dropped over *Tirpitz* from specially adapted Avro Lancaster bombers. These were planes that had much greater potential for dealing with *Tirpitz* than any aircraft the Fleet Air Arm possessed.

After hearing what was feasible, Air Chief Marshal Sir Arthur ('Bomber') Harris, head of Bomber Command, ruled that the Tallboy bombs were to be dropped by 617 Squadron, whose crews had dropped the bouncing 'dambusting' bombs, and by 9 Squadron. The recently invented Stabilized Automated Bombing Sight, also developed by scientists in Britain, was to be used wherever possible to facilitate bombing with the required precision.

The bombing raid by 617 and 9 squadrons on 15 September 1944 broke the deadlock: in the course of Operation Paravane, Lancaster bombers flown from the island of Yagodnik, near Archangel, holed *Tirpitz*. The operation had to start in Russia because the range would have been too great for Lancasters carrying such a heavy payload if they had had to fly from and return to aerodromes in Britain. Before the passing of the first days of October 1944, reports from Norwegian agents, who were complying with instructions they received from the British Secret Intelligence Service, and Enigma decrypts had confirmed that for the moment at least she was out of action (see Note 2 for details of the damage done to *Tirpitz* supplied by Norwegian agents, and the part they played in making a success of the attack).[2]

On 15 October 1944 she was moved to the south of Haakoy island (Håkøya – see Map 18 inset). There she was anchored with her bow pointing east towards the nearby island where Tromso was located, bringing her within range of Lancaster bombers loaded with Tallboy bombs that could be flown from Scotland, provided the crews could endure 12-hour flights.

Although *Tirpitz* was damaged again in a raid on 29 October 1944

(Operation Obviate), cloudy weather at the time of the operation proved to be an obstacle in the way of the kind of precision bombing necessary to sink her. Another raid that took place on the morning of 12 November 1944 (Operation Catechism) was to have more success.

617 Squadron's leader Wing Commander James 'Willie' Tait, who led the mission, recalled later how the conditions were very different to those encountered during the previous raid. Their optimism leapt when, with not a cloud in the sky, the crews of the approaching British aircraft saw *Tirpitz*, as Tait put it: 'lying squat and black among her torpedo nets like a spider in her web, silhouetted against the glittering blue and green water of the fjord.' (See Chapter 18 inset and 12 in Map 1 for location.)[3] They were also blessed by meeting no opposition from the Luftwaffe. Not one of the fighter aircraft from the German squadrons based in Bardufoss opposed them. There is no knowing what might have happened had the Luftwaffe taken off in time and in force given that the Lancasters, which had been specially adapted in order to give them the necessary range, had minimal ammunition for their inadequate guns, and had fuel tanks installed internally. 'If we'd been attacked and there was a tracer shell, we would have gone up in flames in no time at all,' wrote one of the participating crew afterwards.[4] As it was, going on 30 British aircraft were left to mount their attack, dropping their first bombs shortly after 9.40 a.m. without any effective opposition.

To monitor the explosion of the bombs which were dropped from between around 12,000 and 16,000 feet, one Lancaster was equipped with cameras rather than bombs.[5] The flickering black and white film the cameraman came back with is stirring. Those who view the *Tirpitz* film initially see the flickering flashes that emanated from *Tirpitz*'s numerous anti-aircraft guns as the aircraft approached the battleship. This and the smoke screen that already covers half the ship is succeeded by the sudden flowering of a white cloud of smoke, which belches out from amidships, the first sign she had been hit. What looks like another explosion amidships, and another which appears to be coming from under *Tirpitz*'s Caesar gun turret, well aft of amidships, are also captured on the film, the latter eruptions being accompanied by a simultaneous explosion on the nearby shore to port, which threw debris high into the air. The film finally shows two or three more explosions in the sea on the ship's port side seconds later, but that is all, as even the best of cameras could not record what happened next. By then the entire ship was hidden from view by the smoke.

The suspicion that even after the bombing *Tirpitz* was still afloat disappointed Bruce ('Buck') Buckham, the Australian pilot of the aircraft carrying the film unit. But as he explained afterwards, just before he set off for home, the voice of Lieutenant Eric Giersch, a fellow Australian, came up on the intercom saying: 'Hey Skip, I think she's keeling over. Have a look.' Buckham turned the plane back once again, and when he still could not see, in the words of Hugh Rogers, the British cameraman on board: 'he dipped the starboard wing and lowered his altitude. We could see in the distance that the smoke and steam had gone. Though there was a haze over the aircraft, you could see it was upside down.'[6]

That sighting told them the ship had been hit. What they did not know was how many Germans their squadrons had maimed and killed in the process, or the agonies, both mental and physical, survivors trapped inside the upturned hull would have to endure.

For some of the Germans it was, if that was possible, as bad as anything experienced by those who escaped with their lives when the lower regions of *Nabob* were flooded (see Chapter 40). Petty Officer Ernst Renner, one of the Germans affected, was following one of his men up a ladder leading from the Ammunition Room under one of the 5.9-inch gun turrets on the starboard side of the ship for'ard of the funnel in the hope they might reach a hatchway leading from the turret to the open air, when the ship which after the first hits had been listing more and more to port, all of a sudden turned right over. 'A giant column of water pushed into the tower (the turret) and the man in front of me fell right into this surge,' he reported later. 'He was carried away by the water, washed into the tower, and did not make another sound. He died instantly. Horrified, I screamed to the others: "Quick . . . back to the Ammunition Room!" We climbed back as fast as we could, now upwards since the ship had turned [over].'

They ended up with around 35 other men near one of the ship's boiler rooms. 'One comrade hugged me,' Renner recalled afterwards, 'and said: ". . . I will never see my Mum again." But because they had been lucky enough to reach what amounted to an air bubble, they had the time to unscrew the bolts of a manhole cover above their heads which gave them access to an empty tank. Once inside, they were able to knock on the exterior wall of the hull, enabling rescuers some time later to pinpoint where they were. Eventually the rescuers cut a hole in the hull near them, and they all escaped.[7]

Alfred Zuba, who appears to have been located four decks down when *Tirpitz* flipped over, revealed afterwards how on three occasions he only escaped being drowned inside the battleship by the skin of his teeth. In his account he describes how one minute he found himself stuck on a slippery sloping deck he could not climb up, and the next: 'The water breaks in, gurgling, black and oily and comes up to my chest . . . More and more water comes streaming in, holds me tight and does not let me go . . . At last I find a handhold and pull myself up.'

Shortly afterwards he faced another existential crisis which saw him hanging on to a pipe for dear life as his legs dangled over the water flooding in beneath him. Once again, luck was on his side, and his flailing legs happened to strike a ventilator shaft he could stand on.

After all these exertions in the warren of compartments 'underneath' *Tirpitz*'s 'open air' deck, he and some other men found themselves in a dry compartment near the ship's fuel tanks at the bottom of the ship. Here they were encouraged by the sounds they heard that echoed round the cavity where they sat entombed, although Zuba was only too aware that water was rising in the next compartment, and that once it reached a certain level there would be nothing to prevent it flowing into their space. At one point voices were heard, and Zuba and his companions shouted in unison 'Where are you?' They also heard knocking: 'Bang, bang, bang,' wrote Zuba. 'We answer with a fire extinguisher – bang, bang, bang. Now the bang is quite soft and weak, then it is very light indeed – bang, bang, bang. Always three bangs.'

After a time the officer with them ordered them to remain silent so as not to use up the fast diminishing supply of oxygen. They only survived because they had access to bottled oxygen, and because rescuers using cutting equipment broke in through the hull near where they were sitting. The piece of steel the rescuers cut out from above them thumped down beside them. Zuba would later recall what he saw when he peered through the hole the rescuers had made. 'There are two men,' Zuba remembered. 'They speak to us. They came as if from another world. We can hardly grasp what has happened. "Can we get out?" we ask. They reply in the affirmative.'

However, even after clambering through the hole that had been cut, they had to climb through another series of narrow holes made by the rescuers before finally at long last reaching a place leading to open air.

'We see the sky,' Zuba recalled. 'It is evening. The stars are sparkling. I will never forget that moment.'[8]

Zuba was to be one of some 85 men who were rescued from *Tirpitz*'s interior thanks to the judicious use of oxyacetylene torches under the supervision of Kapitänleutnant Walter Sommer, one of the battleship's engineers.[9] Documents in the German archives would suggest that going on 800 of about 1,700 men who had been on board when the ship was bombed were rescued, which puts the dead in excess of 900.[10]

As for the Lancaster bomber crews, they all made it back to Britain, some after a lengthy detour.

News of the action was quickly disseminated. At 6.50 p.m. that evening (still 12 November) a Mr Martin at the British Embassy in Paris, which Churchill was visiting for the first time after the city's liberation, was handed the following short note written by one of the embassy's staff that contained a report on the raid from Bomber ('Bert') Harris. 'I have just taken the following message for the Prime Minister from C in C Bomber Command: "*Tirpitz* sunk this morning. Bert."'[11]

Churchill sent back his congratulations, before informing Stalin and Roosevelt. 'The news . . . has greatly delighted us,' Stalin replied.[12] 'Great news!' the American president responded, to which Churchill replied: 'Thank you so much. It is a great relief to us to get this brute where we have long wanted her.'[13]

The RAF's series of raids on *Tirpitz* culminating in her sinking was to usher in the final phase of the Arctic convoys, when the danger of attacks by the German fleet really was a thing of the past. It was just unfortunate that one of the first beneficiaries of the decks being cleared following the September 1944 Operation Paravane was the Arctic convoy that was so shaming from the British point of view.

The main cargo for the two liners that formed the core of the very small JW 61A was to be Soviet soldiers, many of whom had been captured by Allied forces after having been press ganged into fighting on the German side in France and in the Middle East. This was well known to those British politicians who decided that even those prisoners who did not want to go back to Russia should be forced to depart. Long before the convoy left Liverpool on 31 October 1944, Anthony Eden had admitted to the British War Cabinet: 'If we do as the Soviet Government want, and return all these prisoners to the Soviet Union, whether they are willing to return . . . or not, we shall be sending some of them to their death.' This might not have been of concern if they all had voluntarily fought for the Nazi regime. However, Eden had added: 'I realize that many of these men may have been compelled to join the German forces under great duress.'[14]

In other words 'good' Russians were to be sacrificed along with the 'bad' in the hope this would prevent complications with their ally, such as the possibility that if Britain did not play ball, the Soviets might in their turn fail to return British soldiers picked up in German prisoner of war camps.[15] It was all the more discreditable since it seems that the Arctic convoy seamen participating in the convoy believed that the British and Russian governments had prior to the passage of JW 61A worked out a deal guaranteeing the Soviet soldiers' safety.[16]

The first effective opposition to an Arctic convoy following the first of the final series of attacks on *Tirpitz* was during the passage of RA 62 (four tankers plus 24 other merchant ships and one rescue ship plus a repaired frigate that had been torpedoed during the early stages of a previous convoy) which departed from Russia on 10 December 1944 (see Note 17 for the limited German successes during previous convoys).[17] It was guarded during what constituted the second half of Operation Acumen (the protection of JW 62 and RA 62) by approaching 30 escorts including 14 destroyers and 9 frigates, plus 2 escort carriers and 1 anti-aircraft cruiser.[18] This huge force came under the command of Rear Admiral Rhoderick McGrigor flying his flag in the carrier *Campania*. However, it was a modest sub-group of the main force, consisting of a corvette and a sloop, whose depth charging may have been responsible for the sinking of a U-boat in the Kola Inlet approaches during a search carried out by British escorts and carrier borne aircraft the day before the convoy sailed.[19]

It may have been this sweep that curtailed the actions of most of the U-boats gathered outside the inlet when the convoy departed. However, at least one managed to remain on RA 62's tail, notwithstanding the low visibility.[20] As Admiral McGrigor's report confirms, the last time the sun rose above the horizon during 1944 in the Arctic was on 1 December, in other words before the convoy set off.[21] Afterwards the best that could be hoped for even at midday was an unrelenting gloomy twilight.

The U-boat in hot pursuit happened to be *U-365*, the same vessel that had had a field day in the Kara Sea against the Russian convoy BD5 (see Chapter 40), albeit now under a different commander, Diether Todhagen.

This U-boat may have been the object that shortly before 5.30 a.m. on 11 December was detected by radar operators in the destroyer *Cassandra*, which was patrolling around 12 miles from the port quarter of the convoy. RA 62 at the time was moving west-north-westward around 200 miles to the north-west of the Kola Inlet (see Note 22 for location).[22] However, the 24-year-old Lieutenant George Leslie, who had only taken over as *Cassandra*'s acting commanding officer shortly before JW 62 left Loch Ewe, ruled it was a false alarm.

Whether or not that was a mistake, shortly before 6 a.m. that morning *U-365*'s crew fired an acoustic torpedo at the destroyer.[23] It blew up near, or on hitting, the British ship beside her forward (A) gun, causing a massive secondary explosion as shells in the destroyer's for'ard mess decks went up.[24]

No-one was more surprised than Able Seaman Morris Birkett, who had been in his hammock near the canteen one deck down from the open-air deck, in the for'ard half of the ship, when the torpedo exploded. He later reported: 'I woke flying through the air, landing flat on my back on the deck.' After he regained his breath, he managed to stand up, and saw 'two figures standing at the open mess door (aft of where he had been lying) . . . beckoning me to come that way.' Only later did he realize how fortunate he was that although concussed, he followed their instructions. As he remarked afterwards: 'some other concussed shipmates had run the wrong way (forward) into the open sea.'[25]

Mercifully, the man who had been standing watch with him before retiring to his hammock in the forward mess deck at about 4 a.m. probably never knew what had hit him. The forward mess deck was near the ship's bow, parts of which had gone up in smoke, leaving the remainder to break off and sink after being swept down *Cassandra*'s port side, making in the words of another seaman 'the sound of screeching and grinding metal.'[26]

Birkett, and those like R. Butler who had been sleeping in his hammock nearby, were lucky not to be blown out of the ship in its wake. Butler recalled: 'I woke in what seemed to be a whirlwind. I dropped out of my hammock, and found all my watchkeeping clothes had vanished with just my seaboots remaining. The piano had gone too!' They had been sucked out of the ship by the pressure unleashed by the explosion.[27]

Lieutenant George Leslie in his report confirmed: 'It was difficult to tell how badly the ship was damaged, as the steam escaping from the capstan pipes had hidden everything forward of B Gun deck.'[28] But he nevertheless managed to come up with a calm authoritative order, which according to Norman Kemp in the wheelhouse was delivered in 'a quiet voice showing no more emotion than if he had been handing round cucumber sandwiches at a vicarage tea party: "Stop both, wheel amidships." '[29]

Although Seaman Dudley Mills had been alerted by what he described as 'an almighty clang, but deadened and not resonant, as if a huge muffled hammer had struck a metal plate', and by the way, as he put it, the ship 'lurched violently', to the extent that he was 'flung' against the radar set in the charthouse, he was totally unprepared for what was to be displayed as he stepped out into the open air. According to his post-war account, he was just in time to see the whole scene illuminated by a flare fired off another ship: 'Looking forward, I could see that the blast shield on B gun deck had been bent back and forced into a vertical position, but the most astounding thing was there was just nothing beyond. No fo'c'sle, no bows, no A gun. Everything had completely disappeared. There was just the sea foaming in the harsh magnesium light. I went back to the charthouse shaken to the core.'[30]

At first there was an expectation among the crew this would necessitate them abandoning ship. But they were eventually stood down after it was discovered that, amazingly, what remained of the ship was still watertight. Bulkheads at the front were holding. *Cassandra* was then towed back to Russia escorted by ships from the 20th Escort Group.[31] It was a sad procession. Sixty-two of *Cassandra*'s crew had perished in the incident.[32]

There might have been further ship losses if the attack by nine Ju 88 torpedo bombers during the afternoon of 12 December had been more committed.[33] However, it was to make those planning convoys sit up, since it was the first time torpedo bombers had raided an Arctic convoy during the year, and it made them wonder whether they should take it as a warning concerning what was to come. This was in spite of the fact it turned out to be more costly for the Germans than the British Fleet Air Arm. German records confirm that six of the Ju 88s failed to return, three of them 'because of the weather', while one of the British planes failed to return to its mother carrier.[34]

But it was to be offensive action on 13 December by two of 813 Squadron's Swordfish flown off the escort carrier *Campania*, after the convoy had passed the Bear Island passage and had turned to the south-west, which was to lead to the only other blood-letting during RA 62. While on the way back to the convoy, after being scrambled at around 3.30 p.m. to follow up a U-boat sighting some 30 miles from the convoy's port side, the radar in the Swordfish accompanying the other Swordfish piloted by the 21-year-old Sub-Lieutenant Bill Henley detected a second U-boat some 12 miles away to the south. Unbeknown to them it was *Cassandra*'s nemesis, *U-365*.

It was fortunate, at least from Henley's point of view, that his wingman's radar worked, because Henley's had failed on taking off from *Campania*. There was no chance of seeing the U-boat by natural light since apart from a very faint glow from the northern lights, it was dark. Likewise they were lucky that Henley still had three depth charges under his Swordfish because his wingman had already dropped his.

After the war Henley described how notwithstanding these obstacles, they nevertheless managed to set up the attack, which started off with both planes flying side by side on a parallel course to the U-boat that was heading south well ahead of them but to the east of their line of advance:

'The technique we operated [was] as if we were working on our own . . . at night: he homed in and dropped flares [on parachutes on the western side of the U-boat] . . . At flare drop, you turned away 45 degrees [in this case the turn was to starboard] and started to dive. After having lost a few hundred feet, [you'd] do a sweeping turn round to port and [after passing ahead of the U-boat] come back towards [what in this case was the eastern side of] the target in a teardrop pattern. You'd get the target between yourself and the [slowly falling] flares.

'As a bit of true cooperation . . . my observer . . . was already hanging over the side, and as I started this dive, he came up with "U-boat bearing red 160" (red in this context means to port). So I carried on down and started the turn to port. As soon as I could, I looked over my shoulder and saw there he was. I'd never seen anything like it before . . . There this U-boat was, going . . . flat out and looking much bigger than I'd seen before . . . I carried on my turn and my observer suddenly said: "He's diving! he's diving!" . . . I . . . answered rather testily, ... and headed back towards the target ... Just before the conning tower went under, I pressed the release button ... and felt the effect as the depth charges came off ... and I pulled up to turn to starboard.

'I then heard the observer in the other aircraft shout: "A beautiful shot!" He'd seen the splashes of the depth charges going into the water. Apparently I'd got a dead straddle on either side [of the U-boat] ... Soon as I could, I looked over my shoulder. The depth charges ... were set to go off quite shallow ... They made an enormous column of water in the air. I could see the wake of the U-boat going right into the middle of this ... The next thing we saw was the rear third of the U-boat sticking out of the water at about 45 degrees. It just seemed to hang there for a while, and then suddenly it went straight down ... Then the flares went out ... They were reputed to burn for 55 seconds. So the sighting, the attack and the sinking [all] took place in [around] 55 seconds.'[35]

Afterwards Henley flew over the area where the U-boat had disappeared, and by the light of the flares dropped from his aircraft, he was gratified to see an oil slick several hundred yards across, along with debris, although there were no objects which could be recognized as having come from a U-boat. Because of this, even after both Swordfish returned to *Campania,* and their crews had reported what they had witnessed, the sinking was only rated 'possible'. Claims that Henley had sunk *U-365* were only accepted after the war.

However, the Seekriegsleitung Kriegstagebuch entry for 14 December confirms that the U-boats' attempt to attack the convoy had been called off because of strong opposition by enemy aircraft.

The convoy's arrival in Loch Ewe on 19 December without any merchant ships having been sunk was regarded by Admiral Rhoderick McGrigor as another landmark achievement, since it showed that provided the temperature did not plummet, aircraft flying off the carriers were capable of operating and defending convoys even during the darkest periods of the year. However, as always there were reservations: the Wildcat fighters supplied could not operate effectively at night, and the Swordfish, which in spite of Bill Henley's efforts to show what could be done with them notwithstanding their limitations, were said to be 'obsolescent', were unable to operate in the strong winds so often seen in the Arctic, and broke down too frequently for comfort.[36]

42

Last Throw of the Dice

Main Actions: 17 February and 23 February 1945
Evacuation of Sørøya; sinking of U-425,
Bluebell and Henry Bacon, JW64 and RA64

(See Map 21)
GMT + 1

After the German failure to mount any opposition against the east and west-going Arctic convoys that had sailed during January 1945, those required to participate in the supply of aid to Russia during the following month could have been excused for thinking that, winter weather permitting, they were onto a winner. However during February 1945, those in Arctic convoys would have to withstand one final determined push by the Germans, who finally had the means to halt the supply of aid to Russia via the northern route. In spite of German forces coming under increasing pressure from the East and West, Hitler had at long last once again permitted a sufficient number of aircraft to be placed in northern Norway to give the Luftwaffe a chance of replicating, or even improving on, what had been achieved in September 1942, during the passage of PQ18 (see Chapter 27).

Unfortunately for the Luftwaffe's aircraft crews, allowance had not been made for the increased strength of the British convoy protection forces, or the deployed German pilots' inexperience. Although on 7 February 1945 no less than 48 German Ju 88s took off from Trondheim

Vaernes and Bardufoss with a view to attacking JW 64 (3 tankers, 2 escort oilers, and 24 merchant ships, 19 of them American), the east-going Arctic convoy which had set out from the Clyde, Scotland four days earlier, the majority of the German crews, hampered by the reduced visibility on account of bad weather, failed to find their target.[1]

Whether or not this affected the outcome of the raid is debatable. The dozen or so German aircraft which did reach the convoy as it proceeded north-eastward, going on one-third of the way between the Faroe Islands and Bear Island (see 1 in Map 21, and Note 2 for approximate location), came off second best against the British forces laid on for Operation Hotbed (the protection of JW 64 and RA 64).[2] These forces included the aircraft carried by two escort carriers (12 Swordfish, 4 Wildcat fighters, and 1 Fulmar night-time fighter operated by 813 Squadron from *Campania*; and 14 Swordfish and 6 Wildcat fighters operated by 835 Squadron from *Nairana*), an anti-aircraft cruiser and 18 other escorts including 9 destroyers.[3]

The First Cruiser Squadron's Rear Admiral Rhoderick McGrigor, once again in charge of the escorts, flying his flag in *Campania*, was pleasantly surprised by what he referred to as the Germans' 'lack of spirit'. He put this down to the demotivating effect of seeing one of their planes shot down at the beginning of the raid by the gunners in the corvette *Denbigh Castle*, which was located in the outer of the two concentric rings of escorts that had been placed around the merchant ships. None of the German aircraft crews managed to penetrate the inner screen, and consequently there were no attacks on the aircraft carriers which were supposed to be the attackers' priority.[4] Even so, at least one German plane retreated trailing smoke at the end of the raid, and seven aircraft failed to make it back to their bases. Most of these losses were the result of friendly fire by German gunners who had not been given sufficient information about the raid.[5] However, one German officer laid some of the blame for the raid's poor showing on the misguided attempt to stiffen his and his comrades' resolve by presenting each crew with four bottles of Cognac prior to 7 February, a gift which backfired because rather than improving their performance, it merely left those who overindulged nursing a hangover.[6]

The deployment of 31 of KG 26's Ju 88s which took off from Bardufoss three days later, with a view to making a second attack on JW 64, was to be even more of a missed opportunity. Although most of the German aircraft duly reached the area south-east of Bear Island where the convoy was sailing towards the east (see 2 in Map 21, and Note 7 for approximate location), the British gunners and fighter crews had been forewarned as a result of one of the Ju 88s arriving around 20 minutes before the others.[7] Because of this mistake, when the main body of German aircraft turned up, British fighter aircraft were already airborne, and the convoy escorts were moving into their anti-aircraft formation. Six German aircraft were shot down, with the Wildcat crews claiming at least two of the victims.[8] Afterwards a member of one of the German aircraft crews stated that so many tracer bullets were fired in quick succession by what he took to be the convoy's anti-aircraft cruiser (*Bellona*) that it was as if he was flying through 'a snowstorm'.[9]

The losses did not stop many of the surviving Germans making exaggerated claims after returning to Bardufoss about all the warships and freighters they believed they had sunk or damaged. Not all of them were credulous however. When Leutnant Hans-Werner Grosse, the commander of one Ju 88 unit, was congratulated for having sunk a destroyer, he retorted that it was most unlikely. After the war, he wrote an account stating that he was glad he had not gone along with the unrealistic boasts of his comrades. In spite of the German claims they had 11 scalps, and notwithstanding what Admiral McGrigor described as the similar 'sweeping' claims made by Germany's 'propagandist-in-chief' Lord Haw-Haw during a typically misleading broadcast, in fact the Luftwaffe had not sunk any ships.[10] Their only clear cut success was the downing of a Wildcat, whose pilot had to be rescued after ditching his plane in the water. Another Wildcat crashed as it landed on *Campania*'s flight deck, but the accident had nothing to do with German prowess. Its engine cut out after it had been hit by flak fired from some of the convoy's freighters, whose gunners had mistaken it for a German plane. Once again the pilot survived.[11]

The only ship from the convoy that would eventually be taken out as a result of German action was *Denbigh Castle*. Eleven of her crew lost their lives when she was torpedoed by *U-992*'s crew during the night of 12–13 February, as ships from the convoy entered the Kola Inlet, at a time when British carrier aircraft were grounded because of the weather (see 3 in Map 21).[12] She was eventually towed to land and beached.

Prior to the setting out of RA64, which was to be protected by the escorts which had survived JW 64, the commanders of four of the Allied destroyers were ordered to go to Soroy (Sørøya), an island off Norway's north-west coast, to pick up Norwegian men, women and children who had taken refuge there in caves and other primitive dwellings. They were refugees, whose homes had been destroyed by the Germans as part of the scorched earth policy they were following during their retreat to Norway's west and south, prompted by the pressure applied by the Red Army's advance from the East.

The rescuing of these Norwegians, referred to as Operation Opendoor, was to be a risky enterprise. Not only did it require the four destroyers to enter fjords on Sørøya's west coast, where their crews might encounter German patrols. But in order to reach Sørøya in the first place, they also had to break through the U-boats assembled around the approaches to the Kola Inlet without the support of aircraft flown off carriers. The carriers and their aircraft were being preserved for the west-going convoy which was to set out after Operation Opendoor was completed.

The operation was all the more daunting because during the afternoon of 14 February, just hours before the commanders of the destroyers were ordered to depart, the Norwegian tanker *Norfjell* and the Liberty ship *Horace Gray*, two of the Allied ships forming part of the small feed convoy sailing from the White Sea to the Kola Inlet to link up with RA 64, had been torpedoed near where *Denbigh Castle* had been hit. After the war it was discovered that the German submarine responsible for both of these 14 February attacks was *U-968*.

Fortunately for those on board the destroyers, Captain John Allison, the 43-year-old commander of the destroyer *Zambesi,* Captain (D) of the 2nd Destroyer Flotilla, who was in charge of the operation, was equal to the task. According to John Brackenbury, who had been one of *Zambesi*'s junior officers, when he was interviewed after the war: 'When we got the orders to go, we formed into a diamond and sped off at 30 knots. We just went flat out, our sheer speed avoiding the possibility of U-boat actions against us.'[13]

'We went steaming round (the north of Norway) and that was very exhilarating,' Rodney Bowden, who had been another of *Zambesi*'s young officers, remembered afterwards. 'Then there was the excitement of going into these islands and quite narrow channels.'[14]

When they arrived near the three pickup points on Sørøya's west coast during the afternoon of 15 February, the ships were split up with *Zealous* going into the northern Sandoyfjord (Sandøyfjorden), and *Zambesi* and *Zest* entering Borrfjord and Nordfjord (Borrfjorden and Nordfjorden) respectively, which are effectively sub-fjords accessed via Galtefjord (Galtefjorden), further to the south (see 4A and 4B in Map 21). The Canadian *Sioux* patrolled seaward of the inlets, with her crew ready to step in should German patrol vessels or aircraft show up.[15]

The crews of the destroyers entering the inlets had similar experiences, but the following report by *Zealous*'s 42-year-old Commander Richard Jessel provides the most compelling account:

'As we steamed up the fjord, everything was very quiet. There was not a sign of life. All we could see was a small boat at the head of the fjord. Things looked suspicious until a man jumped up in the boat and fired a Very light. It was a prearranged signal, and then followed one of the most impressive sights I have ever seen. Down the snowy slopes on skis came the Norwegians, men and women carrying babies and their few humble belongings, and even the youngsters were on miniature skis. They were obviously very glad to see us.'[16]

Another witness from Jessel's ship, who was watching the arrival of the Norwegian refugees, noticed that: 'on their backs some of them carried sheepskins, stitched together with the "wool" inside, in which they carried babies in the manner of Indian squaws.'[17]

The ships had to remain in the inlets for several hours until everyone who wanted to had boarded. There were some 420 men, women and children all told.[18] Afterwards the ships cast off, and retraced their steps, once again travelling at high speed, arriving back in the Kola Inlet on 16 February after the 1,200-mile round trip.[19] The Norwegian refugees were then taken to those of the RA64 ships which were to transport them when the convoy departed the next day.

In an attempt to disrupt the U-boats which were gathered outside the Kola Inlet at dusk, Admiral McGrigor sent out the reinforced 7th Escort Group consisting of three sloops and two corvettes to sweep the approaches. He was asking a lot. Documents made public after the war confirm that the German wolfpack near the inlet was made up of no less than 10 vessels.[20] At around midnight that night (16–17 February) the asdic operator in the sloop *Lark,* which was the starboard vessel in the line of ships sweeping in a westward direction, heard the sinister ping which told him that they had detected a U-boat. A message was sent to the commander of the corvette *Alnwick Castle,* which had been a mile away from *Lark* to port, and together they set out to hunt it down.[21]

They would later discover from Herbert Lochner, the 22-year-old torpedo mechanic who would be the only German survivor of this encounter, it was *U-425,* a run of the mill U-boat, but nevertheless a vessel which especially when working alongside others in a so-called wolf pack, spelt mortal danger for enemy shipping if it was not kept at a distance. It was in fact a type VIIC U-boat, one of the mainstays of the German U-boat arm, measuring around 13 yards long, and 7 yards wide at its beam with the ability to advance at a speed of around 20 knots above the surface and approaching 8 knots when submerged. A crucial characteristic that was to come into play during what ensued was the extra buoyancy tank that had been built into VIICs giving them a higher chance of making it onto the surface than the predecessor models if push came to shove, and its crew found they were having difficulty surfacing.[22]

According to the account Lochner wrote afterwards, he was lying in his bunk when he heard the distinctive sound of one of the ships' propellers passing overhead. Shortly afterwards, depth charges exploded nearby. As he recalled succinctly later, they had seemingly catastrophic consequences: 'The U-boat . . . shuddered . . . The lights went out. Total darkness!'

When the emergency lighting came on, he saw that the reading on the depth gauge was a petrifying 200 metres. Observing his shipmates' anxious expressions, he could see he was not the only one who believed they were in a 'hopeless situation'. He was even more terrified when he heard the order: 'Every man to the bow!' This told him that water had penetrated into the machine room to the rear. The engines were no longer working, and the word went round that acid had been released and gases were accumulating.

However, for him at least there was to be salvation. He had almost given up any hope that he and the other members of the crew would ever have a chance to get out in one piece, when he heard the commander give the 'Full blow!' order, which was an instruction to the engineer to try to blast the water out of the ballast tanks using the compressed air, a move that it was hoped would enable the vessel to reach the surface. It was at this point that the extra buoyancy tank built into *U-425* may have made a difference. Whether or not it did, shortly afterwards, he heard the commander's gratifying: 'Get out!' accompanying the invigorating fresh air which entered the boat when the hatch in the control room was opened.

The fact that he was one of the last to clamber out may have saved his life. When the first Germans emerged onto the outer deck, they were fired at from the circling British warships, and he only escaped being shot, like some of his comrades, because he managed to take cover near the gun platform. Another man near him had been shot in the back. Lochner noticed how this man's blood was dripping into the water.

His previous experiences in the destroyer *Z 24* when *Z 26* was sunk (the sinking described in Chapter 5) also stood him in good stead. He had learned that his chances of surviving would be much higher if he remained on his vessel until the last minute. He waited on the U-boat's deck as long as he dared before jumping into the icy water, and then struck out towards the nearest ship whose lights were by this stage illuminating the scene. He quickly appreciated he was now in a race against time which he was not winning.

'I . . . felt my legs stiffening,' he wrote later. 'The chill was spreading "upwards", and [I realized] the end must surely be imminent. My thoughts went back once again to my beloved in Danzig . . . In my heart I was far away and at home . . . I was filled with an overwhelming sense of peace . . . I knew [what was coming] and saw . . . all too clearly . . . the inevitable [death that] lay before me.'[23]

He must have lost consciousness at this point. Nevertheless he remained afloat, supported by his life jacket, until picked up by the sailors in *Alnwick Castle*.[24] When he came to, the British men around him used sign language which seemed to suggest that all the other Germans they had reached had already expired.

Such a rudimentary method of communication could not begin to impart the horror of what the British seamen had witnessed. When *Alnwick Castle*'s John Durning in his post-war account described the fate of *U-425*'s submariners, he wrote: 'I shall never forget the sound of their voices calling "Kamerad" over the water as they drifted away, and our inability to do anything to help, as the scrambling nets were frozen solidly to the deck.'[25]

As for *U-425* herself, the British sailors made no attempt to board her. At around 1.30 a.m. on 17 February, her stern sank until her bow was pointing up towards the sky, and then she disappeared beneath the waves (see 5 in Map 21 for the approximate location, and Note 26 for the source).[26]

The sinking of *U-425* appeared to be an auspicious prelude to the departure of convoy RA 64 (30 merchant ships, and four oilers and tankers) which started to emerge from the Kola Inlet later that morning (17 February).[27] However, they had not proceeded far to the east when a torpedo fired from *U-968* blew the stern off *Lark*, killing two of the four men who had been stationed there (see 6 in Map 21 for approximate location; and Note 28 for source).[28] The other two men, who were blown into the sea, were rescued by a passing Russian motor boat.[29] As such torpedoings go, the damage and casualties, restricted as they were to two fatalities, were mercifully light. *Lark* would eventually be towed into the inlet, in the words of her captain 'with her tail literally and figuratively in the air', a reference to the remains of her deck aft which was sticking up.[30] But it provided a worrying warning, all the more so because the U-boat which had fired the torpedo was still on the prowl.

Shortly before midday (still 17 February) the crew in that U-boat (*U-968*) struck again, torpedoing the RA 64 American merchant ship *Thomas Scott* on her starboard side within sight of the damaged *Lark* (see 7 in Map 21 for location; and Note 31 for the source).[31] This time there were no fatalities, and the 40 refugees from Sørøya and the crew abandoned ship without mishap. The crew were taken back to the Kola Inlet, but the refugees were transferred to the destroyer *Onslaught,* and were thus able to travel with RA 64 after all. One might even go so far as to say that *U-968*'s crew had done one of the young rescued Norwegian girls a favour: had it not been for the torpedoing, she would probably never have met the British seaman in *Onslaught* who would eventually become her husband.[32]

But from the Allied point of view it can safely be said there was no good side to what happened shortly before 3.30 p.m. that afternoon (17 February). The corvette *Bluebell* had no sooner returned to her inner screen station on the port beam of the convoy, following her participation in the search for the U-boat that had torpedoed *Thomas Scott,* than she was torpedoed, by *U-711,* in her turn.[33] Only there could not have been a bigger contrast between the rather sedate abandoning of the merchant ship and the fate of this corvette and her unfortunate crew.

According to William Henry, Commanding Officer of the Armed Guard on RA64's American freighter SS *Silas Weir Mitchell*: 'A huge column of flame and smoke was . . . [seen] just outside the convoy off our port quarter. When the smoke cleared two minutes later, nothing was observed where the explosion had occurred.'[34] *Bluebell* had completely disappeared (see 8 in Map 21 and Note 35 for approximate location and the source).[35]

Lieutenant Commander Roger Hicks, the 45-year-old commander of the destroyer *Zest* (an RA64 escort) stated it took his ship an agonizing 15 minutes to reach the scene of the disaster, adding that as they drew near: 'Cries were heard from about a dozen men who could just be discerned in the failing light. Although various floats and rafts from the sunk ship were drifting in the vicinity, none was near enough to be of use, and I therefore dropped more, although it seems certain none of the few "survivors" had the strength to even reach them. If I could have stopped, then it might have been possible to rescue the majority of these men, but instead I regretfully continued my course . . . in the hopes of detecting the U-boat.'

He later described how he was only freed up to go back to where the corvette had sunk when another destroyer approached. His account continues: 'The whaler was lowered at 1553, at which time there were [only] 3 or 4 voices to be heard, but from scattered sources. I shouted encouragement to them, but it was not possible to pick up more than one at a time. Three were actually recovered in an unconscious state, but only one revived, although artificial respiration was continued for nearly five hours on the other two.'[36] The revived man was to be the only survivor from *Bluebell*'s crew; none of the other 90 men who had been on board survived.[37]

The explosion represented the ultimate demonstration of the biblical saying an eye for an eye, a tooth for a tooth. First the lives of all but one of *U-425*'s crew had been extinguished (there were 52 fatalities). Then their deaths were 'avenged' by the snuffing out of all but one of *Bluebell*'s crew.

The *Bluebell* explosion terrified the Norwegian refugees in the merchant ships nearest to it which were shaken by the resulting shock wave. The frightened Norwegians included the 19 placed in the Liberty ship *Henry Bacon* (the third ship in the fourth column in the convoy, that is in the port section of the 11-column formation). One of her messmen afterwards recalled how all of a sudden normal conversation among the refugees was transformed into 'complete silence'. All the messman could do was to smile reassuringly at them, as if to say: 'Don't worry, it's going to be OK.'[38]

And to the surprise of many in the RA64 merchant ships and escorts alike, who were expecting more attacks to follow on from those they had already seen, it really was OK, for a while. Apart from an unsuccessful depth charge attack on a U-boat detected by an escort's asdic that evening, there was to be no sign of any opposition for several days. However, those who were pessimists could later claim they were literally correct when they forecast it was the calm before the storm.

Over the next two days (18–19 February) the merchant ships in the convoy were scattered by the first gale to impact the convoy's formation. But when the first airborne attack on the convoy was made by some 35 to 40 torpedo bombers of KG26's 1st and 2nd wings at around 10 a.m. on 20 February, as the merchant ships, by then south of Bear Island, headed eastward, virtually all RA64's freighters were back in their allotted places (see 9 in Map 21 for approximate location).[39] This contributed to the Luftwaffe having no more success during this raid than they had had against JW64. Afterwards crews from British escorts and aircraft claimed to have shot down at least three German aircraft with two more probables, whereas the Germans departed empty-handed.[40] Although some of the Luftwaffe crews believed they had sunk a cruiser and a freighter, they were incorrect.[41]

The exaggerated German claims could not conceal the moral victory achieved by the escorts and aircraft which had protected JW64 and were now keeping RA64 safe. Josef Mang from KG26's 5th Squadron, one of the junior officers whose plane had been hit during the 20 February raid – it limped back to Bardufoss with one of its two engines out of action – admitted after the war: 'We were scared while waiting [for the next operation and] we were very frightened whenever we flew out over the water. It wasn't fun anymore. The danger bore deeper and deeper into our consciousness, and even the teenage go-getters had the jitters because of what was waiting for them. It was fair to say that the fate of their [missing] comrades had showed them that death awaited them in the Arctic: it was just a matter of time. Everybody's turn would come.'[42]

However, before the full effects of the Luftwaffe's failures could play out, another factor was thrown into the mix. On 22 February a second gale blew up whose wind-strength was much stronger than the first, to such an extent it was classed as a Force 12 hurricane.[43] It is safe to say this second gale was one of the most extreme weather events, if not the most extreme, that any Arctic convoy had to pass through. So extreme was it that during the night of 22–23 February, not only were RA64's freighters scattered once again, but Captain Ken Short, the 37-year-old commander of the escort carrier *Campania*, took the unprecedented decision to abandon the convoy, albeit temporarily, on account of the weather. If *Campania* had continued on the newly ordered south-easterly route selected by RA64's Norwegian Commodore Ernst Ullring, there was a risk that the strong wind blasting in from the west would have resulted in the aircraft in the ship's hangar breaking loose. 'Shortly after turning onto the new course (chosen by Ullring) I rolled about 45° both ways,' Captain Short reported (see 10 in Map 21 for approximate location where the carrier temporarily left the convoy).[44]

Nairana's more bullish 45-year-old captain, Villiers Surtees, who was reputed to have a Nelsonic attitude to suggestions or orders from inferior and superior officers alike, refused to follow suit on the grounds that the merchant ships would be sitting ducks when the storm died down if he also left them. This was the case even though at times his carrier was bucking up and down in the huge waves like a rocking horse. According to Stephen Mearns, a fighter pilot based in *Nairana*, 'the whole ship was in an uproar. Aircraft were breaking loose. There were things like forklift trucks in the hangar rushing up and down like battering rams . . . [Fuel] tanks were being ruptured, petrol was spilling all over the place.'

Nevertheless, when Surtees was informed that if he did not heave to, the aircraft and fork lift truck-like vehicles located on the hangar deck underneath the flight deck would be smashed up, he is said to have retorted: 'Don't bother me with all these stupid details. Take the falls off the boats and tie the damn things down!'[45] His crew did their best to comply. However, because of this decision, several planes were damaged, and some of the 'fork lift things' were put out of action. But Surtees achieved his object. True to his word, he was still with the convoy when the hurricane eventually subsided.

Although the new course was supposed to soften the effect of the wind on the merchant ships, some were affected more than others. *Henry Bacon* was particularly vulnerable. Her steering motor mechanism and engines had already stopped working properly during the first gale.[46]

61. Above left: A Blohm & Voss 138 reconnaissance aircraft like the one that on 1 July 1942 appeared above convoy PQ17 (see Chapter 16).

62. Above right: Murmansk, PQ17's original destination, after the bombing that resulted in PQ17 on 1 July 1942 being redirected to Archangel.

63. Above: A photograph of a German bomber as it races in to launch its torpedoes at close range during the big attack on PQ17 on 4 July 1942. It was shot down, as was the plane in *64. on the right* which during the same action is seen to be losing height and smoking after flying too close to two Allied destroyers (see Chapter 1).

65. Above: Russian tanker *Azerbaijan* appears to go up in smoke after being torpedoed during the same 4 July 1942 air raid. Miraculously she remained afloat and reached Russia.

66. Near right: Admiral Sir Dudley Pound, the First Sea Lord, and *67. extreme right* Norman 'Ned' Denning, who had diametrically opposed views on the threat to PQ17 posed by *Tirpitz* (see Chapter 17).

68. Above left: HMS *Keppel's* Captain Jack Broome, the senior officer in charge of PQ17's close escort. *69. Above centre:* Rear Admiral Louis Hamilton, commander of the supporting cruiser squadron, and *70. above right: Palomares'* Captain Jack Jauncey, the senior officer remaining with the convoy. All played their part in PQ17's destruction (see Chapter 18).

71. Above left: Leo Gradwell, the rebellious commander of armed trawler *Ayrshire*. She is seen in photo *72. above right* from *Troubadour*, one of three merchant ships Gradwell insisted on protecting notwithstanding the 4 July 1942 scatter order.

74. Above centre: Howard Carraway, *Troubadour's* armed guard chief, who describes in his diary how his ship was camouflaged on Gradwell's orders with the white paint seen being applied in photo *73. above left.*

75. Above right: Lotus' John Hall, another officer who refused to leave merchant crews to their fate (see Chapter 19).

76. Above left: A PQ17 freighter sinks; *77. above centre:* her survivors in boats. Both photos have, probably incorrectly, been alleged to show the aftermath of *Carlton*'s 5 July 1942 torpedoing.

78. Above right: SS *Washington*'s radio operator Robert Henderson who survived the 5 July 1942 bombing and abandonment of his ship, and wrote an account of his experiences in a lifeboat. Two of *Washington*'s lifeboats following the abandonment are to be seen pictured in *80. below right.*

79. Above left: The last moments of American PQ17 merchant ship *Daniel Morgan*. She was bombed on 5 July 1942 before being sunk by *U-457*.

81. Right: Survivors from *Washington* on a Novaya Zemlya beach following their long journey in lifeboats (see Chapters 18 and 23). Photos *80.* and *81.* are part of a unique series of photos supplied thanks to *Washington*'s Arthur Mcdonald.

82. Left: American ship *Ironclad* in the distance on or after 10 July 1942 in Novaya Zemlya's Matochkin Strait (see Chapter 24). This photograph was taken from *Troubadour*, part of which is visible in the foreground.

83. *Above left*: The abandoned *Paulus Potter* is seen sinking after being torpedoed on 13 July 1942 from *U-255*.

84. *Above right:* The British army officer taken prisoner after the torpedoing of PQ17's *Empire Byron* (see Chapter 18) is brought ashore at Narvik. He is carrying his white coat.

85. *Above left*: A reward for *U-255*'s Reinhart Reche following his successes against PQ17, and 86. *above right:* the reception committee for other U-boat men who had attacked PQ17, on the arrival of the returning U-boats in Narvik.

87. *Above*: Churchill (*on the left*) and America's Averell Harriman (*on the right*) on either side of Stalin when they met in Moscow in mid-August 1942 (see Chapter 26).

88. *Right:* Lady Juliet Duff – seen here pre-war in dressed to kill fancy dress, who during the summer of 1942 highlighted the terrible conditions in Murmansk's hospital where injured Allied seamen were being treated (see Chapter 26).

PQ18: THE GOLDEN COMB ATTACK

89. Near right: The very distinctive 'glass house' front of an He 111 torpedo bomber aircraft, similar to the many that took part in the large-scale air raids targeting PQ18 on 13 and 14 September 1942. Some of the attackers in the air were led into battle by Werner Klümper, pictured *90. top right* (see Chapters 27 and 28).

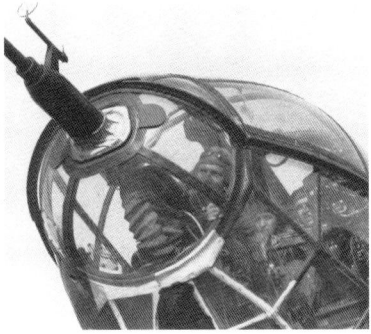

91. Above left: Robert Burnett, the rear admiral in charge of the close escort protecting PQ18.

92. Above: A German photograph showing some of the Luftwaffe planes darting in to deliver their golden comb attack on 13 September 1942, whose climax was the blowing up of an ammunition ship shown in another German photo *93. on the left* (see Chapter 27).

94. Above left: Eskimo sails on regardless in spite of the nearby explosion – probably photographed during one of the big attacks on PQ18 mentioned above and below.

95. Above right: The moment when the American SS *Mary Luckenbach* was vapourized during one of the 14 September 1942 air raids (see Chapter 28). This photo was taken from the escort carrier *Avenger.*

96. *Above left:* The Russian ship *Dekabrist* which was sunk on 4 November 1942 while carrying aid independently to the Soviet Union, resulting in some of the survivors becoming castaways for many months on the deserted Hope Island. The first to be rescued – by the crew of *U-703* led by the commander Oberleutnant Joachim Brünner (pictured 98. *below left*) – was *Dekabrist*'s captain, Stepan Belyaev, whose photo is 97. *above right*, on 25 July 1943 (see Chapters 30–31).

99. *Above right:* A photo of the funeral near the mass grave on the beach at Cape Mineral in Spitzbergen's Isfjord during the first half of 1943, near where the castaways from the wrecked British aid ship *Chulmleigh* had taken shelter from the Arctic conditions for the best part of two months. Those who were rescued at the beginning of January 1943 included the ship's Captain Daniel Williams (in naval uniform on the right side of the grave), as well as Lance Sergeant Richard Peyer (pictured in photo 100. *on the extreme left* with his wife Diana) and Robert Paterson (pictured in photo 101. *near left*) – see Chapter 31.

102. Top left: The heavy German cruiser *Admiral Hipper*, which appeared invincible during the 31 December 1942 German attack on JW51B masterminded by Vizeadmiral Oskar Kummetz (pictured *103. top right*) until its crew were blindsided by the arrival of two British cruisers.

104. Above left: Lieutenant Commander Tom Marchant who took over as commander of the destroyer *Onslow* when *Onslow*'s Captain Robert Sherbrooke was blinded in one eye during an exchange of fire with *Hipper*. *105. Above right:* What appears to be *Onslow*'s B gun and shattered mount after *Hipper*'s gunners had put a shell into it.

106. Above left: Loftus Peyton Jones, the destroyer *Achates*' 1st Lieutenant, who had to take over the command of the ship after a *Hipper* shell hit *Achates* killing her captain. *107. Above centre:* *Onslow*'s Captain Robert Sherbrooke with Rosemary, his wife, on the day when he was formally presented with his Victoria Cross. *108. Above right:* The former Grossadmiral Erich Raeder meets Adolf Hitler about a month after the abortive Battle of Barents Sea attack. Raeder had been effectively demoted and given the post of Admiralinspecteur der Kriegsmarine (see Chapter 33).

109. *Left:* Grossadmiral Karl Dönitz – here seen with Hitler, who is on the right – recklessly insisted *Scharnhorst* (*110. below*) should attack JW55B in spite of opposition from Admiral Otto Schniewind (*111. below extreme left*), head of Marinegruppenkommando Nord und Flottenkommando, and Konteradmiral Erich Bey, pictured *112. below centre*, the stand-in commander on board the battlecruiser.

113. *Above right:* Admiral Sir Bruce Fraser, Commander-in-Chief of the Home Fleet (*on the left*), here seen standing beside Russia's Vice Admiral Arsenii Golovko during the British fleet's 16 December 1943 visit to the Kola Inlet (see Chapter 37).

114. *Above left:* A hole in the cruiser *Norfolk*'s X turret's barbette made by a shell fired out of one of *Scharnhorst*'s 11 inch guns.

115. *Above centre:* British battleship *Duke of York* is cheered as she returns to her base in Scapa Flow having participated in the sinking of the battlecruiser.

116. *Above right:* Blindfolded members of *Scharnhorst*'s crew who had been taken prisoner.

They had been repaired, but during the hurricane, her engines broke down again, leading to her losing contact with the other ships in the convoy.[47] Once again repairs were effected. But not before she had on one occasion rolled over so far that for one ghastly moment, those on board, already weakened by seasickness and by the need to hold on for dear life if they were not to be tossed around their cabins along with their possessions, feared she would never become upright again.[48]

'The . . . (second) gale will live in my memory as the most terrifying experience of my life,' commented Chuck Reed after the war, while harking back to the time when he was an 18-year-old messman in the ship. 'The seas grew to an estimated eighty to ninety feet . . . We all donned life preservers and some donned the rubber Arctic suits.'[49]

However, during the morning of 23 February, by which time the awesome power of the wind had been reduced, *Henry Bacon* was still afloat. Perhaps all would have been well had she been reunited with the other freighters. But the task of returning to the RA 64 fold was complicated by the changes of course ordered by Commodore Ullring as the strength of the storm abated. A 60-degree turn to the south-west was made by the main body of the convoy at around 4 a.m. on 23 February, followed by a further 20-degree turn to starboard some seven hours later (see 11 and 12 in Map 21).[50]

It seems likely that at least one of these commands never reached those on *Henry Bacon*'s bridge.[51] The result was it did not matter how fast her stokers and engineers had her propellers whirring following the emergency repair. As things stood, she would never have caught up with the convoy because the convoy's and *Henry Bacon*'s courses were diverging.

Eventually, puzzled by not coming across the other merchant ships where he expected to find them, *Henry Bacon*'s 62-year-old master Alfred Carini, a diminutive Sicilian-born New Yorker with a lifetime of seafaring behind him, made what with the benefit of hindsight was acknowledged to be a fatal miscalculation. Rather than sensibly concluding that as the wind subsided, the convoy's escort would in all probability want to direct the merchant ships to the south-west, away from the Norwegian coast, at around midday he took the risky decision to head back towards the north in case *Henry Bacon* had ended up as the lead ship, which would have meant the rest of the convoy was behind her.

It was while the ship was still straggling in this way during the early afternoon of 23 February that the fateful decision was made by the commander of some 20 German aircraft, whose crews spotted *Henry Bacon* to the west of the southern tip of the Lofoten Islands, to focus at least some of their efforts on her rather than to carry on searching with a view to finding the bulk of the convoy (for *Henry Bacon*'s approximate location at this point, see 13 in Map 21).[52] Whether the German crews' decision was influenced by the loss of morale mentioned by KG26's Josef Mang (mentioned above) is hard to know. Perhaps the fact that the KG26 unit deployed, the 3rd wing based in Vaernes near Trondheim, were on their first mission since arriving in Norway, had something to do with it.[53]

Whatever the reasoning behind it, the German decision was to cause consternation among the American seamen and gunners tasked with defending *Henry Bacon*. The Liberty ship's Chuck Reed, who acted as a gunner's mate during action stations, recalled afterwards the moment he saw the aircraft approaching: 'I saw someone point astern at what appeared to be a line of ducks coming low over the water.'[54] Another member of the crew stated that the planes in the distance looked like 'a swarm of bees'.[55]

These sightings were swiftly followed by the signature cry that greeted nearly every expected attack: 'Here they come!'[56] At around 2.15 p.m. *Henry Bacon*'s first distress message was sent out to the convoy escorts informing them the ship was under attack, but although those on board the American Liberty ship knew there was little prospect of any British warship intervening, there was no talk of capitulation.[57] The official Operation Hotbed reports, when describing the merchant ships' use of their artillery during the attacks that had taken place prior to this action, were to be highly critical with regard to the gunners' lack of discipline. The gunners had blazed away at friendly aircraft as well as those flown by foe.[58] However, on this occasion, the 26 enlisted men in *Henry Bacon*'s armed guard – who by this stage of the war like the armed guard deployed in most of the Arctic convoys' merchant ships had been liberally supplied with appropriate weapons (8 Oerlikons plus a 3-inch gun near the bow and a 5-inch gun at the stern) – held their fire as instructed while the aircraft circled in the distance. Not one bullet was directed at the German Ju 88s until the first plane advanced to within around three-quarters of a mile. Only then did John Sippola, the ship's Armed Guard Commander, shout out: 'Fire!'[59]

'The first plane . . . made his pass and made off unscathed,' Chuck Reed remembered. But one that followed flew into a curtain of shells and bullets. 'The five-inch . . . gun got one [plane] on the nose and blew him to pieces,' recalled another member of the crew.[60]

Assisted by that demonstration of intent, *Henry Bacon*'s gunners managed for some time to keep the Germans at a respectful distance.[61] While this continued, those on the upper bridge were able to tell the helmsman below them how to change course in good time to avoid torpedoes aimed at them. There was much of this turning and weaving. But after the motor which operated the 5-inch gun stopped working, *Henry Bacon* became vulnerable to attacks from or near her rear end.[62]

It did not take long for the Germans to exploit this. Members of *Henry Bacon*'s crew watched impotently as a German plane flew in close from starboard and dropped its torpedoes. No evasion could be taken this time because the ship's rudder mechanism was no longer responding to the helmsman's urgent attempts to alter the ship's course. One of the torpedoes hit *Henry Bacon*'s starboard side beside her No. 5 hold below the water line and then exploded.[63]

Even for those passengers who had not been able to observe the battle because they were below decks, it was immediately apparent that something terrible had happened. According to Henrik Pedersen, one of the adult Norwegian refugees, the ship 'shook as if hit by an earthquake. We all realized we were hit, and feared we were about to sink.'[64] After investigating, Alfred Carini evidently agreed. He ordered Spurgeon 'Spud' Campbell, the ship's 23-year-old radio officer, to send out a second distress message, which was done at around 2.30 p.m., and then gave the order to abandon ship.[65]

There appears to have been no doubt in Carini's mind over who should be placed into lifeboat no. 1, the first to be launched, on the starboard side of the ship: he ordered that the 19 Norwegian refugees, 16 of whom were women and children, should be helped into this boat. They were to be accompanied by radio officer Campbell, who was instructed to send out mayday signals from the boat, and some half a dozen seamen.[66]

Far more difficult was the decision over who should go into lifeboat no. 2 on the port side, the only other serviceable boat given that lifeboats nos. 3 and 4 had capsized on reaching the water after attempts were made to lower them.[67] Because of these events it was impossible to accommodate in boats all the remaining crew and armed guards.

On learning this was the case, Don Haviland, the 49-year-old Chief Engineer, who along with others was already seated in lifeboat no. 2, announced that he had already lived the best years of his life, and so it did not matter if he did not survive. On saying this, he got out of the boat, leaving a space for a younger man, and joined the Master on the bridge.[68]

When this second lifeboat was launched, those left on board were still hoping that ships from the convoy would come to rescue them before *Henry Bacon* sank. As it turned out their expectations were not unreasonable. It was later revealed that an alert telegraphist in the RA64 destroyer *Opportune* had worked out *Henry Bacon*'s bearing (100°) from one of Campbell's distress signals, and what amounted to a search party was mobilized.[69] At around 2.50 p.m. a Wildcat which had been sent from the convoy to find *Henry Bacon* arrived overhead, and signalled that help was on its way.[70]

However at around 4.30 p.m., there was still no rescue ship in sight when *Henry Bacon* finally sank (see 13 in Map 21, and Note 71 for approximate location).[71] According to Chuck Reed, who had previously left the ship, and was by this time sitting on a large piece of floating timber: 'Her lights were still burning even as her bow approached the perpendicular. As she almost reached a perpendicular position, I heard the whistle blow a long salute, then a boiler erupted with a whoosh, [and] she slid quietly under.'[72]

It is likely that even before *Henry Bacon* sank, the decimation of those who had been unable to find a temporary refuge out of the freezing cold water after abandoning ship was well under way. Another witness has confirmed seeing a number of shipmates supported only by their 'life preservers' dead in the water. The dead included the ship's Chief Mate who was seen 'motionless, his head hung forward, and foam coming from his mouth'.[73]

This is consistent with the following extract from the post-war memoirs of Norwegian refugee Nils Mortensen, based on what he observed as a seven-year-old child from lifeboat no. 1. 'The sea was really cold. Everyone in the lifeboat appreciated that. The water in the boat came up to my knees. My younger brother Eldor, who was sharing a life jacket with my mother, was soaked by the water that came into the boat. My mother slipped and fell into the water at the bottom of the boat.

'One of the men in the boat was seasick and vomited. Another complained about the cold, and another prayed aloud, asking God to send a ship to rescue us . . .

'Some of the crew were in our boat . . . When we got close to something that looked like a body, they yelled at it. However their cries were never answered.'[74]

Spud Campbell would later describe the survivors' guilt he experienced because he had been allocated a seat in a lifeboat while others, including the man who was his best friend, had no alternative but to jump into the water. Campbell admits that he was the sailor whom Nils Mortensen had seen vomiting. He had become uncontrollably seasick while erecting the mast in the lifeboat, with a wire antenna hanging from it, so that he could carry on sending distress signals. He persevered, he said, in the hope that his action would enable rescuers to find them before nightfall, adding: 'It was certain no one [in the water] could live overnight.'[75]

The rescuers only just made his deadline. The light was already fading, when shortly before 5 p.m., the three destroyers sent back some 50 miles to rescue the survivors finally reached them. The destroyers had been delayed by snow squalls. On catching sight of the first warship's mast as it appeared on the horizon, some of the men in lifeboat no. 2, most of whom were armed guards, fired red flares to attract the destroyers' crews' attention.[76]

The flares told the searchers they were on the right track. 'Shortly afterwards a number of boats, rafts and floating wreckage was sighted,' destroyer *Zambesi*'s Captain Allison reported. He decided that in the first instance his ship would pick up the shipwrecked men on the three rafts while *Opportune*'s crew would focus on those in the two lifeboats, leaving the circling *Zest* to check there were no U-boats about.

The following extract from radio officer Spud Campbell's memoirs highlights how even transferring the men, women and children from lifeboat no. 1 to the destroyer was challenging: 'The seas were about 30 feet . . . One instant we would be level with their deck, and then suddenly 30 feet below. Each time we reached the peak level, we would quickly hand [over] a child or mother. This routine continued until all except for our crew and a few of the more able-bodied Norwegians were left. Then we all scrambled onto the deck of the *Opportune*.'[77]

Campbell's account fails to mention the surprise that greeted *Opportune*'s Able Seaman Len Phillips after he had climbed down one of the destroyer's scrambling nets to help the exhausted survivors. After the war he recalled: 'I was handed a bundle, and struggled aboard thinking it was a bundle of belongings until I heard a cry. I opened the bundle, and there was a baby's face looking at me.'[78] (The 'baby' was the two-year-old Sofie Pedersen whose four-year-old sister and parents were also rescued.)[79]

At least the merchant seamen and armed guards in the boats were still mobile. According to *Zambesi's* Captain Allison, the first three men recovered from a Carley float were 'completely numb with cold'. His report states that while his crew recovered nine other men from two rafts, 'the bodies of five others were observed in the vicinity'. His report continues: 'Considerable difficulty was experienced in securing lines to the men, who were quite unable to help themselves.'[80]

Zambesi's John Booth recalled how Gavin Hamilton, the destroyer's first lieutenant, 'in his anxiety to secure a line round one of the survivors, attached a rope to himself and jumped into the water . . . Within a very few moments, [he] was yelling to be hauled out, as the paralysing temperature . . . soaked into his bones.'[81]

By the time darkness proper fell, the three destroyers had between them picked up around 66 of approximately 88 men, women and children who had been on board *Henry Bacon* – the survivors including all 19 of the Norwegian refugees who had been in the ship at the time of the sinking, and those referred to in Allison's report as 'the remaining four live men that could be seen' in the water.[82] At 6.20 p.m. Captain Allison, believing that all those alive had been rescued, issued the order to head back to the convoy, which was reached by all three destroyers at 1 a.m. on 24 February.[83] Tellingly the missing included Captain Carini and 14 members of his crew, and seven armed guards, most of whom would probably have survived had they not willingly sacrificed their lives so that the civilians and the younger men on board the merchant vessel could be saved.

Those in the convoy still had more gales to sail through, but the attack on *Henry Bacon* represented the last opposition put up against RA64 by the Germans. Some of the convoy's merchant ships finally reached the various destinations allocated to them, which included Loch Ewe and the Clyde, on 28 and 29 February, while those ships remaining with the Commodore arrived at Belfast Lough on 1 March 1945.[84] In the meantime most of the *Henry Bacon* survivors, including the 19 Norwegian refugees rescued by *Opportune,* had been dropped off in the Shetland Islands when the destroyer had docked there on 26 February before she rejoined the convoy.[85]

43

Wolves at the Door

Main Actions: 20 March and 29 April 1945
Sinking of Lapwing and Goodall:
JW65 and RA65, JW66 and RA66

GMT + 1: JW65 and RA65
GMT + 2: RA66

By the spring of 1945, it could confidently be asserted that the northern route to the Soviet Union had been secured as much as it ever could be while the Germans still had a functioning U-boat arm. U-boats carried on congregating in the approaches to the Kola Inlet, and were to show that German opposition continued to have a sting in its tail.

The potency of this sting was demonstrated when JW65 (22 merchant ships – 17 of them American, 4 British and 1 Norwegian – 3 tankers and 1 escort oiler, that is 26 ships in total) which had sailed from the Clyde, Scotland during the night of 11–12 March 1945, was forced to approach the Kola Inlet up the usual 40-mile channel from the east, without an 'air umbrella'.[1] Although the support laid on for Operation Scottish (the protection of JW65 and RA65) included a substantial, but not an extraordinarily large, protection force (9 destroyers, 8 corvettes, a sloop and an anti-aircraft cruiser) as well as aircraft flown off two escort carriers, in one of which the 10th Cruiser Squadron's Vice Admiral Frederick Dalrymple-Hamilton flew his flag), the British bombers and fighters were neutered during the early morning of 20 March 1945 when JW65 reached the approaches to the Kola Inlet. It was snowing heavily, causing the aircraft to remain grounded.[2]

The escorts' task was made all the more difficult because the Russian destroyers which were supposed to meet up with the convoy with a view to taking six of the JW65 merchant ships to the White Sea failed to make an appearance.[3] That left the escorts with more ships to protect than was feasible given that so many U-boats had moved in on the 40-mile-long east to west route along which JW65 would have to pass during the last lap of its journey before turning south into the Kola Inlet.[4] It was a case of an overstretched group of escorts having to guide their charges through a double cordon made up of no less than 13 U-boats.[5]

The imbalance provided the opportunity at 9.15 a.m. that morning for U-995's Oberleutnant Hans-Georg Hess, whose vessel lay concealed some 24 miles to the east of the Kildin Island North Light (Severni Kildinski light – Kildin Island being a short distance to the north-east of the Kola Inlet's entrance), to order that a torpedo should be fired at the convoy (see Note 6 for location).[6] It struck amidships on the port side of the American Liberty ship *Horace Bushnell*, the first freighter in the port column, and exploded in her engine room killing five men, but sparing the lives of the other 63 men in the ship.[7]

Water gushed into both the engine room and No. 3 hold through the 35 by 25 foot hole in her hull, but after appearing to be going down rapidly by the stern, the ship steadied and she was eventually first towed and then beached.[8]

But the removal of two of the six convoy escorts guarding the front of the convoy, as it continued on its westward path, to stand in for destroyers diverted to react to the threat posed by the U-boat which had targeted *Horace Bushnell*, together with the moving away of two more escorts to follow up another U-boat contact, left JW65 dangerously exposed.[9]

Taking advantage of the resulting lacuna, when at around 11.10 a.m. that morning JW65 was a few miles to the north-west of the Kildin Island North Light, U-968's Oberleutnant Otto Westphalen, whose torpedoings had created such mayhem during the lead up to RA64 (see Chapter 42), gave the order to fire one of his vessel's torpedoes. The crew in the sloop *Lapwing*, the starboard escort at the front of the convoy, were to be the unfortunate sailors on the receiving end.[10]

As had happened with *Horace Bushnell*, the torpedo hit her amidships. However on this occasion, the effects of the torpedo which slammed into *Lapwing*'s starboard side but which also holed her port side, were devastating. So violent was the explosion, that a sailor watching from the corvette *Allington Castle*, about a mile and a half away on *Lapwing*'s port beam, later reported: 'As the torpedo hit, I heard a thud. I saw steam or smoke rising up as high as the ship's mast. When the steam cleared away, I saw a hole in the port side in the centre of the ship.'[11]

Lapwing's Lieutenant Ian Leitch, who was at the time of the explosion in the sloop's plotting room on the after end of the bridge, later recalled how it 'threw us off our feet and wrecked the . . . plot'.

Even worse, as he reported: 'the door of the compartment jammed, and . . . it was some minutes before the attention of those on the bridge could be attracted . . . A. B. Birtwhistle kicked the panels of the door in from outside and let us out'.

It was lucky he was released when he was. When he looked over the side of the ship, he saw that she was settling quickly. As he reported later: 'Her back was broken, and there was a large hole torn in the upper deck, starboard side, abreast the funnel . . . I considered it unlikely that the ship would remain afloat for more than a few minutes . . .

'I said . . . [to] Surgeon Lieutenant Wilson [who] was on the bridge: "Where is the Captain?" He replied: "He has been knocked out. I am just going to attend to him." I then saw the Captain lying unconscious on the port side of the bridge under the chart table.'

In his report Leitch then described how he reacted: 'Some ratings on B gun deck were cutting free a flotanet from the starboard guard rails, but there appeared insufficient life-saving equipment for the large number of ratings, about one hundred, which had mustered on the forecastle. I shouted to them to cut everything adrift that would float off, such as the whaler's gear, which was slung overhead on the Bofors gun platform support.'

As he descended to the upper deck, he heard ominous sounds: 'loud breaking up noises [that] could be heard from the region of the boiler room'. Evidently he was not alone in thinking that the time had come to abandon ship: 'I saw that the ratings forward were starting to jump over the side as the ship was now settling rapidly, and listing heavily to starboard,' he reported, continuing: 'I assisted [the injured] Sub Lieutenant Baldwin through the guard rails into the water, and then followed myself. A few seconds later, the ship broke in half. The forward part capsized to starboard, and the after part floated vertically stern uppermost. As I swam clear to avoid being fouled by the mast and rigging, I saw the Captain holding on to the port side of the bridge as it turned over, and then drop clear into the water.'[12]

All this was unfolding in plain sight of the men in the corvette *Allington Castle,* who were looking on at what for them was a terrifying series of events. What was to stop the U-boat making their ship its next victim? Long after the war, the corvette's Bill Bridges, who at the time had been 19 years old, could still recall how the torpedoing of *Lapwing* prompted him to inflate his life jacket. 'I could see men sliding down the deck – mostly from the stern part – as she broke in half,' he told me when I caught up with him many years after the event.

Because there are few accounts by participants, it is impossible to gauge how many of those whom Bridges saw falling made it to safety. One can only report the little that is known. 'I found my inflatable lifebelt gave ample buoyancy,' Lieutenant Leitch wrote in his report. 'There was also a vast amount of floating wreckage such as planks, danbuoys, floats and cork life jackets to help support one, although oil fuel made it difficult to grasp them. I clung to a wooden plank, but later transferred to a flotanet attached to a fully manned Carley float, whose occupants were singing cheerfully, and appeared admirably confident of being rescued.'

They certainly needed robust spirits, although the report by *Allington Castle's* Lieutenant Commander Phillips Read states that the sea temperature was a life-saving 3° C, much warmer than the air temperature which was -1 °C.[13]

'Snow then began to fall,' Leitch's report continues, 'and . . . [some time later] I found myself drifting under *Allington Castle's* starboard quarter, but cannot recollect anything after this until I found myself being stripped and cleaned on board her in the seaman's bathroom.'[14]

In a book published after the war, Ian Leitch stated that his report 'more or less tells the sad story. From a ship's company of 220, there were [just] 60 survivors.' The latter included *Lapwing's* captain Commander Edward Hulton.[15]

The fallout from this second torpedoing, which led to more ships being diverted from convoy protection to rescue duties, further reduced the number of escorts with the bulk of JW65. Some escorts were still engaged in the task of rescuing men from *Lapwing*, when at 12.15 p.m. that same day, while the convoy's ships were proceeding in two columns in order to ease their eventual entry into the inlet, the American Liberty ship *Thomas Donaldson* was also torpedoed by *U-968*.[16] At the time, the convoy was around three miles north-west of the Kildin Island North Light.[17]

The torpedo exploded after hitting *Thomas Donaldson*'s starboard side beside her engine room, killing all three men on duty there, who either died instantaneously, or they drowned when the compartment flooded. But apart from three other members of the crew who were badly injured as a result of the blast (so badly in one case that the wounded man subsequently died), the remaining men on board were not harmed, and were able to abandon ship. Once again an attempt was made to tow the ship, but it had to be aborted when the ship sank.[18]

Losing a second fully laden ship so close to the planned destination seems at first sight to have highlighted the fragility of the Arctic convoy system when coming up against groups of U-boats whose crews knew the merchant ships' route. However, those who feared that Germans in the Arctic were about to make a comeback would have to eat their words. The remaining JW65 vessels made it into the Kola Inlet safely, and everything that had gone wrong with JW65, went right with the returning convoy, RA65.

The 10th Cruiser Squadron's Vice Admiral Dalrymple-Hamilton was able to have the merchant ships and escorts constituting the Kola Inlet section of RA65 proceed out of the inlet during the night of 23–24 March 1945 without losing a single vessel. Because the U-boat commanders had no idea there was a newly mine-swept channel that went north-east from the inlet's entrance rather than from west to east like the one used previously, the merchant ships and escorts alike were able to escape up it without being noticed let alone attacked. Their unimpeded progress was assisted by the merchant ships passing Toros Island, on the western side of the inlet's exit (see Map 23), at midnight, a departure time that was unprecedented.

The escape was also helped on its way by four destroyers being sent as decoys, shortly before the convoy emerged from the inlet, down what the Vice Admiral designated the 'standard route', which ran from the mouth of the inlet towards the east, where so much damage had been done by the U-boats on 20 March. These destroyers made their presence known by dropping depth charges and firing starshell, before retracing their steps and then catching up with the convoy proper.[19]

The convoy's escape was also made easier because the number of ships passing up the escape route was reduced thanks to the decision to rendezvous with the White Sea feeder convoy after the U-boats had been evaded. The ships in RA65 (3 tankers and 23 other merchant ships) went on to reach their various destinations without loss.[20]

Although as far as the Allies were concerned that was a blessing, one wonders whether the success of the ruse that had been played so artfully during RA65, a ruse that could not be employed again with the same effect, created unrealistic expectations concerning future operations. Those who suffered as a result of the subsequent decision to sail another pair of Arctic convoys could rightly question whether a judicious cost-benefit analysis was done before the merchant ships and escorts set out. Had such an analysis been carried out without political expediency being included in the mix, it is more than likely that the convoys would have been halted by this time. The fact that they were no longer a necessity on purely military grounds was being openly discussed by Churchill with other members of his war cabinet by the end of March 1945.

Admittedly the 26 protected ships within the east-going JW66, which sailed from the Clyde on the night of 16–17 April 1945, guarded by an equivalent escort to that used in the previous east-going convoy, also arrived at their various north Russian destinations without loss.[21] The naval force for this, the first part of Operation Roundel (the protection of JW66 and RA66), consisted of 2 carriers, an anti-aircraft ship, 9 destroyers and 2 escort groups utilizing a sloop, 7 corvettes and 5 frigates. 16 submarine chasers manned by Russians also accompanied the convoy, and 6 Russian destroyers played their part at the end of the voyage, escorting the White Sea portion of the convoy after it split off from the ships bound for the Kola Inlet.[22] But the 14 U-boats which had assembled outside the Kola Inlet prior to the departure of the west-going RA66 were to highlight the unavoidable dangers still lurking there.[23]

These dangers do not appear to have been much affected by the strategems employed by the 10th Cruiser Squadron's Rear Admiral Angus Cunninghame Graham, the Operation Roundel escort commander. Two days before the convoy departed, he deployed what he called a 'feint'. This involved the Russians switching on the coastal navigation lights, wireless beacons being operated, and depth charges being dropped by small craft. He hoped that by doing this, he would simulate the sailing of the convoy two nights before it really sailed, and that this would 'mislead and tire any U-boats present'.[24]

Then during the afternoon and early evening of 29 April 1945, just hours before the convoy proper sailed, he had the eight warships of the 7th Escort Group and the five frigates of 19th Escort Group sweep the area through which RA66 would pass later that night. While the 19th Escort Group frigates were in a long line sweeping northward, a U-boat was detected at around 7 p.m. between Kildin Island and Syet Navalok (at the head of the western side of the entrance to the Kola Inlet) by an asdic operator in the frigate *Loch Shin*. After this U-boat was blasted to the surface by the pattern of Squid fired from *Loch Shin*, and hit by shells and bullets emanating from the guns in *Loch Shin* and in two other British warships, it hovered, vertical, with 30 feet of bow showing, before sinking back under the water stern first. Answers elicited from the 14 survivors it left behind told their rescuers the sunk vessel was *U-307* (see Note 25 for location).[25]

But what initially appeared to be a victory for the Allies turned out to be pyrrhic. 'No sooner had the furore died down,' wrote G. A. Roy, the 20-year-old gunner who operated the port side Oerlikon aft of the bridge in *Goodall*, the 19th Escort Group's frigate tasked with sweeping northward at the left of the line, '[than] . . . I heard the yardarm pulleys working. I looked up and I saw the black flag flying. I remember thinking "Christ, another ping. They must be thick around here." . . . Then . . . there was a terrific flash followed by flying debris. Something big slammed into my gun shield . . . knocking the magazine . . . off the gun . . . I was left hanging by the straps, spitting blood due to a rap on the head . . . My mate was lying beside the gun platform, his head missing . . . Looking at the funnel I could see the carnage . . . What had been the bridge [was high] on the funnel . . . Bodies and body parts [were] lying about the funnel deck.'[26]

Like many in *Goodall* directly impacted by the blast, Roy had not even heard what his shipmate Freddie Peeters described as the 'almighty explosion' – which according to official reports compiled later occurred at around 7.35 p.m. (29 April).[27] Such an eruption is par for the course when as in this case a torpedo hits a ship beside the magazine under its main armament. The torpedo struck *Goodall* beside the magazine for A and B guns. The sound of the resulting blast was for some literally deafening.

Peeters, who like many of the survivors in *Goodall* was knocked onto the deck by the pressure waves and the violent shuddering of the ship as the torpedo exploded, only lived to tell his tale thanks to a stroke of good fortune. He had minutes earlier exited *Goodall*'s wheelhouse, and climbed down onto the top deck. His first observation on picking himself up and looking around, dazed, was: 'half the ship was missing'.[28] As *Goodall*'s first lieutenant, James Dallaway, would subsequently confirm: 'There was nothing of the fo'c'sle left . . . The bridge had turned right over on top of the funnel and midship Oerlikon gun.'[29]

The following extract from Dallaway's official report explains how he came to take charge of the ship: 'At [the] . . . time [when the torpedo hit], the Captain was on the bridge . . . After the explosion, no trace of . . . the Captain could be seen . . . I presume[d] that he was lost.'[30]

However tragic, that was the least of it. 'Ammunition was exploding all around me,' Peeters reported later, 'and as I crawled aft, I could see limbs lying around. It was terrible. A duffle coat lay near me with just an arm in the sleeve.'[31]

But at least he was out in the open with an escape route in sight. For some time telegraphist Bill Bates was, as he put it, 'entombed' in a three foot square 'cubby' amidships, whose door had been jammed by the explosion. By the time someone outside thought to open up the door so as to let him out, he had been almost asphyxiated by fumes.

It was to be this experience which would haunt him for the rest of his life, rather than the carnage which greeted him as he escaped from his prison. One of the first such sights he came across was the corpse of his 'Oppo' whom he referred to as Blondie.

'As I tried to move him, he seemed to come apart in my hands,' Bates would write later. 'I recall how ashamed I was to feel such revulsion.'[32]

He also saw the remains of the masthead lookout, who had been blasted from his vantage point by the explosion, and had landed on top of the depth charge racks aft. 'He was completely in two,' Bates recalled, 'and he was steaming from his stomach. Somebody a little later pushed him over the side.'[33]

Perhaps it was the fear that worse was to come which served as a distraction, thereby making such macabre scenes bearable. 'Under [what had once been] the bridge was situated the diesel fuel tank,' Dallaway would report later. 'This . . . [caught] fire, and fire [also] broke out in the forward engine room and motor room, the whole midship section and the bridge being soon enveloped in flames . . . The fire was gaining aft, and I realized it would not be long before it reached the after three inch . . . magazine. So I ordered the men into the rafts, and told them to get clear as the magazine was likely to blow up at any moment.'[34]

According to Dallaway, 'three rafts with about 15-20 men in each and one . . . [flotanet] with six ratings started to get clear of the ship, leaving the badly wounded on board with 13 other men. I explained . . . to them that the magazine was in danger, and all available rafts had left, and told them either to jump for it and make their way to the rafts, or remain while we cleared anything that was likely to float.'

But then, as Dallaway would explain, one of those seemingly miraculous events took place that changed everything. 'The ship . . . fortunately drifted so that she lay beam to wind and sea, and I realized that the flames were now athwartships [rather than being blown aft], and the danger to the magazine had passed.'[35]

The wounded were eventually taken off *Goodall* thanks to the bravery and skill of Jimmy Wright, *Honeysuckle*'s 32-year-old lieutenant commander, who ignoring the possibility the frigate might explode, edged his corvette right up to the burning ship. The wounded were followed by the other *Goodall* survivors. Only then was *Honeysuckle* moved away, but not before Wright had had a good look at the explosion's repercussions. He afterwards reported: 'Many dead were lying all over the after part, but it appeared that the majority of the crew lost had been blown to pieces, as a considerable amount of limbs of all descriptions were lying around.'[36]

The crisis did not end there. Shipwrecked sailors and rescuers might have been burnt alive where they floated had speedy preventive action not been taken. The oil that had leaked out of *Goodall*'s tanks had spread far and wide, and had then caught fire.

It was the danger this posed that provided the impetus for the next stage of *Honeysuckle*'s mercy mission. She was driven towards what Jimmy Wright referred to as 'a raft' with 'helpless men on it . . . very close to the fire [on the water] and drifting towards it.' Although the rescue commenced with his ship some 100 yards away from the flames, it took so long to heave all the men onto the corvette that, as Wright reported: 'the fire reached the port bow just as the last survivor was brought on board, and in a matter of a second, the ship was enveloped in flame, and to all intents and purposes the whole ship appeared to be on fire. Emergency full ahead was rung, and trusting the fire had not yet spread to starboard, as it was [impossible] . . . to see more than a few inches owing to the flames and smoke, helm was put hard over to starboard, and [the] ship eventually cleared the fire with all the paint work on [the] port bow alight. This was quickly put out, with no damage other than burnt paintwork the result.'[37]

While this rescuing was taking place, the hunt for the U-boat which had caused all this misery continued. We now know that those blown up in *Goodall* did not die in vain. Her telegraphist's last signal '358 degrees – 20, submarine definite' had already been sent out before his messaging was interrupted by the explosion (the 20 in the signal appears to be shorthand for 2,000 yards).[38] That was more than enough to encourage the crews in her sister ships to set out on a U-boat hunt. Within five minutes of the torpedoing of *Goodall*, an asdic operator in *Loch Shin* confirmed the detection of a U-boat, and three minutes later the frigate's Squid was fired at it.

A succession of attacks followed, culminating in the crew in the frigate *Cotton* spotting oil and wreckage on the surface in the wake of her 8.17 p.m. depth charge attack. When more depth charges dropped in the same area by *Cotton* resulted in the oil slick spreading exponentially, and when a sample taken was confirmed to be diesel, consistent with it being U-boat fuel, it was decided that the U-boat had probably been damaged by the earlier attacks, and finally dispatched by *Cotton* (see Note 39 for location of presumed sinking).[39]

The commanders of the four surviving frigates afterwards agreed that, with the convoy due to come out of the inlet later that night, they must resume their sweep to the north as originally instructed.[40] While some on board the escort group's ships may have assumed they had avenged what the U-boat had done to *Goodall*, their assumption may have been wishful thinking. Analysis after the war tells us that they had sunk *U-286* commanded by Oberleutnant Willi Dietrich rather than Oberleutnant Otto Westphalen's *U-968*, which may have played the principal role in putting paid to some of *Goodall*'s crew's hopes of surviving the war.[41] Going on 100 men from *Goodall* died.[42]

Even Westphalen could not accurately claim he had sunk *Goodall*. She only went down later that night after the crews in the frigates from the 19th Escort Group had found her abandoned wreck as they completed their sweeps outside the inlet. The gunners in the frigate *Anguilla* were ordered to deliver the coup de grâce, and at 1.45 a.m. on 30 April *Goodall* finally blew up, but not before around twenty 3-inch shells had been fired at her.[43]

As for convoy RA66 itself, whose 26 merchant ships finally emerged from the inlet shortly after midnight during the night 29–30 April, it was at one point shadowed by so many reconnaissance planes that the 10th Cruiser Squadron's Rear Admiral Cunninghame Graham felt sure the Luftwaffe must be gearing up for a coordinated attack involving German planes and U-boats. However for whatever reason, no such attack was made, and the convoy's merchant ships, all in one piece, arrived back in the Clyde on 8 May 1945, VE Day.[44]

Thus in the wake of the final throes of the Battle of the Arctic, the passage of the last of the wartime Arctic convoys ended on a positive note for the Allies, but without their being able to say that supplying aid to the Soviet Union via the northern route had ever been a walkover.

44

Conclusion

It is hard to come up with a simple answer to the question: Who won the Battle of the Arctic?

It is clear that if one assesses the Battle of the Arctic as one entity, the Allies accomplished what they had set out to achieve: while not losing more merchant vessels and warships than they could afford, they had supplied just enough aid via the northern route to help the Soviet Union stay in the war, and to keep Stalin onside.

Britain's Official Historian of the war at sea, when assessing the Arctic convoys' performance, stated that, while acknowledging the impressive impact made by German attacks during March to September 1942: 'Taken as a whole, the record of the Arctic convoys was . . . amazingly successful. In the forty outward convoys, 811 [merchant] ships sailed. Thirty-three turned back . . . and fifty-eight were sunk.' In other words over 88 per cent of those merchant ships which set out for Russia in convoys (720 out of 811) reached their destination.[1]

Moreover overall, taking into account attacks during the Arctic convoys' homeward journeys as well as during those east-going convoys mentioned above, only 89 merchant vessels including a rescue ship and a fleet oiler were sunk (in the 34 westbound Arctic convoys, 29 merchant ships out of 717 which sailed were sunk).[2] The number of Allied sailors killed during the convoys was also surprisingly low given the strength of their adversary, although it would have been even lower had the number of fatalities not been swelled by the fact that 18 warships, whose crews were much larger than the numbers in merchant ships, were also sunk. Only 829 of some 2,773 Allied seamen killed during Arctic convoys were from merchant ship crews.[3]

Given the harsh conditions, some might be surprised that the death toll was not much higher. There is little doubt it would have been had the Arctic convoys' protection forces after the disastrous PQ17 not been assisted by the presence of accompanying escort carriers whose aircraft were able to provide the required anti-submarine patrols and fighter defence. It was this, along with the German inability to consistently deploy large numbers of combat aircraft in northern Norway that could be used against the convoys, which were as responsible as any other factors for the upturn in the convoys' fortunes after October 1942.

Equally significant was the German Navy's failure to strike the right balance between risk taking and safety when it came to operating its surface fleet against the Arctic convoys. Hitler's insistence that minimal risk-taking was acceptable was behind much of this. Dönitz's going to the opposite extreme during the lead up to the Battle of North Cape at the end of 1943 was just as counter-productive from the German point of view.

Such a judgement on German errors should be put into context. They were not the only ones who were acting cautiously. Most people would say that Britain's First Sea Lord, Admiral Sir Dudley Pound, who as we have seen was in overall charge of the protection of the Arctic convoys until his retirement on account of a brain tumour in September 1943, was also risk averse, some would say to a fault, in relation to the actions of his warships when it really mattered, during PQ17. So prevalent is this view, that there were no howls of protest when the presenter of a recent documentary on the convoy, backing the critical verdict of Britain's Official Historian of the war at sea, felt it was accurate to imply that Pound, when scattering PQ17 in an attempt to save his warships, was either not being very clever, or was unhinged by a combination of exhaustion caused by insomnia on account of an arthritic hip, and the effects of the brain tumour.[4]

Not everyone agrees with this judgement – hence the controversy that has raged over Pound's scatter order ever since it was issued. No-one rational, given the benefit of hindsight, could say that Pound's decision to scatter the convoy was sensible. Even without hindsight, the manner in which the order was given was clearly ill-advised. A re-examination of all the evidence in Pound's possession when the scatter order was transmitted, however, reveals that given what Pound knew at the time, his going for the scatter option was, notwithstanding the horrific implications for the merchant seamen, reasonable and arguably correct (see Note 5 for the analysis that leads to this conclusion).[5]

Although thanks in part to the restraint imposed by Hitler, the Germans lost a much lower number of vessels than the Allies overall in the Arctic theatre, the number of Kriegsmarine fighting vessels sunk (43 – *Tirpitz*, the battlecruiser *Scharnhorst*, three destroyers and 38 U-boats) far exceeded the 18 Allied fighting vessels sunk during the Arctic convoys.[6]

The amount of aid delivered by the Allies via the northern route is also impressive. Approximately 4 million tons of cargo are believed to have reached the northern Russian ports in Arctic convoys. This apparently included a substantial proportion of the 5,218 tanks (1,388 from Canada), and 7,411 aircraft that are believed to have been supplied to the Soviet Union on Britain's behalf during the war. Aid weighing around 300,000 tons is believed to have been lost as a result of ships in Arctic convoys being lost en route to the Soviet Union.[7] To put this in context, Admiral Schofield, a wartime director of the Admiralty's Trade Division, reckoned that the number of tanks, aircraft and trucks sent during the war to the Soviet Union via all routes was around 12,000, 22,000 and 376,000 respectively. It is likely that the number of aircraft specified by Admiral Schofield is intended to include those flown to the Soviet Union via the so-called Alaska-Siberian route that was up and running with effect from August 1942.[8]

On the other hand, it is possible to argue that the Allied 'victory' during the Arctic convoys, if the above statistics dictate that is how it should be termed, was not clear cut. As described in the previous chapters, the threat of German attacks resulted in the convoys being suspended for long periods during the second half of 1942 and during 1944, as well as during much of 1943. This contributed to the failure by the Allies to deliver a substantial part of the aid they had pledged to make available to the Soviet Union when signing the so-called Second and Third

Protocols, which respectively covered the aid that was to be supplied during the periods running from 1 July 1942 to 30 June 1943, and from 1 July 1943 to 30 June 1944 (see Note 9 for the shortfall during the Second Protocol period).[9]

The delivery of all the aid that did get through raises a number of other questions. First of all, did the western allies donate as much as they could to the Soviet Union, even to the extent that they deprived their own forces of what they needed in order to support the Russians on the Eastern Front? Or did they, as was frequently alleged by Russians in contact with the general heading up Britain's military mission in Moscow, only help the Russians after their own needs were met, in effect donating to Stalin's forces the excess or out of date munitions they would 'otherwise have had to dump in the North Sea'?

It has to be said that once again a nuanced reply is in order. The surviving documents do reveal a slice of something approaching the latter attitude. It came to the fore for example during November 1941, when a question arose during a British War Cabinet Defence Committee meeting over whether Britain could satisfy the monthly quota of tanks agreed in the First Protocol by handing over to Russia the less adaptable Matilda infantry tanks – which were relatively slow and had a restricted range, making them less in demand in the armoured divisions being deployed by Britain against Rommel in Egypt and Libya.

Rather than thinking it might be a good idea to ask the Russians whether, in spite of the Matilda's downsides, it would suit them, the Chief of the Imperial General Staff Sir John Dill, argued that it was in his opinion appropriate to give Matildas to the Russians because as he put it 'we had not made any promise . . . to provide one type of tank rather than another, and from what was known of the Russian tactics, the Matilda would admirably serve their purpose'.

By way of contrast, there was also a push back on other occasions in the opposite direction, with both politicians and leaders responsible for the British army and the RAF accepting during the lead up to the September 1941 Moscow conference, and afterwards, that when it came to the restricted number of tanks and aircraft available, the Russian quotas were sacrosanct even though that meant risks had to be accepted elsewhere. This was a particularly committed course of action by Churchill, his war cabinet and senior armed forces advisers because it was signed up to initially when America could not match what Britain was donating to Russia. This was initially because, strange as it may seem, the US was not able to match the British production rates, and subsequently because after Pearl Harbour, America had to use everthing she was producing to arm her own forces.

The result of the British commitment to Russia was that towards the end of 1941 and in early 1942, before the Americans finally and fully stepped into the breach, a form of 'triage' had to be applied when it came to supplying tanks and aircraft for territories where Britain was committed. The home front was naturally positioned at the top of the hierarchy of theatres, insofar as that was necessary, when it came to deciding which areas should be supplied with the restricted equipment. However its needs were not always allowed to trump Russia's. In spite of the Chief of the Air Staff's comment at the September 1941 Defence Committee meeting that preceded the Moscow supply conference that 'the present proposals for aid for Russia would hit the Royal Air Force very hard, and might cause the strength of Fighter Command (which was responsible for keeping clear the skies over Britain) to fall dangerously low in the Spring', the minutes confirmed that like everyone else attending, 'he thought that we must carry them out'.

Meanwhile India and the Far East (Malaya and Singapore) were to be left even worse off. Condemned as they were to sit at the bottom of the hierarchy that governed which territories would be protected, they were at least until the beginning of 1942, knowingly left well-nigh defenceless against a committed attack by an enemy armed with modern tanks and aircraft.

Even General Sir Claude Auchinleck, the British Commander-in-Chief Middle East, who occupied a high place in the hierarchy by dint of his having been instructed to take prompt offensive action in Libya and Egypt, was held up because of the precedence given to the Russian supply operation.

There would be negative consequences. Auchinleck's November to December 1941 Operation Crusader, partly because of a tank shortage that was exacerbated by his tanks' unsuitability for use in the Western Desert, failed to have the unalloyed success that might have been expected had he also had access to the tanks sent to or retained for Russia. His hopes of attacking again quickly at the beginning of 1942, enabling him to kill off what remained of Rommel's forces, were also stymied because of the delay in getting enough tanks to him. If that had not happened, Rommel might well not have been in post and able to inflict on British forces in June 1942 the ignominious defeat, that included the loss of Tobruk.

That was even harder to bear because it followed the previous disasters in Malaya and Singapore. In spite of the relatively late attempt to supply them, caused once again by the previously available tanks and aircraft being given to Russia, they were captured by the Japanese in February 1942. The consequences of favouring Russia in preference to the Far East could have been even worse if Australia had also been in the Japanese sights. At the beginning of 1942 it was acknowledged that the only way to quickly give Australia all the tanks it had requested was if shipments to Russia were cut back. Eventually a compromise was reached after Churchill had explained to the Australian prime minister why he had been forced to favour Russia at Malaya's and the Far East's expense ('all the teachings of war show that everything should be concentrated on destroying one of the attacking forces', Churchill wrote). The aforementioned compromise included the following measures: delaying the number of tanks being allocated for home defence, persuading Australia to manage with a proportion of the armour they had ordered, and satisfying the Russian First Protocol quota from the tanks coming out of British and Canadian factories in February and March 1942, meaning that these tanks would only be made available rather than transported to Russia during these months.

Such contortions and sacrifices in order not to reduce the Russian monthly quota make it all the more germane to pose the following additional query: was the prioritizing of supplies to the Soviet Union worthwhile? This is tantamount to asking: was the amount delivered via the Arctic convoys, even when added onto aid sent to Russia by the Allies via other routes, sufficient, and did any of it affect the course of the war on the Eastern front?

It has been tempting given the sacrifice of life and limb that was involved in transporting all this aid via the northern route to assume it made a huge difference. No lesser authority than Britain's official historian of the war at sea in 1961 wrote of the aid sent via the Arctic convoys: 'Though we have no knowledge of the part which this huge quantity of British and American war material played in helping the Russian armies to gain their victories on land, it must surely have been substantial.'[10] He is only one of many historians and commentators who have been so impressed by what was delivered, they have claimed the Soviet Union could not have defeated the Germans without it.

However, after the war, encouraged by the understandable desire of the Russian authorities to claim that their forces, which had lost so many men, had saved their own country, there was a kickback within Russia against the notion that the British and American aid had helped the Soviet Union to defeat the Germans. The kickback may well have been all the harder, because many Russians were resentful that the West had delayed opening the demanded Second Front until after the Red Army had repulsed the main German attacks.

Russian desire to denigrate the West's contribution to the Soviet success has been further bolstered by the decision to show the world that the communist system was superior to the Western democracies, even when it came to running a wartime economy that could provide the wherewithal to repulse an invasion.

One of the most recent accounts of the ebbing and flowing of Russian appreciation for the British and American aid up to and including the Vladimir Putin era has been written by Olga Kucherenko, one of the historians who assisted in the putting together of the book referred to as Reynolds and Pechatnov in list number 2. in the Abbreviations section of this book, a work that has been much cited in this book's Notes. She confirms that 'the blueprint for Soviet era literature', which downplayed the impact of Western aid, was the book *The Soviet Military Economy in the Great Patriotic War*, published in 1948, by Nikolai Voznesensky, Chairman of the State Planning Committee. She says that while attributing the increase in Soviet imports to Allied aid, he 'asserted that foreign deliveries accounted for only 4% of the Soviet wartime industrial output'. Stalin is said to have excised the passage in the draft which confirmed the Allies' indisputable contribution to the Soviet war economy.[11]

Olga Kucherenko also refers to the seminal work on the Great Patriotic War published by the Russian Defence Ministry in 2014 which asserted that US aid during the crucial years 1941–2 only accounted for 7 per cent of all the wartime aid the US provided.[12] This is part of the ongoing trend encouraged by Russian leaders, right up to Vladimir Putin – albeit with a softening of the line during Nikita Khrushchev's time as leader and during glasnost – to stress that Western aid when the need was greatest was 'insignificant', she says.

It is very likely such disrespect is, as she implies, a misleading simplification. Why else would the three wise Soviet men she cites have freely admitted after the war that a substantial debt was owed to the Allies? Red Army Marshal Georgy Zhukov has confirmed that the aid assisted the forming of Soviet reserves and the production of Soviet tanks; Anastas Mikoyan, who as People's Commissar of Foreign Trade had been in charge of the wartime transportation of supplies and food, has talked up the value of the provisions and warm clothing supplied as well as the weapons; while Khrushchev was so embarrassed by the enormous number of trucks delivered by the Allies, whose presence was still visible during post-war parades, that on one famous occasion after the war, while he was the Soviet leader, he ordered that in future parades, artillery should be mounted on Soviet trucks, rather than on American Studebakers, in case those watching assumed all trucks used by the Soviet army were foreign.[13]

That did not mean he wanted to cover up the way these trucks had helped the Soviet Union during the war. 'Just imagine how we would have advanced from Stalingrad to Berlin without them!' Khrushchev wrote in his memoirs. 'Our losses would have been colossal because we would have had no maneuverability.'

As I pointed out in Chapter 33, he also confirmed that the Red Army's victory at Stalingrad, where Khrushchev had been a participating officer, was assisted by Allied trucks sent to Russia prior to or during the great Russian November 1942 to January 1943 counter-attack, most of which appear to have been transported to Russia via the northern route. 'It was with American and British trucks that it was able to advance swiftly, [and] complete the encirclement of the German forces,' he wrote.[14]

Although at first sight it is hard to understand how the supply of something as unthreatening as trucks could have had such an impact on a clash between titans, it seems likely that they as much as anything else supplied via the Arctic convoys altered the course of the fighting on the Eastern front. If, as Khrushchev appears to be implying, the Russian counter-attack at Stalingrad really would have stalled without the trucks, it can truly be said that the Arctic convoys did affect the course of the war if not its final result. If the Germans had prevailed at Stalingrad at the end of 1942 and the beginning of 1943, who knows what course the war would have taken afterwards.

Having said that, it would be wrong not to stress that the abovementioned comments by Soviet elders were not just aimed at Allied aid sent via the northern route used by the Arctic convoys. By the end of 1943 most of the aid to the Soviet Union was being sent via the other routes. It was these other routes which conveyed most of the food and trucks which every Russian soldier on the Eastern front after 1943 would never forget.

However, that does not mean the earlier aid, when the Arctic convoys played a dominant role, was not significant. It was certainly appreciated at the time it was sent. Readers may recall from the preceding chapters how during 1942 and late 1943 Stalin, his Ambassador Maisky, and Molotov again and again protested when supplies via the northern route were either suspended or delayed. 'It is obvious that the transport via [the] Persian Gulf could in no way compensate for the cessation of convoys to the Northern ports,' Stalin wrote to Churchill on 23 July 1942, after learning the convoys were to be suspended following the PQ17 disaster (see Chapter 24). 'I never expected that the British will stop dispatch of war materials to us just at the very moment when the Soviet Union, in view of the very serious situation on the Soviet-German front, requires these materials more than ever.'[15]

Similarly passionate admissions that the aid was badly needed were in evidence at the end of September 1941 during the Moscow Conference attended by Beaverbrook and Harriman (see Chapter 2), in February 1942, when as the Soviet counter-offensive petered out, Stalin told Roosevelt that the requested delivery of tanks and aircraft were 'of the utmost importance . . . for our further success', during the days prior to the Russian counter-attack on the Ukrainian city Kharkov in May 1942 (see Chapter 13), and during the defence of Stalingrad in October 1942 (see Chapter 30).[16]

In October 1943, there was more evidence that the cargo carried by the Arctic convoys was helping the Soviet Union. In Stalin's 13 October 1943 telegram to Churchill (mentioned in Chapter 36), the Soviet leader stressed once again that the items he needed would not arrive quickly enough if sent via the Persian route. In the same telegram Stalin explained why the convoys planned by Churchill were so important: 'Delivery of equipment and materials by the Northern route ... were taken into account when planning the supplies for Soviet armies,' he informed Britain's prime minister.[17]

Stalin and Molotov evidently believed that the aid mentioned in Stalin's abovementioned 13 October 1943 telegram, that was to be carried by the convoys during the winter of 1943–4, was important enough to merit what if less had been at stake they would probably have considered an unacceptably humiliating climbdown. That appears to have been what lay behind the charm offensive Molotov embarked on, when on 22 October 1943, he talked to Eden in Moscow about the harsh treatment of Allied seamen in the north Russian ports mentioned by Churchill in his 1 October 1943 telegram to Stalin (also referred to in Chapter 36).[18]

These instances of the Soviets stating that the aid was needed, and that it should be sent via the convoys, make uneasy bedfellows with the claims by Russian economists and historians, writing during the Soviet era after the war, that the convoys carrying the requested aid did not significantly help the Soviet Union.

A similar point appears to be supported by what has been written after the war by a small group of Russian revisionist historians. One of their most devastating underminings of the original Soviet line is to be found in the work of Boris Sokolov. He has argued that the Soviet claims that they were able to make their own aircraft, and consequently did not need to rely on those supplied from America and Britain in Arctic convoys and by the other routes, were based on incorrect information. The Soviet Union would never have managed to manufacture so many aircraft without the aluminium donated by the Allies, he says. He also states that the amount of aluminium the Allies donated during the war was an estimated 125 per cent of the aluminium the Soviet Union possessed without relying on foreign aid.[19]

Even if he is wrong about that, the Soviet stance is open to question because of what he says is another fatal flaw in the Soviet case. The Soviet aircraft would not have been able to keep flying had it not been for aviation gasoline supplied by the Allies. He estimates the Allies supplied 140 per cent of the aviation gasoline produced in the Soviet Union during the war.[20]

Other revisionists prefer to pick apart the Soviet arguments by focusing on how the West were able to promptly supply particular kit that was in short supply albeit for a relatively short period. A taste of this kind of viewpoint is to be found in the work of Alexander Hill, an academic based in Canada. His analysis of the events of 1941 is all the more appealing to British eyes because it touches on the significance of two of the Arctic convoys' poster boys: the Matilda and Valentine tanks, which had featured in Britain's tanks for Russia campaign launched in September 1941 by Lord Beaverbrook (see Chapter 2).

As Hill's writing makes clear, it would be hard to prove the significance of all of the 5,000-odd tanks sent over to Russia by Britain during the war given the large number of home-designed tanks produced by the Soviet Union.[21] Various Russian sources mentioned by Hill state that anything from around 75,000 to 110,000 Russian tanks were produced by Soviet factories or reached the Red Army between 1941 and 1945.[22]

However as Hill points out, figures cited by Colonel-General Grigori Krivosheev, who edited the first comprehensive published analysis of the Soviet Union's losses during the war based on declassified documents, reveal that during the first six months of the war things were very different.[23]

It was in the context of the Soviet Union's inability to reinforce the Soviet arsenal of medium and heavy tanks quickly enough that Britain was able to step into the breach, says Hill. According to General Krivosheev, by the end of 1941 the Soviet Union only possessed some 1,400 medium and heavy tanks.[24] It had to be Britain rather than America during the first six months after the invasion of the Soviet Union because, notwithstanding American commitments under the First Protocol, during the period up to January 1942, Roosevelt's administration struggled to find more than a token number of spare tanks which the US could export.[25]

By the end of 1941, 426 heavy and medium tanks supplied by Britain had been transported in Arctic convoys and dropped off in the northern Russia ports.[26] This represented 426/1,400 = 30.4 per cent of the heavy and medium tanks that Krivosheev claims the Russians possessed at the year end. In other words a substantial proportion at a critical period when the Red Army's ability to throw back the Germans from Moscow was hanging in the balance.

Hill's research shows that some of these tanks were drip fed into several of the Soviet tank battalions defending Moscow. One telegram he cites shows that by 9 December 1941, around 90 British tanks had already been in action, and had confirmed that their two-pounder guns penetrated the side armour of German medium tanks at a distance of 800 metres.[27]

A review of revisionist writing which has to be taken into account when evaluating the value of the aid shipped in the Arctic convoys would not be complete without mentioning the writings of the Russian professor, Mikhail Suprun. Although his work does not expressly debunk the Soviet era contributions, it highlights statistics that he has found in various Russian archives which lead one to query the Arctic convoy disrespecters (see an example in Note 28 which supports the conclusion that Allied supplies during the First Protocol period (1 October 1941–30 June 1942), when a relatively high proportion of total aid to the Soviet Union went via the northern route, was significant.[28]

It has to be said that even this dogged academic, who has devoted years of his life to his campaign to uncover the true effect of the aid given to the Soviet Union, has conceded that there are still many Arctic convoys in respect of which the individual statistics have not yet been discovered either in archives in Russia or in the West. Also the statistics he cites, some of which rely on what he has found in Russia's State Archive of Economics, do not always marry up with what is to be found in Western archives.

This brings to the fore a major obstacle to progress which the revisionists have been forced to grapple with. Nowhere is it described more openly than by the historian Andrew Boyd in his latest book which at the date when I wrote this chapter was the most recent English language book that focuses on the impact of the aid given to Russia during World War 2. In it he writes: 'Assessing tonnage delivered and its origin is difficult because there is no single definitive source. British, American and Russian records . . . differ, cover different time periods and do not always distinguish between initial shipment and delivery or differentiate between the Arctic and other routes.'

In other words while a given source might refer to hundreds of Russia-bound tanks being 'shipped' in America, there is no guarantee that they ever travelled beyond Britain or Iceland, or even that after leaving an American factory they were ever loaded onto a merchant ship at an American port, let alone that they actually reached the Soviet Union.

Just as problematic is the impossibility of assessing the reliability of the statistics relating to arms manufacture in the Soviet Union during the war which appear in General Krivosheev's abovementioned book. Some of the revisionist historians have relied on these figures being accurate when seeking to determine whether tanks, aircraft and other arms and equipment supplied by the Allies were numerous and effective enough to make a difference.

That does not mean that academic enquiry into the impact of the Allied aid during World War 2 is a non starter. It can certainly specify the likely impact of the aid. Like Suprun, Boyd is particularly emphatic about what he thinks was the value of the aid during the first 18 months after the Germans invaded, when he says it accounted for around 10 per cent of new tanks and around 19 per cent of fighter aircraft most of it sent via the northern Russian ports. He also urges the reader not to forget about the value of the supplied trucks, explosives and aluminium, as well as other products such as the copper for producing communications equipment which he says added 50% to what was provided within the Soviet Union during 1942.[29]

However because of the dearth of clear information, and because there appear to be other crucial bits of evidence that have yet to be discovered in archives in Britain and America, the only general statistical points that appear to be supportable at this juncture concerning aid sent via the northern route are what, albeit only in broad terms, can be gleaned from the general trends in the table referred to in Note 30, the highlights of which are laid out below: according to the aforementioned table, the total weight of aid sent from the 'Western Hemisphere' via the Arctic convoys was 4.43 million tons out of a total of 19.59 million tons sent from the Western Hemisphere to the Soviet Union via all routes. After the war the American State Department claimed that the value of the aid the US had given the Soviet Union during the war was around $10.8 billion (see Note 30 for the source, and reliability of the figures in the table, and for a comparison with aid given to Ukraine during 2022–2024).

Analysis of the table leads to the conclusion that while, as the war progressed, the weight of supplies shipped via the Arctic convoys soared above the weight of aid sent during 1941, the annual amount sent via the northern route became a smaller percentage of the total weight sent each year from the West to the Soviet Union. That came about partly because, as stated above, the Arctic convoys were suspended at various times, and partly because there was a massive increase in the amount of aid sent via some of the other routes. Aid sent to the Persian Gulf ports and to the Soviet Far East (Vladivostock) rose very steeply in 1943, and remained at a high level during 1944.

Table. *The percentage of the total aid sent from the Western Hemisphere to the Soviet Union during the war and its immediate aftermath that was sent via the Arctic convoys.*[30]

Year	Short tons sent via the Arctic convoys	Percentage of the weight of aid sent to the Soviet Union that was delivered via the Arctic convoys
1941	170,000	42.7%
1942	1,060,000	38.7%
1943	760,000	14.2%
1944	1,630,000	23.4%
1945	810,000	19.8%

All this is leading up to the point that even if the likes of Zhukov, Mikoyan and Khrushchev are right when they say that the foreign aid given to the Soviet Union played an important part in their country's victory over Nazi Germany, it is only being accurate to acknowledge that the relative contribution of the Arctic convoys compared with transport via other routes diminished rather than expanded after 1942.

That said, when the current regime in Russia alleges by implication, as was stated expressly by some during Soviet times, that during what the Russians refer to as the Great Patriotic War, Britain and America fought to the last Soviet soldier, that is also unfair. Such a charge can certainly not be levelled with any justification in relation to the majority of the men, who in a desperate bid to help the Russians, risked life and limb while participating in the fighting during the Arctic convoys, and in so doing, did their very best to ensure that the Battle of the Arctic was won.

Maps

Maps Note To Reader

The maps on the following pages have been produced using as a base the maps which accompany the Naval Staff History *Arctic Convoys 1941–1945*, which can be found in NA London ADM 234/369, but also using maps referred to under the sub-heading 'Maps' in the Notes, as well as information in the documents cited in the Notes relating to the relevant chapters of this book. When looking at the maps on the following pages, the following points are relevant:

COURSE LINES AND SYMBOLS
In the maps on the pages that follow, unless what is specified below is expressly contradicted by labelling or text on the maps or accompanying key notes:

Ship course lines
a light grey line: shows the approximate progress of an east-going Arctic convoy

a series of adjacent relatively large light grey dots with no continuous line in between them: shows the approximate progress of a west-going Arctic convoy

a dark grey line: shows the approximate progress of one or more Allied warships

a black line: shows the approximate progress of one or more German warships

Air raids
a dark grey aircraft shape, or if provided, the pointer line emanating from such shape with an arrow on the end: shows the approximate location of a British air raid

a black aircraft shape, or if provided, the pointer line emanating from such shape with an arrow on the end: shows the approximate location of a German air raid

Sinking or abandoned vessels

a light grey silhouette of half of a ship with the visible section of its hull sticking up at around a 45° angle from a short horizontal line, or if provided, the pointer line emanating from such a silhouette with an arrow on the end: shows the location where an Allied merchant ship was sunk or abandoned (if this silhouette has x6 beside it, the silhouette is showing the approximate location where 6 merchant ships were sunk or abandoned; different numbers using the same format should be interpreted the same way mutatis mutandis)

a dark grey silhouette of half of a ship with the visible section of its hull sticking up at around a 45° angle from a short horizontal line, or if provided, the pointer line emanating from such a silhouette with an arrow on the end: shows the approximate location where an Allied warship was sunk or abandoned

a black silhouette of half of a ship or half of a U-boat with the visible section of its hull sticking up at around a 45° or 60° angle from a short horizontal line, or if provided, the pointer line emanating from such a silhouette with an arrow on the end: shows the approximate location where a German warship or U-boat was sunk or abandoned

U-boats

a black silhouette of a whole U-boat whose hull is not sticking up at around a 60° angle from a short horizontal line, or the pointer line emanating from such a silhouette with an arrow on the end: shows in the former case the approximate location where a U-boat was waiting for a convoy, and in the latter case the approximate location where the U-boat attacked an Allied ship (a rectangle around a group of such U-boat silhouettes represents the edges of the approximate area where U-boats waiting for an Arctic convoy were operating)

Firing and radar

a series of tiny adjacent dots arranged in a straight line which emanates from a different line which latter line according to the above text represents the progress of one or more Allied or German warships, and where the former line consisting of tiny dots has an arrow on the end that points towards another line which according to the above text represents the progress of one or a group of Allied or German ships belonging to the former warships' enemy: the place where the series of tiny adjacent dots starts shows the approximate location where the former warship(s) fired at their enemy's ships

a series of tiny adjacent dashes arranged in a straight line which emanates from a different line which latter line according to the above text represents the progress of one or more Allied warships, and where the former line consisting of tiny dashes has an arrow on the end that points towards another line which according to the above text represents the progress of one or a group of German warship(s): the place where the series of tiny dashes starts shows the approximate location where the former Allied warship or group of warships was located when its radar detected the position occupied by German warships

MAP HEADINGS
The chapter numbers specified within the headings for this book's maps indicate the principal chapters to which the maps relate. If chapter numbers appear in a map's heading with no specification of time zone, times specified on that map follow the time zone used in those chapters. However the places drawn on the maps should also be used to help readers follow the action in other chapters (see at the beginning of each chapter the map numbers specified under the title for each chapter).

POSITIONS SHOWN ON THE MAPS
Because official sources specifying locations and progress of vessels and aircraft in many cases only give approximate details, and also because different sources often give conflicting locations and progress, locations and progress of vessels and aircraft marked on the following maps can only be approximate. Where the best that can be gleaned from the sources and maps in official documents is the general direction of travel rather than the approximate course or position, the wording on the map specifies this is the case.

During the war in order to hide the location of their vessels from the Allies the German Navy often disguised particular positions referred to in messages and documents by specifying where they appeared on its grid system rather than mentioning the latitude and longitude co-ordinates. Where I have relied on a reference in a German document that mentions a location in this way, I have specified in the Notes the grid reference specified in the document followed by the approximate latitude and longitude co-ordinates referred to.

NAMES OF PLACES
In this book's maps I have in most cases adopted the spelling of place names which is most frequently used in this book's main text. In such text I have stuck to one of the versions commonly seen in official English language reports or messages during World War 2. However where a place in a particular country that plays a prominent part in the story is mentioned for the first time, I have also specified in brackets a spelling which either conveys how the location is spoken by locals (this is useful for Russian names which locals would write in Cyrillic script that would be unintelligible to most English speaking readers) or how they write it – in most cases this has been achieved by using the spelling in one of the editions of what is now referred to as the United Kingdom Hydrographic Office's *Admiralty Sailing Directions: Arctic Pilot* volume 1, the book designed to guide seafarers as they enter coastal waters in the

Arctic. In maps that exclusively show a part of Norway, I have used the correct Norwegian spelling.

COUNTRY BORDERS

The maps on which the maps in this book are based do not precisely specify where the borders between countries are located. That is also the case on the maps in this book.

A particular example of this relates to the border that is shown on some of the maps in this book between Finland and the Soviet Union in the vicinity of the Rybachy Peninsula (north-east of Petsamo). The front line in this location changed at various times during the war. Rather than seeking to record each such change, the maps in this book that show this area record the approximate border that is recorded in a map entitled 'Finland & North-Western U.S.S.R.' in NA London WO 106/5729 which purports to show the approximate location of the border near the end of December 1941.

Maps Referred To In This Book

Map 1

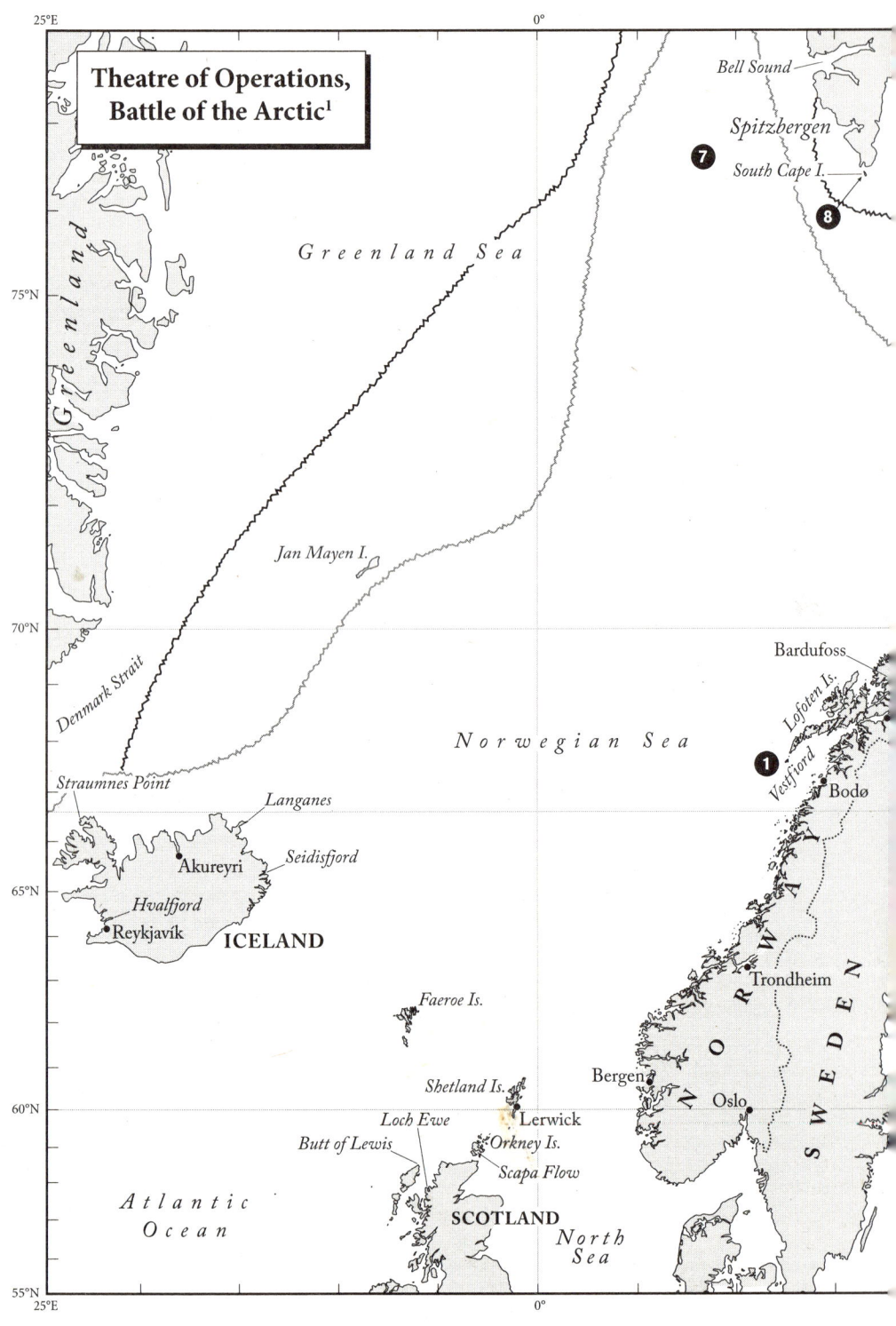

Theatre of Operations, Battle of the Arctic[1]

25°E

0°

Bell Sound

Spitzbergen

❼

South Cape I.

❽

Greenland Sea

75°N

Greenland

Jan Mayen I.

70°N

Denmark Strait

Norwegian Sea

Straumnes Point

Langanes

Bardufoss

Lofoten Is.

❶

Vestfjord

Bodø

Akureyri

Seidisfjord

65°N

Hvalfjord

Reykjavík

ICELAND

Trondheim

N
O
R
W
A
Y

S
W
E
D
E
N

Faeroe Is.

Shetland Is.

Bergen

Loch Ewe

Lerwick

Oslo

60°N

Butt of Lewis

Orkney Is.

Scapa Flow

Atlantic Ocean

SCOTLAND

North Sea

55°N

25°E

0°

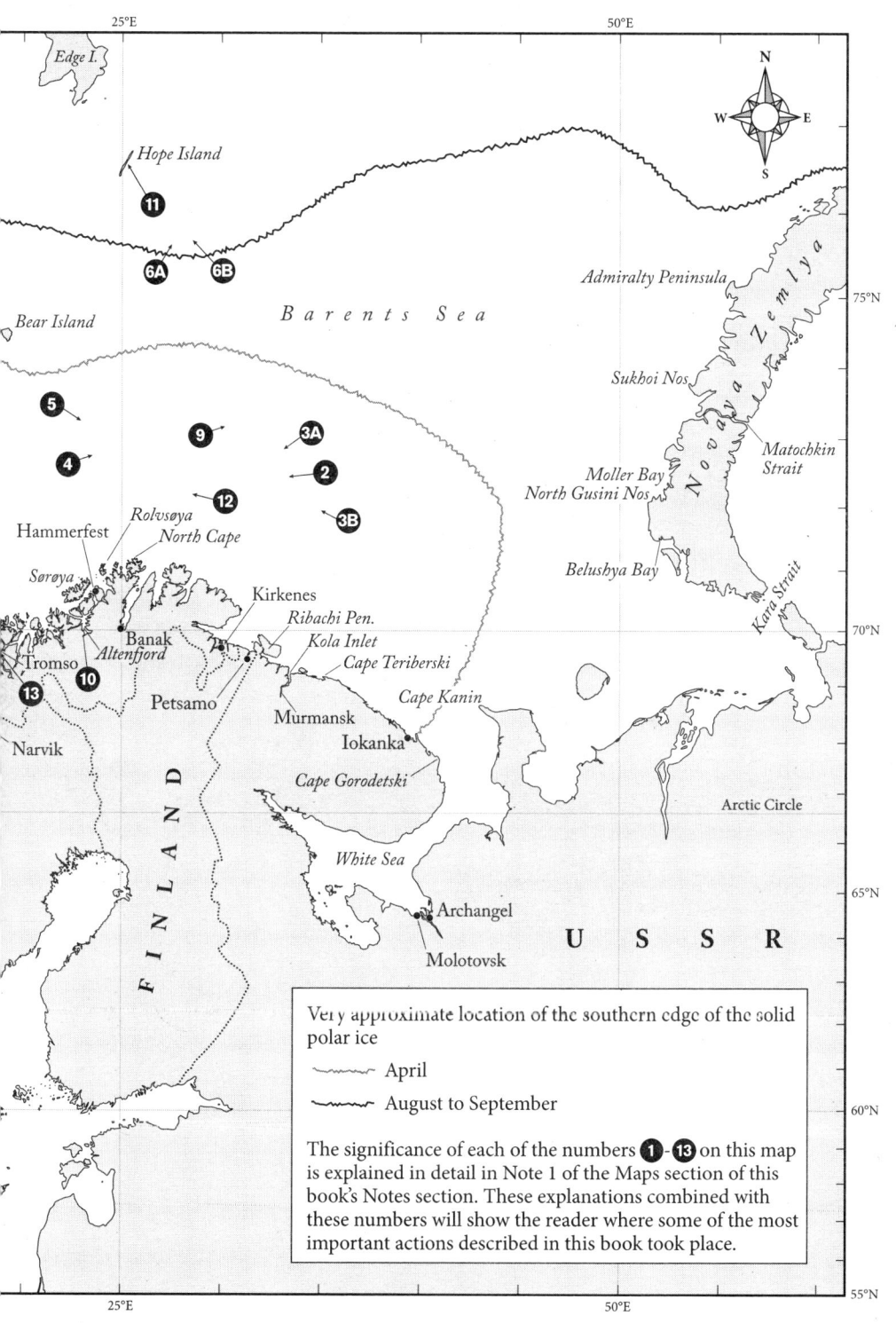

25°E   50°E

N
W   E
S

Edge I.

Hope Island

11

6A   **6B**

Admiralty Peninsula

75°N

B a r e n t s   S e a

Bear Island

Sukhoi Nos

5

9   **3A**

Moller Bay
North Gusini Nos

Matochkin
Strait

4   **2**

12   **3B**

Rolvsøya
North Cape

Hammerfest

Belushya Bay

Sørøya

Kirkenes
Ribachi Pen.

Banak   Kola Inlet
Altenfjord   Cape Teriberski

Tromso   **10**

Cape Kanin

70°N

13

Petsamo

Murmansk

Iokanka

Narvik

Cape Gorodetski

Arctic Circle

F I N L A N D

White Sea

65°N

Archangel

U   S   S   R

Molotovsk

Very approximate location of the southern edge of the solid polar ice

〜〜 April

〜〜 August to September

The significance of each of the numbers **1**-**13** on this map is explained in detail in Note 1 of the Maps section of this book's Notes section. These explanations combined with these numbers will show the reader where some of the most important actions described in this book took place.

60°N

25°E   50°E

55°N

Map 2

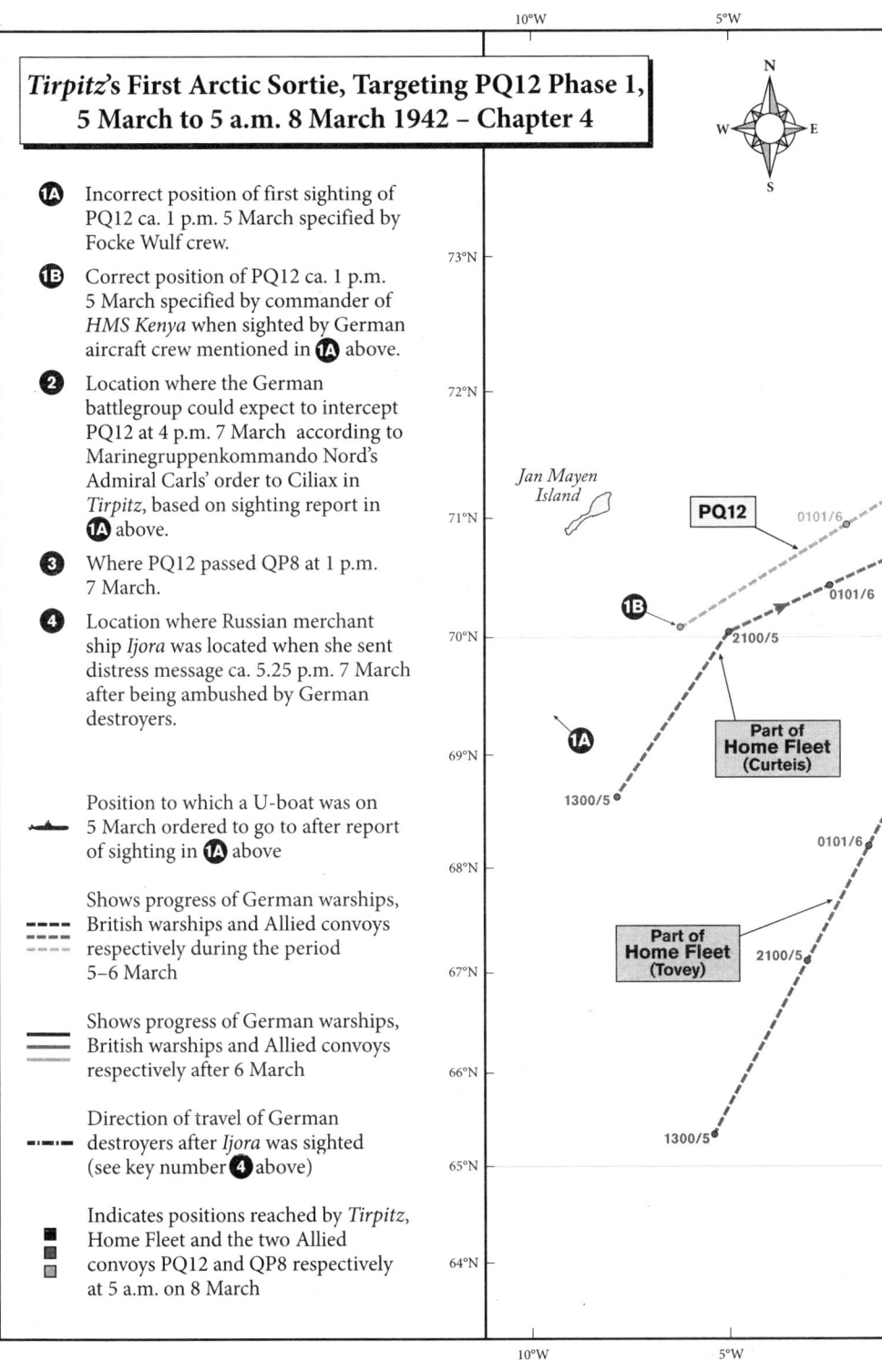

Tirpitz's First Arctic Sortie, Targeting PQ12 Phase 1, 5 March to 5 a.m. 8 March 1942 – Chapter 4

1A Incorrect position of first sighting of PQ12 ca. 1 p.m. 5 March specified by Focke Wulf crew.

1B Correct position of PQ12 ca. 1 p.m. 5 March specified by commander of *HMS Kenya* when sighted by German aircraft crew mentioned in **1A** above.

2 Location where the German battlegroup could expect to intercept PQ12 at 4 p.m. 7 March according to Marinegruppenkommando Nord's Admiral Carls' order to Ciliax in *Tirpitz*, based on sighting report in **1A** above.

3 Where PQ12 passed QP8 at 1 p.m. 7 March.

4 Location where Russian merchant ship *Ijora* was located when she sent distress message ca. 5.25 p.m. 7 March after being ambushed by German destroyers.

Position to which a U-boat was on 5 March ordered to go to after report of sighting in **1A** above

Shows progress of German warships, British warships and Allied convoys respectively during the period 5–6 March

Shows progress of German warships, British warships and Allied convoys respectively after 6 March

Direction of travel of German destroyers after *Ijora* was sighted (see key number **4** above)

Indicates positions reached by *Tirpitz*, Home Fleet and the two Allied convoys PQ12 and QP8 respectively at 5 a.m. on 8 March

Jan Mayen Island

PQ12   0101/6

1B   0101/6

2100/5

Part of Home Fleet (Curteis)

1A

1300/5

0101/6

Part of Home Fleet (Tovey)   2100/5

1300/5

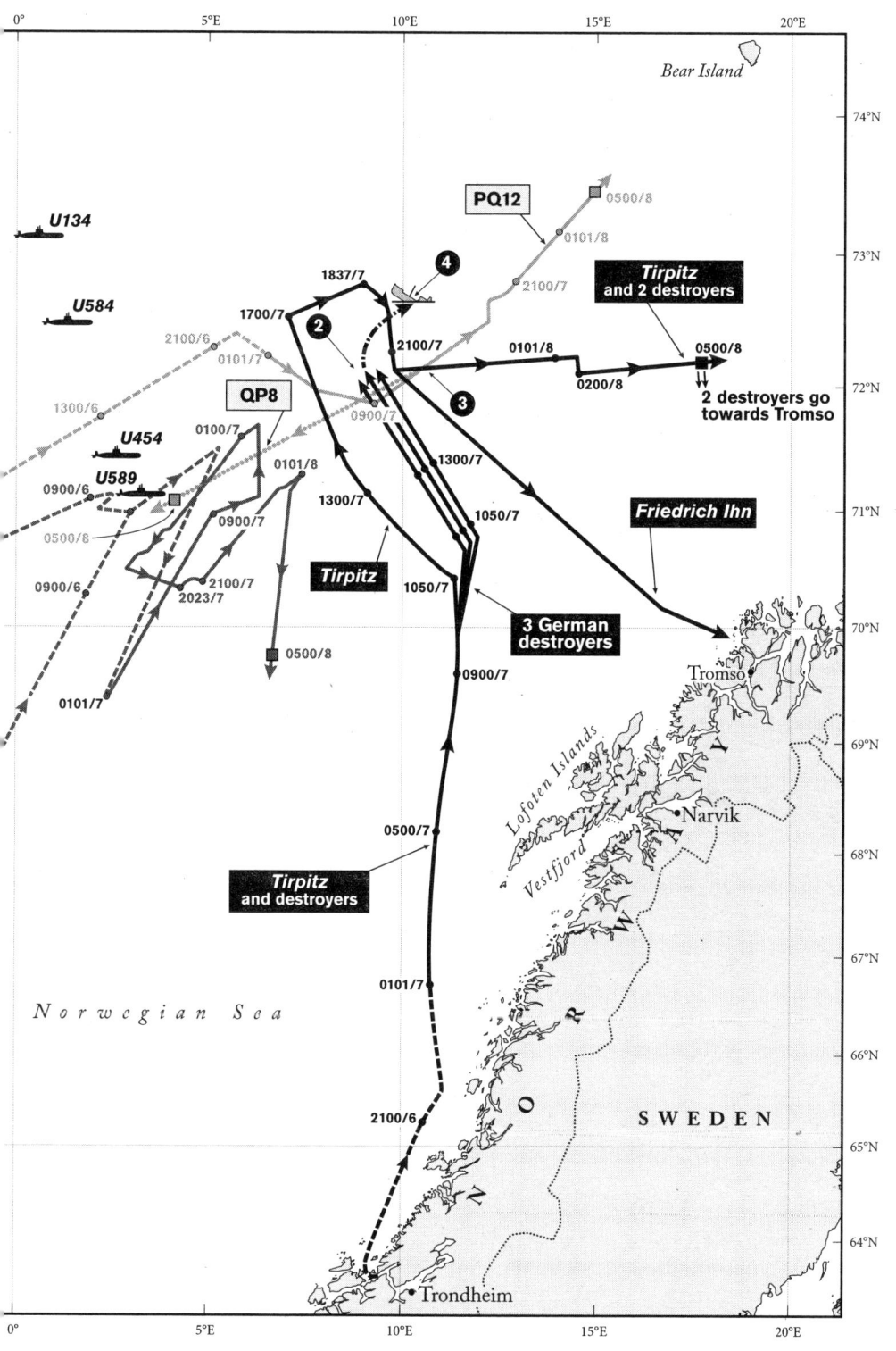

Bear Island

74°N

U134

73°N

PQ12

0500/8

0101/8

2100/7

Tirpitz and 2 destroyers

U584

1837/7

1700/7

4

2

2100/7

0101/8

0500/8

72°N

2100/6

0101/7

0900/7

3

0200/8

2 destroyers go towards Tromso

1300/6

QP8

Friedrich Ihn

U454

0100/7

0101/8

71°N

U589

0900/6

0900/7

1300/7

1050/7

0500/8

1300/7

Tirpitz

0900/6

2100/7

2023/7

3 German destroyers

1050/7

0101/7

1050/7

0500/8

0900/7

70°N

Tromso

69°N

Lofoten Islands

0500/7

Narvik

68°N

Tirpitz and destroyers

Vestfjord

N   O   R   W   A   Y

67°N

0101/7

66°N

Norwegian   Sea

2100/6

SWEDEN

65°N

64°N

Trondheim

0°   5°E   10°E   15°E   20°E

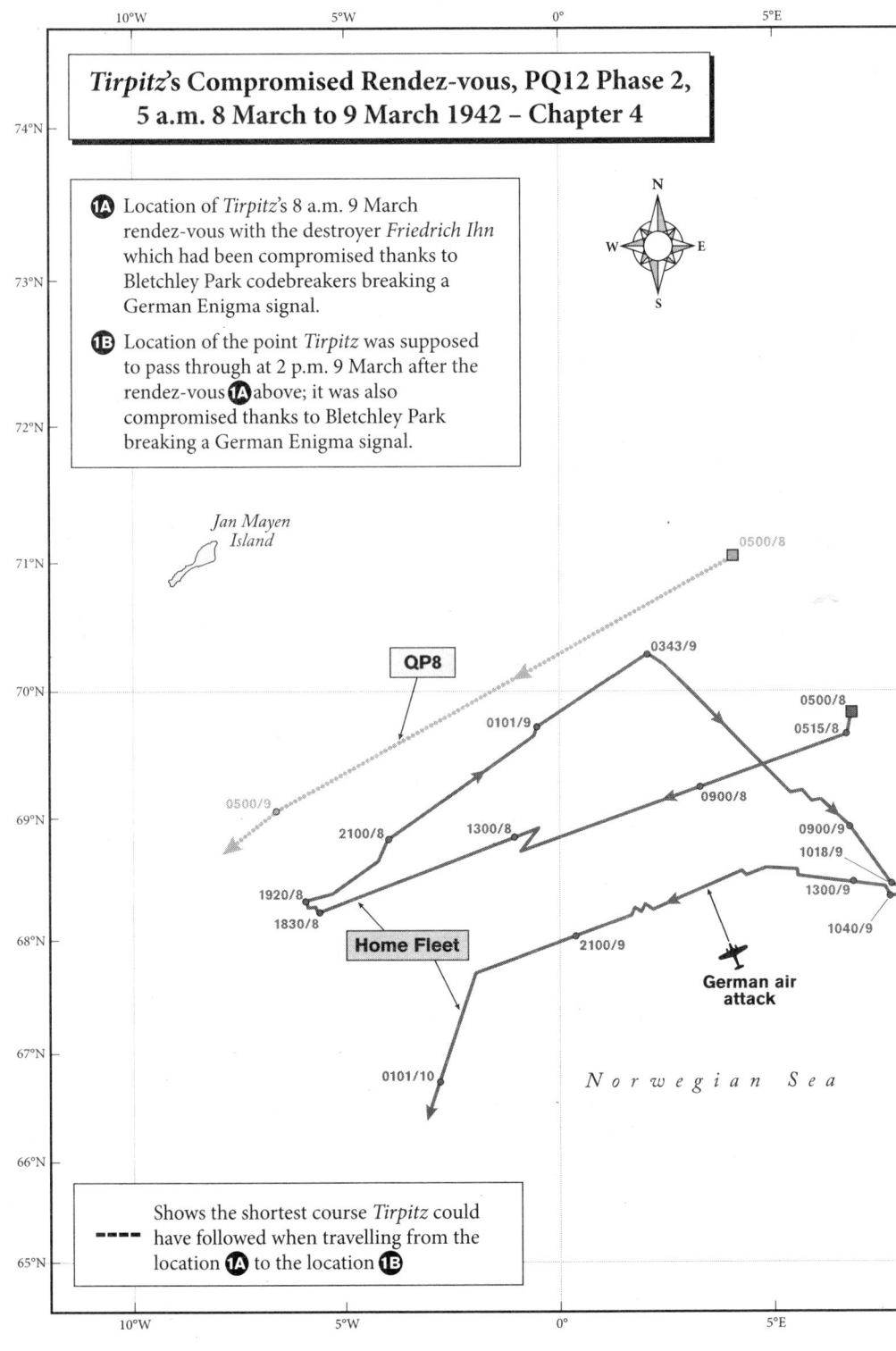

Map 3

Tirpitz's Compromised Rendez-vous, PQ12 Phase 2, 5 a.m. 8 March to 9 March 1942 – Chapter 4

1A Location of *Tirpitz*'s 8 a.m. 9 March rendez-vous with the destroyer *Friedrich Ihn* which had been compromised thanks to Bletchley Park codebreakers breaking a German Enigma signal.

1B Location of the point *Tirpitz* was supposed to pass through at 2 p.m. 9 March after the rendez-vous **1A** above; it was also compromised thanks to Bletchley Park breaking a German Enigma signal.

Jan Mayen Island

0500/8

QP8

0343/9

0500/8

0101/9

0515/8

0900/8

0500/9

0900/9

2100/8

1300/8

1018/9

1920/8

1300/9

1830/8

1040/9

Home Fleet

2100/9

German air attack

0101/10

N o r w e g i a n   S e a

---- Shows the shortest course *Tirpitz* could have followed when travelling from the location **1A** to the location **1B**

74°N

73°N

72°N

71°N

70°N

69°N

68°N

67°N

66°N

65°N

10°W 5°W 0° 5°E

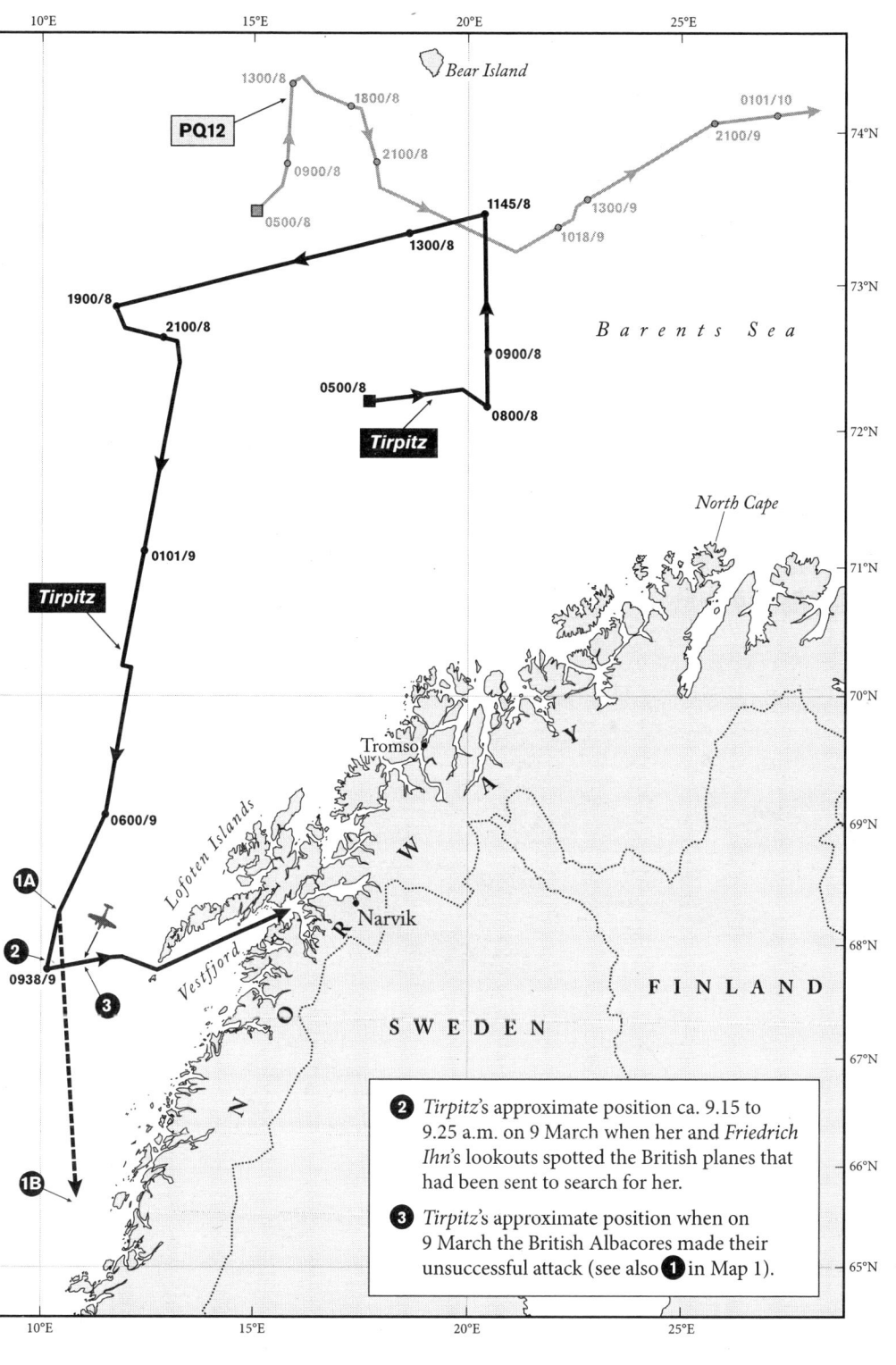

Bear Island

1300/8
1800/8
PQ12
0900/8
2100/8
0500/8
1145/8
1300/8

0101/10
2100/9
1300/9
1018/9

B a r e n t s   S e a

1900/8
2100/8
0900/8
0500/8
Tirpitz
0800/8

North Cape

0101/9
Tirpitz

71°N

70°N

Tromso

69°N

0600/9

Lofoten Islands

1A
2
0938/9
3

Narvik

Vestfjord

68°N

W
R
A
Y

FINLAND

O
SWEDEN

67°N

N

1B

66°N

2 *Tirpitz's* approximate position ca. 9.15 to
9.25 a.m. on 9 March when her and *Friedrich
Ihn's* lookouts spotted the British planes that
had been sent to search for her.

3 *Tirpitz's* approximate position when on
9 March the British Albacores made their
unsuccessful attack (see also **1** in Map 1).

65°N

10°E   15°E   20°E   25°E

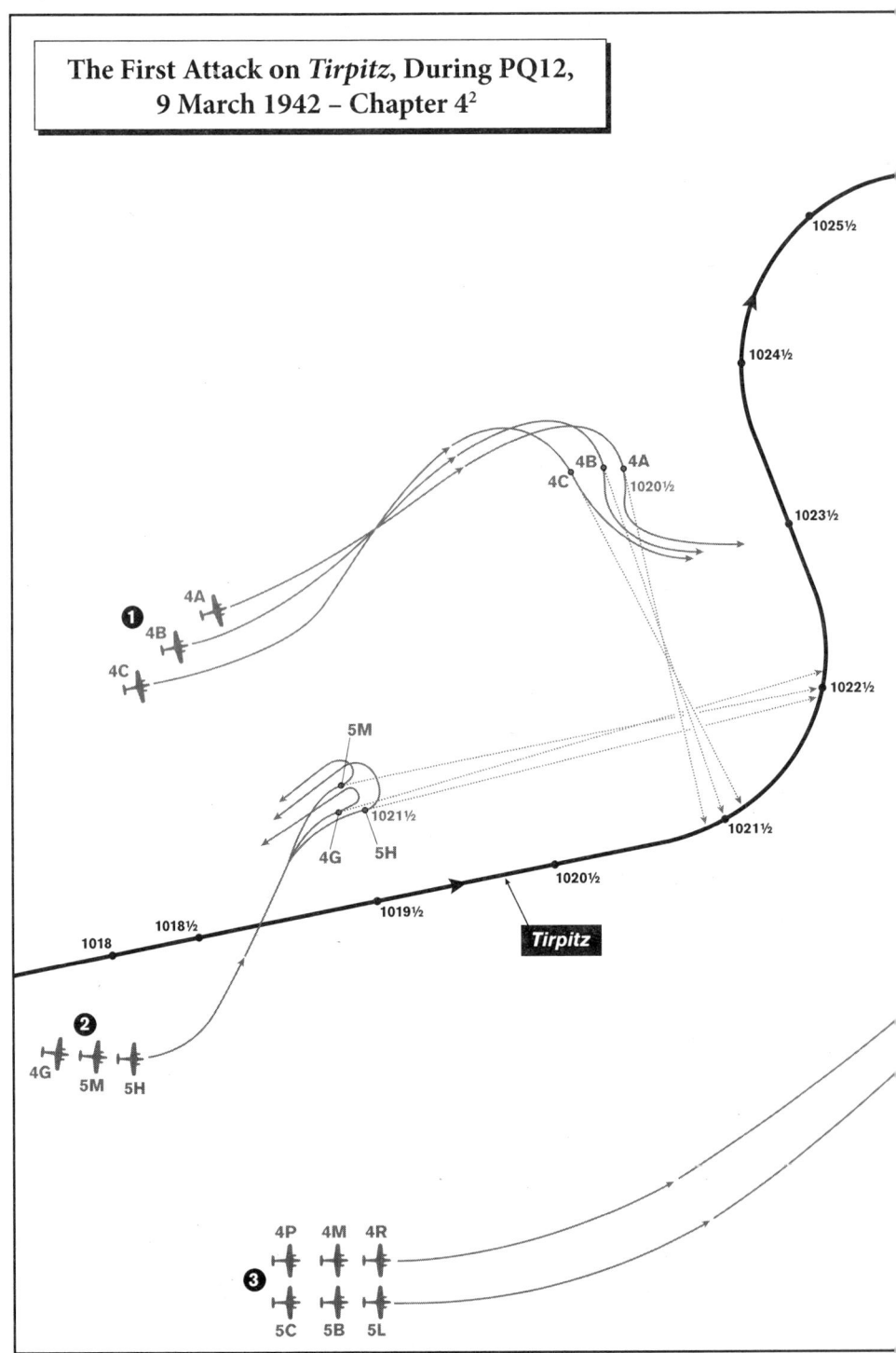

Map 4

The First Attack on *Tirpitz*, During PQ12,
9 March 1942 – Chapter 4[2]

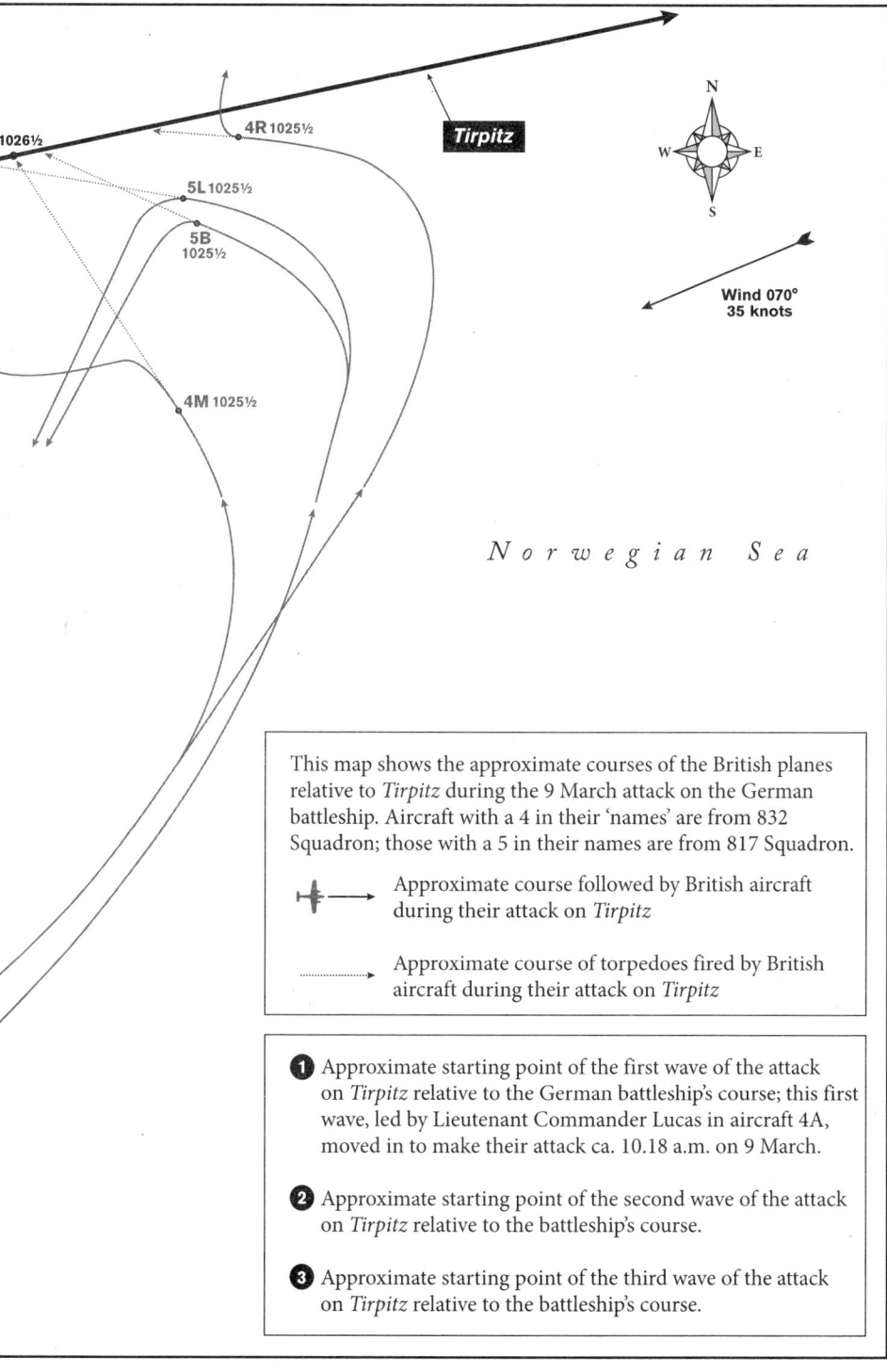

1026½

4R 1025½

Tirpitz

N
W   E
S

Wind 070°
35 knots

5L 1025½

5B
1025½

4M 1025½

N o r w e g i a n   S e a

This map shows the approximate courses of the British planes
relative to *Tirpitz* during the 9 March attack on the German
battleship. Aircraft with a 4 in their 'names' are from 832
Squadron; those with a 5 in their names are from 817 Squadron.

Approximate course followed by British aircraft
during their attack on *Tirpitz*

Approximate course of torpedoes fired by British
aircraft during their attack on *Tirpitz*

1 Approximate starting point of the first wave of the attack
on *Tirpitz* relative to the German battleship's course; this first
wave, led by Lieutenant Commander Lucas in aircraft 4A,
moved in to make their attack ca. 10.18 a.m. on 9 March.

2 Approximate starting point of the second wave of the attack
on *Tirpitz* relative to the battleship's course.

3 Approximate starting point of the third wave of the attack
on *Tirpitz* relative to the battleship's course.

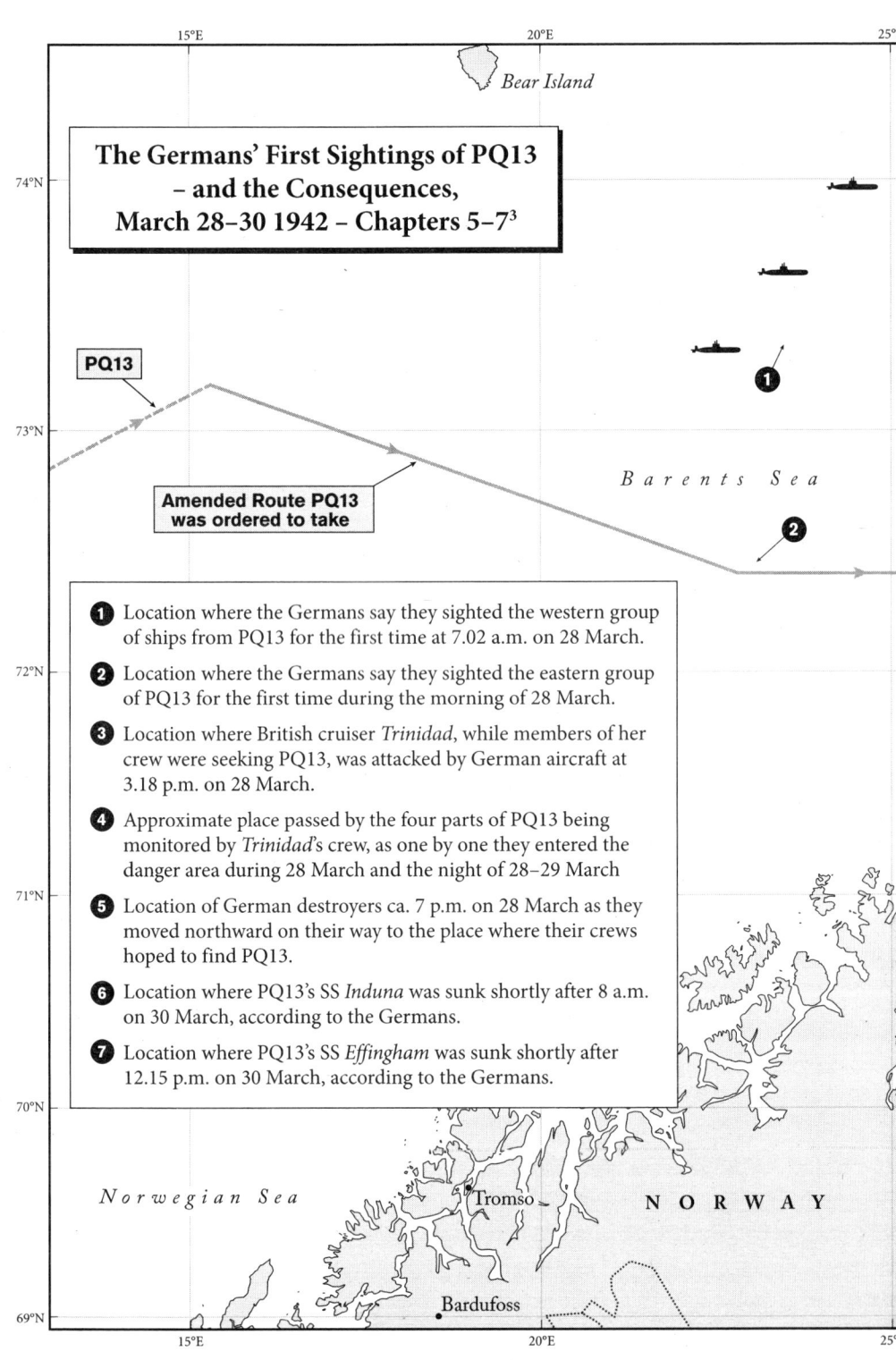

Map 5

The Germans' First Sightings of PQ13
– and the Consequences,
March 28–30 1942 – Chapters 5–7[3]

Bear Island

74°N

PQ13

73°N

**Amended Route PQ13
was ordered to take**

Barents Sea

1

2

① Location where the Germans say they sighted the western group
of ships from PQ13 for the first time at 7.02 a.m. on 28 March.

② Location where the Germans say they sighted the eastern group
of PQ13 for the first time during the morning of 28 March.

③ Location where British cruiser *Trinidad*, while members of her
crew were seeking PQ13, was attacked by German aircraft at
3.18 p.m. on 28 March.

④ Approximate place passed by the four parts of PQ13 being
monitored by *Trinidad*'s crew, as one by one they entered the
danger area during 28 March and the night of 28–29 March

⑤ Location of German destroyers ca. 7 p.m. on 28 March as they
moved northward on their way to the place where their crews
hoped to find PQ13.

⑥ Location where PQ13's SS *Induna* was sunk shortly after 8 a.m.
on 30 March, according to the Germans.

⑦ Location where PQ13's SS *Effingham* was sunk shortly after
12.15 p.m. on 30 March, according to the Germans.

72°N

71°N

70°N

Norwegian Sea

Tromso

N O R W A Y

Bardufoss

69°N

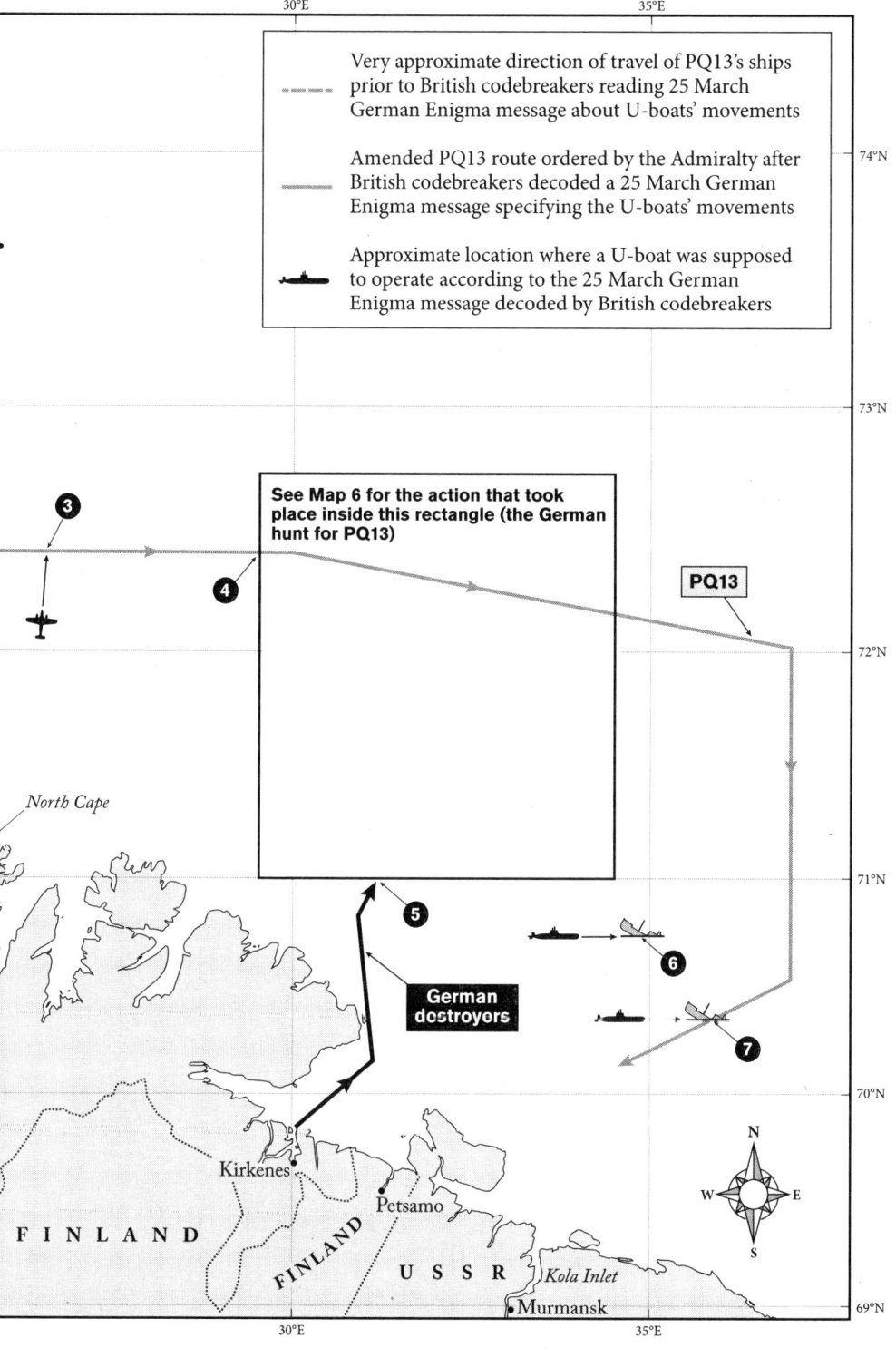

30°E   35°E

74°N

Very approximate direction of travel of PQ13's ships
prior to British codebreakers reading 25 March
German Enigma message about U-boats' movements

Amended PQ13 route ordered by the Admiralty after
British codebreakers decoded a 25 March German
Enigma message specifying the U-boats' movements

Approximate location where a U-boat was supposed
to operate according to the 25 March German
Enigma message decoded by British codebreakers

73°N

**See Map 6 for the action that took
place inside this rectangle (the German
hunt for PQ13)**

3

4

PQ13

72°N

North Cape

71°N

5

6

**German
destroyers**

7

70°N

Kirkenes

Petsamo

N

W   E

S

F I N L A N D

FINLAND

U S S R *Kola Inlet*

•Murmansk

69°N

30°E   35°E

Map 6

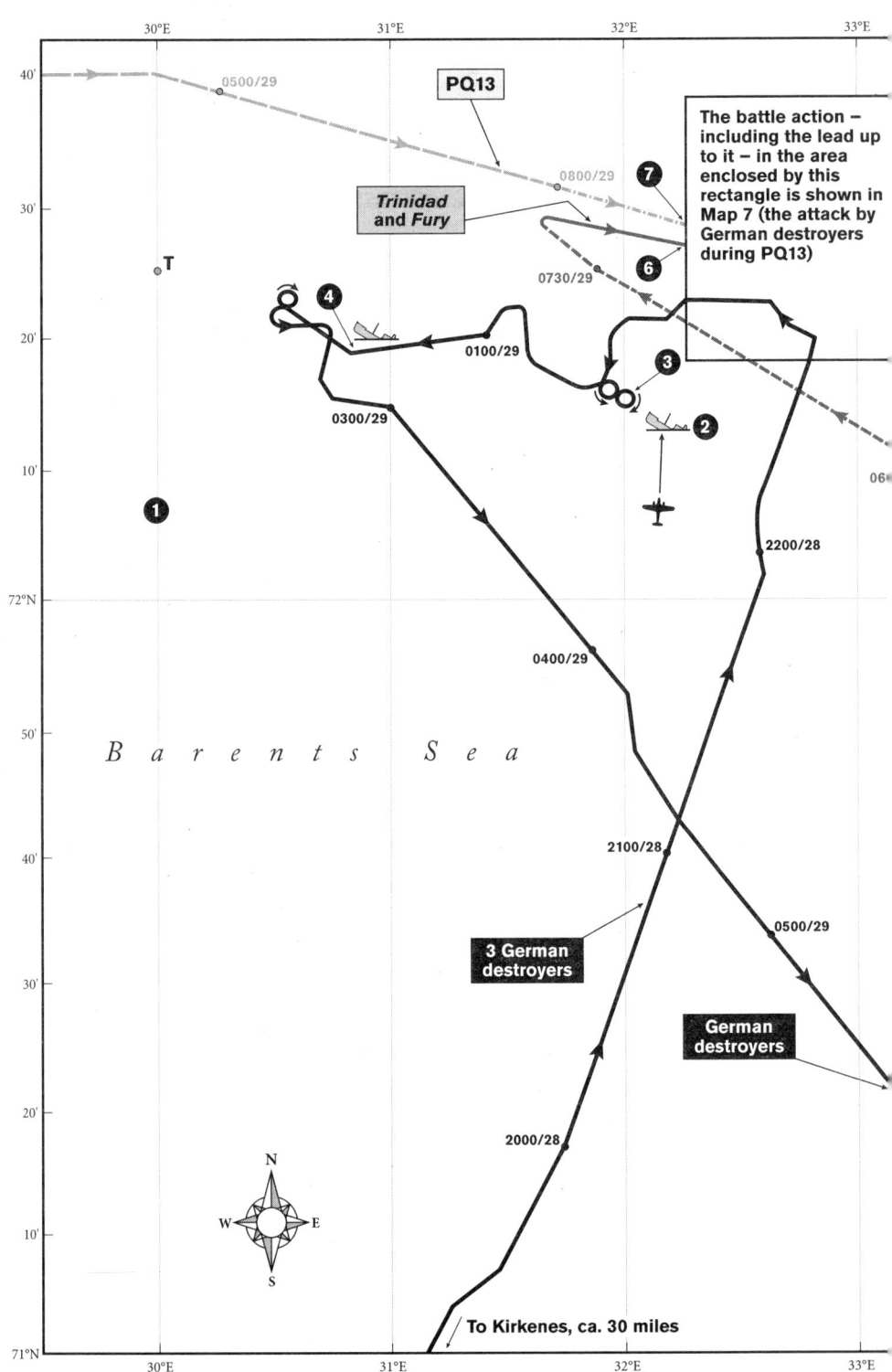

PQ13

Trinidad and *Fury*

The battle action – including the lead up to it – in the area enclosed by this rectangle is shown in Map 7 (the attack by German destroyers during PQ13)

0500/29

0800/29

7

0730/29

6

4

T

0100/29

3

0300/29

2

1

2200/28

0400/29

B a r e n t s   S e a

2100/28

0500/29

3 German destroyers

German destroyers

2000/28

N
W · E
S

To Kirkenes, ca. 30 miles

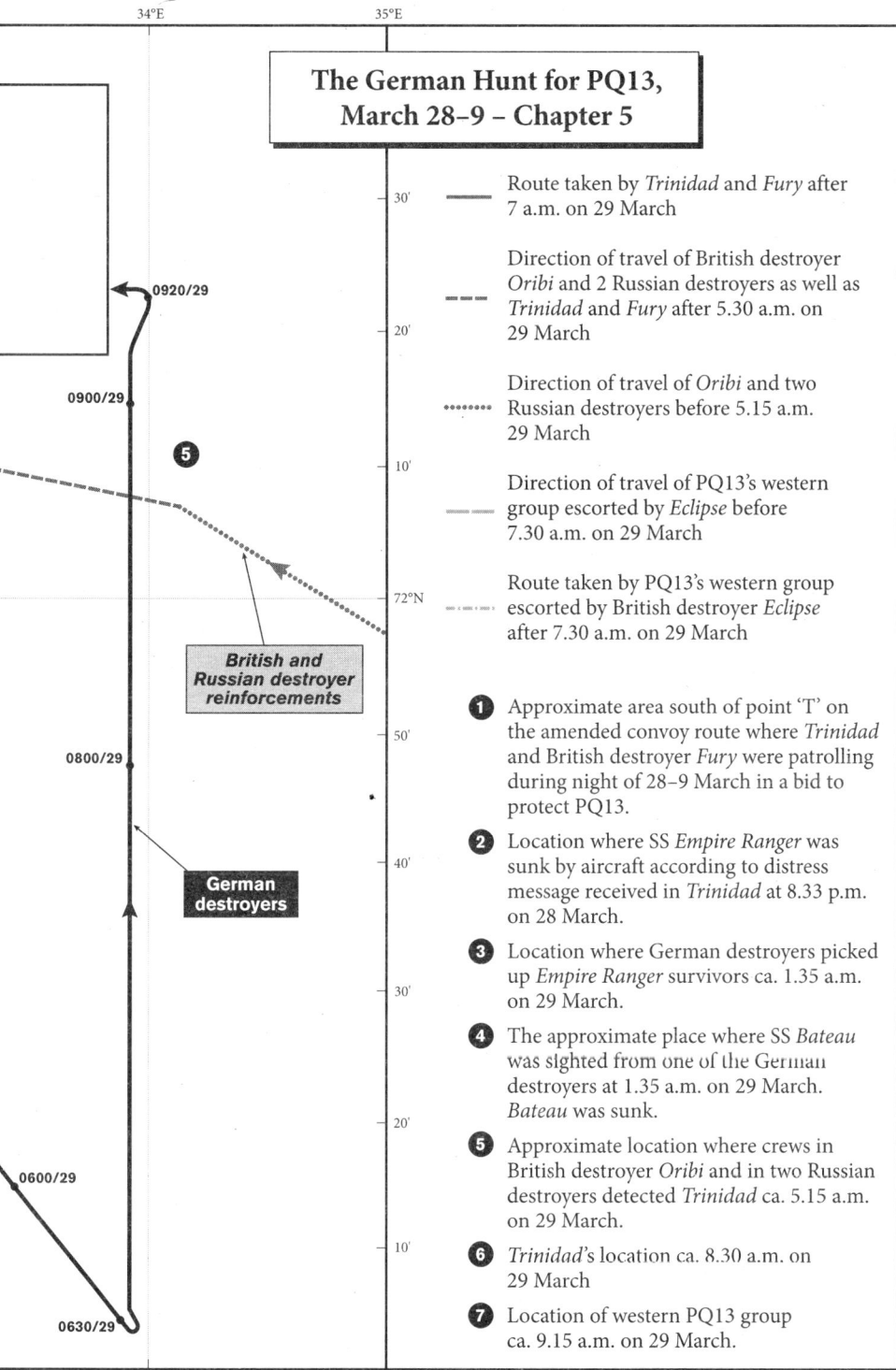

**The German Hunt for PQ13,
March 28–9 – Chapter 5**

34°E   35°E

30′

—— Route taken by *Trinidad* and *Fury* after
7 a.m. on 29 March

0920/29

20′

--- Direction of travel of British destroyer
Oribi and 2 Russian destroyers as well as
Trinidad and *Fury* after 5.30 a.m. on
29 March

0900/29

········ Direction of travel of *Oribi* and two
Russian destroyers before 5.15 a.m.
29 March

5

10′

— — Direction of travel of PQ13's western
group escorted by *Eclipse* before
7.30 a.m. on 29 March

72°N

—·—·— Route taken by PQ13's western group
escorted by British destroyer *Eclipse*
after 7.30 a.m. on 29 March

**British and
Russian destroyer
reinforcements**

1 Approximate area south of point 'T' on
the amended convoy route where *Trinidad*
and British destroyer *Fury* were patrolling
during night of 28–9 March in a bid to
protect PQ13.

50′

0800/29

2 Location where SS *Empire Ranger* was
sunk by aircraft according to distress
message received in *Trinidad* at 8.33 p.m.
on 28 March.

40′

**German
destroyers**

3 Location where German destroyers picked
up *Empire Ranger* survivors ca. 1.35 a.m.
on 29 March.

30′

4 The approximate place where SS *Bateau*
was sighted from one of the German
destroyers at 1.35 a.m. on 29 March.
Bateau was sunk.

20′

5 Approximate location where crews in
British destroyer *Oribi* and in two Russian
destroyers detected *Trinidad* ca. 5.15 a.m.
on 29 March.

0600/29

10′

6 *Trinidad*'s location ca. 8.30 a.m. on
29 March

0630/29

7 Location of western PQ13 group
ca. 9.15 a.m. on 29 March.

34°E   35°E

Map 7

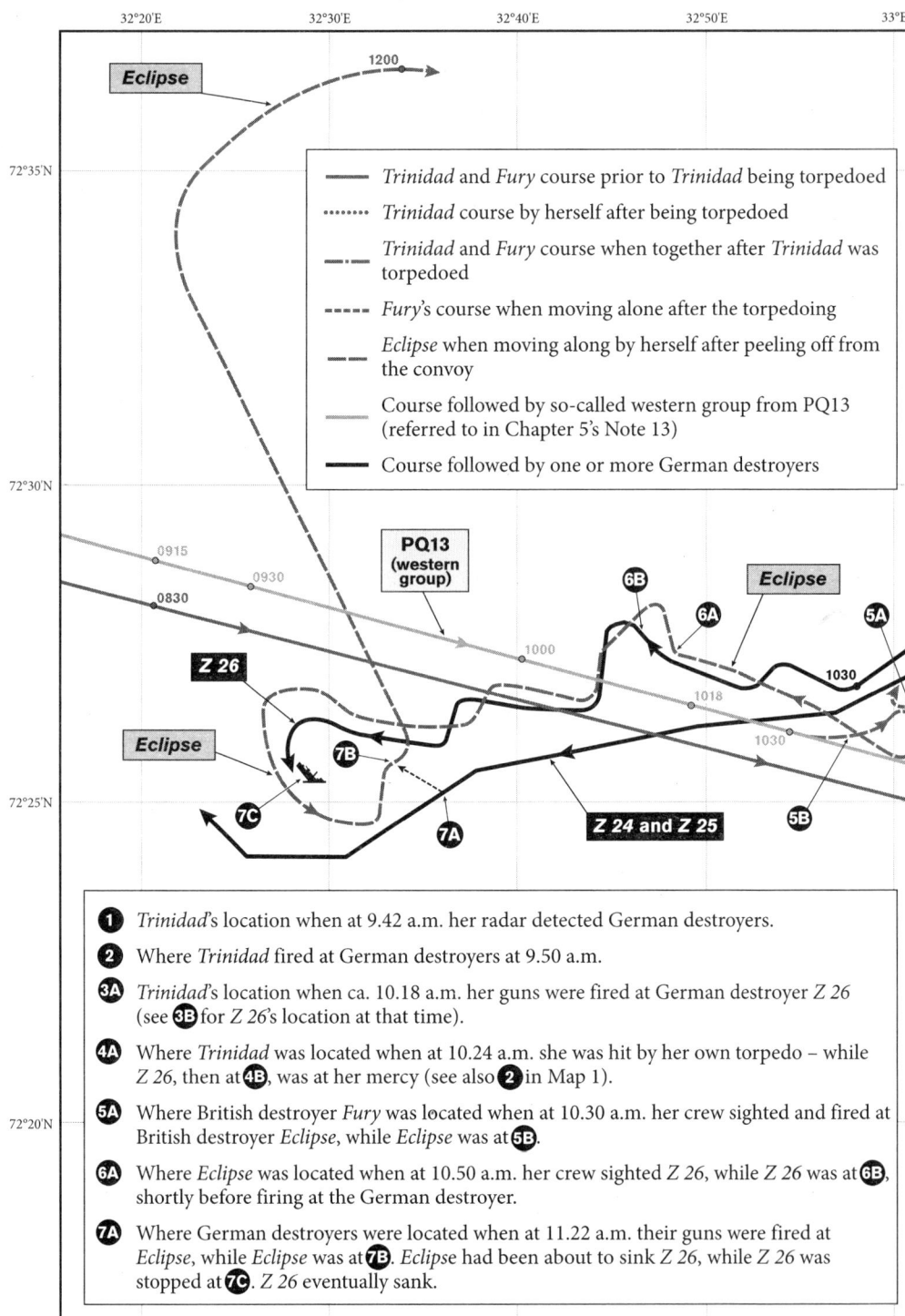

Legend:

——— Trinidad and Fury course prior to Trinidad being torpedoed

········ Trinidad course by herself after being torpedoed

—··—·· Trinidad and Fury course when together after Trinidad was torpedoed

----- Fury's course when moving alone after the torpedoing

— — Eclipse when moving along by herself after peeling off from the convoy

——— Course followed by so-called western group from PQ13 (referred to in Chapter 5's Note 13)

——— Course followed by one or more German destroyers

Eclipse · 1200

72°35'N

72°30'N

0915 · 0830 · 0930

PQ13 (western group)

1000

Z 26

Eclipse

6B · **6A** · **5A**

1018 · 1030

1030

72°25'N

Eclipse · **7B** · **7C** · **7A**

Z 24 and Z 25 · **5B**

1 Trinidad's location when at 9.42 a.m. her radar detected German destroyers.

2 Where Trinidad fired at German destroyers at 9.50 a.m.

3A Trinidad's location when ca. 10.18 a.m. her guns were fired at German destroyer Z 26 (see **3B** for Z 26's location at that time).

4A Where Trinidad was located when at 10.24 a.m. she was hit by her own torpedo – while Z 26, then at **4B**, was at her mercy (see also **2** in Map 1).

5A Where British destroyer Fury was located when at 10.30 a.m. her crew sighted and fired at British destroyer Eclipse, while Eclipse was at **5B**.

6A Where Eclipse was located when at 10.50 a.m. her crew sighted Z 26, while Z 26 was at **6B**, shortly before firing at the German destroyer.

7A Where German destroyers were located when at 11.22 a.m. their guns were fired at Eclipse, while Eclipse was at **7B**. Eclipse had been about to sink Z 26, while Z 26 was stopped at **7C**. Z 26 eventually sank.

72°20'N

72°18'N

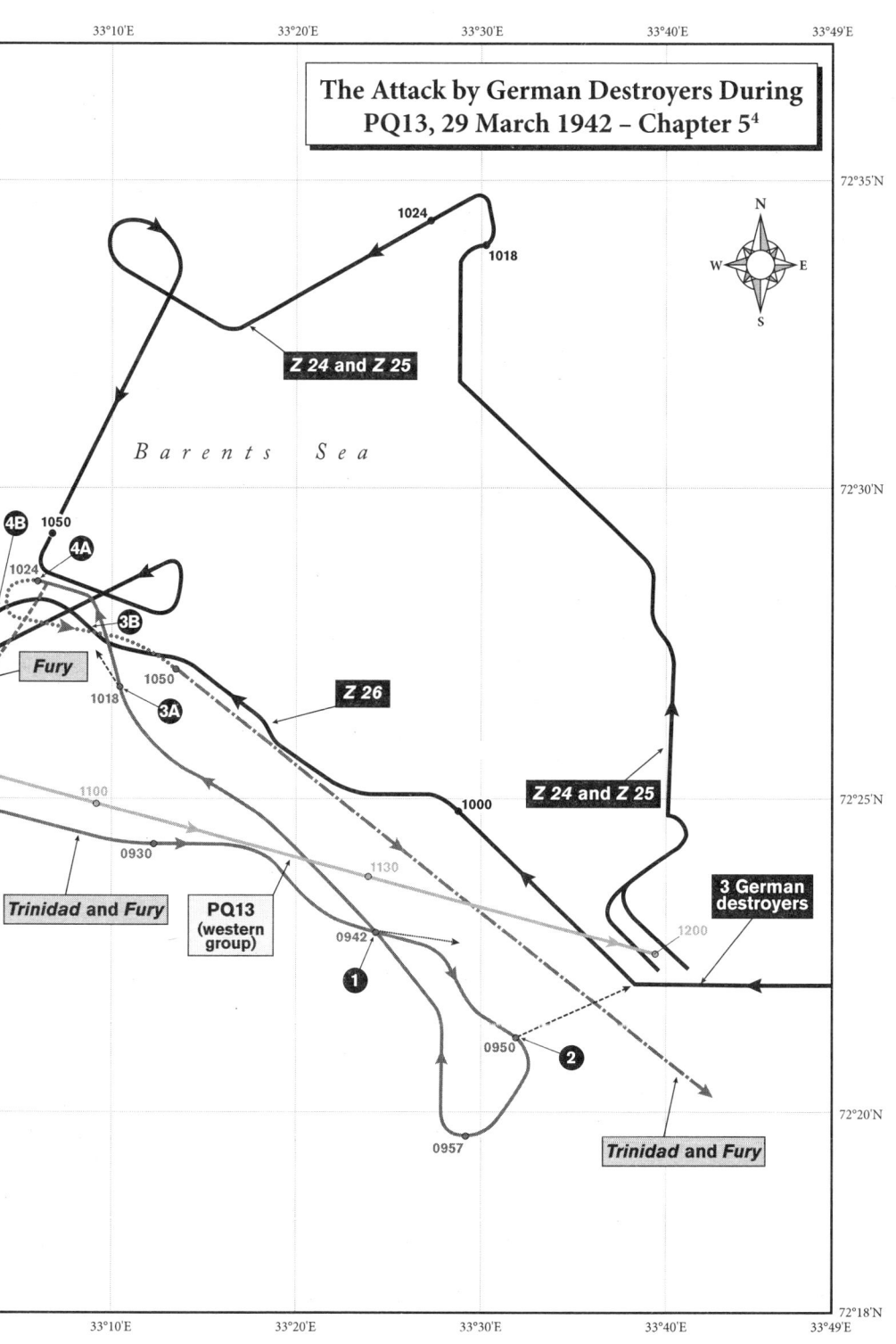

The Attack by German Destroyers During
PQ13, 29 March 1942 – Chapter 5[4]

N
W   E
S

Barents   Sea

Z 24 and Z 25

1024

1018

4B   1050
4A
1024
3B
Fury
1050
1018
3A

Z 26

Z 24 and Z 25

1000

1100

0930

Trinidad and Fury

PQ13
(western
group)

1130

0942

1

3 German
destroyers

1200

0950

2

0957

Trinidad and Fury

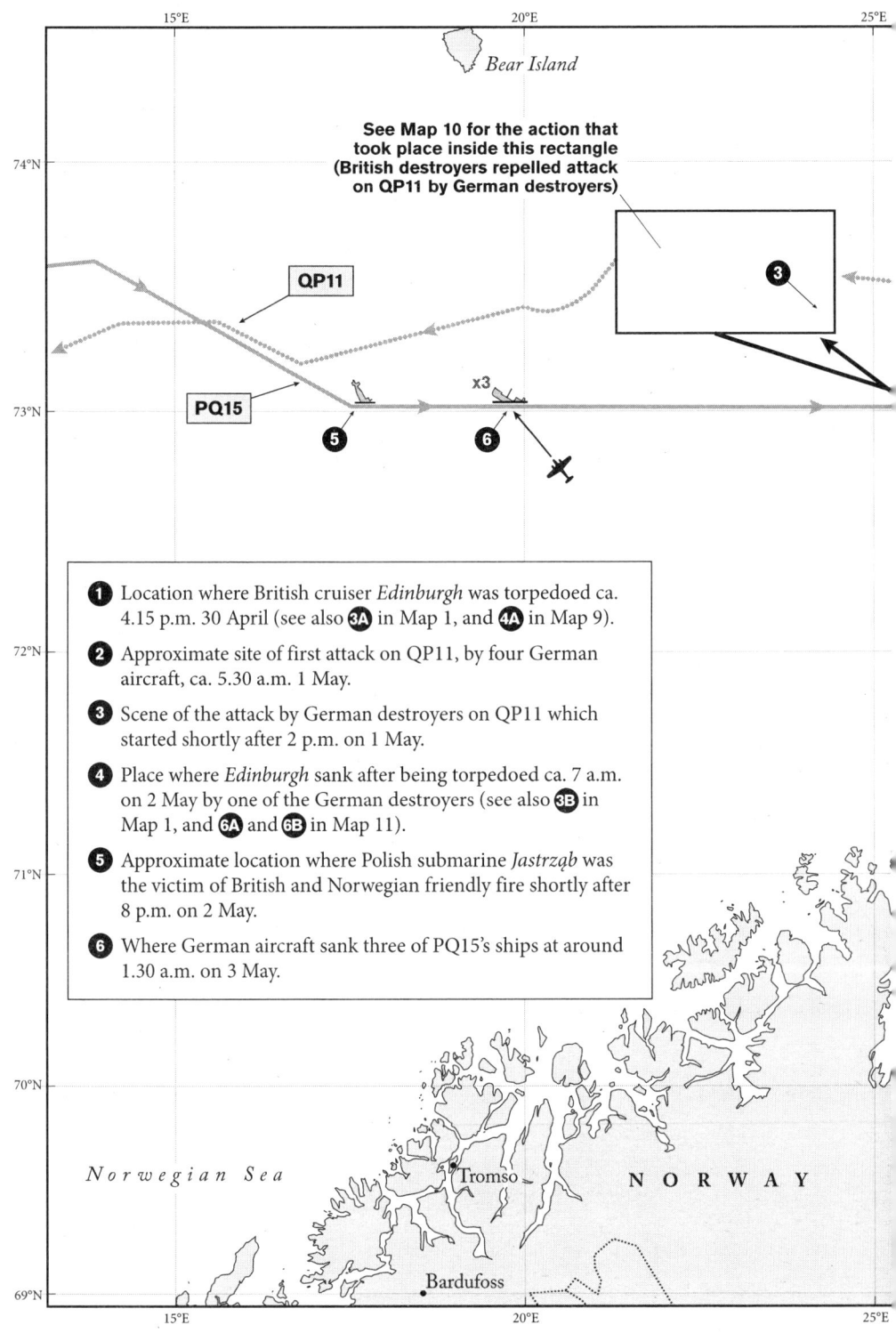

Map 8

See Map 10 for the action that took place inside this rectangle (British destroyers repelled attack on QP11 by German destroyers)

QP11

PQ15

x3

❶ Location where British cruiser *Edinburgh* was torpedoed ca. 4.15 p.m. 30 April (see also ❸Ⓐ in Map 1, and ❹Ⓐ in Map 9).

❷ Approximate site of first attack on QP11, by four German aircraft, ca. 5.30 a.m. 1 May.

❸ Scene of the attack by German destroyers on QP11 which started shortly after 2 p.m. on 1 May.

❹ Place where *Edinburgh* sank after being torpedoed ca. 7 a.m. on 2 May by one of the German destroyers (see also ❸Ⓑ in Map 1, and ❻Ⓐ and ❻Ⓑ in Map 11).

❺ Approximate location where Polish submarine *Jastrząb* was the victim of British and Norwegian friendly fire shortly after 8 p.m. on 2 May.

❻ Where German aircraft sank three of PQ15's ships at around 1.30 a.m. on 3 May.

Bear Island

Norwegian Sea

Tromso

N O R W A Y

Bardufoss

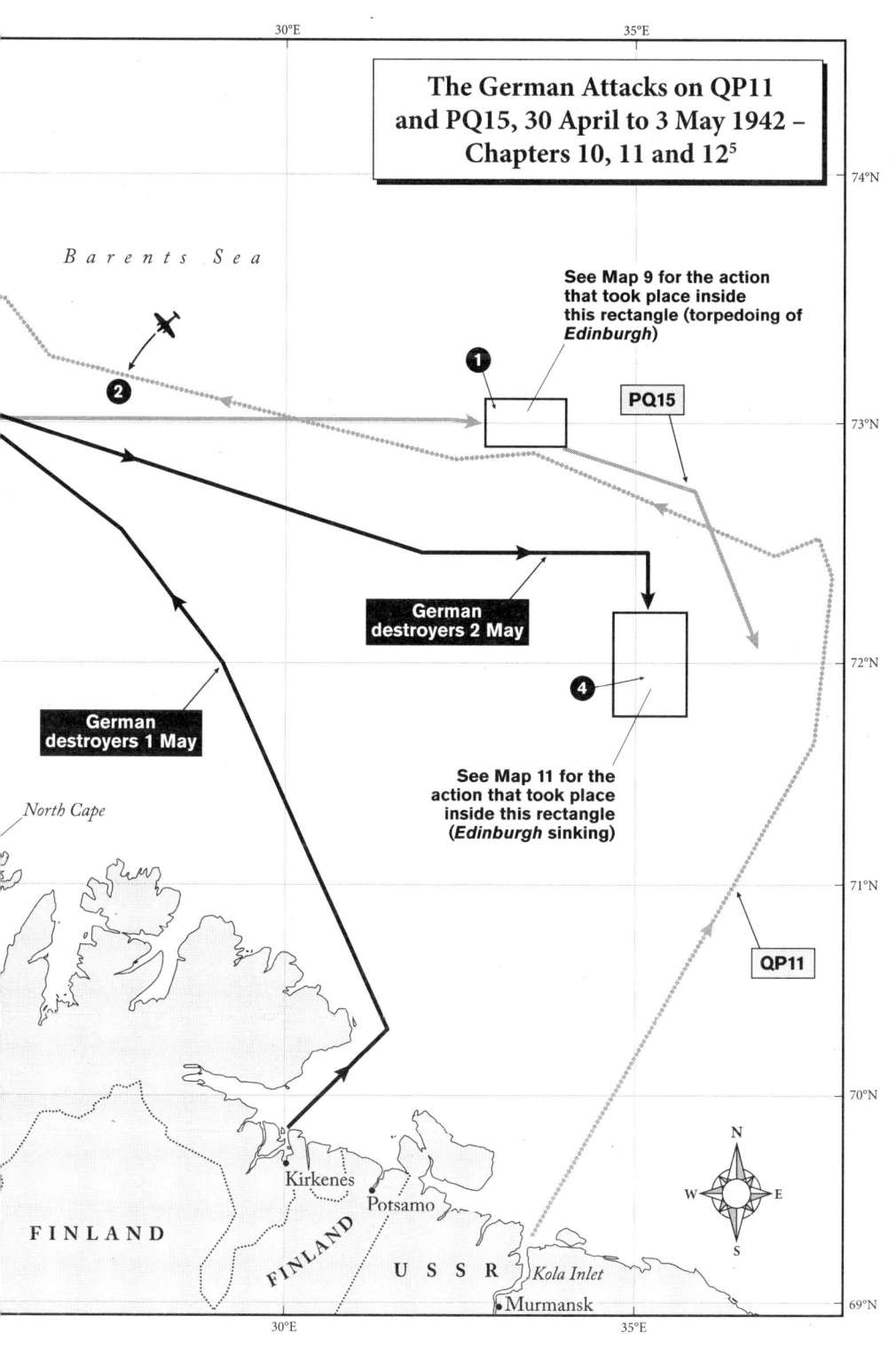

The German Attacks on QP11 and PQ15, 30 April to 3 May 1942 – Chapters 10, 11 and 12[5]

Barents Sea

1

2

See Map 9 for the action that took place inside this rectangle (torpedoing of *Edinburgh*)

PQ15

74°N

73°N

German destroyers 2 May

4

72°N

German destroyers 1 May

See Map 11 for the action that took place inside this rectangle (*Edinburgh* sinking)

North Cape

71°N

QP11

70°N

N

W E

S

Kirkenes

Potsamo

FINLAND

FINLAND

U S S R *Kola Inlet*

Murmansk

69°N

30°E

35°E

Map 9

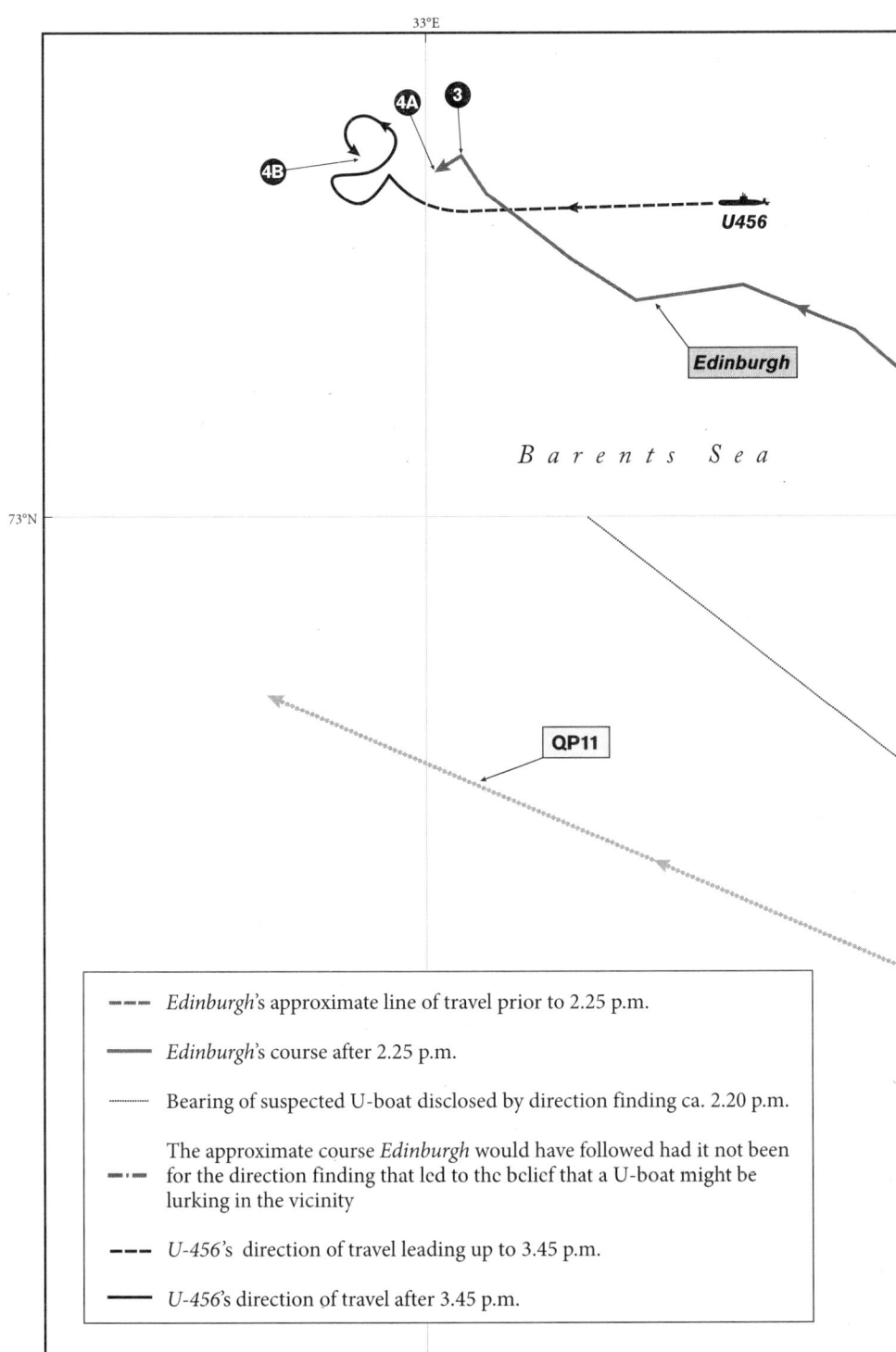

33°E

73°N

U456

Edinburgh

B a r e n t s   S e a

QP11

33°E

- - - *Edinburgh*'s approximate line of travel prior to 2.25 p.m.

—— *Edinburgh*'s course after 2.25 p.m.

········· Bearing of suspected U-boat disclosed by direction finding ca. 2.20 p.m.

—·— The approximate course *Edinburgh* would have followed had it not been for the direction finding that led to the belief that a U-boat might be lurking in the vicinity

– – – *U-456*'s direction of travel leading up to 3.45 p.m.

—— *U-456*'s direction of travel after 3.45 p.m.

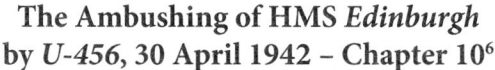

The Ambushing of HMS *Edinburgh* by *U-456*, 30 April 1942 – Chapter 10[6]

The following numbers and text detail the approximate position of and movement by QP11, *Edinburgh*, *U-456*, and another suspected U-boat relative to *Edinburgh*'s location near 73°15′ N 32°50′ E, the place where the Germans stated she was torpedoed at around 4.15 p.m. on 30 April 1942.

1A Position of convoy QP11 at around 2.20 p.m. when direction finding identified the bearing of a U-boat that was believed to be possibly in the vicinity of the location shown on the map as **1B**.

2 Point on course British cruiser *Edinburgh* avoided ca. 2.45 p.m. as a result of the decision to deviate from her planned course because of the belief there might be a U-boat in the vicinity of **1B**.

3 Location where *Edinburgh* made the fatal turn that left the cruiser vulnerable to the attack from *U-456*.

4A Approximate position where ca. 4.15 p.m. *Edinburgh* was torpedoed by *U-456* whose approximate position was at **4B**.

73°N

1B

2

Edinburgh

N
W · E
S

QP11

1A

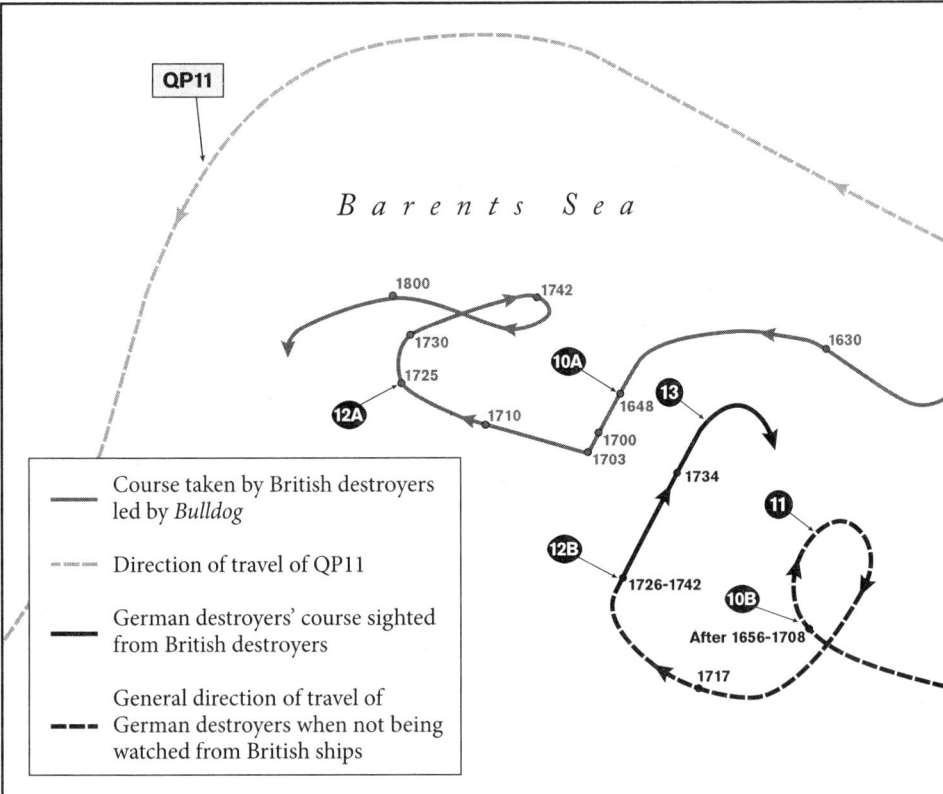

Map 10

B a r e n t s   S e a

QP11

Course taken by British destroyers led by *Bulldog*

Direction of travel of QP11

German destroyers' course sighted from British destroyers

General direction of travel of German destroyers when not being watched from British ships

The following numbers and text detail the approximate positions of and movements by British and German ships relative to the destroyer *Bulldog*'s location – near 73°22′ N 25°32′ E – shortly before 2 p.m. 1 May 1942.

First German attack

1A *Bulldog*'s position to the north-west of QP11's location – which was approximately at **1B** ca. 1.45 p.m. when *Bulldog*'s commander was informed that three German destroyers had been sighted.

2A British destroyers' position north-west of the German destroyers – which were approximately at **2B** – when at around 2.07 p.m. both sides opened fire for the first time.

3 Position of German destroyers when they turned away ca. 2.10 p.m., putting an end to the first engagement.

4 Place where Russian merchant ship sank after being torpedoed at around 2.25 p.m.

Second German Attack

5A Location of British destroyers when their crews sighted German destroyers – which were at approximate position **5B** to the south-east – ca. 2.33 p.m., prompting the second exchange of fire.

6 Position of German destroyers when they turned away ca. 2.45 p.m. following the second engagement.

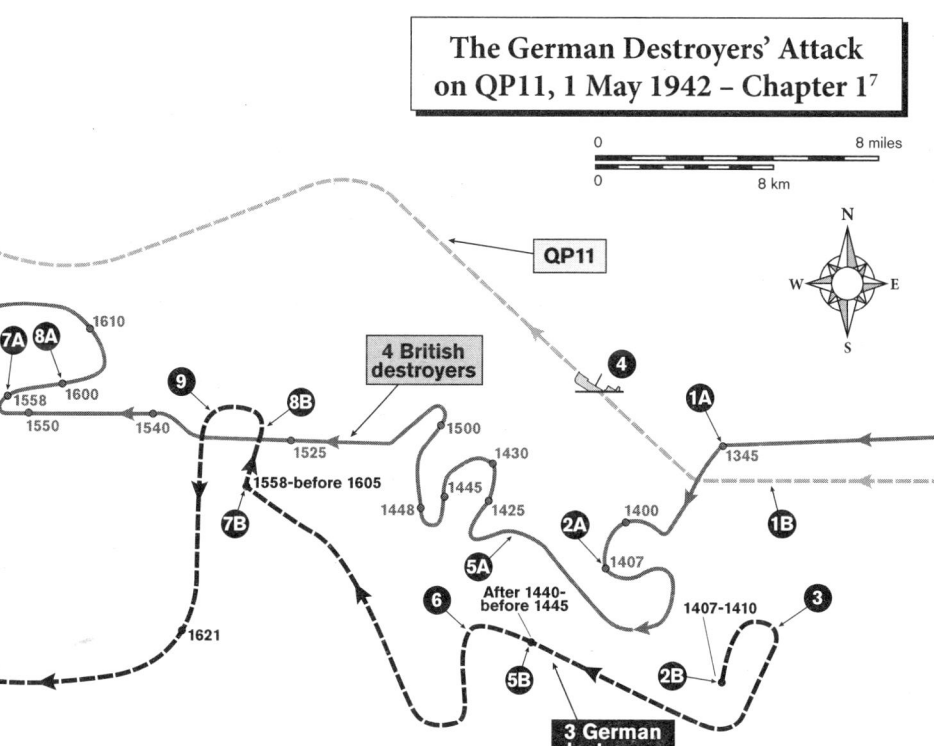

The German Destroyers' Attack on QP11, 1 May 1942 – Chapter 1[7]

Third German Attack

7A Location of British destroyers when German destroyers – in the approximate position **7B** – were sighted at 3.58 p.m., prompting the beginning of the third engagement.

8A Location of British destroyers at 4 p.m. when they and the German destroyers – which were in the approximate position **8B** – opened fire during the third engagement.

9 Location of German destroyers when ca. 4.10 p.m. they turned away, ending the third engagement.

Fourth German Attack

10A Location of British destroyers ca. 4.48 p.m. when their crews sighted the German destroyers – which were at approximate postion **10B** – starting the fourth engagement.

11 Location of German destroyers when they turned away ca. 5.05 p.m., ending the fourth engagement.

Fifth German Attack

12A Location of British destroyers when ca. 5.25 p.m. the German destroyers – whose approximate position was at **12B** – tried to break through to QP11 one last time.

13 Location of the German destroyers when ca. 5.42 p.m. they turned away for the last time, ending the fifth engagement.

Map 11

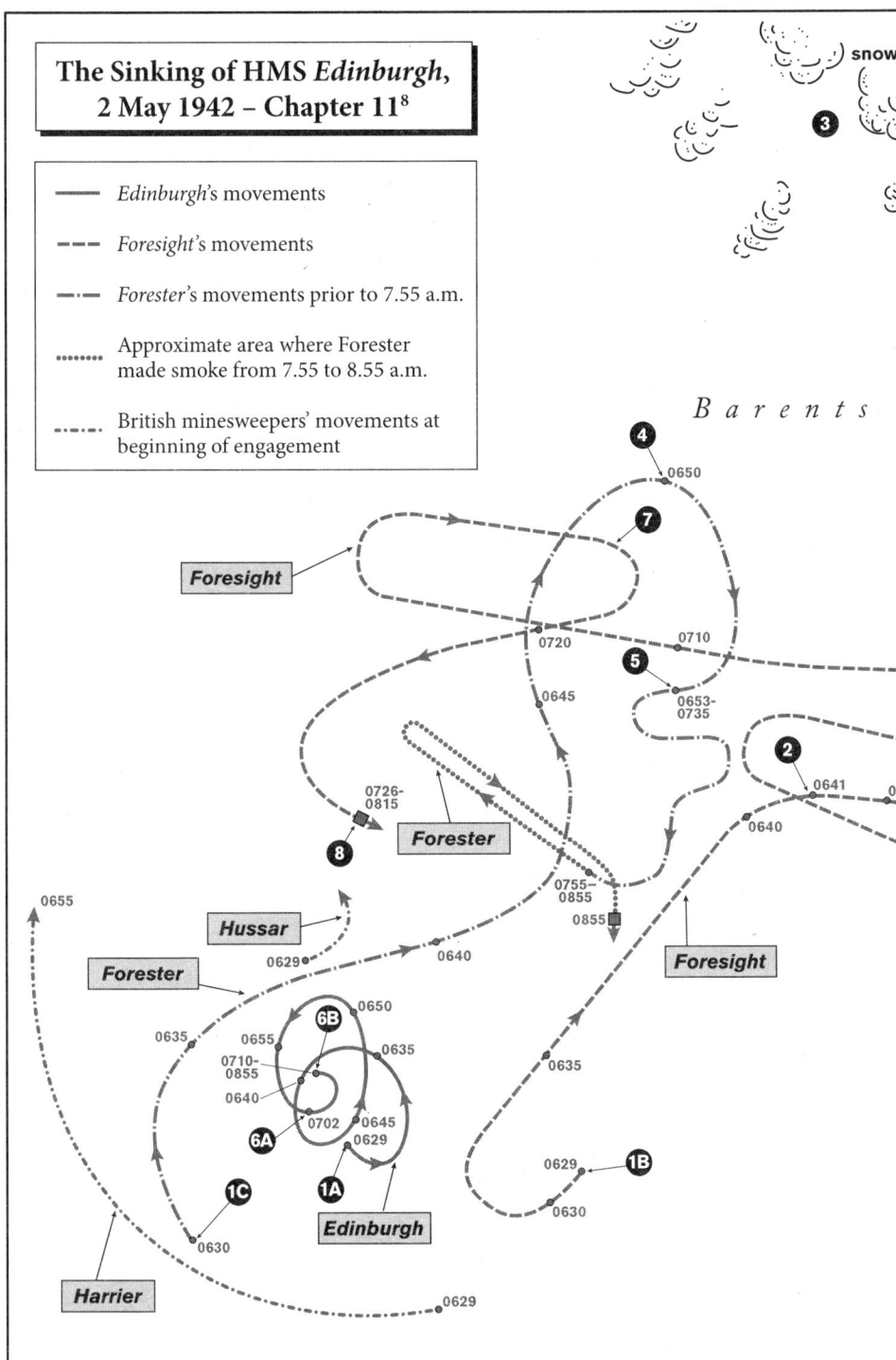

The Sinking of HMS *Edinburgh*, 2 May 1942 – Chapter 11[8]

——— *Edinburgh*'s movements

– – – *Foresight*'s movements

–·–·– *Forester*'s movements prior to 7.55 a.m.

········· Approximate area where Forester made smoke from 7.55 to 8.55 a.m.

–··–··– British minesweepers' movements at beginning of engagement

snow

3

B a r e n t s

4 0650

7

0710

0720

5

0645 0653–0735

2

0641

0640

0726–0815

8

Forester

0755–0855

0855

Foresight

0655

Hussar

0629 0640

Forester

0635

Foresight

0635

0635

6B 0650

0655 0635

0710–0855

0640

6A 0702 0645 0629

1C

1A

0629 **1B**

0630

Edinburgh

0630

Harrier

0629

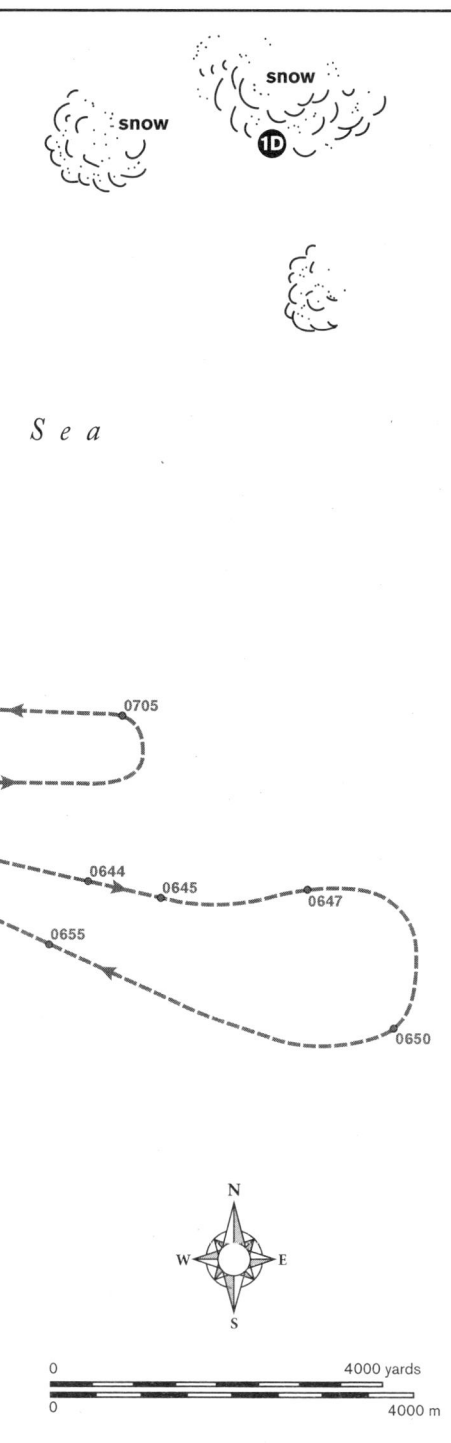

_S e a_

The following numbers and text detail the approximate positions of and movements by British and German ships relative to the approximate position where the cruiser _Edinburgh_ sank – 71°51′ N 35°10′ E – ca. 8.52 a.m.

1A **1B** **1C** **1D** Very approximate positions of _Edinburgh_, the British destroyers _Foresight_ and _Forester_, and the German destroyers respectively at around 6.30 a.m. when engagement started.

2 _Foresight_'s location when ca. 6.40 a.m. her crew started firing at German destroyers to the north.

3 Very approximate position of German destroyer _Hermann Schoemann_ after she was hit ca. 6.40 a.m.

4 _Forester_'s location when at 6.50 a.m. she was hit after advancing to try to torpedo German destroyers to the north.

5 Place where the damaged _Forester_ stopped between ca. 6.53 and 7.35 a.m.

6A Where _Edinburgh_ was located when torpedoed ca. 7.02 a.m., and **6B** where she was abandoned ca. 7.20–7.45 a.m. and sunk ca. 8.52 a.m. (see also **3B** in Map 1, and **4** in Map 8).

7 Location where at 7.18 a.m. _Foresight_ fired torpedoes at stopped German destroyer _Hermann Schoemann_ to the north.

8 Location where damaged _Foresight_ stopped between ca. 7.26 and 8.15 a.m.

Map 12

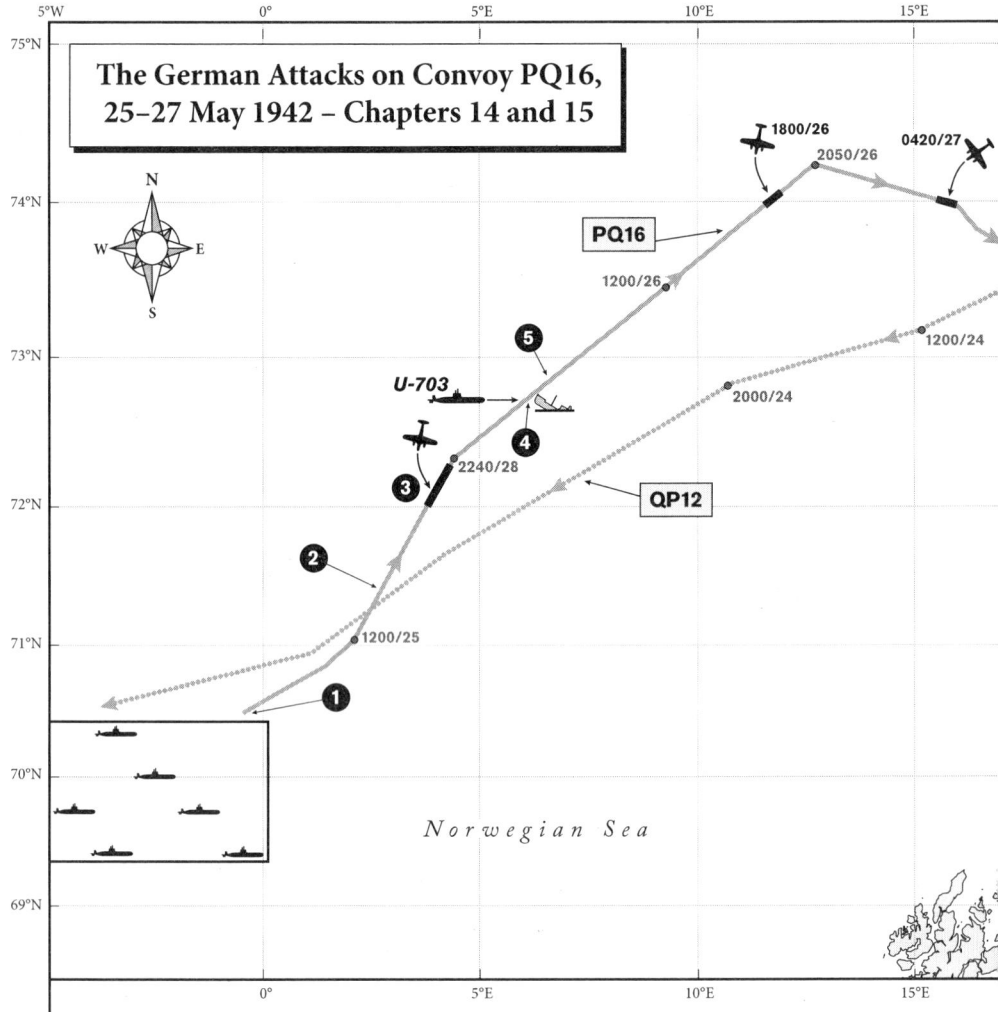

The German Attacks on Convoy PQ16, 25–27 May 1942 – Chapters 14 and 15

❶ Place where British cruisers joined PQ16 close escort ca. 5.30 a.m. on 25 May.

❷ Approximate place where a U-boat was sighted by a look out in a PQ16 escort for the first time ca. 2.38 p.m. 25 May.

❸ Location where the Luftwaffe attacked PQ16 for the first time ca. 8.35 to 10.30 p.m. on 25 May resulting in damage to SS *Carlton*.

❹ Site where SS *Syros* was torpedoed by *U-703* at 3.05 a.m. on 26 May.

❺ Approximate place where British cruisers left PQ16 at ca. 3.30 a.m. on 26 May.

❻ Location of series of attacks between ca. 11.15 a.m. and 2.20 p.m. on 27 May in the course of which the Luftwaffe damaged ORP *Garland*, SS *Starii Bolshevik* and SS *Alamar* (eventually sunk by British escort), and sank SS *Mormacsul* between around 1 to 1.30 p.m.

❼ Location of raid ca. 2.49 to 3.10 p.m. on 27 May in the course of which the Luftwaffe sank SS *Empire Lawrence* at around 2.49 p.m.

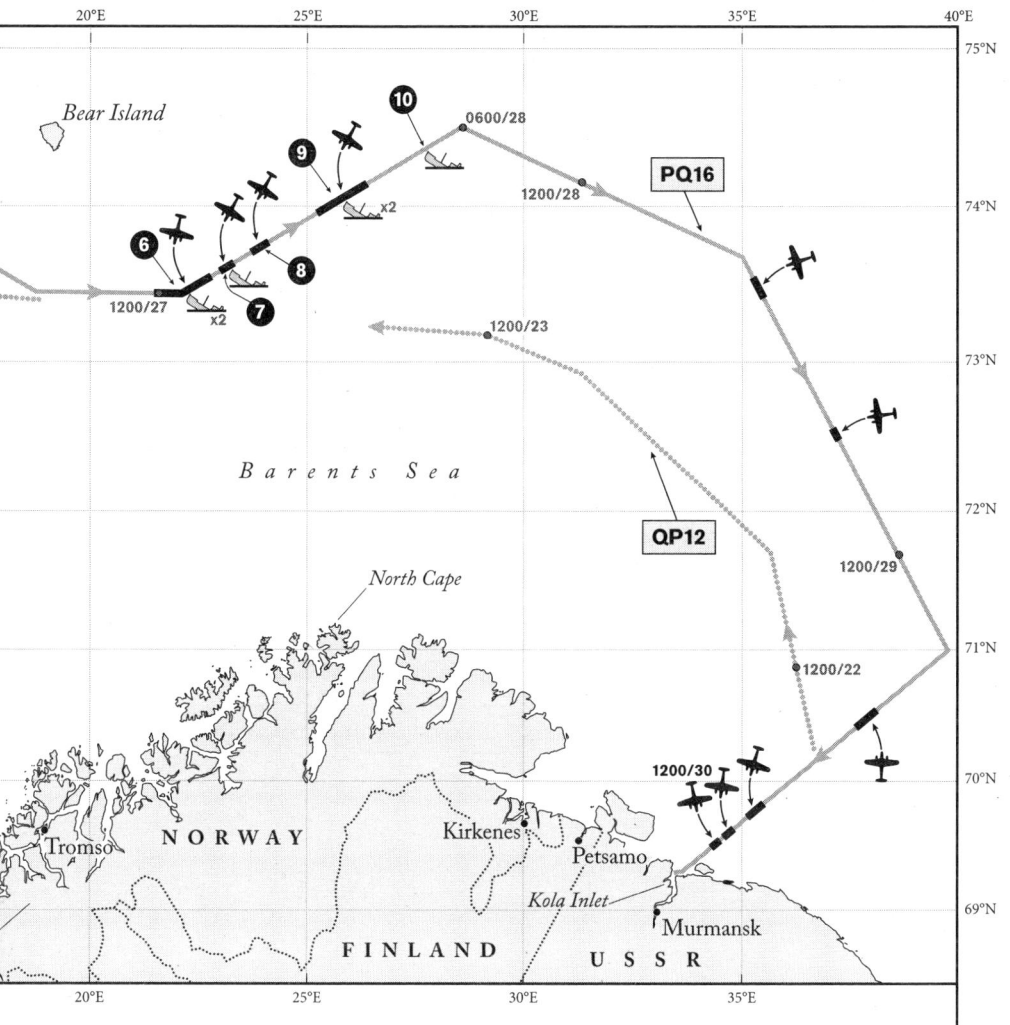

8 Location of raid ca. 4.27 to 4.50 p.m. on 27 May in the course of which the Luftwaffe damaged SS *Ocean Voice* and SS *City of Joliet* ca. 4.30 p.m.

9 Convoy's location at beginning of raid made ca. 7.25 to 9.30 p.m. on 27 May in the course of which the Luftwaffe damaged SS *Lowther Castle* and SS *Empire Purcell* – which later sank.

10 Very approximate position where *City of Joliet* (apparently sinking) was abandoned.

Location of Gruppe Greif U-boats when PQ16 sailed

Map 13

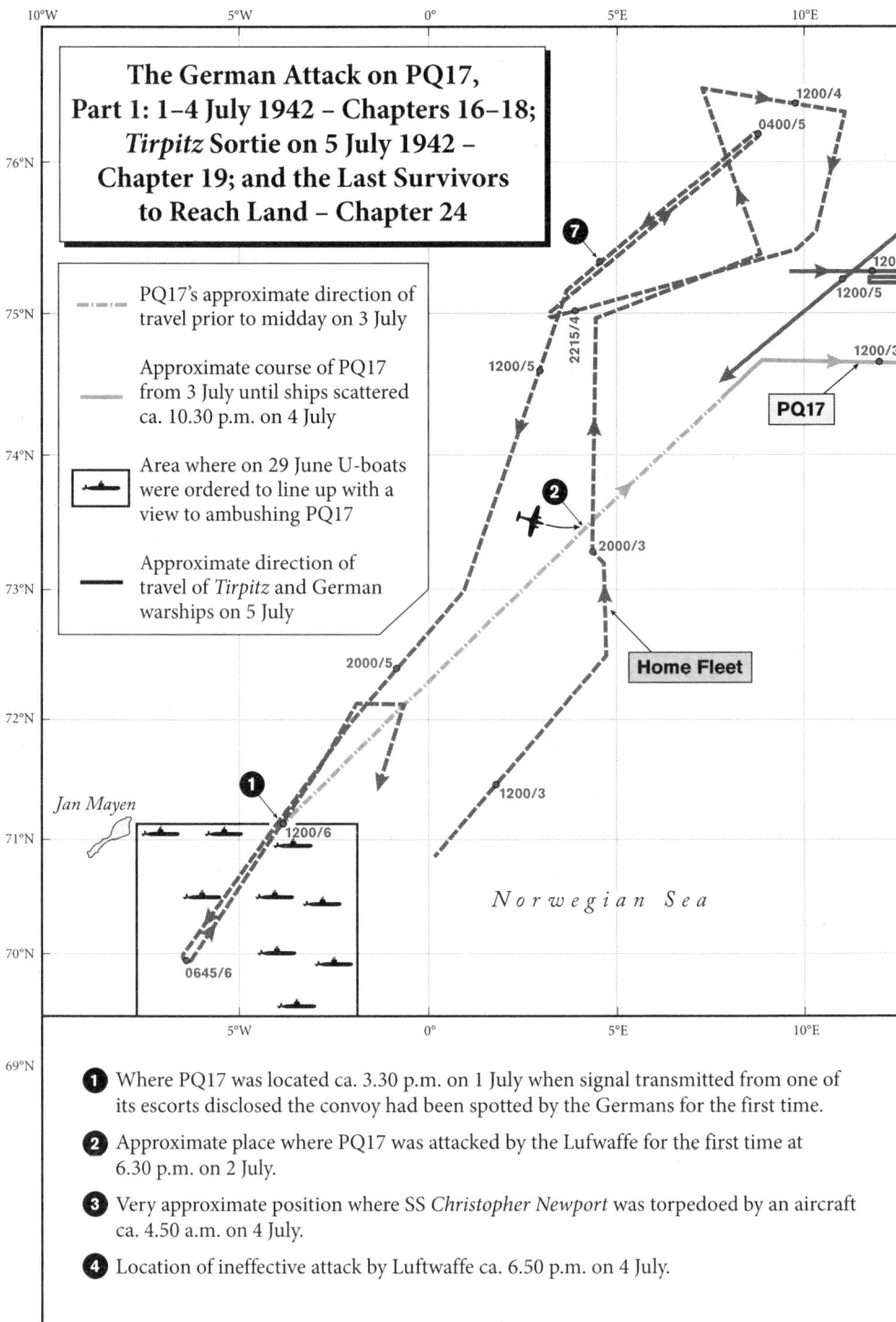

The German Attack on PQ17,
Part 1: 1–4 July 1942 – Chapters 16–18;
Tirpitz Sortie on 5 July 1942 –
Chapter 19; and the Last Survivors
to Reach Land – Chapter 24

PQ17's approximate direction of travel prior to midday on 3 July

Approximate course of PQ17 from 3 July until ships scattered ca. 10.30 p.m. on 4 July

Area where on 29 June U-boats were ordered to line up with a view to ambushing PQ17

Approximate direction of travel of *Tirpitz* and German warships on 5 July

PQ17

Home Fleet

Jan Mayen

Norwegian Sea

1200/4
0400/5
1200/3
1200/5
1200/3
1200/5
2215/4
1200/5
2000/3
2000/5
1200/3
1200/6
0645/6

❶ Where PQ17 was located ca. 3.30 p.m. on 1 July when signal transmitted from one of its escorts disclosed the convoy had been spotted by the Germans for the first time.

❷ Approximate place where PQ17 was attacked by the Luftwaffe for the first time at 6.30 p.m. on 2 July.

❸ Very approximate position where SS *Christopher Newport* was torpedoed by an aircraft ca. 4.50 a.m. on 4 July.

❹ Location of ineffective attack by Luftwaffe ca. 6.50 p.m. on 4 July.

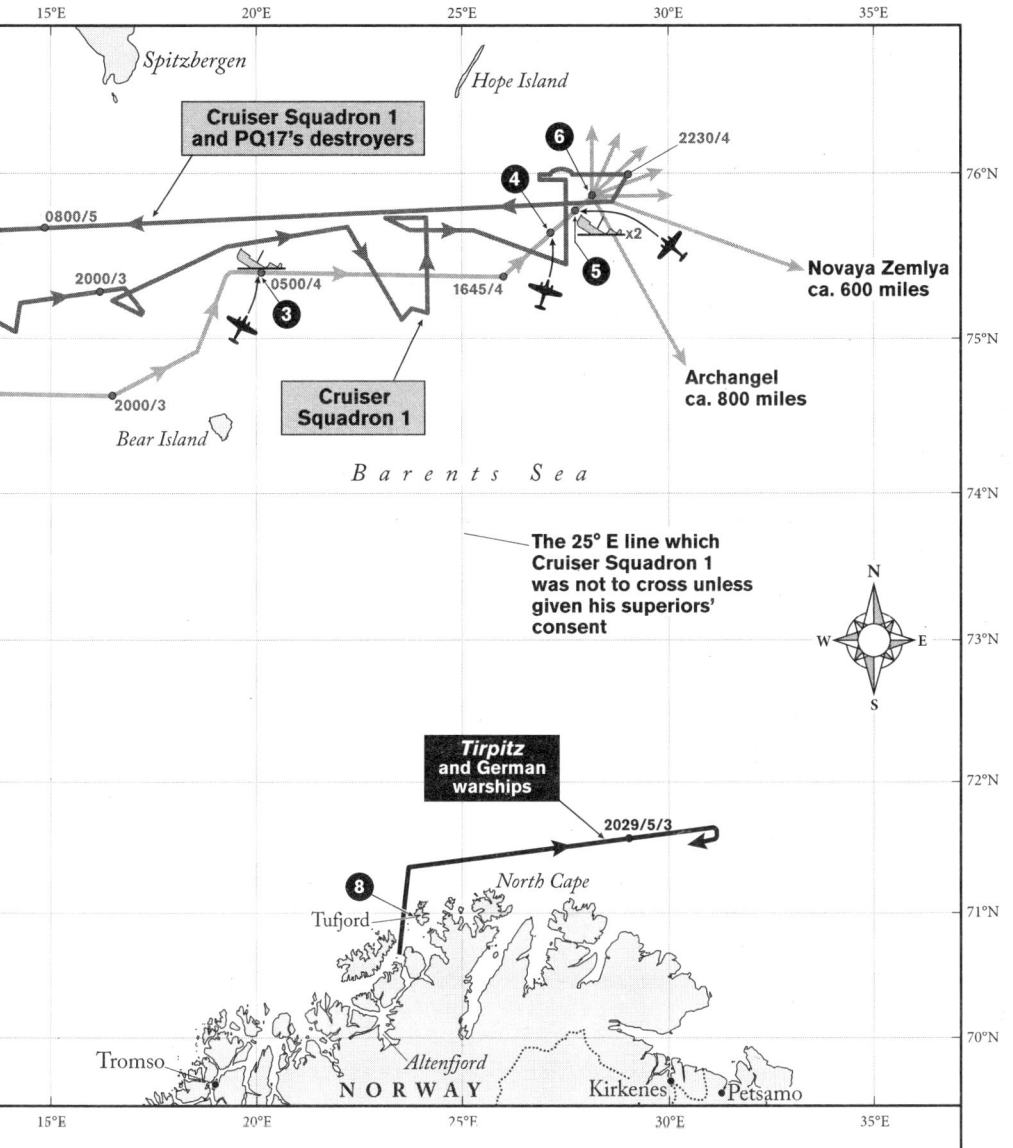

15°E 20°E 25°E 30°E 35°E

Spitzbergen

Hope Island

Cruiser Squadron 1 and PQ17's destroyers

76°N

0800/5

6

2230/4

4

5

x2

Novaya Zemlya
ca. 600 miles

2000/3

0500/4

1645/4

3

2000/3

Cruiser Squadron 1

Bear Island

Archangel
ca. 800 miles

75°N

B a r e n t s   S e a

74°N

The 25° E line which Cruiser Squadron 1 was not to cross unless given his superiors' consent

N

W—E   73°N

S

Tirpitz **and German warships**

72°N

2029/5/3

8

North Cape

Tufjord

71°N

Tromso

Altenfjord

N O R W A Y   Kirkenes   Petsamo

70°N

15°E 20°E 25°E 30°E 35°E

5 Approximate location of the big attack by German aircraft ca. 8.21 p.m. on 4 July in the course of which SS *Navarino*, SS *William Hooper* and Soviet tanker *Azerbaijan* were torpedoed. SS *Navarino* and SS *William Hooper* were later sunk.

6 Place where PQ17's merchant ships scattered ca. 10.30 p.m. 4 July.

7 Location where the Home Fleet was detected at 6.45 a.m. on 5 July from a German aircraft for the first time that day.

8 Fishing village Tufjord, on Rolvsøya island, reached by SS *Carlton*'s survivors in their lifeboat on 24 July, the last boat from a sunk or abandoned PQ17 ship to make it to dry land.

Map 14

20°E   25°E

Edge I.

Halvmaneoya

Spitzbergen

Ayrshire and 3 merchant ships

Hope Island

The Loss of 21 Allied Ships After the Scattering of PQ17, 5–13 July 1942 – Chapters 18–20 and 22–24

1 Location where according to the Germans SS *Empire Byron* was torpedoed and sunk by *U-703* ca. 8.30 a.m. on 5 July, the first German scalp after the scattering of PQ17.

2 Place where according to the Germans SS *Carlton* was sunk by *U-88* ca. 10.15 a.m. on 5 July.

3 Site where according to the Germans SS *Honomu* was sunk by *U-456* ca. 2.45 p.m. on 5 July.

4 Where SS *Peter Kerr* was abandoned ca. 5 p.m. on 5 July after being attacked by aircraft.

♢ Bear Island

5 Where SS *Earlston* was sunk ca. 5 p.m. on 5 July after being attacked first by aircraft, and then by a U-boat.

6 Place where the tanker RFA *Aldersdale* was abandoned ca. 5.20 p.m. on 5 July after being attacked by aircraft. She was later sunk.

7 Location where rescue ship *Zaafaran* was abandoned following 5.20 p.m. 5 July attack by aircraft.

8 Approximate area where between ca. 5.45 and 7.15 p.m. on 5 July first SS *Bolton Castle* was sunk, then SS *Washington* and finally SS *Paulus Potter* were abandoned following attacks by aircraft.

North Cape

9 Place where ca. 5.55 p.m. on 5 July SS *Pan Kraft*'s crew abandoned ship after an aircraft attack.

10 Approximate area where SS *Fairfield City* was abandoned and sunk between ca. 6.45 and 7.40 p.m. on 5 July after an aircraft attack.

11 Approximate area where, according to the Germans, SS *Daniel Morgan*, which had been damaged during attacks by aircraft, was dispatched by *U-88* after 9.10 p.m. on 5 July.

N O R W A Y

12 Approximate place where, according to the Germans, SS *River Afton* sank ca. 9.22 p.m. on 5 July after being torpedoed by *U-703*.

13 Location where SS *John Witherspoon* was sunk by *U-255* ca. 4.45 p.m. 6 July.

S W E D E N

14 Very approximate estimate of where SS *Pan Atlantic* was sunk by aircraft at 6.18 p.m. on 6 July.

15 Location where SS *Alcoa Ranger* was torpedoed and sunk by *U-255* between ca. 9.30 a.m. and midday on 7 July.

16 Site of torpedoing and sinking of SS *Hartlebury* by *U-355* ca. 6.35 to 6.45 p.m. on 7 July.

17 Where SS *Olopana* was torpedoed and sunk by *U-255* ca. 1 a.m. on 8 July.

18 Approximately where HMS *La Malouine* rescued *John Witherspoon*'s survivors from their boats ca. 5.20 a.m. on 9 July.

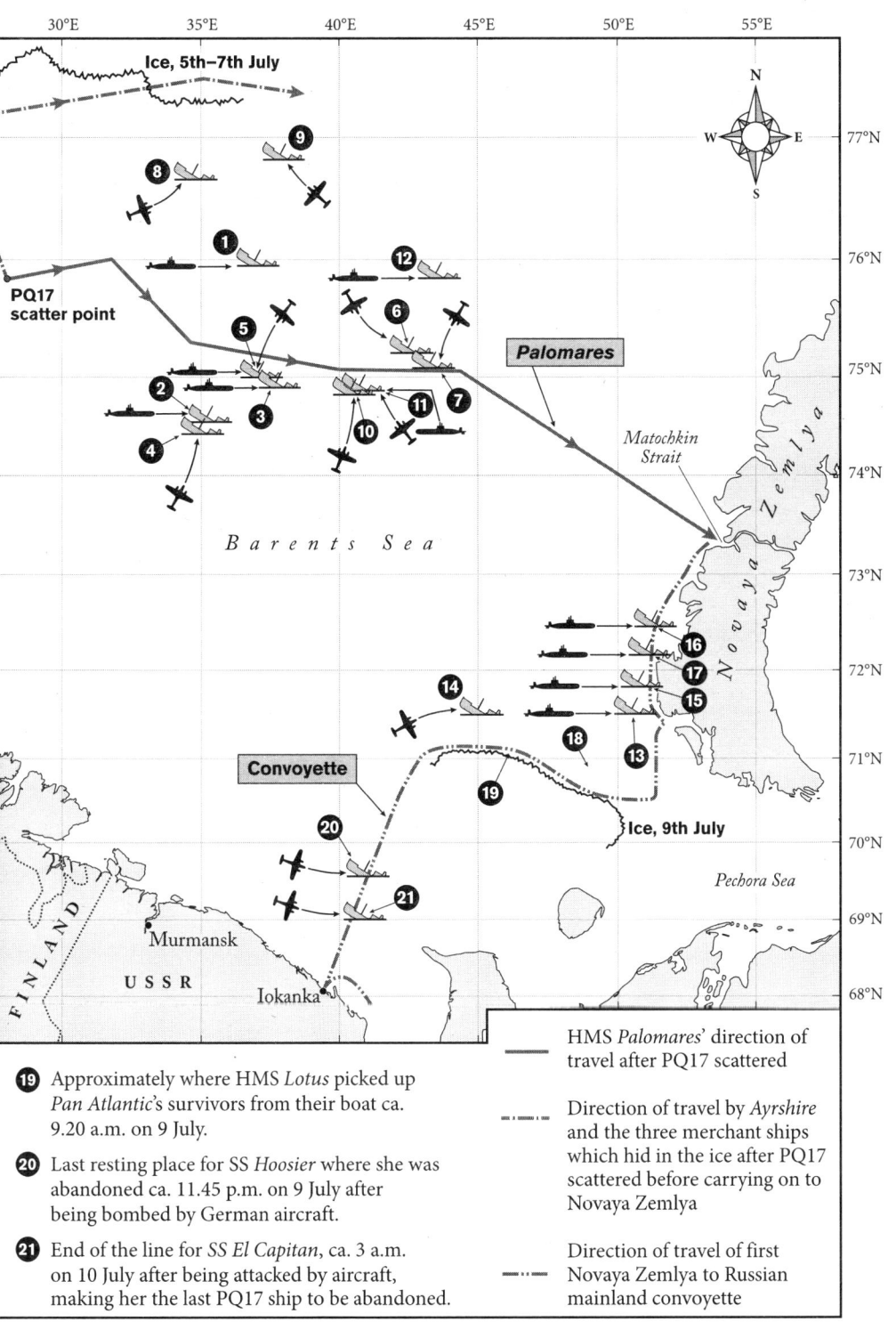

30°E	35°E	40°E	45°E	50°E	55°E

Ice, 5th–7th July

N
W **E**
S

77°N

PQ17
scatter point

76°N

Palomares

75°N

Matochkin
Strait

74°N

B a r e n t s   S e a

73°N

72°N

71°N

Convoyette

Ice, 9th July

70°N

Pechora Sea

69°N

F I N L A N D

Murmansk

U S S R   Iokanka

68°N

19 Approximately where HMS *Lotus* picked up
Pan Atlantic's survivors from their boat ca.
9.20 a.m. on 9 July.

20 Last resting place for SS *Hoosier* where she was
abandoned ca. 11.45 p.m. on 9 July after
being bombed by German aircraft.

21 End of the line for SS *El Capitan*, ca. 3 a.m.
on 10 July after being attacked by aircraft,
making her the last PQ17 ship to be abandoned.

HMS *Palomares*' direction of
travel after PQ17 scattered

Direction of travel by *Ayrshire*
and the three merchant ships
which hid in the ice after PQ17
scattered before carrying on to
Novaya Zemlya

Direction of travel of first
Novaya Zemlya to Russian
mainland convoyette

Map 15

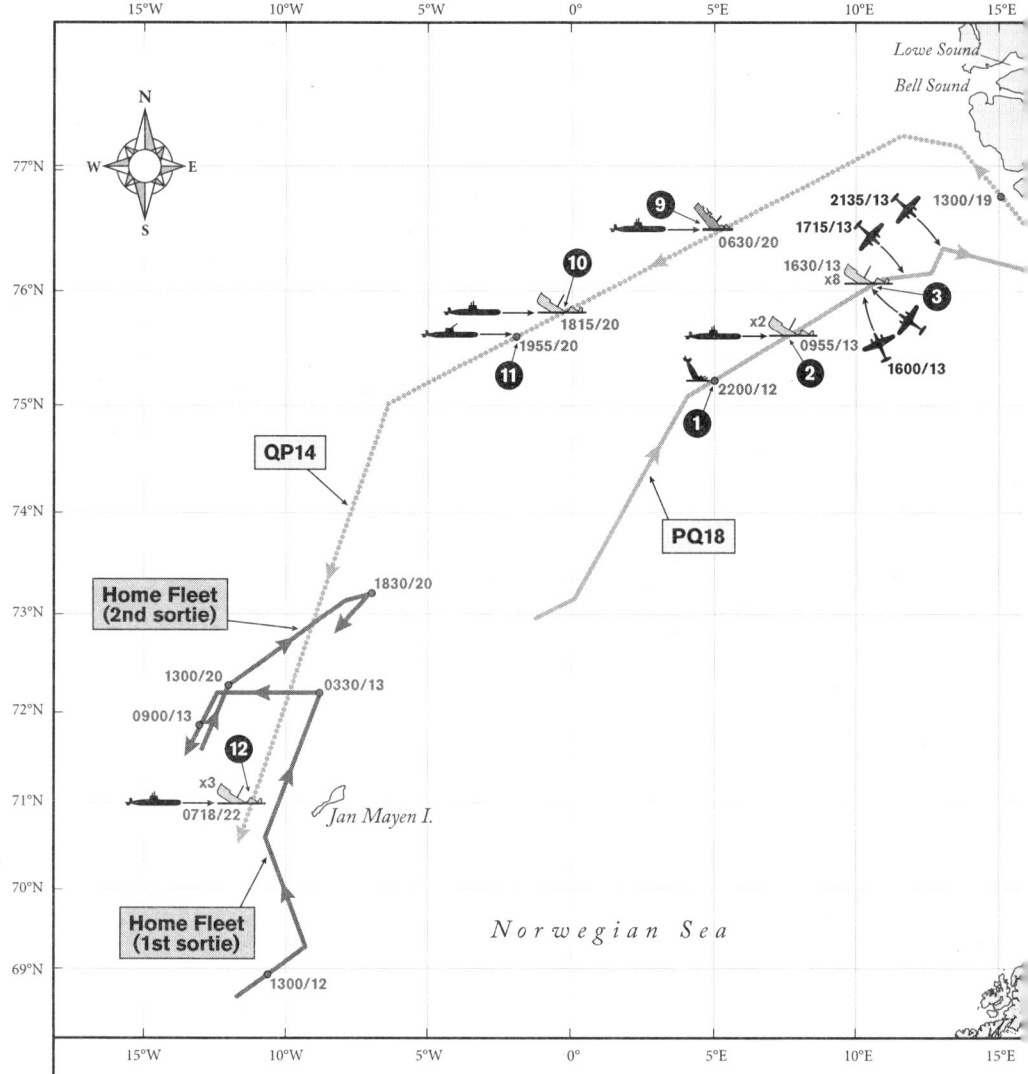

PQ18 Action

1 Place where *U-88* was sunk by HMS *Faulknor* ca. 10 p.m. on 12 September.

2 Location where SS *Stalingrad* and SS *Oliver Ellsworth* were sunk ca. 9.55 a.m. on 13 September.

3 Approximate area where eight of PQ18's ships were abandoned or sunk in the wake of the Luftwaffe raid ca. 4.30 p.m. on 13 September.

4 Approximately where *U-457* torpedoed *Atheltemplar* ca. 4.30 a.m. on 14 September.

5 Site of sinking of *U-589* by HMS *Onslow* between ca. 11.55 and 2.10 p.m. on 14 September.

6 Approximate location of the main Luftwaffe attacks on 14 September in course of which *Mary Luckenbach* was 'sunk' ca. 3.10 p.m.

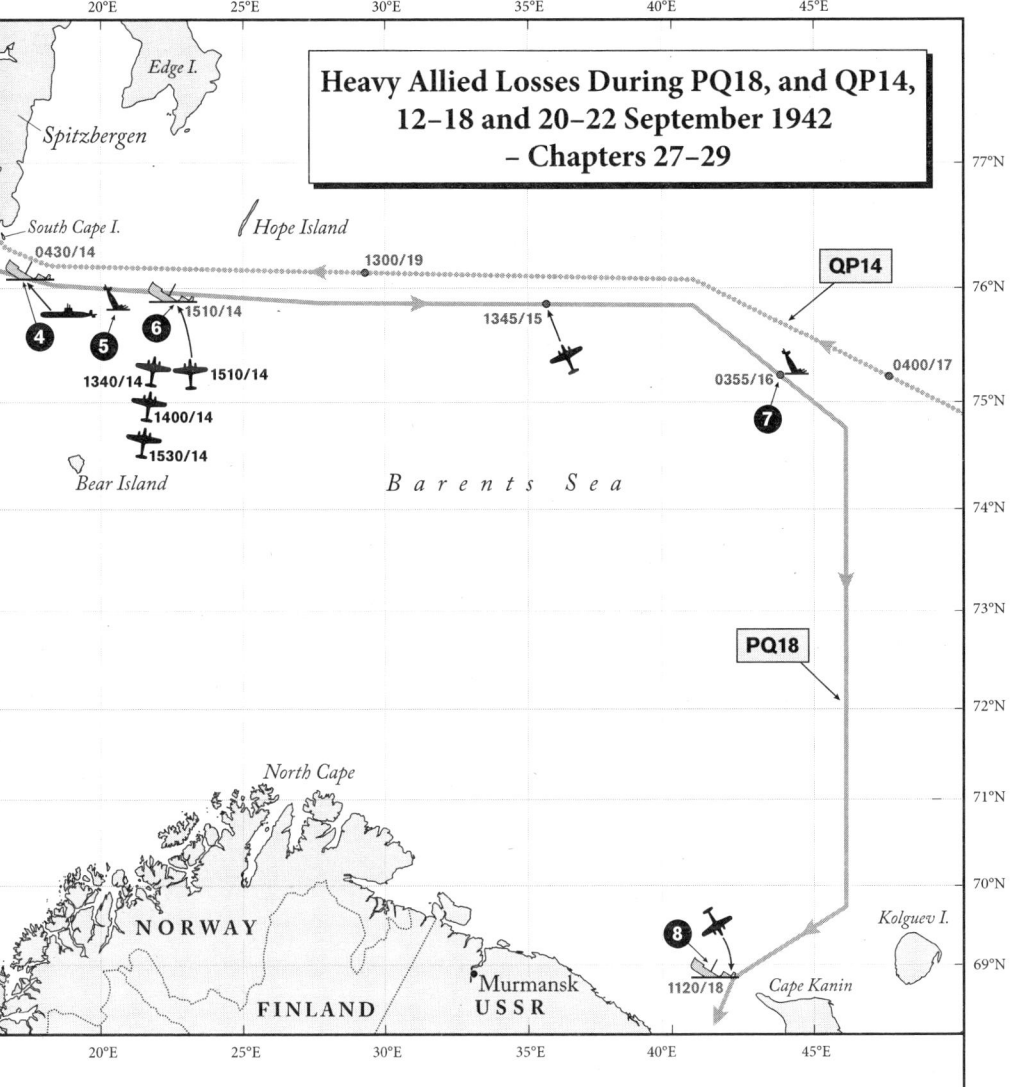

Heavy Allied Losses During PQ18, and QP14,
12–18 and 20–22 September 1942
– Chapters 27–29

7 Approximate location where HMS *Impulsive* sank *U-457* ca. 3.55 a.m. on 16 September.

8 Approximate location where Luftwaffe torpedoed SS *Kentucky* ca. 11.20 a.m. on 18 September.

QP14 Action

9 Site where minesweeper *Leda* was sunk by *U-435* ca. 6.30 a.m. on 20 September.

10 Place where *U-255* torpedoed SS *Silver Sword* ca. 6.15 p.m. on 20 September.

11 Location where the destroyer HMS *Somali* was torpedoed by *U-703* ca. 7.55 p.m. on 20 September.

12 Where *Bellingham*, *Ocean Voice* and *Grey Ranger* were torpedoed by *U-435* between 7.18 and 7.24 a.m. on 22 September.

Map 16

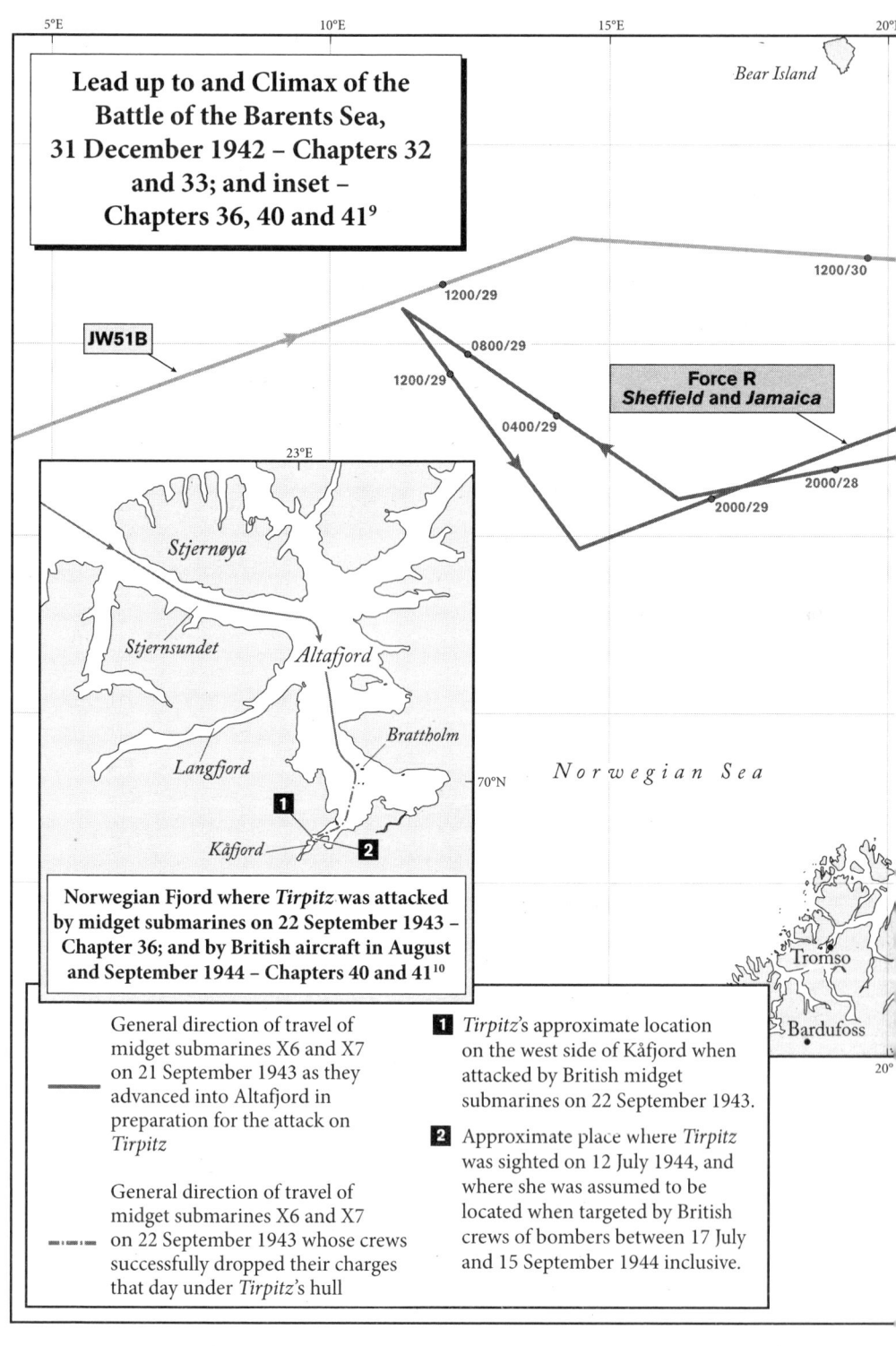

Lead up to and Climax of the Battle of the Barents Sea, 31 December 1942 – Chapters 32 and 33; and inset – Chapters 36, 40 and 41[9]

Bear Island

JW51B

1200/30

1200/29

0800/29

1200/29

0400/29

Force R
Sheffield and *Jamaica*

2000/28

2000/29

23°E

Stjernøya

Stjernsundet

Altafjord

Brattholm

Langfjord

70°N   *Norwegian Sea*

1

Kåfjord   **2**

Norwegian Fjord where *Tirpitz* was attacked by midget submarines on 22 September 1943 – Chapter 36; and by British aircraft in August and September 1944 – Chapters 40 and 41[10]

Tromsø

Bardufoss

20°

General direction of travel of midget submarines X6 and X7 on 21 September 1943 as they advanced into Altafjord in preparation for the attack on *Tirpitz*

General direction of travel of midget submarines X6 and X7 on 22 September 1943 whose crews successfully dropped their charges that day under *Tirpitz*'s hull

1 *Tirpitz*'s approximate location on the west side of Kåfjord when attacked by British midget submarines on 22 September 1943.

2 Approximate place where *Tirpitz* was sighted on 12 July 1944, and where she was assumed to be located when targeted by British crews of bombers between 17 July and 15 September 1944 inclusive.

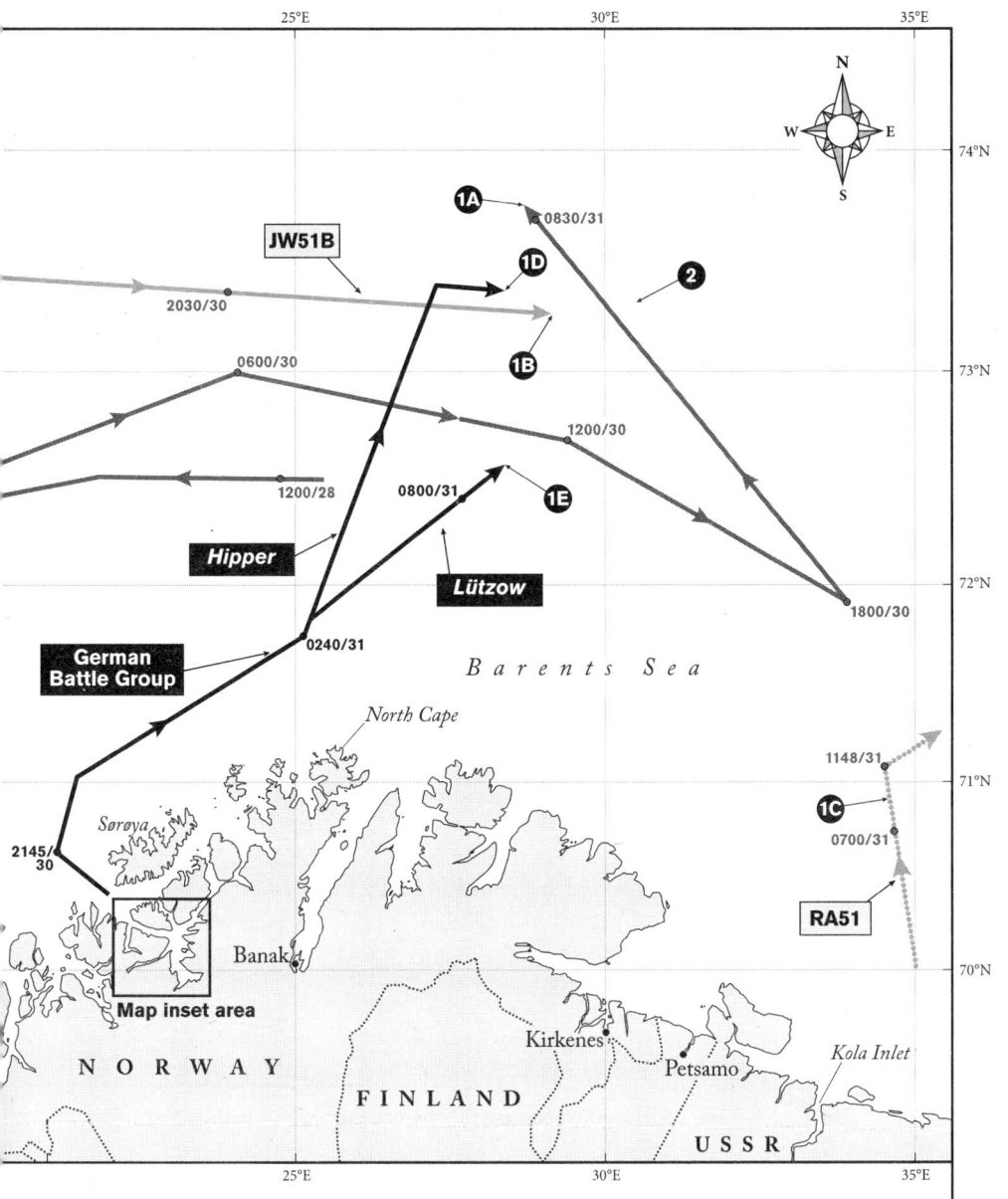

1A Approximate place where Rear Admiral Burnett's Force R was operating between 8.45 and 9.45 a.m. on 31 December, during which period the following units passed through the approximate positions specified below: JW51B: **1B**; RA51: **1C**; *Hipper* and supporting destroyers: **1D**; and *Lützow* and supporting destroyers: **1E** .

2 Approximate place where ca. 11.30 a.m. 31 December Force R ambushed *Hipper*, the German cruiser (see also **8** in Map 1, and Map 17 for the combatants' relative positions at the time of the ambush).

Map 17

The Battle of the Barents Sea, 31 December 1942 – Chapter 33[11]

The positions in this map are all relative to the position for Force R at dawn on 31 December specified by Rear Admiral Burnett: 73°47′ N 28°54′ E[12]

1A, **1B** and **1C** Approximate locations ca. 8.45 a.m. of Force R, JW51B, and British trawler *Vizalma* and a merchant ship respectively relative to each other (the **1A** and **1B** locations were around 25 miles apart).

2 Location where at around 9.45 a.m. *Achates* was damaged for the first time by a shell fired from *Hipper*.

3 Where *Onslow* was ca. 10.19 a.m. when hit by a shell fired from *Hipper*.

4 Approximate place where *Bramble* was located when hit for the first time by a shell, fired from *Hipper* ca. 10.36 a.m. *Bramble* was later sunk.

5 Location where ca. 11.15 a.m. *Achates* was hit by a shell fired from *Hipper*. *Achates* later sank.

6 Very approximate location where the three undamaged British destroyers sailed as they shielded the convoy after ca. 10.45 a.m.

7 Very approximate indication showing where *Obedient*'s aerials were hit by a shell fired from *Hipper* ca. 11.30 a.m.

8 Location where *Hipper* was damaged by shells fired by Force R's *Sheffield* and *Jamaica* after being ambushed by the British cruisers shortly after 11.30 a.m.

9 Approximate place where *Friedrich Eckoldt* was shot up by Force R ca. 11.45 a.m. She later sank.

British ships' direction of travel

●—●—●—● *Obdurate*'s course at the beginning of the battle

━··━··━ *Achates*' when *Hipper* fired at her the first time

━ ━ ━ ━ *Onslow*'s, initially when alone, and subsequently when joined by three other destroyers, after German attack started

●—●—●—● *Onslow*'s and *Orwell*'s after the other British destroyers which had been accompanying them turned to the south in order to approach the convoy

············· *Obedient*'s and subsequently *Obdurate*'s after leaving *Onslow*, and turning south to support the convoy

━·━·━ *Bramble*'s when *Hipper* fired at her

━━━━━━━ *Obedient*'s, *Obdurate*'s and *Orwell*'s after 11 a.m.

German ships' direction of travel

━·━·━ *Friedrich Eckoldt*'s during encounter with British cruisers

━··━··━ *Richard Beitzen*'s during British cruisers' counter-attack

━━━━━━━ German destroyers forming part of *Hipper*'s group at the beginning of the battle

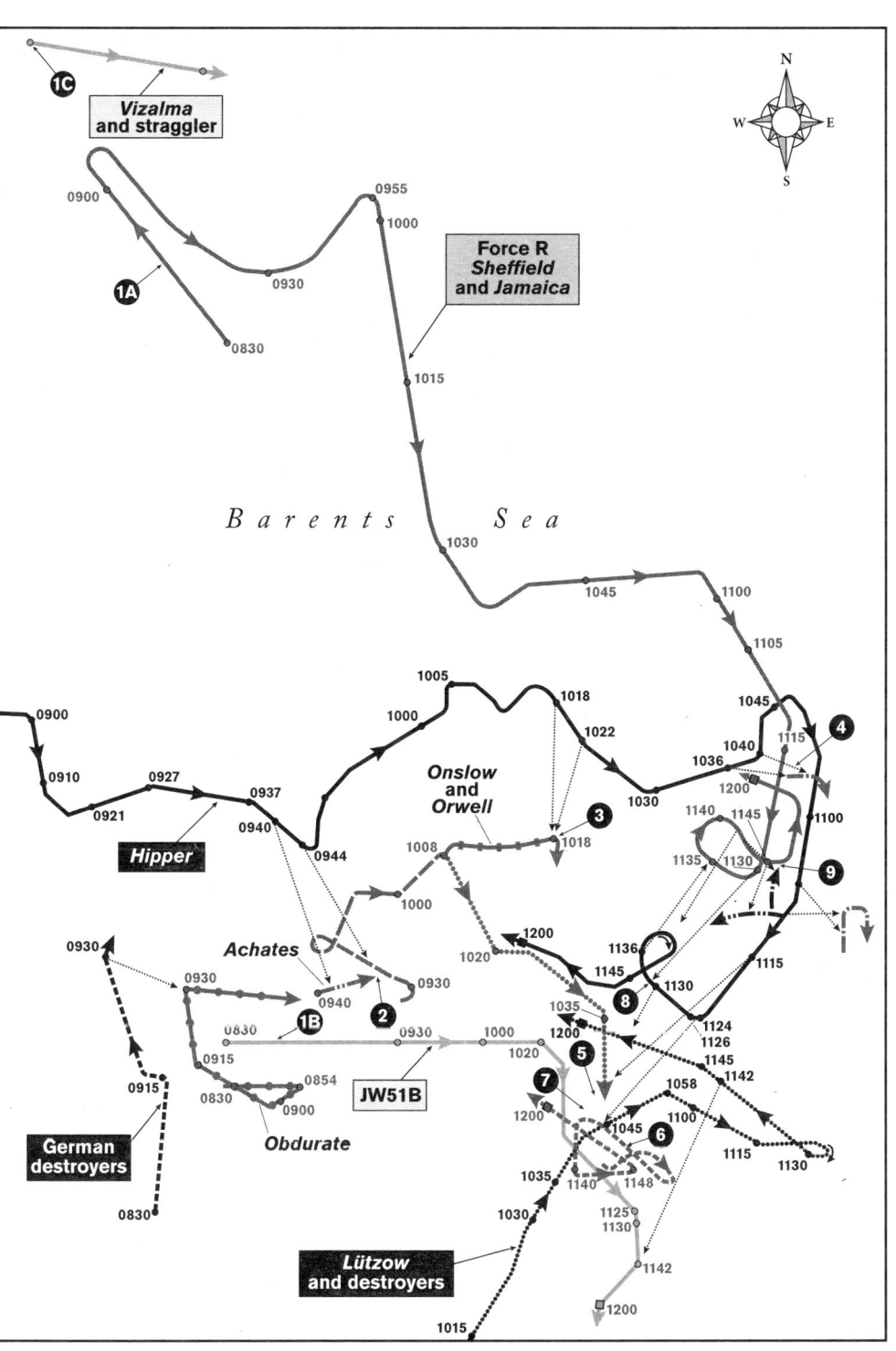

1C
Vizalma
and straggler

0900
0955
1000
0930
1A
0830

Force R
Sheffield
and *Jamaica*

1015

B a r e n t s   S e a

1030

1045   1100

1105

1005   1018   1045
1000   1022   1115   **4**
0900   1040
0910   1036
0921   0927   0937   *Onslow*   1200
                and   1140   1145   1100
0940   *Orwell*   1135   1130
0944   1008   **9**
Hipper   1018
1000   **3**
1020   1200   1115
Achates   1136   1145
0930   0930   1124   1130   **8**
0930   1035   1126
1B   0940   **2**   1200   1145   1142
0830   1200   **5**   1058
0915   0930   1000   1045   **6**   1100
0854   1020   **7**   1140   1115   1130
0830   0900   1200   1148
Obdurate   1035   1045   1130
German   1140
destroyers   1125
0915   1030   1130
0830   1142

Lützow
and destroyers   1200

1015

JW51B

Map 18

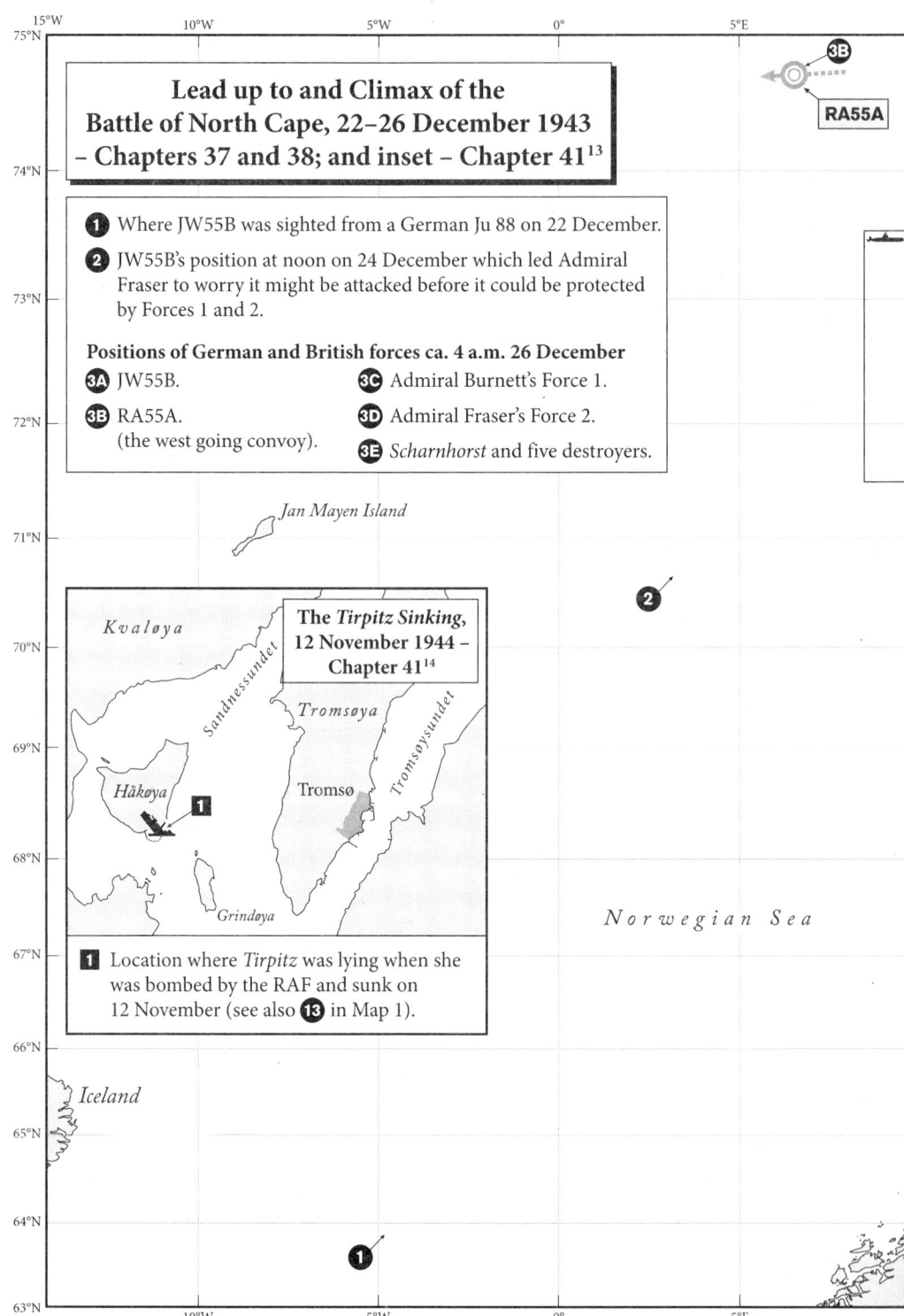

**Lead up to and Climax of the
Battle of North Cape, 22–26 December 1943
– Chapters 37 and 38; and inset – Chapter 41[13]**

1 Where JW55B was sighted from a German Ju 88 on 22 December.

2 JW55B's position at noon on 24 December which led Admiral
Fraser to worry it might be attacked before it could be protected
by Forces 1 and 2.

Positions of German and British forces ca. 4 a.m. 26 December

3A JW55B.

3B RA55A.
(the west going convoy).

3C Admiral Burnett's Force 1.

3D Admiral Fraser's Force 2.

3E *Scharnhorst* and five destroyers.

3B

RA55A

Jan Mayen Island

Kvaløya

Sandnessundet

Tromsøya

**The *Tirpitz Sinking*,
12 November 1944 –
Chapter 41[14]**

Tromsøysundet

Håkøya **1**

Tromsø

Grindøya

Norwegian Sea

1 Location where *Tirpitz* was lying when she
was bombed by the RAF and sunk on
12 November (see also **13** in Map 1).

Iceland

2

1

Note: check angles given in brief for course bearings. Seem a little different to the original.

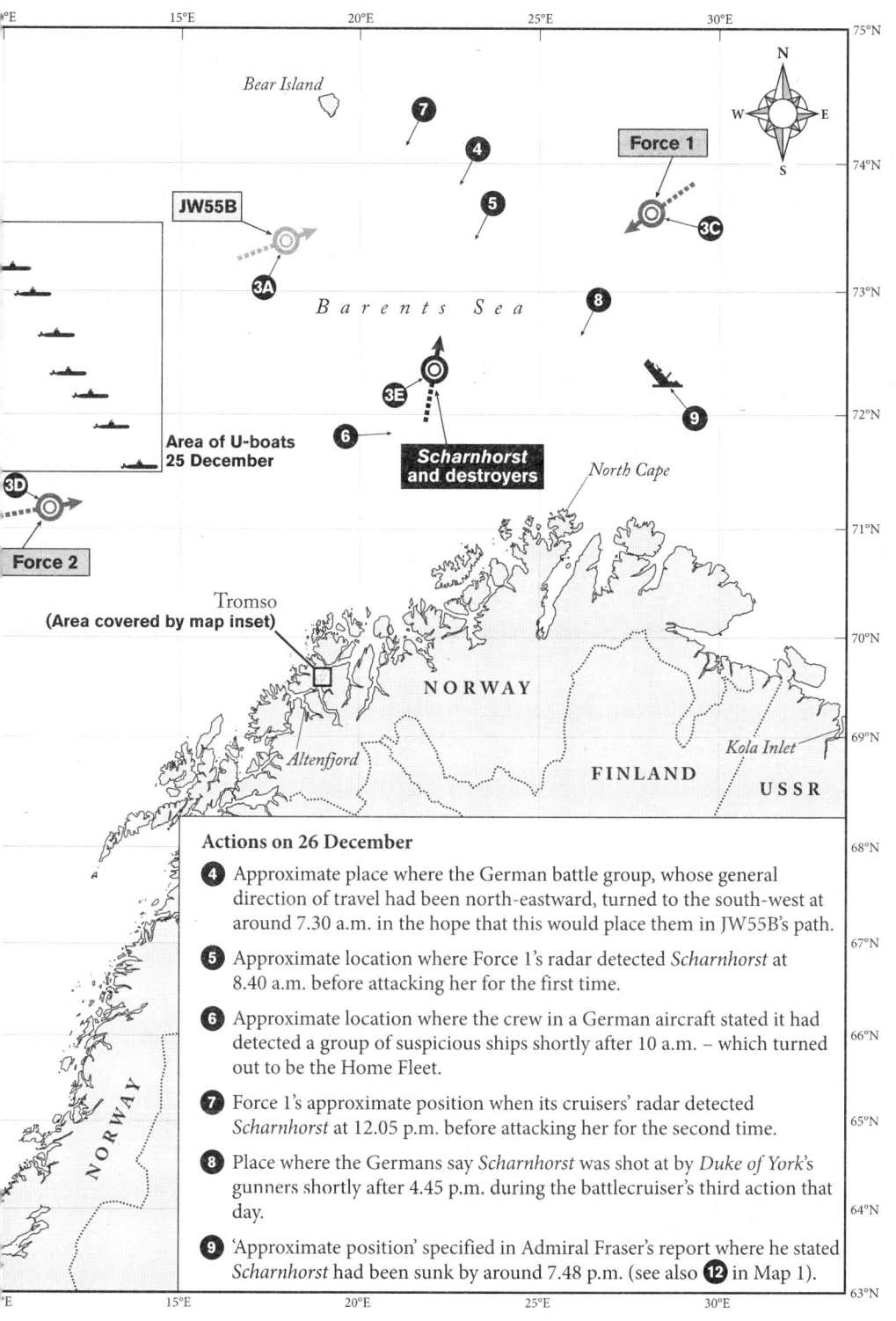

N
W ● E
S

Bear Island

7

4

5

Force 1

JW55B

3A

3C

B a r e n t s   S e a

8

3E

9

6

Scharnhorst and destroyers

North Cape

Area of U-boats 25 December

3D

Force 2

Tromso
(Area covered by map inset)

N O R W A Y

Altenfjord

Kola Inlet

FINLAND   **U S S R**

Actions on 26 December

4 Approximate place where the German battle group, whose general direction of travel had been north-eastward, turned to the south-west at around 7.30 a.m. in the hope that this would place them in JW55B's path.

5 Approximate location where Force 1's radar detected *Scharnhorst* at 8.40 a.m. before attacking her for the first time.

6 Approximate location where the crew in a German aircraft stated it had detected a group of suspicious ships shortly after 10 a.m. – which turned out to be the Home Fleet.

7 Force 1's approximate position when its cruisers' radar detected *Scharnhorst* at 12.05 p.m. before attacking her for the second time.

8 Place where the Germans say *Scharnhorst* was shot at by *Duke of York*'s gunners shortly after 4.45 p.m. during the battlecruiser's third action that day.

9 'Approximate position' specified in Admiral Fraser's report where he stated *Scharnhorst* had been sunk by around 7.48 p.m. (see also **12** in Map 1).

Map 19

First Two Actions During the Battle of North Cape, 26 December 1943 – Chapter 37

All positions on this map are relative to the position of Force 1 ca. 8.40 a.m. 26 December 1943 (see **1A** below) – which according to Vice Admiral Burnett was around 73° 35' N 23° 21' E (see **5** in Map 18)[15]

1st Action on 26 December

1A, **1B** and **1C** Relative positions of Admiral Burnett's Force 1, *Scharnhorst* and JW55B respectively at 8.40 a.m. when, as *Belfast* approached JW55B, the British cruiser's radar detected *Scharnhorst*.

2A Location of Force 1 at 9.29 a.m. when one of its cruisers fired at *Scharnhorst*, which was at **2B**.

2nd Action on 26 December

3A Location of Force 1 at 12.05 p.m. when *Belfast*'s radar detected *Scharnhorst*, which was at **3B**.

4A Location of Force 1 shortly before 12.30 p.m. when its cruisers fired at *Scharnhorst*, which was at **4B**.

---   *Scharnhorst*'s direction of travel

———   *Scharnhorst*'s course

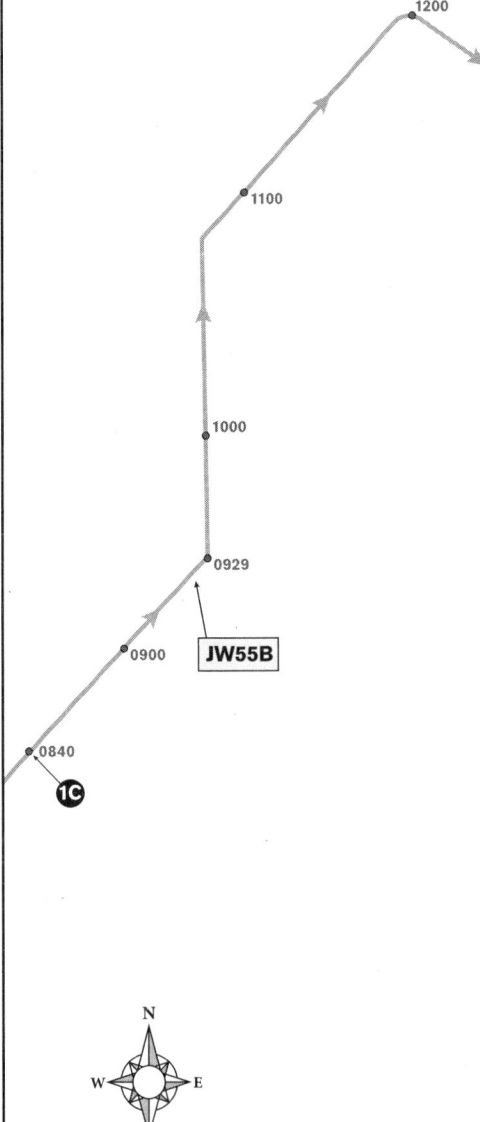

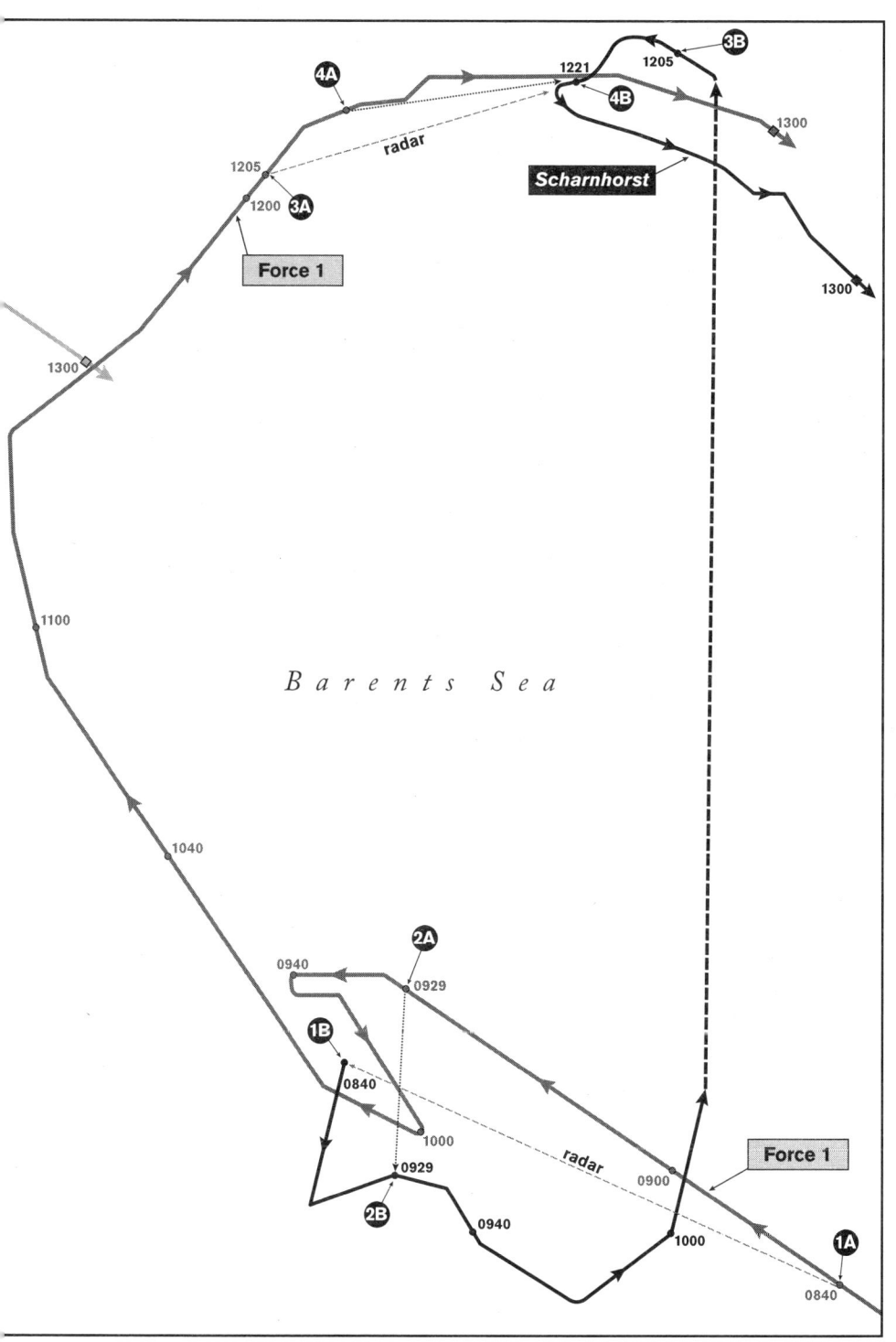

Force 1

3A
4A
1205
1200
1221
1205
3B
4B
Scharnhorst
1300
radar
1300

1300

1100

B a r e n t s   S e a

1040

2A
0940
0929
1B
0840
1000
0929
2B
0940
1000

radar
0900
Force 1
1A
0840

Map 20

Sinking of *Scharnhorst*, 26 December 1943 – Chapter 38

Locations in this map are relative to approximate position where *Scharnhorst* was sunk (see ⑪ in this map, and ⑨ in Map 18)

①A and **①B** Relative positions of 2nd Sub-Division of destroyers (*Scorpion* and *Stord*), and *Scharnhorst* respectively when these destroyers fired torpedoes at *Scharnhorst* at around 6.49–6.50 p.m.

②A and **②B** Relative positions of 1st Sub-Division destroyers (*Savage* and *Saumarez*), and *Scharnhorst* respectively when these destroyers fired torpedoes at *Scharnhorst*, at around 6.55–6.56 p.m.

③A and **③B** Relative positions of battleship *Duke of York* and cruiser *Jamaica*, and *Scharnhorst* respectively when the two British ships fired at the German battlecruiser at 7.01 p.m.

④A (Position to north of map area indicated) and **④B** Relative positions of *Belfast* and *Scharnhorst* respectively when the British cruiser fired at *Scharnhorst* at 7.15 p.m.

⑤ Approximate place where *Jamaica* branched off from *Duke of York* at 7.19 p.m. to put in the torpedo attack described beside **⑥A** below.

⑥A and **⑥B** Relative positions of *Jamaica* and *Scharnhorst* respectively when the British cruiser at 7.25 p.m. fired torpedoes at the battlecruiser.

⑦A and **⑦B** Relative positions of *Belfast* and *Scharnhorst* respectively when at 7.27 p.m. the British cruiser fired torpedoes at the battlecruiser.

⑧A and **⑧B** Relative positions of *Opportune* and *Virago*, and *Scharnhorst* respectively when between 7.31 and 7.34 p.m. the two British destroyers fired torpedoes at the battlecruiser.

⑨A and **⑨B** Relative positions of *Musketeer* and *Scharnhorst* respectively when at 7.33 p.m. the British destroyer fired torpedoes at the battlecruiser.

1740

Scharnhorst

1830

1840

Savage and Saumarez

Duke of York and Jamaica

1900

③A

1850

1820

Scorpion and Stord

0		2 miles
0		2 km

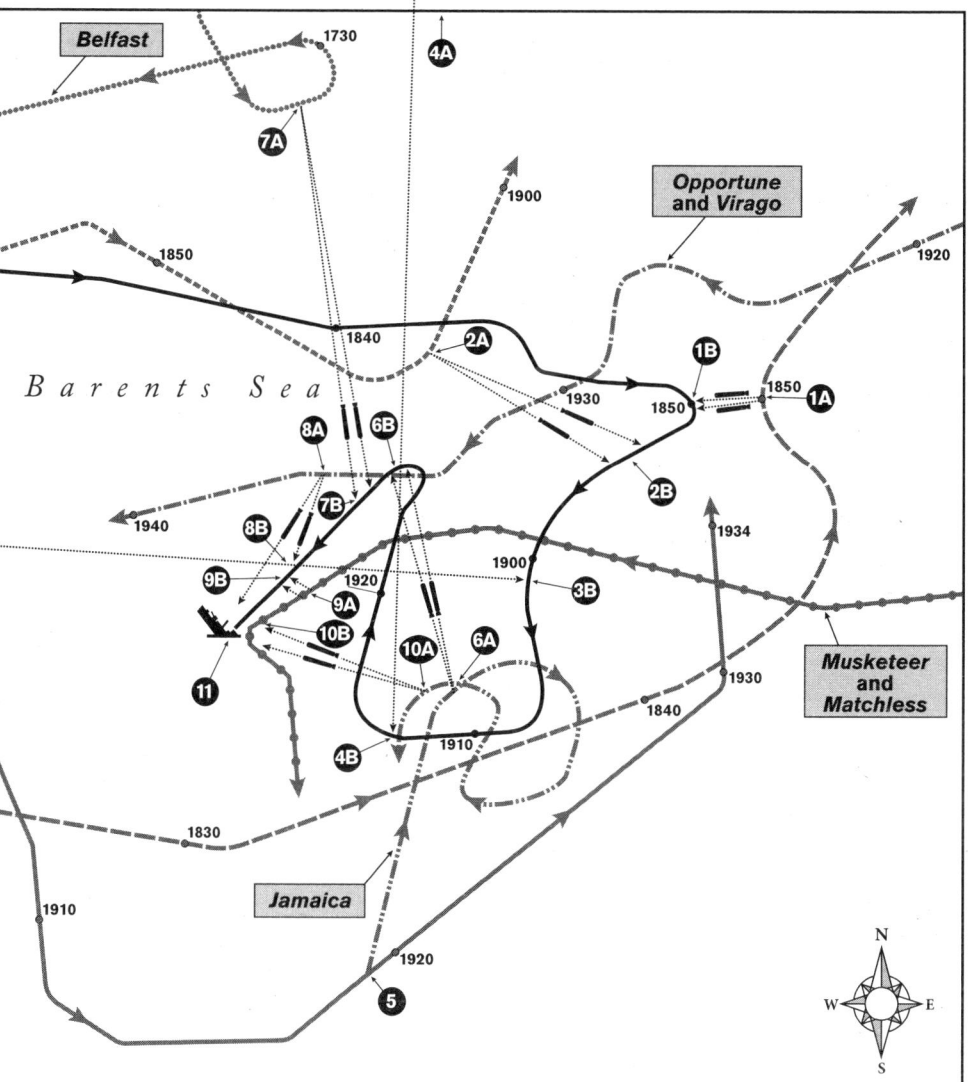

Belfast

1730

4A

7A

Opportune
and Virago

1900

Barents Sea

1850

1840

2A

1B

1850

1A

1930

1850

8A

6B

2B

1940

7B

1934

8B

9B

1900

3B

1920

9A

10B

Musketeer
and
Matchless

10A

6A

11

1930

4B

1910

1840

1830

Jamaica

1910

1920

5

N

W   E

S

10A and 10B Relative positions of *Jamaica* and *Scharnhorst* respectively when at 7.37 p.m.
the British cruiser fired torpedoes at the battlecruiser.

11 Approximate location relative to the action outlined above where *Scharnhorst* sank.

------- *Savage's* and *Saumarez's* joint course   ············· *Belfast's* course

━ ━ ━ *Scorpion's* and *Stord's* joint course   ━ ·· ━ *Opportune's* and *Virago's* course

━ ·· ━ ·· ━ *Jamaica's* course after split from   ●━●━● *Musketeer's* and *Matchless'* course
Duke of York at key number 5

Map 21

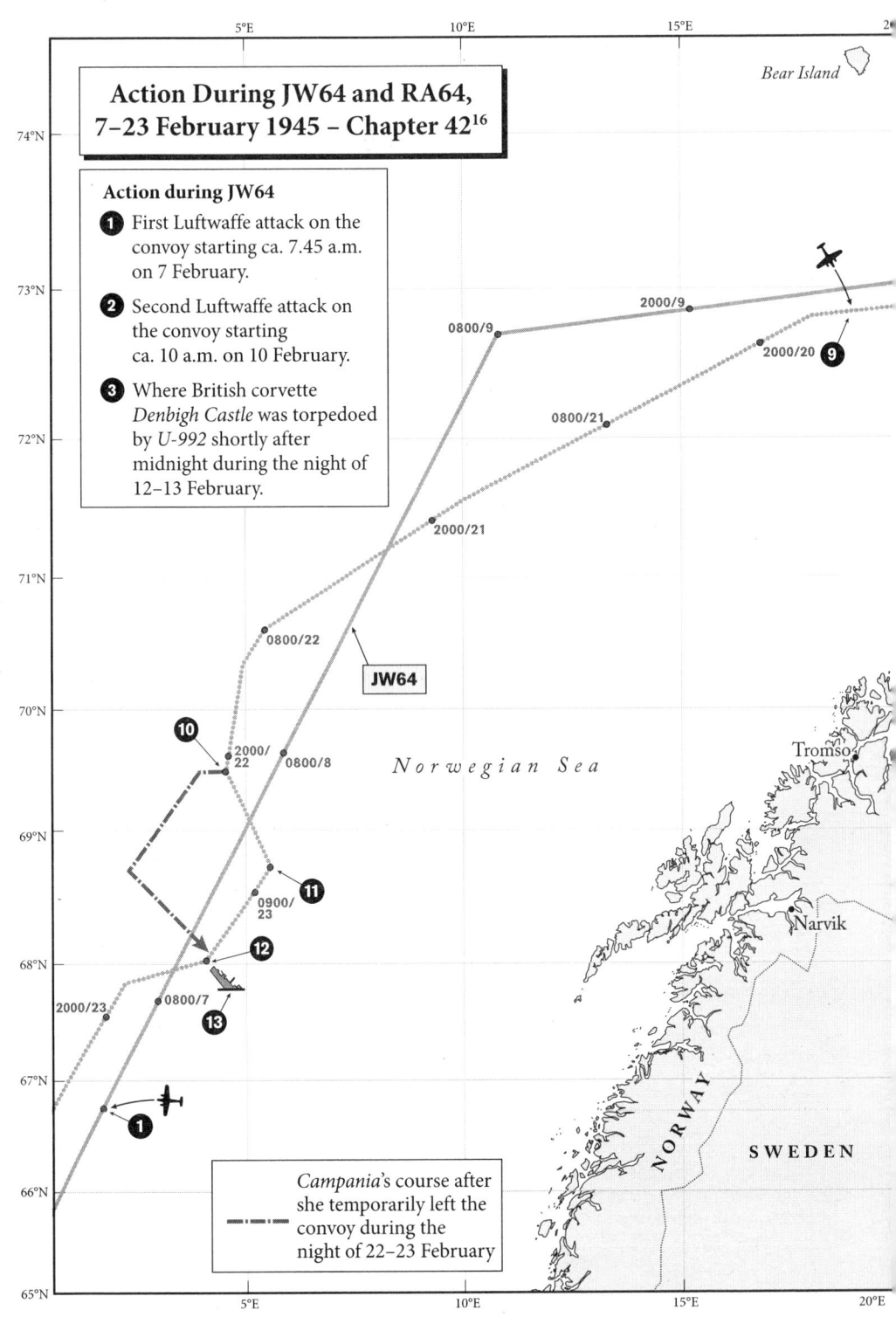

Action During JW64 and RA64, 7–23 February 1945 – Chapter 42[16]

Action during JW64

1 First Luftwaffe attack on the convoy starting ca. 7.45 a.m. on 7 February.

2 Second Luftwaffe attack on the convoy starting ca. 10 a.m. on 10 February.

3 Where British corvette *Denbigh Castle* was torpedoed by *U-992* shortly after midnight during the night of 12–13 February.

Bear Island

2000/9
0800/9
2000/20 **9**
0800/21
2000/21
0800/22

JW64

Norwegian Sea

Tromso

10
2000/22
0800/8

0900/23
11

12
2000/23
0800/7
13

Narvik

1

Campania's course after she temporarily left the convoy during the night of 22–23 February

NORWAY

SWEDEN

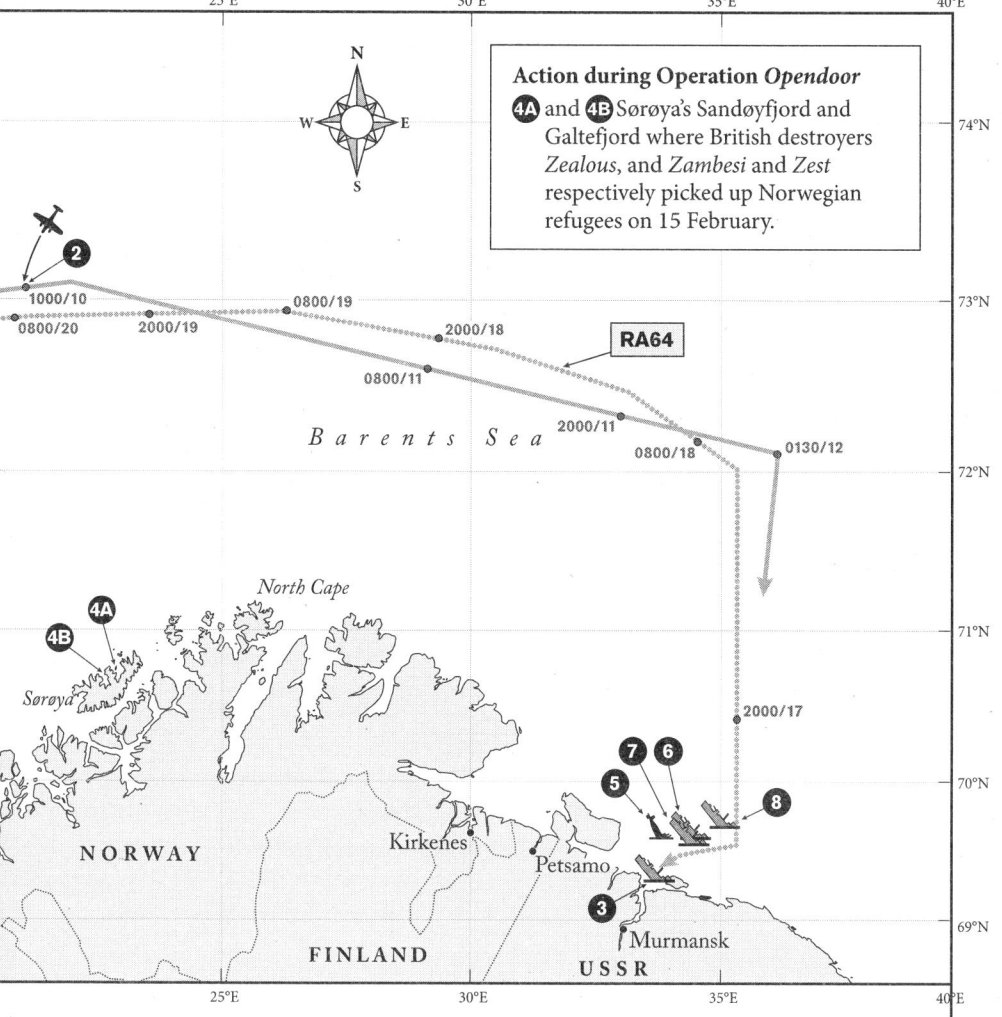

Action during Operation *Opendoor*

4A and **4B** Sørøya's Sandøyfjord and Galtefjord where British destroyers *Zealous*, and *Zambesi* and *Zest* respectively picked up Norwegian refugees on 15 February.

2

1000/10
0800/20   0800/19   2000/19   2000/18   **RA64**
            2000/19   0800/11
                                    2000/11   0130/12
B a r e n t s   S e a   0800/18

North Cape   2000/17

4A
4B
Sørøya

NORWAY   Kirkenes   **7** **6**
                            5   **8**
            Petsamo
                        3
FINLAND   Murmansk
            U S S R

Action on 17 February during lead up to RA64

5 Where *U-425* was sunk shortly after 1.30 a.m.

6 Location where British sloop *Lark* was torpedoed by *U-968* ca. 10.25 a.m.

7 Site where SS *Thomas Scott* was torpedoed by *U-968* ca. midday.

8 Place where British corvette *Bluebell* sank after being torpedoed by *U-711* shortly before 3.30 p.m.

Action during RA64

9 Location of 20 February attack ca. 10 a.m. by the Luftwaffe

10 Place where there was a parting of ways ca. 9 p.m. 22 February: escort carrier *Campania* went to the west, while the convoy proceeded south-eastward.

11 Location of convoy's change of direction ca. 4 a.m. 23 February.

12 Location of convoy's change of direction ca. 11 a.m. 23 February.

13 Where the Luftwaffe torpedoed SS *Henry Bacon* ca. 2.20 p.m. 23 February, which subsequently sank.

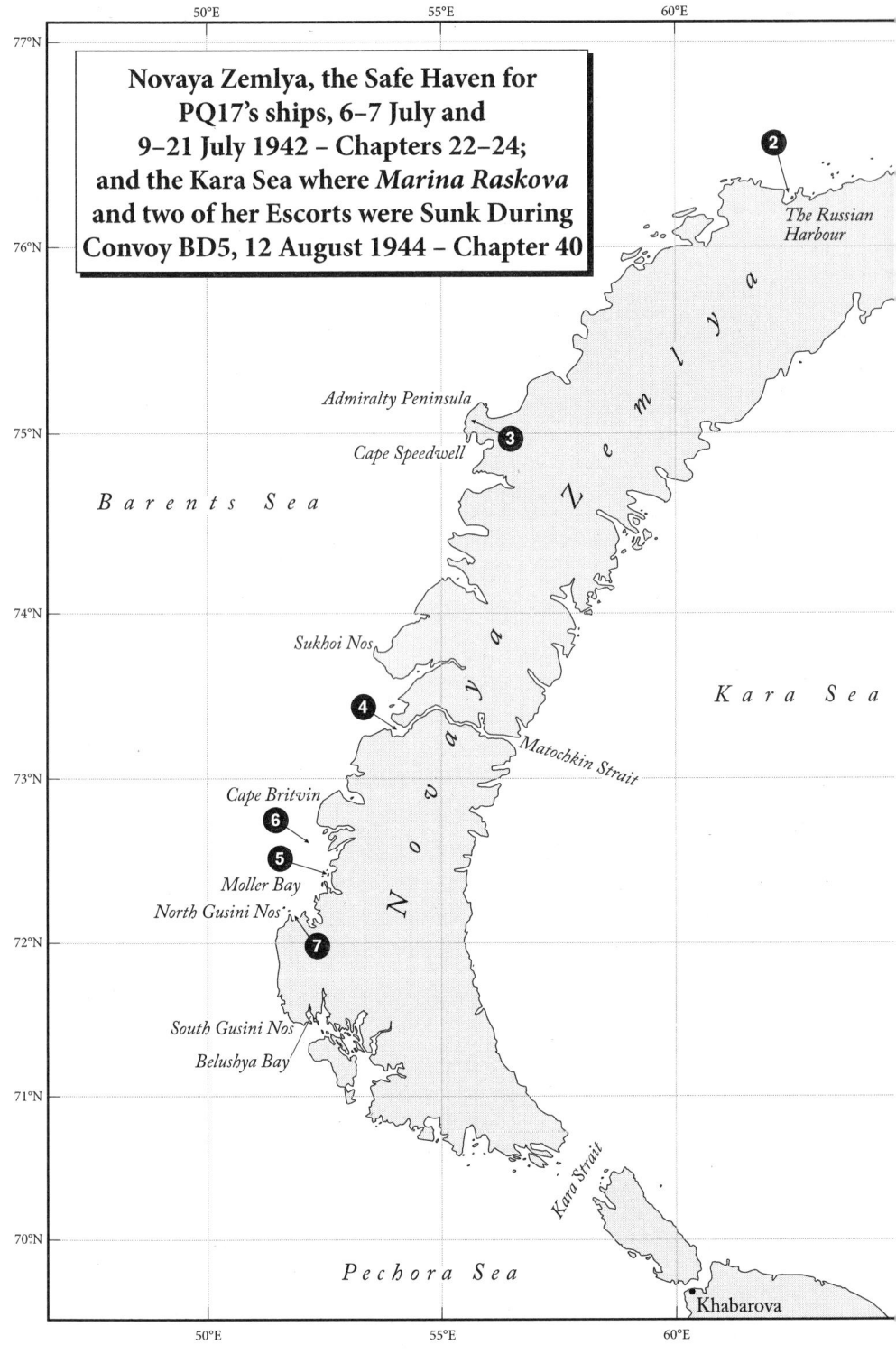

Map 22

**Novaya Zemlya, the Safe Haven for
PQ17's ships, 6–7 July and
9–21 July 1942 – Chapters 22–24;
and the Kara Sea where *Marina Raskova*
and two of her Escorts were Sunk During
Convoy BD5, 12 August 1944 – Chapter 40**

77°N
76°N
75°N
74°N
73°N
72°N
71°N
70°N

50°E
55°E
60°E

*The Russian
Harbour*

Admiralty Peninsula

Cape Speedwell

B a r e n t s   S e a

Sukhoi Nos

K a r a   S e a

Matochkin Strait

Cape Britvin

Moller Bay

North Gusini Nos

South Gusini Nos

Belushya Bay

Kara Strait

P e c h o r a   S e a

Khabarova

N o v a y a   Z e m l y a

1596–7

1 Site of Het Behouden Huys (the so-called Saved House) mentioned in Chapter 30 where 16th-century Dutch explorer Willem Barentsz and his shipmates lived from August 1596 until June 1597 after their ship became stuck in the ice near the northern end of Novaya Zemlya's east coast.

1942

2 The Russian Harbour, the first port of call for the Soviet ship *Azerbaijan* after the 4 July scattering of PQ17 described in Chapters 17–18.

3 Admiralty Peninsula, the most popular landfall target for those PQ17 ship captains who, after the convoy was scattered, sought a haven on Novaya Zemlya's coast.

4 Matochkin Strait, the Novaya Zemlya haven where many of PQ17's ships' captains sought refuge after the convoy was scattered.

5 Moller Bay's Karmakulski island, in the shadow of which the master of CAM ship *Empire Tide* sought refuge for his vessel and crew following the scattering of PQ17.

6 The approximate place where PQ17 British merchant ship *Hartlebury* was torpedoed by a U-boat during the early evening of 7 July around 17 miles south-west of Britvin Beacon (near Cape Britvin).

7 Approximate site where PQ17's SS *Winston Salem* ran aground on the shoal to the east of North Gusini Nos. She remained there from 8 until 22 July.

1944

8 Location where SS *Marina Raskova* was torpedoed from *U-365* on 12 August.

Map 23

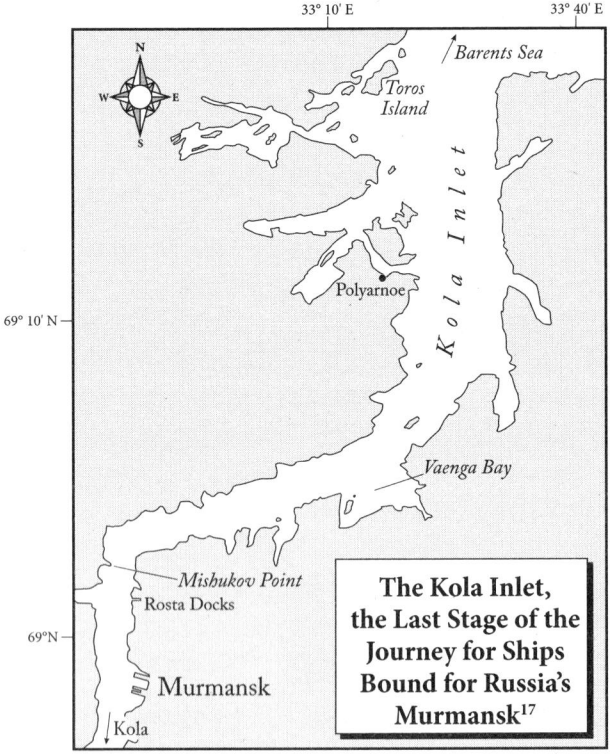

Barents Sea

Toros Island

K o l a   I n l e t

Polyarnoe

Vaenga Bay

Mishukov Point
Rosta Docks

The Kola Inlet, the Last Stage of the Journey for Ships Bound for Russia's Murmansk[17]

Murmansk

Kola

33° 10' E   33° 40' E

69° 10' N

69°N

Map 24

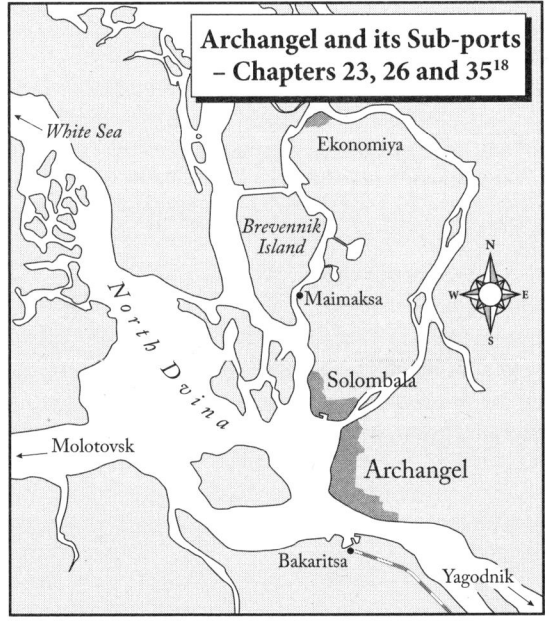

Archangel and its Sub-ports – Chapters 23, 26 and 35[18]

White Sea

Ekonomiya

Brevennik Island

•Maimaksa

N o r t h   D v i n a

Solombala

Molotovsk

Archangel

Bakaritsa   Yagodnik

Glossary

The following words and expressions used in this book are intended to have the following meanings:

GERMAN

Admiral Nordmeer: Admiral Northern Waters, who at times was in charge of U-boat operations in the Arctic.

Befehlshaber der Kampfgruppe: German Commander of Battlegroup.

Befehlshaber der Kreuzer (abbreviated form BdK): German Commander of Cruisers.

Befehlshaber der Schlachtschiffe (abbreviated form BdS): German Commander of Battleships.

Flottenchef: German Fleet Commander.

Führer der Unterseeboote Norwegen: Commander of U-boats Norway.

Grossadmiral: Commander-in-Chief of the German Navy.

Kampfgeschwader (abbreviated form KG): Literally a Luftwaffe battle squadron, but a less confusing explanation in English given that a Staffel is the German equivalent of a British squadron, and a Kampfgeschwader usually contained three wings each consisting of 3 squadrons i.e. 9 squadrons in total, would be a battlegroup.

Kriegsmarine: German Navy during the war.

Kriegstagebuch (abbreviated form KTB): War diary.

Marinegruppenkommando Nord: Naval Group Command North, the headquarters under the Commander-in-Chief of the German Navy, responsible for the Arctic.

Seekriegsleitung (abbreviated form Skl): German Naval Staff, the German equivalent of the British Admiralty. Its Teil A KTB quoted in this book is for the Skl's Operations Division.

ENGLISH AND OTHER

Able-Bodied Seaman (abbreviated form AB): On a merchant ship, an experienced seaman.

Asdic: British sonar equipment that detected U-boats by sending out sound waves. The waves bounced back if they hit a solid object. It took its name from the Anti-Submarine Detection Investigation Committee.

Beam: Width of a vessel at the widest point. A reference to an incident 'on a ship's beam' refers to it taking place beside the ship's widest point. A reference to a ship being on her beam ends means the ship has keeled over so far she is about to capsize.

Bearing: The clockwise angle between north and the object (also referred to sometimes as the absolute bearing to distinguish it from the relative bearing which means the clockwise angle between a vessel's forward direction and the object).

Calibre: The calibre of the smaller guns, such as machine guns fired from merchant ships, refers to the diameter of the projectile fired by the gun.

CAM ship: Catapult aircraft merchant ship.

Captain (D): Captain of destroyers, referring to the senior officer in a destroyer flotilla.

Director Control Tower in a warship is where one finds the telescopes that are connected with computers that calculate a target's bearing and elevation. The tower was normally high up on the ship's superstructure.

Donkeyman: Seaman on a merchant ship responsible for the winch engine used to load and unload cargo.

DDIC: Admiralty's Deputy Director Intelligence Centre (during July 1942 it was Rear Admiral Jock Clayton – who played a significant supporting role concerning PQ17, referred to in Chapter 17).

Displacement: In this book references to a warship's displacement are to her standard displacement, which in broad terms means the weight of the water displaced by the ship when placed in the water fully equipped but with no fuel on board. This in its turn an indication of the ship's weight.

Fireman: Sailor who tends the fire needed for the running of a merchant ship's boiler (in a Royal Navy vessel he would be called a stoker).

Fog Buoy: A buoy towed by a merchant ship when visibility is low to enable the crew in the ship behind her in a formation to know her location.

Greaser: Sailor on a merchant ship who lubricates the engines.

Hawser: Thick rope suitable for towing a ship.

HF/DF: High frequency direction finding (nicknamed huff-duff), a form of radio direction finding used by the Allies, including by their crews in warships, to work out the bearing of radio signals transmitted from German vessels at sea. It was particularly useful when it came to tracking down where U boats were located.

Hog Islander: A standard construction ship built in the Hog Island, Pennsylvania shipyards during and just after World War 1.

Jolly boat: a small utility boat on board a ship used for various tasks (it is usually smaller than a standard lifeboat which is typically larger so when a ship is sinking as many of her crew as possible can be saved).

Glossary

Keelson: structural support inside a boat running on top of the boat's keel.

Lend-lease: The arrangement used by Roosevelt to enable American supplies to be handed over to allies such as the Soviet Union without their having to pay immediately, or in some cases ever, for various reasons. For example either because the items were to be given back to America after the war if not destroyed during the fighting, or because America was to be paid in kind, or because the items were used by America's allies in the common cause.

Monkey Island: On a merchant ship refers to the open deck above her navigating bridge, which serves as a lookout point.

Open A arcs: when used with reference to main armament guns means positioning the ship so that the main armament can be fired at the target without being obstructed by the ship's own structure.

ORP: Okręt Rzeczypospolitej Polskiej (Republic of Poland's ship).

Poop: Deck at the back of a ship (strictly a raised deck).

Port: The left side of a ship or convoy.

SBNO North Russia and SBNO Archangel: Senior British Naval Officer North Russia and Senior British Naval Officer Archangel respectively.

Squid: An anti-submarine weapon that consisted of three mortars that could simultaneously fire three depth charges, sometimes referred to as 'a pattern of Squid', ahead of the ship in which it was mounted.

Starboard: The right side of a ship or convoy.

Thwart: A piece of wood running between the two sides of an open boat acting as a seat and a structural support.

Tons: In this book references to tons are to long tons (2,240 pounds), the measure most commonly used in Britain, unless short tons (2,000 pounds), the measure most commonly used in America, are specifically mentioned.

Tonnage: A merchant ship's gross register tonnage, which is often the measure referred to when expressing World War 2 merchant ships' relative sizes, is the volume of the inside of the ship expressed in cubic feet, including areas that cannot carry cargo such as the engine room, divided by 100 cubic feet. Deadweight tonnage by way of contrast is the ship's cargo, fuel, provisions and people carrying capacity expressed in tons.

Ultra: A British radio signal usually sent from the Admiralty on a one-time pad (a pre-arranged encoding setting that was only used once, and was as a result unbreakable in real time by the Germans even when they broke the regular naval codes) containing information derived from decrypts of German radio messages encoded prior to transmission using an Enigma machine. Ultras were sent to British admirals at sea so that they had the most up to date naval intelligence possessed by the Admiralty in London.

Appendices

The Appendices on the following pages specify convoy formations in order of appearance in the book rather than in date order.

The following abbreviations which appear under the names of the ships in the convoy formations have the following meanings:

Br means British
Du means Dutch
Pan means sailing under the Panamanian flag
R means Russian
US means American

Appendix A

PQ17's Formation[1]

Laid out below is PQ17's formation, excluding two of the rescue ships, during the night of 1–2 July 1942 – prior to the departure of the oiler *Gray Ranger*, and prior to any attacks.

LEFT SIDE

14	13	12	11
William Hooper	*Ironclad*	*Hoosier*	*Paulus Potter*
Br	US	US	Du
24	23	22	21
Troubadour	*Bolton Castle*	*El Capitan*	*Washington*
Pan	Br	Pan	US
34	33	32	31
Donbass.	*Olopana*	*Pan Kraft*	*Hartlebury*
R	US	US	Br
44	43	42	41
Silver Sword	*Bellingham*	*Navarino*	*Pan Atlantic*
US	US	Br	US
54	53	52	51
Winston Salem	*Alcoa Ranger*	*Gray Ranger*	*River Afton*
US	US	Oiler	Br

BACK →

			FRONT
64	63	62	61
Azerbaijan	*Empire Tide*	*Earlston*	*Peter Kerr*
R	CAM ship	Br	US
	Br		
74	73	72	71
Aldersdale	*Ocean Freedom*	*Benjamin*	*Empire Byron*
Oiler	Br	*Harrison*	Br
		US	
84	83	82	81
John Witherspoon	*Honomu*	*Fairfield City*	*Christopher*
US	US	US	*Newport*
			US
94	93	92	91
Zamalek	*Daniel Morgan*	*Carlton*	*Samuel Chase*
Rescue ship	US	US	US

RIGHT SIDE

Appendix B

PQ16's Formation[1]

Laid out below is PQ16's formation prior to the first attacks on 25 May 1942 by the Luftwaffe, according to documents in London's National Archives.

LEFT SIDE

14 Carlton US	13 Steel Worker US	12 Alcoa Banner US	11 Empire Lawrence CAM ship Br
24 John Randolph US	23 ?*	22 Richard H Lee US	21 Empire Baffin Br
34 Hybert US	33 West Nilus US	32 City of Omaha US	31 Lowther Castle US
44 Empire Purcell Br	43 Michigan Pan	42 Nemaha US	41 Empire Selwyn Br
54 American Press US	53 Alynbank AA ship	52 Heffron US	51 Ocean Voice Br
64 ?*	63 Arcos Pan	62 City of Joliet US	61 Atlantic Br
74 Syros US	73 Alamar US	72 Minotaur US	71 Empire Elgar Br
84 Mormacsul US	83 Starii Bolshevik R	82 Shchors R	81 Chernyshevski R
94 American Robin US	93 Exterminator Pan	92 Pieter de Hoogh Du	91 Revolutioner R

BACK (left) → FRONT (right)

RIGHT SIDE

* The documents I found in the National Archives London which specify the PQ16 formation include one ship in position 23 that could not participate, and exclude *Mauna Key* and *Massmar* although the latter two ships, as specified in other documents, did travel to Russia as part of PQ16.[2] It is possible they were placed in positions 23 and 64 (the latter position had no ship allocated to it in the formation documents I saw in the National Archives London).

Appendix C

PQ18's Formation[1]

Laid out on p.659 is PQ18's formation prior to the first attacks on 13 September 1942 by U-boats and the Luftwaffe, according to documents in London's National Archives.

LEFT SIDE

15 *Copeland* Rescue ship US	14 *Andre Marti* US	13 *McCormick* US	12 *Kentucky* US	11 *Empire Baffin* Br
	24 *Ulster Queen* AA Ship	23 *White Clover* US	22 *Petrovsky* R	21 *Komiles* R
	34 *Hollywood* US	33 *Exford* US	32 *St Olaf* US	31 *Empire Snow* Br
45 *Atheltemplar* Br	44 *Meanticut* US	43 *Esek Hopkins* US	42 *Patrick Henry* US	41 *Empire Beaumont* Br
	54 *Black Ranger* Oiler	53 *Empire Morn* CAM ship Br	52 *Schole* US	51 *Empire Tristram* Br
65 *Gray Ranger* Oiler	64 *Schoharie* US	63 *Campfire* US	62 *Lafayette* US	61 *Temple Arch* Br
75 *Tbilisi* R	74 *Goolistan* Br	73 *John Penn* US	72 *Nathanael Greene* US	71 *Ocean Faith* Br
	84 *Alynbank* AA ship	83 *William Moultrie* US	82 *Virginia Dare* US	81 *Dany Bryn* Br
	94 *Africander* Pan	93 *Mary Luckenbach* US	92 *Wacosta* US	91 *Empire Stevenson* Br
105 *Oliver Ellsworth* US	104 *Sukhona* R	103 *Stalingrad* R	102 *Macbeth* Pan	101 *Oregonian* US

BACK ← → FRONT

RIGHT SIDE

Abbreviations

In the Notes and elsewhere in this book I have wherever possible used abbreviations for frequently mentioned archives and sources. The names of the lists of these abbreviations are laid out below. The lists can be found in the following pages.

Lists of Abbreviations

1. Abbreviated Archive and Collection Names:
   The first mention of each of these names in the notes for each chapter is in bold type.

2. Abbreviated Sources (excluding German war diaries and American merchant vessel reports):
   The first mention of each of these names in the notes for each chapter is in capital letters.

3. Abbreviated Names of German War Diaries and American Merchant Vessel Reports:
   The first mention of each of these names in the notes for each chapter is in underlined capital letters.

1. Abbreviated Archive and Collection Names

In the Notes and elsewhere in this book the following abbreviated archive and collection names shall have the following meanings:

'**Acta Norvegica Arkiv**': Privately run collection of German and English World War 2 documents that relate to Norway. Kjetil Korsnes, Associate Professor at Nord University, Bodø, one of its backers, sent the relevant documents to me. Its other founder is Olve Dybvig.

'**AFHRA**': Air Force Historical Research Agency archive stored at the Maxwell Air Force Base in Montgomery, Alabama. It was brought to my attention by Adam Claasen, *Hitler's Northern War: The Luftwaffe's Ill-Fated Campaign, 1940–1945*.

'**Alan Blyth Collection**': Documents and testimony, mostly relating to PQ13, collected by Alan Blyth, a nephew of *Induna*'s radio officer Norman Blyth who died when the ship was sunk during PQ13 (see Chapter 6).

'**Arctic Convoy Museum**': Museum near Loch Ewe, one of the main Arctic convoy assembly points during World War 2. It houses a collection of documents relating to the Arctic convoys.

'**Churchill Archives Centre**': Archive at Cambridge University's Churchill College in Cambridge.

'**David Irving's Papers**': The documents author David Irving used to write his controversial book *The Destruction of Convoy PQ17*; they were made available by Acta Novegica Arkiv (see above), which in its turn sourced them from the library at the Norwegian Universitet i Tromsø.

'**GAAO**': Gosudarstvennyi Arkiv Arkhangel'skoi Oblasti (Archangel State Archive). Relevant documents from this Archive were brought to my attention by Ivan Katyshev from Archangel's Northern Maritime Museum.

'**GAOPDiFAO**': Gosudarstvennyi Arkiv Obshchestvenno-Politicheskikh Dvishenii Formirovanii Arkhagel'skoi Oblasti (Archangel State Social Political Archive). Relevant documents from this Archive were brought to my attention by Ivan Katyshev from Archangel's Northern Maritime Museum.

'**IWM Documents**': Imperial War Museum, London archive for documents.

'**IWM Sound**': Imperial War Museum, London archive for recorded verbal interviews.

'**Luftflotte 5's Daily Reports**': Täglicher Morgen und Abendmeldungen des Luftflottenkommandos 5, in the Deutsche-Russisches Projekt zur Digitalisierung Deutscher Dokumente in Archiven der Russischen Föderation site on the internet brought to my attention by aircraft expert and historian Peter Taghon.

'**Marine Forum Archive**': Archive maintained by the journal *Marine Forum* based in Wilhelmshaven, Germany.

'**Militärarchiv Freiburg**': The section of the German Bundesarchiv in Freiburg, Germany where readers can find documents relating to the German armed forces.

Abbreviations

'**NA London**': National Archives near Kew Gardens, London, England, formerly known as the Public Record Office, where most declassified official British documents relating to historical subjects can be found.

'**NA Maryland**': National Archives at College Park, Maryland, America which is near the border separating Maryland and Washington D.C.

'**National Maritime Museum**': Archive at the Caird Library, in the National Maritime Museum, London.

'**NA Maryland Microfilms**': Microfilms held by the National Archives Washington, which has given them numbers that follow the prefix T-1022. Most quoted in this book have been sent to me by Acta Norvegica Arkiv (see above).

'**NA Washington**': National Archives in Washington D.C.

'**NHB**': Naval Historical Branch, Portsmouth, England, whose documents were brought to my attention by its Senior Researcher, Aedan Butler.

'**Sikorski Museum**': Archive at the Polish Institute and Sikorski Museum, London.

'**U-boot Museum**': Deutsches U-Boot Museum in Cuxhaven-Altenbruch, Germany.

2. Abbreviated Sources (excluding German War Diaries and American Merchant Vessel Reports)

In the Notes and elsewhere in this book the following sources shall have the following meanings:

'**Blair's Book**': Clay Blair, *Hitler's U-Boat War*, in two volumes.

'**British Arctic Convoys History**': *The Royal Navy and the Arctic Convoys*, the published version of the Naval Staff History, *Arctic Convoys, 1941–45, Battle Summary No. 22*, NA London ADM 234/369.

'**British Intelligence Official History**': F. H. Hinsley with E. E. Thomas, C. F. G. Ransom, and R. C. Knight, *British Intelligence In The Second World War*, in several volumes.

'**British Naval Aviation History**': The Naval Staff History, *The Development of British Naval Aviation 1919–1945*, vol. II, in NA London ADM 234/384.

'**British War At Sea Official History**': Captain. S. W. Roskill, *The War At Sea 1939–1945*, in several volumes.

'**Carraway's Diary**': Howard Carraway's diary, written as if it was a very long letter to his wife, Avis, to tell her about his experiences in the merchant ship SS *Troubadour* – courtesy of his son Mac Carraway and daughters Nancy Carraway Leonard and Cathleen C. Farmer, and Florida State University's Institute on World War II & Human Experience.

'**Churchill's Book vol. 3**': Winston Churchill, *The Second World War, vol. III, The Grand Alliance*.

'**Churchill's Book vol. 4**': Winston Churchill, *The Second World War, vol. IV, The Hinge Of Fate*.

'**Churchill's Book vol. 5**': Winston Churchill, The Second World War, *vol. V, Closing The Ring*.

'**Churchill and Roosevelt Correspondence Book**': Warren F. Kimball, *Churchill & Roosevelt: The Complete Correspondence vol. 1 Alliance Emerging*.

'**Luftflotte 5's War Diary**': The document entitled 'German Air Attacks On PQ Convoys: Extracts from war diaries of Luftflotte 5': Translation number VII/60: Translations Second World War Vol. III, NA London AIR 20/7702, brought to my attention by Stuart Hadaway at the Air Historical Branch/British Ministry of Defence.

'**Reynolds and Pechatnov**': David Reynolds and Vladimir Pechatnov, with assistance of Iskander Magadeyev and Olga Kucherenko, *Kremlin Letters: Stalin's Wartime Correspondence with Churchill and Roosevelt*.

'**Rohwer's Hummelchen's and Weis's Chronology**': Jürgen Rohwer, Gerhard Hummelchen and Thomas Weis, *Chronology Of The War At Sea 1939–1945*.

'**Tirpitz Official History**': History of Tirpitz in 2 volumes entitled 'TIRPITZ An account of the various attacks carried out by the British Armed Forces and their effect upon the German Battleship' completed in 1948, NA London ADM 234/349 AND 350.

'Tovey's Despatch': Tovey's account 'Convoys To North Russia, 1942' in the 17 October 1950 Supplement to the 13 October 1950 edition of *The London Gazette*, NA London ADM 1/20021.

'Woodman's Book': Richard Woodman, *The Arctic Convoys 1941–1945*, the classic book on these convoys.

3. Abbreviated Names of German War Diaries and American Merchant Vessel Reports

GERMAN WAR DIARIES

The following underlined German war diaries, which are referred to in the Notes and elsewhere in this book, have been sourced from the archives specified below beside them; the archives so specified are either the Militärarchiv Freiburg, or Acta Norvegica Arkiv (see Abbreviated Archive and Collection Names list). In the case of microfilm from the National Archives Washington, my source has been Acta Norvegica Arkiv.

NOTE 'KTB' is the abbreviated form of Kriegstagebuch ('war diary' in German).

KTB der 4 Zerstörerflottille
16–27 December 1943, Militärarchiv Freiburg RM 58/18

KTB des Admiral Nordmeer
1 March to 21 April 1942: Militärarchiv Freiburg RM 45 III/276
22 April to 30 June 1942: Miltärarchiv Freiburg RM 45 III/277
1 September 1942 to 1 January 1943, Militärarchiv Freiburg RM 45 III/279
1 to 15 March 1943, Militärarchiv Freiburg RM 45 III/280
16 to 31 December 1943, Militärarchiv Freiburg RM 45 III/281

KTB des Befehlshabers der Kreuzer
30 December 1942 to 4 January 1943 – über Regensbogen, Militärarchiv Freiburg RM 7/1040

KTB des Befehlshabers der Schlachtschiffe
1–15 March 1942: Militärarchiv Freiburg RM 50/182

KTB des Führer der Unterseeboote Norwegen
15–31 January 1943 PG 31827
1–15 February 1943 PG 31828
1–15 March 1943 PG 31830
16–31 December 1943 PG 31849
16–31 January 1944 PG 31851
1–15 February 1944 PG 31852
16–29 February 1944 PG 31853
1–15 March 1944 PG 31854
16–30 April 1944 PG 31857
16–31 August 1944 PG 31864
1–15 September 1944 PG 31865

KTB der Kampfgruppe
1 November 1943 to 30 June 1944, Militärarchiv Freiburg RM50/184

KTB des Kreuzers Admiral Hipper
16 December 1942 to 2 January 1943, Militärarchiv Freiburg RM7/1040

KTB des Kreuzers Lützow
30 December 1942 to 3 January 1943, Militärarchiv Freiburg RM134/224

KTB des Marinegruppenkommandos Nord
16 March 1942: NA Washington Microfilm, T-1022 3947, PG 34854
1–11 July 1942: NA Washington Microfilm T-1022 3948, PG 34862
16–31 July 1942: NA Washington Microfilm T-1022 3950, PG 34863
30 December 1942 to 2 January 1943, Militärarchiv Freiburg RM 7/1040

KTB des Marinegruppenkommandos Nord und Flottenkommandos
16 to 31 December 1943, Militärarchiv Freiburg RM35 I 149

KTB des Schlachtschiffes *Tirpitz*
1–15 March 1942: NA Washington Microfilms, T-1022-2905, PG 48531

KTB der Skl Teil A
This is the KTB der Seekriegsleitung Teil A (War Diary for the German Naval Staff, Operations Division, Part A). Where possible the English translation of this war diary in NA Washington Microfilms, T-1022-1660-1685, has been consulted. It has been supplied by Acta Norvegica Arkiv

KTB *U-88*
4 May to 11 July 1942, PG 30082/3 Acta Norvegica Arkiv

KTB *U-209*
2 June to 28 July 1942, PG 30197/5, Acta Norvegica Arkiv

KTB *U-255*
20 June to 14 July 1942, Militärarchiv Freiburg RM 98/448
9–25 September 1942, PG 30231/4 Acta Norvegica Arkiv
10 February to 15 March 1943, Militärarchiv Freiburg RM 98/448

KTB *U 278*
20 December 1943 to 19 February 1944, PG 30369/1 Acta Norvegica Arkiv

KTB *U-307*
16 April to 5 May 1944, PG 30390/06 Acta Norvegica Arkiv

KTB U-334
15 April to 6 July 1942, PG 30405/3 Acta Norvegica Arkiv

KTB U-354
10 October to 30 November 1942, PG 30420/2 Acta Norvegica Arkiv
1 December 1942 to 1 January 1943, PG 30420/3 Acta Norvegica Arkiv

KTB U-355
1 June to 12 July 1942, PG 30421/2 Acta Norvegica Arkiv

KTB U-360
20 November 1943 to 28 January 1944, PG 30426/3 Acta Norvegica Arkiv

KTB U-365
23 July to 25 August 1944, PG 30431/5 Acta Norvegica Arkiv

KTB U-376
11 March to 1 April 1942, PG 30438/2 Acta Norvegica Arkiv

KTB U-403
20 March to 21 April 1942, PG 30457/2 Acta Norvegica Arkiv

KTB U-408
17 July to 26 September 1942, PG 30466/3 Acta Norvegica Arkiv

KTB U-435
23 February to 5 April 1942, PG 30489/07 Acta Norvegica Arkiv
5-26 April 1942, PG 30489/08 Acta Norvegica Arkiv
31 August to 3 October 1942, PG30489/10 Acta Norvegica Arkiv

KTB U-454
24 July 1941 to 20 January 1942, PG30507/1 Acta Norvegica Arkiv

KTB U-456
20 April to July 1942, Militärarchiv Freiburg RM 98/950

KTB U-457
30 May to 16 July 1942, PG30510/2 Acta Norvegica Arkiv
8–16 September 1942, PG 30510/4 Acta Norvegica Arkiv

KTB U-586
13 October to 5 November 1942, PG 30618/6 Acta Norvegica Arkiv

KTB *U-703*
7–30 May 1942, PG 30711/3 Acta Norvegica Arkiv
30 May to 15 July 1942, PG30711/4 Acta Norvegica Arkiv
11-26 September 1942, PG 30711/6 Acta Norvegica Arkiv
15 May to 3 August 1943, PG 30711/8 Acta Norvegica Arkiv
3 August to 10 October 1943, PG 30711/9 Acta Norvegica Arkiv
29 February to 8 March 1944, PG 30711/10 Acta Norvegica Arkiv

KTB *U-716*
11 December 1943 to 7 March 1944, PG 30722/1 Acta Norvegica Arkiv

KTB *U-968*
13 November 1944 to 20 February 1945, PG 30801/7 Acta Norvegica Arkiv

KTB *U-990*
22 January to 28 February 1944, PG 30815 Acta Norvegica Arkiv

KTB Zerstörergruppe Nordmeer
9 April to 9 May 1942, Militärarchiv Freiburg RM 58/41

KTB des Zerstörers *Friedrich Ihn*
1–15 March 1942, Militärarchiv Freiburg RM 94/84

KTB des Zerstörers *Z 24*
1–31 March 1942, Militärarchiv Freiburg RM 94/106

KTB des Zerstörers *Z 25*
1–31 March 1942, Militärarchiv Freiburg RM 94/110
1–2 May 1942, Militärachiv Freiburg RM 94/111

KTB des Zerstörers *Z 29*
16-31 December 1943, Militärarchiv Freiburg RM 94/123

War Diary for Luftflotte 5 (in English)
Extracts from war diaries of Luftflotte 5 dated May–September 1942, document V11/60, Translations Vol. III Second World War, NA London AIR 20/7702

AMERICAN MERCHANT VESSEL REPORTS
The following underlined abbreviations which are used in the Notes and elsewhere in this book refer to the sections of NA Washington and NA Maryland specified below beside the abbreviations.

US Armed Guard Reports: NA Maryland RG38 Records Of The Office Of The Chief Of Naval Operations, Naval Transportation Service, Armed Guard Files 1940–1945.

US Casualty Records: NA Maryland RG24 Records Of The Bureau Of Naval Personnel: Casualty Branch: WWII Casualty Lists And Related Records.

US Casualty Reports: NA Washington RG 26 Records Of The US Coast Guard, War Casualties Section, Casualty Reports 1941–1946.

US Medical Reports: NA Maryland RG 52 Records Of The Bureau Of Medicine And Surgery, Records Relating To Rescued Survivors Of Wrecked Ships And Aircraft 1942–1945, Shipwreck Survivors Of S/S Vessels Box 2 Entry 40.

US Merchant Ship Losses Reports: NA Maryland RG 38 Tenth Fleet, ASW Analysis & Stat. Section, Series XIII, Report And Analysis Of U.S. And Allied Merchant Ship Losses 1941–1945.

US Merchant Vessels Sinking Reports: NA Washington RG 26 WW II Reports Concerning Merchant Vessels Sinking.

US Naval Attaché Reports: NA Maryland RG 38 Records Of The Office Of The Chief Of Naval Operations, Office of Naval Intelligence, Naval Attaché – Moscow, USSR.

Notes

Chapter 1

1. PQ17's formation before any of the convoy's ships were attacked is specified in the PQ17 formation diagram in **NA London** ADM 199/757 ('PQ17's Formation Diagram'), which is reproduced in this book's Appendix A.

2. Sound of the planes: *River Afton*'s Captain Harold Charlton's undated account, supplied by Richard Woodman, author of WOODMAN'S BOOK; time planes appeared: p. 70 of undated account by Douglas Fairbanks junior ('Fairbanks' Account'), **National Maritime Museum** MS 82/066; and 6 July 1942 'Report of operations with Commander Cruiser Squadron One, Cruiser Covering Force of PQ17' by American Destroyer Squadron Eight's Captain Don Moon in USS *Wainwright* ('Wainwright's Report'), **David Irving's Papers**.

3. Group of merchant ships present during the big attack: all those in Appendix A, except for *Gray Ranger* which had previously departed, and *Christopher Newport* (previously sunk); ship sunk before big attack, and direction of travel: 8 July 1942 report by destroyer *Keppel*'s Commander Jack Broome ('Keppel's Report'), **Churchill Archives Centre** BRME 8/1.

4. The 5 July 1942 entry in the KTB DER SKL TEIL A refers to 23 aircraft, as does the 5 July 1942 morning report in **Luftflotte 5's Daily Reports**.

5. Appendix I to the 6 July 1942 report by Rear Admiral Louis Hamilton, commander of the First Cruiser Squadron ('Hamilton's 6 July 1942 Report'), who flew his flag in the cruiser HMS *London,* BRME 8/1 Churchill Archives Centre, states the main attack by German aircraft on 4 July 1942 took place at 75°43' N 27°45' E.

6. Keppel's Report.

7. Concerning the German aircraft shot down during the 2 July 1942 attack referred to in this chapter's main text, Keppel's Report states: 'Unless this aircraft died from fright, I think it should be credited to (the destroyer) U.S.S. *Rowan* who was seen at this time putting up a fine display of A.A.

fire while approaching the convoy to fuel.' The same report concerning the destroyer USS *Wainwright*'s performance at and after *ca.* 6.50 p.m. 4 July 1942 in response to the second of the three main attacks by German aircraft that day stated: 'I was most impressed and grateful for the way she sped round the convoy worrying the circling aircraft, and it was largely due to her Fourth of July enthusiasm that the attack completely failed.'

8. 27 July 1942 report by Captain S. D. N. Lawford, commander of the anti-aircraft ship *Pozarica*, Churchill Archives Centre BRME 8/1, refers to six Heinkel 115 seaplanes.

9. Keppel's Report confirms the torpedoed ship was *Christopher Newport*.

10. Ibid.

11. PQ17's Formation Diagram.

12. CARRAWAY'S DIARY.

13. Hauptmann Eicke's account ('Eicke's Report') on p.138 of Rudi Schmidt, *Achtung - Torpedos los!* ('Schmidt's Achtung'), brought to my attention by Christer Bergström, one of the co-authors of *Black Cross Red Star: Air War Over the Eastern Front vol. 3*.

14. 8 October 1942 report by *Navarino*'s Captain A. Kelso, NA London ADM 199/2141.

15. Ibid.

16. Carraway's Diary.

17. Robert Henderson's diary, courtesy of his wife Lyndell and daughter Sue.

18. The chapter 'De mannen van de Paulus Potter' (The Men of Paulus Potter) in Anthony Van Kampen, ed., *Scheepsverklaring* p.190. It was brought to my attention by Jos Odijk.

19. Carraway's Diary.

20. For example 7 October 1942 'Report Of An Interview With The Master, Captain J. Pascoe: s.s. "Bolton Castle"', NA London ADM 199/2141; and report by M.I. Pavlov, skipper of *Donbass*, **GAOPDiFAO**, Archive Section 296, Inventory 1, Book 1210.

21. Keppel's Report.

22. Report by captain of *Azerbaijan*, in GAOPDiFAO, Archive Section 296, Inventory 1, Book 1210.

23. Eicke's Report on pp.138–9 of Schmidt's Achtung.

24. Roger Hill, *Destroyer Captain* ('Hill's Book') p. 49.

25. Fairbanks' Account, pp. 71–2.

26. Leutnant Georg Kanmayer's account in Schmidt's Achtung pp. 140–1; Hill's Book pp. 40–50; Keppel's Report; and Wainwright's Report.

27. Schmidt's Achtung p. 142.

28. Ibid p. 137.

29. Keppel's Report specifies PQ17's course. Hamilton's 6 July 1942 Report states PQ17 was scattered at 75°50' N 28°30' E.

30. Hill's Book p.51. What is written in Jack Broome, *Convoy Is To Scatter* ('Broome's Book') p.187 implies that it might have been a single flag raised by *Keppel*'s signalman which puzzled Hill rather than, as specified in Hill's account, the string of flags raised by the signalman in *River Afton*, the Commodore's ship.

31. Broome's Book p. 191.

32. Hill's Book p. 51.

33. Broome's Book p. 194.

34. Ibid. pp. 194–5.

35. Ibid. p. 195.

36. Ibid. pp. 189 and 200.

37. Fairbanks' Account pp. 73–4.

38. Carraway's Diary.

39. S. A. Kerslake, *Coxswain In The Northern Convoys* pp. 75–6.
40. Head of the Political Department of the Northern Sea Fleet Koltiakov to the head of the Political Department Commissar of the USSR Comrade Belakov on 17 August 1942, GAOPDiFAO Section 296, Inventory 1, Book 1210.

Chapter 2

1. WOODMAN'S BOOK pp. 36–7; and BRITISH NAVAL AVIATION HISTORY p. 176.
2. British Naval Aviation History p. 176.
3. Hubert Griffith, *R.A.F. In Russia* ('Griffith's Book') p. 5.
4. Ibid. p. 22.
5. Ibid. p. 21.
6. Morris O. Mills, *PQ13: Unlucky For Some* p. 35.
7. British Naval Aviation History pp. 176–7.
8. Ibid. p.176; and Griffith's Book pp. 44–88.
9. 22 June 1941 entry Gabriel Gorodetsky, ed., *The Maisky Diaries: Red Ambassador to the Court of St James's 1932–1943* ('Maisky Diaries') p. 366.
10. CHURCHILL'S BOOK vol. 3 pp. 331–2.
11. Robert Hugh Jones, *The Roads To Russia* ('Jones' Book') p. 35.
12. Churchill's Book vol. 3 p. 340.
13. REYNOLDS AND PECHATNOV p. 28.
14. Ibid. p. 30.
15. Robert E. Sherwood, *The White House Papers of Harry L. Hopkins* ('Hopkins' Book') pp. 317–8.
16. Jones' Book p.34; Joan Beaumont, *Comrades In Arms: British Aid to Russia 1941–1945* pp. 26–8.

17. Martin Gilbert, ed., The Churchill Documents 1941 ('Churchill Documents') p. 991.
18. Ivan Maisky, *Memoirs of a Soviet Ambassador: The War 1939–43* ('Maisky's Memoirs') pp. 180–1.
19. Hopkins' Book pp. 325–8.
20. Quote from *The American Magazine* (date not specified) in ibid. pp. 344–5. Dates of Hopkins' meetings with Stalin, ibid. pp. 330 and 332.
21. Ibid. 341.
22. Ibid. p. 344.
23. Churchill's Book vol. 3 p. 381.
24. Hopkins' Book pp. 385–396 and 399.
25. Churchill Documents. pp. 1065–6.
26. Reynolds and Pechatnov pp. 40–1; British guilt at not complying with second front request, and Moscow informed: Maisky Memoirs pp. 185–7.
27. 4 September 1941 entry in Maisky Diaries p. 386; and Maisky's Memoirs pp. 190–1.
28. Reynolds and Pechatnov pp. 43–4.
29. W. Averell Harriman and Elie Abel, *Special Envoy to Churchill and Stalin 1941–1946* ('Harriman's Book') p. 87.
30. Tanks for Russia Week, referred to in the 22 September 1941 entry in Maisky Diaries p. 391.
31. Harriman's Book pp. 87 and 89.
32. Antony Beevor, *Stalingrad* ('Stalingrad Book') pp. 28–9 and 33.
33. Harriman's Book p. 89.
34. Ibid. p. 87.
35. Ibid. pp. 90–1.
36. Stalingrad Book pp. 33–4.
37. Harriman's Book p. 97.
38. Ibid. pp. 87–8.
39. Ibid.; and *Soviet Supply Protocols*, a publication by the US Department of State, pp. 1–12.
40. Anne Chisholm and Michael Davie, *Beaverbrook: A Life* p. 417; and

Woodman's Book p. 42. Convoys in the first series of east-going Arctic convoys were all given the prefix PQ after Paul Quellyn-Roberts, the Admiralty officer who in 1941 was responsible for their administration. Convoys in the first series of west-going Arctic convoys were given the prefix QP, the reversal of the letters to show that the convoys were travelling in the opposite direction. This has been confirmed by Paul Quellyn-Roberts' son Paul junior, who was introduced to me by Sir James Vernon.

41. Churchill's Book vol. 3 pp. 418–19.

42. Distance from American east coast to Murmansk: 8 May 1942 report by *Dunboyne's* Armed Guard commanding officer Ensign Rufus Brinn, <u>US ARMED GUARD REPORTS</u>. Stalin's objection to routes: Hopkins' Book pp. 330 and 340.

43. 27 June 1942 Agreement and 16 August 1941 Agreement, in both cases between Britain and the Soviet Union, a copy of which are in Appendix 2 and 3 respectively of the 'Report On Fulfilment Of The Moscow Protocol October 1941-June 1942', **NA London** PREM 3 401/7. Concerning non-military aid supplied by Britain, 40 per cent of its value had to be paid in cash, and 60 per cent in five equal annual instalments, the first to be paid 3 years after the purchase and the last 7 years after the purchase.

44. Jones' Book p. 261 describes how President Harry Truman's administration after the war sought to extract payment for a proportion of $2.6 billion, the latter figure being what the Americans believed to be

the value of civilian-type supplies that remained in Soviet custody. The above figure was in its turn a proportion of the $10.8 billion worth of aid which the Americans believed they had supplied under lend-lease.

45. P. M. H. Bell, *John Bull and the Bear* (<u>'Public Opinion Book'</u>) p. 59.

46. Minutes of 20 October 1941 Defence Committee meeting, NA London CAB 69/8 and 19 October 1941 Memorandum, NA London CAB 69/3.

47. Public Opinion Book p. 64, referring to the 20 October to 3 November 1941 reports produced by the Home Intelligence Division of the Ministry of Information.

48. Ibid.

Chapter 3

1. WOODMAN'S BOOK pp. 36–54.

2. Undated note headed 'Final Figures Of Arrivals And Losses For Each Convoy Up To And Including P.Q.16' with 29 July 1942 letter from the Offices of the War Cabinet's G. Fitch to N. Gifford, Commercial Secretary, Kuibyshev, **NA London** CAB 111/109; and report by Anastas Mikoyan, People's Commissar for Foreign Trade, following a 9 January 1942 conference in Moscow (<u>'Mikoyan's Arrears Report'</u>), quoted in Alexander Hill, *The Great Patriotic War of the Soviet Union, 1941–1945: A documentary reader* pp. 171–2. Hill credits G. N. Sevost'ianov, *Sovetsko-amerikanskie otnsoheniia, 1939–1945* p. 192.

3. 24 January 1942 letter headed 'General Ismay' and attached table, NA London CAB 111/108.

4. Mikoyan's Arrears Report.

5. Antony Beevor, *Stalingrad* p. 41.
6. 13 January 1942 Ivan Maisky to Eden letter, NA London CAB 111/108.
7. The sources relied on for the description of the types of men in the Merchant Navy and US Merchant Marine include: British: *Merchantmen At War: The Official Story of the Merchant Navy: 1939–1944* pp.14–16; and Morris O. Mills, *PQ13: Unlucky For Some* pp. 54–94; American: Robert Carse, *A Cold Corner Of Hell* pp. 27–8 and 33–4.
8. William A. Carter, *Why Me Lord?* pp. 104–5.
9. Dalton Leslie Munn, *Diary of Squandered Valor: First Convoy to Murmansk* p. 2.
10. Ibid. p. 8.
11. Ibid. p. 40.
12. Ibid. pp. 9 and 16.
13. Ibid. p. 18.
14. 15 June 1942 sworn statement signed by *Silver Sword*'s C.W. Calbeth; and 31 October 1942 letter from a representative of Sword Line Inc. to the United States Coast Guard, US MERCHANT VESSELS SINKING REPORTS. Entry P-2 Box 45.
15. Woodman's Book p.53.
16. 22 January 1942 report by *Trinidad*'s Captain Leslie Saunders ('Trinidad's PQ8 Report'), NA London ADM 199/72.
17. ROHWER'S HUMMELCHEN'S AND WEIS'S CHRONOLOGY p. 134.
18. 11 November 1942 'Report of an Interview with the Master – Captain R.W. Brundle. S.S. Harmatris. P.Q.8.' ('Harmatris' Report'), NA London ADM 199/1709.
19. 3 February 1942 report by Captain Donald Bain, Captain (D) Sixth Destroyer Flotilla, HMS *Somali* with header 'Attack On Convoy P.Q.8 On January 17/18TH. 1942' ('Somali's PQ8 Report'), NA London ADM 199/72.
20. 17 January 1942 entry in KTB *U-454*.
21. Harmatris' Report.
22. Testimony of Captain Donald Bain, Lieutenant Commander John Cooke and Lieutenant William Whitworth, Minutes of Proceedings, 11-12 March 1942 Board of Inquiry into *Matabele* sinking ('Matabele Inquiry'), NA London ADM 1/11951; Somali's PQ8 Report; and 8 February 1942 report by Captain Donald Bain commander of HMS *Somali* with header 'Torpedoing And Sinking of H.M.S. Matabele' ('Somali Matabele Report'), NA London ADM 199/72.
23. Testimony of survivor Ernest Higgins, Appendix 1 to Somali Matabele Report ('Matabele Survivors' Report').
24. Admiralty's 1909A 17 January 1942 signal, Trinidad's PQ8 Report; and Extract of Somali Log in Appendix 3 to Somali's PQ8 Report.
25. Trinidad's PQ8 Report.
26. Testimony of Ernest Higgins, Matabele Survivors' Report.
27. Ibid.; and Matabele Inquiry.
28. Ibid.
29. 19 January 1942 report by Commander Eric Hinton commanding officer of HMS *Harrier* to Captain (D) 6th Destroyer Flotilla, HMS *Somali*, NA London ADM 199/72.
30. Ibid.
31. Matabele Survivors' Report.
32. William Burras, Matabele Inquiry.
33. Document entitled 'R.N. Casualties In N. Russia Convoys' sent with

undated note, written after the 31 December 1942 Battle of the Barents Sea, from the office of the Director of Naval Intelligence, NA London ADM 199/604.

34. 17 January 1942 entry in KTB *U-454*.

Chapter 4

1. 4 January 1942 letter from Tovey to Admiralty Secretary which appears to be a draft of the final letter which was dated 29 January 1942, both in **NA London** ADM 199/757.

2. Jak Mallmann Showell ed., *Fuehrer Conferences On Naval Affairs 1939–1945* pp. 246–7 and 259; and NA London AIR 20/1332.

3. BRITISH WAR AT SEA OFFICIAL HISTORY vol. 2 p. 119.

4. TIRPITZ OFFICIAL HISTORY.

5. 25 February 1942 letter from Tovey to the Admiralty, NA London ADM 199/347.

6. PQ12's merchant ships: undated summary of sailing and arrival dates in Russian ports, NA London ADM 237/163. QP8 merchant ships: 1 March 1942 SBNO North Russia telegram, NA London ADM 199/347.

7. 27 February and 3 March 1942 messages from Tovey to Vice Admiral Curteis, NA London ADM 199/347.

8. 1 March 1942 message from SBNO North Russia to the Admiralty, NA London ADM 199/347.

9. WOODMAN'S BOOK p. 72.

10. 5 March 1942 entry in <u>KTB DES ADMIRAL NORDMEER</u>.

11. Ibid.

12. 6 March 1942 entry in <u>KTB DER SKL TEIL A</u>.

13. Account by Dick Raikes, **IWM Documents** 6349.

14. 12.50 a.m. 7 March 1942 message from the Admiralty to Tovey (specified sending time being 2350A 6 March) referring to *Seawolf*'s signal, NA London ADM 199/347; and BRITISH ARCTIC CONVOYS HISTORY p. 8.

15. Account by Charles Friend ('Friend's Account'), IWM Documents 86/37/1.

16. 7 March 1942 entry in '<u>832 Squadron's War Diary</u>', NA London ADM 207/28.

17. Report by Admiral Sir Jack Tovey headed 'Operations In Support Of Convoys PQ12 & QP8', enclosed with 13 March 1942 letter ('<u>Tovey's 2nd PQ12 Report</u>'), NA London ADM 199/347.

18. Dalton Leslie 'Dal' Munn, *Diary of Squandered Valor: First Convoy to Murmansk* pp. 48–51, diary entries for 4–6 March 1942.

19. 'Summary of Captain Denny's Report of Proceedings (Kenya's 0355/A of 14.iii.42)' ('<u>Kenya's Report</u>') in **NHB**.

20. Ibid.; and British Arctic Convoys History p. 9.

21. 7 March 1942 message from the Admiralty to PQ12 escorts, timed 1519A (4.19 p.m., GMT + 2), which according to Kenya's Report appears to have been received in *Kenya* at 5 p.m. (GMT + 2) 7 March 1942.

22. 7 March 1942 entry in KTB der 5 Zerstörerflottille, **Militärarchiv Freiburg** RM 58/23; 6 March 1942 entry KTB der Skl Teil A; and Anlage 1 to the <u>KTB DES BEFEHLSHABERS DER SCHLACHTSCHIFFE</u> for 1–15 March 1942.

23. The 5 March 1942 entry in the KTB des Admiral Nordmeer covering 1–12 March 1942 refers to the sighting of PQ12 by the German aircraft; and that KTB's Anlage 18a states the sighting took place at the position referred to as AA 9918 on the German grid map (approximately 69°39' N 09°30' W); whereas *Kenya*'s Report states that the aircraft approached the convoy at 70°05' N 06°09' W. The latter location is around 90 miles to the north-east of the location reported by the German aircraft crew.

24. 7 March 1942 entries in: KTB *DES ZERSTÖRERS FRIEDRICH IHN*; KTB DES ZERSTÖRERS *Z* 25; and in KTB der 5 Zerstörerflottille, Militärarchiv Freiburg RM 94/84, RM 94/110 and RM 58/23 respectively.

25. *Kenya*'s Report; *Onslow* message to Tovey timed '1632' (1732: GMT + 2) 7 March, NA London ADM 199/347; Tovey's 2nd PQ12 Report.

26. Admiralty message sent at 1518A (4.18 p.m.: GMT + 2) 7 March 1942, NA London ADM 223/109.

27. 7 March 1942 1652A (1752 p.m.: GMT + 2) and 1934A (2034: GMT + 2) messages from Admiralty to Tovey, NA London ADM 223/109.

28. BRITISH INTELLIGENCE OFFICIAL HISTORY vol. 2 pp. 207–8.

29. Part II Commander-in-Chief Home Fleet war diary covering 1–15 March 1942 ('Home Fleet PQ12 War Diary'), NA London ADM 199/427.

30. 7–8 March 1942 entry in 832 Squadron's War Diary.

31. 10 March 1942 report by Tovey ('Tovey's 1st PQ12 Report'), NA London PREM 3/191/1.

32. Home Fleet PQ12 War Diary.

33. 6–8 March 1942 entries in KTB des Befehlshabers der Schlachtschiffe.

34. Decrypt 239, NA London DEFE 3/88.

35. 8 March 1942 entry in KTB des Befehlshabers der Schlachtschiffe.

36. Decrypt 267 DEFE 3/88 contains Bletchley Park's codebreakers' translation of the all-important signal from Carls to Ciliax timed 2332 which was intercepted by the British at 2354 (both GMT + 2, 8 March), and sent to the Admiralty at 0155 (GMT + 2, 9 March). The decrypt stated: 'Hereby acknowledge short signal concerning break off of operation and rendezvous in square AF 3185' (the reference on the German grid map to the approximate position 68°15' N 10°38' E). Decrypt 268, DEFE 3/88, which was sent to the Admiralty at 0202, contains a similar signal sent from Carls to two of the German destroyers with the added confirmation the rendezvous was to be at 0800 (GMT + 2, 9 March). The Ultra passing on the information in these signals to Tovey was timed 0148A (0248 GMT + 2) 9 March 1942, ADM 223/88 and ADM 223/109. All documents in this note are in NA London.

37. Tovey's 1st PQ12 Report.

38. The Ultra, in NA London ADM 223/109, which prompted Tovey's turn towards the north-east was timed 1500A (1600 GMT + 2) 8 March 1942.

39. British War At Sea Official History vol. 2 p. 122.

40. Ultra timed 02 48A 9 March 1942 (3.48 a.m. GMT + 2), NA London ADM 223/109, based on decrypt 273, NA London DEFE 3/88. The latter stated *Tirpitz* would pass through AF 6183, the reference on the German grid map to around 65°38' N 10°52' E, at 1400 (GMT + 2) 9 March.

41. Message from Bovell to Tovey timed 5.37 a.m. (GMT + 1), that is 6.37 a.m. GMT + 2, NA London ADM 199/347.

42. 9 March 1942 entry in 832 Squadron's War Diary.

43. Friend's Account.

44. The following appendices to the 15 March 1942 letter written by *Victorious*' Captain Henry Bovell ('*Victorious*' Letter'), NHB and NA London ADM 199/167: Appendix 1 containing 'Narrative' ('*Victorious*' Narrative'); and Appendix VII containing '*Victorious*' List Of Aircraft Crews'; 832 Squadron's War Diary; and 9 March 1942 entries in: KTB DES SCHLACHTSCHIFFES *TIRPITZ*; and KTB des Zerstörers *Friedrich Ihn*.

45. *Victorious*' Narrative; *Victorious*' List Of Aircraft Crews; and 832 Squadron's War Diary.

46. Tovey to *Victorious* message timed 7.21 a.m. (GMT + 1; 8.21 a.m. GMT + 2), NA London ADM 199/347.

47. Time *Tirpitz* sighted: 10 March 1942 report by observer Sub-Lieutenant W.H.C. Browne in Appendix VI to *Victorious*' Letter; and Anlage 8 to 5 to 13 March 1942 KTB des Befehlshabers der Schlachtschiffe.

Friedrich Ihn's position relative to *Tirpitz* and location when the first aircraft from the British search force were sighted – AF 3443 right top (approximately 67°48' N 10°15' E) – 9 March 1942 entry in KTB des Zerstörers *Friedrich Ihn*.

48. Ludovic Kennedy, *The Life and Death of the Tirpitz* ('Kennedy's Tirpitz Book') p. 41.

49. Anlage 7 to 5 to 13 March 1942 KTB des Befehlshabers der Schlachtschiffe.

50. 'Remarks Of The Striking Force Leader' ('Lucas' Remarks'), in Appendix IV to *Victorious*' Letter.

51. Friend's Account.

52. Ibid.

53. Lucas' Remarks.

54. Time attack by British aircraft started: 9 March 1942 report by Lieutenant D. George ('Lucas' Observer's Report'), Appendix V to *Victorious*' Letter. Location of attack: AF 3461 left bottom (approximately 67°42' N 11°00' E), 9 March 1942 entry in KTB des Zerstörers *Friedrich Ihn*.

55. Kennedy's Tirpitz Book p. 42.

56. Lucas' Remarks. Map 4 is taken from Appendix III to *Victorious*' Letter.

57. Kennedy's Tirpitz Book p. 44.

58. Time attack by British aircraft ended: Lucas' Observer's Report. Location of attack by aircraft: 9 March 1942 entry in KTB des Zerstörers *Friedrich Ihn*.

59. 'Kurzbericht über den L.T. Angriff am 9.3.42 . . ', **NA Washington Microfilms**, T-1022 2905 PG 48531.

60. Kennedy's Tirpitz Book p. 45.

61. 11 March 1942 entry in 832 Squadron's War Diary.

62. Kenya's Report; Home Fleet PQ12 War Diary; and 14 March 1942 telegram from SBNO North Russia, NA London ADM 237/163.
63. Tovey's 2ⁿᵈ PQ12 Report.
64. 9 March 1942 Bovell to Tovey, NA London ADM 199/347.

Chapter 5

1. Report by Admiral Sir Jack Tovey headed 'Operations In Support Of Convoys PQ12 & QP8', enclosed with 13 March 1942 letter, **NA London** ADM 199/347.
2. Based on Jak Mallmann Showell ed., *Fuehrer Conferences On Naval Affairs 1939–1945* pp. 265–6; and the translation headed 'Report by the Commander-in-Chief, Navy to the Fuehrer at Headquarters "Wolfsschanze" the evening of 12 March 1942', NA London AIR 20/1332.
3. 26 April 1942 Commodore D.A. Casey 'Report on Convoy P.Q.13 from Reykjavik 18th March 1942' with accompanying note headed 'Position Of Convoy PQ. 13 At 0700. G.M.T', NA London ADM 199/347; and 4 April 1942 report by HMS *Trinidad's* Captain Leslie Saunders ('Trinidad's PQ13 Report'), NA London ADM 199/347 and **Alan Blyth Collection.**
4. John Dodds' diary supplied by his son Nick and daughter Jane.
5. The 150 miles figure: Trinidad's PQ13 Report referring to 28 March.
6. Dodds incorrectly believed there were only 18 merchant ships in the convoy.
7. 30 March 1942 report by *Sharpshooter's* Lieutenant Commander David Lampen ('Sharpshooter's Report'), NA London ADM 199/72 refers to QP9's 19 ships, contradicting a QP9 formation diagram in the same file showing 16 merchant ships.
8. Sharpshooter's Report.
9. 23 and 24 March 1942 entries in KTB DES ADMIRAL NORDMEER.
10. Decrypts 505 and 506 containing Carls to Gruppe Zieten 25 March 1942 orders, NA London DEFE 3/90.
11. 2315A 26 March 1942 message sent by the Admiralty which was received by Captain Saunders at 0015A on 27 March 1942 according to Trinidad's PQ13 Report.
12. PQ13's route was altered for the first time on 23 March 1942 pursuant to a 1336A message from the Admiralty, according to Trinidad's PQ13 Report.
13. The 28 March 1942 entry in the KTB des Admiral Nordmeer states the first sighting from *U-209* was at AC 4525 on the German grid map (approximately 73°21' N 23°30' E). Other evidence suggests the merchant ships sighted from *U-209* were from the group escorted by the destroyer *Eclipse,* referred to in Chapter 5's main text as the western group. The 31 March 1942 report by *Eclipse's* commanding officer, in Appendix I to Trinidad's PQ13 Report, combined with the convoy formation sketch headed 'Convoy. Cruising Order. PQ13 . . .' in NA London ADM 237/164, suggests that: by 9 a.m. on 28 March 1942 *Eclipse* was escorting: *Eldena, El Estero, Empire Cowper, Gallant Fox, Mormacmar* and *Scottish American*;

and by the time *Trinidad* first fired at the German destroyers on 29 March 1942, *Eclipse* was also escorting *New Westminster City*, the trawler *Paynter* and the whaler *Sumba*.

14. 28 March 1942 entry in *U-209*'s KTB, PG 30197, **Acta Norvegica Arkiv**.

15. The 28 March 1942 entry in the KTB des Admiral Nordmeer, and 'Lagebetrachtung zur Operation gegen den Geleitzug "PQ 13"' in that KTB specify that the sighting was at AC 4816 on the German grid map (approximately 72°27' N 23°50' E). Other evidence suggests the merchant ships sighted from the aircraft were the following six, referred to in Chapter 5's main text as the eastern group (when first sighted, they were to the south-east of those specified in Note 13, but they would subsequently move to the east of those specified in Note 13, leading to their eastern group name): *Ballot, Dunboyne, Effingham, Empire Starlight , Induna,* and *Mana*.

16. 28 March 1942 entry in KTB des Admiral Nordmeer.

17. Trinidad's PQ13 Report; and Decrypt 747, NA London DEFE 3/91.

18. For example decrypt numbers 31, 33, 37, 38, 39, 47, NA London DEFE 3/91.

19. Decrypt number 64, NA London DEFE 3/91, was sent from Bletchley Park to the Admiralty at around 3.30 p.m. on 29 March 1942, i.e. after the battle with the British warships.

20. 28 March 1942 entries in KTB DES ZERSTÖRERS Z 24 and KTB DES ZERSTÖRERS Z 25.

21. 'Gefechtsbericht des Zerstörers Z 24 über das Gefecht am 29.3.42 mit Sicherungsstreitkräften eines englischen Geleitzuges im Nordmeer' ('Z 24's Battle Report'), **Militärarchiv Freiburg** RM 94/106; and KTB des Zerstörers Z 24.

22. 28 March entries in KTB des Zerstörers Z 24, and KTB des Zerstörers Z 25.

23. Hans-Jürgen Meyer-Brenkhof's account, written after the war by which time his rank was Oberleutnant zur See, supplied by his son Jürgen ('Meyer-Brenkhof's Account')

24. *Trinidad*'s PQ13 Report refers to 72°13' N 32°10' E, the coordinates in *Empire Ranger*'s distress signal, received at around 8.30 p.m. on 28 March.

25. Ernst Pfefferle, ed., *Kameraden zur See* vol. 7 pp. 100–103, chapter written by Viktor Gernhard, Geleitzugkampf im Eismeer. Das Ende von Z 26 ('Viktor Gernhard's Report'); and 28 March 1942 entry in KTB des Zerstörers Z 25.

26. 28 March 1942 entry in KTB des Zerstörers Z 24.

27. Ibid.

28. Meyer-Brenkhof's Account.

29. Viktor Gernhard's Report; and 6 men rescued: 29 March 1942 entry in the KTB des Zerstörers Z 25.

30. *Bateau* casualties: 14 June 1942 report by the US Coast Guard's examining officer Frank Hicken, US CASUALTY REPORTS Box 6 A1 Entry 195.

31. 29 March 1942 12.35 a.m. signal in Appendix 75 to the 13 March to 2 April 1942 KTB des Admiral Nordmeer, recorded in the 2 a.m. 29 March entry in the KTB des Zerstörers Z 24.

32. 29 March 1942 entries in KTB
des Zerstörers *Z 24*; and KTB des
Admiral Nordmeer for 13 March to
2 April 1942, and the latter's Anlagen
81 and 84.

33. 29 March 1942 entry in the KTB des
Zerstörers *Z 24*.

34. Meyer-Brenkhof's Account.

35. *Z 24*'s Battle Report.

36. 29 March 1942 entries, and maps, in
KTB des Zerstörers *Z 24* and KTB
des Zerstörers *Z 25*; Trinidad's PQ13
Report; and 17 April 1942 report by
Trinidad's Captain Leslie Saunders
('Trinidad's PQ13 Battle Report'),
NA London ADM 199/347.

37. Report that escort was to the south
of the convoy: *Z 24*'s Battle Report.

38. Radar not working in two German
destroyers: 28 March 1942 entry in
KTB des Zerstörers *Z 25*; and
undated 'Gefechtsbericht *Z 25* über
den Ansatz der 8 Zerstörerflottille
gegen einen gemeldeten Geleitzug
im Seegebiet nördlich
Nordnorwegen', Militärarchiv
Freiburg RM 94/110.

39. *Z 26*'s radar detected *Trinidad* before
the cruiser opened fire: undated
'Vorläufiger Gefechtskurzbericht 8.
Z.-Fl. Auf Grund mündlicher
Aussagen Kmt. "*Z 25*" und I.O. "*Z*
26"', Appendix 111 to the KTB des
Admiral Nordmeer for 13 March to
2 April 1942.

40. Trinidad's PQ13 Battle Report; and
Frank Pearce, *The Ship That
Torpedoed Herself* ('Trinidad's
Book') p. 67.

41. Trinidad's PQ13 Battle Report; and
Trinidad's PQ13 Report. These
reports also confirm the Soviet
ships were *Sokrushitelni* and
Gremyaschi.

42. Ibid. These reports state that
Trinidad's position when her guns
opened fire was approximately 72°21'
N 33°32' E.

43. Trinidad's PQ13 Battle Report.

44. Viktor Gernhard's Report.

45. Leslie Saunders' memoirs 'His Coats
of Navy Blue' ('Saunders' Memoirs'),
Alan Blyth Collection, and supplied
by Captain Saunders' son Iain.

46. Trinidad's PQ13 Battle Report; and
the 1 April 1942 report by *Fury*'s
Lieutenant-Commander
C. Campbell ('Fury's PQ13 Report')
which is in Appendix III to
Trinidad's PQ13 Report.

47. Trinidad's PQ13 Battle Report.

48. Trinidad's PQ13 Report; and
Trinidad's PQ13 Battle Report.

49. Saunders' Memoirs.

50. Ibid.; and Trinidad's Book p. 75.

51. Board of Inquiry report 'Extracts
from Enclosure No. 1 Plymouth
Letter . . . of 11th June 1942', NA
London ADM 267/71; and 11 June
1942 'Finding and Minutes Of Board
of Inquiry Held To Investigate The
Circumstances In Which H.M.S.
"Trinidad" Was Torpedoed On 29th
March 1942 . . .' ('Trinidad Board of
Inquiry Finding and Minutes'), NA
London ADM 1/12032.

52. Saunders' Memoirs. *Trinidad* was
torpedoed at 72°27' N 33°10' E
according to her signal in
Trinidad's PQ13 Battle Report's
Appendix VI.

53. Trinidad's Book p. 77, and Appendix
VII of Trinidad PQ13 Battle
Report.

54. Trinidad's Book p. 81.

55. George Lloyd account dated 11 April
1992, brought to my attention by his
nephew Bill Lloyd.

56. Appendix VIII to Trinidad's PQ13 Battle Report.

57. Fury's PQ13 Report.

58. Report by *Eclipse*'s Lieutenant Commander Edward Mack dated 7 April 1942 ('Eclipse's Battle Report'), NA London ADM 199/347. *Trinidad*'s first enemy report timed 0851A 29 March 1942 is mentioned in the aforementioned report's Appendix VIII.

59. Eclipse's Battle Report.

60. Ibid.

61. *Fury*'s John Manning in a letter dated 23 July 1991, Alan Blyth Collection.

62. Eclipse's Battle Report.

63. Ibid.

64. Josef Hirsch's account brought to my attention by Josef Neuberger.

65. Meyer-Brenkhof's Account.

66. Ibid.

67. Appendix V to Eclipse's Battle Report.

68. Narrative in Appendix I to Eclipse's Battle Report.

69. Ibid.; and Viktor Gernhard's Report.

70. Appendix IV to Eclipse's Battle Report; and signal timed 1958C from *Eclipse* in Appendix VIII to Eclipse's Battle Report mention ten men needing to go to hospital including seven cot cases.

71. Viktor Gernhard's Report.

72. Meyer-Brenkhof's Account.

73. Viktor Gernhard's Report.

74. Meyer-Brenkhof's Account.

75. 29 March 1942 entries in KTB des Zerstörers *Z 24* and *Z 25*.

76. Viktor Gernhard's Report.

77. Ibid.; and KTB des Zerstörers *Z 25*.

78. Trinidad's PQ13 Battle Report; and Fury's PQ13 Report.

79. Evidence of Able Seaman Edward Harris and Electrical Artificer James Goodwin in the Trinidad Board of Inquiry Finding and Minutes; Appendix XI to Trinidad's PQ13 Battle Report; and Trinidad's Book pp. 94–6.

Chapter 6

1. 19 January 1942 letter from Bernard Covington, supplied by his son via Eric Berryman (see Acknowledgements).

2. Morris O. Mills, *Convoy PQ13: Unlucky for Some* ('Mills' Book') pp. 17–19.

3. Ibid. pp. 89–90.

4. Ibid. pp. 90–92.

5. Statement by Lieutenant-Commander Colin Campbell, the commander of HMS *Fury*, during 7 April 1942 'Board of Enquiry' to enquire into the loss of HM Whaler *Sulla*, **NA London** ADM 1/12142, also part of **Alan Blyth Collection**.

6. Mills' Book p. 94.

7. 26 April 1942 report of proceedings by PQ13's Commodore D.A. Casey, NA London ADM 199/347; 16 June 1945 'Summary of Statements by Survivors of the SS Raceland' ('Raceland Summary'), US CASUALTY REPORTS Box 6 A1 Entry 195; and internet site covering the *Raceland* sinking prepared by Leif Myrhoej, nephew of Eskild Lauth, a member of *Raceland*'s crew who did not survive.

8. Information from Lise Lindbaek, *Tusen Norsk Skip* pp. 185–7; Richard Larsson, *Porsgrunn I Krig Og Fred* p. 38; and Raceland Summary.

9. 4 April 1942 report by *Oribi*'s Commander John McBeath ('Oribi's PQ13 Report') in Appendix II to the

4 April 1942 report by *Trinidad*'s Captain Leslie Saunders ('Trinidad's PQ13 Report'), NA London ADM 199/347.

10. Mills' Book pp. 95–6; and Oribi's PQ13 Report.

11. 8 May 1942 report by Ensign Rufus Brinn, designated 'Commanding Officer, Armed Guard, of SS *Dunboyne*', US ARMED GUARD REPORTS Box 175 UD93.

12. 1 April 1942 report by Commanding Officer of *Fury*, Appendix III to Trinidad's PQ13 Report.

13. *Induna*'s movements are taken from the 13 May 1942 'Report of an Interview with the Second Officer Mr E. Rowlands: SS Induna', NA London ADM 199/2140 ('Rowlands' Report'); and Austin Byrne's account, **IWM Sound** 11063 ('Byrne IWM').

14. Byrne IWM.

15. 30 March 1942 entry in KTB DES ADMIRAL NORDMEER covering 13 March to 2 April 1942, and that KTB's Anlage 109.

16. Byrne IWM.

17. Austin Byrne in Byrne IWM makes it clear he either never knew or after the war did not recall the name of the *Ballot* seaman in his lifeboat. However the statement on a list of war graves in Murmansk, in the Alan Byrne Collection, which states that 'R. Bennett' died on 2 April 1942, the day when according to Byrne the American seaman passed away in the hospital in Murmansk, suggests that this is the *Ballot* seaman in question's name.

18. Ibid.

19. Rowlands' Report.

20. Byrne IWM.

21. William Short's account, IWM Sound 11276 ('Short IWM').

22. 30 March 1942 entry in the KTB U-376; and Byrne IWM. The 30 March 1942 entry in the KTB U-376 states that the torpedoing of an unidentified ship (which appears to have been *Induna* – although ROHWER'S HUMMELCHEN'S AND WEIS'S CHRONOLOGY p. 153 only states that U-376's and U-435's torpedoes sank *Induna* and *Effingham* on 30 March 1942 without specifying which U-boat was responsible for the sinking of which merchant ship) – took place shortly after 8 a.m. at the position shown as AC 8333 on the German grid map (approximately 70° 45' N 34°50' E), the position for the torpedoing marked on Map 5. It should be noted however that this is different from the position specified in the 26 April 1942 report by PQ13's Commodore D.A. Casey, NA London ADM 199/347, and Rowlands' Report – 70° 55' N 37°18' E – which were the coordinates in the two *Induna* distress signals received by the Commodore's ship *River Afton* at 8.18 and 8.27 a.m. 30 March 1942.

23. Short IWM.

24. The 8 May 1942 statement by *Effingham*'s master, Charles Hewett, US MERCHANT SHIP LOSSES Box 222 states the torpedoing was at 70° 28' N 35° 44' E; and the KTB U-435 states the coup de grâce shortly after 12.15 p.m. 30 March 1942 was at AC 8646 on the German grid (approximately 70°21' N 35°50' E).

25. 11 May 1942 letter from Maynard B. Barnes, First Secretary of American Legation, Reykjavik to

Secretary of State, in *Effingham* section of US Merchant Ship Losses Box 222.

26. 30 March 1942 entry, <u>KTB *U-435*</u>.
27. Charles Hunnefield's diary brought to my attention by his daughter Darlene and son-in-law Paul via Eric Berryman.

Chapter 7

1. 26 April 1942 Commodore D.A. Casey 'Report on Convoy P.Q.13 from Reykjavik 18 March 1942' ('<u>PQ13's Commodore's Report</u>'), **NA London** ADM 199/347. The coordinates referred to in *Induna's* distress messages are described in Chapter 6's Note 22 along with the conflicting German specification.
2. 13 May 1942 'Report of an Interview with the Second Officer Mr E. Rowlands S.S. Induna' ('<u>Rowlands' Report</u>'), NA London ADM 199/2140 says there were 32 men in the boat, whereas William Short's account, **IWM Sound** 11276 ('<u>Short IWM</u>') refers to 34 occupants.
3. Short IWM.
4. Ibid.; and Rowlands' Report.
5. Short IWM.
6. Report by James Campbell ('<u>Jimmy Campbell's Account</u>') brought to my attention by his daughter Patricia, and the **Alan Blyth Collection**.
7. Short IWM.
8. Austin Byrne's account, IWM Sound 11063.
9. Ibid.
10. PQ13's Commodore's Report.
11. Article by Gus Lacy junior in the 9 June 1942 South Boston News ('<u>South Boston News Article</u>'), Bernard Covington's documents ('<u>Covington's Documents</u>'), supplied

by Covington's son via Eric Berryman.

12. Undated letter from John Guthrie to Alan Blyth, Alan Blyth Collection.
13. *Effingham's* Crew List with a 14 April 1942 letter from the US Coast Guard, in <u>US MERCHANT VESSELS SINKING REPORTS</u> Box 14, Entry P2, states Joseph de Silva, the Chief Cook, had a 'dark' complexion.
14. Charles Hunnefield's diary ('<u>Hunnefield's Diary</u>') brought to my attention by his daughter Darlene and son-in-law Paul.
15. BRITISH ARCTIC CONVOYS HISTORY p. 32; and PQ13's Commodore's Report.
16. 2 April 1942 report by *Ballot* master Henry Bejer and Chief Officer H. Stromberg, <u>US MERCHANT SHIP LOSSES REPORTS</u> Box 214.
17. 9 April 1942 report by Commander Eric Hinton, Senior Officer, Sixth Minesweeping Flotilla ('<u>The Minesweepers' Report</u>'), NA London ADM 199/347.
18. Bill Short's written account, brought to my attention by his daughter Helen, confirms the number of survivors in the boat; and Rowlands' Report.
19. Short IWM.
20. 21 September 2007 edition of *Izvestia* newspaper, brought to my attention by Bill Short's daughter Helen.
21. Jimmy Campbell's Account.
22. South Boston News Article; and Rowlands' Report.
23. The Minesweepers' Report; and undated despatch in Covington's Documents.
24. 21 July 1944 Report On U.S. Merchant Vessel War Action

Casualty, based on information
from *Effingham*'s master, <u>US
CASUALTY REPORTS</u> Box 5.

25. Rowlands' Report.
26. Lise Lindbaek, *Tusen Norsk Skip*
pp. 185–9; and 7 April 1942 entry in
the war diary for the chief of Naval
Defence, Tromso, referred to in the
internet site covering the *Raceland*
sinking prepared by Leif Myrhoej
('The Raceland Site').
27. 2 April 1942 entry in the war diary
for the chief of Naval Defence,
Tromso, referred to in The
Raceland Site.
28. 9 April 1942 telegram, in Covington's
Documents.
29. Undated newspaper article 'cutting',
Covington's Documents.
30. Undated letter from 'Annie' to
Bernard Covington's parents,
Covington's Documents.
31. Undated note written by Bernard
Covington's mother, Covington's
Documents.
32. 4 May 1942 telegram, Covington's
Documents.
33. 29 June 1942 letter Bernard
Covington to his parents,
Covington's Documents.
34. 24 May 1942 entry in Hunnefield's
Diary.
35. 30 March 1942 entry in <u>KTB DER
SKL TEIL A</u>.
36. 30 March 1942 report by *Kenya*'s
Captain Michael Denny, NA
London ADM 199/72.

Chapter 8

1. Morris O. Mills, *Convoy PQ13:
Unlucky for Some* ('Mills' Book')
p. 99; 26 April 1942 report by PQ13's
Commodore D.A. Lacy, **NA
London** ADM 199/347.

2. SBNO North Russia's Report for
June 1942, NA London ADM
199/1104.
3. Undated 'Report of an Interview
with the Chief Officer, Mr A.S.
Galer. S.S. New Westminster City'
('New Westminster City's Report');
time of German attack: 16 July 1942
'Report Of An Interview With The
Master, Captain . . . Stein S.S.
Empire Starlight', both NA London
ADM 199/2140.
4. Edward Starkey, 'To Murmansk and
Back: My Arctic Run' for the Hull
Chess Club brought to my attention
by his daughter Marie; and New
Westminster City's Report.
5. Edward Starkey's account, **IWM
Sound** 15448.
6. Mills' Book pp. 103–104.
7. Undated report Morris Mills sent to
Alan Blyth in 1994, **Alan Blyth
Collection**.
8. Mills' Book pp. 104–106.
9. Austin Byrne's account, IWM
Sound 11063.
10. 'Hospital Facilities In North Russia
1941/2' ('McMillan's Article'),
including extracts from an article by
G. H. G. McMillan, previously
published in the *Journal of the Royal
Naval Medical Service*, The Arctic
Lookout Winter 1996: No. 26 pp.
20–1. The article contains a quote
from Austin Byrne.
11. William Short's account, IWM
Sound 11276 ('Short IWM').
12. Mills' Book p. 108.
13. Short IWM.
14. Mills' Book pp. 108–109.
15. Surgeon Lieutenant Ballantyne,
Ashanti's medical officer: Tovey's 30
July 1942 telegram, NA London
ADM 116/4972.

16. Surgeon Lieutenant Ballantyne's 23 July 1942 report 'Medical Services in the Kola Inlet existent on the arrival of Convoy P.Q.16.' ('Ballantyne's Report'), NA London ADM 116/4972.

17. Ibid.

18. *Edinburgh*'s Surgeon Lieutenant Lillie ('Lillie's Account') in McMillan's Article.

19. Ballantyne's Report; and Mills' Book pp. 106–7.

20. Lillie's Account

21. Ballantyne's Report.

22. Mills' Book p. 109.

23. Undated untitled report in US NAVAL ATTACHÉ REPORTS, Box 23, File 2/5 Medical.

24. 22 September 1942 Boston Globe article about *Ballot*'s Peter Hyde, brought to my attention by Bobbie Berryman (see Acknowledgements).

25. Short IWM.

26. 8 July 1971 letter from Geoff Jelbart, Alan Blyth Collection.

27. Undated written account by Bill Short, brought to my attention by his daughter Helen.

28. Report by James Campbell supplied by his daughter Tricia, and the Alan Blyth Collection.

Chapter 9

1. 1 April 1942 Minutes of Chiefs of Staff Committee, **NA London** CAB 79/20.

2. The undated documents in NA London ADM 237/165 stating that 26 merchant ships sailed in PQ14 should be treated with caution because other documents and publications contain conflicting statistics; WOODMAN'S BOOK p. 104 for example refers to 25 PQ14 merchant ships. Concerning the 8 PQ14 ships which carried on post 11 April 1942: see undated report by Vice Commodore Captain W.H. Lawrence, Master of *Briarwood*, NA London ADM 199/721; and 26 May 1942 'Report of an Interview with the Master Captain H. J. M. Downie Convoy P.Q.14' ('Empire Howard's Report'), NA London ADM 199/1709.

3. 20 April 1942 'Report of Proceedings of Escort Group with Convoy P.Q.14', NA London ADM 199/721 written by the destroyer *Bulldog*'s Commander Maxwell Richmond ('Bulldog's PQ14 Report').

4. Ibid.; and 15 April 1942 entry in KTB DES ADMIRAL NORDMEER which refers to the sighting of PQ14 in the location referred to as AB 5611 on the German grid (approximately 73°27' N 08°10' E).

5. Ibid.

6. Empire Howard's Report. The 16 April 1942 entry in KTB *U-403* whose crew fired the torpedoes states they did so at AC 4175 on the German grid map (approximately 73°51' N 21°10' E).

7. Empire Howard's Report.

8. Empire Howard's Report states that 56 men were in the ship when she was torpedoed, 16 were 'missing' after the ship sank, and 9 died after being picked up.

9. Empire Howard's Report.

10. The article in the *Journal of Royal Naval Medicine* 1991: 77: 139–149: 'Circum-Rescue Collapse' by F. St. C. Golden, G. R. Hervey and M. J. Tipton mentions the fallen blood pressure hypothesis. The article in the *Journal of Wilderness Medicine* 5, 88–98 (1994), which mentions the danger of drinking when cold, is:

'Alcohol ingestion and temperature regulation during cold exposure' by Beau J. Freund, Catherine O'Brien and Andrew J. Young.

11. No darkness: Bulldog's PQ14 Report.

12. Ibid.; and 27 April 1942 report by 18th Cruiser Squadron's Rear Admiral Stuart Bonham Carter ('Edinburgh's PQ14 Report'), NA London ADM 199/721.

13. Ships in QP10: Commodore D.A. Casey's 26 April 1942 'Report on Q.P.10. Sailed from Murmansk 10.4.1942' ('Commodore's QP10 Report'); and his 26 April 1942 report of proceedings ('Commodore's QP10 Proceedings') which referred to the former report, both NA London ADM 199/347.

14. 27 April 1942 report by the destroyer *Oribi*'s Commander John McBeath ('Oribi's QP10 Report'), NA London ADM 199/347.

15. 22 April 1942 report by the cruiser *Liverpool*'s Captain William Slayter ('Liverpool's QP10 Report'), NA London ADM 199/347.

16. Ibid.

17. Austin Byrne's account, **IWM Sound** 11063; Liverpool's QP10 Report.

18. Liverpool's QP10 Report.

19. 5 May 1942 'Report of an Interview with the Master, Captain J. H. Wigham S.S. Empire Cowper', ('Empire Cowper's Report'); and 28 April 1942 'Report Of An Interview With The Master, Captain H.W. Williams s.s. "Harpalion" ('Harpalion's Report'), both NA London ADM 199/2140.

20. Empire Cowper's Report; and the enclosure 'Track Chart of Convoy QP.10' ('QP10's Track Chart'), NA London ADM 199/358 which is said

to go with Oribi's QP10 Report. According to the Commodore's QP10 Proceedings, *Empire Cowper* was torpedoed at 70°40' N 36°25' E.

21. Empire Cowper's Report.

22. 19 January 1992 letter to Alan Blyth from Thomas Errington, **Alan Blyth Collection**.

23. Undated report by *Empire Cowper*'s Captain J. H. Wigham, NA London BT 381/2203.

24. J. K. Neale's account, **IWM Documents** 2130.

25. Oribi's QP10 Report.

26. Empire Cowper's Report.

27. Empire Cowper's Report; and 28 April 1942 report by HMT *Paynter*'s Lieutenant Richard Nossiter, NA London ADM 199/347.

28. Three German aircraft were shot down, and others were damaged during the afternoon of 11 April 1942 according to British witnesses: Oribi's QP10 Report. But the British claims should be treated with caution given that the 11 April 1942 Evening Report and 12 April 1942 Morning Report in **Luftflotte 5's Daily Reports** only refer to the shooting down of two Ju-88s.

29. 25 April 1942 'Report of Attacks on Convoy Q.P.10 11-13th April, 1942' by *Punjabi*'s Commander John Waldegrave ('Punjabi's QP10 Report'), NA London ADM 199/347; and Oribi's QP10 Report.

30. Punjabi's QP10 Report.

31. Oribi's QP10 Report.

32. Oribi's QP10 Report. The 13 April 1942 entry in the KTB *U-435* appears to state her crew torpedoed *El Occidente* at AC 4662 on the German grid (approximately 73°09' N 28°30' E), in line with the 10 May 1942

'Summary of Statements by Survivors, SS El Occidente' ('El Occidente's Report'), US ARMED GUARD REPORTS Box 190 UD93, which states she was torpedoed at 73° 28' N 28° 30' E. Both are consistent with QP10's Track Chart.

33. Chapter: Smert' Kieva i Empair Bairon (Death of 'Kiev' and 'Empire Byron') by G.A. Rudnev, pp. 167–177 of *Severnie Konvoi: Issledovaniya, vospominaniya, documenti, Vipusk 2* (*Northern Convoys: Research, memoirs, documents, vol. 2*).

34. Enclosure No. 2 to the 20 April 1942 report by *Speedwell's* Lieutenant Commander Joseph Youngs, NA London ADM 199/347; and El Occidente's Report.

35. Oribi's QP10 Report.

36. John Dodds' diary supplied by his son Nick and daughter Jane.

37. 13 April 1942 Evening Report, Luftflotte 5's Daily Reports; and QP10's Track Chart.

38. Oribi's QP10 Report; Commodore's QP10 Report; 21 April 1942 'Report on Voyage of Convoy Q.P.10' by Commanding Officer of HMS *Fury*, NA London ADM 199/347; 22 May 1942 'Report of Interview with the Master, Captain A.P. Collister. S.S. Beaconstreet', NA London ADM 237/174; Harpalion's Report.

39. Oribi's QP10 Report.

40. Commodore's QP10 Report.

41. Liverpool's QP10 Report.

42. Edinburgh's PQ14 Report.

43. 18 April 1942 entry in the KTB DER SKL TEIL A.

Chapter 10

1. Minutes of the Chiefs of Staff Committee, 128th Meeting, 23 April 1942, **NA London** WO 193/580.

2. War Cabinet Conclusions, 52 (42), 24 April 1942, NA London CAB 65/26.

3. 26 April 1942 Roosevelt to Churchill, CHURCHILL AND ROOSEVELT CORRESPONDENCE BOOK, p. 473.

4. 28 April 1942 Churchill to Roosevelt, ibid. p. 474.

5. Anne Chisholm and Michael Davie, *Beaverbrook: A Life* p. 434.

6. 10 May 1942 'Report of Proceedings of Escort Group with Convoy Q.P.11' by Commander Maxwell Richmond, Commanding Officer HMS *Bulldog*, NA London ADM 199/721.

7. TOVEY'S DESPATCH.

8. Frank Pearce, *Last Call For HMS Edinburgh* ('Edinburgh's Book') pp. 53–4.

9. Barry Penrose, *Stalin's Gold* pp. xii–xiii.

10. Edinburgh's Book p. 54.

11. 8 May 1942 report by Rear Admiral Stuart Bonham Carter ('Bonham Carter's QP11 Report'); and 5 May 1942 report by Captain Hugh Faulkner ('Edinburgh's Report'), both in NA London ADM 199/165.

12. Enclosure No. 6 to Edinburgh's Report.

13. Morris O. Mills, *Convoy PQ13: Unlucky for Some* ('Mills' Book') p. 117.

14. Ibid. p. 118.

15. Ibid. pp. 118–9.

16. 29 April 1942 entry in KTB DES ADMIRAL NORDMEER.

17. Undated report by SS *Briarwood's* W. H. Lawrence, NA London ADM 199/1709.

18. Bonham Carter's QP11 Report.
19. 30 April 1942 entry in KTB *U-456*; translation of such entry in Daniel Morgan and Bruce Taylor, *U-Boat Attack Logs* pp. 230-1. Distance from Murmansk: BRITISH ARCTIC CONVOYS HISTORY p. 37.
20. 30 April 1942 entry in KTB *U-456*.
21. Bonham Carter's QP11 Report; and Edinburgh's Report.
22. The 30 April 1942 entry in KTB *U-456* gives the location of the torpedoing as AC 5519 on the German grid map (approximately 73°15' N 32°50' E), and the time as 4.18 p.m.; whereas Bonham Carter's QP11 Report states his ship was torpedoed at 4.13 p.m.
23. Enclosure 1 to Edinburgh's Report states that the first torpedo seems to have hit *Edinburgh* near the ship's station 80, which is at the after end of the stokers' mess deck. The stokers' mess deck appears to have been located on the ship's lower deck, which is the second deck down from the open air forecastle deck.
24. Norman Sparksman, *Jottings of a Young Sailor* p. 36.
25. Ibid. pp. 36–7.
26. Edinburgh's Report.
27. Jocelyn Salter's account ('Salter's Account'), **IWM Sound** 9304.
28. Edinburgh's Report.
29. John Kenny's account, **IWM Documents** 92/27/1.
30. Alan Higgins, *You're In The Navy Now* pp. 21–2.
31. Alan Higgins when interviewed by me in June 2020, facilitated by his daughter Susan.
32. Mills' Book pp. 120–2.
33. Edinburgh's Book pp. 66–7.
34. Salter's Account; and Edinburgh's Report.
35. Edinburgh's Report.
36. Jack Thwaite, 'A Signalman in HMS *Edinburgh*: the story of the "gold ship"', IWM Documents LBYK 95/384, also brought to my attention by his daughter Sue.
37. 30 April 1942 entry in the KTB des Admiral Nordmeer.
38. 1 May 1942 entry in KTB ZERSTÖRERGRUPPE NORDMEER.
39. Ibid.; and 1 May entry in the KTB des Admiral Nordmeer.
40. 3 May 1942 entry in KTB DER SKL TEIL A.
41. 1 May 1942 entry in KTB Zerstörergruppe Nordmeer.

Chapter 11

1. 10 May 1942 report by *Amazon*'s Lieutenant Commander Nigel Roper ('Amazon's QP11 Report'), **NA London** ADM 116/4544 brought to my attention by David Slade; and 5 May 1942 report by *Snowflake*'s Lieutenant Harold Chesterman, NA London ADM 199/721.
2. 10 May 1942 Report by *Beverley*'s Lieutenant Commander John Grant ('Beverley's QP11 Report'), NA London ADM 199/721.
3. Amazon's QP11 Report.
4. 10 May 1942 'Report of Proceedings of Escort Group with Convoy Q.P.11.' by *Bulldog*'s Commander Maxwell Richmond, NA London ADM 199/721 ('Bulldog's QP11 Report').
5. Recommendation for award to be given to Petty Officer Charles Green, 'Enclosure No.4 in 888/11.F. 0212/35 of 3rd July 1942', NA London ADM 116/4544.

6. Ibid.

7. Amazon's QP11 Report.

8. Bulldog's QP11 Report; and 6 May 1942 report by *Beagle's* Commander Ralph Medley ('Beagle's QP11 Report'), NA London ADM 199/721.

9. Amazon's QP11 Report.

10. 13 August 1942 'Report Of Interview With The Master, Captain W. H. Lawrence O.B.E. S.S. Briarwood', NA London ADM 199/1709.

11. 10 May 1942 'Narrative' by *Bulldog's* Commander Richmond, NA London ADM 199/721; Beverley's QP11 Report; and Beagle's QP11 Report.

12. 1 May 1942 entry KTB ZERSTÖRERGRUPPE NORDMEER.

13. BRITISH ARCTIC CONVOYS HISTORY p. 39.

14. Undated report by *Foresight's* Commander Jocelyn Salter delivered to Admiral Bonham Carter on 8 May 1942 ('Foresight's Report'), NA London ADM 199/165.

15. 5 May 1942 report by Captain Hugh Faulkner ('Edinburgh's Report'); and 8 May 1942 report by 6th Minesweeping Flotilla's and *Harrier's* Commander Eric Hinton ('Harrier's Report'), both in NA London ADM 199/165.

16. Foresight's Report.

17. Ibid.

18. Edinburgh's Report.

19. Gunnery report in Enclosure 8 to Edinburgh's Report; Appendix 1 to the 18 June 1942 letter from Admiral Jack Tovey to the Secretary of the Admiralty (Honours and Awards), NA London ADM 116/4544; and Rear Admiral Bonham Carter's 'Notes Made Onboard Harrier On The Way Back to Kola' ('Bonham Carter's Notes') in Appendix II to the 8 May 1942 report by Rear Admiral Stuart Bonham Carter ('Bonham Carter's QP11 Report'), NA London ADM 199/165.

20. Undated 'Gefechtsbericht "Hermann Schoemann" über Ansatz Zerstörergruppe "Nordmeer" gegen havarierten "Belfast"-Kreuzer bzw. Ost-West-Geleitzug' written by Korvettenkapitän Heinrich Wittig ('Hermann Schoemann's Report') attached to 6 May 1942 letter circulating it, **Militärarchiv Freiburg** RM 58/41.

21. 6 May 1942 'Narrative of Action on 2nd May 1942' by Lieutenant Jack Bitmead ('Forester's Report'), NA London ADM 199/165.

22. Edinburgh's Report; and Bonham Carter's Notes.

23. Jack Thwaite memoir 'A Signalman in HMS Edinburgh: the story of the "gold ship"' p. 33, **IWM Documents** LBYK 95/384.

24. Harrier's Report.

25. Alan Higgins, *You're In The Navy Now* pp. 26–7; and Alan Higgins when interviewed by me in June 2020.

26. Enclosure 1: Damage Control section of Edinburgh's Report.

27. Forester's Report.

28. Forester's Report and Foresight's Report.

29. Account by Joseph Fowells ('Fowells' Report'). brought to my attention by his son Richard and grandson Chris.

30. Forester's Report, Foresight's Report; and Harrier's Report.

31. Foresight's Report.

32. Fowells' Report.

33. Foresight's Report; Forester's Report and Fowells' Report.
34. 22 October 1942 recommendation for the award of the Albert Medal to Stoker Petty Officer John P. Bain; the 6 January 1943 confirmation the Medal should be awarded; and the details in the document recommending that his rescuer Lt Pughe Davies Lewis should be honoured, NA London ADM 116/454; and Foresight's Report.
35. Hermann Schoemann's Report.
36. Bonham Carter's QP11 Report.
37. Harrier's Report.
38. Morris O. Mills, *Convoy PQ13: Unlucky for Some* p. 125.
39. Fowells' Report.
40. Bonham Carter's QP11 Report – which states he estimated *Edinburgh* sank at 71°51' N 35°10' E; and Bonham Carter's Notes.
41. Foresight's Report; Forester's Report; and Harrier's Report.
42. Hermann Schoemann's Report; 2 May 1942 entry in the KTB Zerstörergruppe Nordmeer; 2 May 1942 entry in KTB DES ZERSTÖRERS Z 25; and Edinburgh's Report.
43. Undated report headed 'H.M.S. Forester and Foresight Shell Damage', NA London ADM 267/23.
44. Jocelyn Salter account, **IWM Sound** 9304.
45. Undated report by SS *Briarwood*'s W.H. Lawrence, NA London ADM 199/1709.
46. 2 May 1942 entry in KTB Zerstörergruppe Nordmeer.
47. 2 May 1942 entry in KTB DES ADMIRAL NORDMEER.
48. 8 May 1942 entry in KTB DER SKL TEIL A.

Chapter 12

1. Number of PQ15 merchant ships: Commodore Herbert Anchor's 26 April 1942 Report of proceedings; and list of PQ15 ships ('PQ15's Ship List'), both **NA London** ADM 237/166.
2. PQ15's Ship List.
3. Manifest of aid carried by American SS *Topa Topa*, NA London ADM 237/166.
4. The War Transport Minister was Lord (Frederick) Leathers.
5. 28 April 1942 letter from Churchill to Roosevelt, CHURCHILL AND ROOSEVELT CORRESPONDENCE BOOK p. 474.
6. 21 May 1942 report by PQ15 Commodore H. J. Anchor refers to two trawlers, while his undated note headed 'Important Incidents' refers to a trawler with a different name to those in the aforementioned report. Both reports are in NA London ADM 237/166.
7. 6 May 1942 report by the 10th Cruiser Squadron's Rear Admiral Harold Burrough ('10 Cruiser Squadron's PQ15 Report'), NA London ADM 199/721.
8. Ibid.
9. 11 May 1942 report by Lieutenant Commander Roger Hill, commander of HMS *Ledbury*, NA London ADM 199/721; and 10 Cruiser Squadron's PQ15 Report.
10. The 1 May 1942 'Report of Collision or Grounding' with the minutes of the 7–8 May 1942 Court Martial relating to the 'Loss of H.M.S. Punjabi in collision with H.M.S. King George V: 1 May 1942' ('the Punjabi Court Martial Minutes'), NA London ADM

156/227, states the collision occurred at 66°52' N 08°02' W.

11. Robert Ellis' account ('Ellis' Account') supplied by his granddaughter Caroline.

12. 5 May 1942 report by Sub-Lieutenant A. M. Synnot with the Punjabi Court Martial Minutes.

13. Ellis' Account.

14. 2 May 1942 report by *Punjabi*'s Commander John Waldegrave in the Punjabi Court Martial Minutes.

15. 'Part II Of The Commander-In-Chief, Home Fleet's War Diary Covering The Period 16th to 30th April 1942' and subsequent days, NA London ADM 199/427.

16. Jugement in the Punjabi Court Martial Minutes.

17. 27 September 1989 letter from Stanisław Olszowski to Theresa Cass, Archivist at Naval Submarine Base, New London, Groton, Connecticut, USA ('Olszowki's Letter'), brought to my attention by Anna Pacewicz; About ORP Jastrząb featuring answers given by Stanisław Olszowski to questions posed, in Nasze Sygnaly Nr. 173 January to June 1993 pp. 56-63 brought to my attention by Wanda Troman; and 'Findings of Board of Inquiry Into Loss of O.R.P. Jastrząb' ('Jastrząb Inquiry') held on 13–16 July 1942, **Sikorski Museum**, MAR AV 30/2.

18. 10 Cruiser Squadron's PQ15 Report.

19. Ultra timed 1 May 1942 1347B, NA London ADM 223/110.

20. The following documents specify where, near PQ15, *Jastrząb* was detected and attacked: the 7 May 1942 report by H. Nor. M.S. *St. Albans*' Commander Skule

Storheill ('St Albans' Jastrząb Report') specifies 73°01' N 17° 32' E; whereas the 3 May 1942 report by *Seagull*'s Lieutenant Commander Charles Pollock ('Seagull's Jastrząb Report') specified 72°58' N 18°09' E, both in NA London ADM 199/721.

21. Snow falling as *St Albans* passed: Romanowski testimony in minutes of 13 July 1942 'Board of Inquiry into the loss of Polish Submarine Jastrząb', Sikorski Museum MAR AV 30/2.

22. Bołeslaw Romanowski, *Torpeda W Celu* (Torpedo On Target) ('Romanowki's Book') pp. 254–9.

23. From the Frying Pan Into The Fire: ORP Jastrząb: The Last Patrol by Stanisław Olszowski ('Olszowki's Last Patrol'), in Nasze Sygnaly Nr. 161 January to April 1988 brought to my attention by Wanda Troman.

24. The Unsuccessful Patrol by Andrzej Guzowski in Nasze Signaly Nr.137 March to August 1977 pp. 3–6; Romanowski's Book; Olszowski's Letter; Olszowski's Last Patrol; and Seagull's Jastrząb Report.

25. St Albans' Jastrząb Report.

26. 8 May 1942 report by the minesweeper *Bramble*'s Captain Harvey Crombie ('Bramble's Report'), NA London ADM 199/721.

27. Jastrząb Inquiry.

28. Ibid.

29. St Albans' Jastrząb Report.

30. 10 Cruiser Squadron's PQ15 Report.

31. Ibid.

32. R.F.C. Struben account ('Struben's Account'), **IWM Documents** 3375; and Bramble's Report.

33. Struben's Account.
34. Bramble's Report states the location of the attack was 73°00' N 19°40' E.
35. Report by *Somali*'s Captain Jack Eaton ('Somali's PQ15 Report'), NA London ADM 199/721.
36. 'Report Of Interview With The Master Captain J. Barnetson. S.S. Cape Race' ('Cape Race's Report'), NA London ADM 237/166.
37. 4 June 1942 'S.S. Botavon Report of an Interview with the Master Captain J.H. Smith' ('Botavon's Report'), NA London ADM 199/2140
38. W. L. Cruickshank account ('Cruickshank's Account'), IWM Documents 96/21/1.
39. Struben's Account.
40. Cape Race's Report.
41. 23 June 1942 'Report Of Interview With The Master Captain H. Austin. S.S. Southgate', NA London ADM 237/166.
42. Struben's Account.
43. Cruickshank's Account; and Botavon's Report.
44. Cruickshank's Account; and 9 June 1942 'S.S. "Jutland" Report of an Interview with the Master, Captain J. Henderson' ('Jutland's Report'), NA London ADM 199/2140.
45. Ibid.
46. Cape Race's Report; and 14 August 1942 'Report Of An Interview With The Second Engineer, Mr. G. Waddingham s.s. Cape Corso' ('Cape Corso's Report'), NA London ADM 199/2140.
47. Struben's Account; and 5 June 1942 report by Captain Dan McGrath, commander of HMS *Ulster Queen*, NA London ADM/721.
48. Jack Whyte's account brought to my attention by Norman Angell, son of *Cape Corso* crew member Arthur Angell, who was killed when the ship was torpedoed.
49. Kenneth Allen statement given to Amy Cotton, sister of Seaman Hayes, who was killed when *Cape Corso* was torpedoed.
50. Cape Corso's Report.
51. Botavon's Report; and Jutland's Report.
52. Botavon's Report.
53. Jutland's Report.
54. Struben's Account.
55. 28 April 1942 Admiralty message, NA London ADM 199/110.
56. Struben's Account; and 22 April 1942 report by *St Albans*' Commander Storheill, NA London ADM 237/166.
57. Struben's Account; and concerning the deteriorating weather: Bramble's Report.
58. Somali's PQ15 Report.

Chapter 13

1. 30 April 1942 Roosevelt to Churchill, CHURCHILL'S BOOK vol. 4 p. 231.
2. 2 May 1942 Churchill to Roosevelt, ibid. p. 232.
3. 2 May 1942 Roosevelt to Churchill, CHURCHILL AND ROOSEVELT CORRESPONDENCE BOOK p. 483.
4. 6 May 1942 Stalin to Churchill, REYNOLDS AND PECHATNOV p. 108.
5. Antony Beevor, *Stalingrad* pp. 65–7 and 72.
6. 9 May 1942 Churchill to Stalin, Reynolds and Pechatnov pp. 108–9.
7. 13 May 1942 Stalin to Churchill, Churchill's Book vol. 4 p. 233.
8. 9 May 1942 Churchill to Stalin, ibid.

9. 10 May 1942 report by *Bulldog*'s Commander Maxwell Richmond, **NA London** ADM 199/721.

10. Jocelyn Salter account, **IWM Sound** 9304.

11. Captain Leslie Saunders' memoirs ('Saunders' Memoirs'), **Alan Blyth Collection,** and supplied by Captain Saunders' son Iain.

12. Rear Admiral Bonham Carter's 14 May 1942 'impressions' ('Bonham Carter's Trinidad Sinking Report') with 21 May 1942 letter to Tovey, NA London ADM 116/4544.

13. Frank Pearce, *The Ship That Torpedoed Herself* ('Trinidad's Book') p. 140.

14. Bonham Carter's Trinidad Sinking Report; and 26 May 1942 report by *Trinidad*'s Captain Leslie Saunders ('Trinidad's Sinking Report'), NA London ADM 116/4544.

15. 23 May 1942 report by Captain Jack Eaton, Captain (D), Sixth Destroyer Flotilla in *Somali* ('Somali's Trinidad Report'), NA London ADM 116/4544.

16. Diary by Midshipman Thomas Baird, later Vice Admiral Sir Thomas Baird ('Baird's Diary'), brought to my attention by him, and his friend David Dickson.

17. Somali's Trinidad Report.

18. Trinidad's Book p. 140.

19. Ibid. p. 141.

20. Ibid. p. 143.

21. Baird's Diary.

22. Somali's Trinidad Report.

23. Trinidad's Sinking Report.

24. Baird's Diary.

25. Trinidad's Book pp. 145–7.

26. Saunders' Memoirs.

27. Trinidad's Book p. 154.

28. Trinidad's Sinking Report.

29. Saunders' Memoirs.

30. Trinidad's Book pp. 162–3.

31. Baird's Diary. Trinidad's Sinking Report states *Trinidad* was bombed and sunk at approximately 73°03' N 23°26' E.

32. Saunders' Memoirs. The following source appears to state that 93 of *Trinidad*'s officers and ratings were killed if one takes into account all those who lost their lives when she was torpedoed and later bombed and sunk: document entitled 'R.N. Casualties In N. Russia Convoys' sent with undated note, written after the 31 December 1942 Battle of the Barents Sea, and circulated by the office of the Director of Naval Intelligence, NA London ADM 199/604.

33. Trinidad's Book p. 167.

34. Saunders' Memoirs; Trinidad's Report; and 3 October 1942 letter to the Deputy Master, Royal Mint confirming the award of the Albert Medal, NA London ADM 116/4544.

35. Somali's Trinidad Report.

36. Ibid.

37. Ibid.

Chapter 14

1. PQ16's formation diagram is in this book's Appendix B.

2. 16 May 1942 minutes of War Cabinet Chiefs of Staff Committee, **NA London** CAB 79/21.

3. 19 May 1942 Churchill to Stalin, REYNOLDS AND PECHATNOV p. 111.

4. Graeme Ogden, *My Sea Lady* ('Ogden's Book') pp. 18–19 and 94.

5. Ibid. pp. 5–6.

6. Ibid. p. 94.

7. 29 May 1942 Report of Proceedings by Rear Admiral Harold Burrough,

commander 10th Cruiser Squadron ('10 Cruiser Squadron's PQ16 Report'), NA London ADM 199/757.

8. Ogden's Book p. 95.

9. Ibid. pp. 94–5.

10. Ibid. p. 97.

11. 30 May 1942 report by PQ16 Commodore N. H. Gale, NA London ADM 199/757.

12. Ibid.; and list of ships that sailed in PQ16, NA London ADM 237/167. See also this book's Appendix B (PQ16's formation) and its Notes.

13. Ogden's Book p. 99.

14. Alexander Werth, *The Year of Stalingrad* ('Werth's Book') pp. 27–8.

15. 18 and 22 May 1942 entries of KTB DES ADMIRAL NORDMEER; and 5 June 1942 message from SBNO Archangel to Admiralty, NA London ADM 237/167 specifying PQ16's route.

16. 6 June 1942 Report of Proceedings by *Ashanti*'s Commander Richard Onslow ('Ashanti's PQ16 Report'); and 10 Cruiser Squadron's PQ16 Report, both NA London ADM 199/757.

17. Ogden's Book p. 102; and Ashanti's PQ16 Report.

18. Ibid.

19. Ogden's Book pp. 102–3. The German word Schlachter means butcher.

20. William Edward Grenfell's account ('Grenfell's Account'), **IWM Sound** 15450.

21. 29 May 1942 report by Captain (D) Third Destroyer Flotilla in destroyer *Inglefield* specifies number of QP12 ships, and its escort: 6 destroyers, 4 trawlers, and an anti-aircraft ship after the local escort and the two

Russian destroyers dropped out, which they did before reaching the meridian of North Cape, NA London ADM 199/347.

22. Ashanti's PQ16 Report.

23. 10 Cruiser Squadron's PQ16 Report.

24. Captain W. L. Cruickshank's account ('Cruickshank's Report'), **IWM Documents** 5145.

25. R. F. C. Struben's account, IWM Documents 3375.

26. Cruickshank's Report.

27. Ashanti's PQ16 Report states the attack commenced at 72°03' N 03°14' E.

28. Werth's Book pp. 30–1.

29. 10 Cruiser Squadron's PQ16 Report.

30. Grenfell's Account.

31. B. Pawłowicz, *O.R.P. Garland: In convoy to Russia* ('Pawłowicz's Book') p. 27.

32. Grenfell's Account.

33. Pawłowicz's Book p. 27.

34. 10 Cruiser Squadron's PQ16 Report.

35. Werth's Book p. 31.

36. Ashanti's PQ16 Report, including its Appendix I, and the latter's Annexe I and the screening diagrams referred to in such Annexe I.

37. Werth's Book p. 31.

38. Ashanti's PQ16 Report.

39. Ibid.

40. Undated report by *Hyderabad*'s Lieutenant Stuart Hickman, NA London ADM 237/176.

41. Ashanti's PQ16 Report; location: 10 July 1942 report by SS *Syros*' 2nd Officer James W. Davidson (Syros' 2nd Officer's Report'), US MERCHANT VESSELS SINKING REPORTS Box 47 Entry P-2.

42. Romuald Holubowicz's account ('Holubowicz's Account'), IWM

Documents 2159, with permission from his daughter Diana Holubowicz. The 10 June 1942 report by J.G. Grotenrath, commanding officer of the Armed Guard in SS *City of Joliet,* US ARMED GUARD REPORTS Box 134 UD 93, confirms the torpedo hit *Syros* on her port side. The document headed 'Appendix X. Anti-Submarine Operations', which is Appendix I to Ashanti's PQ16 Report, states *Syros* was torpedoed at 72°43' N 06°20' E.

43. 26 May 1942 entry in <u>KTB *U-703*</u>.
44. Holubowicz's Account.
45. Syros' 2nd Officer's Report.
46. Ashanti's PQ16 Report.

Chapter 15
1. PQ16's formation diagram is in this book's Appendix B.
2. 29 May 1942 Report of Proceedings by Rear Admiral Harold Burrough, commander of the 10th Cruiser Squadron, **NA London** ADM 199/757.
3. Alexander Werth, *The Year of Stalingrad* ('Werth's Book') pp. 27–8.
4. 6 June 1942 Report of Proceedings by *Ashanti*'s Commander Richard Onslow ('Ashanti's PQ16 Report').
5. LUFTFLOTTE 5'S WAR DIARY.
6. Ashanti's PQ16 Report.
7. Enclosure F with 2 June 1942 report by *Alynbank*'s Captain Henry Nash ('Alynbank's PQ16 Report'), NA London ADM 199/757 states that series of attacks starting at around 11.15 a.m. on 27 May 1942 commenced when the convoy was at 73°35' N 20°25' E.
8. Ibid.
9. Luftflotte 5's War Diary.

10. Werth's Book p. 34; and Appendix II to Ashanti's PQ16 Report.
11. 28 July 1942 report by *Garland*'s Lt Commander H. Eibel, **Sikorski Museum**.
12. B. Pawłowicz, *O.R.P. Garland: In Convoy to Russia* pp. 38–46.
13. Ashanti's PQ16 Report.
14. 30 May 1942 message from O.R.P. *Garland* to the SBNO North Russia, NA London ADM 358/4083.
15. Loftus Peyton Jones, *Wartime Wanderings 1939–1945*, p. 83 brought to my attention by his son Professor James Peyton Jones.
16. Werth's Book p. 34.
17. Ralph Ransome Wallis, *Two Red Stripes* ('Martin's Surgeon's Book') pp. 83 and 93–5.
18. Undated report by Ensign William Gibson, 'Officer in Charge, Armed Guard Unit, S.S. Alamar', <u>US NAVAL ATTACHÉ REPORTS</u> Box 25, Entry UD 44.
19. 10 June 1942 report by Ensign Frank P. McConnell, Commanding Officer Armed Guard Unit SS *Mormacsul*, <u>US ARMED GUARD REPORTS</u>, Box 482 Entry UD 93.
20. Graeme Ogden, *My Sea Lady* ('Ogden's Book') p. 108.
21. 31 May 1942 'Report of Escorts of Convoy "P.Q.16" 13th May – 30th May 1942' by commanding officer HMS *Trident*, NA London ADM 199/1864.
22. Account by Commander Edward Grenfell ('Grenfell's Account'), as he was at the time of his post-war interview, **IWM Sound** 15450. Ashanti's PQ16 Report's Appendix II states the *Empire Lawrence* bombing was at 73° 27' N 22° 40' E, and specifies convoy's course.

23. Ogden's Book p. 109.
24. Grenfell's Account.
25. Werth's Book p. 35.
26. Ogden's Book pp. 109, and 34. Ogden's first lieutenant was Geoffrey Angus.
27. Grenfell's Account.
28. Werth's Book pp. 35–6.
29. Undated report by *Hyderabad*'s Lieutenant Stuart Hickman ('Hyderabad's Report'), NA London ADM 237/176; and 28 July 1942 'Report Of An Interview With The 2nd Officer Mr. N.S. Hulse. S.S. Empire Lawrence', NA London ADM 199/2140.
30. Ogden's Book p. 109.
31. Martin's Surgeon's Book p. 98.
32. 10 June 1942 report by *City of Joliet* Armed Guard Commander J.G. Grotenrath, US Armed Guard Reports Box 134 UD93. Time of bombing specified in Commodore N.H. Gale's 30 May 1942 report of proceedings ('PQ16's Commodore's Report'), NA London ADM 237/167. Location of bombing raid: Ashanti's PQ16 Report's Appendix II: 73°43' N 23°51' E.
33. Werth's Book pp. 36–7.
34. Number of German aircraft deployed: Luftflotte 5's War Diary; corroborated by the 27-29 May 1942 entries in **Luftflotte 5's Daily Reports**. The 3 June 1942 entry in KTB DER SKL TEIL A confirmed Luftwaffe's reports of sinkings were exaggerated.
35. Werth's Book p. 37.
36. 27 May entry in KTB DES ADMIRAL NORDMEER.
37. Ashanti's PQ16 Report's Appendix II states that the raid during which

Empire Purcell and *Lowther Castle* were hit commenced at around 73°49' N 24°38' E.
38. Werth's Book p. 38.
39. Thomas Edward Chilvers' diary, MSS 87/090, JOD/325, **National Maritime Museum**.
40. 21 July 1942 'Report Of An Interview With The Chief Officer Mr. J.G. Lomas. S.S. Lowther Castle', NA London ADM 199/2140.
41. Account by Roy Dykes given to me by Ian Claxton, author of *Honeysuckle's War: The Story of a Corvette* ('Dykes' Account'); and an interview with Roy Dykes posted on YouTube.
42. 15 July 1942 'Report Of An Interview With The Master Captain R. Stephenson. S.S. Empire Purcell', NA London ADM 199/2140.
43. Hyderabad's Report.
44. Dykes' Account; and Hyderabad's Report.
45. Hyderabad's Report.
46. PQ16's Commodore's Report; Ashanti's PQ16 Report; and Alynbank's PQ16 Report.
47. Ashanti's PQ16 Report.
48. Werth's Book p. 38.
49. 19 July 1942 Patrol Report by *Seawolf*'s Commanding Officer for period 13 May to 30 May 1942, NA London ADM 199/1836.
50. Ashanti's PQ16 Report, account by J. Lussey from *Alynbank*, **IWM Documents** 92/27/1, and 2166; and 28 and 29 May 1942 entries in KTB des Admiral Nordmeer.
51. Hyderabad's Report; and 2 June 1942 report by Armed Guard commander in SS *West Nilus*, US NAVAL ATTACHÉ REPORTS Box 25 UD 44.

Chapter 16

1. PQ17's formation diagram is in this book's Appendix A.
2. Tovey's 19 June 1942 letter to the Admiralty, **NA London** ADM 199/757. Although 28 merchant ships arrived in Russia, 29 remained afloat (*Carlton* had returned to Iceland).
3. TOVEY'S DESPATCH.
4. 12 January 1953 letter from Tovey to the official historian Stephen Roskill, **Churchill Archives Centre**, ROSK 4/29.
5. Jak Mallmann Showell, ed., *Fuehrer Conferences On Naval Affairs 1939–1945* pp. 284–7. Details about German aircraft based on Brian Filley, *Junkers Ju 88 in Action Part 1* and other sources brought to my attention by Peter Taghon; and Alexander Steenbeck, *Die Spur des Löwen.*
6. Ibid.; and 9 June 1942 message from the staff of the Oberbefehlshaber der Luftwaffe to the Seekriegsleitung, **Militärarchiv Freiburg** RM 7/1024.
7. Ned Denning's 'PQ17' account, **National Maritime Museum** DEN 6/1 File 38 MS/84/192.
8. Henry Denham, *Inside the Nazi Ring* pp. 87–90; and BRITISH INTELLIGENCE OFFICIAL HISTORY vol. 2 p. 213.
9. Militärarchiv Freiburg RW 49/551; and the Cobweb file in NA London KV2/1137, both brought to my attention by Alf R. Jacobsen and his book *X-Craft Versus Tirpitz: The Mystery of the Missing X5* pp. 41-57. Cobweb's real name was Ib Riis.
10. Report by Vladimir Nikolaevich Izotov, captain of *Azerbeijan*, ('Izotov's Report'), **GAOPDiFAO** Section 296, Inventory 1, Book 1210 pp. 63-73.
11. Report by Douglas Fairbanks Junior ('Fairbanks' Report'), **National Maritime Museum** MSS 87/090.
12. Douglas Fairbanks Jnr., *A Hell of a War* ('Fairbanks' Book') pp. 128–9.
13. Izotov's Report. Rear Admiral Louis Hamilton said he, Jack Broome and PQ17's Commodore Dowding spoke at the convoy conference, 11 July 1942 'Report Of Proceedings Of The Cruiser Force Covering Convoy P.Q. 17', Churchill Archives Centre ROSK 19/5. Fairbanks' Report states that Hamilton warned that the cruisers might not be seen by the convoy very often.
14. 13 July 1942 report by PQ17's Commodore John Dowding, NA London ADM 199/757.
15. PQ17 ships taken from: diagram in NA London ADM 237/168; and 8 July 1942 report by *Keppel's* Commander Jack Broome ('Keppel's Report'), Churchill Archives Centre, ROSK 19/5.
16. Fairbanks' Book pp. 132–3.
17. 4 October 1942 report by Ensign E.S. Neely, the commanding officer armed guard: SS *Richard Bland*, US ARMED GUARD REPORTS UD93 Box 547; and Keppel's Report.'
18. Keppel's Report.
19. Godfrey Winn, 'P.Q.17' ('Winn's Book') p. 61. Date taken from the Narrative attached to the July 1942 letter (date of document partly cut out of document) from *Palomares'* commander John Jauncey, Churchill Archives Centre ROSK 19/5.

20. Winn's Book p. 63.
21. Ibid.
22. Keppel's Report.
23. Winn's Book pp. 66-7.
24. 30 June 1942 entry in <u>KTB DES ADMIRAL NORDMEER</u>.
25. Anlage 12 to KTB des Admiral Nordmeer for 16–30 June 1942 containing confirmation of where Gruppe Eisteufel U-boats were to line up on 29 June 1942.
26. Time aircraft sighted: Keppel's Report. Location of PQ17 when sighted by aircraft: AB 7167 on the German grid (approximately 71°09' N 4°50' W), 1 July 1942 entry in the KTB des Admiral Nordmeer.
27. Winn's Book p. 67.
28. Keppel's Report.
29. Fairbanks' Report.
30. Winn's Book p. 68.
31. The approximate location of the 2 July 1942 attack on PQ17 is specified as being 73°30' N 4° E in Appendix I to the 6 July 1942 'Report of the Operations Of The Cruiser Force Covering P.Q. 17' (<u>'Hamilton's 6 July 1942 Report'</u>), Churchill Archives Centre ROSK 19/5.
32. Keppel's Report; Hamilton's 6 July 1942 Report; Christer Bergström, a co-author of *Black Cross Red Star: Air War Over the Eastern Front vol.3* bringing to my attention Walter Lehwess-Litzmann, *Absturz ins Leben* p. 189.
33. Winn's Book p. 74.
34. Ibid.
35. Keppel's Report.
36. The signal from the Admiralty's Operational Intelligence Centre at 4.59 p.m. 3 July 1942 said no warships were in Trondheim harbour; this was corroborated by the photographs taken, according to the signal, at 7.47 p.m. 3 July 1942. A signal sent to PQ17's escorts at 10.22 p.m. 3 July 1942 confirmed the Admiralty's appreciation the German warships had moved to the north, threatening the convoy. All in NA London ADM 237/168.
37. Winn's Book p. 75.
38. Hamilton's 6 July 1942 Report.
39. Rear Admiral Hamilton's 9 July 1942 'Report On Withdrawal Of First Cruiser Squadron And Scattering Of Convoy P.Q.17', Churchill Archives Centre ROSK 19/5.
40. 27 June 1942 Admiralty instructions in Tovey's Despatch; and Captain Jack Broome, *Convoy Is To Scatter* pp. 110–12.
41. Tovey's Despatch confirms the Home Fleet covered PQ17 during the morning of 4 July 1942, at the end of which according to Hamilton's 6 July 1942 Report it was not far short of 24°10' E, where it was at 1.35 p.m. on 4 July 1942. Home Fleet ships deployed: Part II Commander-in-Chief Home Fleet's War Diary 1–15 July 1942, NA London ADM 199/427.

Chapter 17

1. PQ17's formation diagram is in this book's Appendix A.
2. The coordinates given by the 14 July 1942 report by the Master of *Christopher Newport* (<u>'Christopher Newport's Master's Report'</u>), **NA London** ADM 199/757; and the 11 July 1942 report by Admiral Hamilton, **Churchill Archives Centre** ROSK 19/5 are: 75°49' N

22°15' E and 75°05' N 20°00' E respectively.

3. Christopher Newport's Master's Report. The ship's cargo is specified in 11 August 1942 'Convoy Room (PQ Section) Trade Division' list, NA London ADM 237/168.

4. 3 November 1942 'Summary of statements by survivors of the S/S Christopher Newport', US MERCHANT SHIP LOSSES REPORTS Box 218.

5. Report by Vladimir Nikolaevich Izotov, captain of *Azerbaijan*, **GAOPDiFAO** Archive Section 296, Inventory 1, Book 1210 pp. 63–73.

6. Godfrey Winn, '*P.Q.17*' ('Winn's Book') p. 83.

7. Douglas Fairbanks Jnr., *A Hell of a War* p. 137.

8. Hugh Sebag-Montefiore, *The Battle For The Code* pp. 198–9.

9. Patrick Beesly, *Very Special Intelligence* ('Beesly's Book') pp. 11–19.

10. Robin Brodhurst, *Churchill's Anchor* p. 201.

11. Ibid. pp. 113 and 121–3.

12. Arthur Hutchinson letter dated 16 October 1966, Churchill Archives Centre, MLBE 1/14.

13. Beesly's Book p.139; and Admiral Sir Henry Moore's 24 April 1967 letter ('Moore's PQ17 Letter'), Churchill Archives Centre MLBE 1/14.

14. 10.17 a.m. 3 July 1942 message sent by the OIC's Deputy Director Intelligence Centre, NA London ADM 223/111. The 'decrypts' of the messages to Schniewind summarized in the Ultra are in NA London DEFE 3/110 p.396 (sent to Schniewind at 11.03 p.m. 2 July 1942)

and p.394 (sent to Schniewind at 3.26 a.m. 3 July 1942).

15. Reports of reconnaissance at 2 p.m. 3 July 1942 sent out by OIC's D.D.I.C. at 4.59 p.m. 3 July (visual observation: no warships in Trondheim); and 7.47 p.m. 3 July 1942 (photographs show warships have left Trondheim), both in NA London ADM 237/168.

16. 12.30 p.m. 4 July 1942 order from Admiralty to CS 1, Appendix II to Hamilton's 6 July 1942 report ('Hamilton's 6 July 1942 Report'), Churchill Archives Centre ROSK 19/5.

17. 3.12 p.m. 4 July 1942 order from Tovey to CS 1, in ibid.

18. 6.09 p.m. 4 July 1942 message from Hamilton to Tovey and Admiralty, in ibid. Position inferred from: Hamilton's 11 July 1942 report, Churchill Archives Centre ROSK 19/5; and report by Douglas Fairbanks Junior, **National Maritime Museum** MSS 87/090.

19. Ned Denning's 'PQ17' account ('Denning's PQ17 Account'), National Maritime Museum DEN 6/1 File 38 MS/84/192 states that Pound received Hamilton's 6.09 p.m. 4 July 1942 message while Denning and Pound were conferring in the OIC for the first time that evening. If Denning's recollection is correct, that puts their first meeting at some point between 6.09 p.m, and around 6.50 p.m. 4 July 1942, the latter time being the approximate time when the decrypts of the signals using the settings in force between midday 3 July to midday 4 July started to be

20. Ibid.
21. Ibid.; Patrick Mahon, 'The History of Hut Eight' p.56, **NA Maryland** RG 457 Box 4685; and Hugh Alexander, 'Cryptographic History of the Work on the German Naval Enigma' p. 32, supplied to me by Hugh Alexander's son Sir Michael Alexander.
22. 6.58 p.m. 4 July 1942 message from Duty Captain to CS1, NA London ADM 237/168; and Denning's PQ17 Account.
23. Decrypt sent to the OIC at 6.59 p.m. 4 July 1942 containing 7.40 a.m. 4 July 1942 message from Flottenchef und Befehlshaber Schlachtschiffe to Befehlshaber der Kreuzer, NA London DEFE 3/110 p. 896.
24. Decrypt sent to the OIC at 6.51 p.m. 4 July 1942 containing 12.40 a.m. 4 July 1942 message from Fliegerführer Lofoten, NA London DEFE 3/110 p. 894.
25. Denning's PQ17 Account.
26. If Denning's PQ17 Account is correct, his second discussion with Pound during the evening of 4 July 1942 was after the time when the decrypt in Note 23 was sent to the OIC (6.59 p.m.), and it is likely it was before the 7.18 p.m. 4 July 1942 Ultra referred to in Note 29 below.
27. The words in rounded brackets, within the sentence at the end of which this chapter endnote number 27 appears, have been inserted by me since although Denning was attempting years afterwards to recall and to specify what he knew at the time of the meeting in question, unless Denning had access to decrypts not in NA London DEFE 3/110, the decrypts available to him at this point would not have been sufficient to support the assertion quoted without the reservation in the brackets.
28. Denning's PQ17 Account.
29. 7.18 pm 4 July message from the OIC's Rear Admiral Clayton to Tovey and CS1, NA London ADM 223/111.
30. The 4 July 1942 German message in the decrypt in DEFE 3/110 p. 927 which was forwarded to the OIC at 8.03 p.m. 4 July 1942 appears to be one of the first messages using the post midday 4 July 1942 settings seen by the OIC.
31. Decrypt sent to the OIC at 8.15 p.m. 4 July 1942 containing 2.58 p.m. 4 July 1942 message from Admiral Nordmeer to *U-457*, NA London DEFE 3/110 p. 927. The decrypt which stated that CS1 only consisted of cruisers and destroyers was sent to the OIC at 8.08 p.m. 4 July 1942; it contained the 2.55 p.m. 4 July 1942 message from Fliegerführer Lofoten referring to a sighting at 2.22 p.m., NA London DEFE 3/110 p. 919.
32. Decrypt sent to the OIC at 8.31 p.m. on 4 July 1942 containing the message from Admiral Nordmeer to Eisteufel boats originated at 11.30 a.m. 4 July 1942, NA London DEFE 3/110 p. 937.
33. Denning's PQ17 Account.
34. Moore's PQ17 Letter.
35. David Irving, *The Destruction of Convoy PQ17* p.117; and David Irving's note of his 8 June 1963 conversation with Admiral Sir John

Eccles, who in 1942 had been at the meeting described in his capacity as Director of Operations Division (Home), **David Irving's Papers**.

36. Denning's PQ17 Account.

37. 9.11 p.m. 4 July 1942 signal, NA London ADM 237/168.

38. 9.23 p.m. 4 July 1942 signal in ibid.; and Moore's PQ17 Letter.

39. 9.36 p.m. 4 July 1942 signal, NA London ADM 237/168; and Moore's PQ17 Letter.

40. Denning's PQ17 Account.

41. Hamilton's 6 July 1942 Report states the convoy was at 75°50' N 28°30' E when it was scattered.

42. Ransome Wallis, *Two Red Stripes* p. 72.

43. 8 July 1942 report by *Keppel's* Commander Jack Broome, Churchill Archives Centre ROSK 19/5 ('Keppel's Report'); Captain Jack Broome, *Convoy Is To* Scatter ('Broome's Book') p. 173; and Broome's draft deposition ('Broome's Deposition') for the Irving libel court case, Churchill Archives Centre BRME 5/3.

44. Broome's Deposition.

45. Broome's Book p. 182. In 1970 Broome successfully sued David Irving and his publisher for damages concerning the depiction in David Irving, *The Destruction of Convoy PQ17* of Broome's actions during PQ17.

46. Keppel's Report.

47. Broome's Book p. 183.

48. Broome's Book pp. 190–1.

49. Broome's Book p. 193; 13 July 1942 'Report Of Convoy From Iceland To Time Of "Scatter" Signal. 4th July' by Commodore J.C.K. Dowding, NA London ADM 199/757.

Chapter 18

1. Captain Jack Broome, *Convoy Is To Scatter* ('Broome's Book') p. 194; and Hamilton's 6 July 1942 'Report Of The Operations Of The Cruiser Force Covering P.Q. 17', **Churchill Archives Centre** ROSK 19/5.

2. John Dodds' diary, brought to my attention by his children Nick and Jane.

3. Broome's Book p. 107.

4. Post-war interview given by Admiral Sir William O'Brien, as he then was (the recording is on Legasee, the online Veterans Video Archive), combined with his comments in the deposition he made for the Broome v David irving libel trial, Churchill Archives Centre. BRME 5/11.

5. 27 July 1942 report by *Pozarica's* Acting Captain Edward Lawford, **NA London** ADM 199/757.

6. Report by captain of *Azerbaijan* ('Izotov's Report'), in **GAOPDiFAO** Section 296, Inventory 1, Book 1210.

7. Godfrey Winn, *'P.Q.17'* p. 85.

8. 11 July 1942 'Report of proceedings: S.S. Zamalek: Archangel' by her Master Captain Owen Morris, NA London ADM 199/757.

9. 13 July 1942 'Rescue Ship Zaafaran. Report Of Proceedings From The Time Of Dispersal Of The Convoy Till The Sinking Of My Vessel' by Master Charles McGowan, NA London ADM 199/757.

10. Broome's Book p. 167.

11. Izotov's Report; 14 July 1942 report by *Britomart's* Commander S.S. Stammwitz; and 14 July 1942 report by *Halcyon's* Lieutenant Commander Colin

Corbet-Singleton, NA London ADM 199/757.

12. Izotov's Report.

13. Ronald Crees' account ('Crees' Account'), **IWM Sound** 10718.

14. CARRAWAY'S DIARY.

15. William Carter, *Why Me Lord?* p. 177.

16. Carraway's Diary.

17. Ibid.

18. According to the 5 July entry in the KTB *U-703*, *Empire Byron* was torpedoed at AC 2629 on the German grid (approximately 75° 57' N 36° 50' E), contradicting the 23 July 1942 report by *Empire Byron*'s John Wharton ('Empire Byron's 1st Report'), NA London ADM 199/757, which states the location was 76°18' N 33°30' E.

19. 13 October 1942 'Report Of An Interview With The Master Captain John Wharton: s.s. Empire Byron' ('Empire Byron's 2nd Report'), NA London ADM 199/2141.

20. Ibid.

21. Ibid.

22. Ibid.

23. The 5 July 1942 entry in the KTB *U-703* appears to confirm these explosions were caused by *Empire Byron*'s boiler blowing up.

24. Empire Byron's 2nd Report.

25. Ibid.; and bracketed words from Empire Byron's 1st Report.

26. Empire Byron's 2nd Report.

27. Empire Byron's 1st Report.

28. Empire Byron's 2nd Report.

29. 11 August 1942 'Convoy Room (PQ Section) Trade Division' list, NA London ADM 237/168.

30. Decrypt of 10.15 a.m. 5 July 1942 message from Bielfeld, commander of *U-703*, NA London DEFE 3/111 p. 234.

31. The 4 July 1942 entry in KTB *U-88* states that *U-88* sank *Carlton* at AC 2974 on the German grid map (approximately 74°33' N 35°10' E).

32. 11 August 1942 'Convoy Room (PQ Section) Trade Division' list, NA London ADM 237/168.

33. LUFTFLOTTE 5'S WAR DIARY.

34. Cargo statistics from 11 August 1942 'Convoy Room (PQ Section) Trade Division' list, NA London ADM 237/168. Details of specified attacks on PQ17 ships taken firstly from the following casualty reports addressed to the British Naval Control Service Officer, Archangel, NA London ADM 199/757: concerning *Aldersdale*: from 20 July 1942 report by master of *Aldersdale*, and 13 July 1942 report by Commanding Officer *Salamander*; concerning *Daniel Morgan*: 15 July 1942 report by George Sullivan master of *Daniel Morgan* ('Daniel Morgan's Casualty Report'); concerning *Earlston*: 30 July 1942 report by 2nd Officer Evans; concerning *Fairfield City*: 3 August 1942 report by Leon Walters master of *Fairfield City*; concerning *Honomu*: 4 August 1942 report by *Honomu*'s 2nd Officer Hodgin; concerning *Peter Kerr*: 22 July 1942 report by master of *Peter Kerr*; concerning *Zaafaran*: from 11 July 1942 report by Owen Morris Commanding Officer *Zamalek*. Details of abovementioned attacks also taken from following German KTBs' 5 July 1942 entries: via Acta Norvegica Arkiv: concerning *Daniel Morgan*: KTB *U-88*; concerning *Earlston*: KTB *U-334*; concerning *Honomu*: KTB *U-456*. The 7 July 1942 entry in KTB *U-457* confirms

Aldersdale was finally torpedoed and sunk that day.

35. 5 November 1942 'Summary of Statements by Survivors of American SS Daniel Morgan', US ARMED GUARD REPORTS Box 157.

36. Daniel Morgan's Casualty Report; and 15 August 1942 report by Lieutenant Morton Wolfson, Commanding Officer of *Daniel Morgan*'s Armed Guard Unit, US Armed Guard Reports Box 157.

37. Cargo statistics from 11 August 1942 'Convoy Room (PQ Section) Trade Division' list, NA London ADM 237/168.

38. Crees' Account.

39. *Washington*'s Robert Glenn Henderson's diary, brought to my attention by his widow and daughters.

40. Crees' Account.

41. William Kenyon's account, IWM Sound 9040.

42. 5 July 1942 'Report Of An Interview With The Master, Captain J. Pascoe: s.s. "Bolton Castle"', NA London ADM 199/2141.

43. 3 August 1942 report by *Washington*'s master Julius Richter, NA London 757; and 21 July 1942 report by Ensign Charles M. Ulrich, Commanding Officer of the Armed Guard, SS *Washington*, US Armed Guard Reports Box 674 Entry UD 93.

44. Crees' Account.

45. Ibid.

Chapter 19

1. 5 July 1942 signal sent by DDIC (Admiral Clayton) at 2.38 p.m. to Tovey and Hamilton. '1200B' means

midday according to GMT + 2 timing (see this book's Note for Readers).

2. 3 July 1942 entry in KTB des Befehlshabers der Kreuzer über Unternehmung Rösselsprung, PG 48723 in Microfilm 3007, **Acta Norvegica Arkiv.**

3. 20 July 1942 'Abschlussbericht Rösselsprung', Anlage 12 to 12–31 July 1942 KTB des Marinegruppenkommandos Nord, NARA Microfilm 1022–3950, PG 34863, Acta Norvegica Arkiv; and 'Translation of the final report on Operation Rösselsprung (Attack on PQ.17) submitted by Admiral Carls (Gruppe Nord) on the 12.7.1942' **Churchill Archives Centre** BRME 6/2. The two documents in this note are hereinafter together referred to as 'the Final PQ17 Report'. The importance of this report was first brought to my attention by Bill Geroux, author of *The Ghost Ships Of Archangel.*

4. 5 July 1942 entry in KTB DES MARINEGRUPPEN KOMMANDOS NORD specifies the Home Fleet was spotted from the German aircraft at 6.45 a.m. 5 July at AB 2732 on the German grid map (approximately 75°15' N 4°30' E); whereas the Final PQ17 Report states that at one point during period 6.45 to 8 a.m. 5 July, the Home Fleet was at 75°50' N 03°30' E, that is around 450 miles from the convoy.

5. Decrypt of 11.45 a.m. message from Schniewind to Carls, **NA London** DEFE 3/111. See Maps 1 and 13 for Rolvsøya's location.

6. 5 July 1942 entries in *Z 30*'s and *Friedrich Ihn*'s KTBs, **Militärarchiv Freiburg** RM 94/124 and RM 94/84 respectively.

7. Decrypt of Schniewind message to Carls originated at 11.45 a.m. 5 July 1942 which was forwarded to the Admiralty at 2.20 p.m. that day, NA London DEFE 3/111 p. 237.

8. 3.17 p.m. 5 July 1942 Ultra sent by Admiralty to Tovey, NA London ADM 223/111. The enclosure to Tovey's 11 July 1942 report, Churchill Archives Centre ROSK 19/5, does not refer to this Ultra. But it does comment that after receiving an Admiralty suggestion sent to him at 7.10 p.m. 5 July to steer east in order to persuade *Tirpitz* not to attack PQ17, that it was essential to continue to the south-west so that his destroyers could be refueled.

9. Two cases of ships diverting to pick up survivors on 5 July 1942 are described in: the 13 July 1942 report by the Commanding Officer of the minesweeper HMS *Salamander*; and the 11 July 1942 report by rescue ship *Zamalek*'s Captain Owen Morris, both in NA London ADM 199/757.

10. 10 November 1969 deposition by *Pozarica*'s Captain Edward Lawford relating to the David Irving libel trial, Churchill Archives Centre BRME 5/2.

11. 26 July 1942 report by Temporary Lieutenant Vivian Bidwell commanding officer of *La Malouine* ('La Malouine's PQ17 Report'), NA London ADM 199/757.

12. Lieutenant John Hall's account brought to my attention by his son Christopher. The location specified in *Pan Kraft*'s SOS signal was '76°50'

N 38°00' E according to the undated 'Report of Proceedings P.Q.17 H.M.S. "Lotus"' ('Lotus' PQ17 Report'), NA London ADM 199/757. *Pan Kraft* is in some documents referred to as *Pankraft* or *Pan Craft*.

13. La Malouine's PQ17 Report.

14. 1904 5 July 1942 signal from SBNO North Russia, NA London ADM 237/168. According to the undated Narrative by *Palomares*' Captain John Jauncey, Churchill Archives Centre ROSK19/5, what was apparently a copy of this signal was received on his ship at 7.25 p.m. 5 July 1942; it may well have been received on *Lotus* at about the same time.

15. Lotus' PQ17 Report; and 12 July 1942 'Letter of Proceedings' by 'Commanding Officer H.M.S. "Lord Austin"', NA London ADM 199/757.

16. 2 November 1942 'Summary of Statements made by Survivors of SS Pankraft,' ('Pan Kraft's Survivors' Report'), US ARMED GUARD REPORTS.

17. Aircraft numbers used during 5 July 1942: 5 July 1942 entry in KTB DER SKL TEIL A.

18. Pan Kraft's Survivors' Report; and 4 August 1942 report by *Pan Kraft*'s Master, both NA London ADM 199/757.

19. 11 August 1942 'Convoy Room (PQ Section) Trade Division' list, NA London ADM 237/168.

20. Lotus' PQ17 Report.

Chapter 20

1. 2.30 a.m. 6 July 1942 signal from '1st S.L.' (Sea Lord i.e. Pound), **NA London** ADM 237/168.

2. 8 October 1942 'Report Of An Interview With The Master, Captain H.W. Charlton. Convoy P.Q.17 S.S. River Afton' ('River Afton's 2nd Report'), NA London ADM 199/2141.

3. The 5 July 1942 entry in KTB U-703 states River Afton was torpedoed at AC 3568 on the German grid (approximately 75°39' N 43°30' E), which is almost in line with the location 75°57' N 43°00' E specified in the 15 July 1942 'P.Q.17 Master's Statement: S.S. "River Afton"' by Harold Charlton ('River Afton's 1st Report'), NA London ADM 199/757. However, these locations do not in all respects line up with the location in River Afton's SOS message: 73°43' N 43°18' E, picked up in the PQ17 merchant ships Ocean Freedom and Azerbaijan, as specified in 'S.S. "OCEAN FREEDOM" List of Distress Messages received after convoy P.Q.17 was scattered . . .' with Ocean Freedom's 21 July 1942 report, NA London ADM 199/757; and as specified in the document headed 'Signals picked up by the radio set in Azerbaijan' ('Azerbaijan's Signals Report') with the report by Azerbaijan's Izotov, **GAOPDiFAO** Section 296, Inventory 1, Book 1210 pp. 62–4.

4. Quotation partly from River Afton's 1st Report, and partly from River Afton's 2nd Report.

5. George Jamieson account, **IWM Documents** 11412.

6. This quote uses words from: River Afton's 1st Report; and River Afton's Harold Charlton's private account brought to my attention by Richard Woodman ('Charlton's Personal Account').

7. 5 July 1942 entry in KTB U-703.

8. River Afton's 2nd Report.

9. 13 July 1942 'Report of events in S.S. River Afton after convoy scattered' by Commodore J.C.K. Dowding ('Dowding's Post-Scatter Report'), NA London ADM 199/757.

10. Quotes from Percy Grey and Benjamin Coffee in this chapter are from the 12 and 13 April 2018 articles by Dorothy Ramser in The Shields Gazette.

11. Dowding's Post Scatter Report.

12. River Afton's 1st Report.

13. Charlton's Personal Account.

14. Ibid.

15. See Note 10.

16. Dowding's Post-Scatter Report.

17. Ibid.

18. Lieutenant John Hall's account brought to my attention by his son Christopher.

19. River Afton's 2nd Report.

20. Charlton's Personal Account.

21. Undated 'Report of Proceedings P.Q.17. H.M.S. Lotus' by Lotus' Lieutenant John Hall, NA London ADM 199/757.

22. 11 August 1942 'Convoy Room (PQ Section) Trade Division' list, NA London ADM 237/168.

23. Azerbaijan's Signals Report.

24. CARRAWAY'S DIARY.

25. Ibid.

26. Azerbaijan's Signals Report.

27. Carraway's Diary.

28. Walter John Baker, The Convoy is to Scatter p. 51 brought to my attention by William Geroux, author of The Ghost Ships of Archangel, and Baker's granddaughter Clare Howard.

29. Dick Elsden sequence of events supplied by his daughter Su, to whom I was introduced by BBC producer Gemma Hagen.
30. Carraway's Diary.
31. William A. Carter, *Why Me Lord?* pp. 177–8.
32. Carraway's Diary.

Chapter 21

1. 9 July 1942 report by the destroyer *Inglefield's* Commander Arthur West.
2. 2 July 1942 'North Russia – 11th Monthly Report – June 1942' in war diary for SBNO, North Russia, **NA London** ADM 199/1104.
3. 26 June 1942 report by *Gossamer's* Lieutenant Commander Thomas Crease ('Gossamer's Report'), NA London ADM 116/4544, brought to my attention by his son Paul and by Susan Griggs, daughter of *Gossamer* crew member John Maddern.
4. Geoff Jelbart's account recorded by his son John; his 29 May 1943 letter to his mother which John Jelbart brought to my attention; Gossamer's Report; 'R.N. Casualties In N. Russian Convoys' with undated Naval Intelligence Division letter sent after the Battle of the Barents Sea ('The Naval Casualties Summary'), NA London ADM 199/604.
5. 14 August 1942 minute by Admiral Henry Moore, Vice Chief of the Naval Staff, NA London ADM 199/347.
6. 12 July 1942 Report by Rear Admiral Frederick Dalrymple Hamilton, Admiral Commanding Iceland (C) ('Admiral Iceland's Report'), NA London ADM 199/347.
7. Ibid.
8. Graeme Ogden, *My Sea Lady* ('Ogden's Book') p. 136.
9. Admiral Iceland's Report.
10. The Naval Casualties Summary.
11. François Flohic, *Ni Chagrin Ni Pitié* ('Roselys' QP13 Account') p. 122.
12. Norman Pickles' account ('Pickles' Account'), **IWM Sound** 16757; and the torpedo seen by Ogden: Ogden's Book p. 137.
13. Romuald Holubowicz account, **IWM Documents** 2159, and account supplied by his daughter Diana; 22 July 1942 report by John C. Guibert, 'Commanding Officer Armed Guard Unit, S.S. Hybert', US ARMED GUARD REPORTS Box 315 UD93; and undated report by Joseph L. Dalton, Master of *Hybert*, US MERCHANT VESSELS SINKING REPORTS Box 20 Entry Point P-2.
14. Undated report by John J. Connor, Acting Third Assistant Engineer on SS *Massmar*, US Merchant Vessels Sinking Reports Box 32 Entry P-2; and 22 July 1942 report by Ensign William C. Gibson Jr., the Officer-in-Charge of the Armed Guard Unit assigned to *Alamar*, US Armed Guard Reports Box 8 UD93.
15. Concerning sunk or abandoned QP13 ships: 22 July 1942 report by *John Randolph's* Armed Guard commander Ensign Alexander Anderson: part of ship sank, 5 men lost; 22 July 1942 report by *Hybert's* Armed Guard commander Ensign John Guibert: ship sank, 0 men lost, both aforementioned documents in US Armed Guard Reports; 18 August 1944 Report On U.S. Merchant Vessel War Action Casualty based on information from

Heffron's master Edward Geddes, US CASUALTY REPORTS: ship abandoned, 1 man lost. Following QP13 ships damaged but not sunk or abandoned: *Mauna Kea*: 26 July 1942 report by her Armed Guard Commander Ensign Robert Crawford; and *Exterminator*: 9 July 1942 report by her master R. Kolsoe ('Exterminator's Report'), both latter two documents US Armed Guard Reports, Boxes 460 and 216 respectively, UD93.

16. Aleksandr G. Somkin, *Mi pomnim vas . . . (We remember you . . .)*, p. 37.
17. Admiral Iceland's Report.
18. Roselys' QP13 Account pp. 122–3.
19. Pickles' Account.
20. Admiral Iceland's Report.
21. Exterminator's Report; and 28 July 1942 'Report of Homeward Bound Voyage enroute Murmansk, Russia to U.S.A.' by Ensign John M. Nisbet, Commanding Officer, Armed Guard Unit, SS *Mormacrey*, US Armed Guard Reports Box 481 UD93.
22. Report of Proceedings of QP13 by convoy commodore N.H. Gale, NA London ADM 199/347.

Chapter 22

1. 5 July 1942 entry in KTB DES MARINEGRUPPENKOM-MANDOS NORD.
2. Ibid.
3. 5 July 1942 entry KTB DER SKL TEIL A.
4. 1.17 p.m. 6 July 1942 Ultra, **NA London** ADM 223/111; and decrypt of Schniewind's 2219 5 July 1942 Enigma message, NA London DEFE 3/111.
5. 7.46 p.m. 6 July 1942 message Admiralty to PQ17 escorts, NA London ADM 237/168.

6. 21 July 1942 report by Master of *Ocean Freedom*, NA London ADM 199/757; undated report by *Palomares*' Captain John Jauncey ('Palomares' Report'); and 27 July 1942 report by *Pozarica*'s Captain Edward Lawford ('Pozarica's Report') both in **Churchill Archives Centre** ROSK 19/5.
7. Godfrey Winn, '*PQ17*' ('Winn's Book') p. 109. He appears to be referring to the Guba Pomorskaya (Pomorskaya Bay) settlement on the south side of the strait near its western entrance.
8. Ibid.
9. Ibid. p. 110; and Pozarica's Report.
10. Winn's Book p. 110.
11. 7.46 and 7.47 p.m. 6 July 1942 Admiralty messages to PQ17 escorts, NA London ADM 237/168.
12. Palomares' Report.
13. Undated report by J. S. Clark, Master of *John Witherspoon*; and 16 July 1942 report by Master of *Pan Atlantic*, both in NA London ADM 199/757; and 6 July 1942 entry in KTB U-255, which specified sinking of *John Witherspoon* was at AT 7216 on the German grid (approximately 71°33' N 50°50' E). *Pan Atlantic* fatalities and sinking location, very approximately 71°00' N 45°00' E, respectively 29 October 1942 'Summary of Statements by Survivors of the MS Pan Atlantic . . .' and undated summary concerning *Pan Atlantic* sinking, both US MERCHANT SHIP LOSSES REPORTS.
14. Palomares' Report.
15. 7 July 1942 entry in KTB U-255: *Alcoa Ranger* sinking: AT 4875 on German grid (approximately 71°48'

N 50°40' E), in line with *Alcoa Ranger*'s Master's 20 July 1942 report; and 8 July 1942 entry in KTB *U-255*: *Olopana* sinking: AT 4827 on the German grid (approximately 72°21' N 51°10' E), in line with *Olopana*'s Master's 22 July 1942 report. Both masters' reports NA London ADM 199/757. *Olopana*: 5 killed: 27 November 1942 US Coast Guard report, <u>US MERCHANT VESSELS SINKING REPORTS</u>; *Alcoa Ranger*: 0 killed: 11 November 1942 Summary of Statements by Survivors of the SS Alcoa Ranger . . .', <u>US ARMED GUARD REPORTS</u>.

16. 28 July 1942 report by Master of *Empire Tide* ('<u>Empire Tide's Report</u>'), NA London ADM 199/757.

17. Report by captain of *Azerbaijan*, **GAOPDiFAO**, Archive Section 296, Inventory 1, Book 1210.

18. 11 August 1942 'Convoy Room (PQ Section) Trade Division' list, NA London ADM 237/168; 13 October 1942 'Report of an Interview with the Master, Captain George W. Stephenson. S.S. Hartlebury' ('<u>Hartlebury's 3rd Report</u>'), NA London ADM 199/2141, also brought to my attention by Lee Stephenson, Peter Armstrong's nephew; 21 July 1942 report by Captain Stephenson ('<u>Hartlebury's 1ˢᵗ Report</u>'), NA London ADM 199/757; and Palomares' Report.

19. Hartlebury's 1ˢᵗ Report; and Hartlebury's 3ʳᵈ Report. The 7 July 1942 entry in <u>KTB *U-355*</u> states that *Hartlebury* was sunk at the location on the German grid referred to as AT 4589 (approximately 72°39' N 51°50' E).

20. Hartlebury's 1ˢᵗ Report; and Hartlebury's 3ʳᵈ Report.

21. Ibid.

22. Needham Forth's handwritten personal account ('<u>Forth's Handwritten Account</u>') made available by his daughter Catriona, whose whereabouts were traced by his former neighbour Joan Hudson.

23. Needham Forth in BBC documentary 'PQ17: An Arctic Convoy Disaster' presented by Jeremy Clarkson, first broadcast in 2014 ('<u>Forth's TV Interview</u>'); and knife incident mentioned in Hartlebury's 1ˢᵗ Report.

24. Forth's Handwritten Account.

25. Forth's TV Interview.

26. Forth's Handwritten Account.

27. 23 July 1942 report by *Hartlebury*'s first mate S. Gordon ('<u>Hartlebury's 1st Mate's Report</u>'), NA London ADM 199/757; and Hartlebury's 1ˢᵗ Report.

28. 7 July 1942 entry in KTB *U-355*.

29. Forth's Handwritten Account.

30. Peter Armstrong's account ('<u>Armstrong's Account</u>'), supplied thanks to an introduction from his granddaughter in the course of an interview with the author on 10 May 2019 when he was 94 years old, suggests that he believed there were at first 13 men on his raft. However Captain George Stephenson in Hartlebury's 1st Report states there were at first 14 on Armstrong's raft and 17 in Forth's lifeboat.

31. Armstrong's Account.

32. Hartlebury's 3ʳᵈ Report.

33. 4 August 1942 report by Master of *Winston Salem*, NA London ADM 199/757.

34. Armstrong's Account.

35. Forth's Handwritten Account.
36. Hartlebury's 3rd Report.
37. Forth's Handwritten Account.
38. Ibid.; corroborated by Hartlebury's 1st Mate's Report.
39. Forth's Handwritten Report.
40. Hartlebury's 3rd Report.
41. Ibid.
42. Hartlebury's 1st Report.
43. Hartlebury's 3rd Report. The reference to Pomorski Bay appears to be to a bay near the Malyye Karmakuly settlement mentioned in this chapter's main text, possibly a bay which can be accessed from the nearby river (Reka Pomorskiy). The *Hartlebury* survivors were taken to the settlement on 16 July, Empire Tide's Report.
44. Needham Forth's typed account supplied by his daughter Catriona, after being traced by Joan Hudson (mentioned above).

Chapter 23

1. 13 July 1942 report by *Pozarica*'s Captain Lawford ('Pozarica's Report'), **Churchill Archives Centre** ROSK 19/5.
2. Godfrey Winn, '*PQ17*' ('Winn's Book') pp. 119–20.
3. Report by *Palomares*' Captain Jauncey ('Palomares' Report') and accompanying map, **NA London** ADM 199/757.
4. Pozarica's Report.
5. 14 July 1942 report by *Britomart*'s Lieutenant Commander Spencer Stammwitz; and 21 July 1942 report by *Ocean Freedom*'s William Walker ('Ocean Freedom's Report'), both NA London ADM 199/757.
6. 3 August 1942 report by *Benjamin Harrison*'s master, NA London ADM 199/757.
7. Winn's Book pp. 123–4; and Pozarica's Report. Palomares' Report' states that the aircraft dived beneath the clouds whose altitude was 'approximately' 5,000 feet, and never released their bombs beneath 4,000 feet.
8. LUFTFLOTTE 5'S WAR DIARY states that 38 aircraft participated in the attack. The aircraft belonged to the 2nd wing of KG30 based in Banak.
9. Winn's Book p. 125.
10. July 1942 report by Louis D. Marks, Commanding Officer of Armed Guard Unit aboard *El Capitan*, US NAVAL ATTACHÉ REPORTS Box 25 UD44; and 2 November 1942 'Summary of Statements by Survivors of the SS Hoosier', US MERCHANT SHIP LOSSES REPORTS Box 230 AI 350.
11. Map with Palomares' Report shows *Hoosier* abandoned at 69°35' N 41°91' E; *El Capitan* abandoned at 69°08' N 40°50' E.
12. Winn's Book pp. 125–6.
13. Pozarica's Report.
14. Winn's Book pp. 126–7.
15. 11 July 1942 Report by *Zamalek*'s master Owen Morris, NA London ADM 199/757.
16. Winn's Book p. 127.
17. 20 July 1942 report by Ensign H. Kroetz, Armed Guard Commander SS *John Witherspoon*, US ARMED GUARD REPORTS UD93; Undated report of proceedings by *Lotus*' Lieutenant John Hall, NA London ADM 199/757 (concerning *Pan Atlantic* boat).
18. Winn's Book p. 117.
19. Luftflotte 5's War Diary.

20. Ocean Freedom's Report; and 11 August 1942 'Convoy Room (PQ Section) Trade Division' list ('PQ17 Aid List'), NA London ADM 237/168.

21. 14 July 1942 report by Lt. John E. Sexton, Commanding Officer Armed Guard SS *Samuel Chase*, US Armed Guard Reports Box 580 UD93; and PQ17 Aid List.

22. Winn's Book p. 134; and 10-11 July 1942 entries in La Malouine's George Bagnall's account, **IWM Documents** 23380.

23. 10 July 1942 report by *Bellingham's* Commanding Officer Armed Guard Lieutenant Willard Brown, US naval attaché reports Box 25 UD44; and PQ17 Aid List.

24. 11 July 1942 report by *Rathlin's* master Augustus Banning, NA London ADM 199/757.

25. 9 July 1942 Anastas Mikoyan to Stalin and Molotov, Collection 82. Inventory 2 Case 7 Page 81 Russian State Archive of Social and Political History, brought to my attention by Professor Mikhail Suprun.

26. This statistic has been extracted from the reports in the National Archives London and the National Archives Maryland and Washington relating to all the sunk or damaged PQ17 merchant ships.

27. 7 October 1942 'Report Of An Interview With The Master Captain J. Pascoe: s.s. Bolton Castle' ('Bolton Castle's Report'), NA London ADM 199/2141.

28. Ronald Crees account, **IWM Sound** 10718 ('Crees' Account').

29. Medical Research Council, *A Guide To The Preservation Of Life At Sea After Shipwreck* p. 20.

30. Ibid. p. 9.

31. Anthony Van Kampen, ed., *Scheepsverklaring*: 'W. J. Sissingh, De mannen van de Paulus Potter', brought to my attention by Jos Odijk.

32. Robert Henderson's diary, courtesy of his widow Lyndell and his daughter Sue.

33. Ibid.

34. Ibid.

35. Ibid.

36. 4 August 1942 report by Master *S.S. Winston Salem*, NA London ADM 199/757.

37. Crees' Account.

38. Ibid.

39. Bolton Castle's Report.

Chapter 24

1. 26 July 1942 report by *Ayrshire's* Lieutenant Leo Gradwell ('Ayrshire's 2nd PQ17 Report'), **NA London** ADM 199/757.

2. CARRAWAY'S DIARY.

3. Ibid.; and Ayrshire's 2nd PQ17 Report.

4. Ayrshire's 2nd PQ17 Report; and 1 August 1942 report by William Carter, the Armed Guard Officer SS *Ironclad*, US NAVAL ATTACHÉ REPORTS Box 25.

5. Carraway's Diary; Salvesen's details from William Geroux, *The Ghost Ships Of Archangel* p. 8; and 11 August 1942 'Convoy Room (PQ Section) Trade Division' list ('PQ17 Aid List'), NA London ADM 237/168.

6. PQ17 Aid List.

7. The 'settlement' appears to have been the settlement of Lagernyy.

8. Ayrshire's 2nd PQ17 Report; text of Gradwell's 13 July 1942 message, NA London ADM 199/757; and

Gradwell's private account, brought to my attention by Bill Geroux, and also supplied by Gradwell's daughter Mary.

9. 15 July 1942 letter from Rear Admiral Bevan to Gradwell, supplied by Gradwell's daughter Mary.

10. Undated 'Report Of Proceedings P.Q.17: H.M.S. Lotus' by her Lieutenant John Hall, referring to action commencing 16 July 1942, ('Lotus' 2nd PQ17 Report'); and 26 July 1942 report by *La Malouine*'s Lieutenant Vivian Bidwell ('La Malouine's 2nd PQ17 Report'), both NA London ADM 199/757.

11. Ayrshire's 2nd PQ17 Report.

12. Carraway's Diary.

13. Ayrshire's 2nd PQ17 Report; Lotus' 2nd PQ17 Report; and La Malouine's 2nd PQ17 Report.

14. Carraway's Diary.

15. Lotus' 2nd PQ17 Report; and 28 July 1942 report by *Empire Tide*'s Frank Harvey, NA London ADM 199/757.

16. Ibid; and La Malouine's 2nd PQ17 Report.

17. 4 August 1942 report by *Winston Salem*'s master William Lovegreen, NA London ADM 199/757; 1 August 1942 report by Robert Chitrin, Armed Guard Officer SS *Winston Salem*, US ARMED GUARD REPORTS Box 718 UD93; and PQ17 Aid List.

18. PQ17 Aid List.

19. 16 July 1942 report by Commanding Officer *Dianella*, NA London ADM 199/757; 6 July 1942 Admiralty order to pick up survivors, NA London ADM 237/168.

20. 21 July 1942 report by Commanding Officer HMS *Halcyon*, NA London ADM 199/757, which states the *Honomu* rafts were found at around 73°41' N 37°12' E; the 28 July 1942 entry in KTB *U-209*, which states the *Honomu* lifeboat was found at around AC 8126 on the German grid (approximately 71°33' N 30°50' E); the following documents with the 12 and 6 March 1945 letters from the War Shipping Administration: statements by *Honomu*'s radio operator Irving Elliot and master Frederik Strand, which confirm 11 out of 19 men in the lifeboat died before the remainder were rescued, US MERCHANT VESSEL SINKING REPORTS Box 20.

21. Charles Mulchy's diary brought to my attention by his son Timothy.

22. Charles Blockston interview, in documentary *Murmansk-Konvoiene* shown on Norsk Rikskringkasting (NRK), brought to my attention by Bjørn Tore Rosendahl, researcher at the Norsk Senter For Krigsseilerhistorie, Arkivet, Freds-og menneskerettighetssenter (Centre of the History of Seafarers At War, Arkivet, Peace and Human Rights Centre), Kristiansand, Norway.

23. 10 March 1945 'Summary of Statements by Survivors of the SS Carlton', US Armed Guard Reports Box 29 UD93.

24. 13 July 1942 entry in KTB *U-255*.

25. 6 July 1942 entry in KTB DER SKL TEIL A.

26. Ibid. 13 July 1942 entry.

27. LUFTFLOTTE 5'S WAR DIARY.

28. 12 July 1942 entry in KTB der Skl Teil A; 20 July 1942 'Abschlussbericht Rösselsprung', Anlage 12 to 16–31 July 1942 KTB des Marinegruppenkommandos Nord;

and 'Translation of the final report on Operation Rösselsprung (Attack on PQ.17) submitted by Admiral Carls (Gruppe Nord) on the 12.7.1942', brought to my attention by author Bill Geroux.

29. 30 July 1942 verdict on behalf of Rear Admiral Fricke, **Militärarchiv Freiburg** RM 48/266.

30. Head of the Political Department of the Northern Sea Fleet Koltiakov to the head of the Political Department Commissar of the USSR Comrade Belakhov on 17 July 1942 in **GAOPDiFAO**, Archive Section 296, Inventory 1, Book 1210.

31. Head of the Political Department of the Northern Sea Fleet Koltiakov to the head of the Political Department Commissar of the USSR Comrade Belakhov on 17 August 1942, ibid. Koltiakov's criticism of *Olopana's* crew appears not to be justified by the evidence: the 22 July 1942 report by her master, NA London ADM 199/757 states that when first attacked by aircraft he and the crew agreed to stand and fight until the vessel was sunk or 'abandoned' (probably meaning until she had to be abandoned). The report went on to state that although there was a partial abandonment when aircraft attacked again, the men came back on board after the aircraft departed and *Olopana* was only abandoned after she was torpedoed by a U-boat.

32. 19 July 1942 letter from Admiral Nicolai Kuznetsov to Molotov, Collection 82. Inventory. 2 Case 866 pp. 24–31 Russian State Archive of Social and Political History, brought to my attention by Professor Mikhail Suprun.

33. 13 July 1942 War Cabinet Defence Committee, NA London CAB 69/4.

34. CHURCHILL'S BOOK vol. 4 pp. 238–9.

35. REYNOLDS AND PECHATNOV, pp. 124–6.

36. Antony Beavor, *Stalingrad* p. 79.

37. Reynolds and Pechatnov p. 129.

38. Ivan Maisky, *Memoirs Of A Soviet Ambassador* pp. 292–3; and Gabriel Gorodetsky ed., *The Maisky Diaries* ('Maisky Diaries') p. 453.

39. 24 July 1942 Confidential Annex, 95th War Cabinet Conclusions, Minute 2, NA London CAB 65/31. Report On Fulfilment Of The Moscow Protocol . . .", PREM 3 401/7.

40. 27 July 1942 Confidential Annex, 96th Conclusions, Minute 4, NA London CAB 65/31; and 11 August 1942 'Convoy Room (PQ Section) Trade Division' list, NA London ADM 237/168. In the latter document the cargo on the Panamanian flagged *Troubadour* was included in the US delivered figures, and the cargo on the Dutch *Paulus Potter* was included in the UK lost figures.

41. British and American documents in the British and American archives disclose that 157 men were reported to have been killed including one man who died after being flown to Archangel. However a small number of discrepancies make it safer to give an approximate figure. Fulfilment of First Protocol: The 17 September 1942 'Report On Fulfilment Of The Moscow Protocol October 1941 – June 1942', NA London PREM 401/7 appears to confirm that although the tanks and aircraft paid for or

supplied on Britain's account which had been delivered to the Soviet Union numbered 1,442 and 1,337 respectively by the time the report was written, that is less than the 2,250 and 1,800 specified in the Protocol for the period until the end of June 1942, the number made available by the end of June 1942 was 2,443 and 1,836 respectively, in other words complying with the obligation in the Protocol which only obliged Britain to make these items available. The apparent shortfall was made up of 470 tanks and 288 aircraft lost when ships were sunk with them on board, and 531 tanks and 211 aircraft that were being transported by sea. Rough preparatory notes for the above report suggest that 100 of the tanks en route to Russia were being sent via Persia, NA London CAB 111/27.

42. Maisky Diaries p. 456.
43. 31 July 1942 telegram from Churchill to Stalin, Reynolds and Pechatnov p. 132.
44. 31 July 1942 telegram from Churchill to Stalin, ibid. p. 133.
45. 31 July 1942 telegram from Stalin to Churchill, ibid. pp. 133–4.

Chapter 25

1. Godfrey Winn, 'P.Q. 17' ('Winn's Book') pp. 131–3. The signaler: George Bagnall account, **IWM Documents** 23380.
2. S. A. Kerslake, Coxswain *In The Northern Convoys* ('Kerslake's Book') pp. 92–3. The jetty described by Kerslake appears to be one of many alongside the sawmills lining the banks of the Dvina channel known as Maimaksa.

3. 24 January 1942 letter from HMS *Bramble*'s Captain Harvey Crombie, **NA London** ADM 223/249.
4. Samuel Frankel interview recorded on behalf of US Naval Institute's Oral History programme.
5. William Carter, *Why Me Lord?* p. 234; corroborated by Vice Admiral Sir Lennon Goldsmith report filed with his 14 March 1943 report on Convoy RA53, NA London ADM 199/73.
6. Kerslake's Book p. 93.
7. Winn's Book pp. 150–1.
8. R. Struben account, IWM Documents 3375.
9. Winn's Book p. 147.
10. Ibid. p. 148.
11. John Beardmore account, IWM Documents 92/45/1.
12. Winn's Book pp. 149–50.
13. SS *Paul Luckenbach*'s Virgil Sharp report, brought to my attention by Ian Millar.
14. William Geroux, *The Ghost Ships of Archangel* p. 195, and confirmed by Jim North when he was interviewed by me in 2019, following an introduction by William Geroux.

Chapter 26

1. W. Averell Harriman and Elie Abel, *Special Envoy to Churchill and Stalin 1941–1946* ('Harriman's Book'), p.154; and Sir Archibald Clark Kerr's account ('Kerr's Diary'), **NA London** FO 800/300.
2. Details of the meetings between Churchill and Stalin, NA London PREM 3/76A/12.
3. Harriman's Book p. 156.
4. Ibid. p. 185.
5. CHURCHILL'S BOOK vol. 4 p. 437.

6. Kerr's Diary, which includes an 11 and 12 June 1942 draft of an account of his meeting with Stalin that he sent to the Foreign Office's Christopher Warner; his 29 March 1942 telegram to the Foreign Office mentioning Stalin's satisfaction with British aid, NA London WO 193/645A; Clark Kerr's character, as well as Clark Kerr's description of his meeting with Stalin, and Churchill's visit to Moscow: Giles Milton, *The Stalin Affair: The Impossible Alliance that Won the War* pp. 121–5 and 144–165.

7. Night of 15–16 August 1942 meeting, NA London PREM 3/76A/12.

8. Churchill's Book vol. 4 pp. 446–7. A lively account of the meetings in Russia during Churchill's visit is to be found in Giles Milton, *The Stalin Affair: The Impossible Alliance that Won the War* pp. 147–165.

9. 28 August 1942 entry in the war diary of the British Naval Mission Moscow ('Moscow Naval Mission War Diary'), NA London ADM 199/1102.

10. 15 July 1942 letter from Lady (Juliet) Duff to Clementine Churchill, NA London PREM 3 396/2.

11. 16 July 1942 letter from Clementine Churchill to Lady (Juliet) Duff, ibid.

12. 26 July 1942 letter from J. N. Henderson at the Ministry of War Transport to T. L. Rowan, ibid.

13. 4 and 21 August 1942 Lady Duff letters to Clementine Churchill, ibid.

14. 24 July 1942 letter from Commander Richard Onslow to Admiral Tovey, ibid.

15. 30 July 1942 message from Admiral Tovey to the Admiralty, ibid.

16. 4 August 1942 message from SBNO Archangel, NA London ADM 116/4972.

17. Ronald Crees' account, **IWM Sound** 10718.

18. 23 July 1942 'Report of burial of Edward Hall, deceased plus observations made', section P2/5 Medical, US NAVAL ATTACHÉ REPORTS Box 23.

19. 22 November to 25 December 1941 entries, V.N. Il'in, V.A. Radishevskaya and T.V. Titova eds., *Voina: Zapechatlennie dni 1941–1942 War: Captured Days 1941–1942*; interviews with others who experienced Archangel famine: Elizaveta Khatanzeiskaya's article 'Everyday Life in Wartime Arkhangelsk: The Problem of Starvation and Death during the Second World War (1939-1945)', in open access Septentrio Conference Series site on internet. Deaths in Archangel: Mikhail Suprun, 'Lend-Lease food aid to Russia/ USSR during the Second World War', *Journal of Slavic Military Studies* 2023, 36: 1, 96-108. Absence of dogs: 17 April 1942 entry in war diary for 126 Base Unit, NA London WO 176/391. Soup kitchens: CARRAWAY'S DIARY.

20. 20 August 1942 letter from J. N. Henderson at the Ministry of War Transport to F. D. Brown, NA London PREM 3 396/2; and Surgeon Captain J. L. S. Coulter, *The Royal Naval Medical Service Vol.II: Operations* p. 440.

21. 10 September 1942 '13th Monthly Report 26th July to 31st August 1942', war diary of SBNO North Russia, NA London ADM 199/1104.

22. 21 August 1942 letter from Lady (Juliet) Duff to Clementine Churchill, NA London PREM 3 396/2.
23. 17 September 1942 letter to the Foreign Office, NA London ADM 116/4972.
24. Martin Gilbert, *Road to Victory: Winston Churchill 1941–1945* p. 218; and 10 and 28 August 1942 entries in the Moscow Naval Mission War Diary.

Chapter 27

1. PQ18's formation diagram is in this book's Appendix C.
2. 7 August 1942 Minute 1, Confidential Annex, for War Cabinet's 107th Conclusions, **NA London** CAB 65/31.
3. Naval Staff History, *The Royal Navy and the Mediterranean Convoys* pp. 83–97.
4. REYNOLDS AND PECHATNOV p. 151.
5. 29 September 1942 report entitled 'Operation E.V.' by Rear Admiral Robert Burnett ('Scylla's Report'); and 22 September 1942 Report of Proceedings by HMS *Malcolm*'s Commander A. Russell ('Malcolm's PQ18 Report'), both NA London ADM 199/758.
6. Appendices I to III to Rear Admiral Burnett's 29 August 1942 order headed 'Operation E.V.', itself being Appendix 13 to Scylla's Report.
7. 'Cruising Order: Mercantile Convoy "P.Q.18"', NA London ADM 199/758.
8. 6 October 1942 Report of Proceedings by Commodore Boddam Whetham ('Commodore's

Proceedings'), NA London ADM 199/758.
9. L. Dmitriev, 'West of Bear Island', *Labour* 30 November 1967, cited in *Gangut*, issue 3 1992 p. 113.
10. A. Iatkovskii, 'The 18th breaks out', *East Siberian Pravda*, 31 January 1974, cited in *Gangut* issue 3 1992 p. 113.
11. 6 September 1942 entry in KTB DER SKL TEIL A.
12. 7 September 1942 entry in ibid.
13. 8 September 1942 entry in ibid.; and Malcolm's PQ18 Report.
14. 12 September 1942 and following days' entries in KTB DES ADMIRAL NORDMEER; and Malcolm's PQ18 Report.
15. Location of depth charging that turned out to be sinking of *U-88* was stated to be 75°04' N 04°49' E in 'Summary Of A/S Operations During Operation "EV"', Appendix 10 to Scylla's Report ('PQ18's Anti-Submarine Report').
16. Ibid.
17. The 13 September 1942 entries in KTB *U-408* and KTB des Admiral Nordmeer claimed respectively that at around or shortly before 10 a.m. 13 September 1942 a merchant ship was sunk by *U-408* at AB 2569 on the German grid map (approximately 75°39' N 07°50' E) and another was sunk by *U-589* at AB 2566 on the German grid map (approximately 75°45' N 07°50' E) without giving enough details to be sure which U-boat sank which of the two PQ18 vessels sunk at around this time.
18. 25 September 1942 report by Lieutenant John Laird, Commanding Officer Naval Armed

Guard Unit, SS *Virginia Dare*
('Virginia Dare's Report'), <u>US
ARMED GUARD REPORTS</u>
Box 672.

19. 'Stalingrad's Last Journey' by V. F.
Vorobiev, *Gangut*, 3, 1992, brought
to my attention by Captain of the 3rd
rank (equivalent to British
Lieutenant Commander) Cyril
Besson; and Enclosure II to 26
September report by 6th
Minesweeping Flotilla's Commander
Alan Jay ('Minesweepers' PQ18
Report'), NA London ADM
199/758.

20. 20 September 1942 report by Ensign
Jeremiah Mahoney, commander of
the Armed Guard in SS *William
Moultrie* ('William Moultrie's
Report'); and 26 September 1942
report by John F. Kelly,
Commanding Officer Naval Armed
Guard, SS *Oliver Ellsworth* ('Oliver
Ellsworth's Armed Guard Report'),
US Armed Guard Reports
respectively Boxes 696 and 504; 5
November 1942 'Summary of
Statements by Survivors of SS Oliver
Ellsworth' ('Oliver Ellsworth's
Survivors' Report'); and 16 October
'Intelligence Report' concerning
Oliver Ellsworth based on interview
with ship's master Otto Buford
('Oliver Ellsworth's Intelligence
Report'), both in <u>US MERCHANT
SHIP LOSSES REPORTS</u> Box
240; and 26 September 1942 report
by corvette *Bryony*'s Lieutenant
Commander John Stewart, NA
London ADM 199/758.

21. Oliver Ellsworth's Intelligence Report.

22. Oliver Ellsworth's Armed Guard
Report states the hero was the
armed guard Charles Ratz.

23. Ibid.

24. Oliver Ellsworth's Intelligence
Report; Oliver Ellsworth's Survivors'
Report: and Enclosure I to
Minesweepers' PQ18 Report.

25. Malcolm's PQ18 Report; and Scylla's
Report.

26. PQ18's Anti-Submarine Report.

27. British source: 'Brief Narrative of
Voyage' by Rear Admiral Boddam
Whetham ('Commodore's
Narrative'), which appears to be
referred to in the Commodore's
Proceedings; Number of planes,
German sources: 27 He 111 I/KG26
aircraft from Bardufoss under
Werner Klümper; and 16 Ju 88 III/
KG26 aircraft from Banak, i.e. in
total 43 aircraft, attacked PQ18 in
the big raid on 13 September 1942:
'Der Einsatz des KG26 als
Torpedotraemer in Norwegen, by
Werner Klümper ('Klümper's
Account'), **AFHRA** Reel K1028-F;
and 14 September 1942
Marinenachrichtendienst report
('Luftwaffe's 13 September 1942
Report'), **Militärarchiv Freiburg**
RM7/1026. Location of attack:
76°44' N 08°30' E specified in
'Appendix A' referred to in undated
document 'Convoy P.Q. 18
Summary of Air Attacks –
September 13–21 1942', which was
itself referred to in the 13
November 1942 report by the
Director of Gunnery & Anti-
Aircraft Warfare, all in NA London
ADM 199/758.

28. Memoirs of Lieutenant Commander
John Manners, as he was at the date
when the memoirs were written,
brought to my attention by his son
Errol and daughter Diana.

29. 20 September 1942 report by Commander Anthony Colthurst, commander of HMS *Avenger* ('Avenger's Report'), NA London ADM 199/758.

30. 15 September 1942 letter from Rear Admiral Boddam Whetham ('Commodore's Letter') in Appendix 11 to Scylla's Report.

31. 5 January 1943 'Report of Interview with the Master, Captain C. Patton: S.S. Ocean Faith' ('Ocean Faith's Report'), NA London ADM 199/1709.

32. Virginia Dare's Report.

33. Lieutenant Commander John Manners when interviewed by me in 2018.

34. Virginia Dare's Report.

35. Horace Bell's account sent to his son on 1 November 1942 ('Copeland's Bell Account'), and preserved in his file in the **Arctic Convoy Museum**.

36. 28 September 1942 report by Ensign Thomas D. Carter, Commanding Officer Armed Guard, *Sahale*, US NAVAL ATTACHÉ REPORTS Box 25.

37. Copeland's Bell Account.

38. Undated report by Ensign Daniel Rooker, Commanding Officer Naval Armed Guard SS *Campfire*, US Armed Guard Reports.

39. Ocean Faith's Report; 19 September 1942 report by Lieutenant Albert Maynard, Armed Guard Officer in *Schoharie*, US Armed Guard Reports Box 597; and Commodore's Narrative.

40. Copeland's Bell Account.

41. Virginia Dare's Report.

42. Copeland's Bell Account.

43. 4 November 1942 'Summary of Statements by Survivors of the SS Wacosta', US Armed Guard Reports Box 674, Entry UD93; and 25 August 1944 War Action Casualty report based on information from *Wacosta*'s master, US CASUALTY REPORTS Box 5.

44. 10 November 1942 'Summary by Survivors of SS Macbeth'; and 4 November 1942 'Summary of Statements by Survivors of the SS Africander', respectively in US Armed Guard Reports Boxes 44 and 6, Entry UD93.

45. 30 September 1942 'Report Of An Interview With The Master, Captain D. J. Jones: S.S. Empire Beaumont' ('Empire Beaumont's Report'), NA London ADM 199/2142.

46. 13 November 1942 report by H. McDermott, Commanding Officer of the Armed Guard, SS *John Penn*, US Armed Guard Reports.

47. Minesweepers' PQ18 Report.

48. 4 November 1942 'Summary of Statements by Survivors of the SS Oregonian', US Armed Guard Reports Box 506 UD93.

49. Empire Beaumont's Report.

50. William Moultrie's Report.

51. Avenger's Report.

52. Klümper's Account.

53. Luftwaffe's 13 September 1942 Report.

54. Commodore's Narrative.

55. 6 October 1942 message from SBNO Archangel to SBNO North Russia, NA London ADM 199/758.

56. Commodore's Narrative.

57. Commodore's Letter.

58. Commodore's Narrative.

59. 9 October 1942 'Letter of proceedings of H.M.S. Ulster Queen with Convoy P.Q.18', NA London ADM 199/758; and PQ18's Anti-Submarine Report.

Chapter 28

1. Bullshit Bob: account by Lieutenant Commander John Manners, as mentioned in the previous chapter, the first lieutenant in the destroyer *Eskimo* during PQ18.

2. 29 September 1942 report entitled 'Operation E.V.' by Rear Admiral Robert Burnett ('Scylla's Report'), **NA London** ADM 199/758.

3. Ibid.

4. 8 and 9 September 1942 entries <u>KTB DER SKL TEIL A</u>; 28 September 1942 report by Ensign Thomas D. Carter, Commanding Officer Armed Guard Unit, SS *Sahale* ('Sahale's Report'), <u>US ARMED GUARD REPORTS</u>, Box 571; 14 September 1942 entry in <u>KTB U-457</u> states *U-457* torpedoed *Atheltemplar* at AB 3643 on the German grid (approximately 75°51' N 17°50' E), whereas Appendix 10 to Scylla's Report entitled 'Summary of A/S Operations During Operation "EV"' ('PQ18's U-boat Report') specified 'approximately' 76°17' N 16°40' E.

5. 6 October 1942 'Report Of An Interview With The Master – Captain Carl Ray M.V. Atheltemplar', NA London ADM 199/2142; and Enclosure I to 26 September report by 6th Minesweeping Flotilla's Commander Alan Jay, NA London ADM 199/758. The abandoned *Atheltemplar* appears to have been sunk by *U-408* during the afternoon of 14 September, 14 September 1942 entry in *U-408*'s KTB PG 30466/3 **Acta Norvegica Arkiv**.

6. PQ18's U-boat Report states the sinking of the U-boat which turned out to be *U-589* was at 75°40' N 20°32' E.

7. Ibid.; and 13 and 17 September 1942 entries in <u>KTB DES ADMIRAL NORDMEER</u>.

8. Horace Bell's account sent to his son on 1 November 1942 ('<u>Copeland's Account</u>'), and preserved in his file in the **Arctic Convoy Museum**. Approximate location of Luftwaffe's 14 September attacks: 75°57' N 22°07' E, specified in 'Appendix A' referred to in undated document 'Convoy P.Q. 18 Summary of Air Attacks – September 13–21 1942', which was itself referred to in the 13 November 1942 report by the Director of Gunnery & Anti-Aircraft Warfare, all in NA London ADM 199/758.

9. Ibid. There is a conflict between the two principal German sources recording which Luftwaffe unit and how many aircraft attacked in the first wave which reached PQ18 around 1.35 p.m. 14 September 1942, and which Luftwaffe unit and how many aircraft attacked in the second wave which reached PQ18 around 3.10 p.m. 14 September 1942. However there are corresponding details in both Scylla's Report, which refers to the first wave consisting of two groups of 14 and 8 aircraft (i.e. 22 aircraft) some of which tried to attack *Avenger*, and in 'Der Einsatz des KG26 als Torpedotraemer in Norwegen', by Werner Klümper ('<u>Klümper's Account</u>'), **AFHRA** Reel K1028-F, which states that his 1st wing KG26 attacked before any other Luftwaffe unit with 22 aircraft, and acted as specified in Scylla's Report.

10. 'Summary of Air Attacks Of P.Q.18' in Scylla's Report's Appendix 3 ('PQ18's Air Attack Report'); and 20 September 1942 report by *Avenger's* Commander Anthony Colthurst ('Avenger's Report'), NA London 199/758.

11. Sahale's Report; undated report by Ensign Daniel Rooker, Commanding Officer Naval Armed Guard SS *Campfire* ('Campfire's Report'), US Armed Guard Reports Box 88.

12. Scylla's Report.

13. Avenger's Report.

14. Both Klümper's Account, and the 12 October 1942 report by Luftflotte 5's commander Generaloberst Hans-Jürgen Stumpff: 'Zusammengefasster Bericht über Bekämpfung PQ18 und Aufklärung QP14 in der Zeit vom 5.9.42 – 21.9.42' ('Luftflotte 5's Report'), in a document labelled 'Skl Akte VIII, 14, Unternehmungen, u Eispalast u Meisen-Balz (PQ18)', **Militärarchiv Freiburg** RM7/1026 appear to be saying that 4 German aircraft were shot down during the 14 September attack's first wave, although the latter source states that the losses were sustained by the 3rd wing KG26 rather than by Klümper's 1st wing KG26. Klümper's Account states an additional 10 1st wing KG26 aircraft were so badly damaged during the 14 September raid, they could not be used in subsequent attacks.

15. Scylla's Report.

16. Ibid.

17. Scylla's Report refers to an air raid by high level bombers at around 2.05 p.m. on 14 September.

18. Ibid.

19. Hitler's instruction to Luftwaffe: Luftflotte 5's Report. Defective German intelligence: Klümper's Account.

20. Klümper's Account.

21. 25 September 1942 report by Lieutenant John Laird, Commanding Officer Naval Armed Guard Unit, SS *Virginia Dare* ('Virginia Dare's Report'), US Armed Guard Reports Box 672. *Virginia Dare's* and other merchant ships' very approximate positions within PQ18 on 14 September: diagram with Sahale's Report; it put *Virginia Dare* in convoy position 83 (8th column, row 3).

22. Copeland's Account. The witness in relation to *Mary Luckenbach's* position was Lieutenant R. M. Billings, 24 September 1942 report by Lieutenant R.M. Billings, Armed Guard Commander, SS *Nathanael Greene* ('Nathanael Greene's Report'), US NAVAL ATTACHÉ REPORTS.

23. Thomas Wells' account, **IWM Documents** 09/15/1.

24. This paragraph is based on: 'Report of Interview with the Master Captain C. Patton: S.S. Ocean Faith' ('Ocean Faith's Report'), NA London ADM 199/1709; Sahale's Report; the following in US Armed Guard Reports Boxes 597, 672 and 696 respectively: 19 September 1942 report by Lieutenant Albert Maynard, Armed Guard Officer: SS *Schoharie*; 'Virginia Dare's Report'; and 20 September 1942 report by Ensign Jeremiah Mahoney, Commander Armed Guard Unit SS *William Moultrie* ('William Moultrie's Report').

25. The five ships were those named in the following reports: Ocean Faith's Report; *Dan-Y-Bryn*: 'Report of Interview with The Master Captain H. Macleod: S.S. Dan-Y-Bryn' ('Dan Y Bryn's Report'), NA London ADM 199/1709; Nathanael Greene's Report; Virginia Dare's Report; and William Moultrie's Report.
26. Dan-Y-Bryn's Report.
27. Ocean Faith's Report.
28. *Nathanael Greene*'s Lieutenant Billings' sketch with Nathanael Greene's Report suggests his ship was on *Mary Luckenbach*'s port side.
29. Nathanael Greene's Report.
30. Ibid.
31. Robert Hughes, *In Perilous Seas* p. 111.
32. Copeland's Account.
33. Robert M. Browning, *United States Merchant Marine Casualties in World War II* p. 171.
34. Scylla's Report.
35. Avenger's Report; and map forming part of Appendix 3 to Scylla's Report.
36. The figures in the main text are given respectively in the 14 September 1942 entries in the KTB des Admiral Nordmeer, and in **Luftflotte 5's Daily Reports**.
37. PQ18's Air Attack Report states that the American SS *Kentucky* was abandoned after being bombed by the Luftwaffe at around 68°25' N 42°45' E.
38. Scylla's Report; Avenger's Report.
39. Klümper's Account; and 9 October 1942 report by *Ulster Queen*'s Acting Captain C. K. Adam.
40. 22 September 1942 report by *Kentucky*'s Ensign William Farrar, US Armed Guard Reports UD93.
41. PQ18's U-boat Report; and 15 and 17 September 1942 entries in KTB des Admiral Nordmeer.

Chapter 29

1. 27 September 1942 report by QP14 Commodore John Dowding, **NA London** ADM 199/721 ('QP14's Commodore's Report').
2. 13 September 1942 entry in KTB DER SKL TEIL A.
3. Conversation with van Laar, in Jelte Rep, *SOS Paulus Potter* ('Rep's Book') pp. 179 and 185 – brought to my attention by Jos Odijk.
4. 23 July 1952 letter from Sissingh to *Nieuwe Rotterdamsche Courant* newspaper as mentioned in Rep's Book – pp. 179 and 184.
5. 15 July 1942 report by Guy Maund, NA London ADM 199/2492.
6. 29 September 1942 report by *Bramble*'s Captain Harvey Crombie, NA London ADM 199/758.
7. QP14's Commodore's Report.
8. CARRAWAY'S DIARY.
9. Ibid.
10. 29 September 1942 report entitled 'Operation E.V.' by Rear Admiral Robert Burnett ('Scylla's Report'), NA London ADM 199/758.
11. 18 and 19 September 1942 entries in KTB DES ADMIRAL NORDMEER.
12. Scylla's Report.
13. 20 September 1942 entry in KTB U-435 states that she torpedoed the ship that turned out to be *Leda* at 76°27' N 05°32' E.
14. S.A. Kerslake, *Coxswain In The Northern Convoys* ('Kerslake's Book') pp. 98–9.
15. These words are taken partly from Lieutenant Commander A. H.

Wynne-Edwards' evidence ('Wynne-Edwards' Testimony') in the 'Minutes Of Proceedings at a Board of Inquiry . . . into the circumstances attending the loss of His Majesty's Ship "Leda" on 20th September, 1942' ('Leda Inquiry Minutes') whose findings are dated 28 September 1942, and partly from his 21 September 1942 report ('Wynne-Edwards' Report') with these minutes, both in NA London ADM 199/163.

16. Testimony of Lieutenant Harry Pratt in the Leda Inquiry Minutes.

17. Testimony of Lieutenant Nicholas Lambrick in ibid.

18. Ibid.

19. Kerslake's Book p. 99.

20. Wynne-Edwards' Report.

21. Wynne-Edwards' Testimony. The following source stated that 44 Leda officers and ratings were killed: document entitled 'R.N. Casualties In N. Russia Convoys' ('The Navy Casualty Report') sent with undated note, written after the 31 December 1942 Battle of the Barents Sea, from the office of the Director of Naval Intelligence, NA London ADM 199/604.

22. Ibid.

23. 28 October 1942 report by Admiral Bruce Fraser, NA London ADM 199/163.

24. 25 September 1942 report by Somali's Lieutenant Commander Colin Maud ('Maud's Somali Report'), NA London ADM 199/163.

25. The 20 September 1942 entry in KTB U-255 states that the ship that turned out to be Silver Sword was torpedoed at AB 1648 on the

German grid (approximately 75°39' N 00°30' W).

26. 2 November 1942 'Summary of Statements by Survivors of the USA S/S Silver Sword', US MERCHANT SHIP LOSSES REPORTS Box 10.

27. 1 November 1942 'Summary of Submarine Operations During Passage of P.Q.18', NA London ADM 199/1834.

28. Scylla's Report.

29. The 20 September 1942 entry in KTB U-703 stated she torpedoed the ship that turned out to be Somali at AB 1836 on the German grid (approximately 75°09' N 01°10' W).

30. 20 September 1942 entry, KTB U-703; Maud's Somali Report; Appendix 1 to Scylla's Report headed: 'Loss of H.M.S. Somali: Extract from Report by Captain (D), 6th Destroyer Flotilla', by Ashanti's Acting Captain Richard Onslow ('Onslow's 1942 Somali Report').

31. Thomas Wells' account, IWM Documents 09/15/1.

32. Testimony by Lieutenant Walter Williamson, Flotilla Anti-Submarine Officer in Somali; Lieutenant G. Ritchie, Officer of the Watch in Somali; Able Seaman G.W. Windsor, an asdic rating in Somali, all in the minutes of the 27 September 1942 board of inquiry relating to Somali ('Somali Inquiry Minutes'), NA London ADM 199/163.

33. Lieutenant Walter Williamson evidence, the Somali Inquiry Minutes.

34. Ibid.; and undated report by an unidentified Ashanti officer

('Ashanti Officer's Account'), sent to Admiral Lord (Terence) Lewin, who at the time of *Somali*'s sinking was Sub-Lieutenant Lewin in HMS *Ashanti*, brought to my attention by Lord Lewin's son Tim.

35. 'A Tale of Two "Tribals"' 'written years after the events described by the officer, who at the time of these events was Acting Captain Richard Onslow ('Onslow's Post-War Account'), brought to my attention by Tim Lewin, and Richard Onslow's son Richard.

36. Ashanti Officer's Account.

37. Onslow's Post-War Account.

38. Onslow's 1942 Somali Report.

39. Maud's Somali Report.

40. Onslow's Post-War Account; and Onslow's 1942 Somali Report.

41. Ibid.

42. Maud's testimony ('Maud's Testimony'); and Onslow's testimony, in both cases in the Somali Inquiry Minutes.

43. Report by Lieutenant M. J. Lee ('Lee's Somali Report') in the Somali Inquiry Minutes.

44. Onslow's 1942 Somali Report.

45. Onslow's Post-War Account.

46. Maud's Somali Report; and Maud's Testimony.

47. Onslow's Post-War Account. It should be noted that Maud's Somali Report and Maud's Testimony combined with Onslow's 1942 Somali Report, all of which were contemporaneous, have led me to accept that the extremely bad weather arrived just after *Somali* began to sink, rather than prior to the beginning of the sinking as described in Onslow's Post-War Account.

48. A compilation of words from both Onslow's 1942 Somali Report and Onslow's Post-War Account.

49. Onslow's Post-War Account refers to these words being spoken by 'the Pilot'; I have assumed from the context this must be the officer from *Somali* who Onslow states came on board *Ashanti*.

50. Onslow's Post-War Account.

51. Lee's Somali Report.

52. Maud's Somali Report.

53. Onslow's Post-War Account.

54. Ibid.

55. Lee's Somali Report.

56. Maud's Somali Report.

57. Ashanti Officer's Account.

58. Onslow's Post-War Account.

59. Ashanti Officer's Account.

60. Onslow's 1942 Somali Report.

61. Onslow's Post-War Account.

62. Onslow's 1942 Somali Report.

63. Onslow's Post-War Account.

64. Lee's Somali Report states that *Lord Middleton*'s crew picked up 19 men but one of them died after being 'rescued'; and The Navy Casualty Report.

65. Onslow's Post-War Account.

66. Scylla's Report.

67. 3 November 1942 'Summary of Statements by Survivors of U.S.A. SS Bellingham' ('Bellingham's QP14 Report'), US ARMED GUARD REPORTS Box 57 Entry UD93; and Scylla's Report. The 22 September 1942 entry in KTB *U-435* states the three ships were torpedoed at AA 9286 on the German grid (approximately 70°57' N 11°10' W).

68. 16 October 1942 'Report of an Interview with the Master, Captain Harold James Kay: S.S. Ocean Voice'

('Ocean Voice's QP14 Report'), NA London ADM 199/1709.

69. Bellingham's QP14 Report; and *Gray Ranger's* undated 'List of the Crew which is undated but stamped with the date 30 March 1943, NA London BT 38/2175.

70. Ocean Voice's QP14 Report; and undated report by *Zamalek's* Captain Owen Morris ('Zamalek's Report'), NA London ADM 237/177.

71. Rep's Book pp. 189–90.

72. 23 September 1942 entry in KTB des Admiral Nordmeer.

73. QP14's Commodore's Report; Zamalek's QP14 Report; undated report by *Benjamin Harrison's* Lieutenant Paul W. Thompson; and 1 October 1942 report by *Deer Lodge's* Ensign Thomas Delate, latter two reports US Armed Guard Reports Boxes 61 and 166 respectively.

74. Undated report by *Troubadour's* Ensign Howard Carraway; and 16 December 1942 report by *Winston Salem's* Lieutenant Robert Chitrin, US Armed Guard Reports Boxes 661 and 718 respectively.

Chapter 30

1. REYNOLDS AND PECHATNOV p. 155.

2. Ibid.

3. Ibid. pp. 158–9.

4. Antony Beevor, *Stalingrad* pp. 161–5 and 220–2.

5. First Churchill to Roosevelt telegram in series discussing post-PQ18 Arctic convoys: 22 September 1942, CHURCHILL AND ROOSEVELT CORRESPONDENCE BOOK pp. 605–6.

6. 5 October 1942 from Roosevelt to Churchill, ibid. pp. 616–7.

7. 7 October 1942 Churchill to Roosevelt telegram text ('Churchill's 7 October 1942 Telegram') with 6 October 1942 War Cabinet Conclusions 134 W.M.42, **NA London** CAB 65/28.

8. Admiralty Note with ibid.

9. Ibid.

10. Churchill's 7 October 1942 Telegram.

11. Ibid.; and Roosevelt to Churchill 7 October 1942, Churchill and Roosevelt Correspondence Book p. 624.

12. Reynolds and Pechatnov p. 160.

13. Roosevelt to Churchill 8 October 1942, Churchill and Roosevelt Correspondence Book p. 630.

14. 8 October 1942 Churchill to Stalin, Reynolds and Pechatnov p. 160.

15. Ibid. p. 162.

16. Ibid. pp. 167–8.

17. Ibid. pp. 165–6.

18. Harry Hutson, *Arctic Interlude: Independent To North Russia* ('Hutson's Book') pp. 141–4; and 13 November 1942 report by *Richard H. Alvey's* Ensign Robert S. Platt, US NAVAL ATTACHÉ REPORTS Box 25.

19. 2 November 1942 entry in KTB U-586 states the sinking was at AA 9469 on the German grid (approximately 70°15' N 13°10' W).

20. Ibid.

21. 4 November 1942 entry in KTB U-354 states the torpedoing was at AA 9513 on the German grid (approximately 70°45' N 12°10' W).

22. 14 November 1942 report by trawler *St Elstan's* Lieutenant R. M. Roberts, in Hutson's Book pp. 117–118; and 21 January 1943 'Summary of

Statements by Survivors of the SS William Clark', US MERCHANT SHIP LOSSES REPORTS Box 252.

23. 6 November 1942 entry in KTB *U-625*, a translation of which is laid out in Hutson's Book p. 105, states these events were at AB 3388 on the German grid (approximately 76°15' N 18°30' E).

24. 12 November 1942 'Armed Guard Report: S.S. Hugh Williamson' by Ensign Roger Philip Wise, US NAVAL ATTACHÉ REPORTS, Box 25 UD 44.

25. Ibid.

26. Hutson's Book pp. 141–4 and 179.

27. Ibid.

28. Details of *Donbass* sinking brought to my attention by Captain of the 3rd rank Kirill Lukyanov after he referred to *Donbass'* Captain Tsilke's account in Konstantin Badigin, *On The Sea Roads*.

29. The sources in this chapter's Note 29 confirm the sailing of *Dekabrist* was at the end of October 1942 without agreeing on the exact date.

30. 4 and 5 October 1942 entries in KTB DES ADMIRAL NORDMEER.

31. The experiences of the *Dekabrist* survivors described in this chapter are taken from the following sources: what some commentators believe to be a corrected version of the diary of Stepan Belyaev, *Dekabrist*'s captain, which was published in the 21, 23, 26 and 28 January 1960 editions of *Vodnyj Transport* (Maritime Transport); an abbreviated version of the account by *Dekabrist*'s doctor Nadezhda Natalich which was published in *Polyarnaya Pravda* (Polar Truth) on 20 July 1979; pp. 176–180 of *Polyarniy Krug* (*The Polar Circle*), compiled by A.V. Shumilov: chapter: Perezhitoye: iz vospominaniy sudovogo medika parohoda "Dekabrist" (A testimony of what was experienced: from the memoirs of the ship's doctor on the vessel "Dekabrist") by Nadezhda Natalich. The Norwegian translations of all the abovementioned articles which are filed in the archives of the Norsk Polarinstitutts Bibliotek were brought to my attention and translated into English by Håvard Hansen in November 2022 while he was working as a weather observer at the Hope Island meteorological station. An extract from the Belyaev articles, and the Natalich article are also to be found in the U-boot Museum.

32. Report by *John Walker*'s Lieutenant Milton A. Stein, US Naval Attaché Reports Box 25.

33. Ibid.; and 4 October 1942 entry in KTB des Admiral Nordmeer.

34. Hutson's Book pp. 42–3.

35. G. A. Rudnev, *Na Morskih Dorogah Voini* (*The Naval Paths of War*) p. 142.

36. Charles T. Beke, ed., *Voyages By the North-East Towards Cathay and China Undertaken by The Dutch in the Years 1594, 1595 and 1596 by Gerrit De Vere* pp. 99 and 194. The literal translation is the Saved House but given the context, I felt House of the Saved captures an alternative meaning that might also have been intended.

Chapter 31

1. Section of 17 June 1943 'Report Of An Interview With The Master,

Captain D.M. Williams and 3rd Officer, Mr. D.F. Clark: S.S. Chulmleigh' ('Chulmleigh Report') written by Captain Williams ('Williams' Report'), **NA London** ADM 199/2143.

2. Chulmleigh Report; and the account by Richard Peyer ('Peyer's Account') brought to my attention by his son; and the report by Captain Williams' nephew, which contained Peyer's Account, brought to my attention by the daughter of Robert Paterson, Chulmleigh's Radio Officer.

3. Peyer's Account.

4. Williams' Report.

5. Tuna's war diary, NA London ADM 199/1844.

6. Williams' Report.

7. Ibid.

8. Peyer's Account.

9. Section of Chulmleigh's Report written by David Clark ('Clark's Report').

10. Williams' Report.

11. Peyer's Account.

12. Ibid.

13. Williams' Report.

14. Clark's Report.

15. Peyer's Account.

16. The approximate location is specified in an undated remnant of a telegram sent to the Admiralty after the survivors were found, NA London BT 381/2129. The Norwegian archaeologist Per Kyrre Reymert, formerly the director of archaeology at the Svalbard Museum in Longyearbyen, Svalbard, and the author of Fangsthytter på Svalbard 1794-2015 (Hunting cabins on Svalbard 1794-2015), a book about the huts on Svalbard including Spitzbergen, has informed me that the hut where the Chulmleigh survivors were found was at Kapp Mineral, around one and a half miles north-east of Kapp Linné. It was burned down some time after the rescue. When the son of Chulmleigh sailor Andrew Hardy visited the site more recently, he found the foundations of the burned down hut, the dip in the ground left after the Chulmleigh sailors' remains were exhumed from the mass grave where they had initially been interred, so that they could be reburied in Tromso, and the remains of a lifeboat that may well have been the boat used by the survivors before they reached the huts.

17. Clark's Report.

18. Ibid.; and Williams' Report – which is also the source of all subsequent quotes and information attributed to him in the main text.

19. Dates of events during the survivors' stay in the hut should be taken as approximate; they are based on estimated dates worked out using the timings in Peyer's Account, Williams' Report and Clark's Report and the documents relating to Chulmleigh in NA London BT 381/2129 including the 20 July 1942 'List of the Crew' ('Chulmleigh's Crew List').

20. Williams' Report.

21. Peyer's Account – which is also the source of all subsequent quotes and information attributed to him in the main text; and Chulmleigh's Crew List.

22. Robert Paterson's account ('Paterson's Account') in the article headed 'Seaman's Epic Experience On Arctic Isle' in 25 June 1943

edition of *The Shetland Times* brought to my attention by Richard Peyer's son.

23. Brought to my attention by Douglas C. Smith in his article in *Shetland Life* 'Chumleigh Revisited', and by the son of *Chulmleigh* seaman Andrew Hardy.

24. Paterson's Account.

25. Ibid.

26. Thoralv Lund, *Kalde Krigsår: Den Norske Innsets På Og For Svalbard 1940–1945 (Cold War Years: The Norwegian Efforts On And For Svalbard 1940-1945)* pp. 117–118, brought to my attention by Svalbard Museum's archivist Haakon Kvaale; and an account based at least in part on the experiences of the Norwegian Thoralv Lund, who cared for those in the Barentsburg settlement during the war; it was brought to my attention by *Chulmleigh*'s Andrew Hardy's son, as were many of the sources used by me to tell the *Chulmleigh* story.

27. Williams' Report.

28. Ibid. Clark's amputated fingers: article headed 'Another Epic Of The Sea' in 10 November 1943 edition of the *Western Morning News.*

29. Ibid.

30. Undated cutting apparently from the *Daily Express* brought to my attention by Richard Peyer's son.

31. 25 July 1943 entry in <u>KTB U-703</u>.

32. Leutnant Heinz Schlott's undated account, *U-703* file, **U-Boot Museum.**

33. 9 May 1980 letter from *U-703* crew member Hans Noack to Reinhart Reche ('<u>Noack's Letter</u>'), *U-703* section of Selinger collection, in the U-Boot Museum. The location

of the huts occupied by the Russians, and the distance between them, is taken from the privately published book *Hopen 2014: Ishavøy og meteorologisk stasjon*, by Oddmund Søreide and Tor Børsting, brought to my attention by Håvard Hansen.

34. 7 October 1943 entry in KTB *U-703*.

35. Noack's Letter.

Chapter 32

1. CHURCHILL'S BOOK vol. 4 p. 537.

2. REYNOLDS AND PECHATNOV p. 179.

3. 6 December 1942 report by *Sahale*'s Ensign Thomas D. Carter, <u>US ARMED GUARD REPORTS</u> Box 571 UD93.

4. 17 November 1942 Report of Proceedings and attached narrative by Convoy's Commodore William Meek ('<u>QP15's Commodore's Report</u>'), **NA London** ADM 237/166.

5. V. Shackleton's account, **IWM Documents** 96/22/1. QP15 shipping: QP15's Commodore's Report.

6. The 23 November 1942 entry in the <u>KTB DES ADMIRAL NORDMEER</u> states *Goolistan* and *Kusnetz Lesov* were respectively torpedoed by *U-625* at AB 3592 on the German grid (approximately 75°33' N 16°30' E) and by *U-601* at AB 3569 on the German grid (approximately 75°39' N 16°50' E), both of which locations are north-west of Bear Island; and QP15's Commodore's Report.

7. 'The Search For Sokrushitelni Is To Be Terminated' by V.I. Usov, *Gangut* journal edition 1 pp. 86–9, brought

to my attention by Captain of the 3rd rank Kirill Lukyanov.

8. 'Sokrushitelni's Last Journey' by P. I. Nikiforov ('Nikiforov's Account'), *Gangut* journal edition 7 pp. 118–25, 1994, brought to my attention by Captain of the 3rd rank Kirill Lukyanov; and Arseni Golovko, *With The Red Fleet* pp. 133–40.

9. Nikiforov's Account.

10. TOVEY'S DESPATCH.

11. Appendix I to the 12 January 1943 report by *Obedient*'s Lieutenant Commander David Kinloch ('Obedient's JW51B Report'), NA London ADM 199/73.

12. Number of escorts: Appendix I; and number of merchant ships and their relative location: Appendix III, both appendices forming part of ibid.

13. Force R's movements 18-27 December 1942: War Diary of the Commander-in-Chief Home Fleet 16-31 December 1942, NA London ADM 199/427.

14. Force R's approximate position at 8.45 a.m. 31 December 1942 according to Burnett's 6 January 1943 report ('Force R's Report'), NA London ADM 199/73, was 73°47' N 28°54' E; Force R's prior movements shown in Map 16 are based on the BRITISH ARCTIC CONVOYS HISTORY'S Plan 14.

15. Force R's Report.

16. 25 miles to the north of the convoy: Report entitled 'Action In Defence Of Convoy J.W. 51B' with 25 January 1943 Tovey memorandum, NA London ADM 199/73.

17. 30 December 1942 entries in KTB U-354; KTB des Admiral Nordmeer; and KTB DES

MARINEGRUPPENK OMMANDOS NORD. *U-354* reported the convoy was sighted at the place described on the German grid as AB 6388 (approximately 73°33' N 18°30' E).

18. 30 December 1942 entry in KTB *U-354*.

19. Vizeadmiral Theodor Krancke's report, ('Krancke's Report'), **NA Maryland**, RG38, Records of the Chief of Naval Operations, Entry UD-WW 24: Translated German War Diaries, 1941-45 Box 143.

20. 30 December 1942 entries in KTB des Admiral Nordmeer; and KTB *U-354*.

21. 30 December 1942 entry in KTB DES BEFEHLSHABERS DER KREUZER.

22. 30 December 1942 entry in KTB DES KREUZERS ADMIRAL HIPPER.

23. Krancke's Report.

24. The approximate location can be gleaned from the following slightly different coordinates taken from the following sources: The 31 December 1942 entry in the KTB des Befehlshabers der Kreuzer states the alarm was given at 7.58 a.m. that morning when *Hipper* was at AC 4395 on the German grid (approximately 73°39' N 28°30' E), but 'Skizze 1' entitled 'Gefechtskizze Kreuzer "Admiral Hipper" für das Gefecht am Geleitzug am 31.12.1942', with the KTB des Kreuzers Admiral Hipper, suggests the alarm was given with *Hipper* at around 73°25' N 27°40' E.

25. 30–31 December 1942 entries in the KTB des Befehlshabers der Kreuzer.

26. Ibid.
27. 2 January 1943 report on behalf of the destroyer *Onslow* ('Onslow's JW51B Report'), NA London ADM 199/73.
28. 30 December 1942 entry in KTB *U-354*.
29. Dudley Pope, *73 North: The Battle of the Barents Sea* p. 151.
30. Appendix I to Obedient's JW51B Report; and British Arctic Convoys History p. 93.
31. Appendix I and VII to Obedient's JW51B Report.
32. Alan Ross, *Blindfold Games* ('Ross' Book') p.164.
33. Appendix I to Obedient's JW51B Report.
34. Ross' Book p. 165; and Appendix VII to Obedient's JW51B Report.
35. *Achates'* Lieutenant Loftus Peyton Jones' 2 January 1943 report ('Achates' JW51B Report'), NA London ADM 199/73; and Obedient's JW51B Report.
36. George Charlton's account, brought to my attention by Michael Foight, Director of Distinctive Collectives and Digital Engagement at Villanova University's Falvey Memorial Library in America.
37. Loftus Peyton Jones, *Wartime Wanderings* ('Peyton Jones' Book') p. 121, brought to my attention by his son James, and the abovementioned Michael Foight.
38. Tom Marchant's account ('Marchant's Account'), IWM Documents 99/42/1.
39. Ross' Book p. 165.
40. Appendix I to Obedient's JW51B Report.
41. Achates' JW51B Report; Peyton Jones' Book p. 122; and transcript of Peyton Jones' evidence with 8 January 1943 report of the Board of Inquiry concerning the loss of HMS *Achates*, NA London ADM 199/73. The convoy did not turn to the south-east until around 10.15 a.m.: Appendix IV Obedient's JW51B Report.
42. Peyton Jones' Book pp. 122–3.
43. Undated 'Artilleristischer Bericht über das Gefecht am 31. Dezember 1942' ('Hipper's Regenbogen Artillery Report'), filed with the undated 'Gefechtsbericht Kreuzer "Admiral Hipper" über das Gefecht mit engl. Sicherungsstreitkräften am 31. Dezember 1942' ('Hipper's Regenbogen Report') written by Kapitän Hans Hartmann, which is in its turn referred to in the 31 December 1942 entry in the KTB des Kreuzers Admiral Hipper.
44. Hipper's Regenbogen Report.
45. British torpedoes' range: Marchant's Account.
46. Time when *Hipper* closed in on *Onslow* and the movements of the other destroyers; and distance separating ships: respectively Appendix I to Obedient's JW51B Report; and Hipper's Regenbogen Artillery Report.
47. Ross' Book p. 167. Time when *Hipper* fired on the right bearing for *Onslow*: Appendix I to Obedient's JW51B Report; and Hipper's Regenbogen Artillery Report.
48. Appendix I to Obedient's JW51B Report.
49. Marchant's Account.
50. Ross' Book p. 167.
51. Ibid.
52. Appendix I to Obedient's JW51B Report.

53. Marchant's Account; Onslow's JW51B Report states *Hipper* hit *Onslow* at 10.19 a.m. 31 December 1942.

54. Account by the officer who in 1942 was HMS *Orwell*'s Lieutenant Commander Nigel Austen ('Austen's Account'), IWM Documents 11/34/1.

55. Appendix I to Obedient's JW51B Report.

56. Austen's Account.

57. Appendix I to Obedient's JW51B Report.

58. Austen's Account.

59. Hipper's Regenbogen Report.

60. Hipper's Regenbogen Artillery Report. *Bramble*'s mission: Appendix III to Obedient's JW51B Report.

61. Appendix VII to Obedient's JW51B Report.

62. 8 January 1943 Board of Inquiry report into loss of HMS *Bramble*, NA London ADM 199/73.

63. Hipper's Regenbogen Report.

Chapter 33

1. Tom Marchant's account, **IWM Documents** 99/42/1.

2. Ibid.

3. Thomas Hanley's account, **IWM Sound** 12812.

4. Alan Ross, *Blindfold Games* pp. 161–3 and 168.

5. 31 December 1942 entry in <u>KTB DES KREUZERS LÜTZOW</u>.

6. 31 December 1942 entry in the <u>KTB DES BEFEHLSHABERS DER KREUZER</u>; and undated 'Gefechtsbericht Kreuzer "Admiral Hipper" über das Gefecht mit engl. Sicherungsstreitkräften am 31. Dezember 1942' ('Hipper's

Regenbogen Report') written by Kapitän Hans Hartmann, <u>KTB DES KREUZERS ADMIRAL HIPPER</u>.

7. Undated 'Artilleristischer Bericht über das Gefecht am 31. Dezember 1942' ('Hipper's Regenbogen Artillery Report'), filed with <u>Hipper's Regenbogen Report</u>.

8. This sentence, taken from Loftus Peyton Jones' testimony at the January 1943 Inquiry into the sinking of *Achates*, has been inserted into the quotation from Loftus Peyton Jones, *Wartime Wanderings* ('Peyton Jones' Book') specified in Note 9 below.

9. Peyton Jones' Book p. 124; and *Achates'* Lieutenant Loftus Peyton Jones' 2 January 1943 report ('Achates' JW51B Report'), **NA London** ADM 199/73.

10. Peyton Jones' Book p. 125.

11. Achates' JW51B Report.

12. Peyton Jones' Book p. 125.

13. Ibid. pp. 125–6.

14. G.F. Barker, Villanova University's Falvey Memorial Library in America brought to my attention by Michael Foight, Director of Distinctive Collectives and Digital Engagement at the Library.

15. Achates' JW51B Report; and position of *Achates'* ERA Mess: Testimony of Chief Stoker Wilfred Brown, with 8 January 1943 report of the Board of Inquiry concerning the loss of HMS *Achates*, NA London ADM 199/73.

16. George Charlton, Villanova University's Falvey Memorial Library in America, brought to my attention by Michael Foight,

Director of Distinctive Collectives and Digital Engagement at the Library.

17. Peyton Jones' Book p. 126.
18. Ibid. p. 125.
19. Hipper's Regenbogen Artillery Report; 5 January 1943 report by convoy Commodore Robin Melhuish, NA London ADM 199/73; and Appendix I to the 12 January 1943 report by *Obedient's* Lieutenant Commander David Kinloch ('Obedient's JW51B Report'), NA London ADM 199/73.
20. Their delay through being out of position, as mentioned in Chapter 32, had been exacerbated by Rear Admiral Burnett temporarily mistaking two JW51B ships – the British trawler *Vizalma* and a straggling merchant ship – to his north for the enemy (their approximate position relative to Force R at dawn on 31 December 1942 can be seen in Map 17). He only turned towards the convoy to his south at around 9.50 a.m. after he had seen the flashes of the guns in that direction as the Germans attacked JW51B, Burnett's 6 January 1943 report ('Force R's Report'), NA London ADM 199/73.
21. Force R's Report; Petty Officer Fuller's account ('Fuller's Account'), **IWM Documents** 2425. Although *Sheffield's* 'Gunnery Report On Action With German Surface Craft 31st December 1942' ('Sheffield's Gunnery Report'), Enclosure 1 to Force R's Report, states that *Sheffield* was 16,900 yards away (over 9 miles) from *Hipper*, *Jamaica's* Gunnery Control Officer's Narrative (Enclosure 5 to Force R's Report)

says *Jamaica* was 12,400 yards away (7 miles). Tovey stated in his 9 February 1943 report in NA London ADM 199/73 that *Sheffield's* specification of the distance was probably erroneous.

22. Fuller's Account.
23. Henry Brown, who served in one of *Sheffield's* aft gun turrets during the engagement, **Arctic Convoy Museum.**
24. *Sheffield's* Gunnery Report.
25. Hipper's Regenbogen Artillery Report.
26. Hipper's Regenbogen Report
27. Force R's Report.
28. 31 December 1942 entry in KTB Kommando 5 Zerstörerflottille KTB, **Militärarchiv Freiburg** RM 58/23.
29. Force R's Report; and map in its Enclosure 2.
30. Fuller's Account.
31. Anlage 3e to KTB DES KREUZERS ADMIRAL HIPPER.
32. Fuller's Account; and *Sheffield's* John Somers' post-war account, brought to my attention by his nephew Alan, which confirms *Friedrich Eckoldt* was on *Sheffield's* starboard side when the cruiser passed the German destroyer.
33. Herbert A. A. Twiddy, *My Teenage War And Later Career* pp. 19 20.
34. Appendix I to Obedient's JW51B Report.
35. 20 January 1943 Official Admiralty Communiqué relating to loss of *Bramble*, NA London ADM 199/73; and Hipper's Regenbogen Report.
36. 31 December 1942 entry in KTB des Befehlshabers der Kreuzer; and Force R's Report.

37. Peyton Jones' Book pp. 128–9.
38. Sidney Kerslake, *Coxswain In The Northern Convoys* ('Kerslake's Book') p. 114.
39. Peyton Jones' Book p. 130.
40. Kerslake's Book p. 114.
41. Peyton Jones' Book pp. 130.
42. Survivors lists attached to Achates' JW51B Report. Number of dead: 'Fidus Achates', an unpublished book edited by David and Joan Wood, IWM Documents 12796.
43. Officers Steward Allan Jones and Canteen Manager G. Drummond, posthumously mentioned in despatches, Appendix XI Part II to Obedient's JW51B Report, NA London ADM 1/14229.
44. Peyton Jones' Book pp. 131–2.
45. Appendix VI to Obedient's JW51B Report.
46. Surgeon Captain J.L.S. Coulter, *The Royal Naval Medical Service Volume II Operations* ('Medical History Vol. II') p. 448.
47. Ibid.; and Part I of Home Fleet Destroyer Command War Diary for period from 16 to 31 December 1942, NA London ADM 199/429.
48. Surgeon Commander J.L.S. Coulter, *The Royal Naval Medical Service Vol. I Administration* pp. 405–6, and p. 441 which states Russian permission to open the hospital was granted on 5 October 1942.
49. Tovey's Report 'Action In Defence of Convoy J.W.51B' circulated on 25 January 1943, NA London ADM 199/73.
50. 23 January 1943, 'Abschliessender Bericht über das Gefecht im Nordmeer am 31. Dezember 1942', Militärarchiv Freiburg RM 7/129.

51. Nikita Khrushchev, *Memoirs* vol.1: *Commissar* p. 226. Number of trucks sent to Russia prior to the surrender of the Germans in and around Stalingrad: I have struggled to find precise figures that clearly include all trucks sent to Russia which were made in America as well as in Britain. A document referring rather misleadingly to 'Military Stores from United Kingdom production . . ', in NA London CAB 111/110, when interpreted in the light of other documents in NA London CAB 111/109, including one headed 'Final Figures Of Arrivals And Losses For Each Convoy Up To And Including P.Q.16', and the 29 July 1942 Office of the War Cabinet letter that accompanied it, appears to confirm that 3,037 trucks arrived in Russia during 1941–2, including 2,636 either made in the UK, or made in America for the British-Russia account, which were carried in the Arctic convoys that sailed prior to the sailing of PQ17.
52. Vizeadmiral Theodor Krancke's report ('Krancke's Report'), **NA Maryland**, RG38, Records of the Chief of Naval Operations, Entry UD-WW 24: Translated German War Diaries, 1941-45 Box 143.
53. Krancke's Report.
54. Grand Admiral Erich Raeder, *My Life* p. 370; Jak Mallmann Showell, ed., *Fuehrer Conferences On Naval Affairs* 1939–1945 pp. 306–8.
55. Krancke's Report.
56. Decision to surrender: memoir of German 194 Regiment's general Friedrich Roske, quoted in Iain MacGregor, *The Lighthouse Of Stalingrad* p. 265.
57. Antony Beavor, *Stalingrad* p. 396.

Chapter 34

1. REYNOLDS AND PECHATNOV p. 190.
2. 9 January 1943 Churchill note to Eden, **NA London** FO 954/3B/261.
3. 10 January 1943 Churchill to Stalin, Reynolds and Pechatnov pp. 194–5.
4. BRITISH ARCTIC CONVOYS HISTORY pp. 138 and 141.
5. WOODMAN'S BOOK p. 332; and 27 and 29 January 1943 entries in KTB DES FÜHRER DER UNTERSEEBOOTE NORWEGEN. The sunk merchant ship on 3 February 1943 was RA52's *Greylock*, 9 February 1943 report by RA52's Commodore R. Melhuish, NA London ADM 199/73.
6. Details supplied by Russ Riddell senior's son Russ and granddaughter Jennifer.
7. RA 53 consisted of 17 US, 9 British, 3 Panamanian and 1 Soviet merchant ships, Convoy formation, NA London ADM 237/956.
8. 14 March 1943 report by Captain I.M.R. Campbell, Captain (D) Third Destroyer Flotilla ('Milne's Report'), NA London ADM 199/73.
9. Ibid.; two NA London ADM 199/73 documents: 18 March 1943 'Report Of Proceedings . . . Passage Of Convoy R.A. 53' by *Scylla's* Commanding Officer ('Scylla's RA53 Report'); and list of convoy's daily positions filed with 14 March 1943 report by RA53's Commodore Vice Admiral Sir L. Goldsmith ('RA53's Commodore's Report'); and 2-5 March 1943 entries in KTB des Führer der Unterseeboote Norwegen.
10. The 5 March 1943 entry in KTB U-255 states the torpedoing took place at AB 5939 on the German grid (approximately 72°21' N 10°50' E).
11. Ibid.; and 17 March 1943 report by Arthur C. Krohn, Commander of Armed Guard in SS Executive ('Executive Armed Guard Report'), US ARMED GUARD REPORTS Box 215 UD93.
12. 5 March entry in KTB U-255.
13. Undated and unsigned report which 1st Mate Gordon McAllister told his sons Gordon junior, Doug and Kevin was written by him ('Executive 1st Mate's Report'), US CASUALTY REPORTS Box 3 A1 190; and Executive Armed Guard Report.
14. Executive Armed Guard Report.
15. Executive 1st Mate's Report; 14 March 1943 'Report Of Proceedings For The Passage Of Convoy R.A. 53' by the Captain (D) Eighth Destroyer Flotilla in *Faulknor* ('Faulknor's RA53 Report'), NA London ADM 199/73.
16. 17 March 1943 report by Lieutenant William Carter concerning *Richard Bland* ('Carter's Richard Bland Report'), US Armed Guard Reports Box 547; and William A. Carter, *Why Me Lord?* ('Carter's Book') pp. 10–12.
17. Carter's Book pp. 15–17. Weather: Milne's Report.
18. Milne's Report; and 12 March 1943' of Proceedings by Lieutenant-in-Command of St Elstan' ('St Elstan's RA53 Report'), NA London ADM 199/73.
19. The 24 June 1943 'Supplement to Summary of Statements by Survivors of the SS Puerto Rican' ('Puerto Rican Survivors Summary

Supplement'), <u>US CASUALTY RECORDS</u> Box 38. The 9 March 1943 entry in the <u>KTB U-586</u> states the torpedoing was at AE 3574 on the German grid (approximately 67°21' N 08°22' W). But it is quite likely that *Puerto Rican*'s SOS recorded in Faulknor's RA53 Report which refers to 66°44' N 10°41' W was more accurate given that St Elstan's RA53 Report confirms that, while responding to the SOS, she passed a very large expanse of oil at 66°44' N 10°36' W and found a waterlogged boat in the vicinity.

20. 21 May 1943 report of August Wallenhaupt interview ('Wallenhaupt's Interview'), US Casualty Records Box 38.

21. 'Torpedoed in the Arctic' by Carl B. Wall in 24 June 1944 edition of the magazine *Liberty* ('Wallenhaupt Liberty Article'), US Casualty Records Box 38.

22. Wallenhaupt's Interview.

23. Wallenhaupt Liberty Article.

24. Ibid.

25. Wallenhaupt's Interview.

26. Wallenhaupt Liberty Article.

27. Faulknor's RA53 Report.

28. Carter's Book p. 18.

29. The 10 March 1943 entry in the KTB *U-255* appears to say the torpedoing at 4.36 p.m. was at AE 2824 on the German grid (approximately 67°03' N 14°22' W). This is close to the location picked up by the telegraphist in Faulknor from *Richard Bland*'s SOS: 66°53' N 14°10' W, Faulknor's RA53 Report. Westward course: 27 April 1943 'Summary of Statements by Survivors SS Richard Bland' ('Richard Bland's Survivors

Report'), US Armed Guard Reports Box 547.

30. Carter's Book p. 19.

31. Ibid. pp. 9-10; and Carter's Richard Bland Report.

32. The 10 March 1943 entry in the KTB *U-255* states the torpedo was fired at 7.47 p.m.

33. Temperature: 3rd Mate Richard Braithwaite's undated sworn statement, US Casualty Records Box 38. Sludge: Carter's Book p. 24.

34. Carter's Book pp. 26–8.

35. Carter's Richard Bland Report.

36. 22 April 1943 report by Lieutenant William Carter, US Armed Guard Reports Box 547.

37. 24 August 1943 note from Navy Department Board of Decorations and Medals, US Armed Guard Reports Box 547.

38. George Carlson account courtesy of his daughters Hannah, Pat and Sue.

39. Richard Bland's Survivors Report.

40. St Elstan's RA53 Report.

41. Wallenhaupt Liberty Article.

42. Carter's Book p. 246.

43. Wallenhaupt's Interview; and Wallenhaupt Liberty Article.

44. Wallenhaupt Liberty Article.

45. 'Puerto Rican Survivors Summary Supplement'.

46. Scylla's RA53 Report; and Faulknor's RA53 Report.

47. 19 March 1943 note from NOB Iceland, US Casualty Records Box 38.

48. RA53's Commodore's Report.

Chapter 35

1. 30 March 1943 message Churchill to Stalin, REYNOLDS AND PECHATNOV pp. 225–6.

2. Gabriel Gorodetsky, ed., *The Maisky Diaries*, p. 503.
3. Ibid. p. 504.
4. Reynolds and Pechatnov p. 227.
5. Professor A. N. Yakovel with V. N. Haustov, V. P. Naumov, and N. S. Plotnikova, eds., *Lubyanka: Stalin and NKVD-NKGB-GUKR Smersh* ('Lubyanka Book') pp. 433–5, brought to my attention by Liudmila Novikova, 'Criminalized Liaisons: Soviet Women and Allied Sailors in Wartime Arkhangel'sk' ('Criminalised Liaisons Article'), Journal of Contemporary History 2020 vol. 55 issue 4, pp. 745–63.
6. 3 July 1943 comments at meeting of the bureau of the Archangel Communist Party committee, **GAOPDiFAO** Section 296, Inventory 1, Book 1445, p. 32, brought to my attention by the Criminalised Liaisons Article. Malkov complaint: Transcript of the 14 November 1941 meeting of the Archangel regional party activists, GAOPDiFAO Section 296, Inventory 1, Book 934, p. 84; British laughing at empty shop shelves: V.N. Il'in, V.A. Radishevskaya, T.V. Titova, eds., *Voina: Zapechatlennie dni 1941–1942* (*War: Captured Days 1941–1942*) 16 August 1941 entry; foreign seamen looking down on Russians: report 'On board the U.S.S.R. leading Destroyer "Baku" 22nd October to 31st October 1943' with 7 November 1943 letter from unnamed lieutenant, NA London ADM 199/2492; Billie Moore's diary, **IWM Documents** 20866; venereal disease concerns: 12 October 1943 report by Captain

A.B. Taylor, RAMC, **NA London** WO 222/1552; frozen Russian corpses, and channel cut in ice on Dvina icing over quickly: Christopher Stiff account, IWM Documents 8572.1; cut with razor blade: 29 June 1945 letter from William McCormick and Warren Asplin to US Naval Attaché, Murmansk, US NAVAL ATTACHÉ REPORTS Box 26.
7. 22 May 1944 report by Lieutenant A. Penn ('The Archangel NKVD Report'), NA London ADM 199/2492.
8. Gluzman's report about the Interclub in 1943, **GAAO** Section 1649, Inventory 2, book 3 pp. 34–7. NKVD agents in institutions: The Archangel NKVD Report.
9. WOODMAN'S BOOK pp. 333–5.
10. Gluzman report covering 8 January to 29 December 1945 ('Gluzman's Summary'), **GAAO** Section 1649, Inventory 2, book 6; and behaviour like in captialistc pub: Gluzman report covering 1943, Section 1649, Inventory 2, File 3.
11. 4 July 1943 resolution by Malkov, against Anastasia Sidorenko, **GAOPDiFAO** Section 296, Inventory 1, Book 1458, page 20.
12. 5–10 December 1943 entries in the British Naval Mission, Moscow war diary, NA London ADM 199/1102; and 5 December 1943 30 Mission to Admiralty telegram, NA London WO 193/668.
13. Document headed 'In A Russian Prison and Labour Camp', NA London ADM 199/2492.
14. Lubyanka Book p. 435. Gluzman's comment that foreigners were kept under observation in the Interclub:

December 1943–4 Interclub report by Gluzman, GAAO Section 1649, Inventory 2, Book 3 p.37.

15. 6 March 1943 message from Clark Kerr to Molotov; 10 March 1943 Eden note, attached to Note by Secretary to Chiefs of Staff Committee, referring to message sent to Molotov pursuant to 25 February 1943 decision; and memorandum shown by Eden to Maisky on 26 February 1943, NA London ADM 199/604, CAB 80/68 and FO 954/3B/331 respectively.

16. Extract from the Minutes of the 9 March 1943 Chiefs of Staff Committee, NA London WO 193/669.

17. 12 March 1943 Memorandum from Eric Brind, Assistant Chief of Naval Staff, and Norman Bottomley, Assistant Chief of Air Staff (Operations) for the Chiefs of Staff Committee, NA London CAB 80/68.

18. 6 March 1943 Archibald Clark Kerr to Molotov, NA London ADM 199/604.

19. 18 August 1943 'Memorandum Regarding Vexatious Formalities . . .' ('Vexatious Formalities Memo'), NA London ADM 199/606.

20. 2 August 1943 note by Lieutenant Commander K. Henderson, Naval Base Archangel, US NAVAL ATTACHÉ REPORTS Box 23.

21. British troubles in Russia linked to No Second Front: 24 July 1943 report by Rear Admiral Ernest Archer, NA London ADM 199/606.

22. 12 September 1943 report by Rear Admiral Ernest Archer, NA London ADM 199/2492.

23. 12 September 1943 report by Rear Admiral Douglas Fisher, Head of British Naval Mission Moscow: 'Request from Soviet Government for Two British Officers and a British Army Officer to leave the Country', NA London ADM 199/2492.

24. 24 July 1943 report by Rear Admiral Ernest Archer, NA London ADM 199/606.

25. 17 July 1943 entry in British Naval Mission Moscow war diary, NA London ADM 199/1102.

26. Vexatious Formalities Memo. Reduction of *Dover Hill seamen*'s sentences: 19 October 1943 entry in Naval Mission Moscow war diary, NA London ADM 199/1102..

27. 11 August 1943 note by Humphrey Waldock, Head of M.(I), NA London ADM 199/606.

28. Extract from Chiefs of Staff 26 July 1943 meeting; and 28 July 1943 note by Humphrey Waldock, Head of M. (I) 'Difficulties In North Russia', both in NA London ADM 199/606.

29. 8 August 1943 telegram from Eden to Clark Kerr, NA London ADM 199/606.

Chapter 36

1. Operation Source has featured in the following books: Alf Jacobsen, *X-Craft Versus Tirpitz: The Mystery of the Missing X5*; Frank Walker and Pamela Mellor, *The Mystery of X-5*; Niklas Zetterling and Michael Tamelander, *Tirpitz: The Life and Death of Germany's Last Super Battleship*; Patrick Bishop, *Target Tirpitz*; Paul Watkins, *Midget Submarine Commander: The*

Life of Rear Admiral Godfrey Place VC.

2. Battle Summary No. 29 by Tactical and Staff Duties' Division (Historical Section) p. 5, **NA London** ADM 234/348.

3. 23 September 1943 Archibald Clark Kerr to Foreign Office, NA London FO 954/3.

4. Ibid.

5. BRITISH INTELLIGENCE OFFICIAL HISTORY vol. 3 part 1 p. 261; 12 October 1943 report by Admiral (Submarines); and 26 July 1945 report by Rear Admiral G.E. Creasy ('1945 Operation Source Report'), both NA London ADM 199/888.

6. 1945 Operation Source Report, which refers to 'Kaa Fjord'. However some British documents refer to Kaa Fiord or Kaafiord.

7. Lieutenants Donald Cameron and Godfrey Place were awarded the Victoria Cross in February 1944, NA London ADM 199/888.

8. British Intelligence Official History vol. 3 part 1 pp. 256–8.

9. 1 October 1943 Churchill to Stalin, CHURCHILL'S BOOK vol.5 pp. 234–7; and NA London ADM 199/606.

10. Churchill's Book vol.5 pp. 237–9.

11. 15 October 1943 Churchill to Eden, ibid. p. 239.

12. 16 October 1943 Churchill to Roosevelt, ibid.

13. Ibid pp. 241–2.

14. Anthony Eden, *The Eden Memoirs: The Reckoning*, pp. 412–3.

15. The Third Protocol was signed in London on behalf of the US, Canada and UK on 19 October 1943.

16. 22 October 1943 Eden to Churchill via Clark Kerr, Churchill's Book vol.5 pp. 243–4; and NA London ADM 199/606.

17. 22 October 1943 Eden to Churchill via Clark Kerr, NA London ADM 199/606.

18. 23 October 1943 Eden to Churchill via Clark Kerr, NA London ADM 199/606.

19. 28 October 1943 entry in British Naval Mission, Moscow war diary, NA London ADM 199/1102.

20. 7 November 1943 telegram from Clark Kerr quoting Molotov's memorandum, NA London ADM 199/606.

21. Stalin's 13 October 1943 letter to Churchill, REYNOLDS AND PECHATNOV pp. 322–3 had only stated he had no objection to minor violations being dealt with by the British.

22. Admiral Fisher's 27 October 1943 message citing Clark Kerr's advice to let matters take their course; and hoping for improvement in better atmosphere, Clark Kerr 6 November 1943 telegram, both in NA London ADM 199/606.

23. Document headed 'In A Russian Prison and Labour Camp', NA London ADM 199/2492; and 24 May 1944 entry in British Naval Mission, Moscow war diary, NA London ADM 199/1102.

Chapter 37

1. 21 December 1943 report by Admiral Sir Bruce Fraser, **NA London** ADM 199/2492.

2. All Ultra messages in this chapter are taken from Appendix 14 in the BRITISH INTELLIGENCE

OFFICIAL HISTORY vol. 3(1) pp. 537–41. The 22 December 1943 entry in the KTB DES ADMIRAL NORDMEER states that the first sighting of the convoy, that was JW55B, was on that day at AE 6983 on the German grid (approximately 63°51' N 04°52' W).

3. 28 January 1944 report by Admiral Sir Bruce Fraser ('Fraser's JW55B Report'), NA London ADM 199/913.

4. Ibid.; and the destroyer *Onslow*'s Captain James McCoy's Report of Proceedings ('Onslow's JW55B Report') in Appendix II to McCoy's 9 January 1944 letter ('McCoy's JW55B Letter' – mistakenly dated 9 January 1943), NA London ADM 199/77.

5. Escort list with Commodore Maitland Boucher's 20 December 1943 Report of Proceedings, NA London ADM 199/77.

6. 1 January 1944 report by Vice Admiral Burnett entitled 'Destruction of German Battle Cruiser "Scharnhorst" On St. Stephen's Day 1943' ('Burnett's Battle of North Cape Report') NA London ADM 199/913; his 20 December 1943 report; and his 3 January 1944 report, both in NA London ADM 199/77.

7. Fraser's JW55B Report.

8. 23 November 1943 entry in KTB DER KAMPFGRUPPE.

9. Schniewind's 24 December 1943 'Lagebeurteilung und Vorschlag' ('Schniewind's First Proposal'), Anlage 8 to KTB DES MARINE-GRUPPENKOMMANDOS NORD UND FLOTTENKOM-MANDOS for 16–27 December 1943.

10. 24 December 1943 message from Kampfgruppe to Gruppe Nord and Admiral Nordmeer, in Anlage 13 to KTB des Marinegruppenkommandos Nord und Flottenkommandos for 16–27 December 1943.

11. Dönitz's 26 February 1943 meeting with Hitler, Jak Mallmann Showell, ed., Fuehrer Conferences on Naval Affairs 1939-1945 pp. 311–12.

12. 24 and 25 December 1943 entries in KTB DES FÜHRER DER UNTERSEEBOOTE NORWEGEN.

13. 25 December 1943 entry in ibid.

14. 25 December 1943 entries in: KTB des Marinegruppenkommandos Nord und Flottenkommandos; and KTB DER SKL TEIL A.

15. 25 December 1943 order from Dönitz ('Dönitz's Attack Order'), in Anlage 9 to KTB des Marinegruppenkommandos Nord und Flottenkommandos.

16. Schniewind's First Proposal.

17. 25 December 1943 message from Schniewind to Dönitz, in Anlage 10 to KTB des Marinegruppenkommandos Nord und Flottenkommandos.

18. 25 December 1943 entry in KTB des Führer der Unterseeboote Norwegen; and 26 December 1943 entry in KTB des Marinegruppenkommandos Nord und Flottenkommandos.

19. Dönitz's Attack Order.

20. 26 December 1943 entry in KTB des Marinegruppenkommandos Nord und Flottenkommandos.

21. 25 December 1943 entry in KTB der Skl Teil A.

22. 2.17 a.m. 26 December 1943 Admiralty message to Fraser and Burnett, NA London ADM 223/188.

23. 2.18 a.m. 26 December 1943 Admiralty message to Fraser and Burnett, ibid.; and decrypt of 5.15 p.m. 25 December 1943 message from 'Scharnhorst' to 'V 5903', NA London ADM 223/36.

24. When *Scharnhorst* left Lang Fjord, the watching Norwegian agent quickly telephoned his contact, and dropped into the conversation, mentioning his Christmas greetings, the pre-agreed code to announce the battlecruiser's departure. It went something like 'I shall be at home . . . but Grandmother is travelling'. Unfortunately the subsequent attempt to pass this on to the Admiralty appears not to have reached the Admiralty in time to make a difference (Tony Insall, *Secret Alliances* p. 325 points out that the British director of naval intelligence in January 1944 stated that information obtained from the *Scharnhorst* seamen captured after the ship was sunk showed that the Norwegian agents' information was correct; although the written record of this intimation does not disclose what information was being talked about, this might have been a reference to the eventual receipt of the notification from the Norwegian agents that *Scharnhorst* was leaving Lang Fjord as she set out to attack JW55B). Story of the Norwegian agents based on Alf R. Jacobsen, *Scharnhorst* ('Jacobsen's Scharnhorst Book') pp. 153-4; interview with Harry Pettersen for the documentary film *The Scharnhorst Mystery* produced by Alf Jacobsen first shown on BBC's

Timewatch in 2001 ('Jacobsen's Scharnhorst Documentary'); 31 July 1944 report by Torstein Råby supplied by Frode Færøy at Norway's Resistance Museum.

25. Burnett's Battle of North Cape Report states that on 26 December 1943 twilight in the relevant area lasted from around 9.40 a.m. to 1.15 p.m.

26. Fraser's JW55B Report.

27. Fraser's 0401 and 0628 26 December 1943 signals, in Appendix III to McCoy's JW55B Letter.

28. Fraser's JW55B Report.

29. Burnett's Battle of North Cape Report.

30. 26 December 1943 entry in KTB DER 4 ZERSTÖRERFLOTTILLE.

31. The location where the German battlegroup turned to the south-west – with the destroyers separated from *Scharnhorst* – was in the vicinity of 73°50' N 22°40' E, the map and 26 December 1943 entry in the KTB DES ZERSTÖRERS Z 29; and the 26 December 1943 entry in the KTB der 4 Zerstörerflottille.

32. Burnett's Battle of North Cape Report; Fraser's JW55B Report.

33. *Norfolk's* 'Gunnery Narrative', Appendix 3 to Burnett's Battle of North Cape Report.

34. Fraser's JW55B Report. The 6 October 1944 account by *Scharnhorst's* Matrosengefreiter Günther Sträter ('Sträter's Account'), **Marine Forum Archive**, states that during this first encounter, the battlecruiser's guns were fired although all the gun teams could aim at was the flash made by the enemy's guns.

35. Karl Doenitz, *Memoirs: Ten Years And Twenty Days* p. 380.
36. Burnett's Battle of North Cape Report.
37. Helmut Backhaus interview in Jacobsen's Scharnhorst Documentary; and extra information from the Backhaus interview in Jacobsen's Scharnhorst Book p. 174.
38. Burnett's Battle of North Cape Report.
39. John Winton, *The Death of the Scharnhorst* ('Winton's Scharnhorst Book') pp. 89-90, and 160 - the comment was by Admiral Sir Frederick Parham, as he became after the war; Burnett's Battle of North Cape Report specifies the time of receipt of Fraser's 10.58 a.m. 26 December 1943 signal mentioned in Fraser's JW55B Report.
40. Fraser's JW55B Report. The 26 December 1943 entry in the KTB des Marinegruppenkommandos Nord und Flottenkommandos states that the German aircraft crew saw the suspicious ships at AC 4776 on the German grid (approximately 71°51' N 20°50' E), which is going on 200 miles to the south-west of where the same KTB's same day's entry stated that the first of the day's engagements was fought according to Bey: AC 4133 on the German grid (approximately 74°21' N 22°50' E).
41. 26 and 27 December 1943 entries in KTB des Marinegruppenkommandos Nord und Flottenkommandos; and Cajus Bekker, *Hitler's Naval War* pp. 356–7.
42. 26 December 1943 entry in the KTB des Marinegruppenkommandos Nord und Flottenkommandos.
43. The detection of *Scharnhorst* prior to second engagement: Burnett's Battle of North Cape Report, which states the detection was approximately at 74°11' N 22°18' E.
44. Ibid.
45. *Sheffield*'s 'Gunnery Narrative' dated 29 December 1943, Appendix 3 to Burnett's Battle of North Cape Report.
46. Ibid.
47. 18 July 1948 letter from *Scharnhorst*'s Oberbootsmannsmaaten Willi Gödde to Kapitän zur See Helmuth Giessler, Marine Forum Archive.
48. Paymaster Commander Walker, Winton's Scharnhorst Book p. 99.
49. 'General Remarks On Gunnery', Appendix 2 to Burnett's Battle of North Cape Report.
50. Account by *Norfolk* gunner Leonard Wardle, brought to my attention by Ken Moth, the son of *Norfolk* stoker Bert Moth mentioned below.
51. Report by ordinary seaman Terry Hulbert, BBC WW2 People's War archive, available on the internet, brought to my attention by Bill Forster.
52. Chief Engine-room Artificer Davies, in Gordon Holman, *The King's Cruisers* p. 163.
53. Bert Moth account ('Moth's Account'), BBC recording made on 4 January 1944, **IWM Sound** 2449, brought to my attention by his son Ken Moth.
54. Number of *Norfolk* men killed: Fraser's JW55B Report.
55. Moth's Account.
56. Reverend Ken Mathews, 'Christmas In Battle', *Northern Light* journal December 1997, issue 51 p. 19, brought to my attention by Ken Moth.

57. 26 December 1943 entry in KTB des Marinegruppenkommandos Nord und Flottenkommandos, referring to the message Bey sent at 12.40 p.m.
58. Undated 'Narrative' on behalf of destroyer *Musketeer*, NA London ADM 199/913.
59. Burnett's Battle of North Cape Report.
60. Fraser's JW55B Report.
61. Sträter's Account.
62. Fraser's JW55B Report.
63. Admiral Sir Frederick Parham as he then was, IWM Sound 13407.
64. 26 December 1943 entry in KTB der 4 Zerstörerflottille.
65. Lord Fraser, as he then was, *The Life and Death of the Scharnhorst*, BBC documentary presented by Ludovic Kennedy ('Kennedy's Scharnhorst Documentary').
66. Lieutenant Vivian Cox, Kennedy's Scharnhorst Documentary.
67. *Duke of York*'s 'Gunnery Narrative' ('Duke of York's Gunnery Narrative') with Fraser's preliminary Report dated 31 December 1943, NA London ADM 199/913.
68. Captain Guy Russell's exchange with Fraser, Winton's Scharnhorst Book p. 111.
69. Fraser's JW55B Report; and Enclosure number 3 to the destroyer *Scorpion*'s Lieutenant Commander William Clouston's 30 December 1943 report, NA London ADM 199/913.
70. Undated report 'Gefecht im Nordmeer am 26.12.1943', **Militärarchiv Freiburg** RM7/1684 states approximate location of the third engagement was at 72°39' N 22°18' E.

71. 10 November 1984 letter from Captain A.G.F. Ditcham as he then was to John Winton, ROSK 5/77, Roskill's papers, **Churchill Archives Centre;** Ditcham's age: A.G.F. Ditcham, *A Home On The Rolling Main* p. 165.
72. Lieutenant Bryce Ramsden's account, 'Sinking The Scharnhorst: 26th December 1943', *Blackwood's Magazine* vol. 256, November 1944 No. 1549 p. 346.
73. Gunnery Officer Lieutenant Commander Crawford, Winton's Scharnhorst Book p. 115; and Duke of York's Gunnery Narrative.
74. 'Preliminary Report On The Interrogation Of Survivors From The German Battleship "Scharnhorst" . . .'; and 'Report On The Interrogation Of Survivors From The German Battle Cruiser "Scharnhorst" . . .', respectively in NA London ADM 1/16833 and ADM 199/913.
75. Winton's Scharnhorst Book p. 117.
76. Fraser's JW55B Report; and Duke of York's Gunnery Narrative.
77. Fraser's JW55B Report.
78. Winton's Scharnhorst Book p. 119.
79. Ibid.
80. Duke of York's Gunnery Narrative.
81. 1840 26 December 1943 message from Fraser to Burnett, NA London ADM 199/913.

Chapter 38

1. Account by Admiral Sir Henry Leach, as he then was, ('Leach's Account') when interviewed for the documentary film *The Scharnhorst Mystery* produced by Alf Jacobsen, first shown on BBC's Timewatch in 2001 ('Jacobsen's Scharnhorst Documentary'). Leach was the First

Sea Lord and Chief of the Naval Staff who in 1982 advised British prime minister Margaret Thatcher that with the Navy's help British forces could retake the Falklands. His father Captain John Leach was killed when the battleship *Prince of Wales* was sunk in December 1941 (mentioned in Chapter 17).

2. 6 October 1944 account by Matrosengefreiter Günther Sträter ('Sträter's Account'), **Marine Forum Archive**.

3. Leach's Account.

4. 28 January 1944 report by Admiral Sir Bruce Fraser ('Fraser's JW55B Report'); German prisoners' reports cited in 'Gunnery Narrative' with Fraser's preliminary Report dated 31 December 1943, all in **NA London** ADM 199/913; and 'Information Captured From Prisoners Of War Ex Scharnhorst, Enclosure No.2 in H.F.1415/17 at 1st January 1944', NA London ADM 1/16833.

5. 30 December 1943 report by *Scorpion's* Lieutenant Commander Bill Clouston ('Scorpion's Report'), NA London ADM 199/913; and Fraser's JW55B Report. *Scharnhorst's* stern thrust upwards: one of the *Scharnhorst* survivors' reports mentioned in this chapter's Note 29.

6. Enclosure No. 3 to ibid.; and 1 January 1944 report by HNoMS *Stord's* Lieutenant Commander S. Storheill ('Stord's Report'). Commander Campbell Clouston's death is described in my book *Dunkirk: Fight To The Last Man* pp. 443–4.

7. A.G.F. Ditcham, *A Home On The Rolling Main* ('Ditcham's Book') p. 175.

8. Ibid. pp. 178–82; Scorpion's Report.

9. John Winton, *The Death of the Scharnhorst* ('Winton's Scharnhorst Book') p. 127.

10. Quote supplied by *Scorpion's* Rex Chard, a sub-lieutenant at the time of the battle, on being interviewed by me in 2001, after his testimony was brought to my attention by Jacobsen's Scharnhorst Documentary.

11. Scorpion's Report; and Fraser's JW55B Report. The latter states the approximate position where *Scharnhorst* was sunk was 72°16' N 28°41' E. This is going on 100 miles north-east of North Cape.

12. Ditcham's Book, pp. 179–80; and slightly different wording in Winton's Scharnhorst Book p. 128.

13. Scorpion's Report.

14. Stord's Report.

15. The 9 January 1944 report by *Saumarez's* Lieutenant Commander Eric Walmsley, NA London ADM 199/913, states his ship's torpedoes were fired when *Saumarez* was just 1,200 yards from *Scharnhorst*; Fraser's JW55B Report says the distance was 1,800 yards.

16. Fraser's JW55B Report.

17. Appendix I to the 30 December 1943 report by *Savage's* Commander Michael Meyrick ('Savage's Report'), NA London ADM 199/913.

18. Fraser's JW55B Report.

19. Savage's Report.

20. Enclosure 8 to *Saumarez's* Lieutenant Commander Walmsley's 2 January 1944 letter, NA London ADM 267/110.

21. Kenneth Evans' account ('Evans' Account'), **IWM Sound** 13954.

22. Fraser's JW55B Report.

23. Lieutenant Bryce Ramsden's account 'Sinking The Scharnhorst: 26th

December 1943', *Blackwood's Magazine* vol. 256, November 1944, No. 1549 pp. 348–9.

24. Report and Torpedo Narrative by *Jamaica's* Captain John Hughes-Hallett, in Appendices A and C to his 1 January 1944 letter number 05/705 (together referred to as 'Jamaica's Report'), NA London ADM 199/913.

25. Fraser's JW 55B Report; and 1 January 1944 report by Vice Admiral Burnett entitled 'Destruction of German Battle Cruiser "Scharnhorst" On St. Stephen's Day 1943', including the 29 December 1943 torpedo report in the report's Appendix 4. NA London ADM 199/913.

26. 1 January 1944 report by Commanding Officer of *Matchless*, NA London ADM 199/913.

27. Fraser's JW 55B Report.

28. Ibid.

29. This quotation and subsequent descriptions of how sailors in *Scharnhorst* were affected by the shelling and torpedoing, as well as descriptions of Kapitän Hintze's actions, except for where specific reference is made to other sources, are based on the 'Preliminary Report On The Interrogation Of Survivors From The German Battleship "Scharnhorst" . . .'; and 'Report On The Interrogation Of Survivors From The German Battle Cruiser "Scharnhorst" . . .', respectively in NA London ADM 1/16833 and ADM 199/913. These reports are together or separately referred to in Chapter 38's main text and Notes as 'the *Scharnhorst* survivors' reports'.

30. Helmut Feifer's account and thoughts are from Jacobsen's Scharnhorst Documentary produced by Alf Jacobsen; and Alf Jacobsen, *Scharnhorst* ('Jacobsen's Scharnhorst Book') pp. 206–7.

31. Jacobsen's Scharnhorst Documentary.

32. *The Life and Death of the Scharnhorst*, BBC documentary presented by Ludovic Kennedy.

33. Jacobsen's Scharnhorst Documentary.

34. Jamaica's Report.

35. Scorpion's Report.

36. Jacobsen's Scharnhorst Documentary, supplemented by my 2001 interview with Dick Squires, whose testimony was brought to my attention by Jacobsen's Scharnhorst Documentary. Fraser's JW 55B Report specifies the 'approximate position' of sinking was 72°16' N 28°41' E. However Jacobsen's Scharnhorst Book states that he and his advisers in the year 2000 found the wreck of the battlecruiser at 72°31' N 28°15' E.

37. Jacobsen's Scharnhorst Documentary.

38. My 2001 interview with John Wass whose testimony was brought to my attention by the Jacobsen Scharnhorst Documentary.

39. Fraser's JW 55B Report.

40. Jacobsen's Scharnhorst Documentary.

41. Sträter's Account.

42. Jacobsen's Scharnhorst Documentary.

43. 8.18 p.m. Fraser to *Scorpion*, Enclosure No. 3 to Scorpion's Report.

44. 8.20 and 8.30 p.m. *Scorpion* to Fraser, in ibid.

45. 26 December 1943 Fraser to 'Scapa' message timed '2035', NA London ADM 199/913.

46. 26 December 1943 Admiralty to Fraser message timed '2136A', ibid.

47. Information from *Scorpion*'s signal log, recorded by telegraphist John Wass.

48. Number rescued: Fraser's JW55B Report.

49. Jacobsen's Scharnhorst Book p. 219.

50. 20 December 1943 report by JW55B's commodore Maitland Boucher, NA London ADM 199/77.

51. G. H. G. McMillan, 'Care of World War II convoy casualties in the Kola area of North Russia. Part 2 – The Royal Naval Auxiliary Hospital, Vaenga', *Journal of the Royal Naval Medical Service* 1996, 82, 61-79, a copy of which is in the **Arctic Convoys Museum**.

52. Evans' Account.

53. Karl Doenitz, *Memoirs: Ten Years And Twenty Days* p. 385.

54. 28 December 1943 report by Schniewind, Anlage 17 to 16–31 December 1943 KTB DES MARINEGRUPPEN-KOMMANDOS NORD UND FLOTTENKOMMANDOS.

Chapter 39

1. 9 February 1944 report by First Cruiser Squadron's Vice Admiral Arthur Palliser; and Admiralty's Anti-U-Boat Division's 15 May 1944 'Analysis Of Operations In The Vicinity Of Convoys J.W.56A, J.W.57B and R.A.56' ('Operation FW Anti-U-boat Report'), both in **NA London** ADM 199/77.

2. 2 and 25 January 1944 entries in KTB DES FÜHRER DER UNTERSEEBOOTE NORWEGEN.

3. 25 January 1944 entry in ibid.; and 26 January 1944 entry in the KTB U-360, which states U-360 torpedoed the destroyer at the location referred to as AC 4452 on the German grid (approximately 73°09' N 21°30' E). The map entitled 'Convoy J.W.56A And J.W.56B' in Plate 7 of the Operation FW Anti-U-boat Report ('Operation FW Map') shows the convoy's direction of travel when the torpedoing took place.

4. 30 January report by *Obdurate*'s Lieutenant Commander Claude Sclater ('Obdurate's JW56A Report'), NA London ADM 199/77.

5. Convoy's direction of travel: Operation FW Map.

6. The 25 January 1944 entry in KTB U-278, which states the merchant ship was hit at the location referred to on the German grid as AC 4572 (approximately 73°22' N 22°30' E); and 16 March 1944 report by US Cadet-Midshipman John S. Morgan; and 8 March 1944 'Summary of Statements by Survivors of the SS Penelope Barker' ('Penelope Barker Survivors' Report'), both of the latter reports in US ARMED GUARD REPORTS Box 521.

7. Unsigned and undated copy of report by Alex R. Boris, *Penelope Barker*'s 2nd Mate ('Penelope Barker's 2nd Mate's Report'), US MERCHANT VESSELS SINKING REPORTS Box 37, Entry P-2.

8. 17 February 1944 report by US Naval Port Officer, Belfast, US MEDICAL REPORTS Box 2 Entry 40.

9. Penelope Barker's Survivors' Report.

10. 'Extract from an NNI-142-X, US Naval Port Officer, Belfast, N. I. 12 February 1944', US Armed Guard

Reports Box 521; Penelope Barker's 2nd Mate's Report; and Obdurate's JW56A Report.

11. The 26 January 1944 entries in the KTB *U-360* and KTB *U-716* state that *U-360* and *U-716* each torpedoed a merchant ship from JW56A at around 12.15 a.m. on 26 January 1944. The entries specify that the torpedoings were respectively at the locations referred to on the German grid as AC 4529 and AC 4552 (approximately 73°45' N 24°48' E and 73°22' N 24°15' E respectively). The entries do not make it possible to work out which ship each U-boat torpedoed, or which of the two locations specified is more accurate. The Operation FW Anti-U-boat Report states the sinkings were approximately at 73°22' N 24°45' E.

12. John Crawley, 'The Fort Bellingham: A View From HMS Offa', *The Arctic Lookout* journal Winter 1996 – Number 26 p. 45.

13. Undated Report of Proceedings by *Offa*'s Lieutenant Commander Rowland Leonard, NA London ADM 199/77.

14. 14 March 1944 'Report of an Interview with the Master – Captain J. N. Maley' (the master of *Fort Bellingham*), NA London ADM 199/77.

15. Ibid.

16. 10 April 1944 'Summary of Statements by Survivors of SS Fort Bellingham', US CASUALTY REPORTS Box 195.

17. Undated report by JW56A's commodore Ivan Whitehorn, NA London ADM 199/77.

18. For example 28 January 1944 0431A Ultra specifying position of 7

U-boats in JW56B's path, NA London ADM 223/189.

19. 12 February 1944 report by the destroyer *Milne*'s Captain Ian Campbell (Captain (D) 3rd Destroyer Flotilla) ('3rd Destroyer Flotilla's Report'); and 22 January 1944 report by Commodore Maurice Mayall and Formation Diagram, both NA London ADM 199/77.

20. 8 February 1944 report by the destroyer *Hardy*'s Captain William Robson (Captain. (D) 26th Destroyer Flotilla), NA London ADM 199/957.

21. 3rd Destroyer Flotilla's Report; and 29 January 1944 entry in KTB des Führer des Unterseeboote Norwegen.

22. Ibid.; and 22 January 1944 report by Commodore Maurice Mayall and Formation Diagram, NA London ADM 199/77.

23. 3rd Destroyer Flotilla's Report.

24. *U-314* was the U-boat sunk, 11 February 1944 entry in the KTB des Führer der Unterseeboote Norwegen.

25. The Operation FW Anti-U-boat Report states *Hardy* was torpedoed at around 73°37' N 18°56' E.

26. 30 January 1944 entry in KTB *U-278*.

27. Sub-Lieutenant Lloyd Stainer account, **IWM Documents** 13762.

28. 2 February 1944 message from '*Hardy*' to the Admiralty; and undated Official Admiralty Communiqué, both in NA London ADM 358/3414.

29. 22 March 1944 report by Vice Admiral Irvine Glennie ('Vice Admiral's Operation FX Report'); Vice Admiral Glennie's 14 February 1944 Operation FX order with 'Plan of Convoy'; Vice Admiral Glennie's 18 February 1944 message to escorts

amending aforementioned order; and Admiral Fraser's 17 April 1944 letter relating to Operation FX ('Fraser's FX Report'), all in NA London ADM 199/327.

30. Fraser's FX Report; Part I Home Fleet Destroyer Command War Diary 16–29 February 1944, NA London ADM 199/1426; 11 March 1944 report by destroyer *Milne's* Captain Ian Campbell; undated report by frigate *Strule's* Commander Lewis Majendie; all NA London ADM 199/327; and BRITISH NAVAL AVIATION HISTORY p. 205.

31. 13 March 1944 report by *Chaser's* Captain H. McClintock ('Chaser's Report'), NA London ADM 199/327.

32. British Naval Aviation History pp. 205–6.

33. 23 to 26 February 1944 entries in KTB des Führer der Unterseeboote Norwegen.

34. The 25 and 26 February 1944 entries in KTB *U-990*, state that the torpedoing took place at what is referred to as AB 9423 on the German grid (approximately 70°45' N 12°50' E, two-thirds of the way along the invisible line stretching from Jan Mayen Island to Altenfjord – see Map 1). Convoy's course: transcript of testimony by the destroyer *Serapis'* Captain Peter Cazalet ('Cazalet's Testimony') in 'Minutes of Evidence Taken at Inquiry Held To Invest[igate] The Circumstances Attending The Loss Of *H.M.S. Mahratta*' ('Mahratta Inquiry Minutes'), NA London ADM 199/327

35. Cazalet's Testimony.

36. Lieutenant Commander Bekenn's testimony ('Bekenn's Testimony') in the 'Mahratta Inquiry Minutes'.

37. Post-war account by Captain Dennis Foster, as he then was ('Foster's Account'), in his unpublished memoir, referred to with the consent of his son Jonathan.

38. Bob Whinney, *The U-Boat Peril: An Anti-Submarine Commander's War* pp. 118–19. A record of what appear to be morse code signals sent from *Mahratta* after the torpedoing, which is in Cazalet's Testimony, contains similar content to what Whinney claims he heard over the radio telephone.

39. Foster's Account. Captain Peter Cazalet's evidence to the Inquiry appears to suggest that the messages 'heard' by Foster may have been read by someone in *Wanderer* after they had been sent by *Mahratta's* telegraphist using morse code.

40. James Row in *Arctic Convoys*, 27 July 2013 documentary on BBC Radio Wales cited in 'A Welshman's Introduction To War: Letters from the Arctic Convoys' by S. J. Davies, an article available at the University of the West of England Research Repository. It should be said there is nothing similar to this in the Mahratta Inquiry Minutes.

41. Jack Humble's words in this chapter's main text ('Humble's Account') is mostly from *The Arctic Convoys*, an episode of Witness written and presented by Alex Last, broadcast on the BBC's World Service on 10 May 2013. The account in the text also includes some words from the article headed 'Arctic convoy veteran recalls miraculous

rescue after his ship was torpedoed as he celebrates 90th birthday' written by Gavin Engelbrecht, which was published in the *Northern Echo* newspaper on 19 January 2016.

42. Humble's Account; and testimony of *Mahratta*'s Petty Officer Robert Hall, Mahratta Inquiry Minutes.

43. Bekenn's Testimony.

44. Vice Admiral's Operation FX Report; and Official Admiralty Communiqué, NA London ADM 199/957.

45. Article by Noel Simon, *The Arctic Lookout* journal Winter 1998, no. 33 p. 34.

46. 24 and 25 February 1944 entries in KTB des Führer der Unterseeboote Norwegen; and Vice Admiral's Operation FX Report.

47. 27 February 1944 entry in KTB des Führer der Unterseeboote Norwegen.

48. 2 March 1944 entry in ibid. The sunk U-boats were *U-601* and *U-713*.

49. British Naval Aviation History pp. 206-7. The sunk U-boats were *U-366*, *U-472* and *U-973*, 4, 7 and 11 March 1944 entries in the KTB des Führer der Unterseeboote Norwegen. *Empire Tourist* was sunk on 4 March 1944 by *U-703* at what is described in the German grid as AC 4438 (approximately 73°15' N 22°11' E), 4 March 1944 entries in KTB des Führer der Unterseeboote Norwegen; and in <u>KTB *U-703*</u>.

50. WOODMAN'S BOOK p. 385.

51. Fraser's FX Report.

52. British Naval Aviation History p. 206; and Chaser's Report.

53. Ibid.

54. Number of merchant ships in JW58: Formation with 5 April 1944 report by Commodore John Dunn ('<u>JW58</u> Commodore's Report'), NA London ADM 199/327. Number of JW58 escorts: March 1944 War Diary of the Commander-in-Chief Home Fleet, NA London ADM 199/1427.

55. 5 April 1944 report by Captain G. Willoughby, Commanding Officer of *Activity*: and Enclosure to Appendix D of 5 April 1944 report by Captain J. H. Huntley, Commanding Officer of *Tracker* ('Tracker's JW58 Report'), both in NA London ADM 199/327. 819 Squadron operated from *Activity*, and 846 Squadron from *Tracker*.

56. Admiral Fraser's 1 June 1944 letter to the Admiralty concerning Operation FY ('Fraser's FY Letter'), NA London ADM 199/327.

57. 2 April 1944 message, British Naval Aviation History p. 121.

58. Fraser's FY Letter; and Tracker's JW58 Report. The U-boat sunk was *U-288*, David Hobbs, *The Fleet Air Arm And The War In Europe 1939-1945*.

59. Tracker's JW58 Report.

60. The 25 June 1944 report by Clarence Howard-Johnston, Director of Anti-U-Boat Division, NA London ADM 199/327, pointed out that 3 U-boats were sunk during 27 hunts in the course of JW58 and RA58, a rate of 11 per cent, half what might have been expected in the Atlantic.

61. Remarks with 11 April 1944 letter from 2nd Escort Group's Captain F. Walker, NA London ADM 199/327.

62. JW58 Commodore's Report.

63. April 1944 entry in the war diary of the Commander-in-Chief Home Fleet, NA London ADM 199/1427; and Tactical, Torpedo and Staff Duties Division, Historical Section, Naval Staff, 'Battle Summary No. 27

Naval Aircraft Attack on the Tirpitz ("Operation Tungsten") 3rd April 1944' pp. 4 and 8, NA London ADM 234/345.

64. 19 April 1944 entry Part II Home Fleet Destroyer Command War Diary, NA London ADM 199/1426; undated report by Commodore John Dunn ('RA59 Commodore's Report'); and Diagram with 10 July 1944 'Analysis of Operations in the vicinity of Convoy R.A. 59' by Anti-U-Boat Division ('RA59 Anti-U-Boat Report'), latter two documents in NA London ADM 199/351.

65. 5 May 1944 Report of Proceedings by the carrier *Fencer*'s Captain W. Bentinck ('Fencer's Report').

66. RA59 Anti-U-Boat Report. The sunk U-boats were *U-277*, *U-674* and *U-959*, British Naval Aviation History p. 224.

67. 5 May 1944 report by *Activity*'s Captain G. Willoughby, NA London ADM 199/351; and Fencer's Report.

68. 28-30 April 1944 entries in KTB des Führer der Unterseeboote Norwegen.

69. The 30 April 1944 entry in KTB *U-307* states this occurred in the area referred to on the German grid as AB 6349 (approximately 73°51' N 17°50' E).

70. 30 April 1944 entry in KTB *U-307*.

71. 5 May 1942 report of proceedings by Commanding Officer HMS *Walker*, NA London ADM 199/351; and RA59 Commodore's Report.

72. 4 May 1944 report by the Commanding Officer of HMS *Whitehall*, NA London ADM 199/351.

73. 24 May 1944 Sworn statement by Daniel A. Sperbeck Master SS *William S. Thayer*, US MERCHANT VESSELS SINKING REPORTS Box 53 Entry P-2.

74. Chapter: Na pravah passazhirov (On the rights of passengers) by G. Polyakov on pp. 222–3 of *Bratsvo severnikh konvoev 1941–1945* (*Brotherhood of the northern convoys 1941–1945*), compiled by R.V. Gorchakov.

75. Appendix II to 17 May 1944 report by Rear Admiral Commanding First Cruiser Squadron, NA London ADM 199/351.

76. 3 June 1944 'Summary of Statements by Survivors of the SS William S. Thayer', US MERCHANT SHIP LOSSES REPORTS.

77. Fencer's Report. Its 2 May 1944 entry confirms there was 'no night'.

78. 5 June 1944 'Operation FZ: Report of Proceedings' by Admiral Fraser, NA London ADM 199/351.

Chapter 40

1. 'Erinnerungen an die Unternehmungen mit U 367 von Februar 1944 bis Oktober 1944' by Kapitänleutnant Haimar Wedemeyer ('Wedemeyer's Account'), *U-365* file in U-**Boot Museum**.

2. 18 September 1944 Report by head of Northern Governmental Sea Shipping Company Novicov to People's Commissar of the USSR's Sea Fleet Shirshov, **GAAO** Section 367, Inventory 11, Book 76, pp. 1–4.

3. Chapter: Tragediya v Karskom more (Tragedy in the Karsky Sea) by Y.D. Kapralov on p. 117 of *V konvoyakh i*

odinochnikh plavaniyakh (*In convoys and in solo voyages*) compiled by V.V. Kolt ('Kolt's Book').

4. Wedemeyer's Account. The 12 August 1944 entry in <u>KTB U-365</u> states the torpedoing took place at around AT 6434 (around 73°21' N 67°10' E).

5. 4 September 1944 report by Alexandrovich Karelski ('Karelski's Account'), GAAO Section 367, Inventory 11, Book 76, p. 47.

6. Ibid.

7. T5 torpedo fired at *T-118*: 12 August 1944 entry KTB *U-365*.

8. Kolt's Book pp. 119 and 121.

9. Wedemeyer's Account.

10. Ibid. Wedermeyer's short report in Appendix II/4 to the 16 to 31 August 1944 <u>KTB DES FÜHRER DER UNTERSEEBOOTE NORWEGEN</u> states the torpedo that hit *T-114* was fired at 11.45 p.m. 12 August 1944.

11. 14 October 1944 report by Fedor Rodionov GAAO Section 367, Inventory 11, Book 76, p. 38.

12. Kolt's Book p. 121.

13. Ibid. p. 125.

14. Karelski's Account; and report by Clavdia Nekrasova, GAAO Section 367, Inventory 11, Book 76, pp. 82–4.

15. 13 August 1944 entry in KTB *U-365*.

16. Wedemeyer's Account.

17. Ivan Vondrukhov's report, GAAO Section 367, Inventory 11, Book 76; chapter: Svidetel' gibeli parohoda 'Marina Raskova' (Witness of the death of the vessel 'Marina Raskova') by T.A. Sanakina on p. 180 of *Zashitniki Otechestva*, (*Defenders of the Motherland*) ('Motherland Book').

18. Ibid.

19. Motherland Book p. 175.

20. Kolt's Book. p. 126.

21. Ibid. p. 130.

22. Ibid. p. 131.

23. Ibid. pp. 131–2.

24. Motherland Book pp. 176–8.

25. Number of escorts: Part I of Home Fleet Destroyer Command War Diary 16–31 August 1944, **NA London** ADM 199/1426; and 14 September 1944 report by 10th Cruiser Squadron's Vice Admiral Dalrymple-Hamilton, NA London ADM 199/351.

26. U-boats' position: 1–21 August 1944 entries in <u>KTB DES FÜHRER DER UNTERSEEBOOTE NORWEGEN</u>; and 5 September 1944 report by *Vindex*'s Captain Horace Bayliss ('Vindex's Report'), NA London ADM 199/351.

27. 21 August 1944 entry in KTB des Führer der Unterseeboote, which states the torpedoing took place at the location in the German grid referred to as AB 5450 (approximately 73°03' N 03°30' E).

28. 9 September 1944 findings of 'the Board of Enquiry' concerning loss of *Kite*, NA London ADM 1/16879.

29. Petty Officer John Payne's testimony in the 'Minutes of Board of Enquiry' concerning *Kite*, NA London ADM/1 16879.

30. 11 September 1944 report by the destroyer *Keppel*'s Commander James Tyson, NA London ADM 1/16879.

31. Vindex's Report.

32. The 3 November 1944 report by Admiral Sir Henry Moore, Commander-in-Chief Home Fleet ('Moore's Goodwood Report'), stated the fly off point was 71°35' N 21°55' E. The 1 October 1944 report by the First Cruiser Squadron's Rear Admiral Rhoderick McGrigor describes the Operation Goodwood

attacks ('McGrigor's Goodwood Report'), both NA London ADM 199/942. Distance from Altenfjord: 23 August 1944 entry in KTB des Führer der Unterseeboote Norwegen.

33. 23 August 1944 entry in KTB des Führer der Unterseeboote Norwegen; and 1 September 1944 report by *Kent*'s Captain Geoffrey Hawkins, NA London ADM 199/942.

34. 23 August 1944 entry in KTB des Führer der Unterseeboote Norwegen, which states that the torpedoing of the carrier was at the location referred to on the German grid as AB 9333 (approximately 71°39' N 19°50' E).

35. Betty Warrilow, *Nabob: The First Canadian Manned Aircraft Carrier* ('The Nabob Book') p. 97; and 2 September 1944 report of proceedings by *Nabob*'s Captain Horatio Lay ('Nabob's 2nd Report'), NA London ADM 199/942.

36. Minutes of proceedings of the 'Enquiry Into Damage to H.M.S. Nabob By Enemy Action', NA London ADM 199/957.

37. The Nabob Book pp. 4 and 92.

38. 2 September 1944 report of proceedings by *Nabob*'s Captain Horatio Lay ('Nabob's 2nd Report'), NA London ADM 199/942.

39. Donald Macintyre, *U-Boat Killer* ('Macintyre's Book') p. 168.

40. Appendix 1 to the 31 August 1944 report by D. Macintyre, Senior Officer, 5th Escort Group with Minutes of 'Board of Enquiry – Loss Of H.M.S. Bickerton', NA London ADM 1/18925.

41. Nabob's 2nd Report.

42. Macintyre's Book p. 169; and Moore's Goodwood Report.

43. Macintyre's Book p. 169; and The Nabob Book p. 5.

44. BRITISH INTELLIGENCE OFFICIAL HISTORY vol. 3 (2) p. 277. According to the TIRPITZ OFFICIAL HISTORY vol. 1 one of the 1,600 lb bombs that hit *Tirpitz* on 24 August 1944 hit the port side of the upper deck abreast the forward conning tower, then penetrated through the armour deck to the lower platform. A German report said its failure to explode was 'an extraordinary stroke of luck' since the result of an explosion would have been 'immeasurable'.

45. Moore's Goodwood Report; and McGrigor's Goodwood Report.

46. 27 August 1944 report by Captain Horatio Lay, NA London ADM 199/957.

47. Vindex's Report.

48. Account by Lieutenant Commander John Mosse ('Mosse's Account') brought to my attention by his son Peter.

49. Ibid.

50. 'Hunt And Possible Destruction Of A U-boat By H.M.S. Mermaid In Position 72°49' N 30°41' E On The 24 August 1944' by *Mermaid*'s Lieutenant Commander John Mosse, supplied by his son Peter but also in NA London ADM 199/351.

51. 30 August 1944 entry in KTB des Führer der Unterseeboote Norwegen.

52. JW 59 arrival date: War Diary of the Commander-in-Chief Home Fleet for the month of August 1944, NA London ADM 199/1427.

53. The location is specified in the report by *Mermaid*'s Lieutenant Commander Mosse entitled 'Hunt

and Destruction of a U-boat by
H.M. Ships "Keppel", "Whitehall",
"Peacock", and "Mermaid" In
Position 69°35' N 4°45' E on
2ⁿᵈ September 1944, Whilst With
Convoy R.A.59A.', supplied by
Mosse's son Peter but also in NA
London ADM 199/351.

54. Vindex's Report.

55. Mosse's Account.

56. 2 September 1944 report by
Peacock's Lieutenant Commander
Dick Stannard, NA London ADM
199/351.

57. Ibid.; and attached 3 September 1944
report by *Peacock*'s surgeon
lieutenant.

58. 3 September 1944 entry in KTB des
Führer der Unterseeboote
Norwegen.

59. Mosse's Account.

60. Vindex's Report.

61. 23 August 1944 entry in KTB des
Führer der Unterseeboote
Norwegen.

Chapter 41

1. Churchill's 27 January 1942 note to
the First Lord of the Admiralty
refers to *Tirpitz* as 'the beast', **NA
London** PREM 3/191/1.

2. BRITISH INTELLIGENCE
OFFICIAL HISTORY vol. 3
(2) p. 277; and Tony Insall, *Secret
Alliances* pp 323–4 and 327–8 states
that: for example on 1 October 1944,
a Norwegian agent informed the SIS
that the Operation Paravane
bombing had made a 17 metre hole
in *Tirpitz*'s hull partly above and
partly below the water line
stretching from the bow towards the
stern; the agent reported the hole
was 'so large that motor boats could

go in'. After this bombing, the SIS
congratulated the Norwegians for
enabling the attack to go ahead
when the weather was good,
reflecting that the Norwegian agent
Torstein Raaby had sent the SIS,
amongst other helpful intelligence, a
weather report every two hours
during the lead up to the operation,
a very courageous act considering
the Germans had access to direction
finding equipment. The TIRPITZ
OFFICIAL REPORT vol.1
confirmed that a Tallboy bomb hit
the starboard deck on the extreme
starboard side some 50 feet abaft the
bow, passed through the flare of the
forecastle into the water and
detonated below keel level close to
the ship. The damage resulted in the
front 120 feet of the ship being
flooded below the waterline.

3. James (Willie) Tait account, **IWM
Sound** 2519. The 29 October 1944
bombing thanks to a near miss near
the battleship's port quarter
impacted the *Tirpitz*'s port shaft and
rudder, and caused around 100 feet
of the after end of the ship to be
flooded, TIRPITZ OFFICIAL
HISTORY vol. 1.

4. Frank Tilley interview, International
Bomber Command Centre Digital
Archive, University of Lincoln.

5. The film that was taken seems to
corroborate the description of the
damage to *Tirpitz* described in
the Tirpitz Official History
(see Note 6 below).

6. Interview with Hugh Rogers,
International Bomber Command
Centre Digital Archive, University
of Lincoln. The Tirpitz Official
History vols.1 and 2 state that *Tirpitz*

appears to have been hit twice amidships on her port side aft of her funnel, and the same side was damaged by a near miss. The same source appears to suggest it was likely that the eruption emanating from *Tirpitz*'s Caesar gun turret was not directly caused by a hit but was either the result of an internal explosion not easily attributable to a particular bomb or was caused by a near miss.

7. *Hunting Tirpitz: Royal Naval Operations Against Bismarck's Sister Ship* pp. 284–5, commissioned by Britannia Royal Naval College's Britannia Museum.

8. The English version of Albert Zuba's account, possibly a translation by a third party, brought to my attention by Dr Robert Owen, 617 Squadron's Official Historian, in whose archive it is stored. Extracts from Zuba's account also appear in several books including Patrick Bishop, *Target Tirpitz*.

9. 4 December 1944 'Bericht über Aussergefechtsetzung des Schlachtschiffes "Tirpitz" am 12.11.44 (Liegeplatz bei Tromsö Netzkasten Haakoy)' by Kapitänleutnant Alfred Fassbender, **Militärarchiv Freiburg** RM 7/1056.

10. 17 November 1944 telegram from 'Skdt Tromsoe', Militärarchiv Freiburg RM 7/1056.

11. 12 November 1944 message from the British Embassy's Peter Scarlett relaying Sir Arthur Harris' notification to Churchill, NA London PREM 3/191/1.

12. 13 November 1944 Stalin to Churchill, ibid.

13. 13 November 1944 Roosevelt to Churchill, and 15 November 1944 Churchill to Roosevelt, ibid.

14. 3 September 1944 Memorandum by Anthony Eden, NA London CAB 66/54.

15. 12 October 1944 telegram from Eden to the Foreign Office, NA London CAB 121/297.

16. William Birch account, IWM Sound 12723.

17. 20 December 1944 report by RA62's Commodore Ernst Ullring, and RA62 formation document, NA London ADM 199/602. German U-boats had very limited successes against Arctic convoys between Operation Paravane and RA62, the subject of this chapter: On 29 September 1944 during RA60 US Liberty ship SS *Edward H. Crockett* and SS *Samsuva* were abandoned after being torpedoed. The numbers killed were 1 and 3 respectively, 2 November 1944 'Summary of Statements by Survivors of the SS Edward H. Crockett'; and undated report by *Rathlin*'s G.L. Campbell, NA London ADM 217/113. On 1 November 1944, during lead up to RA61, frigate *Mounsey* was torpedoed but made it back to Kola Inslet under own steam. 10 of her crew were killed, Casualty list and 2 November 1944 SBNO North Russia message, NA London ADM 358/4408.

18. War diary of the Commander-in-Chief Home Fleet December 1944, NA London ADM 199/1427.

19. 19 December 1944 report by First Cruiser Squadron's Rear Admiral Rhoderick McGrigor ('1st Cruiser Squadron's RA62 Report'), NA London ADM 199/602.

20. ROHWER'S HUMMELCHEN'S AND WEIS'S CHRONOLOGY p. 375.
21. 1st Cruiser Squadron's RA62 Report.
22. Lieutenant Leslie testimony ('Leslie's Cassandra Testimony') in Minutes of 21 December 1944 board of inquiry concerning damage sustained by HMS *Cassandra* ('Cassandra Inquiry Minutes'), NA London ADM 199/1013. The 11 December 1944 entry in KTB DER SKL TEIL A states the torpedoing took place at the location marked on the German grid as AC 5763 (approximately 72°15' N 31°50' E).
23. 11 December 1944 entry in KTB der Skl Teil A.
24. Lieutenant John Brook testimony, Cassandra Inquiry Minutes.
25. Morris Birkett account in Peter Erwood, ed., *A Long Night For The Canteen Boat* ('Cassandra Book') p. 9.
26. Able Seaman Robert Fisher, ibid. p. 10.
27. R. Butler, ibid. p. 10.
28. Lieutenant George Leslie's report attached to his 16 December 1944 letter, NA London ADM 199/1013.
29. Norman Kemp, Cassandra Book p. 11.
30. Dudley Mills, ibid. p. 13.
31. Report with 15 December 1944 letter from 20th Escort Group's Commander George Thring, NA London ADM 199/1013.
32. Leslie's Cassandra Testimony.
33. 12 December 1944 entry in KTB der Skl Teil A.
34. 1st Cruiser Squadron's RA62 Report; and 12 December 1944 entry in KTB der Skl Teil A.
35. Bill Henley account, IWM Sound 19105, with editing thanks to Appendix 7 to 21 December 1944

report by *Campania*'s Captain Kenneth Short, NA London ADM 217/532, and the diagram illustrating the attack in the report's Appendix VII.
36. 1st Cruiser Squadron's RA62 Report.

Chapter 42

1. Alexander Steenbeck, *Die Spur des Löwen* ('KG26's History') p. 269; JW64's ship list in Convoy Form A1 attached to the 13 February 1945 report by JW64's Commodore Ernst Ullring ('JW64's Commodore's Report'); 2 March 1945 report by Captain Villiers Surtees, Commanding Officer of *Nairana* ('Nairana's Hotbed Report') and 1 March 1945 report by Captain Kenneth Short, Commanding Officer of *Campania* ('Campania's Hotbed Report'), latter three sources all in **NA London** ADM 199/759.
2. Plan 1, headed 'Passage of J.W. 64 . . .', ('The JW64 Plan') referred to in Rear Admiral Rhoderick McGrigor's 28 February 1945 report ('1st Cruiser Squadron's Hotbed Report'), NA London ADM 199/759 suggests the attack took place at around 66°40' N 01°30' E.
3. Escorts: War Diary of Commander-in-Chief Home Fleet for February 1945, NA London ADM 199/1440; and the 28 February 1945 report by the destroyer *Onslow*'s Captain Hugh Browning, Captain (D) 17th Destroyer Flotilla ('17th Destroyer Flotilla's Hotbed Report'), NA London ADM 199/759. 1st Cruiser Squadron's Hotbed Report; Campania's Hotbed Report; Nairana's Hotbed Report; JW64's Commodore's Report; and

BRITISH NAVAL AVIATION HISTORY p. 300.

4. KG26's History p. 269.

5. 1st Cruiser Squadron's Hotbed Report; and KG26's History pp. 268–9.

6. Leutnant Hans-Werner Grosse quoted in KG26's History p. 268.

7. The JW64 Plan suggests this second air raid took place around 73°00' N 21°00' E.

8. Campania's Hotbed Report; and KG26's History pp. 270–1.

9. Leutnant Hans-Werner Grosse in KG26's History p. 270.

10. Ibid.; and 1st Cruiser Squadron's Hotbed Report.

11. Campania's Hotbed Report.

12. Ibid.; and 17 February 1945 report on *Denbigh Castle* casualties, NA London ADM 358/3080.

13. John Brackenbury in the film *Through Hell and High Water* directed by Elly M. Taylor ('Elly Taylor's Film').

14. Rodney Bowden in ibid.

15. 2 March 1943 report by *Zambesi's* Captain John Allison ('The Opendoor Report') brought to my attention by the **NHB**.

16. 19 March 1945 *Daily Record* article headed 'Hunted From Cave To Cave For 3 Months', brought to my attention by Matthew Drennan, an amateur historian who has undertaken to write up the story of how Norwegian refugees were during the war brought over from Norway to Neilston, East Renfrewshire, Scotland, and housed there in a camp until it was safe for them to return home.

17. 1 April 1945 letter from Colin Christensen brought to my attention by Matthew Drennan, and quoted with the consent of the Christensen 'Whanau' (Maori word for family) including his son.

18. The Opendoor Report.

19. 1st Cruiser Squadron's Hotbed Report; and The Opendoor Report.

20. ROHWER'S HUMMELCHEN'S AND WEIS'S CHRONOLOGY pp. 393–4.

21. Report (date obscured) headed 'Narrative of the sinking of U-boat 425 by H.M. Ships "Lark" and "Alnwick Castle" on 17th February 1945' by *Lark* Anti-Submarine officer Lieutenant Anthony Parsons; and 3 March 1945 note by *Cygnet's* Commander Anthony Thorold correcting Parsons' aforementioned report, both NA London ADM 199/759.

22. Herbert Lochner's 'In A Sinking Submarine' in the Winter 1993 edition of the Journal of the Royal Naval Amateur Radio Society Newsletter p.23.

23. Ibid.

24. The 19 February 1945 report by *Alnwick Castle's* Lieutenant Commander Herbert Stonehouse ('Alnwick Castle's Report'), NA London ADM 199/759.

25. Notes written by John Durning, supplied by his daughters Frances and Susan.

26. Alnwick Castle's Report. The location of sinking in Map 21 is taken from the Plan 3 ('The RA64 Departure Plan') headed 'Approaches To Kola Inlet Showing RA64 Departing 17th February 1945' referred to in 1st Cruiser Squadron's Hotbed Report.

27. Ships list with Commodore Ernst Ullring's undated 'Report from Commodore of Convoy from

Murmansk at 1000 BST. on 17th.
February' ('RA64 Commodore's
Report'), NA London ADM 199/759.

28. The location of the torpedoing is taken
from The RA64 Departure Plan.

29. 17 February 1945 entry in KTB
U-968; and 22 March 1945 document
referred to as 'Minutes of the
Proceedings at a Board of Enquiry . . .
to investigate the circumstances
attending the damage to H.M.S.
"Lark" on 17th February 1945'
concerning the damage to HMS
Lark, NA London ADM 1/18932.

30. 20 February 1942 report by *Lark*'s
Commander Hedworth Lambton,
NA London ADM 1/18932.

31. 1st Cruiser Squadron's Hotbed
Report; and undated report by Jack
A. Teston, *Thomas Scott*'s Master,
US MERCHANT VESSELS
SINKING REPORTS. The
location of the torpedoing is taken
from The RA64 Departure Plan.

32. Elly Taylor's Film.

33. Rohwer's and Hummelchen's
Chronology p. 334.

34. 1 March 1945 report by William
Henry, who sailed in *Silas Weir
Mitchell*, brought to my attention by
Ian Millar.

35. The location of the torpedoing
is taken from The RA64
Departure Plan.

36. 26 February 1945 report by *Zest*'s
Lieutenant Commander Roger
Hicks, NA London ADM 267/118.

37. Undated official Admiralty
communiqué, NA London ADM
358/3080.

38. The messman was Joseph Psybysz,
Donald R. Foxvog and Robert
I. Alotta, *The Last Voyage of the SS
Henry Bacon* ('Henry Bacon's

Book') p. 113. Number of *U-425*
fatalities: Herbert Lochner account in
the booklet 'Der Landser Grossband',
a copy of which is in the *U-425*
section of the **U-boot Museum**.

39. Location of convoy during 20
February 1945 air raid: taken from
Plan 2 headed 'Passage Of R.A 64 . . .'
('The RA64 Plan') referred to in the 1
Cruiser Squadron's Hotbed Report.

40. 1st Cruiser Squadron's Hotbed Report.

41. Ibid.; and KG26's History p. 272.

42. Josef Mang, KG26's History p. 272.

43. The Section 1 General Narrative
attached to the 17th Destroyer
Flotilla's Hotbed Report; and the list
headed 'Weather Experienced'
attached to the February 1945 report
by the Commanding Officer of the
destroyer *Whitehall*, both in NA
London ADM 199/759.

44. Location where *Campania*
temporarily left the convoy, based
on The RA64 Plan. Campania's
Hotbed Report.

45. Stephen Mearns' account, **IWM
Sound** 11088.

46. Henry Bacon's Book pp. 118–21.

47. Ibid. p. 127.

48. Ibid. pp. 127–8.

49. Ibid. p. 126.

50. The convoy's changes of course in
Map 21 are based on The RA64 Plan.
They are in line with the
confirmation in Campania's Hotbed
Report that RA64 turned onto a 165°
course at 9.12 p.m. 22 February, the
RA64 Commodore's order to the
convoy's merchant ships to turn at 4
a.m. to 225° after he had received
Bellona's Captain Gerald Tuck's 3
a.m. 23 February 1945 agreement;
and Tuck's 10.40 a.m. 23 February
1945 order telling the Commodore to

turn the convoy at 11 a.m. to 245°, both the latter two orders in Tuck's 28 February 1945 report's Appendix C, NA London ADM 199/759.

51. Henry Bacon's Book p. 125 states that the ship's 3rd Mate recalled the receipt of an order to change course, which according to his recollection was to 240°, but there is no record of anyone in the ship knowing about a second change of course.

52. Location based on The RA64 Plan. The 1st Cruiser Squadron's Hotbed Report states that survivors claimed they had been attacked by 19 aircraft.

53. KG26's History p. 277.

54. Henry Bacon's Book p. 129.

55. Ibid. p. 132.

56. Ibid. p. 130.

57. Time of first distress signal: 5 April 1945 'Summary of Statements by Survivors of the SS Henry Bacon . . .' ('The Henry Bacon Survivors' Report'), Henry Bacon file in the **Arctic Convoy Museum**; and 1st Cruiser Squadron's Hotbed Report.

58. 1st Cruiser Squadron's Hotbed Report.

59. Henry Bacon's Book p. 135; The Henry Bacon Survivors' Report; and 16 May 1945 war action casualty report based on information supplied by Joseph Scott, Henry Bacon's 3rd Mate ('Henry Bacon's War Action Casualty Report'), US CASUALTY REPORTS Entry A1 191 Box 5.

60. Henry Bacon's Book p. 135.

61. Ibid.

62. Ibid. pp. 135–6.

63. Ibid. p. 141; and Henry Bacon's War Action Casualty Report.

64. Henry Bacon's Book p. 142.

65. Time of second distress signal: The Henry Bacon Survivors' Report. Carini's action after torpedo hit:

E. Spurgeon Campbell, Waves Astern ('Campbell's Book') p. 82.

66. Henry Bacon's Book pp. 148–9; Campbell's Book pp. 82–3. Lifeboats used: 28 May 1945 report by Joseph Scott, Henry Bacon's 3rd Mate, US Casualty Reports Box 3.

67. 28 May 1945 report by Joseph Scott, Henry Bacon's 3rd Mate; and May 1945 Examining Officer report, both in US Casualty Reports Box 3.

68. Henry Bacon's Book p. 155; and Campbell's Book p. 87.

69. Account by Opportune's Commander Robert Ryder ('Ryder's Account'), brought to my attention by his son Lisle and grandson Philip. Bearing: 1st Cruiser Squadron's Hotbed Report.

70. Henry Bacon's Book pp. 171 and 181; and Nairana's Hotbed Report.

71. Henry Bacon seems to have sunk at around 67°40' N 05°19' E, the location specified in the RA64 Commodore's Report.

72. Henry Bacon's Book p. 163.

73. Ibid. pp. 159–60 report based on testimony of baker George Bartin.

74. Nils Mortensen, Refugees in Their Own Country p. 70.

75. Campbell's Book pp. 83–4.

76. Appendix 2 to 5 March 1945 report by Zambesi's Captain J. Allison, Captain (D) 2nd Destroyer Flotilla ('2nd Destroyer Flotilla's Henry Bacon Appendix'), NA London ADM 199/759; and Henry Bacon's Book p. 184.

77. Campbell's Book p. 85.

78. Justin F. Gleichauf, Unsung Sailors p. 184.

79. Undated copy of an article from The Family magazine, Henry Bacon file in the Arctic Convoy Museum.

80. 2nd Destroyer Flotilla's Henry Bacon Appendix.
81. John Booth's account brought to my attention by *Zambesi*'s Roy Elwood.
82. Henry Bacon's War Action Casualty Report; and 2nd Destroyer Flotilla's Henry Bacon Appendix. Henry Bacon's Book pp. 247–9 states that of the 88 on board 60 survived and 28 died.
83. 2nd Destroyer Flotilla's Henry Bacon Appendix.
84. RA64 Commodore's Report.
85. Ryder's Account.

Chapter 43

1. Ships in convoy: JW65 Formation diagram read in conjunction with diagram in JW65's Commodore William Meek's 20 March 1945 report, both **NA London** ADM 199/759.
2. Escorts: March 1945 section of War Diary for the Commander-in-Chief Home Fleet, NA London ADM 199/1440; and 30 March 1945 report by the destroyer *Myng*'s Captain P. Cazalet, Captain (D) 23rd Destroyer Flotilla ('23rd Destroyer Flotilla Operation Scottish Report'), NA London ADM 199/759; report attached to 31 March 1945 letter from the carrier *Trumpeter*'s Captain Kenneth Colquhoun, NA London ADM 199/759.
3. 31 March 1945 report by the 31 March 1945 report by the 10th Cruiser Squadron's Vice Admiral Dalrymple-Hamilton ('10th Cruiser Squadron's Operation Scottish Report').
4. Ibid.
5. ROHWER'S HUMMELCHEN'S AND WEIS'S CHRONOLOGY p. 399.

6. 8 May 1945 'Summary of Statements by the Survivors of the SS Horace Bushnell' ('Horace Bushnell Survivors' Report'), US ARMED GUARD REPORTS Box 310 states torpedoing was at 69°23' N 35°17' E.
7. U-boat: Rohwer's Hummelchen's and Weis's Chronology p. 399; and Horace Bushnell Survivors' Report.
8. Horace Bushnell Survivors' Report; and 23rd Destroyer Flotilla Operation Scottish Report.
9. 23 Destroyer Flotilla Report.
10. 10th Cruiser Squadron's Operation Scottish Report; and 15 April 1945 report by corvette *Allington Castle*'s Lieutenant Commander Phillips Read ('Allington Castle's Report'), NA London ADM 199/759.
11. *Allington Castle*'s Bill Bridges, speaking to me.
12. Undated report by *Lapwing*'s Lieutenant Ian Leitch ('Leitch's Report'), brought to my attention by John Kirke, nephew of Eddie Sheridan, one of those who died when *Lapwing* sank.
13. Allington Castle's Report.
14. Leitch's Report.
15. Ian Leitch account in Ian Hawkins, ed., *Destroyer*, p. 436; the number of survivors, taking into account the eight who died after being rescued, is confirmed in Allington Castle's Report.
16. 1 May 1945 report by *Thomas Donaldson* master Robert Headden ('Thomas Donaldson Master's Report'), US MERCHANT VESSELS SINKING REPORTS Box 47 Entry P-2; still rescuing *Lapwing*'s survivors: Allington Castle's Report; 2 columns: diagram with Commodore Meek's 20 March 1945

report on *Thomas Donaldson* sinking; and 21 March 1945 report by corvette *Oxlip*'s Lieutenant Commander John Craig, both latter documents NA London ADM 199/759.

17. 10th Cruiser Squadron's Operation Scottish Report.

18. Thomas Donaldson Master's Report.

19. 10th Cruiser Squadron's Operation Scottish Report. .

20. 1 April 1945 report by RA65's Commodore W. Meek; and RA65 ship list, both in NA London ADM 199/759; and WOODMAN'S BOOK p. 435.

21. 26 protected ships: 15 May 1945 report by the destroyer *Zephyr*'s Captain John Allison, Captain (D) 2nd Destroyer Flotilla, NA London ADM 199/1339. A 28 March 1945 note addressed to Churchill confirms the Chiefs of Staff opinion that the Arctic convoys were no longer a necessity on military grounds, NA London CAB 120/688.

22. Escorts: War diary of Commander-in-Chief Home Fleet April 1945, NA London ADM 199/1440.

23. Rohwer's and Hummelchen's Chronology.

24. 9 May 1945 report by 10th Cruiser Squadron's Rear Admiral Angus Cunninghame Graham ('10th Cruiser Squadron's Operation Roundel Report'), NA London ADM 1/30417.

25. Section II of report by *Loch Shin*'s Commander John Kitcat, Senior Officer 19th Escort Group ('19th Escort Group's Report'), attached to his 6 May 1945 letter, which gives the location of the sinking as 69°25' N 33°39' E, NA London ADM 199/1339.

26. G.A. Roy's account in Vic Ould, *Last But Not Least* ('Goodall's Book') pp. 61–2.

27. 19th Escort Group's Report.

28. 'Freddie Peeters' account, Goodall's Book p. 58.

29. Record of part of an enquiry with the reference M.O. 8383/45 on it, brought to my attention by Robert Wilson, nephew of Lieutenant Robert Whyte, who was killed by the explosion.

30. Report by Lieutenant James Dallaway ('Goodall's Report'), Goodall Book pp. 16–17 and 19–21; also brought's to my attention by the abovementioned Robert Wilson.

31. Freddie Peeters' account, Goodall's Book p. 58.

32. Bill Bates' account, Goodall's Book p. 27.

33. Bill Bates' account, **IWM Sound** 22327.

34. Goodall's Report.

35. Ibid.

36. 30 April 1945 report by *Honeysuckle*'s Lieutenant Commander Jimmy Wright, NA London ADM 199/1339.

37. Ibid.

38. 19th Escort Group's Report.

39. Ibid. states the location of the presumed sinking was: 69°29' N 33°37' E, that is, a short distance to the north-west of where Note 25 above states *U-307* was sunk.

40. Ibid.

41. Rohwer's and Hummelchen's and Weis's Chronology p. 412.

42. List of the dead and wounded in *Goodall*, NA London ADM 358/4448.

43. 19th Escort Group Report.

44. Dispatch Of The Commander-in-Chief Home Fleet covering up to the end of May 1945, NA London ADM 199/1440; 10th Cruiser Squadron's Operation Roundel Report.

Chapter 44

1. BRITISH WAR AT SEA OFFICIAL HISTORY vol. 3 part 2 pp. 261–2. BRITISH ARCTIC CONVOYS HISTORY p. 129 points out that the figures for east-going convoys exclude ships that sailed to Russia independently.

2. British Arctic Convoys History p. 129. British War At Sea Official History vol. 3 part 2 p. 262 points out that the specified number of sunk ships excludes the 5 merchant ships and 1 minesweeper sunk in Russian ports or waters after arrival in Russia.

3. Merchant seamen killed: British Arctic Convoys History p. 129. British War At Sea Official History vol. 3 part 2 p. 262 states 2,883 Allied seamen were killed during the Arctic convoys; whereas the British Arctic Convoys History p. 129 states the total killed amounted to 2,773 men.

4. British War At Sea Official History vol. 2 p. 140; and Jeremy Clarkson, presenter of BBC's 'PQ17: An Arctic Convoy Disaster'.

5. BRITISH INTELLIGENCE OFFICIAL HISTORY pp. 220–2 explain why it can be argued that given his knowledge at the time Pound was acting reasonably when he decided to scatter PQ17 at the meeting convened during the evening of 4 July 1942. Some of the reasoning in those pages leading to that conclusion, backed up by additional points disclosed in this book, are laid out below:

a. When Pound attended the meeting, he should have realized that Denning may well have correctly concluded that *Tirpitz* would only be permitted to attack PQ17 if the Germans knew the Home Fleet was too far away to intervene, and if the Germans realized there really was no battleship near the convoy. At the time of the meeting, Pound did not know the Germans' current knowledge concerning the location of the Home Fleet and regarding the claim by the crews of German reconnaissance aircraft that there was a battleship near the convoy. However given the constant daylight, it was reasonable for Pound to assume it was likely that the Home Fleet would be sighted by German reconnaissance plane crews sooner rather than later, if it had not already happened. It was also reasonable for him to assume it was probable that the Germans would soon realize that there was no Allied battleship near the convoy, if that had not already been discovered. Evidence had already been shown to Pound revealing that questions were being asked about whether there really was a battleship near the convoy: as mentioned in Chapter 17, an Enigma decrypt that was among the decrypts sent over from Bletchley Park to the Admiralty after 8 p.m. on 4 July contained a notification that the German aircraft crew which had initially stated that the Allied group near the convoy included a battleship, had subsequently reported that it just consisted of cruisers and destroyers. In other words during the meeting on 4 July, it was not unreasonable for Pound to assume that the Germans would realize the obstacles standing in the way of an attack on the convoy would be removed at any minute if they had not already fallen by the wayside, and that the *Tirpitz*-led battlegroup would soon be on her way to attack the convoy if she had not already departed with that in mind. He would also have been justified in concluding that the German battlegroup would be supported by the pocket battleships *Lützow* and *Admiral Scheer*. At the time he made his decision, he could not have known *Lützow* had been forced to drop out.

b. Because Pound had been warned that messages sent in the Arctic might not be intercepted quickly or at all, and some intercepted encoded messages would not be decoded quickly, there was always the possibility that a message sent by the Germans ordering or announcing *Tirpitz*'s departure from Altenfjord would not be seen or might not be decrypted quickly by Bletchley Park's codebreakers. In other words it was reasonable for Pound to assume that he might not be tipped off before *Tirpitz* reached the convoy. He could not be certain the crews in the British submarines off Norway would sight the German battlegroup before it approached PQ17. The possibility that an

intercepted German Enigma message might not be decrypted quickly was highlighted by what actually occurred on 5 July: as mentioned in Chapter 18, the German message confirming that the *Tirpitz* battlegroup was about to sail was sent just minutes before midday on 5 July when the new Enigma settings began to be used. If that German message had been initiated and sent more than 15 minutes later, the signal would not have been decrypted until the next settings were worked out by British codebreakers many hours later. In those circumstances Pound might not have been tipped off about *Tirpitz*'s sortie until it was too late to save the convoy and its escorts.

c. It was reasonable for Pound to assume that if the *Tirpitz* battlegroup had attacked the convoy before he was tipped off, it would have been quite likely that many if not all of the supporting Allied warships would have been damaged or sunk, which was something Pound could not allow to happen given the impact this might have had on the keeping open of Britain's lifeline to and from America, as well as on the keeping open of the route to and from Malta at the same time as aid was being supplied to Russia. Britain could not afford to lose all or most of the convoy's escorts, which could have been the consequence of allowing the German battlegroup to attack PQ17. This leaves aside the British and American public's damaging loss of confidence in the Royal Navy that would probably have been the result of such a disaster. The loss of confidence would have been all the more impactful given that, as mentioned in Chapter 17, Pound had made a similar mistake before, which had ended in the sinking of two of Britain's capital ships. Pound's stance was all the more supportable because past sinkings of warships and merchant ships prior to the PQ17 scatter order had demonstrated that the fatalities were likely to be much higher for each warship sunk than for each merchant ship sunk. This was borne out by what actually happened in the Arctic during and after PQ17: as specified in Chapter 24, around 155 men lost their lives following the sinking or abandonment of 24 of the 'civilian' PQ17 ships whereas the sinking of just one destroyer during the 1944 convoy JW57, as described in Chapter 39, resulted in more than 200 fatalities.

d. When the meeting was convened, Pound would surely have realized that if he did not scatter the convoy on 4 July, it was quite likely that circumstances would arise the next day that would force him to scatter it then. These circumstances did indeed come into existence during the early afternoon of 5 July when as mentioned in Chapter 19, Bletchley Park sent to the Admiralty the decrypt confirming that the *Tirpitz* battlegroup was setting out that afternoon to attack the convoy.

e. What is written above leads to the conclusion that Pound's decision to scatter the convoy on 4 July was arguably the only logical step he could have taken, however tempting it is to look for a scapegoat for the terrible losses that occurred after PQ17 was scattered.

6. British War At Sea Official History p. 262.

7. Tons transported and lost in Arctic convoys: British Arctic Convoys History p. x, relying on the 6 September 1950 assessment report by the Ministry of Transport's Michael Constance ('The Ministry of Transport's Assessment Report'), NA London ADM 1/20021; and the cited number of tanks and aircraft sent by Britain to the Soviet Union is based on the answer prime minister Clement Attlee gave when responding to a 1946 parliamentary question. It should be added that the answer as quoted in the British Arctic Convoys History pp. x–xi does not clearly state the tanks and aircraft mentioned were all sent via the Arctic convoys. While a substantial number may have been sent via the northern route, that is not clearly stated. The British War At Sea Official History vol. 3 part 2 p. 262, suggests that rightly or wrongly the book's author believed that some 5000 tanks and 7000 aircraft were sent in the Arctic convoys. The comments in Note 30 should be taken into account when referring to the figures covered by this Note.

8. B. B. Schofield, a director of the Admiralty's Trade Division, specified these figures in his *The Russian Convoys* pp. 215 and 224–5 without naming the primary source; he states he is relying on the 16 April

1946 verbal statement by Britain's prime minister Clement Attlee in the House of Commons and the '3rd report on Mutual Air, 1946'; and what he refers to as 'Lease Lend reports 19, 20, 21 and 22 to US Congress. They should perhaps be regarded as his best estimates, based on statements and documents supplied by the administrations in Britain and America.

9. The second Protocol specified a hope that 3.3 million short tons of aid would be sent to Russia via the northern route between 1 July 1942 and 30 June 1943. The 25 October 1943 Report On The Implementation Of The Second Soviet Protocol With Comparisons Between The Second And Third Protocols, NA London PREM 3 401/19 states that only 344,200 short tons were sent to Russia via the northern route during the abovementioned period. It also states that the total sent via all routes during such period was 2,972,000 short tons compared with 4.4 million short tons pledged.

10. British War At Sea Official History vol. 3 part 2 p. 262. The sources relating to the impact on the western allies of prioritising giving aid to Russia are in the following NA London files: in CAB 69/2: Commander-in-Chief Middle East General Auchinleck inability to comply with instruction to attack quickly in Autumn of 1941: 1 August 1941 Defence Committee minutes; Chief of Air Staff Sir Charles Portal's agreement Russian supplies should be prioritized: 19 September 1941 Defence Committee minutes; Chief of Imperial General Staff Sir John Dill's opinion that Russians should be given Matildas: 17 November 1941 Defence Committee minutes. In CAB 69/3: number of British tanks and aircraft restricted due to US cutbacks: 22 September 1941 Report by Chairman of the British Representatives after the Conference on the British-United States Production and Assistance to Russia; India defenceless: Annex to 25 October 1941 Defence Committee minutes; Malaya and Singapore defenceless: 20 December 1941 War Cabinet Chiefs of Staff Committee minutes. In CAB 69/4: General Auchinleck unable to comply with instruction to attack quickly in 1942: 20 March 1942 telegram from Sir Stafford Cripps with 26 March 1942 Defence Committee documents; Churchill 19 January 1942 telegram to Australia's prime minister John Curtin: Defence Committee documents 21 January 1942; compromise concerning tanks for Australia: Chief of Imperial General Staff Sir Alan Brooke's conclusions in Annex in 31 January 1942 Defence Committee documents. Western allies accused of giving aid only fit for throwing in North Sea: undated 'Final Report by Lieutenant General M.B. Burrows', head of 30 Military Mission, Moscow starting in March 1944, NA London ADM 223/252.

11. Olga Kucherenko chapter 'Lend-Lease in war and Russian memory' ('Kucherenko's Lend Lease Appreciation Chapter') in David L. Hoffmann, ed., The Memory of the Second World War in Soviet and Post-Soviet Russia; and S. Monin, 'Vtoraia Mirovaia Voina. Mify o

Lend-Lize', in *Liudi I Teksty: Istoricheskii Al'manakh* 12 (2019): pp. 146–64.

12. *Velikaia Otechestvennaia Voina 1941–1945 (The Great Patriotic War 1941–1945)* vol. 9 p. 601, brought to my attention by Kucherenko's Lend Lease Appreciation Chapter.

13. Kucherenko's Lend Lease Appreciation Chapter; and Nikita Khrushchev, *Memoirs* vol.1 *Commissar* p. 226.

14. Nikita Khrushchev, *Memoirs* vol.1 *Commissar* p. 226.

15. 23 July 1942 telegram Stalin to Churchill, REYNOLDS AND PECHATNOV p. 129.

16. 18 February 1942 telegram from Stalin to Roosevelt, ibid. p. 85.

17. 13 October 1943 telegram Stalin to Churchill, ibid. p. 322.

18. 23 October 1943 Eden to Churchill via Clark Kerr, NA London ADM 199/606.

19. Boris Sokolov, 'The Role of Lend Lease in Soviet Military Efforts, 1941–1945', *The Journal of Slavic Military Studies*, 7, 3, 567–86.

20. Ibid.

21. British Arctic Convoys History pp. x–xi quotes the British prime minister Clement Attlee while answering a parliamentary question in the House of Commons on 16 April 1946 stating that Britain had supplied 5,218 tanks to the Soviet Union during the war including 1,388 from Canada. Attlee did not specify his source.

22. Alexander Hill, Associate Professor, Military History, University of Calgary, *Journal of Military History* vol. 71 no. 3 (July 2007) pp. 773–808 in 'British Lend-Lease Aid and the Soviet War Effort, June 1941-June

1942' ('Hill's Soviet War Effort Article').

23. Hill is referring to Colonel-General G.F. Krivosheev, ed., *Soviet Casualties And Combat Losses In The Twentieth Century* ('General Krivosheev's Book').

24. General Krivosheev's Book p. 252.

25. The report by Anastas Mikoyan, People's Commissar for Foreign Trade, following a 9 January 1942 conference in Moscow, quoted in Alexander Hill, *The Great Patriotic War of the Soviet Union, 1941–1945: A documentary reader* pp. 171–2. Hill credits G. N. Sevost'ianov, *Sovetsko-amerikanskie otnsoheniia, 1939–1945* p. 192, although it was previously referred to, and its source in Russian archives disclosed, in Mikhail Suprun, *Lend-liz I Severniye Konvoi 1941-1945 (Lend Lease and the Northern Convoys 1941-1945)* ('Suprun's Lend Lease Book') p. 49.

26. 29 July 1942 letter from the Offices of the War Cabinet to the Commercial Secretary based in Kuibyshev, Russia and the statement sent with it entitled 'Final Figures Of Arrivals And Losses For Each Convoy Up To And Including P.Q.16', NA London CAB 111/109, which states that 426 tanks were sent in Arctic convoys PQ2 to PQ6 inclusive. The 9 February 1942 telegram headed 'From the Foreign Office To Washington', NA London CAB 111/109, confirms the abovementioned 426 tanks sent via the Arctic convoys were Valentines and Matildas.

27. 9 December 1941 telegram from 30 Military Mission to the War Office citing a report from the Russian tank

directorate, NA London WO 193/580 brought to my attention by Hill's Soviet War Effort Article.

28. Suprun's Lend Lease Book pp. 120–122 states that the 4,697 tanks given by the Western allies to Russia during the First Protocol period (up to 30 June 1942) was 33% of the number of tanks produced by Russia during the country's first year in the war, and 96% of the number of tanks produced by Russia during the country's first six months in the war. The equivalent figures for the 3,296 aircraft given to Russia by the western allies during the First Protocol period was 17% and 34%, he says. He is not saying these tanks and aircraft were all received in Russia by 30 June 1942. But what he does say is that even the smaller number of tanks, armoured cars and aircraft actually delivered to North Russian ports via the Arctic convoys by that date (he says 2,314 tanks, 1,550 armoured cars and 1,903 aircraft were delivered before July 1942) was an important contribution: prior to July 1942, the Arctic convoy shipping delivered approximately the same numbers of these items as Russia possessed at the beginning of 1942, he says.

Using such comparisons to highlight the significance of what the Western allies supplied is inventive. But because he is often having to comment on the usefulness of the aid without complete data, which through no fault of his own may only become available when more documentation is declassified, some of his commentary is most valuable for its general tenor, rather than for the precise statistics.

It is interesting for example to hear him praising the Western allies for supplying, partly via the northern route in the Arctic convoys and partly via the other routes, machine tools and the raw materials necessary to maintain Russian production, as well as radio and communications equipment to help the Red Army keep in touch on the battlefields.

He also has emphasized the significance of the enormous quantities of food after the Soviet Union was deprived of its 'bread basket' in the Ukraine, that the western allies sent via the various routes, the bulk of it during mid-1943 to mid-1945 (canned meat, sugar and flour are the individual items believed to have represented the largest share of these food supplies by weight). He has estimated that wartime food supplies from the West, some of it sent in ships in the Arctic convoys, were enough to feed the Red Army during all the years the Soviet Union was participating in the Second World War (Mikhail Suprun, 'Lend-Lease food air to Russia/ USSR during the Second World War', *The Journal of Slavic Military Studies*, 2023, 36:1, 96–108).

29. Andrew Boyd, *Arms For Russia & The Naval War In The Arctic 1941–1945* pp. 173–182, 491–2 and 532.

30. The weight figures in the table are based on those in 'Table 16' headed 'Shipments From The Western Hemisphere To The U.S.S.R. By Route, June 22, 1941–September 20

1945' in Hubert P. van Tuyll, *Feeding The Bear* ('The Bear Book') p. 164. The Table 16 figures, which are also cited in Robert Jones, The Roads To Russia ('The Jones Book') p. 290, are said to be based on the US Department of State, Protocol and Area Information Staff of the USSR Branch of the Division of Research and Reports, 'Report on War Aid Furnished by the United States to the U.S.S.R.' (Foreign Economic Section, Office of Foreign Liquidation, November 28 1945, 29); and T. H. Vail Motter, *The Persian Corridor and Aid to Russia*, pp. 481–3. The Bear Book does not disclose whether or not the Table 16 figures include aid not produced in America It should be noted that The Ministry of Transport's Assessment Report's figures for the year by year Arctic convoy shipments show similar trends to the figures in the abovementioned Table 16 figures, and a similar total for the entire war, but different figures for each individual year. This reinforces the point that unless and until primary sources are discovered which reveal the true statistics, the Table 16 figures and The Ministry of Transport's Assessment Report figures as well as the figures referred to in this Chapter's Notes 7 and 8 should be regarded as estimates. The Jones Book p. 261 cites the US State Department's 1951 claim that $10.8 billion of US aid was sent to the Soviet Union during and shortly after the war. Various reports can be used to estimate what the $10.8 billion figure quoted is worth in today's terms taking into account inflation. If one accepts that the appropriate inflation multiplier is around 20, that puts the value of the aid in today's terms at around $215 billion (The 20 multiplier is at the bottom end of the range indicated by the US Bureau of Labor CPI Multiplier which appears to refer to a multiplier of ca. 17, and the Bank of England's Inflation calculator which appears to refer to a multiplier of ca. 36). The very approximate unverified figures that have been cited for what the US has donated to Ukraine during 2022-2024 are some $119 billion (source the Kiel Institute). Because none of these figures have been backed up with documentation, they should be regarded at best as very rough estimates.

Maps

1 The coast lines in Map 1, which is based on the theatre map in the BRITISH ARCTIC CONVOYS HISTORY, are very generalized, and they should not be taken to be anything other than approximations.

A note in the text box on Map 1 states that the explanations of the numbers that are to be seen on this map are to be found in this note. These explanations are laid out below. Each of the numbers laid out below has text beside it which explains the significance of the corresponding number on Map 1.

Please note that the numbers below are formatted differently to those on Map 1, in that those below, unlike those in Map 1, are not white numbers set in blacked in circles.

1 Location where after searching for PQ12 *Tirpitz* was

unsuccessfully attacked by British aircraft on 9 March 1942, as described in Chapter 4.

2 Where the cruiser HMS *Trinidad* was located when while protecting PQ13 she was hit by her own torpedo on 29 March 1942, as described in Chapter 5.

3A Place where during the passage of QP11 the cruiser HMS *Edinburgh* was torpedoed on 30 April 1942, as described in Chapter 10, before she was sunk on 2 May 1942 in location **3B,** as described in Chapter 11.

4 Location where during the night of 14-15 May 1942 *Trinidad* was bombed, before she was finally sunk, as described in Chapter 13.

5 Approximate location of PQ16 on 27 May 1942 when 8 of the Allies' ships were sunk or abandoned, or so severely damaged that they could not remain with the convoy, in the course of a series of raids by the Luftwaffe, as described in Chapter 15.

6A Where PQ17's ships were bombed during the big air attack on 4 July 1942, as described in Chapter 1, shortly before the convoy was scattered at **6B,** as described in Chapter 17.

7 Site where 8 of PQ18's ships were either sunk or abandoned during and after a raid by the Luftwaffe on 13 September 1942, as described in Chapter 27.

8 Approximate place where SS *Chulmleigh* was abandoned during the night of 5-6 November 1942 after sailing onto the reef on the west side of Spitsbergen's South Cape Island, as described in Chapter 31.

9 Place where the two British cruisers *Sheffield* and *Jamaica* were located when their gunners ambushed the German heavy cruiser *Admiral Hipper* at the climax of the 31 December 1942 Battle of the Barents Sea, as described in Chapter 33.

10 Approximate site, in Kaa Fjord (the Altenfjord sub-fjord), where on 22 September 1943 *Tirpitz* was damaged by charges dropped under her hull from two British midget submarines, as described in Chapter 36; and where, in a slightly different spot, on 15 September 1944 *Tirpitz* was damaged again, this time by bombs dropped by the RAF, as described in Chapter 41.

11 Where the survivors of SS *Dekabrist* who had been castaways on Hope Island for around eleven months were finally rescued by *U-703's* crew on 7 October 1943, as described in Chapter 31.

12 Approximate location where on 26 December 1943 the German battlecruiser *Scharnhorst* was sunk by the British Home Fleet, as described in Chapter 38.

13 *Tirpitz's* last resting place, a short distance to the

south-west of Tromso, where
she capsized and sank during
a bombing raid by the RAF
on 12 November 1944, as
described in Chapter 41.

2 Map 4 is based on Appendix III to
Victorious' commanding officer's letter
dated 15 March 1942, in the **NHB**.

3 In addition to the sources in
Chapters 5–7, Map 5 is also based on
the 28 March 1942 entry in the <u>KTB
DES ZERSTÖRERS Z 25</u>, and its
'Wegekarte Z 25 vom 28 III – 29 III',
both in **Militärarchiv Freiburg** RM
94/110.

4 In addition to relying on sources in
Chapter 5's notes, Map 7 is
principally based on maps entitled
'Track Chart Of Engagement
Between H.M.S. Trinidad & German
Destroyers Barents Sea Sunday 29th
March 1942' and 'Convoy PQ13
Action With German Destroyers
Barents Sea Sunday March 29th 1942',
both in **NA London** ADM 199/348;
and the map entitled 'Gefecht mit
englischen Sicherungstreitkräften
am 29.3.42 im Nordmeer.
Wegekarte Zerstörer Z 24' in
Militärarchiv Freiburg RM 94/106.

5 As well as taking into account the
sources in Chapter 10's and 11's
notes, Map 8 is principally based on
the map entitled 'Track Chart Of
Convoy QP11 HMS Bulldog S.O
Escort 28th April To 7th May 1942',
NA London ADM 199/165.

6 In addition to relying on sources
specified in Chapter 10's notes, Map
9 is principally based on the map
entitled 'Movements of H.M.S.
Edinburgh between 1415 and 1615
(Zone -2) 30th April 1942' in NA
London ADM 199/165; and map

entitled 'Angriff U456 am 30.4.1942
auf einen britischen Kreuzer der
Belfast-Klasse (2 Treffer) in KTB des
Unterseebootes U456, Militärarchiv
Freiburg RM98/950.

7 Map 10 relies on several of the
sources in Chapter 10's notes, but it
is principally based on the 10 May
1942 report by *Bulldog's* Commander
Maxwell Richmond; the 6 May 1942
report by *Beagle's* Commander
Ralph Medley; and 'Track Chart Of
Action Against Three Enemy
Destroyers Off Bear Island', all in
NA London ADM 199/721.

8 In addition to relying on sources in
Chapter 11's notes, Map 11 is
principally based on maps entitled
'Action Between H.M.S. Edinburgh
& Escort & Three German
Destroyers In Barents Sea 2nd May
1942'; Action Between H.M. Ships
Edinburgh Foresight & Forester &
Three German Destroyers On
Saturday the 2nd Day Of May 1942
From 0630-0820'; and 'H.M.S.
Forester Track Chart May 2nd 1942,
all in NA London ADM 199/165.

9 In addition to relying on other sources
in Chapter 32's notes, Map 16 is
particularly based on the map in NA
London ADM 199/73 that is in
Enclosure 2 to the document referred
to in that chapter's notes as '<u>Force R's
Report</u>'; and the maps in Militärarchiv
Freiburg RM7/1040 that take into
account Hipper's Regenbogen Report
and Hipper's Regenbogen Artillery
Report, as those reports are defined in
Chapter 32's notes.

10 This inset within Map 16 is based on
the Naval Staff Battle Summary 29,
The Attack On The Tirpitz By Midget
Submarines (Operation "Source")

22nd September 1943, Plans 3 and 5, NA London ADM 234/348', and the despatches submitted by Rear Admiral C.B. Barry on 8 November 1943 and by Rear Admiral G.E Creasy on 26 July 1945, both published in Supplement to The London Gazette of 10 February 1948, NA London AIR 2/9875; and the plan entitled 'Bomber Command Attack on Battleship Tirpitz in Kaa Fjord Photos taken on 15.9.44' opposite p. 62 of the report entitled 'Tirpitz: An account of the various attacks carried out by the British Armed Forces and their effect upon the German Battleship Volume 2', NA London ADM 234/350.

11 As well as being based on other sources in Chapter 32's and Chapter 33's notes, Map 17 is particularly based on the plan labelled 'Gefechtsskizze Unternehmen "Regenbogen" am 31.12.42' in Militärarchiv Freiburg RM 7/1040.

12 The co-ordinates cited in the preliminary note that precedes this Map 17's key numbers' texts are based on what is mentioned in Force R's Report (defined above in Note 9 of the Maps section of this book's notes).

13 In addition to relying on sources in Chapter 37's and Chapter 38's notes, Map 18 is also based on 'Wegkarte des Zerstörers "Z 29" beim Unternehmen gegen engl. Geleitzug vom 25-27.12.1943' with the 16-31 December 1943 KTB DES ZERSTÖRERS Z 29.

14 Map 18's inset is based on the map entitled 'Bomber Command Attack on Battleship TIRPITZ in Kaa Fjord', NA London AIR 34/141.

15 The co-ordinates in the preliminary text preceding the text linked to the key numbers in Map 19 are based on Burnett's Battle of North Cape Report, as defined in Chapter 37's notes.

16 In addition to relying on sources in Chapter 42's notes, Map 21 relies on Plans 1, 2 and 3 referred to in 1st Cruiser Squadron's Rear Admiral Rhoderick McGrigor's 28 February 1945 report headed, Operation Hotbed – Passage of J.W.64 and R.A.64', NA London ADM 199/759.

17 Map 23 is based on sketch in a diary compiled by Lieutenant Commander P.W. Dolphin while he was serving as a midshipman aboard the cruiser Trinidad, **IWM Documents 09/54/1.**

18 Map 24 is based on a sketch with the war diary for the British 126 Base Unit, NA London WO 176/391.

Appendix A

1. Based on the formation diagram in NA London ADM 199/757.

Appendix B

1. Based on the PQ16 formation sketch in NA London ADM 199/757, and another slightly different PQ16 formation sketch and a document specifying which PQ16 ships reached Russia in NA London ADM 237/167.

2. 6 June 1942 reports by Mauna Key's Ensign Robert G. Crawford, and Massmar's Ensign William A. McDowell Commanding Officers Armed Guard, US ARMED GUARD REPORTS Boxes 460 and 458 respectively.

Appendix C

1. Based on the PQ18 formation sketch in NA London ADM 199/758.

Bibliography

I have specified a country as the publication location for books in this section which have been privately published. If first publication of a book took place during the same year in London as well as in another country, I have in this section specified London as the place of publication unless it is obvious that a publisher in the other country commissioned the book. Books with no disclosed author, or books in which the chapter quoted is by a person who is not the book's compiler, are listed at the beginning of the list below.

Bratsvo severnikh konvoev 1941-1945 (Brotherhood of the northern convoys 1941-1945), compiled by R.V. Gorchakov: chapter Na pravah passazhirov (On the rights of passengers) by G. Polyakov, Archangel, 1991

Hunting Tirpitz: Royal Naval Operations Against Bismarck's Sister Ship commissioned by Britannia Royal Naval College's Britannia Museum, Plymouth, 2012

Polyarniy Krug (The Polar Circle), compiled by A.V. Shumilov: chapter: Perezhitoye: iz vospominaniy sudovogo medika parohoda "Dekabrist" (A testimony of what was experienced: from the memoirs of the ship's doctor on the vessel "Dekabrist") by Nadezhda Natalich, Moscow, 1982

Severnie Konvoi: Issledovaniya, vospomininaniya, documenti, Vipusk 2 (Northern Convoys: Research, memoirs, documents, vol. 2): chapter Smert' Kieva i Empair Bairon (Death of "Kiev" and "Empire Byron") by G.A. Rudnev, Moscow, 1994

The Royal Navy And The Arctic Convoys: A Naval Staff History, Abingdon, 2007

V konvoyakh i odinochnikh plavaniyakh (In convoys and in solo voyages) compiled by V. V. Kolt: chapter Tragediya v Karskom more (Tragedy on the Karsky Sea) by Y. D. Kapralov, Archangel, 1985

Velikaia Otechestvennaia Voina 1941–1945 (The Great Patriotic War 1941–1945) vol. 9, Moscow, 2014

Zashitniki Otechestva (Defenders of the Motherland): chapter Svidetel' gibeli parohoda "Marina Raskova" (Witness of the death of the vessel "Marina Raskova") by T. A. Sanakina, Archangel, 2004

Beaumont, Joan, *Comrades In Arms: British Aid to Russia 1941–1945,* London, 1980

Beesly, Patrick, *Very Special Intelligence: The Story of the Admiralty's Operational Intelligence Centre 1939-1945*, London 1977

Beevor, Antony, *Stalingrad*, London, 1998

Beke, Charles T. and Beynen, Koolemans, eds., *The Three Voyages of William Barents to the Arctic Regions, 1594, 1595 and 1596 by Gerrit De Vere*, London, 2016

Bell, P.M.H., *John Bull and the Bear: British Public Opinion, Foreign Policy and the Soviet Union 1941-1945*, London, 1990

Bishop, Patrick, *Target Tirpitz: X-Craft, Agents And Dambusters – The Epic Quest To Destroy Hitler's Mightiest Warship*, London, 2012

Boyd, Andrew, *Arms For Russia & The Naval War In The Arctic 1941–1945*, Barnsley, 2024.

Brodhurst, Robin, *Churchill's Anchor, The Biography Of Admiral Of The Fleet Sir Dudley Pound*, Barnsley, South Yorkshire, 2000

Broome, Captain Jack, *Convoy Is To Scatter*, London, 1972

Browning, Robert M., *United States Merchant Marine Casualties in World War II*, North Carolina, 2011

Bunker, John, *Heroes in Dungarees: The Story Of The American Merchant Marine In World War II*, Annapolis, Maryland, 1995

Campbell, Spurgeon, *Waves Astern: A Memoir of World War II and the Cold War*, Bloomington, Indiana, 2004

Carse, Robert, *A Cold Corner Of Hell*, New York, 1969

Carter, William, *Why Me Lord?: The Experiences of a U.S. Navy Armed Guard Officer in World War II's Convoy PQ 17 on the Murmansk Run*, USA, 2007

Chisholm, Anne and Davie, *Beaverbrook: A Life*, London, 1993

Churchill, Winston, *The Second World War*:
> vol. III, *The Grand Alliance*, London, 1950
>
> vol. IV, *The Hinge Of Fate*, London, 1951
>
> vol. V, *Closing The Ring*, London, 1952

Claxton, Ian, *Honeysuckle's War: The Story of a Corvette*, England, 1999

Coulter, Surgeon Captain J. L. S. *The Royal Naval Medical Service*:
> Volume I: *Administration*, London, 1954
>
> Volume II: *Operations*, London, 1956

Denham, Henry, *Inside the Nazi Ring: A Naval Attaché in Sweden 1940-1945*, London, 1984, London, 2013

Ditcham, A. G. F. *A Home On The Rolling Main: A Naval Memoir 1940-1946*, Barnsley, South Yorkshire, 2013

Doenitz, Karl, *Memoirs: Ten Years And Twenty Days*, London, 2000 (original German version: Bonn, 1958)

Eden, Anthony, *Memoirs: The Reckoning*, London, 1965

Erwood, Peter, ed., *A Long Night For The Canteen Boat: The Torpedoing and Salvage of HMS Cassandra 11th December 1944*, Fleet Hargate, Lincolnshire, 1996 (edition I used 2003)

Fairbanks, Douglas Jr., *A Hell of a War*, London, 1995

Foxvog, Donald R. and Alotta, Robert I., *The Last Voyage of the SS Henry Bacon*, St Paul, Minnesota, 2001

Bibliography

Flohic, François, *Ni Chagrin Ni Pitié, Souvenirs d'un marin de la France libre,* Paris, 1985

Geroux, William, *The Ghost Ships Of Archangel: The Arctic Voyage That Defied The Nazis,* New York, 2019

Gilbert, Martin, *Road to Victory: Winston S. Churchill 1941–1945,* London, 1986 (edition I used London, 1989)

Gleichauf, Justin F. *Unsung Sailors, The Naval Armed Guard in World War II,* Annapolis, Maryland, 1990

Golovko, Arseni, *With The Red Fleet: The War Memoirs Of The Late Admiral Arseni G. Golovko,* London, 1965 (Russian edition previously published in Moscow, 1960)

Gorchakov, R.V., ed., *The Brotherhood of the Northern Convoys: On The Rights of Passengers* chapter by Poliakov, G.

Gorodetsky, Gabriel, ed., *The Maisky Diaries: Red Ambassador to the Court of St James's 1932–1943,* London, 2015

Griffith, Hubert, *R.A.F. In Russia,* London, 1942

Harriman, Averell and Abel, Elie, *Special Envoy to Churchill and Stalin 1941–1946,* London, 1976

Hawkins, Ian, ed., *Destroyer: An anthology of first-hand accounts of the war at sea 1939-1945,* London, 2003 (edition referred to by me: Conway, a division of Anova Books Company Ltd, 1999)

Higgins, Alan, *You're In The Navy Now: A teenage recruit sees front-line action in WWII,* England (no publication date recorded in book)

Hill, Alexander, *The Great Patriotic War of the Soviet Union, 1941–1945: A documentary reader,* Abingdon, 2009

Hill, Roger, *Destroyer Captain,* London, 1975 (edition referred to by me: Grafton Books – a division of Collins Publishing Group – paperback, London 1986)

Hinsley, F.H. with other authors, *British Intelligence In The Second World War: Its Influence on Strategy and Operations*
> *Volume 2, London 1981*
> *Volume 3 Part I, London, 1984*
> *Volume 3 Part II, London, 1988*

Hobbs, David, *The Fleet Air Arm And The War In Europe 1939-1945,* Barnsley, 2022

Hoffmann, David L., ed., *The Memory of the Second World War in Soviet and Post-Soviet Russia:* 'Lend-Lease in war and Russian memory' chapter by Olga Kucherenko, Abingdon, Oxfordshire 2022

Holman, Gordon, *The King's Cruisers,* London, 1947

Hughes, Robert, *In Perilous Seas,* Tunbridge Wells, Kent, 1990

Hutson, Harry C., *Arctic Interlude: Independent To North Russia,* Bennington, Vermont, 1997

Il'in, V.N., Radishevskaya, V.A., Titova, T.V., eds., *Voina: Zapechatlennie dni 1941–1942 (War: Captured Days 1941–1942),* Archangel, 2005

Insall, Tony, *Secret Alliances: Special Operations And Intelligence In Norway 1040–1945 – The British Perspective,* London, 2019

Irving, David, *The Destruction of Convoy PQ17,* London, 1968

Jacobsen, Alf R., *Scharnhorst,* Oslo, 2001 (edition referred to by me: Sutton Publishing Ltd, Stroud, Gloucestershire, 2003)

Jessop, Keith, *Goldfinger: The True Story of One Man's Discovery,* London, 1998 (edition referred to by me: Pocket Books, an imprint of Simon & Schuster UK Ltd, 1999)

Jones, Robert Huhn, *The Roads To Russia: United States Lend-Lease To The Soviet Union,* Oklahoma, USA, 1969

Kerslake, S. A. *Coxswain In The Northern Convoys,* London, 1984

Khrushchev, Nikita, *Memoirs of,* Volume 1: *Commissar*[1918-1945], Pennsylvania, 2004 (Russian version first publication 1999)

Kimball, Warren F., ed., *Churchill & Roosevelt: The Complete Correspondence:*
   I Alliance Emerging, Princeton, London, 1984
   II Alliance Forged, London, 1984

Krivosheev, Colonel-General G. F., ed., *Soviet Casualties And Combat Losses In The Twentieth Century,* London, 1997

Lindbæk, Lise, *Tusen Norske Skip,* Norway, 1945

Lund, Thoralv, *Kalde Krigsår: Den Norske Innsets På Og For Svalbard 1940–1945 (Cold War Years: The Norwegian Efforts On And For Svalbard 1940–1945),* Norway 1990

MacGregor, Iain, *The Lighthouse Of Stalingrad: Hidden Truth At The Heart Of the Greatest Battle Of World War II,* London, 2022

Macintyre, Captain Donald, *U-Boat Killer,* London, 1956

Maisky, Ivan, *Memoirs of a Soviet Ambassador: The War 1939-43,* London, 1967 (Russian version first publication Moscow, 1965)

Mallmann Showell, Jack, ed., *Fuehrer Conferences On Naval Affairs 1939–1945,* 1947, England (edition referred to by me The History Press, Stroud, Gloucestershire, 2015)

Medical Research Council: *A Guide To The Preservation Of Life At Sea After Shipwreck,* London, 1943

Mills, Morris O., *PQ13: Unlucky For Some,* Bramber, West Sussex, 2000

Milton, Giles, *The Stalin Affair: The Impossible Alliance that Won the War, London,* 2024

Ministry of Information: *Merchantmen At War: The Official Story of the Merchant Navy: 1939-1944,* London, 1944

Moore, Arthur R., *A Careless Word . . . A Needless Sinking,* New York, 1983

Mortensen, Nils, *Flyktninger I eget land,* Molde, Norway, 1995

Motter, T. H. Vail, *The Persian Corridor And Aid To Russia,* Washington, 1952

Munn, Dalton Leslie, *Diary of Squandered Valor: First Convoy to Murmansk,* USA, 2012

Ogden, Graeme, *My Sea Lady: HMS Madeleine: February 1941 to February 1943,* London, 2013

Ould, Vic, *Last But Not Least: H.M.S. Goodall Torpedoed 29th April 1945,* England, 2013

Pawłowicz, B., *O.R.P. Garland: In Convoy to Russia,* Surrey, 1943

Pearce, Frank, *Last Call For HMS Edinburgh: A story of the Russian convoys,* London, 1982
   The Ship that Torpedoed Herself, Plymouth, 1975

Penrose, Barrie, *Stalin's Gold: The Story of HMS Edinburgh and Its Treasure,* London, 1982

Peyton Jones, Loftus, *Wartime Wanderings 1939–1945,* England, 1993 (edition referred to by me: 2019)

Bibliography

Raeder, Erich, *My Life*, Annapolis, Maryland, 1960 (edition referred to by me: Arno Press Inc., New York, 1980)

Ransome Wallis, R., *Two Red Stripes: A Naval Surgeon at War*, Shepperton, Surrey, 1973

Rep, Jelte, *S.O.S. Paulus Potter*, The Hague, 1984

Reynolds, David & Pechatnov, Vladimir, with assistance of Iskander Magadeyev and Olga Kucherenko, *The Kremlin Letters: Stalin's Wartime Correspondence with Churchill and Roosevelt*, London, 2018

Rohwer, Jürgen, Hummelchen, Gerhard, and Weis, Thomas, *Chronology of the War at Sea 1939–1945*, London, 2005 (original edition by first two cited authors first published 1972)

Roskill, Captain S.W., *The War At Sea:*
   Volume II: The Period Of Balance, London, 1956
   Volume III : The Offensive, Part I: 1ˢᵗ June 1943-31st May 1944, London, 1960
   Volume III: The Offensive, Part II: 1ˢᵗ June 1944-14ᵗʰ August 1945, London, 1961

Ross, Alan, *Blindfold Games,* London, 1986

Rudnev, G. A., *Na Morskih Dorogah Voini (The Naval Paths of War)*, Vladivostok, 1995

Schmidt, Rudi, *Achtung – Torpedo Los! Der strategische und operative Einsatz des Kampfgeschwaders 26 – Löwengeschwader – Das Torpedogeschwader der deutschen Luftwaffe im Zweiten Weltkrieg,* Koblenz, Germany, 1991

Schofield, B.B., *The Russian Convoys,* London, 1964 (edition referred to by me: Pan paperback, London, 1971)

Sebag-Montefiore, Hugh, *The Battle For The Code,* London, 2000
   Dunkirk: Fight To The Last Man, London, 2006

Sherwood, Robert E., *The White House Papers of Harry L. Hopkins: An intimate history, Volume I September 1939-January 1942,* London, 1948

Somkin, Aleksandr, *Mi pomnim vas . . . (We remember you . . .)*, Archangel, 1995

Sparksman, Norman, *Jottings of a Young Sailor,* Ely, Cambridgeshire, 2008

Steenbeck, Alexander, *Die Spur des Löwen,* Lübeck, 2013

Suprun, Mikhail, *Lend-Liz I Severniye Konvoi 1941-1945 (Lend Lease and the Northern Convoys 1941-1945)*, Moscow, 1997

Tuyll, Hubert P. van, *Feeding The Bear: American Aid to the Soviet Union, 1941-1945,* Connecticut, 1989

Twiddy, Herbert A.A., *My Teenage War And Later Career,* England, 2009

Van Kampen, Anthony, ed., *Scheepsverlaring,* Amsterdam, 1952

Warrilow, Betty, *Nabob: The First Canadian-Manned Aircraft Carrier,* Ontario, Canada, 1989

Werth, Alexander, *The Year Of Stalingrad: An Historical Record And A Study Of Russian Mentality, Methods And Policies,* London, 1946

Whinney, Bob, *The U-Boat Peril: An Anti-Submarine Commander's War,* Poole, 1986

Winn, Godfrey, *'P.Q.17',* London, 1947

Winton, John, *The Death Of The Scharnhorst,* Chichester, 1983

Woodman, Richard, *The Arctic Convoys 1941-1945,* London, 1994

Yakolev, Professor A. N., with Haustov, V. N., Naumov, V. P., and Plotnikova, N. S., eds., *Lubyanka: Stalin and NKVD-NKGB-GUKR Smersh,* Moscow, 2006

List of Illustrations

List of Illustrations

Acknowledgements

The seed that set off my interest in the attacks on Arctic convoys – and the Battle of the Arctic – was sewn over 25 years ago when I met Sir Harry Hinsley, a professor at England's Cambridge University. It was in connection with a book I was hoping to write about the breaking of the German Enigma code. He told me about his personal participation, when working as an intelligence officer at Britain's Bletchley Park codebreaking centre, in the attempt in July 1942 to use decrypts of German Enigma messages to protect Arctic convoy PQ17.

Enthused by his dramatic telling of the PQ17 story, my next step along the long road that ended with my decision to write a book about the Battle of the Arctic was to visit the Maritime Museum at London's Greenwich, where I read the account by Ned Denning, an officer who had during World War 2 worked at the British Admiralty, and who had also participated in the attempt to protect the convoy.

The information I gleaned from these two men was to form the basis of the PQ17 chapter in the book I eventually had published under the title *Enigma: The Battle For The Code*. But it was only years later, after writing two other books, that I happened to read Alistair MacLean's gripping novel *HMS Ulysses* about the adventures on a British anti-aircraft cruiser while escorting merchant ships to Murmansk, and my thoughts turned to writing about Arctic convoys again.

My very first breakthrough when seeking to determine whether it would be possible to find vivid testimony that might match the kind of action described in Alistair MacLean's novel was having the good fortune to be introduced to Alan Blyth, an Arctic convoy enthusiast. His uncle, Radio Officer Norman Blyth, had died when the merchant ship SS *Induna* was torpedoed during Arctic convoy PQ13. This family connection had prompted him to find out as much as he could not only about the *Induna*, but also about the other ships in the convoy. He had at one time intended to write a book about PQ13. But by the time I contacted him, he had changed his mind although he was sitting on a mass of valuable material. When I contacted him, he very generously immediately offered to let me use it. He also introduced me to *Induna's* Austin Byrne, who by then was the doyen of the Arctic convoy survivors. Another helper I encountered thanks to

Alan Blyth was Jos Odijk from Holland, whose uncle, Niek Odijk, died when SS *Raceland* was sunk during PQ13. Jos brought to my attention relevant Dutch books and documents, and helped me search for the families of veterans.

Round about the same time, I was also introduced to Tim Lewin, whose late father, Lord (Terence) Lewin, had been Chief of the Defence Staff under Margaret Thatcher when the decision was taken to recapture the Falkland Islands. During the war Lieutenant Lewin, as he then was, had served in the destroyer *Ashanti* on various Arctic convoys. Tim, who had been asked by his father to do what he could to ensure that the contribution of Arctic convoy veterans to the war effort should be recognized, agreed to assist me, making available relevant documents, and introducing me firstly to his Russian colleague, Katya Fowler, who helped me communicate with museum staff in Archangel, and secondly to all his many Arctic convoy contacts.

Tim Lewin's most helpful Arctic convoy contacts included:

- George Milne, the then chairman of what is now known as the Arctic Convoy Museum near Aultbea, north-west Scotland, who in his turn introduced me to Bruce Hudson, the then vice chairman. Bruce made sure I was able to access the museum's extensive archives and journals.

- Commander Eric Dietrich-Berryman, in America, who helped me contact the families of American merchant seamen, leading to the discovery of precious previously unpublished letters and diaries. When Eric tragically died before my research was completed, his wife Bobbie Berryman stepped into the breach, carrying on where Eric left off. She also introduced me to Brother Dunstan Robidoux, a Benedictine friar, who in his turn suggested that his friend Bob Urban, a coast guard veteran, might be willing to find relevant documents for me in the National Archives, Maryland. Bob readily agreed, and both with and without Brother Dunstan, he unearthed many relevant documents and photographs.

- Colonel Wojciech Aksamit, based in Poland, who has helped me identify the most relevant books concerning Polish men who participated in the convoys, and who has translated the most important passages of those works written in Polish which he recommended.

- Valentina Golysheva, based in Russia, a professor of English Philology who has worked at Archangel's Northern Arctic Federal University, and who has written several books about the Arctic convoys. Her father, Georgy Golyshev, died following the abandoning of *Marina Raskova*. She not only told me about the sinking but helped me discover what happened. It is thanks to her that the sinking of this ship and its aftermath is covered in this book.

Other Americans who have given invaluable assistance are:

- Ian Millar, a retired lawyer in America, who as well as campaigning over many years to persuade the US authorities to give awards to American

Arctic convoy veterans, has interviewed many veterans in order to enable him to write up and publish their experiences. He has generously shared with me not only the documents he has collected but also his photograph collection.

- Dick Carter, the son of the American armed guard officer William Carter, who wrote a first hand account, published in a book entitled *Why Me Lord?*, describing his participation in dramatic events during two Arctic convoys. Dick, who had publishing experience and was instrumental in getting his father's account published in an attractive format, as well as telling me about the book, sent me the edition of Life Magazine that covered Arctic convoy PQ17, and also introduced me to the American historian Bill Geroux (see below).

- William (Bill) Geroux, one of whose books *The Ghost Ships Of Archangel* has vividly chronicled some of the most interesting aspects of PQ17, has generously shared with me all of his relevant sources and contacts both in America and even more significantly in Russia (see below).

Russians to whom I was introduced by Bill Geroux include:

- Mikhail Suprun, a history professor who has worked at Archangel's North-ern Arctic Federal University and who has written several books and articles about the Arctic convoys and lend-lease (America's provision of aid to Russia during the war). It would not be exaggerating to describe him as the Russian guru when it comes to assessing the impact of the wartime aid to the Soviet Union. He has sent me copies of various relevant documents, answered my many questions, and equally importantly introduced me to his former student Katya Emelyanova, who has worked tirelessly on my behalf in Archangel, and in the process sent me copies of many relevant documents and books she found in Archangel archives and libraries.

- Ivan Katyshev, who at the time worked at the Archangel Northern Maritime Museum. He sent me many relevant documents that came originally from the Archangel archives.

Other assistance relating to Polish seamen has been provided by:

- Wanda Troman. She not only supplied articles relating to the sunk submar-ine *Jastrząb* that I would never have found without her assistance but she also very kindly translated them. Very sadly she has not lived to see the publication of this book.

- Anna Pacewicz, whose father served in the Polish ship *Garland* after the destroyer's involvement in the Arctic convoys. Anna and her contact Barbara Lesisz-Dembinska, whose uncle served in *Garland* during the Arctic convoys, have helped me find a book and photographs relating to *Garland's* participation in PQ16.

Assistance from Norwegians has been provided by:

Alf Jacobsen, whose own research as an investigative journalist and TV producer enabled him to help me in many ways. One of his many books describes the events leading up to the sinking of the German battlecruiser *Scharnhorst,* which is featured in this book. He also produced a Timewatch documentary for the BBC about the sinking of that ship during Arctic convoy JW55B. He brought to my attention documents concerning the Arctic convoy spy, and introduced me to Kjetil Korsnes, an associate professor at Nord University located in Bodø, Norway who is the lead administrator of Acta Norvegica Arkiv, a private archive which contains amongst other documents copies of most of the German war diaries which are relevant to the Battle of the Arctic. He has sent me copies of anything from the archive which I have requested.

Assistance concerning Svalbard has come from:

Håvard Hansen, who while working as a meteorological representative at the meteorological station on Hope Island, found the accounts by the shipwrecked captain and doctor from *Dekabrist* who were castaway on the island, as well as unearthing a privately published book that specifies the location of the huts they occupied. He also supplied photographs of the remains of one of the huts and of the monument on the island, erected after the war, commemorating the Dekabrist crew's sacrifice.

Per Kyrre Reymert, author of a book on trappers' cabins on Svalbard, has confirmed where on Spitzbergen the *Chulmleigh* survivors, featured in this book, were rescued. He has also sent me photographs showing the mass burial of those who died that took place after the rescue.

Other assistance from Russia has come from:

Natalia Ershova, a Russian Murmansk resident who teaches English. She has supplied sources relating to Murmansk, including about the hospital. Some come from the archive relating to the Arctic convoys that are in a local gymnasium.

Assistance from Germany has been provided by:

Jürgen Meyer-Brenkhof, a retired German Fregattenkapitän, who I first came across thanks to an article he wrote in a German journal about the fighting during convoy PQ13, an action that had interested him because of his father Hans-Jürgen Meyer-Brenkhof's involvement. He sent me his father's account of the incident, and has answered my many questions about German vessels and nautical matters that I have sent to him.

Dirk Sieg, from the Wertegemeinschaft Marine-Offizier-Vereinigung (the German marine association) in Bonn, brought to my attention relevant German sources some of which had appeared in the journal Marine Forum.

Before mentioning the other main helpers with this book, I would like to credit the special contributions made by both Richard Kemp, a retired solicitor, and my son Saul Sebag-Montefiore. Their assistance with many aspects of the necessary research has been so intensive and rigorous that at times their contributions have been sufficient for them to be classified as co-authors, with Richard focusing in particular on searching for Arctic convoy veterans' accounts, and Saul concentrating on information contained in documents in archives in America and Germany as well as in Britain, and in books and other publications, as well as on all matters Russian. He has also sought out the best available photographs.

The following personnel assisted me considerably by helping me extract the most useful information from their collections:

In Britain

British Library:
- Books: Andrew Gough, Srikanth Mattewada, Kathryn Mouncey and Jeremy Nagle.
- Maps: Nicola Beech and Carlos Garcia-Minguillan.

Churchill Archives Centre, Cambridge: Allen Packwood, Director.

Imperial War Museum:
- Head of Documents and Sound: Anthony Richards.
- Curator, Second World War: Robert Rumble.
- Reading Room: Documents, Books and Sound: Jane Rosen.
- Sound in course of digitization: Margaret Weller, Head of Visual Resources and Maria Castrillo, Head of Collections Access & Research.

Ministry of Defence:
- Air Historical Branch: Stuart Hadaway.
- Naval Historical Branch: Aidan Butler.

National Archives:
- Production Co-Ordination Manager: David Priest.
- Resource, Access & Advice Programme Manager: Debbie French.
- Document services adviser: Greg Cole.

National Maritime Museum:
- Caird Library and Archive: Gareth Bellis, Senior Manager, and Magdalena Schedl, Library Assistant.
- Curator, Historic Photographs and Ship Plans: Andrew Choong Han Lin.
- Assistant Curator, Historic Photographs and Ship Plans: Alex Grover.

Polish Institute and Sikorski Museum:
- Archives director: Dr Andrzej Suchcitz.
- Films and photographs: Wojtek Deluga.

Second World War Experience Centre, Otley, West Yorkshire: Office Manager: Anne Wickes.

In America
Air Force Historical Research Agency, Alabama: Archivist Leslie Smith.

Falvey Memorial Library, Villanova University, Pennsylvania: Director of Distinctive Collections and Digital Engagement: Michael Foight.

Institute on World War II and the Human Experience, Florida: Administrative Assistant: Anne March.

National Archives
  - Maryland: Archivist: Nathaniel Patch; and Textual Reference Operations: Richard Peuser and Amy Reytar.
  - Washington: Archivist: Chris Killillay.

Naval History and Heritage Command: David Colamaria, Photo Archivist.

US Navy Armed Guard World War 2 Veterans Association: Charles Lloyd.

In Norway
Centre for the History of Seafarers at War: Archivist: Bjørn Tore Rosendahl.

In Svalbard
The Svalbard Museum, Longyearbyen: Archivist and historian: Haakon Unhammer Kvaale.

In Germany
Bundesarchiv: Militärarchiv Freiburg: Christiane Botzet.

U-boot Archiv, Cuxhaven: Annemarie Bredow, Rainer Stührenberg, and Kai Steenbuck.

I have also been helped by the following advisers, researchers and translators:
Tobias Barland, Merlijn Feenstra, Katharina Froelich, Polina Gern, Tobias Henriksen, Anna den Hollander, Josephine Hülsen, Paul Hünsche, Maria Jouravleva, Janina Klement, Daniel Konn-Vetterlein, Hauke Kottek, Lyuba Lukashenko, Ferdinand Mowinckel, Elizaveta Nidzelskaya, Tony Olszowski, Charlotte Pechau, Fred Powell, Frederik Risse, Luisa Rombach, Madita Schröder, Sebag-Montefiore family members: Abraham and Simon, Anna Springer, Brandon Tachco, Jill Van Duin, Valeriia Verbovaia, Anastasia Vikhanova, Kai Wittmacher, Clive Wolman, Garrett Wralstad, Theodore Xing, Mikael Zakharov.

Although I have tried to use as many primary sources as possible, no book such as this can give a comprehensive airing to the available information without relying to some extent on what other historians have written. In this book's introduction, I have already paid tribute to Richard Woodman's book *Arctic Convoys 1941–1945*. When I

Acknowledgements

met him he very generously shared with me all the relevant notes and source material he had retained.

Other authors who have given me substantial assistance in addition to writing the books cited in the Bibliography include: Adam Claasen, author of *Hitler's Northern War: The Luftwaffe's Ill-Fated Campaign,* who shared with me various sources from Germany and America including a detailed account by a Luftwaffe commander; Christer Bergström, author of a series of books entitled *Black Cross Red Star,* who brought testimony by Luftwaffe personnel to my attention; John McKay, author of *Surviving the Arctic Convoys: The Wartime Memoirs of Leading Seaman Charlie Erswell,* who has shared with me the large collection of Northern Light journals Charlie Erswell gave him; and Peter Taghon, the author of many books about World War 2 including several about the Luftwaffe, who brought to my attention Luftwaffe daily reports available on the Deutsch-Russisches Projekt internet site.

My agent, David Godwin, helped me pitch to HarperCollins the idea of writing a book about the Battle of the Arctic, and has played an active role during the writing of the book concerning its structure.

Arabella Pike, the responsible editorial director at HarperCollins, insisted the scope of the book should be ambitious, covering the whole period from 1941–5 rather than the more limited period that had featured in some previous works on this subject, and has given me the time to accomplish that goal.

The complicated task of making both the text and sources reader friendly has been expertly managed by copy editors Tom Whiting, and HarperCollins' senior editor Alex Gingell who has also acted as project manager, and in such capacity has done everything possible to make sure all the different elements of the book have fallen into place on time. They include the corrections at the proof stage by proofreader Anne Rieley, which could not have been done more sensitively and efficiently, and the intricate maps designed by Martin Brown, which can only be described as an author's dream. Sam Harding has made sure the selected photographs were delivered on time and laid out in the most attractive way possible.

Index

All ships and other vessels appear under the sub-heading 'ships and other vessels'. All Arctic convoys in this index appear under sub-heading 'convoys, Arctic or Russian'.

Index